The Seafaring
Dictionary

The Seafaring Dictionary

*Terms, Idioms and Legends
of the Past and Present*

DAVID S.T. BLACKMORE

Foreword by Vice Admiral J.A. Baldwin, Jr.,
U.S. Navy (Ret.)

McFarland & Company, Inc., Publishers
Jefferson, North Carolina, and London

LIBRARY OF CONGRESS CATALOGUING-IN-PUBLICATION DATA

Blackmore, David S.T.
The seafaring dictionary : terms, idioms and legends of the past and
present / David S.T. Blackmore ; foreword by J.A. Baldwin, Jr.
p.   cm.
Includes bibliographical references and index.

ISBN 978-0-7864-4266-9
softcover : 50# alkaline paper ∞

1. Naval art and science — Dictionaries.
I. Title.
V23.B583   2009   623.803 — dc22   2009001471

British Library cataloguing data are available

Cover images ©2009 Shutterstock

Manufactured in the United States of America

*McFarland & Company, Inc., Publishers
Box 611, Jefferson, North Carolina 28640
www.mcfarlandpub.com*

TABLE OF CONTENTS

FOREWORD

Vice Admiral J.A. Baldwin, Jr., U.S. Navy (Ret.)

In contrast to the thrust of this volume, which in the main looks to the past for origins, definitions, and anecdotes, David Blackmore and I met in a thoroughly modern way — through the internet. David had received my email address from a mutual friend, and thus began a valued association.

Indeed, associations engendered by the sea and by having gone to sea make it easier for most sailors to communicate because of their acquired vocabulary, and made our collaboration easier as well. While most professions have their own lexicon, "sailor speak" seems to me to be older, broader, and deeper than others.

The importance of this was made clear to me during my plebe year at the U.S. Naval Academy by a crusty retired chief petty officer whose mission it was to impart some salt along with his wisdom to the landlubbers in my class. His view of the need for using a different vocabulary — port, starboard, forward, aft, galley, head, overhead, and the like — was so that a sailor would "think ship" in everything he or she thought and did. And so it was.

If you have half as much fun delving through *The Seafaring Dictionary* as I did rummaging around in the interstices of the draft and thrashing out with David the different usages between the U.S. and Royal navies, then you will have an interesting read and learn something to boot.

Nantucket, Massachusetts
September 1, 2008

PREFACE

The writer writes in order to teach himself,
to understand himself, to satisfy himself.
— Alfred Kazin, 1963

An author who speaks about his own books is almost
as bad as a mother who talks about her own children.
— Benjamin Disraeli, 1873

I will go back to the great sweet mother
Mother and lover of men, the sea.
— Algernon Charles Swinburne, 1852

What qualifies a retired oil company executive to compile a book such as this? Well, I've been connected with ships and the sea for as long as I can remember. Born in the shadow of Salisbury Cathedral in England, I was taken on my first ocean voyage (to Egypt) when just a few months old, returning by sea several years later. I have no recollection of either passage, but perhaps I got a little salt in my blood.

Back in England my family spent every July and August at Sheringham, a then-tiny fishing village in Norfolk, where crab and lobster fishing, along with long-lining for cod, herring, and mackerel made the local fishermen major suppliers to the London fish markets. At that time there were over 200 boats, today, only eight remain.

There, I met Tiny, a pure-bred Cairn terrier puppy who had been born at sea when her dam whelped unexpectedly early. On virtually every one of the sixty or so halcyon days we spent there every year, Tiny and I were on the wharf before dawn begging a ride. The fishermen must have looked on the little boy with his dog as some kind of good luck mascots, because they were always ready to take us on board. Days spent handling the lines in bouncy little boats on the seldom-smooth North Sea gave me sea legs that I have never lost.

At ten I joined the Sea Scouts, learning how to box the compass, tie knots and splices, and other bits of oceanic lore, plus countless hours (and countless blisters) rowing whaleboats up and down the Thames River. By then my family had deserted Sheringham in favor of the little seaport of Mevagissey in Cornwall, from where I spent most of my summers sailing solo around the rocky wave-beaten headlands. (Solo because, sad to say, Tiny had gone to doggy Fiddler's Green, where I think of her perpetually performing her self-appointed duty — standing stiff-legged on the heaving bow as forward lookout, enjoying the salty spray on her face.)

At fourteen I temporarily deserted the sea to become a founder member of the Air Cadet Corps, where I found the recruitment propaganda of naval aviation more compelling than the rival claims of the Royal Air Force. Then came the Battle of Britain and Nazi invasion threat, during which I spent my days as a bicycle courier for Civil Defense and many nights equipped with rifle and bayonet on sentry duty with the Home Guard (which was happy to overlook the age regulations to recruit 15-year-olds at one end of the spectrum and octogenarians at the other).

Two years later, I graduated high school

and tried to enlist, but the Royal Navy and Royal Marines both told me to go away and come back after my eighteenth birthday, so I signed on as a deck officer cadet in the Merchant Navy. I was appointed to newly launched *mv Hardingham,* an 8,000-ton freighter equipped with anti-aircraft artillery worthy of a destroyer. There were only two cadets, so we worked a grueling back-to-back four hours on and four off.

Sailing on the North Sea in the spring of 1942 (the worst year for Allied maritime losses) my ship was bombed twice by the German Luftwaffe and once by the RAF (whose ship-recognition was never very good). The explosions were close enough to soak me with spray, but otherwise did no harm.

In that summer, the manpower shortage was so acute that — with barely a year of sea time between us — my fellow cadet and I were appointed acting third officers for a short passage up the Irish Sea, he conning the ship during the evening watch and I in the forenoon (not a very challenging task in convoy, which requires station-keeping but no navigation).

During one of these watches, I stood on the bridge looking at a torpedo track coming straight for me (fascinated, more than terrified). The "fish" stuck our side with a crash that the engine room staff said sounded "like a thousand kettle-drums" down in their hole, but it was a dud that failed to explode.

A little later in mid–Atlantic, the rising sun revealed another torpedo swaying to-and-fro within inches of the hull, trapped in the mesh of our AND (anti-submarine net device). This time it was live and armed, but we cast it loose and sank it with a burst of 20mm cannon fire.

The final episode of that eventful year was a shelling by French Foreign Legion shore batteries while in the Mediterranean during the November invasion of North Africa. We felt they were shooting at us, but the shells landed so far away that they probably had another target. Anyway, having survived all this without a scratch, I decided my charmed life could not go on forever and it would be much

wiser to sail in something with guns and armor.

My transfer to the Royal Navy was at first denied on the grounds that merchant seaman was a "reserved occupation," but I managed to pull a few strings and was selected for training as an aircraft engineer at Manadon Royal Naval Engineering College (the British Annapolis). Nearing graduation, I was seconded to the Welsh Guards training battalion to learn how to lead an infantry platoon in combat. I never did discover why, although there were vague mutterings about having to defend the perimeter of a MONAB (mobile operational naval air base) against Japanese counterattacks. The Hiroshima bomb was dropped ending the Pacific War before I had to do anything so hazardous.

Since then, my sea time has been confined to passenger liners and cruise ships, and they hardly count, being closer to floating hotels than "real" ships. However, while at Manadon I had acquired an enduring love of naval affairs and military history, which I studied voraciously during a business career that took me to many parts of Europe, Africa, and North America, ending in Calgary as director of strategic planning for a major resources company.

After early retirement I changed my hobby into a profession by studying history at the Canadian universities of Queens and Waterloo, graduating from the latter on the dean's honors list. Shortly afterward, my wife and I visited Turkey where, standing on the Hill of Hisarlik and looking at the Field of Troy, I remembered how the poet Homer sang in antiquity, "The cruel war-god has darkened the banks of Scamander River with the blood of our dead"— then I raised my eyes across the Dardanelles, to the cliffs of Gallipoli, where naval aviator Charles Samson observed in 1915, "The sea, for a distance of about fifty yards from the beach, was absolutely red with blood."

Sadly, I realized thirty-three centuries had done nothing to curb humanity's lethal instincts towards its own species. Turning to

Paula, I commented on the amazing sweep of history around, across, and along these waters. Always pragmatic, she shot right back, "Well, don't just talk about it, write about it." And so began my new career as naval historiographer.

During my research, I consulted numerous dictionaries and other sources of nautical terminology; together with books on ghost ships and paranormal maritime events; volumes devoted to marine monsters and sea serpents; others on nautical customs and superstitions; many on naval traditions and courtesies; and lots of glossaries of naval slang. I even found works showing how words and phrases in common everyday use come from the sea.

How convenient it would be, I thought, if these disparate subjects could be brought together for easy reference in a single accessible volume. Hence *The Seafaring Dictionary*, which is a representative (but by no means exhaustive) overview of naval speech and maritime matters. It is intended to give enjoyment to readers and browsers, provide a source of reference for people who want to understand nautical speech and customs, and even be helpful to professional seafarers who cannot always be familiar with the vocabularies of today's specialized maritime occupations, let alone those of bygone ages.

The literature of the sea fills entire libraries and could never be done justice in a single volume. So, in the final analysis, any selection from this vast treasure house of nautical words and phrases is bound to be subjective. I am painfully aware of the vast number of terms, events, superstitions, and the like that have perforce been omitted from this work. The least I can hope for is to give the reader an overview and "feel" for the subject. The best would be to inspire the reader to delve into this vast body of information to learn more about the demanding and often perilous seafaring life.

A large number of words or phrases found in other nautical fact books have been omitted in the interest of saving space. Some were rarely used in their day and are now completely forgotten. As an example, "Stabbed with a Bridport dagger" was British sailing navy slang for being hanged. This intriguing idiom originated because the better-quality ropes used for executions were made at a ropeworks in the small Devon town of Bridport.

My aim has been to make each of the roughly 9,000 entries as accurate and entertaining as possible. Many are brief and factual but, when appropriate, I have inserted anecdotal material of colorful or intrinsic interest. Moreover, no good tale has been omitted because it is untrue, although I have indicated whenever something is apocryphal or questionable.

I enjoyed invaluable technical advice from Vice Admiral J.A. Baldwin, Jr., U.S. Navy (Ret.) and Commander Alastair Wilson, Royal Navy (Ret.). If, despite their expert reviews, errors or omissions have slipped through, the fault is entirely mine and I accept full responsibility for them. I do, however, ask any reader who uncovers a mistake or misinterpretation to let me or my publishers know.

If you, the reader, get even a fraction of the enjoyment from this book that writing it has given me, then my efforts will be more than rewarded. Thank you and good reading!

INTRODUCTION

Who commands the sea has command of everything.
— Themistocles, 5th century BCE

Ships are to little purpose without skillful Sea Men.
— Richard Hakluyt, 1589

There is witchery in the sea, its songs and stories.
— Richard Henry Dana, 1840

The purpose of this compendium is to bring together a range of nautical information that would otherwise require an extensive library. It is a mixture of lexicology, factual information, and wild superstition, covering not only what seafarers say, but what they think and believe, how they describe their physical equipment, and what laws, customs and traditions determine how they do their work.

Water covers more than 70 percent of the planet's surface and, until mid–20th century, oceans were the only path for intercontinental travel. Airlines have now taken over passenger traffic, but ships still carry virtually all of the world's rapidly expanding trade. So it is far from surprising that so much of the world's history has been written on the seas, or that so many words have nautical origins. Most of these words are English, but here was a time when they might have been French.

During the early eighteenth century, Britain faced a Marine Royale (French Royal Navy) that had a superb aristocratic officer corps, a maritime regiment of what were arguably the world's most professional naval gunners, and ships that were better-designed and faster. France suffered serious naval setbacks during the Seven Years' War (1756–63), especially at the Battle of Quiberon Bay in November 1759. The *Marine* should have been able to recover, but the purges and excesses of the Revolution sent almost the entire officer corps into exile or to the guillotine, while the superb naval artillery regiment was denounced as "an aristocracy of the sea" and disbanded.

Relatively inexperienced lieutenants found themselves promoted to command or even flag rank. Merchant mariners were recruited to fill the gaps, but had no understanding of naval tactics. Many of the enlisted force deserted, and the remainder, racked by mutinies and discontent, were an undisciplined rabble. Since then world oceans have been dominated by English-speaking powers, though not without serious challenges from time to time.

- Napoleon Bonaparte — who had little appreciation of maritime matters, even though he had originally been an aspirant navale (naval cadet) — tried to re-invigorate the Marine Nationale, which was strengthened by an alliance with Spain's Armada. However, at the Battle of Trafalgar in 1805, Admiral Horatio Nelson all but annihilated a combined Franco-Spanish fleet, guaranteeing British naval domination until 1914.
- During World War I, the Imperial German Navy posed a serious threat by a guerre de course of unrestricted submarine warfare.

Only the introduction of a convoy system saved Britain from being starved into surrender in spite of the Royal Navy's surface hegemony.

- A post-war arms race ended with the 1930 Treaty of Washington, which gave the United States and Britain naval parity, a situation that prevailed until World War II.
- Despite strong challenges by German and Italian air and naval forces, Britain held precarious control of all contested waters until joined (unofficially at first) by naval forces from the technically neutral United States.
- Between its raid on Pearl Harbor in December 1941 and the Battle of Midway in June 1942, the Imperial Japanese Navy enjoyed fleeting local hegemony in the Indian and Pacific oceans.
- Since then the United States Navy has been predominant worldwide in spite of strenuous efforts by the Soviet Union to overtake it during the Cold War.

With a common language and shared maritime heritage going back to the Tudor navies of the sixteenth century, Britain and the United States share a range of nautical traditions and terminology. However, usage occasionally differs — usually very little, but sometimes quite a lot — not only between the two countries, but internally between naval, coastguard, and merchant seamen, not to mention river pilots, fisher folk, and yachters. When there are differences in language or customs, the British convention usually precedes the American because of earlier usage.

Specialized Maritime Vocabulary

Navigable waters cover almost three-quarters of the surface of our planet. They are home to seafarers who, being isolated from land for long periods, developed a language of their own. As well as technical terms, the maritime vocabulary (let's call it "navalese") borrows from normal speech frequently giving common words uniquely nautical meanings.

Every profession has its jargon — anyone who has been to court or in hospital knows that "legalese" and "medicalese" can be as unintelligible to the layperson as Egyptian hieroglyphs — but such terms are not designed to keep things secret from the uninitiated. Rather, they allow complex technical concepts to be communicated briefly and accurately between doctor and nurse or lawyer and judge.

Seamen are no different, using specialized terminology to convey instructions and ideas. Their language is a complex mixture of the strange and familiar, including words taken from many English dialects, coined words, slang words, words used by mariners speaking other tongues, the names of occupations and equipment, and descriptions of work and leisure activities. Like medicalese and legalese, navalese can sometimes be as esoteric and incomprehensible as Sanskrit or Aramaic. At others it uses words which, although uniquely maritime, are familiar to almost everyone — mast, sail, and oar, for example.

The seafarer's vocabulary includes a complete zoo of creatures, including Bear, Beetle, Camel, Cat, Crow, Dog, Dolphin, Donkey, Fish, Fox, Hog, Horse, Lizard, Monkey, Mouse, Pig, Pussy-cat, Turkey, and Worm; plus a number of human body parts, such as arm, arse, belly, breast, buttocks, cheeks, crotch, eyes, foot, hand, head, knee, navel, rib, shoulder, skin, throat, tongue, and waist.

The nautical lexicon includes terms current in Chaucer's time alongside others invented on laptop computers. Many are slang, argot, or acronyms comprehensible only to the initiated, while phrases in common use sometimes have different and special meaning to seamen. Moreover, mariners themselves can be confused by contradictory conventions that, for example, call movement from west to east "westerly" if referring to an ocean current, but "easterly" if speaking of wind.

Shared Everyday Terminology

An amazing number of maritime words and phrases have found their way into common English idiom, frequently with their nautical origins obscured. Many can be authenticated, but readers should be aware that any phrase with even a hint of salt water is likely to be arrogated by "Opanova"—a hypothetical *Organization of People Ascribing Nautical Origins to Virtually Anything.*

Other expressions have moved in the opposite direction, often having totally different meaning to mariners. Some of the many nautical objects with everyday names include apron, bonnet, cradle, crib, diamond, jewel, pudding, ribband, saddle, shoe, stays, and whip.

Wherever possible, word origins are indicated although, even when propounded by eminent lexicographers, many are little more than educated guesswork and conflicting sources are sometimes postulated or imputed. Ancient racial antipathies are reflected in the use of nouns like Chinese, Dutch, or Spanish as adjectives to qualify ineffective practices or nasty things. Where an original seaman's phrase contains profanity it has been allowed to stand without imposition of censorship.

With few exceptions, the glossary is confined to words and phrases used by English-speaking mariners. Numerous other seafarers — French, German, Greek, Italian, Japanese, Russian, Spanish, and others — have their own terminology, but the English lexicon alone is said to number between five million and ten million words, many of which have nautical origins or connotations, or are combined into mariners' phrases. With such an immense — almost unmanageable — field, the selection of items to be covered is inevitably arbitrary and subjective, with many being left out by design or oversight.

In addition to vocabulary and terminology, the listings include professional, occupational, environmental, and historical information in the general areas given below:

Maritime artifacts: Since the days of Egyptian pharaohs, naval architecture and equipment have been at the forward edge of contemporary high technology. Over the millennia, tens of thousands of examples of human ingenuity and workmanship have been produced for maritime use. Obviously, only a few hundred can be mentioned here, along with something of their background and history. These include such physical objects as astrolabe, compass, guided missile, and stabilizer.

Weather factors: Nothing is more important to mariners than the impact of winds and waves, tides and currents. In addition to describing ship motions in response to actions of the sea, a number of conventions for the measurement of weather conditions are described, including the Beaufort wind scale, Douglas wave and swell scale, Fujita tornado scale, and Saffir-Simpson hurricane scale.

Propulsion systems: Rather more space has been devoted to sails and rigging than to modern systems such as steam, diesel, and CODAG-electric, simply because recent developments will be more familiar to contemporary readers.

Customs and traditions: Customs can be defined as shared practices and conventions that are treated as unwritten laws by a group or organization; while traditions consist of knowledge, opinions, and rites, passed from generation to generation, with the authority of long-standing acceptance and consent. Because seafarers spend more time afloat among their own kind than they do ashore with the rest of society, they have tended to develop their own set of customs and traditions. Examples of the questions answered herein are — Why are swords held cutting edge up when making an "arch of steel" at a naval wedding? How did the drink called grog get its peculiar name? Why were so many dockside taverns named "Pig and Whistle"?

Salutes and courtesies: All societies and organizations have social conventions which stem from tradition. This is especially true of the military and naval services, where customs and courtesies have evolved to meet the need for order and to foster mutual respect and fraternity. Courtesies are generally defined as acts of consideration, respect, and recognition, but military courtesies, which include salutes of various kinds, go beyond basic politeness to play important roles in building self-respect, morale, pride of service, discipline and, ultimately, mission effectiveness. In addition to information on the origins and significance of hand, gun, and flag salutes, we learn such things as why senior officers enter a boat or vehicle last and leave it first.

Music and dance: Singing and instrumental music have always been important facets of seafaring life, falling into seven general categories — music for dancing, marching, honoring individuals, and passing orders; plus working, religious, and patriotic songs. In the days when navigation depended on massive squares of canvas handled by human muscle power, labor was synchronized and made easier by work-songs known as chanteys. Sailors with fine singing voices found they could avoid some of the nastier shipboard tasks by volunteering as chanteymen, singing melodies that helped to soften the rigors of shipboard life. Listening to the songs was enjoyable and relieved boredom, especially when a fiddler accompanied the singer. Moreover, the cadence of calls and responses helped synchronize the movements of repetitive tasks. Many a captain kept his crew agile and entertained by ordering them to dance the hornpipe.

Laws and conventions: Because the high seas are beyond territorial jurisdiction, seafarers have found it essential to develop codes of maritime law that are at some times enforced by common consent, at others by Admiralty Court. The reader will find brief descriptions of ancient codes such as the Rôles de Oléron and modern ones like the United Nations Convention on Law of the Sea.

Institutions: Numerous organizations are needed to keep national and global maritime services ticking over properly. In addition to departments of government, these include insurance underwriters such as Lloyds of London; ship classification agencies like Det Norske Veritas; charitable organizations such as the Chatham Chest; and international forums on such things as pollution (Marpol) and safety (Solas).

Mutiny: Organized and open revolt against constituted authority by seamen against their officers was common in the days of sail, but typically occurred in port or just offshore, rather than on the high seas. Usually, mutinies were more like modern labor strikes than the fictional stereotype. Crews would refuse to sail in ships viewed as unsafe, or to carry out duties until wages owed were paid. Often they offered to transfer en masse to a safer vessel, and they were usually ready to sail if a battle impended. The Great Mutiny of 1797 was this type of action in which two Royal Navy fleets went on strike until conditions were improved. The Mare Island Mutiny of 1944, in which fifty U.S. Navy sailors refused to work in unsafe conditions was similar, as was the RIN Mutiny of 1946.

Three "conventional" mutinies at sea are also discussed — those aboard the Dutch ship VOC *Batavia*, and the British HMS *Bounty* and HMS *Hermione*. As far as the author can determine, nobody has ever been formally charged with committing mutiny aboard a commissioned USN vessel. Indeed, the movie *Caine Mutiny* opens with the statement "There has never been a mutiny in a ship of the United States Navy." However, readers can determine for themselves if the USS *Somers* incident involved mutiny, quasi-judicial murder, illegal procedures, or a combination of all three.

Biography: With one exception, none are included. However the mutiny on HMS *Bounty* has been so misinterpreted and the character of Captain William Bligh so maligned in film and fiction that it seemed appropriate to set the record straight.

Military affairs: In addition to brief histories of the origins and development of forces such as the British Royal Marines and the United States Navy, readers will find information on naval bureaucracies, on supporting branches such as chaplain and medical corps, and outlines of current doctrines such as network centric and swing.

International cooperation: Much of the peacetime work that navies do can be considered constabulary. Together with miscellaneous law enforcement agencies, they fight smuggling, piracy, terrorism, weapons proliferation, drugs trading, human trafficking, illegal immigration, organized crime, and other forms of illicit commerce and maritime mayhem. Existing arrangements include the International Ice Patrol and Operation Active Endeavour; while an imaginative future proposal is known as the Thousand Ship Navy.

Tactics and maneuvers: Naval tactical doctrine has ranged from ram-and-sink, via grapple-and-board, to duels between floating gun batteries, but the commander of an Athenian galley would have had at least some comprehension of fleet movements in the World War I Battle of Jutland. By then, however, seamen had discovered how to glide silently under the waves and soar triumphantly above them, bringing entirely new dimensions to naval conflict in World War II, during which opposing fleets sometimes never even sighted one another. Maneuvers discussed include the fifth century *periplus,* twentieth century Thach weave, and a series of person overboard rescue turns.

Amphibious operations: British military historian Basil Liddell Hart writes, "Amphibious flexibility is the greatest strategic asset that a sea power possesses," and both Britain and the United States took full advantage of that asset during the twentieth century. Of the seven examples discussed, three were disastrous — Gallipoli (1915), Dieppe (1942) and Anzio (1944) — while North Africa (1942), Sicily (1943), Normandy (1944), and Okinawa (1945) were successful.

Major conflicts: This is not a history book but aspects of the Pacific War are discussed because it involved not only the logistic feat of moving hordes of men and tons of matériel across the entire length of the world's largest ocean; but also all five of the carrier-against-carrier battles ever fought; the largest surface battle in history; the first engagement in which opposing surface forces never saw each other; and the greatest ever series of night encounters.

Pivotal maritime events: Over the millennia, hundreds (perhaps thousands) of naval events have been termed "decisive," but usually in the sense of having had a major impact at a particular time and place, without significant long-lasting effects. For example; the Battle of Lepanto in 1571 temporarily destroyed Ottoman sea power and ended the seaborne threat to Europe, but the land threat continued for another century until the Siege of Vienna in 1683. Similarly, if Nelson had lost the Battle of Trafalgar in 1805, the British Channel Fleet was still "in being" with the potential to break up any Napoleonic invasion armada. As another example, if Japan had won the Battle of Midway in 1942 it would only have gained a brief respite before being overwhelmed by United States industrial might.

Truly "pivotal" events — which the author defines as changing the course of world history — are far less frequent. In fact, only the following six seem to deserve that designation. Other historians will doubtless disagree with these choices, but the compiler enjoys right of selection.

1. The march of the "Sea People" virtually destroyed the Mycenaean and Hittite empires, wiped out important city-states such as Ugarit, and fatally weakened the Egyptian superpower. With no competitors left, they might have dominated the Aegean and Mediterranean, but their defeat at the naval Battle of the Nile Delta in 1176 BCE, left the way clear for the rise of Greece, Etruria, Carthage, and Rome, and the development of Western civilization as we know it.

2. Had Persian Emperor Xerxes won the naval Battle of Salamis in 480 BCE, the Athenian experiment in democracy would have been stifled, perhaps along with the important Greek contribution to Western philosophy,

art, and architecture. Moreover, with Greece out of the way, Persia might have succeeded in adding the European continent to its vast Asian empire, with incalculable impact on the course of human history.

3. During the fifteenth century, Chinese fleets visited Africa, Arabia, Australia, Europe, India, Japan, Southeast Asia, and (possibly) North America. With an unlimited pool of manpower, and a naval technology that was centuries ahead of the rest of the world, they could easily have dominated or colonized the entire globe, had their adventures not been halted by the Ming Naval Decrees of 1500.

4. The relatively small and indecisive naval Battle of Virginia Capes in 1781 was pivotal because it secured independence for the United States. If Britain had regained control of the sea, and the armies of Clinton and Cornwallis had linked up, their combined forces might well have crushed Washington's army and his French allies.

5. The unintended and accidental naval Battle of Navarino Bay in 1827 irreparably crippled Ottoman sea power; established Greece as an independent Kingdom; won autonomy for Balkan States; and paved the way for Russian imperial expansion.

6. The naval Battle of Tsushima in 1905 established Japan as an international player and the superpower of East Asia. It told the oppressed peoples of the region that Europeans were not invincible, leading to the independence movements of the twentieth century. Moreover, it seriously weakened the prestige of the Russian Tsar, paving the way for revolution a decade later.

Superstition: Unique occupational hazards, the uncertainties of life at sea, the occasional disappearance of an apparently sound vessel, and frequent exposure to poor visibility and mirages have combined to make seafarers some of the most superstitious and gullible of people. Maritime beliefs are as deep as the ocean itself, and include so many hazards, taboos, and superstitions that the reader may wonder why any sane individual ever ventured out to sea. Just a few of the disparate items with weird connotations are birds, buckets, drinking glasses, fridays, naked women, pigs, and whistling.

Paranormal Events: Modern as well as ancient reports of mysterious disappearances, transmutations, and alien visitations abound; together with yarns and legends about strange water deities, ghost ships, fearsome monsters of the deep, and beautiful mermaids — all of which have been widely exploited by the media, novelists, and the popular imagination. Many such tales can be dismissed as the outcome of hazy conditions, fevered imaginations, excessive drinking, superstitious awe, or just plain confusion. But some have been found to have rational explanations, while others have been substantiated by credible eyewitnesses, including naval officers, scientists, oceanographers, naturalists, and other responsible individuals with impeccable credentials.

Gods of the sea: Oceans, seas, rivers, and lakes have always been mysterious and magical places to humans, who have peered into their stygian depths and contemplated which spirit might control them and what strange beings might inhabit them. Virtually every pagan culture has one or more gods devoted to water, some symbolizing cleansing and purification, some being protectors of seamen, and others being evil spirits threatening destruction. Greco-Roman deities such as Portunus and Poseidon (Neptune) have persisted in European tradition. Other sea-dwelling or sea-related beings have established themselves in myth, including Davy Jones, Sinbad the Sailor, and Britannia.

Ghost ships: There are several types of these maritime apparitions in naval lore. Some are thought to warn of coming disaster, while others recall earlier tragedies. The *Block Island Phantom* does both. Some, such as the *Cursed Corsair*, the *Flying Dutchman*, and the Japanese *Yureisen*, are ethereal phantoms that appear out of nowhere as sinister and dangerous apparitions. Others were real ships like *Mary Celeste*, discovered intact with crew mysteriously vanished (often confused with *Marie Ce-*

leste, the subject of a Conan Doyle horror story). And some appear to be explicable phenomena such as the *Chaleur Bay Phantom* and *Jenny the Glacial Ghost.*

Sea serpents and monsters: Strange creatures have been reported in all the world's seas and oceans, being variously described as swimming dragons, writhing serpents, multi-armed horrors, and dinosaur survivors. Reports have generally been dismissed as myth, legend, misidentification of known species, or the ramblings of over-imaginative seafarers, often ignoring the evidence of credible eyewitnesses such as those mentioned. Indeed, it is easy to misinterpret things seen at sea — on land, objects can be compared to nearby trees or structures; but on water only the waves offer size comparison, and their movement alone can suggest an undulating body in motion.

For example, the 1848, Pekin Monster turned out to be a six-meter (20-foot) length of seaweed with its root shaped like a shaggily maned head. Another sighting, by ship's surgeon Arthur Adams in 1860, was later found to be "a long dark root, gnarled and twisted ... secured to ... a fishing net, with a strong tide ... giving it an apparent lifelike movement." Something as mundane as a pod of dolphins, swimming in a straight line one behind the other could be interpreted as the multiple dorsal fins of a lengthy sea serpent.

Sightings of strange sea creatures seemed to diminish in the twentieth century, which many interpreted as the reflection of seamen becoming better educated and less superstitious. However, a wind-powered vessel could glide stealthily over the water, adding nothing to the ambient noise except the gentle slapping of its bow-wave. In contrast, powered ships have clanking engines, rumbling propulsion systems, whirring propellers, and disturbed wake. Water is an excellent transmitter of sound, so sea creatures would receive ample warning to swim away or sound deeply, leaving the ocean as apparently empty as a snake-infested forest whose denizens have slithered away at the noise of approaching footsteps.

There is a huge body of conjecture concerning real or yet undiscovered creatures that might have been mistaken for sea monsters. These include at least four bony fish, a crocodilian, and three invertebrate cephalopods whose visual characteristics might fool even experienced observers into thinking they had seen a monster. There is also an order of marine mammals which may have given rise to the mermaid legend. These are discussed in the appendices.

Alphabetical sequencing of the glossary should make it easy for readers to locate physical objects such as capstan or topgallant; naval customs like saluting and flogging; military units like the United States Coast Guard or Royal Marines; shipping registries like the American Bureau of Shipping; legal systems such as the Laws of Wisby; and other similar references. However, it is less satisfactory for intangible or mythical items that the reader might never find without some guidance. Accordingly, the index lists:

- People mentioned in the text.
- Ships mentioned in the text.
- Supernatural personages.
- Ghost ships and paranormal phenomena.
- Sea serpents and monsters.

The Dictionary

The knowledge of naval matters
is an art as well as any other.
— Pericles, 432 BCE

A Nautical Dictionary, or
Cyclopaedia of Naval Science and
Nomenclature is a desideratum
— Major Shadwell Clarke, 1836

Many branches of knowledge are
demanded of the intelligent seaman
— Admiral W.H. Smyth, 1865

No group of workingmen harbours
as many superstitions within its
collective breast as do sailors
— Peter Jeans 2004

Every profession has its own argot,
A virtual other language by which its
practitioners communicate among themselves
— Deborah Cutler, 2005

A

A-: Prefix indicating "at," "in," "on," or "towards." For example; aboard, asea, ashore, and alongside, which are self-explanatory; also ahead or astern meaning forward or backward, abaft meaning behind, etc. (Probably derived from the French "à.")

A1: This term, which is in general use to signify first-class or excellent, comes from the highest insurance rating awarded by Lloyd's Register of Shipping.

AAA: Anti-aircraft artillery.

AAFSF: Amphibious assault fuel supply facility.

AAM: Anti-aircraft missile.

AAV: Armored amphibious vehicle.

AB: [1] Able Seaman. [2] Aviation Boatswain's Mate (USN).

Aback: [1] When, instead of a following wind blowing into square sails, a headwind presses them against the mast they are said to be aback. [2] When a ship suddenly stops due to the foregoing, it is said to be taken aback. [3] The triangular Marconi (Bermudian) rig doesn't press on the mast, but can still be taken aback when tacking.

Abaft: Towards the back, closer to the stern.

Abaft the beam: Between beam and stern.

Abandon: [1] To desert a vessel on account of the danger in remaining aboard. [2] To relinquish to underwriters all claim to property which may be recovered from shipwreck, capture, or any other peril stated in the policy.

Abandon ship!: This command for all hands to leave the vessel is normally issued by the captain or senior surviving officer when a ship is foundering.

Abatement: A demand for a reduction of freight when unforeseen causes have delayed or hindered the performance of a charter-party.

Abeam: Abreast of the vessel, directly at right angles to the side.

Abergele apparition: For centuries, and as recently as May 2008, people claim to have seen an antique ship sailing along the coast off Abergale in Wales. Eyewitness reports are strikingly similar. For example, on 31st January 2006, Craig of Abergele reported, "I saw that ghost ship. It looked like a galleon but straight away in like 7 seconds it disappeared into thin air" while, on 25th September that year, David Patterson of Rhyl said, "it looked like an old galleon ... (but) disappeared after a few seconds." Local tradition holds that the apparition is twelfth century *Gwennan Gorn*, a ship associated with a fascinating and amazing legend of pre–Columbian discovery that may or may not be true.

In 1170, Madoc, Prince of Snowdon in Wales, and his step-brother Rhiryd, Lord of Clochran in Ireland, rendezvoused at sea and set out westward into the unknown. Both Madoc's *Gwennan Gorn* and Riryd's *Pedr Sant* are said to have been "built of sturdy oak from ancient forest trees, with nails of stag's horn to protect the craft from the fatal attraction of magnetic islands." Some years later, Madoc returned, told of the discovery of a new land, recruited colonists, fitted out an expedition of ten ships, and returned to North America. Legend says the settlers gradually moved up the Alabama and Coosa Rivers to the Chattanooga area, building forts along the way. The one at DeSoto Falls, Alabama, is said to be almost identical in setting, layout, and method of construction to Dolwyddelan Castle in Wales.

Three centuries on, the Spanish reported with surprise that some of the natives were already worshipping the Christian Cross when they arrived. Later, explorers discovered an unusual tribe living on the banks of the Missouri. They were blue-eyed with fair skin; their hair was blonde, red or brown; and instead of canoes they fished from boats made like the coracles of Wales. Calling themselves Mandans, their language contained so many Welsh words that, in 1669, the Rev. Morgan Jones claimed he was able to preach the Gospel in Welsh to them. In a letter dated 1810, Governor John Seiver of Tennessee reported a conversation he had with Oconostota, ruling chief of the Cherokee Nation, who said his grandfather told him: "White people formerly inhabited the country ... called Welsh, they had crossed the Great Water and landed first near the mouth of the Alabama River."

Aberration: In celestial navigation, the apparent displacement of a heavenly body due to the observer's motion.

ABFS: Amphibious bulk fuel system.

Able: Skilled or proficient (abbreviation of capable).

Able Seaman: In 1653, the Royal Navy recognized the value of seamen who had at least two years of sea service and were "able to hand, reef, and steer" by giving them special status and 25 percent higher pay. The shorter title "AB" is widely believed to be an abbreviation of "able-bodied," but in actuality is the first two letters of "able." The USN originally applied the same criteria to the appointment of ABs, but no longer awards the rating which is still used in the British Merchant Navy, the United States Merchant Marine, and the Royal Navy (where an able seaman ranks above ordinary seaman and below leading seaman and is thus the second lowest rate).

Formerly, a ship's master had absolute discretion to rate or disrate ABs irrespective of ability, but nowadays a candidate needs to be certificated. In 1838, the United States Coast Guard introduced a program to ensure that each American mariner had the "experience, training, physical ability, and character to serve safely and competently aboard vessels."

This evolved until there are now one international and three domestic credentials issued by the USCG, including the certification of AB's as meeting the requirements of the International Convention on Standards of Training, Certification, and Watchkeeping for Seafarers, which is followed by most of the world's merchant shipping. Certificated ABs in the British

Merchant Navy and United States Merchant Marine are the mainstays of a modern merchantman's deck crew. To qualify, a person must have at least three years of relevant sea service, plus:

> The ability to splice wire or fiber line, to work aloft and over the side of the ship, to operate the deck machinery such as windlass or winches, to paint and mix paint, to know the principles of cargo stowage, to be a good wheelsman and competent lookout, to overhaul and install any running or standing rigging on the ship, and be able to sew, repair and mend canvas.

An AB must also be competent to handle a lifeboat under oars or sail, know its safety equipment, and be capable of assuming the duties of coxswain in charge. In contrast to these stringent merchant requirements — and reflecting the 21st century relaxation of long-established standards — the Royal Navy now gives recruits the AB rating as soon as they have completed basic training.

ABM: Anti-ballistic missile.

Aboard: [1] In or on a vessel. [2] Nearby or close to (e.g., "bring the lighter aboard for loading").

Abort: To abandon or cancel a mission.

About: Usually preceded by "come." [1] To turn onto a new course or tack. [2] To move across the wind in relation to the bow.

Above-board: Fair, open, and without concealment. There are two possible nautical derivations: [1] Early trading ships would hide illegal cargo below the ship's deck. Legal goods could be placed in plain view, that is above the boards of the deck. [2] When hoping to get close to a potential victim without arousing suspicion, the majority of a heavily-armed pirate crew would crouch behind the bulwark while a few unarmed ruffians remained on deck pretending to be friendly merchant mariners. The forthright appearance of the ones who were, literally, above the boards may have given the term its onshore meaning.

Abox: Said of square-rig yards that have been laid square to the foremast in order to heave-to.

Abreast: Side-by-side, abeam.

Abroad: A flag was formerly said to be abroad when hoisted. The term is obsolete.

ABS: American Bureau of Shipping.

Absent without leave: Unauthorized absence from the place of duty. (Former USN terminology was "absent without official leave," and its acronym was often used verbally and pronounced "a-wol.")

Absentee pennant: Flown to indicate that the captain or embarked flag officer is not on board.

A'burton: Said of casks stowed athwartships in line with the deck beams.

Abyss: That part of the ocean that is deeper than 300 fathoms (550 meters/1800 feet).

Abyssal hills: A tract of small elevations on the floor of the abyss.

Abyssal plain: The flat, deep ocean floor. It is almost featureless because a thick layer of sediment covers the hills and valleys of the ocean basin below it.

AC: [1] Aircraft. [2] Aircraft carrier [not in naval use]. [3] Air Traffic Controller [USN]. [4] Hull classification symbol of a fleet replenishment collier.

ACB: USCG designation of an icebreaker.

Accident boat: A small boat kept swung out for rapid lowering in the event of a person overboard. Also rescue boat.

Accommodation ladder: Portable flight of steps suspended from a ship's side to give access for boat crews or to a wharf. It consists essentially of upper and a lower platforms connected by a ladder. The lower end being raised and lowered by the falls of a davit. Landlubbers frequently but mistakenly call the accommodation ladder the gangway (cf. brow, gangplank).

Account: *See* On the Account.

Accouterments: Equipment other than clothing and weapons.

ACDS: Advanced Combat Direction System.

Ace: A pilot who has shot down numerous enemy aircraft (five in USN, unofficial designation in RN).

Ace high: USN designation of a tropospheric forward-scatter communications system.

Acey-deucey: A board game similar to backgammon, popular in the USN.

ACG: Hull classification symbol of an amphibious Force Flagship.

Acknowledge: Proword confirming a message has been received.

ACLS: Automatic Carrier Landing System.

ACM: Air combat maneuver.

Acockbill: Describes [1] An anchor hanging at the cathead ready to let go. [2] Square-rig yards angled randomly as a sign of mourning. *See also* blue paint, mourning salute, yards apeak.

Acon: A flat-bottomed Mediterranean boat used to carry cargo over shoal water.

Acoustic baffle: Sonar arrays are extremely sensitive to underwater noise and have to be protected from propeller cavitation, wake disturbance, machinery noise, and other sounds generated by the vessel. To this end a sound-attenuating shield or baffle is placed between hull-mounted sonar and the propulsion system (*see* baffle zone).

Acoustic mine: Device which is detonated by sound waves such as those generated by a ship's propellers.

Acoustic speed: The maximum speed at which a submarine can travel without being sensible to conventional sound detection systems.

Acoustic torpedo: A sound-guided torpedo — "passive" versions home in on sounds emanating from the target; "active" versions rely on the reflected sound of their own emissions.

Acoustic warfare: [1] The use of underwater acoustic energy to search for, locate, intercept, record, analyze, and exploit hostile radiated acoustic energy. [2] To mount countermeasures that prevent or impede enemy use of the underwater acoustic spectrum.

Acrostolium: A symbolical ornament on the prows of ancient vessels; precursor of the modern figurehead.

ACS: [1] Air-capable ship. [2] Auxiliary crane ship.

Act of God: Marine insurance term meaning any natural event which could not have been reasonably foreseen.

Acting: Prefix to a grade, rank, rate, or title, indicating that it is temporary and that the incumbent may not be fully-qualified for the post.

Acting Sub-Lieutenant: Appointed by order rather than commissioned, this subordinate officer rank was introduced by the RN in 1860 to replace those of Acting Mate and Passed Midshipman. After completion of qualifying courses they were commissioned as Sub-Lieutenants. Their status was somewhat nebulous until 1894 when Admiralty Order in Council No.41 defined them as being "To all intents and purposes Sub-Lieutenants ... being merely styled 'Acting' until they have passed the final examination for Lieutenant." The title fell into abeyance after the First World War, but in 1955, probably to introduce a closer equivalent to USN Ensign, the Royal and Commonwealth navies re-instated it as a substantive rank, separate from and junior to Sub-Lieutenant. In 1993, the RN abolished the rank in regular service, but it continues in the Royal Naval Reserve and in the Canadian and Australian navies. A similar rank exists in the Pakistani Navy.

Action information center: *See* combat information center.

Action stations!: RN call for the ship's company to go to battle positions (cf. General Quarters).

Active duty: Full-time service as opposed to reserve, retired, or inactive.

Active Endeavor: The mission of NATO's Operation Active Endeavour is to intercept, escort, protect, disrupt and deter criminal activity that may support terrorist activities. Navies from Germany, Greece, Italy, Netherlands, Spain, Turkey, the UK and U.S. patrol the eastern Mediterranean, monitoring thousands of ships against narcotics trafficking, human smuggling, arms and radioactive materials. Attempts to extend the operation into the Black Sea (which serves many insurgent groups as a main smuggling route) have so far been vetoed by Turkey and Russia — the former to avoid diluting the terms of the Montreux Treaty, the latter to keep NATO away from its southern frontier.

Active list: RN document recording officers on active duty.

Active service: RN term for assignment to a combat zone.

Active sonar: Anti-submarine technologies that emit pulses of sound (known as "pings") into the ocean, and then listen for reflections (echoes) in order to paint a snapshot picture of all objects within their range. Cf. passive sonar.

ACV: Air Cushion Vehicle.

AD: Aviation Machinists Mate [USN].

ADAC: Acoustic Data Analysis Center.

Adam's ale: Slang for fresh drinking water, which was a much valued commodity during the long voyages undertaken by sailing ships, during which water in casks was certain to turn putrid.

ADC: [1] Aide-de-Camp. [2] Air Defense Command [U.S.]. [3] Analogue-Digital Converter.

ADCOM: Administrative Command [USN].

Addled: [1] In common language, to be muddled, confused, or rotten. [2] Obsolete, seaman's term for "fresh" water that had gone putrid in the cask. From Old English adela = filth.

Address: Officers up to the rank of lieutenant-commander are properly called "Mister" although, as a matter of conversational politeness or in ignorance, Lt-Cdrs are sometimes addressed as "Commander" by civilians. Captains are addressed as "Captain," and all flag officers as "Admiral." The proper title for the commander of a merchantman is Master, but Captain is often used as a matter of courtesy. Similarly, the commander of even the smallest naval vessel is normally addressed as "Captain" irrespective of rank. Between 1870 and 1914 it was also customary to address the executive officers of RN ships as "Captain." In the RN, a Master at Arms is always addressed as "Master," never as "Chief" or "Sir" irrespective of rank.

ADF: Automatic direction finding.

Adjacent zone: Waters immediately beyond territorial limits over which a nation claims customs enforcement or fishing rights.

Adjustable pitch: Ability to alter the pitch of an aerial or marine propeller to improve efficiency and to increase or decrease speed. Also controllable pitch, and more fully described under variable pitch.

Administration: The management of logistics, repairs, maintenance, training, and other naval activities not directly concerned with strategy or tactics.

Administrative shipping: Support vessels capable of transporting troops and cargo from origin to destination, but that cannot be loaded or unloaded without non-organic personnel and/or equipment (e.g., cargo handling personnel, stevedores, piers, barges, cranes, materials handling equipment, etc.).

Administrative weapons specialist: USN enlisted derogatory slang for a Yeoman or other sailor with purely administrative duties. Not usually used when the sailor in question has a regular warfare or weapons qualification.

Admiral: This term is derived from the Arabic amir-al-bahr meaning commander of the sea. The Genoese dropped bahr (the word for "sea") and combined the first two into amiral, which became Almirante in Spanish and Admiral when taken into English. Today, an admiral is the senior naval officer commanding a fleet or other large unit and holds four-star rank, the equivalent of army general. A supreme naval position, titled Admiral of the Fleet, Fleet Admiral, or Admiral of the Navy, is sometimes held by the senior flag officer of a naval service and is usually symbolic and honorific, having virtually no more authority than any other admiral.

Admiral of the Fleet: This British rank probably originated in the Middle Ages, but the first recorded appointment was in 1690. When the Royal Navy was divided into three squadrons (*see* Admirals in the Royal Navy) the Admiral of the Fleet was supreme commander of the assembled squadrons, each of which was commanded by a full admiral. Until 1827 the head of the Royal Navy was called admiral of the fleet, then the position became First Sea Lord. The rank was placed in abeyance in 1996, but incumbents nonetheless retain the title for life. *See also* fleet admiral.

Admiral of the Navy: This United States Navy rank, generally considered to be six-star equivalent, was created specifically for Admiral George Dewey by Act of Congress in March 1903, with the proviso that it would exist for his lifetime. The award was retroactive to 1st May 1898 when then Commodore Dewey fought the Battle of Manila Bay, commanding a fleet of modern armored cruisers which so far outgunned his opponent's antiquated and decrepit wooden ships that the encounter was more of a slaughter than a battle. Dewey died in 1917 and the rank lapsed accordingly.

***Admiral Popov*:** The first of two extraordinary Russian warships built in the 1870s to the revolutionary circular design of Vice-Admiral A. A. Popov. The 3,533-ton vessel was completely round, armed with two 12-inch (300 mm) guns in a central circular rotating barbette, a design intended to provide a stable firing platform. She was powered by eight engines driving six propellers. Not surprisingly, the ships were unseaworthy and almost unmanageable.

Admirals in the Royal Navy: The first English admiral is believed to have been William de Leyburn, appointed by King Edward I in 1297 with the title Admiral of the Sea of the King of England. The subordinate positions of vice and rear admiral were not introduced until the 16th century; initially as appointments to command the white (van) and blue (rear) squadrons rather than official ranks. By 1743, squadrons had become much larger, so each was divided into three sections and for the next sixty-two years there were rear-admirals, vice-admirals, and admirals in each of three colors (*see* British ensigns). Promotion was based on seniority, and the only way to advance was for a vacancy to be created by promotion, death, or resignation. The nine-step flag rank hierarchy was based on a combination of grade and squadron, running from rear-admiral of the blue as the most junior flag officer, to admiral of the red as the senior:

Rear Squadron	Lead Squadron	Center Squadron
1. Rear-Admiral (blue)	2. Rear-Admiral (white)	3. Rear-Admiral (red)
4. Vice-Admiral (blue)	5. Vice-Admiral (white)	6. Vice Admiral (red)
7. Admiral (blue)	8. Admiral (white)	9. Admiral (red)

Then, as explained by Michael Lewis in The Navy of Britain (London, George Allen & Unwin, 1948), a clerical mistake introduced a tenth grade:

> The man who commanded the whole also commanded the central — and therefore the most important — squadron, the Red.... He was therefore, in practice both Admiral of the Fleet and Admiral of the Red. But since it is always a man's tendency to use the highest title to which he has a right, he almost always called himself by the former name.... The tenth kind of flag officer — Admiral of the Red as distinct from Admiral of the Fleet — was only introduced, as the result of an error, in 1805.

In 1864, the color-coding was abandoned and the number of flag ranks was reduced to the current three, excluding the now dormant Admiral of the Fleet.

Admirals in the United States Navy: Having just overthrown a monarchy, and being imbued with ideals of equality, Congress was initially reluctant to introduce the title of admiral which it felt would create an "aristocracy of the sea" unsuitable for a nascent republic. Until the huge naval expansion of the Civil War there were no flag officers, with captains in command of squadrons being temporarily awarded the courtesy title of commodore.

Permanent commodores (1-star) and rear admirals (2-stars) were introduced in 1862, followed by vice admirals (3-stars) in 1864, and full admirals (4-stars) in 1866. In 1891, however, the two senior ranks were allowed to lapse. Eight years later, the permanent rank of commodore was abolished leaving only rear admirals, who were divided into upper and lower halves, with pay differences, but both wearing two stars.

In 1915, with World War I raging, the commanders-in-chief of the Atlantic, Pacific and Asiatic fleets were awarded the temporary rank of admiral, and their seconds-in-command that of vice admiral. A year later the Chief of Naval Operations was also given temporary admiral rank. However, the Navy Register continued to list these officers in their permanent grade of rear admiral. It was not until July 1941, with World War II looming over the United States, that Congress authorized President Roosevelt to award permanent commissions to three and four star admirals. In April 1943, the rank of commodore (1-star) was re-established for the duration of the War, after which it again lapsed. *See also* Commodore Admiral and table 15.

Admiral's watch: Informal USN term for the second dog watch when the embarked flag officer traditionally visits the bridge to chat with the vessel's commanding officer.

Admiralship: The combination of character traits and professional skills that allows a naval commander to develop successful strategies and tactics.

Admiralty: [1] Formerly, the department of state responsible for the British Royal Navy (*see* Board of Admiralty). [2] The building housing officials of that department. [3] Maritime law.

Admiralty court: A tribunal administering maritime or admiralty law, including matters pertaining to shipping, collision, piracy, disposition of prizes, etc.

Admiralty law: A uniform, supranational, comprehensive body of maritime jurisprudence progressively codified over millennia. *See* laws & conventions of the sea, maritime law and United Nations Convention on the Law of the Sea.

Admiralty Midshipman: Formerly one who, having served his time and passed the lieutenant's examination, was appointed to a ship by the admiralty, in contradistinction to those who were rated by the captain.

Admiralty sweep: A wide, cautious turn, made to come alongside another vessel or a jetty.

Admonitions, Reprimands, and Cautions: These are non-punitive disciplinary actions that highlight minor wrongdoings, the only difference being degree of censure. A reprimand is the more severe and a caution the least. Records of admonitions and reprimands can be filed and later used to justify more serious measures, such as non-judicial punishment, demotion, or dismissal. Cautions, however, are more informal and do not form part of the individual's record. *See also* captain's mast, non-judicial punishment, non-punitive disciplinary action, and Uniform Code of Military Justice.

Adornment: The "gingerbread" woodwork on the stern of old ships.

Adrift: [1] Loose from moorings. [2] Out of place. [3] Late or tardy.

Advance: [1] Distance traveled along the original course from the time the rudder is turned until the vessel is steady on its new course. [2] Increase in rate or rank.

Advection fog: Mist created by the interaction of a horizontal flow of warm moist air with a colder water surface.

Adventure: [1] A hazardous undertaking of uncertain outcome. [2] A long-standing commercial term for a speculative financial enterprise, typically involving goods consigned to a ship's master, to be traded opportunistically wherever the best price could be obtained. Merchants who consigned cargo in this way were known as adventurers (or sometimes venturers).

Advisory: A warning of potential bad weather.

ADZ: Amphibious defense zone.

Adze: An ancient cutting tool that has a thin arched blade set at right angles to the shaft (unlike the blade of an ax which is set in line with the handle). It is used by carpenters, coopers, and shipwrights for shaping rough-hewn timbers. Generally, the user stands astride the work, swinging the adze downward towards the feet, chipping off pieces of wood while moving backward to leave a relatively smooth surface behind. The modern form originated before the 12th century, but similar tools are found in pre-dynastic Egypt and Neolithic man used a flint version.

AE: [1] Aircraft Engineer. [2] Hull classification symbol of a fleet replenishment ammunition ship.

Aegis: A highly automated shipborne combat weapons control system. Modern anti-ship missiles, coordinated to arrive simultaneously on a designated target, can be launched from air, surface, and submarine platforms lying well beyond the horizon. Recognizing that countering this threat demands exceptional firepower, reaction time, and operational availability, the USN developed a system which integrates sensors and weapons to detect and engage multiple (up to 200) airborne targets simultaneously, at heights from wave-top to directly overhead, and at speeds from sub- to supersonic — christening it Aegis after the mythical protective breastplate worn by Greek gods Zeus and Athena. Capable of operation in all weather conditions, resistant to chaff or jamming, Aegis can currently provide area defense for an entire strike group, together with a clear picture for the effective deployment of aircraft. The system is being enhanced to provide theatre-wide protection against ballistic missile attacks by terrorists or rogue states.

AEM: [1] Mechanic [USN]. [2] Air Engineering mechanic [RN].

AEO: Aircraft Engineering Officer [RN].

Aerofoil: A surface designed to produce lift when air passes over it. Aircraft wings and propellers, and helicopter blades are examples. Also Airfoil.

Aerography: USN term for weather forecasting.

AEW: Airborne Early Warning.

AFB: Air Force Base (U.S.).

Affectionate friends: According to an anecdote related by Admiral William Henry Smyth in his 1867 Sailor's Word Book, the former Board of Commissioners of the (Royal) Navy was the only government organization snobbish enough to have a special form of address for "officers who were not of noble families (n)or bore titles" calling them with tongue in cheek "affectionate friends." However, when a distinguished naval captain, himself a knight, closed a letter to the Board with that salutation the Commissioners were offended and ordered him to "discontinue such expression." The captain acknowledged, but ended with "I am, gentlemen, no longer your affectionate friend." Smyth recounts that the practice then ended abruptly.

Affirmative: A proword meaning "yes" or "What you said is correct" (cf. negative).

Affreightment: An expression used to describe a contract in which a shipowner (sometimes known as the "carrier") agrees to carry the goods of a shipper (also called the freighter) on a specified voyage or over a period of time in return for payment of a specific price (sometimes called freight). *See also* charter party.

Afloat: Buoyantly riding on water.

Afloat prepositioning: Refers to the forward deployment — near a potential crisis area, or to support amphibious operations — of merchantmen tactically-loaded with equipment, supplies, and ammunition.

Afore: Obsolete term for before.

Afoul: Entangled.

AFS: Hull classification symbol of a fleet replenishment combat stores ship.

Aft/After: At or towards the back of a vessel. In nautical terminology, aft is an adverb and after is an adjective as in "let us go aft to the after cabin."

After ladder: Stairs leading to a sailing ship's officers' quarters and only used by them.

Afterguard: [1] Sailing warship term for seamen and landsmen assigned to sail-handling on poop and quarterdeck. [2] Term for the owner, captain, or navigator of a yacht. [3] Infrequently used to refer to a merchantman's officers.

Aftermost: Nearest the stern.

Afternoon effect: Reduction in sonar effectiveness caused by the sun warming the sea surface.

Afternoon watch: The work shift beginning at 1200 and ending at 1600 (noon to 4 PM). Also noon watch.

Against the sun: [1] A counter-clockwise horizontal circular motion. [2] Said of rope laid-up left-handed. Cf. with the sun.

A-Gang: USN slang for engineering department personnel responsible for auxiliary equipment such as air-conditioning, water distillation, etc.

Age of Sail: This term could be considered an oxymoron, since ships with sails have existed from pre-history to the present day. However, a Eurocentric view holds that the "great" age of sail began in the mid–15th century — when Europeans began to embark on worldwide voyages — lasting until the mid–19th when iron and steam superseded wood and wind in commercial trade and naval warfare.

Age of tide: The time lapse between a transit of the moon and the resultant tide. Also retard of tide.

Aghulas current: A current that flows through the Mozambique Channel to the Aghulas Bank and then southward.

Agility: Said of the ability of forces to react faster than their enemy can.

Agonic line: A line on the earth's surface connecting points of zero magnetic variation.

Aground: Sitting on the bottom (cf. Ground).

Aguardiente: [1] In Spain and Portugal, an inferior brandy, often supplied to British warships before rum became standard issue. [2] In Spanish America, a coarse, potent liquor, based on sugar cane and sometimes flavored with anise. (Contraction of Spanish agua = water + ardiente = burning.)

AH: [1] Aircraft Handler [RN]. [2] Hull classification symbol of a hospital ship [USN].

Ahead: [1] Forward, in front of the bow. [2] Engine room command to drive the ship forward.

Ahoy!: The standard nautical hail used to gain attention. Believed to be descended from a Viking warcry, it now says essentially "Hello there!"

Ahull: Said of a sailing vessel under bare poles with helm lashed.

Aid to navigation: Any fixed device such as a buoy, light, or sound signal, to assist mariners or warn them of potential hazards such as reefs (cf. navigational aids).

Aide-de-camp: Confidential assistant on the personal staff of an admiral or official.

Aiguille: A small fishing boat formerly used in the Garonne region of France.

Aiguillettes: Ornamental braided loops or cords worn as identification by aides-de-camp, the style designating the rank or status of their principals.

Aileron: Either of two moveable control surfaces on opposite sides of an aircraft wing which move asymmetrically (one going up when the other goes down) to control rolling and banking.

AIMS: American Institute of Merchant Shipping.

Air and naval gunfire liaison company: A group of U.S. naval and marine personnel that controls naval gunfire and close air support from an amphibious beachhead.

Air bedding!: Command to bring bedding on deck for exposure to sun and wind.

Air boss: The watchkeeper responsible for safe operations on an aircraft carrier's flight deck, including the placement of aircraft, operation of catapults and arresting gear, and firefighting when required.

Air bunting!: Command to hoist signal flags for drying in the wind.

Air burst: A nuclear explosion high enough to avoid interaction with ground or water, thereby reducing fallout.

Air capable: Said of a vessel that can launch or land aircraft or provide them with logistic support. May be equipped with cranes for seaplane recovery, or have a landing pad from which helicopters or v/stol aircraft can be launched and recovered without the need for flight deck, catapults or arresting gear.

Air course: A longitudinal ventilation channel running along the side of a wooden sailing vessel to prevent mildew and rot of frames and planking.

Air cover: The use of military aircraft to provide protection against attack by enemy aircraft during ground or naval operations.

Air cushion vessel: *See* Ground-effect vessel.

Air frame: The structural components of an aircraft, excluding its engines.

Air gap: *See* Atlantic air gap.

Air independent propulsion: Before the advent of nuclear power, submariners were eager to free their boats from the need to surface or use snorkels to access the atmospheric oxygen demanded by the internal combustion engines that charged their batteries.

This requirement still exists with small submersibles for littoral operations where nuclear would be too expensive. During the 1930s the German Kriegsmarine experimented with hydrogen peroxide (H_2O_2) as an oxidant, but it proved too unstable creating a safety hazard. Currently, developers are pursuing four generic approaches to augment or replace diesel-electric propulsion systems:

1. Closed-cycle diesel engines with stored liquid oxygen.
2. Closed-cycle steam turbines.
3. Stirling-cycle engines with external combustion.
4. Hydrogen-oxygen fuel cells.

Air traffic controller: Naval air traffic controllers perform duties similar to those of civilian counterparts and play a key role in the effective use of Naval airpower. They may be enlisted/ratings, or limited duty commissioned officers.

Aircraft: Generic term for any vehicle capable of flight, whether heavier or lighter than air.

Aircraft carrier: A major capital ship using aircraft as its offensive weapon. Usually has a hangar for storing aircraft and a flight deck equipped with launching catapults and arresting gear.

Aircrew: The pilot and other personnel manning an aircraft.

Airdale: USN slang for a naval aviator. Also Airedale.

Airhead: Refers to an area in hostile territory seized and held during the assault phase of an airborne operation. *See also* beachhead, bridgehead, lodgement.

Airlock: A pair of doors giving access to a pressurized space. When opened and closed in sequence, they preserve interior pressure.

AIS: Automatic Identification System.

Ait: A small riverine island. Mainly British and pronounced "ate."

AK: [1] Aviation Storekeeper (USN). [2] Hull classification symbol of a commercial cargo ship.

AKA: [1] Also Known As. [2] Former Hull classification symbol of an attack cargo ship.

Alabama: [1] The most famous of Confederate raiders was CSS *Alabama*, one of three warships built secretly in England. She sank, burned, or captured sixty-four Union merchantmen and whalers before being sunk by USS *Kearsage* outside Cherbourg, France, on 19 June 1864. After the Civil War, Britain had to pay $15-million compensation for the damage inflicted by English-built Confederate raiders, the settlement being known as "the *Alabama* claims." [2] USS *Alabama* was the battleship that led the U.S. Fleet into Tokyo Bay to receive the Japanese surrender in 1945. Decommissioned in 1947, she is now the centerpiece of Battleship Memorial Park in Mobile Bay.

Alamottie: Another mariner's name for the stormy petrel.

Alaska current: A counter-clockwise current that follows the coast of Canada to Alaska.

Albany beef: British seamen's slang for sturgeon caught in the Hudson River and served to Royal Navy ships during the American War of Independence. The term caught on and was used until the late 19th century.

Albatrosses: There are many varieties of this member of the petrel family including the mollymawk and wandering albatross. The latter is the largest of all flying birds, with a wingspan of up to five meters (15 feet), weighing up to 11 kilograms (24 lbs), and flying at up to 53 km/h (33 mph). Completely oceanic, they land only to lay eggs and raise chicks. Sailors believe that killing one is an horrendous maritime crime which will bring disaster to the ship committing the murder. This is because seamen have long believed that when a shipmate dies, his body goes to Davy Jones' locker, but his soul is transferred to an albatross whose supernatural nature seems to be confirmed when it is seen to remain aloft without flapping its wings for days on end (using the technique of "dynamic soaring" to exploit and glide over cross-currents of air). Since World War II, the albatross has been losing its fight for existence. Pirate fishermen troll for toothfish, their principal food, with long lines that trap and drown the birds as well as destroying their food supply. (*See also* Mother Carey's chickens.)

Aldis lamp: A hand-held Morse code signaling device used by ships and aircraft.

***Alecton*'s monster:** In November 1861, cruising off the Canary Islands, under sail with her auxiliary propulsion machinery silent, the crew of *Alecton*— a French Navy paddle-wheel "aviso" (courier boat)— sighted a strange creature with a long tail, multiple arms, and eyes the size of dinner plates. Cannon and musket fire missed the animal, but they chased and came close enough to harpoon it, then throw the bight of a rope around its mantle. However, when they tried to haul the creature inboard, the rope cut through its soft tissue and all they recovered was the tail, which *Alecton*'s captain delivered to the French consul at Tenerife who forwarded it to the Academy of Sciences in Paris.

Being unable to identify the specimen, the Academy's scientists ridiculed *Alecton*'s report as either fabricated or the result of mass hallucination. One academician, Arthur Mangin, proclaimed that no man of science should give credence to such stories, because, "...the existence of such a creature would contradict the great laws of harmony and equilibrium which have sovereign rule over living nature...." In fact, it may well have been a giant squid (*see* appendix).

Alee: [1] Downwind. [2] Position of the Helm when turning to leeward.

Aleutian current: An easterly-flowing North Pacific current that divides to form the north-flowing Alaska Current and the south-flowing California Current.

Alfa: NATO phonetic notation for the letter "A." Also Alpha, but *see* table 11.

ALG: Hull classification symbol of an amphibious force flagship.

Algal bloom: *See* red tide.

Alidade: Telescopic-sighted instrument used by navigators to measure angles or bearings.

Alist: Leaning to one side, listing.

Alive: Alert. The command "look alive!" means "get with it" or "pay attention."

All A'taut-O: Obsolete description of rigging that is properly installed, shipshape and taut.

All balls: USN enlisted slang for an all-male crew.

All hands: [1] The entire ship's company, its crew. [2] Boatswain's pipe calling the entire crew either to pay attention to a following announcement, or to muster immediately on deck.

Alleyway: British Merchant Navy term for a ship's interior corridor. The RN uses "alley" and the USN term is "passageway" (*see* Burma road and ships versus houses).

Allision: Term in admiralty law referring to the collision of a moving vessel with a stationary object.

All's well!: Oil-burning navigation lights used to be checked every hour and reported with the cry "lights burning bright and all's well." Today, provided there have been no untoward incidents, the traditional cry at the end of each four-hour watch is still "eight bells and all's well." However, similar or identical calls had long been made ashore by night-watchmen, so attempts to attribute the phrase to a nautical origin are probably inappropriate.

Almagest: A comprehensive treatise on astronomy and geography developed by Ptolemy at the Alexandrian observatory during the second century B.C.E.

Almanac: An annual publication containing lists, charts, tables, and other information for navigators. Some, such as the British HM Nautical Almanac cover only astronomical data for ocean navigation with a sextant. Others, such as the American Reed's Nautical Almanac include additional information about tides, tidal currents, sunrises, sunsets, and other critical items.

ALNAV: USN prefix indicating the following message applies to all naval personnel.

Aloft: [1] Upward on masts or rigging. [2] Above the upper deck (cf. topside). [3] Used in a figurative sense for heaven (he's gone aloft).

Aloft there!: Deck officer's attention-getting hail to men on the yards and in the rigging.

Alongshore: Along or beside the shore (cf. longshore).

Alongside: At or beside something (another ship, a pier, etc.).

Alongside replenishment: Since World War II, the most common method of replenishment at sea. The supply ship holds a steady course, the receiving ship comes alongside and conforms to the other's speed. A messenger line is then used to pull across transfer lines and a telephone link. The operation is risky. With two or three ships running side-by-side, even a slight speed or steering error could be disastrous. *See also* vertical replenishment and astern fuelling.

Aloof: Obsolete sailing ship term for lying at a distance off to windward, now in general use to signify distant or unsympathetic.

Alow: Obsolete Old English term for on or near the deck. The converse of aloft.

Alphabets: *See* phonetic alphabet, signal flags, and tables 8 and 11.

Always afloat: A Charter Party term specifying that the vessel must not enter any berth where she would be aground part of the time.

AM: Former Hull classification symbol of a minesweeper.

Amain: An archaic term meaning with full force, at once, or suddenly.

Ambergris: A secretion in the intestines of sperm whales that is sometimes found floating on the sea or washed up on the shore. This solid, waxy, flammable substance with a sweet, earthy smell is used as a fixative in perfumery. During the Renaissance, it was molded and dried, to be worn as beads or jewelry.

AMC: American Maritime Congress.

American Bureau of Shipping: Founded in 1862 and based in Houston, Texas, with regional offices in London, Singapore, and Dubai, ABS is one of the "big three" in ship classification, the others being Lloyd's Register and Det Norske Veritas.

America's Cup: An ornate silver trophy, presented to the winner of the world's most prestigious sailing competition which circles nine times around the Isle of Wight off the south coast of England. Originally called the Royal Yacht Squadron Cup, it was renamed after the U.S. schooner *America* which won the first contest in 1851. From then until 1983 it remained in American hands; the longest winning streak in sporting history.

Amidships: [1] In general: At, near, or toward the center of a ship relative to its length or breadth (i.e., halfway between bow and stern or halfway between the sides). [2] Specifically: Halfway from the forwardmost point on the waterline to the rearmost point on the waterline. [3] Of the helm: When the rudder blade is aligned precisely with the keel. [4] Formerly: The timbers at the broadest part of the vessel. Also Midships, Amidward.

Amidward: The 18th century term for amidships.

Ammunition: The explosive and propellant components of military projectiles, including bullets, bombs, cartridges, fuses, grenades, mines, missiles, powder, primers, pyrotechnics, rockets, shot, shrapnel, and the like.

Amphibian: [1] A small self-propelled craft, equipped with wheels or air cushions enabling it to move on land as well as water. [2] An aircraft capable of operating from land or water.

Amphibious assault: An operation in which an attack is launched from seaward against a hostile shore. After marines or sea-transported soldiers have secured a beachhead, the attack becomes a conventional military ground operation.

Amphibious demonstration: An amphibious operation conducted as a feint to deceive enemy forces and divert them away from other operations.

Amphibious flagship: During World War II, wanting to remove tactical force commanders and their staffs from overcrowded combat ships, the USN converted a number of merchantmen and naval vessels to serve as floating command posts during large-scale amphibious operations in the Pacific. *See also* command ship and LCC.

Amphibious lift: The carrying capacity of assault shipping assigned to an amphibious operation, expressed in terms of personnel, vehicles, and weight (or measurement) of supplies.

Amphibious operation: A military operation that uses the flexibility and mobility of water transport to launch (preferably surprise) assaults, raids, or demonstrations from ships at sea against hostile or potentially hostile ground forces, or to extract friendly forces from a hostile shore The complexity of such operations demands closely coordinated efforts by specially trained sea, air, and ground forces.

Amphibious raid: A type of amphibious operation involving swift incursion of a hostile objective, followed by scheduled withdrawal after temporary occupation.

Amphibious ready group: A USN formation usually consisting of a helicopter carrier and several amphibious assault ships with embarked marines.

Amphibious ship: A vessel designed to transport supplies, put them on shore, and support forces engaged in amphibious operations. Capable of being loaded or unloaded by naval personnel without external equipment or assistance. May have a floodable well deck.

Amphibious transport dock: A ship with embarked landing craft, amphibious vehicles, and helicopters to land troops, equipment, and supplies.

Amphibious warfare: The use of naval forces to project military power onto a hostile shore, requiring the coordination of aviation, firepower, transport, and logistics.

Amphibious withdrawal: The seaward extraction of friendly forces from a hostile or potentially hostile shore. This is the most complex of all military maneuvers.

Amphibiousness: The ability to operate on land or water.

Amphitrite: This Greek goddess, who was one of the Oceanides, personifies the sea, of which she is queen. She is usually depicted in a seashell chariot drawn by marine animals, and Homer calls her "She who beats the billows against the rocks, and has the creatures of the deep in her care." According to legend, she was abducted by dolphins and carried to Poseidon who married her. She is an important figure in the "crossing-the-line" ceremony. Amphitrite is not to be confused with Aphrodite, who is not a sea-goddess despite the legend of her origin.

AMR: Auxiliary Machinery Room.

AMVER: Automated Mutual-Assistance Vessel Rescue System.

Analemma: The figure eight scale on terrestrial globes showing the declination of the sun and time equation on a daily basis.

Anan: An ancient nautical response, no longer in use, signifying "I did not understand your order, sir."

Anaumachion: The ancient Greek punishment of infamy, for the crime of refusing to serve in the fleet.

Anchor: [1] A device fastened to a chain or line, consisting either of a hook which embeds itself in the sea floor or of a heavy weight to hold the ship in place. The concept is said to have been developed in China for Emperor Yu (2205–2197 B.C.). [2] To place such a device. (From the Anglo-Saxon ancor.)

Anchor ball: A black ball or circle displayed in the forepart of a ship to indicate it is at anchor.

Anchor bed: Permanent chocks which hold a stored anchor in place.

Anchor bell: A warning bell rung by anchored ships during poor visibility.

Anchor bend: A knot used to fasten an anchor to its cable.

Anchor buoy: A small float attached to the anchor by light line to indicate its position.

Anchor cable: A cable attached to an anchor for raising and lowering it. It is generally conceded that a vessel should never ride to a shorter scope of cable than six times the depth of water. That is to say, if anchored in ten fathoms of water she should not have out less than sixty fathoms of cable for ordinary security. *See also* anchor chain.

Anchor chain: A chain attached to an anchor for raising and lowering it. The links act as weights which help keep the ship in position, and also hold the anchor close to the ground so that it digs in better than with a cable. RN terminology is anchor cable, or chain cable.

Anchor ice: Ice forming on and attached to the sea floor.

Anchor lights: *See* riding lights.

Anchor watch: [1] A detail of seamen in overnight readiness for emergency when the ship is moored or at anchor. [2] Crew member(s) detailed to watch the anchor chain and ensure the anchor is not dragging. Often an officer on the bridge takes crossbearings for the same purpose.

Anchorage: A coastal area with secure holding for anchors.

Anchoromachus: A barge-like boat of the middle ages, used for transporting anchors and naval stores.

Anchor's afoul!: Report that the anchor cable is caught around the fluke, or that another object is caught around the anchor.

Anchor's apeak!: Report that the anchor is under the hawse.

Anchor's atrip!: Report that the anchor has broken out of the ground.

Anchor's aweigh!: [1] Report that the anchor has been hoisted clear of the bottom, at which point the vessel is underway, but does not necessarily have way on. [2] Unofficial anthem of the USN (*see* March Music).

Anchor's clear!: Report that the anchor is not foul or otherwise obstructed.

Anchor's in sight!: Report that the anchor is visible coming out of the water. Immediately followed by a report that the anchor is either clear or fouled.

AND: Anti-torpedo net device.

Anderson turn: *See* Person Overboard.

Andrew Millar: A notorious Crimp (person who entrapped seamen to be pressed into naval service, usually offering to advance money, then plying the victim with liquor, persuading him to sign articles while intoxicated, and delivering him on board stripped of all valuables). So many sailors came into the service through his efforts that it seemed as though he personally owned it. To this day, Royal Navy personnel informally call their service "The Andrew."

Anemometer: An instrument for measuring wind speed.

Aneroid: A mechanical barometer.

Angary: The right under International Law of a belligerent to destroy, seize, force into service, or otherwise use the vessels or goods of neutral nations, subject to compensation of the owners.

Angle bar: An angled metal bar forming the gutter or waterway leading to the scuppers.

Angle of attack: [1] The angle between the sail and the apparent wind direction. [2] The angle between the rudder or centerline and the water flow. [3] The difference between where an aircraft's wing is pointed and the direction of the air flowing over it.

Angle of heel: The degree of list. An early indicator of the need to reef the sails.

Angle of repose: The greatest degree to which a cargo can tilt without shifting.

Angled deck: Developed by Captain (later Rear Admiral) D. R. F. Campbell RN, and adopted by the USN, the angled flight deck has enormous operational advantages. It allows aircraft to be launched while others are landing, and it clears the forward section of the flight deck for use as an aircraft park. It also allows aircraft missing the arrester wires to take off and fly around for another try — previously they would either crash into a barrier, or miss it to destroy parked aircraft or injure flight deck personnel.

Angles and dangles: USN submariner slang for placing the boat in extreme up/down attitudes shortly after leaving port to see if anything breaks loose. Loose objects can then be stowed or tightened to avoid unwanted noise while on patrol.

ANGLICO: Air & Naval Gunfire Liaison Company.

Anglo-German Naval Agreement: In June 1935, without consulting the other signatories of the Treaty of Versailles, Britain attempted to appease Hitler by negotiating a bilateral agreement giving Germany the right to build a navy beyond the limits of the Treaty. The total tonnage of the Kriegsmarine (fighting navy) was allowed to increase to 35 percent of that of the Royal Navy, and remain permanently at that level. More significantly, Britain agreed that Germany could build a U-boat fleet equal to the total submarine tonnage of the Commonwealth — a decision it would regret (*see* Battle of the Atlantic).

Annunciator: A device [1] Indicating which of several electric circuits is active. [2] On a ship's bridge for signaling orders to the engine room. [3] To alert gun crews that target designations are forthcoming.

Answer: To respond. Said of a vessel when it reacts to movement of helm and rudder.

Answering pennant: A pennant with red-white-red-white-red vertical stripes. When at the dip it signifies a message has been received. When hoisted to the truck it acknowledges the message has been understood.

Antarctic: The area lying south of an imaginary line drawn along the northern limit of the South Frigid Zone (approximately latitude 66°33'S).

Anti-aircraft artillery: weapons capable of rapid traversing and firing at high angles of elevation against aircraft. Sometimes called Triple-A or abbreviated to AAA.

Anticyclone: An intense wind system rotating outward from an area of high barometric pressure; turning clockwise in the northern hemisphere and counter-clockwise in the southern (cf. cyclone).

Anti-flash gear: RN term for clothing with anti-flash and splinter-resistant properties for wear in combat. The USN term is "battle dress."

Antifoulant: Preparation painted on a hull to discourage barnacles, teredo worms and other undesirable growths.

Antigallicans: Additional backstays rigged temporarily on square-rigged merchantmen when running before the trade winds. They were unnecessary on warships, which were more heavily stayed in the first place.

Antilles current: This flow originates in the West Indies and joins the Florida Current to form the Gulf Stream.

Antipodean day: The twenty-four hours gained when eastbound or lost when westbound on crossing the International Date Line, which follows (approximately) the meridian of 180°.

Antirecovery device: A mechanism incorporated into a mine or missile which causes it to detonate if disturbed.

Antisubmarine air support: Flight operations to protect a specific force or convoy against hostile underwater forces. Close air support is normally provided within 80 nautical miles of the protected force. Distant air support is further from, but still directly related to, the specific force.

Antisubmarine barrier: A line of static devices or

mobile units formed to detect, deny passage to, or destroy, hostile underwater forces.

Antisubmarine rocket: A self-propelled, surface-launched, nuclear depth charge or homing torpedo (*see* ASROC).

Antisubmarine screen: An arrangement of ships and/or aircraft for the protection of a force or unit against underwater attack.

Antisubmarine torpedo: A torpedo with conventional or nuclear warhead capable of being launched from air, surface, or subsurface and guided by wire and/or passive or active acoustics.

Antisubmarine warfare (ASW): The use against hostile submarines of weaponry, listening and tracking devices, and other techniques.

Antisweep mine: A small explosive device designed to make minesweeping more difficult. When the sweep wire makes contact the mine slides along it until it strikes and is detonated by the sweep.

Anti-torpedo net device: A net suspended from booms on British merchantmen during World War II. It was intended to catch or explode torpedoes at a safe distance from the hull (the author can confirm that it worked, if not this book might never have been produced!). Usually known as AND Gear.

Any port in a storm: This metaphor, which equates to "beggars can't be choosers," obviously has a nautical origin.

Anzio landing: The Allied amphibious assault on Anzio, Italy in 1944 was code-named Shingle. The invasion force arrived without detection and landed with virtually no opposition. However, as was demonstrated at Calamita Bay in 1854 and Gallipoli (Suvla Bay) in 1915, a strange lethargy sometimes comes over the commanders of unopposed landings. Only two understrength and exhausted German divisions were nearby and the road to Rome lay open, but U.S. generals Clark and Lucas decided to wait for heavy weapons, tanks, supplies, and reserve troops to land. Churchill was exasperated, saying "I thought we were hurling a wildcat onto the shore, but all we got was a stranded whale!" By the fourth day, the panicked Germans had rushed reinforcements from northern Italy, southern France, Yugoslavia, and Germany itself. Although aware of this, Lucas was still intent on building up his own force. When Supreme Allied Commander, British General Alexander, urged him to advance, he replied "I will not be stampeded." It was not until the ninth day that he launched his offensive, and by then it was far too late. Counter-attacks drove the Anglo-Americans back to their beachhead where, for three months, they suffered the privations of trench warfare, under continuous observation, swept by gunfire, and pummeled by aerial bombardment.

AO: [1] Hull classification symbol of a fleet oiler. [2] Aviation Ordnanceman (USN).

AOA: Amphibious objective area.

AOL: Absent over leave. USN term now preferred to AWOL.

AP: [1] Armor piercing. [2] Anti-personnel. [3] Admiralty Pattern [RN].

APA: [1] Army pre-positioned afloat. [2] Former Hull classification symbol of an attack transport.

APD: Former hull classification symbol of 32 destroyers converted for amphibious raiding operations during World War II.

Apeak: [1] Straight up-and-down, as of an anchor cable or chain. [2] At the masthead.

APF: Afloat pre-positioning force.

Aphrodite: This goddess of erotic love (who is not to be confused with Poseidon's wife Amphitrite). was a nymphomaniac who had affairs with virtually every male god in the Greek pantheon, as well as most of the great heroes, and a large number of ordinary mortals. There are conflicting myths about her genesis. Homer says she was the daughter of the chief Greek god Zeus and an oceanide named Dione; but Hesiod tells us she sprang from frothy bubbles which gathered about the severed genitals of Uranus as they floated on the sea towards the Island of Cyprus (her name supports Hesiod's version, because aphros means sea foam in Greek).

APO: Afloat pre-positioning operations.

Apogee: The point in a missile trajectory or satellite orbit that is furthest from the earth (cf. Perigee).

Aport: To the left.

Apostles: A pair of large bollards found on the main deck of square-rigged sailing vessels.

Apparel: This formal word for costume, together with the modern charter-party term apparel and tackle, encompassing a ship's appurtenances (sails, rigging, anchors, and the like) goes back to the seventh century, at which time items of equipment were collectively apparel after the French appareil meaning apparatus or machinery.

Apparent wind: Refers to Wind speed and direction as they appear to a shipborne observer, being a vector of the true wind and the motion of the ship.

Apple stern: A rounded stern sometimes found on Dutch sailing vessels.

Apple-pie order: Neat and precise. There are numerous theories as to the origin of this phrase, two of the most likely being cap-à-pie from the French for head-to-toe (describing a knight in perfect armor) or nappe pliée, also French (describing well-folded linen).

Appointment: In military or governmental service, refers to the designation or assignment of a person to perform a duty, or hold an office, station, or position.

Appurtenances: Under Admiralty Law, all equipment and tackle belonging to and essential to the use of a vessel for its intended purpose. The marine insurance term is apparel.

Apron: [1] A strengthening timber between the lower part of the stem and the foremost part of the keel in a wooden vessel. [2] A gentle, smooth slope on a sea floor, usually at the base of a steeper slope. [3] A sloping underwater extension of an iceberg.

[4] Part of a wharf extending on piles beyond the land-fill. [5] A World War I line of tethered barrage balloons.

APS: Afloat pre-positioning ship.

Aqualung: An underwater breathing device, invented by Captain Jacques Cousteau and French engineer Emile Gagnon in 1943 to enable divers to operate independently of surface support. This was one of the earliest examples of scuba, which has since been considerably improved to allow dives of longer duration and greater depth. Also hyphenated (Aqua-lung) and two words (Aqua Lung).

Aquatic: [1] Pertaining to water. [2] Growing in water (e.g., aquatic plants or mosquito larvae). [3] Living or swimming in water (aquatic mammals or reptiles). [4] Frequenting the margins of waters (aquatic birds). [5] Taking place in or on water (aquatic sports).

AR: Hull classification symbol of a repair ship.

Arbalest: [1] Stone-throwing naval artillery of the classical era. [2] A medieval missile launcher designed on the principle of the crossbow. Also arbalest.

Arch of steel: The tradition of brother officers forming two lines and raising swords to create an archway at a shipmate's nuptials is said to symbolize their commitment to protect the couple throughout their married life. The weapons are presented with cutting edges upward in the guard position, facing away from the newly-weds as they walk underneath. Although not traditional, non-commissioned personnel sometimes form such an arch with bayonets or cutlasses.

Archipelagic sea lanes passage: The right of continuous and expeditious transit through and over archipelagic waters via routes normally used for navigation and overflight.

Archipelago: A group of related islands forming a geographical entity.

ARCS: Admiralty Raster Chart Service.

Arctic: The area north of the arctic circle.

Arctic circle: An imaginary line drawn along the southern limit of the North Frigid Zone (approximately latitude 66°33'N).

Arctic current: Another name for the West Greenland Current.

Arctic sea smoke: *See* "steam fog."

Ardent: Obsolete term describing a sailing vessel whose head tends to come into the wind when close-hauled.

ARG: Amphibious Ready Group.

Argo: [1] An international oceanographic project designed to observe the effect of climate change on the world's oceans in real time. Three thousand submarine robots called Argo floats, launched in 2007, drift along at 1,000 meters, rising to beam data to satellites and on to control centers in France and the U.S. [2] In Greek mythology, *Argo* was the name of the ship Jason and the Argonauts used to find the Golden Fleece.

Argosy: Poetical name for a large merchantman, especially one with rich cargo. Originally ragusy after Ragusa (now Dubrovnik) a wealthy maritime city

state from the 14th to 18th centuries. Not in nautical use.

***Arizona* Memorial:** This Pearl Harbor relic commemorates the site where World War II began for the United States and is the final resting place for 1,777 of USS *Arizona*'s crew killed during the surprise Japanese attack on December 7, 1941. Article 1282 of Navy Regulations directs all persons on deck between sunrise and sunset to come to attention and render hand salutes when passing the semi-submerged battleship. In fact most USN and USCG warships and many foreign ones go beyond individual honors and man the rails as they pass. Although *Arizona* is not a commissioned vessel of war she has special dispensation to fly the national ensign on a staff attached to the severed remains of her mainmast.

Arm: [1] To equip with weapons. [2] To prepare a weapon for use. [3] The area between crown and fluke of an anchor. [4] The upright member of a davit. [5] To apply soap or tallow to a sounding lead to pick up a bottom sample. [6] A deep and narrow sea inlet.

Arm badges: There are specific rules concerning on which sleeve rate and rating badges are to be worn. [1] The Royal Navy introduced substantive petty officer rate badges to be worn on the left sleeve In 1827, then added non-substantive specialty rating (trade) badges to be worn on the right sleeve in 1860. [2] The U.S. Navy changed the positioning of rate badges several times:

- Regulations of February 1841 introduced the petty officer's badge (known familiarly as the crow). Boatswain's Mates, Gunner's Mates, Carpenter's Mates, Ship's Stewards, and Ship's Cooks, were to wear an eagle and anchor on the right sleeve. Quartermasters, Quartergunners, Captains of Fore-Castle, Corporals and Captains of the Hold were to wear the same device on the left.

- Regulations of December 1866 specified that petty officers of the starboard watch should wear their rate badges on the right sleeve, while those of the port watch should wear them on the left. At this time specialty marks were added to the enlisted men's uniform, consisting of the tools or instruments used in performing specific duties.

- Regulations of January 1913 cancelled the identification by watch and ordered petty officers of the seaman branch to wear their rate badges on the right, all other petty officers on the left.

- In April 1949 right arm rates were disestablished by the USN.

Armada: The Latin armata (fighting force) — from which is also derived the English term army — is the source of this Spanish term for the national navy or a large fleet.

Armador: A Spanish privateer.

Armament: [1] The weapons or weapon systems with which a warship or other military unit is equipped. [2] The military strength of a nation. [3] Sailor slang for the genitals.

Armed forces: The military forces of a nation. Its naval, air, and land services.

Armed Guard: Naval gun crews assigned to protect U.S. merchant vessels in time of war (cf. DEMS).

Armed to the teeth: This descriptive metaphor probably originated with naval or piratical boarding parties who clamped weapons between their teeth to leave both hands free for gripping enemy rigging or bulwarks.

Armor: Protective material for ships, aircraft, vehicles, or personnel.

Armor belt: A strip of lightly-armored compartments girdling a ship's hull just above and below the waterline. When struck by a torpedo, the outer armor detonates the device before it penetrates the inner plating, thereby minimizing damage. Also known as side protection or torpedo belt.

Armored cruiser: Former USN designation of a battlecruiser.

Armorer: [1] The Petty officer responsible for the upkeep and issue of a vessel's small arms. [2] A manufacturer or repairer of weapons.

Armory: [1] Place where weapons are stored, an arsenal. [2] Place where weapons are manufactured.

Arms: [1] The heraldic symbols of a family, state, etc. [2] weapons considered collectively. *See* pole arms, side arms, small arms, stand of arms.

Arms control: *See* Anglo-German Naval Agreement, Versailles Treaty, and Washington Naval Agreement.

Armstrong: [1] Merchant mariner slang, referring to a ship without mechanical aids, forcing the crew to use their strong arms to work it. Also handraulic. [2] A term peculiar to air support radar indicating both the command and the response for arming and fusing circuit activation.

Array: Two or more components feeding a common system (e.g., hydrophones for sonar, antennae for radar).

Arresting gear: A system of cables running across the flight deck of an aircraft carrier; attached to a below deck complex of pulleys, blocks, and hydraulics designed to engage the tailhook of a landing aircraft, apply graduated resistance, and bring it smoothly to rest (also arrester gear). There are four arresting wires (cross deck pendants) and, if it's done right, the point of the tailhook lands in the middle of them — the ideal is a "three-wire landing." The failure of an arresting wire or its attached fittings could produce a catastrophic accident, involving loss of a multi-million dollar aircraft, high risk of death or severe injury to pilot and crew, and endangerment of sailors on the flight deck. *See also* deck landing modes.

Arrêt de Prince: *See* restraint of princes.

Arrive: This word began as a nautical term meaning to make landfall at one's destination. It is derived from the French à rive meaning "to the shore."

Arse: [1] The area at the choke end of a block through which the fall emerges. [2] The human buttocks or, more crudely, the anus.

Arsenal: A storehouse for munitions. Originally a nautical term referring to the docks and wharves of a seaport. From the Italian arsenale = wharf.

Articles: [1] The employment contract between a merchantman's master and its crew, specifying rates of pay, hours of work, scale of rations, etc. [2] Formerly, an agreement between members of a pirate ships' company, outlining the terms and conditions of service, including the election or deposition of officers, rules for handling the ship, terms of engagement in combat, division of booty, compensation for injuries, punishment of crimes, and the like. Piratical articles were almost invariably far more democratic than would have been found in contemporary civil or military society. [3] Articles of War.

Articles of War: In 1653, the British Admiralty issued a disciplinary code entitled Articles of War, intended to standardize shipboard punishment, which had previously been largely at the discretion of individual captains. These were incorporated in the Naval Discipline Act of 1661, and amended by acts of Parliament in 1749 and 1757. Thirty-five articles defined what constituted a crime on naval vessels, and prescribed the appropriate punishment, which was death in about one-third of the cases. They fall into seven principal categories, covering a wide range of activities (not all of which are listed):

1. Offenses against God and religion (blasphemy, observance of faith).

2. Offenses against Crown or Government (arson, desertion, disobedience, espionage, mutiny, treason).

3. Offenses against humanity (fighting, murder, quarrelling, sodomy, theft).

4. Conditions of service (treatment of prisoners and prizes, carriage of merchandise, complaints about victuals, waste of ammunition).

5. Failure of responsibility (errors, incompetence, infractions of duty).

6. Actions in combat (cowardice, lack of initiative, indecision).

7. A "catch-all" clause, known colloquially as "The Captain's Cloak," gave considerable scope to local discretion, saying:

> All other crimes not capital committed by any person or persons in the fleet, which are not mentioned in this act, or for which no punishment is hereby directed to be inflicted, shall be punished by the laws and customs in such cases used at sea.

The Articles were treated with the gravity of Holy Writ, being read publicly at the commissioning of new warships, and to the entire ship's company at timely intervals, usually by the captain when church was rigged on a Sunday. They were amended many times, and remained in effect after the consolidation of Britain's armed forces in 1971. In 2004 they were changed to reflect European Union human rights requirements, and in 2005 they were consolidated under the Army, Air Force and Naval Discipline (Continuation) Order. Comparable regulations for the United

States Navy, called Articles for the Government of the Navy, were superseded by the Uniform Code of Military Justice in 1951.

Artificer: The generic naval rate for a skilled mechanic, engineering technician, artisan, or other craftsperson. Many specialties include air engineering, carpentry, marine engineering, ordnance, radio and radar, etc.

Artillery: This is a collective term for heavy projectile-firing weaponry of all kinds, including over the ages arbalests, ballistas, catapults, onagers, smoothbore cannon, rifled guns, howitzers, and missile-launchers. It excludes personal missile weapons such as bow, javelin, pistol, rifle, and sling; also intermediate crew-portable weapons such as the Roman arrow-firing scorpione and the modern heavy machine-gun.

AS: Hull classification symbol of an aviation ship.

As the crow flies: When visibility became too bad to see the shore, it is said that Norse navigators would release one of the birds from the crow's nest. Like Noah's dove it invariably headed straight for the nearest land, giving them a bearing to follow. The term entered common usage as referring to the fastest or most direct route between two places.

As you were!: The order given to revoke a preceding drill command or to resume the position held before moving.

ASAP: As soon as possible.

Ascending mine: A submerged floating mine that rises or cuts its cable, based on elapsed time or when it detects a potential target.

Asdic: British World War I submarine detection device, using a trainable sound transmitter and receiver to calculate the range and bearing of a target. The first such device and forerunner of sonar, it was developed by and named after the initials of Allied Submarine Detection Investigation Committee.

Asea: At sea.

Ashcan: USN slang for a depth charge.

Ashore: [1] Of a ship = aground. [2] Of a seaman = on leave or liberty. [3] In general = on land.

ASL: Archipelagic sea lane.

ASM: [1] Air to Surface Missile. [2] Hull classification symbol of an assault ship, multi-purpose.

Aspect ratio: [1] The depth of a rudder relative to its fore-and-aft length. [2] The height of a ship's hull relative to its beam. [3] The length of the luff of a sail relative to the length of its foot. [4] The ratio of the span of an aerofoil to its mean chord.

ASROC: USN abbreviation of **A**nti-**S**ubmarine **Roc**ket referring to an all-weather anti-submarine missile system, developed in the 1950s for deployment on surface ships, mostly cruisers and destroyers.

Assault area: The area in amphibious operations that embraces transport and landing ship areas, lines of departure, boat lanes, landing beaches, and fire support areas.

Assault craft: Vessels or amphibious vehicles employed principally for landing troops and equipment during the assault phase of amphibious operations.

Assault group: Sub-division of an attack force, consisting of naval units designed to protect, transport, place on shore, and support a landing force.

Assault phase: [1] In a seaborne operation; the period between landing the amphibious task force and consolidation of an initial beachhead. [2] In an airborne operation; the period between air delivery of the assault echelon and consolidation of an initial airhead.

Assets: [1] In naval and military terminology; All the personnel, weapons, equipment, devices, and capabilities available to a commander. [2] In espionage; Controlled spies working in enemy territory. [3] In accounting; Anything on a company's books considered as having a positive monetary value. [4] In bankruptcy law; The property owned by a person and available to settle debts. [5] In general; Useful or valuable qualities, persons, or things.

Astern: [1] Behind the vessel. [2] To move backward (go astern).

Astern all!: The shout of a harpooner telling the boat's crew to backwater when a whale is struck.

Astern refueling: The transfer of fuel at sea during which the receiving ship keeps station astern of the delivering ship. *See* underway replenishment, replenishment at sea.

Astrolabe: A Medieval navigation instrument used to determine a ship's latitude from the position of heavenly bodies. A primitive form is said to have been invented as early as the second century BCE by the Greek astronomer Hipparchus, but it was improved considerably by Islamic navigators before reaching European mariners in the 14th century. It consists of a rotating arm attached to the centre of a metal circle divided into 360 degrees like a protractor. An attached framework, with spikes representing fixed stars, rotates over a plate engraved with a grid showing coordinates for geographic latitude. When zero on the scale is aligned with the horizon and the arm is pointed at a star or other celestial body, the elevation of that object can be read off the scale. After adjusting the instrument for time of day, the position of the star can be read off the grid. Conversely, the instrument can be adjusted to the measured position and time read off the grid. Accuracy was limited by the dimensions and tolerances of the instrument, and by the fact that its measurements were relative to the scale rather than the horizon. These shortcomings caused the astrolabe to be superseded by the Jackstaff in the 16th century and by the sextant during the 1700s.

ASW: [1] Anti-submarine Warfare. [2] Average surface wind.

ASW screen: Ships and aircraft patrolling ahead of a main force to protect it against underwater attack.

AT: Aviation Electronics Technician [USN].

At ease!: USN command for those standing at attention to assume a more relaxed but still formal posture. (The equivalent British command is "stand at ease!")

At loggerheads: To quarrel or be at strife with someone. There are two credible explanations of the origin of this term. [1] In the 15th and 16th centuries, a loggerhead was a big long-handled ladle used to pour boiling liquids onto a grappled enemy. When both sides were doing this, they were literally at logger-heads. [2] Later, the loggerhead was a heavy iron ball mounted on an iron shaft, used to heat pitch for caulking. Being readily available on deck, a couple of them could be seized as weapons in disputes between seamen, who thus found themselves at loggerheads.

At rest!: USN command to adopt an informal stance. Posture is relaxed, right foot remains in place, but body movement and quiet talking are permitted. (The equivalent RN command is "stand easy!")

At sea: [1] Marine insurance term indicating a ship is free from its moorings and ready to sail. [2] Away from port. [3] In common speech, confused.

Ataut: [1] Said of rigging that is in place and tightly drawn without give or slack. [2] Said of a vessel that is shipshape. From the ancient phrase "all ataut-o."

ATB: All the best [salutation].

ATC: Air Traffic Control.

Ategar: A hand-thrown dart used in Saxon naval combat. From the Saxon aeton = fling + gar = weapon.

ATG: Amphibious task group.

Athwartships: [1] At right angles to the centerline of a vessel. [2] Said of a cocked hat with its points facing the wearer's sides.

Atlantic (battle): The Battle of the Atlantic lasted throughout the European phase of World War II, from the fall of 1939 to the spring of 1945. There were a few surface actions, but it was essentially a contest between Allied antisubmarine forces and German U-boats attempting to sink the ships on which Britain's survival and the eventual liberation of Nazi occupied Europe depended. After the fall of France, advance bases on the Atlantic coast allowed the U-boats to penetrate deeper into the Atlantic air gap and mount highly effective night attacks by surfaced wolfpacks. A series of convoy battles in March 1943 turned the tide, but the U-boats were only contained and were still at sea when the war ended. They had sunk 2,753 merchantmen totalling 14.6 million gross tons, plus about 90 warships, but 733 submarines — about two-thirds of the total — had been destroyed.

Atlantic air gap: That area too distant from North America, Iceland, or Great Britain to be covered by air support during the Battle of the Atlantic (1939–1945). There, German U-boats enjoyed freedom of surface movement and assembled in extremely large wolf-packs that overwhelmed convoy escorts. Despite desperate pleas from the Admiralty, the Royal Air Force consistently refused to divert long range aviation from strategic bombing to convoy protection. Shipping losses in the gap, which had been heavy at all times, became cripplingly so during the winter of 1942–43,

leading the RAF to finally provide suitable aircraft. More importantly, escort carriers began to be deployed in hunter-killer groups and, by 1944, virtually every convoy enjoyed air cover.

Atmosphere: [1] The envelope of air surrounding the globe. [2] A unit of pressure equal to 76 centimeters (29.9 inches) of mercury, or 1033.2 grams/sq. centimeter (2116.3 pounds/sq. foot). (Cf. hydrosphere, lithosphere.)

Atoll: A horseshoe-shaped or circular coral reef encircling a lagoon.

Atrip: Said of [1] A sail, hoisted to the cap, sheeted home, and ready to be trimmed. [2] A yard, swayed up and ready to have the stops cut. [3] An anchor, that has just broken ground and is aweigh.

Attached: A person or unit (ship, squadron, task element, etc.) formally assigned to a specific unit or command on a temporary or permanent basis.

Attack center: A submarine's combat engagement center.

Attack force: All the ships, aircraft, and personnel assigned to an amphibious assault.

Attack submarine: A military submersible designed and armed to locate and destroy hostile shipping, usually with torpedoes. *See also* hunter-killer.

Attend the side: To provide a guard of honor, the Officer of the Day or Watch assembles the quartermaster, corporal of the watch, side boys, and quarterdeck messengers at the gangway to greet or say farewell to a visiting officer or dignitary. Also known as tend the side (USN) or man the side (RN), and see side honors.

Attention: A military drill posture in which the heels are touching with feet turned out equally at 45-degrees; legs are straight without stiffening or locking the knees; body is erect with chest lifted; shoulders are square and even; arms hang straight down, thumbs along the seams of the trousers or skirt and palms facing the leg; head is kept erect and to the front with the line of sight parallel to the ground. Silence and immobility are required.

Attention-getting signals: *See* table 10.

Attention to port (or starboard)!: This command calls all on deck to come to attention, face a passing ship being honored, and salute if so ordered.

Attrition: [1] Becoming fewer in number and decreasing in power as a result of long-drawn-out combat or other causes. [2] The act or process of gradually wearing out, especially due to friction.

ATVB: All the very best [salutation].

Australia current: Part of the South Equatorial Current that branches off near the Fiji Islands to flow to the east coast of Australia.

Authentication: A communications procedure designed to confirm genuine signals, and hence identify spurious ones.

Automated Mutual-Assistance Vessel Rescue: A U.S. Coast Guard system that coordinates ocean search and rescue efforts. Based on a worldwide plot of merchant vessel locations.

Automatic fire suppression: A damage control system which detects, isolates, and contains outbreaks of fire with minimal human intervention.

Automatic pilot: A device that controls the course of a ship or aircraft so that it follows a pre-determined path. Known colloquially as "Iron Mike" by U.S. naval aviators.

Automatic station-keeping: A system of surface and submerged sensors that detect forces such as wind, currents, and wave-action. The ship's computers use this data to activate thrusters which keep it in position.

Autonomous operation: A mode in which the unit commander assumes full operational responsibility for a ship or other unit which has lost contact with higher echelons.

Autopilot: *See* automatic pilot.

Auxiliary: [1] A non-combatant naval vessel such as a tug, transport, hospital ship, or supply ship. [2] Machinery used to power non-propulsion equipment such as pumps, winches, and the anchor engine. [3] The stand-by propulsion engine of a sailing ship. [4] A support group, such as the U.S. Coast Guard Auxiliary.

Availability factor: The percentage of operationally ready aircraft on a carrier or shore station. (*See* Aviation readiness.)

Avast!: Emergency command to stop an action, often abbreviated (as in 'vast heaving, which means stop pulling).

Average: Marine insurance term referring to the equitable apportionment between owners and insurers of loss or damage to ship or cargo. For example, goods thrown overboard to lighten ship in foul weather are jetissoned for the good of all, and the loss thus sustained is covered by a general average (contribution from all the parties concerned).

Avgas: Fuel for aircraft. Abbreviation of **Av**iation **Gas**oline.

Aviation: The skill or practice of operating aircraft. *See also* naval aviation.

Aviation Midshipman: This almost-forgotten and little-understood USN title existed for about five years during the immediate post–World War II period. The appointment was devised as a means of rapidly replacing seasoned combat pilots who were then returning to civilian life by the thousand. Aviation midshipmen wore wings but no rank insignia, did not get service credit, and were not commissioned as ensigns until completion of two years service, during which time they were assigned to the fleet and treated as officers. Some flew combat missions in the Korean War (where three were killed in action), several became astronauts (including Neil Armstrong, first person on the moon), and eighteen eventually reached flag rank.

Aviation readiness: A process to ensure the combat-worthiness of naval aviation by providing the right logistic support elements at the right time within current budgetary constraints. Elements include such items as maintenance efficiency, personnel training and support, material and equipment supply, physical facilities, computer resources, etc.

Aviation Readiness Evaluation: A bi-annual evaluation preceding the certification of air-capable USN ships.

Aviation support: When Army Aviation or Air Force units are embarked on United States Navy or Coast Guard air-capable vessels, the ship provides the combined benefits of landing zone, maintenance and work areas, fuel farm, air operations planning facilities, and command and control, while also providing for sustainment, creature comforts, and daily necessities. The shipboard environment demands the ultimate in teamwork. At any time there can be an event that may affect every person embarked. Navy and Coast Guard regulations set forth the authority of the ship's Commanding Officer (CO) with respect to aircraft embarked in or operating from the ship. The joint force commander's operation order will define command relationships apply throughout the assigned mission from initial embarkation until final debarkation but, in all cases, the ship's CO retains authority over embarked units in all areas involving safety of the ship or its crew.

Aviator: One who flies in an aircraft as pilot or crew.

Avionics: Electrical and electronic devices used by aircraft.

AW: All Weather.

AWACS: Airborne Warning and Control System.

Awake: Obsolete term meaning ready for use.

Award flags & pennants: USN ships that have been awarded citations or commendations are authorized to fly identifying flags or pennants from sunrise to sunset when not underway. These are flown on the foremast on a single halyard in the following order of seniority:

1. Presidential Unit Citation
2. Joint Meritorious Unit Award
3. Navy Unit Commendation
4. Meritorious Unit Commendation
5. Battle efficiency pennant

Each of the foregoing awards is described separately. Medals are awarded to individuals serving in the honored unit and carry the same seniority. Flags or pennants are also awarded in recognition of excellence in submarine or surface warfare, and for achievements in non-combat areas such as safety, environmental protection, and energy conservation.

Awash: [1] Level with or scarcely above the water. [2] Overflowing due to waves breaking on board in a heavy sea.

Away: [1] To prepare a boat for service, e.g., "call away the barge." [2] Assemble a group of USN enlisted seamen, e.g., "call away damage control party" (the RN would "muster" the party). [3] Former query, not in current use, as to the bearing of a sighted object, e.g., "Where away?"

Aweigh: Just clear of the ground, referring exclusively to the anchor (cf. atrip, weigh).

AWOL: Formerly, Absent Without Official Leave.

AX: Aftercastle.

Axis: [1] A reference line for the positioning of ships relative to the center of a task force or other formation. [2] The imaginary line around which a rotating body (such as the earth) turns. [3] World War II term for the military alliance of Germany, Japan, and Italy.

Axle-tree: *See* gun-carriage and transom.

Aye: [1] The correct and seamanlike naval acknowledgement of an order. "Aye" signifies it has been understood, while "Aye-Aye" means it is understood and will be obeyed. From an archaic form of "yes." [2] A boat recognition call in the RN, signifying the presence of an officer.

Azimuth: [1] In navigation; the angle measured clockwise between north and the celestial body being sighted. [2] In gunnery; the angle of horizontal deviation measured clockwise from north or south.

Azimuth ring: *See* pelorus.

Azores current: A slow and constant branch of the North Atlantic Current, which itself is part of the Gulf Stream.

B

Baboon watch: USN slang for those assigned to anchor or harbor watch while the rest of the crew relaxes or goes ashore on liberty.

Bac: [1] A French ferry-boat. [2] A punt used by shipwrights for carrying tar, pitch, etc.

Back: [1] Wind changing direction anti-clockwise. A backing wind portends weather worsening in the Northern Hemisphere, but improving in the Southern (cf. veer). [2] To trim sails so as to catch the wind on the wrong side and check the vessel's movement. [3] USN command to reverse engines to go astern. [4] The surface of a propeller blade which faces forward.

Back the anchor: To increase the holding power of an anchor by planting a smaller one ahead of it, and connecting the two with chain or cable.

Back to battery: [1] USN term describing the re-alignment of a gun muzzle to its firing position. [2] USN slang for a return to duty after illness or injury.

Back Water: [1] Command to oarsmen to reverse the usual method of rowing, usually to slow down the boat. [2] Water thrown back by the turning of a paddle-wheel or propeller.

Backfreight: Payment for the cost of returning goods due to the fault of either consignees or consignors.

Background: Sound or noise that interferes with radio or sonar reception.

Backhaul: A return trip carrying merchandise rather than ballast.

Backing & filling: Said of a sailing ship that is marking time; staying more or less in the same place by alternately spilling wind and allowing the sails to draw.

Backrope: A guy that secures the dolphin striker, counterbalancing the pull of the bowsprit.

Backrush: Alternate name for backwash.

Backset: [1] A surface current contrary to the main flow. [2] An eddy.

Backspring: Mooring line leading aft from the bow to a cleat or bollard ashore.

Backstaff: Obsolete instrument for determining the sun's altitude while facing away from it, thereby avoiding eye damage. Invented in 1590 by John Davis and sometimes called Davis' quadrant.

Backstay: Standing rigging running from an upper masthead to the sides or stern, serving to protect the mast against forward pull.

Backwash: [1] Water retreating from a broken wave (cf. backrush). [2] Mud and water thrown up by a ship's propellers in shallow water. [3] To clean a filter by reversing the flow of fluid through it.

Backwater: [1] Water held back by a dam or reservoir. [2] Water held back by a tide. [3] An isolated, backward, or peaceful place. [4] The boondocks (USN) or Ulu (RN).

Backwind: Wind deflected backward by a sail.

Backwinding: Turning mainsail or jib so that the wind blows into its rear side, thereby slowing the vessel. Pronounced to rhyme with "sinned" not "whined."

Bad conduct: Behavior violating regulations or disturbing others. If consistent, it justifies a "bad conduct" discharge from the USN or an "SNLR" (services no longer required) discharge from the RN. Neither is quite as prejudicial as a dishonorable discharge. A USN bad conduct discharge may only be awarded by a general or special court-martial.

Bad hat: This British slang for a dishonorable or untrustworthy person goes back to the days when seamen were expected to make their own headgear from tarred canvas or woven straw. The clumsy sailor who could not come up with something well-made became known initially as a bad hatter, a term which was later abbreviated and acquired its present meaning.

Bad relief: A person who is late in taking over the watch.

Badan: Small sailboat used in the Gulf of Oman. Characterized by straight stem and sharp stern with a false sternpost.

Badgerbag: Nickame for Neptune.

Badra: An Australian double-rigged fishing dugout.

Baffle: [1] A plate or plates installed to reduce the destabilizing fore-and-aft movement of tanked fluids. [2] To confuse or deflect radar or sonar signals: [3] An acoustic baffle.

Baffle zone: An cone-shaped area in the water roughly 30° on either side of the stern of a ship or submarine where its acoustic baffle and propeller noise create a blind area known as the sonar gap in which a hostile submarine can hide to avoid detection (submariners call this area "The Baffles"). *See also* clearing the baffles and crazy Ivan.

Bagged cargo: Refers to commodities that are usually packaged in sacks or bags (e.g., sugar, cement, onions, grains, flour, etc.).

Baggywrinkle: Protection against wear or chafing. Made from old rope and used where the sail might rub against the rigging. (*See also* Bolster.)

Baghla: A fast-sailing two-masted lateen-rigged vessel used in the Red Sea, Persian/Arabian Gulf, and Indian Ocean for both commerce and piracy. Also Bagala.

Bagpipe: A mizzen is "bagpiped" when it is laid aback by bringing the sheet to the shrouds.

Baie de Chaleur Fireship: The large inlet of Baie de Chaleur lies at the boundary of the Canadian provinces of Québec and New Brunswick and has been listed as one of the "thirty most beautiful bays of the world." It is the site of the 200-year-old legend of the ghostly apparition of a triple-masted ship with red and orange flames bursting through its decks and sailors scrambling up its burning rigging. There are numerous quasi-historical interpretations of the phantom's origin, including:

• A French frigate, burning its crew alive after being set alight by British gunfire.

• A Portuguese slave-trader, attacked and set afire by vengeful Indians.

• A pirate ship, condemned to the flames as Divine retribution for having abducted and ravaged a beautiful young bride.

Literally thousands claim to have seen it over the centuries and—since the name is French for "Bay of Heat"—it seems likely the phenomenon had been seen by the explorers who named it. Some form of flickering ethereal light undoubtedly does occur there, and in January 1981 a local high school teacher took a reasonably clear photograph. Most probably, it is an as yet unexplained natural phenomenon such as self-ignition of rotting vegetation, release of natural gas from nearby oilfields, or an unusual form of corposant.

Bail: To scoop water from a boat by bucket or other utensil. From old French nautical term baille = tub, bucket or pail.

Bail out: [1] To parachute-jump or eject from an aircraft in distress. [2] To empty a boat of water by bailing. [3] To rescue someone from a predicament.

Bait: To entice or deceive an enemy, especially a submarine, into exposing itself to detection.

Balance: [1] A submarine using a density layer to hover with no way on is "balanced." [2] A sailing vessel which remains on course with little or no assistance from the helm is "in balance."

Balandra: [1] A type of Spanish schooner. [2] A Philippine sailing dugout with double outriggers.

Balandrina: A sloop-rigged Peruvian fishing boat.

Balcony: An open gallery projecting over the stern of older sailing men-o-war. Usually ornately decorated with much carving known as gingerbread work and many glazed windows. The latter made the ship vulnerable to raking from astern. Also stern gallery.

Baldheaded: Said of a sailing ship underway without topmasts or headsails.

Bale: [1] A bundle of merchandise wrapped or bound with rope or wire for shipping as cargo. [2] Alternate spelling of bail.

Baleira: A Brazilian whaling boat propelled by sails or oars.

Balener: A whaling vessel similar to a brig. From the French baleine = whale.

Balinger: [1] A 15th century European sloop-of-war. [2] A trading vessel found in the Philippines and Moluccas.

Balk: [1] A roughly-squared timber beam formerly imported from the Baltic and used for house construction as well as shipbuilding. [2] To refuse or to hinder. From Old Norse bálkr. Also baulk.

Ball: [1] Short form of cannon ball. [2] *See* anchor ball, tide ball, time ball.

Ballahou: [1] A fast-sailing West Indian schooner, with no topsails, forward raked foremast and backward sloped mainmast. [2] The term was sometimes applied to men-of-war in which the masts were not properly stayed, or which were slovenly in other respects.

Ballam: A dugout fishing boat used on the Malabar Coast of India.

Ballast: [1] Heavy material such as gravel or pig iron stowed low in a ship to improve its stability. [2] Water or other liquid used for the same purpose (*see* ballast bag, ballast tank). [3] To ballast a merchantman requires disposing the ballast so that the ship will maintain her proper equilibrium, and be neither too stiff nor too crank. It is not merely the weight of ballast which has to be considered, but also its distribution relative to the weight and distribution of cargo. [4] In a man-of-war the ballast is permanent, and arranged to balance the guns and other top-weights carried.

Ballast bag: A waterproof bag laid on the floor of a hold, and filled or emptied by means of a pump and hose.

Ballast-shooting: The illegal practice of throwing ballast overboard while in port.

Ballast tank: [1] On surface vessels, a container for liquid ballast, which can be pumped from tank-to-tank to adjust trim and buoyancy, or be discharged overboard via a pipe, which is usually, but not necessarily, underwater. [2] A submarine uses ballast tanks to submerge and auxiliary trim tanks, to control its buoyancy. When the boat is surfaced, the ballast tanks are filled with air and the submarine's overall density is less than that of the surrounding water. As the vessel dives, its ballast tanks are flooded with water while, simultaneously, the air is vented, giving it negative buoyancy so that it sinks. A supply of compressed air is maintained on board, for life support as well as to blow water out of the ballast tanks for surfacing.

Ballista: Ancient naval stone-throwing artillery. *See also* scorpione.

Ballistic bulkhead: A strengthened barrier to protect crew and equipment from the effects of gunfire.

Ballistic correction: [1] Adjustment to the aim of a gun. [2] Regulation of a gyro-compass.

Ballistic damping: A gyro-compass error caused by the momentum of its damping fluid during a sudden change of course or speed.

Ballistic missile: A guided missile which flies like a bullet, without relying on aerofoil surfaces for lift. (*See* cruise missile.)

Ballistic missile submarine: A military submersible designed and armed to attack strategic land targets with conventional (e.g., Tomahawk) or nuclear missiles.

Ballistic wind: The effective wind, determined by computation, whose action on a projectile during flight will be the same as the combined actions of the true winds in each of the strata through which the projectile's trajectory passes.

Ballistics: The science and study of the motion of projectiles. From the Greek ballista = throw.

Balloen: The great Siamese (Thai) state-galley. Built to imitate a sea-monster and pulling seventy to a hundred oars on each side.

Balok: A lug-rigged Malayan trading vessel.

Baltic bow: One which recedes sharply to ride over ice and crush a pathway by the ship's own weight.

Baltic Exchange: The world's oldest global marketplace for the matching of ships and cargoes, founded in 1744 at the Virginia & Baltick Coffee House in London and still UK based. It provides six daily indices of shipping markets, runs related training courses, and resolves maritime disputes.

Baltimore Clipper: A lengthy, tall, and speedy 19th century schooner with sharply raked stem and masts, used extensively by American slavers and smugglers.

Baluk: A six-oared Istanbul harbor rowboat.

Bamboozle: Was originally a piratical term for hoisting a false national flag to deceive potential prey into thinking they were friendly. It has entered common usage to mean getting the better of someone by trickery.

Bandanna: This bright cotton scarf, popular with sailors and pirates as a head covering or neckerchief, was originally purchased by seamen from Hindu merchants whose name for tie-dyed material was bandhnu.

Banderole: A small streamer flown at the masthead to indicate wind direction.

Bangkong: Variation of the prahu, favored by Dyaks.

Bank: [1] A navigable but shallow elevated seafloor, usually on a continental shelf. [2] The side of a lake or river. [3] A bench for rowers in a galley. [4] A row or tier of oars. [5] A row or tier of guns. [6] To cover

a boiler's coals with ash to reduce draft and slow down the combustion process. [7] To rotate a flying aircraft about its longitudinal axis.

Bank effect: Phenomenon encountered in narrow channels, where the nearest bank tends to create a cushion which repels the bow, and a suction which attracts the stern, making steering difficult.

Bank fires: To conserve fuel by allowing the furnace to burn down low, then cutting off the supply of oxygen by covering the fires with ashes and closing the doors of the furnace and ash-pit. Since the fuel is still smoldering, fires can be spread and steam rapidly generated when required.

Banyan: [1] Formerly a meatless day aboard ship. [2] A wide-spreading fig tree whose high branches extend horizontally for 18 to 24 meters (60–80 feet) and then drop tendrils to the ground where they take root, forming a tent-like enclosure. The name originally applied to a specific tree, under which the Hindu merchant caste (Vāṇiyo, pronounced banio) had built a pagoda. In tropical service, parties were often held in its shade; hence Banyan Party became RN slang for a picnic ashore, later spreading to the USN.

Baptism: A ceremony performed on those crossing the equator for the first time (*see* crossing the line).

Bar: [1] A shoal across the mouth of a tidal estuary. [2] A unit of atmospheric pressure. [3] A turning-bar.

Bar shot: A pair of cannonballs or half-balls joined by a bar. When fired from cannon, it would open up and spin around its center to slice through enemy rigging (cf. chain shot, star shot).

Baratarian: A Pirate-Privateer-Smuggler operating in the Mississippi Delta and the Gulf of Mexico.

Barbary Coast: [1] The littoral of North Africa, extending from Egypt to the Atlantic, inhabited chiefly by and named after the Berbers. [2] the waterfront district in San Francisco. Renowned for the many saloons, gambling dens, and brothels established during the gold rush of 1849 and mostly destroyed by the earthquake of 1906.

Barbary piracy: Piracy and the slave trade had long been major sources of revenue for states on the Barbary Coast. During the sixteenth and seventeenth centuries, Corsair galleys and sailing ships ranged well beyond the Mediterranean, terrorizing European shipping along the Atlantic seaboard. Between 1569 and 1616 they are reported to have taken 466 ships off the British Isles, and in 1631 they sacked Baltimore in Ireland, taking its entire population away. Only a lucky few were ransomed; 20,000 Christians were sold in Algiers' slave bazaar during first half of the seventeenth century, and there were many other markets.

Barbary States: Formerly, Algiers, Morocco, Tripoli, Tunis, and some minor states along the Barbary Coast, nominally under Ottoman rule, but effectively independent under rulers known as Pasha, Dey, or Bey.

Barbary Wars: By the late eighteenth century, most European nations found it easier to pay exorbitant

"Tribute" (protection money) than try to stamp out the Corsair trade. Only the French and British Mediterranean fleets were powerful enough to win their merchants a degree of immunity without payment. With its Declaration of Independence, not only did the fledgling American Republic lose the protection of the Royal Navy, but Britain actively encouraged the Corsairs to attack vessels wearing the rebel Stars and Stripes. Soon, the United States was paying one-fifth of its annual revenue as "tribute" to the Barbary States, but the Corsairs had no compunction about breaking treaties and capturing ships whenever they felt like it. In 1803, Congress resolved "More effectually to protect the commerce of the United States against the Barbary Powers" and this led to several Barbary Wars. (*See* United States Navy, United States Marine Corps, and Mameluke sword.)

Barbecue: When they roasted a whole goat or ox, boucaniers said they were cooking it "from beard to tail" which, in French, is barbe-a-queue.

Barber: A form of frost smoke in which vapor tends to hug the water in eddies, resembling soap-suds.

Barbette: An armored column which both supports a rotating gun mount and protects its ammunition hoist.

Barca-longa: [1] A large Spanish coasting vessel with two or three pole-masts and lug-sails. Very common in the Mediterranean and off South America during the 17th and 18th centuries. [2] The name is also applied to Spanish gunboats.

BARCAP: Barrier Combat Air Patrol.

Bare boat: Charter party term indicating that only the vessel is chartered. The charterer appoints master and crew, and assumes all operating expenses.

Bare poles: Masts with sails removed or fully-furled.

Barge: [1] A boat used by an admiral or the senior officers of a warship. [2] A long flat-bottomed, often non-powered, vessel for carrying freight on inland waters. [3] An ornamental ceremonial boat.

Barge boards: English term for bilge boards, so-called because they were a feature of Dutch barges.

Bark: A small three-masted ship, square-rigged on fore and main masts, with fore-and-aft sails on the mizzen.

Barkentine: Similar to a bark, but square-rigged only on the foremast.

Barker: 18th century slang for a pistol. Hence, barking-irons = dueling pistols.

Barnacle: A small shellfish prone to attach itself to the underwater hull of ships.

Barograph: An instrument for recording atmospheric pressure; usually on a paper drum.

Barometer: An instrument which indicates, but does not record, atmospheric pressure.

Barque: *See* Bark.

Barquentine: *See* Barkentine.

Barracks: RN term for the Royal Marines mess and quarters in a warship.

Barrage balloons: Unmanned, lighter-than-air, gas-filled blimps, anchored by steel cables to winches on the ground. Their purpose was to create genuine and psychological hazards which would deter low-level air attack. During World War One they were tethered together by steel cables to form a barrier called an "apron." In the Second World War they were flown individually — by merchant ships in convoy, and over the approaches to ports and other military or civilian targets.

Barratry: [1] Fraud or gross negligence by a ship's master or crew. [2] Generally, any act committed with criminal intent by a master or crew. [3] Specifically, willful and illegal sinking, casting away, or damaging any part of a ship or its cargo while at sea.

Barrel: [1] A cylindrical container, usually bulging at the middle, consisting of wooden staves bound with metal hoops. [2] The tube, forming the main part of a gun, through which shells or bullets are discharged. [3] A volumetric measure (42 U.S. gallons = 35 imp gallons = 159 liters) used in the petroleum and shipping industries.

Barricoe: A small cask, keg, or barrel. From the Spanish baréca. (*See also* breaker.)

Barrier/Barricade: A net suspended transversely across an aircraft carrier's deck, to prevent aircraft which miss the arrester wires from crashing into parked planes or going over the side.

Barrier CAP: A combat air patrol forward-deployed to intercept incoming air attacks before they reach the carrier group.

Barrier ice: Ice which has broken off the outer edge of an ice sheet.

Barrier patrol: A detachment of warships, possibly accompanied by aircraft, deployed to intercept hostile air, surface, or submarine forces before they reach a designated line.

Barrier reef: A partially-submerged coral outcrop, running roughly parallel to the shore and separated from it by deep water.

Bartley's ordeal: In February 1891, James Bartley, an apprentice seaman, was on his first voyage aboard the whaler *Star of the East*. Near the Falkland Islands, the lookout spotted a sperm whale and two boats were launched. One succeeded in harpooning the animal, but the second was upended by the creature's thrashing tail and its crew tossed into the water. One drowned body was recovered, but Bartley had disappeared.

The dead whale was hauled to the side of the ship, where the crew set to work carving up the carcass by lantern light. Next morning they winched the stomach on deck and slit it open. To their amazement, Bartley was inside, alive but raving. By the end of the third week he was sufficiently recovered to recount being engulfed by total darkness and slipping along a smooth passage until he came to an open space. He felt slimy stuff around him and realized he'd been swallowed by the whale. There was enough trapped air to breathe, but the animal's high body heat sucked the energy out of him and he passed out.

After reaching England Bartley was treated at a London hospital, and the only lasting effect of his fifteen hours inside the whale's stomach was losing all the hair on his body, while his skin was bleached to the color of parchment (some accounts say he also lost his eyesight). He never made another ocean trip, but settled down as a cobbler in his native city of Gloucester, England. His tombstone in a local churchyard is said to carry a brief account of his experience and a footnote reading: "James Bartley—1870–1909. A Modern Jonah."

This story was headlined in newspapers and found its way into numerous other publications, both secular and religious, the latter including serious Bible commentaries on the Jonah story. But did it really happen? Sperm whales are certainly capable of swallowing a human being because they gulp their prey whole. In 1955 a 405-pound squid was removed intact from the belly of one and on another occasion a sixteen foot long shark was found. Edward B. Davis, a professor at Messiah College in Grantham, Pennsylvania, decided to check it out. He extensively researched the story and summarized his findings in an 1891 article in "The American Scientific Affiliation."

Records showed that *Star of the East*, British registry, John B. Killam, Master, set sail from New Zealand in December 1890 and arrived at New York in April 1891, so she could have been near the Falklands in February. But otherwise, he found no credible evidence to support the story. The ship was not a whaler, and no James Bartley was on the crew list. Moreover, no London hospital was able to confirm reports that any patient had been treated for the effect of gastric juices on his skin. The final and most damaging evidence was provided by captain Killam's widow who, in a letter, published in 1907 in *The Expository Times*, said:

> There is not one word of truth to the whale story. I was with my husband all the years he was in the Star of the East. There was never a man lost overboard while my husband was with her. That sailor has told a great sea yarn.

Base ring: *See* carriage.

Base speed: The speed made good by a zigzagging vessel.

Baseline: A line dividing internal waters from territorial sea. It generally follows the low-water line, except in highly-indented coasts where it jumps from one headland to another. The right of innocent passage in foreign waters terminates at the baseline, and maritime zones are measured from it.

Baseplate: *See* bedplate.

Basic seamanship: When an apprentice seaman first comes on board he or she has to begin by learning three fundamentals of the mariner's trade. These are [1] To know the ropes. [2] To box the compass, and [3] To identify the marks and deeps of the leadline by sight and by feel.

Basilisk: Ancient name for a long 48-pounder naval gun adorned with fanciful reptiles known as basilisks whose exhalation was supposed to be deadly.

Basin: [1] A body of water enclosed by quays, where ships can remain afloat regardless of the state of the tides. [2] A depression in the earth's surface, wholly or completely surrounded by higher ground and usually containing a lake, sea, ocean or river.

***Batavia* mutiny:** The Dutch East India Company's VOC *Batavia* left Holland on her maiden voyage to Batavia (now Jakarta, Indonesia) in company with seven other ships of various sizes. She was the finest Indiaman afloat and the Company's treasure ship. In command of the fleet was Francesco Pelsaert, a senior merchant. The VOC's policy of appointing a business man to command was hated by the ship's master, Adriaen Jacobszoon. Moreover, the men were enemies from a previous journey, and their relationship became more and more acrimonious as the journey progressed.

Conspiring with his first mate, Jeronimus Corneliszoon, Jacobszoon conceived a plan to hijack the ship and either turn to piracy, or perhaps start a new life using the treasure ship's gold and silver. To that end he deliberately steered the ship off course and away from the rest of the fleet but, on 4 June 1629, before they could mount their mutiny, he ran *Batavia* onto Morning Reef, near Beacon Island, in the Western Australian archipelago known as Houtman Abrolhos (appropriately, Abrolhos is a Portuguese lookout's cry, meaning "Beware!")

Water was desperately short on the islands, and Jacobszoon agreed to join Pelsaert and search for some on the mainland. After failing to find any, they set sail for Batavia, arriving on 7 July after an epic voyage. Corneliszoon, the senior officer left behind on Beacon Island, instituted a reign of terror, taking charge of all weapons and the remaining water, ordering the execution of anyone who might challenge his authority or be a burden on their limited resources. The mutineers became intoxicated with rape, savagery, and killing as daily "entertainment." Most women were murdered after being used, but a few of the more comely were saved "for common service."

Eventually, the mutineers were rounded up, questioned by waterboarding, and tried in a formal court convened by Pelsaert on the island. Some were hanged, on the spot, including Corneliszoon, who first had both his hands chopped off. Others were taken to Batavia to face execution there. On the way, two lesser mutineers, Wouter Loos, a soldier, and Jan Pelgrom de Bye, a cabin boy, were marooned on the Australian mainland, near the mouth of the Murchison River, thereby becoming Australia's first European settlers. (Early British explorers encountered unusually light-skinned Aborigines in that area., but other European shipwreck survivors could have made contact with and been adopted into a local clan.)

In Batavia, on Pelsaert's indictment, Jacobszoon

was arrested for navigational negligence but, despite being tortured, he refused to admit planning the mutiny, and thereby escaped execution. What finally happened to him is not known, but it is suspected he died in prison. Pelsaert was held partly responsible for what had happened. His finances and belongings were seized and he died a broken man within a year.

Bathymetric chart: A map showing bottom contours by means of lines and color-coding.

Bathymetric current: A deep flow that does not reach the surface.

Bathymetry: The measurement of water depth. May include other qualities such as salinity, temperature, and bottom contour. From the Greek bathos = deep.

Bathyscaphe: A small submersible designed for deep ocean exploration.

Bathy-thermograph: A device for measuring water temperature at various depths.

Batsman: Person who directed pilots landing on an aircraft carrier before the introduction of automated techniques for high-speed aircraft. So-called because he signaled the incoming pilots with a pair of hand-held paddles similar to table-tennis bats. Known colloquially as "bats," but properly called Landing Signal Officer in the USN and Deck Landing Control Officer in the RN.

Battalion Landing Team: For amphibious landings, the United States Marine Corps assembles task organized teams, typically consisting of an infantry battalion reinforced with an artillery battery; a platoon each of tanks, amphibious assault vehicles, and light armored reconnaissance vehicles; and combat engineers.

Battard: An ancient lightweight cannon.

Batteau: Former type of North American riverboat, usually pole-propelled.

Batten: [1] A thin strip of wood or synthetic material inserted in a sail to keep it flat. [2] A strip of wood or metal used to secure the tarpaulin cover of a hatch [3] To put battens in place, in the case of hatches by hammering a wedge in between the coamings and the batten.

Batten down the hatches: A hatch (or hatchway) is an opening in the deck which allows people or cargo to move from one level to the next. It is surrounded by coamings (raised frameworks to prevent deck water pouring in) and covered with trapdoor-like covers. When foul weather is expected the hatch is "battened down" by stretching a tarpaulin across the covers and securing it with battens. The phrase has been taken into common usage to mean preparing for a difficult problem or crisis.

Batten pocket: A pouch in a sail to hold stiffening battens.

Battery: [1] Two or more artillery pieces of the same caliber, or used for a shared purpose (e.g., anti-aircraft). [2] The entire armament of a warship. [3] A set of interconnected galvanic cells capable of holding an electrical charge and providing a source of supplementary energy (e.g., in a diesel-engined submarine).

Battery reference plane: An arbitrarily chosen plane, usually within the ship, from which angles of elevation are measured. *See* deckplane and naval surface fire control.

Battle bowler: World Wars I and II RN slang for an anti-shrapnel steel helmet, whose shape resembled a bowler hat. (Also tin hat.)

Battle dress: USN term for flash-protective and splinter-resistant clothing for wear in combat. The RN term is "anti-flash gear."

Battle efficiency: Ability to meet exacting standards of combat readiness. The USN holds an annual battle efficiency competition and the winning unit is entitled to paint a white "E" on each side of the bridge and fly a triangular red pennant with a black ball. A ship which wins the five consecutive competitions replaces the white "E" with a gold one, and flies a triangular blue pennant with a yellow ball. *See also* prize money.

Battle fatigue: *See* combat fatigue.

Battle flags: In the days of sail it was common practice for warships to wear at least two and often three oversized ensigns, one on each mast. This served to identify their nationality in the smoke and confusion of combat; also to prevent an enemy from assuming they had struck their colors if one was shot away. The practice gradually fell into disuse but, as recently as the Battle of the River Plate in 1940, the command "Hoist battle ensigns!" was issued, mainly as a means of encouraging crew morale and raising their fighting instinct. To avoid confusion, it is still the practice for a flag officer's command flag to be kept aloft even if he is killed or incapacitated during combat.

Battle group: *See* strike group.

Battle honors: The names of fleet or individual actions in which a warship has taken honorable part. In the RN they are usually displayed on a Battle Honours Board, mounted on the quarterdeck and include honors won by earlier ships with the same name. They are known as Battle Stars in the USN (*see* Award Flags & Pennants). The rules governing their award are strictly governed in both navies.

Battle lamp/lantern: Battery-powered light which turns on automatically if the ship's power is cut off in action. Known as Emergency lighting in the RN.

Battle lights: Dim red lights used below decks in order to preserve the night vision of seamen going out on deck.

Battle line: A row of warships formed to engage an enemy in surface warfare. The formation originated in the seventeenth century and has been essentially obsolete since the Battle of Jutland in 1916, although it was employed during the Battle of Surigao Strait in October 1944. (Also called line of battle.)

Battle messing: The process of feeding personnel on ships during prolonged periods at general quarters or action stations.

Battle Stars: *See* battle honors.

Battle station: Crew member's place of duty during combat (cf. action station, general quarters).

Battlecruiser: Heavily-armed but lightly-armored early 20th century class of warship. Intended to be fast enough to escape anything more powerful and powerful enough to overcome anything it could catch. The same concept applied to the American super frigates and the German pocket battleships.

Battleship: [1] A sailing ship-of-the-line. [2] The most heavily-armed and armored of power-driven warships (cf. Dreadnought).

Battleship row: The area of Pearl Harbor that was the primary target of the surprise Japanese air raid that precipitated the United States into World War II. (*See* Taranto.)

Battlespace: The U S Department of Defense defines "battlespace" as:

The environment, factors, and conditions that must be understood to successfully apply combat power, protect the force, or complete the mission. This includes the air, land, sea, space, and the included enemy and friendly forces; facilities; weather; terrain; the electromagnetic spectrum; and the information environment within the operational areas and areas of interest.

Battlewagon: Colloquialism for battleship.

Baulk: The British form of balk.

Bay: A body of water partially enclosed by land. Larger than a cove and smaller than a gulf.

Bay boat: A Chesapeake Bay oyster dredger, usually a bugeye or skipjack.

Bay of Pigs: An area on the southern coast of Cuba (Bahia de Cochinos in Spanish) that was the site of a CIA inspired counter-revolutionary amphibious assault by Cuban émigrés against the Marxist Castro régime. Most of the 1,400 invaders were captured or killed.

Bayonet: A close-combat weapon of last-resort; shaped like a knife, dagger, or spike and designed to fit on or over the muzzle of a rifle or similar weapon, effectively turning it into a spear. It is believed to be named after the French town of Bayonne where, during a 17th century insurrection, Basque peasants ran out of powder and rammed hunting knives into the mouths of their muskets.

BB: [1] Hull classification symbol of a battleship. [2] Breakbulk.

BC: Bottom current.

BCD: Bad conduct discharge.

BCU: Beach clearance unit.

BDA: Battle (or Bomb) Damage Assessment.

BDL: Beach discharge lighter.

BDR: Battle damage repair.

Beach: [1] Sandy or pebbly strip of shore between low and high water marks; sometimes extending inland to the point where topography changes or vegetation begins. From the Anglo-Saxon bece = brook or stream. [2] To run a ship aground. [3] The section of shore designated for amphibious landing (e.g., Gold, Juno, Sword, Omaha, and Utah Beaches, in Normandy June 1944). [4] The beach is a Mariners' term for land.

Beach marker: Colored dye, panel, or other device delineating the specified limit of an amphibious landing beach.

Beach netting: Steel mesh laid on an amphibious landing beach to improve the traction of vehicles.

Beach party: The naval personnel in a landing party.

Beach ranger: [1] A term formerly applied to a seaman who had been discharged for bad conduct but continued to hang around the waterfront. [2] A term sometimes applied to waterfront prostitutes.

Beachcomber: [1] A wave (comber) crashing onto the shore (beach). [2] A vagrant who subsists by searching (combing) the beach for articles of value.

Beachhead: The area of a hostile shore seized and held by an amphibious landing party. Frequently, but incorrectly called a bridgehead. *See also* airhead, lodgement, amphibious.

Beachman: [1] A West African who acts as interpreter to shipmasters, and assists them in conducting trade. [2] A West African boatman who lands people through heavy surf.

Beachmaster: An Officer who goes ashore after the assault phase to assume responsibility for the logistics of amphibious operations.

Beacon: A fixed aid to navigation, either lighted or unlit.

Beak: Ram on the prow of a fighting galley.

Beaked whales (Ziphiidea): Are one of the least-known families of large aquatic mammals. Several species have only recently been identified, and it is entirely possible more remain undiscovered. They are creatures of the ocean deeps, diving for long periods (85 minutes have been recorded) and to great depths (1,000 fathoms or more) making them the deepest-diving air-breathing animals. They are highly sensitive to underwater sound and have been reported to mass strand during naval sonar exercises.

Beakhead: [1] Projection under the bowsprit and beyond the bows of a sailing vessel. [2] Space immediately ahead of the forecastle, often used as a toilet via a grating open to the sea below (cf. head).

Beakhead beam: *See* catbeam.

Beam: [1] A ship's width at its widest point. [2] A horizontal timber supporting a deck or flat: [3] The rays, waves, or signals emitted by radio, radar, or sonar. [4] The ray of light emitted by a searchlight.

Beam ends: A vessel is said to be "on beam ends" when she is heeled so far over that her deck beams are almost vertical.

Beam reach: Sailing at right angles to the wind.

Beam sea, tide, or wind: Waves, tidal currents, or winds coming at right angles to the ship.

Beamy: Describes a vessel which is unusually wide compared to its length.

Bear: [1] Heavy coconut matting which was weighted with sand or shot and dragged across a wooden deck to scour it. [2] To lie in a certain direction (bearing) from the ship. [3] To carry. [4] To support, sustain, or hold up. [5] To wear as a mark of authority or distinction.

Bear a hand!: Request or Command to provide assistance.

Bear down: [1] To approach from upwind. [2] To change course further downwind. [3] Command to work harder. [4] Instruction to contract the abdominal muscles and diaphragm during childbirth.

Bear off: To steer away from something, especially the shore or another vessel. Also bear away.

Bear up!: Nowadays, this is an admonition to keep one's spirits up and not despair, but it was originally a naval command to alter course towards the wind, or an object by keeping the tiller to windward.

Beards: *See* facial hair and permission to grow.

Bearing: [1] Direction or position relative to the ship. [2] The support and guide for a reciprocating, oscillating, or rotating shaft, pivot, or wheel.

Bearing drift: The shift in bearing of a vessel in motion relative to another. If there is no bearing drift and the range is decreasing, collision is inevitable.

Beat: [1] To sail as close to the wind as possible. [2] Work to windward by successive tacks (also beat up).

Beat to quarters: 18th century Royal Navy command to prepare for combat, announced by drums beating to the rhythm of "Heart of Oak" (*see* march music).

Beating the booby: Sailing ship slang for swinging the arms from side to side to create warmth by accelerating blood circulation.

Beaufort Scale: In 1805 Royal Navy Commander Francis Beaufort devised a 12-point scale for the indication of wind-strength based on observation of the speed of a square-rigged frigate running before the wind with sails clean-full (bellying) for forces 2 through 4 and, for higher forces, the amount of sail which could safely be carried in pursuit of an enemy when sailing full and bye (as close as possible to the wind without having the sails shiver).

In 1838, by then Rear-admiral and Hydrographer of the Navy, Beaufort persuaded the Admiralty to adopt his scale "For all Her Majesty's Ships and Vessels of War." Then in 1853, the First International Meteorological Conference, held in Brussels, adopted Beaufort's scale as the standard format for recording weather conditions in ships logbooks. In 1912, with fewer and fewer seamen sailing in square-riggers, the scale was revised to a system based on the visual condition of the sea; in 1926 wind speed ranges in knots were applied to each force; and in 1946, the World Meteorological Organization (WMO) added five more hurricane force wind speeds. (*See* table 1 for details.)

Becalmed: Said of a sailing ship which is motionless for lack of wind.

Becket: [1] A loop or eye at the end of a rope or block. [2] An eye in the fluke of an anchor, used to secure it while underway. [3] Formerly, anything used to confine loose ropes, tackles, oars, or spars until they are wanted. [4] In tailoring, the "slots" on trousers or raincoat through which a belt is passed. [5] In RN slang, beckets means pockets in clothing.

Bedini: A trading dhow used on the Gulf of Oman.

Bedplate: A plate, platform, deck, or frame supporting all or part of an engine, pump, or other machine. Also soleplate.

Bedundered: Formerly said of a seaman who had been deafened and stupefied by the roar of repeated broadsides.

Beedle: A large mallet used in caulking. Also Beetle.

Beeper: Slang term for a device used to control a pilotless aircraft or drone.

Beer: Before brandy or rum was issued to sailors, beer was the accepted ration, but it seems to have been of very low quality. In his 1634 *Advice of a Seaman*, Nathaniel Knott wrote, "Whilst it is new, it shall seemingly be worthy of praise, but in one month wax worse than stinking water." It was no better 127 years later, when William Thompson wrote, "It stank as abominably as the foul stagnant water which is pumped out of many cellars in London at the midnight hour." Nevertheless, most captains considered a good supply to be essential — when asked how long a cruise could continue, the great explorer Martin Frobisher is said to have replied "As long as the beer lasts."

Beetle crushers: RN slang for the heavy boots worn by Royal Marines.

Before: Ahead, in front of.

Before the mast: Said of seamen (who originally berthed in the forecastle ahead of the foremast).

Before the wind: Sailing with the wind coming from astern or across one of the quarters.

Belay: [1] Order to ignore or cancel the preceding command (e.g., belay that!). [2] To fix or secure something, especially a running rope. [3] To stop doing something (nautical slang).

Belaying pin: A short round bar of wood or metal, inserted into a rail to secure a line and provide a form of quick-release device, since removing the pin releases the line.

Belfast bow: A bow that rakes forward above the waterline to give more cargo space.

Belfry: A protective canopy over a ship's bell.

Bell-bottoms: Wide trousers flared from the knee down to enable seamen to roll them up when swabbing decks or doing other wet jobs. This was not the original purpose; in the days when sailors tailored their own clothes they made the trouser legs wide all the way down, so as not to waste any of the cloth they had bought. Only later was the utility of a flare discovered.

Bell buoy: An anchored buoy with a warning bell

which is frequently wave-activated, but may be mechanically-rung in quiet waters.

Bell routine: For timekeeping at sea, the ship's bell is rung every half hour during each watch; starting with one bell at the end of the first thirty minutes, and ending with eight bells at the end of each four-hour watch. A light stoke on the bell, known as the "little one" is sometimes struck five minutes after the beginning of a night watch. Its origin and significance are obscure.

At midnight on 31st December, sixteen bells are traditionally struck; eight by the oldest person aboard, irrespective of rank, to signify the old year's passing, followed by an additional eight, struck by the youngest to welcome the incoming new year.

In the days before reliable chronometers, every day at sea, just after seven bells of the forenoon watch, the captain and his senior officers would assemble to calculate the ship's latitude. At the moment when the sun was observed to be at its zenith, signifying local noon, the navigator would sing out "There he goes!," whereupon the half-hour glass would be turned and eight bells rung, re-setting ship's time for the next twenty-four hours. (*See also* timekeeping and watchkeeping.)

Bells: The rules of navigation (table 7) require regular bells to be sounded when anchored, aground, or fogbound. *See also* bell routine.

Belly: [1] The bulging part of a sail as it captures the wind. [2] The bulbous part of a trawler's fishing net.

Belly robber: Naval slang for a Chief Steward or Purser who kept the crew on short rations in order to line his own pockets.

Belly rope/strap: Rope or strap passed around a boat to carry a kedging anchor suspended below the keel.

Below: Beneath the main or weather deck (i.e., in a cabin or inside a hold).

Bench: Fore-and-aft seat in a small boat (cf. thwart, sheet).

Benchhook: Also called a sailhook or stretching hook and, colloquially, "third hand." Used to hold canvas for stitching, pulling it taut with the left hand and sewing with the right.

Benchmark: [1] Specifically, a fixed point of reference used in surveying, navigation, or weapon alignment. [2] Generically, any standard or average against which similar items can be compared. [3] In information technology, a program or set of programs which can be run on different computers to give an approximate measure of their relative performance.

Bend: [1] To attach a sail, line, cable, or signal flag with a knot. [2] The knot itself (e.g., Sheet Bend; Carrick Bend). [3] A curve in a river.

Bends: A painful ailment afflicting divers due to over-rapid decompression.

Beneaped: Formerly said of a vessel that went aground at the height of the spring tide and was thus forced to wait two weeks until the subsequent high tide. Vessels beneaped at an equinox might have to wait six months.

Benguela Current: A slow-moving northwest flow along the coast of West Africa to join the South Equatorial Current.

Bergy bits: Pieces of ice which have broken off a glacier, usually about the size of a small house.

Bering Current: Flows northerly through the Bering Strait.

Berm: [1] The flattish strip at the back of a beach, formed of material deposited by wave action. [2] A narrow embankment.

Bermuda rig: A fore-and-aft rig developed in Bermuda during the 17th century and widely used by modern cruising and racing yachts. It is distinguished by sharply raked masts and a tall triangular mainsail with one point going straight up. Also Marconi rig.

Bermuda Triangle: In contrast to the ancient origins of most myths and legends, that of the roughly triangular imaginary area bounded by the southern coast of Florida and the islands of Bermuda and Puerto Rico is relatively modern. Its notoriety is based on the large number of ships and aircraft which have vanished there since 1800 without any trace of wreckage or survivors. Also known as the "Devil's Triangle," it is one of only two places on earth where a magnetic compass points due north with no variation toward the magnetic pole. (The other, which lies off the east coast of Japan, is also renowned for mysterious disappearances and Japanese and Filipino seamen call it the "Devil's Sea.")

Proposed explanations of these disappearances include extraterrestrial interference by visitors from outer space, interference by underwater-dwelling survivors from the lost continent of Atlantis, and the action of physical forces hitherto unknown to science, including cosmic electro-magnetic effects, and time-distorting tunnels. The U.S. Coast Guard, however, is not impressed with supernatural explanations — pointing out that the combination of natural forces and human unpredictability outdoes even the most far-fetched science fiction.

The Caribbean-Atlantic area has long been recognized for freakish weather, sudden fierce but local storms and waterspouts, and as a breeding ground for hurricanes. As early as 1596, Sir Walter Raleigh complained of the region's "hellish sea, thunder, lightening, and storms." In addition, the interaction of strong currents with deep marine trenches and shallow reefs or shoals puts the ocean floor topography in constant flux, so that the development of new navigational hazards is rapid, while the swift and turbulent Gulf Stream can quickly erase any physical evidence of disaster.

Skeptics point out that many of the reported events actually occurred outside the triangle; some were preceded by reports of instrument failure or loss of power, and others happened during periods of unusual fog or strange sea conditions. In fact, scientific analysis shows that the number and frequency of disappearances is not abnormal. Nonetheless, the belief in paranormal influences is widespread and persistent.

Berserker: One of a band of Norse or Viking shock troops, famed for extreme ferocity and frenzy in combat. The name translates roughly as "bearskin man" and berserkers did indeed wear bear or wolf skins over light chain mail armor. They used a variety of weapons, the most feared being a deadly throwing ax. Numerous speculations of their fearless and furious behavior include the influence of herbal drugs mixed with alcohol, belief in "possession" by the spirit of the wild animal whose pelt they wore, and a psychological state induced by rituals and ceremonies.

Berth: [1] Place for a ship to moor or anchor: [2] Place for crew to sleep. [3] To provide either of these. [4] A shipboard job (e.g., I've got a berth on a Cruise Liner). [5] To give something a wide berth is to allow it plenty of space.

Berthon boat: A collapsible craft made with double canvas linings stretched on a folding wooden frame to form watertight envelopes that assist buoyancy and give protection should the outer canvas be accidentally torn. Invented by Edward Berthon in 1850. Seeing it on display at the Great Exhibition of 1851, the Prince of Wales commented that a cannonball would easily penetrate the canvas. To the amusement of Queen Victoria, Berthon replied, "What, sir, could not be penetrated by a cannonball?." In 1873 the Royal Navy adopted Berthon boats for destroyers, other small craft, and (later) submarines where storage space was at a premium. It is frequently reported that RMS *Titanic* carried four Berthon boats, but these were actually similar, but larger and single-skinned, Englehardt boats.

Beset: Trapped in ice with no rudder control.

Best bower: Sailing ship term for the starboard of two bow anchors. The one on the port side was called the "small anchor," even though it was the same size.

Betty Martin: The origin of the 18th century seafarer's expression of disbelief "All My Eye and Betty Martin" is obscure. The first part clearly comes from the ancient French dismissive phrase "mon oeil" and the translation "my eye" is still used to indicate skepticism. The British prefixed it with "all," and for some uncertain reason later added the suffix "Betty Martin." There are at least three explanations for this, none of which seems credible or satisfactory.

- The *Oxford English Dictionary* cites the earliest appearance of the phrase as being in a 1781 letter from Samuel Crisp to his sister Sophia, which refers to it as "A sea phrase that Admiral Jemm frequently makes use of." From this, it has been postulated that a Betty Martin was an item of nautical equipment whose name has long been forgotten. But it would be most unusual for such a term to totally disappear from the extensive records and dictionaries of the time. There is no Admiral Jemm in the 1660–1815 *List of Royal Navy Sea Officers*, but Mass-

achusetts historian J.L. Bell says "Admiral Jemm" was used by English author and diarist Fanny Burney as an affectionate nickname for her brother James, who was only a captain at the time, but was "yellowed" to rear-admiral on retirement.

- Some suggest there was a real Betty Martin, variously reported to be either a contemporary London actress or a notorious waterfront prostitute. However, it is unclear why seamen would have added her name to a perfectly good expression already in common use.

- It has been proposed that the entire phrase is a corruption of Roman Catholic prayers overheard and misunderstood by a Protestant English sailor visiting a foreign port. When asked what it was like ashore, he is supposed to have replied "All I heard them say was 'My eye and Betty Martin.'" The most commonly accepted version of this garbled prayer comes from a French book of hours, dated 1500, in the Royal Danish Library which reads, "Ora pro mihi, beate Martine," meaning Pray for me, blessed Martin. However the Latin is ungrammatical and the supplication does not appear in any liturgy. An alternative is "Mihi, Beate Mater," meaning (roughly) Grant my wish, Holy Mother. Neither seems very credible, although "mee hye" is how my eye would have been pronounced by a cockney-speaking seaman.

Between a rock and a hard place: This phrase, meaning to have no acceptable alternatives, is sometimes said to refer to Odysseus' dilemma when rowing between Scylla (a monster on the rocky cliff) and Charybdis (a dangerous whirlpool). More probably it is simply a colorful idiom without any nautical connection.

Between decks: The space between any two decks (not to be confused with 'tween deck which is any deck below the main deck, nor the plural 'tween decks meaning inside the ship).

Between the devil and the deep (blue sea): It is widely believed that this idiom (to which "blue sea" is a recent addition) refers to a sailor being lowered over the side to caulk the space between keel and garboard strake (one of two long seams known as "devils" because they were so difficult to maintain). However, that derivation is apocryphal, because the phrase was in use ashore long before it found its way aboard ship and, in any case, the garboard seam was so far down that it could only be caulked when the ship was careened or dry-docked. In fact, the idiom should be taken at face value. The Devil is evil and deep water is dangerous, so being between them means facing undesirable alternatives.

Between two fires: Now used to indicate that someone is being verbally or physically assaulted from several sources, the term undoubtedly originated with the sailing ship naval tactic of doubling (placing ships on both sides of an opponent during combat).

Between wind and water: [1] Refers to the waterline. This area is alternately submerged and raised as the ship rolls, so a cannon ball striking a wooden hull in this area could sink it. [2] Hence, a metaphor for being in a hazardous situation. [3] Coincidentally, in Chinese Feng Shui (literally wind-water), correct positioning between the two is essential for balancing the Chi (life force).

BGC: Boat group commander.

Bib: Sailing ship sailors seldom cut their hair which grew long enough to blow in the face when aloft or get caught in equipment and machinery. To overcome these problems, they would braid their tresses into pigtails and hold them in place with tar. However, even top-quality "Stockholm Tar" left stains on the backs of shirts and made a mess of the collars of their best dress when going ashore, so they took to arranging a protective scarf or bib around the back of the neck. By the time this evolved into the traditional square collar seen on the uniforms of naval ratings or enlisted personnel, pigtails were no longer in fashion. The three stripes, which appear on both RN and USN seamen's bibs, have nothing to do with Nelson's three victories as is popularly believed.

Bible: Slang for a large holystone. Cf. prayer-book.

BIBO: **B**ulk **I**n, **B**ags **O**ut in reference to bulkers that are specially equipped to bag dry cargo while loading. One such ship can load and package 300 tonnes of bulk sugar into 50 kg sacks every hour.

Big chicken dinner: USN enlisted slang for a bad conduct discharge ("That'll earn him a big chicken dinner").

Bight: [1] Any part of a line between its two ends. [2] A bend or loop in a line. [3] A bend or curve in the shoreline. [4] The body of water enclosed by such a bend. [5] A bay or gulf.

Bigwig: This derisory term for a senior officer has carried on from the days when status was reflected in the size of the incumbent's wig. The term may or may not have originated at sea before transferring to common English.

Bilander: Small two-masted sailing vessel, square-rigged on foremast, lateen-rigged on main. Used on canals in the Low Countries and in the Mediterranean.

Bilbo: A 16th century term for a flexible type of cutlass. Named after Bilboa where some of the finest Spanish blades were forged.

Bilboes: Long bars padlocked at one end, on which iron leg-shackles could slide. Used to confine prisoners on board ship.

Bilge: [1] The lowest, almost flat part of a ship's interior space nearest the keel where water is likely to accumulate. [2] The filthy water that collects in that area. [3] a colloquialism for nonsense.

Bilge blocks: Supports for a vessel in dry dock. Also keel blocks.

Bilge boards: Retractable keels on both sides of small sailing boats to reduce leeway due to wind pressure. *See also* barge boards.

Bilge keel: Small fin extending fore-and-aft along a ships bilge to reduce rolling.

Bilge pump: Pump to remove water from the bilges. May be mechanical, electric, or manual.

Bilge rat: Derogatory slang used by USN deck seamen for a person who works in the engineering spaces of the ship. Also snipe.

Bilged: [1] Stove-in at or near the bilge. [2] USN slang for being failed, as in "He was bilged on the inspection," or the act of denying as in "I bilged his promotion."

Bilgewater: Filthy water accumulated in the bilge.

Bill: [1] The point of an anchor fluke. [2] A slender promontory. [3] An assignment of duties (e.g., the watch bill). [4] A pike or halberd.

Bill of Health: Certificate that a ship's port of departure was free of contagious disease, and that the crew was healthy at time of sailing.

Bill of Lading: Detailed listing of cargo, comprising a receipt for the goods, a transportation contract, and a definition of legal title to the property.

Billboard: [1] The anchor bed; a sloping and slightly projecting platform at the bow, serving to protect it against damage by the anchor bill and to support the anchor when not in use. [2] A ship's notice board. [3] An outdoor advertising sign, especially theatrical. It is unclear whether the latter use of the term has a nautical origin or was independently derived.

Billet: A job, appointment, or place assigned to a member of the ship's company.

Billhead: A carved ornamental scroll or volute terminating the upper end of a stem or cutwater and serving in place of a figurehead.

Billow: A soft upward-curving surge or wave. A poetical term rather than a nautical one.

Bimmy: Slang for a teaser.

Binge: [1] To rinse out a cask . [2] An eating or drinking spree. Possibly derived from seamen assigned to cask cleaning gulping down any food or spirits left at the bottom before rinsing it out.

Bingo: The NATO command "Bingo!" — which is always accompanied by a bearing, distance, and destination — orders a pilot to divert to an emergency landing field or airport known as the "Bingo Field," while "Bingo Fuel" refers to the minimum quantity required to safely reach that field.

Binnacle: Housing for the compass.

Binnacle list: A record of sick crew members. The name derives from the former practice of maintaining such a list beside the compass, where it could be updated by the Officer of the Watch for review by the captain. The name lives on in a USN medical report (Navmed 6320/18) recommending that binnacle-listed personnel be excused from duty for 24 hours, subject to approval from the commanding officer.

Binoculars: A pair of identical telescopes, mounted side-by-side and aligned to point accurately in the same direction, allowing the viewer to use both eyes when viewing distant objects. Most can be hand-held, but much larger types are pivot-mounted.

Biological weapons: The offensive use of living organisms (such as anthrax) to create injury, incapacitation, or death. Cf. chemical weapons.

Biologics: The sounds generated by marine life as picked up on sonar. *See* bloop.

Bioluminescence: Emission of light by marine organisms when stirred up by wave motion or the bow wave of a ship or its propellers. Popularly, but incorrectly, known as phosphorescence.

Biometrics: Also known as biomimicry, is a relatively new engineering science which examines nature for biological solutions that can lead to the development of mechanisms or capabilities which achieve human goals. A good example is the GhostSwimmer.

Bird farm: Formerly, USN surface seamen's derogatory slang for an aircraft carrier. Seldom used since aircraft gained prestige and replaced guns as the primary naval weapon.

Birds Free: Permission to fire missiles is granted.

Bird's nest: A small round seat or tub placed at the masthead to provide a lookout position higher than the crow's nest.

Birds Tight: Permission to fire missiles is withheld.

Bireme: An ancient battle galley, propelled by two banks of oars. Probably invented by Phoenicians in the 7th or 6th century BCE, the design rapidly spread all around the Mediterranean. It was gradually superseded by the trireme, beginning in the mid–5th century BCE.

Biscuit: Ships bread, made from well-kneaded flour, mixed with the least possible quantity of water, and slowly baked into flat, hard, doughy cakes.

Bisquine: A French lug-rigged fishing boat with two or three masts, the foremost being placed well forward in the eyes of the ship.

Bite: An anchor is said to bite when its flukes dig in without dragging.

Bittacle: An ancient spelling of binnacle.

Bitter end: [1] The absolute end of a piece of line or cable. [2] The last link of an anchor chain in the chain locker.

Bitts: [1] Heavy timbers to which a wooden ship's anchor chains are attached. [2] Strong spool-shaped posts projecting, usually in pairs, above the deck of a ship, for securing cables or towing lines. [3] Bollards.

B/L: Bill of Lading.

Black Book of Admiralty: Semi-official name for the earliest codification in English of Admiralty Law, compiled in 1336 to consolidate a collection of earlier maritime law and customs. Its lengthy official title was: "Rules for the Office of Lord High Admiral; Ordinances for the Admiralty in Time of War; The Laws of Oléron for the Office of Constable Marshall; and Other Rules and Precedents." These included the authority of ship captains to enforce discipline and mete out punishments, which then included hanging, marooning, keelhauling, flogging, starvation, and

drowning. Being bound in black leather, and having such an unwieldy title, it soon became known colloquially as "The Black Book" and was an important reference for the High Court of Admiralty for almost five hundred years. *See also* Blue Book.

Black cargo: Goods banned or blacklisted by a cargo workers union.

Black dog: [1] To "give a black dog for a white monkey" is an old naval way of expressing a fair exchange. [2] Winston Churchill called depression "The black dog."

Black-down: To coat hull or rigging with blacking as a protective against salt water damage.

Black gang: U.S. and RN slang for stokers and other engineering personnel who always appeared dirty due to ubiquitous coal dust. The term is still sometimes used, although the days of coal-firing are long gone (cf. Snipe).

Black Jack: [1] Nautical slang for bubonic plague. [2] Slang for the Jolly Roger (pirate flag).

Black-shoe: USN slang for an officer of the surface fleet (cf. Brown-shoe).

Black tot day: *See* rum ration, and spirits in the USN.

Blackbirder: Slang for a vessel or person engaged in the slave trade or transporting indentured labor.

Blacking: A mixture of coal dust, coal-tar, and pitch, blended with salt water, boiled, and applied while piping hot as a protective coating for yards, masts, standing-rigging, and hulls.

Blackwall frigate: 18th–19th century merchantman, built on the lines of a frigate with high bulwarks to the main deck, little sheer, limited cargo space, and staterooms for passengers in the poop. (Blackwall was a London shipyard.)

Blackwall hitch: Way of attaching a rope to a hook, so that it is loose until weight is applied but gets tighter as the load increases.

Blade: [1] The flat end of an oar, thrust into the water when rowing. [2] A flat or shaped surface that rotates in air or water to provide thrust for a propeller or paddle-wheel, or to produce power from a turbine. [3] The flat surface of a rudder. [4] The flat cutting part of a sword, cutlass, or knife.

Blank: A cartridge with no bullet, or a cannon fired without shot.

Blanket: Move to windward of another sailing vessel so as to block its wind.

Blasphemy: The punishment of blasphemers has had ups and downs with changing standards of propriety. Under the twelfth century Code of Oléron, profane speech at sea brought no more than a fine in silver coin, but by the late sixteenth century ethical criteria had begun to harden and the culprit had his tongue scraped and was gagged. In the puritanical seventeenth century, it was ordained that blasphemy be punished by burning the offender's tongue with a red-hot iron. Then, in the eighteenth century, religious fervor diminished, and sentences also declined. The

1757 British Articles of War left the punishment for a court to decide:

> All flag officers, and all persons in or belonging to His Majesty's ships or vessels of war, being guilty of profane oaths, cursings, execrations, drunkenness, uncleanness, or other scandalous actions, in derogation of God's honor, and corruption of good manners, shall incur such punishment as a court-martial shall think fit to impose, and as the nature and degree of their offence shall deserve.

The United States' *Colonial Naval Rules* of 1775 were more specific:

> If any shall be heard to swear, curse, or blaspheme the name of God, the Commander is strictly enjoined to punish them for every offense by causing them to wear a wooden collar or some shameful badge for as long as he shall judge proper.

Blazer: This name for a plain or striped colored jacket, usually worn with contrasting trousers, owes its origin to Captain J.W. Washington of HMS *Blazer* who, in 1845 (before uniform clothing was introduced into the Royal Navy) dressed his boat crew in matching blue-and-white striped jackets.

BLCP: Beach lighterage control point.

Bleed the monkey: In this case, the monkey (a generic term for something small) was a tall pyramid-shaped bucket, used to transfer grog from the point of issue to the seamen's mess, and the expression means to sneak a drink before delivering it. (Also Suck the Monkey.)

Bligh: The events of 28 April 1789 and Captain William Bligh's subsequent magnificent feat of small boat navigation are tales too often told to bear repeating, except for some explanatory remarks (*see* Bounty mutiny). It is less well-known that Bligh went on to a distinguished naval career. He fought HMS *Director* with distinction at the Battle of Camperdown, and commanded HMS *Glatton* at the Battle of Copenhagen, where he was the only captain in his squadron in position see both the Admiral's and Vice Admiral's signals (*see* blind eye). By choosing to repeat the latter, he ensured that all the vessels behind him kept fighting, and was personally praised by Nelson for his contribution to the victory. Later, as Governor of New South Wales, he gained the respect of local settlers and Lord Castlereagh commended his "zealous and patriotic exertions."

Nevertheless his achievements were marred by involvement in three more insurrections. In April 1797, his ship was one of those whose crews joined the Spithead mutiny and, a month later, was involved in events at the Nore (*see* Great Mutiny). In 1808 he tried to end the corrupt practices of officers of the New South Wales garrison who had monopolized the import of spirits and re-sold them at 200 percent to 300 percent profit. This culminated in the "Rum Rebellion" led by Major George Johnston and wool merchant John Macarthur who forcibly deposed Bligh and imprisoned him for two years. On his release he was cleared of all blame and promoted to Rear Admiral of the Blue, while Johnston was cashiered. He died a well-respected Vice Admiral of the Blue in 1817 and it was not until later that his reputation was sullied.

Blimp: A small, non-rigid, gas-filled airship.

Blind eye: At the Battle of Copenhagen in 1801, Admiral Sir Hyde Parker hoisted signal "43" (break off the action). Vice Admiral Horatio Nelson, who sensed victory was at hand, raised his telescope to his blind eye, said he could see no signal, and told his flag captain not to strike "signal 16" (engage the enemy). The phrase "Turn a blind eye" later entered colloquial speech meaning to overlook an indiscretion.

Blind zone: An area in which signals or echoes cannot be received.

Blink: Light reflected from ice, snow, or white sand.

Blip: Informal term for the spot of light on a radar or sonar screen, indicating the presence of a contact.

Blister: [1] A bulge built into the side of a warship to protect against mines and torpedoes. Many can be flooded or pumped to adjust stability. [2] A bulge in the fuselage of an aircraft, housing guns or equipment.

Block: A pulley, or multiple pulleys, mounted in a case.

Block and tackle: A system of pulleys and ropes. *See also* sheave, and block and tackle individually.

Block Island Phantom: The Dutch ship *Palatine*, out of Amsterdam, and bound for Philadelphia, had had a harrowing crossing. After murdering the captain, a mutinous crew had terrorized and robbed the 300 well-to-do immigrant Hollanders on board. The drunken seamen were far off course when, just before Christmas 1752, they ran *Palatine* onto the shoals of Block Island, where most of the passengers drowned. Soon local wreckers swarmed on board the abandoned vessel and, after taking everything of value, set it on fire to remove evidence of their crime. A rising tide refloated the burning vessel which drifted into Long Island Sound but, as it went, a terrified shrieking could be heard and a young woman appeared on deck from wherever she had been hiding from the rapacious crew and wreckers. She stood on the deck screaming for help until it collapsed and she disappeared in a shower of bright red sparks. Shortly afterward *Palatine* foundered, leaving nothing but a few charred timbers behind. Since then many people have claimed to have heard female screams and seen the specter of a burning vessel floating in Long Island Sound, sometimes near the December anniversary of the event, sometimes as the portent of a coming gale.

Blockade: Closing a port, harbor, coastline, or shipping lane to prevent passage, entrance, or exit by hostile and (possibly) neutral vessels.

Blockade-runner: A vessel which risks all hazards to pass through a blockade.

Blockship: A vessel deliberately scuttled to restrict access to a channel or harbor entrance.

Bloke: RN lower deck slang for the executive officer of a large ship holding the rank of Commander. (XOs of lower rank are called "Jimmy-the-One.")

Blood money: [1] Compensation paid to the relatives of a slain person. [2] Payment for information leading to the arrest of smugglers or pirates. [3] Bounty paid to a crimp or tavern keeper for assisting in the impressment of sailors.

Bloom: A proliferation of algae and/or higher aquatic plants in a body of water; often related to pollution, especially when pollutants accelerate growth. *See* algal bloom, plankton bloom, and red tide.

BLOS: Beyond line of sight.

Blow the gaff: To disclose secret information. The word "gaff" has nothing to do with the spar or boathook of the same name, but is a variant of "gab" (as in "gift of") which in turn is derived from the Middle English gabbe meaning idle chatter.

BLS Beach landing site.

BLT: Battalion Landing Team.

Blubber: This is the layer of fat from which whale oil is derived, found between the skin and muscles of whales and other cetaceans.

Blubbing: In common usage, the term means crying or shedding tears, but it is one of the few words to come from the whaling industry. When blubber is cut, oil seeps from it in small globules which run down the animal's skin like tears, leading whalers to call weeping blubbing or blubbering.

Blue Book: [1] Generically, any report published by the U S government. [2] Specifically, Regulations for the United States Navy, listing the lineal precedence and seniority of its officers. Cf. Black Book of Admiralty.

Blue ensign: One of three United Kingdom naval flags carrying the Union in the hoist canton (upper left quadrant). *See* British ensigns.

Blue light: A pyrotechnic used by pilot boats to attract attention.

Blue paint: During 17th century, being attacked by "blue devils" (possibly derived from the leaping blue flames of burning brimstone) described a bout of despondency or despair. Later, the expression was abbreviated and "blue" as a stand-alone adjective implied melancholy. Hence, when a sailing ship returned to its home port after a long voyage, it was customary to give people on shore advance notice of the death of the captain or a mate by flying a blue flag and, often, painting a blue stripe along both sides of the hull. If the dead man was especially loved by the crew, they would carry the stripe around the bow and over the figurehead (which had powerful significance for seamen). The practice has long since died out, but the concept of blue being the color of depression lives on when people who are sad say "I'm feeling blue" or Afro-Americans sing "The Blues."

Blue Peter: A square blue flag with a white center ("P" in international code) is displayed to indicate a ship is about to depart. Peter was originally the pho-netic notation for letter "P" and, although it has been changed to Papa, the name of the flag remains. *See also* morning colors.

Blue Riband: The concept of honoring the fastest average speed achieved during an Atlantic crossing arose on 18th April 1838 when *Sirius* averaged 8.03 knots, only to be beaten next day by *Great Western* at 8.66 knots (*GW* had set sail four days after *Sirius*, but arrived only four hours later). The media interest in this quasi-race led a group of shipping magnates to decide that it would be excellent public relations to give the passenger liner making the fastest crossing the unique distinction of flying a large blue ribbon as a pendant on her mainmast. Crossing times rapidly diminished, as can be seen in the following table showing the dates and vessels first exceeding selected speeds:

Speed	Westbound	Eastbound
10	1838 *Great Western* @ 10.43 knots	1843 *Great Western* @ 10.17 knots
15	1875 *City of Berlin* @ 15.21 knots	1873 *Baltic* @ 15.09 knots
20	1889 *City of Paris* @ 20.01 knots	1889 *City of Paris* @ 20.03 knots
25	1908 *Lusitania* @ 25.01 knots	1909 *Mauretania* @ 25.16 knots
30	1936 *Queen Mary* @ 30.14 knots	1935 *Normandie* @ 30.31 knots
35		1952 *United States* @ 35.59 knots
40		1998 *Cat-link V* @ 41.3 knots

During the late 19th and early 20th century winning this privilege became a matter of intense national pride and rivalry, but it lost its significance with the arrival of mass air transport and has not been officially awarded since 1952. (*See also* Hales Trophy.)

Blue shirt: [1] Personnel working on a USN aircraft carrier flight deck wear colored shirts for easy identification; blue shirts chock and chain aircraft on the flight deck. [2] USN slang for any enlisted person below Chief Petty Officer (E.7) at which grade and above khaki shirts are worn.

Blue tile country: An area on the main starboard passageway of an aircraft carrier where the Strike Group flag officer and his staff live and work. In many ships the deck is indeed painted blue here.

Blue water operations: Naval activity on the high seas — about 1,200 kilometers (750 miles) from land. *See also* brown water, green water.

Bluejacket: A naval rating or enlisted person (after the first official uniform for seamen).

Bluenose: [1] A seaman who has served north of the Arctic Circle. [2] Any ship or seaman from Nova Scotia.

Bluewater: Said of [1] A seaman with oceangoing experience. [2] A navy with oceangoing capability.

Bluff: [1] An almost-perpendicular headland, cape,

or cliff. [2] A ship with broad, blunt, clumsy bows (probably from Old Dutch blaf = flat). [3] To mislead by a display of strength, self-confidence, or the like (probably Dutch bluffen = brag).

Blunderbuss: This was a small, compact, large bore, weapon with a unique funnel-shaped barrel, designed (like today's shotguns) to deliver a large quantity of small projectiles over a wide area. It was more like a hand-held cannon than a musket, not fired from the shoulder, but braced against the hip to steady its enormous kick Such a weapon was excellent for personal security, but had no real value on land battlefields, being ineffective beyond about forty feet. However, infantry combat had little in common with the tactics of a naval boarding party. At a range of about thirty feet it spread a six to ten foot cone of shot that was devastating on the deck of a warship. (The name is probably derived from the German donnerbusche meaning thunder gun.)

BM: [1] Boatswain's Mate. [2] Ballistic missile. [3] Beachmaster.

BMCT: Begin morning civil twilight.

BMNT: Begin morning nautical twilight.

BMU: Beachmaster unit.

Boanga: An oared Malayan pirate vessel.

Board: [1] In general, the side of a hull. [2] Specifically, the uppermost plank of a bulwark. [3] To enter or go on board a vessel; whether by invitation, by armed force, or for inspection (e.g., by Customs).

Board of Admiralty: In 1546, King Henry VIII created a Council of the Marine (later to become the Navy Board) to oversee administrative affairs of the naval service, leaving policy direction and operational control in the hands of the Lord High Admiral — until 1628 when King Charles I transferred the latter powers to a committee known as the Board of Admiralty. For the next two centuries, the Navy was run by these two boards, but they were frequently at odds with each other and, in 1832, a reforming political head of the Navy abolished the Navy Board, bringing its functions under the Board of Admiralty, which consisted of Sea Lords (always admirals) and Civil Lords (usually politicians). The professional head of the Royal Navy was (and still is) called First Sea Lord. The political head, who was President of the Board and a Cabinet Minister, was known as First Lord of the Admiralty.

The United States briefly had a Board of Admiralty, founded in 1780. But it was renamed Department of the Navy in 1798. In 1949, it was absorbed by the Department of Defense. In a similar consolidation, fifteen years later in 1964, the British Admiralty came under the jurisdiction of the Ministry of Defence.

Board of Investigation: A military judicial body consisting of one or more persons (usually officers). It is lower than Court of Inquiry and has no power of subpoena.

Board of Ordnance: This agency traces its evolution to the 1370s, when the Privy Wardrobe, one of the departments of the Royal Household, with offices in the Tower of London, was designated to administer weapons, arsenals and castles. The Tower became the most important arsenal in the kingdom, with its own workforce of armourers, bowyers, fletchers, etc. Prior to the establishment of a standing army or navy, it was the only permanent military department in England.

In 1544, King Henry VIII created the Office of Ordnance, which became the Board of Ordnance in 1597. There was still no standing army, and its principal duties were to supply guns, ammunition, stores and equipment to the "Navy Royal." The Great Master of Ordnance ranked immediately below the Lord High Admiral.

In 1683, the Board became a Civil Department of State, under a Master General, responsible for supplying both Navy and Army with military hardware. In 1855, the War Office (army) took over control of the Board, but the Admiralty did not establish its own Naval Ordnance Department until 1891. *See also* Bureau of Ordnance.

Boarding net: [1] Net hung over the side to assist people (often embarking soldiers) to climb the side. Also called scrambling net. [2] Netting hung from the masts of a sailing vessel to prevent an enemy alongside from boarding.

Boarding party: An ad hoc group of seamen and marines, formed to board another vessel.

Boarding pike: A long, sharp, pointed spear used to repel hostile boarders. *See* half pike and pole arms.

Boat: [1] Small vessel for specialized use (e.g., fishing boat) or carried for use by a larger one (e.g., lifeboat). The U.S. Coast Guard defines a boat as being less than 300 tons, anything larger being a ship. [2] Traditional term for tugs, submarines and Coastal Forces or amphibious craft regardless of size. [3] Term used by landlubbers for any waterborne craft.

Boat ahoy!: Traditional hail or challenge to an approaching boat.

Boat barn: Submariner's slang for a submarine pen.

Boat boom: A spar which can be swung out at right angles to the hull as a mooring point for small boats when a ship is at anchor. Also riding boom.

Boat cloak: A sleeveless outer garment, worn to protect uniforms from spray while in small boats, and usually left with the coxswain until the return trip. Originally a mandatory part of an officer's uniform, it was a combination of cape with coat, but later consisted of cape only. This was lined with white satin for naval officers and crimson satin for marines. RN and USN designs were similar with the latter being defined in Article 3501.4 of Uniform Regulations as:

> Made of dark blue woolen fabric, three-quarters of a circle, with a circular bent collar, an extending 2 inches below the kneecap. May be water repellent. Cloak is closed at the neck with hooks and eyes and on the chest by one set of silk or mohair fasteners.

The cloak was officially discontinued by the USN in March 2000. It remains optional in the RN, but is very seldom worn. In the 1840s Lieutenant (later Captain) Peter Halkett, RN invented what was literally a boat-cloak. Made of Mackintosh India-rubber cloth, it could be inflated to form a canoe-like life raft, while an accompanying umbrella could be used as a sail. It was displayed at the Great Exhibition of 1851 and taken on several Arctic expeditions, but never came into naval use.

Boat deck: Superstructure deck for lifeboat storage on a passenger ship. Normally the boats are lowered until level with the deck below, from where passengers clamber into them.

Boat drill: A mandatory assembly of passengers and crew for familiarization with lifeboat stations and to practice donning life preservers. The lifeboats are normally lowered, but not boarded. Provisions of the Canada Shipping Act (here abbreviated) are typical of those applied throughout the industry:

- Before commencement, the master must ensure that all passengers are notified that a drill will take place and that there is no actual emergency.
- The master must ensure that drills, in so far as is practicable, are carried out as if there were an actual emergency.
- The master must ensure that any equipment or installations used during a drill are immediately returned to their full operational condition and are ready for immediate reuse.
- If the general emergency alarm signal or the fire alarm signal is sounded, passengers must proceed to their designated muster stations and the crew members must report to their designated muster stations and prepare to perform their assigned duties.

Boat etiquette: Traditionally, small boats are boarded in reverse order of rank, and exited the other way around. By going first, juniors are on board to steady the craft and provide a helping hand to seniors when they climb down the ship's ladder or step off a quay. The convention also ensures that seniors do not have to wait in the boat while subordinates clamber on board at one end or disembark at the other. This works especially well when the senior officer is visiting a ship. On arrival, the captain can greet the visitor and lead him to his cabin without disembarking juniors getting in the way while, on departure, it allows the senior to linger in conversation after the juniors have boarded. By extension, the same courtesy applies to automobiles and aircraft, where the senior is always last to enter and first to leave. In the RN it is customary that, when a flag or commanding officer leaves his command, the boat taking him ashore be crewed entirely by officers.

Boat fall: A purchase for hoisting a boat to its davits.

Boat gongs: In the USN, when the coxswain of an approaching boat identifies the rank of its most senior passenger (*see* boat recognition) word is passed

"(title) arriving." A bell is then struck as many times as the number of sideboys required to greet the visitor — eight for a vice admiral or above, six for a rear admiral, four for a captain or commander, and two for any other commissioned officer — with one more bell being sounded as the visitor steps aboard. The tones are sounded in pairs as are the half hours of a watch. For example the captain commanding destroyer squadron twenty-five would be announced as "DesRon25 arriving," followed by "Ding-ding ... Ding-ding," plus a final "Ding" as his foot touches the deck. This procedure is reversed upon departure.

Boat group: The basic unit of landing craft in an amphibious operation.

Boat lane: The pathway from line of departure to landing beach designated for landing craft to follow during an amphibious assault. The width of a boat lane is determined by the length of the corresponding landing beach.

Boat oars!: Command to place the oars fore-and-aft across the thwarts, ready to be shipped. *See also* oars, ship oars, toss oars, trail oars.

Boat paint: In the Royal Navy, flag officers' barges are blue, a commander in chief's is green, and all other boats are painted grey or at the captain's discretion. By tradition dinghies are not painted, but varnished over plain wood.

Boat recall: Small boats are called back to the mother ship by a pre-arranged flag or pennant, usually accompanied by a sound signal.

Boat recognition: The United States and Royal Navies share some of the conventions for responding to a sentinel's call of "boat ahoy!" challenging an approaching boat. If not intending to come alongside, the coxswain replies "Passing." Otherwise, the single word "Flag" signifies the presence of an admiral. If a captain (ship commander rather than rank) is carried, the coxswain replies with the name of his ship. When the passengers include a commissioned officer, the response is "Aye-Aye." (If the boat carries a very distinguished civil passenger — a bishop, for example — an astute coxswain will use the "Aye-Aye" response to ensure that the visitor is properly received.)

Other responses differ. In the RN the response "No-No" indicates that no one senior to midshipman is on board, but in the USN this indicates the presence of a petty officer, while "Hello" is used when only junior enlisted personnel are aboard. In addition the USN uses "Fleet" for a fleet, force, or group commander; and "type/Ron/number" for a squadron commander. For example, "DesRon25" would identify the commander of destroyer squadron 25. Each navy has its own responses for senior officials and heads of state.

Boat station: [1] In a warship, the allotted position in a boat for each member of its crew. [2] In a merchant vessel, the assigned place on deck for each passenger to board a lifeboat.

Boat waves: Successive lines of landing craft taking part in an amphibious assault.

Boathook: A wooden pole ending in a metal cap and hook, used for holding-on (with the hook) or fending-off (with the butt-end). Also gaff.

Boatman: A person who hires out boats or provides transport by boat. (Cf. waterman.)

Boats: Traditional slang name for a boatswain.

Boatswain: This is the oldest extant naval title, dating back to the 6th century Anglo-Saxon Batswegen (boat-servant) who was essentially the ship's master responsible for its sailing and navigation. In 1040, the title was brought back (as boatswain) for one of four non-military warrant officers created for warships provided and crewed by the Cinque Ports.

In days of sail the boatswain had to be a first-class seaman, able to command the respect of highly-skilled professional sailors. He was responsible for sails, rigging, anchors, cables, and boats; could stand watch, but was not eligible to command ships. The sailmaker and boatswains mates reported to him. U.S. Naval Regulations of the late 19th century specified:

> A candidate for a boatswain's appointment must be of correct habits, not less than 21 nor more than 35 years of age; must have been at least seven years at sea, and have served at least one year as a petty officer; he must be a thorough practical seaman, and understand cutting, fitting, and rigging according to regulations, the weighing, catting, fishing, securing, and transportation of anchors and the working of cables, the erection and securing of sheers, the handling of purchases, masting, securing yards, etc., and be able to write sufficiently to keep an account of stores.

Nowadays, in naval service, the boatswain is the warrant or petty officer responsible for a vessel's equipment and deck crew. In merchant service he is a petty officer who performs somewhat like the foreman in an industrial plant, being the principal contact between the deck crew and the Chief or First Mate. The title is frequently but differently abbreviated — to Bosun in the USN, Bos'n in the RN, or Bos'un in merchant service.

Boatswain's call or pipe: This high-pitched metal whistle is unique to sea services, where it is used to convey orders and honor visitors. For centuries it was the sailing ship's PA system, emitting shrill penetrating notes that could be heard by topmen high in the rigging and seamen down in the deep, dark orlop. The current instrument has been used in English ships since at least 1248, when it was used to call crossbowmen to action stations, but it has much earlier origins. In the Classical era, Greek and Roman galleys cadenced the stroke of their oars by drum and flute or whistle.

Because it has always served to pass orders, it has often been worn as an honorable symbol of authority. From 1485 to 1562 the "Whistle of Honour" was a golden version suspended from a golden chain and worn as a badge of office by the Lord High Admiral of England. Silver versions known as "Whistles of Command" were used throughout English fleets for the transmission of orders by shipmasters, boatswains and coxswains. Today, wearing one is restricted to quartermasters and boatswain's mates. All its parts have nautical names; the mouth is the "gun"; the ball is the "buoy"; the leaf is its "keel"; and the suspending ring is the "shackle."

In the USN the instrument is known as the boatswain's "pipe," and the message or order it conveys is a "call." In the RN the terms are reversed, with the instrument called boatswain's "call," while "sounding" (playing) it is known as "piping," and the message is a "pipe." Neither service ever uses the term "whistle."

Some calls/pipes have to be followed by an explanatory verbal command, but many are time-honored and understood as orders by themselves. This was a great advantage in 17th/18th century navies when many members of a ship's company might be foreigners with little understanding of languages other than their own. When the pipe is not self-explanatory, the crew is called to attention and the verbal order is preceded by "D'ye hear there" in the British and "Now hear this" in the U.S. navy.

Boatswain's chair: A rope-suspended plank on which a person can be hoisted aloft, transferred across open water to another vessel, or swung over the side for work such as painting.

Boatswain's locker: Compartment where deck gear is stored. Usually forward.

Boatswain's Mate: A petty officer who reports to and assists the boatswain.

Boatswain's pipe: *See* boatswain's call.

Boatwright: A person who builds or repairs boats.

Bobbing the light: A technique for determining if an observer is within the geographic range of a navigation light. If the light disappears when the observer ducks down to a lower line-of-sight, it is at the limit of its range.

Bobstay: A cable, chain, or rod holding down the end of a bowsprit.

BOG: Beach operations group.

Bogey: An unidentified or potentially hostile aircraft (Battle of Britain RAF slang, now in common use in both RN and USN). Also Bogy or Bogie.

Boiler: The pressure vessel in which water is converted into steam for propulsion, heating, and auxiliary purposes. Common forms are "fire tube" and "water tube." The term is used to loosely to include the firebox and ancillary equipment.

Boiler room: *See* furnace room.

Boll: A half-decked, single-masted Dutch fishing boat, gaff-rigged with fore-and-aft sails.

Bollard: Thick low post mounted on a wharf or pier, to which ships mooring lines are attached (cf. bitts).

Bollock block: A block at the head of a topmast, through which the tye of a topsail yard is rove.

Bollocking: RN slang for a severe reprimand (cf. bottle).

Bolo: USN term for a heaving line. Also bola.

Bolster: In sailing ship days, this referred to a piece of soft wood or bag of tarred canvas placed to prevent chafing of stays against the mast when the ship pitched. The modern term is baggywrinkle.

Bolt: The short arrow-like missile fired by a crossbow.

Bolter: Slang for an aircraft which touches down on a carrier but misses the arrester gear and, thanks to an angled flight deck, takes off for another try.

Boltrope: A rope to which the edge of a sail is stitched to prevent splitting. It is made of the best hemp and finest yarns, and is the most superior kind of cordage.

Boltsprit: Antique term for a bowsprit.

Bomb: [1] A hollow projectile containing an explosive or nuclear charge for dropping from aircraft or firing from mortars. [2] To drop such a projectile. [3] A bomb vessel. [4] A great success (Brit.). [5] A great failure (U.S.). Probably from Latin bombus or Greek bombos = a deep hollow sound.

Bomb vessel: Formerly, a small ketch-rigged warship carrying one or more high trajectory heavy mortars for firing at shore targets. The foremast was removed and the hull strengthened to take the heavy weapons and absorb their recoil. These purpose-built vessels often landed their mortars and operated as sloops, sometimes re-installing the foremast for that purpose.

The concept originated in 1681 when the French Navy mounted a pair of forward-pointing mortars side-by-side on the foredeck. These could only be aimed by turning the entire ship with a spring anchor, but later that year the Royal Navy improved the design by mounting the mortars on revolving platforms at the centerline. Space was created by stepping the remaining masts farther aft than normal, thus making the vessels difficult to handle. The rigging of the forward mast was often made of chain to protect it from muzzle blast.

Bomb vessels saw their first action in the British bombardment of Algiers in 1682. They were traditionally given names suggestive of explosive or frightening qualities, especially volcanoes and underworld characters. They were often used for polar expeditions because their sturdy hulls fared well in ice. Two of them — HMS *Erebus* and HMS *Terror* — accompanied Sir James Clark Ross on his 1841 discovery of Ross Island, which is formed by three volcanoes. Ross named the one active volcano Mount Erebus, and the bigger of two dormant volcanoes Mount Terror. With no more ships to give him inspiration, he named the third one Mount Bird.

Bombard: [1] To attack with artillery, bombs, or mortars. [2] A 15th century large-bore, short-barreled cannon.

Bombay Marine: The maritime force of the British East India Company. *See* Indian Navy.

Bonded: Stores kept in or delivered from a Customs-controlled (bonded) warehouse. They may not be opened or consumed until the vessel is in international waters.

Bone: [1] The white foam or spray thrown out under the bow of a fast-moving vessel, which is said to "have a bone in her teeth." [2] 18th century RN slang for pilfer, steal or scrounge. The word comes from the name of the boatswain in Admiral Cornwallis's flagship, who became notorious for making good deficiencies in his stores by stealing from other ships. The admiral is reported to have said after one such flagrant event: "I trust, Mr. Bone, you will leave me with my anchors."

Bongo: A boat made of a hollowed-out bonga tree. Formerly popular in what are now the southern United States.

Bonnet: A supplementary sail laced to the foot of a square-sail or jib.

Booby: This tropical sea bird liked to perch on the yards of sailing ships where, because it had few predators and no fear, sailors could approach near enough to easily catch it. This led Spanish seamen to call it bobada (stupid) and the word was adopted into English as both the name of the bird and slang for a fool. The bird's puffed out chest also reminded sex-starved seamen of a woman's breasts, which they colloquially called boobs. All three terms found their way into common usage.

Book: [1] To be listed as a member of the ship's company is to be officially "on the books." [2] The colloquial phrase "in the black book" (meaning to be in disfavor or deserving punishment) is almost certainly derived from the Black Book of Admiralty.

Boom: [1] A floating barrier protecting a harbor or containing something. [2] The sound of distant gunfire. [3] A spar extending the foot of a sail. [4] A boat boom. (From the Dutch boom = tree.)

Boom vang: A device to hold a boom down and maintain the shape of its sail. Cf. martingale.

Boomer: USN slang for a ballistic missile submarine.

Boondocks: USN slang for any remote or isolated place. The word (which derives from the Tagalog word bundok = mountain) was brought to the United States by military personnel returning from the brutal and bloody colonial Philippines campaign of 1899–1902. The RN equivalent is "ulu" from the Malayan for headwaters. Hence, "out in the boondocks" = "up the ulu."

Boot camp: USN term for recruit training. Named after the leggings called "boots" worn by trainees during the Spanish-American War.

Boot stripe: A stripe painted along the waterline to delineate side paint from bottom paint. Called boot-topping in the RN.

Boot topping: [1] The RN term for a boot stripe. [2] The activity of painting a boot stripe.

Bootlegger: This term for an illegal trafficker in alcohol originated with seamen who smuggled perfume or liquor by stuffing bottles into their high seaboots when going ashore or embarking.

Bootneck: RN slang for a marine. After the heavy leathern stock worn by 18th century soldiery. The USN equivalent is leatherneck.

Booty: Plunder gained by war or piracy. Originally restricted to things that could be picked up by hand on the open deck, but now more general. From the Viking byti = loot.

Bording: A flat-bottomed Baltic coastal cargo vessel.

Bore: [1] The inside of a gun barrel. [2] Its diameter or caliber. [3] A tidal wave rushing upstream from an estuary, an eagre. [4] To proceed steadily or laboriously (e.g., a destroyer boring through heavy seas, or an icebreaker boring through an icefield). [5] To make a hole or tunnel by drilling, digging, or burrowing. [6] A dull or tedious person.

Boreas: Greek god of the cold and powerful north wind, whose name was still common among seafarers in the 19th century. Ancient artists usually depicted him as an old man with shaggy hair and beard, whistling through a conch shell, clad in a short pleated tunic and wearing a billowing cloak. Often he had serpent tails instead of feet. *See also* gods of the wind.

Boss: The rounded hub of a propeller.

Bosun: *See* boatswain.

Botte: The Anglo-Saxon word for boat.

Bottes-carle: The Anglo-Saxon word for a coxswain. It translates as "boat-person."

Bottle: RN slang for a reprimand (cf. bollocking, gig).

Bottom: [1] A vessel's lower hull, from bilge-to-bilge, including the keel. [2] The sea bed or floor. [3] To sink to and rest on the sea bed (of a submarine).

Bottom board: A removable grating in a small open boat.

Bottom bounce: The technique of increasing effective sonar range by allowing transmitted sound waves to ricochet off the ocean floor.

Bottom effect: The "drag" on sonar or other sound waves caused by contact with the floor in shallow-water.

Bottom mine: An explosive device that detonates when its pressure sensitive sensor detects a passing vessel. It lies on or is anchored to the sea bed at depths of about 30 fathoms (55 meters/180 feet) for attacks on surface vessels, or down to about 110 fathoms (200 meters/660 feet) when submarines are the prey. Rocket mines and torpedo mines are specialized varieties.

Bottomry: A form of mortgage executed by a master who is unable to contact his owners but needs funds for repairs, or to continue and complete a voyage. Either the vessel and its cargo, or the ship alone can be hypothecated as security. *See also* respondentia.

Bottoms: Term sometimes used to count an assembly of disparate types of vessel (e.g., there were 15 bottoms in the anchorage).

Boucan: [1] A grill or barbeque used to smoke meat. [2] Strips of cured meat similar to biltong.

Boucanier: The user of a boucan grill. Applied to French religious and political refugees who eked out a living on the island of Hispaniola by hunting cattle and selling their hides, tallow, and cured meat to passing ships. Boucaniers were far from prepossessing. Their faces were almost hidden by long tresses and thick beards. They stank to the heavens, and were so heavily-tanned that they might have been smoked on their own curing fires. Clothing was usually a blood-stained, fat-impregnated, cotton vest or coarse linen shirt. Their rawhide leggings had been donned while still reeking and worn until they stiffened to the proper shape. When Spain destroyed their herds and drove them from their homes, many boucaniers settled on the island of Tortuga and turned to piracy. The name was eventually anglicized to buccaneer and applied to all 17th century Caribbean pirates. *See also* Filibuster.

Bounce line: The point off a hostile beach at which underwater demolition teams launch their rubber boats, usually at night.

Bound: [1] Proceeding in a specific direction or to a specific destination (e.g., bound for New York). [2] A constraint (e.g., fogbound, icebound, tidebound). [3] A leap forward. [4] To be fettered, fastened, tied, restrained, or obligated.

Boundary current: A warm, deep, narrow, fast flowing current that occurs along the side of an ocean basin. Fast-flowing Western Boundary Currents are an important factor in climate control, bringing warm water northward from the equator. In contrast, Eastern Boundary Currents are generally broad and shallow, creeping slowly along carrying cold water towards the tropics.

Boundary wave: A subsurface wave between different density layers. Often much larger than wind-driven surface waves. Also called an internal wave.

Bounded sea: Any sea space surrounded by land with restricted entry and exit routes and limited operating space.

Bounty: [1] A premium or reward offered by a government for specific actions. [2] An incentive to enlistment. [3] A death benefit paid to widows of seamen.

***Bounty* mutiny:** Thanks to novelists and Hollywood, this event is popularly believed to have been a reaction to the cruel behavior of a despotic shipmaster. In fact, Lieutenant Bligh tended to scold when other captains would have flogged, and to flog when others would have hanged. He only imposed one sentence on the outward journey, writing in the log, "Until this afternoon I had hoped I could have performed this voyage without punishment to anyone." He was uncommonly concerned with the physical health of his men, but he had little empathy for their sensitivities, his temper was ferocious, and his tongue-lashings became legendary. The public insults of a captain who had long been his personal friend deeply affected Master's Mate Fletcher Christian, who was already psychologically disturbed by having to leave his Tahitian wife-mistress. He planned to desert but at the last minute instigated mutiny instead. *See also* Bligh.

Bouquet mine: An anti-minesweeping device, consisting of a sinker or anchor with a number of buoyant mines attached. One is raised to a pre-determined depth, while the others are held near the bottom. If the mooring of the raised one is cut, or the mine is detonated, another rises from the sinker to take its place.

Bourrelet: One of the features of a naval projectile, being a machined surface that acts as bearing for the projectile during its travel along the bore of a gun. Some projectiles have a single bourrelet forward; others also have one or two at the rear.

Bow(s): The angled forward end of a boat or ship, as it widens from the stem.

Bow-chaser: A gun mounted so as to fire forward of the ship (cf. Stern-chaser).

Bow door(s): [1] On landing craft, a bottom-hinged door is dropped to form a ramp for the disembarkation of troops and vehicles. [2] On landing ships or ro-ro ferries, a pair of side-hinged doors opens for the same purpose.

Bow insignia: Symbols attached to the bows of a boat, indicating the rank of the officer on board. *See* visual recognition of approaching boats.

Bow line: A mooring line attached to the bow. Not to be confused with bowline.

Bow number: Identification number painted on the bow of U.S. warships. Also hull number or official number.

Bow thruster: A tunnel-mounted propeller which pushes the bow laterally to assist maneuvering in tight spaces (pronounced bau-thruster).

Bower: Either of two anchors carried at the bow. They are called "best" and "small," not because of size, but because that to starboard is the most-used (or best) while the one to port has only occasional (small) use.

Bowing & scraping: This term for extreme humility originated in the 18th century when a small triangular sail, called a skyscraper, was sometimes set at the peak of the mast (above the skysail which itself sat above the royal). By analogy, a naval officer's cocked hat, being worn at the peak of his body, was known colloquially as a scraper. Supplementing the conventional salute to a superior by bowing as well as removing the hat consequently came to be associated with unusual servility.

Bowline: [1] A knot which neither jambs nor slips (pronounced bo-lin). Not to be confused with bowline (bau-line). [2] A rope made fast to the weather leech of a square-sail to keep it as flat as possible when close-hauled.

Bowline-on-a-bight: A bowline tied using doubled line when a free end is not available.

Bowman: [1] The foremost oarsman, who manages the boathook (pronounced bau-man). [2] An archer (pronounced bo-man).

Bowplane: A forward-mounted fin which can be rotated to help a submarine rise or dive.

Bows-on: Heading directly towards.

Bowse: To tighten with a tackle.

Bowser boat: A vessel equipped with tanks for re-fuelling boats or seaplanes.

Bowsheets: A platform or seat at the front of a small boat (*see* sheets).

Bowsprit: A heavy spar pointing forward from the stem of a vessel, supporting parts of the standing rigging, and usually carrying its own sail or jib (pronounced bo-sprit).

Bowsprit-ends: Former RN name for the jackstaff.

Bow-wave: The transverse wave created by the stem of a vessel cutting through the water. Reducing the size of bow waves is a major goal of naval architects because they create friction which has a negative effect on fuel economy. A blunt bow produces a large wave, while a bulbous bow reduces its size (cf. wave-resistance).

Box: [1] A container with firm flat sides, used for certain types of solid cargo. [2] *See* box the compass, boxhaul, and carrier box.

Box the compass: To recite all thirty-two points of the compass clockwise from north (*see* table 17). This is one of three basics an apprentice seaman would have to master, the others being to know the ropes and to recognize the marks and deeps of the lead line. (From the Spanish boxar = go around.)

Boxhaul: A maneuver in which sails are backed, helm is put hard-alee, and the ship gains sternway to turn on her heel. Only performed in cases of extreme emergency, since no sailing ship seaman was comfortable running astern.

Boy: From its earliest days, ships of the Royal Navy carried male children, who served in many capacities, including powder-monkey and apprentice seaman. The official rating of Boy Seaman evolved during the eighteenth century and eventually created a pool of men, trained in the ways of the Navy (but knowing virtually nothing else). In 1903, the rating of Boy Artificer was introduced, to provide training in the emerging technologies of steam, aircraft, and signals. The recruitment and training of boys continued until its abolition in 1956.

Boy was an enlisted rating in the United States Navy from 1797 until 1893. Meanwhile, an apprentice system, introduced in 1875, had begun to form a major part of the training program for enlisted men. Its purpose was to attract high caliber youngsters to enlist as Apprentice Boys for instruction in seamanship, gunnery and the rudiments of a general education. This program was discontinued in 1904.

Boyer: A Flemish boat with high bow and stern works.

BP: [1] Beach party. [2] Black powder.

BPF: British Pacific Fleet (World War II).

Brace: [1] To stiffen or support something (from this is derived the term "brace yourself," meaning prepare to meet a challenge or disappointment). [2] A device that holds something firmly. [3] To swing or turn the yards of a square-rigged vessel. [4] A brace is also running rigging consisting of a line rove through a block and stropped to the end of a square-rig yard to control its horizontal movement so that the sails catch the wind as efficiently as possible.

Bracket: Gunnery term referring to establishing the range of a target by firing one shot short and another beyond. A correction equal to half the distance between the two will then bring the shot to fall closer to the target, perhaps to straddle it or score a hit.

Brackish: [1] Slightly salty or briny. [2] a mixture of fresh and sea water.

Braid: [1] To weave the strands of a rope together (cf. splice). [2] Gold decoration on an officer's uniform.

Braided line: This type of line does not stretch to the degree that twisted rope does, and is more difficult to splice. However, it goes through a pulley or block very well because of its rounded shape, and is stronger than equivalent sized twisted line. However, it tends to snag when used as docking line if the pilings are rough. Several types are available:

• Hollow Braid has no core. It is very flexible but can flatten during use and is only found in small sized rope.
• Braid on Braid has a braided core inside a braided sheath. It will stretch less, and has less flexibility, than a hollow braid.
• Multibraid is braided with 2 pairs of Z-laid and two pairs of S-laid strands. It is flexible and does not kink.
• Parallel Core has a braided sheath over a core of straight or lightly twisted yarns. it is very strong.

Brail(s): [1] Rope(s) passed through blocks and fastened to the leech of a fore-and-aft sail. [2] To haul on these so as to reduce sail.

Branding: At one time, those dishonorably-discharged from the Royal Navy were physically branded "D" for deserter or "B" for bad character. Later, the name was applied to a dishonorable-discharge certificate or "ticket" which had its corner cut off, thereby "branding" the recipient.

Brash: [1] Small fragments of crushed ice collected by the wind. [2] Timber that does not splinter when stressed (usually a sign of rot).

Brass hat: slang term for a senior officer (entitled to wear gold braid on the cap). Collectively "the brass."

Brass monkey: According to some sources, the phrase "Cold enough to freeze the balls off a brass monkey" is not a crude reference to simian anatomy, but concerned a device for storing ready-use cannonballs near each gun without having them rolling dangerously around the deck. The foundation is said to have been a square plate with sixteen cannonball-shaped indentations on its face, made of brass because iron balls would have rusted to an iron one, and called a monkey because that term then signified small. Nine balls could be nested in the gaps between the sixteen sitting directly on the plate, four could fit on top of the nine, and a thirtieth ball could rest on those four, forming a neat and stable pyramid.

According to this theory, a problem arose when temperatures fell, because the coefficients of linear expansion of brass and iron are different, thus causing the indentations to contract faster than the balls resting in them. Hence when it got "cold enough to freeze the balls **off** a brass monkey" the bottom layer would slide off, spilling all thirty balls across the deck. This theory fell down when engineers calculated the difference in contraction over any probable temperature range would be far too small to dislodge the balls. Undeterred, supporters of the theory suggested that a drop in temperature would cause condensation to form on the metals, which would then turn to ice and lock the balls in position, so the phrase should really be "freeze the balls **onto** a brass monkey."

These ingenious theories are questionable, firstly because no contemporary nautical glossary mentions the device, secondly because none of the vast collections of maritime artifacts includes one, and thirdly because round shot was normally carried in wooden racks or stacked on rope garlands, and there would have been no reason to use expensive brass when these cheaper materials worked perfectly well. Probably the phrase is nothing more than a traditional, crude, and colorful idiom describing exceptionally bitter weather.

Brass rags: In the days when sailors were required to provide their own cleaning materials, it was a sign of friendship for two of them to share gear, especially their brass-cleaning rags. Those who did so were called raggies and when the friendship broke up they were said to have "parted brass rags."

Brassard: An identifying armband (e.g., for members of shore patrols).

Bravo: NATO phonetic notation for the letter "B" (*see* table 11).

Bravo Zulu: Phonetic rendering of the NATO signal code "BZ" meaning "Well done" (*see* table 11).

Brazil Current: A warm and saline branch of the south equatorial current that flows southward along the coast of Brazil.

Breach: Said of [1] A sea crashing over the side of a vessel and breaking: (if the waves roll over the vessel without breaking it is said to be a clear breach. [2] A whale leaping out of the water, falling back at an angle, splashing and making a loud noise. (This may be a form of communication with other whales, or may clean off some of the encrustations of parasites such as barnacles and lice.) [3] A gap or opening made by breaking or battering a wall or fortification. [4] Non-fulfillment of an obligation (e.g., breach of contract; breach of promise). Cf. breech.

Break: [1] To unfold and display a flag that was still

furled when previously-hoisted. [2] The point of discontinuity between two levels on the deck of a ship. One deck stops and a ladder leads to another at a lower level. [3] An improvement in the weather. [4] To reduce in rank or rate. [5] To fold over and form a breaker (said of a wave). [6] To part the surface (said of an ascending submarine).

Break ground: [1] Said of an anchor as it comes clear of the bottom. [2] Seabee term for starting a construction project.

Break out: [1] To open something or make it available. [2] To release an anchor from the bottom. [3] Stevedore term for the removal of cargo from the hold to the lifting area below the hatch (i.e., to un-stow).

Break step: To stop marching in cadence.

Breakaway: To disconnect and retrieve all lines and hoses used for refueling at sea.

Breakaway music: A modern U.S. Naval practice, intended to motivate sailors. When underway replenishment is complete and the breakaway begins, the receiving ship's "signature song" is played in recognition of a difficult job well done.

Breakbulk: [1] To begin the discharge of cargo. [2] To assemble numerous small shipments at a central point so that economies of scale can be realized. [3] Short for breakbulk cargo.

Breakbulk cargo: [1] Any commodity whose weight, dimensions, or incompatibility with other cargo require it to be shipped by special means. [2] See general cargo.

Breakbulk ship: A ship equipped with cargo-handling gear and conventional holds for the stowage of breakbulk cargo, which may be stored above as well as below deck. Breakbulk ships are sometimes capable of carrying a limited number of containers, above or below deck.

Breaker: [1] A heavy wave, rising up, curling over, and dissolving into foam near the shore. As the wave moves into shallower water, friction with the sea bed starts to slow it down. The energy released causes a steeper sea, often higher than the wavelength can support. A marked increase in roughness and much breaking of waves is then likely to occur. [2] large swells may also become unstable and form deep water breakers or combers in mid ocean. [3] A small cask, keg, or barrel. From the Spanish baréca, hence also "Barricoe."

Breaking strength: The quoted strength of rope or cable is usually determined using new product, under laboratory conditions, pulling — at a slow, steady rate, in a straight line, and in accordance with prescribed test procedures — until it snaps. In real life, however, forces often change direction and intensity, while factors of wear, tear, and type of service can cause the rope to fail at much reduced loads. Accordingly, the safe working load of any rope is much lower than its nominal strength.

Breakwater: [1] A low forward bulkhead on the upper deck of a ship. [2] A structure used to reduce the force of incoming waves on a shore.

Bream: To burn weeds off a wooden ship's hull while in dry dock.

Breast: [1] To head directly into the waves. [2] The end of a block opposite to that through which the fall runs.

Breast & sleeve insignia: USN personnel wear various gold, silver, or pewter insignia over the left breast to indicate special qualifications such as aviation, surface, or submarine warfare. Some are worn above medal ribbons, others below. Special service badges such as command-at-sea or presidential service are worn on the right breast while on that duty; afterward they are transferred to the left below the medal ribbons. The RN uses only the submariner's "dolphins" in this fashion. RN aviators wear their wings on the left sleeve, above their distinction lace. Royal Naval and Royal Marine personnel wear parachute wings on the left sleeve just below the shoulder.

Breastband: Safety belt worn by a leadsman in the USN.

Breastbeam: A timber at the forward end of quarterdeck or after end of forecastle.

Breastline/Breastrope: A lateral mooring line to prevent movement away from the dock.

Breech: [1] The rear end of a gun enclosing the chamber of a muzzle-loader, or where the shells and cartridges of a breech-loader are inserted. [2] A trunk connecting two boilers to a single funnel, resembling a pair of breeches or an upside down "Y." [3] the lower end of a pulley block. Cf. breach.

Breech block: A locking device that seals the firing chamber of a gun.

Breech-loader: A gun loaded from the breech (cf. muzzle-loader).

Breeches buoy: Short canvas trousers attached to a lifebuoy, suspended from a highline by block-and-tackle, and used to transfer people from ship-to-ship or from shipwreck-to-shore.

Breeching ropes: *See* Gun tackles.

Brendan the Navigator: Legend has it that this sixth century Irish Abbot had a vision of the "Land of Delight" across the Western (Atlantic) Ocean. His first attempt to find it was unsuccessful, so he and the monks of his crew prayed and fasted for forty days before setting out again. Their second voyage is said to have lasted seven years and taken them to many unidentified islands. These may have included the Orkneys and Shetlands; while places as far south as Madeira and the Canaries, and as far west as the Azores have also been suggested. However, based on prevailing winds and the sailing qualities of an Irish curragh as tested by British scholar-adventurer Tim Severin, their most probable route would have been via the Hebrides and Faroes to Iceland, and possibly on to Newfoundland.

Whatever their ultimate landfall, they claimed to

have found a large land mass which they called "The Promised Land of the Saints" at the far side of the Western Ocean. This was shown (in various locations) on maritime charts for several centuries and, along with Viking reports of "Vineland," may have helped convince Christopher Columbus there was land across the Atlantic.

Some skeptics refused to believe that a fragile oxhide curragh could have survived an open sea crossing, but Severin's expedition proved it possible. Others pointed to implausible statements that they claimed proved the story to be mythical. But "crystals that rose to the sky" could well have been icebergs; the "flaming, foul-smelling rocks" with which they were pelted could easily have come from Icelandic volcanoes; and their being "raised up on the back of sea monsters" could simply mean that a whale breeched under their little craft. Far from being a medieval fantasy, the Navigatio Santi Brendani Abatis (Voyage of Saint Brendan the Abbot) could be the distorted report of an actual exploration. Brendan himself lived well into his nineties, and must be having a busy afterlife as he is considered the patron saint of boatmen, watermen, mariners, sailors, travelers, and whales.

Brethren of the Coast: This is said to have been a loose confederation of Caribbean buccaneers based on Tortuga Island during the "Golden Age." Some such organization may have existed, but the name is probably one of several 19th century fictional inventions such as walking the plank.

Brevet: Military or naval commission in a higher grade or rank, usually without pay and with limited authority. Sometimes granted for the duration of hostilities, at others as a retirement honor. No longer used in the British armed forces.

Brevity code: An insecure method which serves to shorten messages but does not conceal their content.

Bride of the Adriatic: Since the 11th century, the marriage of Venice to the sea has been celebrated on Ascension Day. Originally, the elected chief magistrate, known as the Doge, was rowed out to the Adriatic in his magnificent state barge *Bucentaur* to throw a golden ring into the waters, symbolizing the city-state's marriage to Neptune who granted his bride supremacy at sea. The ceremony continues to this day, with the Mayor replacing the Doge.

Bridge: [1] A raised transverse platform from where a powered vessel is controlled, docked, and navigated; usually includes chart room and pilot house. [2] The open area on top of a submarine's sail or conning tower. [3] To ride the waves from crest-to-crest without sinking into the troughs.

Bridgehead: Refers to an area in hostile territory that has been captured and is held awaiting further troops and supplies. *See also* airhead, beachhead, lodgement .

Bridle: A line or wire rope secured at both ends, used to distribute the load of another line or object attached to its mid-point. Used especially when towing another ship or catapulting an aircraft.

Bridport dagger: The rope used for a naval hanging (*see* Preface).

Brief: To instruct assigned personnel before they begin a mission or operation (cf. debrief).

Brig: [1] A small two-masted square-rigged ship with a fore-and-aft sail on the lower part of the mainmast. Brigs often carried long sweeps so that they could maneuver in calm weather. [2] USN term for a ship's prison, formerly but no longer used in the RN. One theory holds that the name refers to a jail for brigands, but it more probably originated when Admiral Nelson used brigs to transport prisoners of war from the Mediterranean to English prisons or hulks.

Brigantine: A small two-masted ship, square-rigged on the foremast and main topmast, and fore-and-aft on the lower mainmast.

Brightwork: [1] Polished metal shipboard fittings. [2] Scoured woodwork, plain or varnished, but excluding painted surfaces.

Brine: [1] Water saturated or strongly impregnated with salt. Used before refrigeration to preserve foodstuffs, especially meats, during long voyages. [2] Sea water.

Bring about: Change onto a new course.

Bring 'em near: 18th century term for a telescope.

Bring to: Check movement by arranging sails so that they counteract each other.

Bring up: Stop quickly by running aground or dropping an anchor with way on.

Briny: [1] As a verb = saline. [2] As a noun = the sea (British slang).

Bristol fashion: In the heyday of sail, the port of Bristol on the Severn Estuary in south-western England had a worldwide reputation for proficiency in shipbuilding and repair. Hence the term "Shipshape and Bristol Fashion" came to be applied to vessels which were exceptionally well-maintained, clean, trim, and tidy.

British ensigns: From the 17th to the 19th centuries the British fleet was divided into three squadrons which took their names from the color of distinguishing ensigns worn at the maintop in combat. Originally the order of seniority was red-blue-white, but that was changed to red-white-blue in 1653 during the First Anglo-Dutch War. Thereafter, in the line of battle the red squadron stood at the center and was commanded by the admiral. The white squadron took the van under command of the vice-admiral, while the blue squadron lay at the back under the rear-admiral. These were appointments rather than ranks, and an individual might, for example, be in overall command as Admiral of the Red in one engagement but commanding the White or Blue squadron (as vice- or rear-admiral) in the next. In 1743 permanent flag ranks, still color-identified, were introduced (*see* Admirals in the Royal Navy).

Color-coding ended In 1864, when the entire navy

adopted the white ensign (as Nelson had recommended decades before). Thereafter, the blue ensign was reserved for government departments and vessels crewed or commanded by members of the naval reserve, while the red ensign was made officially available to the general public as well as merchantmen (which had been using it unofficially for some time). Special warrants were issued authorizing various yacht clubs to use one of the three ensigns, usually with a "defacing" badge or emblem superimposed.

Broach: [1] Of a sailing vessel; to head into a quartering wind due either to waves striking the stern or to bad helmsmanship. [2] Of any vessel; to veer unintentionally broadside-on to wind and waves and be overwhelmed. [3] Of a submarine; to break without rising completely to the cruising position. [4] To tap a barrel or break into cargo.

Broad: [1] In hydrology: a wide river that is shallow over long stretches. [2] USN slang for a female.

Broad in/on: [1] "Broad **in** the beam" refers to a wide-hulled ship. [2] "Broad **on** the beam" signifies 90° from dead ahead on either side. [3] "Broad on the bow" means a relative bearing of 45° (to starboard) or 315° (to port). [4] "Broad on the quarter" means midway between abeam and astern (135° from dead ahead).

Broad pennant: The distinctive mark of a commodore, worn at the masthead of his command ship.

Broad reach: Sailing away from the wind, but not directly downwind.

Broadside: [1] The side of a ship, above the water between bow and stern. [2] All the guns on one side of a ship. [3] Their simultaneous firing. [4] The weight of shot then fired. *See also* naval tactics in the age of sail.

Broadside on: [1] Facing a ship's side. [2] With waves on the beam.

Broke: Today an officer convicted by court-martial is dismissed, but in earlier days he was sentenced to be broke(n). As most had been at sea since the age of twelve or thereabouts, they had few skills for survival in civilian life and many soon found themselves penniless. Thus, the term came into general use to mean bankrupt or short of funds. *See also* break.

Broken water: Ripples, eddies, or small waves on otherwise smooth seas.

Broker: [1] In general: An agent employed to effect bargains and contracts, as a middleman or negotiator, for a fee or commission. The broker does not take possession of the subject matter of the negotiation, and generally contracts in the names of those who employ him, rather than his own. [2] In insurance: An agent procuring marine insurance on vessels, or against fire. [3] In shipping: One who acts as agent in buying and selling ships; also in procuring freight, arranging loading and discharge, etc.

Brokerage: The fee or commission paid to a broker.

Broom at the masthead: [1] In the days of sailing ships, a long-handled broom worn at the masthead signified that the vessel was for sale and bids would be welcome. [2] There is a tradition (possibly apocryphal) that Dutch Admiral Michael Adriaansoon de Ruyter hoisted a broom on his flagship to signify he had swept the British fleet aside during his daring raid in the Thames Estuary in 1667. [3] In the modern USN a broom is sometimes raised to the masthead to show that the vessel has been awarded a battle efficiency pennant.

Brow: The Navy term for a gangplank used to bridge the gap between ship and shore or between two vessels. Often equipped with handrails and wheels to allow movement when the tide rises or falls.

Brown Bess: Familiar nickname for the regulation-issue, large-caliber (0.75 inch) British flintlock musket, a short version of which was in naval and marine service from about 1730 to 1863.

Brown paper warrant: One issued on a captain's authority and revocable by him.

Brown shirt: Personnel working on a USN aircraft carrier flight deck wear colored shirts for easy identification. Brown shirts are worn by plane captains and flight deck petty officers.

Brown-shoe: Former USN slang for officers in naval aviation (cf. Black-shoe). Seldom used since khakis were introduced and all officers wear brown shoes.

Brown water operations: Naval activity along the littoral in navigable riverine and estuarine areas and extending perhaps 150 kilometers (about 100 miles) offshore. This is the area in which navies interact with land forces, coastal traffic, and much of a nation's economic activity by making close offshore and inshore approaches to hostile or friendly land masses. *See also* blue water, green water, and littoral operations.

Brunswick's "Kraken": Shortly after World War II, Captain Arne Grønningsæter reported that, during the 1930s, the Royal Norwegian Navy's auxiliary tanker *Brunswick* had been attacked three times off Samoa by a giant squid. In each case the creature had pulled alongside, paced the ship for a while and then, possibly mistaking it for a whale, wrapped its tentacles around the hull and attempted to overturn or pull the vessel down. It eventually slipped off the greasy steel plates and was minced by the ship's propellers, but might well have succeeded if it had attacked a wooden vessel of one-tenth the burden. This story raises three questions.

- How could the creature have mistaken a 15,000 ton tanker for a 200 ton whale?
- Why did a (presumably) sound-sensitive animal ignore the noise of *Brunswick*'s propulsion system to approach the ship?
- Why did Captain Grønningsæter wait two decades before reporting the incident?

The first two remain open, but it seems reasonable to assume that the captain waited until retirement, fearing ridicule that would harm his naval career. (*See also* Kraken, monsters of the deep, and the appendix.)

BSA: Beach support area.

BTU: British Thermal Unit.

Buccaneer: Specifically refers to a pirate operating in the Caribbean during the so-called "Golden Age" (1680–1730). Sometimes incorrectly used as a generic term for any pirate. *See* Boucanier.

Bucentaur: The large and splendid state galley of Venetian Doges. *See* Bride of the Adriatic.

Buck: The phrase "pass the buck," meaning to evade responsibility by shifting the blame to someone else, has two possible origins. [1] During the heyday of poker in the 19th century, a marker called "the buck" was placed beside the player next due to deal. Accepting the buck was to accept responsibility for dealing. [2] The card players may have got the idea from an earlier egalitarian USN tradition that is still followed. At formal dinners, a marker, also called "the buck," is placed on the wardroom table to indicate which officer is to be served first. This buck is moved around the table before the next dining-in, so that a different officer has that privilege at each meal. [3] No one knows where the term came from, but it has been suggested that the original markers were silver dollars — raising the question, was the marker named after the coin, or the coin after the marker?

Bucket: To lose a bucket over the side was considered a major calamity, far beyond its obvious utility on shipboard since, for some unrecorded reason, anyone who deliberately or accidentally pushed or kicked one overboard was believed to be inviting Death on board. This superstitious seafarer's fear of disaster probably underlies the phrase "kick the bucket."

Bucko: [1] American Merchant Marine slang for the mate of a sailing ship who was frequently a brutal and violent slave-driver, especially while striving for speed in the grueling passage around Cape Horn. [2] British Merchant Navy slang for a manly and swaggering sailor.

Buffer: RN slang for the Chief Boatswain's Mate.

Bugeye: A Chesapeake Bay oyster dredger, descended from both the Log Canoe and the Baltimore Clipper. About 60 feet (18 m) long, with a graceful clipper bow, ample midship section, and sharp stern. It was originally built of nine long logs, but later used frame and planking construction. Two tall masts, raked sharply aft, carried sails that were sharp-headed long before Marconi rig was introduced.

Bugle: Although the boatswain's call (or pipe) is the principal "sound signal" used on smaller naval vessels, the bugle is traditionally used to convey orders on shore stations and on ships large enough to carry marine detachments. Originally called the buglehorn it first appeared in England during the 13th century, and traces its roots to the Latin buculus meaning ox or young bull. The modern instrument, which owes its development to the British infantry and came to the navy via the marines, is made of copper or brass with a conical bore of increasing diameter. Pitch is controlled by varying the shape of the player's mouth. The British bugle, introduced in 1870, is twice-coiled, as is the regulation American instrument of 1882. This design is short and easy to handle on shipboard.

The high-pitched notes of wind instruments can penetrate the noise of battle, so their use to issue commands has a long history. There are many references to horns and trumpets in the Old Testament, including (Numbers 10:9) "And if ye go to war ... sound an alarm with the trumpets." At least forty-three signals were used in the Roman Legions — in *De Re Militari* (A.D. 390) Vegetius wrote; "The music of the legion consists of trumpets, cornets and buccinae. The trumpet sounds the charge and the retreat ... but in time of action, the trumpets and cornets sound together." The first reliable record of horn commands in the post-classical era, comes from William of Brittany, who wrote of the Battle of Bouvines in 1214; "the trumpets sounded terrifyingly, inviting the warriors to promptly charge the enemy" (Phillipiad XI:64)

Bugle calls: In the 16th century English army, trumpets were used for cavalry commands and drums for infantry, but gradually the bugle took over from the latter (a Royal Marines bugler is still called a drummer). To avoid confusion between different units, British bugle calls were standardized late in the reign of King George III. In the United States, some bugle calls were inherited from the British, most were adopted from the French by the Continental Army, and a few are home-grown.

The wide range of bugle calls for command and control are made easier to remember by "mnemonics" (systematic methods for helping the memory when recall is required). In this case, words or rhymes are developed which are both relevant to the activity and have a cadence matching the rhythm of the bugle notes. There may be many calls during a day, but some of the most important are those which begin and end it, known respectively as "Reveille" and "Last Post" (Brit.) or "Taps" (U.S.).

The custom of rousing troops with music goes back to the Roman Legions who were awakened by horns playing a hymn to the goddess Diana — even though English-speaking nations name their wake-up calls after the French word réveiller (to awaken) the French still call theirs "La Diana." Music of the American "Reveille" was composed in 1890 by John Philip Sousa, then leader of the Marine Corps Band, to words written by Robert J. Burdett. The best-known mnemonic phrase comes at the end of each stanza:

> I can't get 'em up! I can't get 'em up!
> I can't get 'em up in the morning!
> I can't get 'em up! I can't get 'em up!
> I can't get 'em up at all!

The British army bugle call which most lay-people call "Reveille" is correctly known as "Rouse." The real reveille is seldom played because it is so long. Neither of these is played in the Royal Navy, which uses a third bugle call named for some obscure reason Charlie Reveille. One Royal Marine drummer (i.e., bugler) told the author he thought this might be because it is the third wake-up call and Charlie is the third letter of the phonetic alphabet. Another suggested that the opening mnemonics were originally "Charley! Charley!" rather than "Wakey! Wakey!" but no one seems to know for sure. There are numerous unofficial mnemonics, many totally unprintable. The most generally accepted version beginning with:

Wakey! Wakey! Time to get out of bed!
Wakey! Wakey! Rise up and shine!
Wakey! Wakey! Get up and wash yourself!
Wakey! Wakey! Lash up and stow!

Americans mark the end of the day with "Taps" which probably got its name either from a British infantry signal for the spigots on beer barrels to be closed (*see* tattoo) or from the drum tapping which was an alternative to a bugle call. There are conflicting stories about how the current version came about, both set in 1862. One says that Union Army Captain Robert Ellicombe rescued a mortally-wounded Confederate soldier, only to find it was his musician son who had enlisted on the other side without telling his father. In the boy's pocket were some musical notes he had been working on and Ellicombe had them played at the funeral. However, the story generally accepted by the U.S. military says that General Daniel Butterfield, a brigade commander in the Union Army of the Potomac, found the borrowed French bugle call "L'Extinction des Feux" too formal and summoned Bugler Oliver Norton to play revisions he had made to an earlier tune. The result was so hauntingly beautiful that it rapidly spread throughout the army, and was even usurped by some Confederate units. After the Civil War, it was officially adopted by the navy, and is now used by all U.S. armed forces. Unofficial mnemonic words are in part:

Day is done, gone the sun.
From the lakes, from the hills, from the sky.
All is well, safely rest.
God is nigh

The British "Last Post" originated as part of the 17th century Tattoo ceremony. As night approached, the duty officer, orderly sergeant, and a drummer-bugler made the rounds of all sentry posts to ensure they were properly manned. When they began, "First Post "was sounded on the bugle. The party then went from station to station, accompanied by the beating drum until another bugle call signaled that the "Last Post" had been reached. Unofficial mnemonics begin:

Come home! Come home!
The last post is sounding for you to hear
All good soldiers know very well
There is nothing to fear
While they do what is right

Both the "Last Post" and "Taps" are "closure music," and have been widely-used at funerals and remembrance ceremonies. On those occasions, they are often followed, after a moment of silence, by Reveille or Rouse to symbolize rebirth.

Built: Said of a vessel that is fully-constructed but has not been launched (cf. complete).

Bulb: A cylindrical or spherical underwater protuberance at the fore-end of a vessel to reduce bow wave and modify the flow of water around the hull, reducing drag while increasing speed, range, and fuel efficiency. Also bulbous bow.

Bulk cargo: Goods shipped unpackaged in loose condition, usually in specialized ships (tankers or bulkers). May be liquid such as petroleum products, wine, cooking oils, or chemicals; or dry such as grain, sugar, sand, ores, coal, or chemicals.

Bulker: A merchant ship designed to carry dry cargoes, shipped in large quantities that do not need to be packaged. The principal bulk products are coal, iron ore, bauxite, phosphate, nitrate and grains. The standard bulker design is a single double bottomed hull with a large holds, hopper tanks, and topside tanks. As with oil tankers the engine room, navigating bridge, and crew quarters are nearly always located at the stern of the ship, making the two vessels look very similar. The simplest way of telling them apart is that the deck of a tanker is covered with pipes, while that of a bulker has raised hatches. Large hatchways are essential for efficient cargo handling, but pose the risk of catastrophic flooding. Bulker cargoes are often dense, corrosive, or abrasive, and prone to shifting which can cause the ship to capsize or break in half. Hence, loading and discharging is time-consuming and dangerous. International regulations require the captain and terminal master agree on a detailed plan before operations begin. *See also* BIBO carrier, gearless bulker, OBO carrier, and self-discharging bulker.

Bulkhead: Interior wall in a ship, dividing it into compartments.

Bull: [1] To ram a buoy. [2] Naval slang for a ship's policeman. [3] A slang expletive describing a ludicrously false statement; nonsense.

Bull Ensign: USN slang for the senior Ensign on board (reputedly named after Admiral "Bull" Halsey who assigned specific duties to that officer). *See also* George Ensign.

Bullet: A small, solid, round or cylindrical, projectile with a round or pointed end, fired from a personal firearm such as rifle, pistol, or machine gun.

Bullhorn: A powerful directional electric megaphone.

Bullnose: A closed chock at the apex of a vessel's bow, looking like a flared nostril.

Bullrope: [1] The most weight-bearing line in a cargo hoist. [2] The line used to hoist a topgallant or topmast.

Bull's eye: [1] A thick convex glass disc fitted to a door, deck, or skylight c to admit light. [2] A similar disc used to concentrate the rays of artificial light from a lamp or candle.

Bully: [1] Coercion or intimidation by fear or violence. [2] Corned meat. [3] Excellent, splendid (U.S. slang).

Bully beef (or mutton): Originally a naval and military designation of meat that had been corned or pickled to preserve it for use in the field or at sea. It is derived from the French bouilli = meat left over after lengthy simmering to produce the soup known as bouillon.

Bully boy: [1] In normal conversation this term refers to a hired ruffian. [2] It is also a term of endearment, as in "my bully boy" (from the Old Dutch boele = sweetheart). [3] In naval poems and chanteys it originally meant "beef-eating seaman" in reference to the pickled meat served at sea. [4] The dictionary definition of bully includes dashing, jovial, blustering, quarrelsome, and good friend, all of which could be considered to refer to "Jolly Jack Tar."

Bulwark: Part of a ship's side projecting above its upper deck to prevent people falling overboard and provide protection from the waves.

Bumboat: A boat peddling goods to a ship at anchor. May be a corruption of boom boat (i.e., one allowed to tie up to the boom for trade).

Bummaree: A variant of bottomry.

Bumper: A protective guard hung over the side of a ship and left in place when underway (*see* fender).

Bumph: RN slang for toilet paper and hence administrative paperwork.

Bumwad: USN slang for toilet paper.

Bundleman: Former slang for a married sailor. When paying off, seamen were allowed to buy provisions at bargain prices, so one with a family to support could be recognized by the bundle he carried ashore.

Bunga-Bunga: Seldom used today, this RN slang for a hoax is based on an anecdote (possibly apocryphal) telling how the Channel Fleet, lying in Weymouth Bay, was alerted to the arrival of a Siamese prince on an official tour of inspection. The side was manned to greet the distinguished visitor with all the courtesies appropriate to his rank. The prince could speak no English and had no interpreter, but praised everything he was shown with the comment "bunga-bunga." Only after he and his entourage had been piped over the side and taken ashore was it revealed that they were students from Oxford University responding to a dare.

Bunk: A built-in bed, often arranged in tiers one above another.

Bunker: [1] A bin, tank, or compartment for fuel storage. [2] To load coal or oil as fuel.

Bunkers: Fuel to be consumed by the engines of a ship.

Bunket: The blade of a paddle-wheel. (Also float.)

Bunt: The middle section of a sail.

Bunting: [1] Decorative streamers or flags. [2] The cotton or woolen material for flag-making.

Buntline: The line used to haul the foot of a square-sail up to its yard.

Bunts: RN slang for a signalman (short for "bunting-tosser").

Buoy: An anchored float serving as a navigational marker, or ship's mooring (pronounced "boy" or "boo-ee"). Basic navigational shapes are "nun" (cone-topped), and "can" (flat-topped). A "lateral system" includes one or more buoys equipped with lights, bells, gongs, or whistles.

Buoyage: [1] The act of placing buoys. [2] An established system of buoys. *See also* uniform buoyage systems.

Buoyage region: The International Association of Lighthouse Authorities designates virtually every system of maritime buoyage as belonging to one of two regions. The coastal countries of North and South America and Japan form Region "B," while almost all other coastal countries are in Region "A." The shape of buoys is the same in both regions but, confusingly, inbound ships are required to keep red-painted ones to port in region "A" and to starboard in region "B."

Buoyancy: Ability to float on water. A vessel floats when the weight of water it displaces is equal to the weight of the craft. This displacement of water creates an upward thrust called the buoyant force, which acts in opposition to gravity tending to pull the ship down. Unlike a ship, a submarine can control its buoyancy, thus allowing it to sink and surface at will.

BUPERS: Bureau of Naval Personnel (USN).

Burden/Burthen: The cargo capacity of a ship. Originally based on how many 252-gallon tuns of wine it could hold. (*See* tonnage.)

Burdened vessel: One which must give way to the "privileged vessel" under the Navigation Rules (table 7).

Bureau of Ordnance: In 1862, the functions of twenty-year-old U.S. Navy Bureau of Ordnance and Hydrography were split between separate and independent Bureaus of Ordnance and Navigation, with the former responsible for the procurement, storage, and deployment of all naval weaponry.

During the early 20th century, the Bureau's development of guided missiles led to friction with the Bureau of Aeronautics , which was responsible for the development of Naval aircraft, including pilotless (unmanned) "drones." In 1959, the Navy decided to end the conflict by merging the two organizations into a new Bureau of Naval Weapons. This, in turn, was disestablished in 1966 and replaced by the Naval Air Systems Command. *See also* Board of Ordnance.

Burgee: A small flag used for identification by yachts and yacht clubs.

Burgoo: A sea dish from the age of sail, consisting of buttered oatmeal porridge, seasoned with salt and sugar. From Hindi bar-goo = holy cow-dung.

Burial at sea: In this simple but dignified ceremony the body is sewn into a canvas sheet or bag, traditionally the deceased's own hammock. The sewer was formerly awarded one guinea for each corpse sewn up. The last stitch of the huge sailmaker's needle traditionally goes through the nose of the corpse to ensure no spark of life remains — this practice probably originated in the early 1790s, when Captain William Hargood of HMS *Hyæna*, who had succumbed to a fever, was being prepared for burial, but came back to life when the needle accidentally pierced his nose. (Hargood recovered to lead a distinguished career. At the Battle of Trafalgar, his ship HMS *Belleisle* fought on after being completely dismasted, leading Nelson to exclaim "Nobly done, Hargood!" Later, he became honorary Colonel-Commandant of the Royal Marines and naval Commander in chief at Plymouth.)

Heavy weights (originally cannonballs) are placed inside the bag to prevent the body from being raised to the surface by the gases of decomposition. The burial ship's ensign and those of nearby vessels are half-masted while the captain or chaplain reads the burial service. Then the body is piped over the side as it slides gently from under an ensign draped over it. After the funeral it's an RN custom for the master-at-arms or coxswain to auction off the decedent's kit. (*See* Personal Effects Disposal.)

Burma Road: RN colloquialism for the main corridor in a warship. Named after a World War II supply route used to deliver Allied aid to China.

Burn bag: A receptacle for classified or secret papers that are to be burned or otherwise destroyed.

Burrel: A form of langrage.

Bursar: The original title of the ship's officer responsible for supplies and accounting was clerk of the bursar, later abbreviated to bursar, and finally changed to purser. The word comes from the Latin busarius, meaning purse or purse-keeper.

Burton: [1] A small two-block tackle. [2] RN slang for lost or destroyed, as in the phrase "Gone for a Burton" (a brand of ale).

Buscarle: An Anglo-Saxon ship captain. (*See* Saxon Seapower.)

Bushing: A metal bearing for a shaft.

Busk: To cruise as a pirate in search of prey.

Buss: [1] A two-masted fishing vessel, sometimes armed for naval service. [2] Originally an Anglo-Saxon cargo vessel with an exceptionally spacious cargo hold.

Bust: [1] To break something. [2] To reduce in rank. [3] A failure. [4] A drinking spree.

Butcher's bill: Slang for battle casualties in general, but especially referring to the terrible carnage during conflict between wooden warships, typically inflicted more by splinters than by shot.

Butt: [1] A large cask or barrel. [2] The squared-off end of a plank. [3] The bottom of a mast.

Butter Bars: USN enlisted slang for an Ensign (based on the color of his rank insignia).

Buttock: [1] The beam where the hull rounds down to the stern.

Buy boat: A large vessel, at least 50 feet (15m) long, that cruised up and down Chesapeake Bay, buying the daily catch from oyster dredgers and taking it to market for resale, thus enabling the working boats to stay out longer. These vessels are still in service to carry and plant seed oysters on behalf of the state.

Buy the farm: This euphemism for being killed originated during World War I when the United States Navy issued life insurance policies to enlisted seamen. At a time when the vast majority had rural origins, they saw the face value of these policies as enough to pay off the mortgage on their families' acreage.

Buys-Ballot's Law: Rule-of-thumb which allows mariners to estimate the location and direction of a storm center. Dutch meteorologist C.H.D. Buys-Ballot (1817–90) showed that this will lie about 90° to the right of an observer facing the wind in the Northern Hemisphere, or to the left in the Southern. Periodic observations will then indicate its relative movement, and on which side of its track the observer is located.

Buza: A Viking cargo ship, similar to a knorr but with higher gunwhales.

BVR: Beyond visual range.

By and large: Command to sail to the wind and off it. This imprecise helm order has come into general use to mean "on the whole."

By guess and by God: This expression, which today means embarking on an enterprise without adequate preparation, was originally applied to navigation by dead (deduced) reckoning. This involved approximating the ship's position by calculating the distance run on various headings, adjusting for estimated winds and currents, and modifying the result according to the navigator's experience. In the final analysis, this was little more than guesswork, leaving it up to the Supreme Being to guide the ship safely.

By the: [1] "By the head" = bow lying deeper than the stern. [2] "By the stern" = drawing more water aft than forward. [3] "By the wind" = sailing close-hauled. [4] "By the lee" = sailing downwind with the wind blowing over the leeward side. [5] "By the board" = (a) In the water close to the ship's side; (b) To go over the side; (c) To be forgotten.

By your leave: USN courtesy request to overtake a senior officer while walking. The senior returns the junior's salute and responds "permission granted" or "carry on."

Byrdingur: A Viking coastal cargo vessel.

C

Cabane: A flat-bottomed passenger boat, formerly popular in the Loire Estuary.

Cabin: Shipboard accommodation for officers or passengers (cf. Stateroom).

Cable: [1] A measure of distance equal to (a) In general use, 100 fathoms = 600 feet = 182.9 meters (b) In the RN, 1/10 nautical mile = 608 feet = 185.3 meters (c) In Australia and (sometimes) the USA, 120 fathoms = 720 feet = 219.5 meters. [2] A large rope or hawser of wire or hemp. [3] Electric wiring. [4] A message sent by submarine cable.

Cable-laid: Three triple-stranded ropes laid together.

Cable markings: Colored stripes or twist of wire on the anchor chain to indicate how much of it is out.

Cable ship: Vessel specifically designed for laying, maintaining, and repairing submarine telegraph cables.

Cable-tier: The compartment where cables are coiled for storage.

Caboose: Most people think of this as referring to the crew compartment which used to be required by law to be attached to the rear of all North American trains. However the word originated at sea from Low German kabhaus which referred to a wooden cabin on the weather deck of a ship. The term was later picked up by Dutch mariners who called a deck-mounted galley the kabuis. Transliterated into caboose, the term was for a while used in the British merchant marine, from where it was adopted by the railroads, probably because the rail vehicle (also known as "brake car" in the U.S. and "guard's van" in Britain) served as a kitchen for the train crew. The term is still used in the Royal Navy (where it is pronounced "caboosh"), referring specifically to a compartment for storing cleaning materials, and generically to any small compartment. For example, the shipwright's workshop is known as "chippy's caboose."

Cabotage: The coastal carriage of goods or passengers between ports in the same country. The French word for "coastal navigation."

Caddie of Cadboro Bay: The existence of a sea serpent in the waters off South Vancouver Island is recorded by the Salish Indians, in folk tales which speak of T'Chain-Ko, a strange but friendly aquatic creature. The first reports, made by white settlers in the 1920s, have been followed by some 200 reported sightings up to the present day. As well as individual sightings, the creature has been seen by groups of up to 30 people. Once called the Sea Hag, it is now popularly known as Caddie. Described as being the size of a whale, it is said to be long and thin, with a slender neck, supporting a horse- or camel-like head topped by a jagged mane-like crest, well-defined nostrils, no visible ears, a lengthy beard and whiskers, long sharp fangs, a snakelike tongue, and huge bulbous black eyes, glowing with reddish-green luminosity.

Eyewitnesses have called the beast's visage everything from loveable to horrifying. They include such reputable persons as Major W. H. Langley, a well-known barrister and amateur marine biologist; F. W. Kemp, an official of the Provincial Archives; J. T. Brown, Chief Justice of Saskatchewan; and Captain Paul Sowerby of West Vancouver. On another occasion, fisherman David Webb reported in some detail:

> I was fishing out of Cadboro Bay in 1941 ... and a southeast gale started blowing so I decided it was time to go into the harbour.... Suddenly, near where I moored my boat, I saw a strange animal come up

out of the water a thing with about a five or six foot neck on it. It had a head something like a camel.... Judging by the length of the neck, I imagined it to be another 20 feet or so in the water, but I couldn't see below the surface.... I have seen sea lions, basking sharks, whales, but I have never seen anything like this in my life.

Other sightings of a smaller but similar creature without whiskers or mane are believed to have been of the creature's mate, dubbed Amy. In 1968, Captain Bill Hagelund claimed to have captured a 40 cm (16 inch) infant of the same species. He planned to take the creature to the Pacific Biological Station, but released it when he feared its frantic struggles would result in death. In 1992, after extensive study, marine scientists Paul Leblond of the University of British Columbia and E.L. Bousfield of the Royal British Columbia Museum notified the American Society of Zoologists of the probable existence of a surviving marine dinosaur, which they baptized with the scientific name Cadborosaurus Willsi, category Cryptid — Cadboro, after the bay; Saurus, meaning lizard-like; Willsi, after Archie Wills the newspaper editor who first drew world attention to the creature; and Cryptid, meaning species for which there is no confirmation —*see* cryptozoology.

Cadence: The uniform measure or beat essential for pulling oars or for marching.

Cadet: This title for an officer in training comes from the Latin capitellum (lesser captain). It applies to students at the United States Coast Guard Academy, to apprentices in the British Merchant Navy, to junior students at the British Royal Naval College (where senior students may be rated midshipman) and to students under the USN aviation cadet program.

Cag: Informal nickname for the commander of a USN carrier air wing. Acronym of the obsolete title "Commander Air Group."

Caique: [1] A small single-masted Levantine sailing vessel with a sprit mainsail and square topsail. [2] A Turkish 10–12 oared skiff used on the Golden Horn of Istanbul.

Caisson: [1] A watertight chamber in which underwater work can be done. [2] A floating vessel used as a floodgate in docks. [3] An ammunition chest or wagon. (Also spelled cassoon and sometimes so pronounced.)

Cakes and wine: USN slang for the bread and water served to prisoners under punishment.

Caldera: A collapsed or partially-collapsed seamount, commonly of annular shape.

Calender: To press sailcloth between hot steel rollers to flatten it and make it more durable.

Caliber/Calibre: [1] The internal diameter (bore) of a gun barrel. [2] The external diameter of a bullet or shell. [3] Quality or strength of character (e.g., a high-caliber candidate).

California Current: A southeastward flow along the coast of Baja California which swings westward to form part of the north equatorial current.

Calk: Alternate spelling of caulk.

Call: [1] In the RN, the boatswain's call or whistle. [2] In the USN, a tune played on that instrument. [3] Also in the USN, an informal visit by an officer to another warship. [4] In both RN and USN, a social visit to another officer.

Call away: Pipe ordering a crew to prepare for a specific evolution such as "call away boat crew," or "call away working party."

Call mission: An air support sortie mounted extemporaneously by naval aircraft in response to a request by the supported unit.

Call sign: Radio, visual, or flag signal identifying a vessel or aircraft by letters and numbers.

Callianti: A long, slow rowing style, in which the oarsmen rise from their thwarts with each stroke. Popular in Malta, Italy, and elsewhere in the Mediterranean.

Calm: Force 0 on the Beaufort Scale (winds less than 1 knot = 1.15 mph, or 1.85 km/h). Sometimes flat calm.

Calve: [1] Of an iceberg or glacier, to shed ice into the sea. [2] Of a marine mammal, to give birth.

Cam: A disc or cylinder irregularly-shaped so that its motion (usually rotational) gives a rocking or reciprocating motion to parts in contact with it.

Cam cleat: A pair of spring-loaded cam-shaped cleats which close automatically to secure a line.

CAM ship: The "Catapult Aircraft Merchantman" was a British World War II attempt to cover the Atlantic air gap by equipping merchantmen with bow-mounted catapults to launch fighter planes against German long-range aircraft that located convoys and directed U-boats to them. The CAM ship had no flying-off or landing deck, so the pilot had to ditch near a recovery vessel and the plane would be lost. Thirty-five conversions were made, the first five being taken into the Royal Navy, while the rest sailed with their regular merchant crews. The aircraft were flown by RAF pilots from a specially formed Merchant Ship Fighter Unit. In the two years they were in service (1940–41) twelve CAM ships were sunk through enemy action. Eight catapult launchings were made, and six enemy aircraft were shot down. This short-term emergency solution was discontinued after arrival of the MAC ship.

Camber: The curvature or arch of a weather deck which causes water to drain athwartships into the scuppers and thence overboard.

Camel: [1] A hollow vessel of wood or metal which can be submerged and attached to a sunken vessel. When pumped out, its buoyancy will lift the other vessel. (Named after the Camel Dock at Amsterdam, where the technique was first used early in the 14th century.) [2] A protective float placed between ships or between a ship and a quay.

Canadian Navy: A half-hearted attempt to found a Canadian maritime force was made in 1881 when the country was just 14 years old. A steam-powered wooden vessel was purchased but allowed to rot at moorings, and it was not until 1910 that the Royal Canadian Navy was officially created. When World War II broke out, that force amounted to six destroyers, four minesweepers, and three auxiliaries, but when it ended, it was the world's third largest, with 434 vessels in commission. In 1968, Canada's Armed Forces merged, with the naval component being named Maritime Command. It is now 28th in the world.

Can buoy: A flat-topped buoy.

Can-do: [1] Slang abbreviation of "it can be done" or "I can do it." Probably derived from pidgin Chinese. [2] In the USN the term is used to praise a ship which is efficient or an individual who gets things done.

Canal: A man-made waterway. Transiting vessels may be raised and lowered in locks to connect with different levels of water.

Canal effect: *See* "channel effect."

Canaries Current: A broad, shallow, slow-moving drift current that flows southwestward from the Bay of Biscay along the coast of Africa to Senegal where it turns westward towards the Canary Islands.

Canister: A container of musket balls or other small projectiles (langrage), fired from a cannon as an anti-personnel weapon or to sever rigging. Also called case-shot, and similar to grape shot or shrapnel.

Cannibalize: To remove serviceable parts from one aircraft, ship, or piece of equipment in order to repair another.

Cannon: [1] In the 18th–19th centuries, a large, smoothbore, muzzle-loading gun mounted on a wheeled carriage. Usually classified by the weight of round-shot it fired, but *See also* "Great Gun." The word comes from the Latin canna = tube, and a muzzle-loading cannon is essentially a tube sealed at one end to form a chamber. The preferred naval term is gun. [2] Today, any large tubular firearm, with a caliber in excess of 20 mm, designed to fire over considerable distances.

Cannon firing: *See* gun firing.

Cannonade: Continuous heavy gunfire (cf. bombardment).

Cannon ball: [1] A large round solid metal projectile. The preferred naval term is shot. [2] U.S. Naval Academy slang for baked candied apples served to midshipmen on special occasions. A dozen are served to each table and tradition holds that any volunteer who manages to eat all twelve is granted "carry on" privileges (freedom from harassment by upperclassmen) for the rest of the semester.

Canoe: A small narrow boat with pointed ends, usually propelled by paddles.

Canoe stern: A pointed stern, similar to that of a canoe.

Cant: [1]To tilt, tip, or place in an oblique position (e.g., for careening). [2] Insincere, pious, or moralistic speech.

Canton: Any quarter of a flag, but most commonly the upper corner at the hoist, which is also known as the union.

Canvas: [1] A strong coarse cloth, made from hemp or flax. [2] Slang for a sail.

Canyon: A relatively narrow, deep, steep-sided depression on the sea floor, the bottom of which usually deepens continuously. Characteristically found on continental slopes.

Cap: [1] A metal collar for joining two spars or masts. [2] The top of a mast (cf. truck). [3] A covering for a ropes-end, usually made of leather or tarred canvas. [4] *See* combat air patrol.

Cape: A headland or promontory jutting into the sea.

Cape Agulhas: The southernmost point of the African continent. The name, which is Portuguese for "needles," refers to the rocks and reefs that have wrecked many ships. Its meridian of 20°E is the official boundary between the Atlantic and Indian oceans.

Cape Breton Current: A flow originating in the Gulf of St. Lawrence and flowing through the southwestern part of Cabot Strait to merge with the Labrador Current Extension.

Cape Hatteras Mystery: On January 29, 1921, the five-masted schooner *Carroll A. Deering* passed the Cape Lookout Lightship whose keeper reported that the crew seemed to be milling about aimlessly. Next day, the ship passed the SS *Lake Elon* whose log noted *Deering* seemed to be steering a peculiar course. The day after that, C.P. Brady of the Cape Hatteras Coast Guard Station spotted a vessel aground and helpless on the shoals with decks awash. Due to heavy seas, boats failed to reach the wreck, whose sails were set, while lifeboats and anchors were missing. Finally, on the morning of February 4, USCG cutter *Manning* and the wrecker *Rescue* reached the battered ship. Captain James Carlson boarded and confirmed it was the *Deering*. He found food laid out in preparation for a meal, but no sign of the crew or their personal belongings. Key navigational equipment and the ship's papers were also missing. No trace of any of them has ever been discovered.

Cape Horn: A promontory at the southern tip of South America, famous for the severity of its storms and the difficulty of making an east-west passage under sail.

Cape of Good Hope: A rocky headland on the Atlantic coast of South Africa. Although it is about 150 kilometers (90 miles) from the southernmost point of Africa (Cape Agulhas), it is the place where a West-to-East circumnavigation becomes more eastward than southward. Thus, rounding the cape in 1488 was a psychologically important milestone in the Portuguese effort to establish a trade route to the Orient.

Caper: [1] A lightly-armed 17th century Dutch privateering vessel. [2] To run and jump joyously.

Capesize: A vessel too large to pass through the Suez Canal and hence forced to circumnavigate the South African Cape of Good Hope. Cf. panamax, mallacamax.

Capital ship: A large warship with heavy striking power. Usually larger than 10,000 tons. Originally a battleship or battlecruiser, now includes aircraft carrier.

Capitaner: The Command ship of a Mediterranean galley fleet.

Caprail: The top of a bulwark.

Capsize: To overturn, usually inadvertently. Prior to the 19th century, the preferred term was "overset."

Capstan: A vertical revolving drum or winch used for hauling the anchor or other cables (cf. Windlass). Formerly turned by bars inserted in its rim, now powered.

Capstan drill: The former practice of making boys and younger seamen jump repeatedly off the drum of a capstan while keeping their legs straight. For some obscure reason, this was supposed to deepen their high-pitched voices.

Captain: [1] A commissioned naval officer ranking below one-star flag officer and above commander. [2] A commissioned military officer equivalent to a naval lieutenant. [3] The courtesy title of the officer commanding any naval vessel regardless of rank. [4] A courtesy title for the certificated master of a merchantman. [5] Used in the sense of foreman to describe some of the petty officers in a man-of-war — for example, Captain of the Foretop, or Gun Captain.

Originally, the basic military unit, whether serving on land or in a ship, was a company of troops. Each was commanded by a "captain" who still commands a company in armies. In navies, however, ships grew bigger and required ever larger crews. Hence, the command responsibility of a capital ship grew closer to that of a regiment than of a company. As a result, in RN and USN usage, "captain" is unique in being both a title and a rank. The naval **rank** of captain is equivalent to that of army colonel, but is also the **title** of the person commanding a vessel of any size or type, no matter what their rank. No other person on board may use that title, which is one reason why a captain of Royal Marines is addressed as "major" when afloat.

Many other navies have escaped this dual meaning by developing rank titles that indicate the kind of vessel to be commanded. For example, in French, "Capitaine de Vaisseau" is the equivalent of full captain, "Capitaine de Frègate" equates to commander and "Capitaine de Corvette" to lieutenant commander. *See* table 16.

No matter whether the ship is large or small, taking command is an awesome duty. The captain has full and final responsibility for security of the vessel, for navigating and fighting it, and for the discipline, health and efficiency of its crew. An admiral may order the captain to do something, but has no more authority than any other passenger to say how it is to be done. The title has its root in the Latin capitus meaning headman or chief which, in turn, comes from caput meaning head.

Captain of the Fleet/Fleet Captain: This title was

first used by the Venetians for the officer in command of their entire galley fleet. Only a noble was entitled to that rank, but a commoner could become Armir-riao (admiral) commanding a division of the main fleet. During the 18th century an overworked Royal Navy flag officer sometimes unofficially appointed one of his officers to act as his chief of staff, with the post being variously titled Assistant to the Admiral, First Captain, Adjutant of the Fleet, or Captain of the Fleet.

This arrangement, and the latter title, became official in 1782 when King George III proclaimed that a Captain of the Fleet, no matter what his substantive rank, should hold effective seniority below the most junior rear admiral and be entitled to the pay and allowances of a rear admiral so long as he held the post. This settled a longstanding dispute over the relative standing of a captain of the fleet, but did not define his specific responsibilities and authority. These were not officially detailed until 1913, when Kings Regulations & Admiralty Instructions, Chapter XII defined that officer's "General Duties":

> Item 521: The Captain of the Fleet is, under the direction of the Commander in chief, or Senior Flag Officer of the fleet, to attend to the various details and arrangements for the management of such fleet and for the maintenance of it in the most efficient state possible, giving, as may be necessary, with the sanction of the Commander in chief or Senior Flag Officer, such orders for the above subjects as circumstances may require; and all orders so given by him are to obeyed by every person in the fleet as well as by officers superior to him as by those inferior.

In about 1920, the post of Chief of Staff was introduced to assume responsibility for operational matters. Since then the Captain of the Fleet has been limited essentially to personnel matters.

The United States Navy used the title unofficially before, during, and after the Civil War, and so did the Navy of the Confederate States during that conflict. Early in World War II, the Navy Department proposed introducing the five-stripe rank of Fleet Captain, positioned between captain and rear admiral but, when the rank of Commodore was reintroduced in 1943, the proposal was modified to give five-stripe rank to the commanders of vessels such as carriers and battleships that had multiple four-stripe captains on board. That proposal was withdrawn a year later, having never been implemented.

Captain of the Heads: Slang term for the seaman assigned to cleaning toilets.

Captain of the Port: The title of a U.S. Coast Guard officer responsible for maritime law enforcement in a designated area (cf. port admiral).

Captain's Clerk: From the earliest days of English seapower, captains needed someone to copy outgoing letters and maintain files of records and correspondence. If they could find a literate seaman who could "write a fair and round hand" they might appoint from the lower deck; otherwise they would hire from civil life. Initially, the clerk seems to have been a member of the captain's personal staff rather than one of the crew but, so far as the author can ascertain, was unofficially given petty officer status. Sometime in the 18th century, the post became official and at least a year in that position was mandatory before appointment to the rank of bursar or purser. The closest modern equivalents are yeoman in the USN and writer in the RN. Also Quill-pusher (slang).

Captain's daughter: Lower deck slang for the cat-o'-nine-tails. *See* non-naval flogging.

Captain's Mast: A hearing at which the officer commanding a U.S. naval or coast guard vessel awards non-judicial punishment or non-punitive disciplinary measures for minor offenses, commends work exceptionally well-done, and listens to complains from enlisted personnel. A mast may be held by a more senior officer, in which case it is called admiral's mast or flag mast. The RN term is captain's table.

Captain's Servant: In addition to voluntary enlistment on the lower deck in the hope of advancement, there were two routes by which young men of "good family" could enter the Royal Navy to be trained for commissioned rank. One, beginning in the reign of Henry VIII (1491–1547), was as Captain's Servant. The other, instituted in 1676, was to obtain a "King's Letter." The former usually signed on between the ages of nine and twelve, but entry as young as five was not unusual. Britain's greatest naval hero, Horatio Nelson, began his career in 1771 as a twelve-year-old "servant" to his uncle who commanded 64-gun HMS *Raisonnable*.

Initially, every post-captain was allowed an unlimited number of "servants" who were carried on the books for pay and victuals, with the captain usually pocketing the former. This was so seriously abused that, towards the end of Queen Elizabeth's reign, a limit was imposed of two for every fifty or part of fifty in the ship's company. Captain's servants were not menial domestics as the name implies, but dependant protégés. Seamanship training was informal, rough, and rudimentary, frequently involving little more than assisting ABs to perform their duties. The older boys received navigational instruction from the sailing master or one of his mates. The system lasted roughly two hundred years before being abolished.

Captain's Table: The Royal navy term for captain's mast.

CAPTOR: This abbreviation of en**ca**psulated **tor**pedo is the USN designation of the Mk.60 deepwater moored torpedo launcher or torpedo mine.

Caramousal: A 16th/17th century Turkish merchantman with a narrow pink-like stern. Used especially for grain transport.

Caravel: A small 15th century two or three-masted trading and exploration vessel, that could be either lateen or square-rigged on the forward masts, but was normally lateen-rigged on the mizzen. When lateen-rigged, a caravel could speedily navigate rivers and shallow coastal waters. When square-rigged it was a fast oceangoing sailer. (Two of Christopher Columbus' ships—*Pinta* and *Nina*—were caravels, but his flagship *Santa Maria* was a carrack.)

Carbine: [1] A long firearm, shorter and lighter than a musket. Developed for mounted troops, but preferred over muskets for naval use, being easier to manipulate in boats or on fighting tops. [2] The modern carbine is lighter and shorter than a rifle, resulting in reduced range and power, but still providing a compact weapon with more stopping power than the traditional pistol. This makes it especially useful for special operations. Pronounced carb-eyen or car-bean.

Carcatus: The legal term for a fully-freighted ship.

Cardinal points: The four principal points of a compass (N, S, E, W). *See* table 17.

Cards: For a long time decks of cards were forbidden at sea. Because of their connection with fortune telling they were thought of as the Devil's picture books. Some said that tearing up a deck, and tossing it overboard, would produce a favorable change in the wind.

Careen: To heel a ship so that one side of its hull can be cleaned, maintained, or repaired in the absence of a dry dock. Derived from the Latin for keel = carina (cf. grave).

Career tracking: In most navies, surface warfare officers follow career specialties until they reach flag rank, the three main areas of expertise being deck (seamanship and navigation), engineering, and weaponry. Officers on each track are expected to acquire broad understanding of the other two, but to concentrate on mastering the increasingly complex details of their specialty. One of the major exceptions is the United States Navy, which expects all its line officers to be trained in and rotate through each of these functions. This tends to produce very capable and well-rounded generalists, but fewer experts in any one field of endeavor — this is especially true of shiphandling, where some destroyer and cruiser captains lack the experience and confidence to dock these maneuverable vessels under their own power and engage tugboats and pilots even to enter easy berths on calm days.

Cargo: [1] Refers to goods carried as freight by ship or aircraft (the term is not normally used for road or rail transportation). From the Spanish cargar = load . [2] A term used by religious cults of the Southwest Pacific which anticipate the millennium when the spirits of the dead will return bearing vast quantities of "cargo" (beneficial modern merchandise).

Cargo boom: A heavy-duty boom used like a crane for handling freight.

Cargo box: *See* shipping container.

Cargo classification: To sort military cargo by type or function for tactical loading.

Cargo cluster: An assemblage of ultra-bright lights that facilitates cargo handling at night.

Cargo net: Meshed rope netting used to lift and load or off-load cargo.

Cargo preference: Official policy giving preferential treatment to cargoes carried by a nation's own merchant marine. Also known as "flag discrimination."

Cargo space: Defines all areas available for stowing cargo, as opposed to engine room, crew quarters, passenger space, etc.

Cargo ton: A measure of volume equal to 100 cubic feet (2,832 liters). *See also* freight ton.

Caribbean Current: An ocean current flowing westward through the Caribbean Sea to the Yucatan Channel.

Carney: RN lower deck slang for hypocrisy, deception, or double-dealing. Based on 18th century Captain Carney, who was said to have been charming when recruiting seamen ashore, but became a brutal disciplinarian once afloat.

Carpenter: [1] One of four non-military warrant officers created in the 11th century for warships provided and crewed by the Cinque Ports. Unlike other warrant officers, who had risen from the lower deck, the carpenters in sailing ship navies had usually served a shipwright's apprenticeship in a dockyard before going to sea. There they were responsible for maintenance of the hull, masts, spars, and other woodwork. [2] By the 20th century, their work was no longer confined to timber, so Royal Navy carpenters were initially re-titled Warrant Shipwrights, and later Marine Engineering Artificers (Hull), with responsibility for all hull structures (including watertight integrity) and domestic fittings (water, sewage, etc.). [3] The title is obsolete in the USN, but lives on in the RN for a senior petty officer responsible for securing hatches, sounding shipboard tanks, and maintaining wooden fittings. [4] The duties of a modern merchantman's carpenter are numerous, extending far beyond what the job title implies ashore. In addition to all wood work on board, he or she is responsible for the secure lashing of deck cargo; the placement of hatch battens; keeping lifeboat davits in good order; repairing blocks; shoring or bracing weak or damaged bulkheads; rigging collision mats, building soft patches as required, and replacing broken rivets. Also assumes command of emergency crews in case of accident or collision.

Carpet: [1] Some sources claim that the phrase "on the carpet"—meaning to be severely reprimanded by someone in authority — originated because only the Master's cabin was carpeted. However, a nautical origin is suspect since the phrase could refer to almost any manager's office. [2] "Carpet bombing" refers to a tactical air assault on a strategic area using a great number of unguided gravity bombs.

Carrack: An armed merchantman; similar to a caravel, but larger and more robust with heavy cannon on tall fore- and stern-castles. In 1560 English admiral John Hawkins discovered that lowering the exceptionally high forecastle made the ship faster and more maneuverable, thereby creating the forerunner of the galleon.

Carragh: The Irish word for coracle.

Carriage: [1] The conveyance of goods. [2] The fee charged for such conveyance. [3] Formerly, a wheeled wooden support for a muzzle-loading cannon (*see* gun-carriage). [4] That part of a modern gun mount that supports the actual gun. Its lower element consists of a rotating platform known as the base ring, while the upper element is a massive pair of brackets that hold the trunnion bearings.

Carrick bend: A knot used to join different sizes of cables or hawsers or two same-size hawsers when the join will have to pass round the capstan.

Carrier: [1] A person, company, or vessel undertaking to transport goods or passengers for a fee. [2] A widely-used colloquialism for aircraft carrier.

Carrier Air Group/Wing: The former USN term for two or more squadrons of naval aircraft under the administrative and tactical control of one commanding officer (*see* Cag) was Carrier Air Group. It is now known as a Carrier Air Wing.

Carrier box: When a large convoy is accompanied by an aircraft carrier, the last three positions in the commodore's column and the adjacent columns on either side are left vacant to provide space for aircraft launching and landing.

Carrier qualification: Training and tests which make pilots and aircraft eligible to land on aircraft carriers. Pilot re-qualification is required when carrier landings are not regularly performed. Properly called deck landing qualification.

Carrier Strike Group: Former name of a task force built around an aircraft carrier, usually accompanied by guided-missile cruisers, antisubmarine and air defense destroyers or frigates, and attack submarines. Now called simply strike group.

Carronade: A short-barreled, very large caliber, muzzle-loaded gun for use at short ranges. Named after the foundry at Carron in Scotland. Prior to 1817, carronades were not counted when rating warships.

Carry: [1] To take a vessel by boarding (or a fortress by assault). [2] The range of a gun. [3] To transport goods or passengers to a specified point.

Carry away: To break or snap off.

Carry on: [1] Originally, a sailing ship command to hoist all possible canvas. [2] In modern naval usage, the command to resume whatever was previously being done: [3] In common usage, to manage something or persevere.

Cartel: [1] A ship commissioned to exchange prisoners or messages between hostile powers. Apart from one signal flare pistol, she may carry no weapons, ammunition, or cargo, and usually wears the ensigns of both parties. [2] An informal agreement between carriers aimed at maintaining artificially high prices.

Cartography: The art and practice of creating maps capable of communicating information effec-

tively and quickly. Since planet Earth is a three-dimensional curved surface that must be represented in two dimensions, cartographers (mapmakers) have to develop map projections that minimize distortion. The word comes from the Greek chartis = map + graphein = write.

Cartouche: Panel on a chart or map enclosing its name and scale. French for cartridge.

Cartridge: [1] A case containing the propellant charge for a gun or firearm. One of the jobs of a seaman sentenced to punishment was the sewing of cartridges for the guns. [2] The paper used by hydrographic surveyors for their fair charts.

Carvel-built: A boat whose side planks are flush against each other (cf. Clinker-built).

Cascabel: A knob behind the breech of a muzzle-loading cannon. It usually narrowed to a neck and there was sometimes a flat disc-like section known as the filet between it and the breech.

Case shot: *See* canister.

Casemate: An armored enclosure for a warship's guns.

Cashier: To dishonorably discharge an officer.

Casks: These barrel-like containers were widely used in the days of wooden ships, and developed a terminology of their own. The curved pieces of wood forming the sides of a cask are called staves, and their ends projecting above the head are called chines. The stopper closing the hole in its side is the bung, and its rounded belly is the bilge. The rack on which they are stored is the gantry, designed to hold them "Bung up and bilge free" (with the stopper on top to avoid leakage and the belly clear of the deck). In the Royal Navy the chines were color-coded, with rum casks painted red, lime juice casks green, and vinegar casks white.

Casrep: USN abbreviation of "**cas**ualty **rep**ort."

Cast adrift: To set loose without anchor, mooring., or any form of motive power.

Cast off!: Command to throw off mooring lines to get underway. *See also* "take in."

Cast ship: To turn a complete 360° without changing position. Achieved by alternately backing and forwarding engines, with appropriate rudder movements.

Cast the lead: To take soundings by throwing the leadline.

Castaway: [1] A shipwrecked sailor, as opposed to one who has been marooned or landed deliberately. [2] An outcast. [3] Formerly, a drunk.

Castle: Structure at the bow, stern, or masthead of a ship, originally a fighting platform.

CASU: Carrier Aircraft Service Unit. A self-contained USN mobile unit, designed to operate from advance Pacific island bases, to provide full support to carrier air groups while they were separated from their carriers.

Casualty report: [1] Surgeon's report of personnel killed or wounded by accident or in combat. [2] A report of material breakdown or equipment not working properly.

Cat: [1] To raise an anchor to forecastle level at the cathead. [2] The cat-o'-nine-tails. [3] Slang for an aircraft carrier's catapult. [4] A floating platform to keep the ship away from a jetty. Contraction of "catamaran" and preferred over "camel" by the RN. [5] Also in the RN, a "paint cat" is a floating platform with a variable scaffolding tower used in painting a ship's side.

Cat purchase: A two or three-fold block, fitted with an iron strop and hook, used to cat (draw) an anchor up to the cathead, which also carries three sheaves. *See* cat davit.

Cat ship: A Norwegian vessel formerly used in the coal and timber carrying trade. Distinguished by its narrow stern, projecting quarters, deep waist, and lack of any figurehead.

Cat the anchor: Keep the anchor clear of the hull by hanging it on the cathead before securing it for sea in its anchor-bed.

Cat yawl: Similar to a catboat but bigger with a second mast stepped abaft the rudder post.

Catamaran: [1] A type of raft with two or more floats. [2] A boat with twin hulls linked by a deck or crossbeams. From the Tamil katta = tied + maran = wood.

Catapult: [1] A device for launching aircraft from an aircraft carrier. [2] Ancient artillery throwing arrows, stones, or other missiles. From the Greek kata = hurler.

Catbeam: The longest beam in a wooden ship, usually made from two beams bolted together. Sometimes called beakhead beam.

Catboat: This American "Cape Cod" design is traditionally fitted with a gaff-rigged sail on a single mast set well forward in the boat, though some are Marconi-rigged. Some have passenger cabins, while others are fully or partially decked. Centerboards are standard, but keeled versions exist. "Cats" are shallow draft and broad beamed — the classic beam measurement being half the waterline length — which makes them very stable.

Catch a crab: To dig an oar so deeply into the water that the rower cannot recover it quickly enough to avoid being knocked over backward by the boat's momentum.

Catch a turn!: Command to belay rapidly for temporary holding.

Cat-davit: A device used to swing an anchor to the cathead. *See* cat purchase.

Catenary: The sag in a line or chain that is suspended between two points. The deeper the curve the more the catenary. When its cable is almost straight the anchor is easily snubbed or lifted from the ground, but with a full catenary it lies along the bottom so that any pull tends to dig the flukes in deeper. The word is derived from the Latin for chain, and one of the main reasons chain is used for anchor cables is that its weight tends to form a natural catenary.

Caterpillar drive: In his novel, *The Hunt for Red October*, author Tom Clancy gives a Russian submarine a revolutionary stealth propulsion system which he called "caterpillar drive." It is described as a hydro-jet system in the book, but in the film it is shown as being magnetohydrodynamic.

Catfall: The rope used to raise an anchor. It is rove through the blocks of the cat purchase and the cathead sheaves.

Cat-harpings: Defined in Admiral Smyth's *Sailor's Word-Book* as: "legs which cross from futtock-staff to futtock-staff, below the tops, to girt in the rigging, and allow the lower yards to brace sharp up." A more modern definition, "short ropes or iron cramps used to brace the shrouds towards the mast so as to give freer sweep to the yards," may be easier to follow.

Cathead sheaves: Triple sheaves attached to the cathead through which the catfall is rove.

Cathead-stopper: A length of rope or chain rove through the ring of an anchor to secure it for sea.

Catheads: Large wooden beams projecting on either side of the bows to which an anchor is raised and secured. They are set as square as possible to the deck and bolted to it above the catbeam. The end of each cathead was traditionally carved into the semblance of a lion's head.

Cathole: One of two holes in the stern of a sailing man-o-war level with the capstan, through which a stern hawser could be passed to heave the ship astern.

Cat-o'-nine-tails: The origin of the name for this fearsome flogging device is uncertain. One theory is that the scars left on the victim's back looked as though he had been mauled by a cat's claws. Another says it dates back to Pharaonic Egypt, where the cat was a sacred and beneficial animal and each lash (made of cat skin) represented one of its nine lives. Being scourged was then believed to transfer the cat's goodness from the lashes to the victim.

The naval version consisted of a handle made of thick rope with nine triple-knotted tails or thongs, each about 24 inches (61 cms) long, attached to it. The finished article weighed about 14 ounces (400 grams). Each was traditionally made by its intended victim for one-time use. Even so, it was no crude, hastily-assembled and roughly-tied instrument. Making a good one was considered a test of seamanship and self-respect, so most were beautiful examples of skilled ropework. Construction began by selecting four feet (1.2 meters) of three-stranded 1.5-inch (38-mm) diameter line. It was unlayed for half its length and each of the strands was divided into three parts. Then the nine parts were braided into tails, which were knotted at the tip and tarred (to inflict punishment for theft, a particularly offensive crime on board ship, each of the thongs was knotted three times to cause additional pain). Then, the unraveled half was whipped and covered with red (or sometimes green) baize to serve as the handle and, finally, the traditional blood-red baize carrying bag was sewn.

Later the "cat" became a ready-made naval issue,

losing its individuality and fine finish. Often a wooden baton replaced the rope handle and a faintly discernible strand of red cotton ran through each tail as an example of the Admiralty's marking of rope to prevent theft. A quasi-scientific test of the instrument's power was carried out by the Anatomy Department of the University of Edinburgh Medical School, using an exact replica of an original rope-handled cat. Pieces of knot-free pitch pine (chosen because of its elasticity) were lashed by a 5'10" (178 cm) man of average build and musculature. A single blow shattered a three-quarter inch (1.9 cm) square piece, while a one-inch (2.54 cm) square piece broke on the second stroke.

Catspaw: [1] A wind ripple on the surface of an otherwise calm sea. [2] A hitch made by double twisting the bight of a rope to form a pair of eyes through which a hook can be inserted.

Catwalk: A narrow platform or walkway across or around some form of obstruction, for example the raised structure connecting the amidships bridge structure to the forecastle and poop deck of a three-island freighter, or the walkways around and just below the flight deck of an aircraft carrier.

Caulk: To waterproof by packing seams with oakum or other fibrous material and sealing them with pitch (known as "pay"). Pronounced "cork." Also calk.

Caulk-off: Sailor slang for stealing a nap on deck. So-called because the culprit would often be betrayed by streaks of caulking on his back. Modern RN usage omits the "off."

Caulking iron: A chisel-like tool used when hit by a caulking mallet to drive fibers into the wedge-shaped seam between planks.

Causeway: [1] A raised road or track across a body of water. [2] A long, narrow, barge-like craft, used to assist the discharge of cargo during amphibious operations.

Caution: A non-punitive disciplinary action. *See* admonition, reprimand, and caution.

Cavitation: The formation and collapse of air bubbles created by a ship's propeller. This reduces effective thrust, creates noise detectible by an enemy, and may cause structural damage.

Cay: A small low-lying islet. Also Key.

Cease fire: A truce, armistice, or cessation of hostilities.

Cease firing!: Naval gunnery command to stop shooting. (*See also* check firing.)

Cease loading!: Naval gunnery command to stop inserting rounds into the weapon.

CEC: Civil Engineer Corps (USN).

Ceiling: [1] An overhead lining or floor covering in a cargo hold or other interior space. [2] The maximum height an aircraft is capable of attaining. [3] The distance between the surface of earth or sea and the lowest cloud bank.

Celestial equator: The plane of the terrestrial equator extended to the celestial sphere.

Celestial navigation: The science of determining position by means of heavenly bodies rather than by surface landmarks as in pilotage.

Celestial sphere: A conceptual ball of infinite radius, concentric with the earth, and rotating around an axis aligned with the terrestrial poles. This imaginary sphere is bisected by a projection of the earth's equator into space, dividing it into north and south celestial hemispheres. All heavenly bodies, no matter how distant, can then be thought of as lying on the sphere, allowing astronomers to keep track of the sky despite the earth's constant movement.

Centerboard/Centreboard: A plate which can be lowered through the keel of a small sailboat to prevent leeway. Sometimes written as two words with either spelling.

Centerline/Centreline: A straight line running fore-and-aft from stem to stern midway between the sides of the hull.

Certificate of Inspection: A document issued by a competent maritime authority certifying a vessel's compliance with all laws and regulations.

Certificate of Origin: Document issued by a consular authority at port of shipment, giving the consignee certain privileges at port of discharge.

Certificate of Registry: A document confirming the national registry of a vessel.

Certificated: A ship, seaman, or officer having a document confirming seaworthiness or proficiency.

Cessation: A temporary or complete end to hostilities. An armistice, truce, or cease-fire.

Cetaceans: Mammals that evolved from terrestrial habitats to become fully adapted to aquatic life, living, breeding, resting, and carrying out all other functions in the water. They are nearly hairless, but insulated by a thick layer of blubber. The order contains upwards of ninety species, and is divided into one extinct and two extant suborders. Archaeoceti (ancient whales) are believed to be extinct, but if there are survivors it is possible they could be mistaken for sea serpents (*see* appendix). The extant sub-orders, both thought to be descendants of archaeocetes, are Mysticeti (baleen whales) and Odontoceti (toothed whales). The latter includes beaked whales, dolphins, and porpoises. All are noted for their high intelligence.

CFR (Cost and Freight): *See* Incoterms.

Chafe: To damage rope, canvas, hull, or any other object by rubbing against another object.

Chaff: Strips of metal, foil, or glass fiber with a metal content, cut into various lengths and having varying frequency responses, that are used to reflect electromagnetic energy as a radar countermeasure. Chaff is usually dropped from aircraft, but can also be deployed from shells or rockets.

Chafing gear: Canvas, cloth, rubber, leather, or other material wrapped around a line to protect it from wear and abrasion.

Chain: [1] A series of metal links (rings) passing through one another to form a flexible tie with high tensile strength. [2] A group of related islands forming a more-or-less straight line (if the line is curved they form an arc).

Chain locker: The Compartment in which the anchor chain is stored.

Chain of command: The military hierarchy via which orders are passed downward by superior ranks, and requests passed upward from junior ranks.

Chain pipe: A trunk running from the windlass to the chain locker (also deck pipe).

Chain reaction: [1] A self-sustaining nuclear event. [2] The sequential explosion of a series of proximate mines or other munitions, caused by the deliberate or accidental detonation of one of them (as in countermining).

Chain shot: A pair of cannonballs or half-balls linked together with a short length of chain. When fired they spin to wreak havoc on masts, sails, and rigging (cf. bar shot, star shot).

Chain slings: Short lengths of chain used to raise and lower the yards of a square-rigger.

Chainplates: Iron strips bolted to a wooden sailing ship's sides, with deadeyes on their upper ends to which shrouds are secured.

Chains: [1] The position or platform in the bow from where the leadsman takes soundings. [2] A platform outboard of the bulwarks to which the lower shrouds of sailing ships are attached. Also chainwale.

Chainwale: *See* Chains. Pronounced "channel."

Challenge: [1] A signal requiring another ship, aircraft, or unit to respond with an authenticating or identifying code. [2] The demand made by a sentinel or lookout for boats or persons approaching to identify themselves.

Challenger Deep: Situated in the Mariana Trench, and named after the British survey ship *Challenger II* which discovered it in 1951, this is the deepest known point in the earth's oceans. The bottom here is 5,973.35 fathoms (10,924 metres; 35,840 feet) below sea level. This is about 23 percent more than Mount Everest, the highest point on land, is above sea level.

Chamade: Formerly a drumbeat signaling the desire to parlay.

Chamber: [1] The enclosed part of the bore of a muzzle-loading cannon that holds the charge. [2] The compartment in a firearm (such as the breech of a rifle, or the cylinder of a revolver) that holds a cartridge preparatory to firing.

Chancery: *See* in chancery.

Chandelle: An abrupt climbing turn in which an aircraft almost stalls while exploiting its own momentum to achieve a higher rate of climb.

Chandler: A dealer in maritime supplies and provisions.

Changey-changey: Lower deck RN slang for barter. From Chinese pidgin English.

Channel: [1] The navigable part of a waterway. [2] A length of water, wider than a strait, linking two seas or oceans. [3] A gutter.

Channel effect: Phenomenon similar to bank effect encountered in shallow channels, where interaction with the bottom makes steering difficult. Also called canal effect.

Channel fever: The sense of euphoria and excitement that grips homeward-bound seafarers on the final stretch. Originally used by British seamen on entering the English Channel.

Chantey/Chanty: A seaman's working chant of calls and responses. From the French chantez = sing (pronounced shanty). In the days when navigation depended on massive squares of canvas manhandled by human musclepower, work was synchronized and made easier by these work-songs. Sailors with fine singing voices found they could avoid some of the nastier shipboard tasks by volunteering as chanteymen, singing melodies which helped to soften the rigors of shipboard life. On one hand, listening to the songs was enjoyable and relieved boredom, especially when a fiddler accompanied the singer. On the other, the rhythm of calls and responses served to synchronize the movements of repetitive tasks.

As early as 1493, a Dominican friar named Felix Fabri reported hearing mariners on a Venetian galley singing as they worked, writing: "There is a concert between one who sings out orders and the laborers who sing in response." This technique is similar to the cadence calls of military units, except that chanteys came in several categories. "**Short-haul**" songs were used when the job would be over after a few quick pulls on a line. An example is "Boney" (referring to Emperor Napoleon) where the crew would pull as they hollered each response:

Singer:	Boney was a warrior
Crew:	Away, hey, yah!
Singer:	A warrior and a terrior
Crew:	Jean-François!

"**Long-haul**" chanteys were sung when the job was expected to be a prolonged. Usually the crew would only pull at the second response, thus giving themselves a brief rest between hauls. For example:

Singer:	Blow the man down, me boys, blow the man down!
Crew (hauling):	Away, hey, blow the man down
Singer:	Oh, blow the man down, bullies, blow 'im right down!
Crew (resting):	Oh, gimme some time to blow the man down.

The other important working chanteys were "**stomp-and-go**" (also "***stamp-and-go***") songs, to be sung while walking steadily around the capstan. Because there was no hauling to be timed, the crew sometimes sang a short chorus as well as calls-and-responses:

Singer:	I'll sing you a song, a good song of the sea
Crew:	Away, Rio
Singer:	I'll sing you a song, if you'll sing it with me
Crew:	And we're bound for the Rio Grande. Away Rio. Away Rio

Singer:	It's fare ye well my pretty young girl
Crew:	And we're bound for the Rio Grande
Singer:	We'll man up the capstan and run her around... etc.

There were also "*pumping*" chanteys for clearing the bilges; and "*forecastle*" chanteys, which were not working rhythms at all, but songs to while away the time off watch or in port. One of the latter (that may also have been sung while holystoning) was the alphabet song, in which each stanza (often improvised by each seaman in turn) is bawdier that the one before:

A is for anchor as everyone knows, and
B is the sharp bit, that we call the bows!
C is the captain that spoils all the fun,—and
D is for damn him he's watered me rum.

So hey derry, ho derry, hi derry dee.
No man on the land's like a sailor at sea.
So turn the glass and ring the bell, keep sailing
along,
When it's time for our grog, then it's time for this
song.

E is for ensign, At the stern it's now seen,—and
F is for fo' rard there to liberty clean. Then
G is the gangway, where to shoreward we go!—and
H is the Harlot, whose body we'll know.

Chapeling: When a sailing ship came to against the helm, or was taken aback by a shift of wind, or by negligence of the helmsman, she could be recovered on the same tack without bracing the head-yards, by making a complete circle. This maneuver was called chapeling ship, or building a chapel.

Chaplain: A priest, rabbi, minister, or other ecclesiastic attached to a ship or military unit. Seafaring is extremely hazardous, and the presence of spiritual guides or mentors has long brought comfort to mariners. As early as the Bronze Age merchant sailors of Crete celebrated an unnamed seagoing goddess, who is depicted as traveling in a boat. However, there is no evidence that her priestesses actually went to sea with the Minoan Navy. It is however probable that the great Phoenician and Carthaginian navigators were accompanied by priests of Asherah (Our Lady of the Sea), while Roman fleets were invariably accompanied by priestly augers who had no spiritual or counseling duties, their task being to read omens and predict the outcome of any campaign or battle.

Today's seagoing clergy are normally endorsed by their religious superiors and are given naval orientation and chaplaincy indoctrination before being posted to their initial ship, shore station, or marine detachment. They conduct religious services, provide social, ethical and moral counseling, and give spiritual and emotional support to their "parishioners" (the ship's company and their dependants). In most navies they are expected to provide pastoral care and solace to members of other denominations or faiths when no appropriate counselor is available. Chaplains are designated non-combatants under the Geneva Convention.

• The Royal Naval Chaplaincy Service: As early as the seventh century, Anglo-Saxon kings sent Roman Catholic priests to sea to "Exercise the ministry of the Gospel through Word and Sacrament." After the Reformation, English naval chaplains were exclusively Church of England (Anglican) priests, but they were not officially regulated until 1677 when it was required that they should be warranted by the Admiralty and also hold a certificate of spiritual fitness from either the Archbishop of Canterbury or the Bishop of London. In 1808 they were granted wardroom status and in 1843 became commissioned officers — without distinction of rank, — being assumed to hold the rank or rate of whomever is being counseled. To be more accessible and encourage confidence, they have the option of wearing civilian clerical dress or naval uniform without insignia. Today, the Royal Naval Chaplaincy Service recruits ordained clergy of virtually all English and Scottish, Catholic and Protestant, Christian denominations. When required, the Ministry of Defence provides naval units with civilian chaplains of the Buddhist, Hindu, Jewish, Muslim, and Sikh, Faiths.

• The United States Navy Chaplain Corps: Counts its origin from 28 November 1775, only 38 days after the Continental Navy was formed. Early chaplains were recruited more for teaching ability than ecclesiastical duties. They were mainly Methodist or Episcopalian, and ordination was not mandated until 1841. The first Roman Catholic priest was commissioned in 1888 and the first Jewish rabbi in 1917. Today officers of the Chaplain Corps hold naval rank and include clergy from over 100 denominations and faith groups. They offer spiritual care to Naval, Coast Guard, and Marine personnel, and are supported by enlisted RP (Religious Program) specialists. Specialty chaplain insignia identify Christians (Catholic, Orthodox, and Protestant) with a Cross; Buddhists with an 8-spoke Prayer Wheel; Muslims with the Crescent, and Jews with Mosaic Tablets surmounted by the Mogen David. As in the British Service, officers of the Corps are expected to work collegially in a pluralistic environment, cooperating with chaplains of other religious faiths. Also like the British, they have the option of wearing clerical dress rather than uniform, but the privilege is less often exercised than in the RN.

Chaplain of the Fleet/Chief of Chaplains: This office originated in 1695, when the chaplain of Admiral Rooke's flagship was appointed by the Admiralty Board "...to inspect and oversee the lives and behaviors of the rest of the chaplains of His Majesty's fleet in the Mediterranean." Six years later King William III authorized the appointment of a "Chaplain Generall of the Fleet," but when the office was implemented by Order in Council the title was changed to "Overseer and Inspector of Naval Chaplains." In 1712, King William's title of Chaplain General was reinstated. Over the next 115 years the office was abolished and reinstated several times.

In 1857, the Chaplains of all Royal Navy ships were directed "To correspond with (the Senior Chaplain at Greenwich Naval Hospital) on all matters relating to the religious instruction given by them to the ships companies and generally regarding their sacred duties." This marks the beginning of the modern Chaplaincy Service. Two years later the office was defined by Order in Council as "Head of the Naval Chaplains" with the title of Chaplain **to** the Fleet. Today, the Service is headed by a Director General, known as Chaplain **of** the Fleet, who is normally an Archdeacon of the Church of England, or the equivalent in other denominations. The USN Chaplain Corps is headed by a Chief of Chaplains who ranks as Rear Admiral.

Characteristics: The distinguishing qualities of a navigation aid or buoy, including shape and color, whether fixed or flashing, and flashing sequence.

Charge: [1] The explosive or propellant with which a gun or shell is loaded. [2] To load a gun or a vessel. [3] A formal accusation of infraction of discipline or crime. [4] To store electrical energy in a battery. [5] To pressurize a pneumatic or hydraulic system. [6] A figure, badge, or heraldic symbol on the field of a flag.

Charlie: [1] NATO phonetic notation for the letter "C." [2] Naval aviation term directing an aircraft into the carrier landing pattern.

Charlie Noble: This mariner's nickname for the galley funnel undoubtedly refers to a real person who was fanatical about keeping the brass or copper stovepipe brilliantly polished. Unfortunately it's not absolutely certain who that was and, confusingly, the name is sometimes spelt Charley Nobel. Uncertainty is increased because he has been "positively identified" as being both British and American; in merchant and in naval service; and as cook, mate, and master. Despite these ambiguities, the most likely candidate seems Captain Charles Noble who served in the British merchant service during the 1850s.

Charlie reveille: *See* bugle calls.

Chart: A geographical, hydrographical, or marine map designed for navigation. Nowadays frequently kept in electronic form.

Chart datum: [1] The water level below which depths on a chart are measured, and above which heights of tide are expressed. [2] The geodetic reference used to establish spatial relativity of objects depicted on a chart. Despite their shared name, these are separate entities.

Chart room: A small room adjacent to the bridge in which charts are stored and navigators work. Also charthouse.

Charter: To lease or hire a vessel.

Charter Party: The legal contract covering af-freightment, in which shipowner and freighter or shipper agree that: the vessel "Being tight, staunch and strong, and in every way fitted for the voyage" shall load specified cargo at a designated port and proceed — with all possible despatch to a designated place and there deliver the cargo to the freighter or his assigns. — The document should include at least:
- Name and tonnage of the vessel.
- Name of its master.
- Name of the freighter.
- Time and place for loading.
- Time and place for discharge.
- Price of the freight.
- Demurrage or indemnity in case of delay.
- Any other terms agreed by the parties.

Chase: [1] To pursue another vessel. [2] The vessel being pursued. [3] The tapering outer part of a gun barrel, lying ahead of the trunnions.

Chaser: A cannon mounted to fire ahead when pursuing another vessel (bow-chaser), or behind when being followed by an enemy (stern-chaser). Also chase-gun.

Chasse Marée: A lugger-rigged two or three-masted French coastal vessel. Used by fishermen to carry fresh-caught fish to market. Often used by smugglers and as a naval courier or aviso.

Chatham Chest: This is one of the earliest of maritime charitable organizations, established in 1590 by Queen Elizabeth I, to pay gratuities known as "smart money" to seamen who had been hurt or wounded in royal service. It was funded by compulsory payroll deduction from every seaman and apprentice according to their wages.

Chearly!: Obsolete command to do something heartily or quickly.

Check!: [1] Command to stop or slow down. [2] To ease a line a little and then belay it.

Check firing!: Command ordering a temporary halt in naval gunfire. *See* cease firing!

Check valve: One that allows liquid to flow in one direction but not in the other.

Checkers/Draughts: The game, known as checkers by Americans and draughts by the British, was so much enjoyed by sailing ship seamen that it was not unusual to find a checkered board carved into the wood of a fighting top so that those on duty could play (when they should have been keeping lookout).

Checklist: A written sequence of procedures to ensure nothing is overlooked when performing a complex or vital task.

Cheek block: A block with one end permanently attached to something such as a mast.

Cheeks: The side pieces of a gun carriage. Each cheek of Spanish and most other European carriages was usually made from a single great plank, but English and American construction called for a built-up cheek of several planks, jigged or mortised together to prevent starting under the strain of firing.

Cheese: A tight coil of rope lying flat on the deck with the end in its center.

Chemical weapons: Toxic substances — solid, liquid or gaseous — used to cause injury, incapacitation, or death. They are classified as weapons of mass destruction by the United Nations, and their production and stockpiling was outlawed by the Chemical Weapons Convention of 1993. Cf. biological weapons.

Cheerful but subdued: The RN ceremonial drill book description of the aspect the honor guard and mourners should assume at naval funerals.

Cheese Whizzo: Derogatory USN enlisted slang for a Commissioned Warrant Officer (based on the initials of the job title).

Cheops ship: *See* Khufu ship.

Cherry-picker: USN flight deck slang for a device used to clear crashed aircraft. *See* crash dolly, jumbo.

Chesapeake Bay (battle): *See* Virginia Capes (battle).

Chesapeake incident: On 22nd June 1807, HMS *Leopard* intercepted USS *Chesapeake*, forced her to heave to by firing across her bow, then boarded, and seized four seamen, claimed to be deserters from the Royal Navy. The incident was one of the factors contributing to the War of 1812.

Chesapeake log canoe: This design was used by the indigenous Indians and later developed into a family of vessels that included the bugeye and skipjack. It was built of five 30–40 foot (9–12 m) logs hand hewn into a dugout with a fixed bowsprit, raked mast, and narrow open deck.

Chew the fat: Even after long-term boiling in the galley kettles, salted pork or beef was tough and difficult to swallow. The worst part was the fat, which sailors would often cut off and save to gnaw sitting on deck during their time off watch. The ship's officers would correctly tell passengers they were chewing the fat, but from a distance it looked as though they were sitting around gossiping, so the phrase came into common usage to mean idle chatter.

Chief Engineer: The title of what could be considered a merchantman's technical manager, responsible for structural integrity of the vessel, the operation and upkeep of machinery and mechanical equipment, fuel bunkers, and related anti-pollution measures. Like the ship's master, its chief engineer stands no watches, which are kept by assistant engineer officers. In highly-automated ships, however, machinery spaces are monitored by data loggers and left unmanned, thus allowing junior engineers to follow daywork routines, only standing watches when in coastal waters, during pilotage, or under adverse weather.

[It is interesting to note that, when the RN Corps of Naval Engineers (then civilian employees)was formed in 1835, the profession was so little regarded that even the chief engineer ranked below the carpenter, with other grades of engineer having even less status. Today, the senior engineer officer of a Royal Navy

ship (known colloquially as "The Chief") is commissioned and has much greater status.]

Chief of Naval Operations: Created in 1915, the CNO is the senior flag officer and professional head of the United States Navy. He or she takes precedence over all other officers in the naval service except when an admiral is Chairman or Vice-Chairman of the Joint Chiefs of Staff. With administrative rather than command responsibility, the CNO is a member of the Joint Chiefs of Staff, and is responsible to the Secretary of the Navy for management of the Navy and its operational efficiency. The RN equivalent is Chief of Naval Staff—(*also see* First Sea Lord). A Vice–CNO is appointed from officers on the active-duty list eligible for command at sea and serving in grades above captain. The VCNO holds the temporary rank of admiral for the duration of the appointment.

Chief of the Boat: The senior enlisted person in a USN submarine.

Chief Officer: The second-in-command of a merchantman, responsible for deck operations and cargo stowage (also called Mate, First Mate, or First Officer).

Chief Petty Officer: A naval non-commissioned officer rate. [1] In the USN it is in pay grade E-7, senior to petty officer first class, junior to Senior Chief Petty Officer, and equivalent to Gunnery Sergeant in the Marine Corps. [2] In the RN it is in NATO rank code OR-7, senior to Petty Officer, junior to Warrant Officer, and equivalent to Colour Sergeant in the Royal Marines.

Chief Warrant Officer: A former enlisted petty officer or chief petty officer, expert in a technical specialty. CWOs take the same oath and receive the same commission as regular commissioned officers, ranking "with but after" ensigns, and are saluted by warrant officers and all enlisted personnel. They can and do assume limited command responsibility, but are primarily technical experts, providing valuable skills, guidance, and expertise in their particular field. CWOs differ from limited duty officers only in degree of authority and responsibility. After 3 years of active duty, a CWO may apply for the designation of LDO and, if accepted, he or she is appointed as lieutenant, junior grade.

Chiefs of Staff Committee: The British equivalent of the U.S. Joint Chiefs of Staff. Formed in 1924 to give military advice to the Prime Minister, and provide administrative and tactical coordination, and strategic direction to the British armed forces.

Chinch: *See* chinse.

Chine: [1] The line along a hull where sides and bottom meet. [2] The rim of a cask formed by projecting staves. [3] A water channel above the deck on wooden ships. [4] In south-central England, a steep-sided river valley leading to the sea though easily-eroded cliffs (Anglo-Saxon cinan = gap).

Chinese jibe: An unintentional jibe in which the boom and bottom of a gaff- or lug-sail changes side leaving the top behind. A frequent problem with Chinese junks.

Chinese landing: USN terminology for [1] Coming bow to stern with another vessel. [2] Coming alongside down-current. [3] Landing an aircraft downwind.

Chinse: To seal a small seam by working in oakum with a knife or chisel. A temporary measure when the opening would not stand the force of full caulking.

Chips/Chippy: Nicknames for a carpenter or shipwright.

Chit: A memorandum, note, voucher, or requisition (from the Hindi citthi = pass).

Chock: [1] Deck-mounted guide for an anchor chain or mooring line. [2] Wedge-shaped block to stop aircraft or cargo from moving. [3] One of several blocks supporting a boat under repair.

Chock-a-block: This term describes the situation when two blocks (pulleys) in a tackle have been pulled so close together that no further movement is possible. In Britain and Australia the term has come into slang use to mean "overcrowded," "full up," or "fed up."

Chocker: British slang for "fed up." Probably an abbreviation of chock-a-block.

Chockman: Flight deck person who places chocks under aircraft wheels.

Choke: To deliberately foul a line in a block to temporarily secure the fall. Short form of "choke the luff."

Choke point: A narrow passage, such as a strait, creating a bottleneck through which shipping must pass. The most significant are:
• Bab-el-Mandeb: between the Arabian and Red Seas.
• Gibraltar Strait: between Atlantic Ocean and Mediterranean Sea.
• Hormuz Strait: at the entrance to the Persian/Arabian Gulf.
• Malacca Strait: between Malaysia and Indonesia.
• Panama Canal: connecting the Pacific and Atlantic Oceans.
• Suez Canal: connecting the Red and Mediterranean Seas.
• Turkish Straits: linking the Black and Mediterranean Seas.

Chop: [1] Short, steep, irregular waves (*see* choppy). [2] To signify approval of something by initialing it (from the Chinese for a seal denoting authority). [3] USN term for the transfer of a ship or unit from one command to another. [4] Slang for food (from West African Pidgin-English).

Chop-chop: Asian Pidgin-English for "quickly-quickly" (from the Chinese k"wai-k"wai = nimbly-nimbly).

Chop line: The boundary between two USN commands.

Chopper: Colloquialism for helicopter.

Choppy: [1] Of the sea: Having many small waves; rough. [2] Of the wind: Abruptly shifting; variable.

Chow: USN slang for a meal (from the Mandarin Ch'ao = to cook or fry).

Christening: [1] Landlubbers say a ship is christened, seamen say she is named. [2] In some navies a chaplain, using the ship's bell inverted as a baptismal font, may christen children of members of the ship's company. Afterwards, the consecrated water is returned to the sea.

Chronometer: An especially accurate and highly consistent marine timepiece designed to facilitate course-plotting. Before the fifteenth century, the only reliable means of navigation was to follow known features on the shore. Then acquisition of the compass from China via Arabia, and the astrolabe from Islam allowed European mariners to calculate their approximate north-south position (latitude) while out of sight of land. However, in the absence of a reliable means of measuring time, their east-west location (longitude) could only be "guesstimated" through a complex process known as dead reckoning. The resultant errors caused numerous shipwrecks.

In 1713, the British Parliament offered the then immense reward of £20,000 for any means of determining longitude with an error of less than thirty miles (48 kms) after six weeks at sea. This demanded precise timekeeping to within three seconds per day while pitching and tossing and traveling from frigid arctic to steaming equator; a degree of accuracy which had seldom been achieved by the finest stationary clocks in temperate zones. Sixty years later, the prize was won by John Harrison, a Yorkshire carpenter and self-taught horologist. His first machines were costly, complicated, and delicate; but soon he and Pierre Le Roy of Paris (independently) developed more rugged marine timekeepers with all the essential features of a modern chronometer.

By then, invention of the sextant had provided a more accurate means of calculating latitude. Thus, by the great naval wars of late 18th and early 19th centuries, shipmasters could set out on long voyages with confidence in making an accurate landfall or rendezvous. Today, after more than two centuries of use, chronometers are being replaced by electronic timekeepers.

Church pendant/pennant: Worn by RN and USN ships holding religious services, these are the only flags which may be flown above the national ensign, and then only during church services.

CIF: *See* Incoterms.

Cimarrónes: Spanish for mountain-dwellers, applied to runaway African or (sometimes) American Indian slaves, many of whom took to piracy. In the 1570s, the Cimarrónes of Panama allied with Sir Francis Drake who described them as "A black people which about eighty years past fled from the Spaniards their masters, by reason of their cruelty, and are since grown to a nation." Also called maroons.

Cinderella liberty: USN enlisted slang for shore leave ending at midnight.

Cinque Ports: A group of ports (pronounced "sink") on the SE coast of England granted special privileges during the 11th century, including exemption from the jurisdiction of Admiralty Courts, in return for coastal defense and providing warships. The original five were Hastings, Romney, Hythe, Dover, and Sandwich. Rye and Winchelsea were added later.

Cipher: A text in which symbols or substitutions replace ordinary letters in order to conceal its meaning from those who do not possess the key. *See also* code, cryptography.

Circumnavigation: A voyage around the world or a feature such as a cape or promontory.

Civil Engineer Corps: A staff corps of the United States Navy that includes the Seabees. Its officers are professional engineers, architects, acquisitions specialists, and construction managers. They plan, design, acquire, construct, operate, and maintain naval shore facilities.

Clamp down: USN term for light cleaning with a dry mop, as opposed to swabbing with a wet mop.

Clamshell bucket: *See* grab bucket.

Clandestine: Said of an operation conducted in such a way as to ensure secrecy or concealment. A clandestine operation differs from a covert operation in that emphasis is placed on concealment of the operation rather than on concealment of the identity of its sponsor.

Clap: Seaman's slang for venereal disease (from Old French clapier = low-class brothel).

Clap on: [1] To add a temporary feature, such as an extra sail. [2] Command to catch hold of a rope and haul it.

Class: [1] A group of warships or racing yachts sharing design and other characteristics. *See also* sister ships. [2] Ships of the same type (e.g., tankers, break-bulk vessels).

Classified: A general term defining information which must be controlled in the interest of national security. *See* "confidential," "secret," and "top secret."

Claw off: Beat to windward to escape a lee shore.

Clean full: Sailing so as to keep the sails full and bellying in the wind.

Clean into: Former RN command to change into the rig (uniform) specified in the instruction. This led to the ridiculous order "clean into coaling rig" to do the dirtiest job on shipboard.

Clean ship: Refers to [1] A vessel whose lines are clear and unobstructed from bow to stern so that she moves smoothly through the water. [2] A bulk oil carrier whose cargo tanks are free of all traces of heavy fuel or crude oils previously carried.

Clean slate: This term — which now implies the removal of (unfavorable) items from a person's record — probably originated at sea in the days of sailing ships when changes of course were temporarily recorded on a slate. At the end of each watch the data was logged and the slate was wiped clean.

Clear: [1] To obtain approval of something. [2] An open message not in cipher or code. [3] To authorize access to classified information . [4] To safely pass over or by an obstruction or hazard such as a reef. [5] To round a cape or promontory or pass a landmark. [6] Free-running, not fouled. [7] To remove stoppages or fouling of a gun. [8] To remove ammunition from a gun. [9] To complete all formalities necessary to enter or leave a port. [10] To remove all cargo from a ship. [11] To drive or force out (e.g., clear the seas).

Clear anchor!: Report to the commanding officer that the anchor is in sight and free from any entanglement.

Clear away!: Command to lay out rope in a coil that will run freely.

Clear datum: Said of a submarine which leaves an area after being detected.

Clear days: A charter party term referring to the number of days (first and last excluded) available for work.

Clear for action!: Command [1] In the days of sailing ships with broadside gun batteries, to open up the gun decks by removing all interior bulkheads and canvas screens, rolling and lashing hammocks to be placed in nettings above the bulwarks, etc. [2] Today, to remove all encumbrances from the decks, and prepare for an engagement (cf. clear ship, strip ship).

Clear for Guam: To set sail for an unknown destination. At the height of the Australian gold rush, ships which carried prospectors to Melbourne had to leave in ballast to search for return cargoes. Australian Customs regulations required that vessels clearing outward declare their destination. Since this was usually unknown it became customary to "Clear for Guam"—an island in the Western Pacific Ocean with the status of United States unincorporated territory.

Clear ship: Prepare for combat by removing the jackstaff and other spars not required for navigation, clearing flammable items from the deck, and laying out ready-use ammunition (cf. strip ship, clear for action).

Clear the decks!: Command to remove all unnecessary gear and objects from the open decks in preparation for foul weather.

Clear the yardarm: [1] In common usage: To absolve oneself of blame, either before or after an embarrassing incident, mistake, or omission has occurred. [2] In communications parlance: Make no signals (outstanding hoists are not executed).

Clear visibility: Weather conditions allowing visual range of at least 10 nautical miles.

Clear water: Ice-free Polar seas.

Clearance: A document indicating that a vessel has completed all Customs requirements and is free to leave.

Clearance bearing: A pre-calculated bearing to a charted object, warning of a navigational hazard on the vessel's course. The American term is "danger bearing." Also called "clearing bearing," "limit bearing" or "index bearing."

Clearing baffles: Good submarine warfare tactics

require the vessel to turn sharply and abruptly to one side or the other at irregular intervals so that its sonar can scan the previous baffle zone for any hostile submarine which might be hiding there. This maneuver is properly known as clearing the baffles and colloquially as a crazy ivan. Modern boats usually deploy a towed sonar array within the baffled area, thereby making the maneuver redundant.

Clearview screen: A fast-rotating glass disc that throws off spray or rain water to allow bridge officers to see ahead.

Cleat: [1] A fitting to which a line can be secured without needing a hitch. [2] To secure a line to such a fitting.

Clench: [1] A knot made by a half hitch with the end of the rope fastened back by seizing. [2] To secure a nail or screw by beating over the protruding point. [3] To settle definitely and conclusively, to make final. [4] To grip, grasp, or close tightly. Also clinch, and both forms are used in common speech (e.g., "When she clinched the deal, it made him clench his teeth").

Clew: [1] The lower corners of a square sail. [2] The lower corner of the leech of a lugsail or a triangular sail.

Cliff: A steep or vertical rock face, especially one facing the sea.

Clinch: [1] That part of a cable, or rope that is fastened to the ring of the anchor. [2] Alternate spelling of clench.

Clinker: [1] A chunk of soot emanating from the stack or exhaust of a ship. [2] The stony residue from burnt coal. [3] Code-name for a system which senses the heat generated by a submarine's wake.

Clinker knocker: RN slang for a stoker.

Clinker-built: Boatbuilding style in which side planks overlap (cf. Carvel-built).

Clinking glasses: 18th century superstition held that a seafarer drowned each time a drinking glass was knocked and "rang." However, he could be saved if the sound was silenced with a finger and someone simultaneously cried out "save the sailor." Some believed that two soldiers would then be taken instead. This widespread civilian courtesy is still occasionally frowned upon by seamen.

Clinometer: An instrument for measuring the inclination of a vessel's roll, heel, or list. Also, but slightly incorrect, inclinometer.

Clipper: A 19th century fast-sailing merchantman, fully-rigged with an exceptionally large sail area, designed for speed rather than cargo capacity, with a long, low, narrow hull, sharply concave knife-edged bow, and three to seven tall square-sailed masts. Built specifically for the East Indian tea trade, they were the fastest commercial sailing ships ever built. Speeds in excess of 15 knots were usual, and in 1854 *Sovereign of the Seas* reported making 22 knots while running down to Australia.

Clipper bow: A forward-curved stem and sides with lots of flare. Also schooner bow.

Close: To approach another vessel or place (pronounced "cloze").

Close aboard: [1] The distance at which naval honors should normally be rendered (600 yards or meters for a ship, 400 for a boat). [2] Said of enemy fire which falls near the ship (pronounced as written).

Close air support: Aerial action to assist ground forces in combat. Requires careful coordination to avoid "friendly fire" casualties.

Close-hauled: Steering towards the wind as much as possible.

Close-quarters: [1] Fighting yardarm-to-yardarm or man-to-man on deck. Although long in naval use and sometimes said to have a naval origin, the phrase almost certainly began ashore as an infantry term for hand-to-hand combat. [2] Loopholed bulwarks across the upper decks of merchantmen for defense against pirates. [3] A barrier across the deck of a slave-trader to guard against an uprising. [4] Any small confined place or position.

Close reach: The point of sail between a beam reach and close-hauled.

Close-reefed: Said of square-rig topsails when all possible reefs have to taken in to minimize sail area.

Close support: Gunfire by a supporting unit against targets or objectives engaged by another unit that are sufficiently near to that unit as to require coordination with the supported unit's fire, movement, or other actions.

Close-up: [1] The act of hoisting a flag or sail to the highest position (pronounced "cloze"). [2] Said of flags or sails which are as high as possible (pronounced as written). This term derives from visual signaling. When the flagship hoisted a signal the addressee hoisted the same signal at the dip to confirm it had been seen. After looking it up in the signal book the hoist was brought "close-up" to indicate it was fully understood. When the admiral's hoist was hauled down, the addressee immediately lowered the signal and executed the order.

Closed-cycle diesel: An engine that can be operated underwater to provide air-independent propulsion by running on an artificial atmosphere synthesized from liquid oxygen, an inert gas, and recycled exhaust products. The exhaust — largely carbon dioxide, nitrogen, water vapor, and argon — is cooled, scrubbed, and separated, with the argon being recycled and the remaining products mixed with seawater and discharged overboard. The engine can also be operated conventionally when on the surface or while snorkeling.

Closed-cycle steam turbine: In this form of air-independent propulsion, steam is generated by the combustion of ethanol and liquid oxygen at a pressure of about 60 atmospheres. Pressure-firing allows exhaust carbon dioxide to be discharged overboard at any depth without an exhaust compressor.

Closed-up: To be au fait with a situation, to understand what is going on (pronounced "clozed").

Cloth: Refers to the canvas of a sail. For example, a ship with wide sails was said to "spread much cloth."

Clothing: [1] During the seventh century sails were known as "clothing" after the cloth from which they were made. [2] Today the term is used for insulating material wrapped around pipes and then covered with lagging. [3] Garments collectively.

Cloudburst: Brief but very heavy rainfall, unofficially specified as more than 100 mms (4 inches)/hour.

Clove hitch: A knot formed of two half-hitches made in opposite directions. Often used for securing mooring lines.

Club-haul: A seldom-performed and hazardous emergency maneuver in which the lee anchor is dropped to bring the ship's head to the wind, at which moment the cable is cut and sails are trimmed on the new tack. Only performed in the most perilous and rarest of situations (such as in 1814 when HMS *Magnificent* was caught between two reefs in the Basque Roads).

Clue: Either of the lower corners of a square sail.

Clutter: Radar distortion due to precipitation, electronic interference, or wave reflection.

Coach: The cabin or compartment just ahead of the Great Cabin in a sailing man-o-war. Used by the flag-captain when carrying an admiral.

Coaling bag: A large canvas bag used by the USN to transport supplies during replenishment at sea.

Coaming: A raised frame to keep water from running into a hatch or opening in the deck to flood the space below. There is a rabett (incised shelf) in the upper inside edge to receive a hatch cover or grating. In the days of fighting sail, loopholes in the coamings allowed muskets to be fired from below to clear the deck of boarders. Also (incorrectly) combing.

Coast: The land near to the sea, the seashore.

Coast Guard: The U.S. Coast Guard is primary guardian of United States maritime borders, charged with preventing illegal incursions into the exclusive economic zone (EEZ), and halting the inflow of illegal drugs, migrants, and contraband. It is unique in operating as both a civil authority and a branch of the national armed forces, reporting to the Secretary of Homeland Security in peacetime, and to the Secretary of the Navy in war.

Coast is clear: This was originally a smuggler's term indicating there were no revenuers lurking ashore or coast guard vessels nearby.

Coastal current: A stream flowing parallel to the shore outside the surf line (cf. longshore current).

Coaster: A vessel engaged in coastwise trade, normally unsuitable or uncertified for blue-water service.

Coastguard: The British Coastguard is part of the civilian Maritime & Coastguard Agency and is primarily concerned with search and rescue at sea, ensuring that passage is safe, and preventing coastal pollution.

Coastie: Slang for a member of the U.S. Coast Guard.

Coastwise: Shipping routes which remain within twenty nautical miles of the shore.

Cobbing and firking: These were unofficial punishments awarded by "messdeck court-martial" to cooks who spoiled a meal or consistently served unpalatable food. **Cobbing** involved all members of the mess beating the offender with socks filled with sand or a flat piece of wood called a cobbing-board, while **firking** was similar treatment using the staves of the small cask called a firkin. Those who did not remove their hats when the watch was called were also subject to cobbing. The practice got out of hand and was officially forbidden in 1811.

Coble: A flat-bottomed, square-sterned boat used by Yorkshire turbot fishers.

Cock: The naval term for a tap or faucet.

Cockbill: To place the yards of a square-rigger at random angles (acockbill) as a sign of mourning.

Cocked hat: [1] In navigation, three observed position lines should properly pass through a single point to make the fix, but if there is any compass error, or if a sight has been less than perfect, the lines will form a triangle known as a "cocked hat." [2] Headgear, pointed at front, back, and crown, universally worn by naval officers until World War II, and still occasionally at formal events with full-dress uniform. Also (incorrectly) called a tricorne. [3] The phrase "knocked into a cocked hat" means to be soundly and swiftly defeated.

Cockpit: [1] Originally a compartment below the waterline of a man-o-war, used as junior officers' quarters and a dressing station for men wounded in combat. [2] Nowadays, the space containing helm and compass in a small boat. Also [3] the crew compartment in an aircraft.

Cock-up: RN slang for a bungle.

CODAD propulsion: This acronym of **C**ombined **D**iesel **A**nd **D**iesel refers to a propulsion system using two diesel engines, connected by a gearbox and clutches that allow either or both of them to power a single propeller shaft.

CODAG propulsion: **C**ombined **D**iesel **A**nd **G**as turbine, refers to a propulsion system for ships which need a maximum speed (using the combined system) that is considerably faster (usually 50 percent) than their cruising speed with diesel power alone. Linking the two power sources requires complex and potentially troublesome gearing, so an alternative is to let each system use its own drive shafts to turn smaller propellers. However, this is less efficient and the propellers of the idling system cause drag. CODAG propulsion is employed by Norway's Nansen Class frigates and Germany's Köln Class frigates.

CODAG–Electric propulsion: In this variation, each of the CODAG power sources is connected to a generator, and the propellers are driven by electric motors. This design is employed by RMS *Queen Mary 2* which mounts the propulsion motors inside pods and places the gas turbines directly under the funnel where fresh air is more easily accessed than in the engine room.

CODAG–WARP propulsion: In this system the second acronym does not come from Star Wars, but refers to **W**aterjet **A**nd **R**efined **P**ropeller. Two diesel engines drive two propellers in a CODAD arrangement, with a water jet powered by a gas turbine at the centerline. When idling the water jet causes no drag and — since its nozzle can be placed further aft and higher — it does not affect the size of the propellers.

Code: [1] A systematic collection of laws. [2] A text in which whole words or phrases (rather than individual letters) have been substituted in order to conceal its meaning from those who do not possess the key. *See also* cipher, cryptography.

Code flag: A red-and-white striped pennant used to signal that International Code (table 8) will be used for the subsequent message.

Codger: This term for an odd or eccentric person, especially one who is old and miserly, was originally a seaman's name for a lazy or easy-going shipmate who would never move faster than he had to.

Cofferdam: [1] A sealed double bulkhead used for insulation or to prevent the escape of vapors or liquids. [2] A watertight chamber or enclosure for construction or repairs.

Coffin ship: Colloquial description of a vessel of dubious safety or seaworthiness.

Cog: A capacious sailing merchantman of the Baltic and Mediterranean. Characterized by high sides, flat bottom, and single square-sail. Popular from 10th to 15th centuries.

COGAG propulsion: A combination power plant consisting of **C**ombined **G**as turbine **A**nd **G**as turbine in which one is employed for cruise economy, and is supplemented by a second, larger one, to provide boost power.

COGOG propulsion: A combination of gas turbines in which one is used for cruise economy, and a second larger one provides boost power. It differs from a COGAG configuration in that the smaller turbine must be physically disengaged when the boost turbine is employed, hence the acronym comes from **C**ombined **G**as turbine **O**r **G**as turbine.

Coil: [1] To lay down a line in fakes. [2] To loop a line for storage. [3] Anything arranged in concentric circles. [4] A standard 120-fathom length of line as purchased.

Coin: *See* quoin.

Coir: Fiber made from coconut husk, used to make buoyant matting and low-grade rope. Pronounced coyer.

Coir rope: Is the weakest of all cordage, but it has the advantage of being so light that it floats on water. It is also flexible and very springy, but rots if stowed while wet, and does not stand up well to chafe or weather. It is half the weight, and one-fifth the strength, of equal size manila or sisal rope.

Cold iron: *See* cold ship.

Cold move: To shift a cold ship by means of tugs, or wires and dockside capstan.

Cold ship: A vessel with no source of power for propulsion, heat, communication, or any other purpose. Also cold iron, dead ship.

Cold shot: [1] A catapult launch lacking sufficient power to propel the aircraft to flying speed, causing it to crash. [2] Unheated cannon balls.

Cold War: A state of political tension and military rivalry between nations that stops short of full-scale combat. Especially the nuclear standoff between the United States and Soviet Union following World War II.

Collateral duty: A function assigned to a person whose primary task is unrelated.

Collier: A vessel designed to carry coal as its sole cargo.

Collision: The impact (usually violent) of one moving body (e.g., a ship) with another, or with a fixed object (e.g., a wharf). *See* Colregs.

Collision Avoidance System: An electronic system designed to prevent collisions in confined waterways.

Collision bulkhead: A watertight enclosure extending from keel to main deck to prevent the entire ship from being flooded in the event of head-on collision.

Collision mat: A heavy pad for covering underwater holes in the hull caused by battle or collision damage. The pressure of sea water holds it in place. (Cf. fother.)

Colors/Colours: [1] The Flag or ensign, indicating a vessel's nationality. [2] A ceremonial bugle call made when raising the national flag in the morning and (USN only) lowering it in the evening. The RN term for the latter is "sunset."

Colregs: This abbreviation of **Col**lision **Regu**lations refers to rules formalized at a 1972 Convention on International Regulations for the Prevention of Collisions at Sea (*see* table 7). Based on concepts of seamanship and nautical wisdom that had evolved over centuries of seafaring, Colregs became effective in July 1977, and are periodically updated. They are binding on the vessels of all States while in international waters. In inland waters, vessels obey the regulations of the State having jurisdiction, but these are usually based on and similar to Colregs.

Although mandatory, these international rules do not stifle initiative, because Rule 2 makes it clear that blindly following them does not exonerate any master or navigator from personal responsibility for prudent and responsible behavior; even to the extent of ignoring the rules when circumstances dictate alternative emergency action. In addition to steering and sailing regulations, Colregs prescribe lights and shapes that respectively identify the types and relative positions of watercraft by night and by day; sound and light signals (table 9) which allow masters or pilots to communicate their vessel's present situation and imminent maneuvers; and a wide range of methods for mariners to signal distress (*see* table 10).

Colt: *See* Starter and Unofficial Beating.

Column: [1] One of the dimensions of a convoy, which is traditionally assembled in a rectangular formation of columns running from front-to-back (counted from the left); and lines running from side-to-side (counted from the front). For example, the second ship in the first column would be in Station 12, while the third ship in the fifth column would be in Station 53. [2] The USN and NATO term for line-ahead (single file). *See also* "open order column."

Comb: [1] To roll and break (used of waves). [2] To make a thorough search (e.g., He combed through the file, looking for the contract).

Combat Air Patrol: A defensive umbrella of fighter aircraft, deployed over a naval force or operating area for the purposes of combating hostile air attacks and of destroying scout aircraft before they can gather or transmit intelligence information. Usually known as "the Cap."

Combat Direction Center: *See* combat information center.

Combat Engagement Center: The nerve center of an RN warship in combat. Formerly known as Gun Direction Room.

Combat Information Center: The communications and electronics hub of a warship, staffed and outfitted to collect, display, evaluate, and disseminate tactical information from radar, sonar, and other equipment, for use by the commanding officer or embarked flag officer during an engagement. During normal operations, CIC supports the bridge and the OOD by tracking and identifying surface and air contacts, coordinating with shoreside command centers, and communicating with other vessels. Also called Action Information Center and, on aircraft carriers, Combat Direction Center.

Combat loading: Embarking troops and equipment in the order required for rapid and effective disembarkation during an amphibious assault (cf. commercial loading; tactical loading).

Combers: Deep water waves with foamy crests (cf. breakers).

Combined operations: [1] Military action in conjunction with allied forces. [2] Operations involving at least two of a nation's land, sea, and air forces.

Combing: *See* coaming.

Come about: To bring a boat from one tack to the other by turning into the eye of the wind.

Come home: Said of an anchor when its flukes are not holding and it drags.

Comingle: To mix two or more petroleum products. Usually the result of improper handling procedures.

Comito: The title of a galley officer whose rank and status diminished over time. In antiquity the title signified an admiral, in the Byzantine navy it referred to a captain, and by the Renaissance it meant first mate.

Command: [1] The authority exercised by virtue of rank or assignment. [2] A ship or unit under the jurisdiction of an individual commander. [3] An instruction requiring immediate execution (cf. order).

Command and control: [1] This phrase has long been used generically to describe the exercise of authority and direction by a properly designated commander over assigned forces for the accomplishment of a mission. [2] Recently, it has acquired the specific meaning of a data system for the direction of tactical, strategic, or combat activities in "real time" as is demanded by the speed of 21st century warfare. A commander in the field or at sea uses such a system as the tool to direct and coordinate forces in order to accomplish the assigned mission and cope with the inevitable uncertainties of battle. The more remote from the scene of action, the more dependant he or she is on communications.

The activity is usually abbreviated C^2, but has recently been referred to as C^3 (C^2 plus communications) or even as C^4I (adding computers and intelligence). These additions seem superfluous because without accurate information and speedy data processing, no commander can make meaningful decisions; without rapid, effective, and dependable communication he or she is unable to pass timely instructions to subordinates; and without some form of feedback from those subordinates effective control is impossible.

Command of the Sea: Accrues when a seapower is able to protect its own commerce by keeping open trade routes, while denying or controlling the use of such routes by hostile powers. The means of achievement are threefold: [1] Aerial and surface combat, to destroy enemy naval forces. [2] Blockade, to neutralize enemy naval and merchant shipping, by confining them to their ports, or destroying them if they venture forth. [3] Amphibious operations, when necessary to invade enemy territory. In the 21st century, all three are increasingly dependent on the Command of Space. [4] Another possibility, attempted by Germany in both World Wars, is to mount a guerre de course.

Command ship: Encouraged by the success of amphibious force flagships in World War II the post-war USN planned to convert several incomplete heavy cruisers and small aircraft carriers to tactical command ships equipped with advanced communications and extensive combat information spaces. Only a few were actually completed and commissioned in that role, which became extinct in 1980.

Commandant: [1] The highest ranking officer in the United States Marine Corps. By statute a four-star General and member of the Joint Chiefs of Staff, the Commandant reports directly to the Secretary of the Navy (a political appointee) not to the Chief of Naval Operations. [2] The officer in command of a naval base irrespective of rank.

Commander: [1] A person who exercises authority. [2] The officer in tactical command (OTC) of a group of specifically designated warships. [3] A naval rank instituted by the Royal Navy in 1814 to replace the former Master and Commander and then achievable only by being appointed to the command of a vessel smaller than a post-ship but larger than a lieutenant's command. It soon became an essential stepping stone to post-captain. In 1827, the first lieutenants (seconds-in-command) of battleships were also made commanders. [4] A naval rank instituted by the United States Navy in 1837 to replace the former Master Commandant (table 15). Today, commanders rank below captain and above lieutenant-commander.

Commanding Officer: The senior commissioned, warrant, or petty officer of a vessel, air squadron, unit, post, base, station, or other shore establishment. Also Officer-in-Command.

Commando: British name for an elite amphibious raiding force. Adopted from the South African Boer term for an irregular cavalry unit which, in turn, was taken from the Portuguese for a small military command. *See* special forces.

Commendatory Mast: USN term for a ceremony at which the commanding officer congratulates or decorates members of the command. *See also* captain's mast.

Commerce: Trade: business transactions; the buying selling, and movement of merchandise on a large scale between countries or regions.

Commerce raiding: *See* Guerre de Course.

Commercial loading: Embarking troops and equipment to ensure optimum use of available space without regard for combat readiness, as opposed to tactical or combat loading.

Commissary: Shore-based grocery and general goods store for USN personnel and dependants.

Commission: [1] To place a warship on active service. [2] The period during which a warship is assigned to specific duties. [3] A document conferring officer rank on an individual (excluding warrant, petty, and other non-commissioned officers). [4] A percentage of the selling price paid to a salesperson as payment for making the transaction. [5] A fee charged by a broker or agent for service in facilitating a business deal. [6] An official investigative body. [7] To contract for the production of something (e.g., a work of art).

Commission of War: Authorization to operate as a private warship (privateer) against enemies of the issuing authority, empowering the person to whom it is granted to carry on all forms of hostility which are permissible at sea under the usages of war. Frequently, but slightly incorrectly, called a Letter of Marque.

Commission Pennant: Under Article 1259 of Navy Regulations, a United States warship flies a special pennant from the main truck, day and night; from the moment it is commissioned until the moment it is decommissioned, except when displaced by an admiral's flag or a command pennant. When a pennant is to be changed, the new one is closed up before the old is struck. The pennant is blue from the hoist for one-

quarter of its length with seven evenly spaced white stars (there were originally thirteen, but the number was reduced when the pennant was shortened). The remaining three-fourths is divided horizontally, red over white. The Royal Navy's equivalent is known as the Masthead Pendant.

Commodity: General commercial term for any product or raw material available for trade.

Commodore: [1] A Royal Navy one-star flag rank created in 1999. [2] The commander of a convoy of merchantmen. [3] The senior captain of a line of merchant vessels. [4] The president or head of a yacht squadron or boat club. [5] Formerly, an RN or USN officer appointed to assume operational command of a group of specifically designated warships (today, this appointment would be termed "officer in tactical command").

During the 17th century Anglo-Dutch Wars, wanting to create additional squadron commanders without having to pay admiral's salaries, the Dutch Navy introduced the position of Komondeur which was a title rather than a rank. In 1689 the Dutch Stadholder, Prince William of Orange, became King William III of the United Kingdom, and a year later gave the title to the senior captains of detached squadrons, and the commanders of shore establishments where no flag officer was present. As in the Dutch prototype, these were only temporary appointments, and incumbents retained their seniority on the captains' list. In 1747, although commodores were still neither permanent nor a rank, captains serving as such were given the status of brigadier general in the first official British list of army-navy equivalents. During the Napoleonic Wars — when admirals were appointed strictly on seniority — the office of commodore allowed commanders-in-chief to reach far down into the captain's list, to give young and energetic officers the chance to prove themselves in command of squadrons, or even small fleets.

In 1805, RN commodores were divided into First Class, who were virtually junior admirals and entitled to flag captains, and those of the Second Class who captained their own ships as well as commanding a squadron. Both remained temporary appointments until 1996, when the second class was abandoned and the first was made substantive with one-star rank. The ups-and-downs of commodores in the U.S. Navy from temporary appointment to permanent rank are outlined above under "Admirals" and below under "Commodore Admiral." The title has now reverted to its original 18th century usage as the courtesy title of a senior captain commanding a squadron.

Commodore Admiral: This is perhaps the rarest of all naval titles, having been held by only a handful of USN officers appointed during the last eleven months of 1982. The rank was created to appease army and air force complaints that both upper and lower halves of rear admiral wore two stars, giving naval captains the advantage of skipping one-star rank. Congress established the rank of Commodore Admiral with a single star, but faced immediate and numerous objections that this violated centuries of naval tradition. In response, the "admiral" was dropped at the beginning of 1983. Two years later, the rank was abolished and rear admiral lower half was re-designated one-star (with no change in pay grade).

Common carrier: Refers to an individual or company engaged in transporting goods or passengers for profit.

Communication countermeasures: Techniques designed to detect, intercept, confuse, interfere with, or otherwise disrupt hostile communications. *See also* radar countermeasures, radio countermeasures, and electronic warfare.

Communication system: A system or facility capable of providing information transfer between persons and equipment, usually consisting of communication networks, transmission systems, relay stations, tributary stations, and terminal equipment capable of interconnection and interoperation so as to form an integrated whole.

Communications: [1] General: The transfer of information according to agreed conventions. [2] Information technology; the representation, transfer, interpretation, and processing of data between and among persons, places, and machines: [3] Military: The conveyance of information of any kind, but especially orders and decisions, from one command, person, or place to another, usually by means of electronic equipment.

Companion: [1] Formerly an opening that allowed light to enter cabins below the quarterdeck. [2] The cover over a cabin hatchway. From the Dutch kampanje = quarterdeck.

Companionway: A hatch or opening with a ladder giving access to a lower compartment (traditionally, the captain's or embarked flag officer's quarters). Also companion ladder.

Company: The oldest military unit, typically consisting of 75–200 soldiers or marines. Most contain from three to five platoons, the number varying by country, service, and structure. Several companies form a battalion, and several battalions a regiment (*see* military organization). The current meaning as the subdivision of an infantry regiment dates from about 1590, but the word "compaignie" appears as early as twelfth century French to describe a body of soldiers of any size. *See also* ship's company.

Compartment: Any space enclosed by bulkheads.

Compass: A direction-finding instrument showing the heading of a ship. Magnetic compasses orient themselves to the earth's magnetic field and can only show magnetic north. A gyrocompass depends on the tendency of freely-spinning rotors to maintain spatial orientation, and can be set to indicate true north.

Compass bowl: A round dish in which the compass card is mounted.

Compass card: A circular card, divided around its rim into the cardinal or inter-cardinal points of the compass, or into degrees. A lubber's line on the fixed compass bowl is aligned to the bow, and hence its intersection with the card shows the vessel's heading. To a shipboard observer the card seems to rotate when the vessel turns, but in fact it remains aligned to the north while the ship turns around it. Also compass rose.

Almost without exception, the northward direction on a compass card is indicated by a fleur-de-lys — a stylized lily flower, formerly the emblem of French royalty. Few mariners would be able to explain why, but the practice dates back to the twelfth century when the French called their water compasses "Mariniere." In 1258, the Florentine Brunetto Latini wrote; "Even as our august King is our guide on the land, so does the fleur-de-lys on the Mariniere guide the seafarer by constantly pointing to Boreas (the ancient Greek god of the north wind) no matter how the ship may go."

Compass compensation: Adjustments to a magnetic compass to counteract the effects of degaussing.

Compass course: The angle between the direction of compass north and the ship's fore-and-aft line, measured clockwise from compass north.

Compass error: Consists of two components. [1] Variation, which is caused by the difference between the geographic and magnetic poles, and changes with the observer's position on the earth's surface; and [2] Deviation, which is due to the magnetic effect of the iron in the ship itself.

Compass needle: A device used to determine geographic direction, usually consisting of a small bar magnet horizontally mounted or suspended and free to pivot until aligned with the earth's magnetic field.

Compass points: Before the arrival of modern instruments accurate enough to be calibrated from 0° to 360° (with finer readings possible) compasses used a less-precise 32-point system. Each of these points covered an arc of 11 1/4° and had a unique name as follows: North, North by East, North-Northeast, Northeast by North, Northeast, Northeast by East, East-Northeast, East by North, East, and so on around the other three quadrants (*see* cardinal points and intercardinal points). To recite them in sequence was to box the compass (table 17).

Compass rose: [1] A circle divided into 32 points or 360 degrees, numbered clockwise from true or magnetic north, printed on a map or chart for purposes of navigation or orientation. [2] A compass card.

Complaint: Refers to the creaking noise made by spars or timbers when under stress but in no danger of breaking.

Complement: [1] The number of officers and crew required for safe operation and navigation of a merchantman. [2] The number of officers and ratings/enlisted required and authorized to form a warship's company at full operational readiness.

Complete: Traditionally a ship is not "complete" until she has been launched. A finished but unlaunched vessel is "built."

Composite sailing: *See* sailings.

Con: [1] To pilot or direct the steering of a ship. [2] In American terminology, the location from which the ship is conned. Also conn. From Anglo-Saxon con-nan = skillful or cunning.

Condemnable: Said of goods declared to be contraband and thus subject to seizure and condemnation. Goods contaminated by infection are also condemnable.

Condemnation: [1] General: an expression of strong disapproval, severe reproof; or strong censure. [2] Ecclesiastical: a formal curse, often accompanied by excommunication. [3] Civil law: the act of (a) forfeiting land for public use, or (b) judging a food product unfit for consumption or a building unsafe for use. [4] Admiralty law: The sentence of an admiralty court declaring a captured vessel to be a lawful prize. Without such a ruling, the vessel may not legally be sold. Goods declared contraband are also subject to condemnation.

Condition: *See* "material condition" and "readiness condition."

Cone of Silence: [1] Space directly above a radio transmitter where its signal is indistinct or cannot be heard. [2] Space directly below a sonar where submarines cannot be detected.

Confederate States Navy: An armed naval force formed in 1861 to harass the Union's maritime trade and establish local control of the coasts of southern states. Confederate raiders destroyed 257 Union ships and forced some 700 others to switch flags to avoid attack.

Confidential: The lowest classification of material or information which would be harmful to national interests if disclosed. *See also* "secret" and "top secret."

Confidential Report: A periodic assessment of Royal Navy officers' performance, made by the commanding officer and forming the basis for promotion to higher rank. The USN equivalent is called Fitness Report.

Conformality: A term used in cartography. When the scale of a map at any point is the same in all directions, the map projection is said to be conformal. Shape is preserved locally, and meridians and parallels intersect at right angles. No projection can be simultaneously conformal and area-preserving.

Confused sea: Force 9 on the Douglas Scale.

Conning tower: [1] A watertight compartment inside the sail of some submarines, from which periscopes can be raised to direct the boat and launch torpedo attacks. [2] Frequently, but incorrectly, the sail itself. [3] The place from which armored ships of an earlier generation were supposed to be controlled in combat. (In practice the surrounding iron structure made it difficult to correct the magnetic compass, while the tower was ill-ventilated with poor external visibility, often leading the responsible officers to move outside.)

Consign: To hand over or deliver goods or merchandise, usually for shipment by a common carrier.

Consignee: The person or organization to whom something is consigned.

Consignment: [1] Something that is consigned. [2] The act of consigning something. [3] Something sent to an agent for storage, sale, or shipment. *See also* on consignment.

Consignor: The person or organization making a consignment.

Consolato de Mare: An important sourcebook of maritime legislation that made a major contribution to the codification and development of shipping law and laid the basis for present-day maritime law. It was first published in Spanish at Barcelona in 1494, but achieved its widest circulation in Italian (specifically Venetian) editions during the 16th and 17th centuries. In addition to legal detail, it provides extensive information on the practical running of a ship, maritime organization, and taxes and tariffs. *See* Laws and Conventions of the Sea.

Consort: A vessel keeping company with another.

Constant helm: *See* "sinuating."

***Constitution*:** Was one of six "super-frigates" authorized for construction by the Naval Act of 1794 (*see* warship rating). Launched in 1797, and known affectionately as "Old Ironsides," she is frequently claimed to be the oldest commissioned warship in the world, but in fact that honor belongs to HMS *Victory* who is 32 years older. However, the latter is in dry dock, while *Constitution* is still afloat.

Constrained by draft: A classification under the Navigation Rules (table 7) of a power-driven vessel whose size (beam or draft) restricts its ability to deviate from its course in a waterway.

Construction Battalion: A formation of the USN's Civil Engineer Corps, specially trained for building ports, airfields, and other facilities in combat areas. Its officers enjoy line status, and members are often called Seabees after the initials CB. Motto "We Build, We Fight." *See also* Song of the Seabees.

Constructive presence: A doctrine of international law which allows a coastal state to exercise jurisdiction over a foreign-flagged vessel that is hovering to seaward of its territorial waters while acting in concert with another vessel which is violating the coastal state's laws while inside its territorial waters (e.g., a mother ship that remains in international waters after launching a fast-running boat to carry contraband ashore may be boarded and seized by the coastal state).

Contact: A Radar or sonar echo, that is neither a false reading, nor evaluated as clutter, but has not been identified as a specific target.

Contact mine: This is the original type of moored mine and is still in naval use. Usually it consists of a round, oval, or cylindrical explosive-packed container with positive buoyancy, tethered to the sea bed by a cable that holds it below the surface at approximately keel depth. Protuberances around the top and sides of the container, known as Hertz horns, contain glass vials filled with acid. When a ship's hull makes contact with one of these horns the vial is crushed allowing acid to flow into an electrolyte-free lead-acid battery and activate it. The energized battery then detonates the explosive charge. *See also* Mine (Naval).

Container: A cargo box or shipping container.

Container ship: A vessel designed to accommodate large standardized cargo boxes in stacks.

Contiguous Zone: Is defined in international law as an area extending no more than 12 miles from the outer limit of a nation's territorial sea.

Continent: A large, contiguous, discrete landmass separated from other landmasses by expanses of water. By this geographical definition, there are five, namely Africa, America, Antarctica, Australia, and Eurasia. However, seven are generally identified by convention, with the westernmost peninsula of Eurasia considered to be the continent of Europe, and the two Americas treated as separate entities.

Continental Navy: This was the name of the maritime force of the United States from 1776 until 1794 when the United States Navy was founded. Also known as Navy of the Thirteen United Colonies, it had an inauspicious beginning and a generally undistinguished War of Independence. Commissions were awarded as political patronage with little consideration of seafaring or military experience. Drunkenness and desertion were as common in the wardroom as on the lower deck.

There was no time for purpose-building, so most of the ships were merchantmen with gunports hastily sawn into their hulls. American shipwrights had virtually no experience of warship design and made many mistakes. None was delivered on time, and those that were launched often lay at the docks waiting for ordnance, rigging, stores, and crews. When equipment did arrive, much of it was substandard. Only two of the frigates survived the War; seven having been captured and inducted into the Royal Navy, while four more were scuttled to avoid a similar fate. The last one, USS *Alliance*, was abandoned on a mudbank in the Delaware River, where her rotting hulk remained until the 1920s.

Overall, Continental privateers did better than the navy; about 2,000 Letters of Marque were issued and their holders wreaked havoc on British trade. However, two Continental Navy officers managed to seriously damage the Royal Navy's feeling of invincibility. Captains Lambert Wicks in 18-gun brig *Reprisal* and John Paul Jones in 18-gun corvette *Ranger* raided and took prizes off the English coast, and shortly afterward Jones obtained command of *Bonhomme Richard*, a French East Indiaman converted to 42-gun frigate. In her, Jones circumnavigated the British Isles, creating turmoil along the English, Irish, and Scottish coasts, and topping it off with a victorious single-ship action against HMS *Serapis*, a new, faster, purpose-built 44-gun frigate.

Continental Shelf: A zone of relatively shallow water, usually less than 100 fathoms (200 meters/600 feet) deep, extending from the low water mark to the point where rapid deepening occurs.

Continental Slope: The descent of the sea bed from the continental shelf to the abyss.

Continuous fire: All guns firing independently, as fast as they can re-load rather than in timed salvoes.

Continuous voyage: When a blockading power has reason to believe that a neutral vessel heading for a neutral port and carrying contraband of war intends to trans-ship that cargo for onward carriage to the enemy, it can invoke the doctrine that the two voyages are in fact one and seize both the vessel and its cargo.

Contraband: Goods prohibited by law from import or export.

Contraband of war: Under international law, a belligerent power may seize goods essential or useful in the prosecution of war from a neutral who is attempting to deliver them to the opposing power. Such goods and (often) the vessel carrying them are subject to lawful confiscation (seizure). All classes of goods that are contraband of war have not been precisely defined. Offensive matériel such as arms and ammunition are clearly included, but the status of food and other goods indirectly supporting military action is often in doubt. At the beginning of World War II the belligerents agreed lists of absolute and conditional contraband, but later the total absorption of national economies in warfare eventually led to interdiction, to the extent possible, of all shipping destined for the enemy.

Control room: The nerve center of a submarine, containing the devices and instrumentation for submerging, surfacing, steering, and operational control.

Control ship: [1] One that directs the boats of an amphibious assault. Also "marker ship." [2] One that sets course and speed during underway replenishment. Also "control vessel."

Control surfaces: [1] The diving planes, hydroplanes, rudders, and sailplanes used to direct the motion of submarines and surface vessels. [2] The ailerons, elevator, and rudder that allow a pilot to adjust and control the flight path of an aircraft.

Controllable pitch: Ability to alter the pitch of an aerial or marine propeller to improve efficiency and/or increase or decrease speed. Also called adjustable pitch, and more fully described under variable pitch.

Controlling depth: The least depth of water in a channel or approach to a port or anchorage. This determines the maximum draft of vessels entering.

Convening authority: A person or body authorized to organize courts-martial, courts of inquiry, and boards of investigation.

Conventional weaponry: All military hardware other than nuclear, chemical, or biological.

Convey: [1] To take or carry from one place to another; to transport. [2] To legally transfer ownership or title. [3] To communicate or make known (convey sympathy). [4] To serve as a medium of transmission (convey electricity by wire).

Conveyance: [1] A vehicle or vessel. [2] A means or method of transporting something: [3] The action of transporting or moving something: [4] An instrument by which title to property is transferred.

Convoy: [1] A group of merchantmen traveling together for mutual security. [2] To provide an armed escort to such a group.

Cook: This is one of the oldest naval rates, having been created in the 11th century as one of four non-military standing warrant officers appointed to serve in warships provided and crewed by the Cinque Ports. Originally an appointee required previous experience in food preparation ashore, but the post gradually diminished in importance until, by the eighteenth century, it had become a sinecure for superannuated, wounded, or disabled seamen, appointed as a reward for faithful service without regard for culinary ability. For a while, the crews suffered accordingly but, during the Napoleonic Wars, it became obvious that a warship's combat capability depended on the proper nutrition of its ship's company, so cooks gradually became professionals again. In modern navies, senior cook-stewards at the chief petty or warrant officer level are culinary specialists, expected to meet the highest of hotel and restaurant standards in supervising all aspects of onboard food service.

Cook-off: USN term for the unwanted explosion of a projectile due to excessive heat build-up in a gun barrel.

Cooler: Slang for cells or a jail. *See* Brig.

Cooper: This rating (usually nicknamed Jimmy Bungs) made and repaired the casks, barrels, firkins, and tubs which were essential to the victualing and operation of sailing warships.

Coordinated Universal Time: This is a high-precision standard which conforms to International Atomic Time (TAI) and replaced Greenwich Mean Time (GMT) on 1972–01–01 00:00 (*see* table 12). It forms the basis for legal civil time all around the globe and has been adopted by virtually all military forces. Seconds in UTC are uniform in length, but the system is based on the earth's angular rotation, which is not quite steady and requires the insertion of leap seconds at irregular intervals. A date and time written as above without qualification (or with "J" appended) is usually assumed to be local. However appending a capital "Z," which stands for the Prime or "Zero" Meridian at Greenwich, England, and is phonetically pronounced "Zulu," indicates UTC. *See also* Date & Time Notation and Time Zones.

Coordinates: Intersecting lines of latitude and longitude which define an exact position on the surface of the globe.

Copernicus: In 1990, the USN recognized we had crossed the threshold into the Information Age and were facing a Revolution in Military Affairs that moved information and information dominance to center stage, holding that the first to implement offensive and defensive information tactics into the warfighting arsenal would gain a significant advantage over less-integrated opponents. Copernicus is the Navy's code-name for an initiative intended:

> To make command, control, communications, computers and intelligence (C⁴I) systems responsive to the warfighter; to field these systems quickly; to capitalize on advances in technology; and to shape doctrine to reflect these changes.

Copper-bottomed: [1] A wooden ship whose bottom has been covered with a thin sheet of copper to inhibit the formation of barnacles and seaweed or infestation by the teredo worm. [2] Sailor slang for safe and secure. [3] Financial term for solid and reliable.

Coracle: An ancient round Celtic boat made of skin-covered wickerwork. Also curragh.

Coral: A material made by tiny carnivorous animals called polyps that live in immense colonies. The polyp is related to the anemone, and consists of a stomach and a mouth surrounded by tentacles. These tentacles resemble feet ("polyp" is a Greek word meaning many feet). The tentacles are covered with tiny stinging cells and, when a small creature brushes against them, it is killed and brought into the stomach to be digested.

Each polyp also extracts calcium from the water to build a protective limestone case. After it dies, the case remains and forms the foundation for another polyp to build on. Colonies form different shapes according to their environment — smooth and rounded where wave action is strong, and branched in calmer, deeper water. When these limestone formations aggregate, they are called a coral reef.

Corals grow in clear, fairly shallow water, and are highly sensitive to environmental change. They cannot grow in polluted water, or in water carrying soil from the land, or if the salinity of the water drops. They will be swamped by algae if there are too many nutrients in the water, and will also die if the water temperature changes by more than a degree or two beyond their preferred 18° to 33° C range.

Coral reefs: Are the largest structures created by any group of animals in the world (humans included). They are found in a variety of forms as follow:
- Apron: A sloping reef, extending outward and downward from the shore.
- Atoll: A more or less circular reef extending all the way around a lagoon. Formerly the barrier reef surrounding a now sunken island.
- Bank: Is essentially a large patch reef and may be linear or semi-circular in outline.
- Barrier: A reef separated from a mainland or an island by deep water. It is formed when the land sinks or the sea rises, causing the polyps to build upwards. The Great Barrier Reef is the largest natural feature on earth stretching more than 2,300 kms along the northeast coast of Australia.
- Fringing: A reef that is directly attached to the shore, or separated only by a shallow, narrow channel or lagoon.

- Patch: An isolated, often circular reef, usually within a lagoon or embayment.
- Ribbon: A long, narrow, somewhat winding reef, usually associated with a lagoon.
- Table: A small, isolated organic reef which has a flat top and does not enclose a lagoon.

Coral reefs have existed on earth for over 200 million years, but a combination of temperature change, pollution, overuse by divers, and harvesting for jewelry has already led to the destruction of many; leading scientists predict that over 50 percent may be destroyed by the year 2030.

Coral Sea: This May 8, 1942, battle was the first fought entirely by naval aviation during which the opposing warships never sighted each other. Although losses were even (one carrier sunk and another seriously damaged on each side) it was a tactical victory for Japan, but a strategic one for the United States. A Japanese attack on Port Moresby was thwarted and their invasion forces turned back. On the other hand, two additional modern USN carriers at next month's Battle of Midway might have contributed to a more decisive victory.

Corbita: A Roman merchantman with a stout wooden hull secured by mortise and tenon. It carried a large square-sail on the mainmast, with a pair of small triangular sails above it on either side of the mast. One or two helmsmen handled each of two steering oars. A long forward-sloping mast, carrying an artemon, was forerunner of the long bowsprit of a 19th century clipper. The after castle was frequently decorated with a large goose or swan's head.

Cord: Several yarns hand-twisted together.

Cordage: [1] Ropes, lines, cords, hawsers, and cables taken as a whole. [2] The non-metallic running rigging of a ship.

Corinthian: Nineteenth century term for an amateur yachtsman who sailed without a professional skipper.

Coriolis effect: The movement of air (and hence storms) is deflected clockwise in the northern hemisphere and counter-clockwise in the southern by a hypothetical force postulated in 1843 by French mathematician Gaspard Coriolis. Although the angular speed of terrestrial rotation is constant, its linear speed varies with latitude, being fastest at the equator and diminishing towards the poles. This has a geostrophic effect on the air, also tending to amplify surface currents by imposing circular motion on surface water, clockwise in the northern hemisphere and anti-clockwise in the southern.

Corned: [1] Ground into grains and sorted as to size (e.g., gunpowder). [2] Preserved and seasoned (e.g., beef or mutton). [3] Slightly intoxicated (slang).

Corocoro: An Indonesian pirate vessel of up to 100 tonnes, propelled by sail and/or oars on outriggers.

Corpen turn: USN term for a change of course in which ships in company move their rudders sequentially in so as to maintain the same relative bearings to each other, as opposed to a regular turn during which they maintain true bearings. The term is an abbreviation of Course Pennant. (In the RN, this maneuver is called a wheel.)

Corporal: [1] In the Navy, a ship's policeman responsible to the master-at-arms for small-arms training, attending the gangway when entering port, and ensuring that no alcohol is illegally brought on board. [2] In the Army and Marines, a non-commissioned officer, subordinate to sergeant.

Corposant: A luminous electrical discharge, accompanied by ionization of the surrounding atmosphere, manifesting itself as glowing brushlike jets around ships' masts, aircraft wings, the tops of tall buildings such as church steeples, and even the horns of cattle. Also called Corona Discharge, Saint Elmo's Fire, or Jack O'Lantern.

Corpsman: A paramedical enlisted member of the United States Navy Hospital Corps specially trained in combat first aid.

Corsair: A privateer licensed by one of the Barbary States to attack the vessels of Christian powers.

Corsaire: A French privateer of the 18th–19th centuries.

Corvette: [1] In the sailing ship era, a sixth-rate naval vessel usually carrying 9-gun broadsides on an open flush-deck. [2] In the transitional navy of the late Victorian era, an unarmored cruising vessel, carrying all her guns on an open weather deck. Later, reclassified as a 3rd class or light cruiser. [3] In modern navies, a small escort vessel.

Corvus: A Roman spiked boarding plank, mounted on a swivel base and secured vertically against a mast. When dropped onto an enemy deck, the spike held firm, allowing marines to swarm across. The name is Latin for "raven" (*see also* grab).

COSAG propulsion: A power plant consisting of a **C**ombination **o**f **S**team **A**nd **G**as turbines. For normal operations, the steam turbine is employed while the gas turbine provides boost power as needed.

Coston gun: A firearm invented by Benjamin Franklin Coston and used to shoot a messenger line to another ship or to stranded people. It was also used as a signaling device, igniting a flare that remained in the gun which was waved at arm's length. *See* Very pistol.

Cot: Bed used by sailing warship officers, consisting of canvas stretched on a wooden frame and containing a mattress. More comfortable than a hammock, but slung like one to permit rapid removal when the ship cleared for action (from Hindi khat = bed).

Cotidal chart: A map of the shoreline connecting places where high tide arrives simultaneously.

Coubais: A heavily-ornamented 40-oared Japanese barge or galley.

Council of the Marine: *See* Board of Admiralty.

Counter: That part of a vessel which overhangs and projects abaft the sternpost (cf. cruiser stern).

Counter-flood: To allow water into one compartment to compensate for the imbalance caused by previous flooding of another compartment. This emergency measure rightens the vessel, but reduces its overall buoyancy.

Counterbattery fire: Fire directed against active hostile artillery or fire-control systems.

Counterbrace: To turn the yards of a square-rigged vessel so that the sails face in a contrary direction and stop the ship.

Countercurrent: A current that flows in opposition to the main current or stream (cf. eddy).

Counterforce: [1] General: A force or action that opposes or checks another. [2] Specific: The employment of strategic air and missile forces in an effort to destroy, or render impotent, selected military capabilities of an enemy force, especially as an opening action in hostilities. This tactic, which is called counterforce, is generally associated with nuclear warfare. Cf. first strike.

Countermeasures: Actions taken to eliminate or reduce the effectiveness of enemy equipment or operations.

Countermining radius: The distance between mines that will avoid the explosion of one setting off a chain-reaction among the others.

Country: USN term for a specified area within a ship (e.g., "admiral's country," "officer's country," etc.). Also Territory.

Coupling: A metal fitting at the end of a hose, designed to connect with a matched fitting on a standpipe, hydrant, or another hose.

Course: [1] The direction in which a vessel is being steered; usually designated as true, magnetic, or grid. The type of compass may also be referenced as in "Steer 030 true pgc" (per gyro-compass). [2] A term sometimes used for the actual path followed by a vessel, but the preferred nautical term is "track."

Course made good: Progress along the direct track from point of departure to destination irrespective of course changes made along the way.

Courses: The name for sails suspended on the lowermost yards of a fully square-rigged ship (thus main-course, fore-course, and mizzen-course). A trysail is also a course when used in place of one of these sails during a storm. The term was sometimes extended to include the main staysails of brigs and schooners. A ship driven by one or more of these with no other sails set used to be called "under courses" but the term is now seldom used.

Court-martial: One of three levels of trial held under naval or military law. The lowest level is termed "summary" and deals with relatively minor misdeeds; an intermediate level is called "special"; and the highest, covering serious misdemeanors up to and including capital offenses, is a "general court martial."

Court of Inquiry: An investigative court that reviews and reports on questionable activities involving naval personnel or property. Consists of three or more officers and has subpoena authority. Senior to board of investigation and junior to court-martial.

Courtesy: An act of civility or respect, traditionally given or done as a polite gesture:

Courtesy flag: A small national ensign of the host country, flown at the starboard yardarm or spreader (crosstree) as a token of respect while visiting a foreign nation. Concurrently, the national ensign of the visitor is flown on the ensign staff at the stern.

Cove: [1] A small, sheltered inlet, bay, or creek (Old English cofa = cave). [2] An ornamental groove incised high along a vessel's sides and usually painted or gold-leafed. Also cove stripe. [3] Slang for a fellow or chap (Romany cofa = man).

Cover: [1] To protect or screen (e.g., airpower covering ground forces). [2] The correct nautical term for headgear.

Covering fire: To provide gunfire support to a force or an operation.

Covert: Said of an operation that is planned and executed so as to conceal the identity of, or permit plausible denial by, the sponsor. A covert operation differs from a clandestine one in that emphasis is placed on concealing the identity of the sponsor rather than the operation.

Cow hitch: [1] Any improvised fastening or interweaving of line which is not a recognized maritime knot. [2] Any bend or hitch which is improperly tied and slips.

Cowl: A scoop-like device which directs fresh air into a vessel for ventilation, or to provide combustion air to the boiler rooms below.

Cowling: A removable streamlined covering for an aircraft engine.

Coxswain/Cockswain: This is another ancient title, referring to the sailor who takes charge of a ship's boat and its crew, and usually handles its steering. The word is a combination of the Anglo-Saxon cok meaning a small boat with swain meaning husband. It is pronounced "cox'n." In both USN and RN, coxswain still carries its original meaning and refers especially to the sailor commanding a captain's gig or admiral's barge. In the RN, it is also the rating of the senior petty officer on board a submarine or a small ship (such as a corvette), who performs as the vessel's quartermaster and assumes disciplinary duties that are performed by the master-at-arms and chief boatswain's mate in larger ships.

CPO: Chief petty officer.

CQD: [1] Close Quarters Defense. [2] The first radio (Morse Code) distress signal, introduced in February 1904, and replaced by SOS in July 1908.

CQR anchor: A single plow-shaped fluke mounted on a pivoting shank. Widely used by yachts, especially for holding in mud or weed (CQR is a verbal pun on "secure"). Also plow anchor.

Crab: [1] To drift sideways under wind or current. [2] To adjust course to remain on track under the influence of wind or current.

Crack: First-class or excellent (e.g., A crack ship is uncommonly smart in evolutions or discipline).

Crack on: Add sail to the limit of masts, yards, and rigging.

Crackerjack: [1] A sea dish from the age of sail, made from of salt meat mixed with broken ship's biscuit and sundry other ingredients as available. Also cracker hash. [2] USN slang for an enlisted seaman's uniform.

Cradle: [1] A framework on which a hull rests during construction or repair in a shipyard. [2] A shaped frame to support a small boat: [3] An artillery device on which a recoiling gun slides while its mount remains stationary.

Craft: [1] A generic term for one or more water vehicles. This is the widest of four such terms, embracing boats, ships, and vessels and covering all other forms of water transportation such as rafts. [2] A trade. [3] Art or skill.

***Craig-Gowan*'s monster:** In 1905, steam trawler *Craig-Gowan* was off Scotland's Rattray Head when her skipper, Captain Ballard, was alerted to the presence of a large creature following the ship. He later reported:

> On reaching the deck ... I saw a very large animal of a dark color, which seemed to be racing with us, but was about fifty feet to windward.... I at once saw that the animal was not a whale but some sea monster, the like of which I have never seen in my life. As it rose several portions of the body were visible at one time. It seemed to snake its way through the water, showing repeated portions of its brown body. The animal was now uncomfortably near. We could even see that the skin was covered with some substance like a rough coating of hair.

Ballard tried to drive off the creature with the trawler's furnace rake, but he monster raised its fore part clean out of the water, made direct for the trawler, and...

> ... I plainly saw the monster rise up until its head was over our gaff peak, when it lowered itself with a motion as sudden as lightning carrying away all the peak halliards and sending the gaff, sail and all, down on deck.

By the time the crew had squared away, the creature had disappeared.

Cramp: [1] A metal device that can be screwed up to clamp things together. [2] A painful involuntary muscle-spasm, especially dangerous to swimmers.

Crane: Any of various shipboard or land-based machines for lifting or moving heavy weights by means of a movable projecting arm or a horizontal beam traveling on an overhead support.

Crank: Unstable. Top-heavy and prone to capsize (cf. tender).

Crannequin: A portable device for applying tension to a crossbow.

Crash dolly: Term for a wheeled device or crane used to move crashed aircraft from the flight deck. (Affectionately called "Jumbo" in the RN.)

Crate: A (usually) slatted wooden box, custom-made to pack fragile goods for transportation.

Crazy Ivan: Submariner's Cold War slang for the abrupt and unexpected turns made by Soviet submarines when clearing the baffles in search of a shadowing American or NATO boat.

Creek: [1] In USA, Canada, Australia, a watercourse smaller than a river. [2] In Britain, a narrow inlet in the sea-coast smaller than a cove.

Creep: To search for a sunken object by dragging a grapnel along the bottom.

Creeping attack: An antisubmarine technique in which a relatively distant ship echo-ranges the target and relays the information to a consort which remains silent so that the target is unaware of its approach until actually attacked.

Crest: [1] The highest point of a wave, which may or may not be foamy. [2] The heraldic device identifying a ship or person.

Crew: [1] The group of sailors who work a ship, excluding its captain or master. In this sense the term applies mainly to merchantmen, the preferred naval term being ship's company or (informally) the troops. [2] A group detailed to specific duty such as gun crew or boat crew. [3] The personnel of an aircraft.

Crime: [1] General: The breach of a rule or law for which a punishment may ultimately be prescribed. [2] Military: Special codes supplement "regular" crimes with specific ones such as mutiny, and a number of misdemeanors (still classified as "crimes") such as desertion, insubordination, mutilation, and unauthorized absence. [3] International law: Acts such as crimes against humanity, war crimes, hate crimes, etc. [4] Religion: Offenses against codes of religious morality, such as Islamic Sharia or Christian Canon Law.

Crimp: [1] A crease formed in sheet or plate metal as a fastener or to reduce flexibility. [2] To press something into a locking seam (e.g., to close the soft metal mouth of a detonator over the raw end of a length of safety fuse). [3] Slang for impede or hinder as in "it will put a crimp in their plans." [4] A person who entrapped or kidnapped seamen to be sold to merchant captains (*see* sailor-monger). [5] The act of crimping.

Crimping: During the late eighteenth and early nineteenth centuries the competing manpower needs of naval, merchant, and privateer captains encouraged illicit recruiters known as "crimpers" or "crimps" to trade in this scarce commodity for profit. Becoming the private enterprise equivalent of the Navy's Impress Service, they supplied merchantmen and privateers with prime seamen in return for head money or a lien on future wages, as well as pocketing any valuables the man might be carrying. Often a crimp plied the victim with liquor and persuaded him to sign articles while intoxicated.

Sometimes crimps acted as money lenders, encouraging a man to spend himself into debt, and then facing him with the alternatives of jail or signing on. Frequently they offered a small bounty to the owners of taverns, brothels, and waterfront boarding houses who turned over merchant sailors or fishermen when they were too drunk to offer serious resistance.

At Liverpool, a sisterhood of crimp-prostitutes was said to decoy naval ratings ashore, and then sell them for three pounds a month on their future wages. The going rate for a man with naval experience was at least twenty guineas, so crimps also visited naval hospitals, debauching convalescent seamen with alcohol, and bribing them with promises of high wages if they deserted naval service to sign on with a privateer or merchantman on recovery. This was such a serious drain of naval manpower that it led Admiral Holbourne to declare "The crimp is worse than the deserter and ought to be hanged in his stead."

Cringle: A fitting which allows a line to be fastened to a sail.

Crippen's Curse: In July 1910, Canadian Pacific liner *Montrose* was about to leave Antwerp, when a late-arriving couple bought tickets for Québec. Their behavior soon aroused Captain Henry Kendall's suspicions. At mealtimes the father would transfer tasty morsels from his own plate to the son's and on deck they wandered around holding hands. In the first-ever use of wireless-telegraphy for police purposes Kendall told Scotland Yard he believed "Mr. Robinson" was the notorious Harvey Crippen — an American doctor wanted in England for the brutal murder and dismemberment of his nagging wife* — while the youth was his poorly-disguised paramour Ethel le Neve.

Detective Chief Inspector Walter Dew promptly set off in pursuit aboard White Star liner *Laurentic*. He was three days behind, but Kendall slowed down, allowing the faster vessel to pass and land the policeman at Father Point. In order to get on board without being seen and recognized by Crippen (whom he had previously interrogated) the inspector donned a pilot's uniform and took an oar in the pilot boat.

As the handcuffed felon was being hustled down the accommodation ladder, he turned to the captain, screaming: "You'll suffer for this treachery sir! You'll soon join me in Hell." Four years later, Kendall was in command of *Empress of Ireland* when she was rammed and foundered at almost exactly the place where Crippen had been arrested. The superstitious believed the curse had been fulfilled. But it had been against the captain rather than his ship, and he survived to the ripe old age of 91.

*Crippen eventually went to the gallows, but was probably unjustly convicted. In 2008, almost a century later, American forensic toxicologist John Harris Trestrail and associates, using modern techniques that include mitochondrial DNA, have shown that the "wife's" body parts were actually those of a male, unrelated to Crippen, allegedly planted by the police to secure conviction of the man they believed guilty.

Critical: Said of a nuclear reactor when it is producing enough neutrons to be self-sustaining.

Cromwell Current: A sub-surface Pacific current flowing from east to west below the north equatorial current.

Cross: To sail or steam across another vessel's bow.

Cross deck pendant: The correct but seldom used term for an arresting wire.

Cross fire: Lines of gunfire converging from different directions.

Cross jack: The lowermost square-sail on the mizzen mast of a ship or bark with four or more masts (pronounced crojack).

Cross seas: Confused waves going in different directions due to varying winds.

Cross signal: To answer another ship's two-blast whistle signal with a single blast or vice versa. If this signaled intention was carried out, a collision would be inevitable (*see* table 9).

Cross staff: Early navigational device for determining the angle of elevation of heavenly bodies.

Cross the line: To sail over the equator. Traditionally celebrated with an initiation ceremony (*see* line-crossing).

Cross the tee: A classic surface warfare tactic, in which one battle line crosses the enemy line at right angles, thus being able to concentrate all its broadsides on the leading ship, while itself exposed only to the forward-firing guns of that ship. Last employed at the Battle of Surigao Strait in 1944.

Cross wind: A wind blowing across the line of advance of a ship or aircraft.

Crossbar shot: An American invention. When folded, it looked like conventional bar shot and could be loaded into cannon. But it expanded on leaving the muzzle, to form a cross with one-quarter of a ball at each of its radial points. Spinning violently, it could be fired low as an anti-personnel weapon, or high as a rigging-cutter. *See also* Star shot.

Crossbeam: The transverse member connecting the hulls of a catamaran or trimaran.

Crossbearings: Two or more bearings taken from a vessel to determine its position. (*See* Cocked Hat.)

Crossbones: A pair of thigh bones, placed crosswise, usually below a skull, symbolizing death. A favorite device on pirate flags, but more common in fiction than life, because most pirates preferred a personalized emblem (*see* jolly roger).

Crossbow: A bow fixed transversely across a wooden stock with a groove for a bolt or arrow, and equipped with a trigger mechanism to release the missile. Often incorporating or accompanied by a device such as a crannequin for bending the powerful bow. Frequently used in pre-gunpowder and early-gunpowder sea battles.

Crosscurrent: A current running across the main flow.

Cross-cut: Said of a sail with seams at right angles to the leech.

Crossdeck: [1] To temporarily transfer personnel to another ship for training or experience. [2] To land an aircraft from one carrier on another — this used to be a routine exercise between allies, but has become less common with more specialized aircraft and flight operations procedures.

Cross-hairs: Ultra fine wires in the focal plane of an optical instrument or gunsight, serving to define line of sight or point of aim. Also cross-wires.

Crossing the line: *See* line-crossing.

Cross-trade: Trade between two nations, carried by the ships of a third nation.

Crosstree: [1] One of a pair of horizontal timbers at the top of a lower mast, supporting the topmast: *See also* hounds, trestletrees. [2] British term for a strut for separating the shrouds on a mast (the American term is spreader).

Crosword coincidence: In the weeks immediately before the 1944 Allied amphibious invasion of Normandy, consecutive crossword puzzles in the London *Daily Telegraph* contained clues to which the answers were top secret code words — Overlord (the invasion itself), Neptune (the naval operational component), Mulberry (prefabricated harbors), and Omaha and Utah (the American landing beaches). Convinced there had been a major breach of security and the clues had been planted by a spy, Military Police and Scotland Yard detectives grilled a bewildered (and innocent) amateur crossword composer who just happened to have used those words.

Crow: USN slang for the eagle emblem worn by petty officers.

Crowdie: A seaman's delicacy made from milk, thickened with meal, and eaten with butter and treacle.

Crown: The point where the arms of an anchor join the shank.

Crown-and-Anchor: Board game, formerly popular with British naval ratings but now banned due to excessive gambling.

Crow's nest: A platform or shelter for a lookout near the top of a mast. Viking longships are believed to have carried crows in cages attached to their mastheads (*see* as the crow flies). Later, when sailing ships began to carry lookouts in a tub strapped to their main masthead, this inevitably became known as the "crow's nest." Whaling ships often carried a second smaller tub mounted even higher on an upper mast and called the "bird's nest."

Crud: [1] A corrosive deposit inside a nuclear reactor, which can break loose and cause a temporary increase in radioactivity known as a "crud burst." [2] A person or thing that is loathsome, despicable, disgusting, or worthless. [3] A slang term for filth or muck. [4] A game played on a billiard table.

Cruise: [1] To be detached from a main fleet to roam in search of hostile forces and return to alert the main body. A favored frigate captain might be "given a cruise" to harass trade and take prizes to his own (and the admiral's) pecuniary advantage. [2] To travel to a specific region as a pleasure trip. [3] To make an extended voyage with no specific destination. From the Dutch kruise(n) = cross.

Cruise missile: An aerofoil-equipped guided missile, that flies aerodynamically rather than as a projectile (cf. ballistic missile).

Cruise ship: A passenger vessel used almost exclusively for pleasure, normally making extended circular voyages, stopping at various points of interest, and returning to disembark passengers at the port of departure. Modern cruise ships are some of the biggest non-naval vessels afloat, combining the attributes of luxury hotel, upscale shopping mall, theater complex, gambling casino, theme park, and spa.

Cruiser: [1] Formerly, any warship sent on detached operations (*see* cruise). [2] The biggest surface warship after the capital ships. Classified as light (six-inch guns or smaller) or heavy (eight-inch or larger). [3] Any boat or power yacht designed and used for cruising.

Cruiser stern: A broad, almost flat stern, with no counter and wider at the waterline.

Crush depth: The depth at which a submarine's pressure hull will cave in.

Crusher: Lower deck RN slang for a regulating petty officer (*see also* master-at-arms).

Crutch: A support for a spar that is not in use.

Cryptanalysis: The processes, procedures, and methods used to uncover the clear meaning of enciphered or encoded texts.

Cryptid: *See* cryptozoology.

Cryptography: The science of turning plain language into unintelligible text for secrecy and security. Typically the development of codes or ciphers.

Cryptozoology: Generally considered a pseudoscience, cryptozoology refers to the study of hidden animals (Greek kryptós = hidden + zôon = animal + logos = knowledge or study). It involves the search for living examples of animals believed extinct, as well as undiscovered creatures for whom anecdotal evidence exists in the form of myths, legends, or unconfirmed sightings. Its practitioners are known as cryptozoologists and the animals that they study are called cryptids.

The discipline, has not been embraced by the scientific community, which claims that many self-styled cryptozoologists are amateurs who make fundamental errors of reasoning and fact, or tend to give undue weight to unreliable eyewitness accounts. Scientists generally agree that thousands of unknown animals await discovery, but argue that mega-fauna are unlikely to exist in sufficient numbers to sustain a breeding population without being detected. Cryptozoologists counter that they have been seen and reported, albeit mostly by non-scientists, moreover, that much of the planet remains unexplored, especially ocean deeps, while the comparatively recent discoveries of coelacanth, giant squid, and megamouth shark confirm that large sea creatures can remain undetected for centuries (*see* appendix).

Cuckold's knot: The hitch used to secure a rope to

a spar, consisting of a single loop with overlapping parts seized together (also cuckold's neck).

Cuddy: [1] A small cabin or compartment at the bow or (usually) stern. [2] The galley or pantry on a small sailing ship. [3] The dining compartment for officers in a larger sailing merchantman. [4] Lower deck RN slang for an admiral's or captain's quarters. [5] The platform on a fishing vessel where nets are coiled.

Culverin: A long-barreled 16th Century cannon firing an 18-pound ball. Frequently cast in the form of a dragon.

Cummerbund: The sash worn with dress uniform in both RN and USN. It originated with the waistband (kamarband) worn by Persian and Hindu warriors to hold their swords and other weapons.

Cumshaw: [1] In the USN, work performed without authorization, or equipment obtained through unofficial channels (cf. Rabbit). [2] In the RN, a gift or gratuity. The word is a corruption of kam siā = "grateful thanks" in the dialect of Xiamen, a port in southeast China. It was probably picked up by British sailors who heard it from dockside beggars and thought they were asking for handouts. [3] In general, its meaning ranges from bending the rules to blatent bribery.

Cunningham: A line used to control the shape of a Bermuda-rig sail.

Cuntline: [1] The space between the bilges of casks stowed side-by-side. When casks are tiered they are said to be stowed "bilge-to-cuntline." [2] The groove in a twisted line. (In response to "political correctness" the first vowel is sometimes incorrectly changed to an "a.")

Cup of Joe: In 1913, United States President Woodrow Wilson appointed Josephus Daniels as Secretary of the Navy. Daniels, a teetotaler, immediately embarked on a host of reforms, among which was the banishment of liquor from all United States Navy ships. From that time forward the strongest drink available afloat has been a cup of coffee which, inevitably, was nick-named after its introducer.

Current: [1] A steady flow of water in a definite horizontal direction. [2] The speed of such a flow. *See also* Oceanic Circulation.

Current flow: It is conventional to define currents by the direction they are flowing towards rather than from as is the case with wind direction.

Current sailing: *See* sailings.

Cursed Corsair: This Spanish tale is far more gruesome than that of the more famous Flying Dutchman. On the morning after a terrible storm, Dahul Raïs looked out from the port of Algiers and saw a tempting Christian prize. A Spanish brig traveling from Barcelona to Palermo had been dismasted by the tempest and was drifting towards the Algerian coast. His swift galley soon reached and boarded the helpless craft, plundering baggage and a rich cargo destined for Sicily.

The Spanish crew hoped robbery would satisfy the bloodthirsty corsair, but Dahul's lust had been aroused by an exceptionally attractive young woman cowering behind the terrified passengers and he ordered her brought to him. The ship's chaplain, a Jesuit priest, stepped boldly forward, urging the corsair not to ravish the mother of a newborn babe. The Raïs was impressed by this effrontery and laughingly said he would leave the woman alone, and free all the other passengers unharmed — provided the courageous priest agreed to his demands.

The Jesuit said would do whatever was asked of him, but balked when ordered to remove his cassock, foreswear Christianity, embrace Islam, and join the Corsair's crew. Dahul was enraged by the broken promise and ordered all the passengers bound while the priest was nailed to the mast. Then he had the woman's baby brought on deck, ordering "Fetch me the cook, we'll have roast Spanish piglet for supper! The woman can wait until after we've eaten." When the baby had been cooked and carved, the corsair told the crucified priest to say grace: Instead, the Jesuit raised his eyes to heaven and called on the Almighty for delivery from these grisly captors.

Immediately, the waves were stilled, the corsairs were miraculously transferred back to their own galley, and a powerful voice rolled out of the sky, saying: "Oh Dahul, you shall wander the sea until the end of centuries, never approaching the shore, and seeing all other ships fly before you!" Since then Mediterranean mariners report seeing a corsair galley, sailing at tremendous speed through calm and storm, surrounded by fearful flames rising from waterline to masthead, while the ghastly howls of torturing ghouls are almost drowned out by the horrendous screams of Dahul and his crew.

Customary dispatch: [1] Naval command to do something at the habitual (expected) speed. [2] Charter party term requiring discharge and loading to be made with speed and diligence according to the regulations of the port in question.

Customary phraseology: Naval commands are always issued in standardized format using specific words. This is to ensure that orders are clearly and immediately understood and promptly obeyed, even in the noise and confusion of combat. For example, in the USN, "Starboard ahead one-third, port back one-third" would be an engine order. Steering orders, by contrast, are not given as port or starboard, but as right or left: "right standard rudder," for instance. Thus, from the conning officer's first word, the entire bridge watch knows whether the change is to engines or steering and in what direction, and can start reacting even before the order is completed.

Customs: Government officials charged with regulating the entry of goods, services, and supplies into a country, charging duty as applicable.

Customs of Amsterdam: *See* laws and conventions of the sea.

Customs of the Service: Unwritten but traditional naval practices.

Cut: A passage or channel, usually dug out, but possibly eroded.

Cut and run: When faced with an emergency, such as a rapidly approaching storm or enemy vessel, the captain would sometimes order the mooring cable to be severed with an ax so that he could set sail as quickly as possible. The term endures on shore, with the meaning of hurriedly backing away from an awkward situation.

Cut of the jib: The phrase "I don't like the cut of your jib," signifying dislike or even hostility, can be traced to the days of sail when a vessel's nationality could usually be determined from the shape and configuration of its sails and rigging. As a rule of thumb, English ships normally carried a single large jib, while a Spaniard's was noticeably smaller, and a Frenchman would often fly two.

Cut the painter: To die. A painter is a line attached to the bow of a boat for securing it to a quay. If it was cut, the boat drifted quietly away and its crew was left stranded on the dock. By analogy, a seaman's lifeline was his metaphorical painter, so if it was severed his soul drifted quietly to heaven while his body was left dead on earth. Sometimes used as the threat of a more violent death; as in "I'll cut your painter!"

Cutlass: A naval sword, with a basket guard giving maximum protection to the striking hand, a slightly curved, sharp-edged blade suitable for both thrusting and slashing, and short enough for use at close-quarters (from the French coutelas = small knife, but known colloquially in the French Navy as cuillère-a-pot = ladle). The weapon was officially dropped from the RN arsenal in 1936, but is known to have been used during World War II. It remained a USN stores item until 1949, and is still sometimes carried as a symbol of office by regulating petty officers during recruit training.

Cutter: [1] A small single-masted vessel, fore-and-aft rigged, with a gaff mainsail, two or more headsails, a bowsprit with jib, and a mast set further aft than in a sloop. May also be Marconi rigged. [2] A ship's boat, powered by oars, sails or motor, smaller than a whaler but larger than a yawl or jollyboat. [3] An armed patrol craft used by the U S Coast Guard and similar services.

Cutting-in: A sailing whaler's term. After the animal had been killed it was tied up alongside the cutting stage to be flensed. This was an exceptionally tedious, messy, and dangerous task, not only because rolling of the vessel dunked the stage with danger of being swept overboard, but also because blood in the water attracted hordes of sharks. Nowadays the carcass is winched up a slipway onto the flensing deck of a factory ship (*see* Processing a Whale).

Cutting iron: A tool used to trim threads of oakum which might get caught to pull out sections of caulking.

Cutting-out: Entering a hostile port or anchorage to seize and remove an enemy ship, usually by stealth and surprise.

Cutting stage: A platform lowered from a whale ship's rail for use by the flensing crew.

Cutting the line: The doctrine of Line-ahead governed naval warfare through most of the 18th century, but was challenged by Sir John Clerke of Eldin, a Scottish landlubber who was obsessed with naval matters. Using cork models and mathematical techniques he developed a number of tactical theories, one of which recommended directing the attacking vessels at right angles to the enemy line — a radical and potentially dangerous maneuver which temporarily caused the enemy to cross the tee of the attacker — breaking through to concentrate overwhelming firepower on a section of the hostile line (especially the rear since the center and van would then have to turn and sail against the wind to engage).

In 1780 Clerke began to discuss his conclusions with various naval officers and issued a series of pamphlets (published ten years later in book form). After hearing these ideas British Admiral Rodney is reported to have said to Henry Dundas, the future Lord Melville, "There is one Clerk, a countryman of yours, who ... appears to know more about the matter than any of us. If I ever meet the French fleet, I intend to try his way." Rodney did meet the French in the April 1782 Battle of the Saintes, during which he took advantage of a change in the wind to break through in three places and achieve a decisive victory. (Clerke's ideas had previously been tested by the brilliant French admiral Pierre André de Suffren during the Battle of Sadras in February 1782 when he managed to double the British line, but the outcome then had not been decisive.) *See also* fighting instructions.

Cutwater: The leading edge of a bow, its stem.

CW candidate: This RN term refers to ratings selected for Commission and Warrant training. The USN equivalent is officer candidate.

CWO: [1] Commissioned warrant officer. [2] Chief warrant officer.

Cycle: [1] The time interval in which a series of events or phenomena is completed, and then repeats, uniformly and continually in the same order. [2] A periodical space of time marked by the recurrence of something peculiar; as the cycle of the seasons or year.

Cycloidal drive: *See* Voith-Schneider Drive.

Cyclone: An intense tropical windstorm rotating inward towards an area of low-pressure; turning clockwise in the southern hemisphere and counterclockwise in the northern due to the Coriolis effect. (*See* tropical rotating windstorm.)

D

D: Prefix used to designate the day on which an operation is scheduled to be launched. Thus "D-7" means one week before the operation, "D" is the date of the operation, and "D+3" would be three days after it. *See also* "H."

DADT: Don't Ask, Don't Tell. Controversial U.S. DoD policy concerning sexual orientation.

Dædalus' Creature: One of the most famous sea serpent sightings was reported by Captain Peter M'Quahe of the frigate HMS *Dædalus*. On 6th August 1848, off the Cape of Good Hope, the midshipman of the watch reported a strange object approaching. The captain and five others moved to the gunwale, where they watched the creature for twenty minutes using telescopes. M'Quahe later reported that all seven witnesses saw...

> ... an enormous serpent with head and shoulders kept about four feet constantly above the sea and at the very least sixty feet of the animal à fleur d'eau (just above the water) ... so close under our lee quarter that, had it been a man of my acquaintance, I should have recognized his features with the naked eye.... The diameter of the serpent was about 15 or 16 inches behind the head, which was without a doubt that of a snake ... its colour a dark brown with yellowish-white about the throat.

When eminent scientists poured scorn on the sighting, Captain M'Quahe issued a public rebuttal saying, "I adhere to the statements ... in my official report to the Admiralty." (*See also* appendix.)

Daggerboard: A centerboard which slides vertically rather than on a pivot.

Dahlgren gun: A smoothbore, barrel-shaped, naval gun developed in 1850 by Commander (later Rearadmiral) John Adolphus Dahlgen of the USN Ordnance Department. (*See also* Paixhan.)

Damage area: The space around a minesweeper in which a mine detonation is likely to impede ongoing operations.

Damage claims: Under Admiralty Law, when both vessels are established to be at fault, each is guilty of contributory negligence and neither can obtain judgment against the other. Instead, damages are divided equally between them.

Damage control: A self-explanatory naval term referring to actions which enable a wounded vessel to float, move, and fight. These include the preservation or re-establishment of watertight integrity, stability, maneuverability, and offensive capability; the control of list and trim; the rapid repair of material damage; limiting the spread of and providing protection against fire or flood; limiting the spread of, removing contamination by, and providing protection against chemical, biological, radiological, or other toxic agents; and facilitating the care of wounded personnel.

Damage Control Central: A protected compartment in a warship from where action can be taken to preserve the vessel's integrity and fighting capability.

Dan buoy: [1] A temporary marker carrying a flag or light, placed to show the boundary of an area swept clear of mines. [2] A float, often equipped with a staff-mounted radar reflector and/or strobe light, used by commercial fishermen to mark the location of gear.

Dandy: [1] British term for a yawl or ketch-rigged boat. [2] A man who affects extreme elegance in clothes and manners; a fop. [3] Something very good or agreeable (slang).

Dandyfunk: An oven-baked sea dish from the age of sail, consisting of broken ship's biscuit mixed with molasses, sometimes with jam or fat added.

Danforth anchor: A brand of lightweight anchor with pivoting flukes, capable of holding in most types of bottom.

Danger angle: A Navigational warning, referring to the angle subtended by two fixed points on shore, or by the top and base of a landmark. It is safe to steer a course between the maximum and minimum angles observed from the vessel.

Danger bearing: A pre-calculated bearing to a charted object, warning of a navigational hazard on the vessel's course. Also called "clearing bearing," "limit bearing" or "index bearing." The British term is "clearance bearing."

Danger buoy: A float marking a submerged hazard to navigation. Those with a red upper ring are to be left to starboard of a vessel approaching from seaward, those with black or green top rings should be left to port.

Danger signals: Under nautical Rules of the Road, five or more short blasts of the ship's whistle or short flashes of light warn of possible collision or other emergency. *See also* table 9.

Dangerous Semicircle: The more-violent half of a circular storm, where winds are complemented and accelerated by the movement of the cyclone, which tends to bring vessels into its path. The dangerous side is to the right of clockwise moving winds in the southern hemisphere and to the left of counterclockwise winds in the northern. *See also* navigable semicircle.

Danube rudder: *See* salmontail.

Daphne's Serpent: In September 1848, less than two months after the *Dædalus* incident, the brig USS *Daphne* was about 1200 miles north of the *Dædalus* sighting when, as reported by Captain Henderson, he and nine of his crew saw a sea serpent with a dragonlike head rise from the water and stare at them with huge glaring eyes. It seemed about to attack the brig, but Captain Henderson ordered the quarterdeck cannon to be loaded with nails and old iron and fired at the monster. It immediately plunged, exposing an undulating body estimated to be at least 100 feet long, and made off at 15 to 16 knots.

Darken ship!: Command to extinguish all lights which might be visible from outside the vessel.

DAS: [1] Deep Air Support. [2] Days at Sea.

Date and time notation: While an American would immediately recognize "03/04/08" as symbolizing March 4, citizens of the Commonwealth would be equally confident it stood for April 3 (but none would know if the year was 2008, 1908, or even earlier). Most Europeans and many Asians, accustomed to totally different formats, would find it basically unintelligible, but might tentatively interpret it as April 8 (in 1903 or 2003). Commercial organizations with global operations attempted to overcome these sequencing incompatibilities by requiring months to be presented alphabetically (usually abbreviated to allow standard field lengths). But computer programmers preferred a numerical format that avoided wasting space on tables for alpha-numeric conversion.

In the mid–20th century, many of them saved space and encoding time (both then very costly) by using only the last two digits of the year. This came to a head in what was known as the "Y2K Crisis," when it was realized that many computers around the world would interpret "00" as 1900 rather than 2000. Doomsday predictions for 1 January 2000 included newborns being registered as 100 years old, elderly people recorded as dying on the day they were born, ATMs seizing credit cards as long-since expired, and the interest on loans issued on 31 December 1999 being calculated on minus 36,524 days instead of plus one.

Ultimately the crisis was a blessing in disguise, as it forced the International Standards Organization to develop ISO 8601, promulgated in 1988 to pre-empt the "Y2K" problem, along with many others by using the format year/month/day. Its salient points are given in table 12.

Date line: *See* International Date Line.

Date-Time Group: A set of characters, usually in prescribed format, placed in the header of a message, as an indicator of when and where it originates. For example, in NATO protocol, "071945N" means the message was sent on the 7th day of the month (07), at 7:45 P.M. (1945 hours), in time zone November (near the Azores Islands). *See* coordinated universal time.

Davits: Small cranes used for lowering or raising a boat or other load, often mounted in pairs.

Davy Jones: The fiend who presides over all the evil spirits of the ocean and is often seen perched in the rigging on the eve of hurricanes or other maritime disasters. In 1751 naval surgeon and author Tobias Smollett painted this word picture: "Know him by his saucer eyes, his three rows of rotting teeth and tail, and the blue smoke which comes out of his nostrils." The origin of the legend is obscure, but the name seems to have originated in the Caribbean during the 17th century and probably comes from "duffy" a West Indian slave word for ghost or devil and "jonah" referring to the biblical bringer of ill fortune at sea. Hence Davy Jones means Ghost of Jonah.

Davy Jones' Locker: The ocean floor was Davy's storage place or locker, the destination of all things jettisoned and final resting place of people drowned or buried at sea. (It has been suggested that this phrase originated independently of the fiend's name and is a corruption of Deva Lokka, the Hindu goddess of Death.) Seamen believed that Davy could not keep the bodies of truly devout Christians sealed in his locker, having to relinquish their souls to Mother Carey's Chickens who carried them to fiddler's green, but this conflicts with the albatross superstition.

Day: In modern usage every kind of solar time has its zero or stating point at midnight, but this has not always been so. In recent times there have been four conventions for measuring the start and finish of a day. [1] The civil or calendar day began at midnight, as it still does. [2] Until January 1, 1925, the astronomical day began at noon, 12 hours *later* than the start of the calendar day of the same date. [3] Until October 11, 1805, the nautical day also began at noon, but 12 hours *earlier* than the calendar day, and a full day (24 hours) earlier than the astronomical day of the same date. [4] The sidereal day is not a solar measurement like the first three, but rather the time required for a complete rotation of the earth in reference to any star or to the vernal equinox at the meridian, equal to 23 hours, 56 minutes, 4.09 seconds in units of mean solar time.

Day of departure: Ancient maritime superstition held that no voyage should begin on a biblically inauspicious day, but should preferably be deferred until the omens were favorable. [1] The first Monday in April was a no-no, being both Cain's birthday and the day on which he killed his brother Abel. [2] Any Friday was especially ill-omened, because that was supposedly the day on which Jesus was crucified. An old seafarer's rhyme says:

> On a Friday she was launched
> On a Friday she set sail
> On a Friday met a storm
> And was lost in the gale

[3] On the other hand, December 31 was considered lucky, since that is when the Bible says Judas Escariot hanged himself. [4] And, drawing from pre–Christian belief, Wednesday was propitious since it is named after and dedicated to Wotan (Odin), erroneously believed to have been the Viking protector of seafarers (actually he was chief of all the gods and the seafarers' guardian was Njord).

Day shape: *See* shapes.

Daybeacon: A fixed unlighted daytime aid to navigation (also daymark).

Dayman: A non-watchkeeping member of a ship's company (also day worker, idler).

Days of grace: The period of time allowed in time of war for; [1] A neutral vessel to clear a port before being blockaded by a belligerent. [2] A belligerent warship to stay in a neutral port for essential repairs.

Dazzle paint: Former method of disguising a warship by lines painted randomly on hull and superstructure. Designed in World War I by British marine artist Noman Williamson and intended to break up the vessel's profile, making it hard to determine size, speed, class, course or range. Now generally replaced by camouflage paint.

DC: Damage control.

DCO: Damage control officer.

DCPO: Damage control Petty Officer.

DCT: Depth charge thrower.

DD: [1] The traditional and authorized RN notation that an officer or seaman has been "discharged dead." [2] Hull classification symbol of a destroyer.

D-Day: [1] June 6, 1944, the day of the Normandy invasion, on which Allied troops invaded France and fought in heavy battles against Nazi troops. [2] Generic term designating the unnamed day on which any military operation commences or is scheduled to begin (*see* D).

DDG: Hull classification symbol of a guided missile destroyer.

DE: Former Hull classification symbol of an ocean escort destroyer.

Deactivate: [1] To close down a unit that is no longer needed. [2] To lay up a ship for possible future use. *See also* Mothball, In Ordinary, Inactivate.

Dead: Adjective meaning [1] Exactly (e.g., dead ahead; dead astern; dead on target; dead level). [2] Completely (e.g., dead stop; dead calm). [3] Extremely (e.g., dead easy).

Dead as the Dodo: Refers to the dodo bird, which was driven to extinction by the predation of seamen.

Dead-end: To secure the end of a rope, usually on a cleat.

Dead freight: Unused cargo space reserved by a shipper on which freight must be paid.

Dead horse: It was customary for merchant seaman to be given a cash advance against their first month's wages, in order to buy clothing and necessaries for the voyage. "Working the dead horse" was their slang for the subsequent period of laboring against pay which had already been drawn and spent. When they began to earn money again, they celebrated the end of their unpaid month by "Flogging the dead horse." This involved hoisting a straw-filled canvas horse into the rigging and belaboring it to pieces, all the while singing the "Dead Horse Chantey," of which there are numerous versions, one of them being:

> The horse is gone and will come no more.
> Goodbye old horse!
> They say so and they hope for.
> Goodbye old man!

> They'll hoist him to the fore yardarm.
> Goodbye old horse!
> There he won't do sailors no more harm.
> Goodbye old man!

Dead in the water: Said of a vessel which is not moored, anchored, or made fast, but remains stationary with no way on.

Dead load: A wheeled device used to simulate an aircraft when catapult-testing.

Dead marine: An empty wine, beer, or liquor bottle is familiarly known as a "dead marine" or "dead soldier." This is one of the very few colloquialisms

whose origin can perhaps be traced. Rear-admiral HRH the Duke of Clarence (later King William IV) is alleged to have been dining aboard his flagship when he pointed at a pile of empty wine bottles and ordered his steward to "Clear away those dead Marines." A major of Marines immediately objected to the slur on his Corps and the astute duke replied that "Like Marines these bottles have given their lives nobly in the cause of duty and, given the chance, would willingly do so again."

The authenticity of this anecdote is suspect because none of its sources cites the name of the flagship or the date of the incident. Moreover there is a more earthy alternative explanation. According to the lore of the Royal Navy's lower deck, an empty bottle resembles a dead marine because it is of no further use to anyone; if thrown overboard, a bottle floats neck down, and so does a marine due to the buoyancy of air trapped in his huge boots.

The term seems to have been introduced independently in Australia long after it was in circulation elsewhere. Because beer bottles were returnable to licensed recyclers called Marine Dealers, it seemed natural to the Aussies to call the empties "dead marines."

Dead men: Refers to the ends of gaskets and points that have been left dangling under the yards, but should have been tucked in when the sail was furled.

Dead reckoning: An estimate of position arrived at by calculating course, speed, and drift, without the benefit of observations. Abbreviation of deduced reckoning. (*See also* estimated position.)

Dead rope: Loose ends of rope not attached or led through a block.

Dead sheave: A half block with no rotating parts.

Dead ship: One with no power. Also cold ship or cold iron.

Dead slow: The lowest speed which can be maintained without losing steerage way.

Dead space: [1] An area or compartment which cannot be used, especially in a hold. [2] An area within the range of sight, radar, or a weapon, which is obscured by an obstacle or inherent limitation.

Dead ticket: A discharge certificate issued to clear a ship's books of the name of a deceased crew member.

Dead water: Eddies forming along or behind a ship's hull.

Deadeye: Either of a pair of circular wooden blocks, having holes through which a lanyard is rove. One is fixed to the ship, while a strop from a stay or shroud is attached to the other. Tension in the shroud or stay can be adjusted by pulling or slackening the lanyard.

Deadhead: [1] To sail without cargo, usually on a return trip. [2] A non-paying passenger. [3] A useless member of the crew. [4] A partially-submerged log or pile. [5] A bollard. [6] A wooden block used as an anchor marker.

Deadlight: [1] The hinged metal cover of a port or

scuttle. [2] In American usage, a thick glass pane set in hull or deck to admit light.

Deadman control: A device which works only so long as its operator maintains pressure on a pedal or handle and stops immediately that pressure is relieved.

Deadweight: The difference between the displacement of a merchantman when light and when fully laden.

Deadweight tonnage: The weight in long tons of cargo, passengers and provisions which brings a vessel from its light displacement to its summer load-line (also deadweight capacity). *See* tonnage.

Deadwood: Blocks of timber used to fill voids between keel and stem or sternpost without adding structural strength.

Deaf as the mainmast: Is the nautical equivalent of "deaf as a doorpost," except that it was said of a sailor who did not readily catch an order or respond to it, even if his hearing was otherwise acute.

De-arm: To change a weapon from "ready" to "safe." *See also* disarm, unarm.

Debacle: This word for a sudden downfall or utter defeat has French nautical origins. Débâcler meaning to clear (literally unbar) referred to the break-up of ice on a river or navigable channel.

Debark: To put or go ashore, usually by walking. Variation of disembark.

Debrief: [1] To interrogate personnel returning from a mission to determine the conduct and results of the operation. [2] To remove the bark from a felled tree when making a spar or mast.

Decco: To take a look at something. Adopted by the British Army from the Hindi dekko = look, and thence to the Royal Navy.

***Décidée*'s Monster:** In April 1904, the officer commanding screw-gunboat *Décidée* submitted the following official report to the flag officer commanding the French Indochina Station.

> I was standing on the bridge when my attention was directed to a round dark mass in the water some three hundred meters to port. I took it to be a rock but, on seeing it move, presumed it to be an enormous turtle four or five meters in diameter. Soon afterward it rose out of the water, and from the undulatory movement that followed, I understood I was in the presence of an enormous sea monster, shaped like a flat-bodied serpent about one hundred feet in length.
>
> It appeared to have a soft black skin covered with marbled spots, and the head, which rose about sixteen feet out of the water, closely resembled that of an enormous turtle with huge scales. It blew two jets of water to a height of about fifty feet. It moved slowly through the water at a speed of about eight knots, and when one hundred and fifty meters from the gunboat, plunged beneath it like a submarine, reappearing on the surface about four hundred meters away.

A number of the officers and crew watched the monster, which gradually disappeared from view. After it

had gone Lieutenant Lagresville, one of the officers of the gunboat, said that when cruising off this coast in 1898, in the gunboat *Avalanche*, he had seen a similar — possibly the same — creature. (*See also* appendix.)

Decipher: To convert an enciphered message into intelligible text. *See also* decode, decrypt.

Deck: The term comes from the Dutch dek, meaning roof or covering and was originally used in the same sense in English. Only later did it come to mean a floor or platform connecting the sides of a ship and dividing it into layers. Unlike flats, decks are fundamental structural elements of the vessel.

Deck ape: USN slang for a deckhand.

Deck beam: Any transverse beam supporting a deck.

Deck boy: An unqualified member of a merchantman's crew who must acquire six months sea time before being rated ordinary seaman.

Deck cargo: Goods carried on the deck and open to the weather.

Deck engineer: The member of a merchantman's crew responsible for the maintenance and repair of deck machinery such as capstans and winches.

Deck gang: The officers and seamen assigned to work the ship as opposed to in the engine space or specialty services (also Deck Department, or just plain Deck).

Deck Landing Control Officer: One who directs pilots landing on an RN aircraft carrier. The USN term is Landing Signal Officer. *See also* batsman, deck landing modes, and mirror landing aid.

Deck landing modes: The most demanding task facing a naval aviator is landing on an aircraft carrier in anything but the smoothest seas. Landing on a stationary runway is hard enough. Added to that task are the pitching and rolling motions of the ship, the vortex of air caused by the island, and the need to position the tailhook accurately on the third arresting wire. No wonder a deck landing has been compared to a "controlled crash." There are six ways in which a pilot can land on a flight deck, three conventional and three electronic "modes":

- Unassisted: Without any guidance, deck landing is difficult and hazardous even for experienced fliers, and theoretically suicidal for neophytes — although land-based military pilots flying aircraft without tailhooks have occasionally succeeded during calm weather.

- With a batsman: This tried and true method (*see* landing signal officer) was employed from the 1920s until the advent of jet aircraft whose high landing speeds made human reaction capacity too slow.

- With a mirror aid: The approach is semi-automated, but still depends on skill and observation. Moreover, since the pilot is watching the meatball rather than the deck, the solid thump of every landing is a surprise.

Today's Naval air traffic controllers guide aircraft onto the deck relying on electronic technology:

- In Mode I, a radar-controlled Precision Approach Landing System takes over to provide a hands-off touch down. Pilots have an aversion to relinquishing their controls to a computer, but automatic carrier landing systems are important when all other methods fail.
- In a Mode II approach, pilots approach using a crosshair display, and get confirmation of their readings from the carrier air traffic control center computer.
- Mode III, involves an air traffic controller or landing signal officer "talking down" the pilot, by providing him or her with precise instructions for a safe landing.

Deck landing qualification: Is part of normal training to enable air crews to obtain or retain the considerable skills needed to land aboard a ship at sea. For navy and marine pilots it entails taking off from the flight deck, flying around the ship and landing again for a short time before taking to the air again. Following DoD doctrine that stresses "unified air, land, sea, and special operations" Army and Air Force aviators are sometimes assigned missions that require landing on, and operating from, U.S. Navy or Coast Guard air-capable ships (*see* aviation support). This dictates that non-naval aviation units complete preparatory and sustainment training for operations in the maritime environment, including naval radio procedures, hand and arm signals, light signals and how to exit an aircraft under water. After the academic portion of their training, pilots have to make five real or simulated deck landings to acquire deck landing qualification.

Deck load: Cargo stowed on the weather deck.

Deck log: A rough book maintained by the officer of the watch, recording events such as changes of course or speed, arrivals and departures, deaths and injuries, soundings and sea conditions, land or sea marks passed or sighted, and any other unusual happenings. Later transcribed to a fair copy, but always taking precedence if the two disagree.

Deck Officer: [1] A merchant officer certificated to assist the master with navigation at sea, and to supervise the handling of cargo when in port. [2] A USN officer qualified, or under training to stand deck watches (the RN term is Seaman Officer).

Deck passenger: One who travels without a berth or cabin.

Deck pipe: *See* chain pipe.

Deck status light: A tri-colored light which displays an aircraft carrier's status and ability to support flight operations.

Deck Steward: The merchant petty officer responsible for deck chairs and serving refreshments to passengers on the promenade and open decks of liners and cruise ships.

Deckhand: A seaman who works on the deck or in the wheelhouse under direct orders of the boatswain. *See* deck ape.

Deckhead: British term for an interior ceiling in a ship (the American term is overhead).

Deckhouse: A small superstructure or cabin on a ship's weather deck containing the helm and navigational instruments.

Decking: Material for covering a deck to make it more waterproof and durable, or less slippery.

Deckplane: The standard fire-control reference on a warship, taking the place of the horizon which is unreliable at sea. *See* battery reference plane.

Declassify: To declare information no longer secret.

Declination: In navigation, the angular distance of a heavenly body north or south of the celestial equator.

Decode: To convert a coded message into intelligible language. *See also* decipher, decrypt.

Decorate: In military terminology, decorate means to bestow medals or other honors on someone.

Decorations: *See* medals.

Decrypt: To decipher a cryptographic message.

Deduced reckoning: *See* dead reckoning.

Deducted space: The enclosed spaces in a ship that are deducted from gross tonnage to calculate net tonnage.

Deep: [1] Any of the intermediate levels between fathom marks on a leadline. [2]*See* oceanic deep. [3] A generic term for the ocean.

Deep air support: Aerial action at such a distance that the possibility of "friendly fire" casualties is not a consideration (cf. close air support).

Deep scattering layers: Strata of ocean organisms which scatter or echo sound waves such as sonar. The organisms migrate downward to 150–200 fathoms during the day, but come close to the surface at night.

Deep sea exploration: The investigation of physical, chemical, and biological conditions on the abyssal sea bed, an area we know less about than the surface of Mars. Beyond the continental shelf, the bottom slopes into deeper water known as the abyssal plain. This is a vast, mostly flat, and generally unexplored area comprising about 40 percent of the ocean floor and lying between one and three thousand fathoms (6,000 to 18,000 feet/1,830 to 5,490 meters) below the surface. At these depths it is permanently dark, bone-chillingly cold, and pressure can reach more than 1,125 kg/sq.cm (16,000 pounds/sq.in). Sensing from air and space provides an overview, and photographs taken by cameras towed along the bottom can be studied to determine places worthy of examination. but detailed observation relies on submersible vehicles.

Remotely Operated Vehicles (ROVs) and Unmanned Underwater Vehicles (UUVs) excel at large area exploration, but periodically have to have their batteries recharged or replaced. Oceanographers have begun to replace them with "sea gliders" that do not have engines and propellers, but "fly" through the water on stubby wings, moving vertically by changing buoyancy. Their electricity demands are minimal, giving them much longer endurance. But as yet there is no substitute for human eyes, so manned submersibles usually make the final observations. However, with the expanded use of fiber optics, satellites, and more advanced remote-controlled robots, scientists may eventually be able to explore from computer screens in laboratories without having to venture into the depths themselves.

Deep-sea line: (pronounced dipsyline). The heavy leadline used for sounding deep waters before the advent of echo sounders. The standard weight was 50 pounds (22.7 kg) and the line was normally 100 fathoms, but occasionally longer. William Falconer's description in his 1780 *Dictionary of the Marine* is still appropriate:

The deep-sea-lead is marked with two knots at 20 fathom, 3 at 30, 4 at 40, and so on to the end. It is also marked with a single knot in the middle of each interval, as at 25, 35, 45 fathoms, &c. To use this lead more effectually at sea, or in deep water on the sea-coast, it is usual previously to bring to the ship, in order to retard her course: the lead is then thrown as far as possible from the ship on the line of her drift, so that, as it sinks, the ship drives more perpendicularly over it. The pilot, feeling the lead strike the bottom, readily discovers the depth of the water by the mark on the line nearest its surface. The bottom of the lead being also well rubbed over with tallow, retains the distinguishing marks of the bottom, as shells, ooze, gravel, &c. which naturally adhere to it.

Deep six: USN slang for throwing something overboard (cf. jettison). Based on the leadsman's call "by the deep, six" made when the water is more than six but less than seven fathoms deep.

Deep tank: A compartment for the carriage of liquids, usually extending from the double bottom to the lower deck and equipped with baffles to minimize surging.

Deep-waisted: Refers to a vessel whose poop and forecastle are much elevated above the weather deck.

Deepwater circulation: Movement below the upper layer influenced by surface currents is driven by density (a function of temperature and salinity) and by gravity which pulls the water downhill into ocean basins. These currents, which flow under the surface of the ocean, hidden from immediate detection, are sometimes called submarine rivers, but are properly named thermohaline circulation (thermo = heat, haline = salt), or meridional overturning circulation, or density-driven circulation. Over a very long period of time, thermohaline circulation mixes the waters of all the oceans and turns them into a global system. It is this system that climatologists fear may be impacted by global warming and alter worldwide climates (*see* Argo).

Popularly described as the "great oceanic conveyor belt," it originates in the North Atlantic where evaporation increases the salinity and hence the density of surface water, which is also cooled by water from the Arctic Ocean. Sinking to the abyssal plain, it moves south along the coasts of the Americas to Antarctica, where it joins another deep current caused by evaporation in the Drake Passage off the southern tip of South America. This dense water then splits into two streams that cross the Indian Ocean and resurface in the Pacific about 1200 years later. The colder, denser water eventually warms and returns to the surface layer.

Deepwater layer: The water between the thermocline and the sea floor, representing some 90 percent of all ocean water. It is extremely cold (close to 0°C), non-circulating, and almost devoid of oxygen. Nevertheless, recent studies show that it houses a wide range of living creatures and organisms. Also called the hypolimnion.

Deepwater mooring: *See* offshore mooring.

Deepwater zone: *See* density levels.

Defaulter: A person accused of committing a naval or military offense.

Defcon: Defense readiness condition (USN).

Defensively Equipped Merchant Shipping: British World War II term for merchant vessels equipped with weapons crewed by Royal Navy ratings and/or members of the Maritime Royal Artillery. *See* Armed Guard for a comparison with American practice.

Defilade: Protection against horizontal fire provided by a hill or other obstruction.

Defilade fire: Gunnery term for the plunging fire needed to over-pass a defilade.

Deflection: [1] Gunnery term for the angle between the line-of-sight to the target and the line-of-sight to which the gun must be pointed to compensate for movement, wind, etc. [2] Deviation of a compass needle caused by local magnetic influence, especially on a ship.

Degauss: To permanently wrap a steel vessel with electrical cable running fore and aft. This can be activated when required to reduce the ship's variable magnetic field and minimize the threat posed by magnetically-activated mines and torpedoes. Rhymes with delouse (cf. deperm).

Degrees of freedom: A term referring to the six possible motions of vessels in response to action of the sea, three of which (pitch, roll, and yaw) are rotational oscillations and three (heave, surge, and sway) are linear displacements. (*See also* ship motions.)

Delivered Ex-Quay (DEQ): An Incoterm similar to DES, except that the seller must clear the goods for import and pay discharge costs. Risks and costs are transferred to the buyer when the goods are on the quay.

Deliverer: Medieval term for a carpenter or artificer employed to construct castles on the decks of merchantmen being converted for war.

Delta: [1] Alluvial deposit at the mouth of a river or tidal inlet. [2] NATO phonetic notation for letter "D" which, when used as a single-letter signal, signifies "Stand clear — I am maneuvering with difficulty" (*see* table 8). [3] A triangular-shaped aerofoil.

Demi-culverin: A 16th century cannon firing a 9-pound ball.

Demise Charter: Seldom-used term for a Bareboat Charter.

Demonstration: A feint or deceptive military operation.

Demotion: A disciplinary reduction in grade, rank, or status.

DEMS: Defensively Equipped Merchant Shipping (British).

Demure: [1] Applied to persons in the sense of modest, shy, quiet, sober, or sedate. [2] Formerly used to describe a quiet untroubled sea. From Old French demoure.

Demurrage: [1] The detention of a vessel beyond the agreed time for loading or discharging. [2] The rate or amount paid to a shipowner for revenue lost due to such a delay.

Density: The weight of water divided by the amount of space it occupies. This is determined by the combined effect of temperature, salinity, and atmospheric pressure. Cold, salt-laden water is denser than warmer, fresher water and will sink below it. *See* Density levels.

Density current: *See* turbidity current.

Density levels: Ocean waters can be divided into three layers, depending on their density. At the top is the surface or mixed zone. This is unstable due to atmospheric interference. For example, evaporation could increase its salinity, or a cold front could reduce its temperature. In the middle is a transition zone known as the pycnocline layer (Greek pycno = dense + cline = slope). This forms a barrier between the layers above and below, allowing little movement between them. At the bottom is the deepwater zone, which is cold, saline, dense and more or less stable, never interacting with the atmosphere (except in polar regions where the pycnocline is not always present).

Departure: [1] The act of leaving. [2] The time of leaving. [3] Starting a voyage or a new course of action. [4] Divergence or deviation from an established rule, plan, or procedure. [5] Distance traveled due east or west along a parallel of latitude. [6] Bearings of prominent landmarks taken as a ship clears harbor for a voyage. *See also* day of departure, line of departure, and point of departure.

Departure buoy: The last and furthest from shore of a series of buoys marking a channel. Also sea buoy.

Deperming: Removal of a steel vessel's permanent magnetism by energizing coils of electrical cable temporarily wrapped, vertically and athwartships, around its hull. Unlike degaussing, where a cable is attached to and travels with the ship, this is a one-time procedure performed in port.

Deploy: [1] To spread out and position ships for combat or amphibious assault. [2] To dispatch for duty in foreign waters.

Depression: [1] Meteorology: An area of low barometric pressure — a bad weather system in which winds circulate clockwise in the Southern and anticlockwise in the Northern Hemisphere (*see* Coriolis effect). [2] Physical Geography: A depressed or sunken area lower than the surrounding surface. [3] Astronomy. The angular distance of a celestial body below the horizon. [4] Economics: A period during which business, employment, and stock-market values decline severely or remain at a very low level of activity. [5] General: The state of being depressed — sadness; gloom; dejection.

Depth charge/bomb: An explosive container set to detonate at a predetermined depth or when in proximity to a submarine. A depth charge is dropped or thrown from a warship, while a depth bomb is usually delivered by aircraft. (*See also* antisubmarine rocket.)

Depth measurement: Sounding by leadline, while still practiced, has largely been replaced by: [1] An instrument known as an echo sounder. This sends a pulse of sound energy downward from a transducer on a ship's hull; when the pulse strikes the bottom or a submerged object it bounces back as an echo, the timing of which can be converted to depth measurement. [2] A sounding sonar, which works in the same fashion but uses ultrasonic waves rather than audible sound. [3] In a submarine, a depth gauge measures the pressure of overlying water to determine its depth.

DEQ: Delivered ex–Quay.

DER: Former hull classification symbol of a Destroyer Escort Radar Picket.

Derelict: [1] A vessel abandoned in open water, to which its crew has no hope or intention of returning. It may be boarded and claimed as salvage, provided no cat, dog, or other domestic animal is still on board and alive, in which case the owner may reclaim the ship on payment of salvaging costs. [2] Land left dry by a permanent change in the water line. (Latin derelictus = abandoned.)

Dereliction of duty: Failure to perform assigned duties, whether willful or negligent.

Derrick: A fixed-base crane with a pivoted arm, used as a lifting device to raise or lower cargo (named after the portable gallows designed by Thomas Derrick, a 17th century hangman).

DES (Delivered Ex Ship): *See* Incoterms.

Deserter: A person who has deliberately run away from military service with no intention of returning.

Desertion: The crime committed by a deserter.

Desig: A USN signal flag indicating that the following hoist is to be read literally, rather than as code.

Designator: A four-digit USN code identifying an officer's qualifications and specialties (if any).

Destination: The point at which a voyage ends or is scheduled to end.

Destroyer: A versatile class of high-speed warship that evolved from the torpedo-boat destroyer. These vessels are themselves armed with torpedoes, enabling them to operate offensively and attack much larger opponents. Modern destroyers are equipped with ASW and AAA weaponry and operate: [1] Offensively with strike forces and hunter-killer antisubmarine groups. [2] Defensively to screen convoys and task forces against submarine, air, or surface attack . [3] In support of amphibious operations.

Destroyer Escort: The USN's World War II designation of an ocean escort frigate.

Destructor: A device to destroy classified documents or secret equipment in danger of compromise or enemy capture.

Det Norske Veritas: Established in 1864, DNV is one of the "big three" in ship classification, along with the American Bureau of Shipping and Lloyd's Register, but it also has many other interests. With some 300 offices in 100 countries, it is a leading provider of services for managing risk in maritime, rail, and automotive transportation, and in the oil and gas industries.

Detachable link: A connector designed to join two sections of anchor chain. Unlike a shackle, it can pass through the hawsepipe or round the capstan like any other link.

Detached: [1] A ship is detached from its fleet or station when assigned elsewhere. [2] In the USN, an officer is detached when ordered away from a ship or unit (enlisted personnel are assigned or transferred). [3] In the RN, the term refers to a person assigned to serve temporarily in another ship or unit while retaining attachment to the regular ship or unit.

Detachment: A group or unit separated from a larger force for a specific assignment or operation.

Detail: [1] A person or (usually small) group assigned to a specific task. [2] To issue orders appointing such a group.

Deviation: The error in a ship's compass due to its own magnetic field.

Deviation Clause: A Charter Party item permitting a ship's master to visit ports other than the contractual destination.

Devil: Any of various long seams that are difficult to caulk due to shape or position (e.g., between keel and garboard strake, or between deck planking and an adjacent waterway).

Devil to pay: Despite claims of a naval origin, this phrase almost certainly originated on shore during the 15th century, as a forecast of future retribution for an action about to be taken, the reference being clearly to the inevitable outcome of a Faustian bargain with Old Nick. After the cliché had been established, the punning instinct of seamen probably led them to apply it to one of the most despised and unpleasant of shipboard duties, frequently considered a minor form of punishment.

The long outermost deck seam in a wooden ship was one of several known to seamen as a difficult (the devil) to caulk with pitch (pay). The job involved squatting uncomfortably in the bilges for hours on end, pressed tight against the bulwark, without enough space to properly hammer in the oakum. The later addition of "and no pitch hot" was probably re-verse-transferred back to the shore after the alternate nautical meaning had been established.

Dew point: A meteorological term for the temperature at which atmospheric water vapor begins to precipitate.

DF: Direction finding/finder.

Dghaisa: A Maltese harbor boat in which the oars are pushed instead of pulled. Pronounced "di-sar."

DGUTS: USN admonition to persevere (a very informal abbreviation of "Don't give up the ship" used only in private correspondence).

Dhobi/Dhobey: To wash or launder clothes (from Hindi dohb).

Dhow: A flat-bottomed sailing vessel, usually lateen-rigged with two or three forward-sloping masts. Used by Arab traders on the African, Arabian, and Asian coasts of the Indian Ocean.

DI: Drill Instructor [USMC].

DIA: Defense Intelligence Agency [US].

Diaphone: A foghorn producing a low-pitched two-toned signal as an aid to navigation. Many older devices, especially those on land, used diaphones to produce the distinctive deep and penetrating tone followed by an audible "grunt" that most people associate with foghorns and the sea.

Dicing: Naval aviator's slang for high-speed, low-altitude photographic operations.

Dieppe Raid: An Allied assault on this small French port in August 1942 was intended to probe German defenses and test Allied amphibious tactics. It discovered the former to be formidable and the latter abysmal. Tactical intelligence was woefully inadequate, and planning was inept. Inter-service cooperation barely existed. Promised close air support did not materialize and, with nothing larger than a destroyer, naval gunfire alone was inadequate. Approximately 75 percent of the attack force (5,100 Canadians, 1,000 British commandos, and a handful of U.S. Rangers) was killed, wounded, or captured.

Diesel-electric: A propulsion system consisting of a diesel engine connected to a generator whose electricity powers the propellers.

Diesel engine: A form of internal-combustion engine in which the heat generated by compression of air in a cylinder ignites the fuel. Named after its inventor, German engineer Rudolf Diesel, who was presumed drowned after disappearing from the Antwerp-Harwich ferry in 1913.

Difficulty: According to Admiral Smyth's 1887 *Sailor's Word-Book*, "this word is unknown to true salts." (*See* impossible.)

Digestive systems: An old saying holds that midshipmen have guts, wardroom officers have stomachs, and flag officers have palates.

Dilbert: USN slang for a stupid or ineffective aviator (Dilbert was the anti-hero of World War II instructional cartoons for naval airmen).

Dingbat: In England this term refers to something undefined, a thingamabob; in the United States it means a foolish or flighty woman; and in Australia and New Zealand it applies to a mad or eccentric person, especially one with delirium tremens. Each of these terms can trace its origin to sailor slang for a mop made of teased-out old rope's ends, whose strands flopped around uncontrollably when swabbing the decks.

Dinghy: [1] Formerly a single-banked ship's boat with four oars and a spritsail. [2] Now any small oared, sailed, or motor-driven boat used as a tender. [3] A rowing boat used on Indian coastal and inland waters for the transport of passengers and freight (from the Hindi dingi).

Dining-in: The RN has long-standing traditions and the USN an official directive (OpNavInst 1710.7) prescribing procedures for the formal dinner known as "Dining-in" or "Mess Night." Officers wear dress uniforms and civilians black tie. Unlike military and air force mess dinners where the commanding officer presides, the ship's captain is considered a guest in the wardroom and the second-in-command is mess president. A vice-president, known as "Mister or Madam Vice," acts as organizer of the function and enforcer of wardroom rules. (*See also* Passing the Port, and Toasts.)

Dining-out: Similar to dining-in except that officers' civilian spouses are invited to attend.

Dip: [1] To partially lower the national ensign and then raise it as a form of salute. [2] A correction for the height of eye above the water when making a sextant observation. [3] Downward inclination of a compass needle due to the earth's magnetic field. [4] To lower the shorter end of a lugsail yard so as to shift it to the opposite side of the mast when tacking. [5] A heavenly body crossing the meridian is said to "dip." [6] Any flag or pennant not fully-raised is "at the dip" (the author recalls being summoned to the bridge and his captain demanding "who is dead?" followed by "you hoisted the ensign at the dip" when in fact it was only about two inches below the cap!).

Dire straits: Geographers and mariners use the Middle English word "strait," meaning confined or narrow, to describe a narrow passage connecting two larger bodies of water. Combined with the Latin word for fearful or unlucky, the phrase now refers to being in position of danger, difficulty, distress, or need.

Direct drive: Said of a reciprocating engine connected directly to the propeller shaft without gearing. With this arrangement, engine and propeller revolutions are the same.

Direct fire: Gunfire aimed by line-of-sight at the target (cf. defilade fire, indirect fire).

Direct steering: With the Helm directly connected to the rudder having no intermediate ropes, chains, shafting, or steering engine.

Dirk: A small dagger-like naval sword worn by midshipmen and others in full dress uniform. Originally the Scots word for a long dagger.

Dirt sailor: USN enlisted seaman slang for a Seebee (considered to spend all his time on the muddy shore, never going to sea)

Dirty: [1] Rainy, squally, stormy, or otherwise foul weather. [2] Confused or baffled wind on the leeward side of a sail.

Disabled: Unable to proceed and not under command.

Disarm: [1] To deprive of weapons. [2] To lay down weapons, either voluntarily or following defeat. [3] To remove the fuse from a bomb, shell, or mine. [4] To de-arm or unarm.

Disburse: To distribute, pay out, or expend money.

Disc area: The zone swept by the tips of rotating propeller blades.

Discharge: [1] To unload cargo. [2] To fire a gun or missile. [3] The flow of electricity between two points of different electrical potential. If the supply of electrical charge is continuous, so is the discharge; otherwise it is temporary, and serves to equalize the potentials. [4] To release a rating or enlisted person from service, with or without honor. The USN awards five classes of discharge, namely: Honorable, General, Other than honorable, Bad conduct, and Dishonorable. (*See also* DD.)

Discharge Certificate: An essential document which confirms the sea-time and experience of merchant officers and seamen.

Discrepancy: An navigation aid which is not "watching properly" (out of position).

Discrepancy buoy: A temporary replacement for a navigation aid that is not in its assigned position.

Disembark: To put or go ashore from a vessel. Also debark.

Dish up: In general use this means putting food onto a plate before a meal, but in the RN it means clearing away and washing dishes after eating.

Dishonorable discharge: The most severe form of separation from naval service. May only be ordered for warrant officers and enlisted personnel convicted of serious offenses by a general court-martial. The equivalent punishment for commissioned officers is "dismissal." *See* rogue's march.

Dismantle: To remove all guns, stores, masts, spars, and rigging from a sailing warship in preparation for laying it up "in ordinary."

Dismast: Loss of a ship's mast(s) by storm, collision, accident, or battle damage (cf. unstep).

Dismiss!: The command giving a person or assembly permission to leave or disperse.

Dismissal: To discharge or remove an officer from service, usually without honor following court-martial (cf. cashier, dishonorable discharge).

Displacement: Weight of a vessel expressed as either the number of long tons, or the cubic feet of water, displaced by the hull (1 ton = 35 cu.ft of seawater or 35.9 cu.ft of fresh).

Displacement hull: A type of hull that plows through the water rather than skimming the surface (planeing hull) or hovering above it (ground-effect vessel).

Displacement speed: The maximum economical speed attainable by a displacement hull vessel. This is a function of hull shape, waterline length, displacement, and drag. Additional power may increase this speed by a small amount but is not economical (cf. hull speed).

Displacement tonnage: Displacement when loaded to the summer load line. The normal measure of warship size. *See* tonnage.

Display: [1] The visual representation on a cathode ray tube of the output of an electronic device. [2] USN ships "display" their flags, RN ships "wear" them, and merchantmen "fly" them.

Disposition: The arrangement of ships or aircraft for a specific mission or purpose.

Disrate: To reduce a rating or enlisted seaman to a lower rate. *See* downgrade.

Distress: [1] General: That which occasions suffering, pain, misfortune, affliction, or misery. [2] Physics: The process whereby materials are worn down by time and natural forces. [3] Maritime: A state of danger or necessity (e.g., leaking, dismasted, or without provisions or water). [4] Law: The seizure and detention of goods as a pledge or to satisfy a claim. [5] Medicine: Extreme pain or suffering of body or mind. [6] Woodwork: The art of aging furniture and other objects. (Middle English destresse, from Vulgar Latin districtia.)

Distress signals: *See* table 10.

Ditch: [1] Slang name for the sea. [2] To land a crippled aircraft on water. [3] To throw something overboard (cf. deep six; jettison).

Ditty bag/box: A small bag or box used by seamen to hold sewing materials and odds and ends. From Anglo-Saxon dite = tidy.

Diurnal: Occurring once a day, having a daily cycle.

Dive: To submerge, said especially of submarines.

Dive tonnage: The difference between a submarine's displacement when surfaced and submerged.

Diver: Refers to a person who plunges and moves below the surface of the water. *See* diving.

Diving: Refers to [1] plunging into water (especially headfirst). [2] Submerging and moving underwater. This may be done in several different ways.

- In self-contained diving swimmers hold their breath and surface for air.
- In snorkeling the diver breathes through a short tube and cannot go deeper than it is long.
- When hookah diving the person breathes through a mask connected to a small air pump on the surface by a hose that restricts movement.
- In scuba diving air is supplied from portable tanks via complicated delivery valves. Movement is unrestricted, but underwater time is limited by tank capacity.
- With full surface support the diver wears the classic helmet and suit, connected to a copious air supply from the surface. An air hose and a safety tether limit movement, but allow much deeper dives and longer time underwater.

Diving planes: Horizontal aerofoil-like surfaces used to control vertical movement of a submarine. May be mounted on the bow, stern, or conning tower (sailplane). Also called hydroplane.

Diving trim: The condition of a submarine when its trimming tanks contain the amount of water requisite to maintain submerged stability and buoyancy.

Division: [1] An administrative and tactical Marine or Army unit, bigger than a brigade but smaller than a corps, normally commanded by a major-general. [2] The basic administrative unit into which a warship's personnel are organized. [3] In the USN, a tactical group of four or more warships forming part of a fleet or squadron.

Divisions: Every division aboard a warship assembled on parade.

Dixie Cup: USN enlisted slang for their white uniform hat.

DLCO: Deck Landing Control Officer [RN]

DLQ: Deck landing qualification

DMB: Datum marker buoy

DND: Department of National Defence (Canada)

DNI: Director of Naval Intelligence (U.S.).

DOA: [1] Date of arrival. [2] Dead on arrival.

Doa: A Persian coastal trader.

DOB: Date of birth.

Dock: [1] A wharf, jetty, pier, or quay. [2] The water next to one of them. [3] An artificially enclosed basin for loading, unloading, or repairing vessels. [4] To enter such a space.

Dockage: [1] The charge for berthing at a dock. [2] The docking fee.

Docker: One who works on the docks, a stevedore or longshoreman. Also dockhand, dockworker.

Docking fee: The fee charged by a tugboat for helping a vessel to dock.

Docking telegraph: Formerly a set of telltale dials advising the docking officer of the speed of engines and direction of rudder. Nowadays replaced by wireless voice communication.

Dockyard: [1] Waterside area with docks and equipment for outfitting, building, or repairing ships. [2] In Britain, especially for naval use (cf. Navy Yard).

DOD: Date of departure.

DoD: Department of Defense (U.S.).

Dodger: A canvas wind screen.

Dodo bird: A large flightless creature which once inhabited islands in the southwest Indian Ocean. Having no natural predators, it was easily captured by foraging sailors who hunted it to extinction in the 17th century. The Portuguese to call it frango doudo (= stupid chicken), and the name stuck.

DOG: Deployable Operations Group [USCG].

Dog: [1] A lever, bolt, or other device for securing a hatch, scuttle, or watertight door. Also dog-bolt, snib. [2] To activate such a device. [3] A hinged catch or pawl that fits into a notch of a ratchet to move a wheel forward or prevent it from moving backward. [4] A metal support, especially one with fangs fastening a log in a saw pit. [5] The last support to be knocked away when a ship is being launched. [6] Formerly, an iron hook or bar, with a sharp fang at one end that could be easily driven into a plank or spar and used to drag it along the deck or lift it out of a hold. (*See also* top dog, underdog.)

Dog tag: U.S. military slang for a metal identification label worn on a chain around the neck.

Dog Zebra: USN term for the "darken ship" condition, during which all hull openings marked "DZ" (dog zebra in the World War II Allied phonetic alphabet — today it would be "delta zulu") must be closed.

Dogger: A ketch-like Dutch vessel designed for fishing on the Dogger Bank.

Doggie or Dogsbody: A ship's boy or midshipman under training, who found himself at the beck and call of every petty and commissioned officer.

Dog's breakfast (or dinner): Naval colloquialism for a nasty mess.

Dogwatch: One of two short (2-hour) shifts of duty intended to ensure that seamen do not always have to work the same 4-hour shifts (*see* watch).

Doldrums: Belt of calms and light baffling winds lying on both sides of the equator and between the northern and southern trade winds.

Dolphin striker: A strut, stayed in place by martingales and backropes, reinforcing the bowsprit or jib-boom against the upward pull of headstays.

Dolphins: [1] Pilings in a harbor, used for mooring. [2] Slang for submariners' insignia consisting of heraldic dolphins flanking the prow of a World War II submarine (USN) or an anchor surrounded by a crown (RN). [3] An aquatic mammal. Ancient Mediterranean myth holds that, when the island of Atlantis sank into the sea, some of its human inhabitants, especially those who were advanced metaphysicians, miraculously learned to breathe underwater and became dolphins. Being cousins of humankind, they have always been highly protective of mariners in difficulty.

DOM: Day of month.

Domestic registry: A Merchantman which flies the same national flag as its registry (cf. Flag of Convenience).

Don: The title of a Spanish aristocrat, formerly used by British seamen to refer to a Spaniard of any rank.

Donkey: A small engine used for hoisting or hauling.

Donkey's breakfast: Seaman's slang for the straw which formerly stuffed the mattresses of those who had beds instead of hammocks.

Don't give up the ship: On June 1, 1813, two 38-gun frigates met in a duel off Boston. In size, tonnage, and armament the ships were evenly matched, so the outcome depended on morale, experience, and training, where there were marked differences.

- Sir Philip Bowes Vere Broke had been in command of HMS *Shannon* for over six years, during which he had obsessively trained his gun captains and crews to fire individually as their weapons came to bear — some being detailed to aim at the enemy's helm and quarterdeck to destroy command and control, others at its gunports to inflict maximum damage on offensive capability. Confidence was high, and the British crew was anxious to come to grips with the Americans.

- In contrast, James Lawrence, who had recently been promoted to captain, had just taken command of USS *Chesapeake*, a ship with a bad luck reputation, and a surly rag-tag crew who did not know their captain and had not had time to train together as a team. Some even staged a minor mutiny, refusing to man the guns until the purser issued chits for prize money they claimed was owing to them.

In the first exchange of fire, virtually everyone on *Chesapeake*'s quarterdeck was killed or wounded, including the captain, his executive officer, the lieutenant of marines, three midshipmen, and both helmsmen. Lawrence's wounds were mortal but, as he was being carried below, he shouted defiantly "Tell the men to fire faster and not to give up the ship; fight her until she sinks ... (or) blow her up." Brave words were not enough. Within 15 minutes, half of *Chesapeake*'s crew and every one of her officers had been killed or wounded. The butcher bill was exceptionally high, probably because *Chesapeake*'s upperworks had been built of easily-splintered pine when more shot-resistant oak was not available. Despite defeat and death, Lawrence entered the immortal pantheon of naval heroes since his dying order became the unofficial motto of the United States Navy.

Don't spoil the ship: *See* spoil the ship.

Doppler effect: The change in frequency of an electronic wave due to the relative motion of receiver and transmitter. This phenomenon is used in anti-submarine warfare and to measure the speed of a vessel over the sea floor.

Doppler radar: A device which uses the Doppler effect to differentiate fixed and moving targets.

Dorade: A ventilator cowl designed to keep water out.

Dory: An exceptionally seaworthy small flat-bottomed boat with high bows and freeboard. Of American origin and formerly much favored by fishers and whalers.

Dosimeter: A badge or device carried by personnel working near nuclear equipment, giving a direct reading of the individual's exposure to radiation.

Double: [1] To attack an enemy vessel from both sides simultaneously. [2] To sail around a headland, cape, or peninsula. [3] To overlap two sections of a mast or spar. [4] To cover a ship's hull with extra planking when the original has loosened. [5] When preceded by "on the" or "at the" a command to move at a running pace.

Double block: A pulley with two sheaves side-by-side (cf. fiddle block).

Double bollard: One with two columns on a single base.

Double bottom: A watertight false bottom running fore-and-aft above the real one, effectively forming a sort of miniature hull within the main structure to increase its strength and ability to survive damage. In case of grounding or minor underwater damage, only the space between the bottoms will flood, leaving occupied areas intact. The space between the bottoms is often sectioned by watertight bulkheads to provide compartments for ballast, fuel, or fresh water.

Double capstan: A capstan constructed so that it can be worked from either of two decks.

Double drift: A method of calculating wind direction and velocity by observing the drift of a vessel on two different headings.

Double Dutch: Unintelligible gibberish. Another term that originated during the Anglo-Dutch Wars.

Double paddle: An oar with blades at each end, as used in a kayak.

Double purchase: A tackle composed of a fall rove through two single-sheaved blocks with its standing end attached to one of them so as to gain a mechanical advantage. Formerly used as a gun tackle.

Double shot: The loading of two balls into a single cannon. This 17th–19th century practice was more lethal, but reduced range and accuracy. Hence it was usually restricted to actions at close-quarters.

Double Spanish Burton: A tackle having the load suspended from one of two single running blocks, which is supported both by the fall which is rove through it, and by one end of a runner which is rove through the standing block and supports at its other end the running block.

Double-banked: [1] Two rowers pulling on the same oar. [2] Two rowers side-by-side pulling individual oars. [3] A galley with two rows of oars. [4] A frigate with a second set of broadside guns on a spar deck above the main gun deck.

Double-bitted: Said of a cable that makes two turns around the bitts instead of one.

Double-breeching: Additional ropes on a gun's recoil system, for extra security in heavy weather.

Double-decker: A ship with two decks above the waterline.

Double-ender: [1] A powered vessel, such as a ferry, capable of going in either direction equally well. [2] A sailing vessel with both bow and stern coming to a point.

Double-fluked: An anchor hinged at the crown so that both flukes dig into the ground simultaneously.

Double-headed shot: Similar to bar-shot, except that the heads are hemispherical rather than round.

Double-siding: Painting a row of dummy ports below the real ones, to make a single-decker look twice as powerful. A ruse frequently practiced by the Bombay Marine. *See also* gundeck stripes, quaker, mask paint.

Double-up: To use two sets of mooring lines.

Doughboy: [1] A seafarer's dumpling made from flour and slush. [2] An outdated slang term for an American infantryman, used in the Mexican-American War and World War I.

Doughnut: Legend has it that a 19th century New England sea captain called Hansen Gregory wanted some way of feeding the helmsman during long night watches, so he instructed his cook to deep-fry rings of dough flavored with molasses. When delivered to the man at the wheel, they could be slipped over the spokes where they would be handy for consumption hot and fresh, or could be saved for eating cold later. The circular shape was later adopted on shore, where round balls of fried dough were already known as Dough Nuts.

Douglas scales: In 1917 Royal Navy Captain (later Vice-Admiral) H.P. Douglas devised two nine-level scales for expressing the condition of waves and swell. The first, which he termed Wind-Sea, expresses the size of waves attributable to immediate and local wind effects. The second, which he named Swell, refers to waves generated by distant weather conditions and characterized by regular period and flat crests. These scales were adopted by the 1929 International Meteorological Conference at Copenhagen in an attempt to improve on the complexity of the Pierson-Moskowitch sea spectrum, and the rather vague wave descriptions in the Beaufort Scale. Taken together the two Douglas scales indicate the state of roughness of the sea. Details are given in table 2.

Douse: [1] To extinguish a lantern [2] To take in or lower a sail [3] To abruptly slacken a line.

DOW: Died of Wounds.

Down: In the direction toward which a current is flowing or a wind is blowing.

Down and out: Nowadays meaning destitute, lacking friends, money, or prospects, this phrase comes from one of the many shouts boatswains used to roust sailors out of their hammocks. The cry "out or down!" meant that the man had better turn out, or the bosun would cut the lanyard of his hammock. Once this had been done, the unfortunate man would be both down and out of bed.

Down by: Riding lower forward (down by the bow or head) or aft (by the stern).

Down the hatch: Although its origins are obscure, this drinking expression obviously began as a merchant seaman's comparison of a hatchway waiting for freight to a mouth waiting to receive a drink.

Down-Easter: A full-rigged 19th century New England ship. Slower than a clipper, but still relatively speedy.

Downgrade: To reduce in rank or rating; to disrate.

Downhaul: [1] A line attached to the bottom of a boom and used to flatten the sail. [2] The line used to pull down a jib or staysail.

Downtime: [1] A period when equipment is out of service due to failure of parts, lack or power, or other factors [2] A period when personnel are idle due to lack of assigned work.

Downwind: In the same direction as the wind is blowing.

Doxy: 19th century sailor's slang for a dockyard prostitute. From the Flemish dockesy = little doll.

DOY: Day of year.

DPV: Delivery point verification.

DR: Dead Reckoning.

Draft/Draught: [1] The depth of water needed to float a ship or boat. [2] RN term for a group of men transferred from on ship or station to another. [3] The forward curvature of a sail under wind pressure.

Draft/Draught marks: Numerals on both sides of bow and stern indicating how much of the hull is underwater.

Drag: [1] Resistance of a hull to movement. [2] To search the bottom with a grapnel. [3] To move under the influence of wind or current when the flukes of the anchor do not grip the bottom. [4] The amount a ship is down by the stern. [5] A drag chain. [6] U.S. Naval Academy slang for a midshipman's date.

Drag chains: Coils of chain attached to a new vessel's hull so as to slow it down when being launched into a narrow waterway where it might create dangerous waves or even strike the opposite bank.

Drake's Drum: Legend has it that in 1596, when he was dying of yellow fever in the Caribbean, Sir Francis Drake prophesized that if ever England was in serious danger the drum, carried aboard his ship to summon the crew to quarters, would miraculously beat spontaneously to awaken Englishmen to defend their country. In 1897, the poet Sir Henry Newbolt turned Drake's prophesy into a patriotic song:

> Take my drum to England, hang it by the shore
> Strike it when your powder's running low
> If the Dons sight Devon, I'll quit the port of heaven
> And drum them up the channel
> as we drummed them long ago.
>
> Drake he's in his hammock till the
> great armadas come
> (Cap'n art thou sleepin' there below?)
> Slung a'tween the round shot, a'listenin' for the drum
> And dreamin' all the time of Plymouth Hoe.

The music was played on the "great armada" of Allied warships which sailed from Plymouth to the D-Day invasion of Normandy on 6 June 1944.

Drakkar: The largest of Viking fighting ships, propelled by as many as 72 oars and carrying some 300 warriors. Drakkar means "dragon." Commercial cargo-carrying versions were called dreki and knorr.

Draughts: *See* Checkers.

Draw: [1] To haul or pull. [2] To require a specific depth of water to float in. [3] To fill a sail with wind. [4] To requisition something from an arsenal, dockyard, or magazine [5] To remove wad, shot, and cartridge from a loaded cannon.

DRe: Dead reckoning error.

Dreadnought: [1] Generic term for a battleship. [2] Name of a British warship launched in 1906; the first to be heavily armored and carry a battery of uniform caliber heavy guns — a revolutionary design which made all previous battleships obsolete. (Said to have been named after the family motto of her sponsor, First Sea Lord John Arbuthnot [Jackie] Fisher, "Fear God and Dread Nought.")

Dredge: [1] A vessel equipped with machinery designed to scoop or siphon the sea bottom (also dredger). [2] To use such a vessel to deepen a channel, remove silt from waterways, or harvest oysters.

Dredgy: Former name for the specter of a drowned person.

Dreki: A large broad-beamed oceangoing Viking cargo vessel. The name means dragon (cf. drakkar).

Dress: To organize ships or persons in formation or in ranks.

Dress ship: To decorate a vessel with national flags at each masthead and on the flagstaff. When a rainbow of signal flags strung is from the bow, across all mastheads, to the stern, it is known as "full dress." USN ships never dress while underway, but some other navies do, including the RN. The term is derived from the French dresser meaning to put up or erect, but the Marine de Guerre (French Navy) calls it grand pavoisn, meaning great flag display. With random order, there is always the danger of inadvertently inserting readable text or (sailors being sailors) of the yeoman deliberately sneaking in a crude message. To avoid this most yacht clubs and navies specify a standard sequence. Both RN and USN use NATO flags for their dressing lines.

Dressed to the nines: This phrase can be traced to the 17th century, and it has been claimed it refers to wearing a full set of men's clothing (waistcoat, breeches, and great coat). Tailoring these garments (with a minimal amount of waste) required nine yards of cloth. This seems less convincing than the competing explanation that a ship-of-the-line had three masts, each with three principal yards (course, topsail, and topgallant) and, when they were all as elegantly-decorated as possible, it was "dressed to the nines."

Drift: [1] That component of a vessel's or aircraft's movement attributable to the influence of wind, current or tide. [2] A vessel's leeway, expressed in knots. [3] An alternate name for current. [4] The speed of a current expressed in knots at sea, but statute miles/hour in rivers. [5] To float or be driven along by a current of water or air. [6] A short length of anchor chain laid on deck for working purposes. [7] The distance between two blocks in a tackle.

Drift angle: The angle between the path of a drifting vessel and its heading.

Drift ice: Loose floating pack ice which moves under the influence of wind and current and is generally navigable.

Drifter: A fishing boat that allows its net to float along with the current.

Drill: Systemized instruction in naval or military exercises and movements.

Drink: Mariner's slang for the sea.

Drive: [1] Generically, to push in some direction. [2] The force of the wind pushing to leeward. [3] To carry as much sail as is possible in heavy wind. [4] A ship is said to drive if her anchor fails to hold.

Drive shaft: *See* shaft.

Driver: [1] The fifth mast from the bow in a six-masted schooner. [2] A large sail or spanker suspended from the mizzen gaff.

Driving band: One of the features of a gun-fired naval projectile, consisting of a band of copper, alloy, or plastic, seated in a groove cut at the rear of the projectile body. Its purpose is three-fold: [1] To seal against the escape of propellant gas around the projectile. [2] To engage the rifling of the gun's bore and cause the projectile to rotate. [3] To act as a rear bourrelet on those projectiles which have none. Also rotating band.

Driving sail: One which tends to push the hull downward.

Drogher: A small West Indian coastal trader.

Drogue: [1] A canvas or wooden device, resistant to being pulled through the water, attached to a line and dropped ahead or astern of a vessel to hold its bow into the wind during heavy weather, or to minimize drift in water too deep to anchor. Also sea-anchor. [2] A canvas sleeve towed behind an aircraft for target practice.

Droits of Admiralty: [1] Rights claimed by a government over the property of an enemy nation. [2] Ancient English law giving the Lord High Admiral rights, in the name of the Crown, to property found upon the sea or shore, including flotsam, jetsam, lagan, and salvage; wrecked and derelict vessels; prizes taken at sea or by arrêt de prince; many varieties of fish, etc. These rights were surrendered to the public benefit in 1702. Droits, the French word for "rights" is properly pronounced "dwa," but English-speaking seamen usually make it rhyme with "quoits."

Dromon: A large Byzantine battle galley.

Drone: A remote-controlled pilotless aircraft. Now known as an unmanned aerial vehicle (UAV).

Drop: [1] To move gently with tide or current. [2] The depth of a square-sail measured amidships.

Drop keel: A centerboard.

Drop mooring: To drop a bow anchor, drift downstream to drop a stern anchor, and then haul in the bow cable until the vessel is firmly anchored at the chosen position.

Drop rudder: One which can be lowered beneath the level of the keel.

Drop sail: Formerly, to salute by lowering topsails.

Drown: [1] To be killed by the inhalation of water. [2] to submerge or flood something.

Drug trafficking: Buying, smuggling, and selling illegal drugs and narcotics.

Drummer: This is the traditional name for a Royal Marine bugler.

Drumming out: This was an humiliating ceremony applied to those sentenced to dishonorable discharge. If an officer was cashiered, a deserter recaptured, or a seaman declared incorrigible, he would be paraded in front of the ship's company. All buttons and badges of rank would be ripped off. An officer's sword would be snapped in half; a deserter would be flogged and branded "D" on the forehead to prevent re-enlistment; an incorrigible seaman might also be flogged.

Then they would be put ashore, or marched off the station, to the accompaniment of the "Rogue's March" played by drums and possibly a band. Usually the ship's company would turn their backs on the departing person, and sometimes the junior marine drummer would follow behind, repeatedly kicking his backside. By the 20th century the ceremony had been generally discontinued by the Royal and U.S. Navies, but continued in the U.S. Marine Corps until 1962 when adverse media publicity forced its abandonment.

Dry cargo: *See* dry goods.

Dry dock: A gated dock or basin from which water can be pumped or drained (cf. graving dock, wet dock).

Dry-flogging: Punishment applied with the culprit fully-dressed, thereby inflicting less trauma than a flogging on the bare back.

Dry goods: [1] On shore; textile fabrics and related merchandise as distinct from groceries, hardware, etc. [2] To the mariner; non-liquid bulk merchandise such as grains, coal, and mineral ores.

Dry run: A rehearsal.

Dry steam: *See* superheated steam.

DSN: Defense switched network. A U.S. military voice telephone system.

DSRV: Deep submergence rescue vehicle.

DTG: Date-time group.

Duck Up!: When square-sails obstructed the helmsman's view, he would sing out "duck up!" In response the clew-lines would be hauled to raise the lower corners of main- and fore-sail until he could see properly ahead.

Dueling: A number of Royal Navy customs originated when dueling was prevalent and eighteenth century Admiralty instructions clearly stated "Any officer who shall ... refuse to accept a challenge will be deemed to have acted honorably." It was (and still is) considered bad manners to enter a strange wardroom while wearing a sword, since that implies having come to force a quarrel. Drawing the sword brought serious punishment. There are also fines and penalties for placing a bet, or for mentioning a lady's name during formal wardroom proceedings, either of which could give rise to argument.

Duff: A boiled pudding (phonetic corruption of dough).

Duffel/Duffle: [1] Coarse woolen cloth originally from the Flemish town of Duffel near Antwerp. [2] A seaman's kit and personal effects (USN slang).

Duffle bag: A cylindrical canvas bag closed by a drawstring and carried over the shoulder.

Duffle coat: A hooded overcoat of duffel cloth, usually knee-length with toggle fasteners. Originally a naval issue, but adapted for civilian use after World War II.

Dugout: A canoe made by hollowing-out and shaping a tree trunk or large log.

Dumb: Said of a barge or any vessel without propulsion system or steering.

Dumb sheave: A sheave-less block through which a rope is rove.

Dummy funnel: [1] a false smokestack added to a warship to disguise its identity. [2] One added to a passenger vessel to improve its appearance.

Dummy ports: False gunports painted on the hull of a sailing ship to make it look more heavily-armed than it actually was. A 19th century practice of (especially) American, British, Dutch, and French merchantmen intended to deter pirates. *See also* double-siding, gundeck stripes, quaker, mask paint.

Dump: Temporary storage place for ammunition and supplies on shore.

***Dundee Star* Mystery:** This Scottish barque is said to have run aground on Midway Island during a gale in 1887. After the crew abandoned ship, the vessel floated off and disappeared. Four years later, she ran aground again, very close to the spot of her first grounding. Apparently she had spent four years drifting around the Pacific, unmanned and unsighted. This phantom voyage is reported in a number of works on maritime mysteries, but is not confirmed by more serious publications.

Dunes: Wind-formed mounds or ridges of drifted sand along a sea shore. The word survives from Anglo-Saxon.

Dungaree: A sturdy Indian sailcloth (dungri in Hindi). The work trousers worn by seamen were originally cut from time-worn or battle-damaged sails and hence became known as dungarees.

Dungiyah: A broad-beamed, flat-bottomed Arabian vessel trading between the Red Sea and the Malabar Coast of India.

Dunking sonar: An underwater submarine detection device, usually deployed in the water by a helicopter.

Dunkirk: This important seaport in northern France was the site of "Operation Dynamo," the largest amphibious withdrawal under fire from a hostile shore in history. During the 1940 Battle of France, a German army trapped the entire British Expeditionary Force and a number of its allies in a large beachhead around Dunkirk. In the hope of evacuating up to 45,000 troops, the Royal Navy assembled 41 destroyers, plus sloops, minesweepers, and other warships. A large number of civilian craft — yachts, ferries, fishing boats, pleasure steamers, etc. — volunteered to assist under T-124 articles. While the warships embarked soldiers from the port's piers and jetties, the small boats picked up men from ten miles (16 kms) of beaches and ferried them to the bigger vessels.

In the event, the estimate of evacuees was vastly exceeded — in the chaos of withdrawal under fire, accurate figures were not compiled, and several different estimates exist, though all agree on order of magnitude — in round figures, approximately 203,000 British and 135,000 Allied troops were landed in England; the former being almost the entire Expeditionary Force (less casualties). The allies were about 10 percent Belgian, the rest being French support troops — the French combat units, who were valiantly defending the perimeter so that others could escape, were all killed or taken prisoner.

Dunnage: [1] Personal gear or baggage. [2] Loose material used to protect, secure, or ventilate cargo and supplies. From the Dutch dunneje = loosely-packed.

Dutch bar: A structural element spanning the afterdeck of a tugboat and serving to keep the towing hawser above the heads of crew.

Dutch built: Formerly said by English seamen to describe a ship or a person who was broad and bluff without a hint of gracefulness.

Dutch courage: Today, this means alcohol-inspired bravado. The term originated in the 17th century when there were three, essentially naval, Anglo-Dutch wars. During these, English seamen became convinced that the reckless bravery of their opponents could only be explained by the excessive consumption of Geneva gin or Schnapps before combat. (Netherlanders were well aware of the Royal Navy's rum or brandy ration, but they do not seem to have responded with the term "English Valor.")

Dutch landfall: An illusion of land on the horizon.

Dutch pump: A reputed 17th century punishment, which has been described in two different ways. [1] The sailor was thrown overboard and had to tread water (pump the feet) to keep from drowning. [2] The Rasphouse, an old Amsterdam prison, had a punishment cell for lazy prisoners. In one corner was a pump, and in another, a pipe through which a steady stream of water was admitted. The prisoner could stand still and be drowned or pump frantically until the jailer chose to relieve him. This concept is said to have been transferred to sea by holing a small compartment below the waterline.

Dutchman: Old maritime name for a German ship (corruption of Deutsch). An actual Dutch ship was referred to as a "Hollander."

Dutchman's anchor: Former naval term, now obsolete, for anything left behind. Supposed to refer to an apocryphal Netherlands shipmaster who, when asked why he had run aground replied, "I have an excellent anchor but unfortunately left it behind."

Dutchman's breeches: Patches of blue in an otherwise stormy sky.

Dutchman's log: A primitive method of calculating speed by throwing a wooden block into the sea well forward and timing its passage between two marks on the hull.

Duty: [1] Tax on imported goods. [2] An assigned task (e.g., guard duty). [3] Prefix identifying that a person currently has a specific assignment (e.g., duty engineer).

DV: [1] Distinguished visitor. [2] Deo volente (God wills it).

Dvorak Technique: This method of evaluating tropical rotating windstorms (cyclones) was developed in 1973–4 by Vernon Dvorak, of the U.S. National Oceanic and Atmospheric Administration's environmental satellite service. It did not come into general use until the 1980s, but is now the worldwide standard for determining present and near-future intensity. Cyclones tend to be self-amplifying systems that grow predictably until they reach maximum potential intensity. But direct measurements of temperature, wind speed, and pressure are seldom available, so forecasters rely on satellite imagery of cloud patterns — which have visual characteristics, known as signatures, that change predictably — allowing them to use the complicated rules and procedures of Dvorak technique to estimate future changes in intensity over time.

Dwt: Deadweight tonnage.

Dyak: A pirate of Borneo or Sarawak.

D'ye hear there?: [1] Conventional 18th century follow-up to a Command, intended to ensure it had been fully understood. The proper response would have been "anan." [2] Nowadays it is a "heads up" call preceding any routine announcement on an RN warships main broadcast system. Cf. "now hear this."

Dye marker: Brilliant coloring matter which is dropped to spread in or on the water to indicate the position of a person overboard, or a point of action (e.g., where to execute a turn, drop an amphibious craft, etc.).

Dynamic positioning: As the exploitation of sea bed resources moves into deeper waters, it becomes increasingly difficult and costly to employ conventional offshore mooring techniques. One alternative is dynamic positioning, in which thrusters and propellers keep an unmoored vessel in position or on course. A computer-control system calculates the forces that thrusters must produce in order to control the vessel's motion in its three horizontal degrees of freedom — surge, sway, and yaw — while under the influence of winds, waves, and currents. Some vessels, such as dredgers, and cable laying vessels need to follow a pre-determined track. Others, such as those associated with the oil and gas industry, need to weathervane about a specified spot. Operating costs for dynamic positioning are always higher than for passive mooring, mainly because of the human interface required for monitoring and automated control, and may become prohibitive in extreme weather conditions.

Dynamo: [1] A machine or device that converts kinetic energy to electrical energy, generally using electromagnetic induction. The term is usually used for the generation of direct current. *See also* generator, electric motor. [2] Code-name for the Dunkirk evacuation in 1940.

E

Eagre: A tidal bore or flood.

Ear banger: USN enlisted slang for a sycophant or toady.

Earing: A small line used to fasten the upper corners of a square-sail to its yard.

Earring: An item of jewelry worn in the ear or on its lobe. Plain gold earrings have been worn by seamen since the sixteenth century, reflecting an even older fisherman's tradition that pierced ears made a man lively and improved his eyesight. Latterly they became a deep-sea sailor's "insurance policy" against drowning. He would buy a pair of rings (which had to be of pure gold), cut one and push it through his ear lobe, then throw the other overboard as an offering, calling out "Oh Davy Jones! I pray you to protect me." The theory was that the demon would recognize the drowning man's ring as one of a pair he had already accepted and, having had his due, would guide the man to shore.

Ease/Easy: [1] Command to do something slowly. [2] To gradually reduce the amount of rudder as a ship nears the desired course. [3] To slacken a line carefully. [4] A ship is said to roll easy when she does so slowly and smoothly without sudden jerks.

East Greenland Current: Consists of low salinity and low temperature water flowing south along the east cost of Greenland and into the Denmark Strait.

East India Company: The Honourable East India Company, often colloquially referred to as "John Company," was one of the earliest joint-stock companies. A Royal Charter, issued by Elizabeth I on 31st December 1600, gave the company a monopoly on all trade in the East Indies, which gradually evolved from a commercial venture to one that virtually ruled India, with a large bureaucracy, an army, and a navy known as the Bombay Marine. It was dissolved following the Indian Rebellion of 1857.

East Siberian Current: Flows through the Chukchi Sea to join the Bering Current.

Easterly/Westerly: [1] Coming from the east or west (wind, for example). [2] Situated or moving toward the east or west (e.g., side, course, voyage, or current). Even sailors can be confused by these contradictory conventions which call movement from east to west "easterly" if referring to a current, but "westerly" if speaking of wind or the movement of a ship. It is therefore preferable to avoid ambiguity by using the suffix "-ward" for currents, since an eastward current moves toward the east, as does an easterly wind.

Easting: The distance actually made good in an easterly direction on any course that has an easterly component.

Eastward/Westward: *See* Easterly/Westerly.

EAT: Earliest arrival time (ETA is more common).

Eat: [1]To make progress slowly in difficult conditions (e.g., eat to windward): {2} To corrode, as metal, by rust. [3] To wear away or destroy gradually. [4] To eat the wind out of another vessel, is to gain slowly to windward of her.

Ebb: Tide falling and flowing away from the shore (cf. rise).

E-Boat: Allied World War II designation of the German Schnellboot.

ECCM: Counter-electronic countermeasures.

ECDIS: Electronic Chart Display and Information System.

Echo: [1] The reflection of a sound or electronic signal from a target to a receiver (e.g., radar or sonar). [2] The letter "E" in the NATO phonetic alphabet.

Echo sounder: A depth-measuring instrument in which a pulse of energy is converted to sound and transmitted downward to bounce from the bottom or intermediate object back to a transducer.

Echograph: The recording made by an echo sounder.

ECL: Equator crossing longitude.

Eddy: A frequently circular local current of water or air running counter to the main flow (cf. countercurrent, eddy-resistance).

Eddy-resistance: One of the three principal causes of opposition to movement through water and is essentially created by any projection on the surface of the hull that causes swirls and whirlpools to form. It takes energy to make these phenomena and that energy is subtracted from the power available to drive the vessel forward (cf. skin-friction, wave-resistance).

EDD: Estimated delivery date.

EDO: Engineering duty only (USN).

EEC: European Economic Community.

EEZ: Exclusive economic zone.

EFZ: Exclusive fishing zone.

Egede's serpent: Hans Poulsen Egede was a Norwegian Lutheran missionary who went to Greenland in 1721, with the support of the Danish government, to set up missions among the Inuit. He translated Christian texts into the native language and became known as the Apostle of Greenland. In 1741, he published *A Full and Particular Relation of my Voyage to Greenland*, in which he tells of sighting a sea serpent. Translations vary, and this is a composite based on various versions of his description:

> On the 6th of July 1734, when off the south coast of Greenland, there appeared to us a very terrible sea-animal, whose head, when raised, was on level with

our main-top. Its snout was long and sharp, and it blew water almost like a whale. It had broad large paws or flippers and the body was, as it were, covered with a hard scaly skin, very wrinkled rough and uneven. In other respects it was as a serpent; and when it dived, its tail, which was raised in the air, appeared to be a whole ship's length from its body.

A reproduction of Egede's original sketch of the monster now appears in *Dragons, Unicorns, and Sea Serpents* by Charles Gould (Dover, 2002). His depiction of a possible Kraken doesn't quite fit a giant squid or the speculative super-eel (*see* appendix), but could be either if we allow for the unreliability of eyewitness accounts, especially of things seen for only a few seconds while under considerable stress.

Egg code: The World Meteorological Organization system of sea ice symbology is popularly referred to as the "egg code" because it presents data inside an oval designed to make a large amount of information available at a glance. The "egg" is divided into four sections: [1] gives the ice coverage of an area determined by its concentration. [2] breaks down the concentration in terms of thickness. [3] shows the stage of development of the ice as determined by its age, from new and thin to multi-year and thick, and [4] defines the form and type of the ice and its floes.

Egyptian naval architecture: Dispersed in a desert-bound strip along the banks of the mighty River Nile, Egyptians took naturally to the water and were among the first serious shipwrights. Nile winds are so constant that the hieroglyph for northbound movement (even on land) was a boat under sail, while that for southbound travel was one under oars. Bundles of papyrus stalks lashed together were their earliest form of transport. These were cheap and easily manufactured, but had short service lives. During the Predynastic Period, around 3000 BCE, larger reed boats were characterized by sharply-upturned bows and sterns, the classical Egyptian hull shape for centuries to come. They were propelled by paddles or a rectangular sail, and equipped with one or two large steering oars.

By the Old Kingdom (2575–2134 BCE), wood was the preferred construction material, retaining the traditional upward angling above the water line at both ends. The Nile is a tranquil river, even in spate, so shipwrights did not have to provide the rigidity needed to cope with storms or ocean waves. Dispensing with ribs, keel, and planking, they pegged together thick blocks of acacia wood, with a few athwartship beams. As late as the fifth century BCE, the historian Herodotus reported that Egyptian trading craft were "assembled as though building a brick wall."

In the absence of a keel to support the butt of a mast, bi-pod spars were stepped from the side walls of the hull in an inverted "V." These could easily be un-stepped for changes of propulsion between oars and sail. Depending on the size of ship, from one to six large steering oars were controlled by helmsmen standing on the high stern. This design proved so effective that it remained essentially unchanged through the thousand years of the Middle and New Kingdoms (2040–1070 BCE). With minor modifications, it was applied to a wide range of river craft from small skiffs to much larger vessels.

In the early 1950s, a dismantled river boat — probably first used to transport the corpse of Pharaoh Khufu (Cheops) to its place of purification and embalmment, and then stored ready for his voyage to the afterworld — was discovered close to the face of the large pyramid at Giza (see *Khufu* ship). This vessel, which dates to 2528 BCE or thereabouts, has now been reassembled. It is 43.6 metres (143 ft) long with a displacement of about forty tonnes (39 long tons). Egyptians of this period must also have constructed special load-carrying river barges for the transportation of obelisks and immense pyramid building blocks.

The successful river design lacked the rigidity needed by seagoing vessels, but a model found in Pharaoh Sahure's mortuary temple shows that Egyptian naval architects had contrived ingenious methods of preparing vessels for service in open waters. As a substitute for ribs, they provided athwartships support by girdling the entire vessel with a pair of ropes, pulled taut by a third rope zig-zagged between them. Then, in the absence of a keel, they provided fore-and-aft support by running a huge hawser, known as a "hogging truss," over a series of props from bow to stern, tightening it with a pole, like a tourniquet. The sophistication of this design indicates a long period of previous maritime activity. Sahure's ships, which lacked the sharply-angled bow and stern typical of Nile boats, must have been fast and reasonably seaworthy, but could never have been as reliable as keeled vessels.

Eight up!: When signal flag number 8 is hoisted it means "enemy in sight." Hence, "eight up!" whispered by an RN signalman warns that a senior officer is approaching.

Eilean Mòr Mystery: Known as The Hunters because of their toll on shipping, the Flannan Isles are a group of 45 rocks and islets in the outer Hebrides off the northwest coast of Scotland. Only seven are big enough to be called islands, the two largest of these being steep-cliffed Eilean Tighe (house island) and Eilean Mòr (big island). In the 10th century, Scottish monks fleeing Viking raiders arrived on the latter and dedicated a chapel to Saint Flann. Having given the saint's name to the islands, their monastery was abandoned during the 16th century, leaving the island uninhabited until a manned lighthouse was built in 1899.

Early in 1901, Captain Holman, master of the freighter *Tennessee*, complained to the Northern Lighthouse Board that no warning beam had been visible when he passed the islands at midnight on 15th December. Meanwhile, lighthouse tender *Hesperus* had left on a routine visit, arriving off Eilean Mòr on 26th December. Her master, Captain Harvie, was surprised not to be greeted by the usual happily waving keepers. Nor was there any response to blasts of the steam whistle and siren, followed by a signal rocket. Relief keeper Joe Moore landed, but soon returned, pale and agitated, to report that all three keepers had vanished.

Buoymaster Allan Macdonald with seamen Lamont and Campbell then climbed up to the lighthouse 101 meters (330 feet) above sea level. Everything seemed to be in order. The gate was closed and secured, beds had been made, the table was laid for the keepers' dinner, and their lunch plates and pans had been washed and put away. The lamp had been trimmed and its reservoir filled, the last entry in the log, made at 0900 hrs on 15th December, mentioned nothing untoward, while the duty slateboard recorded weather and wind conditions, plus the times the lantern should be illuminated that night and extinguished next morning. However the full fuel reservoir indicated it had never been lit.

An inventory of clothing showed that Thomas Marshall had been wearing full foul weather gear, James Ducat had on a jacket with seaboots, and Donald McArthur was in his shirtsleeves. This seemed to indicate that Marshall had been outside and the others had hurriedly joined him. Then it was noticed that the iron tramway rails and railings between landing platform and lighthouse "had been displaced and twisted in a manner difficult to believe," that the lifeboat normally securely roped to them had been torn away and was missing, and that a rock weighing more than a ton had been displaced.

As with many inexplicable maritime phenomena, speculation was rife. Land-based rumors suggested that one of the keepers had gone mad, murdered the others, and thrown himself into the sea in remorse, or that all the men had been abducted by foreign spies, or that a gigantic seabird had swooped down and taken them. Superstitious and imaginative seamen subscribed to the idea that Davy Jones had been so furious when the newly-constructed lighthouse cheated him of his accustomed harvest of shipwrecked mariners that he had risen out of the sea to register his displeasure by wreaking havoc on the island before abducting the keepers and imprisoning them.

A more mundane explanation — substantiated by the fact that 35 feet (11 meters) of turf had been ripped off the top of a 200 foot (61 meter) headland — is that a powerful rogue wave crashed over the high cliffs and swept on up the steep hill, washing the men away as they rushed out to secure vital equipment at the landing platform. On the other hand, perhaps the wave really was Davy's manifestation and Ducat, Marshall, and McArthur are still languishing in his locker.

Eke: [1] In general use, to supply something lacking or make short supply last longer. [2] In shipbuilding, to lengthen a timber by joining another to it.

El Niño Southern Oscillation Event: A periodic disruption of the ocean-atmosphere system in the tropical Pacific that can have important consequences for weather and climate around the globe, including destructive floods and devastating bush fires. Known as ENSO events, they occur irregularly every 2–7 years due to warmer than usual sea surface temperatures. The name was coined by South American fishers who noted that the phenomenon often appears near Christmastime (El Niño, which means "The Little Boy" is a synonym for Christ Child). An El Niño is often followed by a La Niña event.

Elbow: [1] A sharp change of direction in a river or channel. [2] A promontory. [3] A pipe or pipe connection having a right-angle bend.

Electric drive: A propulsion system in which main engines drive generators that send electrical power to motors which drive the propellers. With this system, overall efficiency can be improved by taking surplus units off-line and running the remaining generators at close to full output. It is also a partial answer to the problem of propulsion machinery and drive shafts that occupy space otherwise available for weaponry and ammunition in warships, or passengers and cargo in merchantmen. Moreover, electric drives can be placed further aft, reducing the length of propeller shafts for in-hull motors, or to zero for those in external pods.

Electric drive is far from new. A battery-powered boat motored along Moscow's Neva River as early as 1834, and by the 1880s electric propulsion was a viable competitor to mechanical drives for passenger liners. When launched in 1932, SS *Normandie* was the largest and fastest ship in the world (*see* Blue Riband), and is still the most powerful steam-turbo-electric propelled passenger vessel ever built. Today's largest is the cruise ship *Freedom of the Seas* whose diesel-electric engines power podded drive propulsion.

As for warships, submarines have, of necessity, always relied on electric propulsion, while the USN enthusiastically adopted the system for surface ships in the early 1900s. Its first aircraft carrier USS *Langley* (the former collier *Jupiter*) had hybrid-electric drive, and the system was installed in *Lexington* Class carriers, and *Tennessee* and *Colorado* Class battleships. Both the United States and Royal Navies have announced that their next generation surface warships will feature electrical propulsion. *See also* CODAG–electric.

Electric motor: A machine that converts electrical energy into mechanical energy. Motors and generators have many similarities, being essentially the same machine operating in the opposite "direction."

Electro-ballistics: The art or science of measuring the velocity of projectiles by means of electricity.

Electromagnetic Railgun: This emerging technology uses high power electromagnetic energy instead of chemical propellants to propel a projectile farther and faster than conventional artillery. Two parallel metallic rails are connected to a power supply. When a conductive projectile is placed on them, it completes the circuit, creating a magnetic field which accelerates the projectile along the rails. No explosives are required to fire the weapon and, since the high-velocity projectiles destroy targets by kinetic energy, no explosive rounds need to be stored in the ship's magazine. A successful experimental firing was conducted at the United States Naval Surface Warfare Center, Dahlgren, Virginia, on January 31, 2008.

Electronic chart display and information system: A specific form of shipborne computer-based navigation information system that complies with International Maritime Organization regulations and can be used in lieu of paper navigation charts in some areas. A true ECDIS displays information from electronic navigational charts and integrates position information from the global positioning System and other navigational sensors, such as radar, fathometer and automatic identification systems. It may also display additional navigation-related information, such as Sailing Directions. The term is often incorrectly used to refer to non–IMO-compliant types of electronic chart display (cf. Raster chart display system).

Electronic countermeasures: That division of electronic warfare involving actions taken to prevent or reduce an enemy's effective use of the electromagnetic spectrum.

Electronic navigational chart: An official database created by a national hydrographic office for use with an Electronic Chart Display and Information System. An electronic chart must conform to International Hydrographic Organization standards before it can be certified as meeting International Maritime Organisation performance requirements (cf. Raster navigational chart).

Electronic warfare: The use of electromagnetic or directed energy to [1] Determine, exploit, degrade, neutralize, or prevent hostile use of the electromagnetic spectrum. [2] Jam or distort enemy communications. [3] Generally mislead the foe, while preserving that spectrum for friendly use.

Electro-Technical Officer (ETO): This relatively new merchant rank refers to a certificated marine engineer with supplementary qualifications in the operation and maintenance of increasingly complex and vital electrical, radar, and computer-control equipment.

Elevation: [1] The vertical angle of a gun barrel above the horizontal. [2] The angle of sight of a heavenly body above the horizontal. [3] The height of a place above sea level.

Elevator: [1] The moving platform used to raise or lower aircraft between hangar deck and flight deck. [2] The hinged horizontal surface used to control the pitch of an aircraft.

ELINT: Electronic Intelligence.

Elliptic stem: A rounded bow, frequently seen on tugboats, where a curve is more suitable for pushing than a sharp stem.

Elliptic stern: A short rounded counter.

Elmo: *See* Saint Erasmus.

***Elokomin* fuelling rig:** An arrangement of hoses

and tackles developed on board USS *Elokomin* to improve fuel transfer while underway.

EM: [1] Enlisted Man (USN). [2] Electrician's Mate (USN).

Embankment: An earth, stone, or concrete construction erected to shut in or confine a river.

Embargo: An order by a state forbidding foreign merchantmen to enter its ports, or preventing any merchantmen from leaving them.

Embark: [1] To enter into a ship as passengers or troops (but not as crew who normally "come aboard"). [2] To put or receive something into a vessel.

Embarked aviation: *See* aviation support.

Embay: To put, force into, or confine a vessel in a bay.

Emcon: Emissions control (in electronic warfare).

Emergency power system: A battery- or generator-operated backup electrical system capable of supplying power to all essential areas of a ship. Normally placed as high as possible in the superstructure so as to be above any water entering a damaged vessel. *See also* uninterruptible power supply.

Emergency speed: The command to run a vessel's propulsion machinery as rapidly as possible, with no consideration of normal safety precautions such as limiting lubricating oil temperature or controlling steam pressure. Such conditions can only be briefly sustained due to the strain on machinery and equipment. (*See* standard speed, full speed, flank speed.)

EMP: Electromagnetic Pulse.

Empress of Ireland: This Canadian Pacific passenger liner was rammed and sunk by Norwegian collier *Storstad* in the St. Lawrence River on 30th May 1914 with the loss of 1,078 lives (73 percent of all those on board). *See also* Crippen's curse.

EMRG: Electromagnetic rail gun.

En flute: Placing a ship en flûte means removing some or all of its artillery (the open gunports being said to look like the finger-holes of a flute). This is usually done either to make room for cargo or troops, or to demonstrate peaceful intent. (The term is French.)

ENC: Electronic navigational chart.

Encapsulated: Said of a torpedo that is enclosed in a deep-water mine to be automatically released for attack when stimulated by a passing vessel.

Encipher: To convert plain text into unintelligible language using a letter-substitution cipher.

Encode: To convert plain text into unintelligible language using a word-substitution code.

Encrypt: Generic term for the conversion of plain text into unintelligible language, including codes and ciphers.

End of mission: In the USN, a command to terminate gunfire on a specific target.

Endurance: The length of time an aircraft can continue flying, or a ship can continue operating, without refueling.

Endurance distance: The total distance that a ship can be self-propelled at a specified speed.

Enfilade: Gunfire directed along the long axis of a target.

Engaged in fishing: Classification under the Navigation Rules covering any vessel deploying fishing apparatus which restricts its maneuverability. Trolling lines and similar non-restrictive gear are excluded.

Engagement: In military terminology, an encounter, conflict, or battle.

Engine: A mechanical contrivance for converting thermal energy into mechanical energy.

Engine room: Space set aside for the operation of main propulsion and auxiliary engines (cf. propulsion machinery, machinery spaces).

Engine-room/engine-order telegraph: *See* Telegraph.

Engineering Duty Officer: A USN line officer restricted to engineering and designated EDO.

Englehardt boat: A collapsible lifeboat with a capacity of about 40 persons, having a slatted wooden bottom and canvas sides that could be collapsed to allow compact stowage. The ill-fated RMS *Titanic* carried four such "collapsibles" three of which were successfully opened and launched. Often confused with the Berthon boat.

Enlist: To engage voluntarily in military service.

Enlisted: Refers to a non-commissioned or warranted person in the United States armed forces (*see* rating). Usually followed by "man" or "woman."

Enlistment: The period of time for which a person agrees to enlist.

Ensign: [1] The flag denoting nationality (cf. colors). [2] The lowest commissioned rank in a British guards regiment. [3] The lowest commissioned rank in the United States and Royal New Zealand navies. Essentially, a naval Ensign is an on-the-job apprentice, similar to and ranking with a Midshipman in the British navy, or an Acting Sub-lieutenant in the Australian and Canadian navies (although none of these is commissioned). In the USN, the most junior ensign on board is colloquially called the George Ensign (from JORG = Junior Officer Requiring Guidance), while the most senior is the Bull Ensign (reputedly after Admiral "Bull" Halsey who assigned specific duties to that officer).

Ensign staff: A short flagpole at the stern of a vessel, on which the national ensign is flown (*see* flag etiquette).

ENSO: El Niño Southern Oscillation Event.

Entrance: The immersed portion of the hull forward of the beam. In general, the slimmer the entrance the faster the ship.

Entrepôt: [1] A warehouse where goods are received for distribution, trans-shipment, or repackaging. [2] In the original French, the term also refers to a port which serves as a centre for import and export.

Entry port: [1] In a merchantman, a large opening in the side for loading cargo or boarding crew. [2] In a three-decker warship, a port cut down to the level of the middle deck. Not to be confused with port of entry.

EOB: Enemy order of battle.

EOD: Explosive Ordnance Disposal.

EOM: End of message.

EOOW: Engineer officer of the watch.

Episodic wave: A freak wave produced by swells which are in opposition to the main tidal current.

Eplimnion: The uppermost layer of sea water. *See* thermocline, hypolimnion, and mixed layer.

Equator: *See* terrestrial equator.

Equatorial currents: North of the terrestrial equator, ocean currents tend to flow clockwise, while to the south they flow counter-clockwise (*see* Coriolis effect). In between are weak countercurrents flowing in the opposite directions.

Equinoctial gale: A storm with violent winds and rain occurring at or near the time of an equinox and popularly, but erroneously, believed to be associated with it.

Equinox: Either of two times a year, midway between the solstices, when the lengths of night and day are approximately equal.

Equipage: [1] In general, requisites for an undertaking. [2] In naval terminology, all non-consumable material needed for a vessel to perform her mission, including personnel, gear, tackle, and other essential equipment (cf. supplies).

Equipment: In logistics, all nonexpendable items needed to outfit or equip an individual or organization.

Erasmus: Was Bishop of Formiae in Italy, who fled to Mount Lebanon to escape the persecutions of Roman Emperor Diocletian. There he is said to have been fed by a raven until captured, tortured, and disemboweled, his intestines being pierced with red hot hooks and wound out of his body onto a nautical capstan while he was still alive. According to legend he survived this and numerous other torments under various Roman emperors to die a natural death in or about 303. He was canonized in 1610 by Pope Paul V. Also known as Saint Elmo, he is the patron of boatmen, sailors, and navigators, with authority over seasickness and storms. Not surprisingly, considering the nature of his martyrdom, he also exercises authority over abdominal pains, stomach problems, and related diseases. (*See also* Saint Elmo's Fire.)

Escape hatch: A watertight cover which allows emergency exit from a compartment when the normal way out is inaccessible.

Escape trunk: [1] A compartment on a submarine capable of accepting a rescue chamber or deep-dive rescue vehicle. [2] A vertical passage with ladders and emergency lighting rising from the lowest deck to allow rapid exit in case of fire or flooding.

Escarpment: An elongated, characteristically linear, steep slope, separating horizontal or gently sloping sectors of the sea floor in non-shelf areas. Often abbreviated to scarp.

Escort: [1] To accompany in order to protect or honor. [2] The ships, aircraft, or personnel providing an escort.

Escort Carrier: Towards the middle of World War II, the large and expensive fleet carriers were supplemented by small versions built on merchantman hulls as an emergency response to the inability of land-based aircraft to patrol or attack U-boats in mid–Atlantic. In the words of British naval aviator Hugh Popham, they were "unlovable little ships, slow (17 knots), jerry-built, utilitarian, and vulnerable, but the amount of work they did was prodigious." As well as being highly successful convoy escorts, "baby flattops," as they were nicknamed, proved invaluable as assault carriers to support amphibious operations, ferried replacement aircraft to theaters of war, and supplemented full-size carriers in combat. Seventy-seven were used by the USN and another thirty-three were leased to the RN and RCN. Also Jeep Carrier (cf. fleet carrier, light fleet carrier, and MAC-Ship).

Escutcheon: A board or raised lettering on the stern of a vessel indicating its name and port of registry.

Esk: A type of Viking longship mentioned in the *Anglo-Saxon Chronicle*. Little is known about it, but the text indicates it had fewer than sixty oars (*see* Saxon seapower). The vessel may have been named after the River Esk in northern England, on which the Norsemen had a settlement called Hvitely (white town) now transliterated to Whitby.

Establishment: The complement or quota of officers and rates assigned to a ship or station.

Estimated position: An approximation based on tides, winds, currents, course, speed, and elapsed time since the last known position. These are more factors than are involved in estimating a position by dead reckoning.

Estuarine: Of or pertaining to an estuary.

Estuary: The wide tidal mouth of a river.

ETA: Estimated time of arrival (also EAT).

ETD: Estimated time of departure.

Evacuation control ship: In an amphibious operation, a ship designated as the control point for landing craft, amphibious vehicles, and helicopters removing casualties from the beaches. Embarked medical personnel perform emergency surgery, and distribute wounded throughout the attack force in accordance with available beds and specialized medical facilities.

Evaporator: A device for vaporizing seawater to make it salt-free.

Evasive action: Tactics such as sinuating or zigzagging designed to confuse a would-be attacker.

Even keel: Floating on the designated waterline so that draft is the same both fore and aft. Is not influenced by heel, which is a sideways list.

Evening watch: The duty shift from 2000 to 2400 (8 P.M. to midnight). Also "first watch" or "first night watch."

Evergreens: Since the 18th century, British warships have hoisted a garland of evergreens to the masthead to signify that discipline has been relaxed and women visitors will be welcomed on board. A similar garland is hoisted on the day any member of the crew is to be married.

Evolution: [1] A movement or one of a series of movements to deploy warships in order of combat. [2] A tactical maneuver. [3] A sequence of actions such as those involved in setting a sail. [4] Gradual development from simple to more complex form.

EW: [1] Electronic warfare. [2] Early warning.

Exceptions clause: A standard provision of charter parties or bills of lading which exempts a shipowner or carrier from liability for losses, damage, or delays due to any one or more of:
• Act or omission of shipper.
• Act of God.
• Acts of public enemies, thieves, or pirates.
• Acts of war.
• Arrest.
• Assailment (assault).
• Embargo.
• Fire or arson.
• Force majeure.
• Hijacking.
• Latent defect.
• Quarantine.
• Restraint of princes or people.
• Riots or civil commotion.
• Seizure under legal process.
• Strikes or lockouts.
• Stoppage or restraint of labor.

Exclusive Economic Zone (EEZ): A sea area beyond and adjacent to a nation's territorial sea, extending up to 200 nautical miles (370 kilometers) from its baseline. In this zone, as defined in The United Nations Convention on the Law of the Sea, a coastal state has

> sovereign rights for the purpose of exploring and exploiting, conserving and managing the natural resources, whether living or non-living, of the waters superjacent to the sea bed and its subsoil, and with regard to other activities for the economic exploitation and exploration of the zone, such as the production of energy from the water, currents and winds.

The Convention also gives jurisdiction over other defined activities such as marine scientific research. The United States has not ratified this section of the UN convention. (*See also* patrimonial sea.)

Exclusive Fishing Zone (EFZ): Since the 1960s it has been generally recognized that a coastal nation can claim extensive, but not exclusive, fishing rights seaward from its baseline. These are normally extensions of and follow the limits prescribed for the nation's exclusive economic zone. Coastal nations such as the United States who have not chosen to ratify the UN convention may unilaterally claim what the U.S. calls a "fishery conservation zone." *See also* right of fishery.

Executive Branch: RN term for officers concerned with working and navigating a ship, as opposed to those of (for example) the engineering, medical, or supply branches. The USN equivalent is Line Officer.

Executive curl: A twist of braid above the uppermost stripe of an RN officer's rank insignia. initially restricted to officers of the Seaman (now executive) Branch. Since 1918, however, non-executive officers have also worn the curl, with their specialties identified by stripes of colored cloth (*see* specialist officers).

Executive Officer: [1] In the USN, this is not a rank but a title, applied to the second-in-command of a ship, shore establishment, or air squadron. The executive officer (usually abbreviated to "Exec" or "XO") is responsible for day-to-day operations, thus freeing the captain to concentrate on planning and directing the mission (the RN equivalent was first lieutenant, but XO is now common). [2] In the RN, the term also refers to an officer fully qualified to navigate and fight a ship at sea and eligible for command of a naval vessel (the USN equivalent is line officer).

Exercise: A rehearsal, drill, or practice simulation. May be as large as fleet maneuvers or as small as lifeboat drill.

Exonerate: [1] To free from responsibility or blame. [2] This term, which has completely lost its nautical meaning, formerly referred to the discharge of cargo. (Latin ex onustus = from freight.)

Expansion hatch: A hatch with high coamings, set above a liquid cargo tank to allow its contents to expand or contract with rise or fall in temperature.

Expansion tank: A small tank, pipe-connected to the main cargo tank, which serves the same purpose as an expansion hatch, but on a larger scale.

Expansion trunk: A trunk rising from the main cargo tank, providing greater expansion space than either an expansion hatch or tank.

Expeditionary Strike Force: One or more carrier strike groups combined with one or more amphibious ready groups, and supplemented by additional ships and aircraft for a particular offensive operation.

Explosion vessel: Similar to a fireship, but crammed with explosives rather than combustibles. Used as early as the 17th century, and as recently as 1942 when the old destroyer HMS *Campbeltown* was rammed into the dock at St. Nazire and exploded.

Explosive: Any substance tending to expand with force and noise due to rapid chemical change.

Exposed waters: [1] United States Coast Guard term for sea areas more than twenty nautical miles (37 kilometers) from the mouth of a harbor providing safe refuge. [2] Any other waters the USCG or another national authority determines present special hazards.

Exposure suit: Special survival clothing designed to partially withstand immersion in cold water.

Extraterritoriality: This exemption from local laws and regulations, similar to that still accorded to diplomats, was formerly extended to the merchantmen of certain powerful nations. Nowadays, all vessels have to obey local laws and regulations as well as those of their flag country.

Eye: [1] A circular or tear-shaped metal fitting (also eyelet). [2] A loop in a rope. [3] A hole in the shank of an anchor. [4] The direction from which the wind is blowing. [5] The circular region of relatively light winds and fair weather at the center of a tropical cyclone.

Eyebolt: A bolt with an eye at one end.

Eyebrow: A metal flange or lip just above a port-(hole) that shields it from water, whether falling as rain or running off the deck. Also rigol.

Eyes: Term for the foremost part of the weather deck, as far forward as it is possible for a lookout to stand. The term may refer to the eyes of the figureheads which used to decorate wooden ships, or to the eyes (oculi) painted on Mediterranean craft from the age of Pharaohs to the present day.

Eyes right/left: In feudal days, military personnel had the privilege of looking their overlords straight in the eye while raising their caps or visors as a sign of respect. By contrast serfs and slaves were forbidden to stare at their "betters" and had to stand aside with heads bowed and eyes averted. In 1740 a military textbook entitled *The New Art of War* stated; "Each officer is to time his salute so as to pull off his hat when the person he salutes is almost opposite him." An integral part of the military salute is still to look directly at the person being saluted. Hence the command eyes right! (or left) is given to columns passing in review.

Eyesplice: A splice at the end of a line which creates a loop for hanging over bollards or cleats. Usually protected by a thimble.

F

FAA: Fleet Air Arm (RN).

Face: [1] USN command to turn on the heel to left or right as ordered (the RN term is turn). [2] The after surface of a propeller blade (confusingly, the forward surface is the "back").

Face curtain: A sheet of heavy fabric installed in an aircraft cockpit. When pulled down it both activates the ejection seat and protects pilot and crew from wind blast.

Face the music: First recorded in the mid–1800s, this phrase, meaning to confront the consequences of one's actions, is believed to refer to the "Rogue's March" which was played when a dishonorably-discharged person was "drummed out" of naval or military service.

Facial hair: [1] In the United States military, moustaches are allowed in all branches, but beards are generally forbidden on the basis of hygiene and the need to seal gas masks. The Navy did allow beards for a time in the 1970s and 1980s, but subsequently banned them again. The Coast Guard allowed beards until 1986. Special Operations Forces have been allowed to wear beards in middle-eastern countries in order to better fit in with the indigenous population. [2] In the British military, Article 1105 of Queens Regulations and Admiralty Instructions forbids the wearing of moustaches *without* beards by officers and men of the Royal Navy (*see* permission to grow). Personnel of the Royal Marines, Army, and Air Force may wear moustaches, but not beards, except in extreme climatic conditions or for medical reasons. Special forces may wear beards when on covert intelligence operations or behind enemy lines. *See also* haircutting.

Factory ship: A floating base for fisher or whaling fleets, fitted with equipment to prepare catch for the market — processing and canning for the former, flensing and barreling for the latter. *See also* processing a whale.

Fag: [1] RN lower deck slang for a cigarette. [2] Derogatory term for a homosexual (short for faggot).

Fag-end: Nautical slang for the extreme end of a rope.

Fag out: [1] To fray the end of a rope. [2] In common usage, to tire or exhaust.

Fair: [1] To adjust or align a hull or its component parts. [2] Wind that blows in the desired direction (called "fair" even if of gale force). [3] Tide which flows in the desired direction. [4] Clement weather. [5] In reasonably good condition.

Fairing: A streamlining structure added to a ship or aircraft.

Fairlead: A fitting through or over which a rope, line, or cable can be led so as to change direction. Unlike a tackle, a fairlead provides no mechanical advantage.

Fairwater: A casting, or an assembly of plate, that improves the flow of water past an area or feature of the hull.

Fairwater cap/sleeve: A conical cap or casting which serves as a fairwater for the propeller shaft.

Fairway: [1] The navigable part of a river or enclosed body of water. [2] The usual course for entering a harbor. [3] The usual path between ports. [4] This nautical term has been adopted by golfers to refer to the mowed area of a course lying between tee and green.

Fake: [1] A single turn or tier of rope. [2] To lay out a rope in a coil or series of loops so that it will run freely without kinking or fouling. Also flake. [3] A coil of rope which has been faked down and is ready for running (aka Flemish coil or French coil).

Falklands Current: A north-easterly flow from Cape Horn into the Atlantic Ocean. Also Maldives Current.

Fall(s): [1] Generally, the line(s) that, together with blocks, constitute a hoisting tackle. [2] Specifically, the running part of the line that is between the blocks.

Fall! A Fall!: Traditional whaler's cry to indicate a harpoon has been effectively delivered.

Fall astern: To drop behind.

Fall in: [1] The Command for troops to assemble in ranks. [2] To "fall in with" is to meet another vessel.

Fall of shot: The point of impact of shellfire. Used to calculate corrections to the aim.

Fall off: To change course to leeward.

Fall out: [1] The Command for troops to disperse from their ranks. [2] Of a hull, to get wider or broaden.

Falling tide: That part of the tide cycle between high and low water when the depth of water is decreasing. The opposite condition is a rising tide.

False colors: Improper national identification. Often used illegally by pirates, but otherwise an accepted ruse de guerre for [1] A merchantman hoping to avoid capture by a belligerent, or [2] A warship running down on an enemy (provided the proper colors are hoisted before combat starts). *See also* bamboozle and flag verification.

False keel: An extension to the keel intended to provide lateral resistance and thus reduce leeway. It also protects the true keel if the vessel runs aground.

False ports: *See* dummy ports.

Fan: To brace the upper yardarms slightly aft to benefit from differences in wind speed at their height above the water.

Fancywork: Ornamental decoration, gingerbread.

Fanning: Sailing slowly in a light breeze.

Fanny: The semi-official name attached to a small round "mess kettle" of about eight pints (4½ liters) capacity issued to British seamen. It had a grisly origin. In April 1867 a nine-year-old girl named Frances (Fanny) Adams was murdered. Her killer cut the body into small pieces, and some of these were rumored to have been found in nearby Royal Clarence Victualing Yard. This was almost exactly at the time that victualing yards began to issue cans of corned mutton to the fleet and, inevitably, the meat was nicknamed Fanny Adams. Sailors found the opened cans (which resembled small paint pots) useful for carrying food and the name carried over to the official issue which appeared later.

Fanny Adams: [1] RN lower deck slang for canned meat or stew. [2] Nothing at all; in phrases such as "Sweet Fanny Adams" or "All my eye and Fanny Adams." *See also* Fanny.

Fantail: [1] A rounded counter extending beyond the sternpost of a vessel to create an exaggerated overhang. [2] USN term for the open after section of a warship's main deck.

FAO: [1] Forward Air Observer. [2]] Forward Artillery Observer. [3] Finance & Accounting Officer.

Fare: [1] An archaic word for "travel" or "wander." Still used in composite words such as seafarer and farewell. [2] The price charged for transportation. [3] A paying passenger on a ship, aircraft, train, or other means of public transport. [4] Range of food, for example, the fare served by a restaurant.

FAS (Free Alongside Ship): *See* Incoterms.

Fashion Show: USN slang for a form of remedial instruction in which a slovenly sailor is required to stand inspection dressed consecutively in each service uniform.

FAST: Fleet antiterrorism security team (USN/USMC).

Fast: [1] Firmly fixed in place (cf. make fast, hold fast). [2] Speedy.

Fast cruise: USN term for a series of drills and exercises which simulate duties and activities while underway, but are carried out at moorings.

Fast ice: Sea ice attached to the shore, to an ice front, or between icebergs.

Fata Morgana: A maritime mirage which makes objects float in the air and seem taller than they really are. The original Fata Morgana, also known as Morgan le Fay, was a fairy enchantress skilled in the art of changing shape. In one traditional story she was King Arthur's sister and learned many of her skills from Merlin the Magician.

Father: Affectionate RN slang for a well-liked commanding flag officer.

Fathom: Many units of measurement are named after body parts. We still measure horses in hands, almost everything in feet, and depth of water by the six-foot span known as a fathom. [1] As a noun, the term is derived from Old Norse fathmr (via Old English fæthm) meaning outstretched arms, and an early Act of the British Parliament quaintly defined it as "The length of a man's arms around the object of his affections." [2] As a verb, the term refers to the nautical practice of casting a leadline to determine the depth of water and nature of the bottom. [3] In common usage, fathom is a metaphor for grasping or comprehending the nature of a problem or difficulty by getting to the bottom of it.

Fathom Marks: *See* leadline.

Fathometer: Proprietary trade name for a type of echo sounder.

Favorable/favourable: Said of a wind or current which assists movement in the desired direction.

Fax: Facsimile.

Fay: A shipbuilding term, meaning to join two pieces together with no perceptible space between them. Formerly applied to timbers, but now extended to cover riveted or welded joints.

Fayfena: A thirty-oared Japanese galley.

FCS: Fire Control System.

Feather: [1] The plume created by a submarine periscope moving through the water. [2] The foamy spray at the stem of a moving craft. [3] To sail so close to the wind that the forward edge of the sail luffs. [4] To turn the blade of an oar parallel to the water during the return stroke. [5] To adjust the pitch of a naval or aviation propeller so that it creates no forward thrust.

Feather merchant: [1] Formerly, described an unscrupulous supplier who added stones or other heavy material to the feathers sold in bulk by weight to the U.S. government for soldiers' pillows and mattresses. [2] In the U.S. Military, a person in a comfortable or easy assignment such as headquarters duty or other staff billet. [3] Often used for any civilian working for the U.S. military. [4] USN derogatory slang for a novice seaman, a newcomer to naval service, or a landlubber. [5] In general, a person who avoids responsibility and effort; a loafer (not in general use outside the USA).

Feedback: Evaluative or corrective information about the effect or result of an action or process.

Feeder current: A current that runs parallel to the beach, drawn by the suction of an outward-flowing rip current.

Feedwater: Preheated distilled water provided to a steamship's boilers.

Feel the way: To navigate strange waters with caution and frequent soundings.

Feint: [1] In general use; something designed to distract or mislead, feigned or counterfeit, a pretence or stratagem. [2] In military parlance, a tactic intended to giving the impression that a certain maneuver will take place, while in fact something else is intended.

Felloe: [1] The rim of a wheel (or segment of the rim) into which spokes are inserted. [2] One of the arched pieces that form the outer ring of a ship's steering wheel, into which both spokes and handles are fitted.

Felucca: A small Mediterranean coasting vessel with lateen sails on one or two masts and a small mizzen.

Fencible: A limited service soldier during the Napoleonic Wars, senior to yeomanry or volunteers, but junior to line regiments and Royal Marines. Only occasionally employed in sea service, but there was a land-based force of sea fencibles.

Fend off: To push away from, or prevent crashing into something.

Fender: A protective guard temporarily placed between a ship's side and another vessel or a pier and removed before getting under way. If left in place it is called a bumper.

Ferja: A Viking boat used for local cargo movement.

Ferret: A ship or aircraft equipped for the detection, location, recording, and analysis of electromagnetic radiation.

Ferrocement: A method of ship construction in which the hull is fabricated by laying a special cement over a basic shape of wire mesh.

Ferry: [1] To transport passengers, vehicles, or cargo. [2] A ship, boat, or raft, frequently purpose-built, employed for the transportation of people, automobiles or goods on a scheduled route across a relatively short body of water. [3] A complete system of boats, terminals and warehouses for the transportation or people, automobiles or goods across broader bodies of water.

Fetch: [1] The distance wind and waves can travel without interference. [2] The distance between the weather shore and the point where waves begin to form. [3] The stretch from headland to headland across a bay or gulf. [4] The distance a vessel must run to reach open water. [5] To begin to move or accelerate. [6] To reach or arrive at a destination. [7] To come to a halt. [8] To sight a landmark or another vessel. [9] To come onto a new tack (16th century, now obsolete).

FEU: Forty-foot equivalent unit (shipping container).

Feu de Joie: This French term for a celebratory bonfire also applies to a military salute performed on special occasions of public rejoicing. It consists of riflemen or musketeers firing sequentially, so that the noise of their shots passes rapidly and steadily from one to the next, down one rank and up another, to produce a long and continuous roll of sound.

FF: Hull classification symbol of a frigate.

FFG: Hull classification symbol of a guided missile frigate.

Fiber: [1] Any substance (such as cotton, flax, or hemp) that can be separated into threads and twisted or braided together (i.e., to make rope). [2] The word has other meanings in anatomy (nerve, muscle, or connective tissue), botany (slender, threadlike root), nutrition (bulk, dietary fiber, roughage), optics (optical fiber), and as a character trait (moral fiber).

Fiber optics: Guiding light by refraction, the principle that makes fiber optics possible, was first demonstrated by French scientists in the 1840s, and in 1870 Englishman John Tyndall discovered that light uses internal reflection to follow a specific path. Practical applications of this principle appeared early in the twentieth century, but it was not until the late 1950s that modern optical fibers appeared.

Unlike copper wire, an optical fiber cable is not electrical in nature, carrying information from one point to another in the form of light. A basic system consists of a transmitting device, to generate the light signal; an optical fiber cable, which carries the light; and a receiver, to accept the transmitted signal. Fiber optic networks are more powerful and versatile than traditional copper-wire networks, operating at very high speeds and providing high bandwidth.

During the second half of the twentieth century, this technology experienced a phenomenal rate of progress, and the U.S. military moved quickly to install fiber optic networks that provide increased information capability to users of high-tech weaponry, command and control systems, global positioning systems, inventory/transportation management programs, personnel/payroll record-keeping, and medical apparatus. Fiber optic systems, using floating radio antennae, provide submerged submarines with two-way communications for the first time in history, while similar technology allows them to deploy a floating optical fiber periscope from well below conventional periscope depth.

Fid: [1] A square bar of iron or wood used to secure or support a spar. [2] A wooden marlinspike. [3] A metal sailmaker's tool used for shaping grommets;

similar to a marlinspike but without the bulbous head.

Fiddle: [1] A small board forming a ledge or barrier to prevent things from sliding off a shelf or table in heavy weather. The name originated when the same purpose was achieved by cords stretched tightly between pegs so that they resembled violin strings. [2] To cheat, swindle, or falsify.

Fiddle block: A pair of sheaves in a single housing, one above the other, the lower being smaller than the upper. It lies flatter and more snugly to the yard than a double block, in which the sheaves are abreast of one another.

Fiddlehead: A billethead shaped like the scroll at the head of a violin. Used when there is no figurehead (cf. scrollhead).

Fiddler: *See* fifer & fiddler.

Fiddler's Green: According to an old jingle, this is a nautical nirvana where dead seamen find unlimited rum, tobacco, and compliant women in a paradise of perfect bliss and beauty.

> Now Fiddler's Green is the place I've heard tell
> Where sailormen go when they don't go to hell
> Just tell me old shipmates, I'm taking a trip mates
> And I'll see them some day in Fiddler's Green

Various superstitions say that their spirits are carried there by soul ships from European waters, and by birds of the petrel family from more distant seas. (*See* albatross, stormy petrel.)

Fid-hole: An opening in the heel of a mast or spar, through which a fid is passed to rest on the trestletrees on either side.

Fidley: [1] An open ventilation area above boilers or machinery spaces. [2] The grating covering such an area. [3] The steel frame around a ladder or hatch (also fiddley).

Field: [1] The background color or area of a flag. [2] A scene of action. [3] A range (field of view/vision).

Field day: Time set aside for housekeeping prior to an inspection (primarily USN).

Field ice: A large ice pack whose limits cannot be seen from shipboard.

Field of view: The area in the eyepiece of an optical instrument in which the image is visible.

Field of vision: The entire area that can be seen by the eyes when they are kept fixed in one direction.

Fife rail: A rail with holes for belaying pins, usually at the base of a mast.

Fifer & Fiddler: These were sailing navy musicians, rated as petty officers, who played to encourage manual labor at the capstan, and when hoisting, warping, or heaving (*see* Chanteys).

Fifie: A wide-beam Scottish herring drifter, with a dipping lugsail on the mainmast and a standing lugsail on the mizzen, both stepped far forward to allow maximum net-handling space at the stern. (Fife is an area of Scotland, situated between the Firth of Tay and the Firth of Forth.)

FIFO: Acronym for "first-in first-out." A warehousing term for a method of storage designed to minimize spoilage.

Figgie-dowdie: RN slang for boiled suet pudding, speckled with bits of dried fruit. "Figgie" obviously refers to the fruit (*see* plum duff), while "dowdie" is thought to refer to the dessert's plain or "dowdy" appearance. Closely-related to spotted dick.

Fighting Instructions: During the latter part of the 17th century, the British Royal Navy developed a system of Permanent Fighting Instructions, which tried to establish uniform and easily-understood doctrines and procedures for dealing with every contingency. However, during the eighteenth century, procedures which were state-of-the-art when codified in 1691 became so rigidly interpreted by "traditional" or "formalist" commanders as to become initiative-freezing dogma — the nautical equivalent of forcing fast-moving World War II generals, such as Rommel or Patton, to practice the static trench warfare of World War I, or face court-martial and execution. Starting in the 1750s a series of British naval officers, proponents of the "melée" (or "gunnery") school, first challenged, then ignored, and finally discredited these inflexible rules. By 1800 the "Permanent" Fighting Instructions were effectively a dead issue. (*See also* naval tactics in the age of sail and cutting the line.)

Fighting sails: When going into close-combat, sails were reduced, usually to courses and topsails only.

Fighting top: A platform on the mast of a sailing warship, from which sharpshooters could fire downward, aiming especially at officers on the enemy quarterdeck.

Figurehead: A carved wooden sculpture that decorates the prows of a ship. The custom originated in antiquity. Minoan, Phoenician, Greek, and Roman craft carried carved idols (acrostolia) with prominent oculi on the bows, believing on the one hand that the eyes would guide the ship and, on the other, that the god depicted would protect the vessel and its crew from the many perils of seafaring. Vikings and Normans carved their upturned stems of their longships into the likenesses of serpents and dragons, hoping to intimidate and terrify their enemies.

In 13th century Europe, a swan figurehead was supposed to help the ship glide gracefully over the water. By this time, seafarers had turned their backs on idol worship, but remained fiercely superstitious, going to great lengths to protect their figureheads which many believed contained the spirit of the vessel, ready to protect them from the perils of the deep and guide them safely to their destination. They firmly believed any harm to the icon would bring disaster to the ship. (*See* figurehead lore.)

During the Middle Ages, oculi and figureheads were eclipsed by the installation of forecastle fighting platforms, but the tradition died hard and figureheads were back by the Tudor era. Earlier, they had been mounted, or carved directly, on the ship's stem but with the forecastle overhanging the bow they were repositioned below the bowsprit. Throughout the 16th and 17th centuries, lions were greatly favored figureheads, but by the 18th they tended to be replaced by classical or mythological figures usually representing the name of the ship, and often the head and torso of a warrior or a partially naked female. Whether the sculpture was full-length, cut off at the waist, a head-and-shoulders bust, or a mere ornament (billethead, fiddlehead, or scrollhead) depended to a large extent on the design of the bow and proportions of the vessel. But, whatever size it was, its eyes continued to be a prominent and important feature, remaining in fashion until the arrival of iron hulls.

By the turn of the 19th century figureheads had become so large and elaborate that they were not only extremely expensive, but were easily damaged in accidents and deteriorated by the weather. The Admiralty first restricted their size (along with the amount of other carved decoration) and officially abolished them in 1840, but they did not disappear completely until the advent of ironclad warships some twenty years later. Figureheads could be seen on merchantmen into the early 20th century, and can still be seen on some private yachts and cruise ships.

Figurehead lore: The figurehead had immense significance for superstitious sailors, who regarded it on one hand as the incarnation of their ship, and on the other as a protector who would placate the gods of the sea. In an era when ships themselves were treated as living things, their figureheads were often endowed with human traits and most seamen believed any hurt to one would be followed by disaster. Although women were considered unlucky aboard ship, the reverse was true of figureheads. Superstitious seamen believed that the sight of a woman's body would calm an angry sea, so female figureheads were popular, almost invariably with one or both breasts exposed.

Figurehead tales: In 1778, during a minor encounter in the English Channel, a British squadron was ordered to turn and retreat without engaging an inferior French force. A boatswain's mate in HMS *Royal George* promptly ran to the bows and lashed a folded hammock over the eyes of the figurehead, which depicted George II in gilded Roman armor mounted on a rearing steed. An officer asked him what he thought he was doing, and the sailor is said to have replied "We ain't ordered to break the old boy's heart, are we? If he was to turn and see this day's work, not all the patience in heaven would hold him a minute."

In 1781, HMS *Atlas* was under construction when it was discovered that, due to a design error, the bowsprit could only be installed if part of the figurehead of Atlas with the terrestrial globe on his shoulders was cut away. The part which was excised included Britain's North American colonies, and superstitious seamen considered this an omen. Sure enough, two years later, the United States won their War of Independence.

Thirteen years later, on the "Glorious First of June," the figurehead of HMS *Brunswick* represented the duke of that name, wearing cocked hat and kilt. When a French cannonball shot away the duke's hat, the crew was appalled and its fighting spirit noticeably fell away. Morale was restored when the captain gave his own cocked hat to the carpenter with orders to nail it on the duke's head.

Filadiere: A flat-bottomed French boat of the Garonne region.

File: [1] Military term for a single column of personnel one behind the other when on parade or in formation (cf. rank). [2] A dossier or collection of documents. [3] Computer data stored under one identifier. [4] A tool for smoothing surfaces.

Filibuster: [1] Currently, the obstruction of legislative action by prolonged speaking in a senate or assembly. [2] Formerly, an irregular military adventurer engaging in unauthorized warfare against a state. [3] A buccaneer. Early Caribbean pirates favored a small, swift craft with superior handling qualities which the Dutch called a vlieboot, naming its sailors a vliebuiters. The French adapted this to call seagoing pirates filibustiers, in order to distinguish them from shore hunting boucaniers although, in fact, the pursuits were interchangeable. Boucanier, anglicized to buccaneer, eventually became the generic name for Caribbean pirates during their "Golden Age" (roughly 1680–1730), while filibustier was anglicized to filibuster and then to freebooter.

Fill: To trim a sail or change course to catch the wind better.

Filling-room: A lead-lined compartment in a sailing man-o-war, in which powder was broken out to fill cartridges.

Fimbriation: A narrow decorative edging or border on a flag, usually gold, white, or silver.

Fin: [1] A stabilizing or steering projection on boats or submarines. [2] A vertical airfoil, fixed or movable, whose chief function is to give stability to an aircraft in flight. [3] A winglike, membranous organ on the body of a fish, dolphin, etc., used in swimming, turning, and balancing.

Final destination: In naval control of shipping, the ultimate objective of a convoy or individual vessel irrespective of whether or not routing instructions have been issued.

Find: To equip or fit out a ship.

Finger signals: [1] When the appropriate boat recognition device is not available, or is obscured, a USN coxswain will indicate the presence of a flag officer by holding up the same number of fingers as there are stars in the officer's rank. [2] Finger signals are also used by RN coxswains, especially for the exchange of courtesies between boats. A flag officer is obvious from the color of his barge; otherwise the coxswain indicates the rank of his most senior passenger by raising four fingers for a captain and three for a commander (representing the number of stripes in the lace of their rank markings).

Fire!: Command to discharge ordnance or launch missiles. (The preferred RN term is shoot!)

Fire bulkhead: Must be capable of resisting temperatures up to 1,500°F (850°C) for at least an hour.

Fire classification: The USN and NATO divide fires into four classes:
- Alpha: Fires of simple combustibles such as wood, paper, or textiles, which leave residual ash.
- Bravo: Fires involving liquid or semi-liquid substances such as paint, gasoline, oil, and grease.
- Charlie: Electrical fires.
- Delta: All other types of fire.

Fire control: Centralized direction of a ship's armament. The material, personnel, methods, communications, and organization necessary to direct a gun or battery in such a way that projectile(s) fired will hit the designated target. *See* battery reference plane, deckplane, and naval surface fire control.

Fire-eater: Obsolete term for one who relishes the thought of going into combat.

Fire main: A saltwater piping system used throughout a warship for damage control and washing decks or bulkheads.

Fire support: The use of artillery or aircraft to assist advancing ground forces.

Fire swab: A mop or bunch of rope yarn soaked in water and used to swab up any loose grains of powder or to cool a cannon in action.

Fire tube: Refers to a type of boiler in which hot gases from the fire pass through tubes producing low pressure steam. This type of boiler was used on small vessels and steam locomotives, and extensively in stationary applications. Marine units were often called "donkey boilers" (*see* donkey engine) and used mainly for auxiliary power. Main propulsion steam engines are almost exclusively of the water tube variety.

Firearm: Any weapon which discharges projectiles by ignition, from the smallest pistol to the largest gun.

Firebox: The chamber of a boiler's furnace in which fuel is burned.

Fireman: [1] In general, a person who tends fires; a stoker. [2] In the USN, an enlisted person ranking below petty officer third class, whose general duties are concerned with ships' engines, boilers, etc. [3] In merchant service, A non-certificated seaman who stands engine room watches in care of oil-burning equipment.

Fireman's chair knot: *See* man-o'war sheepshank.

Firepower: The destructive capacity of a military unit or gun.

Fireroom: A compartment for boilers and related equipment (cf. furnace room).

Fireship: A vessel crammed with combustibles to be set afire and released to sail or drift down on a hostile fleet to create chaos and, hopefully, set fire to enemy ships. A very ancient practice going back to at least the Hellenistic era. (*See also* explosion vessel.)

Firewall: A fire-resistant bulkhead isolating an aircraft's crew compartment from its engines.

Firing cannon: *See* gun firing.

Firing party: A detachment of seamen, marines, or soldiers selected to fire over the grave of a person being buried with military honors. *See also* funerary salutes.

Firing squad: A detachment detailed to carry out a sentence of execution by shooting.

Firing tube: *See* priming tube.

Firkin: [1] A small wooden barrel or covered vessel. [2]. Any of several former units of capacity, usually equal to about ¼ of a barrel or 9 gallons (34 liters). *See* Cobbing & Firking.

First call: A warning bugle sounded five minutes before colors, quarters, or tattoo.

First Lieutenant: [1] USN name for the executive officer's deputy, responsible for a vessel's deck seamanship and topside cleanliness. [2] U.S. Army, Marine, or Air Force officer next below captain. [3] In the sailing RN and USN this title applied to a warship's senior lieutenant, who did not usually have to stand a watch, nor command a division of guns as the others did. During combat, his station was on the quarterdeck, ready to assist the captain, or to take over if necessary. [3] In the 20th century RN, it referred to the ship's second-in-command no matter what his or her rank. The first lieutenants of larger ships were usually commanders and referred to as such in conversation. [4] Today the 400-year-old title is increasingly being replaced by the USN term executive officer.

First light: The moment at which morning twilight begins (technically, when the center of the rising sun is 12° below the horizon).

First Lord of the Admiralty: Formerly, the political head of the Royal Navy (cf. First Sea Lord).

First Mate: The second-in-command of a merchantman, responsible for all deck operations and cargo stowage (also Mate, First Officer, or Chief Officer).

First Navy Jack: A jack consisting of a rampant rattlesnake and the words "Don't Tread on Me" superimposed on thirteen alternating red-and-white stripes. [1] Used by the Continental Navy from 1775 until replaced by the Union Jack in 1777. [2] Revived to be flown by all USN ships during the bicentennial year of 1976. [3] A year later, authorized to be worn by the USN ship with the longest period of active service. [4] In 2002, ordered by President Bush to be flown by all USN ships for the duration of the "War on Terror."

First open water: Charter Party term defining the time at which a port is sufficiently clear of ice for a vessel to enter.

First-rate: This adjective, which today refers to something of the best or highest available quality, was originally used by the Royal Navy to identify the largest and most powerful of its sailing warships (*see* Warship Rating). Second-rate and third-rate, used as adjectives for things of inferior quality, come from the same source.

First Sea Lord: The professional head of the Royal

Navy (cf. Chief of Naval Operations, First Lord of the Admiralty).

First strike: A preemptive surprise attack employing overwhelming force to destroy the enemy's arsenal to the point where the opposing side is unable to continue fighting. This tactic is generally associated with nuclear warfare.

First watch: The duty shift between 2000 an 2400 (8:00 P.M. to midnight). Also known as "first night watch" and as "evening watch."

Firth: Scottish name for a Fjord, often lying between high hills rather than mountains as in Scandinavia.

Fish: [1] A long strip of wood or iron used to strengthen a spar or joint. [2] To apply such a strip. [3] To hoist an anchor until its flukes reach the gunwale. [4] Slang for a torpedo (also tin fish). [4] a creature that lives in water, characteristically having gills for underwater breathing, fins, and a streamlined body. [5] To catch or try to catch such a creature (also fishing).

Fisher: "Politically correct" variation of "fisherman."

Fisherman: A person engaged in fishing.

Fisherman's bend: A knot used to fasten a rope to a spar, anchor, or other object. Its simplicity has led it to be called "king of knots."

Fishing: The activity of catching creatures living in water.

Fishing Zone: *See* exclusive fishing zone.

Fist: Radio operator's term for the distinctive and recognizable "touch" of an individual operator on the sending key. Cf. signature.

Fitness report: Periodic assessment of USN officers' performance, made by the commanding officer and forming the basis for promotion to higher rank. The RN equivalent is called Confidential Report.

Fitting out: [1] Installing propulsion machinery, masts, and other fixed equipment in a new hull after launching. [2] Bringing aboard all the items authorized for a vessel about to depart on a cruise or active service.

Fittings: Refers to miscellaneous small but essential parts and devices required for the operation of a vessel and care of its crew.

Fives and dimes: U.S. slang for a watch rotation with five hours on and ten off (for other work and training as well as meals and relaxation). With three sections, each stands watch at a different time of day and night, repeating every three days.

Fix: An accurate navigational position determined by observation.

Fixed ammunition: A projectile with the cartridge case crimped around its base (cf. separated ammunition).

Fixed light: A navigation light showing a steady beam with no interval of darkness.

Fixed pitch: Said of an aerial or marine propeller that does not change its pitch. This can be more efficient than variable pitch, but only at the speed (rpm), horsepower, and load condition for which it was specifically designed. In those conditions, the propeller can utilize all the power the propulsion system can produce, otherwise it cannot. Also uniform pitch.

Fjord/Fiord: A long and deep arm of the sea between high steep-sided mountains. From the Scandinavian (cf. Firth).

Flag: A piece of rectangular or square cloth, usually bunting, attachable at one edge to a pole or rope, used to identify national or corporate identity or as a signal. *See also* ensign, pennant, fly, display, and wear.

Flag bag: USN term for the place where signal flags are stored. No longer an actual bag, but usually a compartmented metal container.

Flag bridge: A bridge set aside on larger warships for exclusive use by an embarked flag officer and staff.

Flag Captain: The title given to the officer appointed to command, fight, and navigate a flagship, leaving the flag officer free to focus on strategy and the fleet.

Flag command: A unit, station, activity or area for which a flag officer is responsible.

Flag discrimination: *See* "cargo preference."

Flag etiquette: [1] USN ships never display their ensigns at night, and in daytime only when specified by Navy Regulations (cruising in sight of land, falling in with other ships, coming to anchor, during combat, etc.). [2] 1808 King's Regulations were essentially the same, ordering "colours never to be hoisted at sea except on meeting with other ships, or for the purpose of being dried." [3] Nowadays, RN warships wear their ensigns twenty-four hours a day; in harbor, at the ensign staff, where it is also worn at sea, except in bad weather or wartime when it is worn at the peak of a gaff, usually on the mainmast. [4] In combat it is traditional to fly two or more ensigns. This goes back to the age of sail, when masts were targets and a hit on one could drop a single flag and seem to imply surrender; the additional one(s) ensured the colors would keep on flying. The usual rule that no flag should be above the national flag does not apply on board ship. Since the position of honor is the quarterdeck, an ensign there is always superior to a flag anywhere else on the ship, even if higher up.

Flag hoist: *See* hoist.

Flag Lieutenant: Is the title given to the personal aide-de-camp to a flag officer.

Flag mast: *See* captain's mast.

Flag of convenience: The national flag of a country worn by a vessel whose owner is not a citizen of that country but has registered there in order to avoid stricter laws or higher taxes at home.

Flag Officer: An admiral, commodore, or other commissioned officer entitled to fly a special flag indicating rank. *See* Flags of Rank.

Flag salutes: Early in the 13th century, it became customary for converging warships to signify peaceful intent by lowering their topsails or letting fly their sheets, thus making themselves less maneuverable. As gestures of respect and submission, merchantmen saluted warships in the same way. Over the next 200 years the practice of dipping the ensign instead became generally accepted. There are no formal treaties or regulations regarding such salutes, which are merely a matter of international courtesy and custom. However, when the Royal Navy enjoyed undisputed command of the sea, it insisted on being saluted by all foreign vessels. As early as 1638, Captain Richard Bullen of HMS *Nicodemus* was severely punished for failing to force a passing French ship-of-war to salute.

Flag share: An admiral received one-eighth of all prize money awarded within his command, even if the actual capture was made by a different admiral.

Flag signals: Flags have been used to convey commands at sea since the classical era. For example, in his military treatise *Tactica*, East Roman (Byzantine) Emperor Leo VI (886–912) gives an indication of the sophisticated signaling system used to control and maneuver large galley fleets in action:

> All will watch the flagship and guide themselves by her and watch for new orders. Each order must be issued by some particular signal previously agreed upon. Either the flag is held upright, or leaning to right or left, or held high or low, or made to disappear. The shape of the signal may be altered, or only the color.... The battle signal should be red, raised on a long staff. You should practice the different signals ... so that mistakes will not be made.

Nine centuries later little had changed. Early 18th century signaling systems still relied on the placement of individual flags. Thus, for example, a flag at the fore peak ordered the fleet to close its order, while the same flag at the mizzen peak meant weigh anchor. This relatively clumsy system demanded a lot of flags (one-half to one-third as many as the number of orders to be transmitted) and were sometimes modified by audible signals. For example, in Admiral Rodney's system, which is preserved by the Historical Society of Pennsylvania, a red pendant at the mizzen peak required the fleet to wear ship — in succession if the flagship fired a single cannon, or simultaneously if two were fired. (The designer of the code had clearly not considered how these signals were to be distinguished when the flagship was already engaged and firing.)

By mid-century, most navies, led by the French, changed to numerically coded systems. A set of ten basic flags representing numbers from 0 to 9 and raised in hoists of three could send 1,000 different signals. For example the hoist of flag four, over flag five, over flag two, would tell the receiver to look up the message or instruction numbered 452 in the signal code book. Repeater and designator flags extended the range of information which could be sent. Today, the International Signaling Code (table 8) consists of 26 alphabetical flags, 10 numeral pendants, an answering pendant, and three substitutes or repeaters.

Flag verification: A provision of International Law which allows a warship to stop and board any vessel suspected of wearing false colors.

Flags: Nickname for a signalman in both USN and RN.

Flagship: [1] A warship from which the senior officer of a fleet, squadron, convoy, or other assembly of ships exercises command. [2] A passenger liner commanded by the line's senior captain or commodore.

Flags of distress: [1] A ship's national flag or ensign flown upside down was formerly an internationally-recognized signal of distress (it is difficult to understand how this could be done with a vertically-striped tricolor). [2] A weft at the masthead was also considered a distress signal, but this also is no longer recognized. [3] Today International Code flags N (November) and C (Charlie) flown together indicate the vessel is in distress (*see* tables 8 and 10). [4] The United States Coast Guard prescribes an orange flag bearing a black square over a black disc for use by small craft in inland and territorial waters.

Flags of rank: The practice of flying a personal flag to indicate the rank or position of a fleet commander or senior official dates back to the Middle Ages, but formal instructions were not issued until 1530 (to Henry VIII's navy). Nowadays, the appropriate flag of rank is broken at the aftermost masthead as soon as command is assumed and is only hauled down when there is a change of command or under specific circumstances outlined in naval regulations.

- U.S. Navy Flag Officers: Personal flags are rectangular with white stars on a blue ground for officers qualified for command at sea, and blue stars on a white ground for officers of staff corps or on restricted duty. The latter may be worn by boats or flown at shore establishments but are never hoisted on ships. The number of stars matches the officer's rank insignia, namely: Fleet Admiral, a circle of five white stars on a blue field: Admiral, four stars distributed evenly on the field in a diamond pattern: Vice Admiral, three stars arrayed as an apex-up triangle: Rear Admiral, two stars in a vertical line centered on the flag: Rear Admiral (lower Half), a single star centered on the flag.

- Royal Navy Flag Officers: The personal flag of an Admiral of the Fleet is the Union Flag with dimensions of 1:2 rather than the usual 2:3 of British admirals' flags. Originally, all Admirals used a red Saint George's cross centered on a white ground. It was flown by a rear-admiral at the mizzen, vice-admiral at the fore, and admiral at the main. When 3-masted ships disappeared, a full admiral retained the plain Saint George's Cross, with subordinate ranks identified by red roundels. A Vice Admiral has the same flag with a single red ball centered in the upper hoist canton, while a Rear Admiral's flag has red balls centered in both the upper and lower hoist cantons. A Commodore, who ranks as a one-star, has a swallow-tailed broad pendant with a red Saint George's Cross on a white ground.

- Commanders in Chief: The flag worn on a British warship whenever the Lord High Admiral (currently the monarch) is embarked was designed in 1929 and is a golden anchor displayed horizontally on a crimson ground with twin gold ropes, coiled but not fouled. In the United States, the President's flag (designated by Executive Order 10860 which came into effect on July 4, 1960) is a dark blue rectangle bearing a shield of thirteen red and white stripes on the breast of an eagle holding the national motto in his beak, a sheaf of arrows in his right talon, and an olive branch in his left. Behind the eagle is a "radiating glory" and the whole is surrounded by a circle of fifty stars.
- Other Personal Flags: The CNO's flag is blue over white, divided diagonally from lower hoist to upper fly, with the device of the office centered on the flag. This is an eagle with the U.S. shield on its breast and holding an anchor horizontally in its talons. Four stars in a diamond pattern, white on the blue and blue on the white indicate the CNO's rank. The British equivalent, officially known as Chief of Naval Staff (but sometimes using the former title of First Sea Lord), has no individual flag, but unofficially flies an admiral of the fleet's flag even though he does not hold that rank, which is in abeyance. The Vice–CNO has a personal flag divided into four by crossed diagonal lines, colored blue in the hoist and fly, and white in the upper and lower sections, but otherwise identical to the CNO's.

Flagstaff: [1] A tall pole on which a flag is displayed: [1] A vertical staff at the stern of a vessel for displaying the national ensign. [2] A vertical staff at the bow of a small naval boat.

Flagstaff insignia: These are devices attached to the top of USN flagstaffs to indicate the rank of a senior officer or civil official. A star signifies commander or civil equivalent; a ball captain or equivalent; a halberd a flag or general officer; and an eagle an official entitled to a 19-gun salute.

Flak: Colloquialism for anti-aircraft fire, derived from the World War II German acronym for "**Fl**ieger **A**bwehr **K**anone" (aircraft defense cannon).

Flake: A variant of "fake."

Flameout: Failure of a jet aircraft's engine due to extinction of the flame in the combustion chamber. This can be caused by a number of factors, including lack of fuel, oxygen starvation, ingestion of foreign object debris, etc.

Flammable: Easily or spontaneously set on fire. This variant came into widespread use because the original term "inflammable" was all too frequently mistaken for non-flammable or fire-resistant.

Flank speed: A USN term for a speed one quarter more than standard speed except for cruisers, destroyers, light minelayers, and fast aircraft carriers where it is ten knots more than standard speed. *See also* full speed, emergency speed.

Flannel: [1] RN slang for bluff and bluster, full of conceit. [2] Using long-winded but meaningless speech to talk one's way out of a difficult situation (mainly British). [3] A glib, insincere, boastful, or ingratiating talker (called a "flannel-mouth" in the United States). [4] A soft wool or cotton fabric.

Flap: [1] One of a pair of hinged surfaces on the trailing edges of an aircraft wing which, when deployed, increase lift or drag by changing the camber of the aerofoil. Usually used to slow the aircraft when landing. [2] A hinged plate used as a cover or as a simple valve. [3] A chaotic situation, or state of panic (slang).

Flare: [1] Upward and outward curvature of a hull above the waterline. [2] A pyrotechnic distress signal (*see* Very light).

Flareback: [1] Combustion of hot gases in a boiler's firebox spreading outward into the boiler room. [2] Flame and hot gas emitting from the breech of a gun when it is opened after firing.

Flash: The highest precedence that can be assigned to a USN or NATO message.

Flash burn: Injury caused by sudden, brief but intense heat, typically from a conventional or nuclear explosion.

Flash pan: *See* pan.

Flashing light: A navigation light which blinks on-and-off with the period of light being shorter than that of darkness.

Flashless powder: A charge for large-caliber naval guns designed to minimize muzzle-illumination when firing at night.

Flashplate: A metal plate on which the anchor chain rests. The name refers to the fact that it creates sparks when the chain runs out.

Flashproof gear: Clothing specially-designed to resist flash burns.

Flat: A partial deck between two full decks. Often made of plates or gratings.

Flat aback: [1] A square-sail with the wind beating on its forward side. [2] RN term for a seaman's cap worn (against regulations) on the back of the head.

Flat calm: No wind. *See* calm.

Flat top: Slang term for an aircraft carrier. Also flattop.

Flats: A broad expanse of shallows and marshland.

Flatted cargo: Cargo placed at the bottom of the holds, covered with planks and dunnage, and held for future use, frequently serving in lieu of ballast. There is usually space above for the loading of vehicles that may be moved without interfering with the flatted cargo. Also called understowed cargo.

Flatten in: To trim the sheets.

Flax: Fibers from any of several small plants, which can be fabricated into fine linen, sail canvas, or strong cordage.

Fleet: [1] At least five ships working together under unified command (cf. Flotilla, squadron, task group, etc.). [2] An organization of ships, aircraft, marine forces, and shore support facilities under a single commander in chief. [3] The generic term for a national navy. *See also* United States numbered fleets.

Fleet Admiral: In the United States, the definitive five-star ranks General of the Army and Fleet Admiral were created in 1944, to honor a limited number of victorious senior commanders of World War II. With the advice and consent of Congress, President Franklin D. Roosevelt appointed four army and four naval officers to serve in the five-star grade for life. The admirals were William F. Halsey Jr., Ernest J. King, William D. Leahy, and Chester W. Nimitz. An overlooked fifth World War II general was promoted in 1950 by President Truman, and Revolutionary War commander in chief George Washington was posthumously given the rank by President Ford in the centennial year of 1976. No other appointments have since been made, and the titles are effectively in abeyance. *See also* Admiral of the Fleet.

Fleet Air Arm: From 1937 to the end of World War II, the Royal Navy tried desperately to throw off this hated Royal Air Force designation in favor of air branch or naval aviation, but the old term was used consistently by the media, gaining general public acceptance. Reluctantly the Admiralty gave in and the name became official in 1946.

Fleet Captain: *See* Captain of the Fleet.

Fleet Carrier: World War II term used to distinguish full-size aircraft carriers from the smaller light fleet and escort carriers.

Fleet-in-being: Refers to a naval force that exerts influence without seeking battle. By simply remaining in port, it forces a (usually superior) enemy to deploy forces to guard against it. Such a stance can be an effective element in a strategy of sea denial, but not in one of sea control.

Fleet Marine Force: A balanced force of land, air, and service elements of the U.S. Marine Corps, forming part of a naval fleet with the status of a type command.

Fleet Rehabilitation & Modernization: A former USN program intended to extend the useful life of World War II destroyers by converting them from surface warfare to antisubmarine role.

Fleet train: Auxiliary vessels carrying replacement personnel, fuel, ammunition, food, repair facilities, spare parts and replacement aircraft, which follow a fleet to re-provision it, enabling it to stay at sea for long periods.

Fleet up: USN term for an advancement in position or importance. Usually within the same ship or unit to replace a casualty or transfer.

Flemish coil: A stacked or vertical coil of rope in which each fake rides on top of the previous one in order to ensure that the coil will run clear.

Flemish down: To lay down coils of rope or line in decorative figures-of-eight.

Flemish horse: A short foot-rope at the outer end of a yardarm for the man at the earing.

Flemish mat: A flat or horizontal coil of rope, starting with a tight fake at the center with each successive fake butting close against the previous one. Used mainly for its decorative appearance.

Flense: [1] Whaler's term for stripping blubber from a whale (*see* whale processing). [2] Sealer's term for skinning a carcass.

Flettner rotators: During the 1920s, German engineer Anton Flettner developed a method of ship propulsion based on the Magnus effect. Magnus had noted that when air flow is perpendicular to a vertical cylinder, the air current simply splits to pass on both sides of the cylinder. However, if the cylinder is rotating, the air current on one side is augmented by the cylinder's rotation; while the current on the opposite side is slowed down. This creates a pressure differential, which results in a force pushing in one direction.

Flettner's experimental prototype, a converted schooner named *Baden-Baden*, made a successful trans–Atlantic crossing, arriving at New York in May 1926. This led the German Naval Transport Service to commission *Barbara*, a 92 meter (300 foot) vessel, with three Flettner rotators mounted vertically on the weather deck. Each was 17 meters (55 feet) tall and 4 meters (13 feet) in diameter, driven at 250 rpm by an electric motor. For six years, *Barbara* carried freight and passengers between Hamburg and Italy. However, with an abundance of low cost fossil fuels, the rotator system was unable to compete with conventional engines and fell into disuse.

Flettner then turned his attention to aerodynamics, using the Magnus principle to create lift. His prototype rotary wing aircraft flew in 1932 and, seven years later, the Kriegsmarine (Nazi German Navy) ordered a more advanced model, the Fl-282 Kolibri. It flew anti-submarine patrols from surface warships in the Baltic, Mediterranean, and Aegean Sea, thus becoming the world's first operational military helicopter.

Recently, with rising costs and restricted fuel supplies, interest in the marine system has revived. In August 2008, Enercon, one of Europe's biggest wind turbine manufacturers, launched *E-ship 1* (this name was only meant to identify the project, but it caught on so well that Enercon decided to use it for the actual ship). Fuel savings of 30–40 percent are expected, thanks to the auxiliary power of paired 27-meter (89-foot) high, 4-meter diameter, Flettner rotators, mounted two forward and two aft. A ship equipped with turbosails looks virtually identical to one with Flettner rotators, but operates on a different principle. It is hard to believe that either of these vessels — having tall wind-catching elements that cannot be furled — would fare well in a storm.

Flight: The basic aviation tactical unit, consisting of at least two (usually four or six) naval aircraft.

Flight deck: The flat weather deck of an aircraft carrier which serves as aircraft park, launching pad, and landing strip (*see also* angled deck).

Flinders bar: A bar of soft iron placed in the binnacle of a magnetic compass to neutralize the deflection caused by induced magnetism. Named after 18th century RN Captain Mathew Flinders (*see* quadrantal deviation).

Flintlock: This early product of the industrial revolution replaced the slow-match and greatly increased the speed of naval gunfire. The device consists of a spring-powered hammer into which a flint is inserted. When the hammer is released by pulling a lanyard the flint strikes a steel element known as the frizzen, creating a spark which ignites a small quantity of gunpowder sitting in a pan above the touch-hole (vent), this in turn ignites the main charge.

In 1778, Captain (later rear admiral) Sir Charles Douglas, recommended the use of flintlocks for naval ordnance and, when the Admiralty rejected the idea, bought musket locks at his own expense and installed them on his own ship. By 1790 the Admiralty had finally been convinced of the superiority of this form of ignition and installed them throughout the navy. (Army gunners were yet more conservative and — even though the infantry introduced "Brown Bess" flintlock muskets in the early 1720s — flintlocks were not adopted for land artillery until thirty years after the navy, and even then the gunners retained their portfires as backup.)

FLIR: Forward-looking infrared.

Float: [1] To remain on the surface of a liquid. [2] A buoyant platform attached to a wharf or bank as a landing stage. [3] Any floating device. [4] A hollow structure fixed underneath a boat or aircraft to keep it from sinking. [5] The blade or bunket of a paddle wheel.

Float coat: Jacket worn by the flight deck personnel of an aircraft carrier. Should a wearer be blown overboard during flight operations, the coat will inflate automatically when it hits salt water. The garment is color-coded to identify the crewmember's job. Also flotation jacket.

Floating dock: [1] A wharf built on pontoons. [2] A dry-dock facility that can submerge to accept a vessel and, after that vessel has been shored, be pumped out to rise for repairs below the waterline.

Floating dump: Emergency supplies preloaded in landing craft, amphibious vehicles, or in landing ships. Floating dumps are not brought ashore until requested by the assault force commander.

Floating fiber optic scanner: A device that allows a submarine to scan the surface without the need for an optical periscope. While the boat remains at depth, scanning equipment — which includes high-definition color and monochrome television cameras, thermal imager, eyesafe laser rangefinder, electronic support measures sensor, communications receiver, and global positioning system receiver — is raised to the surface on a buoyant platform tethered to the submarine by a reinforced fiber optics cable that transmits visual images to large-screen displays in the boat's control room.

Operating depth is constrained only by the strength of the pressure hull and the length of the tether.

Floating production, storage, and offloading system: This involves anchoring a vessel near one or more producing platform(s) to accept crude oil for processing, and store it until it can be offloaded into tankers for transfer to facilities on shore. Often called by the abbreviation FPSO, these systems are especially effective in deepwater locations where an underwater pipeline would be infeasible, or when oil deposits are too small to justify the cost of a pipeline. *See also* offshore mooring.

Floating reserve: Troops kept on board ship in case they are needed to reinforce a beachhead.

Floatplane: A seaplane equipped with buoyant pontoons as landing gear.

Floe: *See* ice floe.

Flo-Flo ship: *See* heavy loads and vehicles.

Flog the dead horse: This term, which has come to mean expending energy without reward, comes from merchant seamen's slang for a period of laboring to earn pay which had already been drawn and spent. (*See* Dead Horse for details.)

Flog the glass: *See* watchkeeping manipulation.

Flogging excess and abuse: Before 1735, Royal Navy sailors were literally flogged to death. A dozen lashes was the norm, but many captains routinely ordered a hundred or more, and a thousand lashes was the penalty for mutiny. "Flogging around the fleet" was the sentence for attempted desertion or striking an officer. The offender was tied to an upright in the ship's boat and rowed from ship to ship, pulling alongside the gangway so that each ships' bosun could inflict the prescribed number of lashes (at least twelve at each stop), usually to the accompaniment of drum rolls. When a crime was especially nasty, the bosun might be instructed to tie a fourth knot, known as a "thieves' knot," in each of the cat's nine tails, thereby increasing the victim's suffering. *See also* Non-Naval Flogging.

Flogging in Naval Service: With origins going back to the galleys of the Roman Navy (but not the Greeks or Carthaginians, whose oarsmen were volunteers), flogging was by far the most common form of nautical punishment from the eleventh to twentieth centuries. The practice, administered by an instrument known as the cat-o'-nine-tails, was said to "make a bad man worse and break the heart of a good one." In the Royal and United States Navies flogging was a formal occasion. At six bells of the forenoon watch, musket-armed marines would assemble on the quarterdeck, and all the ship's officers would gather wearing full-dress uniforms with swords. When all was ready, and the ship's company had been assembled to "witness punishment," the victim was tied hand and foot and lashed to a grating or to the rigging, or sometimes "spread-eagled over the barrel" (of a gun) to expose his naked back or buttocks. The captain would then read the section of the Articles of War covering the offense to be punished, ending with "Bosun, do your duty!" The bosun would then "let the cat out of the bag" and set to his task, accompanied by rolls on the drum.

Before long, the nine separate lashes would be matted with the victim's blood, forming a single heavy lash which could cause serious damage, so a compassionate bosun would periodically "comb the cat" with his fingers to separate the tails. If several dozen lashes had been decreed, each set would be administered by a fresh bosun's mate. Left-handed ones were especially popular with sadistic captains because they could "cross the cuts" of the preceding bosun and really mangle the flesh. They needed space to lay on their strokes so, when the area was too tight, or too close to standing rigging, there would be "no room to swing a cat." *See also* juvenile punishment.

Flogging in the United States Navy: At its formation, the USN initially followed British practice which by then was limited to twelve lashes (except by Admiralty warrant). Punishments awarded by USN captains during 1848–9 included:

Throwing soapsuds in the eyes	→	6 lashes
Missing muster	→	8 lashes
Swindling a shipmate	→	9 lashes
Profane language	→	11 lashes
Endangering the ship with fire	→	12 lashes
Beating a colored seaman	→	12 lashes

In 1840 William M. Murrell published *Cruise of the Frigate Columbia*, in which he recounts how he himself received twelve lashes for failing to properly mark a piece of clothing, and for accidentally spilling ink on the deck; while other men received twelve lashes for trivial offenses such as having dirty pots or failing to close the door of a toilet. Murrell condemned such flagrant abuse of authority, but believed that flogging should be retained for offenses such as stealing.

In 1841 another former enlisted seaman named Solomon Sandborn published *An Exposition of Official Tyranny in the United States Navy* which set forth instances of the abuse of various regulations by officers and called for the abolition of flogging. Other former enlisted men also published accounts of their naval service and of abuses of authority by officers.

Flogging limitation: Abuse in the Royal Navy ended in 1735, when maximum punishments were clearly spelled out in Admiralty regulations. After that, even the most brutal Royal Navy captain could order no more than 12 lashes without requesting and receiving an Admiralty Warrant which, after 1866, was itself limited to 48 strokes. The British precedent was recognized in Article Four of Rules for Regulation of the Navy of the United Colonies, issued by the Continental Congress on 28 November 1775:

> No commander shall inflict any punishments upon a seaman beyond twelve lashes upon his bare back with a cat-o'nine-tails; if the fault shall deserve a greater punishment, he is to apply to the Commander in chief of the Navy in order to the trying of him by a Court-Martial.

Public opinion, especially in the North, tended to associate flogging with the treatment of convicts and slaves, and thus contrary to the democratic spirit of the times. Warnings against excessive use of the "cat" were written as early as 1797 by Captain Thomas Truxtun, and in 1808 by Surgeon Edward Cutbush. An unsuccessful proposal to abolish naval flogging altogether was introduced in Congress in 1820 by Representative Samuel Foot, but in the 1840s a number of civilian groups began to petition Congress to abolish the practice entirely. This led the Secretary of the Navy to ask a number of naval officers if flogging could be eliminated without damage to the Navy, but only eight percent thought the practice should be discontinued. Flogging was outlawed in the American armed forces by Act of Congress in 1851, but only "suspended" by the British Parliament in 1881, not being officially abolished until 1939 on the eve of World War II.

Flood: [1] Inflowing tide. [2] To admit seawater to a compartment, especially to extinguish fire.

Flood tide: A tide which is flowing shoreward or has reached its peak.

Flooder: In naval mine warfare, a device fitted to a buoyant mine which, at a preset time, floods the case and causes the mine to sink to the bottom.

Floodgate: A gate or sluice designed to regulate the flow of water by shutting it out, admitting it, or releasing it.

Floor: [1] The bottom of the ocean, the sea bed. [2] The deck of a ship. [3] Said of a submarine when it settles to lie on the bottom.

Floorheads: The outboard ends of floor timbers.

Flooring off: Stowing the lower tier of cargo in a hold.

Floors: Timbers on which the bottom of a wooden ship was framed. All the floor timbers were first laid across the keel. Next, the first futtocks were erected on either the forward or after sides of the floor timbers (either with, or without spacer chocks) and bolted to them. Then the second futtocks were chock-bolted to the floorheads and through-bolted to the upper sections of the first futtocks and so-on until the full frame was erected. The keelson was then placed on top and bolted to the floor timbers.

Florida Current: An Atlantic Ocean current that flows easterly through the Florida straits to join the Gulf Stream.

Flotilla: From the Spanish for little fleet. [1] Generically, any small fleet. [2] In the USN, formerly a tactical unit of two or more squadrons under a flagship. [3] In the RN, a squadron of destroyers.

Flotsam: Floating wreckage or debris (cf. jetsam, lagen).

Flow: Said of an incoming tide.

Flowers: Probably because of their association with funerals, it was long considered bad luck to bring flowers on board ship. Modern cruise ships and liners ignore this superstition.

Flt: Fleet.

Fluke: [1] The spade-shaped or pointed tip of an anchor which digs into the sea bed. [2] An unexpected shift in wind direction. [3] Either of the two triangular segments of a whale's tail.

Fluky: Said of a light and constantly variable wind.

Flummery: A sailing ship seaman's dish, made from soured oatmeal.

Flushdecked: Having a continuous weather deck with no breaks at poop, deckhouse, or forecastle.

Flute: [1] A variation of Fluyt. [2] Obsolete slang term for a Royal Marines officer who, for some obscure reason, was by tradition the only person aboard to own or play that instrument. [3] *See* en flute.

Fluyt: Popular Dutch-designed 17–18th century cargo ship. Carvel-built, with a flat bottom and curved sides bent to wrap around the stern. Square-rigged on fore and main masts, with a lateen sail on the mizzen. Could carry 20–40 cannon, but was frequently unarmed to maximize carrying capacity.

Fly: [1] The length of a flag from the hoist to its outer edge. [2] If an ensign, the length from union to outer edge. [3] The outer edge itself. [4] The half of a flag furthest from the pole or mast. [5] A masthead wind direction indicator. [6] Merchantmen "fly" their flags (as opposed to RN ships which "wear" them, and USN ships which "display" them).

Fly-boat: [1] A small, fast, sailing vessel. [2] A flat-bottomed Dutch sailing vessel, distinguished by a high stern resembling a Gothic turret.

Fly-by-wire: A system in which primary maneuvering control of submarines is achieved by replacing traditional hydraulic and mechanical systems with computers and software that transmit command signals, via redundant fiber optic cable networks, to control surfaces. With this system, the four traditional submarine watch stations can be reduced to two chief petty officers serving as pilot and co-pilot. In place of traditional wheeled control yokes, each pilot operates a flat-panel touch screen (or joystick) to input orders. Control algorithms in the computer system then direct the submarine to the desired course and depth. Secondary mechanical indicators — a gauge for depth measurement, an inclinometer to indicate pitch, and a clinometer to show heel or roll — are only required to backup primary digital indicators on the flat panel displays.

Flyer: Colloquialism for a clipper or other fast-sailing boat.

Flying boat: An aircraft with a boat-like fuselage which allows it to take off and land on water.

Flying bridge: A bridge above the navigation and flag bridges on a ship, or above the conning tower of a submarine. Usually open to the weather.

Flying colors: After combat, a ship which struck its flag had surrendered, whereas one with its colors still flying had won. Hence the use of this term to signify success or victory, whether in sport or after some kind of trial.

Flying Dutchman: This famous maritime apparition, which has become the generic term for any ghost ship, is essentially a reprise of the medieval German tale of the North Sea Wraith. It is unclear whether "Dutchman" refers to the ship or its master. If the latter, some sources point to the real Captain Bernard Fokke (*see* Libera Nos Specter), while others give him fictitious names such as Ramhout van Damme, Joost van Straaten or, most frequently, Hendrick (or Cornelius) Vanderdecken ("of the deck").

Versions of the story are varied and legion, but most tell of a hard-driving 17th century Dutch sea captain, who encountered a brutal storm off the Cape of Good Hope, but refused to enter the safe anchorage of Table Bay. After days of battling fierce winds, there was a terrible crunch as the ship struck a submerged rock. As she went down the master stood on deck screaming blasphemously, "I shall round this cape, even if I have to sail until doomsday! God himself cannot stop me!"

Over the ensuing centuries, thousands of sailors claim to have seen the dreaded vessel. Even today, superstitious mariners believe that those who look into the eye of a storm off the Cape of Good Hope may be confronted by a phantom Indiaman, its luminous hull surmounted by mists instead of sails. Unless they quickly look away, they will be damned to join the Dutchman's ghostly crew, sailing for eternity into the teeth of the raging storm.

> Here comes the Flying Dutchman
> Comes fast through hissing spray
> And driven by the tempest he heads for Table Bay
> With bird-like speed he's borne along
> before the howling blast
> But never can cast anchor, for the Bay's already passed
> (Old English Folksong)

The term has become generic. Spectral ships, moving rapidly under sail on windless days, have also been called "Flying Dutchmen," with the first printed reference being in George Barrington's *Voyage to Botany Bay* (1795):

> In the night watch some of the people saw, or imagined they saw, a vessel standing for them under a press of sail, as though she would run them down: the story spread like wild-fire, and the supposed phantom was called the Flying Dutchman.

One of the more famous sightings was by Prince George (later King George V) and his elder brother Albert when they were midshipmen, cruising around the world in a wooden training frigate. They were accompanied by their tutor, Canon John Neale Dalton who, in 1886, published *The Cruise of HMS Bacchante 1879–1882*, in which he claims they were off the coast of Australia on the night of 11/12 July, 1881 when:

> At 4 A.M. the Flying Dutchman crossed our bows. A strange red light as of a phantom ship all aglow, in the midst of which light the masts, spars, and sails of a brig ... stood out in strong relief as she came up on the port bow.... Thirteen persons altogether saw her.

More recently, on 3rd August 1942, HMS *Jubilee* was heading for Simonstown, the Royal Navy base near Cape Town, when an unidentified schooner was sighted, moving rapidly under full sail, even though there was no wind. The officer of the watch, Lieutenant Davies, altered course to avoid a collision and entered the event in the ship's log. Sharing the watch was Sub-lieutenant Nicholas Monsarrat, the novelist, who said the incident inspired his two-volume work *The Master Mariner* (published posthumously) which tells of an Elizabethan seaman doomed to sail the world's seas until the end of time.

Flying jib: [1] The outermost headsail. [2] A light sail set on the foretopgallant royal stay.

Flying jib-boom: A spar extending beyond the jib-boom.

Flying moor: A flamboyant shiphandling evolution in which the vessel drops one anchor, steams upstream to drop the second, and then heaves in the first chain to reach its centered position. Formerly popular with destroyer captains.

Flying sail: Any sail that is set from the deck without attachment to a yard or mast.

FMCS: Freight Movement Control System.

FMF: Fleet Marine Force (USMC).

FN: Fireman (USN).

FNOC: Future Naval Operations Concept (RN).

Foam: A substance that is formed when bubbles of air (or a gas) are trapped in a liquid (or solid). *See* sea foam.

FOB: Free On Board. *See* Incoterms.

Fo'c'sle: Abbreviation of forecastle.

FOD: [1] Foreign object damage, caused by [2] Foreign object debris.

Fod walk: A safety procedure in which carrier crews line up from side-to-side and walk the entire length of the flight deck, picking up any and every item which might cause "Foreign Object Damage" by being sucked into a jet engine, or cause personal injury when blown by jet blast.

Fog bank: A dense haze with at least one clearly-defined edge, looking like a thick cloud resting on the horizon. Often the precursor of wind, especially in high latitudes.

Fog buoy: A floating device towed behind a leading vessel so that another, immediately astern, will be able to keep station in bad visibility. Also called towing spar.

Fog signals: *See* table 9.

Fogbound: Immobilized by bad visibility.

Fogbow: A dim, broad, arc of white or yellow celestial light similar to a rainbow. Usually seen across the sun in high latitudes when mists are clearing. Also called "white rainbows" or "cloudbows," while mariners sometimes call them "sea dogs."

Folding anchor: One designed so that flukes and shank can be laid back against the stock for easy stowage.

Follower: [1] A person permitted by former naval regulations to accompany a captain when he was transferred from one ship to another. [2] A machine part activated by the movement of another part. [3] A spring-loaded plate in a firearm's magazine that angles cartridges for insertion into the chamber.

Following sea: Waves running in the same direction as the vessel, usually making it hard to steer.

Following wind: Wind blowing in the same direction as the ship is traveling. *See* soldier's wind.

Follow-up: In amphibious operations, the landing of supplies and reinforcements on a beachhead after the initial assault.

Follow-up shipping: Ships not originally part of the amphibious task force.

Food distribution: Today a mess is a military dining hall where communal meals are served, but in sailing ship navies the term referred to a group of men who ate together. The arrangement was not immutable and a member of one mess was free to request transfer to another. One member of each group would be designated "mess cook" with responsibility for the preparation of raw foodstuffs for the galley and, later, the collection and distribution of cooked victuals. No actual cooking was involved and his reward for this duty was usually an extra tot of rum.

According to Janet Macdonald in *Feeding Nelson's Navy* (Greenhill 2006), the mess cook was expected and required to whistle constantly while mixing the ingredients for duff or pudding. This ensured he could not surreptitiously pop a few of the precious plums or raisins in his mouth while stirring them into flour and suet. When portions of food were unequal in size, it was the practice for one sailor to turn his back while another pointed to a serving and asked "Who shall have this one?" The first would then nominate a member of the mess to receive the selected portion.

Food in sailing ships: Much has been written about the abysmal quality of meals served aboard naval and merchant ships during the 18th and early 19th centuries. However, every effort was made to ensure seamen received the nourishment needed to sustain their hard manual labor. Samuel Pepys, when Secretary of the Admiralty in the 1660s, wrote...

> ... seamen love their bellies above anything else and therefore it must always be remembered in the managing of the victualling of the navy that to make any abatement from them in the quality and agreeableness of the victuals is to discourage and provoke them in the tenderest point, and will soon render them disgusted with the King's service more than any other hardship that can be put upon them.

The majority of captains were well aware that in the words of Horatio Nelson "It is easier to keep the men healthy than to cure their ills" and they replenished their stores of fresh water and vegetables as frequently as they could. In most cases, sailors were fed much better than their counterparts on land.

But, even with a well stocked larder, problems arose on long voyages or extended periods of blockade duty.

Once their fodder ran out, the poultry and livestock which provided fresh milk and eggs had to be slaughtered. Salted fish and meats soon began to smell. Without proper refrigeration fresh fruit and vegetables deteriorated rapidly and scurvy became a problem after six or seven weeks at sea. More durable grocery supplies such as rice, flour, and dried pease eventually became infested with worms and weevils, not to mention rat urine and droppings.

Another problem was that the ship's cook, who rated as a warrant officer, was almost invariably a naval pensioner, invalided out of active service due to amputation or injury, who applied for the job to supplement his pension. The culinary abilities of many were limited to boiling meat for stew, or pease to make a soup. The food may have been nourishing, but it was always monotonous and seldom tasty. Each man received about 5,000 calories a day, served in three meals:

- **Breakfast** was usually the cereal dish known as Burgoo. This was boiled oatmeal porridge, seasoned with salt and sugar, and butter if available. Easy to serve and prepare even in rough seas, and palatable if served cold, it provided a solid foundation for the day's work. It would normally be washed down with cocoa, but an alternative was Scottish Coffee, made by stirring into hot water a powder of ship's biscuit charred over the galley fire.
- The main dish at **Luncheon** (always known as dinner) was a hearty soup or stew, sometimes made with salt fish, but usually containing 12 ounces (340 grammes) of salt beef per man on Sunday, Tuesday, Thursday, and Saturday; and the same quantity of salt pork on Monday, Wednesday, and Friday. The soup was often thickened with flour, and raisins. Currents, or suet might also be added, while fresh or dried vegetables would be put in when available. Many seamen suspected the origin of the "beef," giving rise to the chantey cited by Richard Henry Dana in *Two Years Before the Mast*:

  > Old Horse! Old Horse!
  > What brought you here?...
  > Killed by blows and sore abuse,
  > They salted me down for sailors use.
  > The sailors they do me despise,
  > They turn me over, damn my eyes:
  > Cut off my meat, and pick my bones;
  > And pitch the rest to Davy Jones.

- **Supper** was almost always cheese or butter, served with bread or occasionally rice. Early in the voyage, the bread would be "soft" (fresh) with each man getting 1.5 lbs (680 grammes), but this would soon have to be replaced by 1 lb (453 g) of "hard" bread, often called ship biscuit or hard tack.

Foot: The lower edge of a mast or sail.

Foot-it: To sail close-hauled.

Footband: A strip of canvas sewn along the after side of a square-sail to strengthen it.

Footlocker: A trunk kept at the end of a bed or bunk for the storage of personal possessions, especially in a barracks. An army and marines term, not generally in naval use.

Footlocks: Wooden strips on the decks of cattle carriers to prevent animals from sliding in heavy seas.

Footloose: Sailors use this term to describe a fore-and-aft sail set without a boom, so that its foot is unsecured and free to flap around. According to some sources, the nautical term came ashore to describe a person not confined by responsibility and able to travel around freely, but it seems more likely to have developed on land, since "foot" and "loose" in their normal senses have the same connotation.

Foot-rope: A rope suspended below a yard to provide footing for sailors reefing or furling square-sails. Also "horse."

Forage cap: [1] Formerly, a small, low, undress cap of the American Civil War. [2] The British term for a garrison cap, worn by the Army and Air Force, but not in the Navy.

Force: [1] A body of troops, ships, aircraft, or combination thereof. [2] A major sub-division of a fleet, tasked for a specific mission. [3] A measure of wind intensity (*see* Beaufort Scale).

Force Majeure: [1] A clause in commercial contracts which exempts the parties for non-fulfillment of obligations due to forces beyond their control, such as earthquake, tsunami, hurricane, or war. [2] A principle of international law which holds that a vessel forced into a coastal state's waters by virtue of distress, whether natural or man-made, is not subject to jurisdiction of the coastal state during a reasonable period of time necessary to remedy the distress. However, the coastal state does have the right to board the vessel in order to verify its claim of distress.

Forced: The piratical equivalent of impressed, referring to crew members taken aboard against their will after refusing to sign articles.

Fore: [1] Abbreviation of forward. [2] Prefix denoting something located towards the front of a vessel; for example, forecastle, foredeck, foremast, etc.

Fore-and-aft: [1] Lengthwise, parallel to the center line of a vessel. [2] A rig whose sails are mounted on yards running lengthwise along the ship and attached to the masts at their butt ends. This type of sail is easy to manage, because it does not usually need to be re-laid when the ship changes course (cf. square-rig). [3] Said of a cocked hat worn with the peak facing forward (cf. athwartships).

Forecastle: (pronounced foak-sel) [1] A deck above the forward end of the main deck. [2] Formerly, crew accommodation below that deck. [3] The term now applies to the berths for deck crews wherever they may be located. Often abbreviated Fo'c'sle.

Forecastle head: The extreme forward part of the weather deck of a flushdecker or of a forecastle superstructure

Forecourse: [1] The lowermost sail on a square-rigged foremast. [2] A staysail, genoa, or jib set on the forestay of cutter, sloop, yawl, or ketch. Also Foresail.

Fore-deck: The upper deck between foremast and bow.

Forefoot: That part of the stem which joins the keel.

Foreland: A cape, promontory, or headland.

Foremast: The mast nearest the bow.

Foremaster: [1] A seaman assigned to work on the forecastle. [2] A seaman who berths in the forecastle.

Foremost: [1] First in time or place; most advanced; chief in rank or dignity. [2] situated closest to the bow.

Forenoon watch: The nautical work shift beginning at 0800 and ending at 1200 (8 A.M. to noon).

Forepeak: A compartment between the foremost bulkhead and the stem, often used for stowage or ballast.

Forereach: [1] To maintain headway after taking in sail or stopping engines. [2] To overtake another vessel.

Forerunner: [1] A small piece of red bunting set into a logline before the first knot, thus allowing some 12–14 fathoms (70–85 feet) to run out and clear the ship's deadwater before estimating its speed. [2] One of a series of long low swells which sometimes presage a storm. [3] A portent or omen.

Foresail: The sail on the foremast of a schooner, or the lowest square-sail on the foremast of a square-rigger.

Foresheets: Platform or seat at the bow of a small boat (cf. sheets, sternsheets).

Foreshore: That part of the shore lying between low and high water marks.

Forestaff: *See* cross staff.

Forestay: *See* headstay.

Fork in the beam: An old gunroom custom was for the senior sub-lieutenant to take a fork from the table, and thrust it into an overhead beam, as a sign that junior members of the mess were to leave without delay.

Form: The shape of a ship's hull, especially the underwater segment.

Forms of address: *See* address.

Forward: (pronounced forrard) Towards the front of a vessel. Often abbreviated to "fore."

Forward-looking infrared: Also known as thermal imaging, FLIR involves using infrared cameras that detect radiation emitted by objects based on their temperature. Digital techniques are often employed to improve picture quality. FLIR can be used at night and in fog, smoke, or other atmospheric obscurity. The technology is used for individual night vision goggles and by naval vessels, military aircraft, and armored fighting vehicles.

Fother: [1] To thread many lengths of oakum or old rope yarn through a sail or tarpaulin to make it into a hairy mat. [2] To seal a hole below the waterline by hanging such a mat over the side.

Foul: [1] To entangle or twist rope or chain. [2] Bad weather. [3] A weed-and-barnacle covered hull. [4] An obstructed flight deck unsafe for take-off or landing. [5] Wind blowing contrary to the desired direction. [6] A coast beset with reefs and breakers. [7] A gun barrel partially clogged by gunpowder-residue or other deposits. [8] Disgusting.

Fouled: [1] Any piece of equipment that is jammed or entangled. [2] Anything which is dirtied.

Fouled anchor: This traditional maritime heraldic emblem consists of an old-fashioned stocked anchor with a slack length of cable twisted around its stock, shank, and fluke. It originated as the official seal of the Lord High Admiral of Scotland in the 15th century, was adopted by the Lord High Admiral of England about a century later, and is prominent in the insignia of the United States and British as well as many other navies. The device is singularly inappropriate, since an anchor in that condition is a seafaring disaster, commonly known as "the seaman's disgrace."

Fouling: General term for the seaweed and marine organisms which gather on a ship's hull and slow it down.

Found: Equipped. A properly supplied, and appointed vessel is said to be "well-found."

Founder: To fill with water and sink.

FOV: Field of view.

Fox: A small rope of twisted yarns, normally smoothed and parceled with tarred canvas, for use as a gasket or seizing.

Foxtrot: NATO phonetic notation for the letter "F."

Foyst: A form of brigantine.

FPO: Fleet post office.

FPSO: Floating production, storage and offloading.

Frahm stabilizer: This system consists of a U-shaped tank, partially filled with water, located above the ship's centre of gravity and running transversely from port to starboard. It is designed so that the natural period of sloshing is approximately equal to the ship's natural period of oscillation. Roll of the vessel is thus transferred to the water which dissipates it — provided the water's frequency of motion harmonizes with the frequency of the exciting waves. At inharmonious frequencies a tank stabilizer can actually increase roll.

FRAM: Fleet Rehabilitation and Modernization Program (USN).

Frame: [1] Rib-like or longitudinal members forming the skeleton of a ship. [2] A case or border enclosing something.

Framing mold/mould: A full-size pattern or template for laying out the shape of a vessel's frames and other structural parts. *See* lofting, mold/mould maker.

Frap: [1] To wrap with line or canvas for protection. [2] To bind tightly together for strength. [3] U.S. Naval Academy slang for being put on disciplinary report.

Frapping lines: Lines wound around falls to stabilize the boat when being lowered into a rough sea.

Fratricide: *See* friendly fire.

Free: Running with the wind astern or on the quarter. A square-rigged vessel is said to be "running free" when it is unnecessary to fully brace its yards.

Free in and out: Commercial term indicating that the cost of loading and discharging is to be borne by the shipper.

Free pilotage: Authorizes specified classes of vessel to enter a port without having to engage a local pilot.

Free port: [1] A port offering equal facilities to vessels of all flags. [2] A trans-shipment port or part of a port in which imported cargoes can be unloaded, stored, and reloaded for onward shipment without paying a fee. [3] A port or part of a port designated for free trade, in which goods are subject to minimum customs regulation and may be exported without paying duty.

Free ship: Piratical term for a vessel whose articles specify equal shares for all irrespective of rank or rating.

Free trade: A market model in which goods and services flow between or within countries without government interference, or regulation such as customs tariffs or duties.

Freeboard: Height of ship's side from the waterline to the freeboard deck (cf. topside).

Freeboard deck: The uppermost watertight deck.

Freebooter: A pirate. Anglicization of the Dutch vrijbuiter. *See* filibuster.

Freedom of the Seas: A principle of international law which allows neutral vessels to sail anywhere on the high seas beyond territorial waters without interference from belligerent powers. Until the sixteenth century, the seas or parts of them were considered to be owned by any country powerful enough to exercise sovereignty, but in the seventeenth the development of seaborne trade led to the concept of open seas. Since then the basic principles of maritime law have been designed to satisfy and reconcile the requirements of national security with freedom of trade and navigation. Accordingly, only a narrow strip of coastal water is considered under the exclusive sovereignty of the coastal state, while the high seas beyond are freely accessible to all. *See also* exclusive economic zone, exclusive fishing zone, right of fishery.

Freeze the balls off: *See* brass monkey.

Freight: [1] Cargo. [2] The charge for carrying goods. [3] *See* tonnage.

Freight ton: A long ton (2,240 lbs or 1,016 kg) usually considered equivalent to 40 cubic feet (*see* shipping container).

Freighter: [1] Any vessel designed and used primarily for carrying cargo. [2] Any person consigning freight for transportation by sea.

French coil: *See* "Flemish coil."

French flake: *See* "Flemish Mat."

French leave: Colloquialism for being absent without permission.

Fresh breeze: Force 5 on the Beaufort Scale (winds 17–21 knots = 20–24 mph = 26–39 km/h).

Fresh gale: Term sometimes used instead of "Gale" for Force 8 on the Beaufort Scale (winds 34–40 knots = 39–46 mph = 62–74 km/h).

Fresh hand on the bellows: Now meaning a new start, or a change of management, this phrase was originally (according to some sources) the sailing ship seaman's colloquialism for a sudden increase in wind. Far more probably it originally referred to a blacksmith's forge and was later adopted by seamen.

Fresh water: In nautical usage this does not mean salt-free or potable, but is a technical term relating to hull displacement. Fresh water is defined as having a density of one kilogram/liter (62.428 lbs/cuft). This includes slightly brackish water.

Freshen: [1] To relieve stress or danger of chafing by shifting or removing a rope or hawser. [2] Said of a wind gaining strength.

Freshwater mark: Load line marking the maximum draft allowable in fresh water.

Fresnel lens: Numerous small lenses assembled to form a single large lens of short focal length. Developed in the early 19th century by French physicist A.J. Fresnel (pronounced freynel) originally used in searchlights, it was later adapted for the mirror landing aid.

Friday: It is widely believed that the reluctance of seamen to sail on a Friday (*see* "day of departure") reached such epic proportions by the eighteenth century that the British Admiralty decided to take drastic measures to prove the fallacy of the superstition. They are said to have laid the keel of a frigate one Friday, arranged her launch for another Friday, given the command to Captain James Friday, named her HMS *Friday*, and sent her to sea on a Friday. There was only one drawback — ship and crew disappeared never to be seen again, or so the story goes. This tale cannot be verified from Admiralty records and is almost certainly apocryphal. (Former Merchant Navy officer James Logan claims it originated as a hoax perpetuated by Irish comedian Dave Allen on one of his popular BBC radio shows of the 1970s.)

Fried hamsters: USN slang for chicken or beef cordon bleu.

Friendly: A contact positively identified as nonhostile.

Friendly fire: Bombing, strafing, shelling, or small-arms fire which inadvertently strikes one's own or allied forces. Also fratricide.

Friendship sloop: A gaff-rigged centerboard sailboat designed for oystering, lobstering, and fishing. Characterized by a high clipper bow, it originated in, and takes its name from, the seaport of Friendship in Knox County, Maine, USA.

Frigate: [1] A small and speedy 17th century warship. [2] An 18th–19th century triple-masted, square-rigged, sixth to fourth-rate naval vessel, smaller and faster than a ship-of-the-line, carrying 20 to 60 guns usually on a single gun-deck but occasionally double-banked. [3] A British World War II escort vessel. [4] After World War II the USN developed ships midway in size between cruisers and destroyers. Technically light cruisers, these vessels were briefly called frigates. [5] During the 1970s, USN nomenclature was revised to include a distinct class of frigates, smaller than destroyers, reflecting the practice of other navies.

Frock: [1] To allow an officer or enlisted seaman selected for advancement to assume the new insignia and title (but not the pay) before the promotion becomes effective. [2] The white woolen polo-necked sweaters worn by British submariners are known as frocks.

Frock coat: A man's outer garment characterized by knee-length skirts all around the base. Popular for both civil and military dress wear during the 19th century. Although obsolete in RN and USN, frock coats remain part of some contemporary military uniforms, usually single-breasted in army use, or double-breasted for naval wear.

Frockers and cockers: Pre–World War II RN officers' slang for frock coat and cocked hat which, until 1939, were the required uniform (with a sword) for making formal calls on an Admiral.

Frogman: Slang term for a swimmer equipped with wetsuit, fins, mask and breathing equipment. Usually trained in demolition, salvage, or other underwater operations, which are frequently clandestine.

Front: Meteorological term for the discontinuous surface between two air masses of different temperature.

Frost: A covering of minute ice needles, formed from the atmosphere upon exposed objects that have cooled by radiation below the dew point when that is below the freezing point.

Frost smoke: A thick mist rising from the surface when temperatures are close to freezing. (*See* "barber.")

Frustration: A charter party term referring to an unanticipated delay when neither party is at fault and either can void the contract. Properly called Frustration of the adventure.

FST: Fleet surgical team.

FSW: Feet of seawater.

FTN: Fuck The Navy. Term used by sailors having a bad day.

Fubar: Fouled Up Beyond All Repair (pronounced foobar). The "politically correct" first word is often changed by seamen.

Fudge: This term meaning to dodge an issue, cheat on an exam, or renege on a promise is said to refer to a notorious 17th century ship captain known as "Lying Fudge."

Fudge factor: A colloquialism referring to a quantity introduced to compensate for uncertainty.

Fuel: Material such as coal, wood, petroleum products, and the like used as a source of heat or power.

Fuel cell: British scientist Sir William Grove invented this device in 1839. Noting that water could be split into hydrogen and oxygen by electrolysis, he reversed the procedure, creating an electrochemical device that combined hydrogen and oxygen to produce electricity with water and heat as by-products. No other energy generation technology offers the same combination of benefits. The process is clean, quiet, highly efficient, and will generate power for as long as fuel is supplied, but the technology remained experimental until the late 20th century.

Currently (2008) the cruise industry is interested in the possibility of improving passenger comfort with a silent, non-polluting power source that produces no detectable exhaust heat, while most of the world's navies have active fuel cell programs, especially for submersibles. The Hellenic Navy Class 214 submarine has a fuel cell-generated power supply that allows it to cruise under water for up to three weeks without resurfacing. By contrast, conventional diesel-electric submarines typically deplete their batteries after a few days cruising. In addition, the fuel cell makes the submarine virtually undetectable. The U.S. and other Navies are also looking into fuel cell propulsion for surface warships. In addition to the foregoing advantages are reduced fuel consumption and the potential to have a number of separate units to provide redundancy in case of combat damage.

Fuel trunk: A connection used for refueling.

Fu-Fu: A sailing ship seaman's dish of barley and treacle.

Fujita Tornado Scale: Was developed in 1971 by Dr Tetsuya Theodore Fujita of the University of Chicago, in conjunction with Allan Pearson, Director of the National Severe Storm Forecast Center at Kansas City Missouri. Because its seven-level scale relies on after-the-event visual inspection of damage to structures and trees ashore, it is not applicable to waterspouts. However, it does indicate wind speeds up to and beyond those which might be anticipated in phenomena of the tornado type. It is therefore included in table 6 which compares it with the Beaufort, Douglas, Pierson-Moskowitch, Saffir-Simpson, and WMO Scales.

Full: The state of sails when bellied-out by wind.

Full and by: Following a course as close as possible to the wind while keeping the sails full without any shiver.

Full and down: Said of a vessel when all cargo spaces are filled and she is down to her load line.

Full dress: [1] Uniform worn on special and ceremonial occasions (*see* frockers and cockers). [2] A ship that is dressed to the nines is fully-dressed.

Full-rigged: A vessel carrying square-sails on at least three masts.

Full rudder: As far as the rudder can go. The USN steering command is "Left (or right) full rudder." The equivalent RN command is "Hard aport (or a-starboard)."

Full sail/spread: All sails set with none of them reefed.

Full speed: To proceed at the maximum sustainable rate. The USN defines full speed as one eighth more than standard speed except for cruisers, destroyers, light mine layers and fast aircraft carriers, for which it is five knots more than standard speed (*see also* emergency speed, flank speed).

Fully dressed: Said of a ship adorned for a special occasion with ensigns at all masts and a rainbow of signal flags stretched from bow-to-stern over the mastheads. *See also* dressed to the nines.

Funerary salutes: During important military funerals, "minute guns" are fired at 60-second intervals, paralleling the "minute bells" tolled by churches during civil ceremonies. If a band is deployed, its drums are muffled by passing their carrying plaits through the snares or cords at the base of the drums. The firing of three rifle or musket volleys over the grave of a fallen warrior has military rather than naval origins. During the dynastic wars of Europe, a truce for evacuating the wounded and burying the dead would often be called after a fierce engagement. The signal that the field had been cleared of casualties and conflict could be resumed was three rounds of musket fire into the air. (American media frequently refer to a "21-gun salute" at military funerals, presumably because three rounds from seven rifles total twenty-one. However, although three volleys is traditional, no regulation or tradition requires the firing detail to be seven or any other number.) In fact, the custom may have older roots in the primitive idea that loud noises will frighten evil spirits away from a grave.

After the volleys, the bugler will sound the eloquent and haunting tune of "Last Post" at British funerals or "Taps" at American ones. As they do for the living, these tunes symbolize that the day's duty is over and the deceased may rest in peace. Then, following a brief silence, the bugler often sounds "Reveille" to symbolize rebirth in a better world (the term is French and means "awaken again").

Funnel: [1] A ship's smokestack or chimney. Naval architects often gave ocean liners dummy funnels, either for esthetic reasons or to give a greater impression of power and speed. [2] A shaft, flue, or stack for ventilation.

Funnel cloud: *See* tornado and waterspout.

Furl: To roll up and secure a sail or awning. From Old English fardle = wrap or bundle.

Furlough: An approved absence. From German urlaub.

Furnace: An enclosed place in which heat is produced by the combustion of fuel.

Furnace room: The engineering compartment in which the boilers of a steam-powered ship are located, along with the furnaces that heat them. So long as ships were coal-fired the stokers and trimmers had a filthy job in appalling conditions — badly lighted and noisy; intensely hot (around 45°C/112°F); smelling of steam, burning sulfurous coal, and human sweat — physically manhandling tons of dusty coal from the bunkers to the furnace doors and shoveling white hot ash and clinker away from the grates — all the while standing on a heaving, pitching, swaying, and rolling deck.

Furnishings: General term for a ship's moveable equipment, such as anchors, davits, masts, rigging, winches, cables, boats, and the like, but excluding fuel and consumable stores. (*See also* fittings, furniture, supplies.)

Furniture: A marine insurance term referring to removable items of equipment necessary for safe operation and navigation of a vessel such as masts, rigging, tackles, guns, and the like. (*See also* fittings, furnishings, supplies.)

Fuse/Fuze: A combustible, mechanical, magnetic, electric, or electronic means of detonating an explosive charge as a result of time, proximity, or contact.

Futtock shrouds: Part of a sailing vessel's standing rigging. The word is believed to be a contraction of "foot-hooks" because the sailor's toes had to be hooked around the ratlines.

Futtocks: The middle timbers of a wooden ship's frame.

Future Navy: This British concept envisages a versatile and flexible maritime contribution to the overall defense mission, while retaining core emphasis on combat capability. As visualized, the future navy will have global reach and endurance, will adapt to change efficiently and effectively, and will be fully "interoperable" with future army and future air force as well as with other national and international military and civil partners in joint, combined, or integrated operations. Based on the NATO Swing concept, the proposed versatile maritime force will have platforms and equipment that can deliver a range of military capabilities either simultaneously, or thorough operational, tactical, or strategic reconfiguration. Simplicity of equipment operation and procedures, reinforced by effective training, will be essential in the future navy, because each seaman will have to be capable of handling multiple tasks rather than a single specialty.

Fwd: Forward.

FWO: Fleet Watch Officer (USN).

FX: Forecastle.

G

G: Gravitational acceleration force.

GA: General Average.

Gaff: [1] A pole with a barbed tip, a boathook (from Portuguese gafe). [2] A spar on the mainmast of a USN vessel from which the national ensign is flown. [3] A short spar to which the head of a fore-and-aft sail is bent. *See also* Sailing Rigs.

Gaff-rigged: Refers to a fore-and-aft sail shaped like a truncated triangle, with its upper edge made fast to a gaff. The top of a gaff-rigged sail tends to twist away from the wind reducing its efficiency when close-hauled.

Gain the wind: To get upwind of another sailing vessel.

Gained day: The 24 hours which are "won" when crossing the International Date Line in an easterly direction. In the Royal Navy this formerly entitled the crew to an additional day's pay (but of course they lost it going the other way).

Gaiters: [1] A leather covering for the leg, extending from above the instep to below the knee. Normally white in USN, polished black in RN. [2] RN slang for a gunnery instructor, said to be "all gas and gaiters" (cf. gunny, liquorice legs).

Gale: Force 8 on the Beaufort Scale (winds 34–40 knots = 39–46 mph = 63–74 km/h). From the Norse gale = furious.

Galileo: A satellite navigation system, launched by the European Union and the European Space Agency. It will be compatible with the current Global Positioning System.

Galiot/Galliot: A smaller version of the galley powered by oars and a large lateen sail on a single mast. [2] A small ketch-like vessel in the Baltic coastal trade. [3] A powered craft used on the Rhine River and North Sea.

Gall: To chafe or wear (e.g., a hawser, anchor cable, bearing, etc.).

Galleass: A large vessel, driven by lateen sails on three masts and thirty to forty oars. Equipped with a pointed ram at the bow and cannon on raised fighting platforms at bow and stern. An unsatisfactory compromise between rowing galley and sailing galleon.

Galleon: A large armed merchantman with two or three decks, square-rigged on fore and mainmasts, lateen-sailed on the mizzen, plus a large square-sail on the bowsprit. Spanish galleons were heavily armed with (mostly) close-range anti-personnel weapons; English ones carried fewer but longer-range cannon.

Gallery: [1] A projecting balcony or structure on the stern or quarter of a vessel, often enclosed with elaborate glass windows and carved woodwork (gingerbread). [2] A partial deck below an aircraft carrier's flight deck between it and the hangar deck.

Galley: [1] A ship's kitchen, probably a corruption of "cooking gallery." [2] A relatively long and narrow sail and oar-propelled, single-decked commercial or combat vessel, which originated in the Aegean and Mediterranean during the classical era. Sails and masts were normally unshipped and left ashore before combat. Early fighting galleys depended on short bursts of speed to ram enemy vessels with sharp "beaks." Later ones carried heavy forward-firing cannon mounted on a platform at the bow. [3] A large clinker-built open rowing boat, usually with a crew of twelve.

Galley packet: RN slang for a rumor. *See* galley yarn, scuttlebutt.

Galley pepper: Sailor's slang for the soot and ashes which sometimes land on the food while cooking.

Galley ranger: An unpopular sailor who has been rejected by all the messes in a ship and has to eat alone.

Galley staysail: A windsail adjusted so as to ventilate the galley.

Galley yarn: USN slang for a rumor, especially a false one. Also scuttlebutt.

Galligaskins: *See* petticoat-trowsers.

Gallipoli: The Dardanelles Campaign of 1915 was the first modern amphibious operation and introduced a number of innovations. However, with the exception of its closing episode, it was a classic example of how not to run an invasion. In his book *Gallipoli* (MacMillan 1956) Alan Morehead says:

> No similar exploit in the past bore any real comparison ... or had had to face such entrenched positions ... the only operation that could be compared with this lay thirty years ahead on the beaches of Normandy in the Second World War; and planning the Normandy landing was to take not three weeks but nearly two years.

Nevertheless, the operation began encouragingly with feint attacks on 25th April 1915, one of which found the key strategic height of Achi Baba virtually undefended — but the troops' orders were only to create a diversion, so they made no attempt to seize it, staying put until ordered to withdraw. Amid a welter of mismanagement the main attacks were made by British and French troops on the tip of the peninsula, and by Australians & New Zealanders (Anzacs) at its narrow neck.

After four months bogged down in trench warfare near the beachheads, Allied C-in-C Sir Ian Hamilton mounted a new landing at Suvla Bay a few kilometers north of Anzac Cove. For the first time in amphibious warfare using purpose-built, self-propelled, armored landing craft instead of cutters and whalers towed by steam pinnaces.

The new divisions had been hastily-trained for static warfare on the Western Front, where as little as fifty meters was considered a significant advance, while in command was General Stopford, who had never led troops in battle and had been retired for fifteen years. With the old-and-outdated leading the young-and-inexperienced, no one seems to have understood the urgency of rushing to secure a defensible perimeter on high ground. Stopford allowed the first wave to swim and sunbathe on the beach while waiting for the rest to land. They too were soon stalemated.

With all his beachheads pinned down. Hamilton planned to open a new front on the Plain of Troy with six combat-ready divisions from France. However, they were diverted to Salonika, and the blow was exacerbated when three of the divisions already on Gallipoli were ordered to Salonika as well. In October, Hamilton was replaced by General Sir Charles Monro, who made a unilateral decision to withdraw. Winston Churchill bitterly paraphrased Julius Caesar, "He came, he saw, he capitulated!"

The troops had to be lifted from open beaches, during bad weather, in waters suitable for U-boat attack, while exposed to the close-range fire of an undefeated enemy. Planners predicted a minimum casualty rate of 30 percent, with a high probability of exceeding 50 percent. Hospitals in Egypt were alerted to prepare for at least thirty thousand casualties.

Thanks to meticulous planning by Australian General William Birdwood, effective cooperation between naval and military, ingenious deception devices, and a short break in the weather, Anzac Cove and Suvla Bay were evacuated in mid–December with no soldiers killed, and only two lightly wounded. At Cape Hellas, neither the enemy nor the weather was so cooperative. Nevertheless, casualties were far fewer than expected. The German General Staff called the evacuation "A military feat without equal."

The objective of forcing the Straits, knocking Turkey out of the war, reinforcing Russia, and bringing Balkan States in on the allied side was a far-sighted strategic concept which should have been attainable — the official Turkish War History said, "If Sir Ian Hamilton had been given six divisions instead of four at the outset, the invading troops could have forced the Straits."

Gallivat: A small vessel with sails and oars, armed with 4–8 cannon. Used on the Malabar Coast and in the Persian/Arabian Gulf.

Gallows: [1] A support on the open deck consisting of uprights and a cross-piece, used for the storage of boats, spars, and the like. [2] A support for the boom of a sailing vessel.

Gam: A whaling term for a news-exchanging visit between the crews of two or more ships when stopped at sea.

Gammon: To lash a bowsprit to the bows. The actual lashing is called gammoning.

Gangboard: [1] A raised walk on a sailing ship, crossing the waist and connecting forecastle to quarterdeck. [2] The longitudinal timber on an open boat, connecting the foresheets and the after thwart. From Old English gang = alley. [3] Formerly, the merchant sailor's name for a brow or gangplank.

Gangplank: A flat bridge-like structure with cleats, used for boarding or leaving a vessel at a pier (see brow, which is the more correct term).

Gangway: [1] An opening in the bulwark into which an accommodation ladder, brow, or gangplank, fits. [2] Incorrectly, but frequently, the accommodation ladder, brow, or gangplank itself. [3] A seaman under punishment is said to have been "brought to the gangway" when he is lashed to a grating for flogging.

Gangway!: Shouted command to make way and stand clear of a person or thing passing through.

Gannet: [1] A diving seabird with voracious appetite. [2] Slang term for a greedy person or gourmand.

Gantelope: See running the gauntlet.

Gantlet: See gauntlet.

Gantline: A line passing through a single block aloft, used for hoisting.

Gantry: A framework, specifically one for storing casks or barrels in a cargo hold.

Garble: [1] Originally the Middle English word "garbelen" meant to remove impurities from ship-ments of spices. [2] With the meaning changed from removal to insertion, "garbling" referred to the practice of mixing rubbish with bulk cargo to increase its weight or volume. [3] Nowadays a distorted or mixed up message is said to be garbled.

Garboard strake: The first continuous row of planks or plates on either side of a ship's keel.

Gare up: A Suez Canal term. When two ships meet, one will "gare up" (moor to) the bank to allow the other to pass.

Garland: Formerly [1] A rope collar round the head of a mast to keep the shrouds from chafing. [2] A strap lashed to a spar for hoisting. [3] A large rope grommet used to hold shot in place or move it around. [4] A net with a hooped neck, hung from an overhead beam, and used by sailors to store the day's provisions way from cats and insects. [5] Three hoops wrapped together by silk and ribbons to form a wreath, hoisted to the main top-gallant stay on the day of a captain's wedding. [6] A similar wreath hoisted on any other spar or stay to celebrate a seaman's nuptials.

Garnet: [1] A gun tackle with two single blocks. [2] A purchase for lifting goods or freight in or out of a cargo ship.

Garnish: Profuse decoration on a ship's head, stern, or quarters (cf. gingerbread).

Garrison: [1] A military post. [2] The troops stationed there.

Garrison cap: A soft wedge-shaped "fore-and-aft" cap which folds flat. Used by all U.S. armed services. Also "overseas cap." The British equivalent is "forage cap."

Garters: Seaman's slang for the leg-irons used in punishment.

Gas and gaiters: See gaiters.

Gash: Nautical slang for anything spare or superfluous. Hence waste food is put in the gash-bucket, waste paper goes in a gash-bin, and slops are sent down a gash-chute.

Gasket: [1] A light line used for fastening sails when furling. [2] A rubber, metal, or fiber ring, used to seal a piston or to make something watertight.

Gat: A passage or channel extending inland through shoals or banks. From the Dutch for hole as in the Kattegat (Cat's hole) between Sweden and Denmark.

Gate: [1] A moveable barrier across the mouth of a harbor or anchorage. [2] Ancient name for a port or landing place (as in Billingsgate, Margate, Ramsgate, etc.).

Gateship: A vessel used to open or close antisubmarine nets or booms protecting the entrance to a harbor or narrow passage.

Gather way: To start moving or speed up, thereby increasing headway or sternway.

Gator: USN slang for [1] An amphibious warfare ship. [2] One who serves in such a ship (short for "alli-gator"). [3] A ship's navigating officer (from navigator).

GATT: General Agreement on Tariffs and Trade.

Gauge: The position of one vessel relative to the

position of another vessel and the wind. In sailing ship combat, the downwind vessel has the "lee gauge," which favors disengagement (if wanted) and heels the vessel so that gunfire tends to break masts and cut rigging. The upwind vessel has the "weather gauge" which favors offensive action and allows broadsides to be aimed at the enemy hull.

Gauntlet: *See* Running the gauntlet.

GBS: Global Broadcast Satellite.

GCA: Ground-Controlled Approach (of aircraft).

GCI: Ground-Controlled Intercept (of aircraft).

Gear: A catchall nautical term covering [1] Any assembly of sails, lines, tackles, etc. [2] The personal effects of a crew member. [3] A toothed wheel that meshes with another to provide a mechanical advantage, to increase force or speed, or to reverse direction.

Gearless carrier: A large bulker without loading and discharging capability. Although avoiding the expense of installing, operating, and maintaining cranes or conveyors, it is dependent on shore-based facilities and can only dock at large, well-equipped ports.

Gedunk: USN slang, believed to be derived from the sound of a candy bar dropping from a vending machine, and hence, [1] Generic term for ice cream, candy, and the like. [2] A ship's store which sells snacks (often Gedunk Stand). [3] An enticement for female companionship; *see also* pogey bait. [4] A Gedunk Ribbon is a decoration awarded for non-combatant service.

Gender: In naval parlance, ships are almost invariably referred to as female. The origin of this tradition is unknown, but there have been numerous explanations. As early as the second century BCE the playwright Plautus made a feminine connection when he wrote "A man looking for trouble only has to buy a ship or take a wife." Twenty-two centuries later, U.S. Fleet Admiral Chester Nimitz gave an equally cynical explanation, saying "It's because a ship costs so much to keep in paint and powder." Most probably the custom arose in classical times, when each newly-launched vessel was dedicated as a bride to Poseidon (or Neptune). In consequence, ships became feminine in Latin and all the Romance languages and, even though English nouns do not have gender, it would have been natural to follow suit (*see also* Names).

General: A senior military title, equivalent to admiral (*see* table 13).

General Agreement on Tariffs and Trade: This 1947 treaty is designed to provide an international forum that encourages free trade between member states by regulating and reducing tariffs on trade goods and by providing a common mechanism for resolving trade disputes. GATT membership now includes more than 110 countries.

General alarm: A loud bell or klaxon with different patterns that call the crew to battle stations, signal chemical emergencies, or raise collision alerts. All three are tested daily and, to avoid misunderstandings, no similar alarms are permitted on shipboard.

General average: An ancient principle of maritime equity which holds that when a peril threatening a ship's survival has been averted by jettisoning cargo, supplies, or furniture, the voluntary sacrifice has been for the good of all and must be shared pro rata by all parties concerned (shipowners, cargo owners, and owners of freight revenue). The principle was established at least as early as the Laws of Rhodes (ca. 916 BCE).

General cargo: Freight composed of different goods carried in non-specialized containers which may vary in size and shape (e.g., bales, boxes, barrels, bundles, casks, crates, packages, pallets, etc.). Until the early 20th century most goods at sea were carried in this form; few liquids were transported, and those that were usually carried in barrels. Today everything has changed; containerization is common and the general cargo ship has largely been replaced by specialized vessels such as tankers, grain and ore ships, container ships, ro-ro ships, and car carriers.

General Court Martial: The highest-level trial court in the military justice system.

General discharge: One of five USN discharge classifications, awarded to personnel who separate from the service with good conduct but an insufficiently meritorious record to deserve an honorable discharge. *See also* other than honorable, bad conduct, and dishonorable.

General mess: USN eating area for all hands (except those with a designated area of their own such as wardroom, chief petty officers mess, etc.).

General of the Sea: The title enjoyed by admirals under the British Commonwealth (republic) of 1649–60.

General Officer: The army and marine equivalent of a flag officer (i.e., above the rank of colonel).

General orders: Instructions issued by a senior commander to an entire force, fleet, or service.

General prudential rule: Caveat in the Rules of the Road permitting a privileged or stand-on vessel to depart from the rules if necessary to avoid immediate danger.

General quarters!: USN voice or bugle call for all hands to don combat gear and go to battle stations. All guns are loaded and ready-use ammunition is placed to hand (cf. Action Stations).

Generator: A machine or device that converts kinetic energy to electrical energy, generally using electromagnetic induction. The term is generally used for the generation of alternating current. *See also* dynamo, electric motor.

Geneva Conventions: A series of international agreements, first reached at Geneva in 1864, covering the status and treatment of captured and wounded military personnel in wartime. The most recent maritime treaty — The Geneva Convention for the Wounded, Sick, & Shipwrecked Members of the Armed Forces at Sea — was negotiated on 12 August 1949. It specifies the treatment and protection of prisoners of war; wounded and sick enemy persons who are not prisoners of war; religious, medical, and hospital personnel caring for enemy wounded and sick; military hospital ships, and coastal rescue craft and lifeboats. After 9/11 the Bush administration withheld its protection from "unlawful enemy combatants" of the USA. *See also* humanitarian emblems.

Genoa: A large headsail or jib used mainly by racing yachts.

Gentle breeze: Force 3 on the Beaufort Scale (winds 7–10 knots = 8–11.5 mph = 13–18.5 km/h).

Geodesy: The branch of mathematics dealing with the terrestrial globe or large sections thereof.

Geodetic: Of or relating to geodesy. Also geodesic.

Geographic coordinates: The latitude and longitude whose intersection defines the position of a point on the surface of the globe.

Geographic poles: The latitudes of 90° North and 90° South, forming the extremes of the earth's axis of rotation.

Geographic referencing: By definition, all geographic data can be spatially referenced to identify its location on the globe. *See* World Geographic Reference System.

Geographic spatial data: International conventions specify the signs to be used by map and chart makers and geodeticists. Latitude references are signed as positive (+) westward and negative (-) eastward from the meridian of Greenwich to 180°. Longitude references are positive north and negative south of the equator to 90° in each direction. Bearings are measured clockwise from north through 360°. Azimuths are also measured clockwise and continuing to 360°, but beginning at south.

Geographical rotation: Refers to the sequence of ports to be visited by a merchant vessel.

Geographical zones: Based essentially on climate and behavior of the sun, geographers divide the surface of the earth latitudinally into five principal regions, namely:
• North Frigid Zone — north of the Arctic Circle.
• North Temperate Zone — between the Arctic Circle and the Tropic of Cancer.
• Torrid Zone — between the Tropics of Cancer and Capricorn.
• South Temperate Zone — between the Tropic of Capricorn and the Antarctic Circle.
• South Frigid Zone — south of the Antarctic Circle.

Georef: *See* "World Geographic Reference System."

George Ensign: USN slang for the most junior ensign on board a warship. Reputed to be derived from JORG = Junior Officer Requiring Guidance (cf. bull ensign).

Get cracking: Now meaning to push ahead, this term derives from the days of sail, when a shipmaster in a hurry would raise so much canvas that masts and standing rigging became taut to the point of creaking and cracking.

Ghanja: Two- or three-masted lateen-rigged craft used in the Persian/Arabian Gulf and along the East African littoral.

Ghost: [1] To sail slowly when there is no perceptible wind. [2] A secondary, duplicate, or false image on a radar screen due to echoes or interference. Also phantom.

Ghost ships: There are several types of maritime apparition. Some are thought to warn of coming disaster while others recall earlier tragedies. The Block Island Phantom does both. Some, such as the Cursed Corsair, the Flying Dutchman, and the Japanese Yureisen, are sinister specters that appear out of nowhere. Others were mystery ships like *Mary Celeste*, discovered intact with crew mysteriously vanished. And some appear to be explicable phenomena such as the Chaleur Bay Phantom and *Jenny* the Glacial Ghost. Interestingly, some 90 percent of all phantom ship sightings are between the fortieth and fiftieth latitudes.

Ghosts: It was a common belief among sailing ship sailors that any vessel which has been sunk and raised again is haunted by the souls of those who perished when she went down.

GhostSwimmer: A sophisticated biomimetic submarine robot or UAV (underwater autonomous vehicle) developed for the U.S. Navy in 2008 and expected to be deployed in 2009. Based on the tuna fish, its mechanism includes a spine with vertebrae and synthetic muscles that drive fins and a tail, turning waves of body motion into propulsion, just as those components perform the same task for the real fish. The tuna was chosen because its family (*Scombridae*) varies in length from 100 cms (Blackfin) to 450 cms (Northern Bluefin), indicating hydrodynamic design adaptable to a wide range of sizes, and so efficient that it allows tuna to make trans-oceanic migrations at speeds of up to 70 km/h. The system is expected to use less power than conventional propeller-drive, to have approximately three times the endurance, and to be relatively silent and stealthy. The tuna-like size and shape of prototypes will allow them to blend into the underwater background, making them perfect for intelligence-gathering. If these small versions perform as expected, the Navy hopes to adapt the concept for full-size submarines.

GI: Government Issue (U.S.).

Gig: A light oared-and-sailed boat, now frequently powered, usually reserved for personal use by the ship's captain. [2] USN slang for a reprimand (cf. bottle).

Gimbals: A system of rings and pivots which suspends an object such as compass, chronometer, or galley stove so that it can move freely in two planes at the same time, thus remaining horizontal even when its support is tilted.

Gimblet: To rotate a suspended anchor to a desired position. Also gimlet.

Gimlet: [1] The name of a cocktail, now made of gin or vodka and sweetened lime juice, that was effectively invented by Admiral Edward Vernon who used rum in the original recipe (*see* Grog). However, the name refers to Thomas D. Gimlette, a naval surgeon (later Surgeon General) who introduced the cocktail in the late nineteenth century as a means of inducing wardroom officers to take lime juice as an anti-scorbutic. [2] *See* gimblet.

Gin pendant: A green-white-green pendant unofficially flown by an RN ship to indicate: [1] That visitors from other ships in the squadron or flotilla will be welcomed in the wardroom, or [2] That one of the wardroom officers is personally entertaining (birthday, promotion, birth of a baby, etc.).

Gingerbread: The elaborate, usually gilded, carvings decorating the bow and stern sections of warships from the 15th to 18th centuries. Also extremely popular on 19th century riverine steamboats in the United States. The term is said to have come from Germany, where the gingerbread sold at country fairs was traditionally splashed with gilt to make its appearance more attractive.

Gingerbread hatch: Obsolete slang for a luxurious cabin or stateroom.

Girdle: To improve the buoyancy and stability of a wooden ship by adding planking along the waterline.

Girth: The measurement from one gunwale to the other, passing under the keel. Taken at any frame.

Girthline: *See* gantline. Also girtline.

Give way!: Command, [1] To begin pulling the oars of a boat. [2] To stand clear or make room.

Give-way vessel: The one which must yield when meeting, crossing, or being overtaken by another. *See also* Stand-on vessel, privileged vessel.

Glacial Ghost: The whaler *Hope* had chased a quarry as far as the ice cliffs of Antarctica where it managed to give them the slip. They were about to sail away in search of other prey when the great ice barrier began to break up and calve. Large chunks fell away opening up several chasms. Suddenly, to the horror of *Hope*'s crew, a spectral ship sailed out of one of the inlets, sails in tatters and hull splintered, with seven ice-encrusted human figures standing or sitting on deck. Quelling his crew's terrified mutterings of "Flying Dutchman," Captain Brighton ordered a whaleboat to be launched and rowed across to the "phantom." In the master's cabin he found a man sitting at his desk, pen in hand, apparently entering something in the log book. He was, however, as solidly flash-frozen as the men on deck and his wife in the next door cabin. His final entry in the log read "No food for 71 days. I am the only one left alive," and the date of May 4, 1823, indicated that the schooner *Jenny* had been trapped in the ice for thirty-seven and one-half years.

Glacier: A compacted mass of snow and ice that is continuously moving to lower ground or outward from a continental center of accumulation.

Glacier tongue: A seaward extension of a glacier, usually floating.

Glad rags: 19th century sailors were skilled needle workers and would spend many off-watch hours making fine shore-going clothes which they called "glad rags," presumably because they were happy to leave the ship for a while. Also go-ashores.

Glass: [1] A telescope. Often an important symbol of office; also "long-glass." [2] A barometer. [3] Formerly the half-hour glass used to tell time aboard ship, and hence [4] a thirty-minute period of time.

Glass ringing: *See* Clinking glasses.

Glasses: Binoculars.

Glide bomb: An air-launched bomb fitted with airfoils to provide lift.

Glide path indicator: *See* mirror landing aid.

Global Command & Control System: A highly mobile, deployable system for the support of joint or multinational military operations, providing integrated command, control, communication, computer, and intelligence systems.

Global Maritime Distress & Safety System: An internationally agreed set of communication protocols, equipment, and safety procedures, based on a combination of satellite and terrestrial radio services. These have changed distress communication from mainly between ships to mainly ship-to-shore, with alert and location signals being automatically transmitted when the radio operator doesn't have time to issue a mayday or contact the Rescue Coordination Center.

Global Maritime Partnership: In response to the need for and difficulties of international naval co-operation a group of senior United States admirals is currently advocating an ambitious concept that envisions a global coalition of navies, "standing watch over the seas, standing watch over each other" and cooperating in law enforcement with coast guards, port operators, commercial shippers, governments, and non-governmental agencies. Recognizing that, despite their good intentions, there is grave danger this will be viewed as an attempt to make the international maritime community dance to an American tune, they emphasize this is not the case. In an opinion piece published by *The Honolulu Advertiser* on 29 October 2007, Chief of Naval Operations, Admiral Mike Mullen, said:

> Membership in this "navy" is purely voluntary and would have no legal or encumbering ties. It would be a free-form, self-organizing network of maritime partners — good neighbors interested in using the power of the sea to unite, rather than to divide. The barriers for entry are low. Respect for sovereignty is high.

The proposal was originally and evocatively entitled "The thousand ship Navy."

Global Positioning System: A space-based navigation system in which orbiting satellites provide extremely accurate three-dimensional coordinates. It is officially called NAVSTAR-GPS, which is short for (**Navigational Signal Timing And Ranging** —Global Positioning System) but is commonly known as GPS. It was designed for and is operated by the U.S. military, which makes segments of it available for civilian use as a "public good" without charge. It can be conveniently divided into three parts.

• **Control Segment** consists of tracking stations located around the world, under the overall control of a master facility at Schriever AFB in Colorado.

- **Space Segment** consists of at least 24 satellites that orbit the earth twice daily and are known as space vehicles (SVs). These are spaced so that between five and eight can be sighted from any point on earth at any time. After locating at least four of them, a GPS receiver can use a simple mathematical technique called trilateration to deduce its location.
- **Public User Segment** has been intentionally downgraded from military precision, but still allows anyone with a GPS receiver to determine latitude and longitude within 100 meters; altitude within 156 meters, and time of day within 340 nanoseconds.

Like any electronic device, a GPS receiver can fail or malfunction, so the prudent navigator will always carry back-up in the form of traditional devices such as leadline and logline, sextant and navigation tables, chronometer, etc. *See also* Galileo, satellite navigation.

Globe: [1] The terraqueous ball of planet earth (usually preceded by the definite article). [2] A round scale model of the world (preceded by an indefinite article).

Globsters: The name given to mysterious rotting carcasses that have sometimes been taken as dead sea monsters.

GLONASS: An acronym of **Glo**bal **Na**vigation **S**atellite **S**ystem, referring to a Russian version of global positioning that provides three-dimensional position, range, and time references. Like GPS it relies on 24 satellites and offers two levels of service — standard for the general public and high precision for military use.

Glory bar: USN slang for a campaign medal.

Glory hole: [1] The lazarette, or any enclosed space in which small items can be stowed until needed. [2] Jocular name for the steward's or firemen's accommodation.

GM: Gunner's Mate.

GMDSS: Global Maritime Distress and Safety System.

GMT: Greenwich Mean Time.

Go about: To change to the opposite tack by passing the bow through the wind.

Go-ashores: Slang for a seaman's best walking out clothes or "glad rags."

Gob: [1] U.S. civilian slang for a naval enlisted man. The term is never used in the USN which banned it as "undignified" in the 1920s. [2] In the RN, Gobby used to be a derogatory term for a naval reservist assigned to Coastguard service, but is seldom heard today.

Gods of the sea: Many sea-dwelling beings have established themselves in myth, but the Graeco-Roman deities are the ones which have persisted in European tradition. In over-simplified form, their history starts with Oceanus and Tethys, who ruled over all the worlds' watery elements but were later succeeded by Poseidon (Neptune) and his wife Amphitrite. Their son Triton became his father's conch-horn trumpeter

creating the roar of the seas, while another son Proteus was guardian of the seal herds; both being revered as sea-elders able to foretell the future. Leucothea and her son Palæmon were invoked by Roman seamen as powerful protectors against shipwreck. Portunus the god of ports and harbors could ensure safe and prosperous voyages. *See also* water deities.

Gods of the wind: Winds were as important to sailing seamen as the waves were, and all seafaring cultures had their own wind gods and goddesses. The Greeks had five major and many minor ones, most of which were adopted by the Romans under different names. Here we shall consider only Greek mythology, which called the principal wind gods Anemoi, each of which was associated with a cardinal direction and specific weather conditions:

- Aeolus was a son of Poseidon, viceroy of the gods, and regent of all the Winds, which he kept in vast caves on the mythical island of Aeolia.
- Zephyrus personified, the gentle and friendly west wind, bringer of light spring and early summer breezes.
- Eurus was the strong, but unlucky, wind that brought warmth and rain from the east.
- Notus was the warm and moist south or southwest wind, much feared by mariners because he not only brought the fierce storms of late summer and autumn, but his fog, mist, and rain hindered visibility.
- Boreas blew from the north, bringing cold winter air. He is the only one who seems to have been remembered and invoked by European sailors.

Godsend: Wrecker's term for a vessel thrown ashore fortuitously rather than deliberately lured onto the rocks.

Going large: Advancing freely before the wind; the opposite of close-hauled.

Gold braid: Popular term for a naval officer's rank insignia. More correctly, gold lace.

Gold lace: The proper name of the stripes indicating a naval officer's rank. Frequently splashed with sea water by junior officers hoping to achieve a less-inexperienced look. Also Gold braid.

Goldbrick: USN slang for a slacker or loafer.

Golden Age (of Piracy): The 16th to 18th centuries.

Golden Dragon: *See* line-crossing.

Golden rivet: The mythical and magical last item which completes construction of a ship.

Golden Shellback: *See* line-crossing.

Golf: NATO phonetic notation for the letter "G."

Gondola: A small, highly-ornamented, boat with high rising stem and stern. Used on the Venetian canals and propelled with a single oar by a "Gondolier" standing at the stern.

Gone aloft: Slang for a dead shipmate.

Gone by the board: [1] Originally an article intentionally or accidentally dropped over the side (*see* deep six). [2] The term now implies something which has been destroyed, neglected, or forgotten.

Gone goose: Slang for a vessel abandoned and given up in despair.

Gone west: This term signifying death can possibly be traced back to the Viking funeral practice of putting a dead chieftain or great warrior in his longship and setting it to sail towards the setting sun.

Gong: [1] A ship's bell, especially when used as a boat gong. [2] Slang for a decoration.

Good Conduct Badge: The RN name for a service stripe, with one stripe being awarded for each five years of certified good conduct free from disciplinary offenses.

Good Humor Man: USN enlisted slang for a sailor wearing summer white uniform thought to resemble an ice cream vendor's dress. Also Milkman.

Goods: [1] A charter party term that includes everything loaded with the exception of live animals and deck cargo. [2] A marine insurance term covering merchandise but excluding personal effects and supplies.

Goofing stations: [1] RN naval aviators' slang for the catwalks and open gallery on an aircraft carrier's island, where spectators often gather to view take-offs and landings. Cf. vulture's row. [2] A pipe peculiar to the Canadian navy, made to alert off-watch seamen that there is something unusual to be seen from the upper deck. The term originated in HMCS *Labrador*, the icebreaking arctic patrol ship, during her first voyage through the Northwest Passage in 1954. The pipe was made so that they would not miss seeing polar bears, walruses and icebergs close at hand.

Goof-off: A person who habitually evades responsibility.

Goof-up: To spoil things or get into trouble, especially due to carelessness or irresponsibility.

Gooseneck: [1] A universal joint which secures a boom to its mast. [2] A flexible jointed metal pipe, or something similar, curved like the neck of a goose or U-shaped.

Goosewing: [1] The weather clew of a square-sail held taut when the lee clew is furled. [2] Setting the main boom of fore-and-aft sails on the opposite side to the fore-sail or mizzen. [3] A sail which has caught on a spreader during a jibe. [4] A triangular studding sail.

Gorget: A crescent-shaped metal plate (the last vestige of armor) suspended on a neck-chain by officers as a symbol of rank when on duty. Mostly 17th and 18th century, but continued into the 21st by some nations.

Gouge: USN slang for inside information.

GP: General Purpose.

GPS: Global Positioning System (or Satellite).

GQ: General Quarters.

Grab: [1] Formerly, an Indian two-masted, shallow-draft warship with excellent handling qualities, especially in light winds. Armed with forward-firing artillery and a long overhanging bow which could be run over a target's quarterdeck or poop for boarding. The name is derived from the Arabic Ghorab, meaning "raven." [2] A crane fitted with a grab bucket consisting of two half shells hinged at the centre.

Grab bucket: [1] A "grab bucket," with interlocking teeth to aid penetration of the soil, is used for dredging and onshore excavation. [2] A "clamshell bucket" with no teeth, is used for stock-piling bulk cargo such as sand.

Grab ropes: Lines suspended from a boat boom so that occupants of a boat may steady themselves when standing.

Grade: Relative degree of rank or rate.

Grain: An obsolete term for the line extending in front of a vessel; the opposite of "wake."

Granny: A reef knot tied backward so as to be insecure. Not only does it slip, but tends to jam and cannot readily be cast loose. Landlubbers tend to tie it naturally. Also "granny's knot."

Grape: [1] Layers of small iron balls kept in place round a central spindle by holes or indentations in circular iron plates which would just fit the bore of the appropriate cannon. When fired the balls freed themselves from their retaining plates and scattered. Also grapeshot (cf. canister, langrage). [2] Informal term for a flight deck aircraft refueler, who wears a purple (grape-colored) shirt.

Grapnel: [1] A small iron-shafted multi-pronged device which can be used (a) as a boat anchor; (b) to drag the bottom for sunken articles; or (c) as a grappling iron. [2] A device fitted to the mooring of a naval mine, designed to catch and hold a sweep wire when it cuts the mooring. [3] USN term for the painter of a pulling boat.

Grapple: [1] To come to close quarters with an enemy vessel, take hold of it with grappling irons, and pull it alongside for boarding. Along with ramming, this was the preferred method of naval combat until the advent of effective artillery. [2] A grappling iron.

Grappling iron: A clawed device with a rope attached; thrown to catch onto the bulwarks of an enemy ship, pull it close, and hold it for boarding. Also grapple, grapnel, grappling hook.

Graticule: [1] Originally a network of lines on a map or chart, usually marked as parallels and meridians. [2] More usually used today to refer to a "compass-rose" type of grid, marked in degrees from zero to 360°, and showing range in yards or thousands of yards.

Grating: [1] In general: any regularly spaced open grid of essentially identical, parallel, elongated elements, made of wood, metal, or plastic. [2] In optics: A system of close equidistant and parallel lines or bars, especially ruled on a polished surface, used for producing spectra by diffraction. [3] In sailing ships: A strong open woodwork of crossed battens, forming the cover of a hatchway, to allow light and fresh air into the space below. Frequently lifted and used to support a defaulter being flogged. [4] A movable lattice used for the flooring of small boats. [5] Decorative gratings were used to cover fittings on the quarterdeck.

Grave: To run a ship aground so that its hull can

be cleaned, maintained, or repaired at low tide. Also greave (cf. careen).

Gravel: [1] A loose mixture of pebbles and rock fragments coarser than sand. Frequently accumulated in terraces at river mouths, or rounded and polished by wave action and deposited on beaches. [2] Obsolete term for running aground.

Graveyard watch: USN slang for the middle (or mid-) watch (midnight–4 A.M.).

Graving dock: A dry dock used specifically for hull cleaning, painting, and repair.

Gravity tank: A container in which water or other liquid can be stored to flow under its own weight when a valve or tap is opened.

Great cabin: A compartment extending across the stern of a wooden sailing ship. Usually occupied by the ship's captain or embarked flag officer.

Great circle: [1] A circle on a sphere such that the plane containing the circle passes through the center of the sphere. [2] The shortest route between two points on the earth's surface. [3] The basis for the nautical or sea mile.

Great circle navigation: To accurately follow a great circle would require continuous changes of course, so in practice a series of points along the course are established and the rhumb lines between them are followed.

Great gun: Generic term for cannon during the 15th to 17th centuries. Some of the principal names in descending order of size (with their approximate weight of shot in pounds) were: Cannon-Royal (74), Cannon (60), Serpentine-Cannon (42), Demi-Cannon (32), Culverin (18), Demi-Culverin [10], Saker [6], and Minion [5]. Smaller (essentially anti-personnel) ordnance included Falcon, Falconette, Serpentine, and Rabinet. As more and more types and sizes were introduced, this nomenclature became too complicated and, starting in the late 17th century, smoothbore, muzzle-loading guns began to be classified simply by the weight of round-shot they fired.

Great guns: Slang for foul weather (It's blowing great guns!).

Great Mutiny: During 1797, there were rumblings of discontent throughout the Royal Navy due to harsh shipboard conditions and half a dozen primary grievances.

- Despite inflation, pay rates had not been revised for 139 years. An AB in the Navy was paid less than one-third of a merchant AB's wage.
- A ship's purser was allowed to keep two ounces of every pound of meat as a perquisite, resulting in short rations for the troops.
- Due to the introduction of copper-bottoming, crews were required to spend longer periods at sea.
- When in harbor, they were seldom allowed time to visit friends and families
- The distribution of prize money was unjust.
- *The Articles of War permitted unfair and excessive punishments.*

Phase I: In April, at Spithead, an anchorage in southern England, sailors of the Channel Fleet complained of shipboard living conditions; demanding better pay, abolishment of the 14-ounce "pusser's pound," and removal of a handful of unpopular officers. Meanwhile, they maintained regular naval routine and discipline, allowed ships to leave for convoy escort or patrol, and promised to take the fleet to sea if French ships hove into sight. After a month, Admiral Lord Howe, intervened to arrange reassignment of the unpopular officers, increased pay, and abolishment of the purser's pound. He also arranged a Royal pardon for the mutineers. But that was not the end of the discontent.

Phase II: Next month the crews of several ships at the Nore, an anchorage in the Thames estuary, seized control of their ships. These crews were less disciplined than those at Spithead. Some of the more unpopular officers were tarred-and-feathered before being ejected, nearby farms were looted, and local fisher boats were seized or terrorized. However, unlike Spithead, where there was a unified fleet, the ships in the estuary were independent and widely spread out. Some remained loyal and managed to slip away despite gunfire from the rebellious ships who tried to stop them.

The mutineers then elected quotaman Richard Parker to be "President of the Delegates of the Fleet," and he formulated a list of eight demands, the most significant being rectification of the six grievances mentioned above. Parker had previously served as masters mate and probationary lieutenant, but had been court-martialed, disrated, and discharged. Shortly before the mutiny he had accepted £20 for reenlistment. These experiences had made him a radical French sympathizer. Under his guidance, legitimate grievances were escalated into a near social revolution, demanding the dissolution of Parliament and immediate peace with France.

The Admiralty response offered nothing except the concessions already made at Spithead and a pardon in return for immediate return to duty. Parker then declared the fleet to be a "Floating Republic" and mounted a blockade to prevent merchantmen from entering the port of London. The Admiralty responded by cutting off food supplies to the mutinous ships, whereupon Parker hoisted the signal for them to sail to France. He had gone too far — the other ships refused to follow and the mutiny fizzled out.

Aftermath: The government feared a wider uprising similar to the French Revolution, hence retribution was rapid and brutal. Parker was convicted of treason and piracy, and hanged from the yardarm of HMS *Sandwich* where he had started the mutiny. Twenty-nine subordinate leaders were also hanged, while others of the *Sandwich* crew were flogged, imprisoned, or transported to Australia. Crews that had refused to defect to France were pardoned without punishment. News of the mutinies spread around the fleets and led to minor incidents off Spain, Ireland, and South Africa. These were contained by their officers, but a major mutiny occurred in September aboard HMS *Hermione*.

Great White Fleet: Sixteen battleships and four destroyers, all painted white, sent on a world cruise by President Theodore Roosevelt in 1907 as a demonstration of rising United States naval power.

Greek fire: In 672, the Byzantine Navy unveiled a secret chemical weapon, which destroyed an Arab fleet at the Battle of Cyzicus on the Sea of Marmara. Said to have been invented by a Syrian architect named Callinicus, the Byzantines actually called it "Roman Fire," but it is usually known as "Greek." It was an early form of napalm, consisting of a liquid which would ignite spontaneously and continue to burn, even on water, not to mention human flesh. It was as unstable as nitro-glycerin, and even the slightest shock would ignite or explode it. For this reason it was seldom used by field armies, but confined to warships and fixed land fortifications.

It was sometimes encased in clay containers, to be dropped over a wall or thrown by catapult; sometimes discharged from a hand-held spray gun; but the most usual practice was to pack it into brass-bound wooden tubes, known as siphons, and blow it out with high-pressure hoses. The mixture would explode on contact with air and water, and be propelled by its own combustion as well as being sprayed by the pressure in the hose.

For two centuries the formula (now believed to have been a mixture of quicklime, saltpeter, sulfur, pitch, and naphtha) was a closely guarded secret. To reveal it was a capital offense the charge being sacrilege as well as treason. Greek Fire was the decisive factor in one sea fight after another, and was all the more effective because it could be directed sideways or downwards.

Green flash: A phenomenon which occurs at the moment the sun sinks or rises below or above the horizon when atmospheric refraction causes its rays to bend and appear green, or occasionally violet.

Green sea: A wave which comes aboard without spume and in such volume that it appears green.

Green shirt: Personnel working on a USN aircraft carrier's flight deck wear colored shirts for easy identification. Green shirts are worn by catapult and arresting gear crews.

Green water: The area between the outer edge of brown water (roughly 150 kms or 100 miles offshore) and the inner edge of blue water (1200 kms or 750 miles from land).

Greens: USN slang for the green working uniforms worn by aviators and Seabees.

Greenwich: The site east of London where Charles II established a Royal Observatory in 1676. Through it passes the prime meridian.

Greenwich Mean Time: Former universal standard of time based on the meridian of the observa-tory at Greenwich in England. Although officially replaced by Coordinated Universal Time the term and its abbreviation "GMT" are still in common use.

Greenwich Naval Hospital: In 1694, by Royal Charter, King William and Queen Mary founded the Royal Naval Hospital for Seamen (later abbreviated to Greenwich Hospital), its stated aims being in part:

> The reliefe and support of Seamen belonging to the Navy Royall ... who by reason of Age, Woundes, or other Disabilities shall be incapable for further service.... And for the Sustentation of Widows and the Maintenance and Education of the Children of Seamen happening to be slain or disabled.

The first of eventually over three thousand seamen arrived in 1705. Despite their magnificent accommodation (in a former royal palace) there were numerous complaints of poor food and petty humiliations. For even minor offenses the proud old sea dogs were forced to wear their uniform coats inside out, the yellow linings proclaiming their shame to all the world. Numbers fell after the Napoleonic Wars, and in 1869 the hospital closed. However, the institution lived on and still provides charitable support to serving and retired men and women of the Royal Navy and Royal Marines and their dependents. It also runs a co-educational school for the children and grandchildren of naval and other seafaring families.

Grey funnel line: It is traditional for merchant shipping companies to identify their ships by painting the funnels with the line's distinctive color and logo. Royal Navy officers jokingly refer to their service as the "Grey Funnel Line."

Grid navigation: A system, often used in polar waters and polar flying, in which grid coordinates on the chart replace latitude and longitude. A map projection is used in which north and south lie along the great circle which creates the 0° (Greenwich) and 180° meridians, the latter being taken as Grid North. Hence any great circle course approximates a straight line and makes equal angles with all other lines on the grid. Being independent of meridian convergence, a constant heading can be followed from departure to destination.

Gridiron: Formerly, a framework installed just above the low water mark. A vessel could be floated over it at high tide to settle on a cradle as the tide fell, allowing work to be performed on the hull.

Gripe: [1] The joint between keel and stem; the forefoot. [2] The lashing holding a boat on deck or on davits. [3] The tendency of a sailing vessel to be ardent. [4] U.S. naval aviation term for a pilot reporting aircraft material discrepancies. [5] To complain (slang).

Grog: Edward Vernon joined the British Royal Navy in 1700 and was a rear-admiral by the age of twenty-four (14 years earlier than Nelson achieved that rank). He served as a Member of Parliament, but was recalled to naval service in 1739 when the War of Jenkins' Ear broke out. Almost immediately he led his fleet in the capture of Porto Bello, where it found a large cache of gold and silver. Contrary to Admiralty regulations, he divided the money among the sailors of the fleet who would normally have received little or nothing. The delighted sailors affectionately nicknamed him Old Grog because at sea, when out of sight of land or other ships, he wore a timeworn cloak made of grogram (a coarse mixture of wool, mohair and silk stiffened with gum) which was so well-used that it was threadbare.

Later they were less enthusiastic when — concerned by widespread drunkenness, disciplinary problems, and "Observing that recent frequent desertions have principally arisen from men stupefying themselves with Spirituous Liquors"— he ordered their daily allowance of 96-proof liquor to be cut with water in the ratio of 3:1. At the same time he suggested that "Men that are good husbands may from the savings of their Salt and Bread purchase Sugar and Lime to make the water more palatable to them" (*see* Gimlet). They contemptuously called the weakened drink "grog" since it was as thinned-out as his cloak. Shortly afterward diluted liquor became standard throughout the Fleet, although petty officers and above could still draw their ration undiluted. (*See also* Royal Navy rum ration.)

Groggy: This originally meant the result of overindulgence in grog, but now it implies staggering or dazed — usually when weakened by exhaustion, lack of sleep, or blows to the head rather than intoxication.

Groin: One of a series of jetties constructed perpendicular to the shore to protect the beach against erosion.

Gromet: A boy or youthful member of a Cinque Ports crew, responsible for tending the vessel when in harbor.

Grommet: [1] A sealing gasket of oakum and white lead. [2] A strop or ring made by laying a strand of rope three times around. [3] A metal eye set in a sail or other fabric as reinforcement. [4] A stiff ring inside a service cap to keep the top stretched flat (frequently and illegally removed by junior officers wanting to look rakish or sea-beaten).

Groove: An aircraft making a perfect approach to a carrier landing is said to be "in the groove."

Ground: [1] The sea bed. [2] To strike bottom — if accidental, the vessel "runs aground"; if intentional, she "takes the ground." [3] The land surface of the earth. [4] In electrical engineering; (a) A conducting body — such as the earth, an object connected to the earth, or a ship, aircraft, or vehicle — whose potential is taken as zero; (b) The connection of an electrical conductor to such a ground; (c) The device — such as a stake or iron pipe — that makes such a connection.

Ground-control: Guidance of naval aircraft by a controller on the ground or aboard ship to intercept an enemy, reach a target, or to land on the carrier or ashore.

Ground-effect vehicle: A (usually) propeller-driven machine that can move over a relatively even surface such as water, marshland, or flattish terrain, while floating on a trapped cushion of low pressure air provided by two or more downward-thrusting fans. Often called air-cushion vessel, surface effect vessel, or Hovercraft.

Ground log: A weight with a line attached that can be dropped to the bottom in water too shallow for a regular logline; speed over the ground being determined by the rate at which the line pays out.

Ground swell: [1] A wave which passes over a shoal without breaking, being increased in height but slowed down and reduced in wavelength. [2] A large oceanic swell or roller on a calm sea, presaging a gale in otherwise clear weather.

Ground tackle: Equipment used for anchoring and mooring, excluding deck gear.

Ground zero: That point on the earth's surface at or under which a nuclear weapon explodes, or some other disastrous event (e.g., 9/11) occurs.

Groundpounder: One of many slightly derogatory naval slang terms for a marine or infantry soldier, including pongo and grunt.

Group: [1] USN term for a number of ships or aircraft temporarily operating together for a specific purpose (*see* task organization). [2] The collections of letters forming words in a cipher or code.

Group rate marks: USN enlisted personnel in non-rated pay grades (E-1 through E-3) are considered to be apprentices in a "specialty group," working their way towards Petty Officer (for example, a recruit who wishes to be an Electrician's Mate will join the Engineering & Hull Group). The groups are identified by short diagonal colored stripes worn on the upper left sleeve:
- White for deck, administrative, medical, and dental specialties.
- Red for engineering and hull.
- Green for aviation.
- Blue for construction, including Seabees.

E-1's wear no rate mark, E-2's wear two stripes, E-3's wear three. Those who earn a rating through training school or by passing a Navy-wide examination wear the appropriate insignia above the stripes.

Growler: A small piece of floating ice; less than one meter (three feet) above the water but large enough to be a navigational hazard.

GRT: Gross Registered Tonnage.

Grunt: USN slang for an infantry soldier (cf. Pongo, groundpounder).

Guard boat: A small boat assigned to patrol the anchored ships of a fleet, to ensure that lookouts are posted and alert, also that they challenge passing boats and prohibit close approach unless a counter-sign or password is given.

Guard flag: The flag worn by a USN guard ship defining its specific duty.

Guard ship: [1] A vessel assigned specific local duty such as collecting and delivering mail. [2] In former usage, a vessel assigned to protect a harbor.

Guardrail: A protective barrier around a ship's upper deck to prevent people falling overboard.

Gudgeon: [1] A socket on the stern frame of a vessel which secures the rudder while allowing it to pivot. [2] The trunnion of a cannon. [3] A small freshwater fish.

Guernsey: A close-fitting jumper, originally made on the Island of Guernsey and introduced into the Royal Navy during the Napoleonic Wars.

Guerre de Course: A French phrase meaning literally "war of running" and involving hit-and-run attacks on the merchant shipping of an enemy, with the goal of cutting off supplies and damaging the domestic economy. Also known as commerce raiding, it is a strategy usually followed by secondary maritime powers that are unable to concentrate enough force to win a fleet engagement (guerre de main or guerre d'escadre). Famous guerre de course campaigns include:

• British and Dutch actions against Spanish treasure fleets during the 16th century.
• French privateers during the Revolutionary and Napoleonic Wars.
• The United States against Great Britain in the War of 1812.
• Confederate naval raiders against Union shipping during the Civil War.
• Germany's U-boat campaigns in World Wars I and II.
• The USN's submarine campaign against Japan in World War II.

Guiana Current: A northward flow along the northeast coast of South America.

Guide ship: The vessel designated for a convoy or other formation to keep station on.

Guided missile: An aerial projectile whose trajectory can be controlled by internal or remote mechanisms.

Guinea Current: An eastward-flowing countercurrent in the Gulf of Guinea off West Africa.

Guinea-pig: [1] A vessel used in naval mine warfare to determine whether an area can be considered free from mines. [2] Derisive slang for the midshipman of an East Indiaman.

Gulf: An area of sea or ocean partially enclosed by land. Similar to but deeper, longer, and larger than a bay. Frequently with a narrow mouth.

Gulf Stream: A clockwise-flowing system of currents which encircles most of the North Atlantic Ocean incorporating the Antilles and Florida currents and the North Atlantic Drift. Powerful, warm, and fast-moving, it heats the east coast of North America, then heads westward to about 30°W, 40°N, where it splits in two, one stream warming the shores of northwestern Europe and the other recirculating off West Africa.

Gulfweed: Seaweed with berry-like air-floats that collects into island masses in the North Atlantic.

Gull: [1] A deceptive device consisting of a floating radar reflector that simulates a surface vessel. [2] A seabird.

Gun: [1] A generic term for the carriage-mounted cannon of sailing warships. [2] Any piece of ordnance from which missiles are propelled by explosion through a metallic tube.

Gunar: A USN electronic system that controls gunfire by radar.

Gun Captain: The petty officer in charge of a gun crew.

Gun carriage: [1] Generically, any structure on which a gun is mounted and fired, whether wheeled or not. [2] Specifically, a 4-wheeled wooden framework on which a sailing warship's cannon was mounted. The first carriages for ship's cannon sat upon two large cart-wheels, like the guns used on land. But, by the mid–1500s, the English had developed the "truck carriage" which had four small solid wooden wheels, one on each corner. Compared to the earlier two-wheeled design, weight was more evenly distributed, it could be rolled right up to the gunport, and was easier to train left or right using a lever known as a "trailspike." At first the carriages had solid flat beds, but by about 1700 most were fabricated from two thick side pieces known as "cheeks," linked by stout baulks of timber known as "transoms" or "axle-trees," with metal reinforcing bolts to hold the parts together. The cheeks were stepped from front to back, providing points of purchase when the gunners were elevating the barrel of the gun using trailspikes. This design became the standard form of maritime gun carriage throughout the muzzle-loading era, except for the Spanish Armada which used two-wheeled sea carriages until the early 17th century.

Gun crew: From the 16th to 19th centuries, the basic division of labor remained the same, core roles being gun captain, loader, and spunger. The size of the crew ranged from four or five for a small gun such as a six-pounder to up to fifteen to fire and service each heavy cannon in a line of battle ship's broadside. Their roles and responsibilities were:

Rating	Duties
Captain	Command the crew, aim and fire the gun
2nd Captain	Assist the captain and run out the gun
Loader/Rammer	Load the powder and ram home the shot. Help run out and train the gun
Assistant loader	Pass powder and shot to the loader. Help run out and train the gun
Spunger	Spunge and worm the gun. Assist the rammer. Help run out and train the gun
Assistant spunger	Pass spunge and worm to spunger and rammer to loader. Help run out and train
Auxiliaries (up to nine)	Use trailspikes to elevate the gun; manage breeching ropes (which check recoil) and tackles (for running out and training); bring powder and shot from ready-use storage; perform fireman duty

Gun direction room: Former name for the nerve

center of an RN warship in combat, now part of the Operations Room. Known as Combat Information Center in the USN.

Gun director: A shipboard system which tracks a vessel's course and speed relative to enemy ships, and adjusts for wind velocity, air and water temperature, and other factors to calculate elevation and bearing for the guns.

Gun firing: Firing a smoothbore muzzle-loading naval cannon required a great amount of hard work and manpower. The weapon was essentially just a pipe (the barrel), sealed at one end to form a chamber. A wet swab was first thrust down the pipe, to extinguish any embers from a previous firing which might prematurely ignite the next charge. Coarse gunpowder was then put into the open end (the "mouth") either loose with a powder spoon, or pre-wrapped in a cloth or paper cartridge, and pushed down to the chamber with a rammer. A quantity of wadding was then rammed on top of the powder, a cannonball or other form of shot was pushed home on top of the wadding, and another wad was rammed on top of the ball. This not only created a better seal, but also stopped the shot from rolling out due to swaying of the ship.

The gun was then "run out," its crew heaving on the gun tackles until the front of the carriage was hard up against the bulwark, and the barrel protruded through the port. This took the majority of the manpower, since a naval cannon and its carriage could weigh more than two tons and be hard to move if the ship was rolling. A small amount of fine-quality "mealed" gunpowder was then put into the vent (touchhole) and the gun was ready to fire.

Ignition was initially achieved by thrusting a red-hot priming iron (spike) down the vent. This worked well but required an open furnace on the gundeck, creating a fire hazard. The next solution was a slow match applied with a linstock. This also worked well, but progressively eroded the vent, leading to a loss of muzzle velocity due to leakage of propellant gas. In 1697, metal firing tubes were introduced. After removing its paper seal, the tube was placed in the vent and ignited by slow-match or portfire. However, hot and possibly ragged metal tubes lying on the deck after firing were a hazard to the bare feet of gun crews, so they were replaced by goose quills in 1778. However, the quills burned completely on firing, bringing back the problem of vent erosion. Finally, in 1790, the problem was effectively solved by introduction of the flintlock.

Gun mount: The carriage, assembly, or other support on which a gun is positioned.

Gun salutes: Nowadays a ceremonial act of respect between ships or on entering foreign port, the gun salute originated when loading cannon was a slow and laborious business. Hence, discharging all a ship's weapons was a sign of friendly intentions. Traditionally, the junior ship always salutes first, with the courtesy to be returned immediately by the senior. Since the magazines of shore batteries could store more ammunition than a ship could carry, they would normally reply to an incoming vessel's salute with more guns than they received.

Shakespeare wrote "good luck lies in odd numbers" reflecting an ancient superstition that even numbers are unlucky. For this reason, gun salutes are normally rendered in odd numbers. The only exception covers unhappy occasions — homecoming ships formerly fired even numbers to signify that an admiral or captain had died on the voyage and even numbers were fired at funerals. *See also* funerary salutes, national gun salutes, personal gun salutes, and salutes and courtesies.

Gun tackles: Motion of the sea, along with firing recoil, made it necessary to secure and control the muzzle-loading cannon of sailing ships by means of ropes and pulleys known as breechings and tackles.

- **Breechings** were ropes attached to ring-bolts on the ship's side and fastened to the cascabel (hindmost knob) of the gun, serving to prevent it from recoiling further than was necessary for reloading.
- **Side tackles** came in pairs consisting of double blocks attached by ring-bolts to the ship, and single blocks eye-bolted to the left and right cheeks of the gun-carriage. They were used to run the gun out from the recoil-and-reload position, train it left or right, or stop it from running in due to heeling of the ship.
- **Train tackle** was identical, but attached to the axletree, serving mainly to prevent the gun from running out when the ship heeled, but also to bring it in after firing blanks in salute (which created no significant recoil), or when the slant of the deck made a manual pull in necessary.

Gun tub: Chest-high armor around an open gun mount.

Gun vessel: A late 19th century wind and steam powered vessel similar to the former sloop-of-war.

Gunboat: A shallow-draft unarmored boat equipped with one or more forward-firing guns. Used for patrol and escort duties and to cannonade shore positions, especially in support of amphibious landings.

Gundalow: A scow-like 19th century freight-carrying New England barge with round bows and stern and a large triangular lateen-like sail on a very short mast.

Gundeck: [1] Generally; any deck below the weather deck of a sailing warship, containing broadside artillery. [2] Specifically; the main (lowest) gun deck in a line-of-battle ship. [3] In USN slang, to falsify or fabricate entries in official documents, reports, or records, especially of work required but not performed. The origin of the term is obscure, but it probably derived from the practice of creating a false impression of strength by painting a row of dummy ports on the side of a sailing man-o-war between the gundeck and the weather deck.

Gundeck stripes: Sailing warships frequently

painted horizontal stripes along the gundecks of their generally black hulls for both decoration and national identification. Britain favored yellow stripes with black gunport covers. Spain usually used red stripes with black covers. The United States used white with black covers, but occasionally made the stripes yellow as a ruse to deceive the British. France tended towards monocolor hulls with no stripes. Merchantmen often painted one or more stripes with dummy gunport covers as a ruse against attack. This practice was sometimes known as mask painting. *See also* dummy ports.

Gunfire support: Fire provided by naval guns in support of military forces on shore. A subset of surface fire support.

Gung-Ho: This Chinese term for "working together" is used in the U.S. Marine Corps to express the enthusiasm and team spirit expected of its personnel.

Gunkholing: A yachtsman's term for cruising in shoal water and/or overnighting in small coves.

Gunlayers: A two-man team that lays (aims) a manually-controlled gun. The pointer or layer controls its elevation (range) and the trainer sets its deflection (direction of firing).

Gun-lock: The mechanism by which the explosive charge of a firearm is exploded.

Gunner: [1] Generically, a person trained to operate a gun or cannon. [2] Specifically, one of a sailing warship's senior standing warrant officers, examined by, appointed by, and responsible to the Ordnance Board. In addition to the maintenance of cannon and their equipment, the gunner manufactured tackle and breeches for the guns as required, and was responsible for ensuring that powder in the magazines remained dry. He was in charge of the junior officers messing in the gunroom, and supervised the security of small arms (but not their upkeep which belonged to the armorer, nor training in their use which was done by the master-at-arms).

Gunner's Daughter: Slang name for the gun to which ship's boys were "married" (spread over) for caning. *See* juvenile punishment.

Gunner's Mate: [1] Formerly, a petty officer appointed to assist the gunner of a sailing warship. [2] Now, a naval occupational rating that operates, maintains, and repairs all ordnance and related equipment, and ammunition including missiles.

Gunnery: The art, science, and management of firing of large artillery pieces.

Gunnery Officer: Formerly the commissioned officer in charge of and responsible for a vessel's artillery. Now that other types of weapon are widespread the term has been superseded by weapons officer.

Gunning: Obsolete USN term for shooting.

Gunny: [1] USN slang for a Marine Corps Gunnery Sergeant. [2] A coarse jute or hemp fabric. [3] A bag made of such fabric.

Gunport: Early in the sixteenth century, to facilitate the loading of cargo, an ingenious French shipwright named Descharges invented the hublot, an opening in a ship's side fitted with a hinged waterproof door. He probably didn't know it, but he had facilitated revolutions in naval architecture and tactics even greater than the introduction of wind propulsion. Until then, naval combat had been fought like land battles, with ships laying alongside and boarding to fight on deck. Anti-personnel gunpowder weapons had been mounted on forward and after-castles and along the bulwarks, but only light guns could be used for fear of making the vessel capsize.

Scottish shipwrights were the first to realize that, by using hublots for artillery to fire through, they could move the gun-decks down into the bowels of the ship, placing heavier weapons well below the ship's center-of-gravity, where they steadied rather than destabilized. In 1511, the idea was implemented by King James IV of Scotland for his new flagship, *Great Michael*, which, in addition to three long bow guns and about three hundred bulwark-mounted anti-personnel weapons, carried twenty-four large cannon firing broadsides through hublots which the Scots re-named "ports" after the Latin porta (door). This started a naval arms race and, a year later, Henry VIII of England adopted the concept for *Great Harry*, which carried 141 light pieces and forty-three heavy guns.

Shipwrights did not immediately realize that gunports near the waterline posed a dangerous hazard. In 1545, Henry's heavily-gunned *Mary Rose* shipped water through open lower-gundeck ports, heeled over and sank, as did the Swedish *Vasa* in 1628.

Gunport cover: The hinged wooden door that weatherproofed a gunport when not opened for firing.

Gunpowder: A powder made from sulfur, charcoal and potassium nitrate that burns to produce hot gases that can be used as a propellant. First developed by the Chinese many centuries ago, it was not used for anything but entertainment (fireworks) for a long time. The idea of using an explosion to shoot a projectile from a tube is said to have arisen accidentally in the thirteenth century, when an alchemist was trying to turn mercury into gold. According to legend, he caused his mixture to explode, blowing the top off his kettle. In its natural form, gunpowder burns slowly, even when confined in the breech of a gun. But by the end of the 15th century the product was being manufactured in grains of varying size known as "corned" gunpowder. Thanks to air trapped between the grains, this ignited and burned faster, making the explosion more powerful and producing less fouling. Large grained powder was used in the main charge, while smaller grained "mealed" powder was used for priming.

Gunroom: Royal Navy term for an eating compartment. Originally it was the one where commissioned officers dined (midshipmen and master's mates then lived and ate in the cockpit), but from about 1800 the officers' mess became known as the wardroom and the term gunroom was applied to the mess for midshipmen and mates (later sub-lieutenants).

Following World War II midshipmen stopped going to sea in large numbers, so RN ships no longer have gunrooms. However, the midshipmen's mess at Britannia Royal Naval College, Dartmouth still bears that name.

Guns: Slang for a ship's gunnery officer.

Gunsling: [1] A looped strap used to hoist and move gun barrels on board ship (a long 32-pounder barrel weighed some three tons). [2] A strap used to hold a personal firearm horizontally or diagonally across the front of the body.

Gunwale: (rhymes with funnel). The topmost plank of a bulwark, forming its rail. Also Gunnel.

Gunwale tank: A ballast tank positioned just below the weather deck, used to lower the metacentric height of a lightly-laden vessel.

Guppy: USN slang for a snorkel-equipped World War II submarine.

Gusset: A triangular brace, used to reinforce a corner or an angle in a framework.

Gust: A brief but rapid increase in wind speed.

Gut: A narrow channel connecting two bodies of water.

Guy: A wire or rope stay used to secure spars, booms, and the like.

Guyot: A flat-topped seamount, found mainly in the Pacific Ocean.

GWS Sea: Short form of Geneva Convention for the Wounded, Sick, & Shipwrecked Members of the Armed Forces At Sea.

Gybe: *See* jibe.

Gypsy head: A flanged drum on a winch, used for heaving.

Gyre: (pronounced jire) A circular or spiral motion, much larger than a whirlpool or an eddy. It is gyre which gives the Gulf Stream its clockwise course around the North Atlantic. *See also* surface current.

Gyrene: USN slang for a marine (phonetic compound of GI = soldier + Marine).

Gyres: Large ocean currents are constrained by the continental masses that border oceanic basins. These force them into almost-closed, circular or spiral patterns called gyres. Each basin has a large gyre at approximately 30° North and South latitude, driven by the atmospheric flow produced by subtropical high pressure systems. Smaller gyres occur in the North Atlantic and Pacific Oceans centered at 50° North, propelled by the circulation due to polar low pressure centers (pronounced jire). *See also* surface currents, deep ocean currents, and oceanic circulation.

Gyro: Abbreviation of gyroscope.

Gyro angle: In submarine warfare; the relative angle between a boat's keel and the final track of a torpedo to be fired from it, measured clockwise from the bow.

Gyrocompass: A compass having one or more gyroscopes torqued to indicate true north without interference from either the earth's magnetic field or the ship's own electromagnetism. Often linked to repeaters throughout the ship.

Gyropilot: An automatic steering device controlled by a gyrocompass repeater which holds a vessel on course without the intervention of a helmsman.

Gyroscope: A stabilization device based on an electrically-driven rotor whose axis is free to turn, but whose inertia maintains it in a fixed spatial position despite movement of its mounting.

Gyroscopic compass: *See* gyrocompass.

Gyrostabilizer: A heavy (usually about 1 percent of the vessel's displacement) gyroscopic device designed to dampen side-to-side roll.

Gyves: An old term for handcuffs.

H

H-: Prefix used to designate the time at which an operation is scheduled to take place. Thus "H-5" means five hours before the start, "H-Hour" is the opening time, and "H+3" would be three hours after it began. (*See also* "D.")

HA: High Altitude.

Habiliments: Obsolete term for furnishings, equipment, provisions, and weapons.

Hack: "In hack" is USN slang for being confined to quarters as a non-judicial punishment.

Hague Convention: This arose from a 1907 meeting, which agreed, on thirteen protocols of wartime maritime law, covering the status of merchantmen at the outbreak of hostilities, the conversion of merchantmen to warships, rights of capture during naval warfare, and establishment of an international prize court.

Hague Rules: These were developed by a 1921 convention which introduced proposals for the codification of international maritime law, especially regarding steamships. They were widely accepted by maritime nations, including minimum conditions for the carriage of cargo under Bill of Lading.

Hail: [1] Pellets of frozen rain. [2] To belong to or come from a particular place. [3] To call or shout in order to greet, attract attention, or announce arrival.

Haircutting: Ancient nautical superstition, probably Rhodian or Roman, holds that cutting hair or nails constitutes a votive offering to Persephone, goddess of the underworld, and is therefore an insult to Neptune, king of the sea, to whom all mariners are subject. Even today, with the notable exception of cruise ship passengers, many seafarers honor the superstition by waiting until they go ashore to visit a hairdresser or barber. *See also* facial hair.

Halcyon days: This term for a happy, carefree, and prosperous time has a nautical origin. The halcyon is a mythical bird (usually identified as the kingfisher), believed by Greek seamen to breed at about the time of the winter solstice and lay its eggs on a floating nest of seaweed. Incubation took fourteen days, during which time the birds used their mystical powers to charm winds and waves into tranquility, providing a mid-winter window for safe navigation.

Hales Trophy: In 1934 — hoping to encourage innovation in ocean passenger transport and to provide a more tangible token than the ephemeral Blue Riband — British parliamentarian, engineer, and entrepreneur Harold Keates Hales commissioned a handsome souvenir to be awarded to "the ship which shall for the time being have crossed the Atlantic Ocean at the highest average speed." Made of solid silver and heavy gilt, the Trophy weighs almost 100 pounds (45 kgs) and stands some four feet (122 cms) high on an onyx base. It consists of a globe upheld by two winged figures symbolizing Victory and surmounted by a figure representing Speed pushing a triple-stacked liner against the forces of nature. It also features statues of Neptune and Amphitrite together with models of old galleons and modern vessels.

In 1979, United States Lines (which had held the Trophy since 1952) went into bankruptcy and donated it to the Merchant Marine Academy Museum at Kings Point, Long Island. In 1990, however, it was claimed by the British Hoverspeed *Great Britain* which had achieved an average speed of 36.65 knots, beating the SS *United States*' 1952 record by more than a knot. The museum and the maritime community initially denied the demand on grounds that Hoverspeed was a ferry without accommodation for overnight passengers. However, to avoid a costly legal battle, the Museum eventually relinquished the Trophy. *Hoverspeed* held the award for eight years until 1998, when Spanish high-speed ferry *Catalonia* won it with an average speed of 38.877 knots. Six weeks later, and in spite of a two-hour diversion to assist a search and rescue operation, the Danish high-speed ferry *Cat-Link V* took it with an average speed of 41.284 knots. All three of the recent winners were Australian built. For over a decade, the Merchant Marine Museum nostalgically displayed the empty glass case that had previously held the Trophy, but it was re-filled in 2002 when Carnival Cruise Lines provided an exact replica to be held on permanent loan.

Half deck: [1] Any partial deck located between decks. [2] Formerly a deckhouse aft of the mainmast where carpenter and sailmaker were quartered, along with their apprentices. [3] A short deck above the upper deck, but below the quarterdeck. [4] the space aft of the gundeck in a wooden battleship, excluding the captain's or flag officer's quarters.

Half-decked: Said of a small boat that is partially open and partially decked.

Half gale: Formerly Force 7 on the Beaufort Scale, now called "near gale."

Half-hitch: An underhand loop used to temporarily bend a line to a post.

Half-mast/staff: to lower, a flag as a mourning salute. The tradition began centuries ago to allow the invisible flag of Death to fly on top of the mast, thus signifying Death's presence, power, and prominence.

The modern practice seems to have originated in 1612 when William Hall, the master of *Hearts Ease*, was murdered by Eskimos while in search of the northwest passage. On her return to London, the vessel flew her flag so low that it draped over the stern, and the sorrowful aspect of this was recognized as a more fitting indication of mourning than the previously-used black flag. At a distance colors are difficult to distinguish but a lowered flag is instantly recognizable.

Half pay in the RN: To ensure their availability when required, King Charles II introduced the concept of paying a few selected captains 50 percent of their salaries while unemployed. At that time an officer's commission appointed him to a specific ship, so when it paid off (usually after two or three years in service), he became unemployed until able to secure appointment to another ship. However, unlike rated personnel, whose pay ended when they were discharged, officers kept their seniority and, from 1693, were given half-pay as a retainer. After 1860, commissions appointed officers to the fleet rather than to individual ships; however, half pay remained a fact of service until 1919/20 for officers of captain's rank or below, and for flag officers until 1938. Half pay still applies as a fine or punishment for RN officers who have been dismissed from a ship by court-martial, and continues until their re-appointment to another ship.

Half pay in the USN: During the 1790s United States naval personnel disabled in the line of duty were entitled to "a pension not to exceed half pay" and in March 1801 a Congressional Order enacted:

> That the President ... be authorized to discharge ... officers in the navy service of the United States, but such of the aforesaid officers as shall be retained in the service shall be entitled to receive no more than half their monthly pay during the time when they shall not be under orders for actual service.

By mid-century, however, according to the Soylent biography of Admiral Farragut, the practice had been discontinued:

> Officers of the U. S. Navy have one great advantage which British officers are without; when on shore they are not necessarily parted from the service, but are employed in their several ranks in the dockyards, escaping thus not only the ... pecuniary difficulties of a very narrow half pay, but also ... the loss of professional aptitude, and of that skill which comes from unceasing practice.

Half pike: An iron spike attached to a short wooden shaft that can be wielded in confined spaces. Sometimes used by boarders. *See* spontoon, pole arms, and boarding pike.

Half seas over: [1] Said of a vessel which is grounded and awash. [2] Slang for almost intoxicated.

Half speed: To proceed at 50 percent of standard speed. The term is used in merchant service and the RN, but not by the USN.

Half-staff: *See* half-mast and mourning salute.

Halls of Montezuma: The annexation of Texas in 1845 did not end territorial disputes between Mexico and the United States, leading to a formal declaration of war in May 1846. Next year, Commodore David Conner landed 15,000 U.S. troops, a small detachment of Marines, and a large siege train at Veracruz, using flat-bottomed, double-ended rowboats, constructed especially for the purpose. From there they made a fighting advance up the Camino Nacional (route of the conquistadors) toward the capital. The Mexicans made a last stand at Castillo de Chapultepec (known as the Halls of Montezuma).

This castle, built of heavy stone masonry, standing on a steep and rocky, 60-meter (200-foot) high hill, was a splendid specimen of military architecture. Two strongly built 15-foot walls, 10 feet apart, surrounded the complex, and the whole hill bristled with forts and outworks. The 1,000-man garrison included some expert French gunners, plus about 100 cadets from the Mexican Military College.

Fighting extended from September 8 to 13, 1847, with both sides taking some of heaviest casualties of the war. Captain Casey's storming party of 40 Marines led the final assault, taking over 90 percent casualties. Their efforts are memorialized in the "blood stripe" worn on the dress blues uniforms of Officers and NCOs, and in the opening lyrics of the "Marines' Hymn" (*see* march music).

Halyard: A rope or tackle used to hoist a flag, sail, or yard. Probably an abbreviation of "haulyard line." Also halliard.

Hammer: To mount a heavy bombardment from close-range.

Hammock: This old-fashioned swinging sailor's bed made of canvas and slung from hooks on the overhead/deckhead is said to have been introduced to the Athenian fleet by Alcibiades in the fifth century BCE; but the name is more recent, dating to 1493 when Christopher Columbus reported that natives of San Salvador slept in beds which they called hamaca and suspended from trees. These beds were introduced into the Royal Navy about 1600, and shortly afterward it became customary to place rolled hammocks on the bulwarks for extra protection during combat. Until well into the 19th century, they were made from the heavy brown canvas of damaged sails (as were sailors' trousers). Later, the standard RN issue could also be lashed-up to form a life preserver that reputedly could keep someone afloat for up to 24 hours. U.S. Navy enlisted men including petty officers slept in hammocks, each of which was provided with a mattress and two blankets.

Hammock netting: Nets placed above the bulwarks of a sailing warship at focsle, waist, and quarters, to receive rolled and lashed hammocks as a shield against musket fire during combat. In the USN, each hammock was rolled around its mattresses and blankets for even better protection.

Hand: [1] A member of the crew (probably derived from the saying "one hand for the ship and one for yourself"). [2] A side of the vessel (e.g., the starboard hand). [3] To furl a square-sail (able seamen had to be qualified to "hand, reef, and steer").

Hand lead: *See* lead.

Hand-over-fist: Today the phrase implies advancing rapidly towards financial gain or personal success, but it originated in the days of sail when speed and agility in climbing aloft were essential skills and a source of pride for individual sailors. The original English expression was hand-over-hand, describing the action of hauling a line as well as climbing the rigging. However, at some time in the 19th century, American sailors changed it to hand-over-fist.

Hand salutes: These are personal greetings between individuals that began with the army custom of removing the cap. Later, when military headdress became more ornate and difficult to remove, the now familiar raising of an open hand to the head was adopted to represent the first movement of uncovering. Removing headgear, touching its peak, or raising a finger to the uncovered forehead remained the traditional naval mark of respect until Queen Victoria — who did not like to see uniformed personnel with bare heads — ordered it replaced with an army-style salute. However, the navy adopted a flat-handed, straight up-and-down salute, because the British army's open-handed wide swing would be likely to strike a bulkhead aboard ship.

Until 1923, either hand could be used by British seamen, with the left hand preferred, but this was discontinued when using that hand was determined offensive to Indians, Africans, and some Europeans. Left-hand saluting is still practiced in the USN whenever the right hand is injured or encumbered. The British normally remain silent while saluting, but U.S. naval personnel are expected to greet the person being saluted by name or rank. Unlike the United States army and air force, British armed forces and United States naval and marine personnel never salute when seated or if the head is uncovered.

Hand salutes are uniquely military courtesies intended to signify mutual respect between individual warriors. But, sadly, the practice is often misinterpreted as elitist by civilians and some service personnel. In consequence, it is frequently abused. For example, if a newly-commissioned junior officer is saluted by a highly-decorated Master Chief Petty Officer he has two options — he can acknowledge with a casual wave of the hand, implying that he accepts the courtesy as rightful deference to his "superior" rank; or he can return the salute with parade ground éclat, showing his recognition of the other's greater service and experience. (For hand salutes to the quarterdeck, *see* salutes and courtesies.)

Handcuff knot: *See* hobbling knot.

Handle: A part that is designed to be grasped by the human hand (e.g., the grips around the outer ring of a ship's steering wheel).

Handmaiden: Term used in the navy of Elizabeth I for a logistic support vessel or tender, usually a pinnace.

Handrail: A narrow barrier consisting of vertical supports and a horizontal bar to be grasped with the hand for support.

Handraulic: Slang for a ship without any mechanical aids. Also "Armstrong."

Handrope: [1] A line on a raft or lifeboat used for steadying. [2] A rope forming the side-rail of a brow.

Handsomely!: A command to hoist or move something slowly and carefully.

Handspike: An iron-tipped wooden rod used as a lever by seamen and gunners. Also trailspike.

Handy: Easily maneuverable.

Handy Billy: [1] Any of various small tackles used on shipboard, usually combining a single and a double block. [2] A small portable water pump, manual or powered, used for firefighting and damage control. [3] New England name for a traditional powerboat built of wood or fiberglass.

Handysize: Refers to a bulker of between 22,000 and 38,000 deadweight tonnage.

Hang: [1] To execute by tying a rope about the neck and dropping the body so as to snap the neck or cause strangulation (*see* hanging). [2] To attach to something above with no support from below (suspend). [3] To attach with free motion at the point of attachment (hang a door on its hinges). [4] To remain poised or stationary (clouds hang low above). Middle English hangen, from Old English hangian.

Hangar: A large compartment below the flight deck of an aircraft carrier, where aircraft are parked and serviced.

Hanger: An 18th century short and light, naval sword, with a curved blade. Used mainly by warrant officers.

Hangfire: The delayed detonation of an explosive charge, usually due to an overheated gun barrel or defective fuse.

Hanging (naval): Unlike land-based execution where gradual strangulation was humanely avoided by dropping the victim through a trapdoor; naval convicts were traditionally hauled aloft slowly. Eventually, crews became so sickened by the sight of a shipmate kicking and struggling as he fought for breath that it became standard practice to tie a second knot six feet above the hangman's noose, leaving a fathom of rope in a loose bight. The execution party would place the noose around the condemned man's neck and take the slack out of the bitter end, which passed though a block at the yardarm. As soon as the command was given, they would run as fast as possible along the deck until the second knot hit the block and opened, releasing the bight and allowing the victim to fall six feet and snap his neck.

Hanging (pirates): The usual penalty for piracy was shore-based hanging by slow-drop, an exceptionally nasty form of execution known colloquially as

"Dancing the Hempen Jig." The felon's hands were bound or fettered in front, rather than behind the body as was more usual, and he was stood on a stool or barrel rather than the trapdoor used for the more humane long-drop. When the support was kicked out from under, he only fell a foot or two to be suspended by the neck, kicking and struggling. Starved of oxygen, his skin would soon begin to turn purple. Then his tongue would begin to protrude. A few minutes later, the eyes would bulge horribly, or even pop out of their sockets. Most were pronounced dead within ten minutes, but some lasted upward of an hour, in constant agony and humiliatingly soiled by relaxed bladder and bowels. After execution, the pirate's corpse was often suspended near a shipping lane, wrapped in chains or enclosed in an iron cage, and left to rot as a warning to others. Otherwise, he would be buried "between the tides" (somewhere between high and low water marks), face down so that his soul could find no rest.

Hanging compass: One attached to or suspended from the deckhead/overhead and designed to be read from below.

Hanging Judas: Obsolete RN term for any rope that has not been made fast or belayed properly. The inference being it is as treacherous and unreliable as Judas Iscariot.

Hanging pendant: The line that holds an anchor to the belly-rope while it is being carried out suspended from a small boat.

Hanging stage: A platform hung over the vessel's side for workers to stand on.

Hank: [1] A coil of line or cordage. [2] To form such a coil. [3] A fitting on the luff of a sail by which it is attached to the stay.

Hanseatic Ordinances: Trade in the middle ages was a dangerous and risky business, so merchants protected themselves, first by traveling in groups and later forming alliances. The German word for guild or association is hanse, and the Hansa (Hanseatic League in English) was an alliance of merchant guilds from prosperous trading ports throughout northern Europe and the Baltic region, forming an early European free trade zone, with over sixty member cities. Each city had its own merchant guild, but they formed a loose diet (parliament) to govern inter-city trade and develop common policies which, in most respects, were secret, protectionist, and monopolistic. The Hansa was wealthy and powerful between the 12th and 15th centuries, but had passed its zenith by 1597 when its long-established, but previously private, ordinances were first published (at Lubeck). These laws were revised and enlarged in 1614, but gradually fell into disuse.

Harassing fire: Intermittent shore bombardment, intended to inhibit hostile troop movement or regrouping, also to deny the enemy rest or sleep.

Harbor/Harbour: A body of water along the shore, deep enough for anchoring a ship and protected from winds, waves, and currents by natural or artificial features, thus forming a safe haven for seagoing vessels. A harbor equipped with cargo and passenger handling equipment, and providing ship-berthing facilities is called a port.

Harbor duty: Work ashore assigned to superannuated seamen or those unfit for sea service.

Harbor log: That part of a ship's logbook covering only events and transactions that occur while the vessel is in port.

Harbor watch: A detail tasked to look after a vessel while it is moored or docked. *See* anchor watch, baboon watch.

Hard: [1] A firm or paved beach or slope convenient for hauling boats or small vessels out of the water. [2] The pad on which wooden warships used to be constructed. [3] A beach prepared for amphibious maneuvers. [4] Helm order denoting that the tiller should be moved with the utmost energy, hard over in the direction indicated (i.e., Hard aport! Hard astarboard! Hard alee! Hard aweather!).

Hard aground: Stuck on the bottom and unable to move without assistance.

Hard alee: Command to move the tiller of a sailing vessel rapidly to leeward, thus turning the boat to windward.

Hard and fast: Describes a vessel which is grounded and immovable on rocks, a shoal, or a firm beach. Also hard aground.

Hard aport (or astarboard): [1] Position of the helm when the rudder is turned as far as possible to the left (or right). [2] Command to place the helm in that position.

Hard bargain: An intractable seaman, a skulker. Short for King's hard bargain.

Hard bread: [1] Refers to a Jamaican staple made with heavily sweetened flour. [2] The term was in occasional naval use as an antonym to soft bread, but the preferred term was hard tack.

Hard chine: An abrupt intersection of hull and bottom (*see* chine).

Hard horse: Slang for a tyrannical or unreasonable merchant officer.

Hard over: Said of the helm or tiller when it is turned as far as possible in either direction.

Hard tack: Slang for ship's biscuit or hard bread.

HARM: High-speed Anti-Radiation Missile.

Harness cask: A tapered wooden cask with two compartments, each filled with fresh water, formerly used to extract the brine from corned meat. After a few days soaking in the first compartment, the meat was moved to the second to complete the process with fresher water. The proper name is steep tub, but seamen decided the meat was so tough and leathery that it must have came from old cab horses who had been wearing harness when they were pickled.

Harpings: Strengthening structural elements at the bow of a ship (*see also* cat-harpings).

Harpoon: [1] A barbed spearlike missile with a rope attached, fired from a gun or hand-thrown to impale large marine mammals. [2] A surface-to-surface, all-weather, anti-ship missile, equipped with a conventional warhead, active radar guidance, and low-level cruise capability.

Hash: [1] Nautical slang for food. [2] Originally a specific cooking term covering leftovers from the joint, chopped, mixed with cooked vegetables and re-heated, usually baked or browned. [3] Slang term for cannabis.

Hash mark: USN slang for a service stripe.

Hasty pudding: Seafarer's batter made by stirring flour and/or oatmeal in boiling water and sweetened with treacle or sugar.

Hat: Never used in naval parlance, the correct terms being "cover" or "headgear."

Hatch: [1] A watertight trapdoor-like cover for a hatchway. [2] A frequently used, but slightly incorrect, abbreviation of hatchway. [From Old English haecc = opening.]

Hatch beam: Steel support for the edges of a cargo hold.

Hatch boom: A shipboard derrick used to raise or lower cargo to or from deck level, at which point the load is transferred to a yard boom.

Hatch coaming: A raised framework to prevent water pouring into an open hatchway from the deck.

Hatch davit: A small portable hoist used when working with light cargo inside a hold.

Hatch-deck: The lower deck of a gun brig.

Hatch list: An inventory of items stowed in each section of the hold, giving their descriptions, volumes, weights, and consignees.

Hatch-ring: A metal ring used to lift and move a hatch.

Hatchway: [1] A square or rectangular opening in the deck, affording passage up and down from one deck to the next usually via a ladder. [2] A larger opening in the deck through which cargo can be lowered or hoisted. This is the proper name, although the abbreviation "hatch" is frequently used.

Hatchway netting: Nets placed over open hatchways, to allow air circulation while stopping anyone from falling down.

Hatchway screens: Curtains of heavy cloth, often dampened, placed around man-o-war hatchways in action to screen passages to the magazines.

Haul: [1] To pull something. [2] To alter course into the wind. [3] Said of wind changing clockwise.

Haul bowling: The ancient name for an able seaman.

Haul off: To increase the distance from another ship or the land, especially to windward.

Haulser: An obsolete form of hawser.

Haulyard lines: The ancient name for halyards (halliards).

Haven: [1] In general: A refuge from the violence of wind and sea. From the Anglo-Saxon hæfen. [2] In surface warfare: A safe area located in the forward operating area where ships can be staged for provisioning or repair, or to await tasking. [3] In submarine warfare: A depth band in which a submarine will be safe from torpedo attack due to stratum inhibits. (*See also* moving submarine haven.)

Hawse: [1] That part of a ship's bows at and ahead of the anchors. [2] The water between the hull and the anchor chain when the anchor is down. [3] To caulk planking. [4] To ride uneasily while at anchor (also horse).

Hawse bag: A canvas bag stuffed with oakum, pushed into a hawse-hole during heavy weather to prevent water coming in.

Hawse block: A wooden plug, used to seal the hawse-hole in rough weather.

Hawse buckler: A steel plate, used to seal a hawse-pipe in rough weather.

Hawse fallen: Said of a ship in rough seas, when she is pitching bows-under so that water spouts through the hawse holes or pipes.

Hawsehole: An opening or pipe in a ship's side through which the anchor chain or cable passes. When the anchor is hove up and secured, its shank lies in the hawse-pipe or hole.

Hawsepiece: A large timber attached to the bow through which the hawseholes were cut.

Hawsepipe: A cast iron tube which fits into the hawsehole to protect it from wear and tear caused by the anchor chain or cable.

Hawser: Heavy rope (nowadays usually steel) for warping, mooring, or towing. Made of three hawser-laid ropes, laid up in the opposite direction to their own lay so that they form a "cable-laid," or "water-laid" rope. Since virtually all hawser-laid ropes are made-up right-handed ("with the sun"), most cable-laid hawsers will be left-handed ("against the sun") but not by definition. Originally called "haulser."

Hawser-laid: Rope made of three strands which are almost always made up right-handed, although left-handed is sometimes encountered.

Hazard: A danger to navigation, such as a submerged rock or wreck.

Hazardous: Said of cargo, goods, material, or waste products which pose a risk to human health or the environment.

Haze: [1] A mist of suspended water droplets, often contaminated with dust particles. From Middle English Hasu = murky. [2] Originally, to award extra duty as a punishment. [3] Nowadays, to inflict unnecessary humiliation or hardship on trainees or novices as part of their indoctrination (*see* hazing).

Haze Grey and Underway: USN sailor slang referring to arduous sea duty as opposed to ceremonial duties in port, or the "soft life" supposedly enjoyed by aviators and submariners because they work away from wind and wave.

Hazing: The word comes from the Old French haser, meaning to tease, irritate, or annoy; but the initiation of rookie seamen frequently went beyond teasing to become savage, sadistic, and degrading (*see* line-crossing). To a large extent (but by no means universally) orientation is now much gentler, often being no more than a practical joke. The innocent trainee may be told to "Ask the carpenter for a punch," which will usually get him a fist in the solar plexus, or he may be told to do something with a non-existent item. For example:

- "Fetch a hammock ladder from your quarters."
- "Ask the engine room for a bucket of steam."
- "Bring the key of the keelson to the bridge."
- "Get some grease for the relative bearing."
- "Clean the deck with non-skid wax."

Another trick is to post the recruit on the bow with instructions to keep a sharp lookout and report as soon as the "mail buoy" is sighted, so that post bags for the ship can be collected from it.

HD: Heavy Duty.

HE: High Explosive.

Head: [1] The upper edge of a sail or mast. [2] The stem of a ship. [3] USN slang for a ship's toilet (*see also* heads). [4] When hyphenated or conjoined, the top of something (e.g., head-gasket, beakhead, masthead, etc.). [5] To move towards something.

Head down/off: To steer away from the wind.

Head money: [1] A supplement to prize money paid for the capture of enemy warships, based on the head-count of their crews. [2] A bounty paid to anti-slave-trade naval patrols, based on the number of slaves released.

Head on: Said of vessels on reciprocal courses in danger of collision.

Head rail: A curved rail extending from the figurehead to the bow of a sailing ship.

Head reach: [1] To make headway to windward with difficulty (e.g., working off a lee shore during a storm). [2] To gain on, overtake, or escape from another vessel.

Head sail: Refers to any canvas set on the foremast, bowsprit,

Head sea: One which is running contrary to the ship's heading.

Head spar: Any spar forward of the foremast, especially the bowsprit.

Head up: To change direction, moving into the wind (not to be confused with heads up!).

Header: [1] A wind unfavorable to sailing in the desired direction. [2] A framing member inserted to distribute load to other construction members after a main member has been cut. [3] A chamber into which the ends of several pipes are connected so that water or steam may pass from one to the other.

Headgear: Although doffing head covering has long since been abolished as a form of salute, there are occasions when it is still considered appropriate. One obvious example is during religious services. In addition, it is unwritten law that junior and warrant officers remove their caps when in the wardroom, while all officers uncover when passing through captain's country or flag territory (although they do not do so when in full dress and wearing a sword). It is also considered courteous for officers to pass bareheaded through crew quarters at mealtimes, and to remove caps if visiting the sick bay. Unlike the United States army and air force, British armed forces and United States naval and marine personnel never salute when the head is uncovered.

Heading: The direction a ship is pointing, usually expressed as a compass point or in degrees clockwise from north.

Headland: A promontory with high cliffs.

Headroom: The distance between deck and overhead/deckhead.

Heads: Slang for the ship's toilet. Early warships were equipped with a beak or ram with which to impale hostile galleys. Later, around the tenth century, platforms for archers were built above and on either side of the beakhead, forward of the bow. Known simply as heads, these platforms were low enough to ship water from waves striking the bow, so were given reticulated decks to allow drainage. It was not long before crews realized they could defecate through the grids, which would be washed clean by the next wave. Long after fighting heads were replaced by castles and they in turn fell out of favor, a ship's toilet continues to be called "the head" (USN) or "the heads" (RN).

Heads up!: [1] A shouted warning of an overhead danger such as swinging cargo. [2] A demand to clear a passage. [3] An alert to take advantage of an opportunity.

Headsail: A jib or staysail set on the stays between foremast and bowsprit.

Headstay: Standing rigging running from the bow to support the foremost mast. Also forestay.

Headway: Forward motion in the *desired* direction. A vessel moving forward relative to the water, but pushed backward by a faster countercurrent would have negative headway. In sailing ship days headway was tested by throwing a floating object over the bow and watching to see if it passed astern into the wake.

Headwind: A wind blowing from directly in front of the vessel, pushing square sails back against the masts.

Heart of Oak: Official march music of the RN.

Heave: [1] To pull something. [2] To throw something. [3] To come into view. [4] The scend of the waves. [5] One of six possible responses of a vessel to movement of the sea (*see* linear displacement, ship motion).

Heave away!: Command to start pulling or heaving and continue until ordered to stop (*see* 'vast heaving).

Heave down: To careen a vessel, pulling it onto its side by hauling on purchases attached to the masts.

Heave ho!: [1] The cry formerly made by sailors while manually raising an anchor. [2] Colloquially, to give someone "the old heave ho" is to dismiss them.

Heave in: [1] To furl a sail. [2] To apply tension to a cable.

Heave out: [1] To shake out or loosen a sail. [2] To slacken a cable.

Heave out and trice up!: USN command to get up and lash hammocks. Although hammocks are no longer used, the phrase is still called out at reveille aboard USN vessels. The RN equivalent is "lash up and stow!"

Heave short: To haul in the anchor cable until it is almost up-and-down but maintains its grip on the sea bed. This holds the vessel in place, but allows rapid response when the command to up-anchor arrives.

Heave the lead: To take depth soundings by means of a leadline.

Heave the log: To throw a log-chip over the side to determine speed through the water.

Heave to: [1] To bring a vessel to a halt. [2] To hold a vessel as nearly motionless as possible. [3] To turn into the wind so that a sailing ship makes no headway.

Heaves: The rise and fall of waves or swell.

Heaving line: A light line with a weighted end which can be thrown to another vessel or to the shore and used to pull a heavier rope or hawser. Also used by personnel working aloft to haul up tools or components. *See also* "bolo."

Heavy cruiser: Twentieth century term for a cruiser armed with eight-inch guns.

Heavy loads and vehicles: There are seven principal methods of loading and discharging heavy cargo and/or vehicles. They are usually known by their abbreviations (written with or without hyphens):

- Lift-on/lift-off (Lo-Lo): Theses operations follow the conventional practice of using the ship's booms or dockside cranes, to hoist cargo on board and discharge it at the destination.

- Roll-on/roll-off (Ro-Ro): These are ships designed specifically to carry wheeled or tracked cargo such as automobiles, truck trailers, railroad cars, or fighting vehicles. They have doors at bow and stern with built-in ramps that allow vehicles to drive on board at one end and drive away at the other.

- Lift-on/roll-off (Lo-Ro): Involves ships designed for combination operation. They usually have conventional bows and ramped doors at the stern.

- Float-on/Float-off (Flo-Flo): These operations involve specialized vessels that operate like floating dry docks by submerging their open decks until a laden barge, another vessel, or an oil rig can be maneuvered on board, then pumping out ballast tanks to rise before proceeding to destination where the procedure is reversed.

- Lighter aboard ship (Lash): Refers to a system of carrying pre-laden barges or lighters on board specially adapted merchantmen. These are single-decked vessels with large hatches and clear access to the stern. They are equipped with heavy-lift gantry cranes, used to stow barges or lighters athwartships throughout the vessel. At destination, the crane moves the craft from their stowed locations and lowers them into the water at the stern. Some Lash ships are equipped with additional gantry cranes for handling an onboard complement of containers.

- Submersible Lash: These ships have ballast tanks that allow them to partially-submerge, float lighters into the cargo hold through an opening stern door, secure them in place, and raise the ship to its fully-floating position by evacuating the ballast tanks. They are unloaded in the reverse manner. Ships of this type (essentially "Lash-Flo" although the term is not in use) are commonly used in inland waterways, seldom for ocean-going.

- Heavy-lift (HL): These ships are specially designed to carry heavy or oversized objects as cargo on a main deck at least 100 meters (330 ft) long. They are fitted with multiple booms or cranes, each capable of a single lift of at least 100 tons, such as a railway locomotive or main battle tank.

Heavy metal: [1] A colloquialism for large-caliber ordnance. [2] A genre of rock music that developed in the late 1960s.

Heavy seas: Large waves or breakers.

Heavy weather: Stormy conditions, involving in high winds, extreme sea states, and heavy rain, snow, or hail. Weather of this type results in extremely uncomfortable conditions on board ship. Excessive rolls, yaws, and pitches make working and living dangerous. Dinner plates may slide over the fiddles. Objects can slide or fall on personnel, causing injury. Personnel can fall into machinery or equipment. Those working outside can be washed overboard or banged against fixed objects.

Heavy-lift: *See* heavy loads and vehicles.

Hedgehog: An ASW weapon thrown by bow-mounted mortar-like projectors to land ahead of the vessel in an elliptical pattern.

Heel: [1] To lean temporarily to one side (cf. list). [2] The foot of a mast or rudder. [3] The inboard end of a bowsprit. [4] The after end of the keel. [5] A small quantity of liquid left in a tank or other container.

Heel-and-toe: Slang for working watch-and-watch.

Heeling error: Compass deviation caused by the ship's list.

Heeling tanks: Ballast tanks, placed amidships on either side of an icebreaker and used to produce a rolling action that breaks the ship clear of enclosing ice.

HEIC: The Honourable East India Company.

Height of eye: The distance above the water surface of an observer's line of sight. (A standard height of eye of 15 feet is used to determine the range at which a light can be seen.)

Height of tide: The distance between a given datum (usually mean low water) and high water. Not to be confused with depth of water.

Helicopter: A highly maneuverable aircraft which flies by means of horizontally rotating blades.

Helipad: A deck area designated and used for take-off and landing of helicopters.

Helm: [1] A lever (tiller) or wheel controlling the rudder of a ship for steering. [2] The entire assembly comprising a ship's steering mechanism. [3] The person at the wheel, the helmsman. [4] The duty of steering (have the helm). [5] The position of the wheel or tiller with respect to amidships (e.g., helm alee). [6] By extension, any controlling position (the president-elect takes the helm of state). From Old High German helmo = tiller, via Middle English helme.

Helm orders: On a tiller-controlled boat, putting the helm to port turns the rudder to starboard which also swings the bow to starboard. On a vessel with a wheel-driven steering mechanism, the reverse is true, but for many decades tiller commands were used for both types of rudder-control. Hence, confusingly, the command "port your helm" then meant turning the wheel to starboard, which resulted in turning the rudder to starboard and swinging the bow to starboard. At an International Conference in London in 1928, it was determined that helm orders were to indicate the direction in which the ship's head was to be turned, regardless of the steering mechanism. British practice tends to retain the traditional "port" and "starboard," while Americans tend to use the revised "left" and "right."

Whenever a helm order is given, the Helm repeats the order back to the Conn verbatim. This assures the conning officer that the order was heard and understood correctly (e.g., Conn orders: "Right standard rudder, steady course 260." To which Helm replies: "Right standard rudder, steady course 260, aye").

Helmed: An obsolete term for [1] Steered. [2] wearing a helmet or protective hat.

Helmsman: The person responsible for steering a ship. In the USN the principal helmsman is normally paired with a lee helmsman. The "politically-correct" say helmsperson.

Helmsmanship: The art and skill of steering a ship.

Hemiola: [1] A speedy, oar-propelled double-banked pirate ship of the Hellenistic era. For combat, the mast with its single sail and part of the upper bank of oars was removed and stored on deck, clearing space for a boarding party to assemble. Mediterranean pirates found this one-and-a-half decker the perfect commerce raider because it could maintain fighting trim while under sail. [2] A musical rhythm developed independently in both Europe and Africa (from the Greek hemiolios, meaning "one and a half").

Hemp: An herbaceous Asian plant, whose fibers are used to make rope and stout fabrics. It is also the source of narcotics such as marijuana and hashish.

Hemp rope: Is made from the stems of the hemp plant, which is the strongest vegetable fiber used in rope manufacture, and is much softer and more flexible. than most other rope fibers. It is used mainly for light lines and small stuff.

Hen frigate: Merchant sailor's slang for any ship in which the master was dominated by his embarked wife.

Hermaphrodite brig: U.S. term for a brigantine.

Hermione **mutiny:** In 1797 Captain Hugh Pigot, a ruthless disciplinarian, was posted to command 32-gun frigate HMS *Hermione*. On September 21, cruising off Puerto Rico, he ordered the topsails reefed, saying the last man off the mainyard should be flogged. In their panic to get down, three young sailors fell to their deaths and Pigot ordered, "Throw the lubbers overboard" (citations are from *Naval History of Great Britain*, William James, 1837). All the other topmen were then severely reprimanded and threatened with punishment. When some sailors complained, Pigot had them flogged.

> Discontent ... kept increasing until the next evening, when it fatally burst forth. The men in addition to the loud murmurs they uttered, now began throwing double-headed shot about the deck; and on the first lieutenant's advancing to inquire into the cause of the disturbance, they wounded him in the arm with a tomahawk. He retired, for a while, and then returned ... the wretches knocked him down with a tomahawk, cut his throat, and threw him overboard. The captain, hearing a noise, ran on deck, but was driven back with repeated wounds: seated in his cabin he was stabbed by his cockswain and three other mutineers, and forced out of the cabin windows.

The mutineers then murdered the other three lieutenants; the purser, surgeon, and captain's clerk; one of the midshipmen, the boatswain, and the lieutenant of marines, "cutting and mangling their victims in the most cruel and barbarous manner." It was one of the bloodiest and most violent mutinies in Royal Navy history.

The mutineers sailed for La Guaira, Venezuela, where on September 27 they handed the ship over to the Spanish, claiming they had set the officers adrift in the jollyboat, but the truth soon emerged. Rear-admiral Henry Harvey, commander-in-chief, Leeward Islands, fully explained the ghastly circumstances in which the ship had been taken, but the Spanish ignored him and fitted *Hermione* for sea as a Spanish national frigate named *Santa Cecilia*. Two years later she was recaptured by a cutting-out expedition and remained in British service until 1805. Eventually, 33 of the mutineers were captured and 24 of them were hanged. *See also* Great Mutiny.

Hertz horn: The upper half of a naval contact mine is studded with hollow lead protuberances called Hertz horns. When a ship's hull hits one of these horns, its lead casing is crushed, cracking a glass vial filled with sulfuric acid. The acid runs down a tube into an empty lead-acid battery, forming the electrolyte and energizing the battery, which detonates the explosive.

HF: High Frequency.

H-hour: Time of seaborne assault landing. *See* H-.

Hidden harbor: One where the outer points overlap so that the shore line appears continuous from seaward.

High-and-dry: Above the high-water mark.

High latitudes: Regions far removed from the equator and nearing the poles.

High seas: In the first two of the following definitions, the word "high" means "chief" or "principal," but in the third and fourth it means "tall" or "towering." [1] The navigable ocean highways, across which the ships of all nations have the right of innocent passage (territorial waters and exclusive economic zones excluded). [2] In maritime law, areas under the jurisdiction of admiralty courts. [3] Force 6 on the Douglas Scale, meaning waves of 15–24 feet (4.6–7.3 meters) in height. [4] Any large waves.

High water: The maximum height reached by a tide. *See also* height of tide.

High water mark: The line along the shore reached by the mean high water.

Highline: USN term for a line used to support a cargo bag or breeches buoy for the transfer of goods or personnel between two ships under way and running parallel to each other. The RN term is Jackstay, qualified by "light" if made of fiber or "heavy" when made of wire.

Highliner: A fishing boat or skipper that consistently brings in the finest catch of the fleet.

Hike: [1] To hang out over the windward side of a sailboat to counter-balance the force of wind in the sails. [2] Informal USN/USMC term for a route march.

Hindcastle: Ancient term for the poop or quarterdeck. More usually "aftercastle."

Hinterland: [1] The area or region supplying trade goods to and receiving cargo from a port. [2] The land lying behind a coastal district (termed "near" up to 5 miles/8 kms inland, and "far" up to 100 miles/160 kms. Thereafter it is no longer hinterland but "interior").

Hit the deck!: [1] Warning to fall to the prone position when under fire. [2] Command to assume the push-up position during physical training. [3] USN command to rise from bed (*see also* "heave out" and "rise and shine").

Hit the rack/sack: USN slang for go to bed.

Hit the silk: Aviator's slang for making a parachute jump.

Hitch: [1] Any knot which fastens a line to something, holding it firmly yet easily released. [2] USN slang for a period of enlistment.

HMAS: Her/His Majesty's Australian Ship.

HMCS: Her/His Majesty's Canadian Ship.

HMIS: Formerly, Her/His Majesty's Indian Ship, now INS.

HMNZS: Her/His Majesty's New Zealand Ship.

HMS: Her/His (Britannic) Majesty's Ship.

Hobbling knot: A knot tied in the bight having

two adjustable loops in opposing directions. Able to be tightened around a pair of human or animal limbs, and originally used on the legs of horses to limit the distance they could wander overnight. Also known as the handcuff knot, but not always effective for that use, since it does not have inherent locking action and is fairly easy for a human to wriggle out of.

Hobby-horse: To rock up-and-down when heading into waves, usually due to excess weight at bow and stern.

Hobnob: [1] In the 18th century, when sea captains met, they would drink ("hob") and toast ("nob") one another. [2] Today, to associate familiarly (hobnob with one's cronies).

Hody: The traditional dugout outrigger catamaran of the Nicobar Islands. Currently used mainly by fishermen but, long before Europeans arrived in that part of the world, the Nicobars and natives of adjoining archipelagic peoples used this unique sickle-shaped craft to explore the Indian Ocean. (The logo of the Indian Navy's "MILAN" initiative depicts a hody.)

Hog: [1] To support a vessel amidships so that both ends droop (e.g., hull balanced on a midships crest with bow and stern hanging over troughs). The opposite of sag. [2] To scrape a ship's bottom. [3] A hogging brush.

Hogging brush: A heavy-duty broom for cleaning the underside of a submerged hull. Made of birch twigs tightly enclosed between long planks and cut off so as to form a wide brush, it was pushed under the ship by a long pole on one side and pulled upward and across by ropes on the other, thus scouring the bottom.

Hogging line: A line attached to the corner of a collision mat or hogging mat.

Hogging mat: An abrasive mat that is pulled under a ship's keel to remove weeds and barnacles.

Hogging strap: A line used to keep a towing line close to the fantail of the towing vessel.

Hoist: [1] A display of signal flags. [2] The vertical edge of a flag alongside the mast. [3] The half of a flag nearest to the mast. [4] To lift something. [5] A lifting apparatus.

Hoist the pendant: To commission a warship.

Hold: A storage space or compartment in the hull of a ship.

Hold captain: The person responsible for tactical loading and unloading of a ship's cargo hold during an amphibious operation.

Hold crew: Longshoremen working in the ship's hold rather than ashore.

Hold fast: [1] To attach firmly. [2] to stop an operation, to belay it. [3] To refuse to surrender a military position. [4] To refuse to abandon an idea or concept. No to be confused with holdfast.

Hold water: To slow down a rowing boat by holding the flat of the blade against the water.

Holdback: A fitting that restrains an aircraft until it is time for catapult launching.

Holdfast: A brace, catch, clamp, dog, hook, or other device used to secure cargo or equipment. Cf. hold fast.

Holding: Said of an anchor which has embedded itself in the sea bottom and is not dragging.

Holes in sails: In antiquity holes were deliberately cut in the canvas so that evil spirits — believed to dwell in the depths and fly on the wind — could pass through without being trapped on board where they might harm the vessel or its crew.

Holiday: Naval slang for an area missed while performing chores such as painting, scrubbing, dusting, and the like.

Holiday routine: USN term for a rest period when only essential work or drill is carried out.

Hollow shot: A cannon ball with an empty center, introduced for naval use in the early 19th century because — with only two-thirds the weight of solid shot — they required less powder, to inflict the same or greater damage. They did not last long, because it soon became apparent that the hollow could be filled with explosive, thereby becoming a shell with greatly increased destructive power.

Holmes light: In 1876, with J.H. Player as co-applicant, Nathaniel John Holmes patented "Self-igniting and inextinguishable signal lights for marine and other purposes." This widely-used distress signaling device consists of a canister, containing calcium carbide and calcium phosphide, attached to a lifebuoy or float. On contact with water, the phosphide ignites acetylene emitted by the carbonide, producing conspicuous fire and smoke.

Holy Ghost: *See* up spirits!

Holy Joe: USN slang for a naval Chaplain (*see* sky pilot).

Holystone: [1] Wooden decks were cleaned by scrubbing with sandstone blocks which were popularly believed to have been named Holy because they brought seamen to their knees. In fact they were called holey because they are full of cavities. Seamen called the bigger blocks Bibles and the little ones, used to scrub narrow spaces, Prayer-books. [2] To scour the deck with such a stone.

Home: [1] To steer towards a beacon. [2] To close in on a target. [3] Something which has been brought to its proper position (e.g., the anchor is home).

Home port: [1] The port at which a seaman signed on. [2] The port from which a merchantman normally operates (which may or may not be its port of registration). [3] The naval establishment or air station at which a ship or aircraft is normally based. USN usually writes as one word "homeport."

Homeland Security: The United States Department of Homeland Security was created in 2003, to consolidate the then current "confusing patchwork of government activities into a single department whose primary mission is to protect our homeland." A large number of independent agencies were absorbed and merged into four major directorates — Border and

Transportation Security, Emergency Preparedness and Response, Science and Technology, and Information Analysis and Infrastructure Protection — with the Secret Service and the Coast Guard left intact and reporting directly to the Secretary of Homeland Security.

Homeward-bound pennant: A United States warship which has been in service outside home waters for nine months or longer is authorized to wear a special streamer on its homeward voyage. Its length is traditionally one foot for every member of the ship's company who has been on board for at least nine months, provided the length of the pennant does not exceed that of the ship. The pennant is hoisted as soon as the vessel gets under way bound for a U.S. port and it remains aloft until sunset on the day of arrival. After being struck, the starred blue portion is presented to the commanding officer. The remainder is cut into foot-long pieces, with each eligible member of the ship's company getting a piece. (The RN equivalent is paying-off pendant.)

Homing anti-sonar torpedo: This is a torpedo equipped with a passive sonar detection device that treats the "ping" emitted by a hostile vessel or homing torpedo as its target. The hostile sonar's signature is stored in memory, and the torpedo will not be diverted by any other sonar source, but continues to home in on the original target.

Homing guidance: [1] In navigation: A process by which a destination is approached by keeping some parameter constant (such as the relative bearing of a signal emitted from or near the destination point). [2] In military use: A system by which a missile steers itself towards the target by means of an electronic device activated by some distinguishing characteristic. It is termed *Active* if the source for illuminating the target and the receiver for detecting reflected energy are both carried within the missile; *Semi-active* if it carries only a receiver and the target is illuminated by an outside source; and *Passive* if it relies on detecting radiation from the target (such as the transmissions of a radio, radar, or navigational aid; or the infrared emitted by a hot engine or exhaust system). The homing run goes through three phases—*enabling* which takes the missile to the general vicinity of the target, *searching* in which it maneuvers to locate the target, and *homing* during which it actively pursues the target.

Homing torpedo: A torpedo equipped with active or passive sonar or other device that detects and tracks a target by the sounds coming from its propulsion machinery, its magnetic signature, or the turbulence of its wake.

Honors: Collective term covering traditional compliments to greet a distinguished guest, salute a passing vessel, respect the colors, or recognize a special occasion. *See* salutes and courtesies, passing honors, side honors, battle honors.

At 4:30 A.M. on 15th July 1815, Captain Frederick Maitland of HMS *Bellerophon* (affectionately known

to the lower deck as "belly rough'n") faced a difficult problem of protocol. Napoleon Bonaparte, who had abdicated following military defeat at Waterloo, was coming aboard. Should the former Emperor of France he be given full honors as a head of state (manning the yards, firing a royal gun salute, etc.), or should he be considered a prisoner of war entitled to no honors? Taking advantage of the Royal Navy custom of normally rendering honors only between 8 A.M. and sunset, he came up with an astute compromise. It was daylight, but only 6 A.M., so Napoleon was piped aboard and greeted by an honor guard of Royal Marines, who snapped to attention, but did not present arms.

Hood: This 42,100 ton battlecruiser was the pride of the Royal Navy and became to the British public the ultimate symbol of imperial naval power. When she was destroyed by plunging fire through her lightly-armored deck during the Battle of Denmark Strait in May 1941, with the loss of all but three of her 1,420 crew, the psychological impact was immense. Naval storyteller Douglas Reeman writes: "*Hood* had been different. She had been more than just a ship. Huge, beautiful and arrogant ... to the public at large she ***was*** the Royal Navy."

Hook: [1] A curved point of land, often terminating in a spit. [2] A curved or bent piece of metal or other material used to hold, suspend, or pull something. [3] Slang for an anchor.

Hooker: [1] Contemptuous term for an old-fashioned or clumsy ship. [2] Slang for a prostitute.

Hooky: RN slang for a leading seaman, whose badge is an anchor (cf. Killick).

Hooligan Navy: World War II USN pejorative for the Coast Guard.

Hopper: General term for a chute with additional width and depth to provide volume for the temporary storage of dry goods in bulk. The bottom typically has a mechanism to control the flow, thus allowing cargo to be metered into a bulker at the desired rate.

Hopper barge: A dumb barge designed to carry materials, like rocks, sand, soil and garbage, for dumping into the ocean, a river, or a lake, usually for land reclamation. It has several transverse hopper-shaped compartments between its forward and after bulkheads, each equipped with a large door that opens downwards to dump its load. *See also* splitbarge.

Hopper tank: A side compartment at the bottom of a cargo ship's hull. Used to contain water ballast which can be pumped in or dumped to compensate for the changing weight of cargo. *See also* topside tank.

Horizon: The line or circle which forms the apparent boundary between sky and earth or sea from any specific point of observation.

Horizontal stowage: Placing similar items in layers throughout all a merchantman's holds, to enable simultaneous unloading from two or more of them.

Hornpipe: [1] A single-reed wooden pipe of Celtic

origin: with spaced holes and a mouthpiece made of oxhorn. In the 14th century, Chaucer wrote about "hornepypes of cornewayle," but the instrument is much older than that, it's origins being lost in prehistory. [2] A lively jig-like dance. The small space required and the fact that no partner was necessary made it particularly suitable for shipboard use. In his diary, Samuel Pepys called it "The Jig of the Ship" and Captain Cook ordered his crews to dance the hornpipe daily to keep them in good health during long voyages in the cramped space of sailing ships.

Despite claims to the contrary, the jig originally had no nautical connection, having been danced from ancient times as a solo in three-time to the music of the Celtic hornpipe. Later it evolved into a group performance featured in pageants by many different trades, each of which added movements symbolizing their work. Early in the 18th century, it became popular with seamen, who changed the measure to two-time and danced to the music of the ship's fiddler.

During the 19th century the "Sailor's Hornpipe" was a popular feature of theatrical productions in which actors dressed as seamen danced with arms crossed, unfolding them to mimic climbing rigging, rowing a boat, hauling ropes, and saluting. This version was performed well into the 20th century, long after fiddlers had had ceased to be part of a ship's company and seamen had found other diversions.

Horns: [1] The jaws of a boom or gaff which embrace the mast. [2] The outer ends of the crosstrees. [3] Projections on the casing of a contact mine which detonate it when touched or broken (see Hertz horn).

Horse: [1] A foot-rope for topmen to stand on while working aloft (furling, reefing, etc.). [2] A rope to keep spritsail sheets clear of the anchor flukes. [3] A rope made fast to the shrouds to protect the leadsman. [4] A metal rail across the stern of a small sailing vessel to which the sheet of the nearest fore-and-aft sail (mainsail in a cutter, schooner or brigantine; mizzen in a ketch) is hooked, enabling the sheet to traverse when tacking. [5] Part of the caulking operation which involved forcing oakum between the planks with a caulking iron and mallet, preparatory to paying the seam. [6] To ride uneasily at anchor (see hawse). [7] A period of unpaid work (see dead horse). [8] Slang for salted or corned meat (see salt horse).

Horse about: Slang for to play the clown, fool around, or indulge in horseplay.

Horse latitudes: Regions of weak pressure in both northern and southern hemispheres where winds are light and variable. So named because becalmed ships often had to jettison embarked horses which had died of heat or dehydration.

Horse Marine: [1] Today, a person out of his or her proper or natural place. [2] Formerly, a marine mounted on horseback or a cavalryman serving on shipboard, a rare creature at the best of times. A music hall jingle that was very popular in United States vaudeville in the late 19th century was:

I'm Captain Jinks of the Horse Marines
I feed my horse on corn and beans
And often live beyond the means
Of a Captain in the Army.

Horse-up: To harden the oakum in a vessel's seams.

Horseshoe maneuver: A U-shaped tactic for the inspection of a vessel suspected of carrying contraband or terrorists. The inspecting craft, usually a high-speed rigid-hull inflatable boat or Zodiac, approaches the vessel from ahead, passes down and inspects the first side, comes around the stern, and runs up the other side to make sure there is nothing there.

Horsing iron: A tool used when caulking deck seams. Also caulking iron.

Horus: For millennia, the eyes of Horus have had immense significance for Mediterranean mariners (see oculi). This falcon-headed god of ancient Egypt had many manifestations, all of which involved light, the sky, and kingship. The sun was his right eye, and the moon his left. When neither was visible (as on the night of a new moon) he went blind and was known as Mekhenty-er-irty, but when they returned he became Khenty-irty (he who has eyes).

Hospital corpsman: A U.S. Navy enlisted medical rating. In 1861, a Navy Department Order replaced "loblolly boy" with "Nurse," and Navy Regulations of 1876 changed the title to "Bayman," (one who staffed the sick bay). Since 1898, enlisted medical personnel have been called "hospital corpsmen." They assist health care professionals in providing medical care to Navy people and their families, and may function as clinical or specialty technicians, medical administrative personnel and health care providers at medical treatment facilities. They also serve as battlefield corpsmen with the Marine Corps.

Hospital ship: A vessel staffed and equipped to provide medical and surgical care. The use of such vessels is protected under the Geneva Conventions as follows:

Article 22: Military hospital ships, that is to say, ships built or equipped by the Powers specially and solely with a view to assisting the wounded, sick and shipwrecked, to treating them and to transporting them, may in no circumstances be attacked or captured, but shall at all times be respected and protected, on condition that their names and descriptions have been notified to the Parties to the conflict ten days before those ships are employed. The characteristics which must appear in the notification shall include registered gross tonnage, the length from stem to stern and the number of masts and funnels.

Article 43: The ships ... shall be distinctively marked as follows: (a) All exterior surfaces shall be white. (b) One or more dark red crosses, as large as possible, shall be painted and displayed on each side of the hull and on the horizontal surfaces, so placed as to afford the greatest possible visibility from the sea and from the air.... Nevertheless, in the case of countries which already use as emblem, in place of the red cross, the red crescent or the red lion and sun on a white ground, these emblems are also recognized by the terms of the present Convention.

Similar clauses extend the same protections and criteria to non-military hospital ships, with the proviso that "Merchant vessels which have been transformed into hospital ships cannot be put to any other use throughout the duration of hostilities." *See also* humanitarian emblems.

Hostile ice: Submariner's term for an ice canopy too thick to break through and surface.

Hot bunk: Term for a single berth used in rotation by the members of several watches.

Hot fuel: To refuel an aircraft without stopping its engine(s).

Hot pursuit: Doctrine of International Maritime Law which allows a military, police, or coastguard vessel or aircraft to follow a foreign-flagged vessel and arrest it in waters where it would not normally have jurisdiction, provided the following criteria have been met:
- The foreign vessel is suspected of violating a law within the jurisdiction of the pursuing vessel.
- The pursuing vessel visually or audibly (radio signals excluded) orders the foreign vessel to stop while still within its jurisdiction.
- Pursuit begins within the coastal zone of jurisdiction.
- The foreign vessel subsequently flees into international waters.
- Pursuit is continuous without loss of visual or radar contact.
- The foreign vessel does not enter another state's territorial waters.

Hot suit: [1] Fire-resistant protective clothing, worn by flight deck rescue crews. [2] A member of such a crew.

Hotel: NATO phonetic notation for the letter "H."

Hounds: A pair of fore-and-aft members at the lower end of a mast supporting athwartships trestletrees that support the crosstrees that support the heel of the upper mast.

House: [1] A structure built on the main deck of a vessel (pronounced howse). [2] To stow something in its proper place (pronounced howze).

House flag: A flag flown at the mainmast of a merchantman, bearing the emblem and/or in the colors of its owners or operators.

Hove: The past participle of heave.

Hove to: Stopped.

Hovercraft: [1] The registered trademark of a specific manufacturer of ground-effect vehicles. [2] Frequently, but incorrectly, used to refer to any air-cushion vessel.

Hovering: [1] Term for a vessel which lurks offshore for what appears to be a nefarious purpose (e.g., drug smuggling, landing contraband, launching terrorism, etc.). [2] Said of a helicopter which remains airborne over a fixed point.

Hoy: The name originated in the Low Countries, probably in the 15th century, but the size, shape, and purpose of this vessel changed over time and from country-to-country, the most common being [1] In the 16th–17th centuries, a sloop-rigged European coastal trader. [2] In the 18th–19th centuries, a single-masted, square-rigged sailing barge.

HQ: Headquarters.

HT: Hull Technician (USN).

HUD: Head-Up Display.

Hug: [1] To run as close to the shore as possible. [2] To sail as close to the wind as possible.

Huissier: Today, this Venetian-developed military transport vessel would be called a "Landing Ship, Horse." Large for their age (about 2,000 tons), with two or three masts carrying lateen sails, these ships were called usciere after their large ports (usci) designed to facilitate the loading of horses. These were normally cut into rounded sterns, but for assault landings by the Fourth and Seventh Crusades (1202 and 1248) they were placed in the bow to allow mounted knights to ride directly into action. This innovation anticipated the Landing Ship, Tank by roughly three-fourths of a millennium.

HUK: USN designation of an ASW hunter-killer group.

Hulk: [1] Slang for a clumsy or unwieldy vessel. [2] The shell of a wrecked, burned-out, or abandoned vessel. [3] Formerly and figuratively, an old sailor worn out in the service. [4] During the 17th to 19th centuries, the hull of a vessel condemned as unfit for sea service, dismasted and moored for use as a training or receiving ship, or a floating crane (sheer hulk), or a floating storage facility (warehouse hulk), or to house convicts or prisoners-of-war (prison hulk). Lack of space in the dockyards and the ready availability of ships retired from fighting careers were some of the reasons why the Navy used hulks rather than building on land.

Hull: [1] The principal structure, outer shell, or body of a vessel. [2] To puncture the skin of a vessel, usually by gunfire. From the Gothic hulga = husk or shell.

Hull classification: A USN–developed system of alphabetical symbols that identify types of vessel, many of which have been adopted by NATO. For example "FF" signifies a frigate, while "CV" refers to an aircraft carrier. Suffixes include "G" = equipped with guided missiles, "N" = nuclear powered, and the prefix "T" = operated by Military Sealift Command.

Hull down: Over the horizon so that only masts can be seen.

Hull number: *See* official number.

Hull speed: The theoretical maximum speed a vessel can achieve without planeing. This is usually slightly faster than its displacement speed. (A rule of thumb for calculating potential hull speed is to multiply the square root of the vessel's waterline length by 1.34.)

Hull up: Fully visible above the horizon.

Humanitarian emblems: The Geneva Conventions recognize several emblems to be displayed by humanitarian and medical ships, vehicles, and buildings, to protect them from military attack.
- The **Red Cross,** adopted in 1864, is simply a reverse image of the flag of historically neutral Switzerland, originally intended to be a unique, universal, and easily recognizable symbol, free from political or a religious connotations.
- Unfortunately, Muslims objected to an emblem that reminded them of Crusaders, giving rise to the 1929 adoption of the **Red Crescent** as a recognized alternative.
- Then in December 2005, the **Third Protocol Emblem** (diamond-shaped and commonly known as the "red crystal") was adopted for use by cultures wishing to avoid the implied religious connotation of the first two. No country or society is obliged to use the new emblem; but all are required to respect it in the same manner as the other emblems.
- Because the **Mogen David** (Solomon's Seal: a six-pointed star formed from two equilateral triangles) is not recognized outside Israel, that country ensures international protection by using the red crystal, either alone, or surrounding a red Mogen David.
- The **Red Lion and Sun** emblem of Iran is also recognized by the Geneva Conventions, but is no longer in use, having been discontinued by the Islamic Republic in 1980.

Humbolt current: Named after Prussian naturalist Freinrich Heinrich Alexander von Humbolt, this is a cold, low salinity ocean current flowing northward along the west coast of South America, generated by a major upwelling that supports an abundance of marine life.

Hummock ice: A field of pressure ice marked by numerous hillocks or ridges.

Hunky-dory: This phrase meaning things are okay or enjoyable originated as USN slang. When the American fleet visited Yokohama, Japan, Libertymen used to head for a dockside street called Honkidori whose female inhabitants catered to their every pleasure.

Hunter-killer group: A fast antisubmarine naval force comprising an aircraft or helicopter carrier and a number of ASW vessels such as corvettes, destroyers, and frigates.

Hunter-killer submarine: A military submersible designed and armed to detect and destroy hostile submarines, especially those armed with strategic ballistic missiles.

Hurricane: A violent cyclonic storm of force 12 on the Beaufort Scale (wind >64 knots = 73.7 mph = 118.6 km/h). *See also* table 1.

Hurricane deck: A promenade deck mounted high on the superstructure of a passenger vessel.

Husky: Code-name for the Allied invasion of Sicily in January 1943.

Huzzah!: British cry of triumph during the Napoleonic Wars. Derived from the "hudsa" shout of Hungarian light cavalry who were themselves called huszárs. *See* vocal salutes.

HVAC: **H**eating, **V**entilating, & **A**ir **C**onditioning.

HWM: High water mark.

Hydraulic current: A flow generated by the interaction of two out-of-phase tidal bodies in a strait.

Hydraulics: [1] The scientific study of water and other liquids, in particular their behavior under the influence of mechanical forces and their related uses in engineering. [2] A mechanical device or system using hydraulic cylinders and machinery.

Hydrofoil: [1] A winglike blade which creates an upward thrust when moved through water. This lifts the hull of a vessel above the surface, reducing drag and increasing speed. [2] A vessel equipped with such blades.

Hydrographic chart: A marine map showing depths, contours, nature of the bottom, the coastline, and tides and currents.

Hydrography: The science dealing with the physical properties and measurements of oceans, seas, lakes, rivers, and adjoining coastal areas, especially with reference to their use in navigation.

Hydrojet propulsion: *See* Water jet.

Hydrology: [1] In general, the branch of geology dealing with the distribution, properties, and effects of water on or under the surface of the earth. [2] In naval use, the study of the physical properties of salt water. *See also* limnology.

Hydrometer: An instrument used to determine the salinity or specific gravity of sea or brackish water.

Hydrophone: A device for detecting submerged submarines by the sound of their engines or other noise emissions.

Hydroplane: [1] A horizontal rudder (diving plane) mounted on the bow, stern, or conning tower (*see* sailplane) of a submarine to control the steepness of its dive. For example, stern hydroplanes are angled so that the flow of water over them forces the stern upward, angling the submarine downward. [2] A high-powered boat equipped with hydrofoils or a stepped hull, designed to skim the water at high speed. [3] To skim over the water.

Hydrosphere: The earth's liquid water and surrounding water vapor, as distinct from the land (lithosphere) and air (atmosphere).

Hygrometer: An instrument for measuring atmospheric humidity.

Hymns: In 1861, English clergyman John Dykes, a prolific writer of religious music, adapted his composition "Melita" (then the name of Malta) to fit a prayer written a year earlier by another English clergyman, William Whiting, after he had survived a furious storm in the Mediterranean:

> Eternal Father, strong to save,
> Whose arm hath bound the restless wave,

> Who bidd'st the mighty ocean deep
> Its own appointed limits keep;
> Oh, hear us when we cry to Thee,
> For those in peril on the sea!

Both the United States and Royal Navies consider this to be their official hymn, usually sung at the close of Sunday services. It is also played as a background to the Benediction at USN changes of command. "Eternal Father" has tremendous emotional appeal to naval veterans and is often played at funerals, including those of U.S. Presidents Franklin Delano Roosevelt (1945) and John Fitzgerald Kennedy (1963), and British Prime Minister Winston Churchill (1965) each of whom had strong naval connections.

Hyperbaric chamber: A pressure-controlled room used in the treatment of decompression sickness due to deep-water diving or high-altitude flying. Also compression chamber, diving chamber.

Hyperbolic navigation: A system of long-range radio navigation in which a fix is obtained by making use of two or more families of constant phase hyperbolae established by a master and two or more slave transmitters working on different but related frequencies.

Hypolimnion: The lowest of three layers of sea water. *See* deep water layer.

Hypothecation: *See* bottomry.

I

I: Immediate. Military and diplomatic communications precedence higher than Priority and below Flash.

IA: Intelligence Assessment.

IACA: International Association of Classification Societies.

IALA: International Association of Lighthouse Authorities.

IB: [1] Inbound. [2] Inboard.

***Iberian*'s crocodilian:** On 30th July 1915, Kapitänleutnant Georg von Forstner, commanding German submarine *U-28* torpedoed British steamer *Iberian* in the North Atlantic. The sinking vessel suffered a violent underwater explosion and, according to von Forstner's testimony he saw:

> Pieces of wreckage, and among them a gigantic sea animal writhing and struggling wildly, shot out of the water to a height of 18 to 30 meters (60–100 feet). At that moment I had with me in the conning tower my officers of the watch, the chief engineer, the navigator, and the helmsman. Simultaneously we all drew one another's attention to this wonder of the seas.... It was about 18 meters (60 feet) long, was like a crocodile in shape and had four limbs with powerful webbed feet and a long tail tapering to a point.

ICBM: Inter-Continental Ballistic Missile.

Ice: Water or brine frozen or reduced to its solid state by low temperature. It is a white or transparent substance; crystalline, brittle, and viscoidal; that floats because its specific gravity is less than that of water.

Ice anchor: [1] A timber frozen in ice to serve as a mooring post. [2] A hook-like device specially designed for securing vessels in ice or dragging them along with a hawser. Also called an ice drag.

Ice blink: Luminosity at the horizon or on the underside of clouds, warning of a distant accumulation of ice.

Ice canopy: Submariner's term for overhead pack ice.

Ice chart: A graphic representation showing the prevalence of ice, usually with reference to navigable waters and showing factors such as extent of ice cover, thickness, topography, temperature, salinity and the location of icebergs. Navigational sea ice charts are extremely important for operations in the polar oceans.

Ice chart symbology: Codes and symbols are essential for effective use of the limited space available for recording sea ice and icebergs on charts. The World Meteorology Organization system for sea ice symbology is more frequently referred to as the "Egg Code" due to the oval shape of the symbol.

Ice clause: A Charter Party proviso that allows a master to divert to an alternate port when the scheduled destination is icebound.

Ice cover: The ratio of ice to total sea surface in a specified area. Often expressed as tenths. Also ice concentration.

Ice drag: *See* ice anchor.

Ice egg: *See* egg code.

Ice field: An area of floating ice measuring at least 5.4 nautical miles (10 kms) across.

Ice floe: A large flat mass of floating ice, too small to be classified as an ice field.

Ice fog: A concentration of air-suspended ice crystals reducing visibility in otherwise clear and calm weather. Occurs at low temperatures in high latitudes.

Ice free: Said of any harbor or channel where ice formation does not normally impede navigation.

Ice front: The place at which a glacier or ice field thins and ends.

Ice island: An exceptionally-large ice field.

Ice master: A ship's pilot qualified for arctic waters.

Ice pack: An expanse of pack ice. A large mass of floating ice, formed over many years by winds and currents pushing smaller pieces of ice together.

Ice reports: The timely and accurate reporting of ice conditions is the responsibility of national governments, whose capabilities and resources vary widely, and which use different conventions for digitizing and color coding. Hence, as additions to its existing "egg code," the World Meteorological Organization is working to standardize international reporting of such items as ice/water boundary, percent coverage, stage of development, floe size, thickness and strength, topography and roughness, and the location of leads and polynyas.

Ice shelf: The end of an ice sheet or glacier, projecting into coastal waters and forming a steep ice front or cliff.

Ice sheet: A mass of glacier ice that covers an area greater than 50,000 km² (19,305 mile²). The only current such sheets are off Antarctica and Greenland.

Iceberg: [1] Part of a glacier which has broken off and is floating freely at sea. It is defined a "large" if it rises at least 15 meters (50 feet) above the surface and is more than 120 meters (400 feet) long. Many are much bigger, forming floating islands. [2] Code-name for the 1945 invasion of Okinawa.

Iceboat: [1] A sail or power-driven racing boat mounted on runners or skates. [2] A small (5-meter; 16-foot) boat, used as a winter ferry across Northumberland Strait until the early 20th century. The hull was tin-clad for ice protection, with twin metal runners on either side of the keel. It would be rowed or sailed until it reached thick ice; then all male passengers had to disembark, don leather harnesses, and help the crew to haul it across.

Icebound: [1] An area such as a harbor which is obstructed or shut off by ice. [2] Said of a vessel hemmed in by frozen water and unable to move.

Icebreaker: A vessel designed to force navigable passages through ice, usually with extra-powerful engines, shielded propellers, and a convex stem that rides over the ice and crushes it with the vessel's own weight. Some have forward screws which run astern to pull water from beneath the ice and weaken it.

ICRC: International Committee of the Red Cross.

Idler: Although this term now refers to someone who shirks work and takes things easy, it originally had no negative connotation, simply referring to a member of the ship's company who worked a day shift and was not required to stand watch. Idlers included boatswain, carpenter, cook, painter, purser, and sailmaker. They worked as hard as anyone aboard, but only during a daylight shift, and were much envied for their ability to enjoy regular bunktime. The modern term is "dayman."

IFF: Identification, friend or foe.

IFFN: Identification, friend, foe, or neutral.

IFS: Inshore Fire Support.

IGO: I'm departing (informal closing of communication).

IHB: International Hydrographic Bureau.

IHO: International Hydrographic Organization.

Ilanuns: Filipino pirates operating in the South China Sea and Malaccan Strait.

Ill wind: The first known reference to this phrase seems to have been in John Heywood's Book of Proverbs, published in 1562, where he cites, "It ys an yll wynde that blowth no man to good." Although Heywood did not say so, it seems virtually certain that the aphorism had a nautical origin, since a contrary wind for one sailing vessel will always be favorable for another.

Illuminate: To direct radar at a target for weapons guidance purposes (cf. paint).

ILO: International Labour Organization.

I'm all right Jack: Essentially a paraphrase of "look after number one" this phrase originated as 19th century RN slang, and is abbreviated from the more typically seamanlike "Fuck you Jack, I'm all right."

I'm for all waters: Though this expression sounds as if it might have a nautical derivation, it first appears in Shakespeare's *Twelfth Night* (IV.ii).

Immatriculation: The procedure by which a merchantman acquires a nationality. The term is French for "registration."

Immediate: The second-highest order of precedence for a NATO message.

Immediately vital: A cargo which the consignee nation regards as essential for the prosecution of a war or for national survival, to be delivered immediately, notwithstanding any risk to the ship or its crew.

IMO: International Maritime Organization.

Import: To bring in merchandise or commodities from another country.

Impossible: Admiral Smyth calls this "A hateful word, generally supplanted among good seamen by 'we'll try.'" *See* difficulty.

Impost: A tax or customs duty on imported merchandise.

Impressment: To force an individual into naval, military, or piratical service. Prior to the invention of conscription and the draft, many countries used forcible recruitment to fill vacancies in both military and naval service. Abducting fishermen or sailors in ports, or compelling captured crews to "volunteer" for service was common practice among pirates as well as regular navies (*see also* Crimping).

In Britain, compulsory sea service was sanctioned by long-standing tradition going back to at least the eleventh century, and was used extensively during the reign of Queen Elizabeth I and by Lord Protector Oliver Cromwell. But the practice will always be associated with the Napoleonic Wars, during which the Royal Navy had immense manpower needs. Not only did it have to replace battle casualties and heavier losses from disease but, between 1793 and 1800, the fleet expanded by 290 percent (from 45,000 to 130,000 men). As a result, there was intense competition for seamen between the navy, the merchant service, and privateers. Thus — despite generous enlistment bounties, improved conditions of service, and the prospect of prize money — it proved impossible to fill all these vacancies with volunteers, and three other methods were employed.

- The **quota system** proved unsatisfactory, since it wasn't worth the time and effort required to train a novice in what was the most complex technology of the age.
- The **Imprest Service** provided the vast majority of skilled mariners. The popular belief that press gangs seized innocent landsmen and forced them to learn seamanship by brutal indoctrination is a Hollywood-inspired falsehood. Those liable to lawful

impressment were "eligible men of *seafaring* habits between the ages of 18 and 55 years" (author's emphasis). The navy had little interest in people who were would be of no immediate use on board a ship. Slightly more than half of the seamen acquired by this method were classified as "volunteers," but it is probable that most of these had made the best of a bad situation by signing-up after being taken, in order to enjoy the enlistment bounty and a better position on board. Those who believed they had been seized unfairly had the right of appeal, and were often successful.

- The third method was **impressment at sea**. A captain could halt a merchantman and legally compel its master to hand over some of his prime seamen (officers, sailors with less than two-years service, and apprentices were exempt). Such men were valuable recruits, since they had not only been trained at someone else's expense, but were usually schooled in handling weapons for defense against pirates. While still a post-captain, Horatio Nelson used cannon to force homeward-bound East Indiamen to heave-to and transfer men to his ship. Since Britain considered all those born under British rule to be the king's subjects, over six thousand seamen who claimed United States citizenship were impressed in this manner. This was one of the factors leading to the War of 1812.

The Impressment Act was revised in 1835, limiting compulsory service to five years and prohibiting re-impressment. These laws have never been repealed in spite of the fact that impressment has not been used by the Royal Navy since Napoleon's final defeat in 1815.

Imprest: [1] An advance or loan of funds, especially for services rendered to a government. [2] An advance payment of wages (known as "the King's shilling") given to military recruits or impressed seamen so as to make their enlistment legal. From obsolete Italian impresto = loan.

Imprest Service: A service manned by Naval officers and ratings for the express purpose of inducting men without their consent. Press gangs, armed with saps, cutlasses and truncheons, would lie in ambush outside taverns and pubs; brothels, and other places where mariners such as local fishermen or paid off merchant seamen could be waylaid. Wise ones made the best of a bad bargain by taking the king's shilling as a "volunteer." Others were dragged aboard by force. The Army had a similar arrangement.

In: Said of [1] An anchor that has been hove up and secured. [2] Sails which have been stowed or furled. [3] A tide that has reached its highest point.

In!: Command to shorten sail (e.g., "in topgallants!").

In a brace of shakes: This phrase, which means "soon" in everyday speech, has a maritime origin. The fluttering of sails when a sailing ship turned into the wind could be used as a measurement of time, as for example in "I'll be with you in two shakes of the sails."

In company: Said of a group of two or more vessels traveling together.

In irons: [1] Facing the wind with no way on, unable to take off on either tack. [2] Shackled as a prisoner. [3] Sailor's slang for restricted activity due to lack of money.

In ordinary: [1] A warship in reserve (cf. mothball, deactivate, inactivate). [2] An officer on half-pay with no appointment. The term formerly referred to payments under the "ordinary" (regular) naval budget as opposed to an "extraordinary" one, and is now obsolete in both senses. [3] The command "Lie in ordinary!" required topmen to resume their normal positions.

In soundings: Obsolescent term for being in less than 100 fathoms of water, signifying it was practical to cast a standard length leadline.

In step: Term used in towing, when both tug and tow ride over troughs and crests at the same time.

In the Black Book: To be in someone's black book now means to be in disfavor. The term probably originated with the 14th century *Black Book of Admiralty* which specified the punishments to be awarded to miscreants and malefactors at sea.

Inactivate: To remove a vessel from operational status (cf. in ordinary, mothball, deactivate).

Inboard: [1] Between the sides or towards the center of a vessel. [2] When two or more vessels are moored side-by-side, the one nearest the shore is "inboard" of the others.

Inbound: Heading toward the shore, homeward bound.

Inchop: USN term for crossing a "chopline" (boundary) so as to come under different operational control (e.g., "USS Anyship will inchop to 5th Fleet in July").

Inclinometer: [1] An instrument for measuring pitch (the angle a ship or aircraft's longitudinal axis makes with the horizontal). [2] An instrument for measuring the dip of the earth's magnetic force. [3] Often incorrectly used to refer to a clinometer.

Incoterms: A set of thirteen trade terms which define the responsibilities of buyer and seller at various stages of international sales transactions. These were promulgated by the International Chamber of Commerce in 1936, and are updated roughly every ten years to reflect changing commercial environments. Six of these terms are exclusive to marine transportation (in boldface below). The others are intermodal or land-based, but all are listed below for completeness. [In global trade, "delivery" refers to the seller fulfilling the terms of sale or completing contractual obligations. Thus it can occur while the goods are in a vessel on the high seas and the parties involved are nowhere near.]

- **CFR (Cost and Freight):** It is the shipper/seller's responsibility to get goods to the port of destination. "Delivery" is accomplished at this time and the buyer coves insurance from the port of origin or port of shipment to buyer's door.

- **CIF (Cost, Insurance and Freight):** This arrangement similar to CFR, but instead of the buyer insuring the goods for the maritime phase of the voyage, the shipper/seller will do so. As above, "delivery" is accomplished at the port of destination.
- CIP (Carriage and Insurance Paid): This term is primarily used for multimodal transport. It relies on the carrier's insurance, so the shipper/seller is only required to purchase minimum coverage. The buyer's insurance is effective when the goods are turned over to the Forwarder.
- CPT (Carriage Paid To): The shipper/seller has the same obligations as with CIF, with the addition of buying cargo insurance, naming the buyer as the insured while the goods are in transit.
- DAF (Delivered At Frontier): The seller's responsibility is to get the goods to a named border crossing and clear them for export. "Delivery" occurs at this time. The buyer's responsibility is to arrange the pickup of the goods after they are cleared for export, carry them across the border, clear them for importation and effect delivery.
- DDP (Delivered Duty Paid): The shipper/seller is responsible for insuring the goods, and moving them from the manufacturing plant to the buyer/consignee's door, absorbing all risks and costs, including the payment of duty and fees. This arrangement tends to be used in intermodal or courier-type shipments.
- DDU (Delivered Duty Unpaid): This is basically the same as DDP, except that the buyer is responsible for duty, fees and taxes.
- **DEQ (Delivered Ex-Quay):** The seller is responsible for delivering the goods to the quay, wharf or port of destination, while the buyer/consignee is responsible for duties, charges, and customs clearance.
- **DES (Delivered Ex-Ship):** The seller's responsibility is to get uncleared goods to the port of destination. "Delivery" occurs at this time and any charges that occur after the ship docks are the buyer's responsibility.
- EXW (Ex-Works): One of the simplest and most basic arrangements, with the buyer responsible for picking-up the goods at the shipper or seller's factory or warehouse.
- **FAS (Free Alongside Ship):** The buyer bears transportation costs and the risk of loss, while the shipper/seller clears the goods for export. "Delivery" is accomplished when the goods are turned over to the buyer's forwarder for insurance and transportation.
- FCA (Free Carrier): The seller is responsible for arranging transportation, but at the risk and expense of the buyer. "Delivery" is accomplished at a predetermined port or destination point and the buyer is responsible for Insurance.
- **FOB (Free on Board):** Specifically refers to transportation of goods by water. The shipper/seller

moves the merchandise to the designated port or point of origin. "Delivery" is accomplished when the shipper/seller releases the goods to the buyer's agent, at which moment the buyer assumes responsibility for insurance and transportation.

Indemnity: Marine insurance term for security against loss or damage.

Indent: RN term for a stores requisition.

Indenture: A contract binding one person to the service of another (e.g., an apprenticeship).

Independent: A merchant ship under naval control, but sailing alone and unescorted by any warship.

India: NATO phonetic notation for the letter "I."

Indiaman: [1] Properly, a large sailing ship officered and operated by the British East India Company between the 17th and 19th centuries. Used for carrying passengers and cargo, but armed and run like a naval vessel. Many were Blackwall Frigates. [2] Colloquially, any vessel engaged in trade with the Orient. Also East Indiaman.

Indian Navy: The maritime branch of Indian Armed Forces is (in 2008) the world's fourth largest navy. India enjoys a long maritime tradition that goes back to over 4000 years, but the genesis of its modern navy came in 1612, when the East India Company was established and almost immediately encountered local piracy and Portuguese naval rivalry. This forced the Company to establish a maritime force, which has since had many changes of name. In 1686, it was named Bombay Marine, but in 1830 was re-titled Her Majesty's Indian Navy. It reverted to Bombay Marine from 1863 to 1877, when it became Her Majesty's Indian Marine. In 1892, recognizing its service in various campaigns, "Her Majesty's" was replaced by "Royal." When India gained independence in 1947, Royal Indian Marine became Royal Indian Navy, dropping the prefix "Royal" in 1950 when India became a Republic. *See also* Milan, Pakistan Navy, and RIN Mutiny.

Indian Ocean: The third largest of the world's oceanic divisions, covering about 20 percent of the water on the Earth's surface. It is bounded on the north by Asia (including the Indian subcontinent, after which it is named); on the west by Africa; on the east by Indochina, the Sunda Islands, and Australia; and on the south by the Southern Ocean or (according to some authorities) Antarctica.

Indirect fire: Aiming at a theoretical point when the actual target cannot be seen.

Indulgence passenger: RN term for a civilian given passage in a warship or Royal Fleet Auxiliary, usually on compassionate or family grounds.

Inertial guidance: A gyroscopic system which directs the path of a missile without external information or commands.

Inertial navigation: A computer-based system which continuously calculates direction and distance traveled from a specified starting position.

Infection: Doctrine under the maritime law of

prize, holding that permitted goods belonging to the same owner as contraband cargo found in the same vessel, have been "contaminated" and are condemnable as if they too were contraband. This doctrine is not universal and has only been adopted by certain maritime states (notably USA, UK, and Japan).

Inflammable: Easily ignited. Because it is frequently mistaken for a negative (i.e., non-flammable) this term has been generally replaced by "flammable."

Influence mine: A naval mine actuated by sound, magnetism, pressure, or other physical conditions emanating from a target.

Inhaul: [1] Specifically, a line used to pull the clew of a sail away from the head of a boom. [2] In general, any line used to pull something toward the hauler (cf. outhaul).

Inherent vice: [1] The characteristic of goods which might change so as to endanger nearby cargo (e.g., by spontaneous combustion, or the leakage of corrosive fluid). The shipper has a legal obligation to advise the carrier of any such possibility. [2] A loss caused by the intrinsic nature of the thing insured and not the result of a casualty or external cause.

Initial path: In naval mine warfare, a path cleared by a precursor sweep to reduce the danger to following minesweepers.

Inland: Away from the sea. *See* hinterland and interior.

Inland rules: A state's regulations governing the navigation and conduct of vessels in its inland waters, also specifying the visual and sound signals to be used in those waters.

Inland Sea: [1] The waters enclosed by the Japanese islands of Honshu, Kyushu, and Shikoku. [2] The Mediterranean.

Inland waters: Unless otherwise specified by local ordinances, inland waters are those which lie shoreward of a line drawn through the outermost buoy, lighthouse, or other aid to navigation. Not to be confused with internal or territorial waters.

Inlet: [1] An indentation of the shoreline, usually long and narrow. [2] A passage between two nearby islands. [3] A pass through a barrier reef.

INMARSAT: **In**ternational **Mari**time **Sat**ellite system.

Innocent Passage: The right, under the United Nations Convention on Law of the Sea, of traversing territorial waters without entering internal waters or calling at a roadstead or port facility. The passage must be continuous and expeditious, but may include stopping and anchoring in specified circumstances, and it is "innocent" so long as it is lawful and not prejudicial to the peace, good order, or security of the territorial state. The ships of all states, whether coastal or landlocked, enjoy innocent passage; with the exception of submerged submarines which are specifically denied this right (*see also* right of transit).

Inshore current: The motion of water inside the surf line and parallel to the coast (cf. offshore current).

INS: [1] Inertial navigation system. [2] Integrated navigation system. [3] Indian Navy Ship.

Inshore: Close to or towards the coast.

Inshore fire-support ship: A post–World War II addition to the U.S. fleet, designed to provide close support for troops during amphibious assault landings. Now discontinued, its major armament consisted of rapid fire rocket launchers. *See also* littoral combat ship, rocket support ship.

Inside passage: A relatively sheltered route for oceangoing vessels along a series of passages between the mainland and coastal islands off the Alaska Panhandle and British Columbia. It is heavily traveled by ferries, cruise ships, freighters, tugs with tows, and fishing craft.

Insignia: Badges or emblems of rank, authority, honor, or occupation. *See* breast and sleeve insignia.

Insubordination: Willful refusal to obey a supervisor's lawful order given by and with proper authority. This is a crime under military law.

Insular shelf: The island equivalent of a continental shelf.

Integrated navigation system: An inertial navigation system enhanced with star tracker, multi-speed repeater, and instrumentation to provide data on roll, pitch, and heading.

Integrated Undersea Surveillance System: This U.S. Navy network for deep ocean observation during the Cold War consisted of a mobile component, known as the surveillance towed array sensor system, and a fixed sound surveillance system.

Intelligence: [1] Information of military or political value. [2] Gathering such information.

Intercardinal points: Four primary intercardinal points are those lying midway between any two of the cardinal points (i.e., northeast, southeast, southwest, and northwest). Eight secondary intercardinal points lie between these primary points (in abbreviated form they are NNE, ENE, ESE, SSE, SSW, WSW, WNW, and NNW). *See* table 17.

Intercoastal waterways: Refers to U.S. domestic shipping routes between the Atlantic, Pacific, and Gulf coasts (cf. intracoastal).

Interdiction: Attacks on supply lines and infrastructures to prevent or inhibit support or reinforcement of enemy fighting units.

Interior: The land more than 100 miles (160 kilometers) from the shore. *See* hinterland.

Intermodal transportation: Occurs when a single carrier coordinates movement by, and documentation of, different modes of transport (air, sea, road, rail) in order to provide door-to-door rather than port-to-port service.

Internal combustion engine: An auxiliary or main propulsion system powered by the ignition of a combustible mixture inside cylinders.

Internal waters: Are defined in international law as all waters on the shoreward side of the territorial waters baseline.

International Association of Classification Societies: *See* ship classification societies.

International Association of Lighthouse Authorities: A non-profit association founded in 1957 to harmonize aids to navigation worldwide, and to ensure that vessel movement is safe, expeditious, cost effective, and environmentally friendly. Its committees and workshops are aimed at developing common standards for such things as buoyage systems, automatic navigation devices, lightships, and lighthouses.

International Convention for the Prevention of Pollution from Ships (MARPOL): This is the main international treaty concerning regulations aimed at preventing pollution of the maritime environment by ships, whether due to routine operation or accident. It was introduced in 1973, modified in 1978, and is regularly updated.

International Convention for the Safety of Life at Sea (SOLAS): The most important international treaty concerning regulations for protecting the safety of merchant mariners and ships. Its first version was enacted in 1914 in response to the *Titanic* disaster, prescribing the number of lifeboats and emergency equipment to be carried, along with safety procedures. It has since been brought under the auspices of the International Maritime Organization (IMO), which attempts to keep up with changing technology and procedures. However, with many member countries to be consulted, the amending procedure is cumbersome and slow.

International Convention on Standards for Seafarers: *See* Standards of Training, Certification, and Watch-keeping.

International date line: A theoretical line following the 180th meridian with adjustments for inhabited regions. Calendar dates to the east of this line are one day earlier than to the west of it.

International Hydrographic Bureau: The original name of the International Hydrographic Organization, whose present name was adopted in 1970, at which time this name was retained by the small staff at the organization's headquarters in Monaco.

International Hydrographic Organization: This intergovernmental consultative and technical organization, was established in 1921 as the International Hydrographic Bureau. It coordinates the activities of national hydrographic offices, ensures the greatest possible uniformity of nautical charts and documents, develops reliable and efficient methodology for hydrographic surveying, and fosters the development of hydrographic science and descriptive oceanography.

International Ice Patrol: After the *Titanic* collided with an iceberg and sank, a group of thirteen nations with North Atlantic maritime interests agreed that the United States Coast Guard would operate patrols during the iceberg season (normally March–August) locating and tracking icebergs and issuing warnings to ships, Membership later expanded to seventeen nations, who share costs in proportion to their individual percentage of the total cargo tonnage transiting the patrolled area. Originally operated by surface cutters, the patrols are now carried out by radar-equipped aircraft, which track about 1,000 icebergs each year.

International Labour Organization (ILO): Geneva-based UN Agency involved in the appraisal and regulation of conditions in the workplace, including labor rights for seafarers.

International Maritime Law: *See* maritime law.

International Maritime Organization (IMO): Shipping is perhaps the most international of all the world's great industries, and one of the most dangerous. It has long been recognized that the best way of improving safety at sea is by developing international regulations that are followed by all shipping nations. The Convention establishing this London-based UN Agency was adopted at Geneva in 1948, with its remit described as being:

> To provide machinery for co-operation among Governments in the field of governmental regulation and practices relating to technical matters of all kinds affecting shipping engaged in international trade; to encourage and facilitate the general adoption of the highest practicable standards in matters concerning maritime safety, efficiency of navigation and prevention and control of marine pollution from ships.

The IMO first met in 1959 and the key treaties developed by the organization include SOLAS, STCW, and MARPOL.

International maritime satellite: One exclusively dedicated to worldwide maritime support in such areas as distress, medical, weather, and navigation.

International naval co-operation: Much of the work that navies do can be thought of as constabulary. Together with miscellaneous law enforcement agencies, they try to fight piracy, terrorism, weapons proliferation, the drugs trade, smuggling, human trafficking, illegal immigration, organized crime, and other forms of illicit commerce and maritime mayhem. However, international co-operation in these matters is patchy, and frequently obstructed by bureaucracies, judicial issues and political in-fighting. Moreover, language and cultural differences hinder co-operation, while concerns about national sovereignty often make outside help appear threatening to some governments. For example, when naval co-operation is initiated by powers such as the United States or European Union it may be construed as an attempt to impose the proposer's agenda.

Organized criminals, terrorists, smugglers, and pirates have become adept at exploiting these cracks between nations and navies. Hence the need for a transnational co-operative network of navies, coastguards, shipping interests, and law enforcement agencies. An ambitious concept of persuading all naval nations to collaborate in countering global maritime threats was originally called the "thousand ship navy," but this imaginative and evocative name has been replaced by the more mundane Global Maritime Partnership. At time of writing (2008) world-wide maritime co-operation remains conceptual and only local and regional examples exist:

- Operation Active Endeavour, is an initiative of the North Atlantic Treaty Organization that conducts maritime constabulary work in the Mediterranean in collaboration with non–NATO countries as disparate as Egypt, Morocco, Portugal, Russia, Tunisia, and Ukraine. It is one of a number of NATO responses to the September 11, 2001, terrorist attacks on the World Trade Center in New York City.
- NATO, led by the United States, wants to expand Active Endeavour into the Black Sea, but would require exemption from the Montreux Convention. To preempt this Turkey has made the following co-operative and unilateral initiatives.
  - ➤ The Black Sea Naval Task Force, was set up in 2001. This Turkish-led squadron, which comprises all six riparian states — Turkey, Russia, Bulgaria, Georgia, Romania and Ukraine — aims at preventing the illicit trafficking of humans, heroin from Afghanistan, and weapons (from small arms to instruments of mass destruction.)
  - ➤ Three years later Turkey (whose navy is bigger than the other five combined) unilaterally launched Operation Black Sea Harmony to patrol its own Black Sea coast. Recently, Ankara invited other littoral countries to join this security initiative.
- The Caspian Sea Naval Co-operation Task Force is intended to consist of warships from the littoral states of Iran, Russia, Azerbaijan, Kazakhstan and Turkmenistan. Russia promotes this force as the most effective way to counter terrorism, and trafficking in arms, narcotics and weapons of mass destruction. No doubt there is also a hidden wish to keep the United States and NATO out of the landlocked Sea. Iran is lukewarm — Abbas Maleki, Chief of the International Institute for Caspian Studies in Tehran, warns it will be "necessary to determine the legal status of the Caspian Sea before successfully implementing the CasFor project."
- On the other side of the world, United States Pacific Command has sponsored a communications network that links the various navies of the region in an effort to spread effective methods of policing the seas and make co-operation easier.
- China is cultivating naval co-operation with Bangladesh and Burma (Myanmar) to gain access to the Bay of Bengal, and is strengthening its military ties with Sri Lanka, including the development of port and bunker facilities in that island nation.
- In the Strait of Malacca, Indonesia, Malaysia and Singapore have created a highly successful maritime network to counter piracy and terrorist movements.
- In the Indian Ocean, India initiated the Milan naval forum in 1995.
- In the southern hemisphere there are various co-operative naval agreements between South American nations and between them and South Africa.

International Organization for Standardization: The proper and self-explanatory name of the world's largest developer and publisher of international standards, more commonly known as the International Standards Organization. With a Central Secretariat in Geneva, Switzerland, the ISO is a non-governmental organization that bridges the public and private sectors of 157 countries.

International Regulations for Preventing Collisions at Sea: Known colloquially as "Rules of the road" or "ColRegs" these regulations (table 7) reflect the agreement of major maritime powers to adopt rules that are binding on their public and private shipping while on the high seas. They also apply to inland waterways unless superseded by the responsible state. (The United States has its own Inland Rules of the Road.)

International rules: Regulations governing the navigation and conduct of vessels on the high seas (seaward of internal waters), and specifying visual and sound signals to be used in those waters. *See* tables 8–10.

International signaling code: *See* table 8.

International Standards Organization: *See* International Organization for Standardization.

International time-date notation: *See* table 12.

International waters: The open waters of a sea or ocean beyond the territorial jurisdiction of any state or nation. Also high seas.

International waterways: Consist of inter-ocean canals, and straits, inland canals, and rivers which separate the territories of two or more nations. Provided no treaty specifically declares otherwise, both merchantmen and warships enjoy the right of free and unrestricted navigation.

Interrogative: Term used in naval communication to signify failure to understand a message or any other question.

Interrogator: A transmitter that emits a signal to activate a transponder.

Intertidal: Between mean high water and mean low water.

Interval: The space between adjacent groups of ships or boats measured in any direction between the corresponding vessels in each group.

Intervalometer: A device which controls the release of mines or missiles in sequence at specified intervals.

Intracoastal: Domestic shipping along a single coast. Not to be confused with intercoastal.

Inverse Mercator: The projection normally used for navigational charts. It is based on a cylinder tangent to a meridian, in contrast to the more common map projection based on a cylinder tangent to the equator. (*See* Mercator Projection.)

Irish horse: Sailing ship seamen's derisory slang for salt beef.

Irish hurricane: Sailing ship seaman's derisory slang for dead calm.

Irish pennant: Seaman's derisory slang for a line left dangling untidily.

Iron Mike: U.S. naval aviators' slang for an automatic pilot.

Ironbottom Sound: USN slang for the area between Guadalcanal and the Florida islands, so-called because fierce fighting in 1942 sent so many American and Japanese warships to its bottom.

Ironbound: Said of a rocky coast devoid of anchorage or shelter.

Ironclad: [1] A 19th century warship with protective iron plates mounted on a heavy wooden backing. [2] Generic term for any armor-plated vessel. The concept originated in the Far East during the 16th century (*see* turtle ship).

Irons: *See* in irons.

Isherwood-built: A vessel in which the main frames are longitudinal rather than transverse to provide extra ice-breaking capability. Named after Rear Admiral Benjamin Franklin Isherwood, the USN's chief engineer (d. 1915).

Island: [1] A tract of land completely surrounded by water at high tide. [2] The superstructure of an aircraft carrier, rising above the flight deck and enclosing the command and flag bridges, primary flight control, radars, and similar equipment. The island is off to one side of the flight deck so that the takeoff and landing runways remain clear. Starboard was originally chosen because the torque of propeller-driven engines tended to pull aircraft to port. Later it became customary, but the Japanese briefly experimented with islands on the left of carriers expected to, operate in concert with standard right-island ships. No advantages were discovered.

Islet: A very small island, larger than a key or rock.

ISO: *See* International Organization for Standardization.

Isochronal roll: Occurs when the period of each roll is the same.

Isodate: Calendar date expressed in accord with ISO 8601 (*see* table 12).

Isotainer: A shipping container meeting International Standards Organization specifications.

ISR: Intelligence, Surveillance, and Reconnaissance.

ISS: Information System Security.

Isthmus: A narrow strip of land, bordered on both sides by water, and connecting two larger landmasses, especially the land connecting a peninsula to its mainland.

Is-was: Slang designation of any improvised device used to measure or calculate position.

IT: Information Technology.

Iurram: The Gaelic word for sea chantey.

IUSS: Integrated Undersea Surveillance System.

J

Jack: [1] A small national flag or ensign, worn forward by warships, such as the First Navy Jack or Union Jack. [2] A small house flag worn forward by merchantmen. [3] A crosstree at the head of a topgallant mast serving to spread the royal shrouds. [4] To turn a propeller shaft prevent it from bowing when engines are stopped. [5] Formerly, a nickname for a seaman (cf. Tar, Jack Tar). [6] To skin a seal. [7] A type of Newfoundland fishing schooner.

Jack Nastyface: [1] Sailing ship seaman's nickname for the cook's assistant. [2] Pseudonym of William Robinson who wrote Memoirs of an English Seaman (ca. 1836).

Jack o' Dover: A very old sea dish, the composition of which is no longer known. It is mentioned by Chaucer (*Cook's Tale* ca. 1390): "Many a Jakke of Dovre hastow sold, that hath been twies hoote and tweis colde" (Many a Jack of Dover have you sold, that has been twice hot and twice cold).

Jack o' dust: USN and USCG slang for the cook or other rating in charge of food distribution.

Jack o' lantern: Sailor slang for a corposant (Saint Elmo's Fire).

Jack of all trades: Although this phrase is now derogatory, usually followed by "is master of none," it originally had the opposite meaning, referring to an able-seaman who — being a "True Jack Tar" — could turn his hand to any job aboard ship.

Jack Tar: A seaman (*see* tarpaulin).

Jackass: A bark (barque) carrying a fore-and-aft sail on the lower mainmast.

Jackass-rigged: Term applied to any unconventionally rigged vessel.

Jackknife: A large pocket knife whose blade folds into its handle. A safe and convenient alternative to long or sheath knives, which are generally forbidden on British and United States ships. Modern jackknives have rounded tips, but in days of sail it was common practice for the mate to snap off the pointed tip of each seaman's knife as he came on board. Commonly thought to refer to the knife of a Jack Tar, but the name actually honors its inventor, French cutler Jacques de Liege.

Jackscrew: A small portable machine formerly used to stow compressible cargo such as wool or cotton.

Jackstaff: [1] A short pole at the bow for carrying a warship's jack. The Jack was originally carried on the bowsprit and, until 1913, the RN continued to call the jackstaff "bowsprit ends." [2] A navigational instrument, first mentioned in the early sixteenth century, consisting of a long staff with a vertical sliding wooden crosspiece called the transom. The navigator aimed the staff at the Pole Star as if it were a rifle, then slid the transom until the top of it marked the star and the bottom horizon. By measuring how far along the pole the transom was he was able to calculate the angle and hence make a reasonable estimate of the ship's latitude. (At the North Pole the Pole Star is directly overhead [90° above the horizon], while at the equator it is on the horizon [0°].) The jackstaff could more readily adapt itself to swaying of the observer's body in a seaway and progressively superseded the astrolabe until it itself was superseded by the sextant in the eighteenth century.

Jackstay: [1] A rod on a yard, gaff, or boom to which one edge of a sail is bent. [2] A rail for guiding the hanks of a sail. [3] A stiffening stay for a mizzen or gaff-rigged mast. [4] A suspension wire (e.g., for hanging seabags). *See also* highline.

Jacob's Ladder: Slang for a wooden-runged rope ladder. Slung over the side or from a mast for temporary use, it is awkward and difficult to ascend and appears interminable to a climber, hence the reference to the Old Testament ladder which rose all the way from earth to heaven (Gen.28:12).

JAG: Judge Advocate General (U.S.).

Jamaica Discipline: Buccaneer regulations governing the distribution of prizes.

Jamboree: Now inextricably related to the international Boy Scout movement, this was originally a nautical term for a dockside gathering of crews for merrymaking, dancing, and boozing. Its origin is uncertain, but it may be a combination of jam in the sense of crowd and the jolly French dance known as a bourée.

JAN: Joint Army & Navy (U.S.).

JAN Grid: A system used jointly by the U.S. Army and Navy to reference geographical positions around the world.

JANAF: Joint Army, Navy & Air Force (U.S.).

Jane's: Abbreviation of *Jane's Fighting Ships*, the primary source of information on world navies, founded in 1898 by Fred T. Jane and published periodically ever since.

Jankers: RN lower deck slang for undergoing defaulter's punishment.

Japan Stream: An ocean current that flows northeastward from Taiwan, along the coast of Japan, and then splits, with the smaller component passing around the Hawaiian Islands and the larger merging with the Oyashio current to form the North Pacific Current. *See also* Kuroshio.

Jarhead: USN slang for a marine.

Jaunty: [1] RN nickname for the Master-at-Arms. Probably a corruption of the French gendarme, via the intermediate form "John Damme." [2] Slightly derisory term for a vessel bedecked with too many flags. [3] Self-confident, debonair, fashionable, cheerful. From the French gentil = nobly-born.

Jaw-breaker: Sailing ship sailor slang for an unusual word difficult to pronounce. Such words were often adapted to fit the sailors' vocabulary — for example, HMS *Bellerophon* was known throughout the British fleet as "Billy ruffian" or "Belly ruff'n."

JCS: Joint Chiefs of Staff (U.S.).

Jebel Ali: The world's largest man-made harbor and largest port in the Middle East, with berths for 67 vessels. It occupies 168 square kilometers (65 sq. miles) and is located 35 kilometres (22 miles) south of Dubai in the United Arab Emirates.

Jeep carrier: USN slang for an escort carrier. The name is popularly believed to be a phonetic rendering of "GP" (general purpose) but, like the land-based army vehicle, was more probably derived from Eugene the Jeep, a fabulous animal in the "Popeye" comic strip.

Jeers: Heavy tackle used to hoist the lower yards of square-riggers.

Jeheemy: Salvage equipment used to recover boats swamped or stranded during amphibious operations.

Jemmy ducks: Sailor slang for a warship's poulterer.

Jerky: Meat cut into strips and sun-dried, with or without salt. English variation of Charqui, which is an abbreviation of the Spanish quechua ch'arki = dried meat.

Jerque: Search of a vessel by Customs authorities, for undeclared goods.

Jet: *See* water jet.

Jetsam: Material thrown overboard to lighten ship (cf. flotsam, lagen).

Jettison: [1] To voluntarily throw something overboard. From the French jeter la cargaison à la mer = throw the cargo into the sea (*see* deep six). [2] To discard a weapon from its delivery vehicle when normal operation is not possible or intended.

Jetty: A wharf, pier, quay, or mole, built out from the shore and serving as a breakwater.

Jewel block: Part of the running rigging used to hoist studding sails.

Jew's harp: [1] A heart-shaped shackle, especially one used to attach an anchor to its chain. Named after [2] a small lyre-shaped musical instrument held between the teeth and plucked with a finger, often used to accompany chanteys along with the fiddler.

JFSC: Joint Forces Staff College (U.S.).

JG: Junior Grade (USN).

JHSV: Joint high speed vessel.

Jib: A triangular headsail, hoisted between foremast and bowsprit.

Jib-boom: A spar extending the bowsprit of larger sailing vessels.

Jibber-kibber: Wrecker's term for walking a hobbled horse along the cliffs with a lantern on its back. At night the motion, resembling that of a ship's light bobbing on waves, was intended to decoy vessels onto the rocks for plunder.

Jibe: [1] To swing across. [2] To change tack by bringing the stern through the wind (the opposite of tacking, in which the bow crosses the wind). A controlled jibe is called wearing. Also gybe or gibe.

Jibstay: The wire on which a jib is raised.

Jigger: [1] The mizzen mast and sail of a yawl. [2] A handy billy tackle.

Jilalo: A Pilipino passenger craft with outriggers.

Jimmy Bungs: Nickname for a ship's cooper.

Jimmy Legs: USN seaman's derisive term for the master-at-arms (cf. Jaunty).

Jimmy-the-one: RN seaman's term for the First Lieutenant (cf. number one, executive officer).

JIT: Just in time.

Jock: Slang for a Scottish seaman (or any Scot).

Joe: USN slang for coffee (*see* Cup of Joe).

Joggle: [1] An abrupt bend to enable a plate or rod to pass round a projection. [2] Matched positive and negative bends which prevent slippage when joined together.

Join: [1] To enlist in the armed forces, especially as a volunteer. [2] To become a member of the ship's company. [3] To attach, connect, unite, or combine.

Joiner: [1] A carpenter who specializes in finished work. [2] A merchantman connecting with a convoy already at sea.

Joint Chiefs of Staff: A group consisting of a Chairman and Vice Chairman, along with the Chiefs of Staff of the Army and Air Force, the Chief of Naval Operations, and the Commandant of the Marine Corps. Its primary responsibility is to oversee the co-ordination, policy, planning, training, and personnel readiness of the United States military services. In addition, the Chairman acts as the chief military advisor to the President and the Secretary of Defense. The concept arose in 1942, when President Roosevelt and Prime Minister Churchill agreed to establish a supreme military body for strategic direction of the Anglo-American war effort. However, the United States had no equivalent to the British Chiefs of Staff Committee, and had to establish an ad hoc group of service heads. This group worked throughout the war without legislative sanction or even formal Presidential definition, and it was not until 1947 that the National Security Act formally established the Joint Chiefs of Staff.

Joint High Speed Vessel: Launched in 2005, the JHSV program plans to take advantage of inherent commonality of hull forms and purpose by combining independent U.S. Army and Navy programs as a cooperative multi-service venture. Development specifications include speed of 35–45 knots and draft of less than 15 feet. The vessel will have a helicopter flight deck, and a ramp to allow vehicles to drive quickly off the ship, even onto the austere piers and quays common in developing countries. Hence, the JHSV envisions an extremely flexible asset, able to operate in shallow waters, or small or damaged ports, and support a wide range of military or relief operations, provide flexible logistic support, and be the key enabler of rapid transport and deployment of conventional or special forces as well as equipment and supplies.

Joint Meritorious Unit Award (U.S.): Established in 1979, this honor is awarded to each unit of a combined services or allied task force that distinguishes itself by exceptionally meritorious achievement in joint military missions of great significance, whether in combat, during a declared national emergency, or while providing extraordinary services in the national interest. Personnel serving in any of the units at the time the award was earned are entitled to wear the Joint Meritorious Unit Medal.

Jolly: RN slang for a marine, or any soldier serving afloat. Origin uncertain.

Jolly jumper: A sail mounted above the moon-raker.

Jolly Roger: Slang for the pirate ensign. Popularly understood to be a black flag with white crossed bones surmounted by a death's head, this version was only occasionally used. In practice, each buccaneer wanted a distinct personal emblem, so there were numerous variations, almost invariably on black or scarlet grounds, adorned with multiple skulls, jawless skulls, complete skeletons, hourglasses, cutlasses, spears, and other weapons. (During the Golden Age of Piracy, "Roger" referred to a rogue or scoundrel.)

Jollyboat: A clinker built ship's boat, smaller than a cutter, often suspended at the ship's stern. From the Dutch jolle = yawl.

Jonah: This name for a shipmate or passenger who brings bad luck on board is based on a story that appears in the Hebrew Tanakh, Christian Bible, and Islamic Q'ran. Jonah (or Jonas) tries to escape God's command by sailing away, but his disobedience causes the Lord to send "a mighty tempest ... so that the ship was like to be broken" [Jonah 1;4]. The sailors cast lots to determine whose transgressions have brought the storm upon them and throw Jonah overboard. The seas instantly calm, and three days later Jonah comes to the shore, still alive.

What happened during those days is open to conjecture. According to the story, he had been swallowed by a "great fish" (commonly considered to have been a whale, but possibly a large shark) which vomited him up after he begged God for forgiveness. This is far-fetched, but not impossible (*see* Bartley's ordeal) although it is difficult to understand how three days in stomach acid would not have burned out Jonah's eyeballs. Jonah himself never mentions a fish but says to God:

> Thou hadst cast me into the deep, in the midst of the seas; and the floods compassed me about; all thy billows and thy waves passed over me.... The waters compassed me about, even to the soul; the depth closed me round about, the weeds were wrapped around my head. (Jonah 2:3,5).

Based on this, it has been hypothesized that "great fish" was an ancient seafarer's term for a powerful current, which swept Jonah away and carried him to shore.

Jonathon: 18th–19th century RN slang for an American seaman. Also Jonathan and sometimes preceded by "Brother."

Jones Act: U.S. legislation requiring all domestic waterborne trade to be carried in U.S.-flagged, built, and crewed vessels. The federal law also provides for benefits to workers who are injured on seagoing vessels on navigable waters and offshore oil rigs which are not permanently attached to the ocean floor.

Jörmungandr: In Norse mythology this sea serpent was so long that it encircled the entire world and sailors would mistake its humps for a chain of islands (cf. Kraken: Leviathan: Zaratan).

Journal: [1] A term synonymous with log-book. [2] The portion of a shaft or axle contained by a plain bearing.

JSFP: [1] Joint Strike Force. [2] Joint Strike Fighter (U.S.).

JSP: Joint Strategic Planning.

JTG: Joint Task Group.

Judge Advocate: A naval law officer whose duty is to investigate offenses and dispense military justice.

Juliett: NATO phonetic notation for the letter "J." Also (incorrectly) Juliet. *See* phonetic alphabets and table 11.

Jumbo: RN slang for a crash dolly.

Jump ship: To go ashore without permission and with no intention of returning. To become a deserter.

Jumper: [1] A seaman's loose outer blouse or jacket. [2] A line which prevents a boom, yard, or spar from being lifted out of place. [3] A short strut that adds stiffness to a mast.

Junior officer: Term usually applied to commissioned naval officers of ranks up to and including lieutenant. Theoretically the term embraces lieutenant commander, but is seldom applied to that rank.

Junk: [1] An Oriental sailing ship historically with up to nine masts, but nowadays from one to three, carrying lugsails made of bamboo, rattan, or grass matting stiffened with poles. Typically with a flat stem, high stern, retractable rudder and no keel. Junks are the first vessels known to have been constructed with watertight compartments (*see* Ming Maritime Decrees). From the Javanese djong. [2] Old ropes or cables cut up for oakum. [3] Anything regarded as having little value.

Jurisdiction: The geographical area or territorial range over which a state has the right and power to exercise judicial authority and maintain law and order.

Jury: [1] To make temporary, makeshift arrangements to replace lost or damaged spars, rigging, or rudder. The origin of the term is uncertain, but probably derives from the French Journée, signifying the repair could only be expected to last the length of a day. [2] The panel of a court-martial is often (incorrectly) called a jury by laypeople and the media.

Jute: A rough fiber made from an East Indian plant, used to make twine, rope, and sacking.

Juvenile detention: During the 18th century, hulks anchored in Sydney Harbour, New South Wales, Australia, served as youth correction centers. Every boy was closely supervised under strict discipline, strenuous physical drill, and a system of grading. New admissions began in the lowest grade and, through hard work and

obedience, gradually won a limited number of privileges.

Juvenile Punishment: A document in the British Museum recounts the treatment of young boys in the Elizabethan navy:

> Petty pilferings and commissions of that kinde ... were generallie punished with the whippe, the offender beinge to that purpose bounde faste to the capstan; and the waggerie and idlenesse of ship boys paid by the boatswayne with a rodde, and commonlie this execution is done upon Mondaye morninges, and ... some meere seamen and saylers doe believe ... that they shalle never have a faire winde until the poor boyes be duly brought to the chest; that is, whipped every Mondaye morninge.

For minor disciplinary infractions, boys of all social backgrounds were later subjected to bare-bottom beatings, latterly with a cane, but originally with a teaser or bimmy — an eighteen-inch length of rope, knotted at the "receiving end" and dipped in hot tar for stiffness. As reported by S. Humphries in *Hooligans or Rebels? An Oral History of Working Class Childhood and Youth 1889–1939* (Blackwell 1981), such punishment was readily accepted by upper-class youths who had attended "public" (elite private) schools, but resented by those with little or no formal education:

> The most determined resistance ... occurred when boys refused to remove their trousers to be beaten on their bare bottoms ... although these ritual humiliations were for many years an integral part of public school life ... working-class ... children were resolute in their resistance ... would stoically endure traditional punishments of the sort their parents might inflict but refused to submit to the more degrading disciplinary measures.

More serious juvenile offenders received full-scale flogging as their summary punishment, but with a light five-tailed whip, known as the "pussy-cat" and reserved for use on youths. However, if the punishment had been awarded by a court-martial use of the "adult" cat-o'-nine-tails was mandatory. Many boys felt this to be a "badge of honor."

K

Kamikaze: A Japanese compound word that can be translated as "Divine Wind." It refers to [1] Major typhoons in 1274 and 1281 which dispersed Mongolian invasion fleets. [2] Suicide attacks, launched in a desperate attempt to stop or slow down the Allied advance towards the Japanese home islands in the closing stages of World War II. They were mounted by submariners, human torpedoes, speedboats, divers, and even a super-battleship; but by far the most common were mass air attacks, code-named kikusui after the "floating chrysanthemum" imperial symbol. Pilots attempted to crash their aircraft — laden with explosives, bombs, or torpedoes, and frequently with full fuel tanks — into Allied ships, hoping to cause greater damage than a conventional bombing or torpedo attack. The first to be hit by a kamikaze was the Royal Australian Navy's flagship, heavy cruiser HMAS *Australia*, during the Battle of Leyte Gulf.

Karbatz: A Laplander boat.

Karfi: A small Viking warship, usually reserved for a king or great chieftain.

Kayak: The traditional Inuit canoe.

K-Day: The scheduled date for introduction of a convoy system on any particular convoy route.

Keckling: [1] Old rope wrapped around a line to prevent chafing. [2] Newer line wrapped around mooring lines to give them a more finished look.

Kedge: [1] To carry an anchor forward in a small boat, drop it and haul in the line to drag (kedge) the vessel ahead. [2] The anchor used for this purpose.

Keel: [1] The lengthwise timber along the bottom of a wooden ship, on which its framework is built. [2] An assembly of plates serving the same structural purpose on an iron vessel. [3] A poetic synonym for ship ("No keel has ever ploughed that path before," Shelley).

Keelage: A fee levied against ships using a port or harbor.

Keelboat: Shallow-draft fully decked Mississippi river barge, propelled by sweeps or poles.

Keeles: Anglo-Saxon name for a longboat. Also written ceoles and cyulis.

Keelhauling: [1] Modern USN term for receiving an exceptionally severe reprimand. [2] A gruesome punishment dating back to antiquity. Keelhauling was never used in the USN and was discontinued by the RN in 1720, but was practiced by the French and Dutch for at least another thirty years. A stout line was rove through a block on a lower yardarm, passed under the hull, and attached to the culprit's ankles. Another line, running from the yardarm on the other side, was secured around the victim's chest below his arms. His wrists were bound behind his back. On the captain's command, the victim was hoisted over the side by the chest line, which was slowly played out, while the slack was taken up by the ankle line. In this way the victim was dragged underneath the vessel's hull, to appear feet first on the other side. As extra punishment, a cannon was often fired over the delinquent's head "to astonish and confound him" as he emerged from the water and also "to give warning to all others of the fleet to look out and be wary by his harm" (Nathanial Boteler, 1634). In addition to nearly drowning, the victim's thighs, stomach, chest, and face would be severely ripped by barnacles growing on the ship's hull. These wounds often became infected, which sometimes resulted in agonizing death days or weeks after apparently surviving the ordeal.

Keelraking: A particularly vicious, brutal, and almost invariably lethal variation of keelhauling. In this rarely-employed punishment the unfortunate victim was dragged the entire length of the vessel from stem-to-stern.

Keelrope: Another name for limber-rope.

Keelson: Any of various fore-and-aft structural members lying above and parallel to the keel at the bottom of the hull (pronounced "kelsun").

Keep off: To stay clear of something (another vessel, land, etc.).

Keep ship: USN term for normal shipboard routine, when neither exercising nor operating.

Keep station: Maintain position relative to a specified marker, usually another ship.

Keep watch: [1] to be in charge of the ship. [2] To stand watch-duty.

Keks: Lower deck RN slang for underwear (*see* skivvies).

Kellet: A weight which is slid partway down the cable of a cast anchor to reduce drag by laying the outer part of the cable closer to the sea bed, thus causing the stock to move parallel to the floor and the flukes to dig in better. The combined weight of kellet and cable do more to hold the ship in place than the anchor itself (also killick, sentinel).

Kelpie: This malevolent Celtic water sprite was said to haunt Irish and Scottish lochs, lakes, and rivers in the form of a young horse which delighted in drowning unsuspecting travelers.

Kelter: Good order and readiness.

Kenning: [1] Whaling term for basing wages on the performance of assigned duties. [2] Sixteenth-century term for the distance at which high land could be observed from shipboard.

Kenning glass: Obsolete name for a telescope or long glass.

Kentledge: Pig iron ingots placed along each side of the keelson as permanent ballast. The name is sometimes applied to permanent ballast of any shape.

Kerlanguishe: A fast-sailing boat used on the Bosphorus. Named after the swallow.

Kersauson's squid: On a moonless night in January 2003, veteran French yachtsman Olivier de Kersauson, competing in the round-the-world Jules Verne Trophy, was off the Portuguese island of Madeira when his 110-foot trimaran *Geronimo* shuddered as if it had run aground. Some of the crew shone spotlights on the water, and first mate Didier Ragot saw something by the rudder "bigger than a human leg." He called Kersauson who took the flashlight, and saw "Two giant tentacles right beneath us ... really pulling the boat hard." A giant squid had clamped on to the hull. "It was enormous," Kersauson recalled. "I've been sailing for forty years ... but this was terrifying." The yacht rocked violently and the rudder started to bend. Then, suddenly, everything went still, and the creature swam away leaving impressions on the hull from the suckers on its long arms.

Ketch: A small vessel, square or fore-and-aft rigged on a tall mainmast, with a shorter mizzen stepped forward of the rudder post.

Key: [1] A reef or low islet. Also cay, from the Spanish cayo = rock. Usually pronounced "kay," but "kee" in certain place names such as Key West. [2] A quay. [3] A lug or angle-iron connecting the keelson to the floor plate. [4] The means of deciphering a code or cryptogram. Pronounced "kee."

Key of the Keelson: [1] *See* key. [2] *See* hazing.

Khaki: A yellowish-brown color for clothing. Originated in India in 1846 as a form of camouflage when British soldiers unofficially soaked their conspicuous white uniforms in a blend of mud, coffee, and curry powder to blend in with the landscape. Officially approved in 1861. Pronounced kaki in American English, Karki in British usage, after the Hindi and Urdu for dust or earth.

Khufu ship: An intact full-size ceremonial oared barge, discovered in 1954 sealed in a pit near the Great Pyramid at Giza. Typical of Egyptian naval architecture, its more than 1,200 pieces were laid out in logical order for re-assembly and use in the afterlife. Now complete and on display, it is believed to date to the mid-third millennium BCE and is of the type known as a "solar barge" — intended for the reincarnated pharaoh's journey across the heavens with the sun god Ra. However, it appears to have been previously used, and probably carried the embalmed body from Memphis to Giza. It is also possible Khufu used it ceremonially while still alive.

KIA: Killed in Action.

Kick: The swirl left in a ship's wake after a change of course. Used as a reference point for following ships to turn at.

Kiftis: An Indian passenger boat with stem-to-stern cabins along both sides.

Killick: [1] Originally, a stone-weighted wooden anchor. From the Erse kellagh. [2] A type of stocked and shanked anchor for small boats. [3] A Leading Seaman in the RN, so called because his badge of rank is such an anchor. [4] A kellet.

Killter: A sailing ship in prime condition and well rigged was formerly said to be "in fine killter."

Kilo: NATO phonetic notation for the letter "K." *See* table 11.

King post: [1] A short mast supporting a cargo boom. [2] A pillar in a merchantman's hold, between the lower deck and the keelson. It serves to support the deck-beam, and strengthen the vessel, also prevents cargo or materials contained in the hold from shifting to the opposite side when the vessel rolls. A king post under the edge of a hatchway is often furnished with notches that serve as steps to mount or descend. Also samson post.

King spoke: The spoke or handle on an old-fashioned ship's wheel that stands vertically when the rudder is exactly amidships. Usually carved or wrapped to make it easily identifiable when coming out of a turn.

King's hard bargain: Referred to the waste of the sovereign's money when the shilling given to a recruit only purchased a slothful, incompetent, or unruly seaman.

King's Letter Man: In 1676, King Charles II wrote to Samuel Pepys, Secretary of the Admiralty:

> Whereas out of our Royal desire of giving encouragement to the families of better quality ... to breed up their younger sons to the art and practice of navigation.... We have ... been graciously pleased ... to admit the bearing of several young gentlemen to the end aforesaid on board Our ships, in the quality of volunteers.

Pepys accordingly issued regulations covering the official rating of Volunteer-per-Order more popularly known as King's Letter Man (or Boy). These lads, who were the earliest form of naval cadet, had to be under sixteen years of age and were paid £2 per month directly from the Royal purse. Each received a letter from the monarch virtually guaranteeing a commission by the age of twenty, subject only to having served three years afloat, at least one of them with midshipman rating, and passing the lieutenant's examination. In 1703, the required practical experience was doubled to six years, but the system still failed to properly teach most of the young men their profession. A notable exception — who was also the last King's Letter Boy to be appointed — was George Rodney, later to become one of Britain's greatest admirals. In 1732, the program was abandoned and cadets received formal training at a Naval Academy in Portsmouth before going to sea.

King's parade: 18th century term for the quarter-deck.

Kink: An unintended twist or turn in a rope or cable.

Kip: RN slang for a brief sleep or nap. The term originally referred to a brothel, but by the latter part of the nineteenth century had come to mean a common lodging-house. Soon after, the sense transferred from the place of sleep to the act of sleeping.

Kippage: Former name for the equipment and crew of a vessel.

Kiss the Gunner's Daughter: *See* Marry and Gunner's Daughter.

Kit: Clothing or equipment.

Kit up: To outfit or equip (mainly British).

Kitbag: A tubular canvas bag, closed by drawstring, used by seamen to carry personal belongings. Also Seabag.

Kitchen's reversing rudder: In 1916, recognizing that conventional rudders are relatively ineffective at low speed, Royal Navy Admiral Jack Kitchen designed and patented a combination steering-and-propulsion device to provide slow-speed maneuvering capability for small powerboats. In Kitchen's device, a pair of curved plates shroud the propeller. When they are parallel to the propeller race, they cause almost no interference, allowing rapid forward movement, but when both are turned in the same direction, they deflect the race, causing a lateral thrust that turns the boat. And when they are moved so that they reduce the space behind the propeller, they gradually decrease forward thrust until, when fully closed, they direct the flow forward, producing an astern thrust. This ingenious device has never achieved significant maritime success, but Kitchen's principle is widely used in the reverse thrust deflectors of modern jet aircraft.

Kite: [1] A device designed to be flown in the air at the end of a long tether. [2] A light sail used in a gentle breeze, usually to supplement regular working sails (*see* spinnaker). [3] In naval mine warfare, a towed device that submerges and planes at a predetermined depth without sideways displacement.

Kite sail: A large kite used to harness higher winds above the water. Auxiliary kite-sails can be used on all vessels to reduce fuel consumption.

Kite sailing: In this form of propulsion a kite sail provides power for a vessel. The basic principles of kite sailing are the same as those of traditional sailing, except that a kite is used to harness the wind instead of a fixed sail. The advantages include being able to access wind that is free of surface turbulence, and the ability to create "apparent" wind through the movement of the kite — fixed sails move in unison with the craft they are propelling, while a kite can move relative to the vessel, thus creating more apparent wind than a traditional fixed sail, and being capable of sailing any course, including up wind.

A Hamburg-based company has developed a kite sail propulsion system that can be retrofitted to large ships, enabling mariners to re-harness the enormous energy potential of the wind. The minimal operating costs of wind-powered systems make shipping more profitable and more independent of declining oil reserves. The motive force that powered ocean voyages for millennia may yet enjoy a revival.

Knee knocker: Slang for the raised coaming at the bottom of a doorway. Intended to strengthen the bulkhead by minimizing the size of the opening, but also a hazard to knees and shins.

Knees: Timber or metal braces used to strengthen two parts being joined together. When used for the knees of wooden ships, the timbers are carefully selected so that their grain approximates the required angle, thereby minimizing splitting.

Knife & Fork School: USN slang for Officer Initiation School, where professionals entering the service are taught the basics of naval etiquette.

Knighthead: One of several baulks of timber to which the heel of a bowsprit was secured.

Knittle: [1] A small hand-laid line used to sling a hammock from the deck beam. [2] Kittles were knotted two or three times and used to belabor a victim running the gauntlet. The word is derived from the verb "knit" and is pronounced "nittles."

Knock off: [1] To blow a sailing vessel off course. [2] To quit suddenly or stop working. (Some sources claim a nautical origin for this usage, since galleys were rowed to the rhythm of a mallet striking a wooden block, and when the knocking stopped, it was the signal to stop pulling.) [3] To kill or murder someone. [4] To hold up or rob. [5] To copy or imitate, especially without permission.

Knock the gilt off the gingerbread: This expression meaning to spoil the best part of a thing or story has a nautical origin. Knocking the gold trim off a ship's gingerbread not only incurred the displeasure of the captain but, depending on age and condition, could damage the vessel.

Knockabout: A sloop- or schooner-rigged sailing vessel with no bowsprit.

Knocked into a cocked hat: Attempts to give this phrase a nautical origin are fruitless. In the game of ninepins, when six pins had been knocked down, the remaining three sometimes formed a triangle said to resemble a cocked hat.

Knoll: The top of an underwater shoal or hillock, characteristically of rounded profile and rising less than 500 fathoms above the floor. If higher, it is called a seamount or guyot. Knolls sometimes form clusters on the sea floor.

Knorr: A seagoing Viking cargo ship, shorter, beamier, and deeper than a raiding longship. Unlike its fighting version (the drakkar) it had no oars amidships to maximize carrying capacity.

Knot: [1] Any of countless ways of interlacing, twining, or looping cord, rope, or line, for fastening, binding, or connecting them together or to something else. [2] A speed equal to one nautical mile per hour (1.1516 mph; 1.853 km/h). Landlubbers frequently refer to "a rate of knots" or speak of "knots per hour," both of which are considered needless repetition (but see counter-argument below).

Knots per hour: Although most seamen consider this term to be a landlubberly tautology, there is an argument in some nautical circles that, rather than being a **speed**, a knot is actually the **distance** between two divisions on the logline. Therefore a cast could be reported as "a rate of X knots per hour."

Know the ropes: This phrase, today meaning to completely understand a business or operation, started out meaning to know only the bare minimum. One of the first things a novice seaman had to learn was the names and locations of all the complex running and standing rigging (i.e., the ropes). This was no simple task, as he had to be able to find and identify every line and block on a dark and moonless night, but even when he knew all that, he still had a great deal more to learn before being rated "able."

Knuckle: [1] Persistent wake turbulence having caused by the tight turn of a surface ship or submarine. Easily misinterpreted as the target by a sonar operator. [2] Raise the knuckles to the forehead in salute.

Koff: A round-bellied Dutch sailing merchantman, which could carry a large load but was a poor sailer due to its flat bottom.

KR&AI: Formerly, King's Regulations and Admiralty Instructions. Now replaced by QRO.

Krabla: A Russian whaling or sealing vessel.

The Kraken: One of the most terrifying legendary monsters of the deep is the Norwegian Kraken. It is claimed to be the size of a small island (*see* Zaratan). In 1752, Eric Ludvigsen Pontoppidan, Bishop of Bergen, wrote that its arms are so large and powerful that "if they were to lay hold of the largest man-o-war, they would pull it down to the bottom." This may not be as fantastic as it sounds if the report of Captain Arne Grónningsæter (*see* Brunswick's "Kraken") can be believed. In fact, when scaled down to a reasonable size, there are possibilities of truth behind the myth. For example, Egede's Serpent, sighted in 1734, could have been such a creature.

Krang: A whale carcass stripped of its blubber and abandoned.

Kruman: Slave trader's name for African seamen recruited to serve on a slaver making the Middle Passage. Some sources suggest the word is a pidgin English corruption of "crew-man," but in fact Kru is both an ethnic group and a sub-dialect of the Niger-Congo language family, spoken by fishers and seamen along the West coast of Africa. In addition to crewing slave ships, Krumen are reported working on the Suez Canal in 1869, on the Panama Canal in 1880, and at various times as stevedores on the docks. Also Krooman.

Kuroshio: This name which means "black flow" is the Japanese name for the Japan Stream.

Kye: RN slang for extra-strong cocoa mixed with condensed milk and served piping hot to watchkeepers.

Kymatology: Seldom-used term for the study of waves and wave motion.

L

LA: Leading Airman (RN).

La Niña: An ENSO event which occurs irregularly every 2–7 years due to cooler than usual sea surface temperatures. The term, which means "The Little Girl," was coined to represent the opposite of El Niño, which La Niña frequently follows. Pronounced Lah Neenya.

Labor/Labour: To roll or pitch excessively in a seaway; probably pounding, hogging, and sagging.

Lace: [1] A cord, string, or light line. [2] To secure a sail to mast or spar by spirally-wrapping a cord through the eyes on the sail. [3] The proper term for the gold "braid" or "stripes" of a naval officer's rank insignia.

Lacepiece: A timber closely-fitted to the back of a figurehead so as to steady it.

LACH: Lightweight amphibious container handler.

Laches: Legal term for sloppy practice or undue delay in bringing a case to a civil or admiralty court, resulting in its dismissal. Ancient French lachesse = loose.

Ladder: Except on passenger and cruise ships, where conventional terminology is used, all shipboard staircases are called "ladders," whether they are vertical with rungs, or inclined with steps-and-risers.

Ladders: A former USN gunnery technique in which secondary batteries deliberately opened short, then fired salvos as quickly as possible, with small increments in range, until the target had been crossed, then reversed to re-cross the target in the opposite direction.

Laden: An adjective describing [1] A ship charged to full capacity, or [2] How the vessel is loaded (e.g., fully-laden, partially-laden, lightly-laden, or in ballast). *See also* lading.

Lading: [1] A ship's cargo or freight. [2] The act of loading a ship. *See also* bill of lading, overloading, and plimsoll mark.

Lady's ladder: Topman's derogatory term for ratlines set close together and easy to climb.

Lagen: Term in maritime law for cargo ditched (often by intercepted smugglers) with a buoy attached for ease of later recovery. Also Ligan. Cf. Jetsam, flotsam.

Lagoon: An area of relatively-calm shallow water separated from the sea by sandbars or (usually) coral reefs.

Laid down: Said of a ship under construction once its keel has been put in place.

Laid up: Said of a ship which is docked and out of service for a short period (e.g., for the winter), but has not been mothballed for long-term storage.

Laker: A vessel trading exclusively in the Great Lakes of North America.

LAMPS: Light Airborne Multi-Purpose System. An integrated avionics weapon system that extends ASW search and attack capabilities by combining the endurance of surface vessels with the speed and flexibility of deployed helicopters.

Land: [1] Any part of the earth's surface not covered by water. [2] Of a vessel, to come to rest alongside a pier or wharf. [3] Of passengers, to leave the ship for the shore. [4] Of an aircraft, to alight on the ground or on a flight deck.

Land ho!: The hail traditionally given by the first person on board to sight land after an ocean voyage.

Landfall: The first sighting of land after an ocean voyage.

Landing beach: That portion of a shoreline over which an invasion force (usually a battalion landing team) may be put ashore.

Landing craft: A flat-bottomed purpose-built vessel for conveying troops and equipment to an amphibious landing beach usually equipped with a bottom-hinged ramp for rapid disembarkation. These vessels have an ancient history. As early as the fifth century BCE, Darius I of Persia seems to have been the first to commission function-built warships, including prototype landing craft. Fifteen hundred years later, when making opposed amphibious landings, the Byzantine navy's horse-transports rowed directly onto the beach and lowered hinged bow-ramps, allowing already-mounted armored cataphracts (heavy cavalry) to charge ashore without delay. For the fourth Crusade (1202) the Venetian navy refined the concept in the Huissier.

The first modern self-propelled infantry landing craft were deployed at Gallipoli in World War I, and by World War II there were designs to handle various combinations of troops, weapons, and vehicles. These were adapted for special purposes such as fire-support, medical evacuation, and fighter direction. Such craft were only capable of relatively short-duration voyages (*see* landing ship). There are innumerable versions of the modern landing craft, identified by initials starting with "LC." Some, but by no means all, are listed alphabetically herein.

Landing gear: Undercarriage components such as wheels, skis, or floats, that enable a grounded aircraft to move on land, snow, or water respectively.

Landing mats: Prefabricated units which can be joined together to form hard surfaces for landing beaches, emergency runways, etc. Many materials have been used; including wood, bamboo, steel, and aluminum.

Landing operation: *See* amphibious assault.

Landing party: Members of a ship's company detailed to go ashore for some (usually military) duty or operation.

Landing point: In amphibious operations, a location within a beachhead where helicopters or VTOL aircraft can land.

Landing ship: A shallow-draft vessel at least 60 meters (200 feet) long, purpose-built for landing heavy equipment on an invasion beach. Usually with bows consisting of a pair of side-hinged doors to allow easy exit of tanks, vehicles, and equipment. These large vessels were capable of long ocean voyages. During an assault landing, some remained offshore, sending their troops and hardware to the beach in smaller landing craft. Others such as the LST were flat-bottomed, designed to drop their ramps directly on the beach, allowing trucks, tanks, self-propelled artillery, and armored engineer vehicles to drive straight off through the double doors in the bow. Some were modified for service as repair depots or hospital ships; others were floating command posts, staffed by naval, air, and military personnel, to ensure inter-service control and cooperation. The biggest of these vessels was the LSD which had quarters for troops, along with their vehicles and landing craft. It could also provide docking and repair services to small craft, and act as control ship for amphibious assaults. There are innumerable landing ship versions, identified by initials starting with "LS" or "LH." Some, but by no means all, are listed herein.

Landing Signal Officer: A naval aviator who directs landings on a USN aircraft carrier. (The RN originally called this job Deck Landing Control officer, now it is Air Traffic Controller.) From the 1920s until after World War II, LSO's used colored paddles to control the approach and touch-down of airplanes (hence the colloquialism "Batsman"). Their signals gave pilots information on lining-up with the flight deck, height relative to the proper glide slope, airspeed (fast or slow), and whether tailhook and wheels were down. The final signal was a slashing motion at the throat ordering the pilot to reduce power and land. LSO signals were mostly advisory in the U.S. Navy, but usually mandatory in the Royal Navy. Hence, when "crossdecking" they had to agree on which system would be used: The duties of today's LSO are described by the USN (Navair 00-80T-104) as...

... the safe and expeditious recovery of non–V/STOL fixed-wing aircraft aboard ship.... Through training and experience, he is capable of correlating factors of wind, weather, aircraft capabilities, ship configuration, pilot experience, etc.... The LSO is also directly responsible for training pilots in carrier landing techniques. In this regard, he must ... certify their carrier readiness and qualification. The pilot and LSO form a professional and disciplined team, both ashore and afloat.

See also deck landing modes.

Landing stage: A platform attached to the shore at one end and the ship at the other, for use when loading or disembarking passengers and cargo.

Landlocked: Said of a country without access to the sea.

Landlubber: Derisive term for a non-seaman (land + lubber).

Landmark: Any prominent feature on the shore which can be easily identified as a guide for ships at sea.

Landsman: [1] Formerly, a naval rating below ordinary seaman. [2] Now, any inexperienced sailor, unfamiliar with ships and the sea.

Lane: A channel or lead. *See also* sea lane.

Langrage/Langridge: Musket balls, nails, or metal scrap formerly used as the filling for case shot to be fired as an anti-personnel projectile or to damage sails and masts.

Lanyard/Laniard: [1] A short length of cord or line connecting or securing something. [2] A cord attached to the breech mechanism for firing a gun. [3] A cord hung around the neck or looped over the shoulder of a seaman to which a whistle or knife may be attached.

Lap: In naval mine warfare, that section or strip of a minefield assigned to one or more minesweepers for a single run through the field.

Lapland Witch: Formerly, a charlatan at a northern Scandinavian port, who would offer to sell favorable winds to credulous sailors.

Lapstraked: *See* clinker-built.

Larboard: Archaic term for the left (port) side of a vessel when looking forward. Abandoned because of possible confusion with starboard when orders were shouted during a storm or in combat.

Larbolin: Formerly, a member of the larboard (port) watch. A member of the starboard watch was a starbolin, hence the cant rhyme:

> Larbolins stout, you must turn out
> And sleep no more within
> For if you do, we'll cut your clue
> And let starbolins in

"Clue" refers to the combination of small lines from which a hammock is suspended.

Lascar: An East Indian seaman (Hindi lashkari = soldier).

Lash: [1] To bind or secure something by wrapping it with rope or wire and tying off with a knot. [2] To flog someone. [3] Acronym for **L**ighter **A**board **Sh**ip (*see* heavy loads and vehicles).

Lash up and stow!: RN command to bind one's hammock with cord and store it out of the way. The USN equivalent command is "heave up and trice."

Lashing: The rope, line, or wire used to secure something in place.

Lassie: Few people would associate the famous canine movie star with the sea, but there is a direct connection. On New Year's Day 1915, a British fleet was steaming off the Devon coast, when HMS *Formidable*, the fourth of five Royal Navy ships to bear that name, developed engine trouble and fell behind the line. At 2:30 in the morning the crippled battleship was struck by two torpedoes fired from German submarine *U-24*. She sank in less than two hours, to become the first British battleship to be lost in World War I. Only 199 men were saved, out of a complement of 750, and the wreck is an official war grave.

Seventy-one survivors crammed into a pinnace which required constant bailing in ten-meter (30-foot) waves and high winds. All day long and through the following night the little boat was battered by rain and hail, but it was spotted next morning by a Miss Gwen Harding walking along the Marine Parade at Lyme Regis. By this time, fourteen had died and been buried at sea, but a rapidly-mounted rescue operation found fifty-one still alive (three of whom died after being rescued) along with six dead bodies. The corpses were brought ashore and laid out on the floor of the Pilot Boat Inn, where the landlady's collie dog Lassie persistently licked the face of Seaman James Cowan until he miraculously coughed and returned to life. Decades later, the incident (very loosely interpreted) inspired the series of movies and a television program.

Last Post: The British bugle call blown at military funerals and at the sunset ceremony (cf. "Taps").

Lateen rig: A triangular sail on a long yard, angled to the mast. This is the ancient and typical rig of the East Mediterranean Sea, the Persian/Arabian Gulf, and the Indian Ocean, and is one of the lowest windage sails, easy to manage. *See also* sailing rigs.

Lateral marks: Those parts of the lateral system which designate the sides of a channel.

Lateral system: *See* uniform lateral system.

Latitude: The angular distance north or south of the equator expressed in minutes and seconds. The equator is at 0° latitude, the poles at 90° North and South respectively (cf. longitude).

Launch: [1] A large, powered, open boat. [2] The largest pulling or sailing boat of a man-o-war (called the longboat in merchant service). [3] To set a small boat in the water. [4] To float a newly-constructed vessel, usually by sliding it down a slope or slipway. [5] To fire a rocket or torpedo. [6] To catapult an aircraft off a flight deck. [7] To commence a project or expedition. The first two come from the Portuguese *lancha* meaning pinnace: the others from Middle English *lancer*, which derives from the Latin *lancear* referring to a javelin, or a spear with a leather thong that could be thrown (launched) as well as used for stabbing.

Launcher: A device for holding and firing a rocket, missile, depth charge, or other projectile.

Launching rituals: Since the beginning of navigation, newly-built vessels have been held to need protection by and from the gods of the sea. There are records of a ship-dedication ceremony as early as 2100 BCE. A little later, the ancient Chinese developed elaborate launching rituals to propitiate the Mother of the Dragon, and many of them are still performed today. In Europe, Scandinavia, and Tahiti, human sacrifice was thought necessary to propitiate the sea deities, but later generations of priest substituted blood-red wine. The practice, if not the superstition, lives on when the sponsor of a new vessel smashes a champagne bottle against the bow as the hull slides down the ways.

Law enforcement: Military services have their own police and security forces that perform some or all of the following duties:
• Enforce military law
• Develop policies and programs to prevent crime and reduce traffic accidents
• Supervise the arrest, custody, transfer, and release of offenders
• Plan and direct criminal investigations
• Investigate suspected treason, sabotage, or espionage
• Plan the security of military bases and office buildings
• Direct security procedures
• Manage military correctional facilities
• Conduct or assist in ballistics, forgery, fingerprinting, and polygraph examinations
See also naval police and master-at-arms.

Laws and conventions of the sea: Ancient Egyptians, Minoans, and Phoenicians were extensively engaged in sophisticated maritime activity, and must have had governing rules, although none has yet been discovered. By about 800 BCE, however, Rhodian Law had become a long-lasting and major international source of maritime regulation. In the ninth century, the Byzantine adaptation of that law applied internationally across the western commercial world but, by the eleventh century, Italian coastal city-states, such as Trani, Amalfi, and Venice, were compiling their own maritime regulations.

These were consolidated into and superseded by the Consolato del Mare, developed in Spain around 1300, which became accepted throughout the Mediterranean. Meanwhile, a separate code had emerged on the Atlantic coasts of Europe. The Rôles de Oléron were of Anglo-Norman origin, but rapidly became accepted in Castile, England, Flanders, France, Prussia, and Scotland. Their terms were closely followed by the Laws of Wisby, and the Customs of Amsterdam. Later, the Hanseatic Ordinances drew heavily on Wisby.

Even today, these early codes are still occasionally (though rarely) cited as precedent or authority by admiralty courts. They had the immense advantage of applying uniform and consistent rules and principles to international disputes, but the pan–European system began to dissipate when the rise of nationalism in the 17th century led Britain, Denmark, France, Sweden, and others to develop their own ordinances. Disadvantages soon became obvious, and maritime law gradually reverted to today's more-or-less uniform and comprehensive supranational body of jurisprudence. *See also* United Nations Convention on the Law of the Sea.

Laws and usages of war: The idea that the conduct of armed conflict can be governed, or at least limited to mitigate excessive evils, can be found in almost all societies from antiquity onward. (The classical name of the laws of war is jus in bello — a separate body of law, jus ad bellum, determines whether entering into war is justifiable.) There have been many international declarations, conventions, treaties and judgments, encompassing a wide range of matters, such as the rights and duties of neutrals; treatment of POWs and those wounded in battle; negotiation and implementation of truces; limitations on means and methods of combat; and war crimes. As an example, eight of twelve sections in the 1907 Hague Conventions concern the following aspects of naval warfare:

VI — The Status of Enemy Merchant Ships at the Outbreak of Hostilities

VII — The Conversion of Merchant Ships into War-Ships

VIII — The Laying of Automatic Submarine Contact Mines

IX — Bombardment by Naval Forces in Time of War

X — Adaptation to Maritime War of the Principles of the Geneva Convention

XI — Restrictions with Regard to the Exercise of the Right of Capture in Naval War

XII — The Creation of an International Prize Court [Not Ratified]

XIII — The Rights and Duties of Neutral Powers in Naval War

Laws of Wisby: This maritime code was developed at Wisby (or Wisbuy), the capital of the island of Gothland in the Baltic Sea. Claimed to be older than the Rôles de Oléron, many of its clauses are virtually identical and it seems certain that one was copied from the other. During the 12th and 13th centuries, Gothland was a wealthy commercial center and, as a result, the Wisby laws carried great authority in the Baltic region, until superseded by the Hanseatic Ordinances.

Lay: [1] To aim a gun. [2] To plan a ship's course. [3] To place a vessel in a specified position (e.g., lay alongside). [4] To order a person to go to a specific location (e.g., lay aloft, or lay below). [5] To drop an anchor. [6] To place strands together ready to be twisted into rope. [7] To twist the strands to form a rope. [8] The direction in which the strands have been twisted (*see* rope & hawser lay).

Lay aloft!: Command for topmen to climb to their stations.

Lay boat: A boat anchored for some specific purpose, such as marking a location.

Lay-by: A place where vessels can anchor away from traffic and out of the current.

Lay off: [1] To wait at a specific location pending further instructions. [2] To chart or plot a course. [3] To discharge personnel.

Lay out!: Command to topmen to spread out at evenly spaced intervals across the yard.

Lay up: *See* laid up.

Layer: [1] One of the pair of gunlayers who work as a team. [2] A thermocline.

Laytime: Contractual term for the period allowed for loading or discharge of cargo. May be expressed in terms of days, hours, or tons/day.

Lazaret: [1] A between decks paint locker. [2] A small cupboard for anything (especially food) in a merchantman. [3] A storage compartment at the stern of a small craft. [4] A quarantine station for contagious diseases. The first lazaret was established by Venice in 1403 on Santa Maria di Nazareth (today "Lazzaretto Vecchio"), an island in the Venetian Lagoon.

Lazy: Extra or spare (e.g., a "lazy painter" is the rope used for hauling a boat to a boom ladder, while a "lazy guy" is an additional guy on a boom or spar to prevent it swinging).

LCA: World War II Hull classification symbol of a Landing Craft, Assault. Designed to carry an infantry platoon of 30 soldiers, and usually carried on a ship's lifeboat davits.

LCAC: Hull classification symbol of a Landing Craft, Air cushion.

LCAP: Low combat air patrol.

LCB: Line of constant bearing.

LCC: Hull classification symbol of an amphibious command ship.

LCCS: Hull classification symbol of a Landing Craft Control Ship.

LCG: World War II Hull classification symbol of a Landing Craft, Gun. Designed to provide close artillery support for troops landing on a defended beach. A number of variations were produced based on the LCT hull, some carrying light anti-tank weaponry, others small naval guns.

LCH: Hull classification symbol of a Landing Craft, Heavy.

LCI: Hull classification symbol of a Landing Craft, Infantry.

LCI(L): Hull classification symbol of a Landing Craft, Infantry (large).

LCL: Less than container load.

LCM: Hull classification symbol of a Landing Craft, Mechanized.

LCP: Lighterage control point.

LCPL: Hull classification symbol of a Landing Craft, Personnel (large).

LCS: Hull classification symbol of a Littoral Combat Ship.

LCSL: Hull classification symbol of a Landing Craft, Support (large).

LCT: Hull classification symbol of a Landing Craft, Tank.

LCU: Hull classification symbol of a Landing Craft, Utility.

LCVP: Hull classification symbol of a Landing Craft, Vehicle and Personnel.

LDO: Limited duty officer.

Lead: [1] An inshore channel, especially one through an ice pack. Pronounced "leed." Also lode. [2] A leadline. Pronounced "led."

Leading edge: [1] The edge of a sail or mast that faces the wind. [2] The forward periphery of an aircraft propeller blade or wing. [3] The foremost position in a trend or movement; a vanguard.

Leading marks: *See* range beacons.

Leading part: One of three divisions or segments of a line rove through a tackle, being the section beyond the tackle that will be hauled. The others are running part and standing part. (*See also* fall.)

Leading Seaman: A non-commissioned rank or rate in many navies, also known as leading rate. The military equivalent is corporal. In Commonwealth navies a leading seaman rates above able seaman and below petty officer. The insignia is a fouled anchor in British and Australian service; in the Canadian navy it is two point down chevrons. The USN equivalent is Petty Officer 3rd Class (E-4) whose insignia is an eagle over crossed anchors and a single point down chevron. (*See also* table 14.)

Leadline: [1] A weighted line used in fishing for holding down nets or traps. May have a lead filament or core (also called bottom line). [2] A depth-measuring device, originally used by the Vikings, who dropped a lead-weighted line until it touched bottom, and then measured the length played out in terms of the length of outstretched arms, which they called fathmr. Today we call it a fathom. [3] The modern leadline is made of ¾-inch braided cotton twine in standard lengths of 20 fathoms for the traditional

hand-thrown version and 100 fathoms for the deep-sea type. The lead sinkers weigh 7 or 14 pounds (3 or 6 kg) and have a hollow at their ends that can be "armed" (filled) with soap or tallow to pick up a sample of the sea bed. The hand line has nine "marks" designed to be read by feel at night (experienced leadsmen often put them in their mouths, which tend to be more sensitive than work-hardened fingers). The marks are:

- 2 fathoms   Two leather strips
- 3 fathoms   Three leather strips
- 5 fathoms   White cotton calico
- 7 fathoms   Red woolen bunting
- 10 fathoms Leather pierced with a round hole
- 13 fathoms Three leather strips (sometimes blue woolen serge)
- 15 fathoms White cotton calico
- 17 fathoms Red woolen bunting
- 20 fathoms Leather with two round holes or light line with two knots

It will be noted that marks for the second set of ten fathoms are virtually a repeat of those for the first, except that twelve fathoms is skipped and twenty is modified. Intermediate "deeps" are unmarked, to be estimated by the leadsman on the basis of experience. A deep-sea leadline is marked in the same way for the first twenty fathoms. Thereafter it is marked with a knot every five fathoms and a double knot every ten fathoms, terminating with a strip of leather at 100 fathoms.

Leadsman: A seaman who takes soundings by casting the lead. Pronounced "leds-man."

League: *See* nautical league.

Leak: [1] An unintended seepage of water through a crack or hole. Anglo-Saxon lekka = drip. [2] To divulge confidential or secret information.

Leatherneck: U.S. slang for a Marine (cf. Bootneck).

Leave: Permission to be relieved of all duties and be absent from a ship or station for more than 48 hours (cf. liberty, shore leave, French leave, sick leave, long leave).

Leaver: A merchantman that breaks away from a convoy to proceed independently.

Ledge: A compact row of rocks running parallel to the shore.

Lee: [1] The side away from the wind, the downwind side. [2] The protection provided by an upwind object ("In the lee of the islet"). From Old English hlēo = shelter.

Lee gauge: To be downwind of an enemy is to hold the lee gauge.

Lee helm: Sailing with helm alee to compensate for wind pressure.

Lee helmsman: [1] A bridge watchkeeper designated to take the wheel if the helmsman is incapacitated. [2] In the USN the lee helmsman handles the engine-order telegraph and is paired with a regular helmsman. The two normally switch duties every half-hour (at each bell) during their watch.

Lee shore: The coast toward which the wind is blowing — a hazardous one for sailing ships to be near.

Lee tide: A tide running parallel to the wind.

Leeboard: A triangular or pear-shaped board, lowered on the lee side of a keelless sailing barge to minimize drift when beating against the wind.

Leech: [1] The vertical side of a square-sail. [2] The longer side of a lugsail. [3] The vertical edge of a triangular sail.

Leechline: Rope attached to the leech of a square-sail, running through a block under the top, and serving to truss the sail up to its yard.

Leeward: In or moving toward the side away from the wind. Pronounced "loo-ard." From the Old English hlēow-ward (cf. windward).

Leeway: Extent to which a ship is blown to leeward of her intended course.

Left arm rates: *See* arm badges.

Left bank: The ground beside a river on the left of an observer facing downstream.

Left hand lay: An "s-twist." *See* rope & hawser lay.

Left hand salute: *See* hand salutes.

Left in the lurch: Some sources claim that this phrase, commonly meaning to be trapped helplessly while others make their escape, refers to a ship failing to recover from the heavy roll known as a lurch. In fact, it is probably derived from the popular 16th century French game of Lourche. In this game, which is said to have resembled backgammon, anyone who fell so far behind that a win was virtually impossible was said to "demeurer lourche" (live in lurch). The word also occurs in the more recent game of cribbage, where a player who is less than half-way around the board when the winner finishes is said to have been "lurched' and loses double the stake.

Leg: [1] The distance sailed on a tack. [2] The portion of a cruise between ports.

Legs: A fast-sailing vessel is said to "have legs."

Lend a hand: In naval parlance this means "please help." The command to do so is "bear a hand."

Lens: [1] Physics; A transparent optical element, so constructed that it serves to change the degree of convergence or divergence of the transmitted rays. [2] Sea service; The glass sealing a port or window. *See also* Fresnel lens.

LENS: Light Enhanced Naval Surveillance.

Let fly!: Command [1] To release sails. [2] To fire a weapon (slang).

Let go!: Command to release and drop the anchor.

Let go and haul!: Command to simultaneously slacken the weather braces and pull the lee braces, issued when tacking a square-rigged vessel.

Let the cat out of the bag: This phrase, which today implies divulging secret information, originated when a shipboard flogging was about to occur and the boatswain ceremoniously removed the cat-o'-nine-tails from its blood-red storage bag.

Letter book: A file or folder in which are preserved all the correspondence and orders issued by a warship's captain.

Letter of Marque: A commission or license to employ a private armed vessel against enemy merchant shipping. King Henry III of England issued the first such authorizations in 1243. Originally called Letter of Marque and Reprisal it predated privateer Commissions of War and differed from them in that it allowed private individuals to seek redress for wrongs suffered at the hands of others on the high seas. If, for instance, a French ship was attacked and robbed by a Spanish one, the Letter of Marque and Reprisal would reflect the theory of collective responsibility by authorizing its owner to seize goods of equal value from any Spanish ship that might be encountered.

Letterman: *See* King's Letter Man.

Leviathan: Longer than twenty winding rivers joined end-to-end, this primordial water serpent is said to have been formed on the fifth day of creation. Living in the Mediterranean Sea, he is a brilliant and beautiful sight, with dazzling bright eyes and luminous shiny scales. As with other creations, he was originally given a female companion, but she was taken away when the Creator realized that, if something of that size was allowed to multiply, its progeny would soon overfill all the oceans of the world.

Leyte Gulf: The Battle of Leyte Gulf (23–26 October 1944) included four major naval engagements — in the Sibuyan Sea and Surigao Strait; and off Samar Island and Cape Engaño — which, together with other related actions, are generally considered to form the largest naval battle of World War II and, possibly, the largest naval battle in history. The Imperial Japanese Navy mobilized nearly all of its remaining major surface vessels in an attempt to defeat the Allied invasion of Leyte but was repulsed by the U.S. Navy's 3rd and 7th Fleets, suffering extremely heavy losses including the "super-battleship" *Musashi*, two other battleships, four aircraft carriers, and eight cruisers.

LF: [1] Landing force. [2] Low frequency.

LHA: Hull classification symbol of an amphibious assault ship. Embarks and deploys the ground personnel of a landing force.

LHD: Hull classification symbol of an amphibious assault ship (dock).

***Libera Nos* Specter:** Seventeenth century Dutch shipmaster Bernard Fokke was a skilled and audacious mariner, who encased his masts in iron in order to carry a greater spread of canvas than any of his contemporaries. In consequence, his voyages from Holland to Java were so uncannily rapid that seamen believed he must have been in league with and helped along by the Devil. After his Indiaman *Libera Nos* (Deliver Us) disappeared without a trace on the return voyage from Batavia, it was suspected he had offended his supernatural helper and been condemned to sail on forever. This forerunner of the Flying Dutchman is said to travel with a crew of spectral skeletons that bring misfortune to all who see them.

Liberty: Permission to be relieved of all duties and be absent from a USN ship or station for less than 48 hours. The RN uses the term shore leave, but calls those who get it "libertymen" and sends them ashore in a "liberty boat." Authorized absence longer than 48 hours is called leave in both RN and USN.

Liberty Ship: World War II U.S. built merchantman, based on vessels ordered by Britain to replace ships torpedoed by German U-boats. It had five cargo holds, eight watertight bulkheads, and displacement of 14,245 tons. For rapid and inexpensive mass-production, faster than U-boats could sink them, they had welded hulls, made assembly-line style from prefabricated sections. By 1943, three new Liberty ships were completed every day, and the total of 2,751 was by far the largest number ever made to a single design. *See also* Victory Ship.

Liburnian: [1] Originally, a single-banked pirate vessel, developed in the Adriatic around 300 BCE and named after the pirate tribe called "Liburnii." [2] Later, it was adopted by the Roman navy, which used it in the role of frigate for scouting and message carrying. [3] Later still, the Romans used the name for a triple-banked warship of different design.

License: Certificate of competence required by the officers and crew of merchantmen of virtually all maritime nations.

Lie: To take up position in response to commands such as: [1] To topmen; "lie out!" meaning spread themselves along the yards for reefing or furling, or "lie in ordinary" to reverse the procedure. [2] To an approaching boat; "lie off!" meaning remain at a distance until permission to come alongside is given. [3] To a helmsman; "lie to!" meaning hold the ship's head steady in a gale and come almost to a stop, usually facing the wind.

Lien: A legal claim against the property of another as security for the payment of debt. A lien gives the holder the right to sell the property to satisfy the debt if it is not otherwise paid. On the other hand, a lien is removed when the debt is discharged or a contract is paid.

Lieutenant: [1] A deputy or substitute (Latin locum tenens = in place of). [2] A Junior naval or military officer. [3] Used in combination with another military title denotes an officer of the next lower rank (e.g., Lieutenant-general).

This is one of the oldest military titles, and in naval use can be traced back to the twelfth century when a sailing master had full command of the ship, while the captain was responsible for embarked soldiers, with a non-commissioned lieutenant as his military deputy. By about 1580 the captain had assumed command of the ship, with the master as a subordinate responsible for shiphandling and navigation. The lieutenant was expected to replace the captain in case of death or incapacitation, but was still non-commissioned, being appointed with no official rank. Some 50 years later, naval lieutenants had evolved beyond their purely military role to become professional commissioned sea officers.

In about 1677, shortly after his appointment as Secretary of the Admiralty, Samuel Pepys introduced formal examinations which had to be passed to qualify for a third lieutenant's commission. Thereafter advancement depended entirely on seniority. Third and second lieutenants each had specific shipboard duties in addition to their prime responsibilities of standing watch and commanding a division of guns in battle (*see* separate entry for first lieutenant). In the days of rated warships, a first-rate normally carried seven to nine lieutenants (one first, one or two seconds, and five or six thirds). The complement diminished with the vessel's rating (for example a third-rate had five lieutenants, while a sixth rate had only two). Nowadays, a naval lieutenant is senior to lieutenant (jg) or sub-lieutenant, and junior to lieutenant commander. At its inception in 1775, the Continental Navy essentially adopted the then current Royal Navy rank structure, including that of lieutenant (*see* table 15). An Army or marine lieutenant is senior to second lieutenant and junior to captain.

Pronunciation is Loo-tenant in America. Until World War II all British Commonwealth navies said Let-enant, but the influx of temporary non-career officers overwhelmed that tradition and substituted the army's Lef-tenant, the former pronunciation being retained only by the Canadian Armed Forces Maritime Command.

Lieutenant-at-arms: Formerly, a warship's most junior lieutenant, responsible for assisting the master-at-arms in training seamen to handle small arms.

Lieutenant Commander: A commissioned naval officer ranking above lieutenant and below commander. In sailing ship navies, senior lieutenants were often given command of vessels too small to justify a captain or commander. In the RN they were given the courtesy title lieutenant-in-command, while the USN used lieutenant commanding or lieutenant commandant. In 1882, the USN replaced those courtesy titles with the distinct rank of lieutenant commander. Thirty-two years later the RN followed suit inserting a hyphen. Both navies used the rank insignia previously used by a lieutenant with eight years seniority (two stripes with a thinner one in between). The equivalent army and marine rank is major (considered a "field" or senior rank, while Lt.Cdr is theoretically still a junior officer).

Lieutenant, Junior Grade: This USN title was created in 1883 when Congress ruled that the rank of Master (formerly Sailing Master) "be changed to that of lieutenant, the masters now on the list to constitute a junior grade of, and be commissioned as lieutenants, having the same rank and pay as now provided by law for masters." The equivalent RN rank is Sub-Lieutenant, which had been introduced in much the same way 22 years earlier (*see* tables 13 and 15).

Life preserver: A personal floatation device. Also life jacket or vest.

Life raft: An emergency floatation device which can accommodate a number of crew members. Can be manually launched to abandon ship, or simply untied and allowed to float off a sinking vessel.

Lifeboat: [1] A ship's boat for emergency use. Usually slung from davits on the boat deck of a passenger ship. [2] A specially-constructed boat, resistant to sinking or swamping, launched from land to rescue people in distress at sea.

Lifeboat drill: A mandatory test of a passenger ship's emergency procedures that must be carried out before or within 24 hours of sailing.

Lifebuoy: A buoyant ring, usually equipped with a light and a smoke generator, for throwing to someone overboard. A USCG Type IV personal floatation device.

Lifeguard: [1] A surface vessel or helicopter detailed to stand by to recover aircrew forced to land in the sea. [2] A submarine assigned to similar rescue work, normally in an area which cannot be covered by surface ship or helicopter because of enemy proximity.

Lifeline: [1] A line strung along the weather deck for the support and protection of seamen in heavy weather. [2] Formerly, line strung between guns on the gun deck for the support of gun crews in rough weather. [3] A hand-line stretched above square-rig yards for topmen to steady themselves when manning the yards in salute.

LIFO: Last-in first-out. [1] In accounting, the term refers to a method of inventory valuation, in which the last units purchased are recorded as the first units sold. [2] In computing, the term is used when the last data entered is the first to be removed or evaluated.

Lift: [1] A specified quantity or weight of cargo. [2] The capacity of shipping required for an assault landing. [3] A crane, derrick, or topping lift. [4] One of the ropes used to hold the yards of a square rigged ship level. [5] The forward pressure exerted by air flowing over a sail. [6] The upward pressure exerted by air flowing over or an airfoil.

Lift-off: The instant at which an aircraft becomes airborne, a missile leaves its firing tube, or a rocket rises from its launching pad.

Ligan: *See* Lagen.

Light: [1] The correct name for a lighthouse. [2] The proper term for a navigation light. [3] The glass in a port or other opening in the hull, whether hinged or fixed.

Light air: Force 1 on the Beaufort Scale (winds 1–3 knots = 1.15–.45 mph = 1.85–5.56 km/h).

Light breeze: Force 2 on the Beaufort Scale (winds 4–6 knots = 4.6–6.9 mph = 7.4–11.1 km/h).

Light cruiser: Twentieth century term for a cruiser armed with six-inch guns or smaller.

Light fleet carrier: World War II designation of a purpose-built and militarized improvement of the escort carrier.

Light load line: The hull mark indicating waterline level when all cargo has been discharged (*see* Plimsoll marks).

Light lock: A system of doors or passageways which allows personnel to pass to and from darkened spaces without showing light outside.

Light phase characteristic: The distinctive sequences of flashes and dark intervals that identify an aid to navigation.

Light ship: An merchant vessel that is empty except for supplies, fuel, and ballast; carrying no freight or cargo (not to be confused with lightship).

Light signals: *See* sound signals and table 9.

Lighter: [1] A self-propelled barge, usually used to transport goods or people over short distances within a harbor or from ship-to-shore. [2] Sometimes applied to unpowered barges maneuvered by tugboats.

Lighter aboard ship: *See* heavy loads and vehicles.

Lighterage: [1] The fee for transporting goods by barge or lighter. [2] The process of using small craft to transport cargo or personnel from ship to shore. Also Lightering.

Lightening: The transfer (normally carried out at anchor) of liquid cargo from a large tanker to a smaller one, to reduce the draft of the larger vessel and enable it to enter port. Not to be confused with lightning.

Lighthouse: [1] Popular name for an onshore tower or other structure displaying a light or lights for the guidance of mariners and to warn of maritime hazards. Previously attended but now usually automated. [2] The shipboard housing for a port or starboard navigation light.

Lightning: A discharge of atmospheric electricity, accompanied by a vivid flash of light, commonly from one cloud to another, sometimes from a cloud to earth or sea. Standing out as they do above the vast flat expanse of ocean water, marine vessels, especially those with masts, can be prime targets for lightning seeking the most attractive path to ground. The most at risk are people on small boats, which are frequently made of wood or fiberglass that are poor conductors of electricity compared to the human body! Hence the need for lightning conductors.

Lightning conductor: A device designed to protect buildings or ships from the destructive effects of lightning. On watercraft, a metal plate (the "lightning protector") is mounted at the main truck, or high on the superstructure of a vessel that does not have a mast. Electrical conductors attached to the device run downward to a grounding conductor in contact with the water. On wooden ships the ground is usually the copper-bottoming, but for an iron or steel vessel it is the hull itself. For small vessels the grounding conductor may be retractable, part of the hull, or attached to a centerboard.

Lightship: A purpose-built, crewed vessel with distinctive markings, anchored at a specified and charted location, and carrying a light for the guidance of mariners (not to be confused with light ship).

Lightweight amphibious container handler: USMC equipment, usually maneuvered by a bulldozer, that retrieves twenty-foot equivalent containers from landing craft in the surf and places them on flatbed truck trailers on the beach.

Lima: NATO phonetic notation for the letter "L."

Liman: A coastal lagoon, bay, or delta, characterized by a muddy or slimy bottom (from the Russian for estuary).

Limber holes: [1] In a ship, holes on either side of the keelson which allow bilge water to flow freely to the pump well. [2] In a boat, openings between compartments that allow water to flow into the bilge.

Limber rope: A rope threaded through the limber holes along the length of the ship. Pulling it back and forth kept the holes from becoming plugged.

Limey: The Royal Navy, and later British Merchant Marine, virtually eliminated scurvy by requiring its sailors to drink lime juice. This led American seamen to call Britishers Lime-juicers, later abbreviated to Limeys.

Limited duty officer: A former USN enlisted person (usually a CWO, CPO, or PO1) who has earned a commission through superior performance, but is limited to duties in his or her field of expertise. "Limited" refers not to authority, but rather career progression and restrictions. LDOs qualify for the full range of promotions up to rear admiral (lower half) but, unlike unrestricted line officers, cannot normally aspire to command a warship or auxiliary vessel, although such appointments have occasionally been made.

Limnology: The study of the physical properties of fresh water. *See also* hydrology.

Limpet mine: A timed explosive device which can be attached to a ship's hull by a frogman.

Line: [1] Is generally defined as being cordage of less than 1-inch (2.5 cm) in circumference. [2] In the USN it refers to rope that has been unspooled and cut for use. [3] One of the dimensions of a convoy, *see* column. *See also* braided line.

Line abreast: Formation in which ships sail side-by-side on the same course.

Line ahead: Formation in which each ship follows the one ahead (cf. column).

Line crossing: Ceremonies for passing an important landmark have been performed by seamen since at least the days of classical Greece. Several still exist today, one of the most significant being the initiation rite to commemorate a first crossing of the equator. The night before the ship is due to cross, she is boarded "via the hawsepipes" by Bears claiming to be agents of the Watery Realm's Secretary of State and demanding to meet to the captain and deliver a Proclamation announcing a Royal Court to be held on the morrow to determine the eligibility of ship and passengers to continue their voyage. The Bears then exit by the way they came.

Next day, the Bears re-appear to proclaim the arrival of "His Majesty King Neptune, by the Grace of Mythology, Lord of the Waters and Master of the Waves, Sovereign of the Oceans, Governor and Lord High Admiral of the Bath" who — assisted by his wife Amphritite, his crony Davy Jones, and sundry pirates, mermaids, and the like — supervises the "trusty shellbacks" (who have crossed before) as they force the "slimy polliwogs" (who have not) to perform increasingly disgusting and degrading tasks as retribution for their lack of respect for him and his realm.

In earlier times the ceremony could be vicious and brutal, involving such things as beating the polliwogs with cobbing boards and wet knotted ropes, or dragging them in the disturbed wake behind the stern. Deaths were not unknown and hospitalization was common until World War II, when most of the world's navies instituted strict regulations limiting abuse and humiliation. Even today, without the oversight of military discipline, line-crossing hazing can still get out of hand on merchantmen.

After the ceremony the initiates are given elaborate "Royal Certificates" of their newly-acquired status requiring, among other things, "all sharks, dolphins, whales, mermaids, and other dwellers of the deep" to abstain from maltreating them should they fall overboard. Similar maritime fraternities include the "Order of the Blue Nose" for crossing the Arctic Circle, the "Order of the Red Nose" for crossing the Antarctic Circle, and the "Order of the Golden Dragon" for crossing the International Date Line. A seaman who crosses the equator at the date line becomes a "Golden Shellback."

Line gun: A firearm used to shoot a messenger line to another ship or to stranded people. *See also* Coston Gun.

Line of battle: Refers to [1] The disposition of a fleet at the moment of engagement. [2] The line ahead formation favored by sailing navies. [3] Warships considered powerful enough to join that line (*see* Warship Ratings).

Line of bearing: Formation in which ships lie in a straight line at a predetermined angle to their course.

Line of departure: Conceptual line from which successive waves of landing craft leave for an amphibious assault.

Line of fire: The expected path of gunfire or a missile.

Line of sight: [1] The straight line along which an observer looks (also line of vision). [2] Radio-communications term, referring to a line between two points that does not follow the earth's curvature.

Line officer: This USN term (which carries over from the 18th century tactical formation line of battle) refers to someone qualified in all respects to take command of a warship, aviation unit, marine detachment, or other line unit such as a seal team (the Royal Navy uses the term "executive officer"). Line officers in the USN wear a star above their stripes of rank on sleeve or shoulder boards to distinguish them from specialist officers. All USMC commissioned officers, other than those on limited duty, are trained to command combat units, so are considered line officers. *See* career tracking.

Line squall: A violent wind-and-rainstorm advancing along the line of a weather front, and observed as a dark line across the horizon.

Line unit: Term used in the United States Navy, Coast Guard and Marine Corps to describe a surface warship, submarine, ground combat team, or combat aviation unit.

Lineal number: A number defining and determining the precedence and seniority of USN commissioned officers.

Linear displacement: *See* ship motion.

Liner: [1] Formerly, a colloquialism for line of battle ship. [2] Now, any vessel following a regular scheduled route, especially a passenger ship or container ship running between fixed ports.

Linstock: A short staff for holding the slow-match used in gun firing.

Liquorice Legs: RN slang for a gunnery officer (after the black patent leather leggings he wore — *see* gaiters).

List: [1] A prolonged tilting to one side or another caused by internal forces such as shifting cargo or uneven ballast (cf. heel). [2] A document recording names or items.

Listless: Some sources have claimed that this word, meaning languid and without interest in doing anything, originated in the days of sail, when the wind dropped leaving a ship becalmed without the list normally caused by wind in the sails. In fact, it comes directly from Middle English, being a combination of liste, meaning to desire, plus-laes, a suffix signifying without.

Lithosphere: The rigid outer layer of the Earth comprising the continental and oceanic crust and a portion of the upper mantle. It is divided into twelve major plates, the boundaries of which are zones of intense geological activity. *See also* atmosphere, hydrosphere.

A little child shall lead them: This is, of course, a biblical quotation (Isaiah xi.6), but it has been applied to the amphibious assault on Gibraltar in 1704 when nineteen hundred British and four hundred Dutch marines landed on the isthmus connecting the "Rock" with mainland Spain. Well-ensconced Spanish troops bravely repulsed repeated frontal attacks until a young girl told Colonel Edward Fox about a steep but unguarded pathway. Led by the child, the marines clambered up to outflank the defenders and take them by surprise.

Littoral: [1] In general, pertaining to the shore of a lake, sea, or ocean. [2] In terms of battlespace control, the littoral comprises two segments (a) Seaward, the area from the open ocean to the coast, which must

be controlled to support operations on shore, and (b) Landward, the area beyond the coast that can be supported and defended from the sea.

Littoral Combat Ship (LCS): A frigate-type vessel intended for inshore operations in support of intelligence, reconnaissance, anti-terrorism, interception, and special forces missions. In these roles it sacrifices air defense and surface-to-surface capabilities in favor of speed and shallow draft. However, it can be rapidly reconfigured for other roles such as antisubmarine warfare, mine countermeasures, and surface warfare by changing "mission modules" that can be moved on or off the ship in standard shipping containers. The LCS can carry a number of unmanned surface vessels.

Littoral warfare: Combat operations launched from the sea across a shoreline and as far inland as can be attacked, supported, and defended by seaborne assets.

Lively!: Command to [1] do something rapidly, or [2] move quickly.

Lizard: [1] Any short length of rope used for a specific purpose. [2] An iron thimble spliced into a main bowline with one end formed into a hook to take a tackle. [3] The line hung from a lower yard or boom for small boats to make fast to when mooring.

LKA: Hull classification symbol of an attack (amphibious assault) cargo ship.

Lloyd's List: A daily newspaper published by Lloyd's of London and devoted to shipping news.

Lloyd's medals: The decision to award a medal for Saving Life (at Sea) was made by the Lloyd's of London Committee in 1836, and the first award was made in 1837. It was joined by a medal for Meritorious Services in 1893, another for Services to Lloyd's in 1913, and one for Bravery at Sea in 1940. Issued in gold, silver and bronze versions, they have become highly valued and prestigious.

Lloyd's of London: In the late 17th century, Edward Lloyd's coffee house became a convenient meeting place for a society or association of English marine insurance underwriters (known as "names") who met to auction captured vessels and prize goods. Soon merchants with voyages to insure would engage a broker to go from name to name until their risk was fully covered. They relied on the broker to ensure that policies were placed only with underwriters who had sufficient financial integrity to meet their commitments.

In an age when communications were unreliable, Lloyd's gradually became a center for maritime intelligence, information on seagoing vessels, and shipping news generally. Moreover, with half of the entire world's shipping British-flagged, the society became the hub of the international marine insurance market. In 1871 an Act of Parliament gave Lloyd's a formal legal foundation as a business institution with the full weight of the (then super-powerful) British government behind it.

Today insurance continues to be underwritten by individual "names," but all manner of non-marine risks are covered, including such things as cyber-liability and kidnap-and-ransom. A major activity is known as "reinsurance." If an underwriter has unwisely or inadvertently offered coverage beyond the amount he or she would be able to discharge, they can shift part or all of the risk by obtaining reinsurance from others.

Lloyd's Register: In the second half of the 18th century, marine surveyors, based at Lloyd's coffee house in London, developed a system for the independent inspection of ships presented for insurance cover. Produced independently of the underwriters in Lloyds of London, Lloyd's Register is an annual publication listing the specifications of all British-flagged and many other merchantmen, with details of their ages, tonnage, construction, and seaworthiness including ground tackle (anchors, cables, etc.). The condition of the hull was classified A, E, I, O or U, according to the excellence of its construction and its adjudged continuing soundness (or otherwise). Equipment was rated G, M, or B (Good, Middling or Bad) later replaced by 1, 2 and 3, which is the origin of the well-known expression "A1," meaning "first or highest class." *See also* ship classification, and ship classification societies.

LNG: Liquefied Natural Gas.

LNG carrier: A vessel specifically designed for the transport of liquefied natural gas in specialized containment systems resembling huge Thermos bottles. Under atmospheric pressure, natural gas liquefies at –163°C, shrinking to $\frac{1}{600}$ of its original volume. While in transit this temperature is maintained by allowing small quantities of gas to boil off so that the remainder of the cargo is kept cool by the latent heat of evaporation.

LOA: Length overall (i.e., the distance between the forwardmost and aftermost points on the hull of a vessel).

Load: [1] To stow cargo or supplies in a ship, aircraft, or vehicle. [2] The cargo carried or to be carried at one time or in one trip. [3] the amount that can be or is usually carried. [4] the weight or stress that a line or structure can bear. [5] The charge for a firearm. [6] To put ammunition into a weapon.

Load factor: The ratio of possible cargo or passengers to the quantity actually carried, expressed as a percentage. For example, a 10,000-ton capacity merchantman laden with 6,000 tons of cargo, or a 2500-passenger cruise ship with 1500 on board, has a 60 percent load factor.

Load lines: The sides of ships have long carried marks to show how low they may safely rest in the water. As early as the twelfth century, Venetian ships were marked with a cross whose intersection represented the safe water level, while Genoese vessels carried three horizontal bars to indicate the appropriate load level under different conditions. However, these

useful customs died out, and it was not until the 19th century that the use of load lines became widespread (*see* plimsoll mark and overloading).

Load on top: After a tanker's cargo tanks have been steam-washed, residual oil separates to float on the condensed steam which is then drained into the sea. New oil is then loaded on top of the water-free residual oil.

Loader: The member of a gun crew responsible for putting powder, wad, and shot into the barrel of a muzzle loader cannon, ramming home the shot, and helping to run out and train the gun.

Loblolly: Eighteenth century mariner's term for food that had to be eaten with a spoon, such as gruel or porridge.

Loblolly Boy: Obsolete term for an assistant to a naval surgeon. Principal duties were to care for and feed the sick and injured, and the name derives from the porridge the "boys" served to patients. In combat they provided braziers to heat cauterizing irons, pots of hot tar for sealing wounds, and containers for severed limbs. They also helped to hold down patients during amputations. The current U.S. Navy title is Hospital Corpsman, while the Royal Navy rating is Medical Assistant.

Lobscouse: A seaman's dish from the age of sail, consisting of salt meat mixed with broken ship's biscuit, onions, beans or potatoes, and any available spices.

Lobster: Formerly, sailor's derogatory slang for a red-coated British soldier.

Lock: [1] A section of waterway enclosed by gates at each end, within which ships can be raised or lowered by pumping water in or out. [2] A mechanism used to ignite the charge of a firearm (*see* flintlock).

Lock-on: To acquire and track a target with radar, sonar, or the like.

Locker: [1] A chest or compartment for clothes, stores, ammunition, etc. [2] Any place of safekeeping. [3] The lair to which Davy Jones takes drowned seafarers, hence the bottom of the sea.

LOD: Line of departure.

Lode: A water course or way; a reach of water. Variation of lead.

Lodestar: Sailor's name for Polaris, the North Star.

Lodestone: A magnetized natural mineral used as an early form of compass.

Lodgement: [1] In general military use, an enclave made by increasing the size of a bridgehead, beachhead, or airhead. [2] Specifically, in amphibious operations, the area created by consolidation of two or more beachheads as a base for future advances inland.

Lodia: A large White Sea trading vessel.

Loft: [1] A sail loft is a large room or space where canvas is spread out, to be cut and assembled by sailmakers. [2] A rigging loft is a raised area or gallery in a shipyard on which riggers stand to step masts and install rigging. [3] A mold loft is a very large space or building with a smooth floor on which naval architects lay out the lines of a vessel and mold makers prepare full-scale templates of hull shape and structure. [4] A parachute loft is an area in which aviators' parachutes are inspected, repaired, and repacked.

Lofting: *See* mold lofting.

Log: [1] A device for measuring the speed of a vessel, *see* logline. [2] To make a written record of events. [3] The book in which such records are maintained.

Log canoe: [1] A dugout canoe. [2] *See* Chesapeake log canoe.

Logbook: Early ships' records were written on shingles (cut from logs) which were hinged together to open like a book. The name survives for modern paper records.

Log-chip: The name for the wooden block used with a logline. Also log ship.

Loggerhead: [1] In the 15th and 16th centuries, a loggerhead was a big long-handled ladle used for scalding a grappled enemy by pouring hot oil, tar, or water from caldrons set up on deck and heated to boiling point in sand-filled brick pits. [2] Later, the name was applied to a caulking tool consisting of a long iron rod with a ball at the end. The latter was heated until red and then plunged into pitch to soften it. [3] An alternate name for bar shot. [4] A wooden fixture at the stem of a rowing whaleboat around which the harpoon line was controlled. [5] An endangered species of sea turtle. (*See also* at loggerheads.)

Logistical support: Known to the United States armed forces as combat service support, logistical support refers to the provision of supply, maintenance, transportation, medical, and other services required by combat units to continue their missions.

Logistics: [1] The organization and methods of moving, lodging, and supplying troops and materiél. [2] The detailed organization and implementation of a plan or operation.

Logistics Branch: Founded in 2004, this branch of the Royal Navy has a long history under other names. These and its current responsibilities are outlined under logistics officer. The USN equivalent is the supply corps.

Logistics Officer: This Royal Navy title, established in 2004, is the final metamorphosis of a job which may have begun as early as the 14th century and has been variously titled captain's clerk, bursar, purser, paymaster, and supply officer. A logistics officer's responsibilities involve ensuring that her/his ship has all the personnel and equipment needed for operational efficiency, and providing essential services through the ship's chefs, caterers, stores accountants, stewards, and writers. He or she may also be required to advise the commanding officer on personnel matters and questions of probity and propriety. Like all non-combatant naval personnel, the logistics officer has a battle station, usually related to damage control or first aid.

Logline: The sailing ship mariner's speedometer consisting of a block of wood (called log-chip or log-

ship) shaped like a quarter-circle with a lead weight on its circular "stern" and a long light line, wound on a reel, made fast to its pointed "bow" by a triangular towing bridle secured with a wooden peg. When the chip was thrown overboard to drag in the water behind the vessel, the lead weight held it upright and caused the line to unreel as the ship moved along. The logline was knotted at regular intervals of 14.4 meters (47' 3"), with one knot after the first interval, two after the second, and so on. After 28 seconds, timed by a special log-glass (sometimes misnamed "half-minute glass"), the number of knots run out was noted. After the reading had been taken, a twitch on a "stray-line" pulled out the peg, releasing the bridle to make reeling-in easier. Twenty-eight seconds are to one hour what 14.4 meters are to a nautical mile, so the knots run out represented speed in nautical miles per hour. There was also a 14 second glass, for a ship going fast — above about ten knots. The routine was the same, but the number of knots read off was doubled to give the speed. This obviated letting out too much logline, with the attendant time penalty for reeling it in. (*See also* knots per hour.)

Loll: To wallow uneasily as when a vessel is top-heavy or waterlogged.

LO/LO: lift-on/lift-off (*see* heavy loads and vehicles).

London Naval Treaties: *See* Washington Naval Agreement.

Long glass: Venerable mariner's name for a telescope. Originally used to identify ships or read signals, but now more frequently carried as a traditional symbol of office by officers of the day or deck when in port. Traditionally a flag officer carries his under the right arm with the eyepiece facing forward; other officers under the left arm with the eyepiece facing aft.

The long glass still plays an important role during the formal commissioning of a United States naval vessel. As soon as the commanding officer announces he has assumed command, he directs the executive officer to set the watch. The XO responds "Aye-aye sir (or ma'am)," salutes, and turns to the prospective officer of the deck, handing him the long glass symbolic of his office and saying "Set the watch, navigator." After the boatswain's mates have piped, and duty stations have been manned, the OOD makes his first entry in the log and the XO salutes and reports "Captain, the watch has been set." The sponsor of the vessel then orders, "Man our ship and bring her to life," and the crew files aboard to the tune of Anchors Aweigh.

Long leave: Permission to be absent for an extended period.

Long seas: Waves with widely-separated crests.

Long shot: This colloquialism for an endeavor which has little chance of success has been claimed as a naval expression designating a distant target which would be difficult to hit with smoothbore cannon. More probably it originated long before gunpowder weapons, as an archery term with the same meaning.

Long splice: [1] A join connecting two pieces of same-size cordage in such a way that the diameter of the splice is no larger than the original cordage enabling it to pass through a block or thimble (a short splice is faster to make, but thicker). [2] Sailor's slang for marriage.

Long Tom: Slang term for a long-barreled cannon often used as a chase-gun, especially by pirates.

Longboat: The largest pulling boat carried by a merchantman, often weighing several tons. The term is not used in the navy (*see* launch).

Longitude: The angular distance east or west of the standard meridian at Greenwich (cf. latitude).

Longitudinal: [1] Extending in the lengthwise direction, as distinguished from transverse. [2] Said of any fore-and-aft structural member, such as a frame or bulkhead.

Longitudinal stability: The tendency of a vessel to return to its original longitudinal position after being displaced.

Longitudinal waves: *See* wave motion.

Long-legged: Said of a vessel which is [1] speedy, or [2] has a extended unrefueled radius.

Longliner: A commercial fishing vessel employing the longlining technique.

Longlining: Fishing by towing a heavy main line with lighter branch lines carrying baited hooks attached to it. There are two main types. Surface lines can be extremely long and are supported by floats at periodic intervals. Bottom lines are much shorter, anchored at one end and weighted at the other. Longline fishing results in high quality catch, because the fish are not crushed together as they are in net fishing. On the other hand, it tends to produce high mortality among sharks and seabirds.

Longship: The basic Norse warship of the eleventh century. Undecked, double-ended, oared and with a single square-sail.

Longshore: Abbreviation of alongshore.

Longshore current: A water flow parallel to the shoreline and within the surf zone (cf. coastal current).

Longshoreman: A dockyard worker (mainly U.S.). Cf. stevedore, lumper.

Look alive!: Command to be alert and move quickly.

Lookout: A person stationed to maintain a visual watch and report specified events, or sightings such as hazards on the ship's track or strange vessels heaving into sight.

Loom: [1] The shaft of an oar between blade and handle. [2] The reflection or glow of a light which is below or at the horizon. [3] To appear from below the horizon as an indistinct and enlarged "mirage."

Loop: A line, rope, cord, thread, etc. that has curved and doubled over itself leaving a circular opening.

Loophole: An opening in the side of a ship (or wall of a building) through light weapons can be fired.

Loose: To release a rope, or unfurl or cast off a sail.

Loose cannon: In common speech this refers to someone, especially a politician, who is unpredictable, uncontrollable, and likely to speak or act without considering either consequences or the "party line." The origin is obvious — two or more tons of wood and metal trundling up and down the rolling gundeck of a sailing man-of-war was not only a terrible hazard to life and limb, but could seriously damage other guns, or even crash through the side to plunge into the sea.

LORAD: **Lo**ng-**R**ange **A**ctive **D**etection. A sonar system.

LORAN: **Lo**ng-**R**ange **A**id to **N**avigation. A former electronic system which determined hyperbolic lines of position by measuring the difference in time of reception of synchronized pulses from two fixed transmitters. It has effectively been replaced by Global Positioning.

Lorcha: A speedy, armed Chinese sailing vessel, featuring oriental rigging on a western-style hull.

Lord High Admiral: The office of Lord Admiral of England was effectively created early in the 15th century when Thomas Beaufort, Duke of Exeter, was appointed Admiral of the Northern and Western Seas (previously separate) for life. A Lord High Admiral of Scotland was created at about the same time and appears to have initially been an hereditary office for the Dukes of Bothwell. By the Act of Union of 1707 the two offices were combined as Lord High Admiral of Great Britain. Today the office is held by the reigning monarch. *See also* Board of Admiralty.

LO/RO: Lift-on/roll-off (*see* heavy loads and vehicles).

LOS: Line of Sight.

Lost!: Whaler's cry when the quarry sounds (dives) or swims too rapidly to be chased.

Lost day: The 24 hours which "disappear" when crossing the International Date Line in a westerly direction.

Low and aloft: Sailor's term for a vessel carrying all possible sail on both lower and upper masts.

Low latitudes: Those less than 10° north or south of the equator.

Low water mark: The lowest level reached by a falling tide.

Lower-deck: The non-commissioned members of a RN ship's company.

Lower-mast: The lowest of several spars joined to make a tall mast.

Loxodrome: *See* rhumb line.

LPA: Hull classification symbol of an amphibious assault transport.

LPD: Hull classification symbol of an amphibious assault dock. Equipped with helicopters, landing craft, and amphibious vehicles for landing troops.

LPG: Liquefied Petroleum Gas.

LPH: Hull classification symbol of an amphibious helicopter landing platform.

LPSS: Former hull classification symbol of an amphibious assault submarine.

L's of navigation: Traditionally, these were "Lead, Log, Latitude, and Lookout"—the four items considered essential for non-astronomical calculation of course and position.

LS: Leading Seaman (RN).

LSD: Hull classification symbol of a landing ship, dock.

LSH: Hull classification symbol of a landing ship, heavy.

LSI: Hull classification symbol of a landing ship, infantry.

LSL: Hull classification symbol of a landing ship, logistics.

LSM: Hull classification symbol of a landing ship, medium.

LSMR: Hull classification symbol of a landing ship, medium, rocket. An amphibious assault vessel used for shore bombardment using 5-inch rockets.

LSO: Landing Signal Officer (USN).

LST: Officially the hull classification symbol of a landing ship, tank, but their crews insisted the acronym stood for "Large Slow Target."

LSV: Hull classification symbol of a landing ship, vehicle.

Lubber: An incompetent or clumsy seaman.

Lubberland: A mythical place where there is no work to be done and the pursuit of pleasure is everything.

Lubber's hole: An easy means of reaching the platform at the head of the lower masts of a square-rigged ship. It was considered cowardly and unseamanlike to go through it rather than climb around on the futtock shrouds.

Lubber's line: A reference mark in the bowl of a compass, showing the forward direction parallel to the keel and used to steer the ship.

Lucky bag: USN term for the place where lost items can be reclaimed (cf. Scran bag)

Luff: [1] The leading edge of a fore-and-aft sail (usually the shorter side of a lugsail and the angled side of a triangular sail). [2] To bring a sailboat into the wind until the luff begins to tremble.

Luff up: To head into the wind in order to slow or stop a sailing vessel.

Lugger: A small ship carrying two or three masts with lugsails. Used for coastal trade, privateering, and smuggling around England and France.

Lugsail: A quadrilateral fore-and-aft sail tied to and hoisted from a yard, usually suspended about one-third of the way along its length.

Lumper: Obsolete term for a dockyard worker, stevedore or longshoreman. So-called because paid a lump sum when the job was done, rather than an hourly wage.

Lunar day: [1] The elapsed time between two consecutive returns of the moon to the same terrestrial meridian. [2] The tidal day.

Lurch: A sudden long roll in a seaway. *See also* left in the lurch.

***Lutine* Bell:** The French frigate *La Lutine* (*The Sprite*) was captured by the British at Toulon in 1793. Six years later, renamed HMS *Lutine* and carrying a large quantity of gold and silver bullion, she sank in a gale off the Dutch coast, with the loss of all hands except one, who died after being rescued. Lloyd's underwriters, who had insured the ship and its cargo, paid the £1-million claim in full and instituted salvage operations, but it was almost sixty years before some of the bullion was recovered, along with the ship's wooden rudder and its bronze bell.

The former was made into a desk and chair for Lloyd's chairman, while the 106-pound bell (engraved "*St Jean* 1799," so it must have been transferred to *Lutine* from another ship) was hung in Lloyd's underwriting room, where it became the custom to ring it twice whenever a ship was reported overdue. This ensured that all underwriters became aware of the situation simultaneously, and gave them the opportunity of reinsuring with specialist brokers against the event of total loss. If such a loss occurred the bell was only tolled once. That practice has ended, but the bell is still rung on ceremonial occasions and to record special events, including the deaths of President John F. Kennedy in 1963 and Sir Winston Churchill in 1965, and the attack on New York's World Trade Center on 9/11/2001.

LWL: Length along waterline.

LWM: Low water mark.

Lying: Whaler's term for a whale basking on the surface to form an easy target.

Lying to: Said of a vessel which is hove to and stationary.

Lyle Gun: A short-barreled cannon used to throw a line to a boat or person in distress. Invented by David Lyle, a graduate of West Point and MIT, and used from the mid–19th century until replaced by rockets in the 1950s. *See also* Coston Gun.

M

MAA: Master at Arms.

Maash: A large Nilotic trading vessel (*see* Egyptian naval architecture).

MAC ships: Precursors of the escort carrier (MAC stands for merchant aircraft carrier). Six bulkers and thirteen tankers were equipped with flight decks and miniature islands, but no catapult or other aircraft support facilities. The tanker conversions carried three Royal Navy torpedo bombers on deck, the grain ships carried four in a small hangar. They operated with their normal civilian crews, under merchant colors, and carried their regular cargo. In addition to aircrew, the naval party included an Air Staff Officer (Lt-Commander), a surgeon, a landing control officer (batsman), about a dozen gunners, several signalmen, and a few Able Seamen. The naval aircraft carried out antisubmarine patrols, and no convoy with an accompanying MAC ship ever lost a vessel to U-boats.

Machinery control room: [1] In merchant and some older naval ships, the MCR is an elevated space with a grand view over the engine room, providing a platform from which engineering watchkeepers can monitor the machinery and change some engine settings. [2] In modern warships, it is the central area from which engineer officers and technicians control and monitor propulsion, power generation, and auxiliary systems. Engine orders from the bridge are executed in the MCR which also doubles as damage control headquarters, locating and coordinating action against fire, flood and battle damage.

Machinery spaces: Term referring to the engine room, and where applicable furnace room, gearing room, and auxiliary machinery spaces.

Mad: Said of a compass needle whose polarity has been impaired.

Made: In the sailing ship navy, a midshipman was said to be "made" once he had passed the lieutenant's examination. Similarly, a lieutenant was "made" when he won a command. Primary use of the term, however, was when an officer was "made post" and reached the rank of Captain.

Made good: A navigational term referring to distance traveled in the desired direction, ignoring deviations.

Made mast: A wooden mast fabricated from several sections.

Mae West: An inflatable life vest. Named after a full-bosomed 1930s film star. *See* personal floatation devices.

Maelstrom: An exceptionally dangerous whirlpool. Sometimes claimed to be a corruption of Mosktraumen (one of the world's most powerful sea-whirlpools, off the Lofoten Islands) but more probably from Old Dutch maal = swirling + stroom = stream.

MAF: Marine Amphibious Force.

Magazine: [1] A compartment aboard ship, or building ashore, for the storage of ammunition and explosives. [2] A replaceable receptacle for the cartridges of an automatic firearm.

Magazine dress: Spark-proof clothing to be worn in a powder magazine, made chiefly of worsted woolen material, without buttons or anything metallic, worn with cotton canvas slippers.

Magged: Somewhat obsolete term for worn, fretted, and stretched, said of a brace for example.

Magnet chamber: That part of a compass, below the card, which contains magnets to compensate for the vessel's magnetic field.

Magnetic airborne detector: A device carried by low-flying aircraft, that locates a submerged submarine by sensing it's magnetic field.

Magnetic anomaly: A natural and localized variation in the earth's magnetic field due to forces within its crust.

Magnetic compass: A compass using a magnetic needle or card which points in the direction of the north magnetic pole. The "flux-gate" version enhances its features by employing small coils of wire wound around a magnetic core to directly sense the horizontal component of the earth's magnetic field, providing readings in electronic form that can be digitized and used by an autopilot for course correction. Readout may also be analogue.

The principle of magnetism was known in China as early as the third century BCE, and the compass itself was probably invented there during the ninth century of the current era. Its use for navigation is first mentioned by Zhu Yu in 1119; "The navigator knows the geography, he watches the stars at night, watches the sun at day (but) when it is dark and cloudy, he watches the compass." Seventy years later, the compass had appeared in Europe but it is unclear whether it was transferred from China or invented independently. The latter is likely because European instruments used a different number of compass points, and the needle indicated north, whereas the Chinese version pointed south. In an unusual reverse direction of technology transfer, Arabs — who call the instrument al-konbas — seem to have adopted the European design.

Magnetic course: A course based on magnetic compass readings (cf. true course).

Magnetic declination: The angular difference between true north and magnetic north at any given location. This is an earth scientist's term, the preferred maritime usage being magnetic variation, or frequently just plain variation.

Magnetic deviation: The error in a ship's compass due to its own magnetic field.

Magnetic field: Lines of magnetic force that surround a metal object such as a ship's hull. They can be neutralized by degaussing.

Magnetic islands: In *Geographia*, written in the second century of the current era, the great Egyptian geographer Ptolemy reported that ten of the islands in the Maniolae group near India contained large quantities of lodestone (magnetic iron oxide, or magnetite). He claimed that iron-bearing ships which entered their magnetic field would be inexorably attracted towards them, overcoming efforts to sail away. Finally, when they had been drawn close enough, all their iron nails would be pulled out, dumping the luckless crew into the water and leaving them clinging to pieces of frame and planking. (Lodestone mountains do exist, but their fields are far too weak to have any such effect.)

Magnetic mine: A mine designed to be detonated by the magnetic field of a passing vessel. Such weapons tend to disable vessels by buckling plates rather than punching holes in them.

Magnetic north: North indicated by a magnetic

compass, as opposed to true north. Also compass north.

Magnetic poles: The ends of a dipole forming the earth's magnetic field. A line joining the north and south magnetic poles would be inclined approximately 11.3° away from the planet's axis of rotation, whereas a line between geographic poles would coincide with that axis.

Magnetic signature: The distinctive magnetic field of an individual vessel. This must be determined before the vessel can be degaussed.

Magnetic storm: Abnormal solar activity producing streams of radiation which temporarily disrupt the earth's magnetic field and interfere with wireless communication and magnetic devices such as a compass.

Magnetic variation: *See* magnetic declination and variation.

Magnetohydrodynamic drive: *See* MHD propulsion.

Magnetosphere: The extension of the earth's magnetic field into outer space.

Magnus effect: During the 1850s, German scientist Heinrich Gustav Magnus developed a theory to explain anomalies in the curved trajectory of cannonballs. (Similar phenomena are seen in baseball, tennis, cricket, and other ball sports; including golf, where "dimples" on the ball extend the distance of flight.) The commonly-accepted explanation is that the spinning object creates a "whirlpool" in the surrounding air. On one side, rotation complements the windstream, enhancing its velocity. On the opposite side, the motions are opposed and velocity is decreased. Consequently, there is an unbalanced force, creating "pull" at right angles to the wind. (Recent studies show that this explanation is not entirely valid; rather that the Magnus force is due to asymmetric distortion of the boundary layer by the combination of spin and flow.) Magnus effect is fundamental to the operation of Flettner rotators.

Magnus-hitch: A round turn taken around a spar and then jammed by a half-hitch around the spar on the opposite side to the standing part.

Maiden voyage: The first outing made by new vessel.

Mail boat: [1] Any vessel carrying mail on any route. [2] One under post office contract to carry mail on a specific route and schedule.

Mail buoy watch: *See* Hazing.

Main: [1] A prefix indicating a principal component (e.g., mainbrace). [2] Of or pertaining to the mainmast. [3] The Spanish Main. [4] Incorrectly, the sea bounded by the Spanish Main(land). [5] As a literary term, the oceans or high seas ("...the fretful elements ... swell the curled waters 'bove the main." King Lear iii.i.4).

Main deck: [1] The uppermost weatherproof deck extending the full length of the ship from bow to stern. [2] A ship's principal deck.

Main truck: The top of the mainmast, rigged with blocks and halyards for signals. The site for mounting a lightning conductor.

Mainboom: The spar that stretches the foot of the mainsail in a fore-and-aft rigged vessel.

Mainbrace: A purchase attached to the mainyard for trimming it to the wind. *See also* brace.

Maincourse: The lowest square-sail on the mainmast.

Mainmast: [1] The mast of a single-masted vessel. [2] The heavy forward mast of a yawl, ketch, or dandy. [3] The second mast from forward in any other vessel carrying two or more masts.

Mainsail: *See* main-course.

Mainshaft: The principal drive shaft in a ship's propulsion system.

Mainstay: [1] The biggest stay supporting the mast of a square-rigged ship, being up to 20 inches (50 cms) in diameter. [2] Something which is greatly relied upon.

Maintenance carrier: A vessel designed to maintain and repair aircraft. The layout usually includes conventional aircraft carrier features such as flight deck and hangars, with the former supplemented by cranes for hoisting damaged aircraft, and the latter containing extensive workshops and spare parts storage.

Mainyard: The lowest yard on the mainmast, from which the mainsail was hung.

Mainyard man: [1] A topman assigned to work on the mainyard. [2] Obsolete slang term for a seaman on the binnacle list.

Major warship: The Washington Naval Agreement and London Naval Treaties define major surface warships as being battleships, aircraft carriers, cruisers, and destroyers. However, the 1936 Treaty makes an exception for smaller craft that meet criteria defined in Part I, Article 1, Section B(5):

> Minor war vessels are surface vessels of war ... the standard displacement of which exceeds 100 tons (102 metric tons) and does not exceed 2,000 tons (2,032 metric tons), provided they have none of the following characteristics: (a) Mount a gun with a caliber exceeding 6.1 in. (155 mm.); (b) Are designed or fitted to launch torpedoes; (c) Are designed for a speed greater than twenty knots.

After the October 1973 Battle of Latakia, fought entirely with cruise missiles on both sides, it is clear that these weapons also make small warships "not minor."

Make!: The RN command to send a signal (the term "send" is never used).

Make and mend: Time off for a British ship's company to tailor or repair clothing (cf. rope yarn Sunday).

Make bad weather: Said of a vessel experiencing undue pitching, rolling, or leakage during a storm.

Make colors!: USN command to hoist the national flag.

Make fast!: Command [1] To fix something securely ("make fast the rope"). [2] To fasten or tie up to an object ("make fast to the jetty").

Make it so!: Captain's traditional response confirming that the time (of sunrise, noon, or sunset) reported to him by the officer of the watch is to be official ship's time.

Make land(fall): To sight land from the sea.

Make number: Signal the four-letters of the number which identifies a warship.

Make ready: Be prepared to do something.

Make sail: [1] Set the sails. [2] Start a voyage.

Make sunset!: USN command to lower the national flag.

Make up: Said of waves which are increasing or building up.

Make water: To leak.

Make way: [1] To move through the water ("make sternway, headway, or leeway"). [2] Command or request to move aside for something or someone to pass.

Making iron: A grooved caulking tool, used to finish off a seam. Also meaking Iron.

Making off: Whaler's term for slicing flensed blubber into pieces small enough to pass through the bilge holes of storage butts.

Malacca Strait: Connecting the Indian and Pacific Oceans, the Malacca and Singapore straits form a choke point approximately 960 kilometers (600 miles) long, but only 2.8 kilometers (1.5 miles) wide at the Phillips Channel. Over 50,000 vessels pass through annually, carrying about one-quarter of the world's trade goods and half of the world's oil shipments, making it one of the most valuable and vulnerable international sea lanes in the world. Petty piracy has long been a problem in these congested waters, and if terrorists were to launch coordinated attacks, the shock to world commodities markets would be immense.

Malaccamax: The largest vessel capable of transiting the Malacca Strait, where length and width are not constraints, but a 25 meter long shallow section restricts draft to 11 fathoms (20 meters; 66.6 feet).

Mameluke: [1] In most Muslim countries, a slave. [2] In Egypt, a member of a military caste that evolved from a body of mounted soldiers (recruited from Balkan slaves converted to Mohammedanism) and ruled Egypt from 1250 until 1517. They remained powerful until dispersed by Mehemet Ali in 1811.

Mameluke Sword: The common name for a scimitar (pronounced simiter). The name probably comes from the Persian shamshir, and refers to almost any Middle Eastern sword with a curved blade sharpened on the convex side. It evolved from a Turko-Mongol weapon and — although not necessarily in the same line of descent — the cutlass, saber, and samurai sword are of similar design. Many armies and navies have adopted scimitar-like sidearms, including:

• **France**: When Napoleon landed in Egypt in 1798, he was impressed by the magnificence of the colorful Mameluke warriors, especially the elegance of their scimitars. After defeating them at the Battle of the Pyramids, the future emperor and many of his cavalry officers adopted the curved sword as their personal sidearm. Later it was taken up by naval officers:

• **Britain:** Throughout his career The Duke of Wellington carried a Mameluke sword that he adopted while serving in India. In the post Napoleonic period, he was instrumental in introducing the weapon to most Light Cavalry and Hussar, and some Heavy Cavalry regiments, and in 1831 made it the regulation sword for General officers. Between 1842 and 1857 the Mameluke sword was also worn by Royal Navy flag officers, being abolished at the end of the latter year:

• **United States:** A Mameluke sword is the personal sidearm of Marine Corps officers and NCOs. They could initially wear swords of any pattern, so long as the hilts were yellow-mounted, but in 1825 it was mandated that their sidearm should take the form of an Arab scimitar, reputedly modeled after one presented to Marine First Lieutenant Presley O'Bannon by the Bey of Tunis. The story behind this, which began some twenty years earlier, is recounted in Shores of Tripoli.

Man: [1] To provide sufficient personnel to crew a ship or to perform a task (e.g., man the guns). In this sense, the word does not indicate gender, but is derived from the Anglo-Saxon manu, meaning to work or service something. [2] Although ships are usually considered feminine, the word "man" is often applied to them, as in man-of-war, merchantman, Indiaman, etc.

Man-of-war: Generic term for a warship, especially of the age of sail. Also man-o'-war.

Man overboard maneuvers: These are methods of shiphandling to return to the position at which a casualty fell off the ship. Common ones (described under the more "politically-correct" person overboard) are the Anderson, Racetrack, Scharnow, and Williamson Turns.

Man-o'war sheepshank: A sheepshank with a hobbling knot in the middle. This configuration with the half-hitches formed close to the central knot is used in rope rescue, when it is called a Fireman's chair knot.

Man the rail: *See* man the ship.

Man the ship: By 1873, many steam ships no longer had masts and yards, so the salute of manning the yards was modified to manning the ship in which the off-watch ship's company falls in along the sides of the upper deck when entering harbor, or to honor a special occasion, an important visitor, or a passing dignitary. Also called manning the rail (mainly USN) and manning the side (mainly RN).

Man the side: [1] To attend the side [2] To man the ship.

Man the yards: A form of salute that involved topmen assembling on the yards, shoulder-to-shoulder between mast and yardarm, while the rest of the crew congregated on deck, hands grasping the rigging, to show that no guns were manned and no small arms were carried. This demonstration of friendly intent goes back at least to the navies of Henry VIII and Elizabeth I of England. *See also* manning the ship, manning the rail, and manning the side.

Manannan: This Celtic sea god is known as Manannan in Ireland, Manawyddan in Wales, and Manannan MacLir in Scotland. His principal domain is the Irish Sea, where the Isle of Man is named after him. His fast ship *Wave Sweeper* can take him wherever he wants to go without need of crew, but (like Poseidon) he sometimes drives a chariot across the surface of the water instead. He is a "shape-shifter" able to manifest himself in any form he chooses, but is seldom seen at all, because he uses the sea fog as a magic all-concealing cloak.

Manbound: Unable to sail due to lack of crew.

Maneuver/Manoeuvre: The planned and regulated movement or evolution of ships or troops.

Maneuverability: The capability of making rapid controlled changes of course.

Manger: A sunken underside in a chain locker, covered by a perforated grating which allows wet chain to drain into it.

Mangonel: An ancient artillery weapon in the form of an immense crossbow.

Manifest: A document listing the cargo carried by a commercial vessel, including the marking and numbers of each separate package, the names of shippers and consignees, the quantity of goods contained in each package, and an account of the freight corresponding with the bills of lading.

Manifold: A pipe or chamber with several fittings for interconnecting pumps, water pipes, fuel hoses and the like.

Manila rope: Is made from abaca plant fibers (originally shipped from the port of Manila, whence its name). It is impervious to salt water, flexible, durable, strong, stands up well to wear and weather, and is more pliable and buoyant than hemp. Manila rope is suitable for slings, hawsers, light running rigging, and gun-tackle falls.

Manrope: [1] A line used instead of a handrail (e.g., at a gangway or accommodation ladder. [2] A rope or ladder used for climbing the sides or masts of a vessel. [3] A foot-rope under a yard or boom.

Mantillis: A kind of shield anciently fixed above the deck as a cover for archers.

Manzera: A cattle-carrying boat of the Adriatic.

Maon: Formerly, a flat-bottomed Turkish vessel carrying heavy cargoes.

Map projection: A method used in cartography to portray the curved surface of the globe, or a portion of it, on a flat surface. Some distortions of conformality, distance, direction, scale, and area inevitably result. Hence a projection may deliberately maximize distortion of some of these properties in order to minimize errors in others, or it may attempt to achieve a balance that only moderately alters each of them. *See*

also grid navigation, inverse Mercator, Mercator projection, orthomorphic projection, and rhumb lines.

Marad: Maritime Administration, a U.S. government agency.

March music: In ancient times, beating drums set the time for galley oarsmen and marching columns; drums and trumpets were used for signaling; and all manner of instruments served as noise-makers to demoralize the foe. After the Crusades, Europeans replicated Islamic military bands that employed a range of wind, brass, and percussion instruments. Their music served to enhance military drill, since the beat of drums encourages troops to keep in step, while accompaniment by lively airs keeps their spirits up.

- **Marine Marches:** Sailors seldom have to march, so it was left to seagoing soldiers to introduce the first nautical marching music. For a long time, each unit of Britain's Royal Marines had its own unique march, but in the mid–1800s the "Soldiers' Chorus" from Gounod's Faust was unofficially adopted by the entire corps. In 1838, American poet-playwright Epes Sargent presented one of his poems to English composer Henry Russell who later said "I hummed an air or two, ran my fingers over the keys, then stopped, feeling baffled; suddenly an idea struck me and ... that bright little air rang out which is now so well known." Fifty years later, the Royal Marines ditched Gounod and made the "bright little air" its unofficial march, but it did not become official until 11th March 1927. The opening stanzas are:

> A life on the ocean wave,
> A home on the rolling deep,
> Where the scattered waters rave,
> And the winds their revels keep:

> Like an eagle caged I pine
> On this dull unchanging shore:
> Oh! Give me the flashing brine,
> The spray and the tempest's roar!

The United States Marine Corps acquired its first march (officially "Hymn") at about the same time. Reflecting achievements at the siege of Derna (1805) and the capture of Mexico City (1847), the colors of the Corps were emblazoned "From the Shores of Tripoli to the Halls of Montezuma." Some time in the 1850s, an anonymous Marine wrote the "Hymn," transposing the inscription for the sake of euphony:

> From the Halls of Montezuma
> To the Shores of Tripoli
> We fight our country's battles
> On the land as on the sea.

> First to fight for right and freedom
> And to keep our honor clean;
> We are proud to bear the title
> Of United States Marine.

Later, a melody from Jacques Offenbach's 1859 comic opera *Geneviève de Brabant* was adapted to fit the poem, and the march version was born. In

1942, the Commandant of the Marine Corps authorized a change in the fourth line to read "In air, on land, and sea."

The Corps adopted the motto Semper Fidelis (always faithful) in 1883. Six years later, John Philip Sousa, director of the USMC Band, used the phrase as the title of a second march for the Corps. Charles Burr wrote the following lyrics (which the author has trouble matching to the music):

"Semper fidelis" is a fabulous Latin motto
meaning that in centuries of Roman might
the soldier swore that he would fight
For Caesar, never questioning if he might return
or if the enemy when they attack could be driven
aback — and that's what it means.
"We're ever faithful" is the general gist
in countries that are Christian
Though it means almost the same we pledge
no longer to the name
Of Caesar, but to principles of the land
we know and love,
Bestowing the motto in war of our
readiest corps — the mighty Marines.

- **Naval Marches**: In 1759, the Royal Navy facilitated the amphibious captures of Canada, Guadeloupe, and Dominica; and was victorious in the naval battles of Lagos, Pondicherry, and Quiberon Bay, crippling French naval power almost beyond repair. Inspired by these events, famous English actor David Garrick collaborated with Royal Chapel composer William Boyce to produce a song glorifying the "wonderful year":

Come cheer up my lads! 'Tis to glory we steer
To add something more to this wonderful year
To honor we call you, not press you as slaves
For who are so free as the sons of the waves?

Heart of oak are our ships,
Heart of oak are our men;
We always are ready, steady, boys, steady!
We'll fight and we'll conquer again and again.

This was the Royal Navy's unauthorized march for centuries before being officially adopted on 11th March 1927 by Admiralty Fleet Order 626 (at the same time as the Royal Marine's march). When the Royal Navy advances in review order, it does so to the tune of Nancy Lee, of which two verses are:

Of all the wives ye'll ever know,
Yeo ho! Me lads, yeo ho!
There's none like Nancy Lee, I trow,
Yeo ho! Yeo ho! Yeo ho!

While I'm away she'll watch for me,
And whisper low when tempests blow,
For Jack upon the sea,
Yeo ho! Me lads, yeo ho!

The U.S. Navy march was written In 1906 by Lieutenant Charles Zimmerman, bandmaster at the Naval Academy, originally as a football song for the Class of 1907. Midshipman (later Captain) Alfred Miles wrote the lyric:

Stand Navy down the field, sails set to the sky.
We'll never change our course,
so Army you steer shy-y-y-y.
Roll up the score, Navy, Anchors Aweigh.
Sail Navy down the field and sink the Army,
sink the Army Grey.

Get underway, Navy, Decks cleared for the fray,
We'll hoist true Navy Blue So Army
down your Grey-y-y-y.
Full speed ahead, Navy; Army heave to,
Furl Black and Grey and Gold and hoist the Navy,
hoist the Navy Blue

This version was first sung publicly during the 1906 Army-Navy game (when the new song must have inspired the Midshipmen because they shut out the Cadets with a 10 to 0 victory). Since then there have been numerous attempts to make the lyric less football-oriented, the best-known having been written by saxophonist-composer George D. Lottman in or about 1926:

Stand, Navy, out to sea, Fight our battle cry;
We'll never change our course,
So vicious foe steer shy-y-y-y.
Roll out the TNT, Anchors aweigh. Sail on to victory
And sink their bones to Davy Jones, hooray!

Anchors Aweigh, my boys, Anchors Aweigh.
Farewell to college joys, we sail at
break of day-ay-ay-ay.
Through our last night on shore, drink to the foam,
Until we meet once more. Here's wishing you
a happy voyage home.

The music remains the widely-accepted, though still unofficial, United States Navy march. However, at time of writing (2008) there is a proposal to make it official by adding a protocol to Navy Regulations.

The U.S. Coast Guard march is named after its motto Semper Paratus (always ready). The music was composed in 1927 by Captain Francis Van Boskerck to match lyrics he had written five years earlier.

From Aztec Shore to Arctic Zone,
To Europe and Far East,
The Flag is carried by our ships
In times of war and peace;
And never have we struck it yet,
In spite of foemen's might,
Who cheered our crews and cheered again
For showing how to fight.

We're always ready for the call,
We place our trust in Thee.
Through surf and storm and howling gale,
High shall our purpose be,
"Semper Paratus" is our guide,
Our fame, our glory, too.
To fight to save or fight and die!
Aye! Coast Guard, we are for you.

- **Rogue's March:** This is played when a person is dishonorably discharged. An anonymous 19th century soldier wrote the following words to fit the tune:

Poor old soldier,
Poor old soldier,
Tarred and feathered and sent to Hell
Because he wouldn't soldier well

Marconi rigged: A sailing vessel with triangular (Bermuda) sails.

Mare clausum: [1] The Latin term for closed sea, used by Romans to refer to winter months when the fleet remained in port deeming the seas too dangerous. [2] Waters to which a nation with command of the sea denies entry by the ships of other nations. [3] Navigable waters under the sole jurisdiction of one nation. [4] Title of a 1631 pamphlet by John Seldon arguing that waters contiguous to a coastline should be under the dominion of that country. Issued in response to Grotius' "Mare liberum."

Mare liberum: [1] Waters open to navigation by the ships of all nations. (Latin = free sea.) [2] Title of a treatise by Hugo Grotius arguing that no nation had the right to claim any part of the open sea as it own.

Mare nostrum: Latin for "our sea," the Roman name for the Mediterranean. It was adopted by Benito Mussolini the Duce (leader) of Italy from 1922 through World War II, during which the Royal Navy proved the bombastic claim to be baseless.

MARG: Marine Amphibious Ready Group.

Marginal sea: [1] Sea area that extends three nautical miles from mean low water line; deemed to be under the jurisdiction of the coastal state. [2] The waters lying between a chain of islands and a continent (e.g., The Caribbean or South China Sea).

Marianas trench: An oceanic trough extending from southeast of Guam to northeast of the Marianas Islands in the Pacific Ocean. It includes the deepest place in the world (see Challenger Deep).

Marie Celeste: A decade after the *Mary Celeste* incident, in 1883, Arthur Conan Doyle, then a struggling writer who had not yet invented Sherlock Holmes, turned that minor maritime disaster into an enduring supernatural mystery with his short story, written under a pseudonym and entitled "J. Habakuk Jephson's Statement." The fictional vessel, which he called *Marie Celeste*, was taken over by mutineers, who murdered all on board and sailed the ship to Africa. Doyle's vivid account, written as if it were an eyewitness report, somehow became confused with that of the genuine *Mary Celeste*, and the story grew into an enduring maritime legend, at various times incorporating mysterious bloodstains, half-eaten meals, piracy, submarine attack, monsters from the deep, ravening sharks, alien abduction, and even disappearance through time travel.

Marigraph: A device that automatically registers the rise and fall of tides. Also mareograph.

Marina: A boat basin offering dockage and supplies for pleasure craft.

Marine: [1] Of or pertaining to the sea, maritime. [2] A synonym for "navy" (e.g., merchant navy = mer- cantile marine). [3] A soldier trained to serve on both land and at sea (see Marines).

Marine aviation: Officers of the United States Marine Corps began to train with naval aviators in 1912, and two years later established a separate section within the Navy Flying School. But in 1915 the Commandant authorized the creation of an independent "aviation company," making the United States the only seapower to have a dedicated marine air arm (other nations have marine airmen, but they fly as part of naval aviation). In accordance with the tradition "Every man a rifleman," enlisted aviation personnel are trained in infantry combat, and all officers are qualified platoon commanders. The Corps operates both rotary-wing and fixed-wing aircraft that provide transport capability as well as close air support to its ground forces. Officers of the Royal Marines fly with the Fleet Air Arm, but do not have a separate organization.

Marine Electronic Highway: This "Regional Demonstration Project" in the Straits of Malacca and Singapore is scheduled for completion by 2010. Based on electronic navigational charts and global positioning technology, the system will allow faster response to hijackings and incidents such as oil spills, and will help ships in transit to share information, lessening the dangers of collision or grounding. Captain Raja Malik Saripulazan, Director-General of the Marine Department of Peninsular Malaysia, says " maneuvering a VLCC in the Straits will no longer be a nightmare."

Marine Hospital Service of the United States: This service dates its establishment from July 16, 1798, when an act for the relief of disabled and sick seamen was passed by Congress. During the 19th century seven hospitals were built by the Marine Hospital Service (the only one still standing is in Louisville, Kentucky, built in 1845 and considered the best remaining antebellum hospital in the United States). A reorganization in 1870 converted the loose network of local hospitals into a centrally controlled Service, headquartered in Washington, DC. The name was changed in 1902 to Public Health and Marine Hospital Service, and in 1912 to Public Health Service. The latter has a uniformed division known as the Public Health Service Corps.

Marine insurance: A contract whereby one party, for a consideration or premium, undertakes to indemnify the other against certain risks or perils of the sea to which his ship, freight, and cargo, or some of them, may be exposed during a certain voyage or for a fixed period of time. The party who assumes the risk, or undertakes to indemnify, is called the assurer, insurer, or underwriter (the latter referring to the practice of signing at the bottom of the contract). The party protected by the contract is the assured or insured, and the money paid as the price of the indemnity is the premium. The written instrument evidencing the contract is called a policy of insurance. Marine insurance preceded onshore coverage. *See* Lloyd's of London.

Marine railway: A tracked inclined plane equipped with a rolling cradle for hauling ships out of the water.

Marine surveyor: A person qualified to inspect a ship or boat for the purpose of determining its current condition and seaworthiness — in particular if it is safe for use in the conditions for which it was designed — and what maintenance and repairs are required to maintain its integrity. Surveys typically cover the vessel's structure and machinery, and its navigational, safety, radio, and cargo-handling equipment, and may involve verifying compliance with international treaties concerning pollution, security, and safety. *See also* Lloyd's Register.

Mariner: An experienced "blue water" seaman of any rank or rate, but especially one who directs or assists in navigation.

Marines: Naval persons organized and equipped as soldiers and specializing in amphibious operations. According to sailors, the name "marine" is an acronym of Muscles Are Required, Intelligence Not Essential, but this jocular sentiment is refuted by naval personalities, such as Horatio Nelson who remarked "every fleet should have a perfect battalion of marines"; Admiral Lord St. Vincent who said, "without a large body of marines we shall be long, very long, before an efficient fleet can be sent to sea"; and David Dixon Porter (one of the first U.S. Navy officers to bear the rank of admiral) who declared: "If the marines are abolished, half the efficiency of the navy will be destroyed."

The practice is ancient. At least five centuries before the current era, fighting men were part of the regular complement of Phoenician, Persian, and Greek warships. Later, cohorts of troops, known as classiarii, served in the Roman navy. Today, most of the world's marines operate in their traditional roles of preserving discipline on board ship and projecting naval power inland when required. They generally consider themselves to be soldiers who go to sea rather than sailors who fight ashore (*see* naval infantry).

An exception is the United States Marine Corps which no longer provides detachments to serve in individual warships, but is a fully-integrated, rapid-response, combined-arms service, larger than the total armed forces of many a sovereign state, falling administratively under the Navy Department, but independent of the naval chain of command.

Maritime: Connected with, bordering on or pertaining to ships and the sea.

Maritime Administration: This agency of the United States Department of Transportation is tasked to promote the development and maintenance of an adequate and balanced merchant marine, to carry all domestic and a large part of foreign waterborne commerce in peacetime and be capable of serving as a naval and military auxiliary in time of war or national emergency. The Maritime Administration is also required to ensure the availability of adequate shipbuilding and repair facilities, efficient ports, effective intermodal sealift capacity, and reserve shipping for national emergencies.

Maritime & Coastguard Agency: This branch of the British government is responsible for maritime safety policy and the prevention of accidents or loss of life at sea or on the coast. This includes coordinating search and rescue operations, checking that ships conform to national and international safety rules, and preventing coastal pollution.

Maritime Industrial Development Area: A commercial zone with easy access to port facilities, where industries dependent on water transportation are encouraged to congregate.

Maritime law: Is a complete legal system, with three major components or sources — common legal principles (evolved over millennia of civil usage), national statutes, and international conventions. Collectively, these cover the laws of:
• Contract (charter parties)
• Sale (of ships)
• Service (towage)
• Lease (chartering)
• Carriage (affreightment)
• Agency (chandlery)
• Pledge (bottomry and respondentia)
• Hire and employment (masters and crews)
• Risk distribution (general average)
• Compensation (injury or illness)
• Indemnity (marine insurance)

Also known as Admiralty law, it includes such concepts as Constructive Presence, Force Majeure, Hot Pursuit, Innocent Passage, and Right of Visit, as well as defining Contiguous Zones, Exclusive Economic Zones, Territorial Seas, and the like. (*See also* Laws & Conventions of the sea, and United Nations Convention on Law of the Sea.)

Maritime lien: A feature of admiralty law that holds a vessel liable for the non-payment of obligations. This makes it very different from a land lien, since it does not reflect personal liability of the shipowner, or its captain or operator, but holds the vessel itself to be a legal entity with obligations that can be breached. Once issued, a maritime lien can only be foreclosed ("executed" in maritime parlance) by an admiralty court and cannot be modified by agreement between the parties. It follows the vessel wherever it goes and can be enforced by any country which obtains jurisdiction. Claims must be maritime by nature and only certain types apply, the most important (in descending order of precedence) being:
• Seamen's unpaid wages
• Salvage fees
• Tort, including collision and personal injury
• General average claims
• Preferred ship mortgages
• Necessaries, supplies, and repairs
• Towage, lighterage, wharfage, stevedoring, pilotage, and the like

- Cargo damage due to improper loading, storage, or custody
- Unpaid freight
- Breach of Charter Party
- Marine pollution.

Maritime power: A coastal nation possessing a substantial navy.

Maritime signals: *See* tables 8–10.

Mark: [1] One of the fathom indicators on a sounding line. [2] A navigational aid or marker which must be passed on a specific side. [3] A target. [4] An equipment identifier, always followed by a Roman numeral indicating the production version of the specified item, and possibly a modification number indicating the number of changes made to the original design (e.g., "Mark III/2 binoculars" identifies the third version which has been twice modified).

Mark!: A call given to indicate that a prescribed reading must be recorded at the specific time of the call.

Marker: General term covering all forms of navigational aids such as buoys, beacons, and the like.

Marker ship: The vessel providing a reference point and control for an amphibious operation.

Marks and deeps: The depth indicators on handheld leadline, each designated by bits of cloth or leather are called marks. The intermediate fathoms, estimated by the leadsman, are called deeps.

Marl: To wrap a small line around a larger one, securing each turn by a knot so that it remains in place if others are cut. Also marle.

***Marlborough* mystery:** On 13 January 1890, a few days out from Littleton (New Zealand), British ship *Marlborough* was greeted by a passing vessel but then disappeared. After she was posted at Lloyd's as "missing," an inquiry determined that cargo was properly stowed, and the ship was in good trim for her voyage to Scotland. The general opinion was she had been sunk by an iceberg off Cape Horn. Twenty-three years later, in 1913, the *Wellington Evening Post* reported that British ship *Johnson* had discovered an abandoned sailing ship near Cape Horn. After his return to Scotland, *Johnson*'s master told the *Glasgow Herald*...

Off the rocky coves near Punta Arenas ... we rounded a point into a deep cleft rock. Before us, a mile or more across the water, stood a vessel, with the barest shreds of canvas fluttering in the breeze. We signaled and hove to. No answer came. We searched the "stranger" with our glasses. Not a soul could we see; not a movement of any sort. Masts and yards were picked out in the green of decay. ... After an interval, our first mate, with a number of the crew, boarded her.... Below the wheel lay the skeleton of a man. Treading warily on the rotten decks, which cracked and broke in places as they walked, they encountered three skeletons in the hatchway. In the mess-room were the remains of ten bodies, and six others were found, one alone, possibly the captain, on the bridge. There was an uncanny stillness around, and a dank smell of mould, which made the flesh creep.... The first mate examined the still faint letters on the bow and after much trouble read "Marlborough, Glasgow."

In spite of extensive investigation, no explanation of the tragedy has ever emerged.

Marline: A light double-stranded, left-handed cord, sometimes tarred, used to join (seize) ropes or fasten (parcel) canvas to a rope. Pronounced "marlin."

Marlinespike: A straight-shafted pointed instrument used to separate strands of rope or wire for splicing. Also marlin-spike.

Maroon: [1] A firework used as a warning signal. [2] A fugitive black or Indian slave (abbreviation of the Spanish Cimarrónes). [3] *See* marooning.

Marooner: Synonym for a Caribbean pirate of the 17th–18th centuries.

Marooning: A punishment in which the accused was abandoned on an isolated shore or island from whence rescue or escape was unlikely. Usually given no supplies other than a musket and powder flask, a few shot, and a cask of water. A surprisingly large number survived to tell the tale of their privations.

Apart from Richard Lionheart's Ordinance (*see* tarring), marooning was practiced mainly by pirates and privateers, although occasional instances of naval and merchant use have been recorded, these often seeming to be based more on antipathy between the victim and his captain than on any specific offense. The term is believed to have originated when Sir Francis Drake came upon and rescued a group of Cimarrónes who had been abandoned by their Spanish masters at some remote place.

Marpol: *See* International Convention for the Prevention of Pollution from Ships.

Marriage customs: *See* Arch of Steel.

Marry: [1] To join two ends of rope (cf. splice). [2] When ship's boys were to be punished they were tied over (married to) a cannon known as the gunner's daughter. As a result the term came to mean being caned or beaten. *See also* kiss the gunner's daughter.

MARS: Marine Accident Reporting System.

Marsiliana: A square-sterned Venetian sailing merchantman. Named after a small town in Tuscany.

Martial law: A system of rules proclaimed when normal or civil law has broken down due to insurrection, mutiny, natural disaster, or the like. Once the proclamation has been made, military authorities assume the administration of justice and maintenance of law and order, usually with restrictions on normal civil rights. Not to be confused with Military Law which governs the conduct of members of the armed forces.

Martinet: This name for a strict disciplinarian is also the French name for a cat-o'-nine-tails. Both refer to the Marquis de Martinet, who was a first-class military engineer and tactician, but became so hated for his brutality that he was "accidentally" killed by friendly fire during the 1672 Siege of Duisberg.

Martingale: [1] Nautical: A stay running from the

dolphin striker to the bowsprit or jib-boom, serving to strengthen them against the force of the head **stays**. [2] Swordsmanship: A strap attached to the sword handle to prevent it from being dropped if disarmed. [3] Equestrian: A harness strap fastened from girth to noseband to restrain a horse from throwing its head back. The latter is probably the earliest usage, with the word coming, via the Spanish almártiga, from the Arabic for rein or harness.

Maru: A suffix to the name of virtually every Japanese merchant ship. The word refers to the completeness and perfection of a sphere or circle, and has connotations of good luck. Hence it is essentially a prayer to safeguard the round trip from origin to destination and return.

Mary Celeste: On 7th November 1872, a Canadian-built half-brig (brigantine), sailed from New York with a cargo of 1701 barrels of alcohol bound for Genoa in Italy. Her master Benjamin Briggs was an experienced mariner and a known teetaler; his mate Albert Richardson was fully qualified and licensed for command. Also on board were a crew of six, plus Briggs' wife Sarah, and his 2-year-old daughter Sophia. On 4th December British brigantine *Dei Gratia* overhauled *Mary Celeste* about halfway between the Azores and Portugal. Captain Morehouse was about to hail his friend Captain Briggs when he realized the other ship was unmanned and out of control. A painter was seen dangling over the stern.

He boarded the vessel, finding it relatively undamaged and well-stocked with food and water. The cargo was intact except for nine barrels of alcohol which had been stove in and the contents drained into the bilges. The longboat was missing, along with most of the ship's navigation instruments, and there was no sign of anyone on board.

A Court of Inquiry reached no definitive conclusion, but suggested that Briggs — possibly fearing alcohol leaking from the broken barrels might explode — might have abandoned ship, intending to trail astern in the longboat until it was safe to board again, but the painter snapped in a storm, casting them adrift to perish.

Mashoof: A shallow-draft raft-like boat used by the Marsh Arabs of Southern Iraq. Traditionally made of reeds, but nowadays often of wood.

Mask paint: *See* Gundeck stripes.

Mass stranding: Refers to events in which groups of distressed cetaceans (whales, dolphins, porpoises) swim ashore alive and apparently healthy, but usually end up dying on the beach. Such strandings occur regularly in various parts of the world but — unlike "die-off events" which usually have a well-defined cause, such as an epidemic or red tide — deliberate mass stranding is still very mysterious with no universally accepted explanation.

Among suggested possibilities are the creatures' reaction to illnesses; geomagnetic disturbances that upset their biological "travel clocks" disorienting navigational ability; trying to escape predation from other marine creatures; environmental effects such as El Nino, salinity and temperature changes; pollution from river runoff, man-made chemicals, oil spills, and litter; behavioral changes such as new feeding patterns; and human intervention such as fishing activity and sonar testing. (*See* beaked whales.)

Mast: [1] A long upright pole stepped on a ship's keel and rising above the hull to support sails or signal equipment. Taller ones are composed of two parts known as lower-mast and topmast, while extremely high ones will add a third spar called topgallant mast. [2] A non-judicial USN disciplinary proceeding at which the captain or other senior officer reviews charges and awards summary punishment. *See* captain's mast.

Mast step: The place where the butt or foot of a mast is secured, usually on the keel (cf. tabernacle).

Master: [1] One eminently skilled at something (e.g., master craftsman, master shipwright, master gunner, etc.). [2] The proper title of the officer commanding a merchantman (who is often called "captain" as a courtesy). The Master stands no regular watches, but oversees navigation of the vessel when under pilotage, in close waters, or during foul weather. He or she is officially the owner's representative rather than a member of the crew, and as such deals with port authorities, charterers, and the like. Being effectively the vessel's CEO, the Master is responsible for all its operations, including safety, cargo, records, etc., as well as navigation, catering, and engineering. [3] Formerly, the warrant officer responsible for a warship's navigation (*see also* Sailing Master and Master Mariner). The relationship between the ship's master and its captain was described by John Smith in 1627:

> The Captain's charge is to command all and tell the Maister to which port hee will go ... in a fight hee is to give direction to the managing thereof. The Maister is to see to the cunning (conning) of the shippe ... and his mates are to direct the course, command all the sailers, for stearing, trimming the sailes, and sailing the shippe.

Master and Commander: This Royal Navy rank was instituted in 1794, and was then equivalent to an army major. It was awarded only to officers appointed to command a vessel larger than a lieutenant's command, but smaller than a post-ship. In 1814 the title became "Commander" and equivalent to Lieutenant-Colonel.

Master-at-Arms: [1] During the 18th century this junior warrant or petty officer was often a former marine, responsible for training the crew in small arms combat, with subsidiary duty as a shipborne police constable. [2] In modern navies, the MAA is chief of the ship's police force, responsible for maintaining discipline and good order among the ship's company. *See also* law enforcement and naval police.

Master Chief Petty Officer: This is the highest enlisted rate in the USN and USCG. MCPOs carry a specialty rating and are normally assigned to major commands afloat as technical experts in their fields. A master chief who successfully completes additional leadership training qualifies as "Command Master Chief Petty Officer." This is not a higher rate but, instead of practicing a specialty, a CMCPO provides liaison between the Command and its enlisted personnel on issues of quality-of-life, discipline, training, and morale.

Still in the CMCPO rate, but unquestionably the most senior enlisted person in the USN is the "Master Chief Petty Officer of the Navy" (known as "Mickpon"). This unique appointment was created in 1967 to provide a channel for the enlisted force to provide direct input to the CNO and Deputy CNO/Personnel. Based at the Pentagon, the MCPON regularly travels around the fleet obtaining input from enlisted sailors and their families. Since 1988, the MCPON's spouse (if any) has been authorized to travel with her husband, representing the interests of the spouses of enlisted members.

Master Commandant: In 1806, this U.S. Navy rank was awarded to warrant or commissioned sailing masters appointed to the command of ships. It was equivalent to the British "Master and Commander" and, in 1837, it too was renamed "Commander."

Master Mariner: A person certificated to command a merchant vessel. This venerable title originated in the 11th or 12th century, when it referred to a skilled and experienced seaman, probably a former boatswain, qualified as competent to command an oceangoing merchantman. *See* master's ticket.

Master of the Fleet: The senior sailing master on board a flagship. He reported to the flag captain and had general responsibilities for the issuance of stores to the fleet and observing any deviations from rule by the sailing masters of other ships.

Master Seaman: This rank is unique to the Canadian Navy, and was created to accommodate the unified rank structure of the Canadian Armed Forces. It is equivalent to Master Corporal in the Army and Air Force. The rank insignia of a Master Seaman is two chevrons surmounted by a maple leaf. Sometimes referred to as "master killick."

Master's Mate: Originally a senior petty officer and later a junior warrant officer, a master's mate in the Royal Navy was an assistant to the sailing master and more or less his apprentice. By passing appropriate examinations, master's mates could become qualified to command prizes or tenders, and eventually become sailing masters themselves.

- During the Napoleonic Wars, midshipmen tired of the long wait for a lieutenancy began to take master's mates appointments for the greater pay and responsibility. Eventually, this became one of the accepted routes to commissioned rank.
- In 1824 the rating was split, with those who wanted to become sailing masters becoming Master's Assistants, and those who aspired to commissioned rank retaining the previous rating.

- In 1840, the rank of Mate was established as subordinate to Lieutenant, and twenty years later was renamed Sub-Lieutenant, which remains the most junior commissioned rank in the RN.
- In the USN, Master's Mate remained a warrant rank and promotion to commissioned rank was rare. During the Civil War the warranted rank was allowed to lapse and the title became simply "Mate," authorized to be rated from seamen who had served at least two years afloat. This was thus the highest enlisted rate, somewhat like a petty officer, but with status and pay similar to a warrant officer. No appointment was made after 1894 and the rate lapsed as its incumbents faded away.

Master's ticket: Today a master mariner has to be certificated as able to chart a course over open waters, and as being proficient with sextant, chronometer, and barometer. The certificate, which is often called a "Master's Ticket," is usually held by a ship's first mate or chief officer as well as its captain. *See* International Convention on Standards of Training, Certification, and Watch-keeping for Seafarers (STCW).

Masthead: The uppermost part of a mast to which standing rigging is attached.

Masthead light: One of a ship's mandatory navigation lights placed high over the fore-and-aft centerline of the vessel, but not necessarily at the top of a mast. It must shine a bright white light over an arc of the horizon from dead ahead to 22.5° abaft the beam on both sides of the vessel.

Masthead pendant: A Royal Navy vessel flies a pendant at the main truck, indicating it is a private warship (one that does not have a flag officer aboard) in commission. Red, white, and blue versions were officially authorized by the Navy Commissioners in March 1653 (*see* British ensigns), but are believed to have been introduced at least 20 years earlier. Today only the white is in use. The pendant is extremely long relative to its width, tapering to a square tip. The field is white, with a Saint George's Cross at the hoist. Like the U.S. commissioning pennant, it is worn at all times, except when it is replaced by the Royal Standard or a flag of rank.

Mastheading: An obsolete form of naval punishment for (mainly) midshipmen who were sent aloft to the crow's nest (not to the truck, despite the name) where they had to stay without food in all kinds of weather until relieved.

Masting sheers: A sheerlegs mounted ashore or on a hulk, used as a crane to hoist a mast or heavy spar and lower it into place on a ship.

Mat: A fender woven from old rope or yarns (cf. collision mat).

Match: *See* slow match, quick match, gun firing, linstock, and portfire.

Match tub: A container with a perforated cover for holding the slow matches formerly used to fire cannon. Water in the bottom of the tub extinguished sparks falling from the matches. *See also* gun firing.

Matchlock: This was the first mechanism for igniting the charge of a hand-held firearm. By automatically lowering a lighted match into the flash pan, it allowed the firer to grip the weapon with both hands and keep both eyes on the target. The device originated in China early in the 14th century and spread westward. By mid–15th century it had reached Europe via Ottoman Turkey. Then, during the 16th century, Portuguese mariners introduced it to India and Japan. It was progressively replaced by wheellock, snaphance, and flintlock.

Mate: Derived from the Dutch Mateloot = companion (and sometimes replaced by "Officer"), this title refers to: [1] An assistant (i.e., Boatswain's mate, Carpenter's mate, etc.). [2] One of a merchantman's officers including:
- **The First (or Chief) Mate (or Officer)** who is second-in-command to the Master, responsible for all deck operations including supplies, maintenance, cargo handling, and stowage with particular attention to the vessel's stability. At sea, he or she stands the morning and evening (4–8) bridge watches.
- **The Second Mate/Officer** is the ship's navigator, with prime responsibility for the upkeep of charts, monitoring navigation equipment, and (frequently) fire-fighting equipment. Keeps the mid and afternoon (12–4) watches at sea.
- **The Third Mate/Officer** assists the chief and second mates as required, supervises the vessel's loading, and is responsible for emergency survival equipment (lifeboats and rafts, personal floatation gear, etc.). At sea, he or she stands the first and forenoon (8–12) watches.
- Large ships have additional (numbered) junior mates or officers.

Matelot/Matlo: A seaman (English slang, derived from the French Matelot).

Mater Cara: The Latin for "Beloved Mother" (The Virgin Mary) has been anglicized to Mother Carey (which see). *See also* stormy petrel.

Material condition: [1] Generally, the readiness of equipment and systems installed in a warship. [2] Specifically, a USN term denoting the required level of damage control readiness. All doors, hatches, ports, valves and the like are designated W, X, Y, or Z. If, for example, "Condition X-Ray" (the lowest level of readiness) is set, all fittings marked "X" must be closed. "Condition Yoke" is intermediate, and "Condition Zebra" is the highest level, set during General Quarters. "Condition Whiskey" is invoked only to counter chemical, biological, or radiological threats.

Matériel: The supplies, arms, ammunition, and equipment; excluding personnel; required by or furnished to a naval or military force.

Matey: Slang term for a stevedore or other dockyard worker.

Matthew Walker: A decorative knot, tied by unraveling the strands of a line, knotting them, and laying them together again. It keeps the end of the rope from fraying, and provides a secure stopper that cannot be untied without unraveling the rope. It was used on topmast rigging lanyards, the rope loop of bunt beckets, and the beckets of tubs and buckets.

Little is known about the man who gave his name to the knot. He may have been a master rigger in one of the British naval dockyards, but alternative myths and theories abound. One of the more colorful tells us he was a sailor, convicted of some crime by a judge who had formerly been a seaman. Calling on their maritime fellowship, he asked for clemency if he could tie a knot the judge could neither make nor undo. Returning to the privacy of his cell, he un-laid half of a ten-fathom line, put in his special knot, then re-laid the rope to the end. This secured his reprieve, and gave the world an excellent knot.

Maul: [1] A heavy caulking hammer [2] To inflict severe damage on an enemy ship by raking or broadside.

MAW: Marine Air Wing (USMC).

Mayday: Internationally-recognized radio call for immediate help by ships and aircraft. Much more urgent than pan-pan. From the French m'aidez = help me. *See* table 10.

Mayonnaise: There are several explanations of the origin of this name, the most popular being that it arose after the naval Battle of Minorca In 1756. At the beginning of the Seven Year's War, Admiral John Byng sailed from Gibraltar with reinforcements for British-held Minorca. By the time he arrived, the island had been overrun by a French invasion force, which was besieging the garrison at Port Mahon, and a French fleet stood in his way. The ensuing battle was inconclusive, but Byng returned to Gibraltar, making no attempt to land his embarked troops. Fort Saint Philip fell, and Byng was later court-martialed and shot for failure to complete his mission. Meanwhile, the French ground commander, Maréchal Duc Louis de Richelieu, had ordered a victory dinner, for which his chef invented a new sauce of eggs and oil beaten onto an emulsion, naming it Maónnaise, after Maó the Catalan name for Port Mahon.

MB: Marine Barracks (USMC).

MC: Mission critical.

MCA: Maritime & Coastguard Agency (Brit.).

MCAS: Marine Corps Air Station (USMC).

MCS: Hull classification symbol of a mine countermeasures support ship.

MCM: [1] Manual for Courts-Martial. [2] Mine countermeasures. [3] Hull classification symbol of a mine countermeasures ship.

MCPO: Master Chief Petty Officer.

MCPON: Master Chief Petty Officer of the Navy. Pronounced Mickpon.

MDP: Ministry of Defence Police (Brit.).

MDZ: Maritime Defense Zone (USN).

MEA: Marine Engineering Artificer (RN).

Meal pennant: A USN warship at anchor hoists the E (Echo) flag to indicate that its crew is at dinner.

Mealed: [1] Coarsely ground foodstuff; especially the seeds of various cereal grasses or pulse. [2] Corned gunpowder treated with spirits of wine and pulverized into smaller grains, making it cleaner and faster burning for use in priming tubes and pans.

Mean: [1] An average (e.g., mean high water is the average depth of water at high tide). [2] Equidistant from two extremes.

Mean sea level: Refers to [1] The level of the ocean's surface — especially the halfway level between mean high and mean low tide — used as a standard datum for reckoning land elevation or sea depths. [2] More accurately, the average height of the sea surface at all stages over a lengthy period (usually the nineteen-year cycle for sun, moon and earth to return to any given alignment). *See also* sea level.

Measurement of ships: Ships are measured in terms of overall length, waterline length, beam, depth (distance from weather deck to keelson), draft (distance between the ship's bottom and the highest waterline), and tonnage.

Measurement of wind & wave: Wind, which was absolutely vital to sailing mariners, remains a potential hazard and important consideration for navigators in the age of powered and nuclear propulsion systems. In consequence, several conventions for measuring or estimating wind speeds and the waves they generate have been developed. These include the Beaufort, Douglas, Fujita, Pierson-Moskowitch, and Saffir-Simpson scales (*see* tables 1–5).

Measurement ton: Cargo volume equal to 40 cubic feet.

Meatball: [1] World War II slang for the red identification disc painted on Japanese aircraft. [2] USN slang for a battle efficiency pennant. [3] Naval aviator's slang for the orange ball which, when seen at the center of a mirror landing aid and in alignment with horizontal green lights, indicates to the pilot of an incoming aircraft that it is on the proper glide path for a deck landing.

Mechanical advantage: The ratio of the output force exerted by a mechanism to the input force applied to it.

Mechanical sweep: In naval mine warfare, a sweep with the objective of physically contacting the mine or its appendages.

Medals: Flat pieces of metal usually in the shape of crosses, discs, or stars, bearing an inscription or design and (usually) accompanied by an identifying ribbon, serving to recognize accomplishments or commemorate events. Medals for courage or bravery in action are called **Decorations**. Those for presence in a theatre of operations or during a specific operation are **Campaign Medals**, and those issued for other reasons are **Service Medals**. Medals are conventionally worn on the left breast, reputedly because that is where Crusaders wore the sign of the cross, but the USN places Unit Citations on the right.

Medevac: Medical Evacuation.

Medical Assistant: A Royal Navy medical rating, equivalent to the USN's Hospital Corpsman. Medical Assistants serve on all types of ship in the surface and submarine fleet, or ashore in a sick bay, hospital, or other establishment. Until shortly after World War II, Medical Assistants were known as Sick Berth Attendants, and earlier as Loblolly Boys. Medical Assistants who volunteer for service with the Royal Marines must pass the All Arms Commando Course.

Medical services: Modern and effective medical support is a fundamental part of any nation's military capability and effectiveness. To that end, medical and dental services promote and maintain the health, fitness, and well being of naval and marine personnel.

- **Initially**: In both the Royal and United States navies, the medical section of larger ships consisted of the surgeon, who was a physician, and his mate, who might have some medical experience or rudimentary qualifications. They were civilians with status similar to that of modern warrant offices, appointed only for a specific cruise. They were assisted by a number of loblolly boys, who were landsmen with nothing more than on-the-job-training. Article 16 of Rules for the Regulation of the Navy of the United Colonies of North America of 1775. stated:

  > A convenient place shall be set apart for sick or hurt men, to be removed with their hammocks and bedding when the surgeon shall advise the same to be necessary: and some of the crew shall be appointed to attend to and serve them and to keep the place clean. The cooper shall make buckets with covers and cradles if necessary for their use.

- **The USN Medical Corps**: Surgeons became commissioned officers in 1872, but it was not until 1898 that this staff corps was founded, covering a wide range of medical specialties. A century later, facing a shortage of trained physicians, the Uniformed Services Health Professions Revitalization Act (1972) created programs under which medical students are given reserve commissions as Ensign (O-1) which they hold during four years of medical education. Upon graduation, they supersede to the rank of Lieutenant (O-3) and are called to active duty as interns at a Navy or Marine Corps hospital. After a year's internship, they may deploy to the fleet as a General Medical Officer, undergo six months of additional training as a Flight Surgeon or Undersea Medical Officer, or apply to complete a full residency in the field of their choice. *See* Hospital Corpsman.

- **The Royal Navy Medical Service** operates in very similar ways. Medical, Dental and Nursing officers and medical assistants work in primary and secondary health care, ashore and afloat. Experienced doctors enter on Short Service Commissions of three to six years' duration (prior experience being considered when calculating seniority). Undergraduate cadetships are available to medical students, paying a salary as well as course fees. During three months at the Institute of Naval Medicine (Gosport) qualified physicians learn to manage clinical problems in the absence of hospital or specialist assistance, and are introduced to the fundamentals of aviation and underwater medicine. They can then elect to serve as generalists at sea, qualify in aviation or submarine medicine, or undertake further professional training in a specialist field.

Mediterranean moor: A maneuver commonly used when harbor space is limited. Twin anchors are dropped from the bow and the vessel is backed into the seawall with the brow being put over the stern.

Meet her!: A steering command to reduce the swing of a turning vessel without stopping the turn altogether.

MEF: Marine Expeditionary Force (USMC).

Megaton: A measure of the explosive power of a nuclear weapon, equal to one-million tons of TNT.

MEH: Marine Electronic Highway.

Men: the ships company in general, also crew, troops, people.

Mercantile Marine: Obsolete British term for the Merchant Navy.

Mercator projection: Method of charting in which the parallels of latitude and meridians of longitude intersect at right angles. Developed by Flemish cartographer Gerhardus Mercator about 1556 and used in navigation, although the dimensions of polar areas are significantly distorted by this projection. *See also* rhumb lines.

Merchandise: Goods, especially commodities or manufactured wares.

Merchant: [1] A person who buys, ships, and sells commodities for profit. [2] Pertaining to trade or commerce, mercantile, commercial, or industrial. [3] Often used in the sense of "non-military (i.e., Merchant Navy).

Merchant aircraft carrier: *See* MAC ship.

Merchant Marine: [1] American collective term for the vessels of a nation engaged in commercial trade. [2] Frequently used but incorrect term for a merchant mariner.

Merchant mariner: A member of a merchantman's crew. It is little appreciated that merchant mariner was one of the most hazardous occupations in World War II. Although technically non-combatant, the U.S. Merchant Marine and British Merchant Navy each suffered a higher overall casualty rate than their respective armies, navies, and air forces.

Merchant Navy: British collective term for the vessels of the nation engaged in commercial trade. Adopted during World War II to honor the wartime contribution and sacrifice of what had previously been called the Mercantile Marine.

Merchant ship: *See* merchantman.

Merchant Ship Reporting and Control Message System: A U.S. and NATO worldwide system for recording the movement of merchantmen and information relating to their control.

Merchant venturer: [1] A trader willing to accept the risks and dangers of a trading gamble, especially one that sends goods across unpredictable seas. [2] The Society of Merchant Venturers is a private charitable organization in the English city of Bristol, which dates back to the 13th century. At one time it was so powerful that it effectively ran the city. [3] During the 16th century, the Company of Merchant-Venturers traded with distant places, especially Russia and Turkey. The hazards are described by Richard Barnfield in his 1594 poem, "The Affectionate Shepherd":

> The wealthie merchant that dothe crosse the sease
> To Denmarke, Polande, Spaine, and Barbarie
> For all his ritches, lives not still at ease
> Sometimes he feares ship-spoyling pyracie
> Another while deceipt and treacherie
> Of his owne factors in a forren land
> Thus doth he still in dread and danger stand
>
> Well is he tearmde a merchant-venturer
> Since he doth venter lands, and goods and all
> When he doth travell for his traffique far
> Little he knowes what fortune may befalle
> Or rather, what mis-fortune happen shall
> Sometimes he splits his ship against a rocke
> Loosing his men, his goods, his wealth, his stocke

Merchantman: A vessel engaged in commercial trade, excluding vessels operating solely within harbor limits, and river and estuarial craft (also merchant ship, cargo ship, freighter).

Meridian: An imaginary circle on the earth's surface running through the north and south poles. The longitudinal equivalent of a latitudinal parallel.

Meridional overturning circulation: *See* Deep Water Circulation, Oceanic Circulation, and Thermohaline Circulation.

MERINT: USN/USCG term for national security intelligence provided by a merchant ship.

Meritorious Unit Commendation: Each U.S. military service issues its own version of this award. The Naval version, established in 1967, is given for valorous or meritorious achievement in battle or non-combat operations at a level that would justify the award of a Bronze Star to an individual. Naval units awarded an MUC are authorized to fly a red, yellow, blue, and green striped pennant, up to five bronze stars being placed on the central red stripe for additional citations. Those who were on board and actually participated in the action are entitled to wear the MUC medal.

Mermaids: Mysterious female sea creatures are featured in the oral traditions of almost every culture, one of the earliest being the Assyrian goddess Atargatis, who is sometimes depicted as having the body of a fish with a human head and legs. More frequently she has the conventional mermaid form of human above, fish below, which is exactly how the Phoenecian Derketo is described. The 14th century French Melusine is sometimes said to have bifurcated twin fish tails below a female torso.

The Sirens of classical Greece — part woman, part bird — sang so sweetly that sailors forgot their native lands and families, landing to waste away on the Sirens' island, which grew white with their bleaching bones. The mythical Lorelei of the Rhine River, whose beautiful song lured mariners onto her "fateful rock," was a typical blonde-haired, blue-eyed madchen with no bird or fish-like features. Neither of these water spirits really fits the mermaid image.

Reports of mermaid sightings by European explorers and navigators were common, widespread, and amazingly consistent, describing creatures with the tail of a fish or porpoise and the head and torso of a naked young woman. Their hair was variously reported as golden, green, or jet black, but invariably said to be waist-length and brilliant. Beyond the physical similarity of "eyewitness" reports there were huge differences. Many called them beautiful, but others recorded disappointment at their ugliness.

"Mer-myths" (if we may call them such) include tales of compassionate mermaids who rescued drowning seamen and deposited them gently ashore; of frivolous mermaids who gamboled around a ship like playful dolphins; and of amorous mermaids who snatched watchkeepers off the deck at night, carrying them to be sex slaves in deep underwater grottoes. Sometimes, it was said, a mermaid would fall deeply in love with a mortal man, leaving her watery home to adopt human form, marry him, and bear his children, but the day usually came when she heard the ocean's call and slipped away never to return.

There were also stories of malicious mermaids, with siren-like powers to lure seafarers to their deaths; of mermaid seers, who could foretell the future, and mer-witches who could control it. Early European mariners believed that the sight of a mermaid's breast could calm angry seas, while ancient Japanese legend held that eating the flesh of a mermaid would result in immortality and eternal youth.

Mermen: Frequently considered to be the spirits of sailors lost at sea, mermen were usually depicted as ugly old fellows with straggly black beards and hair. No wonder there were far fewer tales of merman sightings — what seaman would not prefer to see a young, attractive, bare-breasted creature combing her long and lustrous tresses?

Mess: [1] A shipboard eating area. [2] A segment of the ship's company eating together, often divided according to rank. [3] Formerly, in the age of sail, a segment of the ship's company drawing victuals in bulk and sharing them out. At that time being invited to join the right (or wrong) mess could have immense impact on a sailor's social life. (The word may be derived from either the Old French mes = portion of food, or the Spanish mesa = table.)

Mess dress: A naval officer's formal uniform for evening wear.

Mess gear/kit/traps: Eating utensils (knives, forks, plates, cups, etc.).

Message: Any thought, idea, or report expressed briefly in plain language, code, or cipher.

Messenger: [1] A seaman who carries messages or runs errands for officers on watch. [2] An endless rope, wound around the capstan, attached to the anchor cable by nippers and used to haul it in, especially when it is too thick and heavy for the capstan (also voyo). [3] A light, weighted line which can be thrown across water and then tied to a heavier line to be pulled after it.

Messmates: Members of the same mess.

Metacenter/Metacentre: Defined in naval architecture as the point of intersection between a line drawn through the center of gravity of a hull (vertical when in equilibrium) and a vertical line through the center of pressure under slight angular displacement.

Metacentric height: Distance between the center of gravity and the metacenter. When the latter is below the center of gravity, the ship is unstable. The greater its distance above the center of gravity, the greater the stability.

Meteorology: The study of the processes and phenomena of the earth's atmosphere, especially insofar as they facilitate forecasting weather conditions.

Metric ton: *See* ton.

Mexico Current: A seasonal extension of the California current that flows southeastward along the coast from late October until April.

MFN: Most Favored Nation.

MGB: RN designation of a motor gunboat.

MHD propulsion: The magnetohydrodynamic drive is a tentative and untried method that creates thrust (known as the Lorentz force) by passing an electric current through seawater in the presence of an intense magnetic field. The seawater effectively becomes the moving conductive part of an electric motor, pushing the water out at the back to accelerate the vehicle. Due to their lack of moving parts, MHD drives are (in principle) reliable, economical, efficient, silent, and mechanically elegant. They may eventually prove a viable alternative to the propeller, but experimental prototype seagoing vessels tested by Mitsubishi during the 1990s failed to achieve the anticipated performance.

MHS: Maritime Homeland Security (U.S.).

MHW: Mean high-water (of tides).

MIA: Missing in action.

Mickey Mouse: [1] USN slang for (a) Rules, regulations, and restrictions which make no sense, or (b) A chaotic and disorganized construction, or (c) Anything as trite and contrived as the silly and childish Disney cartoons featuring this character. [2] In Australia the term has exactly the opposite meaning of good or excellent.

MIDAS: Maritime Industrial Development Areas.

Middle: To fold a rope back on itself so that the two lengths are equal.

Middle ground: A length of relatively shallow water between deeper channels.

Middle passage: This was the longest, toughest, and most horrific segment of the triangular trade.

Africans, purchased from local chiefs and warlords, were literally packed like sardines (*see* spooning) into the holds of specially-designed slave ships, chained together (usually in pairs), only occasionally (if ever) allowed a turn around the decks, and fed barely enough food to sustain life. The passage lasted between five weeks and five months, and every day the stench of fear, unwashed bodies, and human excrement got worse. Malnutrition, scurvy, dysentery, and infectious diseases, along with severe depression took a terrible toll. Nevertheless, there were enough survivors to make the slave trade immensely profitable.

Middle watch: The duty shift from 0000 to 0400 (midnight to 4:00 A.M.). Also midwatch.

Mid-ocean dynamics: Study of the fluctuations of ocean currents using the dynamics of eddies.

Midrats: USN slang for rations served to the middle watch.

Midship oar: [1] The longest of five oars on the port side of a whaleboat. [2] The crew member pulling this oar.

Midshipman: Formerly, a senior petty officer belonging to a group from which commissioned officers would be chosen. So-called because they berthed amidships, between the crew who berthed forward and the commissioned officers who lived aft. To be rated midshipman, a candidate had to have served at least two years at sea, either before the mast or as a captain's servant, the latter position being reserved for "young gentlemen" with patronage connections. After a minimum of six years of sea service a midshipman could take the examination for third lieutenant, but might have to wait many more years before a vacancy arose. Thereafter advancement depended entirely on seniority (*see also* Master's Mate). During the Napoleonic Wars midshipmen tended to fall into three distinct categories:

• Well-connected teenage "gentlemen," confidently expecting to pass the lieutenant's examination and be commissioned.
• Ambitious but embittered 30–40 year-olds, who had either repeatedly failed that exam or, worse, had passed but lacked the essential patron.
• Hard-bitten professional seamen, promoted from the lower deck and not expecting to go further.

Nowadays it is the rank of the most junior British naval officer, equivalent to U.S. Ensign but not commissioned and classified as "Subordinate Officer." The rank insignia, which originated in 1758, is a white collar patch that some say can be traced all the way back to Roman times when a white toga was the badge of aspirants to higher office.

In the United States the title refers to members of the Naval Reserve Officer Training Corps at a U.S. university and to students at the U.S. Naval and Merchant Marine Academies. Navy Regulations give them an ambiguous status, saying "Midshipmen are, by law, officers *in a qualified sense*" (author's emphasis). *See also* Passed Midshipman and Aviation Midshipman.

Midships: Abbreviation of amidships.

Midships your helm!: Command to align the rudder exactly fore-and-aft in line with the keel.

Midwatch: The middle watch.

Midway: The year 1942 was the pivotal year of World War II. The British turned the Nazi tide at El Alamein (after 37 months of defensive war), Soviet Russia won the battle of attrition at Stalingrad (after 16 months of constant retreat), and the United States crippled Japanese naval aviation at the Battle of Midway (after 6 months of humiliating setbacks). The latter was due to a combination of accurate intelligence, superior admiralship, and a tremendous slice of serendipitous luck.

Admiral Isoroku Yamamoto had devised a typically complex Japanese naval plan of stealth, ruse, and division of forces, involving a diversion intended to lure the U.S. Navy north to the Aleutians, an invasion force to occupy the islands inside Midway Atoll and bring the Americans rushing back, a four-carrier strike force to intercept and cripple them, and a powerful seven-battleship main force to deliver the coup de grace.

The United States had broken the Japanese naval code, and decoded messages made it clear that a major operation was being mounted at a place designated "AF." Suspecting this to be Midway, commanders arranged for the garrison there to report breakdown of their water distillation plant in plain language. Two days later Tokyo told the fleet "AF is short of water." Knowing the enemy's destination and objectives allowed Admirals Frank Jack Fletcher and Raymond Ames Spruance to strategically pre-position their task forces for the action which began on 4th June.

Luck favored the Americans when a gap in the enemy reconnaissance let their forces go unseen and then, when they were finally sighted, the Japanese pilot misidentified the carriers as cruisers. Meanwhile, their own scouts had found the Japanese. A low-level American torpedo strike was destroyed by the Japanese combat air patrol, but that left the upper level undefended, allowing U.S. dive-bombers to swoop down on three of the Japanese carriers. The fourth carrier, *Hiryu*, managed to launch a strike that crippled carrier USS *Yorktown* (later sunk by torpedoes from Japanese submarine *I-168*), but she herself was located and dive-bombed. Two of the blazing Japanese carriers sank; the other two were finished off by torpedoes from their own destroyers.

Midway had profound consequences; not only had the Japanese lost two-thirds of their fleet carrier force, but the loss of an élite cadre of highly-trained and experienced naval aviators was even more serious. From then on the naval initiative passed to the United States.

Mike: NATO phonetic notation for the letter "M."

Milan Naval Forum: A 1995 initiative of the Indian Navy, involving a biennial gathering of Indian Ocean navies to discuss common concerns, forge co-operation, and build friendship and mutual understanding. Current participants are Australia, Bangladesh, India, Indonesia, Malaysia, Myanmar [Burma], Singapore, Srilanka, and Thailand. (Milan is Hindi for "tryst" or "meeting.")

Mile: *See* nautical mile.

Military: [1] In general, of, related to, or concerning armed forces as distinct from police or civilians. [2] Specifically, of, related to, or concerning soldiers and the army.

Military deception: Concerns misleading the enemy as to one's capabilities, intentions, and operations; thereby causing him to take specific actions (or inactions) that will contribute to the accomplishment of the mission. Ultimately, the intent is to favorably shape the enemy's behavior, or to cause him to form an inaccurate impression of the battlespace. Notable naval examples, one from antiquity and five during World War II, were:

- 480 BCE; Salamis: The Persian fleet enjoyed a huge numerical superiority, so Greek commander Themistocles planned to lure them into the narrow Gulf of Salamis, where numbers would be less decisive. He had his trusted slave Sicinnus "defect" to the Persian camp, to tell young King Xerxes the Greeks were quarrelling among themselves (true) and would fall apart if attacked (false). Xerxes leaped into the trap. After sending a 200-ship squadron to block the Greek line of retreat at the far end of the Gulf, and a detachment of marines to seize the islet of Psyttaleia at its mouth, he ordered the main fleet to cut off any attempt at escape by embarking at sunset and remaining at sea overnight.

  At dawn, five hundred and fifty triremes in line abreast rowed towards three hundred Greek warships inside the Gulf. But they were tired after their night at the oars and lost cohesion splitting to pass on either side of Psyttaleia. Then, as they emerged on the other side, they saw the second deception — a Corinthian squadron backing-water and hoisting sails in a feigned attempt at escape — each Persian vessel surged forward, racing its neighbor for the honor of being first to strike, further distorting their battle line. The trap was sprung. Greek trumpets blared, and the main fleet surged forward to grapple. The Corinthians downed sail and rowed back to join them, and a detached squadron charged in from the flank to smash through the banks of oars and thrust their wicked beaks into the fragile side planks of enemy ships. The rout was close to total.

- 1942; Operation Torch: When its agents reported large numbers of ships passing through the Strait of Gibraltar for the North African Invasion, the German High Command assumed they were another supply convoy heading for Malta. Hitler, however, believed they were an invasion force. So did Italian dictator Mussolini, who correctly forecast Vichy French North Africa as the objective, but Hitler disregarded his ally and ordered large air and submarine forces to assemble in the Sicilian narrows

to forestall an amphibious assault on Libya. The Allies encouraged this belief with two ruses. First HMS *Janine* (undamaged) radioed a plain language distress message, saying she was sinking hundreds of miles east of where she really was. Then, the Central and Eastern Task Forces steamed well beyond their objectives as though heading for Libya, waiting for darkness before reversing course to head for the real invasion beaches.

- 1943; Operation Mincemeat: The capture of Sicily — which would open the Mediterranean to Allied shipping and give them a foothold in Europe — was such an obvious strategic objective that Winston Churchill said "Everyone but a bloody fool would know it." Accordingly, British naval intelligence mounted an elaborate deception plan. The corpse of a 34-year-old man was given the identity papers of a fictional Major of Royal Marines, placed in a steel canister filled with dry ice, and taken on board British submarine HMS *Seraph*. A briefcase, attached to his wrist by a bank-courier's chain, contained forged official documents and a series of letters from senior officers in England to commanders in the field, covering subjects so "sensitive" that they justified being hand-carried rather than sent through regular channels.

  One of these was a personal letter from the Vice Chief of the Imperial General Staff (Sir Archibald Nye) to "My dear Alex" (Sir Harold Alexander, commander, 18th Army Group). Among other things, Nye discussed two totally fictitious amphibious landings. *Operation Husky* (the real code name for the Sicily invasion) was identified as a major assault on Greece, while a secondary invasion of Sardinia was given the invented code name *Operation Brimstone*. Nye then outlined purported deception plans, ending with "we stand a very good chance of making them think we are going for Sicily." There was also a letter from Admiral Lord Louis Mountbatten (Chief of Combined Operations) introducing his subordinate "Major Martin" to "ABC" (Andrew Browne Cunningham, Allied naval C-in-C in the Mediterranean) and ending with a rather forced joke about "sardines," hoping the Germans would see it as a veiled reference to the "*Brimstone*" operation.

  To give verisimilitude to the impersonation, the stubs of recent theater tickets were stuffed into the marine's battledress pockets along with fabricated personal objects. Several private letters included one from his bank manager demanding payment of an overdraft, while more intimate items included love letters from a fictitious fiancée, her photograph (actually of an Admiralty clerk), and the jeweler's bill for her engagement ring.

  Before dawn on 30 April, *Seraph* surfaced near the town of Huelva, where with the Spanish authorities were known to be friendly to German intelligence. The "major" was removed from his canister and gently pushed overboard. Before tide and currents could wash him ashore as intended, the body was found by a local fisherman and handed over to the Spanish Armada, whose pathologists (as hoped) diagnosed that fluid in his lungs — due to the pneumonia that killed him — was consistent with death by drowning after an airplane crash.

To further the deception, the British Naval Attaché was directed to demand immediate return of the papers. After twelve days, the briefcase was handed over and British forensic experts were able to confirm that the envelopes had been opened and resealed. Mussolini still believed Sicily would be the primary target, but Hitler believed the deception, redirecting reinforcements from Sicily to Sardinia and Corsica, and sending renowned general Rommel to assume command in Greece, where German forces were augmented by an entire panzer division moved all the way from France.

Even after the Sicily landings, the Germans remained convinced the main attacks would come later in Sardinia and Greece, keeping forces there until after the Allied beachhead was secure. This embarrassing "sting" made German intelligence officers so suspicious that they dismissed genuine top-secret documents found in an abandoned landing craft that washed ashore in Normandy shortly after D-Day, and others found in a crashed glider near Arnhem in September 1944.

- 1944; Fortitude North: This deception plan was aimed at keeping the 27 German divisions in Norway from reinforcing Normandy when the amphibious invasion began. A fictitious British "Fourth Army," supposedly headquartered in Edinburgh Castle, swamped the radio waves with messages such as "VII Corps needs instructors in the Bilgeri method of mountain climbing" and "80 Division requires 1,800 pairs of Kandahar ski bindings." Russian agents compounded the deception, and the Nazi troops remained in Scandinavia.

- 1944; Fortitude South: A much larger fictitious unit — "First United States Army Group" (FUSAG), said to be commanded by American General George Patton, whom the Germans considered the best Allied tactician — also used false signals and the messages of double agents to persuade the enemy that the Allies could muster 95 to 97 divisions when only 35 were available. While the real invasion force under British General Bernard Montgomery was secretly assembling in southwestern England, German radio intercept and intelligence organizations were persuaded that FUSAG would mount the main assault on the Pas-de-Calais. Consequently, Hitler considered the Normandy landings only a diversion and withheld strategic reserves, making the German response to the beachhead far weaker than it could have been.

- 1945; Operation Tucson: On 10th July, Task Force 38, the powerful striking force of the United States Third Fleet, bombed Tokyo; then headed north under strict radio silence to strike southern Hokkaido and northern Honshu. Simultaneously, USS *Tucson* (CL-98) turned south. After several hours of high-speed steaming she broke radio silence with the first of several "urgent" messages purporting to come from USS *Missouri* (BB-63) Admiral Halsey's flagship (one of *Missouri*'s radio operators was assigned to *Tucson* so that Japanese intercepts would hear a familiar "fist"). They also used voice communication to simulate conversations between TF-38's carriers and their aircraft; placing each speaker in a separate compartment so that the "background noise" was different. After an air strike on the southern island of Kyushu by carrier-type aircraft (that were actually land-based on Okinawa) *Tucson* faked their return and recovery by TF-38. All of this convinced the Japanese that Halsey was off the southern tip of their homeland to support an amphibious invasion. Troops and aircraft were rushed southward, and TF-38's actual strike in the north achieved total surprise. According to Rear Admiral Robert Carney, Halsey's Chief of Staff, "There was no resistance to the strike at all."

Military independent: A merchantman or naval auxiliary sailing alone but controlled and reported as a military unit.

Military law: The body of laws, rules, and regulations that have been developed to meet the needs of the military. It encompasses conditions of service in the armed forces, the constitutional rights of service members, the military criminal justice system, and the international laws of armed conflict. Not to be confused with martial law. (*See also* naval law, articles of war, and uniform code of military justice.)

Military operations other than war: This concept involves using non-lethal pathways for the resolution of conflict. Maritime forces are capable of providing mobile communication-control centers that coordinate the wide range of diplomatic, military, and non-governmental agencies that respond to political or humanitarian crises in areas such as:
- Arms control
- Counterdrug operations
- Counterterrorism
- Humanitarian assistance and noncombatant evacuation
- Peace enforcement and peacekeeping
- Protecting freedom of navigation and overflight
- Protection of shipping
- Sanctions enforcement
- Support to civil authorities
- Support of insurgency or counterinsurgency

Military organization: The following is an oversimplified outline of army and marine hierarchies, which vary greatly between and within national forces. Each unit in the hierarchy is composed of at least two of the preceding unit, and three is a popular number, because it allows the unit commander to commit two while holding the third in reserve. The basic unit is a *fireteam*, whose size and composition varies, but usually includes four or five soldiers or marines. *Squads* (U.S.) or *Sections* (British) are composed of two or more fireteams; and a *Platoon* includes two or more squads.

The oldest structural component is a *Company*, commanded by a Captain or Major, and composed of two or more platoons. Two or more companies form a *Battalion*, commanded by a Lieutenant Colonel. Two or more battalions may make up a *Regiment*, commanded by a Colonel, or a *Brigade*, led by a Brigadier (Brit.) or Brigadier General (U.S.). A *Division* of two or more brigades or regiments is a Major General's command, while a Lieutenant General commands a *Corps* of two or more divisions. A full General commands an *Army* or *Army Corps* of two or more corps. Finally, only encountered in major conflicts, is the *Army Group*, consisting of several armies and commanded by a Field Marshal (Brit.) or a five-star Army General (U.S.).

Military Sealift Command: A component of U.S. Transportation Command (the British equivalent is Royal Fleet Auxiliary). Responsible for freight and passenger sealift service, including the ocean transportation of ammunition, equipment, fuel, and supplies to U.S. forces worldwide. Vessels may be government-owned (usually with civilian crews) or chartered commercial merchantmen. The command operates in three principal modes:
• *Surge sealift*— Used to move equipment to active theaters of operation around the world.
• *Sustainment sealift*— Serves to keep forces already in the field continuously supplied.
• *Afloat prepositioning*— In which fuel, equipment, and supplies are stored on ships at sea, ready meet the initial requirements of a contingency anywhere in the world.

Military Traffic Management Command: Now called Surface Deployment & Distribution Command.

Milkman: USN enlisted slang for a sailor wearing summer white uniform. Also Good Humor Man.

Mimic: A console displaying information on the status of processes or equipment controlled elsewhere.

Mind your P's and Q's: Numerous explanations of the origin of this phrase have been advanced, none of which is completely convincing; least of all the theory that seamen said it to bartenders to ensure they were not charged for quarts of beer when they had consumed pints. Another possible naval origin (which also seems far-fetched) says it was a warning to sailors not to get tar from their queues (pigtails) smeared on their pea jackets. Even less likely is the suggestion that the term is an abbreviation of "please and thank you." Most probably it was a simple warning to scholars learning to read — or perhaps printer's apprentices learning to typeset — not to confuse the lower case letters "p" and "q." If that's the case one wonders why the idiom is not "mind your d's and b's," which has the benefit of rhyming.

Mind your rudder!: Cautionary command, warning the person at the helm that the vessel has veered off course due to inattention or a crosscurrent.

Mine (naval): An explosive device in a watertight container, floating on, or moored below the surface of the water, or lying on the sea bed. Designed to detonate when a hostile vessel strikes it, generates a pressure wave, or exerts acoustic or magnetic influence on it. Mines can be deployed [1] Offensively, to divert or destroy hostile shipping. [2] Strategically, to lock enemy ships in harbor. [3] Defensively, to protect friendly ports or routes, or [4] Psychologically, to inhibit enemy use of trade routes.

The first recorded mention of naval mining was by 14th century Chinese artillery officer Jiao Yu, whose early examples consisted of explosives enclosed in putty-sealed wooden boxes, equipped with time fuses, or rip cords pulled by a concealed ambusher. An American, David Bushnell invented the first practical Western mine for use against the British during the War of Independence. It was a watertight keg filled with gunpowder that was floated toward the enemy and detonated by a percussion lock if it struck a ship. (*See also* Anti-sweep Mine, Ascending Mine, Bottom Mine, Contact Mine, Limpet Mine, Magnetic Mine, Rocket Mine, and Torpedo Mine.)

Mine clearance & disposal: The processes of detecting and destroying, removing, or neutralizing explosive marine mines.

Mine countermeasures: Any method used to reduce or prevent damage or danger from naval mines.

Mine countermeasures ship: A vessel carrying high-technology sonar and video systems, cable cutters and mine detonating devices that can be released and activated by remote control. It is also capable of conventional minesweeping. A hull of fiberglass sheathed wood to reduces or eliminates the hazards posed by magnetic mines.

Mine countermeasures support ship: A converted amphibious assault ship that provides alongside services and command and control for up to four mine countermeasures ships. It has enhanced C^{4}I capabilities, upgraded close-in weapon systems, various radars, and an embarked helicopter squadron. It provides repair facilities for weapons, aircraft, etc., and can accommodate four explosive ordnance disposal groups with their equipment.

Mine damage: Mines harm ships in three different ways. The injury inflicted depends on the distance of the hull from the detonation and, surprisingly, damage initially tends to increase with distance until the range becomes too great and it falls rapidly to zero.
• Contact damage: When a mine explodes close beside the hull, it blows a hole that floods one or more compartments. Pieces of casing or hull may wound some of the crew, but the ship will possibly stay afloat.
• Bubble Jet impact: If the mine detonates a small distance from the ship, it creates an expanding cavitation bubble with walls that move faster than the speed of sound in water, striking the hull and tear-

ing plates apart. When this initial force has expended itself, the bubble collapses and then re-expands, creating a "shaped water-jet" that blasts in through the original hole and breaches the next bulkhead in line. Such heavy damage almost certainly sinks the ship and may break it apart.

• Shaking injury: If the mine detonates a little further from the ship, the change in water pressure causes the hull to resonate, shaking the entire vessel, ripping engines from their beds, and loosening hundreds, perhaps thousands, of rivets. With a myriad of tiny leaks and no power for the pumps, this can often be the most damaging outcome of all.

Minefield: An area of sea (or land) sown with mines. Offensive naval minefields are placed along trade routes or at or choke points to damage enemy vessels, while defensive ones are placed in home waters to deter hostile intrusion.

Minelayer: A vessel or aircraft designed or converted for the purpose of placing mines.

Minesweeper: A vessel or aircraft designed or modified for the purpose of clearing mines.

Minesweeping: The activity of detecting and destroying, removing, or neutralizing explosive marine mines. Mines cut loose are either collected for intelligence analysis or destroyed by gunfire.

• Contact minesweeping: a special cutting wire is dragged though the water, either between two ships or between a ship and a paravane. When it hits the mooring wire of the mine it severs it.

• Distance minesweeping: A device towed behind the minesweeper emits sounds and magnetism that mimic the signature of a real ship, thereby exploding the mine.

• Airborne minesweeping: Traditionally used towed cutter arrays and sleds equipped for acoustic and magnetic detonation, but flying with a tow is a difficult and highly-skilled activity.

• Advanced airborne techniques: Have no in-water components, contributing to faster sweeps, easing pilot fatigue, and maximizing time on station. They include multiple sonars and electro-optical or laser sensors that scan large areas of ocean quickly, detect floating and moored mines down to at least keel depth, and detonate them with laser-aimed rapid-fire cannon.

Ming Maritime Decrees: 15th century Chinese naval technology was state-of-the-art, including the magnetic compass, stern-post rudder, and fore-and-aft lugsails (much more efficient for beating upwind than the square-rig and lateen sails used by contemporary Europeans and Arabs). In 1403, Emperor Ming Zhu Di ordered construction of a huge Imperial Navy, and embarked on an ambitious program of ocean exploration with a fleet of some 350 warships and support vessels, many of them immense — for example, Nelson's *Victory* was 61 meters long with three masts, whereas the Ming Treasure Ship was 145 meters long with nine masts. It was also virtually "unsinkable" due to compartmentalization by watertight bulkheads. It would be centuries before ships of such size and sophistication were built in the West.

The official Ming history records visits to Java, Sumatra, Vietnam, Thailand, Cambodia, Philippines, Ceylon, India, Bangladesh, Yemen, Arabia, Somalia, and Mogadishu. It also mentions "Franca" (believed to be Iberia and France) and a people called "Hollanders." If they really did meet Europeans, they must have circumnavigated the Cape of Good Hope. In 1434, Venetian merchant Nicolo da Conti claimed to have traveled to Australia with a Chinese fleet. He also presented Chinese maps, now lost, said to show the outline of North America. In 2002 British naval officer and historian Gavin Menzies claimed to have located the remains of nine large Chinese junks wrecked in the Caribbean in 1421, but this has been discounted by most naval historians and archeologists.

Admiral Zheng-He may have circumnavigated Africa before Vasco de Gama, sailed around Cape Horn ahead of Magellan, visited America before Columbus, and reached Australia well in advance of James Cook. Even if he did not, his voyages were magnificent achievements. However, soon after his death in 1435, xenophobic scholar-officials challenged the value of foreign trade, and advocated cultural isolationism. In 1500, they gained the ear of Emperor Ming Xiao Zong, persuading him to order the destruction of Zheng's logs and nautical charts, and make it a capital crime to build or go to sea in any vessel with more than three masts. China's commanding lead was lost, never to be regained. Had it been otherwise the history of the world could have been Chinese dominated.

Minion: A 16th century shipborne cannon firing a four-pound ball about 3 inches in diameter.

Ministry of Defence (MoD): Until World War II, the British armed services — Navy, headed by the First Lord of the Admiralty; Army, led by a Secretary of State for War; and Air Force, under the Secretary of State for Air — operated independently. During the War, Prime Minister Winston Churchill was de facto Minister of Defence, coordinating the activities of these, still nominally independent forces.

In 1946 the three existing service ministers — while retaining their titles and operational control of their respective services — relinquished their Cabinet seats, becoming part of a newly-created Ministry of Defence that is both a policy-making department and Britain's highest-level military command, headed by a Secretary of State enjoying Cabinet status.

In 1964, the MoD assumed operational control of all three services, whose individual ministers were replaced by a single Minister of State for Armed Forces, who is not a member of Cabinet. In 1971, MoD assumed responsibility for procuring military aircraft and guided weapons, formerly a function of the Ministry of Aviation Supply.

Minute: One 60th of a degree. For all practical

purposes, one minute of latitude represents one nautical mile.

Minute guns: Guns fired at 60-second intervals to salute entitled personnel, or to honor the deceased at a military funeral.

MIO: Maritime interdiction operation.

Mirage: An optical illusion caused by atmospheric refraction. The preferred maritime term is loom. *See also* fata morgana.

Mirror Landing Aid: In the 1950s, the high landing speeds of jet aircraft proved too fast for the reflexes of the traditional batsman. This led Royal Navy Commander H.C.N (Nick) Goodheart to produce an automatic carrier landing aid. In essence, this consisted of a gyroscopically-controlled convex mirror (later replaced by a Fresnel lens) on the port side of the flight deck. A glowing yellow-orange image (the "meatball") is visible to an approaching pilot, flanked by a horizontal row of green lights (the "datum") representing the glidepath for a perfect landing. If the ball is above or below the datum, the aircraft is too high or low. If it is far too low, red lights flash in warning of potential crash.

Trials on British carriers HMS *Indomitable* and HMS *Illustrious* in 1953 showed the potential of the system. Two years later tests on USS *Bennington* confirmed its effectiveness. Together with the angled deck (another British invention), the mirror sight (also called glide path indicator) contributed to a tremendous leap forward in the safety of naval flying.

Misfire: Refers to a charge that failed to ignite, or a weapon that discharged at the wrong time.

Miss stays: To fail to turn from one tack to another, come to a standstill, and then fall back on the original tack.

Missile: Any projectile propelled by force of any kind.

Missile tube: The vertical pipe on a submarine, from which missiles are fired.

Missing: A term applied by Lloyd's of London to a vessel reported as overdue by its owners. After being "missing" for a week, the vessel is presumed "lost" and the underwriters assume liability. *See* Lutine Bell.

Mission: The task, purpose, or required outcome of a military operation or assignment.

Mission command: This is a time-honored style or concept of decentralized military command and control in which mutual trust between superiors and subordinates allows the former to set goals while giving the latter free rein to implement them. This worked well for at least three centuries, especially in pre-radio navies when centralized commanders could tell a captain what to achieve and why it was necessary, but once on a remote station the captain had to use his own initiative to decide how best to reach the goal; even to the extent of disobedience — as Nelson demonstrated more than once. In July 1799, then a captain, he wrote, "The orders I have given ... are, in a great measure, contrary to those he (the admiral) gave me; but the Service requires strong and vigorous measures to bring the war to a conclusion."

In contrast, during the 1914–18 war, telegraphic communications allowed "chateau-generals" to ignore Helmuth von Moltke's admonition "No operational plan will ever extend with any sort of certainty beyond the first encounter with a hostile force," and pre-plan the tactical minutiae of local actions in trenches they seldom visited. The author fears the possibility that "information age" concepts such as command and control and network-centric operations will produce centralized naval staffs who will stifle local initiative with a similar "we-know-best" attitude. This may, however, be offset by the concept of power to the edge.

Mission Critical: Any system, component, or action, the failure of which could prevent accomplishment of the mission.

Mitts: Coverings for the hands, worn to defend them from cold or injury, but differing from gloves in leaving thumb and fingers open. Because seamen wearing them can still handle rope, some sources claim a nautical origin, but this is far from proven.

Mixed bag: In naval mine warfare, an assembly of mines of various types, with different firing systems, arming delays, sensitivities, and counter settings.

Mixed layer: Almost all the sunlight falling on the sea is absorbed in the surface water which it heats up. Winds and waves stir up this water distributing the heat so that the temperature tends to be quite uniform for the first few hundred feet, after which it decreases rapidly through a transition layer called the thermocline until it reaches the much colder hypolimnion or deep water layer. The mixed layer is also called surface layer or epilimnion. *See* density levels.

Mizzen: [1] The mast at the back (stern) of a three-masted ship, or of a two-masted one if the forward mast is the main. [2] A term qualifying any of the spars, sails, rigging, or fittings pertaining to that mast (e.g., mizzen staysail). Also mizen.

ML: RN designation of a motor launch.

MLE: Maritime law enforcement.

MLW: Mean low-water (of tides).

MM: Machinist's Mate.

MN: [1] Magnetic North. [2] Merchant Navy (Brit.). [3] Multi-National.

Mnemonic: [1] A memory aid, such as an abbreviation, rhyme or mental image that helps someone to remember something. For example, the word Homes is a mnemonic that conjures up the names of the five Great Lakes — Huron, Ontario, Michigan, Erie and Superior (from the Ancient Greek mnemonikos = of memory, pronounced nem-on-ik, plural nem-on-ix). [2] In military bugle calls, mnemonics are used as reminders of the meaning of the call. For example, mnemonics for the British call to form up in ranks are "Fall in A, Fall in B, Fall in every Companee."

MOB: Man overboard.

MOB point: Designates the reference position to which a person overboard maneuver must return.

Mobile mine: [1] A naval mine propelled to its laying position by torpedo-like propulsion machinery.

At the end of its run, it sinks to operate like any other mine. [2] A mine laid in the normal way, but with its own propulsion system and homing device so that, when actuated by a ship's magnetic signature, it is released to act like a homing torpedo.

Mobile naval air base: Self-explanatory name used by both the USN and RN in the Far East and Pacific during World War II. These self-contained units, normally called "Monabs," were equipped to service and repair aircraft, engines, and components as required for their respective fleets. Some of the British Monabs were also used as airfields and re-titled Mobile Operational Naval Air Base.

Mobile support group: A USN floating naval base which can be forward-deployed to provide logistic support to ships in an anchorage.

Moby Dick: The mythical great white whale featured in Herman Melville's 1851 classic novel was based on Mocha Dick, a scarred bull whale who attacked many whaleboats, the first being near Mocha Island off South America in 1810. His fictitious description of Moby Dick's attack on *Pequod* was doubtless inspired by the true story of Nantucket whaler *Essex*, sunk by a whale in mid–Pacific in 1820.

MOC: Meridional Overturning Circulation.

MoD: Ministry of Defence (Brit.).

MODE: Mid-ocean dynamics experiment.

Moderate breeze: Force 3 on the Beaufort wind scale, with 7–10 kt winds and wavelets just starting to break. (*See* table 1b.)

Moderate rough swell: Force 5 on the Douglas swell scale. (*See* table 2.)

Moderate sea: Force 4 on the Douglas wind-sea scale, with waves 1.25–2.50 m high. (*See* table 2.)

Moderate swell: Force 4 on the Douglas swell scale. (*See* table 2.)

Modification Number: *See* Mark.

Mold/Mould lofting: Shipbuilding, whether in wood or metal, is complicated by the various curves of the hull, the complex angles formed by the joints of structural members, and the need to produce a hull that is perfectly symmetrical and smooth. These make it almost impossible to work from small-scale plans as is normal in most structural projects. Instead, the shipbuilder must lay out a full-size replica of the hull, from which the exact dimensions and shapes of frames, planks, plates, and other structural components can be determined. This process is called lofting. *See also* loft.

Mold/Mould maker: A craftsperson who constructs templates and molds to be used as patterns and guides for the layout and fabrication of structural parts and hull components of a ship. Unless previously done by a naval architect, the mold maker may also lay out the lines of the vessel to full scale on the mold loft floor.

Mole: A breakwater or long pier covering a harbor entrance.

Mollymawk: A medium-sized albatross species that frequently follows ships in the southern hemisphere.

Mom & Dad: USN enlisted slang for the CO and XO (as in "Mom and Dad are making rounds").

Momsen lung: A submarine breathing apparatus which serves as a gas mask if toxic fumes arise while submerged. It also allows its wearer to breathe normally while escaping from a sunken boat and, once on the surface, serves as a life preserver. It was developed in the 1930s by Lieutenant (later Vice Admiral) Charles B. Momsen, USN, in conjunction with Chief Gunner's Mate Clarence L. Tibbals and Frank M. Hobson, a civilian employee of the Bureau of Ships. The guided missile destroyer USS *Momsen* (DDG-92) is named in Momsen's honor. The device was clumsy to use, and the Royal Navy adopted an apparatus-free escape technique in which the sailor would exhale during ascent in order to keep expanding air from rupturing the lungs.

Monab: [1] Mobile naval air base (USN and RN). [2] Mobile naval operational air base (RN).

Money for old rope: Old worn-out line had many shipboard uses and this phrase — meaning to get something for nothing — has nautical origins. After being picked apart, the yarn made oakum for plugging the seams of a wooden vessel; or could be used like cotton wool to make earplugs when exercising the guns; or be stashed near the heads for use as toilet paper. Beyond these, old rope was useless to sailors, but some of them discovered that the surplus could be sold for cash to manufacturers of rag-paper.

Money under the mast: Until the late nineteenth century, it was common practice for shipbuilders to place a coin under the heel of the mainmast before it was stepped for the first time. This was a symbolic payment to the spirits of the deep to buy their protection. The practice is believed to parallel the ancient Greek custom of placing a coin in the mouth or hand of a corpse for payment of the fee charged by Charon the ferryman for carrying the deceased across the River Styx to Elysium.

Monitor: A heavily-armored vessel equipped with large-caliber artillery. Its shallow draft and low free-board restrict it to relatively calm coastal waters. Named after USS *Monitor*, the first of the class, designed by Swedish-born American inventor and naval architect John Ericsson in 1861.

Monkey: [1] Obsolete term for anything small. [2] A small version of the pile-driver, used to hammer in small bolts. [3] *See* brass monkey.

Monkey cask: A small container in which grog was formerly carried.

Monkey gaff: A small spar extending from the aftermast carrying the halyard for the national ensign of USN vessels.

Monkey jacket: A close-fitting serge coat formerly worn by sailors. Being cut short to facilitate climbing the rigging, it was said to resemble the garment worn by organ-grinders' monkeys.

Monkey rail: A light rail attached above an ordinary one.

Monkey's fist: A heavy knot at the end of a heaving line, making it easier to throw. Often tied around a lump of lead wrapped in a rag.

Monkey's tail: A length of rope attached to running rigging or to a bar allowing more people to pull on it.

Monsoon: [1] Refers to strong, often violent, wind systems that change direction with the season and are accompanied by heavy rains. Monsoons blow from cold to warm regions because cold air takes up more space than warm air. They blow from the land toward the sea in winter, and from the sea toward land in summer. The name was derived from the Arabic word mausim, referring to seasonal winds experienced in the Arabian Sea. [2] Although primarily associated with southeast Asia, the hydrological definition includes any major wind and rain system that changes direction seasonally.

Monsoon current: An ocean current that replaces the north equatorial current and equatorial countercurrent during the winter months when monsoon winds are blowing. It flows across the Bay of Bengal and Arabian Sea.

Monsters of the deep: Sea serpents and monsters have been reported in all the world's seas and oceans, being variously described as swimming dragons, writhing serpents, multi-armed horrors, and dinosaur survivors. Reports have generally been dismissed as myth, legend, misidentification of known species, or the ramblings of over-imaginative seafarers, even though some of those claiming to be eyewitnesses have been scientists, naturalists, and experienced naval officers.

The vast majority of the earth's waters are unexplored, except for a few fathoms below the surface, so it is conceivable that unknown creatures dwell in remote areas or in troughs (going down further than the Himalayas rise) which are far less explored and understood than the planets of our solar system. Such creatures might, on rare occasions, find their way to the surface, to be briefly glimpsed before sounding again or dying in the unfamiliar environment. Indeed, new species of marine animals or specimens of animals believed extinct are discovered almost every year.

For example, the giant squid was thought to be a creature of myth and legend until 1878; the coelanth was found alive and well in 1938, seventy million years after it was supposed to have become extinct; and the four to six meter (13–19 foot) long megamouth shark was unknown until one was accidentally caught in 1976. In the ensuing thirty years there have only been 35 reported sightings or captures of this creature. Another new species of shark was identified in Mexican waters as recently as March 2006.

Other prehistoric animals may also have survived far from human eyes. In 1997, U.S. naval underwater sensors, placed to track Soviet submarines, detected an unexplained sound with frequency characteristics typical of marine animals, but not matching any known vocalization pattern. Although certainly of biological origin, the signal was far too loud to be produced by any recognized creature. "The Bloop," as it has been fancifully nicknamed, may well be emanating from an unknown giant beast lurking in the ocean depths.

There is a huge body of conjecture concerning real or as yet undiscovered creatures which might have been mistaken for sea monsters. These include at least four bony fish, a crocodilian, and three invertebrate cephalopods whose visual characteristics might fool even experienced observers into thinking they had seen a monster. There is also an order of marine mammals which may have given rise to the mermaid legend. These are discussed in the appendix.

Montreux Convention: This 1936 treaty is designed to control use of the Turkish Straits (Dardanelles & Bosporus). Its salient points are:
- In times of peace (or war when Turkey is non-belligerent) merchant vessels, under any flag or with any kind of cargo, enjoy of right of transit and freedom of navigation in the Straits.
- When Turkey is at war, neutral merchant vessels enjoy the same freedoms on condition they do not in any way assist the enemy.
- Foreign naval forces in transit through the Straits may not exceed an aggregate of 15,000 tons, and may not comprise more than nine vessels.
- The aggregate tonnage which non–Black Sea Powers may have in that sea in time of peace shall not exceed 30,000 tons.
- Vessels of war belonging to non–Black Sea Powers shall not remain in the Black Sea more than twenty-one days.

Moonraker: A small square-sail set above a skysail. Also moonsail (and *see* skyscraper).

Moor: To hold a ship in place by tying it to a pier, buoy, or another ship.

Mooring: [1] The act of confining a ship to a particular place. [2] That which serves to confine a ship, such as anchors, cables, bridles, etc. [3] A berth or anchorage where a vessel can moor.

Mooring buoy: A firmly-anchored float carrying a heavy shackle to which a vessel may attach itself without dropping its own anchor.

Mooring lines: Ropes, cables, or springs used to make a vessel fast to a wharf. Mooring lines (also called docking lines) are defined by their function and position:
- Bow lines (not to be confused with bowlines) lead forward from the bow.
- Stern lines are led aft from the stern.
- Springs are led forward or aft from a point on the hull, ending ahead of stern lines and abaft of bow lines. Together, they prevent the ship from drifting ahead or astern.
- Breast lines run directly to the shore at right angles to the keel and, assisted by the springs, stop outward movement away from the dock.

Moorings: A vessel is said to be "at moorings" when she is anchored or attached to a mooring buoy in the harbor, rather than moored alongside a jetty. Moorings may be forward and aft, or at bow only (termed swinging). *See also* offshore mooring.

MOOTW: Military operations other than war.

Mop: The tool used ashore for cleaning floors and walls is always called a swab in naval and merchant service.

Morning-call book: A list of personnel who must be roused before the rest of the ship's company, in order to prepare the vessel for early departure.

Morning colors/colours: The naval ceremony of raising the national ensign aft and Union Jack forward at exactly 0800 (8 A.M.) local time when warships are in port. If more than one ship is present, all follow the senior ship's timing immediately and precisely, having been given five minutes warning by the blue peter hoisted at the senior ship's foremast yardarm.

Morning gun: A single shot fired by a flagship to announce official daybreak.

Morning watch: The work shift beginning at 0400 and ending at 0800 (4–8 A.M.).

Morse: A code or "language" consisting of dots and dashes used to send messages by signal lamp or radio.

Mortar: A short, large-bore cannon, designed to lob projectiles at high angles so that they drop almost vertically to break through decks, roofs, etc. In the age of sail, mortars were the only naval ordnance to fire explosive shells rather than solid shot. It was considered dangerous to have large stocks of shells on board and, moreover, below-deck reinforcing supports for mortar platforms occupied most potential magazine space, so bomb vessels were usually accompanied by an ammunition tender.

Moses' Law: A punishment under pirate law, sentencing the miscreant to thirty-nine lashes on the bare back. Presumably the reference was to the 40 days Moses spent fasting in the wilderness before receiving the Ten Commandments, but why the last stroke was withheld is unclear.

Most Favored Nation: A trade agreement by which one country guarantees that the "favored" country will not be subject to worse duties and restrictions than any other country.

Mothball: To protect a ship and place it in reserve (cf. In ordinary, deactivate, inactivate).

Mother Carey's chickens: The seaman's name for stormy petrels. Seafaring tradition holds it extremely unlucky to kill one since each bird is thought to carry the soul of a dead sailor on his way to Fiddler's Green. (There is a similar belief concerning the albatross, another member of the petrel family.) The superstition is clearly described in Chapter 41 of Captain Marryatt's book Poor Jack, which tells of a schooner en route to Antigua but becalmed near the Virgin islands. On board were a young man called Shedden and Etau, a female Obi (powerful sorcerer). Some stormy petrels were flying about the stern and...

... Shedden must needs get at his gun to shoot them.... "There are three down!" cried out some of the other passengers. "How many?" said the old woman, "Then count the sharks which are coming up." "Count the sharks, mother! why count them?

There's plenty of them" replied Shedden, laughing. "I tell you that there will be but three sent," replied the old woman who then sunk down her head and said no more.... In about ten minutes afterwards, three large sharks swam up to the vessel, with their fins above water.... "Then three are doomed," said the old woman, "and here we stay, and the waves shall not run, nor the wind blow, till the three sharks have their food. I say three are doomed!" Next morning ... the three large sharks were still slowly swimming round and round the schooner. All that day it remained a dead calm, and the heat was dreadful, and the people, becoming more frightened, questioned old Etau, but all the answer she gave was, "Three are doomed!"...

That night, Shedden developed yellow fever, joined shortly afterwards by a sailor and a African slave. No one else was taken ill. Shedden jumped overboard and next morning one of the predators had disappeared. Then the sailor died and another shark vanished after his body was committed to the deep. Finally the slave died and was carried off by the third shark...

... old Etau cried out, "Three! the price is paid!" ... every one crowded round the old woman ... and they asked her ... whether they should have any wind? and her reply was, "When the three birds come from the sea to replace those which were killed...." Well, after a time, although we never saw them rise, three Mother Carey's chickens were seen dipping and flying about astern of the schooner; and they told old Etau, who said, "Now you'll have wind ... and plenty of waves to make up for the calm" and so they had, sure enough, for it came on almost a hurricane, and the schooner scudded before it under bare poles until she arrived at Antigua.

Mother of wages: Former sailor slang for freight (see wages).

Motion: A floating vessel has six degrees of freedom to move in response to wave action. Heave, surge, and sway are linear, while pitch, roll, and yaw are rotational.

Motor: [1] A machine that converts electrical energy to mechanical energy. [2] A relatively small but powerful engine (usually internal combustion).

Motor gunboat: A small, fast, shallow-draft patrol vessel, armed with relatively heavy artillery.

Motor launch: A small, general-purpose patrol vessel, of similar size to a large motor torpedo boat, but slower and less heavily armed. Used for antisubmarine and other patrol duties, harbor defense, fishery protection, coastal convoy escort, and minesweeping,

Motor torpedo boat: A small high-speed vessel, equipped with torpedo tubes, rapid-fire weapons and (possibly) missiles. Often used for armed high speed air sea rescue.

Motor vessel/ship: One propelled by internal combustion engines, as opposed to a sails or steam.

Motorboat: A small craft propelled by an internal-combustion engine or other motor. Also called powerboat.

Mouldy: Obsolete RN lower deck term for a torpedo (origin uncertain).

Mount: [1] To place artillery aboard ship. [2] A housing for a gun or guns. [3] To launch a mission.

Mount Vernon: The first U.S. President was buried on this estate (which was originally owned by his half-brother Lawrence Washington, who changed the name from Epsewasson Plantation on his return from serving under Vice-Admiral Edward Vernon as a Captain of Royal Marines aboard the flagship HMS *Burford*). In his autobiography Commodore Charles Morris relates the beginning one of the U.S. Navy's oldest and most honored ceremonies. In May of 1801, then a young midshipman, he was on board USS *Congress* when:

> About 10 o'clock in the morning of a beautifully serene day, we passed Mount Vernon.... When opposite the house, by order of Captain Sever, the sails were lowered, the colors displayed half-masted, and a mourning salute of thirteen guns was fired as a mark of respect to the memory of Washington, whose life had so recently closed, and whose tomb was in our view.

In 1906, President Theodore Roosevelt was much impressed with this ceremony and, learning that the honors were only traditional he immediately made them official with General Order No. 22 of June 2nd 1906. Today's ceremony includes (whenever possible) parading the Marine guard and band, manning the side, playing the national anthem, and tolling the ship's bell. All on deck face the tomb and salute, while buglers sound taps and the ensign is half-masted. Civilian personnel on board customarily uncover and place their hands or hats over their hearts. Smaller naval ships do not have bands or buglers nor do they have a regularly detailed guard. However, each has a national ensign and a bell. The tolling of the latter is thus the most distinctive aspect of the ceremony.

Other tributes have been paid to the USN's first commander-in-chief. In August 1814, Rear Admiral Sir George Cockburn sealifted a British ground force to Benedict, Maryland, from where they marched into Washington, D.C., and set fire to almost all public buildings and a few private residences. Before evacuating, Navy Secretary William Jones ordered the Navy Yard destroyed, saving the British the trouble. After being repaired, the President's Mansion was whitewashed to cover smoke discoloration, thereafter being known as the "White House." Withdrawing from the raid on 26th August, Admiral Cockburn paid his enemy's first president the courtesy of ordering the bell of his flagship HMS *Sea Horse* to be tolled as she came opposite Mount Vernon. (Cockburn later conveyed Napoleon to St. Helena, staying on as the exiled emperor's jailer and the island's governor.) During the Civil War, Mount Vernon was (unofficially) neutral ground. Soldiers in blue and grey left their arms outside the gates and met fraternally at the tomb of the Father of their divided country.

Mourning: *See* a-cockbill, blue paint, mourning salute.

Mourning salute: As a token of grief, the national ensign is raised fully, then lowered from the masthead and secured. The U.S. Army, Air Force, and Marine Corps call the lowered position "half-staff," while the U.S. Navy and all British forces call it "half-mast." Originally the gap was equal to the width of a flag to allow the invisible Flag of Death (which is superior to all human entities) to take its place above the ensign. Nowadays the Royal Navy lowers the ensign by one-third of the length of the pole and the United States Navy by exactly one-half. In non-military usage, anywhere from one-third to two-thirds of the way up the flagpole or ship's mast is acceptable. The modern practice is first mentioned in 1612, but originated much earlier. When striking a half-masted ensign, it is always raised to the truck before lowering. *See* half-mast/staff.

Mouse: [1] To wrap line or wire around the jaw of a lifting hook to prevent the load from slipping out. [2] Formerly used on stays to prevent the eye from slipping up to the mast, but making it extremely difficult to remove the stay from the masthead, when necessary. [3] A pointing device used in computing.

Moustaches: *See* facial hair.

Movement Report System: USN system which maintains current information on the status, location, and movement of flag commands, vessels in commission, and other ships under USN operational control.

Moving submarine haven: An area established via notices issued by a submarine operating authority to prevent mutual interference among moving submarines, or between submarines and ships operating towed arrays or other bodies. The area around a submersible in transit extends 50 miles ahead, 100 miles astern, and 15 miles on each side of the estimated position of the submarine along its stated track.

MoW: Man-of-War.

MPA: Maritime patrol aircraft (USCG).

MPF: Maritime pre-positioned force.

MPG: Military Pay Grade (U.S.).

MPR: Maritime patrol and reconnaissance

MRS: Movement report system.

MS: [1] Mess Specialist (USN). [2] Mission Support. [3] Mission Specific. [5] Manuscript.

MSC: Military Sealift Command.

MSL: Mean sea level.

MSO: [1] Hull classification symbol of an ocean minesweeper. [2] Military Service Obligation (U.S.).

MSP: Maritime Security Program. Designed to maintain the nucleus of a fleet of militarily-useful U.S.-flagged vessels.

MSS: Maritime Safety & Security.

MSTS: Military Sea Transport Service (U.S.). Former name of the MSC.

mt: Metric tonne.

MTB: RN designation of a motor torpedo boat.

mtm: Million Ton-Miles.

MTMC: Military Traffic Management Command. Former name of the SDDC.

MUC: Meritorious Unit Commendation.

Mudhook: Seaman's slang for an anchor.

Muffle: [1] To cover a drum with cloth to soften its sound (at funerals, for example). [2] To wrap canvas or other material around the shafts of oars in order to silence them for surprise assaults or funerals. Without wrapping they might rub against the rowlocks and squeak.

Mufti: British Army term for civilian dress worn by a person usually wearing uniform. Sometimes used in the Royal Navy, but the preferred naval term is "plain clothes."

Mulberry: The code-name for a pair of artificial harbors built to maintain the momentum of Operation Overlord, the 1944 Normandy invasion. Vast quantities of matériel had to be brought ashore rapidly, along with substantial reinforcements, but the invasion beaches were unsuitable for this task. Each Mulberry was assembled from prefabricated concrete, and had 10 miles (15 km) of floating roadways to land men and vehicles on the beach. A large number of old merchant ships was scuttled to protect them from rough weather.

Mulberries were about the size of Dover Harbor, but were thought of as short-term and disposable, designed to last up to three months, or until one or more French ports were captured. In the event, after only ten days, a storm destroyed the American Mulberry at Saint-Laurent-sur-Mer which had not been strongly anchored to the sea bed. However, the more firmly secured British one at Arromanches (known as Port Winston) remained in service for eight months. (Its remains are still visible from the beach at Arromanches.) By D+100 four million tons of supplies, half-a-million vehicles, and over 2.5 million troops had been landed there. (*See also* crossword coincidence.)

Mulct: To impose a fine as punishment for some fault or misdemeanor.

Mule: When aircraft are launching into wind, the maxim for escorting vessels is — "Never stand behind a mule or cross ahead of a carrier!"

Multipurpose vessel: A cargo ship equipped to carry standard shipping containers, with retractable tweendecks that can be moved out of the way so that the ship can carry bulk cargo.

Munition: An explosive, propellant, pyrotechnic, nuclear, biological, or chemical device for use in military operations, demolitions, or on ceremonial occasions (*see also* ammunition, ordnance).

Munitions: Naval or military stores (*see* matériel).

Murderer: Naval slang for a carronade or large blunderbuss loaded with langredge and used as an anti-personnel weapon.

Murmansk Current: A warm southeasterly current of the Barents Sea, responsible for keeping the Russian port of Murmansk ice free in winter.

Musket: A smooth-bore, long-barreled personal firearm.

Musket arrow: A projectile used to transfer messages between ships during the 18th and early 19th centuries.

Musket shot: The range at which sailing ship navies liked to open broadside fire. Usually considered to be 400 yards. *See* "Wait 'til you see the whites of their eyes."

Musketoon: A short-barreled, large-bore, blunderbuss-like firearm, usually loaded with langrage, four or five musket balls, or a handful of pistol shot, and swivel-mounted at the bow of a boat, barge, or pinnace for use as an anti-personnel weapon.

Mustang: In USN slang, a Mustang is a career sailor, commissioned from the enlisted ranks to Chief Warrant Officer or Limited Duty Officer. A mustang has the experience and technical background to perform tasks that call for officer rank and protocol, but are better performed with enlisted experience. The Navy and Marine Corps are the only branches of the U.S. armed forces to have such commissioning programs in place.

Muster: To assemble the crew on deck (*see* open list muster). From the Latin monstrare = to show.

Muster book: A document recording the names of a ship's company.

Muster in/out: To enlist for or be discharged from active duty.

Mute: When a prisoner arraigned before a court-martial is called upon to plead but remains silent this is technically termed "standing mute." A prisoner may also stand mute by "visitation of God" (inability to articulate). Under old English common law, standing mute was deemed equivalent to conviction, upon which judgment followed. Nowadays, the court proceeds as though a plea of "not guilty" had been made. The same course is pursued when the prisoner refuses to plead properly in an attempt to obstruct the proceedings.

Mutilation: The term for a naval crime involving a self-inflicted wound or maiming to avoid service or obtain a discharge.

Mutiny: Organized and open revolt against constituted authority, especially by soldiers or seamen against their officers. Mutiny becomes piracy when it is followed or accompanied by the seizure of physical assets, including the vessel. *See Batavia, Bounty, Hermione,* and *Somers* Mutinies; Great Mutiny, and RIN Mutiny.

Muzzle: [1] The open end or front part of the barrel of a gun or other firearm. [2] To attach a cable to the stock of an anchor by a light line.

Muzzle-loader: A gun loaded from the front (cf. breech-loader).

MV: Prefix designating a motor vessel.

MWL: Mean Water Level.

Myoparo: A small, speedy galley, much favored by Mediterranean pirates during the Hellenistic and Roman periods.

Myrmidon: Obsolete (and somewhat poetical) name for a sea captain. After the people of Thessaly, mythologically said to have been the first to construct ships.

N

Nacelle: The streamlined outer casing of an aircraft engine or compartment.

NAEC: Naval air engineering center.

NAF: Naval Air Facility.

Nail: To nail a gun is to spike it.

Nail colors to the mast: A sailing warship's captain would frequently order this action before combat, either to warn the crew he intended to fight to the death, or to prevent the flag falling in apparent surrender if its halyard was cut by enemy gunfire. It was an easy transition to the modern civilian meaning of taking a firm position which all can see.

Nail trimming: *See* haircutting.

Naked: Said of a wooden-hulled vessel whose copper sheathing has been removed.

Naked female: [1] Sailing ship seamen believed that gales and high winds would subside if confronted by an unclothed woman. For this reason, many figureheads depicted women with bare breasts. [2] There was also an old superstition that a chance encounter with a naked woman while going to board the ship foretold a lucky voyage, the more fortunate the more comely she was (one doubts this happened very often!).

Naming: There are conflicting ship-naming traditions in the merchant and naval services. For centuries, merchant seamen would no more use the definite article when referring to their ship, than they would when speaking of their wife (e.g., "The Mary"), but this convention has been increasingly ignored since the mid–20th century. In the RN and USN, however, the first mention of a ship's name should always be preceded by the definite article "The" or by the defining prefix "HMS" or "USS," although it is acceptable to drop the article or prefix in subsequent references. In RN signals, as a form of shorthand, the ship name alone is taken to refer to its captain (e.g., *Ark Royal* will report to the admiral). Once a ship has been christened (usually at its launch) it is considered extremely bad luck to change the name. *See also* Gender and reptiles.

Nancy Dawson: The tune adopted by the Royal Navy to summon a ship's company to receive their grog ration is also used for the children's song "Here we go 'round the mulberry bush." It was originally a popular 18th century song whose first stanza was:

> Of all the girls in our town,
> The black, the fair, the red, the brown,
> That dance and prance it up and down,
> There's none like Nancy Dawson.

It must have had more appropriate mnemonics in the navy, but the author has been unable to trace them.

Nantucket sleighride: Said of the wild run of a whaleboat being towed behind a rampaging harpooned whale. (Nantucket Island off Massachusetts was a major whaling port in the 19th century.)

Nao: The Spanish name for a carrack.

Napalm: [1] Jellied petroleum used in bombs and flame-throwers. [2] The thickening agent (powdered aluminum soap) used to make this product.

Narrows: A constricted section of navigable waterway.

NAS: Naval Air Station.

National Cargo Bureau: Was created as a nonprofit organization in 1952, to render assistance to the United States Coast Guard in discharging its responsibilities under the 1948 International Convention for Safety of Life at Sea and for other purposes closely related thereto. By assignment from and under authority of the USCG, certificates issued by NCB are accepted as prima facie evidence of compliance with the Dangerous Cargo Act and the Rules and Regulations for Bulk Grain Cargo.

National ensign: The flag identifying a vessel's nationality.

National gun salutes: As mentioned under gun salutes the practice of greeting by gunfire originated in the early days of muzzle-loaded firearms, when it took several minutes to charge and prime a musket and up to twenty to reload a cannon. When entering a foreign port or meeting a foreign vessel it became customary for the ship to discharge seven cannon and the crew to fire muskets into the air, to signify friendly intentions by effectively disarming themselves. Since land batteries could store larger amounts of powder and shot, it was traditional for them to reciprocate by firing twenty-one guns in return (three for each one fired by the ship).

A similar procedure was followed when two warships met. Each would steer towards the other on parallel paths, bows-on so that broadsides could not bear until they passed, sequentially firing the broadside that would face the approaching vessel when they met. The guns were fired one-by-one, at five-second intervals, to prove that none had been covertly kept loaded. Eventually, recharging became much faster (British gunners at Trafalgar were expected to fire once every 90 seconds) so that some weapons could have been reloaded before the feu de joie had finished, making the ceremony entirely symbolic.

For many years the number of guns fired varied from country to country (with monarchies usually receiving more than republics) and the differing conventions caused considerable confusion. Moreover, the practice showed every sign of getting out of control, as shots would sometimes be fired for hours on end and the expenditure of gunpowder was becoming prohibitive. In 1730 the British Admiralty proposed a maximum of twenty-one guns, but this was not mandatory in the RN until 1808. By then Britain was the predominant seapower and forced most weaker powers to follow suit.

The United States followed a different path to the same end. On 16th November 1776, Continental Navy brig *Andrew Doria* visited the island of Sint Eustatius to pick up munitions and other contraband of war which the theoretically-neutral Dutch were clandestinely supplying to the American rebels. Entering the harbor, Captain Isaiah Robinson ordered an 11-gun salute (some accounts say 13), to which Johannes de Graaff, the colonial governor replied with 9 guns, then the salute to a republic. The rebel states gave this great publicity because it was the first international "recognition" of their independence.

The British took the incident far less seriously, although they strongly protested ongoing American trade with the Netherlands Antilles. In 1778, David Murray, Lord Stormont told Parliament, "If Sint Eustatius had sunk into the sea three years ago, the United Kingdom would already have dealt with George Washington." Two years later this trade precipitated the Fourth Anglo-Dutch War, and in February 1781, Admiral Rodney seized Sint Eustatius and its companion island Sint Maarten, removing what had been one of the Americans' most important sources of loans and weaponry, but by then the revolution had enough momentum to carry on.

Andrew Doria's ensign, which governor de Graaff later claimed not to have recognized as that of the rebels, was the Grand Union Flag, consisting of thirteen alternating red and white stripes, with the British Jack in the union. It was not until 14th June 1777 that Congress adopted the Stars and Stripes as the "Official Flag of the Thirteen United States." On that same day, Congress appointed John Paul Jones to command the newly-constructed sloop-of-war *Ranger* Eight months later, on Valentine's Day 1778, *Ranger* entered Quiberon Bay and Jones ordered a 13-gun salute (one for each state in the union) to the French squadron anchored there. In the first foreign recognition of the new American flag Admiral LaMotte Piquet's flagship *Robuste* responded with the 9-gun salute to a republic.

Following Jones' example, United States warships unofficially fired one shot for each state until 1810 when the Department of War made it official. However, by 1841 there were twenty-six states and the number was obviously going to increase, so the United States followed the rest of the world and adopted a national salute of twenty-one guns. (Some Americans now claim that the salute is a tribute to Independence, since 1+7+7+6 = 21 but this is clearly incorrect since the practice was well established internationally before the U.S. adopted it.) *See also* personal gun salutes and salutes and courtesies.

National Oceanic and Atmospheric Administration: Formerly the United States Coast and Geodetic Survey, this agency is an important source of marine charts in the United States.

NATO: North Atlantic Treaty Organization.

Nau: Portuguese name for a carrack.

Naufragiate: A 15th century expression meaning to suffer shipwreck. (From the French naufrage.)

Nausea: [1] Dizziness and the urge to vomit. [2] Originally Greek, and later Latin, for seasickness.

Nautical: Of or pertaining to seas and oceans, ships, seamen, and navigation.

Nautical Almanac: For over 150 years the United States Nautical Almanac Office has published this book in collaboration with Her/His Majesty's Nautical Almanac Office in the UK, to provide the U.S. and Royal Navies with a standard resource for marine celestial navigation.

Nautical day: In order to avoid a change of date during the night watches, and because midday was when the ship's position, course, and run distance were recorded, the mariner's day formerly began and ended with the noon observation. However, a ship at sea was thus twelve hours ahead of the civil day and, to add to the confusion (*see* day), when it entered port the civil day took precedence. On 11th October 1805, the RN switched to the civil day beginning at midnight. The USN automatically followed suit, because it used the British Nautical Almanac until 1852 when the American version was published.

Nautical distance: The length in nautical miles of the rhumb line joining any two places on the earth's surface.

Nautical league: A distance of three nautical miles = 3.45 land miles, or 5.56 kilometers.

Nautical mile: A unit of distance theoretically defined as one minute of arc on a terrestrial great circle. Since earth is not a perfect sphere a minute of arc varies from 1,862 meters at the equator to 1,843 at the poles. The international definition standardizes the nautical mile at the mid-point of 1,853 meters, which converts to approximately 2026.8 yds or 1.1516 statute miles.

NAVAIR: Naval Air Systems Command.

Naval: [1] Of or pertaining to ships and the sea. [2] Concerning the customs, equipment, personnel, and infrastructure of a navy. [3] Sometimes used to differentiate between ships of war and those of commerce.

Naval Air Systems Command: Established in 1966 as successor to the U.S. Navy's Bureau of Naval Weapons (*see* Bureau of Ordnance). According to its website, "NAVAIR provides unique engineering, development, testing, evaluation, in-service support, and program management capabilities to deliver airborne weapons systems that are technologically superior and readily available. Using a full-spectrum approach, the command delivers optimal capability and reliability for the Sailor and the Marine."

Naval architecture: The art and science of designing waterborne craft. Cf. naval construction.

Naval arms control: *See* Anglo-German Naval Agreement, Treaty of Versailles, and Washington Naval Agreement.

Naval attaché: An officer attached to an Embassy as adviser on naval affairs, and to gather information on the host nation's navy. Depending on the state of relations between the countries this might involve anything from friendly exchanges of information to covert activity verging on espionage.

Naval aviation: Refers to the land and carrier-based aircraft operated by a navy. Early growth of the latter capability was nurtured by a small group of

American and British, and to a lesser extent, Japanese pioneers. Each developed in its own unique fashion:

• *In the United States:* On November 14, 1910, a civilian aviator named Eugene Ely took off from a temporary platform erected on the forecastle of light cruiser USS *Birmingham*. His aircraft briefly touched the water, damaging its propeller, but rose again and landed on a sandspit. The flight covered less than two and a half miles and took barely five minutes. Two months later, after landing on a wooden platform built on the after turret of armored cruiser USS *Pennsylvania*, Ely launched from the platform and flew back to shore, proving that the aircraft carrier was a viable concept.

When the U.S. declared war on Germany on 6 April 1917, the Navy had only 54 aircraft, 1 airship, 3 balloons and 287 personnel. Nevertheless, one of its units was the first to reach France, while naval aircraft flew more than 3 million nautical miles and damaged a dozen U-boats. By the end of WWI, personnel numbered 37,400, with 252 land-based aircraft, and 1,865 flying boats and seaplanes. U.S. Naval aviation had grown enormously and was well on its way. But in the inter-war years it was treated as second-class by battleship-minded admirals and not until the Battle of Midway did it come into its own. (*See also* marine aviation.)

• *The Japanese military* followed the development of aviation with great interest, and acquired their first aircraft in 1910. When World War I broke out, Japan joined the Allies and, during the siege of German held Tsingtao (September–November 1914), the seaplane carrier *Wakamiya* launched the first shipborne aerial raids in history. During the late 1920s and early 1930s, while the United States and Britain were disarming, the militarist dominated government spent heavily on its armed forces. When World War II began, Japan's ten aircraft carriers had a combined tonnage three times that allowed under the Washington Naval Treaties. Moreover, unlike most British and American admirals, Isoroku Yamamoto, Commander-in-Chief of the Imperial Combined Fleet, had abandoned belief in the battleship and become an enthusiastic advocate of naval air power. By 1940, Japan had the largest and most powerful navy in the Pacific, and had built the biggest and most effective naval aviation service in the world. Japanese carrier aircraft were arguably the best, while their aircrews were superbly trained, and had been battle tested during four years of war with China.

• *Great Britain* got off to a good start. A Royal Flying Corps (RFC) was founded in April 1912, intended to encompass both naval and military flying. However, even though the soldier-dominated RFC arranged Britain's first flight from a moving ship a month later, the Navy was not comfortable having its aircraft under Army control. Without authorization, it formed its own flying branch, which was officially recognized and named Royal Naval Air Service (RNAS) on July 1, 1914.

A month later, when the First World War began, the RNAS had more aircraft than the RFC, and four years after that it was by far the largest, most experienced, and best equipped aeronaval force in the world. Then — appropriately on April Fool's Day 1918 — disaster struck! The government decided to create the Royal Air Force (RAF). forcing naval aviators to choose between love of the sea and enthusiasm for flying. Most chose the latter, many rising to high rank in the RAF.

The new service was obsessed with the concept of strategic bombing and, apart from fighters for home defense, virtually ignored the requirements of carrier operation, coastal patrol, and army tactical support. British naval aviation had lost its momentum. Insufficient numbers of inferior and unsuitable aircraft were crewed mainly by pilots on two-year assignments, none of whom had joined the Air Force in order to go to sea. Many could not distinguish warships from merchantmen, and by the time they became proficient, they returned to land-based squadrons. Naval officers could apply for flying duty, but many considered it career suicide, especially as they had to accept RAF commissions to do so.

Unlike the United States and Japan, there was no specific naval staff or institution responsible for studying the role of aviation, no naval air lobby to challenge the doctrine of battleship supremacy, and no naval air engineers to mastermind the design and development of carrier aircraft . But the worst shortages were at top and bottom. All the highly-specialized technical cadres were Air Force personnel, while transfer of the first generation of naval aviators to the RAF meant that the Royal Navy had no flag officers, and few carrier commanders, with personal flying experience.

In 1937, after a long and bitter inter-service battle, the Navy regained control of its carrier-borne aircraft but, against all logic, the RAF managed to retain responsibility for anti-submarine coastal patrol. In 1918, the RNAS had contributed 55,000 men and 2,950 aircraft to the fledgling Air Force. Nineteen years later, on the eve of World War II, the "Fleet Air Arm" of the RAF returned 700 personnel and 232 operational aircraft, most of them outdated canvas-covered biplanes, vastly inferior to the land-based and carrier-borne monoplanes of the U.S. and Japanese navies, each of which had kept control of its air component.

During World War II a few high-performance aircraft were adapted for naval service, including the famous Spitfire (re-named Seafire) but it was thanks to the United States lend-lease program, that the Royal Navy was able to obtain the purpose-built modern carrier aircraft that played important roles in every maritime theater of operation.

Naval base: A shore station providing administrative and logistic support to forces afloat.

Naval brigade: A temporary organization of marines and seamen, larger than a landing party, but smaller than a division formed to undertake operations ashore in the role of naval infantry.

Naval construction: *See* Civil Engineer Corps and Royal Corps of Naval Constructors.

Naval Construction Corps: A unit of the U S Navy's Civil Engineer Corps, abolished in 1940 with its officers being given line status but designated "EDO."

Naval Co-operation and Guidance for Shipping: An organization set up by NATO to establish and provide advice for the safe passage of merchant ships worldwide. It provides liaison between military commanders and civil authorities during times of peace, tension, terrorism, crisis, or war. In the latter, it may be responsible for establishing convoys.

Seaborne trade is of fundamental strategic interest to those nations whose economic well-being depends on freedom of movement on the seas. Commercial movement may affect military operations while, conversely, naval operations frequently involve, or have some impact, on merchant shipping . Hence, cooperation between military and shipping interests can minimize delays or confusion and afford protection to merchantmen transiting maritime areas of operation. *See also* Pacific and Indian Oceans Shipping Working Group.

Naval crown: An ancient heraldic device consisting of a coronet adorned with alternating depictions of square-rigged masts and the sterns of antique ships. The design concept is reputed to have originated with Roman Emperor Claudius as a trophy (rostral) to be awarded to the first seaman or marine to board an enemy ship.

Naval district: A U.S. concept under which a designated commandant is direct representative of the Secretary of the Navy and the Chief of Naval Operations for defense, security, and naval operations within a defined geographical area.

Naval dockyard: Generic term for a facility equipped with cranes, drydocks, slipways, warehouses and the like; responsible for building, repairing, modifying, and replenishing naval vessels.

Naval doctrine: With the end of the "Cold War," the advent of global terrorism, an increase in the number of failed or failing states, and accelerating technological development; military and diplomatic organizations find themselves confronted with previously-unconsidered, rapidly-fluctuating challenges. In consequence, twenty-first century strategic and tactical planners are actively developing radical new approaches and concepts. *See* Future Navy, Global Maritime Partnership, Military Operations other than War, Network Centric Warfare, Revolution in Military Affairs, and Swing.

Naval hymn: William Whiting's poem, whose first stanza is: "Eternal Father! Strong to save!" is recog-

nized as the official anthem of both the United States and Royal Navies. *See* Hymns for more information.

Naval Infantry: Competency in limited-scale land warfare — sailors performing as soldiers and sometimes providing land based artillery support — was an integral part of 19th century naval operations. In the Royal Navy, officers and seamen were specifically trained in land-based warfare by the gunnery school at HMS *Excellent* in Portsmouth. In the United States Navy individual ships and flag officers were largely on their own until 1891 when the Bureau of Ordnance issued "Instructions for Infantry and Artillery, United States Navy" which was generally compatible with Army operations ashore.

The Achilles heel of naval infantry was invariably weak logistical support without which they could not sustain themselves for long. During World War I Britain fielded a complete naval division (the 63rd) which fought in France and Gallipoli but, unlike the typical naval brigade, it was created, equipped, and trained on shore rather than formed extemporaneously by the ships of a fleet or squadron.

Naval law: The rules and regulations governing personnel in a national naval service. Not to be confused with maritime or admiralty law. *See* Articles of War.

Naval police: During the 17th century Ship's Marshals, assisted by Ship's Corporals, were accountable for the good order, discipline, and conduct of a ship's company. Then, in 1699, the rate of Marshal was replaced by that of Master-at-arms, reporting to the Lieutenant-at-arms, and responsible for small arms training as well as supervising discipline through the ship's corporals. By 1860, small arms training in the RN had been transferred to a junior lieutenant, and the MAA became head of a new "Police Branch." In 1919, Admiralty Fleet Order 2290 re-named the police branch Regulating Branch, and replaced ship's corporals with Regulating Petty Officers. In 1967, the Royal Navy was the first British armed service to introduce a Drugs Squad. Finally, in 2006, the regulators were re-named Service Police.

The military police of the U.S. Navy also fall into the Master-at-arms rating, which can be traced back to the Continental Navy of 1775. However, it was a collateral duty until 1973, when it became an official rating, open to sailors in the Petty Officer 3rd Class (E-4) grade or above who are able to specialize in a range of law enforcement duties.

Naval ranks & rates: In naval terminology, "rank" refers to the status conferred by warrant or commission. The equivalent term for enlisted personnel (USN) and ratings (RN) is "rate." The term "rating" does not apply to status, but refers to an individuals' job classification or specialty (e.g., able-seaman, boatswain's mate, etc.). Together, rank and rate follow the chain of command and give an indication of relative status. Equivalent British and United States Commissioned Officer Ranks (Air Forces excluded) are shown in Table 13. Ranks and rates are identified by codes in both NATO and United States Armed Forces. These codes with representative job titles (there may be several within each) are shown in Table 14. They fall into four general categories as follows:

1. **Commissioned Officers**
   - NATO codes OF-6 to OF-10, and U.S. codes O-7 to O-11 cover admirals and generals, who sit at the apex of the military hierarchy and are known as Flag Officers and General Officers respectively. (An exception is a Royal Navy captain with six years seniority, who ranks as NATO OF-6 but is not a flag officer.)
   - NATO codes OF-3-to OF-5 and U.S. codes O-4 to O-6 apply to naval officers of mid-grade and marine officers of field grade. (These might better be known as "command" grades.)
   - NATO codes OF-1 & 2 and U.S. O-1 to O-3 are the codes for junior and subordinate grade naval officers and company grade marine officers.

2. **Commissioned Warrant Officers**
   - U.S. WO-2 to WO-5. (These ranks do not exist in most other navies, and are not recognized by the NATO code system.) Commissioned warrant officers derive their authority from presidential commissions but, in contrast to commissioned line officers, who are generalists, they remain specialists.

3. **Non-Commissioned (Petty) Officers**
   - NATO OR-7 to OR-9 and U.S. E-7 to E-9 are senior NCOs with significant command responsibility (U.S. code WO-1, currently dormant, was equivalent to NATO OR-9).
   - NATO OR-4 to OR-6 and U.S. E-4 to E6 cover junior non-commissioned or enlisted personnel with limited command responsibility.

4. **Other Ranks and Rates**
   - NATO codes OR-3 and -4 and U.S. codes E-3 and -4 cover rates with minor or no command responsibility. Most of these will have an rating (occupational specialty), of which there are over fifty in modern navies. NATO codes OR-1 and 2 and U.S. codes E-1 and 2 refer to junior unrated personnel in training.

Naval shower: Water aboard ship is manufactured and strictly rationed, so the proper way to take a shower at sea is to wet the body, turn off the water to wash, and turn it on again to rinse.

Naval special warfare: Refers to operations characterized by stealth, speed, and violent application of force; conducted by small, flexible, mobile units operating from or under the sea in coastal and riverine environments (cf. commando, seal team).

Naval station: Similar to a naval base, but smaller.

Naval stores: [1] Historically, sailing ship necessaries such as cordage, canvas, pine resin, pitch and turpentine. [2] Currently, consumable supplies or commodities used on shipboard, such as food, fuel, clothing, medical items, and ammunition. (In the RN, food and clothing are known as "victualling stores.")

Naval surface fire control: The complexity of fire control systems varies widely depending on the ship, its armament, how many guns are controlled, and other factors. If the firing ship and its target are both stationary, gun settings can easily be determined, but in practice both target and ship are in motion. Hence, range and bearing continually change, demanding constant adjustment of elevation and deflection. Moreover, the roll and pitch of a moving ship require corrections to compensate for deck motion. (One early contrivance was to suspend a round shot from a spar. The gunner fired his piece just before this improvised pendulum was parallel to the mast, meaning the deck was horizontal.) This principle was later incorporated in "stable element" and "stable vertical," devices that act like spinning tops to establish a reference plane from which angles of deflection and elevation can be measured. Another factor is the fact that the velocity of the ship is imparted to the projectile at the instant of firing, with direct effect on its trajectory. *See also* ballistic wind.

Naval tactics in the age of sail: Until the 16th century (with the exception of ramming), naval tactics were virtually non-existent; the purpose of ships being simply to lay alongside the enemy so that embarked soldiers could board to fight a land battle on deck. The arrival of gunpowder initially did little to change things, merely adding light anti-personnel weapons on the weather deck. Then, after invention of the gunport, British seamen seem to have been the first to grasp, dimly at first, the tactical changes made possible by broadside artillery, allowing them to decimate the Spanish Armada.

In mid–17th century, British Parliamentary General of the Sea Robert Blake developed the concept of line-ahead (column), to achieve the twin goals of maximizing firepower and creating an orderly formation responsive to command. This gave the British an immense tactical advantage. A French observer of the Second Anglo-Dutch War (1665–1667) compared the old and new tactical styles, writing:

> Nothing equals the beautiful order of the English at sea. Never was a line drawn straighter than that drawn by their ships; thus they bring all their fire to bear on those who come near them.... They fight like a line of cavalry which is handled according to rule ... whereas the Dutch advance like cavalry whose squadrons leave their ranks and come separately to the charge.

However, the concept was soon imitated by other major powers, and combat at sea became as blunt as a sledgehammer — a matter of two fleets sailing in parallel lines and firing point blank broadsides at each other. French and Spanish tried to fire on the upward roll, to bring down rigging and disable an opponent; while British and Dutch usually fired on the downward roll, so their shot would strike the hull creating a lethal shower of razor-sharp splinters. As long as fleets were reasonably well-matched, such battles were seldom conclusive. (*See* Fighting Instructions.)

The ambiguity of battles with no clear victor intrigued Sir John Clerke, whose writings (*see* cutting the line) greatly influenced British naval officers who — during the French Revolutionary and Napoleonic Wars (1792–1815) — increasingly tended to leave the line of battle, sail directly at the foe, break through the hostile line, and destroy the enemy piecemeal, relying on individual initiative, superior seamanship, and faster gunnery to win the day (*see also* raking).

The tactics of warfare under sail were brought close to perfection by Horatio Nelson at the 1805 Battle of Trafalgar, where they were facilitated by a greatly-improved signaling system invented by Sir Home Popham, but the contest was still a pounding match. Not until seven years later was rate of fire joined by accuracy of aim as the deciding factors (*see* Don't give up the ship). After that, no further improvements in naval tactics were developed until the introduction of ironclad steamships during the late 19th century.

Naval time: In common with other military organizations, naval time is expressed as four digits, based on a 24-hour day starting 0000 and ending 2400. (For example 3:15 A.M. would be "Oh-three-fifteen," while 3:15 P.M. would be "fifteen-fifteen.") *See also* Naval day, Date & Time Notation, Time Zones, and table 12.

Naval titles & hierarchies: During the Middle Ages and Renaissance, navies were essentially part-time services. When war broke out, merchantmen were taken over and fitted with fighting platforms. Their regular crews remained on board under direct command of the master, who received a warrant for royal service and was responsible for navigation and seamanship. When the vessel was ready for combat, a detachment of soldiers marched on board, led by a captain, who held a royal commission as military commander. As such he was senior to the master, directed the fighting and movement of the ship, but had no direct control over the crew or shiphandling.

By the 17th century, national navies had begun to evolve, and ships were being purpose-built for combat, but the old arrangement persisted, with a captain in overall military command, assisted by a master who was a professional seaman. Additional orders of precedence and hierarchical chains of command gradually evolved and can be arbitrarily divided into eight broad categories discussed under naval ranks and rates, and repeated below (with U.S. rank codes):

- Flag Ranks (O-7 to 10)
- Command Ranks (O-4 to 6)
- Other Commissioned Officers (O-3 to 5)
- Subordinate Officers (O-1 and 2)
- Warrant Officers (W-2 to 5)
- Petty Officers (E-4 to 9)
- Rated personnel (E-3)
- Junior Unrated Personnel (E-1 and 2)

Officers in merchant service are civilians and, in many ways, more like business executives than military commanders. The British Merchant Navy and United States Merchant Marine have similar job titles (Master, Mate, Chief Engineer, etc.), but the former has a naval-style rank structure, while the latter considers the jobs to be positions rather than ranks (Merchant Marine Officers do, however, hold naval reserve commissions).

Navarino Bay (battle): In October 1825, during a temporary cease-fire in the War of Greek Independence, a three-nation fleet, commanded by British Vice Admiral Sir Edward Codrington, accompanied by French Vice Admiral Compte Henri de Rigny, and Russian Kontr-Admiral Count Login Petrovich van der Heiden was sent with orders to enforce the armistice but avoid hostilities except in self-defense. They advised the Ottoman commander, Ibrahim Reis-Pasha, they planned to enter the harbor peacefully for further negotiations. However, noting that the Turco-Egyptian guns were run out, the allied ships cleared for action, but kept their cannon inboard with ports in the half-open, fine-weather cruising position. Codrington ordered his Marine band to play cheerful music as they anchored in the middle of a semi-circle of Turkish warships.

A British frigate sent its cutter to ask one of the Turkish ships to make space by moving its anchorage. The boat was unarmed, but a trigger-happy Turkish marine decided it was hostile and fired a single musket shot. His aim was good and he hit the boat's officer. In return the frigate's marines gave covering musket fire and, on hearing their fusillade, an overexcited Egyptian cannoneer discharged his weapon at the French flagship, which replied with a full broadside. Like Nelson's famous engagement at Aboukir Bay, the ensuing battle was a duel between anchored gun batteries, rather than a conventional fleet action. Muzzle-to-muzzle, the two sides blazed away at each other until the Franco-Russian-British Alliance — with fewer, but larger and more heavily-gunned ships — had sunk or destroyed more than three-quarters of the Turco-Egyptians, inflicting tremendous loss of life, but suffering few casualties themselves.

In an unintended action, nominally neutral powers had irreparably crippled Turco-Egyptian sea power and paved the way for Russian imperialism. Six months later, Russia attacked Turkey on the pretext of supporting the still-undecided Greek struggle for independence. With Constantinople threatened, Turkey sued for peace. Under the 1829 Treaty of Adrianople, Russia gained the Mouth of the Danube, and the Eastern Black Sea coast; while Serbia, Wallachia, and Moldavia were granted full autonomy. Then the Great Powers got into the act and, three years later, the Treaty of London recognized Greece as an independent Kingdom.

Navel pipe: A deck fitting that guides the anchor chain into the chain locker.

NAVFAC: Naval facility (especially one associated with SOSUS).

Navicert: A document issued in a neutral country by the consular or diplomatic representative of a belligerent nation, certifying that a vessel of that neutral country is carrying no contraband of war and may therefore travel to another neutral country without being liable to search or seizure.

Navigable: [1] Waters deep and wide enough for a given vessel to pass through or over. [2] Any vessel capable of being steered even if not under sail or power.

Navigable semicircle: The less-violent half of a circular storm, in which the rotary motion and forward translation of the storm tend to counteract each other, and winds are in such a direction as to blow vessels away from the storm track. The navigable side is to the right of clockwise-moving winds in the southern hemisphere and to the left of counter-clockwise winds in the northern. Also navigable quadrant and safe quadrant. The opposite side is understandably known as the dangerous semicircle.

Navigant: An ancient word for a seaman.

Navigation: The science or art of planning, ascertaining, and recording the course of a vessel or aircraft; including fixing present and predicting future location, and collision avoidance. The word comes from the Sanskrit navagati.

Navigation Acts: Several British Parliamentary ordinances issued between 1651 and 1847, designed to expand the country's waterborne commerce and limit trade by its colonies with Britain's commercial rivals.

Navigation certificate: *See* navicert.

Navigation lights: Illumination mandated by Rules of the Road to be shown from sunset to sunrise; during poor visibility; and when deemed necessary to prevent collisions by alerting vessels to each other's presence, indicating their relative bearings, giving hints as to each vessel's size, and determining which has right-of-way. The location, color, range and arc-of-visibility of these lights are clearly specified by law and regulation, and no other lights which might be mistaken for them may be shown at the times mentioned above. The basic lights (also known as running lights) are:

- **Side:** Red to port and green to starboard, showing an unbroken arc of light from dead ahead to 22.5° abaft the beam on their respective sides.
- **Masthead:** White, over the fore-and-aft centerline, showing an unbroken arc of light from 22.5° abaft the beam on one side to 22.5° abaft the beam on the other. Powered vessels over 50 meters in length are required to have a second such light abaft and higher than the first (different regulations apply to vessels less than 20 meters long and also for those less than 12 meters long). The white masthead light is not required for vessels under sail but they may carry a red light above a green one at the masthead, both visible over 360°.
- **Stern:** White, showing an unbroken arc of light over 67.5° on each side of dead astern.

- **Towing:** Yellow, showing over the same arc as a stern light.

Navigation rules: *See* Rules of the Road, Colregs, and Table 7.

Navigational aid: Any instrument, chart, marker, or other device designed to assist in navigation (cf. aid to navigation).

Navigator: A naval or merchant officer who practices, is responsible for, or is skilled in navigation.

NAVSTAR: *See* global positioning system.

NAVSUP: Naval Supply Systems Command (*see* victualing).

Navy: The maritime component of a nation's armed forces, including ships, aircraft, shore-based infrastructure, and personnel including seamen, airmen, specialists, soldiers serving as marines, and naval ancillary services.

Navy Board: *See* Board of Admiralty.

Navy exchange: USN term for a store providing household and personal items for naval personnel and their dependants. Profits are donated to the Welfare and Recreation Fund.

Navy League: The latter half of the nineteenth century saw rapid expansion and development of the British Empire and, with it, the dependence on ocean shipping routes for its trade and defense. At the same time the German Empire was becoming increasingly aggressive. Concern as to the adequacy of the Royal Navy of that day to defend the widely separated Empire and its essential shipping gave rise to the formation in Britain in 1895 of a society with the primary aim of ensuring an adequate naval defense, mainly through the training and indoctrination of young people. This was the Navy League. The movement expanded rapidly and before the end of that year branches had been established in Canada, Hong Kong, Malta, and South Africa. Within five years fifty-three branches had been formed throughout the Empire.

Navy League of the United States: This organization was founded in 1902 with the support and encouragement of ardent navy supporter President Theodore Roosevelt. Despite its title, it is closer to the Royal Naval Association than the British Navy League and, like the former it is military-oriented but run by civilians. Its objectives include the support of men and women of the sea services and their families, and the naval education of civilians including elected officials. Members are not required to have served in the military.

Navy-Marine Corps Relief Society: This is a private non-profit United States charitable organization founded in 1904. Its directors are all active duty or retired members of the sea services or their spouses. Sponsored by the United States Department of the Navy, it operates some 250 offices ashore and afloat. In partnership with the Navy and Marine Corps, it provides financial, educational, and other assistance to needy members of the naval services of the United States, eligible family members, and survivors.

Navy Unit Commendation: Established by the Secretary of the Navy in 1944, this award is given to any ship, aircraft, marine detachment, or allied unit which distinguishes itself in combat with collective heroism that would justify the award of a Silver Star to an individual. It may also be awarded for outstanding noncombat service in support of military operations, at a level which would justify award of the Legion of Merit to an individual. Naval units winning an NUC are authorized to fly a pennant with blue, yellow, red, and green stripes, up to five bronze stars being placed on the central green stripe for additional citations. Those who were on board and actually participated in the action are entitled to wear the NUC medal.

Navy yard: [1] In general, any naval dockyard or arsenal. [2] In the USN, specifically the Navy Yard at Washington, D.C.

NBP: Naval beach party.

NCAGS: Naval cooperation and guidance for shipping.

NCB: [1] National Cargo Bureau. [2] Naval construction brigade.

NCCS: Naval Command & Control System.

NCF: Naval construction force.

NCFSU: Naval construction force support unit.

NCHB: Navy cargo handling battalion.

NCIS: Naval Criminal Investigation Service (U.S.).

NCO: Non-Commissioned Officer.

NCTC: Naval Computer & Telecommunications Command (USN).

NCW: Network-Centric Warfare.

NDRF: National Defense Reserve Fleet (U.S.).

Neap: Tide of least range occurring twice each month (cf. Spring).

Near gale: Force 7 on the Beaufort Scale (winds 28–33 knots = 32.2–38 mph = 51.9–61.1 km/h).

NEC: Navy Enlisted Classification; a system of four-digit codes which identify the special skills or training of USN enlisted personnel.

Necessaries: Term in admiralty law referring to the equipment and supplies that a prudent owner would order for a vessel of the class and in the service specified. The list is exhaustive and would include such things as anchors, cables, fuel, propellers, and rigging for the vessel; clothing and provisions for crew; money to pay wages, bills, and fees; and so on. Necessaries are subject to lien under maritime law.

Neck: A narrow strip of water such as a strait; or of land such as an isthmus.

Negat: Short form of negative used in conjunction with naval signals. For example, "Bravo Zulu" is shorthand for "well done" and hence "Negat Bravo Zulu" means "badly done."

Negative: [1] Command or response meaning not to be done, not granted, or do not agree. [2] Cancellation of a previous Command, as in "negative that." Also negat.

Negative stability: Occurs when a vessel's center of gravity coincides with its metacenter, meaning that the vessel will not return to the upright after being inclined.

Nelson's blood: On 21st October 1805, off Cape Trafalgar, British Vice-Admiral Horatio Viscount Nelson with 27 ships of the line engaged Contre-Amiral Pierre Charles Jean Baptiste Sylvestre de Villeneuve with a combined Franco-Spanish fleet of 33. The British sank or captured 17 of the enemy, losing no ships of their own, but Nelson was mortally wounded by a sharpshooter's bullet, dying shortly after victory was declared.

His body was placed in a large cask filled with rum or brandy to preserve it on the long passage back to England; but on arrival the barrel was almost empty and its lid had blown open due to the gases of putrefaction. This may have been due to leakage; but legend has it that Victory's crew had drilled a small hole so that they could "suck the monkey" and enjoy the liquor. This is highly unlikely, since any sailor who desecrated the beloved hero's remains would have been lynched by the rest of the crew.

However, whether the story is true or apocryphal, an alcoholic who would indiscriminately drink anything was known throughout the 19th century as one who would even "tap the Admiral." That derogatory term is now obsolete, but navy-issue rum was called Nelson's Blood until its issue was discontinued in 1970.

Neptune: [1] The Roman name for Poseidon, brother of the supreme god Zeus, and chief of all the water deities. The symbol of his power was the triple-pointed spear or trident, which he used to shatter rocks, shake the earth, and summon or dismiss storms. He created the horse, including steeds with brazen hooves and golden manes to race his chariot over the waves, which became smooth before him, while monsters of the deep gamboled in his honor. Assisted by Amphitrite and Davy Jones, he plays a prominent role in the Line-crossing ceremony. [2] The code-name given to the naval assault phase of Operation Overlord, the Allied invasion of Normandy on D-Day 1944. *See also* crossword coincidence. [3] The eighth and farthest planet from the Sun in the Solar System.

Neptune's sheep: Slang for waves breaking into foam (cf. sea horses).

Nerus: Nerus belongs to an older generation of Greek gods than Neptune. He lived in a large and comfortable cave deep in the Aegean Sea, had the gifts of prophecy and shape-shifting, and was especially benevolent. Homer referred to him as being "trusty and gentle, who thinks just kindly thoughts." He is sometimes identified with the Old Man of the Sea, but Proteus is a more likely candidate for that personage.

Nest: [1] Two or more vessels moored side-by-side. [2] Method of small boat stowage with one boat fully or partially inside the other.

Net: [1] A crisscross grid of rope or line used for fishing or to secure hammocks, sails, etc. [2] A heavy mesh screen, often suspended from floating booms, placed across the entrance of a harbor for protection against hostile vessels, submarines, and torpedoes, or as AND Gear. [3] Telecommunications links and nodes arranged so that messages may be passed from one part of the network to another. [4] Slang for the Internet. [5] The amount remaining after certain deductions or allowances have been made.

Net sweep: In naval mine warfare, a netlike device suspended between two ships, designed to collect drifting mines or scoop them off the sea bottom.

Net weight: Cargo term for the weight of contents after the tare has been deducted from the gross weight.

Netlayer: A vessel equipped for placing and tending antisubmarine and anti-torpedo nets.

Network: [1] A group of radio stations sharing the same frequency. [2] Interconnected computer systems.

Network-centric: This is a doctrine made possible by the Information Age and related to the Revolution in Military Affairs debate. As defined by the Pentagon in its Report to Congress:

It involves new ways of thinking about how we accomplish our missions, how we organize and interrelate, and how we acquire and field the systems that support us.... This monumental task will span a quarter century or more. It will involve ways of operating that have yet to be conceived, and will employ technologies yet to be invented ... (and) has the potential to increase warfighting capabilities by orders of magnitude.

The concept treats geographically dispersed platforms not as individual weapons, but as components in a vast network that allows messages and data to be exchanged between tactical elements without having to be passed up and down the chain of command. Being inter-connected via high-speed satellite communication networks to form a global inter-service information grid, data will be centrally collated to create a coherent overall picture of the battlefield instantly available to all units, giving each of them enhanced situation awareness and enabling more rapid, more informed, and more effective decision-making (but see author's comment under mission command).

Neutralization: [1] Heavy gunfire to immobilize enemy activity in the area bombarded. [2] To render a mine incapable of firing, even though it may remain dangerous to handle.

NFAF: Naval Fleet Auxiliary Force. A division of Military Sealift Command.

NGF: Naval gunfire.

NGFS: Naval gunfire support.

NGLO: Naval gunfire Liaison Officer.

NGO: Non-governmental organization.

Nicholson tube: An instrument formerly used to measure a ship's speed by reading the inboard pressure in a tube whose end was outboard, underwater and facing forward. *See also* Pitot tube.

Night blindness (Nyctalopia): A sufferer from this vitamin deficiency disease has normal vision in adequate light, but gradually requires more and more time to adjust to diminishing illumination, and in semi-darkness becomes unable to detect moving or contrasting objects that are clearly visible to others. Hence the problem would not become evident until a night lookout failed to spot something important and, even then, the unfortunate sufferer was likely to be punished for inattention rather than given medical attention.

When highly advanced the eyes become visibly ulcerated and the lids develop triangular silver-grey deposits known as Bitot's Spots. The disease was as common as scurvy in sailing ship navies and far more pernicious because it has no noticeable symptoms in its early stages, only beginning to appear after about twenty-four months on an unvaried seafarer's diet. The principal cause is deficiency of vitamin A and/or zinc, both of which are found in egg yolks, butter, cream, liver, and fish oil, while leafy green and yellow vegetables provide the pro-vitamin A carotene. None of these foodstuffs has a long storage life and could only be served for a short while after a ship set sail.

Night glasses: Binoculars with high light-gathering capability.

Night order book: A record of the captain's or chief engineer's instructions concerning activities during the night watches.

Night stick: A club or truncheon carried by USN seamen on shore patrol.

Night vision: The ability to see in dim light. The illumination in submarines and certain areas of surface vessels is red in order to preserve this ability.

Nilas: A highly-saline elastic crust of relatively thin, matte-surfaced ice.

La Niña: *See under* La...

Nine yards: When changing tack a sailing warship would reposition its yards sequentially. In the early stages of this maneuver it was possible to abort without any serious repercussion, but by the time the ninth and final yard of a three-master had been set the ship was fully committed. The modern explanation that the phrase "the whole nine yards"— meaning all or everything — is a construction worker's term, based on the capacity of a cement-mixer, is baseless, since the expression was in nautical use long before that equipment existed.

El Niño: *See under* El...

Nip: A sharp bend in a rope or cable which causes it to jam.

Nipped: Said of a vessel caught between ice on both sides.

Nipper: [1] A short rope, clamp, or stopper for securing an anchor cable to a messenger from the capstan. [2] A young ship's boy responsible for placing such stoppers.

Njord: The Viking god of wind, waves, seashores, seamanship, sailing, and fishing. He is one of the Vanir (older gods as opposed to the Aesir who are a younger generation). His wife, the giantess Skadi, was owed a favor by the gods who said she could choose any male god as her husband, but only by looking at their feet. She chose Njord because his beautiful feet had been washed clean by the sea.

NJP: Non-judicial punishment.

NLOS: Not in line of sight.

NLW: Non-lethal weapon.

NMC: Not mission capable.

NMCB: Naval mobile construction battalion.

NMCI: Navy-Marine Corps Internet (U.S.).

NMETL: Navy Mission Essential Task List (USN).

NMHS: National Meteorological & Hydrological Service (U.S.).

NMU: National Maritime Union (U.S.).

No bottom!: Leadsman's cry when no sounding is reached (i.e., the water is deeper than the leadline is long).

No man's land: This World War I term for the space between the trenches was originally maritime. It referred to the area amidships on a sailing ship, where no man lived since officer accommodation lay aft and crew were quartered in the forecastle.

No! No!: Traditional boat coxwain's response to a night challenge. In the RN this response indicates that no-one senior to midshipman is on board, but in the USN it indicates the presence of a petty officer. *See* boat recognition.

No room to swing a cat: This metaphor, today meaning to be cramped or confined, originated because, in order to conduct a proper flogging, the boatswain needed enough space for the lashes of the cat-o'-nine-tails to swing clear of bulwarks, bulkheads, masts, standing rigging, bystanders, and other impediments. This implied having a clear arc of about eight feet (2½ meters) behind him.

NOA: Notice of Arrival.

NOAA: National Oceanic & Atmospheric Administration.

Nodal point: [1] To the mariner, a point of land from where the current flows up the coast on one side and down the coast on the other. [2] The term node is used in many other fields — including astronomy, computer science, medicine, and photography — to denote a position of change or connection.

NOIC: Naval Officer in Charge (RN).

Noise: Unwanted interference of a radio signal.

Non-commissioned: The term is self-explanatory, and refers to enlisted personnel and ratings.

Non-commissioned officer: An enlisted member of an armed force who has been given junior command authority by a commissioned officer. In the United States and British armies, air forces and marines, all ranks of sergeant and corporal are termed NCOs, as are all ranks of Petty Officer in the United States Navy and Coast Guard. The Royal Navy, however, does not refer to its Petty Officers as NCOs, but calls them Senior Ratings (or Senior Rates).

Non-executive: *See* Specialist Officers.

Non-judicial punishment: Commanding officers in both the RN and USN may, in addition to, or in lieu of, admonition, caution, or reprimand, may within specified limits impose one or more of the following disciplinary punishments for minor offenses, committed by officers or enlisted ratings:

- Restriction to specified limits.
- Suspension from duty.
- Extra duties or fatigues.
- Arrest in quarters.
- Confinement in correctional custody.
- Forfeiture of pay.
- Reduction of rate or pay grade.
- Diminished rations, or bread and water diet.

In virtually all cases, the accused has the right to demand court-martial in lieu of summary punishment. *See also* captain's mast, non-punitive disciplinary action, and Uniform Code of Military Justice.

Non-naval flogging: No official restrictions hindered 17th through 19th century merchant masters, whose power was virtually unlimited. Alexander Pope wrote that a sea captain "possesses more crude, naked power over any one of his seamen than the King over his entire nation." The cruelty of brutish shipmasters often led merchant seamen to desert and seek gentler employment by volunteering for the Navy, or going "on the account." (Pirate Articles, which had to be agreed by the crew, usually specified limits to flogging.) The cat-o-nine-tails (known colloquially as "the captain's daughter") is featured in one of the best-known chanteys for hoisting an anchor:

> What shall we do with a drunken sailor?
> What shall we do with a drunken sailor?
> What shall we do with a drunken sailor?
> Err-lie in the morning
>
> Give 'im a taste of the captain's daughter!
> Put 'im in bed with the captain's daughter!
> Marry 'im off to the captain's daughter!
> Err-lie in the morning
>
> Wey-hay and up she rises
> Heave-ho and up she rises
> Hoo-ray and up she rises
> Err-lie in the morning

But in spite of its fearful reputation and nasty wounds, the rope-based cat was too gentle for some masters. Especially sadistic ones might (illegally) order nails, steel balls, or wire barbs to be inserted in the tips of the tails to maximize pain and injury, while others resorted to leather whips or thick wooden birch-rods which were more damaging and painful. In his autobiographical *Two Years Before the Mast* (1840), Richard Henry Dana described a terrible flogging in the brig *Pilgrim*, during which the captain screamed "If you want to know what I flog you for, I'll tell you. It's because I like to do it! Because I like to do it! It suits me! That's what I do it for!" Nevertheless, in his closing chapter, Dana said he doubted the expediency of abolishing flogging altogether.

Non-punitive disciplinary action: Is defined as one or more corrective measures such as counseling, admonition, reprimand, caution, exhortation, disapproval, criticism, censure, reproach, rebuke, extra military instruction, and withholding of privileges [*U.S. Manual for Court Martial, RCM 306(c)(2)*]. *See also* captain's mast, non-judicial punishment, and Uniform Code of Military Justice.

Non-rated: A USN term referring to enlisted personnel in pay grades below petty officer, these are recruit (E-1), apprentice (E-2), and seaman (E-3). *See also* rank and rate.

Noon: [1] Midday. [2] The time at which the sun's elevation is highest. [3] The moment of the sun's transit of the upper branch of the meridian at any given point on earth.

Noon observation: This is when the ship's time, position, course, and distance made good over 24 hours are calculated. Also known as the noon sighting. This was formerly the beginning of the nautical day.

Noon watch: *See* afternoon watch.

Nore mutiny: *See* great mutiny.

Normandy invasion: Code-named "Overlord," the Allied amphibious assault that began on June 6, 1944 (commonly known as D-Day), remains the largest seaborne invasion in history. The initial landing forces were smaller than those in Operation Husky (Sicily), but eventually increased to 47 divisions (3 million men). It also posed logistical issues greater than any previously encountered.

To compensate for the lack of deepwater ports to handle reinforcements and the vast quantities of supplies, weapons and vehicles needed to support the landing forces, the components of two artificial harbors (code-named "Mulberry") were towed or carried across the English Channel, and an underwater pipeline (code-name "Pluto") was laid to supply gasoline from England to France.

On the outcome of the invasion hung the fate of Europe. If it was repulsed, the United States might well turn its full attention to the Pacific War, leaving Britain with most of its resources exhausted by the effort. Hitler could then turn all his strength against the Soviet Union and conceivably become master of the entire continent before U.S. forces returned (if ever). In the event, a comprehensive military deception (code-named operation fortitude) persuaded Hitler the invasion was only a feint. Elite armored divisions, that could easily have overrun the tenuous Allied beachheads, were held in the Pas de Calais to counter the expected full-scale assault by Fortitude's fictitious army corps.

Following massive overnight air and naval bombardments, and inland parachute and glider landings, over 5,300 ships and 11,000 aircraft, with aerial cover provided by some 5,000 fighters, crossed the English Channel to land troops on five code-named beaches in Normandy. Omaha and Utah beaches were assigned to American troops, Gold and Sword to British, and Juno to Canadians. The landings were an overall success (with minor casualties except at Juno and Omaha) but only the Canadians achieved their D-Day objectives. (*See also* crossword coincidence.)

Norse: Pertaining to ancient Scandinavia, including both its inhabitants and the language spoken there.

Norsemen: A collective term for the peoples of ancient Scandinavia, especially during the Viking period (9th to 11th centuries).

North: One of the four cardinal directions, normally treated (explicitly or implicitly) as the fundamental direction used to define all other directions. *See* Table 16.

North Africa current: The most permanent current in the non-tidal Mediterranean Sea, flowing eastward from Gibraltar to the Sicily Strait.

North Africa Invasion: In 1942, with barely two months of planning, the Allies simultaneously mounted two amphibious operations inside the Mediterranean, and a third on the Atlantic Coast. Code-named Operation Torch, it is the largest and most complex amphibious lift ever convened, involving almost a million soldiers and sailors; some eight-hundred merchantmen; six battleships, five fleet and nine escort carriers, twenty cruisers, eighty-one destroyers, and thirty-eight ocean escort vessels. The initial assaults sailed in nine convoys from Britain, and three from the United States; the slowest leaving on 2nd October, the fastest on 1st November, each scheduled to arrive precisely on time.

While the British convoys were converging on Gibraltar, a large German U-boat wolfpack lay across their path. Suddenly it was directed to move south to intercept another convoy (SL.125) heading north. During a six-day battle, several merchantmen in ballast (without cargo) were sunk, but the diversion had saved the invasion fleet. After the war, the escort commander, British Rear Admiral C.N. Reyne said "It was the only time I had ever been congratulated for losing ships."

Not only was Torch the largest, it was also the longest-range amphibious operation. Never before had a major invasion been launched from bases so far away from their targets. The Eastern Assault Force, commanded by Rear-Admiral Sir Harold Burrough RN, sailed from Britain bound for Algiers. It carried 33,000 British troops in thirty-four ships and had to steam roughly 3500 km (2200 miles). The Central Assault Force, commanded by Commodore Thomas Troubridge RN, headed for Oran (with the author aboard). It consisted of forty-seven vessels, carrying 39,000 U.S. troops and British Commandos. It also sailed from Britain and had to travel some 4000 km (2500 miles). The Western Assault Force was entirely American. It consisted of 35,000 troops in thirty-nine ships, under Rear Admiral Henry Hewitt USN. It sailed directly from the United States to Casablanca, roughly 5,000 km (3000 miles).

Air support for the Casablanca assault was provided inshore by four U.S. assault carriers, offshore by fleet carrier *Ranger*. For the Mediterranean landings it was provided inshore by five British assault carriers, while offshore air cover depended on 3 British fleet carriers. To reassure the French, and assist American troops identify unfamiliar but friendly carrier aircraft, most were painted with the American star, rather than the British roundel.

The entire movement had to pass over waters infested with German U-boat wolf packs, enter Axis-controlled air space, and face large and potentially hostile Vichy French forces ashore and afloat. Elaborate disinformation campaigns were mounted (*see* military deception), successfully leading Hitler to concentrate air and submarine forces off Libya, some 1600 km (1000 miles) east of the invasion beaches. Without German help, Vichy French resistance was fierce but brief.

North Atlantic current: This northwestward extension of the Gulf Stream is a powerful, warm, clockwise-setting ocean current, extending from southeast of the Grand Banks to west of Ireland, where it splits in two, one branch (northeast drift) heading for the Norwegian Sea, the other (southeast drift) towards the Canary islands. This flow has major impact on the climate of Europe.

North Atlantic Treaty Organization: A military alliance established by the signing of the North Atlantic Treaty on 4 April 1949. Signatories included the United States and Canada and eight (now expanded to 24) European nations. Article 1 expressed the non-aggressive nature of the alliance, while Article 5 defined its military purpose:

[1] The Parties undertake, as set forth in the Charter of the United Nations, to settle any international dispute in which they may be involved by peaceful means in such a manner that international peace and security and justice are not endangered, and to refrain in their international relations from the threat or use of force in any manner inconsistent with the purposes of the United Nations.

[5] The Parties agree that an armed attack against one or more of them in Europe or North America shall be considered an attack against them all and consequently they agree that, if such an armed attack occurs, each of them, in exercise of the right of individual or collective self-defence recognised by Article 51 of the Charter of the United Nations, will assist the Party or Parties so attacked by taking forthwith, individually and in concert with the other Parties, such action as it deems necessary, including the use of armed force, to restore and maintain the security of the North Atlantic area.

North Cape current: An extension of the Norway current that flows eastward around northern Norway and northeastward into the Barents Sea.

North Pacific current: Also called North Pacific drift, this warm ocean current is formed by conjunction of the Koroshio and Oyashio currents and flows west-to-east across the North Pacific.

North Sea Wraith: In this medieval German precursor of the Flying Dutchman legend, Captain von Falkenburg was an inveterate gambler and terrible blasphemer. One night Satan, disguised as a fellow seaman, lured him into a dice game, in which he bet and lost his eternal soul. The Devil then condemned him and his ship to sail the North Sea until Judgment Day, driven helpless before the winds, without helm or helmsman. But the Fiend gave him an escape clause — once every century, he may go ashore for one hour: If in that short time he can find a virgin who will take him as husband, he may reclaim his soul and live on land with her.

Northeast Passage: The route from Europe to the Orient passing to the north of Europe and Asia.

Northing: The distance actually made good in a northerly direction on any course with a northerly component.

Northwest Passage: The route from Europe to the Orient passing to the north of Canada and Alaska.

Norway current: Part of the northeast drift (*see* North Atlantic current) that flows northeastward along the Norwegian coast to merge with the North Cape current.

NOSC: Naval Oceans Systems Center. Former name of the Space & Naval Warfare Systems Center (U.S.).

Not under command: Refers to any vessel unable to maneuver or keep out of the way of another.

NOTAL: USN abbreviation of "not to all," indicating that the attached message or document may only be seen by authorized eyes.

Nothing off!: Steering command to keep a vessel as close as possible to the wind.

NOTMAR: Notice to Mariners.

November: NATO phonetic notation for the letter "N."

Now hear this!: Traditional USN preliminary to an announcement intended to get the attention of all hands. The RN equivalent is "d'ye hear there!"

NRT: Net Registered Tonnage.

NS: Prefix designating a nuclear-powered ship.

NSC: [1] Naval Supply Corps. [2] National Security Council (both U.S.).

NSFS: Naval surface fire support.

NSRS: NATO Submarine Rescue System.

NSW: Naval Special Warfare.

NSY: Naval Shipyard (USN).

NTDS: Navy Tactical Data System (U.S.).

NUC: Navy Unit Commendation.

Nuckelavee: This Scottish sea monster is a slippery, skinless, creature with two heads, the smaller one mounted on a hump behind the bigger. When he rises dripping from the grey Scottish waters, they make him look like a formless, slimy, decomposing horse with a rider on its back. His corpselike stench and stinking breath roll like a sea mist onto the land, spreading disease and death over fisher villages.

Nuclear explosion: The rapid release of energy from a high-acceleration nuclear reaction, driven by fission, fusion, or a multistage cascading combination of the two.

Nuclear fission: Although they are tiny, atoms have a large amount of energy holding their nuclei together. Certain isotopes of some elements can be split and will release part of their energy as heat. This splitting is called fission, and a series of fissions is called a chain reaction. The heat released in a self-sustaining chain reaction can be used in lieu of other fuels to boil water and generate steam that turns turbines as a source of power.

Nuclear fusion: The process by which multiple atomic particles join together to form a heavier nucleus accompanied by the release or absorption of energy. This process occurs naturally in stars and has been used in nuclear weaponry, but has not yet been sufficiently controlled to be a source of power.

Nuclear power: [1] A nation armed with nuclear weapons. [2] Power derived from fission or fusion reactors, usually to produce steam for ship propulsion or to generate electricity.

Nuclear weapons: There are two basic types of these infernal devices. [1] Atomic bombs produce explosive energy through nuclear fission reactions. [2] Thermonuclear bombs produce energy through nuclear fusion reactions, and can be over a thousand times more powerful than fission bombs.

Nugger: A small Nilotic sailboat combining square with lateen rig.

Nugget: USN informal designation of a newcomer on their first cruise.

Number: An identification code assigned to both naval ships and merchantmen (*see* official number and hull number). A vessel hoisting the appropriate flags or otherwise signaling it is said to "make her number."

Number-in-Grade: A USN register of precedence among officers of the same rank. The lower the number the greater the seniority.

Number One: RN officer's colloquialism for the First Lieutenant (XO) of a warship (cf. Jimmy-the-one).

Numbered fleets: *See* United States numbered fleets.

Number's up: *See* your number's up.

Nun buoy: A buoy with a cone-shaped top.

Nurse: RN lower deck nickname for the first lieutenant of a ship that is commanded by a captain whom the crew considers incompetent or having insufficient seagoing experience.

NWC: Naval War College (U.S.).

NWTS: Navy Warfare Training System (USN).

Nyctalopia: *See* night blindness.

O

O: The fourth classification in Lloyd's Register, signifying condition so poor as to barely qualify for marine insurance coverage.

Oakum: Unraveled rope fiber, mixed with resin and pitch, for use in caulking the seams of wooden vessels.

Oannes: One of the earliest sea-dwelling deities was this ancient Sumerian god, whose head and body were entirely fish, but had human feet emerging from under his tail, and a man's head which spoke with a human voice sitting on top of his fish head. According to legend he brought civilization to humankind at the beginning of the ages, and since then has risen from the sea every morning to give any who would listen the benefit of his deep wisdom. In the beginning he taught humans how to use writing and devise laws; how to develop arts and sciences; how to build boats and construct cities; how to establish temples; and how to distinguish the seeds of the earth and harvest their fruits. According to Babylonian priest Berossus, "From that time to this nothing material has been added by way of improvement to his instructions."

Oar: A long shaft with a handgrip at one end and a broad blade at the other, used as a lever for the manual propulsion of small boats or galleys. From Old Norse ar.

Oared boats: The small craft, generically called "rowing boats" by landlubbers, are differentiated into several categories by seamen:

- **Rowing boats** have fixed thwarts (seats) and no coxswain.
- **Pulling boats** are similar, except that they are steered by a coxswain.
- **Sculling boats** are equipped with seats that move.
- **Stern-scullers** are propelled by a standing rower driving a single oar over the stern.

Oarlock: U.S. term for a device which holds oars in place and allows them to pivot while being pulled (cf. rowlock, thole pin).

Oars!: Verbal command for a boat's crew to cease rowing and hold their oars horizontally above the water with blades feathered. *See also* boat oars, ship oars toss oars, trail oars.

Oarsman: A person who rows a boat, galley, or other vessel.

OBFS: Offshore bulk fuel system.

Objective: In military terminology; [1] To define the overall goal of a campaign (e.g., to capture the enemy capital, or force unconditional surrender). [2] To describe the purpose of a given mission (e.g., to seize a beachhead, take a hill, reach a river, or rescue hostages). [3] In a narrower sense, it refers to a specific target for neutralization or destruction.

OBO: Describes a bulker which carries a combination of ore, bulk, and oil.

Observation: [1] General; the act of measuring some magnitude with an instrument, such as the time of an occultation (with a clock); the right ascension of a star (with a transit instrument and clock); the sun's altitude, or the distance of the moon from a star (with a sextant); the temperature (with a thermometer); etc. [2] Nautical; A celestial sighting, taken in order to calculate a time or position. [3] The information so acquired.

Observation balloon: An aerial platform for intelligence gathering and artillery spotting, consisting of a fabric envelope filled with hydrogen gas, tethered by a steel cable attached to a winch that reeled an observer to the desired height and down again at the end of an observation session. Military observation balloons first appeared in 1794 at the Battle of Fleurus, were used in the American Civil War and Franco-Prussian War, reaching their zenith in World War I, during which naval observation balloons were used to spot submarines and direct the fire of a battleship's main armament. They were also used for anti-submarine work during World War II.

Obstacle: A chain, boom, sunken vessel, or any other object placed to prevent or hinder an enemy vessel's progress.

Obstruction: [1] A reef, shoal, wreck, or other object making it necessary to change course in avoidance. [2] Something that impedes a radar beam. Because of diffraction there is some illumination behind an obstruction, with lower frequency beams tending to illuminate more of the shadow region than beams of higher frequency or shorter wavelength.

Obstructor: In naval mine warfare, a device laid with the purpose of inhibiting or damaging mechanical minesweeping equipment.

Occulting light: A beacon alternating a period of light with a shorter period of darkness.

Ocean: [1] The vast, uninterrupted, body of salt water that covers some three-quarters of the earth's surface, filling its depressions and surrounding the continents. [2] One of five geographical regions known as the Arctic, Atlantic, Indian, Pacific, and Southern Oceans. *See* seven seas.

Ocean acoustics: Refers to the study of sound and its behavior in the sea. When underwater objects vibrate, they create a sound wave that alternately compresses and decompresses the water molecules. The speed of the wave is the rate at which the vibrations travel through the sea. Because the mechanical properties of the mediums differ, sound moves faster in water (1500 meters/sec) than in air (about 340 meters/sec). It also travels faster in warm water than in cold. Sound waves radiate in all directions away from the source, like ripples on the surface of a pond, and are detected as changes in pressure by the human ear, as well as by man-made sound receptors such as a hydrophone, or underwater microphone. *See also* oceanic sound channel, sound surveillance system, and sound fixing and ranging.

Ocean basin: The great depression that covers about one-third of the surface of the lithosphere beyond the continental shelves. It is occupied by the oceans, and has features, such as abyssal plains, trenches and seamounts.

Ocean convoy: A convoy whose course lies generally beyond the continental shelf.

Ocean currents: Continuous river-like movements of water that can flow for thousands of kilometers, determining the climates of the continents, especially those regions bordering on the ocean. *See* oceanic circulation, surface ocean currents, and subsurface ocean currents.

Ocean Escort: Former USN designation of a frigate.

Ocean liner: *See* Liner (definition 2).

Ocean Sea: The ancient Greeks believed that the river of Oceanus rose in the underworld and flowed in a great circle all around the Earth (to them Europe and Asia Minor). The name stuck to waters beyond the Pillars of Hercules (Strait of Gibraltar), and hence Christopher Columbus was named Admiral of the Ocean Sea (Atlantic).

Oceangoing: The legal and marine insurance term for any vessel designed and equipped for, and normally engaged in, travel on international waters.

Oceanic: Living in, belonging to, produced by, or pertaining to the oceans.

Oceanic circulation: Ocean waters are restless, constantly on the move and affecting not only seafarers, but the climate and living conditions of animal and plant life all around the globe. Their movement — which flows in complex patterns dictated by wind, salinity, density, temperature, bottom contours, gravity (of both earth and moon), and planetary spin — can be divided into surface currents, upwellings, and deep-water circulation.

Oceanic conveyor belt: A popular name for deep-water circulation.

Oceanic deep: A depression in the sea floor deeper than 3,000 fathoms. There are deeps in each of the thirteen oceanic trenches that form the ring of fire, and six of them descend below sea level for more than 5,000 fathoms (9,144 meters: 30,000 feet). This depth can be compared to the height of Mount Everest, the highest point on Earth, whose summit is 8,848 meters (29,029 ft) above sea level. These six are:

Trench name	Fathoms	Meters	Feet
Izu Bonin	5,348	9,780	32,086
Kermadec	5,494	10,047	32,962
Philippine	5,740	10,497	34,438
Kurile	5,764	10,542	34,586
Tonga	5,950	10,882	35,702
Marianas	5,973	10,924	35,839

The hydrostatic pressure at such depths is in the order of 16,000 pounds per square inch (1,125 kg/m^2).

Oceanic sound channel: Sounds in the sea can often be "trapped" within this channel, which is caused by temperature and pressure differences that allow low-frequency acoustic waves to travel long distances without significant loss of energy. Descending through the epilimnion, temperature drops and the speed of sound decreases until — at the bottom of the thermocline — both speed and temperature reach their minimums. This is the axis of the sound channel. Below this level, in the hypolimnion, temperature remains constant, but pressure increases, causing the speed of sound to rise again. Because acoustic waves tend to refract towards the area of minimum speed, a wave will be confined within the sound channel, bending alternately up and down as it travels.

The channel lies between 330 and 660 fathoms (600–1200 feet) below the surface, being deepest near the tropics and moving closer to the surface at high latitudes. By placing hydrophones on the axis of the channel it is possible to detect whale calls, seismic activity, propeller signatures, and other human-made noises from far away, sometimes across entire ocean basins. This is the principle behind the sound fixing and ranging and sound surveillance systems. *See also* ocean acoustics.

Oceanic trench: A long, narrow depression of the sea floor. The scale of oceanic trenches is hemispheric and they are also the deepest parts of the ocean floor. They define one of the most important natural boundaries on the Earth, that between two lithospheric plates. A trench marks the position at which one lithospheric slab begins to descend beneath another. Oceanic plates, being made of denser material, sink more readily than continental plates. Oceanic lithosphere disappears into trenches at a global rate of about a tenth of a square meter per second. *See also* oceanic deeps and ring of fire.

Oceanide: [1] In Greek and Roman mythology, the Oceanides were the three thousand daughters of the Titans Oceanus and Tethys. They controlled all sources of fresh-water, from rainclouds to springs. [2] The modern name for a sea nymph in English French, Greek, Portuguese, and Spanish.

Oceanographer: [1] A practitioner of oceanography. [2] A scientist who researches ocean life.

Oceanography: That body of science concerned with the physical, chemical, biological, and geological properties of the oceans.

Oceanus: This Greek sea-god was lord of the great river called Ocean, which completely surrounded the earth, rose in the underworld of Hades, and housed sun and moon between their setting and rising. He is normally depicted as an elderly man with bull's horns on his head and crabs running around in his hair. The concept probably originated with the Sumerians and Egyptians, whose cosmology saw the earth as a raft floating on primeval waters.

OCS: Officer candidate school (U.S.).

OCTU: Officer cadet training unit (Brit.).

Oculi: Eyes painted on the bows of ships. The practice began in ancient China, where fish eyes were thought to help the vessel find its way, while dragon eyes would scare away evil spirits. In ancient Egypt, the bi-colored falcon eyes of Horus on a boat's bow were assumed to be highly protective, with the white right eye representing solar and masculine qualities, while the black left one stood for the lunar and feminine. Together they exerted the full power of the universe in the form of Ra-Herakhty or Horus of the two horizons. The Egyptian custom was adopted by Phoenicia and then by classical Greece, becoming so enduring that the eyes of Horus can still be found on many Mediterranean vessels even including some giant cruise ships.

OD: Ordinary Seaman.

Odie and Jodie: USN enlisted slang for the OOD and Junior OOD.

Off and on: Now in general use to mean occasionally, the expression was originally nautical to describe keeping close to the shore by sailing alternately away from (off) and toward (on) it.

Off duty: Part of the watch below.

Off soundings: In blue water, beyond the 100 fathom line.

Off station: Said of [1] An aid to navigation which has drifted from its assigned location or been taken out of service for repair. [2] A vessel which has left its position in a formation. [3] A vessel which is away from its assigned patrol area.

Off wind: Any point of sailing away from the wind.

Officer: [1] A person who holds a commission or warrant in a national armed force. In the United States Navy, officers are assigned to one of four "communities" based on education, training and assignment; namely line, staff, limited duty, and commissioned warrant: Royal Navy officers are classified as executive, special duties, and warrant. [2] A person certificated to control or navigate a merchantman (*see* mate). [3] Any person exercising rank and authority without necessarily holding a certificate, warrant, or commission (*see* non-commissioned).

Officer candidate: USN term for an enlisted person training to become a commissioned officer. (The RN term is CW Candidate.)

Officer-in-command: *See* commanding officer.

Officer of the day: RN term for the officer responsible for a naval vessel while in port.

Officer of the deck: USN term for the officer responsible for controlling and navigating a naval vessel during a specified watch at sea, or for the vessel while in port.

Officer of the watch: [1] RN term for the officer responsible for controlling and navigating a naval vessel during a specified watch at sea. [2] USN term for the senior engineering officer on duty.

Officer's call: Bugle call or voice message instructing officers to go to their stations. Usually sounded before "all hands" is called or piped.

Official number: As soon as documentation has been completed every merchantman is assigned a unique number that serves to identify it irrespective of name and description. This number must be burned, engraved, or otherwise marked on the vessel in such a way that alteration, removal, or replacement would be obvious due to hull damage or scarring. Also hull number.

Official visit: A formal courtesy call to a warship, requiring special honors and greeting ceremonies.

Offing: [1] The more distant part of the visible sea. [2] A safe distance from the shore, towards the horizon.

Offload: To unload or discharge cargo.

Offshore: [1] Located or operating at a distance from the shore (e.g., a drilling platform). [2] Near to but going away from the shore (e.g., a boat moving off-shore). [3] Moving from land towards the sea (e.g., an offshore wind).

Offshore current: A non-tidal water movement away from the shore, beyond the surf zone and independent of shoal influence or river discharge (cf. inshore current).

Offshore mooring: This technique, also called deepwater mooring, is used by the oil and gas industry to secure mobile drilling platforms and floating production, storage, and offloading vessels by attaching them to anchors embedded in the sea bed. The mooring system must withstand environmental forces (waves, winds, currents) from all directions to avoid movement that could damage subsurface equipment.

The there is a wide variety of configurations available, but most common is the catenary mooring system in which chains and/or wire ropes are allowed to "sag" under their own weight to lie on the floor. Sometimes, kellets are used to supplement the weight of the lines, at others submersible buoys are used to reduce the vertical load on the surface vessel. At depths greater than 550 fathoms (1000 meters), however, the weight of the line(s) becomes a limiting factor and taut leg mooring is preferred. The major difference is that the catenary line arrives at the anchor horizontally, while the taut line comes in at an angle and subjects the anchor to vertical forces as well as horizontal.

Offshore wind: Refers to the movement of air from land towards the sea.

Oggin: Twentieth century RN lower deck slang for the ocean. It is said to be derived from "hogwash," though the connection seems hard to make.

Ogive: Defined in the *NASA Aerospace Science & Technology Dictionary* as "the nose of a projectile, shaped by rotating a circular arc about an axis that intersects that arc." The most common shape is the tangent ogive, which has the outline of a Gothic arch, with its center of rotation in the plane of the base, thereby blending tangentially (smoothly) into the body contour. Other shapes include the secant ogive, where the center of rotation lies abaft of the plane of the base and hence joins the body contour at an angle, and the parabolic ogive, which is similar to the tangential form except that it is generated by a parabola rather than a circle.

OHMS: On Her/His Majesty's Service (Brit.).

OIC: Officer in charge (or command).

Oil canning: The snapping in-and-out of a thin plating in heavy seas. Various combinations of beams, frames, and stringers may be installed to counteract this phenomenon which is also known as panting.

Oil on troubled waters: This term for calming a difficult situation refers to a disputed remedy for smoothing a rough sea, going back to at least the first century when Plutarch wrote "Why does pouring oil on the sea make it clear and calm? Is it that the winds, slipping over the smooth oil, have no force nor cause any waves?" More recently, on 5th January 1770, a Mr. Tengnagel of Batavia reported:

Near the islands ... we met with a storm ... the captain found himself obliged for greater safety in wearing the ship to pour oil into the sea to prevent the waves breaking over her, which had an excellent effect and succeeded in preserving us.... The East India Company owes perhaps its ship to only six demi-ames of oil-olive.... (But) we have found people here so prejudiced against the experiment as to make it necessary for the officers on board and myself to give a certificate of the truth on this head.

There are records of the technique having been successfully used at least as recently as World War II, but diehard skeptics still deny it would work.

Oilbag: A container which allows oil to drip slowly into the sea. Used in emergencies, especially by small boats. The oil slick tends to prevent waves breaking over the deck. *See* oil on troubled waters.

Oiler: A tanker designed to replenish a warship's fuel while underway.

Oilskin: Cotton cloth treated with linseed or other oil for waterproofing.

Oilskins: Slang for foul-weather clothing.

Oker: A sort of red chalk used by shipwrights to mark timber when hewing and forming it. Also ocher.

Okinawa invasion: In April 1945, the Ryukyu Island chain was the next target for United States island-hopping forces. This would move the USN's Pacific War away from atolls and tropical jungles separated by great ocean expanses, and toward the population centers and cultivated terraces of Asia.

Possession of Okinawa — strategically located a mere 400 miles from Japan — would enable the Allies to cut Japan's access to vital sources of raw materials, while its harbors, anchorages, and airfields could be used to stage ships, troops, aircraft, and supplies for the anticipated amphibious assault on the Japanese homeland.

Code-named Operation Iceberg, Okinawa was the last, largest, and bloodiest amphibious operation of the Pacific War. Admiral Raymond A. Spruance's 5th fleet — which included the British Pacific Fleet (*see* Royal Navy) — was the greatest naval armada ever assembled. Some 1,400 vessels included more than 40 aircraft carriers, 18 battleships, 200 destroyers, hundreds of assorted support ships, and 365 amphibious vessels. More troops were put ashore, more supplies transported, more bombs dropped, and more naval guns fired against shore targets than in any other operation in the Pacific.

- **Ground combat:** On 1st April 1945 two Marine and two Army divisions landed with little opposition. In an attempt to negate overwhelming American air and fire power, the Japanese had chosen not to contest the beaches in favor of defense in depth from prepared positions in caves and tunnels on the high ground inland. Naval gunfire and air bombardment were generally ineffective against these entrenchments' leaving the troops to pit explosives and flamethrowers against determined pockets of resistance.

Monsoon rains turned contested slopes into a muddy morass that mired troops in a noxious stew of maggots feasting on unburied Japanese bodies. Casualties totaled more than 38,000 Americans wounded and 12,000 killed or missing, more than 107,000 Japanese and Okinawan conscripts killed. Perhaps 100,000 civilians perished, many by suicide. The battle ended on 7th September but, long before the firing stopped, engineers and Seabee construction battalions, following close on the heels of the combat forces, were transforming the island into a major base for the projected invasion of the Japanese homeland.

- **The Naval battle:** Delay in securing the island caused consternation among naval commanders since the fleet was exposed to potential surface attack and heavy air bombardment. In fact, the Japanese high command did launch "Operation Ten-Go," a combined air-sea suicide mission. Almost 1,500 kamikaze flights sank 30 American ships and damaged 164 others. Simultaneously, "super-battleship" *Yamato*, accompanied by a cruiser and eight destroyers, was dispatched with orders to beach herself at Okinawa and fight until eliminated. She never got there. Intercepted by Vice Admiral Marc Mitscher's carrier-launched air strikes, and with no protective air cover, she took twelve bombs and seven torpedoes before blowing up and sinking on 7th April 1945. The cruiser *Yahagi* was also sunk, three destroyers were so badly damaged they had to be scuttled, and the four remaining destroyers could not return to Japan. There were few survivors from this last Japanese naval action of the war.

Old horse: Tough, stale salt beef.

Old Ironsides: *See* USS *Constitution*.

Old Man: Popular term, combining affection with a hint of disrespect, for the master of a merchantman or captain of a warship, used regardless of age or gender. Less frequently, a flag officer is referred to as "Old Gentleman." Neither term is used face-to-face.

Old Man of the Sea: In Greek mythology the Old Man of the Sea, often called "The Ancient," is usually identified as the minor deity Proteus, although Nerus and Pontus have also been suggested. The old man's shape-changing capability is illustrated in Homer's Odyssey — after Odysseus and his crew are marooned on an island off Egypt, they disguise themselves as seals in order to extract information from him:

At midday the old man himself emerged, found his fat seals already there, and went the rounds to make his count. Entirely unsuspicious of the fraud, he included us as the first four of his flock. When he had done he lay down to sleep. Then with a shout, we leapt upon him and flung our arms round his back. But the old man's skill and cunning had not deserted him. He began by turning into a bearded lion and then into a snake, and after that a panther and a giant boar. He changed into running water too and a great tree in leaf. But we set our teeth and held him

like a vise. When at last he had grown tired of his magic repertory, he broke into speech and began asking me questions.... I answered, "Tell me ... how I can get home across the playgrounds of the fish."

Hesiod's *Theogony*, also written in the 8th century BCE, relates virtually the same story, except that the Old Man is there identified as Heracles. The tale crops up yet again in the fifteenth century *Thousand-and-one Arabian Nights* where the Old Man is called by his Arabic name of Sheik-al-Bahr (chieftain of the sea).

Old Salt: Colloquialism describing a very experienced, retired, or elderly sailor.

Oldster: Formerly described a midshipman with more than four years seniority who had failed to pass the lieutenant's examination. Oldsters messed with warrant officers rather than in the gunroom with "youngsters."

Oleron: *See* Rôles de Oléron.

On beam ends: Refers to a ship that has heeled so far over that the beams supporting its decks and flats are almost vertical. This is a dangerous situation from which there may be no recovery. The term has entered common parlance to mean being in dire financial straits without further resources.

On board: Anywhere in or on the vessel.

On consignment: Goods consigned to a agent with title held by the consignor until the goods are sold.

On course: Heading in the desired direction.

On deck: [1] Outside, as opposed to below. [2] Awake and on duty, not abed or resting.

On report: Facing a disciplinary charge, mast, or table.

On soundings: In water shallow enough to be sounded by a standard 100-fathom deep sea lead. Also "in soundings."

On station: Said of [1] An aid to navigation that is at its assigned location. [2] A vessel that is at its proper position in a formation. [3] A warship that is in its patrol area or at its assigned base.

On the: Prefix describing where something lies relative to the vessel [1] On the bow = dead ahead. [2] On the port (or starboard) bow = ahead and off to one side. [3] On the beam = at right angles to the ship. [4] On the port (or starboard) quarter = behind and off to one side.

On the account: This term for getting something on credit had a special meaning during the Golden Age of piracy. In that era, journeymen ashore were frequently not paid until the job was done, with their wages being held "on account." Articles of piratical service usually followed a similar principle, specifying "no prey, no pay" or "no purchase, no pay." Purchase was their term for loot, so both phrases meant they would receive no return from their labor until they took a prize. Even after making a capture their shares of the booty would be credited to an account until settlement time. Eventually, "going on the account" became a slang term for engaging in piracy.

On the beach: [1] A seaman who is unemployed or retired. [2] One who has temporarily gone ashore.

On the beam: Positioned at right angles to the ship. Also abeam.

On the bow: [1] When qualified by port or starboard, positioned somewhere between straight ahead and four points to the side indicated: (i.e., between relative bearings 45° and 315°). [2] When not so qualified, straight ahead (but seldom used, the term dead ahead being preferred).

On the double!: Command to do something quickly or move rapidly (also "at the double").

On the line: Said of [1] Naval aircraft spotted ready for launching. [2] Engines or boilers currently in operation. [3] A person or location connected to a communication circuit.

On the quarter: When qualified by port or starboard, positioned somewhere between four points on either side of dead astern (i.e., between relative bearings 135° and 225°).

On the rocks: [1] To have run aground on a stony bottom. [2] Colloquially, to be short of money. [3] to serve undiluted liquor on ice.

On the ship: In the Royal and U.S. navies, and the British Merchant Navy one sails and lives "in" a ship. In the American Merchant Marine and civilian conversation "on" is the preferred term.

On the skids: Before the invention of davits, ships' boats were launched on beams known as skids (from the Scandinavian skith), following a downward path to the water. Hence the analogy that a person on the downward path to ruin, poverty, or depravity is "on the skids."

On the ways: Out of the water for repair or storage on a slipway.

On the wind: Close-hauled.

One good turn deserves another: The current meaning of this phrase, that a kindness should be reciprocated, has moved a long way from its original use by seamen, who found it wise to take a second turn around the bitts when the object being secured was especially valuable.

ONI: Office of Naval Intelligence (U.S.).

Onshore: [1] Towards the shore (e.g., an onshore wind). [2] On dry land.

OOB: Order of battle.

OOD: Officer of the deck (or day).

OOS: Out of service.

OOTW: Operations other than war.

OOW: Officer of the watch.

Ooze: Soft and slimy marine sediment, consisting mainly of the shells of small organisms, offering poor holding ground for an anchor.

Opanova: The acronym for a hypothetical Organization of People Ascribing Nautical Origins to Virtually Anything.

Open berth: A place to moor or anchor within an unprotected roadstead.

Open boat: Any small undecked craft.

Open coast: A littoral with few harbors or anchorages.

Open list muster: One of the purser's more profitable enterprises was to issue pay tickets to non-existent crew members, then sell them to moneylenders at a discount. This practice eventually led to "open list" musters, held quarterly at random, during which each crew member reported name, rank or rating, and shipboard duty directly to the captain, who checked them against the purser's pay records.

Open order column: USN term for a line-ahead formation in which odd-numbered ships are staggered a few degrees to the right, and even-numbered ships to the left.

Open port: [1] A seaport without regulations governing the health of passengers or crew. [2] One that is almost never closed by winter ice. [3] One exposed to the open sea. [4] A scuttle that is not closed.

Open registry: Said of a vessel under a flag of convenience.

Open roadstead: A hazardous anchorage, offering little protection from wind and wave.

Open sea: [1] The sea beyond territorial jurisdiction. [2] Any expanse of water not partially enclosed by headlands or barrier islands.

Open spaces: Enclosed areas above the upper deck which are not fitted with doors or other means of closure.

Open water: [1] *See* open sea. [2] An sea area where ice covers less than 12.5 percent (one-eighth) of the surface.

Operation: A military action or mission. May be offensive or defensive, and defined as tactical, strategic, covert, logistic, or training.

Operations Officer: [1] In the USN, the officer responsible for collecting, analyzing and disseminating operational and combat information (the RN equivalent is Principal Warfare Officer). [2] In the RN, the ship's operational planner, responsible to the captain for the program of the ship.

Operations Room: RN term for the tactical control center of a warship, from where warfare operations and exercises are conducted, combining the functions of the USN Combat Information Center, and the former RN Gun Direction Room (now Combat Engagement Centre).

OPK: Oceanic Peacekeeping.

OPNAV: Collective term for the CNO's staff at the Pentagon (USN).

Oppignoration: Obsolete term for pawning part of a cargo in order to raise funds for the payment of duty on the remainder.

Opposite Number: [1] The person having the same station and duties as oneself but in a different watch. [2] Officers (national or foreign) having corresponding duty assignments within their respective military services or establishments: (3) RN slang for a close friend (usually abbreviated to "oppo").

OPREP: Operational Report.

OPS: Operations.

Optical fiber systems: *See* fiber optics.

Optical Landing System: A gyrostabilized shipboard device which informs an approaching aircraft of deviation from the proper glide path for landing. *See* mirror landing aid.

Optical mine hunting: In naval mine warfare, the use of a towed television camera (or a human diver) to detect and classify mine-like objects on the sea bed.

Optimum height: In naval gunnery, the altitude at which an airburst will produce the greatest damage to a given target.

Optional Cargo: A bill of lading term that allows the shipper or consignee discretion to decide the port at which cargo will be delivered, provided 24 hours' notice is given.

Oramby: Malaccan state barge propelled by 50 to 100 paddlers.

Order: Technically an instruction to do something which, unlike a command, does not require instantaneous compliance. In practice, however, if a recalcitrant sailor seems unwilling to respond, the officer will probably say "That is an order" rather than "That is a command."

Order of battle: The composition, arrangement, disposition, and command structure of a military or naval force.

Order-book: A written record of the instructions issued by a flag or other senior officer.

Orderly: An officer's messenger or personal attendant.

Ordinances or Usages of the Sea: A set of laws promulgated by Richard Lionheart to his Crusader fleet in 1190. (One of his draconian rules will be found under Tarring, others under Punishment.)

Ordinary: *See* "In Ordinary."

Ordinary Seaman (OD): One not rated as Able (proficient). Today, the OD is the humblest of a merchantman's deck crew and may be called upon to do any task that does not require the expertise of an AB. For example, chipping and scaling paint, standing lookout, handling mooring lines, taking a trick at the wheel, cleaning the heads, or waking officers due to go on watch. Thanks to "rate inflation" this rating no longer exists in the Royal or U.S. Navies.

Ordnance: Collective term for heavy weaponry and munitions. *See* Board of Ordnance and Bureau of Ordnance.

Originator: Communications term for the authority initiating a message.

Orlop: The lowest deck above the beams of the hold in a four-decked sailing warship. Being well below the waterline it was used to store ammunition and became a surgery during combat. From the Dutch overloop = running above.

Oropesa: In naval mine warfare, a single-ship sweep in which lateral displacement is caused by an otter, and depth is controlled by a kite at the inboard end and by a float at the outer end. Named after HMS *Oropesa* which developed the technique.

ORP: Ocean reception point.

Orthomorphic projection: A map projection in which the scale, although varying throughout, is the same in all directions at any point, so that very small areas are represented by correct shape and bearings are accurate locally.

Oscar: [1] The NATO phonetic notation for the letter "O." [2] A single Oscar flag is the signal for "person overboard." [3] Nickname for the dummy used in man overboard drills.

Oscillating mine: In naval mine warfare, a hydrostatically-controlled mine which maintains its preset distance below the surface irrespective of the rise and fall of tides.

OTC: Officers' Training Corps (Brit.). *See* ROTC.

OTH: Over the horizon.

Other than honorable: One of five USN discharge classifications, applicable to personnel separated for misconduct or security reasons that are too minor to deserve a bad conduct discharge. *See also* honorable discharge, general discharge, and dishonorable discharge.

Otter: [1] A minesweeping device which keeps the sweep wire extended laterally. [2] A similar device used to hold open the mouth of a fishing trawl.

Outboard: Towards or beyond the side of a vessel.

Outchop: USN term for leaving one fleet or area of operational control for another. Cf. inchop.

Outer Space: [1] Beyond the Earth's atmosphere. [3] The lowest altitude above sea level at which satellites can orbit the Earth (approximately 100 km or 62.1 miles).

Outfit: To provide a vessel with the supplies and equipage needed for its operation.

Outfoot: To move faster than another vessel.

Outhaul: [1] A line used to haul the clew of a sail toward the end of a boom. [2] A line used to pull something away from the person hauling.

Outpoint: To sail closer to the wind than another vessel on the same tack.

Outrigger: [1] A spar-mounted pontoon running parallel to the hull of a small boat to give it stability on the leeward side. [2] A bracket extending the oarlock of a racing shell. [3] A flexible pole at the stern of a fishing boat to hold lines clear of the wake when trolling. [4] Timber used to reinforce rigging when a ship is careened. [5] A projecting beam to support a tackle. [6] A spar used to extend a sail.

Outrow/outsail: To row or sail faster than another boat.

Outside: Passenger liner term describing a cabin with a port or window overlooking the sea.

Over a barrel: This term meaning unable to move, or being in an embarrassing situation, originated when an offender would be spreadeagled over the barrel of a gun for punishment (*see* flogging and marry the gunner's daughter).

Over-the-hill: Slang, said of [1] A deserter; [2] An elderly person.

Over-the-horizon: Said of a radar system that uses the phenomena of atmospheric reflection and refraction to extend its range of detection beyond the visible line of sight.

Overbear: To have the advantage over another sailing vessel by being able to carry more canvas in any given wind.

Overboard: Over the side and into the water. Literally, over the board (of the gunwale).

Overcanvassed: Carrying too much sail for efficient ship handling.

Overcarried: Cargo inadvertently taken beyond its destination, possibly due to overstowage.

Overfall: Dangerously steep breaking waves, due to opposing currents in shallow waters.

Overhang: The area of bow or stern projecting above and beyond the perpendicular.

Overhatted: Carrying too many spars or overmasted.

Overhaul: [1] Nautical term for overtake. [2] To repair something and return it to service. [3] To separate the blocks of a tackle. [4] To slacken a rope by pulling in the opposite direction to that in which it was drawn taut. [5] USN firefighting term for the phase in which all remaining traces of fire are located and extinguished.

Overhead: American term for an interior ceiling in a ship (cf. Deckhead).

Overlay: [1] A transparent sheet placed over a chart to superimpose special information. [2] The number of days for which demurrage can be charged.

Overloading: Until the late nineteenth century ships could be (and often were) laden until their decks were almost awash. Shipwrecks and crew losses became endemic, but any seaman who signed articles had to sail or risk being named a deserter and arrested. In 1856, an inspector of prisons reported that three-quarters of the inmates of jails in south-western England were sailors, imprisoned for twelve weeks for refusing to sail in ships they considered unseaworthy. A decade later, four entire crews were jailed in succession for refusing to sail in a decrepit old tub named *Harkaway*. She finally set sail for the West Indies, manned by a fifth crew, but still hazardously overloaded. Shipowners strongly resisted all attempts at regulation, and it was not until 1876 British vessels were legally required to indicate their safe laden draft. (*See* load lines, plimsoll mark.)

Overlord: Code-name for the Normandy invasion that began on June 6, 1944, commonly known as D-Day. (*See also* crossword coincidence.)

Overmasted: Having masts that are too long or too heavy for the ship.

Over-rated: A seaman who has been given a rate for which his skill or temperament is unsuitable. Captains had the power to rate their own men and sometimes — after a battle or epidemic, for instance — only

partially-qualified men might be left alive to fill important vacancies. A seaman promoted beyond his skill or capability was said to be over-rated. Similarly, one who was qualified for promotion was under-rated. Both terms are now in common use to signify being valued too highly or not highly enough.

Overrigged: Having heavier rigging than is necessary or desirable.

Overrisen: Former description of a ship which rides too high above the water for her length and breadth, making her prone to lurching and rolling. The 80-gun British three-deckers of the Napoleonic Wars suffered from this defect.

Overseas cap: *See* garrison cap.

Overset: An early term for capsize.

Overstow: To load cargo inefficiently so that goods to be unloaded later are placed on top of those scheduled to be off earlier, possibly resulting in overcarriage.

Overt: Said of intelligence activity which is open with no attempt at concealment. The opposite of covert.

Overtaking vessel: Defined under the Navigation Rules as a ship overhauling another from more than two points abaft the beam.

Overwhelm: [1] Colloquially, to overpower by emotion or to crush something. [2] In its original nautical sense the term referred to a vessel being swamped by onrushing and breaking seas. From Old English "ofer" = over, plus "hwylfan" = submerge or capsize.

Owler: An old term for a smuggler who works by night.

Owner: [1] The proprietor of a ship. [2] Slang for its captain or master. [3] A person who has title (legal right of possession) to goods or property.

Oyashio Current: A cold ocean current that flows counterclockwise from the Arctic Ocean, through the Bering Sea, to merge with the Japan stream (kuroshio) and form the North Pacific current.

P

P: Priority. Military/diplomatic communications precedence level above Routine and below Immediate.

PA: Position approximate. Chart notation indicating that the position of a wreck, shoal, or other hazard has not been accurately determined.

Pacific and Indian Oceans Shipping Working Group: A forum in which participating nations discuss and reach consensus on how Naval Co-operation and Guidance for Shipping doctrine and procedures can be applied and exercised in the Pacific and Indian Oceans. In 2008, participants include: Australia, Canada, Chile, Republic of Korea, United Kingdom, United States of America, and South Africa.

Pacific Ocean: The world's largest geographic feature, and the largest of five divisions of the World Ocean, covering about 32 percent of the Earth's surface, making up nearly half of the area covered by the earth's oceans. It is larger than all land areas combined.

It extends from the Arctic in the north to Antarctica in the south, and is bounded by Asia and Australia to the west and the Americas in the east. It is nominally divided by the equator into the North and South Pacific Oceans. Volcanic arcs and oceanic trenches partly encircling the Pacific Basin form the so-called Ring of Fire, a zone of frequent earthquakes and volcanic eruptions. The name (which it seldom deserves) is derived from the Latin for "peaceful," bestowed upon it by Portuguese explorer Ferdinand Magellan.

Pacific War: This brutal conflict of World War II included all five carrier-versus-carrier battles ever fought, the largest surface battle in history; the first battle in which opposing surface forces never saw each other, and the greatest ever series of night encounters. It also saw a record number of amphibious operations, although even Okinawa, the largest, was smaller than Husky, Overlord, or Torch in the European theater.

The War began on 7th July 1937 when the Empire of Japan invaded China, and intensified after 7th December 1941 when, to secure much needed resources, Japanese forces mounted simultaneous assaults on European and United States Asian and Pacific bases. The first and most famous of these was a dawn attack against American bases on Oahu, Hawaii (*see* Pearl Harbor) executed with clock-like precision by the cream of Japan's élite naval aviation. This sneak attack without declaration of war united public opinion in ways that the U.S. government could never have achieved, or Japanese planners could have anticipated, virtually guaranteeing ruthless counter-attacks with no possibility of negotiated settlement.

Having occupied most of Southeast Asia and the Dutch East Indies, Japan advanced against the crucial Australian position at Port Moresby in New Guinea, and planned to seize the U.S. atoll of Midway. While offensive in appearance, these moves were actually defensive, intended to establish a perimeter that the Allies would find impregnable. Both were repulsed by the naval air battles of Coral Sea and Midway, after which the initiative shifted to the Allies. They adopted a triple-pronged strategy:

- United States and Australian ground forces would advance through the Solomon Islands and New Guinea toward the Philippines.
- The U.S. Navy would "island-hop" across the central Pacific towards Japan itself.
- British forces would halt the advance on India, then pursue the enemy into Burma.

The American naval achievement was prodigious: a sweep across thousands of miles of ocean from Coral Sea to East China Sea, with forces that made every previous important naval campaign seem puny and insignificant. In August 1945, the nuclear bombardment of Hiroshima and Nagasaki ended World War II before an even more ambitious amphibious assault on the Japanese homeland had to be mounted.

Pack: Term sometimes used for a group of submarines hunting together (*see* wolfpack).

Pack ice: Floating ice cover found in polar regions. Driven by winds and ocean currents, ice fragments of varying size and age are squeezed together across the sea surface, leaving little or no open water. At maximum expansion during winter, pack ice covers about five percent of Arctic waters and about eight percent of Antarctic waters. *See also* drift ice, fast ice, ice pack.

Packet: A small vessel carrying mail, passengers and freight on a regularly-scheduled fixed route. (From the French paquet = parcel.) Also packet-boat (re-translated to French as paquebot).

PACOM: Pacific Command (USN).

Padding: Communications term for meaningless words or phrases inserted in a message to confuse enemy codebreakers by concealing its beginning, ending, and length. An infamous example during the 1944 Battle of Leyte Gulf read (with padding italicized and in parentheses) "(*Turkey trots to water GG*) Where is rpt where is Task Force thirty-four (*RR the world wonders*)." The decrypting officer removed the padding before "GG" but left that after "RR," upsetting Admiral Halsey who assumed his command decision to pursue enemy carriers was being criticized.

Paddle: [1] A short oar, used without a rowlock, usually held with both hands and moved in a more-or-less vertical arc. [2] To use such an oar to propel a canoe, boat, or raft. [3] The blade, float, or bunket of a paddle wheel.

Paddle beams: Two large timbers projecting over the side of a steamer, between which the paddle wheel rotates.

Paddle box: A wooden frame enclosing one of the wheels of a paddle-steamer.

Paddle-steamer: A steam-powered vessel propelled by paddle wheels. Those with a single wheel at the back are called sternwheelers, those with one on either side are sidewheelers.

Paddle wheel: An engine-driven wheel for propelling a vessel by the action of paddles (known as blades, floats or bunkets) spaced around its circumference; the bottom 25 percent or so of the paddles enter the water more-or-less vertically to give forward thrust.

Padre: Slang for a chaplain (Latin for "father").

Paduan: A small Malayan pirate vessel usually armed with a pair of cannon.

Paint: [1] To coat or cover something with a protective or colorful liquid. [2] To illuminate or track a target with radar.

Painted ports: *See* dummy ports.

Painter: A short line attached to the bow of a small boat for towing or making fast.

Paixhan gun: The forerunner of the Dahlgren gun, developed by French General Henri-Joseph Paixhans about 1825 for the horizontal firing of heavy shells. The invention has also been attributed to Colonel George Bomford, the U.S. Army's chief of ordnance, 1821–42.

Pakistan Navy: The early history of this maritime force is identical to that of the Indian Navy. Then, with independence and partition in 1947, the existing RIN fleet was divided the between the two new countries and the Royal Pakistan Navy was born. In 1956 an Islamic Republic was proclaimed and the prefix Royal was dropped.

Palermo Protocol: These United Nations Rules to Prevent, Suppress and Punish Trafficking in Persons Especially Women and Children, which were adopted in November 2000, are supplementary to the United Nations Convention against Transnational Organized Crime.

Pallet: A portable platform used to move goods, usually by fork-lift truck.

Palm: [1] Flattened end of an anchor arm or inner face of its fluke. [2] A stiff rawhide or metal device serving as a sailmaker's thimble. [3] Blade of an oar. [4] The flat surface at the end of a strut or stanchion.

PALS: Precision approach landing system (*see* deck landing modes).

Pamban: A Vietnamese dugout canoe, made from a single tree and propelled by about twenty paddlers.

Pan: In the heat of battle, it was too difficult to fire a primitive "hand gonne" by using one hand to apply a lighted match to the open "touch hole" in the gun barrel while trying to hold the gun steady with the other. To solve the problem, the touch hole was moved to the side of the barrel, and a cup called the "flash pan" or "priming pan" was placed next to it to hold a small "priming charge" of gunpowder. This was protected from wind and rain by a closable lid. When the powder in the pan was ignited, the flash traveled through the touch hole to ignite the main charge of propellant inside the barrel, thereby firing the gun.

Panama Canal: An artificial waterway crossing the Isthmus of Panama, connecting the Caribbean Sea with the Pacific Ocean, and providing a much shorter route than sailing around Cape Horn. It consists of dredged approaches, artificially created lakes, excavated channels, and three sets of locks at each end. On the Atlantic side, they form continuous steps, but small Lake Miraflores separates the middle and upper locks on the Pacific side. Line handlers attach steel mooring cables, controlled by powerful electric locomotives (called mules) which guide ships through the locks and steady them as the chambers fill with water. Built by the United States between 1904 and 1914, the mountainous terrain of central Panama posed major engineering challenges, such as damming a major river and cutting through a mountain ridge. *See also* Panamax.

Panamax: Describes a vessel whose maximum dimensions just allow it to transit the Panama Canal. (32.3 m wide, 294.1 m long, and 12 m draft). Proposed Canal expansion includes installing new locks and widening the Culebra Cut to accommodate post-panamax and capesize vessels.

Pancake ice: Small circular sheets of newly-formed ice which do not impede navigation.

Panel: A group of officers, selected by the convening authority in U.S. practice, or randomly from the list of officers in British armed forces, to serve (essentially) as the Jury at a court-martial.

Panic party: *See* Q-ship.

Pan-Pan: Alert that the following radio voice message should be given priority as it concerns matters of safety which, however, do not involve immediate danger to ship or crew (for which Mayday or Sécurité should be used). From the French panne = breakdown.

Panting: Describes [1] The in-and-out pulsation of a ship's plating which occurs in heavy weather (also oil canning). [2] The noise made by a boiler starved of oxygen for combustion.

Pantry: [1] USN term for the galley in which officers' meals are prepared. [2] RN term for the area from which meals are served.

Panzerschiffe: This was the Nazi-German designation of the warship commonly known in English as a "pocket battleship." The word translates as "armor-ship," and had been used by the Imperial Austrian Navy as early as the 1866 Battle of Lissa.

Papa: NATO phonetic notation for the letter "P."

Paper Jack: U.S. merchant marine derogatory slang for a master advanced by favoritism rather than for professional ability.

Parachute: [1] A soft fabric dome-shaped device used to slow the descent of a person or object, usually from an aircraft. [2] To use such a device. [3] A semi-rigid wing, that is maneuverable to facilitate a controlled descent (skydiving). From the French para = protect and chute = fall.

Parachute anchor: *See* drogue, sea anchor.

Parachute flare: A pyrotechnic device attached to a parachute. Used to provide intense illumination for a short period.

Parade: [1] A military assembly for inspection or display. [2] That section of a USN warship's deck where divisions muster for inspections.

Parallax: The error which can result from not viewing an instrument directly from its front, due to separation of the indicator (needle) from the scale being read.

Parallel: An imaginary east-west circle on the earth's surface running parallel to the equator. The latitudinal equivalent of a longitudinal meridian.

Parametric roll: A large movement generated in head-on or stern-on sea conditions. Its period is about half the natural roll period and occurs in phase with large pitch angle. This relatively new phenomenon is caused by the wide beams and flared bows of post–Panamax container ships. When the bow is down due to moderate pitching and there is a slight roll, the large flare can be abruptly immersed in a wave crest. The restoring buoyancy force, coupled with the wave excitation force, pushes the ship to one side. Similar action happens on the other side when the bow pitches down in the next cycle.

The effect is unpredictable when multiple waves

and swells are coming from different directions, and even moderately high waves can reach the critical threshold for any specific hull design, especially in head/stern or near head/stern conditions. Maximum roll always occurs when the bow is pitched down, and unusually large roll angles can be quickly generated, oscillating rapidly with about half the ship's natural roll period.

The roll can increase unexpectedly, from minimal to over 30 degrees in just a few cycles. leaving little time for corrective action (changing the heading to beam seas is the quickest). Violent parametric rolls have caused hundreds of containers to break their constraints and be damaged or slide overboard.

Pararaft: A parachute-supported life raft provided to naval aviators.

Parasitic drag: Refers to the resistance of a fluid to movement of an object (such as a ship) through it. This occurs in four principal ways known as eddy-resistance, profile-drag, skin-friction, and wave-resistance.

Paravane: A single or one of a pair of torpedo-shaped devices streamed at the end of long cutting wires on either side of a minesweeper or other vessel at a depth regulated by attached vanes. The cutting wires sever the tethers of moored mines, cutting them adrift to surface and be destroyed by gunfire.

Parbuckle: A sling made from the bights of two ropes and used to move or raise casks or other cylindrical objects.

Parcel: [1] To wrap a rope with heavy cloth to prevent chafing or to provide a smooth surface for serving. The latter is the second of a three-stage process exemplified in the old sailor's rhyme "Worm and parcel with the lay. Then turn and serve the other way." [2] To lay a narrow piece of canvas over a freshly-caulked seam and seal it with hot pitch or tar.

Pardon my rig: It is customary in RN wardrooms for officers to wear uniform unless going immediately ashore or just returned aboard. If planning to remain on board in plain clothes it is "proper" for the officer concerned to say "Pardon my rig, Sir/Ma'am" to the senior uniformed officer present, even if the latter is of junior rank.

Parish-rigged: 18th century English term for a ship which had been cheaply and meagerly outfitted.

Parking harness: Device preventing accidental activation of the controls of a parked aircraft.

Parole: The word of honor or written promise of a prisoner-of-war not to attempt escape or take up arms again. Usually given in return for release from close confinement.

Parrel: A band of rope or an iron collar by which a yard is fastened to its mast, so as to slide freely up or down.

Parrot: The transponder of an IFF (Identification Friend or Foe) system.

Part: [1] To break (e.g., the line parted). [2] One of three divisions or segments of a line rove through a tackle. The standing part extends from the fixed point to the first mobile block; the running part or fall passes over the sheaves, and the leading part lies beyond the tackle and is the section that is hauled.

Particulates: Solid contaminants, especially in fuel.

Parting strop: A strop joining two hawsers and slightly weaker than both. Under excess strain it will break before either of the hawsers is damaged.

Partition: A non-structural bulkhead subdividing a main compartment.

Partizan: [1] A pike with a long, tapering, serrated, double-edged blade. [2] A guerrilla fighter in an organized civilian force fighting covertly to drive out an occupying force. [3] A person who strongly supports a specific cause, party, or person, often unreasonably or emotionally. Also partisan.

Party: A group assembled for a specific task (e.g., repair party, working party).

Pass: [1] To throw or project a line. [2] To lead a line through a block or fairlead. [4] Generally, any navigable channel [3] Specifically, a narrow passage through a reef.

Pass down the line: [1] To successively repeat a signal from the flagship when other vessels in the formation are out of visual contact. [2] In the USN a "PDL book" is kept by each watch station to ensure that subsequent watchkeepers are aware of previously-issued instructions.

Pass the buck: *See* Buck.

Pass the word!: Command to relay a message or instruction to persons who might have been unable to hear an original announcement.

Passage: [1] A voyage from one point to another by sea or air, often including the return trip. [2] The route or course followed. [3] A navigable channel or pass. [4] Permission to travel through territorial waters (right of passage). [5] The purchased right of conveyance as a passenger.

Passageway: USN term for a ship's interior corridor (cf. alleyway).

Passed: Having successfully taken an examination for an appointment or promotion.

Passed Midshipman: Formerly referred to a midshipman who had successfully completed the lieutenant's examination and was awaiting a vacancy (in effect, an Acting Sub-Lieutenant without the title). Such an officer could be appointed to command a prize or tender, but many chose to be rated Master's Mate instead.

Passenger: [1] One who pays for and takes passage aboard a ship or other form of conveyance. [2] One who works on a ship in return for unpaid passage.

Passenger liner: A passenger ship carrying goods, mail, and people on a regularly scheduled route between standard destinations.

Passenger mile: [1] One passenger transported over one nautical mile. [2] A measure of traffic economics calculated by multiplying the number of revenue-paying passengers by the distance traveled.

Passenger ship: A vessel licensed to carry more than twelve passengers (six in some jurisdictions).

Passenger space: An area required to be set aside for the accommodation, safety, and convenience of each permitted passenger. It cannot legally be used for mail, cargo or other goods.

Passing from behind: In the USN, a fast-walking junior overtaking a senior from behind is required to ask "By your leave sir (ma'am)?" and receive the reply "very well" or "permission granted" before passing. In the RN the question used to be "May I cross your bows sir (ma'am)?" with the response being "carry on" but that tradition seems to be dying out.

Passing honors: When warships of the same or foreign navies pass one another, or when a boat carrying an important dignitary passes by, it is customary for all on deck to respond to piped commands in small ships or bugle commands in bigger ones, by coming to attention and facing outboard toward the passing vessel. In the USN, all personnel on deck salute; but in the RN, only the Officer of the Watch, or Captain (if present) renders that honor. *See also* salutes & courtesies.

Passing wine: Both RN and USN follow the same tradition when "dining in." After the port (or Madeira) decanter has been unstoppered, no toasts are proposed or drunk until the decanter has passed around the entire table from right to left and all glasses have been charged. The decanter continues to circulate so that no glass remains empty, but "the port always moves to port," never anti-clockwise, even to a next-seat neighbor. If both port and Madeira are provided, it is traditional for the former to precede the latter as they circulate. The decanters are traditionally stoppered between circuits of the table and during the Loyal Toast.

Passive sonar: Sound-sensing equipment that listens without transmitting, detecting noise emitted by the target rather than a return of its own outgoing signal (as in active sonar). With passive sonar, hydrophones may be towed behind a ship or submarine in order to reduce the effect of noise generated by the watercraft itself. Towed units can be towed above or below the thermocline, to combat thermocline effect.

Passport: [1] A document issued by governments to individuals confirming identity and citizenship and authorizing the holder to travel abroad. [2] A document issued by belligerents to neutral vessels granting permission to proceed unmolested through specified waters in time of war (cf. Sea Letter).

Patache: An armed Portuguese sailing boat of about 300 tons, formerly used as a fleet tender.

Patallah: A large and unhandy Indian cattle boat.

Patch: [1] Communications term for temporary connection to a specific radio station. [2] Sailmaker's term for reinforcing canvas.

Patent anchor: Any of several proprietary stockless anchors.

Patent log: Also called taffrail log or screw log. Any of several speed measuring devices designed to replace the log-chip and line. The original version, patented by Connecticut Captain Truman Hotchkiss in 1864, replaced the chip with a finned torpedo-shaped rotator or spinner which was streamed at the end of a log-line the other end of which was attached to a register showing either speed or distance traveled. Some versions use electronic sensors to indicate the vessel's speed. The line of a patent log did not need to be knotted, but was braided to prevent the rotation from unlaying it or twisting it into knots. This type of device was superseded first by the pitot tube and later by global positioning systems.

Pathfinder: An experienced aircraft crew which leads a strike formation to a target, release point, or drop zone.

Patrimonial sea: This term, which originated with the Santo Domingo Conference of 1972, is frequently used by Caribbean countries to reference exclusive economic and/or fishing zones, but is seldom used elsewhere.

Patriotic songs: In the late 18th and early 19th centuries, the rise of industrialized warfare with large citizen involvement gave rise to patriotic war songs, of which the British "Rule Britannia" and French "Marseillaise" were prototypical. Singing them was supposed to improve martial ardor, raise the spirits of troops and civilians, and encourage national chauvinism. To some extent this was a throwback to the war chants of primitive societies which served not only to intimidate enemies, but also to fortify morale.

• British songs: In the days of Julius Caesar, Britannia was a place (England) rather than a person. Then Emperor Hadrian issued a coin with a female figure, resembling the goddess Minerva but identified as Britannia and wearing a centurion's helmet, wrapped in a toga, carrying spear and shield. In typical Roman fashion this young woman was almost immediately identified as a goddess in her own right. During the Elizabethan Renaissance, she was considered the personification of England and, after union with Scotland, was used a rallying image for all Britons. As British sea power and influence began a gradual resurgence, the national goddess became an increasingly important naval symbol. With her spear replaced by Neptune's trident she was the centerpiece of a London pageant in 1602, appeared on coinage in 1672, and was the subject of a poem by James Thompson entitled "Rule Britannia" and written around 1725:

> When Britain first at Heaven's command
> Arose from out the azure main;
> This was the charter of the land
> And guardian angels sang this strain;
>
> Rule Britannia!
> Britannia rule the waves
> Britons never, never, never
> Shall be slaves!

At that time, the Royal Navy was tactically ahead of all its rivals, but had no real claim to "rule the waves." Both Dutch and French had large navies with arguably better ships, while the Spanish Armada was still a significant factor. British maritime hegemony was almost in sight, but the poem was really intended to be a nostalgic remembrance of the ninth century when Alfred the Great (known as "Father of the English Navy") had humbled the Danes (*see* Saxon seapower). Thompson's poem was set to music by Thomas Augustine Arne in 1740, just at the beginning of the Royal Navy's rise to world domination. Throughout the 19th century and into the 20th "Rule Britannia" was a chauvinistic musical celebration of Britain's overwhelming naval power. Even after the British fleet has been reduced to a shadow of its former self the song remains, unofficially, an alternative national anthem; sharing that status with Arthur Benson's poem, set to Sir Edward Elgar's music "Pomp and Circumstance" for use as a coronation ode in 1902:

> Land of Hope and Glory, Mother of the Free,
> How shall we extol thee, who are born of thee?
> Wider still and wider shall thy bounds be set;
> God who made thee mighty, make thee mightier yet.

- The United States has no fewer than five patriotic songs with anthem-like status. Unlike "Rule Britannia," none has direct maritime connections. For most of the 19th century, "Hail Columbia" was the unofficial national hymn. Originally titled "The President's March," it was composed by Philip Phile in 1789 for the inauguration of George Washington. Lyrics by Joseph Hopkinson were added in 1798.

> Hail Columbia, happy land!
> Hail, ye heroes, heav'n-born band,
> Who fought and bled in freedom's cause,
> Who fought and bled in freedom's cause,
> And when the storm of war was gone
> Enjoy'd the peace your valor won.
>
> Firm and united let us be,
> Rallying round our liberty,
> As a band of brothers joined,
> Peace and safety we shall find.

Another anthem, "America the Beautiful," was written in 1893 by writer-poet Katherine Lee Bates, an instructor at Wellesley College, Massachusetts, and set to music by Samuel Ward in 1910. It too won national support.

> O beautiful for spacious skies,
> For amber waves of grain.
> For purple mountain majesties
> Above the fruited plain.
>
> America! America!
> God shed his grace on thee,
> And crown thy good with brotherhood
> From sea to shining sea.

The melody of the third patriotic song, was originally the German "Kaiserhymne," which has also served as the national anthems of Denmark, Russia, Sweden, and Switzerland, and is still that of the United Kingdom. The lyric was written in 1831 or '32 by the Rev. Samuel Francis Smith of Boston's Park Street Church:

> My country, 'tis of thee,
> Sweet land of liberty,
> Of thee I sing;
>
> Land where my fathers died,
> Land of the pilgrims' pride,
> From every mountainside,
> Let freedom ring!

During the late 19th and early 20th centuries these three hymns competed for national recognition with a fourth written in 1814 by Francis Scott Key and set to the tune of a popular British drinking song by John Stafford Smith.

> O! say can you see by the dawn's early light
> What so proudly we hailed at the twilight's
> last gleaming?
> Whose broad stripes and bright stars through
> the perilous fight,
> O'er the ramparts we watched were so
> gallantly streaming?
> And the rockets' red glare, the bombs
> bursting in air,
> Gave proof through the night that our flag
> was still there.
> Oh, say does that star-spangled banner yet wave
> O'er the land of the free and the home
> of the brave?

In 1889, "The Star Spangled Banner" was recognized for official use by the United States Navy when visiting foreign ports, but the nation itself remained without a hymn of national praise. Meanwhile, a fifth patriotic song gained national recognition. It was written in 1918 by Russian-born composer Israel Baline under his adopted American name of Irving Berlin. Its key lyrics are:

> God Bless America
> Land that I love
> Stand beside her and guide her
> Thru the night with light from above
>
> From the mountains, to the prairies,
> To the oceans bright with foam
> God bless America
> My home sweet home

It was not until March 1931 that a Congressional resolution was signed by President Herbert Hoover, making "The Star Spangled Banner" the undisputed United States national anthem.

Patrol: A force sent out to gather information, or to carry out a destructive, harassing, mopping-up, or security mission.

Patrol craft: *See* motor launch, motor gunboat, motor torpedo boat, patrol torpedo boat, submarine chaser, swift boat, and cutter.

Patrol torpedo boat: This was a USN World War II vessel adapted from the fast rum-runners used to outpace Coast Guard cutters during Prohibition.

Pawl: A pivoted metal bar which engages the teeth of a ratchet wheel allowing a mechanism (especially a capstan) to turn in one direction but not in the other.

Pax: Travel industry shorthand for Passengers.

Pay: [1] To coat with pitch or tar, especially when caulking a seam (*see* horse). [2] To let out or slacken off. [3] To distribute wages earned.

Pay grade: Rate of remuneration for all USN personnel, defined by a letter-number code covering all ranks from recruit (E-1) to admiral (O-10). *See also* rank and table 14.

Pay off: [1] Turn to leeward by movement of the helm. [2] Discharge the entire ships company with full wages. [3] Terminate an individual seaman's service with the payment of outstanding wages.

Pay out: Release a line slowly.

Paying-off pendant: Although there is no proper specification or authorization, it has long been the custom of RN ships returning to pay off after a foreign commission to unofficially wear a long white pendant with a Saint George's Cross at the hoist and a balloon or bladder at the fly to keep it clear of the water. It is hoisted on leaving the foreign station, and worn when arriving at the home port to pay off, as well as when entering and leaving any intermediate stops. Originally, crews stitched all their cleaning rags together and hoisted them to show they were no longer needed. Later, proper pendants were made on board as a communal effort, with each member of the ship's company putting in a few stitches. More recently, they are purchased ashore by the ship's welfare fund. There are several unofficial "rules" (customs, really) concerning the length of the pendant; most of them relating to either the length of the ship or the height of its foremast, which is incremented for each month on a foreign station (often by 12 inches). U.S. naval vessels do not pay off, but continue the tradition with their homeward-bound pennants.

Payload: [1] the weight of cargo or passengers that can be carried by a ship or aircraft. [2] The sum of the weight of explosive material, its container, and activating devices in the warhead of a conventional military missile. [3] The explosive energy in the warhead of a nuclear missile (e.g., a payload of 50 megatons).

Paymaster: [1] USN term for any disbursing officer, especially a member of the Supply Corps. [2] Former RN name for a member of the Paymaster Branch. (*See* Purser, Logistics Officer.)

PC: Patrol craft.

PCE: Patrol craft, Escort.

PCF: Patrol craft, Fast. Also Swift boat.

PCG: Patrol craft, Guided Missile.

PCH: Patrol craft, Hydrofoil.

Pea jacket: Seaman's short coat of coarse woolen cloth, usually double-breasted and navy-blue in color. (from the Dutch Pijekket.) Also reefer.

Peacehead: In the early days of naval torpedoes, an unarmed version intended for training or test firing was referred to as having a peacehead. The explosive payload intended for use in combat inevitability became known as a warhead, and that name survived after peacehead fell into disuse.

Peak: [1] The upper outer corner of a gaffed sail. [2] The point of an anchor fluke that digs into the ground. [3] The narrow part of a ship's hull at bow (forepeak) or stern (afterpeak).

Peak tank: A liquid storage compartment, either low in the bow or, occasionally, the stern.

Pearl Harbor: After the successful British naval air raid on Taranto, Japanese Admiral Isoroku Yamamoto planned a similar attack on the U.S. naval base at Pearl Harbor. The raid, launched on 7th December 1941, from 274 miles off the coast of Oahu, achieved complete surprise. The aircraft came in two waves, at 7:53 and 8:55. By 9:55 it was all over. Three hours later all surviving aircraft had landed and the carriers were heading back to Japan. It is instructive to compare the two actions.

- Italy was in a state of war and Taranto received advance warning of the approaching strike, whereas Pearl Harbor's defenses were unmanned, unsuspecting, and on peacetime Sunday routines.

- The British attack had been mounted by a mere twenty-one obsolete open-cockpit fabric biplanes, launched from a lone carrier, with only two being shot down. Japan launched 354 state-of-the-art aircraft from six carriers, and lost 29.

- Damage inflicted was not proportional to the number of aircraft. Half of Italy's six battleships were sunk at their moorings, as were three cruisers. Japanese aircraft also sank three battleships (*Arizona* was claimed by a midget submarine), crippled four more, and sank three cruisers.

- At Taranto, valuable oil storage tanks were set ablaze; but at Pearl four-and-a-half million tons of fuel storage were not even targeted — neither were the huge supply dumps, dry-docks, and precision machine shops, which would allow the U.S. Navy to make a rapid recovery.

- In both operations, nearby airfields and float plane bases were attacked, but the scale of that assault was greater at Pearl.

Taranto was a strategic success, while Pearl Harbor was a failure. In the Mediterranean, where gunpower was still a major factor, the loss of fifty percent of its capital ships was a crippling blow to Regia Marina, which seldom ventured out of harbor again. In the Pacific, however, naval aviation would be the supreme weapon, and not one American carrier had been in port at the time of the attack.

Pease porridge: [1] A mixture of resin, tallow, and sulfur used during the process of boot topping. [2] Pease pudding.

Pease pudding: Boiled and mashed split yellow peas, salted and spiced. Similar in texture to hummus, with a mild taste, it is usually served with ham. Sometimes known as pease pottage or pease porridge.

Pecuniary liability: A personal, joint, or corporate monetary obligation to make good property lost, damaged, or destroyed due to fault or neglect.

Peeway: USN submariner slang for the main corridor in a nuclear boat.

Pelican hook: A long shackle, fitted with a hinged rod which closes against the end of the shackle and is secured by a sliding ring.

Pelorus: [1] A sighting device fitted over a compass for taking bearings and azimuths. [2] In the RN, this device is called an azimuth ring, while pelorus refers to the main compass repeater mounted at the center of the bridge, on which an azimuth ring is mounted.

Pendant: [1] A line secured to a spar or bulkhead, having an eye or hook at the other end and used to secure something in place. [2] A pennant (mainly British).

Peninsula: An area of land almost entirely surrounded by water except for an isthmus connecting it to a larger body of land.

Pennant: A long narrow flag, sometimes swallow-tailed, often indicating command status, a special occasion (church, homeward-bound, paying-off, etc.), or distinguishing a warship from a merchantman. Also spelled "pendant" but always pronounced "pennant."

Pens: A series of parallel jetties for berthing submarines or small craft.

Penteconter: An ancient battle galley, propelled by fifty oars.

People: An early term for crew or ship's company. Still used occasionally.

Peotta: Former Adriatic craft, propelled by oars and sail.

Perigee: The point in a missile trajectory or satellite orbit closest to the earth (cf. Apogee).

Periko: Bengalese barge-like cargo boat.

Peril: In marine insurance, the term Peril (or Peril of the Sea) does not refer to danger or hazard, but to accident beyond the control of master or crew (known ashore as Act of God). *See also* risk.

Periodic current: An ocean current that changes speed or direction cyclically or at regular intervals, as opposed to a permanent current.

Peripheral vertical launch: A shipboard launching system designed to maintain second strike capability by protecting a missile and its crew from blast and fragmentation.

Periplus: [1] A 5th century BCE tactical naval maneuver in which a galley would circle an enemy vessel to attack it from the rear. From the Greek for sailing around. [2] An ancient manuscript listing the ports and landmarks a navigator could expect to find along the shore and the distances between them.

Periscope: This device for observation from a concealed position has ancient roots, its principle having been demonstrated at least as early as 1430, by Johann Gutenberg, inventor of the printing press, but development of a retractable version for use by submarines is usually credited to American naval architect Simon Lake in 1902. A long (up to 18 meters = 60 feet) and narrow (length : diameter ratio = 50 or more), telescopic tube that is raised from a submerged submarine to see what is happening on the surface. Lenses and prisms collect, reflect, and bend images down the tube to the eye of a sailor in the boat's control room.

The navigation or observation periscope — used to scan the surrounding sea and sky for targets and threats — has a wide field of vision at low-power magnification. The targeting or "attack" periscope has a more focused field of view and higher magnification. These conventional optical periscopes have three inherent hazards:

• The hull must be pierced to allow the periscope tubes to pass through, creating points of potential weakness.

• The boat can remain hidden underwater, but must sacrifice stealth by rising to periscope depth, where the tip of the periscope breaks the surface creating a "feather" that betrays its location to surface vessels or aircraft.

• Unprotected periscope operators are especially vulnerable to hostile laser radiation, which can dazzle or blind them. Protection may take the form of a filter or an optical switch.

Technological developments have eliminated these exposures and modern submarines no longer use optical periscopes. One alternative is the photonic mast, another, the floating fiber optic scanner.

Periscope depth: Refers to a submarine that is completely but shallowly submerged, at a depth where its periscopes and antenna masts are just able to break the surface. This is a hazardous situation, since the boat's "shadow" may be plainly visible from the air, while modern radar can detect even a slender periscope.

Periscope feather: The plume of spray raised by the periscope of a submerged submarine moving through the water.

Perishable cargo: Shipments requiring refrigeration, such as meat, fruit, fresh vegetables, and biologicals.

Permanent ballast: Weighty material carried to improve stability or trim and never removed to provide space for cargo or goods. *See* kentledge.

Permanent current: An ocean current that exhibits little or no seasonal or periodic variation of speed or direction (e.g., Gulf Stream, Japan Stream). *See also* periodic current.

Permanent echo: Any dense and fixed radar return caused by the reflection of energy from the earth's surface. Distinguished from ground clutter by being from definable locations.

Permission to grow: The traditional Royal Navy request to cultivate facial hair is "permission to grow, sir please?" Without this authorization, sailors must be clean-shaven.

Personal effects disposal: If an individual left a British warship and it was obvious they were not going to return, it was customary for the master-at-arms or coxswain to auction off any kit they had left behind. If the discharge was marked "R" (run) indicating the person had deserted, the goods would be sold at give-away prices, but if it was marked "DD" (discharged dead) articles would often sell for more than their original cost, with proceeds going to the widow or estate. In cases of known family hardship, most of the purchased items would be returned to the auctioneer for re-sale at inflated prices. In this traditional way, shipmates could provide for needy dependents without making it seem like charity.

Personal flags: *See* flags of rank.

Personal flotation device: United States Coast Guard term for any apparatus designed to keep a wearer afloat with head above water. The term includes all types of such devices from simple life preservers to complex survival suits. USCG rates five versions:

- **Type I — Offshore life jacket:** Suitable for rough open water, especially where rescue may be delayed. This type provides the greatest buoyancy, and automatically turns unconscious wearers into a face-up position with their head out of the water. It is typically jacket-shaped but sleeveless, usually equipped with emergency light and whistle, and has multiple ties and belts for closure.
- **Type II — Near-shore buoyancy vest:** For use where quick rescue is likely. It is similar to type I, but with lesser buoyancy and reduced ability to turn an unconscious wearer face upward. Usually bright orange for easy sighting.
- **Type III — Flotation aid**: Best for conscious wearers who can keep their own faces out of the water. Typically jacket-style, fitting the wearer closely with many zippers and buckles to close.
- **Type IV — Throwable devices**: For areas where there is constant boat traffic and rescue is likely to be immediate. Commonly ring-shaped and known as lifebuoys, but horseshoe and cushion shapes are also made. It is difficult for an inexperienced rescuer to aim the device properly, especially when throwing in rougher water.
- **Type V — Special purpose:** Intended for specific conditions and activities and to be used only for the designated use. Special purpose PFDs come in a variety of styles, from full-body suits to work vests. Some have a safety harness and provide protection against hypothermia.

PFDs are also known as life preservers, Mae Wests, life vests, life savers, life jackets, and life belts.

Personal gun salutes: Having started as a friendly gesture to other countries (*see* National Gun Salutes) the practice of firing cannon evolved into a ceremonial act of respect for individuals. (In the 16th century, intending to honor Elizabeth I, a warship accidentally fired shot instead of blank rounds, damaging Greenwich Palace, the Queen's residence. Since then naval gun salutes have been prohibited on the Thames River above Gravesend.) In 1875, Britain and the United States agreed on salutes ranging from five to twenty-one guns in increments of two, the number of shots depending on the importance of the occasion and the rank or status of the person being honored. (Even numbers are never fired —*see* gun salutes.)

Heads of state and reigning monarchs each receive 21 guns, while other civilians are saluted in accordance with their protocol status, the lowest being a vice-consul who rates five guns. Naval and their equivalent army or air force officers are saluted in accordance with rank. Nineteen guns are awarded to British Admirals of the Fleet and U.S. Fleet Admirals, Chiefs of Naval Operations, and Commandants of the Marine Corps. Seventeen go to Admirals, fifteen to Vice-Admirals, thirteen to Rear Admirals (upper half in the USN), and eleven to RN Commodores and USN Rear Admirals (lower half). *See also* salutes and courtesies.

Person overboard: This is the "politically correct" version of the traditional mariner's cry "Man overboard"! The victim may have inadvertently gone over the side after being hit by a spar, tripping on a line, being caught off balance by unexpected movement of the vessel, sliding on a slippery deck, or thrown into the water for any number of other reasons. If it is not possible to reach the victim with a pole, lifebuoy, or hand-thrown line, the vessel must return for rescue and recovery. The following maneuvers allow it to reach the point of the accident as quickly as possible depending on the relative location of the casualty, known as the MOB Point.

- **Anderson Turn:** This maneuver is most appropriate in the "immediate action" situation, just after the accident while the MOB is still visible from the deck. The rudder is put full over to turn the vessel in a 360° circle. If the person fell over the port side, the rudder is turned to port, and vice versa. This brings the vessel back to the casualty as quickly as possible. The author has found no record of when this turn was invented or who Anderson was.
- **Williamson Turn:** This turn is appropriate in a "delayed action" situation, when the MOB is out of sight, but known to be relatively near. It starts like the Anderson by turning the rudder towards the side of the accident but, after deviating from the original course by about 60°, the rudder is shifted full to the opposite side to start a forward circle, turning back towards the original course, which the helmsman will ease onto and follow its reciprocal until the casualty is reached. This maneuver was developed in 1943 by Lt. John Williamson, USNR.
- **Scharnow Turn:** This one is appropriate in "person missing" circumstances, when the MOB has disappeared and probably lies far behind the vessel's turning radius. It also starts like the Anderson, but unlike the Williamson continues as a backward circle for about 240°. Then the rudder is shifted to the opposite side and the vessel is steered onto the reciprocal of its original course, reaching it much further astern than would be the case with a Williamson turn. It was developed after World War II by Professor Ulrich Scharnow, a maritime expert and author of several books on seamanship.

- **Global positioning systems:** Often have an MOB button which can be pressed as soon as the cry reaches the bridge. This immediately records the position at which the accident occurred and gives continuous readings of the MOB's bearing and distance from the ship as it returns to pick up the casualty.

Personnel: The body of people, as opposed to matériel, comprising a naval or military force.

Persuader: Sailing ship seaman's slang for the rope's end or "starter" used by a bosun's mate to speed up laggards.

Pesage: The fee or duty charged for weighing cargo. From the French.

Petrel: The name given to various ocean birds belonging, like the albatross, shearwater, and mollymawk, to the order of tube nosed swimmers. Tireless fliers by day, at night they rest on the water, many returning to land only to breed. Wilson's petrel (stormy petrel or Mother Carey's chicken) is a surface skimmer and habitual boat follower. Leach's petrel has a bounding, erratic flight and breeds on islands off the New England coast. Other species include the auk-like diving petrel, the albatross-sized giant petrel or fulmar, and the smaller fulmar petrel. The word comes from the Latin name Petrus, and refers to the birds' habit of hovering just above the ocean waves, thus appearing to walk on the water, as Christians believe Saint Peter did.

Petticoat-trowsers: 17th century seaman's breeches with kilt-like legs. Much favored by buccaneers. Also galligaskins.

Petty Officer: Naval non-commissioned rate, senior to seaman but junior to chief petty Officer.

PF: Former Hull classification symbol of a patrol frigate.

PFD: Personal Floatation Device.

PG: Patrol gunboat.

PGH: Patrol gunboat, Hydrofoil.

PGM: Patrol gunboat, missile.

PGR: Precision graphic recorder. Supplementary equipment used with a hydrographic echo sounder when depth cannot be recorded on the standard expanded scale.

Phalanx: A fast-reaction, rapid-fire, radar-controlled, 20-mm weapon system for last-chance defense against air or surface attacks which have penetrated outer defenses.

Phantom: [1] A false bottom recorded by a depth indicator. [2] A non-existent object "sighted" by radar (also ghost). [3] A ghost ship.

The Philadelphia Experiment: This is alleged to have been a USN attempt to investigate whether Einstein's Unified Field Theory could be used to create "electronic camouflage" which would make vessels invisible to the eye and undetectable by enemy radar. Tons of sophisticated electronic equipment are said to have been installed in place of the forward turret of destroyer escort USS *Eldridge* (DE 173) in order to generate an intense magnetic field. This was expected to bend light or radar waves around the vessel, much as the refraction of air over a hot road creates a mirage. Tests are reported to have taken place at the Philadelphia Navy Yard and at sea.

At 0900 hours on 22nd July 1943 (so the story goes) power was turned on and a greenish fog slowly enveloped *Eldridge* temporarily concealing her from view. When the fog dispersed, leaving only undisturbed water where the vessel had been, the watching naval officers and scientists were ecstatic. It seemed they had achieved not only a "cloak" of radar invisibility but visual disappearance as well. After fifteen minutes, they ordered the generators switched off (as these were on board *Eldridge*, their radio command must have been able to penetrate the magnetic field even if radar could not!). The green fog reappeared, and then slowly dispersed disclosing the ship. Disturbingly, crew members on *Eldridge*'s deck were found to be completely disoriented and nauseous.

Navy scientists decided to repeat the experiment with another crew, using increased power to create a more intense magnetic field. According to legend, the second experiment developed very differently, and far more dangerously than they had anticipated. At 17:15 on 28th October the electromagnetic equipment was switched on again and *Eldridge* gradually began to fade from view. Suddenly, there was a blinding blue flash and the destroyer completely disappeared. Seconds later, she was reportedly seen and identified at Norfolk, Virginia, 400 kilometers (250 miles) away. Four hours after that, when the power on-board was turned off (by whom one might ask, and under whose orders?) the destroyer disappeared from Norfolk as mysteriously as it had arrived and reappeared at Philadelphia.

Believers in the story say the 1,240-ton ship had been dematerialized and transported using alien technology reverse-engineered from a crashed UFO. This time, it is said, several crew members had disappeared, several more had been "fused" to the metal of the ship's structure, and the rest were violently sick with no recollection of what had happened. According to the legend, all who survived were discharged as "mentally unfit for duty" but, years later people claiming to have witnessed the experiment said they had began to "remember" details which had been erased from their memories.

The Office of Naval Research claims that records in the Operational Archives Branch of the Naval Historical Center have been repeatedly searched without turning up any evidence that any such event was ever attempted or achieved. In fact, the Navy states that *Eldridge*'s War Diary indicates she was never in Norfolk or Philadelphia during the time frame of the reputed experiment. Proponents of the story retort that this is another massive governmental cover-up similar to the Manhattan Project which developed the atomic bomb, but this time hiding experiments with alien technology, such as those reputed to have come from the capture of an Unidentified Flying Object at Roswell a few years later. Who knows?

PhM: Pharmacist's Mate (USN).

Phonetic alphabets: [1] Originally, a phonetic alphabet (or more properly phonetic notation) was a system for transcribing the sounds of human speech into writing as a guide to pronunciation. Systems for true phonetic notation include the International Phonetic Alphabet (IPA) and Speech Assessment Methods Phonetic Alphabet (SAMPA) a computer-readable and printable script based on IPA. [2] Later, the name was appropriated by military and aviation interests to describe conventions for the identification of individual letters in radio and telephonic communication. Standardized and easy to remember words represent letters of the alphabet, especially those which might otherwise be misunderstood or confused when verbally spelled out such as "M" and "N" or "F" and "S." Despite their name, such alphabets are not truly "phonetic" since they do not describe the sound of each letter but merely identify it. During World War I there was little inter-service or inter-allied communication, so national armies and navies each developed their own systems. In the Second World War, however, combined operations were frequent and a joint version was adopted in 1942 by all Allied armed forces except the British Royal Air Force which maintained its own system for another year.

In between the wars, the International Telecommunications Union (ITU) introduced the first internationally-recognized phonetic alphabet. In spite of clumsy choice of multi-syllabic words, it was adopted by the International Commission for Air Navigation, and was used by civil aviation until the 1950s, when a new version was developed by the International Air Transport Association (IATA). This version was adopted by the International Civil Aviation Organization (ICAO), the United States Federal Aviation Administration (FAA), and the International Maritime Organization (IMO), making it the most widely used civilian phonetic alphabet. However, it gained even greater prominence when it was taken over by the North Atlantic Treaty Organization for its military communications. In consequence it is generally known as the NATO version.

Although basically English, a few words were modified so that the system would be suitable for French or Spanish pronunciation. For example, the English word Alpha would be pronounced Alpa in Spanish, so Alfa was substituted. Similarly, French speakers would treat a single "t" as silent, so Juliet was replaced by Juliett, but not by the French Juliette which Spanish-speakers would read as Juliet-uh. Also, Papa is pronounced with the accent on the second syllable. There are dozens of similar alphabets in official and unofficial use by various police forces and business organizations, including a number of ad hoc systems created by individual telecommunications operators using familiar words that sound right to them. The style and structure of selected English-language systems can be seen in table 11, which gives historical and current examples of two civil and five military alphabets.

Phosphorescence: [1] The residual glow on a radar screen after the indicator sweep has moved on [2] Incorrectly, bioluminescence.

Photonics mast: A device similar in concept to a submarine periscope, that provides many benefits a periscope is unable to offer. It replaces line-of-sight viewing with equipment, similar to a digital camera, mounted on telescoping arms that are contained entirely within the sail without penetrating the pressure hull. The hull opening for cables is much smaller and more easily sealed, minimizing the risk of water leakage. Moreover, being connected by flexible cables instead of rigid tubes, the control room need not be placed directly below the sail, but can be moved to a lower deck away from the hull's curvature where there is more space. Sailors throughout the boat can view color, high-resolution black and white, or infrared images, on flat-panel displays; and these images can be shared with other ships in the theater, or with command centers ashore. However, photonic masts can not operate at the depths possible for floating fiber optic scanners.

PHS: Packaging, handling, & storage.

Picaroon: A pirate vessel (from the Spanish picaro = pirate).

Picket: [1] A small armed boat performing sentinel duty. [2] A vessel or aircraft assigned to patrol an area away from the main force.

Pidgin: A form of communication consisting of words and phrases from the languages of two people without a common tongue and often quite different from either. Hence, the forms of Pidgin-English spoken in China, West Africa, and New Guinea, are completely different from each other, and all are essentially unintelligible to English-speakers.

Pier: [1] An iron or wooden structure on piles projecting into the sea. [2] The support for a bridge or other structure over water.

Pierhead: The offshore end of a pier.

Pierhead jump: [1] A leap ashore by a would-be deserter. [2] A leap on board by a late-arriving crew member. [3] RN slang for an officer's appointment (usually to somewhere unpleasant) with minimum notice.

Pierson-Moskowitch: *See* sea spectrum and table 3.

Pig: The pig was treated with great trepidation and respect by sailors because it had cloven hooves (like the devil). An ancient superstition of unknown origin, now seldom observed, is that use of the word pig on board ship would bring bad luck, so synonyms such as hog, sow, curly-tail, or porker were always substituted. Combined with the shipboard ban on whistling, this led to many harbor-side taverns being called The Pig and Whistle to help seafarers realize they were ashore and could speak of the one and do the other. (*See* tattooing for a more beneficial pig-related superstition.)

Pig iron: This intermediate product of smelting is very brittle, cannot be forged, and is not useful directly except for limited applications. In the mid–18th century it progressively replaced stone and gravel for ship's ballast (*see* kentledge). The traditional shape of ingot molds was a branching structure that reminded ironworkers of a litter of piglets suckling on a sow. Hence the name.

Pigboat: USN slang for a diesel-electric submarine.

Pigeons: NATO preface to the transmission of a magnetic bearing (course) and distance to an aircraft.

Piglet: Royal Marines derisive slang for a midshipman (cf. snotty).

Pigs: RN lower deck slang for commissioned officers (*see* pigsty).

Pigsty: RN lower deck slang for the wardroom. (The terms pigs and pigsty are normally only used in unhappy ships.)

Pigtail: A braid of hair (usually tarred by sailors) hanging down at the back of the neck. A pigtail (properly queue) was often considered the symbol of sailing ship seamen, especially during the Napoleonic Wars. In those days both pressed men and volunteers were likely to come aboard with lice, so their heads were shaved on arrival. Starting earlier, but especially from the mid-eighteenth century to about 1825, long tresses became a symbol of service and were worn as a matter of pride by both officers and seamen to demonstrate their trade and seniority.

Pike: A shafted spear-like weapon with a pointed iron tip, used to repel boarders. A shorter version is known as a half-pike or boarding pike.

Pile: A flat or cylindrical column, driven into the ground to provide support and protection for a structure such as a pier.

Piled ice: Slabs of ice, stacked one upon another and resembling an iceberg.

Pile-driver: [1] Machine used to hammer piles into the ground. [2] Said of a vessel that is too short to bridge consecutive waves and consequently slams violently into the second of each pair.

Pilferage: A marine insurance term referring to the illicit removal of part of the contents of a shipping package. Stealing the entire package is theft.

Pillow: A wedge or block supporting the inboard end of a bowsprit.

Pillow block: A cast-iron or steel support for a journal or bearing. Also pillar block.

Pilot: [1] A mariner with extensive local knowledge, certificated to guide ship captains through hazardous waters. [2] A book of detailed navigational instructions. [3] A person qualified to fly an airplane. [4] Naval slang for a ship's navigating officer.

Pilotage: [1] The act, occupation, or skill of being a pilot. [2] The fee payable for the services of a pilot.

Pilotage waters: Refers to coastal waterways where pilotage is either [1] Legally required. [2] Recommended because of local hazards: or [3] Available on request.

Pilothouse: The structure or space from which a ship is navigated. Also charthouse or chart room.

Piloting: Navigation by use of visual reference points.

PIM: Point of intended movement.

Pinch: To sail so close to the wind that the sails shiver and the vessel loses speed.

Ping!: [1] Verbal representation of the sound emitted by sonar or other sound-ranging equipment. [2] To emit such a sound.

Pingle: Small coastal sailing vessel of northern England.

Pink: Formerly a small, narrow-sterned, square-rigged, cargo vessel of northern Europe and the Mediterranean. Also pinque.

Pinnace: [1] Lugsail or schooner-rigged, eight-oared, ship's boat. [2] Formerly a small galleon-type warship. [3] Coal-fired powerboat, known as a "steam pinnace."

Pinrail: A stout hardwood rail with holes for belaying pins in its projecting edge, attached to a sailing ship's bulwark below its caprail.

Pintle: The hook or pin on a rudder which fits into the gudgeon and allows the rudder to swing from side to side.

Pipe: [1] To transmit an order by boatswain's call (whistle), when necessary followed by a verbal Command. [2] To give a traditional visitor's salute by boatswain's call. (From the Latin pipare = cheep like a bird.) [3] A measure of wine equal to two hogsheads = 125 gallons or 568 liters. (Probably from the French for a barrel in which wine was shipped.)

Pipe down: When an outside job had been completed, the boatswain would pipe a command for the crew to disperse and retire below deck. Once they had gone, the deck became much quieter, so it was natural for the term to become synonymous with "be silent" and hence a verbal command to "shut up!"

Pipe the eye: Seaman's slang for weeping.

Pipe the side: This uniquely nautical ceremony dates back to at least 1645, when it was ordained that:

> When a barge carrying an important visitor approaches the ship, trumpets are to sound ... until the barge comes within less than musket shot. At that time the trumpets are to cease and all as carry whistles are to whistle a welcome three several times.

Later, visiting dignitaries would be hoisted in a bosun's chair while the boatswain passed orders by pipe (whistle) to the sideboys (hoisting crew). The heavier the person to be raised, the bigger the side-party would have to be, and different pipes (calls) were developed to summon an even number of sideboys depending on the visitor's size. It was quite usual for the person's weight to increase with his status and eventually the practice applied to the visitor's rank rather than avoirdupois.

Nowadays, the call is piped twice, first as the visitor's boat pulls alongside, and again when the dignitary mounts the accommodation ladder and steps inboard. This procedure is reversed when the visitor leaves. When coming aboard via a brow from the quay, there is only one pipe. Traditionally, the side is piped whenever the corpse of a naval officer or seaman is carried on board, taken ashore for burial, or committed over the side to the deep. (*See also* side honors.)

Piping hot: The boatswain used to pipe the call for a representative of each mess to report to the galley and pick up their food. If he was tardy, the meal would be cold, but if he was quick, it would still be as hot as when it was piped.

Piracy: Robbery or other act of violence done upon the high seas or the air above the seas, or through descent from sea or air, by a body of men acting for private ends and independently of any politically organized society.

Piragua: Amazon River dugout canoe made from a single tree trunk.

Pirate: [1] A person who practices piracy. [2] A ship used by pirates.

Pirogue: [1] A flat-bottomed keelless open boat used in the bayous of Louisiana (pronounced pee-row in Cajun). [2] A Caribbean dugout canoe (pronounced as written).

Pissdale: An 18th century urinal, usually located near the officers' quarters and consisting of a tapered lead pipe leading to the sea.

Pistol: A small personal firearm, fired from one hand. Available in many patterns, and bearing a great variety of names. From Pistoja, a town in Italy where such weapons originated.

Pistol-proof: A term used by pirates to describe a shipmate courageous enough to stand for election as captain.

Pitch: [1] A distillation of tar or turpentine, mixed with coarse rosin; hard when cold but semi-liquid when heated and used for caulking. [2] Degree of inclination of a propeller blade relative to its axis of rotation. [3] The distance a propeller would travel in one revolution if there were no slippage. [4] Rotation of an aircraft about its lateral axis. [5] One of the six responses of a vessel to movement of the sea, causing it to plunge, dipping stem and stern alternately into the waves. (*See* ship motion, rotational oscillation.)

Pitch ladle: A long-handled iron bowl with a spout. Used to pour boiling pitch or tar into deck seams to make them watertight.

Pitchpole: Said of a vessel tossed and turned stern over stem by a following wave.

Pitot tube: An instrument widely used to measure the speed of aircraft that has also been installed on ships. Projecting through the bottom of the hull, a co-axial tube is bent at right angles to point forward in the direction of motion. The inner tube is open at its forward end to record dynamic pressure, which is proportional to speed through the water; while the outer one has holes in its side to record static pressure, which depends on the depth and density of the water. When the vessel is stationary, the two pressures are equal, but when it moves dynamic pressure becomes greater, the difference varying with the square of the ship's speed which can be calculated by Bernouilli's Equation. This concept for measuring rates of fluid flow was postulated by French hydraulic engineer Henri Pitot in 1732 and developed into a practical device in 1858 by Henry Darcy, another member of the French Corps of Roads and Bridges.

Pivot: [1] A central pin around which something turns. [2] To rotate on an axis; to turn about a central pin.

Pivot-gun: A small anti-personnel firearm, mounted on a shaft which can rotate in a housing to point in any direction.

Pivot point: The point around which a ship rotates when turning. This is usually about one-third of the vessel's length from the bow when moving forward and about one-quarter of its length from the stern when going backward.

Pivot ship: The ship in a line abreast around which a wheeling maneuver is executed.

Pivotal: [1] Pertaining to a pivot; axial. [2] Fundamental, central, important, significant. [3] *See* the author's specific definition in the Introduction.

Plain clothes: RN term for civilian dress (cf. mufti).

Plain sailing: Sailing on waters free of obstructions or hazards (not to be confused with plane sailing).

Plan of the Day: Developed by the Executive Officer (XO), the POD is the primary means of announcing each day's schedule of important events. Commanders of embarked units should be included in POD development to ensure their people fully understand shipboard responsibilities.

Plan Position Indicator: A radar display that presents a picture of the area surrounding the vessel, showing the range and bearing of nearby objects, either relative to the ship's head or, when gyro stabilization is applied, at the true compass bearing and range. *See* radarscope.

Plane: [1] To gain enough speed to lift the forward part of a vessel's hull so that it rides on the surface of the water with minimum resistance. [2] Abbreviation of hydroplane or diving plane. [3] Abbreviation of aeroplane or airplane.

Plane Captain: USN flight deck enlisted person responsible for the material condition, start-up, movement, launch, and recovery of a specific naval aircraft. These brown shirted airmen are usually the youngest and least experienced in a squadron, too fresh to have yet chosen a rate or occupational specialty, but they carry huge responsibilities, serving as liaison between pilot and ground crew and even having their names and home towns stenciled on their aircraft. They conduct safety checks and inspections, take the pilots through start-up procedures and no aircraft may take off or even taxi without clearance from its plane captain.

Plane guard: A fast vessel or helicopter stationed off the beam or quarter of an aircraft carrier in order to pick up aircrew forced to land in the water.

Plane handler: Enlisted person who moves aircraft on the flight deck of a carrier.

Plane sailing: A form of navigation that ignores curvature of the earth, treating its surface (over small ranges of latitude and longitude) as if it were flat. It is based on the preposition that that the meridian through the point of departure and the parallel through the destination form a right triangle of which the course is the hypotenuse.

Plane scale: A navigator's tool, graduated with scales showing chords, sines, tangents, secants, rhumbs, nautical miles, etc.

Planeing hull: A type of hull that hydroplanes (skims over the surface of the water). Also planing hull (cf. displacement hull).

Planesman: The person responsible for operating the bow and stern diving planes of a submarine.

Plank owner: USN slang for a member of the crew when the ship was first placed in commission. Traditionally, entitled to a souvenir piece of planking when the ship is decommissioned and destroyed. Also plankowner.

Planking: Wooden boards covering a deck or hull.

Plankton: Minute floating forms of microscopic plants and animals that cannot move under their own power to any extent. They form the important beginnings of food chains for larger sea creatures.

Plankton bloom: A large accumulation of plankton giving water a definite color. The majority of these organisms are greenish, but plankton blooms may also appear to be blue-green, black, yellow, red, or brown. Cf. algal bloom, red tide.

Plant: A term covering a vessel's main propulsion system.

Plastic range: The range in which a material will suffer permanent deformation, but not completely fail when external force is applied.

Plate: [1] Term in maritime law covering jewels and treasure shipped as freight. [2] Gold or silver bullion. [3] One of the metal sheets of a ship's hull. [4] A tectonic plate.

Platform: [1] A partial deck below the lowest full deck, usually placed in a section of the hold or over the magazine. [2] A plated engine room deck from which propulsion machinery is controlled. [3] Any military structure, vehicle, or vessel forming the base for a weapon system. [4] Any flat or horizontal surface; especially, one that is raised above a particular level. [5] A framework or staging that can be raised or lowered to form a standing place for workers.

Platform endorsement: Different ship types behave differently under way, so a USN officer qualified to stand watch on one platform has to re-qualify when transferred to another. A platform endorsement is the document certifying such re-qualification.

Plating: The metal sheets forming part of a vessel's hull.

Plebe: A first-year midshipman at the U.S. Naval Academy.

Plimsoll mark: Until the late nineteenth century, the dangerous overloading of merchantmen was common. One of the first attempts to introduce loading marks for safety was made in 1835 by Lloyd's Register, but shipowners violently opposed all attempts at regulation, and it was not until 1876 that parliamentarian Samuel Plimsoll was able to push through a bill requiring all British vessels to be painted with a load line to indicate maximum safe laden draft. In recognition of his long fight and many legal battles, this is known as the "Plimsoll mark" or "line."

Initially, it was left to each owner to determine where the mark should be, and some were so disdainful that they placed it on the vessel's superstructure, sometimes even as high as the funnel. Finally, in 1890, stricter regulations were introduced, making it mandatory to have markings located amidships at the officially approved level on each side. The original and basic mark is a circle crossed by a horizontal line indicating the water level at maximum permitted load. However, because water density varies with climate and salinity, subsequent regulations have resulted in a "ladder" of load lines painted beside the Plimsoll Mark to indicate the safe amount of freeboard under each set of conditions.

Plot: [1] A map, chart, or graph, drawn to scale. [2] To show graphically the coordinates of a direction or location. [3] To mark a ship's position or other data on a chart.

Plow anchor: *See* CQR anchor.

Plow-steel: A high-strength steel, with a carbon content of 0.5 to 0.95 percent, used originally to make the line used to attach a plow to a steam engine, and still the preferred metal for making wire rope. The three primary grades are:

- **Mild:** Can stand repeated strain and stress and has a tensile strength of 200,000 to 220,000 psi (214–235 kg/cm^2). It is used for cable drilling and other jobs where abrasion is a factor, but seldom in marine applications.
- **Regular:** Is tough and strong with a tensile strength of 220–240,000 psi (235–257 kg/cm^2). It is used for hauling and hoisting cargo.
- **Improved:** Is the best wire rope for towing hawsers and is regularly used by naval construction forces. It is stronger, tougher, and more wear-resistant than the other types and can stand strains of 240–260,000 psi (257–278 kg/cm^2).

PLS: Pallet loading system.

Plug-and-play: [1] The ability to add a new component to an electronic system and have it work automatically without having to do any technical analysis or manual configuration. [2] Slang for a person who can be assigned to a task without further training.

Plum duff: A stiff flour pudding, boiled or steamed, and often flavored with currants, citron, and spices ("duff" is a corruption of dough). Desserts containing dried plums (prunes) or figs, were popular in medieval times, but gradually the fruits of choice became currants or raisins. The dishes made with them, however, retained their original names as in plum pudding, plum cake, plum duff, and Figgie-dowdie.

Plumb: [1] To rig a tackle directly over a hatch. [2] To measure depth with a weighted line.

Plummer block: A pillow block supporting the propeller shaft.

Plunging fire: Shell or shot fired from an elevation, or by a howitzer, so that it falls at a steep angle and does not ricochet.

Pluto: Code-name (and acronym of **Pipe Line Under The Ocean**) for a vital component of Operation Overlord, the 1944 Normandy invasion. A reliable supply of fuel was of the highest priority; without it any inland advance would at best slow down and at worst grind to a halt, giving German forces time to regroup and counter-attack. However, tankers and ship-to-shore pipelines would clutter up the mulberry harbors, obstruct the movement of troops and matériél, be subject to vagaries of the weather, and provide easy targets for air attack.

Because storage facilities near the English Channel were also vulnerable to air attack, a secret network of pipelines already carried fuel from safer ports and storage facilities to the south coast, with its terminals and pumping stations disguised as bungalows, gravel pits, garages and even an ice cream parlor. Pluto was linked to this network, ingeniously using submarine cable, minus the core, as the underwater pipe. It was essential in war time to use terminology that would convey nothing to the enemy, so all concerned were encouraged to think and speak of "cables" rather than pipes or pipelines.

The initial installation was laid in a mere 10 hours on D-Day. It consisted of four lines totaling 280 miles (450 kms) of cable/pipe, running from the Isle of Wight to the Cherbourg peninsula. As the Allies advanced eastward, a second Pluto with 17 lines totaling 500 miles (800 kms) was laid from Dungeness in England to Boulogne in France. The latter supplied Allied forces with over a million gallons a day.

PO: [1] Petty Officer. [2] Purchase order.

POB: Persons on board.

Pocket battleship: Popular name for a Nazi-German class of heavy cruiser (schwere kreuzer) designed to by-pass Treaty restrictions by mounting powerful 11-inch (250 mm) guns in a relatively small (10,000 ton) lightly-armored hull. Known to the Germans as Panzerschiffe (armored ships) they followed the pattern set in the 18th century by United States "super frigates" (*see* warship rating), being more powerful than anything speedy enough to catch them, but faster than anything able to outgun them. The Germans initially liked the "battleship" designation because it magnified the power and prestige of these "super cruisers" in the public eye. Later the British used the term to overemphasize the magnitude of their 1939 victory in the Battle of the River Plate.

POD: [1] Port of delivery. [2] Port of disembarkation. [3] Plan of the day.

Pod: [1] A streamlined container attached to a vessel's hull or an aircraft to enclose engines, fuel, or guns. [2] A group of marine mammals such as whales, seals, dolphins, or porpoises.

Podded drive: An electric or hydraulic propulsion system in which shaft, rudder, gearbox, and propeller(s) are enclosed in single or multiple pairs of streamlined pods suspended below the hull. Access to underwater equipment for repairs or maintenance is a problem, although damaged units can fairly easily be replaced and repaired ashore.

The cruise industry has eagerly embraced pod technology because units capable of 360° horizontal rotation (known as azimuth thrusters) provide unlimited direction of thrust and give previously undreamed of maneuverability without the need for tugs. Moreover, since the propulsion system is independent of its power source, engines can be placed at any convenient location that reduces noise within the vessel.

Naval services are less enthusiastic. Flexibility in layout could reduce the vulnerability of equipment to blast or shock but, ironically, the benefit of low **internal** noise, so important in cruise ships, could potentially lead to risk in naval combat. When vibrating equipment, previously masked by the hull, is re-positioned in direct contact with the water, it could transmit a louder **external** signature and, once detected, the pods could be identified as targets.

POE: [1] Port of embarkation. [2] Port of entry.

Pogey bait: USN slang for [1] Candy or sweetmeats. [2] Something to attract female companionship (Pogey is the rough transliteration of a Chinese word meaning prostitute). The term originated before Word War II with U.S. Marines in China, who found that sugar and assorted sweets were almost unavailable on shore, while they had a generous candy ration available for barter.

Point: [1] Any of the 32 horizontal directions shown on a compass card (table 17). [2] To taper the end of a rope for ease in reeving it through a block. [3] A narrow bit of land projecting into the sea. [4] A short length of cord attached to the lower edge of a sail for passing through an eyelet and tying to reef the sail. [5] To sail close to the wind.

Point-blank: Fire aimed directly at a target without deflection or elevation.

Point-blank range: The distance a projectile will carry if laid with zero elevation.

Point oars!: USN command to oarsmen to thrust their blades forward and downward in order to push off when the boat is aground.

Point of contact: A person designated as coordinator, action officer, or focus of an activity.

Point of departure: *See* departure.

Point of destination: *See* destination.

Point of impact: [1] The spot at which a bomb or projectile is expected to impact. [2] The position where air-dropped cargo or a parachutist is expected to land.

Point of intended movement: A theoretical reference point for the planned navigational progress of a vessel regardless of deviations such as zig-zagging, unscheduled changes of course, maneuvers, response to emergencies, or other distractions. The vessels in a dispersed strike group take and hold positions relative to the PIM of the flagship.

Point of no return: The point along an aircraft track beyond which its fuel supply will not permit reaching its carrier or the nearest "bingo field."

Pointer: One of the pair of gunners who work as a team, the pointer (also known as layer) controls elevation and hence the range of shot (*see also* trainer).

Pointing: *See* rope pointing.

POL: Petroleum oils and lubricants.

Polacca: A former Mediterranean vessel with two or three masts. In the Levant they usually carried square sails on the main-mast, and lateen sails on the fore-mast and mizzen, but western versions, particularly those of Provence, carried square sails on all three masts. Also polacre.

Polar Lights: Celestial displays associated with sunspots or magnetic storms. Known as Aurora Borealis in the northern, and Aurora Australis in the southern hemisphere.

Polar surface currents: Polar gyres occur only in the Northern Hemisphere. They are propelled by the counterclockwise winds associated with the development of permanent low pressure centers at 50° North latitude over the Atlantic and Pacific basins. In the Southern Hemisphere, gyre systems do not develop because of the lack of constraining land masses.

Polaris: [1] The North Star. [2] A surface or submarine launched, surface-to-surface, solid propellant ballistic missile.

Pole: [1] A spar, especially one used to position a sail. [2] Any spar higher than a topmast, topgallant-mast, or royal-mast. [3] Either of two points on the earth's surface, marking the ends of the axis around which it spins. [4] To propel a punt, raft, or other craft with a pole.

Pole arms: Also called staff weapons, were used by virtually every culture from the stone age to the 19th century. They are edged or pointed, and may be mounted on either a relatively short handle (up to 5 feet = 1.5 meters) or a much longer shaft (20 feet = 6 meters or more) wielded with two hands. An example of the latter was the boarding pike, normally used to repel boarders, but too unwieldy for use by boarding parties, which sometimes used a shorter version called a half pike, although axes, cutlasses, or tomahawks were more common.

Police: [1] To tidy or clean-up an area (USN). [2] *See* naval police, law enforcement and master-at-arms.

Polishing: U.S. Navy tradition has it that the cook shines the bell and the bugler shines the whistle. This tradition may still be observed in some ships of the modern Navy, but the task is now normally assigned to a member of the division responsible for upkeep of that part of the ship.

Polliwog: A seaman who has never crossed the equator (cf. Shellback).

Polynya: Word of Russian origin signifying an area of open water within an ice field. (cf. lead).

Pond: Slang for the Atlantic Ocean.

Pongo: RN slang for a soldier. Probably derived from the Congolese for an ape = mpongo (cf. Grunt).

Pontoon: [1] A float with watertight tanks which can be pumped out to raise a heavily-laden or sunken vessel (cf. caisson, camel). [2] A similarly-constructed platform to support a bridge or derrick. [3] A lifeboat with buoyancy established by a watertight double bottom. Named after Pontus.

Pontus: An abstract personification of the ocean, sometimes (unconvincingly) given human form and identified as the Old Man of the Sea.

Pooling: The sharing of cargo and the profit or loss thereon.

Poop: A superstructure or partial deck at the stern of a vessel. From the Latin puppis = stern.

Poop lantern: A light formerly carried by flagships to denote the admiral's location at night.

Poop-royal: A short deck above the poop of a man-of-war, serving as accommodation for the ship's masters and pilots. The naval equivalent of a merchantman's roundhouse.

Pooped: Receiving one or more waves over the stern. Potentially very dangerous.

Popple: Seldom-used term for a short and confused sea.

Porkchop: USN slang for an officer of the Supply Corps based on the corps insignia (actually a stylized oak leaf with acorns).

Porpoise: [1] Any of several gregarious toothed cetaceans, related to but distinct from whales and dolphins, characterized by a blunt snout and a triangular dorsal fin. Also called sea hog. [2] Said of a vessel whose bow repeatedly plunges beneath the waves and rises like a porpoise.

Port: [1] The left side of a vessel when looking forward (*see* port & starboard). [2] A gunport. [3] The British Merchant Navy term for an opening or window in the side of a ship (the Royal Navy says scuttle, while the United States Navy and Merchant Marine prefer Porthole). [4] A coastal town or harbor equipped with cargo and passenger handling equipment, and which provides berthing facilities. [5] A place where ships may take refuge from foul weather (hence the phrase "any port in a storm"). [6] A fortified wine traditionally served when dining-in (*see* passing wine).

Port Admiral: This 18th/19th century British title refers to an appointment rather than a rank. Typically given to a superannuated senior naval captain who served as shore commander of a naval port, allocating docking or anchorage space to incoming vessels and responsible for crewing, victualing, refitting, and maintaining all vessels within the harbor.

Port & starboard: Before invention of the rudder, boats and ships were steered by one or two oars secured by leather straps to pegs on the gunwale. Because most seamen were right-handed, it made sense to place them on the right of the ship which — by combining the Old English words stēor meaning steering, and borde meaning side — become known as starboard. The steering oar(s) made it difficult to tie up to a pier or jetty, so it became customary to dock with the left side facing the shore. The Old English for loading was ladde, so that side became known as laddeborde, soon corrupted to larboard to match starboard.

However, those words were too similar-sounding when shouted in the noise and confusion of a storm so, early in the eighteenth century, merchant mariners began using "port" to signify the side facing the quay for unloading when docked. The confusion must have been even more disastrous in the heat of combat, but conservative navies hung on to the old term long after their civilian counterparts had converted. The British Royal Navy did not abandon larboard until 1844 and the United States Navy waited two years longer.

Port capacity: Refers to the estimated quantity of cargo a port or anchorage can clear in 24 hours (usually expressed in tons).

Port light: [1] The red-colored navigation light mounted on the left side of a vessel. [2] The glass (lens) sealing a port or window. [3] A light on a pierhead or at a harbor entry. [4] A cocktail (bourbon, lemon juice, honey, passionfruit, and eggwhite).

Port of entry: One at which a country's customs service provides facilities for processing vessels arriving from foreign ports.

Port of registry: The legally-documented home port of a vessel.

Port watch: [1] Formerly, watches were divided into port and starboard. [2] USN term for the duty detail when in harbor (which may include officers and enlisted personnel who are idlers at sea).

Portable soup: In 1756, a London tradeswoman called Mrs. Dubois won a contract from the Victualing Office to supply "portable soup" to the Royal Navy. This was made by boiling meat, bones, offal, vegetables, and herbs for long enough to reduce the mixture to a thick paste which, when allowed to congeal and dry, formed a solid rubbery slab with a strong meaty taste. For ease of transportation and storage, each slab was cut into cakes and issued to warships embarking on long sea voyages at the rate of fifty pounds per hundred men.

When reconstituted by boiling in water, portable soup formed a thick stock. The vegetable content was intended to be a preventive against scurvy, but in fact prolonged boiling must have destroyed all the original Vitamin C, which is highly heat-sensitive. The product was disliked by seamen, perhaps because of its nasty taste, or perhaps, as Captain James Cook reported, simply due to innate conservatism:

> Every innovation whatever, tho ever so much to their advantage, is sure to meet with the highest disapprobation from Seamen: Portable Soup and Sour Krout were at first condemned by them as stuff not fit for human beings to eat.

Cook did not record how he managed to make his crew eat the soup, but he used psychology with sauerkraut by ordering it to be served to officers only, after which the sailors insisted on having their portion.

Portfire: A device used to ignite the charge of a cannon. It consisted of a half-inch (13 mm) paper tube, filled with a combustible mixture of saltpeter, gunpowder, sulfur, and antimony sulfide, carried in a special holder. A linstock was placed behind each gun crew and its slow match was used to ignite the portfire, which in turn was applied to the vent to set off the charge. At "cease firing" the smoldering tip of the portfire was cut off and extinguished. The device was then ready to be used again. It was probably invented during the late 1750s in the arsenal at Essonne, France, and the name comes from the French porte feu = firecarrier. *See also* gun firing.

Porthole: The USN and USMM term for a small, round, ship's window. Also used by civilians rather than port or scuttle.

Portolano: *See* Waggoner.

Ports of call: If specified in the charter party, ports must be visited in the order listed. Otherwise they should be visited in geographical sequence.

Portugal Current: A slow-moving and variable current that flows southward off the Atlantic coast of Iberia.

Portunus: The Roman god of harbors, who gave us the word "port."

POS: [1] Port of support: [2] Point of sight.

Poseidon: [1] A 2-stage solid-propellant submarine-launched ballistic missile with multiple nuclear warheads. [2] The Greek god of the sea — he and his brothers overthrew the ruling Titans and drew lots to divide the universe between themselves, Hades received the underworld, Zeus the heavens, and Poseidon the seas. He lived in a watery palace at Aegae on the northern Peloponnesus, from where he sortied across the waves in a two-horse chariot. He later became identified with the Roman god Neptune, and his spouse Amphitrite with Neptune's wife Salacia. (The line-crossing ceremony traditionally reverses the spouses to pair Neptune with Amphitrite.)

Posh: The origin of this synonym for luxurious and elegant is popularly believed to have originated when the luggage of wealthy travelers on the Peninsular & Oriental Steam Navigation Company was labeled "POSH" to signify they had paid for cabins on the shady and cooler side while in the inferno of the Red Sea, namely port outbound and starboard homeward. Sadly, P&O cannot verify this ingenious explanation and the word may be an abbreviation of polished or, more probably, was adopted from the Romany (Gypsy) word posh which means money.

Position: The location of an object [1] Relative to a reference point. [2] In terms of its coordinates of latitude and longitude.

Position of honor: The tradition that the right (starboard) side is the honorable one goes back at least to the Greeks and Romans, when the right side of a combat formation was reserved for the strongest warriors so that their fighting arms would be unimpeded by a neighbor. With this in mind, aides and junior officers are required to position themselves to the left of their senior. If there are three, however, the most senior should be in the center, the next on the right, and the junior to the left. An exception is walking along a wall, when the senior should be nearest to the structure whether left or right. Similar rules apply to seating in cars or carriages. When a ship has two gangways, the starboard one is reserved for officers, while crew use the port. The second place of honor is "in front," so seniors are always allowed to precede juniors (for example, through a doorway) except when entering a car or boarding a boat or aircraft, in which case the senior is always last in and first out (*see* boat etiquette).

Post: [1] The place or station of duty. [2] A stout piece of timber or metal set upright in the ground. [3] In the sailing navy, to be "made post" signified promotion to command a frigate or ship-of-the-line.

Post-Captain: This semi-obsolete term was not a title, but referred to a captain of three years seniority, who was entitled to command a rated warship (frigate or larger), and whose name was "posted" in the seniority list of the Royal Navy. A junior post-captain (wearing a single epaulette) would usually command a frigate, while a senior (with two epaulettes) commanded a ship-of-the-line. The commanders of smaller unrated vessels were not "listed," and an officer only "made post" when appointed to command a rated vessel. Once he had "taken post," further promotion was strictly by seniority, moving progressively to higher-rated vessels and eventually, if lucky, to flag officer even if only as a yellow admiral.

In 1956, when the downsizing RN had a surplus of captains relative to potential seagoing commands, they were divided into two parts. Those on the so-called "dry list" were assigned to command shore establishments or given flag-rank appointments in the MoD, while those on the "wet list" were considered potential fleet or squadron commanders and were semi-officially referred to as post-captains. The distinction was unpopular and after a short while it was abolished. Today, the term is occasionally used informally for a "four-stripe" Royal Navy captain with a seagoing command. It has never been used by the United States Navy.

Post-Panamax: A vessel too large to transit the Panama Canal. *See also* panamax, capesize, and malaccamax.

Post-ship: A designation from the age of sail, used for an unrated vessel which, for some reason, was temporarily commanded by a post-captain rather than the usual commander or lieutenant.

Post–Traumatic Stress Disorder: *See* combat fatigue.

Pounder: A suffix denoting the size of a cannon according to the weight of solid shot it fires. *See also* groundpounder.

POW: Prisoner of War.

Powder: Short form of gunpowder.

Powder room: Former name for a warship's magazine.

Powder-monkey: A ship's boy formerly employed to carry gunpowder from the magazine to the guns during combat. Because of limited space and headroom, a child could maneuver between and along decks more easily than a man.

Power to the edge: This concept, sponsored by John Stenbit (U.S. Assistant Secretary of Defense for Networks and Information Integration), is outlined in a 300-page document published in 2003 by DoD's Command & Control Research Program:

> ... technological advances ... will, in the coming decade ... remove the last remaining technical barriers to information sharing and collaboration ... we see the soldiers, sailors, marines, airmen, and civilians of DoD all connected by a network they can trust.... Empowered by access to quality information ... there is no limit to what (these) men and women can accomplish.... (In) a network-centric organization ... the leader for a particular task at a particular time and place emerges. Exactly who "takes charge" will differ as a function of the characteristics of the individuals and the situation. When the most well suited or situated individual or organization is in charge ... it can be said to be a meritocracy.... Empowered individuals ... have a greater "bandwidth" for action than their unempowered counterparts in traditional hierarchies....

See also mission control and network-centric.

Powerboat: A boat propelled by any mechanical power source. Also motorboat.

Powered: Having, using, or propelled by some form of mechanical or physical energy. Often used in combination, as in "nuclear-powered," "powered flight," "battery-powered," etc.

PPI: Plan position indicator.

Prahu: [1] Formerly, an Ilanun double-deck warship, wide in the beam and sharp at the prow. Up to one hundred rowers sat cross-legged on the lower deck, while warriors massed on the upper. [2] Now, the generic Malayan name for a boat of any size.

Pram: [1] Generic term for various small craft used in the Baltic and North Seas (also prame). [2] A small open-decked Norwegian fishing vessel with a pram bow. [3] A ship's dinghy.

Pram bow: A bow into which the side planks are gathered together and the bottom planks are raised, both meeting a small raked transom-like board well above the waterline.

Prao/Proa: [1] A small Malaysian lateen-sailed boat, with a flat lee side balanced by a single outrigger. [2] Any of the small boats used by South Pacific islanders.

Pratique: Permission or clearance to enter port with a clean bill of health, either after inspection by a port official, or release from quarantine.

Prayer book: A small holystone for use in confined spaces. A large one was a bible.

Preamble: The opening clause in a charter party agreement describing the vessel and its principal cargo fittings.

Preassault: An operation conducted in the area of an amphibious objective before the actual assault is launched.

Precedence: [1] Priority in order of rank and seniority. [2] The right to precede others at diplomatic or social functions. [3] The sequence in which messages should be handled — USN, NATO, and diplomatic messages are labeled "flash," "immediate," "priority," and "routine" in descending order of urgency and hence of precedence.

Precipitous: Term sometimes used instead of "very high" for seas of Force 8 on the Douglas Wave Scale (table 2).

Precision approach landing system: *See* deck landing modes.

Preemptive right: A belligerent's prerogative under international law to seize contraband of war from neutral vessels on the high seas, subject to just compensation of the owners.

Prep flag: USN slang for the yellow and green "preparative" pendant flown by all NATO navies as five-minute advance warning of morning and evening colors.

Present arms: *See* small arms salutes.

President: One of the American "super-frigates" which caused the Royal Navy so much grief during the War of 1812 was USS *President.* On 15th January 1815, she was captured by the British who commissioned her into the Royal Navy, making her the fourth British warship of that name. The fifth HMS *President* was a 52-gun fourth-rate, built in 1829. In 1862 she became a drillship for the Royal Naval Reserve (RNR), and was moored in the Thames River next to London's Victoria Embankment. In 1903 she was replaced at that location by a sloop, formerly HMS *Buzzard*, rechristened *President* to maintain continuity. She in turn was replaced in 1921 by HMS *Saxifrage*, also renamed *President. Saxifrage* had been built in 1917 as a Q-Ship and is the last such vessel still in service. Today she is the headquarters of the Royal Naval Reserve Medway Division and also serves as a conference and entertainment center.

Presidential Unit Citation: The senior award for exceptionally distinguished service by a United States military unit, established by Executive Order in 1942, to be awarded in the name of the President to units of United States and cobelligerent armed forces for extraordinary heroism in action against an armed enemy, at a level which would earn the award of a Navy Cross or its equivalent to an individual. Naval units winning the award are authorized to fly a pennant with yellow, blue, and red horizontal stripes. Up to five bronze stars being placed on the central yellow stripe for additional citations. Persons who were on board and actually participated in the action are entitled to wear the Presidential Unit Citation medal.

Press: [1] To cram on as much sail as a vessel's rigging can sustain. [2] *See* impressment.

Press gang: *See* Imprest Service.

Pressed man: A seaman or landsman brought aboard ship by legal force.

Pressure hull: The compression-resistant cylinder which encloses the operating and accommodation spaces of a submarine.

Pressure ice: Sea, lake, or river ice that has been altered or deformed by the lateral stress of any combination of wind, wave, tide, surf, or current.

Pressure suit: Body covering which can be inflated to maintain approximately normal atmospheric pressure (and hence normal bodily function) for an aviator at high altitude.

Prevailing wind: The wind direction which is predominant or normally encountered at a given location.

Preventer: [1] A rope used to ease the strain on another rope. [2] Any device used to limit the swing of a boom.

Pricker: [1] A sailmaker's tool used to make eyes. [2] A needle-like device, pushed through the touch hole of a cannon to make a hole in the cloth or parchment cartridge (*see* gun firing). [3] Slang for a small marlinspike.

Primage: A bonus (usually about one-percent of the value of cargo) formerly paid by shippers to masters to ensue diligence in handling and taking care of their goods.

Prime: [1] To put powder, a priming tube, or a quill into the touch-hole (vent) of a muzzle-loading gun, after it has been loaded with powder and shot (Today, the primer is an integral part of the cartridge). [2] To put a small amount of fluid on to the discharge side of a pump to enable it to more easily draw from the suction side. [3] To prepare a metal surface for painting by the application of a base coat. [4] Excellent, superior, of the highest quality.

Prime meridian: Longitude zero degrees. Generally accepted as the meridian passing over a marker at Britain's Royal Observatory at Greenwich.

Prime seaman: An able-seaman.

Priming iron: An iron spike, heated to red-heat in a furnace on deck and used to ignite the charge of cannon prior to arrival of the slow-match and linstock.

Priming pan: *See* pan.

Priming tube: A short, narrow, metal pipe with a bell mouth. The pipe was filled with quick match, while the cup held a paste of mealed gunpowder, gum, and water. A little dry powder was sprinkled on top and sealed with a paper cover. The tube was inserted into the vent of a cannon, holed with a pricker, and ignited by slow-match or portfire to explode the charge.

The tubes were originally made of tin or copper, but hot expended tubes with sharp edges lying on the deck were a hazard to sailors with bare feet, so goose quills of the same size and shape were substituted. The tube was too short to make contact with the cartridge but, when ignited the quick match exploded instantaneously, producing a powerful spurt of flame which easily penetrated the cartridge bag. *See* gun firing.

Principal Warfare Officer: One of the most demanding jobs in the Royal Navy and an essential step on the way to command of a major warship. The PWO (pronounced Peewoh) is the captain's adviser on warfare, controls the operations room, makes all tactical decisions, and has direct responsibility for fighting the ship, deciding which targets to engage and in what order. The USN equivalent is Operations Officer.

Priority: The second-lowest order of precedence for a NATO message.

Prismatic compass: A hand-held compass on which a prism makes it possible to observe an object while simultaneously reading its bearing. Often provided to small boats.

Prison hulks: Ships too worn-out to use in combat, but still afloat, were a common form of internment in Britain and elsewhere during the 18th and 19th centuries. In *Great Expectations*, Dickens describes "A black hulk lying out a little way from the shore, cribbed and barred, and moored by massive rusty chains."

Such ships were used to detain prisoners-of-war during the American Revolutionary and Napoleonic wars. Private companies owned and operated convict hulks and the harbor location of these floating prisons was also convenient for the temporary accommodation of persons awaiting penal transportation. The conversion of a famous fighting ship into a prison hulk is described by David Cordingly in his book *Billy Ruffian* (Bloomsbury, 2003):

> The crew stripped her of everything that had made her a warship The guns were removed and the stores of the bosun, the cook, the carpenter, the gunner, and the sailmaker were taken out. The rigging was dismantled, and the masts and bowsprit lifted out by the sheer hulk. Out too came the barrels of food and water, the coal for the galley, and several tons of shingle ballast. The last job of the crew was to scrub the hammocks and wash down the decks.... The Pay Captain from the dockyard came aboard and paid the sailors of the ship's company. The marines had already been discharged.... The ship's log-book ... concluded with the words "Sunset, haul down the (commissioning) pendant."

Then shipwrights and carpenters from the dockyard removed her gunport covers, fitted bars in the openings, ripped out her internal bulkheads, and installed long lines of cages below deck. A variation of the prison hulk was the juvenile detention vessel.

Private: [1] Said of a soldier, seaman or marine holding no rank. [2] Non-governmental.

Private armed vessel: A non-governmental vessel which carries weapons and ammunition for defensive purposes only. Under admiralty law such a vessel is non-combatant and does not acquire the legal status of warship or privateer. (*See also* public armed vessel.)

Private vessel: One neither owned nor chartered by a government.

Private warship: Formerly, a sailing man-o'-war not carrying a flag officer.

Privateer: An armed vessel belonging to a private owner, and sailing under a Commission of War or Letter of Marque issued by a belligerent state and authorizing it to commit hostile acts against an enemy. The term is also applied to the ship's captain and individual members of its crew. Privateering is no longer permissible under international law.

Privileged vessel: Former term for the ship having right of way under the Navigation Rules. Now called the "stand-on vessel."

Prize: a captured ship, the value of which is divided into shares as prize money. (The word comes from the French prise = capture.)

Prize court: A tribunal convened under admiralty law to adjudicate seizures on the high seas and determine whether the ship and cargo were liable to capture and whether the seizure was lawfully made.

Prize master: The officer appointed to take command of a prize and sail her to port.

Prize money: Under Maritime Law, the captors of a legally-seized vessel are entitled to a percentage of the value of the captured ship and any goods it might be carrying. [1] The Royal Navy's heyday for such payment was during the Napoleonic Wars. If the prize was a warship, the government bought it at a fair price and added head money for each member of its crew. If it was a merchantman, prize money was the proceeds of selling both the vessel and its cargo. [2] Britain also awarded prize money in both World Wars. [3] In the United States, the principle has been upheld by the Constitution, and federal courts have awarded prize money to USN officers and crews. The last distribution being to USS *Omaha* for the capture in November 1941 of German blockade-runner *Odenwald*, disguised as an American merchantman. [4] The term currently refers to a bonus paid to the crews of USN ships winning a battle efficiency pennant. [5] Pirates referred to prize money as "purchase."

Prize money distribution: [1] Naval entitlement to share prize money has varied from time to time and service to service. As an example, in the RN during the Napoleonic Wars, the money was divided into eight equal parts, with the first share going to the responsible flag officer — unless the ship was under direct Admiralty orders, when it went to the captain, who received the second and third shares in his own right. The fourth share was divided by wardroom officers and the fifth by principal warrant officers. The sixth was split between junior warrant officers, petty officers and their mates, sergeants of marines, and midshipmen. The remaining two-eighths were divided among the crew, according to their ratings (i.e., AB's got more than OD's who got more than landsmen, who got more than boys). [2] Piratical entitlement to participate in the division of booty was normally specified in their Articles. Typically the captain might get two shares of the plunder, other officers one-and-a-half shares each, an able seaman a single share, and the cabin boy a quarter-share, while black slaves would get nothing: Those who had lost a limb or eye would often be given an extra quarter share.

Proa: *see* prao.

Procedures: Standard, detailed steps that prescribe how to perform specific tasks.

Proceed: It is customary for Royal Navy ships to ask the senior officer present for "permission to proceed" when about to set sail. This custom is carried out even when the officer addressed has no authority to refuse. It is recorded that one officer discourteous enough to leave without asking permission was ordered to return to the anchorage, the senior ship going to "Action Stations" and threatening to open fire unless the junior obeyed. It was commanded by an officer of the same rank with only a few days seniority over the other commanding officer, but that was sufficient to entitle him to act as he did.

Processing a whale: *See* whale processing.

Procurement Executive: *See* Royal Corps of Naval Constructors.

Profile-drag: One of the four principal causes of resistance to movement of a vessel through water, deriving essentially from the shape of the hull. A sleek or streamlined form produces less drag than does a larger cross-section, and gradual changes of shape have less effect than abrupt ones. *See also* eddy-resistance, parasitic drag, skin-friction, and wave-resistance.

Progressive flood: Refers to water passing from one compartment to the next, due to [1] Lack of watertight bulkheads. [2] Watertight doors being left open. [3] Short bulkheads that allow water to flow over their tops. The latter type of progressive flood sank *Titanic*.

Projectile: An arrow, bullet, shell, rocket, or any other missile.

Projection: In cartography, a systematic construction of lines on a plane surface, representative of and corresponding to the meridians and parallels of the curved surface of the earth.

Prolonged blast: Occurs when the ship's whistle is blown for between four and six seconds (cf. short blast, and *see* table 9).

Promenade deck: The uppermost deck on a passenger liner, usually railed with no solid bulwarks.

Promontory: A point of high land jutting into the sea, a headland.

Prompt: Said of a ship which is ready to accept cargo.

Proof: [1] To test a gun by firing it. [2] An arbitrary benchmark used by the distillery industry to rate the strength of an alcoholic liquor against a standard of 100 (defined as representing 50 percent alcohol by volume).

Proofing the rum ration: Naturally the Royal Navy wanted to ensure that rum purchased for the fleet was not illegally diluted by a ship's purser before being issued but, until the hydrometer was invented, it was virtually impossible to determine how much water had been added. As an approximation, using a rule-of-thumb technique developed by the Royal Arsenal, each purser was required to draw a sample of the rum to be issued, mix it with a little water and add some grains of black gunpowder. When the sun heated the mixture through a magnifying glass, it was supposed to ignite and gently burn, indicating it was "up to proof." If it was stronger than required, the mixture exploded, but if it failed to ignite, the purser could be fined or otherwise punished for over-diluting. In 1816 the Admiralty tested one-hundred samples by both the gunpowder and hydrometer methods and found the former surprisingly accurate, establishing the specification of naval issue rum at a powerful 95.5 proof.

Propellant: [1] The charge used to expel the projectile from a cannon. [2] the substance (usually fuel and an oxidant) used to give impetus to a rocket or missile.

Propeller: A shaft-mounted mechanical device, having a hub with radiating blades that rotate to provide thrust that drives a ship through water or an aircraft through air. Also screw.

Propeller boss: The hub of a propeller.

Propeller guard: A framework that protects that part of a propeller projecting beyond the ship's hull.

Propeller horsepower: A measure of the power available to drive a propeller after all frictional and other losses have been deducted. *See* shaft horsepower.

Propeller post: A vertical member of the stern frame through which the tailshaft passes. Also sternpost.

Propeller shaft: A long round rotating bar supported on bearings and driven by gears, transmitting torque and motion from a vessel's engines to its propeller. Also tailshaft.

Propeller walk: Sideways movement created by the torque of propeller spin.

Propeller wash: [1] The rough or broken water created by a ship's propeller. [2] The backwash from an aircraft's propeller.

Propulsion: Marine propulsion is the act of moving an object through the water or across its surface. Poles, paddles, and oars were the earliest forms, while sails represented the most significant historical method. Today, common types are underwater propeller, water-jet, paddle wheel and, experimentally, magnetohydrodynamic drive.

Propulsion machinery: The assembly of mechanical devices that serve to drive a vessel forward. *See* propulsion systems.

Propulsion systems: Whether providing thwarts for oarsmen, masts for sails, bunkers and boilers for coal-fired vessels, or generators and motors for electrical propulsion, the primary concern of shipbuilders has always been to accommodate currently available systems rather than create new ones to fit individual hulls.

Even in modern merchantmen powered by diesel engines, gas or steam turbines, or hybrid-electric systems, the size and weight of propulsion machinery dictates ship design, reduces the space available for passengers and goods, and inhibits the loading and discharge of cargo; while in warships, machinery and drive shafts occupy space which could otherwise be available for weaponry or ammunition.

One partial answer seems be integrated electric drive, with which efficiency can be improved by taking surplus machines off-line and running the required generators at close to full output. Moreover, electric drives can be placed further aft, reducing the length of propeller shafts for in-hull motors, or to zero for those in external pods. Both the United States and Royal Navies have announced that their next generation surface warships will feature electrical propulsion. *See also* CODAD, CODAG, CODAG-electric, CODAG-WASH, COGAG, COGOG, COSAG, Cycloidal drive, Diesel-electric, Direct drive, MHD drive, Podded drive, Propulsion machinery, Stern drive, Turbo-electric drive, and Water jet.

Protected waters: Sheltered anchorages with few hazards due to winds or weather.

Protection: Formerly, a certificate giving exemption from impressment.

Protective deck: The most heavily-armored deck of a warship (cf. splinter deck).

Proteus: Was Poseidon's sealherd and one of many gods identified as the Old Man of the Sea.

Provision: To provide supplies of foodstuffs. Also victual.

Prow: The bow or stem of a ship projecting above the waterline.

Proword: Word used in voice communication to express standard messages (e.g., roger, wilco, over, etc.). Abbreviation of procedure word.

Proximity fuse: A device for detonating a mine or missile when near to, but not in contact with, a target.

PSU: Port security unit.

PT: Patrol torpedo boat (USN).

Public armed vessel: A privately-owned craft converted for naval use, commissioned by a state and crewed by its military, but not part of the official navy. (*See* private armed vessel.)

Public Health Service Corps: This service evolved from the United States Marine Hospital Service. Its commissioned officers wear United States Navy uniform, and rank insignia identical to that of naval officers with unique and distinctive Corps devices. Two different sets of rank titles are used. Most common are the standard naval ranks, but there are also titles that identify the specialty of the officer. For example, a Commander (O-5) is also a "Senior Surgeon," and the head of the corps, known as the "Surgeon General," is a Vice Admiral (O-9).

Public reprimand: A humiliating court-martial sentence, falling short of dismissal. Cf. admonitions, reprimands, and cautions.

Public vessel: One owned or chartered by a state for governmental duties and effectively enjoying "diplomatic immunity." Even if suspected of carrying contraband of war, a neutral public vessel, may not be visited, searched, detained, or seized by a belligerent.

PUC: Presidential Unit Citation.

Puddening: A sausage-like pad or fender to prevent chafing or scraping. Often made of twisted rope yarn and seen on the bows of tugboats.

Puff: [1] A sudden, brief, gentle burst of wind. [2] Force 1 on the Beaufort scale (table 1).

Pull your finger out: This colloquialism — meaning essentially "stop procrastinating and get on with it" — originally applied to a specific task in naval gunnery. While powder and shot were being rammed into a muzzle-loading cannon, there was a danger of self-ignition due to the heat of previous firings, so one member of the gun-crew would press his thumb against the vent to keep oxygen out. When the gun was loaded, the command "finger out!" would warn him to withdraw smartly or be burned by the approaching slow-match.

Pull: [1] An oar. [2] To row.

Pulley: One or more grooved wheels set in a block for a rope to pass over; used to change the direction or power of hauling.

Pulling boat: A large boat propelled by rowers with individual or shared oars.

Pulpit: An elevated guard rail at the bow of a vessel.

Pulse: A brief emission of radio energy by a radar system. The detection and ranging part of the acronym is accomplished by timing the delay between transmission of radio energy and its subsequent return.

Pulse duration: The length of time a radar transmitter is energized during each cycle.

Pulsing: In naval mine warfare, a method of energizing magnetic and acoustic sweeps by intermittent or variable current.

Pungy: An adaptation of the marvelously successful Baltimore Clipper design to meet the needs of merchants shipping perishable cargo and luxury goods around the Chesapeake Bay region.

Punishment: Rules of conduct and penalties for flouting them are essential to all forms of society, especially so in ships at sea, which were historically independent of land-based authority, giving ship captains unfettered power over their crews. The earliest extant English-language laws and punishments are the Ordinances or Usages of the Sea promulgated in 1190 by Richard Lionheart (who himself spoke little or no English) for the English Crusader fleet. In part, these stated:

> He who kills a man on shipboard, shall be bound to the dead man and thrown into the sea: if the man is killed on shore, the slayer shall be bound to the dead body and buried with it.... Anyone convicted by lawful witness of having drawn his knife or weapon to strike another or who shall have drawn blood of him, he is to lose his hand. If he shall have only

struck with the palm of the hand without drawing blood, he shall be thrice ducked in the sea.

Punishments of this type remained in force for centuries, but gradually became slightly less draconian. Flogging and execution by hanging were by far the most common disciplinary penalties from the 17th to the early 20th century, but other punishments were available, many of them being close to unofficial sentences of death. *See* blasphemy, cobbing & firking, flogging, juvenile punishment, keelhauling, keelraking, marooning, running the gauntlet, sleeping on watch, Spanish mare, spreadeagling, tarring, yardarm ducking, captain's mast, non-judicial punishment, non-punitive disciplinary action, and Uniform Code of Military Justice.

Punt: [1] A small dinghy-like boat with a flat bottom and square bow and stern. [2] A flat-bottomed, raft-like craft used when painting a ship's side above the waterline. [3] To propel a small craft by means of a pushing pole.

Purchase: [1] Pirate slang for loot, booty, or prize money. [2] The mechanical advantage provided by an arrangement of ropes and pulleys. [3] To loosen the anchor from the ground.

Purple Shirt: Personnel working on a USN aircraft carrier's flight deck wear colored shirts for easy identification. Purple shirts are worn by handlers of aviation fuel, who are known colloquially as "grapes."

Purser: This title for the person responsible for accounts and victualing goes back to the 14th century. It is related to bursar or treasurer, and comes from the Latin bursarius meaning bag or purse.

In the Royal Navy: During the 18th and 19th centuries pursers were unpaid warrant officers of wardroom rank, expected to turn a profit even after buying the job. In the 18th century, a candidate had to serve at least one year as captain's clerk before applying; then a purser's warrant cost him £65 and in addition he had to provide a security deposit of at least £2,100. These were significant amounts when the annual pay of an able-seaman was £14.

They easily recovered these outlays by claiming inflated prices for purchased supplies, overcharging for goods re-sold to the crew, and even taking a 5 percent commission on items seamen purchased directly from slop dealers. One of their more profitable enterprises was to issue pay tickets to non-existent crew, then sell them to moneylenders at a discount (*see* open list musters).

In 1825 the title became Purser and Paymaster, and in 1843 it became a commissioned rank. Nine years later the venerable title finally disappeared to become simply Paymaster. This lasted until 1944 when paymasters became Supply Officers. Finally, in 2004, they became Logistics Officers (but are still referred to colloquially as "pusser").

The United States Navy followed a similar path. Pursers were warrant officers until 1812 when they were commissioned. In 1860 they were re-titled Paymaster

and, in 1870, they were consolidated into the Pay Corps which, in turn, was re-designated Supply Corps in 1919. In today's USN, the purser is a junior supply officer who performs shipboard organizational tasks related to meal and mail services, record-keeping, and the like.

In modern merchantmen, especially passenger liners, the Purser is a three-stripe senior officer (ranking with Chief Officer) who handles passenger relations, general administration, fees and charges, currency exchange, and other needs of passengers and crew. In very large cruise ships the purser's job is often split between several four-stripe officers with civilian-style titles such as Hotel Manager and Passenger Relations Manager.

Purser's pound: Formerly a weight equal to 14 ounces (⅞ pound). The purser was allowed to deduct 2 ounces (⅛ pound) for "wastage" (read profit!). Also pusser's pound.

Pursuit: *See* hot pursuit and right of pursuit.

Pusser: RN slang for [1] An officer in the logistics branch. [2] Anything official, whether tangible or intangible (the U.S. equivalent is "GI").

Pusser's grin: RN slang for a hypocritical smile, sneer, or grimace.

Pussy-cat: *See* juvenile punishment.

Put about: To tack or wear onto the opposite tack.

Put away: To leave the ship by boat.

Put in: To enter a port or harbor, usually on an unscheduled basis to avoid bad weather or make emergency repairs.

Put off: [1] To leave the shore by boat. [2] To defer something.

Pyrotechnics: Ammunition, flares, star shells, or fireworks used for entertainment or military purposes such as signaling and target illumination.

Q

QM: Quartermaster.

Q-Message: A classified NATO communication concerning navigational aids and dangers, or mined areas and swept channels.

QRO: Queen's Regulations and Orders (Brit.).

Q-Route: A pre-planned shipping lane through mined or potentially-mined waters.

Q-Ship: An RN-crewed merchantman used during Word War I to deceive German U-boats. When a submarine surfaced to attack with its deck gun, a "panic party," including seamen dressed as women, took to the boats, tempting the submarine to close in. Hinged bulkheads then opened to reveal hidden armament which destroyed the sitting target. Their success led U-boats to remain submerged for torpedo attack. Q-ships were unsuccessfully deployed by the USN in Word War II. (The "Q" comes from the Latin quaere = query.) *See also* HMS *President*.

Quadrant: A former navigational instrument, consisting of a flat piece of metal cut like a quarter-circle, with a 90° angle at the top and a curved side marked with a scale of degrees at the bottom. A weighted thread hung from the top. The navigator lined up one straight edge with the sun or a star and noted where the thread crossed the scale. Since a celestial body is directly overhead (90°) at the pole and lies on the horizon (0°) at the equator, the angle indicated the ship's latitude.

Quadrantal deviation: Deflection of a magnetic compass due to the induced magnetism of a ship's hull.

Quadrantal spheres: Hollow balls of soft iron placed on either side of a magnetic compass in order to compensate for quadrantal deviation by neutralizing induced magnetism. Sometimes known colloquially as navigator's balls (cf. Flinders bars).

Quadrireme: In classical antiquity, a galley with four banks of oars. The fastest and most maneuverable Roman and Carthaginian naval vessel, it could make lightning turns in ram-and-board combat, and was ideal for pirate-chasing.

Quaker: A dummy wooden gun intended to make a vessel look more heavily-armed. The name is an allusion to the Society of Friends' opposition to war and violence. *See also* dummy ports.

Quarantinable diseases: The World Health Organization defines quarantinable diseases as cholera, plague, and yellow fever. Other infections or contagions which may cause a ship to be detained and isolated include anthrax, leprosy, pandemic influenza, psittacosis, severe acute respiratory syndrome (SARS), and typhus.

Quarantine: [1] The isolation and detention of incoming vessels and their passenger or animal cargo which might be carrying or have been exposed to infectious or contagious disease. [2] The period of such imposed isolation, which is seldom more than the implied 40 days (quarenta is forty in Italian). The practice originated when Venice tried to limit the spread of the Black Death by requiring all incoming vessels to remain at anchor for forty-two days. *See also* Lazaretto.

Quarantine signal: The International Code flag "Q" (a yellow square) is displayed alone or in combination by vessels entering or leaving a port. *See* table 8.

Quarrel: A short bolt fired by crossbow or arbalest.

Quarter: [1] To face the waves somewhere between head-on and abeam. [2] Mercy offered to a ship's company surrendering in combat (probably derived from the custom of allowing officers to ransom themselves by paying a one-fourth part of their annual pay).

Quarter bill: A document defining the action station (general quarters) for each member of a ship's company.

Quarter boat: A small boat carried on davits at the ship's quarter, ready for rapid launching while at sea.

Quarter cloth: A long piece of painted canvas, formerly extended outside the quarter netting from the upper part of the gallery to the gangway. It was usually decorated with martial instruments or allegorical figures.

Quarter gallery: A windowed balcony across the stern of wooden sailing ships.

Quarter gunner: A sailing ship seaman responsible for assisting in the maintenance and handling of four of the ship's great guns.

Quarter netting: Mesh placed on the quarters to hold rolled hammocks as protection against musket fire.

Quarter watch: In exceptionally clear weather with light winds, a sailing merchantman's master might require only half of the port or starboard watch (i.e., one-quarter of the watchkeepers) to be on duty at any given time, so that each has four hours on and twelve hours off.

Quarterboard: A carved plank on a vessel's quarter bearing its name and port of registry. Cf. Escutcheon.

Quarterdeck: [1] When decks were in tiers, a half-deck was half the length of the vessel, and the quarter-deck was half of that. [2] Formerly, a deck above the main deck on the after part of the ship, containing helm and compass, used by captain and officers to control a sailing warship. The weather side was traditionally reserved for the captain when on deck; other officers were free to use it while he was below, but scurried to clear it as soon as he appeared. If there was no weather side, the captain took the starboard. [3] Nowadays, a warship's quarters are frequently cluttered with AAA guns, depth charge racks and other paraphernalia, so the quarterdeck is that part of the main or upper deck designated by the captain for official functions, honors, and ceremonies, and as the station of the officer-of-the-deck. It is usually, but not necessarily, aft near the principal accommodation ladder or brow. [4] The quarterdeck has immense ritual significance to naval seamen —*see* salutes and courtesies.

Quarterdecker: Derisive slang for an officer more concerned with appearance and etiquette than seamanship and combat efficiency.

Quartering: Seas or winds approaching a vessel at approximately 45° abaft the beam.

Quarterman: A junior supervisor or foreman in a naval dockyard.

Quartermaster: [1] The second-in-command to the captain of a pirate ship and, like him, elected by the crew. [2] The army officer responsible for rations and accommodation. [3] In naval use the title was originally Master of the Quarterdeck and referred to a petty officer with all the qualifications of an AB, who attended to the ship's helm, binnacle, and signals and maintained the quarterdeck and its equipment in good order. He was also an assistant to the ship's navigating officer, responsible for updating charts, repairing clocks, servicing navigational instruments, and training helmsmen and lookouts. [4] Today, a United States Navy quartermaster is a senior or chief petty officer who specializes in navigation and is familiar with electronic aids as well as conventional navigational instruments. The quartermaster of the watch maintains a dead reckoning of the ship's position and projected path, plots them on the chart, and maintains the ship's deck log. Reporting to the navigator, he or she supervises and administers the work of the ship's quartermaster force, and is sometimes responsible for supervising its signal force as well. [5] In the Royal Navy and in merchant service, quartermaster is not a rate but a duty for (usually) a senior AB or leading seaman. In harbor the QM stands gangway watch with a bos'n's mate, and at sea is the senior hand in the wheelhouse steering position.

Quarters: [1] The after parts of a ship's sides extending roughly to 45° abaft the beam on each side. [2] In naval use, the positions assigned for combat (*see* general quarters). [3] In military use, the place assigned for rest or sleep. [4] An assemblage of personnel for inspection or special duties. [5] Shipboard living spaces. [6] A Bugle call requiring all personnel not authorized to be absent to return to their quarters for the night.

Quarters!: An exclamation to implore mercy from a victorious enemy.

Quay: A mole, bank, or wharf, usually of concrete or stone, built parallel to the edge of a waterway for use as a landing place and for the discharge of cargo. Pronounced "key" and sometimes so written.

Quebec: NATO phonetic notation for the letter "Q." Pronounced kay-bec.

Queche: A small Portuguese smack.

Queen topsail: A small staysail mounted between the fore and main masts.

Quenching: Air bubbles forming around the outside of the sonar dome, reducing underwater sound reception by absorbing the pulse.

Queue: *See* pigtail.

Quick flasher: A navigation light that flashes about once a second.

Quick match: Formerly, threads of cotton or cotton wick soaked in a solution of gunpowder, mixed with gum arabic and boiling water, and strewn with mealed gunpowder. It burned at the rate of approximately one foot (300 mm) in five seconds and was used as a primer for heavy cannon. *See also* gunfiring, portfire, slow match.

Quickwater: The backwash from propellers when a vessel is going astern. Starting from behind the stern, the quickwater moves forward along the vessel as it loses headway, reaching amidships when the vessel has no way on and is about to make sternway.

Quid: [1] An individual wad of chewing tobacco. [2] British slang for a pound (£1).

Quill: The hollow stem of a large bird's feather, formerly used [1] As a pen, when sharpened to a point. [2] As the firing tube of a ship's cannon.

Quill-pusher: Formerly, a slang term for the captain's clerk. Also quill-driver.

Quilting: Matting used to protect a vessel from ice damage.

Quinquereme: A classical galley with three banks of oars. Two rowers known as thranites pulled a single sweep on the upper level, two zygites on the middle oar, and one thalamite on the lower one. (Latin quinque = five + remus = oar.)

Quintal: [1] Seldom-used commercial term for a weight of 100 pounds. [2] Metric term for 100 kilograms.

Quintant: Formerly, a sextant whose arc was equal to one-fifth of a circle.

Quoddy: A New England lobster fishing boat with a gaff mainsail and jib on a detachable bowsprit. Named after Pasamaquoddy Bay. Pronounce "kwaddy."

Quoin: [1] A wedge used to adjust the elevation of a cannon [2] A block or chock used to prevent casks or other round cargo from shifting. Pronounced "koin."

Quota system: This British naval recruitment scheme, introduced in 1795, required local authorities to provide a fixed number of (supposedly) prime seamen, for which they received a bounty of between £20 and £60 a head, much of which they "earned" by rounding up vagabonds and emptying the jails of felons. Such untrained men (known as "scrovies") could holystone decks, haul ropes, and manhandle guns, but were useless for handling sails and working the ship. *See also* impressment.

Quotaman: One raised for naval service through the quota system.

R

"R": [1] Symbol in the sailing navy muster book meaning "run" (i.e., deserted or missed muster three consecutive times). [2] Routine (military and diplomatic communications precedence).

R&D: Research and development.

R&R: [1] Rest and Recreation. [2] Refit and Repair.

R&S: Reconnaissance and surveillance.

Rabbet: A groove in a piece of wood into which another wooden member fits.

Rabbit: In the RN, work performed without authorization, or equipment obtained through unofficial channels (cf. Cumshaw).

Race: A channel through which tide ebbs or flows as a fast turbulent current.

Racetrack turn: A person overboard maneuver in which the vessel turns onto a reverse course and then turns again to follow the original course until the casualty is sighted and rescued.

Rack: [1] To lash two ropes together. [2] A framework from which depth charges are rolled to drop overboard. [3] USN slang for a sleeping bunk. [4] A fiddle-board.

Rack time: USN slang for time to sleep while off watch.

Racking: Seizing made by passing cord around two lines in figure-eight turns.

Radar: System for detecting the presence, range and direction of objects by emitting pulses of high-frequency electromagnetic waves and measuring the time for an echo to return and the direction it returns from (acronym of **ra**dio **d**etection **a**nd **r**anging).

Radar countermeasures: Means of reducing the effectiveness of hostile radar. These may be electronic such as jamming, physical such as chaff, or inherent such as stealth technology.

Radar dome: The protective housing for radar equipment and antennae; transparent to radio waves (also radome). Cf. sonar dome.

Radar echo: An electronic signal that has been reflected back to the transmitting radar antenna; providing information about the location and distance of the reflecting object.

Radar picket: A vessel or aircraft assigned to patrol an outlying area to supplement the radar coverage of the main force.

Radar reflector: A device designed to increase the returned radar echo. Often provided to lifeboats or rafts to assist search and rescue efforts.

Radar scan: The rotating motion of a radar antenna.

Radar shadow: The area obscured by an obstruction that returns no radar echo.

Radar trap: An atmospheric condition which can seal radar pulses between adjacent layers, sometimes leading to signal disappearance, at others greatly extending its range of detection.

Radarscope: The screen which displays an image of received radar echoes. *See also* plan position indicator.

Radiated noise: Sonic or electronic energy emitted by ships, submarines, or torpedoes, making them more detectable. Cf. signature.

Radiation fog: Condensation of warm water vapor as it passes over a cooler landmass.

Radio beacon: An electronic aid to navigation which emits signals which can be detected by a radio direction finding (RDF) antenna.

Radio central: USN term for a ship's principal communications room, which is usually soundproof and located near the navigation bridge.

Radio countermeasures: Jamming or other means of reducing the effectiveness of hostile radio communication.

Radio direction finder: A navigational device which uses a directional antenna to determine the bearings of radio beacons or commercial radio transmitters whose positions are known. The ship's position can be determined by triangulation.

Radio guard: A ship or shore establishment that assumes responsibility for the radio communication of other ships or facilities.

Radio navigation: The use of radio waves to determine a vessel's course, speed, and position. *See* Loran, radio direction finder, satellite navigation.

Radio silence: [1] A tactical means of escaping hostile detection by closing down all equipment capable of emitting radio signals. [2] A period during which radio "chatter" is prohibited in order to leave channels clear for emergency signals.

Radiolocation: The original name of radar.

Radiosonde: A balloon with an instrument package payload that automatically transmits meteorological information as the balloon ascends.

Radius of action: The maximum distance a ship or aircraft can travel away from its base and return without refueling, allowing for safety and operational factors.

Radome: *See* radar dome.

Raft: [1] Ice floes overlapping so that some are supported by others. [2] A small inflatable craft. [3] A flat floating structure made of wood or other material.

Raid: An operation to temporarily seize an area in order to secure information, confuse an adversary, capture personnel or equipment, or to destroy a capability. The raid ends with a planned withdrawal.

Rail: [1] The rounded cap of a bulwark. [2] A rigid fence-like structure on a weather deck or in a machinery space. [3] A track that provides initial support and guidance to a missile being launched in a nonvertical position.

Railgun: *See* Electromagnetic rail gun.

Railroad tracks: USN enlisted slang for the twin bars of a lieutenant's rank insignia.

Rainbow sideboys: A special formation mounted to render side honors aboard aircraft carriers. It consists of flight deck personnel wearing their different colored shirts or jerseys.

Raïs/Raïs-Pasha: In Ottoman Turkish, a Raïs is a ship-captain while a Pasha is a general. Hence a Raïs-Pasha is an admiral. These titles were used by Turks, Arabs, Egyptians, and Barbary Corsairs. Sometimes spelled Reis.

Raise: [1] To come within sight of something (e.g., land or another ship). [2] To establish radio communication. [3] To bring a sunken vessel to the surface.

Rake: [1] To fire along the entire length of a vessel (*see* raking). [2] The fore-and-aft angle from the vertical of a mast or funnel. [3] The forward pitch of a stem or backward slope of a stern. [4] Term for observing and calling the accuracy of gunfire. [5] A dissolute person.

Raking: Sailing warships were immensely strong along the sides, but weaker forward and aft, being especially vulnerable at the stern where large windows pierced the structure to bring light into officers' cabins and around the gallery. Hence, a favorite tactic in the age of sail was to cross an enemy's stern (or bow) and rake it, causing tremendous damage while the ship being attacked was unable to bring its broadside to bear and could only reply with light chasers. *See also* naval tactics in the age of sail.

Ram: [1] A heavy bronze-reinforced timber projecting from the front of a wooden galley in order to pierce the hull of an opponent. [2] A similar armored projection at the bow of a steel warship. [3] A ram-equipped warship. [4] To attack with a ram. [5] A hydraulic device used to apply heavy pressure. [6] The dangerous underwater projection of an iceberg or ice cliff. [7] To use a rammer.

RAM: [1] Radar Absorbent Material (substance that changes radar waves into small electromagnetic fields and reduces the radar image). [2] Random Access Memory (the most common type of computer memory).

Rammer: [1] A cylindrical wooden block the size of a cannon's bore, fastened to a wooden staff and used as a tool to drive home the charge of gunpowder. [2] A person using such a tool.

Ramp: [1] The bottom-hinged forward section of a landing craft, across which troops or vehicles land on a beach. [2] The after end of an aircraft carrier's flight deck. [3] To sail on a tack with all sails filled. [4] An inclined surface for launching ships, a slipway. [5] Any sloping surface accommodating foot or vehicular traffic (as for boarding a ferry).

RAN: Royal Australian Navy.

Ran: In Scandinavian mythology, Ran was a sea-goddess who dragged down ships and drowned their crews.

Randan: [1] A peculiar mode of rowing using alternate long oars and short sculls. [2] A boat rowed by three persons, with the central person pulling a pair of sculls and those at stern and bow each using a single oar.

Range: [1] The distance to a target or object. [2] The horizontal distance at which something can be effective (range of fire, range of sight). [3] An area designated for target practice. [4] The distance a powered vessel can travel without refueling. [5] To organize the placement of aircraft on a flight deck. [6] To lay out anchor cable or another rope. [7] To follow a course parallel to the shore. [8] To swerve or sheer while anchored. [9] The difference between consecutive high and low tides. [10] A heavy two-armed cleat in the waist of a sailing ship. [11] To come alongside without making physical contact.

Range beacons: Two or more beacons lined up with the taller behind the shorter to indicate a safe course to follow. Called leading marks in Britain and (sometimes) range lights in the USA.

Range light: A second white light, mounted above and behind the masthead light, which allows other vessels to estimate a ship's course.

Range markers: A pair of upright markers or beacons which can be lit at night. Used in amphibious operations to aid in properly beaching landing ships or craft.

Rank: [1] A line of personnel standing side-by-side as on parade (cf. file). [2] Status conferred by warrant or commission. *See* naval ranks and rates, and tables 13–15.

Ransack: [1] To re-arrange the contents of a hold. [2] To loot or pillage. [3] to search thoroughly.

Rasing-iron: A tool for clearing old pitch and oakum from a seam in preparation for re-caulking it. Also reaming-iron.

Ransom: Money paid to secure the release of a captured person or vessel, or to pre-empt the spoil of a captured city.

RAS: Replenishment at Sea.

Raster Chart: A digital facsimile of a paper nautical chart, produced by or distributed on the authority of a government authorized hydrographic office. The image can be zoomed in on for detailed information (cf. Electronic navigational chart).

Raster Chart Display System: A navigational information system displaying Raster charts, with positional information from navigation sensors to assist the mariner in route planning and monitoring and, if required, display additional navigation-related information (cf. Electronic chart display and information system).

Rat guard: A large, hinged, conical, circular disc with a central hole through which mooring lines are run so that rats cannot clamber aboard carrying diseases.

Ratan: Radio And Television Aids to Navigation. Information transmitted from a central station to ships equipped to receive the signals.

Ratbars: *See* ratlines.

Ratchet: A bar or wheel with teeth that engage a pawl either [1] To convert reciprocating to rotary motion: or [2] To allow motion in only one direction.

Ratchet block: A block fitted with a ratchet to prevent reverse motion.

Rate: [1] Seaman's job title, indicating rank in the USN; both trade and rank in the RN (*see* naval ranks and rates). [2] To assign a specific rate to a particular seaman. [3] The division of sailing warships into classes (*see* warship ratings).

Rate of knots: *See* knots per hour.

Rating: [1] In the USN, a general grouping of enlisted personnel according to their naval skills or trade. [2] In the RN, a non-commissioned or private seaman. [3] *See* warship ratings. [4] A yachting rule, based on factors that affect a vessel's potential speed, applied to allow different types to compete on more-or-less equal terms.

Ration: The official daily food allowance for one member of a ship's company.

Rations: The allotted portion of food resources being distributed on a particular day or at a particular time.

Ratlines: [1] Small tarred lines laid like the rungs of a ladder across the shrouds as part of the standing rigging of a sailing ship to serve as steps for sailors ascending the mast. Sometimes, especially on the lower shrouds, they are made of wood and called "ratbars."

The seizings and clove hitches of each ratline are traditionally tied from the top down, with the sailors standing on temporary wooden battens that keep the shrouds at the right distance apart and prevent their weight causing the shrouds to sag. (Pronounced "ratlins.") [2] In U.S. military terminology, an organized effort for moving personnel and/or material by clandestine means across a denied area or border.

Rattan: The cane used by a sailing boatswain (*see also* starter). Made from the East Indian climbing plant of the same name.

RATO: Rocket-Assisted Take-Off (cf. JATO).

Raze: To reduce the height of a ship by cutting off its upper deck.

Razee: A ship which has been razed. In the RN, a razee was usually a line-of-battle ship that had been cut down to become an extra-powerful, shallow-draft frigate. In the USN it was often a frigate converted to a powerful sloop-of-war.

RCDS: Raster Chart Display System.

RCN: Royal Canadian Navy.

RCNC: Royal Corps of Naval Constructors.

RDF: Radio direction finding.

Reach: [1] To sail with the wind abeam or abaft the beam. [2] A straight stretch of river or canal between bends or locks.

Reactivate: To restore a de-commissioned (mothballed, in ordinary) ship to service.

Readiness: A USN term indicating the required condition of a warship relative to its immediate task. Readiness covers a range of items, including availability and crewing of weapons, state of propulsion machinery, maximum speed available, closure of watertight doors or hatches, and many other considerations depending on which of the following six conditions has been declared.

- Condition I: Requires the ship to be closed for combat, with all hands at general quarters (battle stations). Sub-divisions of this condition apply during:
    - (1-a) Amphibious operations
    - (1-aa) Threat of air attack
    - (1-as) Submarine alert
    - (1-m) Minesweeping
    - (1-e) A temporary lull in combat
- Condition II: Still on high alert, but specified combat stations may stand down to minimize fatigue and some watertight doors may be opened.
- Condition III: General state of readiness with only selected weapon systems and combat stations crewed and ready.
- Condition IV: Normal peacetime sea duties. Most combat systems un-crewed.
- Condition V: Normal peacetime harbor routines.
- Condition VI: Relaxed condition at moorings with only minimal personnel on board for fire and security watch.

Ready about!: Command ordering a sailing crew to stand by to move onto the opposite tack.

Ready room: The aircraft carrier compartment in which aircrews are briefed or debriefed.

Ready use: Said of ammunition removed from the magazine and stored near its weapon, making it available for rapid loading, but creating an explosion hazard.

Reaming: Caulker's term for opening-up the seams of planking to better permit filling with oakum (also reeming).

Reaming-beetle: The heaviest caulking mallet.

Reaming-iron: An iron wedge used to open up seams for caulking. Also rasing-iron.

Rear Admiral: This flag rank originally designated the third-in-command of a fleet or squadron, who also commanded the squadron bringing up the rear. *See* Rank, and tables 13–15.

Recall: Signal directing all boats and personnel to return immediately to the ship.

Receiver: A person appointed by admiralty court to arrange the disposition of wrecks for the benefit of shipping interests.

Receiving ship: RN term for a vessel assigned to hold volunteers, pressed men, and supernumerary sailors until assigned to a specific ship.

Reciprocal: A course or bearing 180° opposed to the one specified or being followed.

Reciprocating engine: An engine in which pressure in cylinders drives a shaft via pistons, connecting rods, and cranks.

Reckoning: Calculation of a position (cf. Dead Reckoning).

Recoil: The backward motion imparted to a firearm by the force of its discharge.

Recoil mechanism: A system, usually consisting of springs and/or hydraulic pistons with metered orifices which, slows down the recoil of a gun.

Reconnaissance: The military or naval survey of a place or region to locate an enemy or to gather tactical or strategic intelligence.

Reconnoiter: To make a reconnaissance.

Red Cross: [1] An internationally-recognized humanitarian emblem, worn as a flag and painted on the hull of unarmed hospital ships. [2] The International Committee of the Red Cross (ICRC) is an impartial, neutral and independent organization whose exclusively humanitarian mission is to protect the lives and dignity of victims of war and internal violence and to provide them with assistance.

Red Ensign: One of three United Kingdom naval flags carrying the union in the upper left quadrant. Used by merchantmen and the general public and popularly known as the Red Duster. *See* British ensigns.

Red lead: An anti-corrosion primer for metal hulls.

Red sector: Danger area on a chart.

Red shirt: Personnel working on a USN aircraft carrier flight deck wear colored shirts for easy identification. Red shirts are worn by ordnance personnel, firefighters, and crash or salvage crews.

Red tide: The common name for algal bloom, a phenomenon in which photosynthetic algae thrive and multiply in response to increased intensity of light, plus favorable levels of salinity and nutrients in ocean water. During the growth period (or bloom) each cell may replicate itself a million times in matter of days, to accumulate in dense, visible clumps of algae seeking sunlight. The surface may turn pink, violet, orange, yellow, blue, green, or brown, but red is the most common pigment, giving the phenomenon its name. Cf. plankton bloom.

REDCON: Readiness condition (USN).

Reduce: [1] To degrade a person to lower rank or rate. [2] To ration supplies or provisions. [3] To compel a place to surrender.

Reduction gear: Device which reduces engine speed to propeller speed.

Reed boat: A craft made from grass (in Mesopotamia) or papyrus (in Egypt) at least as early as 5,000 B.C.E. Similar boats are still used by the Marsh Arabs of Iraq and on Lake Titicaca in South America. *See also* Mashoof and Egyptian naval architecture.

Reef: [1] A shallow ridge of submerged rocks, coral, or sand, lying at or near the sea surface that may constitute a hazard to surface navigation. [2] The area of a sail that can be rolled and tied down to reduce its exposure to wind. [3] To reduce the area of a sail by securing it at its reef points or by rolling it around a boom or inside a mast.

Reef knot: A double knot made symmetrically with two half hitches. Designed for tying reef points so that they hold securely but cast off easily, allowing a topman to quickly release the reef.

Reef point: Short length of line sewn into a sail, to be tied around a boom or yard when shortening sail.

Reefer: [1] USN name for a pea jacket. [2] RN name for a double-breasted navy blue uniform jacket. [3] Slang for a cold compartment or refrigerator ship. [3] Formerly, a slang term for marijuana.

Reem: *See* reaming.

Reeve: To thread a length of rope, line, or wire though a block, eye, or other aperture.

Reference position: The estimated navigational position announced daily by the vessel in tactical command of several ships in company.

Reference ship: One designated as the base for determining relative motion. It is considered stationary, while the other vessels move around it (e.g., if the reference ship is moving at ten knots and a maneuvering ship is making 15, their relative speeds will be five knots if they are on the same course, or 25 knots if on reciprocal tracks).

Reflag: To change the national registry of a ship.

Refraction: A wave phenomenon involving change of direction or bending. When a wave of any kind — light, sound, sonar, radar, etc. — passes between materials of different density, its behavior changes as it exits the old medium. and encounters the new one. There is reflection off the boundary and transmission into the new medium. The transmitted wave undergoes refraction when it approaches the boundary obliquely.

Regatta: A boat or yacht race, or more frequently series of races (from the Italian regatta, originally referring to Venetian gondola races).

Registration Certificate: A vessel's official identifying document, showing the issuing government and port of registry; and recording the name, measurements and description of the vessel; along with the names of its master, owners, and any other person or corporation with a custody entitlement.

Registry: The nationality and port of a merchantman's registration, either or both of which must be placed below its name on either a quarter-board or the escutcheon at the stern of the vessel.

Regular: On full-time active duty as opposed to being in reserve or on temporary wartime enlistment.

Regulating Branch: Former title of the British naval police.

Regulation lights: Lights required by the Navigation Rules (*see* table 9).

Reis/Reis-Pasha: *See* Raïs/Raïs-Pasha.

Relative bearing: Position off the port (red) or starboard (green) bow of a ship, expressed in degrees with zero at the bow, 90° on the beam, and 180° at the stern. (e.g., an object directly abeam to the left would be designated as "red nine-zero." *See* true bearing, steady bearing, and hazing.

Relative motion: *See* "Reference Ship."

Relief: [1] A change of watch. [2] A person designated to take over duties being performed by another. [3] The depiction of land surface or sea bed contours on a map or chart.

Relieve: [1] To replace a person on watch or other duty. [2] To take over a station from another ship.

Relieving boards: Planks placed on top of one layer of cargo to more evenly distribute the weight of cargo placed above it.

Relieving tackle: A multi-sheaved purchase that applies extra force to turn the rudder under conditions of stress, also serving to reduce the strain on a steering engine due to rudder kick-back during heavy weather.

Religious service (church) pendants/pennants: By naval custom, these are the only flags which may be worn above the national ensign, and then only during religious services held by an authorized chaplain. [1] The USN has two religious service pennants both with rounded tips and white grounds. The Christian version has a dark blue Latin cross oriented sideways near the hoist, while the Jewish version has dark blue tablets of Moses topped with a Mogen David, similarly oriented. [2] The Royal Navy's Church pendant originated during the Anglo-Dutch Wars, when it was flown by both sides to signify a temporary (usually religious) truce. It consists of the English Cross of Saint George at the hoist and the Dutch red, white, and blue tricolor on a tapered fly (The Kerkwimpel of the Royal Netherlands Navy is, unsurprisingly, identical). [3] Royal Navy signalmen are taught that, if a flag officer unexpectedly comes on board, they can cut off the fly and use the hoist portion in lieu of a personal flag, leaving it plain for an admiral and painting on balls for vice or rear admirals if required. [4] An old navigator's joke holds that hoisting the Church pendant over the interrogative flag can be used to say, blasphemously, "Jesus Christ, Where am I."

Remberge: A long, narrow, English, 15th century oar-propelled fighting barge.

Render: [1] To clarify or extract by melting (render fat). [2] To free up a line, rope, hawser or cable so that it can be let out easily (render the main halyard). [3] To surrender (render the ship to the enemy). [4] To observe traditional naval etiquette (render honors to a visitor). [5] To provide (render assistance). [6] To submit (render an account).

Repeat: To copy a flag hoist [1] So that other ships in company may read it, despite greater distance or poor visibility. [2] Often accompanied by an "awakening" cannon shot, to reprimand a subordinate vessel for not responding to the original signal.

Repeater: [1] A device that remotely displays the readings of an instrument or piece of equipment such as compass or radar. [2] USN name for a substitute pennant (*see* table 8).

Replenishment at sea: The transfer of personnel and/or supplies from one vessel to another while at sea. Also underway replenishment.

Replenishment group: A force consisting of oilers, ammunition, and supply ships with accompanying escort vessels.

Report: A member of the ship's company charged with an infraction of rules and regulations is placed "on report," meaning that their name is recorded for appearance before a senior officer (*see* mast).

Reprimand: A non-punitive disciplinary action. *See* admonition, reprimand, and caution.

Reprisal: [1] A act of retaliation. [2] The use of force short of war to secure the redress of harm or grievance caused by the actions of another nation. *See also* Letter of Marque.

Reptiles: Seamen used to consider snakes, lizards, and other "creepy-crawly" animals dire omens at sea. The superstition seemed to be confirmed when, over time, the Royal Navy lost four *Vipers*, four *Serpents*, two *Snakes*, two *Dragons*, a *Lizard*, a *Cobra*, an *Adder*, an *Alligator*, and a *Crocodile*. Even today, ships are almost never given reptile names.

Request mast: In the Navy, Marines, and Coast Guard, an enlisted may "request mast" in order to present a concern over the heads of immediate superiors.

Rescue basket: A lightweight tubular frame stretcher designed for the safe retrieval of casualties from the sea, especially by helicopter. Also known as a Stokes litter, it is narrow enough to carry a casualty along a ship's passageway.

Rescue chamber: A cable-suspended bell-like device which can be lowered to a stricken submarine and attached to its escape hatch in order to take off entrapped personnel.

Rescue ship: A vessel stationed at the rear of a convoy to pick up survivors of sinkings.

Reserve: A military force that is not on active duty but can be mobilized as needed.

Reserve buoyancy: The volume of watertight hull above the water level. If the ship sinks deeper (due to battle damage, for example) reserve buoyancy will provide spare lifting power — until it reaches zero, at which point the ship will descend to the bottom.

Reserve salute: USN slang for a shrug of the shoulders.

Resistance: The property of opposing movement, for example [1] Electrical conductors offer resistance to the flow of electricity and dissipate some of its energy, usually as heat. [2] Water resists the movement of vessels or other objects by parasitic drag, consuming some of the power available to drive the vessel forward.

Respondentia: A form of cargo mortgage executed by a master who is unable to contact his owners but needs funds for repairs, or to continue and complete a voyage. *See also* bottomry.

Restraint of Princes: Originating in 15th century English maritime law, and frequently referred to by the French "arrêt de prince," the term refers to [1] In charter party exception clauses: Forcible interference by a government which prevents performance of the contract (e.g., trade embargoes, restrictions, blockade, seizure of ships, and confiscation of contraband). [2] Under International Law: A belligerent's right to hold a neutral vessel in port to prevent it carrying intelligence of use to the enemy.

Restricted area: A section of land or water where access is prevented or limited either for security (e.g., an ammunition dump or secret testing area) or for public safety (e.g., a bombing range).

Restriction: [1] A limitation on the movement of a person within a warship or shore establishment, either as a form of punishment or because of illness. [2] A limitation on the movement of goods or of a vessel.

Ret: To soak in water as a means of seasoning (of timber, hemp, etc.).

Retard of tide: *See* age of tide.

Retinue: Term for a flag officer's suite or staff.

Retire: [1] To make a tactical withdrawal. [2] To leave the service at the end of a career.

Retract: [1] In amphibious operations, to pull back from a beachhead. [2] In general use, to recant or disavow a statement. [3] To withdraw (e.g., cats retract their claws).

Retreat: A bugle call, drum beat, or boatswain's pipe announcing sunset. *See* taps, last post.

Reveille: A signal on a bugle, drum, etc. at some fixed time early in the morning to awaken soldiers or sailors.

Revenue Service: Established in 1790 as an armed maritime law enforcement agency of the Treasury Department. In 1915 it merged with the Lifesaving Service to form the United States Coast Guard.

Revenuer: Old term for an official charged with intercepting smugglers.

Reverse engineering: The process of discovering the technological principles of a device, object, weapon, or system in order to replicate it, or make something that performs the same function(s).

Reverse slope: A shore target area on the far side of a hill or mountain which can only be reached by high-angle plunging fire.

Reversible propeller: A propeller with pivot-mounted blades which can be rotated along their long axes to change their pitch. When set to negative values, it creates reverse thrust for braking or moving backward without the need for reversing gears or reversible engines. Because the pitch of the propeller controls the speed of the vessel, engine speed can remain steady, reducing wear on it and on the shaft. Also known a variable or controllable pitch. Such propellers are also used on aircraft.

Reversing current: A tidal current that flows through a channel first in one direction and then the other.

Reviewing authority: A senior officer charged with scrutinizing and approving the findings of a court-martial.

Revolution counter: A display that records shaft revolutions. Also called shaft tachometer.

Revolution in Military Affairs: This U.S. Department of Defense doctrine holds that information technology is ushering in new military concepts as radical in their impact on strategy and tactics as the Swedish adoption of massed volley fire in the 16th century, Napoleon's Levée en Masse in the 18th, or the advent of telegraph and railway in the 19th. By about 2020, the Pentagon envisages:

> A major change in the nature of warfare brought about by the innovative application of new technologies which, combined with dramatic changes in military doctrine and operational and organizational concepts, fundamentally alters the character and conduct of ... military operations.

The revolution will be based on three technological advances.

- New systems of intelligence, surveillance and reconnaissance to provide a complete battlefield picture in real time.
- New and more effective data processing systems to change the nature of command and control.
- Satellite-controlled long-range precision munitions to apply lethal force with extreme accuracy.

The RMA concept was originally developed by the Soviet Union's armed forces, and has been adopted to some extent by every important military power.

Revolution table: A listing of the vessel speeds expected to be achieved at different shaft turning speeds.

Revolution telegraph: A mechanical device used to advise the engine room of the shaft speed (in rpm) required.

RFA: Royal Fleet Auxiliary (Brit.).

RFR: Royal Fleet Reserve (Brit.).

RHIB: Rigid hull inflatable boat.

Rhodian Law: A code of customary sea laws that evolved in ancient times on the Island of Rhodes. By about 800 BCE it had become a major international source of maritime regulation, which was later adopted by the Romans — in the second century of the current era, Emperor Antoninus recognized this by declining to rule on a case of plunder following shipwreck, saying: "I am indeed lord of the world, but the Law is lord of the sea. This matter must be decided by the maritime law of the Rhodians, provided that no law of ours is opposed to it." The Lex Rhodia were largely concerned with merchant shipping and commercial practice, and were surprisingly democratic, sometimes requiring consultation with the crew:

> If a ship is in Haven and stays to await her time, and the time comes for departure, the Master is to take counsel with his companions and say to them — "Sirs, you have this weather." There will be some who will say "The weather is not good" and some who will say the weather is "fine and good." The Master is bound to agree with the better part of his companions, and if he does otherwise he is bound to replace the ship and the goods if they are lost.

Rhodian law was codified by Byzantine Emperor Justinian in the 6th century, with regulations that divided liability for loss of cargo due to piracy, or by jettison during storms, between the shipowner, the owner of the cargo, and the passengers. Rhodian law influenced development of the 12th century Rôles of Oléron, and persisted in the maritime laws of Italian medieval cities until at least the 14th century. *See also* laws and conventions of the sea, maritime law and United Nations Convention on the Law of the Sea.

Rhumb line: This concept was invented by Portuguese mathematician Pedro Nunes in the 1530s. It refers to: [1] An imaginary line on the surface of the Earth intersecting all meridians at the same angle. On a globe, rhumb lines spiral from one pole to the other — except at bearings of 90° (the poles) and 270° (the equator) which are lines of constant latitude. [2] The course of a ship that follows a fixed compass bearing — this is easier to steer than a great circle route, which is shorter but requires constant changes of heading — on a Mercator or grid navigation chart, rhumb lines are straight, because those projections distort the spherical globe to fit a flat surface. (also loxodrome, from the Greek loxos = slanted + drome = path).

RIB: Rubberized inflatable boat.

Ribs: A vessel's frames or timbers that are perpendicular to the keel (as opposed to strakes and stringers that run fore-and-aft.)

Ricochet: The movement of a projectile bouncing off a surface with which it comes in contact.

Ride: [1] To rest on the water, especially when lying at anchor. [2] The manner in which a vessel rests on the water. [3] Said of a rope that overlays another causing a jam.

Ride down!: Command to throw the entire body weight onto a sail in order to stretch it.

Ride out: [1] To sustain a gale or storm, usually without serious damage. Rather than face the danger of being blown onto a lee shore, mariners frequently choose to stand out to sea when foul weather threatens. By hoisting a few small but stout sails, or applying just enough engine power to maintain steerage way, and possibly dropping a sea-anchor or drogue, a vessel can lie offshore in relative comfort and safety. [2] Adopted into colloquial usage, the term means to survive a series of blows or outlast a difficult situation.

Ride to hawse: To ride with two bow anchors down, one from each hawse.

Ridge: [1] A long, narrow wall of first-year ice. [2] An narrow, extended area of high atmospheric pressure. [3] A long, narrow elevation on the ocean floor.

Ridge rope: [1] A lifeline running along the side of a bowsprit. [2] A rope rove through stanchions to form a railing. [3] A rope supporting the sides or center of an awning. [4] A gundeck safety line stretched from gun-to-gun in bad weather.

Riding: *See* position of honor.

Riding anchor: The one that takes the strain when two bow anchors are deployed.

Riding boom: Alternate name for a boat boom.

Riding lights: Lights required when at anchor. Also anchor lights (*see* table 9).

RIF: Reduction in Force.

Rifling: Spiral grooves cut on the interior of the bore of a firearm, giving rotary motion to the projectile and increasing the accuracy of its flight.

Rig: [1] To prepare or set up something. [2] The type, style, or configuration of a ship's rigging (i.e., square, fore-and-aft, or lateen. [3] An RN seaman's clothing. Both "rig" and "rigging" are derived from the Anglo-Saxon *wriggan* meaning "clothing."

Rig for red!: Command to extinguish all internal lights other than red ones, enabling rapid visual adjustment to external conditions when personnel have to go on deck at night.

Rig for visitors!: Command to post sentries, close off restricted areas, detail personnel as guides, and so on.

Rig of the day: The uniform to be worn for the day, or for a specific activity as laid down in routine orders, or by announcement to the ship's company.

Rigger: [1] A shipboard or dockyard specialist in fitting or repairing the running and standing rigging of ships. [2] An aviation mechanic skilled in the maintenance of aircraft controls.

Rigging: [1] Equipping or outfitting. [2] Generic term for the combination of ropes, chains, and tackle used to support and control masts, sails, and yards (not be confused with "rig," which refers to the style of rigging). The function of all rigging is to pull, either to hold something still or to move it. Fixed (standing) rigging applies tension that keeps masts in their proper places, while moveable (running) rigging manipulates the spars and sails attached to those masts.

Rigging loft: *See* loft.

Rigging-mat: A mat seized onto a vessel's standing rigging, to prevent chafing.

Right: To return a vessel to an upright position, whether spontaneously or with assistance.

Right arm rates: *See* arm badges.

Right away!: A sailing ship lookout's cry to indicate the direction of a sighting (e.g., "right away on the port beam").

Right-laid: A rope or strand laid clockwise. Also right-handed, or "with the sun."

Right of angary: *See* angary.

Right of approach: International law allowing a warship to come close enough to a merchant vessel to determine its nationality, but not to board or require the other vessel to heave to.

Right of convoy: A widely-contested concept that a convoy of neutral merchantmen, escorted by one or more warships of their own nationality, shall be allowed to proceed after establishing that none of the merchantmen carries contraband. This right was not recognized by combatants in either of the World Wars.

Right of fishery: The 1982 United Nations Convention on Law of the Sea gave coastal nations exclusive fishing rights within 200 miles (320 kms) of their shores, but beyond that limit all states had the right to unregulated fishing on the high seas. Fish, however, do not respect artificial boundaries and swim from high seas into coastal waters and back again, and from one nation's exclusive economic zone to another's.

Soon coastal states began to complain that unrestricted industrial-scale fish harvesting by "distant nations" was destroying their domestic fish stocks. Towards the end of 1995 a supplementary treaty on the Management & Conservation of Straddling Fish Stocks & Highly Migratory Fish Stocks attempted to establish legally-binding conservation and dispute-settlement rules. Unfortunately, some of the worst offenders have yet to sign and ratify this treaty, leaving the problem only partially resolved. *See also* exclusive fishing zone.

Right of passage: *See* innocent passage.

Right of pursuit: *See* hot pursuit.

Right of search: International law that allows a combatant to stop neutral ships and board them to search them for contraband of war.

Right of seizure: An international law allowing: [1] A local or national government to take possession of a vessel which fails to observe local navigation rules, trade laws, or revenue requirements while in territorial waters. [2] A belligerent to confiscate contraband of war destined for an opposing power.

Right of transit: Permits foreign ships to pass through a territorial strait from one section of the high seas (or exclusive economic zone) to another. Unlike innocent passage, this right applies to submerged submarines.

Right of visitation: This principle of international law allows a warship to board a non-military vessel on the High Seas if it has reason to suspect [1] The vessel is without nationality; [2] it shares the warship's nationality; [3] it is engaged in piracy or slavery; or [4] it is operating an illegal radio or television station. Unless unlawful activity is discovered, the boarding party must leave as soon as it has completed its investigation.

Right of way: The privilege of proceeding ahead of another vessel based on relative position and other maritime conventions. *See* table 7 and stand-on.

Right rudder!: USN command to turn the wheel (and hence the ship's heading) to starboard. *See* helm orders.

Righting moment: The force tending to return a heeled vessel to its upright position.

Rigol: A curved metal element installed above a port/porthole/scuttle to prevent water running down the ship's side from entering the opening. Known colloquially as "eyebrows."

RIN Mutiny: On 18th February 1946, while India was still within the British Empire, ratings of the Royal Indian Navy cruiser HMIS *Talwaar*, moored at Bombay, went on hunger strike in protest against substandard food and adverse conditions. But there were more fundamental issues such as racism and impending independence, and the strike soon escalated to mutiny.

On virtually all RIN ships at Bombay, the Union Flag was struck and replaced by those of either the Congress, Muslim League, or Communist party. Naval personnel stationed in the fortress and in the Naval Barracks hoisted red flags on trucks and started patrolling the city of Bombay. They were supported by a one-day general strike in Bombay which spread to other cities, and was joined by units of the Indian Army, Air Force, and Police.

Alerted to the situation by *Talwaar*'s radio, mutiny broke out on board HMIS *Hindustan* off Manora Island, and spread first to shore establishments at nearby Karachi, finally spreading to seventy-eight RIN warships and twenty shore establishments located at Bombay, Calcutta, Karachi, Madras, Cochin and Vishapatam. Indian naval officers who opposed the strike were thrown off their ships. British armed forces personnel were beaten up.

The mutinies got no support from national leaders. Mahatma Gandhi criticized them for mutinying without the "guidance and intervention ... (of) political leaders of their choice," and the Muslim League issued similar statements. On February 24, black flags were raised from the decks to announce surrender, but not before and number of violent confrontations, including an exchange of gunfire between HMIS *Hindustan* and a troop of British Royal Artillery. Eighteen months later, India achieved independence.

Ring-bolt: An eyebolt with a ring through its eye. Usually found at bow or stern of a small boat and used for towing.

Ring-knocker: USN slang for a Naval Academy graduate who flaunts his class ring to officers commissioned via another (supposedly less-prestigious) route.

Ring of Fire: Popular name for an arc stretching from New Zealand, clockwise around the Pacific Ocean via the eastern edge of Asia, north across the Aleutian Islands, and south along the coasts of the Americas. It contains over 75 percent of the world's active and dormant volcanoes. Around the Ring of Fire, the Pacific tectonic plate is colliding with and sliding underneath other plates. The tremendous amount of energy created by this tectonic activity melts rock into magma that rises to the surface as lava, forming volcanoes.

Ring-rope: A line rove through the ring of an anchor, passed through the hawse-hole, and made fast to the cable, to secure the anchor in foul weather.

Ringer: Lower deck slang denoting an officer's rank (e.g., a captain is a four-ringer). *See also* "striper."

Ringing glass: *See* glass ringing.

Rip: Turbulent water with short steep waves where two tidal currents intersect.

Rip current: A strong, relatively narrow, seaward flow, created by the backwash from surf breaking on a beach. Also known as a riptide and (incorrectly) as undertow (which has a downward component).

Ripping-iron: A tool used for stripping sheathing from a wooden ship's bottom, or tearing oakum out of a seam.

Ripples: Little wavelets or undulations produced by a light breeze. Force 1 on both the Beaufort and Douglas scales (*see* tables 1 and 2).

Rise: [1] A portion of the lower parts of a ship, just outboard of the keel. [2] Tide flowing inward (cf. ebb).

Rising tide: That part of the tide cycle in between low and high water when the depth is increasing. The opposite condition is a falling tide.

Risk: A marine insurance term referring to losses against which the insurer agrees to indemnify the insured. These involve peril of the sea or fortuitous events incident to the voyage. They may be occasioned by storm, shipwreck, jetsom, prize, pillage, fire, war, reprisals, detention by foreign government, losses experienced for the common benefit, or expenses which would not have taken place absent such events.

Cargo insurance covers most perils except strikes, riots, civil unrest, capture, war, seizure, civil war, piracy, loss of market, and inherent vice. Coverage may be comprehensive, or limited to enumerated perils, or for the benefit of particular persons, or for a specific time period. It may be restricted to voyage out, or voyage in, or part of the route, or from port to port. Terrorism may be excluded or subject to supplementary coverage.

Riverine: Of or pertaining to a river.

Riverine operations: Operations conducted by land, naval, and air forces as appropriate, organized to cope with and exploit the unique characteristics of a riverine area, to locate and destroy hostile forces, and/or to achieve or maintain control of the area.

RMA: [1] Revolution in Military Affairs. [2] Formerly, Royal Marine artillery. [3] Royal Military Academy.

RMLI: Formerly, Royal Marine Light Infantry.

RMS: Royal Mail Ship. Starting in 1840, British overseas mail was carried in vessels operated by the Admiralty, but titled RMS rather than HMS. Later, private liners were contracted to perform this duty and for them and their passengers the RMS designation became a mark of prestige with implications of speed and timely arrival. *See* Titanic Mailmen.

RN: Royal Navy.

RNAS: Royal Naval Air Service (*see* naval aviation).

RNC: Raster navigational chart.

RNNS: Royal Naval Nursing Service.

RNR: Royal Naval Reserve.

RNVR: Royal Naval Volunteer Reserve (now folded into RNR).

RNZN: Royal New Zealand Navy.

ROAD: Retired On Active Duty (USN.)

Roadstead: An open anchorage. Also Road.

Roaring Forties: A popular term among sailing ship sailors for the stormy ocean latitudes between 40° and 50° South where strong prevailing westerly winds would rumble and howl in the rigging, accompanied by high seas due to the long fetch of almost completely uninterrupted ocean.

Roast beast: USN enlisted slang for meat that even the cooks can't identify.

Robinet: Ancient naval artillery for throwing rocks and darts.

Rock: A segment of the earth's hard mineral crust projecting above the sea bed and forming a potential hazard to navigation.

Rocket: A self-propelled projectile carrying a propellant, a combustion chamber in which it is burned, and a nozzle through which combustion gases are exhausted provide propulsive force (thrust). It was probably developed in China during the 13th century for use as a signaling device, pyrotechnic, or weapon ("fire arrows" were used during the siege of Kaifung-fu [Peiping] in 1232).

Rocket mine: This is a Russian-designed type of bottom mine that fires a high-speed homing rocket (not a torpedo) upward towards the target. This allows it to attack both submarine and surface vessels from greater depth than a conventional bottom mine.

Rocket ship: A shallow-draft vessel providing heavy and rapid rocket fire as close-support for an am-phibious assault. In Word War II vessels designated Landing ship, Medium (Rocket) carried ten power-driven twin launchers, capable of propelling 380 spin-stabilized five-inch rockets a minute over a maximum range of about 11,000 yards. The LSM(R) could be used for deep support or harassing fire, as well as for beach neutralization where, being equipped with a fire control system, it could aim closer to friendly troops than rocket-equipped landing craft. *See also* inshore fire support ship.

Rocks and shoals: USN slang for excerpts from the Uniform Code of Military Justice which are periodically read to enlisted members of a warship's company. The phrase comes from a passage in Articles for the Government of the United States Navy concerning punishment for anyone who "intentionally or willfully suffers any vessel of the Navy to be stranded, or run upon rocks and shoals...."

Rod rigging: Standing rigging made of stiff steel rods rather than more flexible wire rope.

Roger: [1] Voice communication shorthand (proword) meaning "message received" (cf. Wilco). [2] A rogue or scoundrel (*See* jolly roger).

Roger-dodger: Informal USN voice communication term meaning "okay, will do that."

Rogue waves: Freak waves are the stuff of legend. It is common for mid-ocean waves to reach seven meters (23 feet) in height, and not unusual for extreme conditions to produce waves of up to twice that size. But for centuries mariners have reported a seaman's nightmare — great walls of water, preceded by abyssal troughs — appearing without warning, often in clear weather, running against prevailing winds and currents, and with no connection to tsunamis caused by earthquakes or submarine landslides.

For decades, oceanographers and meteorologists dismissed these reports as pure superstition and maritime myth, on a par with mermaids and the kraken — walls of water simply don't come from nowhere, they said. Over the past sixty or so years, however, there have been many well-documented instances. These include:

• 1943: British liner *Queen Elizabeth* plunges into a trough and is struck by two massive waves in succession. Their impact shatters windows on the bridge 28 meters (92 feet) above the waterline.

• 1966: Italian liner *Michelangelo* is hit by a 21 meter (70 foot) wave which crashes through the bridge and into cabins, killing two passengers and a crew member.

• 1982: Semi-submersible oil rig *Ocean Ranger* is in a storm on the Grand Banks. The rig is designed to withstand winds of up to 100 knots and waves up to 34 meters (110 feet), well above the 80-knot gusts and 18 meter (60 foot) waves of the storm. But suddenly a giant wave, far larger than the others, breaks a port light in the ballast control room, allowing water to flood into the rig which eventually capsizes and sinks with the loss of 84 lives. An investigation decides that, although the rogue wave was the proximate cause, design flaws and inadequate crew training contributed to the loss.

- 1995: British liner *QE2* encounters a wall of water which Captain Ronald Warwick described as "looking like the White Cliffs of Dover" and estimated to be 29–30 meters (94–98 feet) high.
- 2005: Norwegian liner *Norwegian Dawn* is damaged by a 20–22 meter (66–72 foot) wave which seemed to come out of thin air, long after the sea had calmed down. German cruise ship *Bremen* is hit by a 35 meter (115 foot) monster which smashes bridge windows and cuts the ship's electricity supply leaving her drifting helplessly.

The disputes were finally laid to rest in 2004, just before the last two incidents, when data collected by satellites identified many brief-lived giant wave phenomena, indicating that up to ten may be raging through the world's oceans at any given moment. However, even though the existence of such waves has now been established, they cannot be predicted and their cause remains a mystery. Ongoing research includes:

- Forecasting: At time of writing (2008), a European Union project called MaxWave, led by Dr. Susanne Lehner of the German Aerospace Center, with Drs. Wolfgang Rosenthal and Norbert Winkel, is subjecting satellite images of the ocean surface to statistical analysis aimed at developing WaveAtlas — a set of global maps showing extreme wave occurrence, and their height, steepness, and period, with related parameters such as wind speed — as an aid to forecasting the arrival of giant rogue waves.
- Modelling: Conventional linear models of wave build-up cannot explain rogue formation, so mathematicians have begun using the complex theorems of hyperphysics, chaos theory, and quantum mechanics to find a solution. Using the Schrödinger equation — which predicts the probable future behavior of dynamic systems — Professor Al Osborne of the Italian University of Turin, working on behalf of the U.S. Office of Naval Research, has shown that waves of up to four times the average height can rear up from nowhere and as rapidly die down. Dr. Efim Pelinovsky of the Russian Institute of Applied Physics at Nizhny Novgorod has produced similar results using the Kortweg-de Vries equation — which uses the Theory of Solitons and inverse scattering transform.
- Research: Practical experiments have also shown that monster waves are possible. Oceanographers from the Technical University of Berlin, using a computer-controlled hydraulically-powered wave-making machine at Hanover University, have shown that, when slow-moving waves are overtaken by faster waves, they can pile up to create a vertical wall of water. "The exploding wave was so powerful that it broke through the ceiling of the building in which the tank is located," reported Professor Gunther Clauss.

Rogue's march: Music played when a person is dishonorably discharged. *See* march music.

Rogue's salute: RN slang for the single gun fired to signal the opening of court-martial proceedings under the Naval Discipline Act.

Rogue's yarn: Rope with a colored strand making it identifiable if pilfered or stolen.

Rôles de Oléron: This Medieval code, ancestor of today's maritime law, was commissioned by Elinor of Aquitaine on the Island of Oléron in 1152 (The term "rôles" refers to the rolls of parchment on which it was written). Originally in French, it was translated and adopted into English law in 1190 while she was acting as Regent while her husband King Richard Lionheart was in the Holy Land. It was probably copied from Rhodian law, which she would have seen while on crusade with her first husband King Louis VII of France.

Its 47 articles are amazingly modern and comprehensive. They cover the duties and responsibilities of the owners of the vessel, the ship's master and pilots, the crew, merchants consigning goods, and dockyard workers. For example, Article VII denies the captain authority to dispose of the ship, but allows limited bottomry subject to consultation with the crew:

> One man is made maister of a shippe, and the shippe belongeth to many parteners, and departeth from the countre of whiches it is, and commeth to ... a strange countre, the mayster ought not to sell the shyp without he have a procuration or lycence of the ouners. But yf he have need of monnie for the exspences of the shyppe, he may lay to guage (pawn) some of the takelyng (tackle), by the councel of the mariners of the shyp. This is the judgement howe the maister is to governe himself.

Some of the penalties could be quite harsh, for example Article XXIII required a pilot who damaged a vessel through incompetence to repay the merchants for any consequental loss. If he failed to do so, the merchants (or the master) were entitled under Article XXIV to cut off his head. By the time Elinor issued the Rôles, Richard had separately promulgated his own Ordinances or Usages of the Sea.

Roll: [1] To rock from side-to-side in response to waves. One of the six responses of a vessel to movement of the sea, as outlined in ship motion and rotational oscillation. [2] A long continuous beat of the drum, formerly used to summon ship's companies to divisions.

Roll control: Naval architects have made numerous attempts to minimize roll, the most widespread being the construction of bilge keels. These long narrow fins projecting from the hull at the junction of side and bottom are relatively inexpensive but have minimal damping effect. Other anti-roll devices include the passive Frahm tank stabilizer and active gyrostabilizers, but stabilizer fins are probably the most functional and effective.

Roll-in-on: Describes an initial maneuver in aerial combat.

Roll-on/Roll-off: *See* heavy loads and vehicles.

Roll period: The time for a ship to roll from one extremity to the other and back again. Used to determine its metacentric height. The roll motion of a ship can be described by a second order differential equation where the angle of roll is used as the independent variable. On the basis of this equation, it is possible to define a natural roll period. The longer the period, the more unstable the vessel.

Roller: [1] A long steadily-advancing ocean swell, usually smooth and non-breaking. [2] A cylindrical piece of timber which revolves on an axis and prevents the chafing of a cable, hawser, or running rigging.

Romeo: NATO phonetic notation for the letter "R."

Romper: A ship which has advanced more than ten nautical miles ahead of its convoy (*see also* straggler).

Room to swing a cat: *See* punishment.

Rooster tail: The plume of water thrown up by a fast-moving motor boat.

Rope: [1] A number of fibers, twisted or braided together. In most nautical usage, rope is generally defined as cordage greater than one-inch (2.5 cm) in circumference, while smaller cordage is generally called line. However, the USN calls all cordage "rope" as long as it remains on the supplier's spool; once unspooled the USN calls it "line," irrespective of size (with the exception of cordage for specific purposes such as manropes, bell-ropes, wheelropes, footropes, etc.). Natural rope fibers include hemp, manila, sisal, and coir, but wire may also be twisted to form rope. Synthetic fibers, such as nylon, polyester, and polypropylene, are increasingly used for rope manufacture. They are stronger than plant fibers, but melt at lower temperatures. (*See also* rope history, rope characteristics and rope manufacture.) [2] To bind, fasten, or tie with line, rope, or cord (e.g., rope a bale of goods).

Rope & hawser lay: Twisted rope, also called laid rope, is the most prevalent form of cordage. The general principle of rope-making is to gather groups of fibers into yarns, that are twisted together to form strands, several of which are then twisted together in the opposite direction to form a rope. When under tension, the tendency for individual strands to unravel is opposed by the tendency of the rope as a whole to untwist in the opposite direction. Most twisted rope consists of three strands and is normally plain-laid (given a right-handed twist). Large heavy-duty ropes, called hawsers or cables, are made of three or four primary ropes, laid in opposition to their own lay.

The most common lay, with strands spiraling upward to the right, is known variously as right-laid, hawser-laid, z-twist, clockwise, or with-the-sun. The strands of a left-laid rope, also known as s-twist, left-hand, counter-clockwise, or water-laid, spiral upward to the left. When the yarns twist in the opposite way to the strands the lay is said to be regular, when they go the same way they are lang-laid. In reverse-lay the lay of individual yarns alternates between regular and lang. (*See also* cable-laid.)

Rope characteristics: Rope has tensile strength. This allows it to be used for pulling or connecting, but not for pushing, as is too flexible to provide compressive strength. Rope will stretch under load, but normally regains its normal length when loosened. The older and more worn the rope, the less elasticity it will possess and the weaker it will become. Rope under load will tend to twist in the opposite direction to that of its lay and thereby tend to unlay itself, but it should regain its normal form when slackened. However, the strands tend to unlay unless the end of the rope is whipped. When wet, rope will usually shrink in length in proportion to the amount by which it swells in diameter, but it will recover its original length when released from tension and allowed to dry.

Rope history: Lines for pulling, fastening, and lifting, must have been one of mankind's earliest technological innovations, probably beginning with the use of naturally occurring vines. But what seem to be fossilized fragments of primitive laid rope were found in Lascaux cave, dating to approximately 17,000 BCE. By the fifth century BCE, ropes were being made from leather, or animal hair, and the fibers of water reeds, date palms, flax, grass, and papyrus. By about 4,000 BCE, Egypt had developed special tools for reed rope manufacture, but it was not until the third century BCE that "modern" hemp fiber rope was introduced in China. From there, the rope making craft spread across Asia and into Europe.

Rope ladder: A ladder with rigid wood or metal rungs, held together by ropes. Used for boarding ships from pilot vessels and small boats (cf. Jacob's Ladder).

Rope manufacture: The traditional method involves stretching rope yarns along a ropewalk and laying them with a twisting machine (not unlike a large spinning wheel) and a sledge (a traveling structure of considerable weight that anchors one end of the yarn). This machinery first twists each yarn, then twists the yarns into strands, and finally twists the strands into rope.

Rope pointing: Unlaying and tapering the end of a rope by taking out some of the yarns, then weaving the remaining yarns into a point and whipping them with twine or yarn A stick is often put in the upper part to strengthen it or the tip may be finished with a small eye. An ordinary seizing or whipping will prevent the strands from unraveling, but the ends are often too large to pass through a block or eye large enough for the rest of the rope. If properly done a pointed rope overcomes this problem, and is thus useful as well as ornamental,

Rope yarn: A single thread made from fibers loosely twisted together. When several are twisted together they form a strand of cordage, and strands twisted together then become line or rope depending on their size.

Rope yarn Sunday: Time off for a USN ship's company to tailor or repair clothing when at sea, or to take liberty if in port. Paradoxically, it is always on a weekday, never on Saturday or Sunday (cf. make and mend).

Rope's end: A length of rope, knotted, pointed, or whipped, formerly used for unofficial "encouragement" or punishment (*see* starter). Bosun's Mates usually carried one concealed in their hats.

Ropewalk: A long, straight, narrow pathway, usually covered, along which long strands of rope yarn were laid before being twisted into line or rope. *See* rope manufacture and ropeyard.

Ropeyard: A facility for making cordage.

Ro-Ro ship: *See* heavy loads and vehicles.

Rosin: A yellowish or brownish solid, left after distilling oil of turpentine from the crude oleoresin of pine trees and other conifers. Formerly called Greek pitch or colophony, it is a component of caulking pitch, and is commonly used in varnishes, paint driers, printing inks, and for rubbing on the bows of such string instruments (precious metals such as gold or silver are often added to violin rosin, purportedly to enhance sound production, but one suspects mainly to increase profits).

Rotating band: *See* Driving Band.

Rotational oscillation: Three of the six possible ship motions in response to the sea are pivoting movements.

- Roll is due to waves hitting the ship abeam, tipping it over on its side, pivoting around its longitudinal axis until the centre of gravity pulls it up again. An extra heavy roll is seldom due to inherent lack of stability, but probably indicates that the encounter period is close to the natural period of the vessel. (*See also* synchronous roll and parametric roll.)
- Pitch occurs when crests and troughs moving parallel to the ship toss its stem and stern upward and downward. This is effectively roll around the vessel's transverse axis but, because a ship is far longer than it is wide, the effects are quite different. The period is longer and even a small angle is so magnified by the time it reaches the extremities that they may be lifted clear of the water. A raised bow can then slam back, producing a cascade of water across the forward weather deck and, possibly, a "whipping" effect throughout the length of the hull; while a rising stern can lift the propeller out of the water, with a danger of engine damage due to racing. Experiments with anti-pitch fins have met with little success, and changing the vessel's speed or course remains the most effective response.
- Yaw is oscillation horizontally around the vertical axis. In conditions of yaw, the vessel's centre of buoyancy moves steadily forward in the desired direction while its stem and stern skid alternately to port and starboard. Yaw caused by wave action in a seaway is especially difficult to control because wave profiles and pressures are not usually the same to port and starboard and these inequalities are compounded by orbital motion of water in the seaway as wave profiles change. Moreover, at every

half wavelength the water next to the rudder will be moving in the same direction as the vessel, compounding the helmsman's problems.

The winds and waves that cause these motions may come from anywhere and can rapidly change direction, but the ship's period of encounter is more important than the absolute period of the wave-form or its direction. This is because the ship is moving relative to the seaway and will meet crests and troughs more frequently or less depending on its speed, and whether it is headed into the waves, diagonally across them, or broadside on.

ROTC: Reserve Officer Training Corps (U.S.).

Rotor: Contraction of rotator, meaning; [1] The rotary part of an electrical or mechanical device. [2] An assembly of gyratory horizontal airfoils, such as those of a helicopter.

Rotor propulsion: *See* Flettner rotators.

Rotten: [1] A marine underwriting clause that absolves the insurer from liability if the vessel is found to be unseaworthy by reason of rot. [2] A term applied to ice that has become brittle after the brine has settled out leaving it honeycombed and liable to disintegration.

Rough music: This is sailing navy slang for the noise made when discontented, but not yet mutinous, seaman expressed their unhappiness by rolling cannonballs around the gundecks and making other discordant noises.

Round: [1] To pass by or circle something (e.g., a cape). [2] A single cartridge or load of ammunition. [3] A single discharge of a firearm. [4] The outward curve at the foot of a sail.

Round dozen: This is the nautical equivalent of a "baker's dozen," being a punishment sentencing the miscreant to receive thirteen strokes of the cat-o'-nine-tails.

Round in!: Command to bring the blocks of a tackle closer together.

Round robin: Today, this term refers to a method of scheduling sports tournaments so that each contestant plays all of the others before being disqualified. It is also a method of computer programming in which each process is given a "time-slice" in sequence. However, the term first appears in English in 1546. Its meaning then is unknown, but by the 17th century it seems to have applied to a certain type or category of person. The meaning changed again in 1731, when discontented Royal Navy seamen went beyond making "rough music" to submit a petition of grievances. Because of the danger that the first to sign such a remonstrance would be accused of being the ringleader and guilty of counseling mutiny (a capital offense), they adopted an earlier French practice called ruban rond, meaning "round ribbon." This involved signing their names like the spokes of a wheel radiating from its hub.

Round shot: Cannonballs.

Round turn: [1] A complete turn of a line around

a cleat, spar, or another line. Often used with a pair of half-hitches to make fast to a post or bollard. [2] To turn a vessel through a complete circle. [3] USN slang for a reprimand.

Roundhouse: A small structure on the after part of a sailing merchantman's quarterdeck. It was normally square, and the term indicated it was possible to walk round it on the deck.

Roundline: Refers to three-stranded, right-handed line.

Roundly!: Command to do something briskly and efficiently.

Rounds: A tour of inspection by the captain or other officer.

Rouse: [1] To handle a rope, cable, or tackle, using main strength without the help of windlass or capstan. [2] To awaken one or more seamen to turn out for duty.

Route: [1] The course to be followed by a ship, formation, or convoy. [2] The path to be followed by a message, including the method of transmission.

Route march: A long march for recruits in training, frequently over rough ground and carrying heavy equipment as training in physical endurance. Normally, the unit retains its formation but individuals are allowed to break step.

Routine: [1] The lowest precedence classification of a military or diplomatic message. [2] The procedure to be followed in certain circumstances (e.g., Sunday Routine).

Rove: [1] The past tense of reeve. [2] A small plate or ring for a rivet to pass through and be clenched in boat building. [3] To wander.

Rover: A pirate or freebooter (Dutch rover = robber)

Row: To propel a boat with oars.

Rowboat: A civilian term for a boat propelled exclusively by oars. Not in naval use.

Rowing port: One of a row of small openings on the lower deck of a sloop or other small sailing vessel, through which oars or sweeps could propel the craft in calm weather.

Rowlock: British term for a Y-shaped device that holds oars in place and allows them to pivot while being pulled (cf. oarlock, thole pin). Pronounced "rolok."

Royal: [1] A mast set above or forming an extension to the topgallant. [2] A square-sail set on the royal mast. [3] Affectionate slang for a member of the Royal Marines.

Royal Arsenal: In the early 1500s, King Henry VIII established a dockyard at Woolwich, on the Thames downstream from London. Its original facilities included naval stores, victualing, weaponry, and a ropeyard. In 1696 an ammunition factory was built, and In 1717 the Royal Brass Foundry began to cast artillery. The arsenal expanded greatly over time to become the largest military-industrial complex in Europe. It remained in operation until after World War II, and today its land and buildings are being redeveloped as a residential and commercial community.

Royal Corps of Naval Constructors: France formed the Génie Maritime — a professional corps of naval constructors — in 1765, but it was not until 1883 that the British Admiralty followed suit and formed the RCNC. Its members were civilian, but had military rank and were required to wear uniforms in certain postings. They alternated between designing ships at the admiralty and practical work in the dockyards. In 1993, the Ministry of Defence began consolidating the RCNC into a centralized Procurement Executive for all the armed services. This is a civilian agency, separate from the military and organized by function rather than service. Naval units oversee warship acquisition, but actual design is assigned to the shipbuilding industry.

Royal Fleet Auxiliary: A flotilla of supply ships, hospital ships, and repair vessels, tasked with keeping warships of the Royal Navy supplied with armaments, ammunition, fuel, victuals, electronic equipment, and other needs (including amphibious assault craft when needed for operations away from their home bases). The RFA's civilian-crewed merchantmen are owned and operated by the Ministry of Defence (cf. United States Military Sealift Command).

Royal Funerals: *See* state funerals.

Royal Marines: The seagoing and amphibious infantry of the United Kingdom, and its specialists in mountain and arctic warfare. All male marines are commando trained. The RM provides bands for the Royal Navy, with musicians having secondary roles as field hospital orderlies. (*See also* women marines.)

The force originated on 28 October 1664, when King Charles II directed that "Twelve hundred land soldiers be forthwith raised to be distributed into his Majesty's Fleets prepared for sea service." The first Maritime Regiment was formed from the "Trained Bands" of the City of London (from whom the Royal Marines inherited the nickname Jollies). In consequence, since 1746 the Royal Marines have had the unique privilege of marching through the City of London with drums beating, colors flying, and bayonets fixed. Officially the Duke of York and Albany's Maritime Regiment of Foot — but commonly known as the Admiral's Regiment — this initial formation was owned by the army but controlled by the Admiralty. It and other maritime regiments returned to land service in 1715, but twenty-six years later were reinstated for the War of Jenkins' Ear.

In 1747, they were transferred to full Admiralty command, but a year later peace was declared and they were again disbanded. Then, in 1755, Parliament approved the establishment of 5,000 Marines to provide detachments for ships of the fleet (ranging from a hundred or more marines, commanded by a captain or major in a ship-of-the-line, to a sergeant and twenty marines in a small vessel). At that time Marines were expected to assist with running the ship and some qualified as able seamen, then leaving the corps to earn considerably higher pay in that capacity. It was not until the Napoleonic Wars that the Marines finally gained recognition as an elite and potent fighting force.

In 1827 King George IV ruled that they had too many battle honors to be recorded on their regimental colors, ordering that their distinguishing badge should be a Globe "as the most appropriate emblem of the Corps whose duties carried them to all parts of the Globe, in every quarter of which they earned laurels..." The modern Royal Marines had been born. Originally, they were two separate but allied forces, the Royal Marine Light Infantry (Red Marines) and the Royal Marine Artillery (Blue Marines); but they amalgamated in 1923. *See also* horse marines, and United States Marine Corps.

Royal Naval Air Service: *See* Naval Aviation.

Royal Naval Association: This British fraternal society was granted a Royal Charter in 1954. With the motto "Once Navy Always Navy," it aims to preserve naval traditions and the well-being of the Service, to perpetuate the memory of deceased naval personnel, to foster comradeship among those who serve or have served in British and Commonwealth naval forces, and to provide financial relief from conditions of need, hardship or distress suffered by those who serve or have served and their dependants.

Royal Navy: Alfred the Great is traditionally recognized as founder of the English navy (*see* Saxon Seapower) but after his death the force slowly fell into disrepair. In consequence, there was little or no maritime opposition to the invasions of Sweyn Forkbeard in 1003, Knut Sveisson in 1016, or William of Normandy in 1066. After the Conquest, Norman kings required the Cinque Ports to provide and crew fifty-seven ships but otherwise paid little attention to seapower. For almost four centuries there was virtually no permanent force and the fleet waxed and waned with merchantmen being rented or requisitioned when required for combat.

In the early fifteenth century Henry V briefly maintained large and impressive fleets, but after he died most of his ships were sold off. In *The Governance of England*, written in the mid–1470s, Sir John Fortescue warned: "Though we have not alway war upon the sea, yet it shall be necessary that the king have alway some fleet upon the sea for the repressing of rovers, saving of our merchants, our fishers, and the dwellers upon our coasts." He went unheeded and, by the turn of the sixteenth century, Henry VII only had about a dozen warships in service. However, when Henry VIII was crowned in 1509, the growing naval power of Scotland was both an affront to his prestige and a threat to the realm.

Henry quickly built up the Navy Royal as it was then known. By his death in 1547 it had grown to 58 state-of-the-art vessels supported by an administration with storehouses and dockyards, but his successors allowed it to decline again, and Elizabeth I inherited only 27 royal warships in 1558.

At this time, the English — whose early impact on the Spanish Empire had been modest, compared to that of the Scots, French, and Dutch — had achieved a remarkably rapid transformation from coastal traders and fishermen to blue water navigators. English shipwrights were designing heavily-armed galleon-type vessels with fine underwater lines, which made them fast, weatherly, and maneuverable, although at the expense of cargo space.

However, instead of building up the Navy Royal, Queen Elizabeth encouraged private enterprise, in effect piracy, against Spain's new Atlantic empire. When Spain counter-attacked with its Armada of 1588 the fleets of England, both Royal and private, were mobilized to successfully defend the realm.

The Navy Royal changed little in size from Elizabeth's death in 1603 to the accession in 1625 of King Charles I who began to build up his fleet. By 1633 there were 50 king's ships, but financial problems and poor administration saw this reduced to forty-two by 1642 when Civil War broke out and the fleet declared for Parliament.

The Commonwealth (republican) regime then created the most powerful and effectively run fleet Britain had yet seen. This magnificent new force proved itself fighting the Dutch and Spanish and, when monarchy was restored in 1660, Charles II inherited 154 ships crewed and administered by permanent professional officers and bureaucrats.

The Royal Navy had come of age, but still had a powerful French fleet to contend with. The latter fell apart after the excesses of the Revolution and, from the late 18th until the early 20th century, Britain was unquestionably the most powerful maritime force in the world. Then, under the 1922 Washington Naval Treaties it was co-equal with the United States Navy, until World War II brought the latter's exponential expansion to superpower status.

During Word War II naval operations in Atlantic and European waters were overwhelmingly British and Canadian, while the Indian Ocean conflict was entirely British. The Pacific naval war was overwhelmingly a United States commitment but, as the European war wound down, Britain was finally able to muster a Pacific Fleet.

The BPF was the largest force ever put to sea by the Royal Navy, with its "sharp end" consisting of six fleet, four light, and nine escort carriers, supported by four battleships, ten cruisers, two maintenance carriers, hundreds of lesser warships, and a huge fleet train. However, the torch of maritime supremacy had been passed, U.S. naval expansion had been so great that the BPF served under American command as one of seven task forces in the Fifth and later Third Fleet.

Royal Navy Sailors' Fund: This charity was established by the British Admiralty when it ended the daily rum ration on "Black Tot Day" in 1970. It was initially capitalized by the money which would have been used to buy the next two year's supply of rum for the entire Navy, and receives an ongoing inflow of funds from the voluntary donation of a share of the profits of the commercial sale of "Pusser's Rum" which is blended from the same five West Indian rums formerly used for the navy issue. The "tot fund," as it is familiarly known, provides financial assistance to serving seamen of the Royal Navy, and has made donations to the United States Navy Memorial Foundation, the Royal Naval Foundation, and numerous other maritime-connected institutions.

Royal United Services Institute: Claiming to be "the Professional Forum in the UK for those Concerned with National and International Defence and Security," the RUSI is believed to be the oldest organization of its kind in the world, having been founded in 1831 by the Duke of Wellington and granted its Royal Charter in 1860. The latter charges it with "the promotion and study of naval and military sciences and literature."

RP: [1] Radar Picket. [2] River Patrol. [3] Recommended Practice.

RR: Radar reflective.

RRF: Reserve Ready Force (USN).

RRR: Former emergency signal by merchantman under attack by surface raider.

RTM: Ready to move.

RTR: [1] Real-time report. [2] Ready to return.

Rubbing strake: A protective molding running longitudinally along the side of a ship or boat. Also rubrail or wale.

Rudder: A vertical underwater plate or blade with a long shank, forming part of the steering mechanism of a boat or ship. It is usually fastened outside the hull at or near the stern, hinged at its forward edge to the rudder post. The device operates on the principle of unequal pressures, forcing the stern to turn or yaw in one direction by diverting the flow of water in the opposite direction. Research in the early 1980s showed it feasible to use rudder(s) for roll damping, while simultaneously controlling the ship's heading. The Voith-Schneider Drive eliminates the need for a rudder by combining propulsion and steering systems. (From the Anglo-Saxon roth or = turning oar.)

Rudder chains: Copper chains, formerly attached to the after side of the rudder at one end and to the stern at the other, with enough slack to allow free movement of the rudder. They served to save the rudder if it was unshipped by striking a reef or shoal.

Rudder post: The element of the stern frame on which the rudder is hung. *See also* sternpost.

Rudder quadrant: A frame fixed to the head of a ship's rudder shank, to which the steering mechanism is attached.

Rudder stock: The shank of a rudder that extends through the hull to the steering engine.

Ruffles & flourishes: Ruffles are the low continuous vibration of one or more drums, played simultaneously with flourishes, which are fanfares played by bugle or other brass instrument (the sound of a single flourish is roughly "dum-ditti-dum-ditti-daah"). These were originally a British tradition which is now seldom observed but continues in the U.S. armed forces, being sounded to render personal honors to selected individuals on the basis of rank or appointment. They are played only for official arrivals and ceremonies, never on informal occasions, and are always followed by a prescribed march or other music, played when the person being honored arrives, and before the national anthem is played. All uniformed personnel within earshot stand to attention, face the person being honored and hand salute or, if appropriate, present arms. If a senior officer is in the audience when a junior is being honored, the senior faces the junior and salutes along with everyone else. Military personnel out of uniform and civilians remove their hats and place their right hands over their hearts.

The full protocol is extremely complicated, recognizing some thirty-seven groups of civilian and military ranks to be honored. The U.S. Army and Air Force share one table of honors, but the Navy has a slightly different one, according more R&Fs to some and fewer to others; often with different music to follow. Four ruffles and flourishes are the highest civil honor, going to the President (followed by "Hail to the Chief"), former Presidents (the U.S. National Anthem), the Vice-President ("Hail Columbia") and foreign heads of state or government (the appropriate National Anthem). Beyond these, a broad selection of other civilians is entitled to one, two, three, or four sets (followed by "The Stars & Stripes Forever"). In contrast, the entitlements for military officers are simple because the number of ruffles and flourishes is equal to the number of stars in their rank, followed by the General's March (Army and Air Force) or Flag Officer's March (Navy).

Ruin your day: This commonly-used phrase probably originated with 5th century BCE. Greek historian Thucydides who wrote "a collision at sea can ruin your entire day."

Rule of sixty: In ocean navigation a change in bearing of one degree will result in an offset of $\frac{1}{60}$ of distance traveled. For ease of calculation, one can assume the nautical mile to be six thousand feet, making the offset 100 feet per mile. Hence, if a hazard is five miles dead ahead, a course alteration of one degree will avoid the object by approximately 500 feet (the actual clearance would be almost seven feet greater, an insignificant error and on the safe side). A similar rule applies in aerial navigation.

Rules of the road: Every day hundreds, sometimes thousands, of vessels pass through each of the world's major shipping choke points. Accidents would be inevitable in such crowded waters without strict rules of behavior and segregation. Moreover, many other waterways have the potential to be equally congested, chaotic, and hazardous, leading the International

Maritime Organization (IMO) to develop principles and practices providing common standards for the safe navigation of any type of watercraft, whether under sail or power, commercial or military management, and including tugboats, dredges, fishing craft, non-displacement (air cushion) vehicles, and water-capable aircraft. *See* table 7.

Rum rat: Describes a seaman with the ability to "smell out" the location of liquor storage and devise ways of tapping into it without being detected.

Rum ration: For 315 years Great Britain's Royal Navy issued a daily tot of rum to its crews, making this one of the oldest and longest-lasting maritime traditions. Originally, beer was carried to give the men a boost and replace water which deteriorated rapidly and became undrinkable. However, even that went off after a while, and this was compounded when unscrupulous brewers, in cahoots with corrupt pursers, provided sub-standard product, of which one report says; "Sailors were under the necessity of shutting their eyes and ... holding their noses before they could drink it."

To replace this disgusting stuff ships began to load "wine of the country," which meant arrack in Asia, wine in the Mediterranean, and rum or brandy elsewhere. Distilled liquors required less space in the cramped hold and did not spoil like beer or wine because higher alcohol content acted as a preservative. Rum was very inexpensive, being made from molasses which was a waste by-product of sugar manufacture.

After the capture of Jamaica in 1655, West Indian sugar interests gained considerable political influence and, by 1731, had succeeded in making rum the Royal Navy's almost universal drink. At this time the sailors received a whole pint (568 cc's) of 95.5 proof rum every day at noon, more than enough to lead to intoxication and disciplinary problems. In 1740, Admiral Edward Vernon ordered the quantity of rum to be halved and the rest to be cut with a quart of water (a 4:1 ratio) before being issued to seamen. Petty officers and above received their half-ration undiluted and one hour earlier. The addition of lime juice and sugar made the "cocktail" more palatable (*see* gimlet).

In 1850, the rum ration was halved again, but the mixture was made more powerful by changing the dilution to 3:1, and "grog money" was paid to teetotalers. This remained in effect until 1937 when seamen needed less fortification against the rigors of sea service, and more ability to concentrate on increasingly complex technology, so the rum ration was halved again to one-eighth pint, but at a stronger 2:1 mixture.

After World War II weapon systems and nuclear propulsion systems became increasingly complex, demanding intense concentration. First, a number of captains unilaterally moved the issue to the end of the working day rather than the traditional noontime, and then the Admiralty abolished the practice entirely.

The last ration was served on 31st July 1970, now known to the Royal Navy as "Black Tot Day." There was considerable resentment, and not a few old salts elected early retirement. (*See also*: Grog, Nelson's Blood, Spirits in the USN, Splice the Mainbrace, and Proofing the Rum Ration.)

Rummage: [1] This is an ancient nautical term, derived from the French "faire l'arrimage" meaning stow cargo. [2] Nowadays it refers to searching for something, or delving through a collection of miscellaneous articles (as in "rummage sale").

Run: [1] To sail downwind. [2] To abscond or desert. [3] The distance traveled in a given period.

Run aground: To accidentally touch, or become stuck upon, a reef, sandbar, or sea bed.

Run ashore: [1] A trip on land. [2] A short leave or liberty.

Run down: [1] To collide. [2] To sail north or south until the latitude of a port of call is reached, then east or west along that latitude until the port is reached. For some unknown reason, French admiral Jean d'Estrées habitually reversed this procedure, sailing along a latitude (which could be calculated) until he thought he had reached the appropriate longitude (which could only be estimated at that time), then turning north or south towards his destination. On 11 May 1678, he thought he was headed for Curaçao but ran his entire fleet onto Las Aves reef, almost 90 miles (150 kilometers) east of his intended landfall.

Run money: [1] Bounty paid for the capture of a deserter. [2] Extra pay awarded to a merchant seaman for a hazardous voyage.

Run out: [1] To open the gunports and pull the cannon into firing position. [2] To carry out a mooring line or hawser.

Runner: [1] A deserter. [2] A smuggler. [3] A blockade evader. [4] A line rove through a block.

Runner crew: Seamen hired to move a vessel from one place to another after its regular crew has been paid off.

Running: Freely moving, such as a rope through a pulley (cf. standing).

Running boat: A small craft that runs a ferry service between anchored ships and the nearby port or shore.

Running bowline: A type of knot that tightens under load.

Running bowsprit: One which can be reefed by sliding in through fid-holes.

Running free: Sailing with the wind abaft the beam.

Running lights: Variation of Navigation Lights. *See* table 9.

Running part: The moveable segment of a fall in a tackle (cf. leading part, standing part).

Running rigging: Consists of ropes and lines rove through blocks and used to manipulate spars and sails. It may be divided into those used to control the sails (tacks, cunninghams and sheets) and those which raise and lower (jeers, lifts, downhauls, and halyards). One end is fastened and known as the standing part. The other is loose end and known as the fall.

Square-rigged ships have lifts that control the fore-and-aft angle of yards; and braces which adjust their up-and-down angle. Braces demand large hauling crews because, although they carry heavy loads, their controlling tackles have too few blocks to give them adequate mechanical advantage. (*See also* rig, rigging, standing rigging.)

Running the gauntlet: This punishment for theft was seldom fatal. It involved lining up the ship's company in two parallel rows along the length of the vessel and forcing the delinquent, stripped naked above the waist, to walk between them while each man belabored him with a ropes-end or a small twisted cord with two or three knots, called a knittle. To stop him moving too quickly, the Master-at-Arms would walk backwards in front of the victim with a cutlass pointed at his chest.

This might be repeated two or three times, during which an unpopular shipmate, or one whose crime had incensed the crew, might be tripped and severely beaten while lying down. On the other hand, when he was well-liked, or when the seamen did not feel the charge was justified, he might walk through without receiving a single blow. In exceptionally bad cases, the culprit would be given a dozen strokes of the triple-knotted "thieves' cat" before this ordeal. Both gauntlet and its alternative gantelope come from the Swedish gattlogge meaning narrow path. In the USN the pronunciation is "gontlet"; in the RN it is "gant-let" or "gantlope."

Ruse de guerre: Literally, hoax of war. A stratagem or deceptive maneuver taken by a belligerent to fool the enemy in order to achieve a tactical advantage, or gain intelligence. In international law, a ruse de guerre is lawful provided it does not involve treachery and falsehood. The phrase is French.

Rust bucket: Any vessel which has been allowed to corrode and deteriorate.

Rutter: *See* waggoner.

RV: [1] Rescue vessel. [2] Research vessel.

S

SA: Stores Accountant (RN rating) *see also* SK.

Sabot: [1] Formerly, a wooden or metal disc attached to the projectile fired by muzzle-loading cannon. [2] A bushing or carrier used with sub-caliber ammunition. It conforms to rifling, seals against the escape of propulsive gas, centers the projectile in the barrel, and falls away when the assembly leaves the muzzle. (From French for shoe, pronounced "Sabo.")

Sabotage: Willfully injuring, destroying, interfering with, or obstructing physical assets or an operation, especially as an act of war.

SAC: [1] Supreme Allied Commander. [2] Strategic Air Command (USAF).

Saccoleva: A Levantine craft with steep sheer, carrying a huge spritsail.

Sack: USN slang for a bunk bed. Also rack.

SAD: Search and Destroy.

Saddle: [1] A bracket attached to one spar for another spar or boom to rest in (e.g., a saddle on the bowsprit supports the jib-boom). [2] A plate used to shunt coal into side bunkers. [3] A support for a refueling hose.

SAF: Surface action force.

Safe conduct: A written guarantee by a belligerent that a ship or person will be allowed to proceed on a specified voyage without let or hindrance.

Safe working load: Equipment should never be stressed close to its breaking strength, and knowing its limitations can help prevent accidents. Safe working load — defined as minimum breaking load divided by safety factor — refers to the maximum stress that can be applied while obtaining efficient service and prolonging life. Most manufacturers provide tables that show their equipment's safe working load under various conditions, but in their absence rules of thumb must apply. In the case of cordage the load should never exceed one-fifth of its breaking strength or, said another way, the breaking strength should be at least five times the weight the line is expected to hold.

Safety factor: The ratio of the breaking stress of an item to the maximum stress it is designed to handle in ordinary use. Also known as safety factor.

Safety harness: An article of clothing or combination of straps and bands, worn around a person's body and tethered to lines which keep the wearer from falling overboard.

Safety hook: A hook with a spring-loaded hinged catch which effectively turns the hook into an eye and prevents its load from slipping off. Also snap hook.

Safety track: A longitudinal track and runner on the upper hull of a submarine between the forward and after escape hatches. A person working on deck can attach a safety harness to the runner with freedom to move along the deck.

Saffir-Simpson Hurricane Scale: Although the 1926 revision of the Beaufort Scale added visual land effects, these were not completely suitable for determining the potential destructive power of tropical cyclonic windstorms after crossing the coast. In 1969, consulting engineer Herbert Saffir, working with Robert Simpson, director of the U.S. National Hurricane Center, produced a five-level scale for the World Meteorological Office. Each level is based on wind speed, but is essentially concerned with anticipated shore-based damage. See table 5.

Sag: Longitudinal deformation of a vessel under stress, causing the waist to drop below stem and stern when they are supported (e.g., by waves). From the Swedish saka.

SAI: Sea-to-air interface.

Saic: A Greek vessel, like a ketch, but without top gallant or mizzen sails.

Sail: [1] A piece of cloth extended on a yard supported by mast and rigging so as to catch the wind and propel a boat or ship (*see also* sailing rigs, sails, and sail nomenclature). [2] The number of sailing vessels in a squadron or convoy. [3] To set out on a voyage by water. [4] To navigate or travel in a waterborne vessel. [5] The superstructure of a submarine's hull, housing periscope(s), communications antennae, electronic warfare masts, and conning tower. When surfaced, the top of the sail serves as the boat's bridge.

Sail ho!: Traditional cry of a lookout who has sighted another vessel. The traditional response from the watch officer being "where away?" (in which direction?).

Sail loft: A manufactory making sails, tarpaulins, awnings, and other canvas items. *See* loft.

Sail nomenclature: Although there are many different types of sailing rig, the sides and corners of all sails share a common terminology. *See* clew, foot, head, leech, luff, peak, tack, and throat.

Sail palm: An oversized thimble used to drive needles through heavy canvas.

Sailboat: A vessel propelled entirely by sails without auxiliary power. The term applies only to smaller craft.

Sailcloth: Few people would associate the heavy cloth used for sail-making with the drug culture, but canvas is a close relative of marijuana and hashish, all three being derived from hemp (Latin cannabis).

Sailhook: *See* benchhook.

Sailing: [1] Describes a vessel driven by sails. [2] The activity of conning a sailing craft. [3] To be traveling in a sailing craft. [4] The departure of a vessel (she'll be sailing at noon).

Sailing Master: This is among the oldest of naval titles, going back to the 12th century when there were no standing navies and merchantmen were converted into warships whenever needed for national service. As already mentioned, when a military captain took command the civilian master remained on board with responsibility for operating and navigating, but not fighting, the vessel. Later, permanent naval forces were established and the military captain and his lieutenants became competent seamen, but the division between fighting and shiphandling survived.

A Sailing Master, often known simply as "The Master," was a well-educated and certificated professional seaman. He had few military duties, but was responsible for navigation, steering, setting sails, maintenance of ropes, rigging, canvas and anchors, and the stowage of stores and provisions. At sea he stood watches, plotted the ship's position using his own charts and instruments, and supervised observations taken by midshipmen and master's mates. In confined waters he conned (piloted) the vessel.

• **In the Royal Navy** of 1808 the sailing master was the most senior "Warrant Officer of Wardroom Rank," with pay and status comparable to those of a commissioned lieutenant, and eligible to command ships on non-combatant duty. In 1864, senior masters became staff commanders and staff captains, and three years later they and the remaining masters and master's mates were commissioned into the newly-formed Navigating Branch. However, after about 15 years it was decided to phase out that branch. No new appointments to it were made after 1883, when the first Executive Branch lieutenant graduated as a qualified navigator, and the last Navigating Branch staff commander retired in 1913.

• **In the United States**, Sailing Master was the senior warrant rank authorized in 1794 when the Federal Navy was established. Like their British counterparts they were experienced merchant seamen, but unlike them could and did command small combat vessels. In 1837, "sailing" was dropped from the title and some masters were commissioned to rank between ensign and lieutenant, while others remained warrant officers. After 1855, graduates of the Naval Academy were appointed as "Masters in line for Promotion." In 1883, Congress mandated the remaining warrant masters to be commissioned as lieutenants, junior grade and Naval Academy graduates became ensigns (*see also* table 15).

Sailing orders: Instructions to a shipmaster concerning time of departure (sailing), destination, etc.

Sailing rigs: Wind propulsion systems evolved over millennia to become highly-sophisticated assemblages of cloth or canvas, supported by various configurations of masts, spars, lines, and battens. There are two main divisions. They and eight of the many basic subtypes are:

• **Rigs running Athwartship**

1. **Square rig:** Most of the sails hang from spars known as yards, which run across the ship and are attached horizontally to the masts at their midpoints. The yards can be adjusted to suit wind direction, but this requires considerable manual effort, so this rig was mostly used by big ships with relatively large crews, making long ocean voyages where the force and direction of wind were reasonably constant.

2. **Lug rig:** Similar to square rig except that spar(s) are asymmetrically attached to the mast(s) with greater length on one side. This allows the sail(s) to be swung into a more fore-and-aft position to give better upwind performance than with fully square rigged sails.

3. **Junk rig:** A type of square rig, similar to lug rig, developed in the Chinese Far East. Several full-width battens stiffen and support the canvas to give more efficient performance at most points of sailing.

• **Rigs running lengthwise**

4. **Fore-and-aft rig:** One long edge of the sail is attached to the mast, while its lower edge is fastened to a spar called the boom which is hinged

near the foot of the mast. The top of the sail is attached to another pole called the gaff. Fore-and-aft sails are easier to adjust than square ones, making them suitable for craft with small crews, sailing in waters where changes in wind direction or course are frequent.

5. **Bermuda rig:** A triangular fore-and-aft sail is set behind the mast which is frequently slanted backward to improve performance in higher winds. The sail may or may not have a boom at its foot.

6. **Gaff rig:** A four-sided fore-and-aft sail with two supporting spars; a gaff at the top, angled upward and backward from the mast, and a boom at the bottom, perpendicular to the mast.

7. **Lateen rig:** A long triangular fore-and aft sail with one very short side, strung from a long drooping spar which crosses a relatively short mast at an angle of about 45°. Prevalent in the Mediterranean and Arab world, and probably derived from the Romans (the name is believed to be a corruption of "Latin"). Its aerodynamic shape performs well upwind, but tacking is a laborious process which requires moving spar and sail to the far side of the mast.

8. **Sprit rig:** In this variation of fore-and-aft rig, a spar runs from the lower part of the mast diagonally across the sail to support its top outer corner.

Sailing ship: [1] A vessel bigger then a sailboat propelled entirely by sails. [2] Under the Navigation Rules a power-equipped vessel is classified as a sailing vessel when it is being propelled by wind without the aid of its engines.

Sailings: A navigator's collective term for various methods of calculating course, distance, latitude, longitude, and departure. A dozen examples are given, some of which are no longer used.

- **Plane sailing:** Following a course plotted without considering the curvature of the earth.
- **Spherical sailing:** A sailing that does consider the spherical (spheroidal) shape of the earth.
- **Traverse sailing:** Uses the principles of plane sailing to determine the equivalent course and distance made good while following a track consisting of a series of rhumb lines.
- **Middle-latitude sailing:** A method of converting departure into difference of longitude, or vice versa, by assuming that such a course is steered at the middle or mean latitude.
- **Parallel sailing:** Occurs when the course is 090° or 270° true.
- **Meridian sailing:** Occurs when the course is 000° or 180°.
- **Mercator sailing:** Applies when the various elements are considered in their relation on a Mercator projection.
- **Rhumb-line sailing:** The term used when a rhumb line is followed.
- **Great-circle sailing:** Occurs when a great circle track is followed.

- **Composite sailing:** A modification of great circle sailing used when it is desired to limit the highest latitude.
- **Current sailing:** A term occasionally used to refer to the process of determining the effect of a current on the direction of motion of a vessel or its predicted course made good.
- **Dead Reckoning:** Not really a sailing so much as an estimate of position arrived at by calculating course, speed, and drift, without the benefit of observations (*see also* estimated position).

Sailing warship rating: *See* warship rating.

Sailmaker: [1] Ashore: The person in one of the large factories called sail lofts responsible for designing, making and repairing complete suits of sails. [2] Afloat: A junior warrant officer who reported to the boatswain. He and his mates were "idlers" who did not stand watches. They were responsible for maintaining and repairing the ship's sails and making other canvas items such as hatch covers and buckets. They also cut and stitched flags, pennants and the like. They would normally have served an apprenticeship in a loft, so would have had the skill to make complete suits of sails, but there was not enough space to spread them out aboard ship, so new ones were made ashore. [3] Modern: The trade might be expected to have faded away when power-driven ships came into use, but a visitor to the bowels of many a modern warship will find sailmakers making all manner of awnings, covers, and other canvas items. Today they work mainly with electric sewing machines, but still use some of the traditional tools such as benchhooks, fids, sail palms, and sailmaker's needles.

Sailmaker's needle: Similar to a leatherworker's needle, but the triangular point (for piercing without tearing) extends further up the shaft. Used for sewing thick canvas or heavy leather.

Sailor: [1] A sailing ship seaman. [2] Any navigator, mariner, or seaman knowledgeable in the ways of ships and the sea. [3] A seaman below the rank of petty officer. [4] A person who does not suffer seasickness.

Sailor-monger: U.S. legal term for a person who uses alcohol or violence to kidnap seamen and sell them to outgoing ships for financial gain (*see* crimp, press gang).

Sailor's disgrace: *See* fouled anchor.

Sailplane: A rotatable, horizontal control surface, located on a submarine's sail and used to help it rise or dive.

Sails: [1] Lower deck nickname for a ship's sailmaker. [2] Sheets of canvas or other fabric, suspended by an assemblage of spars and rigging in such a way as to transmit the force of the wind to a vessel's hull and thus drive it along. The windward side is under higher air pressure than the leeward and this causes the sail to be pulled forward by the phenomenon known as lift. For maximum efficiency, the canvas should assume the shape of a curve, known as its draft.

The larger the curvature the more powerful the pull and, in very strong winds, it may be desirable to flatten the sail.

Saint Elmo's Fire: A nautical event that occurs when the atmosphere develops an electrical potential, and the phenomenon known as a corposant creates a non-dangerous electrical discharge between solid objects and the surrounding air. The glowing halo and fiery jets sprouting from masts and yards were long regarded with superstitious awe by seamen who believed them a supernatural manifestation of their patron saint (Erasmus), giving them a warning of foul weather.

Saker: An ancient cannon, firing a ball of about 5 pounds.

Salamis (battle): In 480 BCE, according to the historian Herodotus, Persian Emperor Xerxes planned to rule Europe as well as Asia, but was repulsed at this battle (*see* military deception) with tremendous impact on the course of human history. Many historians argue that Greece's ensuing independence laid the foundations for Western democracy, art, and architecture, which would have developed differently under a Farsi-speaking, Zoroaster-worshipping, Persian autocracy.

Salinity: The amount of mineral salts dissolved in water measured in parts-per-thousand. Seawater is typically 35 ± 2 ppt.

Sally: [1] To rock a ship by having the crew rush from side-to-side. Ships are often sallied to release them when icebound or lightly aground on mud. [2] A sortie from a besieged place. (From the Latin salire = leap or rush forward.)

Sally port: [1] A large access hatch in a ship's side. [2] A small, easily secured door in a castle wall or other fortification. [3] A secure entryway consisting of a series of doors or gates ("sally" is derived ultimately from Latin salire = leap and "port" is ultimately from Latin portus = door).

Salmagundi: A food dish that has gone through a series of manifestations. [1] It originated ashore in England, late in the 16th century, being comprised of cooked meats, seafood, vegetables, fruit, leaves, nuts and flowers, dressed with oil, vinegar and spices. There was no single recipe, but it was usually presented as a large salad, drizzled with dressing and producing a wide range of flavors, colors, and textures on a single plate. [2] In the age of sail, the term referred to a favorite seaman's dish of sliced cured turtle meat or fish, boiled with pickled onions and cabbage. [3] Today, most recipes involve ground meat, served on a bed of lettuce with anchovies, eggs, onion, and spices. From Italian salami conditi = pickled sausage.

Salmontail: An extension to the after edge of a rudder designed to increase its effectiveness in narrow waterways. Also Danube rudder and Suez Canal rudder.

Saloon/Salon: [1] A large public room in a passenger ship. [2] The officers' dining room in a U.S. merchantman.

SALT: Strategic Arms Limitation Treaty.

Salt: [1] Slang term for a seaman with many years' experience. Often preceded by "old." [2] A preservative and condiment.

Salt horse: A sailor's nickname for the corned beef, mutton, or pork which was formerly a staple of the sailor's diet. *See* food in sailing ships.

Salting: Filling the spaces between the frame timbers of a wooden ship with coarse salt which attracts moisture, turns to brine, and pickles the wood as a preservative.

Saltpeter: Potassium nitrate, the oxidizing component of black powder gunpowder and several kinds of burning fuse, including the slow match. Also saltpetre from Medieval Latin sal petrae = "stone salt."

Salutes and courtesies: Nowadays, salutes are marks of respect or honor, but most began as symbols of friendship, through some formal act such as raising a hand to the head, discharging a gun or guns, presenting arms, pointing a sword to the ground, lowering the colors, dipping the topsails, or raising oars. This demonstration of peaceful intent seems universal, irrespective of time and place. For example, medieval knights would raise their visors with their fighting hand to expose unprotected faces for recognition, while African tribal warriors used to lower their shields and trail spear points on the ground to show peaceful intent. Tradition holds that the junior person or ship always salutes first, with the courtesy to be immediately returned by the senior. *See also* gun salutes, national gun salutes, personal gun salutes.

When boarding or leaving a USN ship it is customary to salute first the colors on the ensign staff and then turn to salute the quarterdeck. This is not, as is popularly believed, because it used to be the site of a crucifix, but because it is the seat of power and authority. In the RN the boarder merely faces aft and salutes once. In both cases, the OOD acknowledges the salute and gives permission to come aboard.

Saluting ship: USN term for a warship large enough to carry a band and therefore capable of rendering full honors.

Salvage: [1] The act of rescuing a ship or its cargo from perils of the sea. [2] Property so saved. [3] The fee or compensation given to those who voluntarily save a ship or its cargo. From Latin salvagium.

Salvage Master: *See* wreck master.

Salvage-money: A bonus paid to the crew of a vessel which has salvaged another.

Salvo: A discharge of artillery or other firearms fired simultaneously, or in rapid succession at the same target, or as a salute. Whereas a broadside involves all guns firing together, a salvo may only involve some of them.

Salvor: The claimant of salvage-money.

SAM: Surface to air missile.

Samakeen: A Turkish coasting sailing freighter.

Sampan: Any of several types of small open-deck work boats found in China, Japan, and Southeast

Asia, usually propelled by a single stern-mounted scull and roofed with matting.

Samson post: [1] A vertical timber on the forward deck of a boat, used for towing or tying-up. [2] A stanchion resting on the keelson and supporting the deck beams of a wooden ship. [3] A king post.

Sand: A loose granular material that results from the disintegration of rocks, consisting of particles smaller than gravel but coarser than silt. Sand can be described in terms of grain size, color, composition, morphology (angularity and shape) and surface texture. Hence the term means different things to different people. To the seafarer, it is essentially a mineral substance deposited along the shores of bodies of water and in river beds, usually containing shells, fossils, corals, algae, volcanic material, and the remains of marine plants and animals.

Sand bar: A sand barrier formed by the action of tides or currents.

Sand jack: A series of sand-filled containers driven beneath the hull of a vessel as temporary support, later to be drained of sand to lower the hull onto a launching cradle.

Sand strake: *See* garboard strake.

Sandbagger: American type of broad, shallow, partially-decked, centreboard sailing craft, carrying immense sail area for its size.

Sandbank: A large mass of sand forming a shoal.

Sandshot: Cannon balls cast in moulds made of sand. These cheap but irregular-shaped items could damage the bore of a large gun, so they were generally manufactured small enough to be used as case or grape shot.

Sandspit: A small sandy island or peninsula, frequently submerged at high tide and supporting little or no vegetation.

SANF: South African Naval Forces.

Sap: A leather-covered hand weapon; similar to a blackjack and much favored by press gangs.

SAR: Search & Rescue (often pronounced as a word).

Saraband: A popular forecastle dance, derived from the Moors of North Africa.

Sardine can: RN lower deck slang for a submarine.

Sargasso: [1] In general, a tangled mass of seaweed, usually encountered in relatively calm and warm areas of water. From the Portuguese Sargaço = gulfweed. [2] Specifically, in 1492, Christopher Columbus, heading (he hoped) for the fabled riches of Asia, sailed through what he termed the Mar de Sargazo (Sea of Weed) that covers upwards of 518,000,000 square hectares (two-million square miles). As Columbus discovered, even in light winds its extensive patches of floating seaweed are easily parted by sailing ships. Nevertheless, generations of sailors were terrified by the belief that any ship which ventured into the Sargasso would be held in its grip until the crew died of starvation.

Sarre: An early form of long cannon, slightly smaller than a bombard.

Satellite navigation: People have always looked to the heavens to find their way, and they still can. Each of a constellation of man-made satellites emits signals indicating the precise time by atomic clock. A ground receiver has in its memory the orbit of every satellite and can calculate its own exact position by simultaneously reading the signals of four or more. *See* Galileo and Global positioning system.

Saturated steam: Steam at the temperature of its boiling point. Sometimes (somewhat incorrectly) applied to wet steam. *See also* superheated steam.

Sausage: A long gunpowder-filled linen tube, used as the fuse for a mine or fireship, burning slowly enough to allow the igniters to retire and reach safety. The original French term saucisson is also used.

Sawbones: Seaman's slang for the ship's surgeon and his assistants.

Saxon seapower: In 871, a brilliant and energetic 22 year old, later known as Alfred the Great and called "Father of the English Navy," came to the Saxon throne, just as another wave of Viking invaders was threatening to destroy his country. At that time Cornwall, Wales, and north-west England were occupied by Celts (Welsh and Britons), while Scotland still belonged largely to the Picts, except for a small enclave of Scots (from Ireland) in its south-western corner. The rest of Britain had been divided by Scandinavian invaders into a number of warring kingdoms. In the south-east the Jutes held sway in what is roughly modern Kent. Angles controlled Mercia in the center, Anglia in the east, and Northumbria in the north-east, known collectively as Angle-Land (later corrupted to England). Across the south, from Welsh Marches to Thames Estuary, lay Alfred's Saxon kingdom of Wessex.

[The following italicized citations are from the *Anglo-Saxon Chronicle* which can be found at www.britannia.com/history/docs/asintro2.html]

Alfred saw that Wessex would never be safe until he had command of the sea. He not only "*built galleys and longships*" but established ports and maritime districts to support them. Saxons were landsmen, so he crewed his fleet with mercenary Frisians and hired "*pirates*" to teach his people seamanship. With Alfred himself in command, this initial fleet fended off invaders, but suffered a severe setback when "*the navy sailed west about until they met with a great mist at sea and there perished one hundred and twenty ships.*" Later, Danish plunderers "*greatly harassed the land of the West Saxons by piracies on the southern coast, most of all by the esks* (a class of ship) *which they built many years before.*" In response, the king ordered a new fleet constructed, based on an improved class of fighting vessel that he personally designed.

King Alfred gave orders for building long ships against the esks, which were nigh twice as long as the others. Some had sixty oars, some with more; and they were both swifter and steadier, and also higher than the others. They were not shaped either after the Frisian or the Danish model, but so as he himself thought that they might be most serviceable.

In the summer of 897 these new ships engaged and destroyed a Viking fleet along the south coast of England. When Alfred died two years later, the first genuine English navy controlled the Channel. (For subsequent developments, *see* Royal Navy.)

SBR: [1] Special boat squadron (USN). [2] Sea-based Radar (a floating, self-propelled, mobile unit, designed to roam the Pacific Ocean to detect incoming ballistic missiles). [3] Short Barrel Rifle.

SBS: Special Boat Service (Brit.).

Scaling: [1] Cleaning the bore of a cannon. [2] Chipping salt deposits off the inside of a boiler (also de-scaling). [3] Climbing the wall of a fortress.

Scampavia: A low, capacious, armed Venetian barge or pinnace, pulled by 40 oarsmen who slept aboard in bunks under their thwarts. Carried a huge lateen sail on a single mast.

Scan: One complete (360°) turn during the continuous rotational search of a sonar or radar.

Scandalize: To set sails askew or acockbill as a sign of mourning. *See also* blue paint and mourning salute.

Scant: To sail as close as possible to the wind.

Scantlings: The structural dimensions of a ship's hull frames. From Middle English scantilon = to gauge or measure.

Scarfing: Obsolete term for dressing ship.

Scarp: *See* escarpment.

Scarph: To taper or otherwise shape two pieces of timber so that they can be joined together. Also scarf. From the Swedish scarf = join.

Scend: [1] To lurch forward from the motion of a heavy sea. [2] The swell-imparted upward heave or pitch of a plunging vessel. (Abbreviation of ascend.)

Scharnow turn: *See* "Person Overboard."

Schellboot: Before the beginning of World War II the Kriegsmarine (German Navy) developed this fast and seaworthy speedboat under the guise of a pleasure craft that could travel fast even in heavy seas, and had brilliant maneuverability. The design was so successful that it was built as a torpedo or gun boat until the end of the war. The Type S-100 (introduced in 1943) was up 50 percent longer than any Allied boat and, unlike them, was not based on a planing hull but had a deeper rounded bottom, more suitable for heavy seas. Three Daimler-Benz 2500 hp diesel engines gave it an outstanding top speed of 43.5 knots, with an emergency speed of 48 knots. They were approximately twice the size of their American and British counterparts, more seaworthy, and enjoyed two to three times the range (approximately 700 nautical miles). In 1945, future U.S. president John F. Kennedy, himself a former patrol craft captain, inspected an intact "E-Boat" (as it was called by the Allies), writing in his diary, "It was far superior to our PT boat."

Schooner: A fore-and-aft-rigged sailing ship, occasionally carrying square topsails. The classic version has two masts, but up to seven have been used. Precursor vessels were being built in Holland during the late 16th and early 17th centuries, but the current design was refined and improved in British North America in 1713, eventually becoming ubiquitous. The name is said to derive from the Scottish "scoon," meaning to make a stone skip or glide across the water. According to legend, the first of this type was built by Captain Andrew Robinson, at Gloucester, Massachusetts. When the vessel slid off the stocks into the water, a bystander cried out, "Look how she scoons!" and Robinson replied, "Then a schooner let her be."

Schooner barge: A barge formerly found on the east coast of the United States. Essentially dumb, but equipped with small masts that gave it limited maneuverability in the absence of a towing vessel.

Schooner brig: *See* brigantine.

Schooner ketch: A triple-masted schooner with a short mizzenmast.

Schooner on the rocks: Former sailor slang for a slice of meat surrounded by roast potatoes.

Schooner yawl: A fore-and-aft rigged vessel carrying a large mainmast with a short boom and a jigger mast stepped abaft the sternpost.

Schuyt: A Dutch riverine and coastal vessel.

SCM: Summary Court Martial.

Scope: The ratio of anchor cable or chain deployed to depth of water. Normally 3:1 is adequate, but between 5:1 and 10:1 may be required in heavy weather.

Score: An almost obsolete term for the number twenty, or twenty of something (e.g., "Fourscore and seven years" — Abraham Lincoln). Commercial use must have been confusing, because a score could sometimes be effectively 16⅔, as recorded in the following mnemonic:

Five score's a hundred of men, money, or pins;
But six score's a hundred of all other things.

Scorpione: Arrow-firing naval artillery of the classical era. *See also* ballista.

Scotch mist: Light soaking rain.

Scotch prize: Slang for a vessel taken illegally by mistake.

Scottish coffee: Seamen's slang for a beverage made from ship's biscuit, charred over the galley stove, crushed, and stirred into hot water.

Scottish-rigged: A four-masted bark with double topgallants and a pole jigger.

Scour: The erosive force of moving water on bottom sediment.

Scouse: [1] Formerly, a generic term and nickname for a sailing ship sailor. [2] British seaman's slang for a person from the port of Liverpool. [3] Abbreviation of lobscouse.

Scout: [1] To reconnoiter or make a reconnaissance. [2] A person (usually a soldier or marine) or a ship sent out to gather intelligence on a hostile force and its disposition.

Scow: [1] An open flat-bottomed boat used to carry sand, gravel, or other bulk material over short distances. [2] Slang term for a barge or lighter. (From the Dutch schouw.)

Scow schooner: A former San Francisco market boat with two masts on a punt-shaped hull with a centerboard and a false cutwater.

Scram: Emergency shut-down of a nuclear reactor. Reputed to be an acronym of **Safety Cut Rope Ax Man**, which was the actual job title of a lumberjack who stood atop the first experimental reactor, ready to sever the rope supporting a protective cadmium shield if anything went wrong.

Scramble: [1] To make a radio or telegraphic message unintelligible, usually by random changes of frequency. [2] An emergency launch of fighter aircraft.

Scrambled eggs: Naval and military slang for the gold braid on the visor of a senior officer's cap.

Scrambling net: Mesh hung over the side to assist people (often embarking soldiers) to climb the side. Also called boarding net and scramble net.

Scran: A old word for eatables, especially, leftovers.

Scran bag: [1] Originally, a receptacle to store ship's biscuit or the remainder of a meal. [2] Now, an RN lost and found depository. By tradition, articles can only be redeemed by payment in bars of soap. (The USN equivalent is lucky bag.)

Screen: [1] A formation of warships positioned to protect a main force or convoy. [2] The large end of a radar or sonar tube on which an image is projected electronically. [3] A shield or mask used to limit the arc of visibility of a light.

Screw: A propeller.

Screw anchor: [1] A device with broad helical flanges welded to a long shaft, designed to be screwed into ground that is too soft for a normal anchor to hold. Usually power-installed and used to permanently secure a mooring buoy. [2] A small, portable, corkscrew-like device, installed manually for the temporary mooring of yachts and small craft.

Screw log: A rotor trailed astern by a cable attached to an onboard revolution counter scaled to indicate distance traveled (also taffrail log, patent log).

Scrimshaw: [1] The art or technique of engraving or carving the byproducts of marine mammals (most commonly the bones, teeth, or baleen of whales, and the tusks of walruses). The practice began on Pacific Ocean whaling ships between 1817 to 1824, and survived into the 20th century. Because most whalers did not have to stand night watches they enjoyed more free time than other sailors and made scrimshaw as a leisure activity. [2] Handicraft articles so produced.

Scrollhead: A billethead shaped like the scroll of a violin, but turning outward and facing forward as opposed to the inward and aft-facing volute of a fiddlehead. Used when there is no figurehead.

Scrovies: A derisory term for useless vagabonds picked up by crimps or the quota system and passed off as qualified seamen.

SCS: Shipboard Computing System.

Scuba: Acronym of **Self-Contained Underwater Breathing Apparatus.** A portable device that allows independent underwater movement. One or two tanks of compressed air are strapped onto the back of a diver, connected by tubing to a mouthpiece through which the diver breathes at a valve-controlled rate. This allows the scuba diver to stay underwater longer than with the simple breath-holding techniques used in snorkeling and free-diving, and is not hindered by air lines to a remote air source as with hookah or full surface support. Also called by the trade name aqualung.

Scud: [1] Low-lying, fast-moving mist or clouds. [2] To run before a gale with minimum sails set. [3] NATO code-name for an obsolete series of short-range land-based Russian tactical ballistic missiles.

Scull: [1] An oar light enough to be pulled with one hand, and long enough for two to be managed by an oarsman seated at the center of the boat. [2] To propel a boat by the twisting motion of an oar placed over the stern of a boat. [3] To row.

Scunner: A sealer's lookout posted in the foretop to watch for seals or to guide the vessel through ice fields.

Scupper: [1] A small opening to drain water from the open deck. [2] An underwater drain pipe fitted with a non-return valve. [3] To sink a ship deliberately by opening the underwater drains (cf. scuttle).

Scurvy: (From the Anglo-Saxon scurf = scabby.) Until the 18th century, seamen on long voyages were seriously afflicted by this vitamin C deficiency disease, characterized by swollen gums oozing black blood, tooth loss, stinking breath, ulcers, breathing difficulty, and the re-opening of previously-healed wounds. The disease usually appeared after about six weeks at sea, when fresh produce ran out, and by the end of ten weeks it was raging. Prolonged cases frequently resulted in death. It has been reliably estimated that scurvy killed two million seamen during the age of sail — more than the combined total due to combat, shipwreck, and all other illnesses.

On a trip to India in 1499, Vasco da Gama lost two-thirds of his crew to the disease, and in 1520 Magellan lost 80 percent while crossing the Pacific. The connection with diet was well understood by experienced ship captains, who tried to bring as many fruits and vegetables on board as possible. But, on extended voyages, spoilage limited foodstuffs to such things as corned beef or pork, dried peas, oatmeal bread, butter, and cheese, none of which contains significant vitamin C. For a long time it was widely believed that daily consumption of beer would protect seamen against the disease, but it did not.

Then, in 1612, John Woodall, Surgeon-General of the East India Company, persuaded the Bombay Marine to provide lemon juice for its sailors. Five years later, in his book *The Surgeon's Mate*, Woodall described the benefits, saying "Lemmons, Limes, Tamarinds, Oranges and other ... good helps available in the Indies ... do farre exceede any that can be carried tither from England." A decade after that, naval writer John Smith recommended "The juyce of limmons for the Scurvy." All these important observations were ignored by the Royal Navy.

Next, in 1753, James Lind, a physician known as the "father of nautical medicine," published his classic work *A Treatise of the Scurvy*, reporting the medical world's first example of a controlled clinical nutrition study on human patients, which Lind had performed while a Royal Navy surgeon's mate. This provided clear evidence of the curative and preventative value of citrus fruits. Lind's work won the attention of First Lord of the Admiralty George Anson, who, during his circumnavigation of the globe in 1740–44 had lost two-thirds of his crew, mostly to scurvy. Anson secured Lind's appointment to Haslar Royal Naval Hospital at Gosport, where one of his first publications was "An Essay on the Most Effectual Means of Preserving the Health of Seamen of the Royal Navy." This too was ignored.

In 1768, on the recommendation of David McBride, author of *A New Method of Treating Scurvy at Sea*, published four years earlier, Captain James Cook's Pacific expedition was issued with substantial experimental supplies of "malt, portable soup, and sauerkraut," plus a small quantity of lemon juice. The relative Vitamin C content of 100 grams of each of these foods is:

- Malt   negligible (about 0.1 mg)
- Portable soup   Probably close to zero (due to prolonged boiling)
- Sauerkraut   15 mg
- Lemon Juice   230 mg

Cook lost no seamen to scurvy but, because the supply of lemon juice was so limited, mistakenly attributed that good fortune to the efficacy of the first three only. In consequence, Lind's work on lemon juice was ignored by the Royal Navy for decades longer. It was not until 1795 that an Admiralty Order was issued requiring the supply of lemon juice to ships. Almost immediately, this antiscorbutic virtually eliminated the disease, halving the number of sailors sent to naval hospitals. At about the same time, the French Navy decided to replace its traditional daily issue of 750 ml of red wine (which contains just enough vitamin C to partially deter scurvy) with 200 ml of eau-de-vie (brandy, which has none). Having inadvertently moved in the opposite direction, the Imperial Napoleonic Navy re-introduced the disease just as the British Royal Navy escaped from it.

Shortly afterward, the Admiralty bowed to the powerful planters lobby and switched to lime juice which was freely and cheaply available from the British West Indies. However, limes are far less effective deliverers of vitamin C than lemons (roughly 4:1), and the latter juice was re-introduced along with orange juice after a serious scurvy outbreak in 1875. A year later, apparently not cognizant of the superiority of lemons, the British Board of Trade mandated a daily ration of lime juice for every sailor in the merchant fleet. Thus British seamen became known as limeys.

Scuttle: [1] To sink a ship deliberately by opening its sea cocks. [2] To make a hole in something, such as a cask. [3] A small hole or port for light or ventilation. [4] The hinged cover of such a port, a deadlight. [5] A small circular watertight hatch. [5] A conduit to carry water over the side.

Scuttle drill: A duty assigned to junior midshipmen in the days of sail. During heavy weather one would be stationed at each gunroom scuttle, opening it to ventilate the fuggy compartment, standing by to rapidly close and secure it when a wave approached.

Scuttlebutt: [1] Formerly an open-topped cask for drinking water, now a water fountain. In order to prevent seamen from becoming dehydrated, shipmasters would often order a butt or cask to be lashed somewhere on deck with its lid scuttled so that a ladle could be used to scoop out drinking water. [2] A visit to the scuttled butt was a good opportunity for sailors to exchange gossip, rumors, or chatter, and these activities soon took on the slang name of the water cask itself.

SDDC: Surface Deployment & Distribution Command.

SDO: [1] Special duties officer. [2] Ship's debarkation officer.

Sea: [1] A body of saline water, smaller than an ocean, either (a) surrounded by land on most sides (Mediterranean Sea), or (b) part of one of the oceans (Caribbean Sea). [2] An inland body of water (Caspian Sea). [3] The condition of the water (calm sea, heavy sea). [4] An action of the water (ship sea). [5] A large area or great number of something (sea of faces).

Sea anchor: A device such as a heavy spar, or drogue dropped from the bow to keep a vessel headed into the wind or sea, and to reduce drift, usually during a storm.

Sea barge: [1] In naval use, a large logistical support vessel for beach landing operations. It carries such things as heavy lifting equipment, causeway sections, tugboats, pre-loaded barges, and other watercraft. [2] In civilian use, a carrier of pre-loaded self-propelled lighters, equipped with rollers to facilitate loading them onto seagoing container ships.

Sea bed: The floor or bottom beyond the continental shelf.

Sea beggar: One of the Dutch Protestant revolutionary seamen who led a popular 16th–17th century revolt against Spanish rule in the Low Countries. After independence they formed the nucleus of the Dutch Navy.

Sea biscuit or sea bread: *See* hardtack.

Sea born: [1] Produced in the sea (e.g., a coral reef). [2] Created of or by the sea (e.g., an oceanide). [3] Born at sea (e.g., a whale calf).

Sea breeze: A light wind blowing from the sea toward the land.

Sea buoy: *See* departure buoy.

Sea cabin: A commanding officer's quarters, used when in combat or during foul weather, adjacent to the bridge and smaller than that officer's regular accommodation.

Sea Captain: The certificated master of a merchantman. Also shipmaster.

Sea change: This phrase for a major transformation is sometimes attributed to the ebb and flow of the tide, or to the uncertainty of weather at sea. In fact, it comes from Shakespeare, specifically *The Tempest* (I.ii.394) where the sprite Ariel sings:

> Full fathom five thy father lies:
> Of his bones are coral made:
> Those are pearls that were his eyes:
> Nothing of him that doth fade
> But doth suffer a sea-change
> Into something rich and strange.

Sea chest: [1] A seaman's wooden trunk, frequently decorated with pictures of ships and sea creatures. [2] A compartment in a ship's hull below the waterline through which sea water can be admitted or dirty water discharged.

Sea cock: A valve on a pipe open to the sea below a ship's waterline, used to obtain salt water when required, or to scuttle the vessel.

Sea condition: The size of waves and state of weather over the sea. *See* tables 1–4 and sea spectrum.

Sea daddy: Slang for an experienced seaman or marine assigned to help a recruit learn the ropes.

Sea dog: [1] A highly-experienced older seaman. [2] A pirate or privateer. [3] Slang for a fogbow.

Sea echelon: A portion of the assault shipping which withdraws from or remains out of the transport area during an amphibious landing and operates in designated areas to seaward in an on-call or unscheduled status.

Sea Fencibles: This organization was developed for naval defense during the French Revolutionary and Napoleonic Wars. It consisted of fishermen, smugglers, and coastal seamen who volunteered to serve in time of invasion. They were trained to use pikes and to man coastal gun batteries, as well as in the operation of any gunboats that might be available. In return they received protection against impressment. Districts were commanded by naval Captains, with from three to six Lieutenants under them, according to the number of Fencibles enrolled.

Sea foam: [1] An accumulation of fine, frothy bubbles formed in or on the surface of the sea, by the agitation of breaking waves. The appearance and thickness of this foam accumulation varies with the size of the waves and strength of the wind. Hence, foam is an important factor in the visual descriptions of the Beaufort Scale (table 1). [2] A similar phenomenon is seen when plankton washes ashore, dies and disintegrates, creating foam-like bubbles, which are left in tide pools after the ocean retreats.

Sea fog: A cloud of water droplets caused by warm damp air passing over water that is colder than its dew point.

Sea fret: A morning mist or light sea fog.

Sea frontier: USN term established in July 1941 to designate an area command responsible for coastal defense and antisubmarine patrol off the continental United States.

Sea-gait: A long, rolling swell of the sea. Also sea-gate or sea gate.

Sea gate: [1] A gate which serves to protect a harbor or tidal basin from the sea. [2] A channel giving access to the sea. [3] A sea-gait.

Sea girt: Surrounded by sea.

Sea grocer: Another of the many derogatory names for a purser.

Sea horse: [1] Fanciful name for the foam of a wave breaking at sea, said to resemble the white mane of a horse. [2] Any member of the pipefish family. [3] A fabulous sea creature with a fish's tail and the foreparts of a horse. [4] A walrus.

Sea ice: Ice formed from seawater.

Sea-kindly: Said of a vessel that is easy on its crew and undemanding on its gear.

Sea ladder: [1] Metal rungs welded to a ship's hull above the waterline. [2] An aluminum or steel device made of pipes and treads and long enough to reach from the waterline to the main deck of smaller ships. When in use it is bolted to flanges permanently welded to the deck; otherwise it is removed and stowed. (Also called a pipe ladder.)

Sea lane: A permanent or frequently-used shipping route.

Sea lawyer: [1] An argumentative seaman inclined to grumble about or question orders. [2] Person with too fine a knowledge of naval rules and regulations.

Sea legs: Acquired ability to keep balance and avoid nausea while afloat.

Sea Letter: A form of certificate issued in time of war to prove a vessel's neutrality and nationality (cf. passport).

Sea level: Refers to the position of the air-sea boundary, used as a standard in reckoning land elevations or sea depths. The concept is based on the assumption that, because the oceans are interconnected and water tends to find its own level, the ocean surface around the world conforms to the ellipsoid (flattened sphere) shape of the earth. In fact, the waters are in constant motion, influenced by tides, atmospheric pressure, gravitational effects, and wind conditions, while longer-term levels are affected by climate change. Hence it is impossible to determine a figure for the entire planet. Even on a local basis, levels vary quite a lot and the best that can be done is calculate mean sea level at a specific point and use that as a datum.

Sea Lord: A naval member of the former British Board of Admiralty (now Admiralty Board of the Defence Council).

Sea maiden: [1] A mermaid. [2] A sea goddess.

Sea mile: *See* nautical mile.

Sea officer: The 17th century term for a naval officer.

Sea People: A loose confederation of tribes from the eastern Mediterranean, the Aegean, Asia Minor, the Black Sea region and (possibly) survivors of Troy. Their relentless land and sea advance between 1200 and 1176 BCE brought dramatic changes to Asia Minor and the civilized world of that time. Rather than pure military and naval operations, there seems to have been a mass migration of warriors, accompanied by women and children in ox-carts, probably displaced by widespread crop failures and famine. The land army was attacked and routed as it crossed the Egyptian border, but the navy continued towards the Nile delta, intending to force entry up the great river.

In the brutal hand-to-hand fighting which ensued, the Sea People were utterly defeated, vanishing from political records, but leaving a legacy second to none in the history of the western world. Superpower Egypt, which had won the battles but lost the Levant, wasted away to become a shadow of its former self. In the Levant, where several of the tribes settled, Philistines and Phoenicians revived and spread much of the inventiveness in metallurgy, seafaring, warfare and trade that had characterized fallen Troy. Most importantly, by virtually destroying all the major powers of the Mediterranean, the Sea People cleared the way for the rise of Greece, Rome, and ultimately Western civilization itself. Surprisingly, the events of such a pivotal moment in world history are little understood and widely disputed.

Sea pie: A seaman's dish consisting of meat or fish and vegetables layered between bread crusts or ship's biscuit.

Sea pod: A capsule maintained at underwater pressure, in which off-duty deep-sea divers can relax without having to adjust to surface pressure and re-adjust to underwater conditions before their next shift.

Sea return: Radar signals reflected off the faces of breaking waves. This phenomenon hampers target identification and is usually worse upwind.

Sea room: [1] Enough space to maneuver a vessel. [2] Clear of inshore shoals.

Sea rover: A pirate.

Sea serpent: A dragonlike or snakelike marine animal, generally considered mythical. Numerous eyewitnesses have claimed to have seen some such creature, many of them qualified observers including experienced naval officers and marine biologists. Despite many theories about what might have been sighted, their existence has yet to be proven. *See* index for individual monsters, and the appendix for possible explanations.

Sea service: The cumulative amount of time actually spent afloat. *See* service.

Sea shed: A temporary deck installed in a container ship to transport large military vehicles and outsized cargo that will not fit into containers.

Sea smoke: A type of fog created when very cold air moves across cold water to produce "steam."

Sea spectrum: The sea is a spectrum or continuum of waves, each of which has a distinct height (distance between trough and crest) and period (time between succeeding crests). This spectrum can be characterized by the significant wave height and the modal period, as is done by Pierson-Moskowitch (*see* table 3).

Sea state: A numerical or written representation of the roughness of the ocean surface, categorizing the force of progressively higher seas by wave characteristics, and the relationship of wind to waves. The large number of variables involved cannot be quickly and easily summarized, so simpler scales are used to give concise, approximate, descriptions, primarily for reporting in a ship's log or similar record. *See* Beaufort scale, Douglas scale, and tables 1–5.

Sea surveillance: Is defined by DoD and NATO as:

The systematic observation of surface and subsurface sea areas by all available and practicable means primarily for the purpose of locating, identifying and determining the movements of ships, submarines, and other vehicles, friendly and enemy, proceeding on or under the surface of the world's seas and oceans.

See also surveillance and integrated undersea surveillance systems.

Sea swap: Occurs when a U.S. warship remains on foreign assignment but replaces its crew with a fresh one. The exchange does not usually take place at sea, but in a friendly foreign port.

Sea trial: A series of tests conducted at sea by a shipbuilder or dockyard in order to confirm that a newly-constructed or repaired vessel is acceptable to its owners.

Sea wolf: One of the beasts rumored to exist in the 17th and 18th centuries was the sea wolf. According to the lore of the time, as reported by Conrad Gesner in *The History of Four-footed Beasts and Serpents* (1658), "the sea wolf liveth both on sea and land."

Seabag: A tubular canvas bag, closed by drawstring, used by seamen to carry personal belongings. Also kitbag (mainly British).

Seabee: [1] Semi-formal USN nickname for an enlisted person in a construction battalion. [2] Informal designation of USN construction personnel, whether or not attached to a construction battalion. *See also* song of the Seabees.

Seaboard: [1] The line where land and sea meet, the shore or coast. [2] Land bordering or adjoining the sea, the seacoast or littoral.

Seaborne: Carried by or transported on the sea.

Seaclergy: During the 16th–17th centuries, it was widely believed that some aquatic creatures resembled Christian priests. In *Des Monstres* (1578), Ambroise Paré described a "marine monster" resembling a Bishop dressed in full Pontifical garments; while in *Physica Curiosa* (1662), the illustrations of Caspar

Schott show an assortment of sea monsters, including a fish resembling a monk, a marine monster looking like a bishop, and two chimerical creatures with long, fishy tails. Similar depictions appeared in numerous other works, and it has been suggested that religious tensions might have contributed to the depiction of clerical figures as alleged monsters. In 1854, naturalist Japetus Steenstrup compared 16th century illustrations of "sea monks" to that of a giant squid captured in 1853, coming to the conclusion, "The Sea Monk is firstly a cephalopod."

Seacoast: The land adjacent to the sea.

SEACOP: Strategic **Sea**lift **Co**ntingency **P**lanning.

Seafarer: One who fares (travels or wanders) over the sea by way of trade, business, or calling.

Seagoing: [1] A vessel designed for or capable of going to sea. [2] A seafarer. [3] in admiralty law, a vessel ordinarily engaged in deep-sea navigation.

Seagull: [1] USN slang for (a) Chicken served aboard ship, or (b) A woman who follows her man from port to port. [2] Seagull has no meaning in ornithology, but is used by laypeople to refer to all birds of the Laridae family. These are typically coastal or inland, rarely venturing far out to sea. An ancient superstition holds that gulls landing in flocks on a ship, or making a loud noise along the coast, prognosticates a storm. This belief goes back to the classical era, being mentioned by Pliny, while Virgil writes in *The Georgics*:

Scarce can the billow spare the curved keels,
When swift the sea-gulls from the middle main
Come winging, and their shrieks are shoreward borne

Seakeeping: The ability of a vessel to accomplish its defined purpose while maintaining equipment operability and crew comfort.

Seal: [1] A fish-eating amphibious sea mammal with webbed feet and flippers. [2] To hunt such a creature. [3] A member of a seal team.

Seal team: An élite USN special forces unit, employed in unconventional covert operations and guerrilla-style warfare, including reconnaissance, counterterrorism, and hostage rescue. Acronym of **Sea Air Land.**

Sealed orders: Secret instructions given to the commander of a warship not to be opened until a specific time or when the vessel is out of contact with the shore. A security measure to ensure that mission or destination is not disclosed by "loose lips."

Sealer: A ship or person engaged in hunting seals.

Sealift: The movement of military supplies or personnel by ship.

Sealift enhancement: Special features, equipment, and modifications applied to merchant tankers and dry cargo ships, to adapt them for specific military missions.

Sealift readiness: A standby contractual agreement between Military Sealift Command and ship operators for the voluntary provision of private vessels when needed for defense purposes.

Seam: [1] The space between adjacent planks or strakes of a ship — essential to allow for expansion when the wood is wetted and swells, but needing caulking to be watertight. [2] The junction formed by a sailmaker sewing two pieces of canvas together. [3] The joint between two steel hull plates welded or riveted together. [4] A similar line, ridge, or groove made by fitting, joining, or lapping together any two objects.

Seaman: [1] Correctly, a person skilled in every aspect of the seafarer's craft. [2] Colloquially, any person familiar with ships and the sea. [3] A naval rating or enlisted man below petty officer and above apprentice.

Seaman-gunner: A seaman who has received special training in the theory of projectiles, and the manner of constructing and using ordnance, and is qualified to instruct others in these matters.

Seaman Officer: An RN officer qualified, or under training to stand deck watches. The USN term is Deck Officer.

Seamanship: Skill in the operation, management, maintenance, and safety of a vessel in all kinds of weather and under all conditions. Does not necessarily include navigational ability. *See also* basic seamanship.

Seamark: A conspicuous land object visible from the sea and serving as a guide to mariners.

Seamount: A conical underwater mountain rising at least 500 fathoms above the sea bed, with its summit usually about the same distance below the surface. Cf. guyot.

Seaplane: An aircraft designed with a boat-like hull or equipped with floats enabling it to take off from, land on, or float on water. Handling a seaplane on the water requires a great deal of skill and judgment. In addition to flying ability, it is essential that the pilot has water handling skills; what might one day be a simple beaching or docking could change greatly the next morning, depending on wind, water condition, available space, and the like.

Seaport: Any coastal or riverine port capable of handling seagoing ships.

Seapower: [1] Any nation with a navy. [2] One with sufficient strength to assume command of the sea.

Seaquake: Disturbance of the sea due to submarine earth tremor or volcanic eruption.

Search: *See* right of search.

Search and Rescue: A mission mounted to locate and assist a person or vessel in distress.

Seas: [1] The salty waters that cover the greater part of the earth's surface. [2] The hydrosphere as distinct from the lithosphere and atmosphere. [3] Disturbance of the water, as waves or swells. (From Greek seiō = shaken.)

Seashore: Legally defined as the ground between normal high-water and low-water marks.

Seasickness: Nausea and dizziness, frequently accompanied by vomiting, caused by the activity of a vessel. A specific form of motion sickness — suffered every time he went to sea by no other than Vice-Admiral Horatio Nelson! One who can defy this affliction is said to have sea legs — which Nelson always acquired after a few days of misery.

Seasoning: [1] Allowing the frame of a newly-constructed wooden vessel time to settle down and mature by exposure to the air and weather before its planking is installed. [2] Using spices or herbs to improve the flavor of food.

Seaspout: When powerful waves hit a rocky shore, water may be compressed into and forced up a narrow cleft or fissure, forming a jet that shoots across adjacent land, often with a load roar. Not to be confused with waterspout.

Seawall: A barrier or embankment to prevent erosion of the shoreline.

Seaward: [1] At or towards the sea. [2] Away from the land.

Seaway: [1] A designated shipping lane. [2] An inland waterway for oceangoing vessels. [3] A vessel's headway. [4] Moderately heavy waves or swell.

Seaweed: Generic term for marine algae, kelp, and other ocean-growing plants.

Seaworthy: In all respects ready to go to sea, sound, furnished, and fully equipped.

SECNAV: Secretary of the United States Navy. Reports to the Secretary of Defense as civilian head of the Navy, the Marine Corps, and (in wartime only) the Coast Guard.

Second-in-command: Someone who relieves a commanding officer with power to act when the superior is absent. Synonyms are deputy, lieutenant, executive officer.

Second strike: The first counterblow of a war, conducted with weapons designed to withstand an initial assault (first strike) and deliver a retaliatory attack. This tactic is generally associated with nuclear warfare.

Secondary wave: [1] The follow-up to an amphibious landing. [2] An earthquake phenomenon in which rock particles vibrate at right angles to the direction of primary wave travel. It can travel through solids but not through liquids.

Secondary wave breaker system: A series of water waves superimposed on another series and differing in height, period, or angle of approach to the beach.

Secret: Security classification falling between "confidential" and "top secret."

Secretary: [1] A politician who holds significant public office in a national or regional government (e.g., Secretary of the Navy). [2] A former USN rank corresponding to lieutenant, bestowed on the officer employed as the private clerk of a flag officer.

Section: [1] A subdivision of a division of enlisted personnel or ratings. [2] A tactical group of ships (usually half a division) or of aircraft (usually two).

Secure: [1] To prepare a ship for wave action by tying down all loose objects and covering all openings. [2] To fasten two or more objects together. [3] To tighten something (e.g., a hatch cover). [4] To end some condition (e.g., general quarters). [5] To stop using something (e.g., main engines). [6] A former gunnery command to arrange breeching and tackles so that the guns shall be in no danger of breaking loose in a seaway.

Sécurité: Verbal preface to a radio message indicating that it contains important safety information. This is the lowest priority of three prefaces, the others being pan-pan and mayday. (From the French, and pronounced say-cure-ee-tay.)

Security classification: Information, that could seriously damage national defense or foreign relations if disclosed, is classified in rising order of importance as sensitive, confidential, secret, and top-secret.

Sedition: Incitement of discontent or mutiny. A serious offense afloat.

SEDR: Sea Emergency Deployment Readiness (USN).

See service: *See* service.

Seiche: A periodic wave oscillation due to seismic or atmospheric disturbance. Seiches move rhythmically back and forth as they bounce off opposites sides of an enclosed body of water such as a bay. In harbors they may cause ships to break mooring lines (pronounced saysh).

SEIE: Submarine escape immersion equipment.

Seine: A fishing net which hangs vertically with weights on the bottom edge and floats at the top (pronounced sayn).

Seismic wave: A powerful sea wave of long period and amplitude, caused by earthquake, volcanic action, tectonic plate movement, or submarine landslide. Also tsunami.

Seize: [1] To confiscate or take possession by right of law. [2] To capture by force. [3] To fasten two ropes together by wrapping with light line. [4] To wrap the end of a rope to its standing part to form an eye. [5] Of machinery, to stop working due to lack of lubrication (often followed by "-up").

Seizing: The cord, marline, yarn, or wire used to seize ropes.

Seizure: The act or an instance of taking possession. *See also* seize and right of seizure.

Selection board: [1] A panel of senior officers convened to review service records and recommend or reject the promotion of more junior officers. [2] A group assembled to interview candidates for some specific appointment.

Selective unloading: The controlled unloading and movement ashore from assault shipping of specific cargo items at the request of the landing force commander.

Self-righting: [1] Specifically, a rescue lifeboat equipped with air tanks in its elevated bow and stern and stabilized by a heavy keel. [2] In general, any watercraft, personal floatation device, or other mechanism able, or designed, to return itself to the upright position after tumbling or capsizing.

Self-sustaining: Said of [1] A vessel capable of loading and unloading containers at ports not equipped with suitable lifting equipment. [2] A continuous chain reaction in nuclear fusion, creating a great deal of heat as a power source. [3] A nuclear reactor that is producing enough power to operate all of a vessel's auxiliary equipment.

Self-trimming: A vessel whose holds are shaped in such a way that cargo levels itself.

Selkies: In Celtic folklore Selkies (derived from the Scottish selch = seal) are shape-shifters who are able to transform from seals into handsome, graceful, sexually-attractive human beings by casting off their skins. If one of these magical pelts is lost, its owner is doomed to remain in human form, so if a cunning man managed to steal a beautiful selkie girl's skin she was unable to return to the sea and forced to marry him. If a human female wanted an affair with a selkie man, she only had to go to the shore at high tide and shed exactly seven tears into the sea for one to come to her. Sometimes, however, the selkie would not wait to be invited but would creep into a human's bed, leaving before their lover realized who had been there.

Selsyn: See synchro.

Selvage: Finishing on the edge of a canvas to prevent it unraveling. Also selvedge.

Semaphore: A signaling system in which a pair of hand-held flags or lever-operated wooden arms are placed in various positions to indicate numbers and letters of the alphabet. The intention to send a message by semaphore is signaled to the receiver by the triple flag hoist "YZ1" or at close range by the semaphore letter "J" (left hand out to the side and right hand above the head, forming a right angle).

Semper Paratus: Always Ready (Latin), the motto of the United States Marine Corps. See Spars.

Senior Officer Present Afloat: Self-explanatory USN/NATO term designating the individual who will assume administrative and operational command of a group of unrelated ships (gathered in a foreign harbor, for example) in the event that some special or emergency action is required by the group as a whole. Referred to as "Sopa."

Seniority: The difference in rank or priority of appointment of one individual or ship relative to another.

Sennit: [1] Flat braided cordage used to make mats, fenders, stoppers, ornamental ropes, and the like. [2] Plaited straw, grass, or similar material, used for making hats. Also sennet.

Sennit hat: A stiff sun-hat made of braided and coiled straw with a flat crown and brim, worn by naval seamen during the 19th century and until 1921. It was worn in summer with blue uniform, weather permitting, but not at sea unless required as protection from the sun.

Sentinel: [1] A seaman, marine, or soldier posted as a guard. [2] A kellet.

Separated ammunition: Consists of a projectile containing the load and fuses, and one or more cartridges containing primer and propellant. Also called semi-fixed (cf. fixed ammunition).

Separation zone: An area delimiting shipping lanes moving in opposite directions.

Serang: The boatswain of a Lascar crew.

Serendipity: The ability to make valuable discoveries by chance. Few people realize that this word has a loose nautical connection. Sarandib was what Arab and Persian seafarers called Sri Lanka, and it entered the English language thanks to Horace Walpole who, in 1754, wrote "I read a silly fairy tale, called 'The Three Princes of Serendip' (who) ... were always making discoveries, by accidents and sagacity, of things which they were not in quest of."

Serpentine: An early 24-pounder gun, usually decorated with serpents.

Serve: [1] To provide artillery with ammunition. [2] To tightly bind with continuous rounds of small stuff to protect a cable or standing rigging from chafing. The final step in the sequence "worm, parcel, and serve" (see also serving). [3] To carry out duties (especially in a nation's armed services).

Serve one's time: Refers to undergoing a period of probation or apprenticeship, including the slow path to commissioned rank in the sailing ship navy. Typically a youth would embark as a captain's servant, supernumerary to the ship's complement. After about three years, he would be rated midshipman and taken on the books, but it required another three years of sea service to be eligible to sit for the lieutenant's examination. Even if this were passed at the first attempt, he would have to continue serving his time until a vacancy appeared.

Service: [1] Employment in one of the armed forces. [2] **The** service refers to the Navy. [3] **See** service means to experience combat. [4] **Sea** service refers to time afloat.

Service craft: USN term for auxiliary craft such as lighters and tenders which are too small to be commissioned as warships. Elizabethans called them handmaidens.

Service force: USN term for a logistical support unit (cf. fleet train).

Service life extension: An extensive USN rehabilitation program intended to add 10–15 years to a vessel's effective working life. See also Fleet Rehabilitation and Modernization.

Service stripe: USN sleeve marking showing the length of service of enlisted personnel. One red stripe is awarded for each four years irrespective of disciplinary record. A gold stripe is awarded after twelve years without any disciplinary offense. See hash mark and good conduct badge.

Serving board: A flat piece of hard wood having a handle attached, used in serving small ropes.

Serving mallet: A short wooden hammer with a groove on the underside, used in serving larger ropes.

Serving stuff: Small lines for serving ropes. Spunyarn is generally used, but hambroline, houseline, or roundline are sometimes preferred.

Servosystem: A control system that compares actual to required conditions and uses negative feedback to drive the controlled mechanism in the direction necessary to reduce or eliminate the error. Also "servomechanism," often abbreviated to "servo." From the Latin word for "slave."

SES: Surface effect ship.

Set: [1] The direction of flow of a wind or current. [2] The arrangement of spars and sails. [3] To raise a sail. [4] To dig in as an anchor. [5] To establish something (e.g., set the watch). [6] To move a boat, punt, or barge with poles. [7] To adjust the sights of a weapon.

Set in: [1] Likely to remain in a particular condition, unlikely to change (the weather seems set in). [2] To blow toward the shore (a gale could set in with the next high tide). [3] To become established (winter has set in).

Set sail: [1] To begin a waterborne journey. [2] To raise a ship's sails. [3] To loosen or extend a previously set sail.

Set the course: To prescribe the direction to be steered. Also shape the course.

Set the watch: [1] To establish the regular routine of watchkeeping in a ship or shore establishment. [2] Command to return to normal watchkeeping from some other routine (e.g., general quarters).

Setback: [1] General; Something which hinders progress. [2] Gunnery; A term for the inertial force which arms a fuse when a projectile is fired.

Settling tank: A temporary holding tank in which oil-contaminated water is allowed to separate into its component parts, after which the oil is transferred to fuel bunkers and the water is discharged to a bilge or holding tank.

Seven Seas: In antiquity these were Persian/Arabian Gulf, plus the Red, Mediterranean, Indian, China, East African, and West African Seas. The modern version, which should really be called Seven Oceans, covers the North and South Atlantic, North and South Pacific, Indian, Arctic and Southern (Antarctic) Oceans.

Sextant: This navigational instrument, which measures the angle of elevation of a celestial object, was invented independently by American Thomas Godfrey and Englishman John Hadley in or about 1730. It rapidly replaced the astrolabe, being capable of taking sights at wider angles, and providing more precise measurements, by using a long beam of light rather than a short arm with inherent errors. Moreover, even on a moving ship, the horizon and the celestial object seem to remain steady when viewed through opposing mirrors which compensate for movement.

The user looks at the horizon through the clear lower half of a lens, while viewing the sky in the mirrored upper half. When an assistant calls out a time-mark, the user adjusts the image of the celestial body (normally the sun), bringing it down until it just touches the horizon. The angle of elevation can then be read from a vernier scale with accuracy to the nearest ten seconds ($\frac{1}{360}°$) and can be translated into a position by any one of several mathematical procedures.

SFCP: Shore fire control party.

SH: Ship Serviceman (USN enlisted rating).

Shackle: [1] A metal loop or link, usually U-shaped, closed by a threaded pin which slides through a hole on one side and screws into a hole on the other. [2] To link two sections of chain with a shackle. [3] A measure of cable length equal to 15 fathoms (known as a shot in the USN). [4] To place a prisoner in fetters. (Anglo-Saxon sceacul.)

Shadow: [1] To follow covertly. [2] An area on a radar or sonar screen which appears devoid of targets due to the obstruction of an intervening object. [3] A quadrilateral spinnaker.

Shadow pin: A vertical rod at the center of a compass card, the direction of its shadow indicating the sun's azimuth.

Shaft: A reciprocating or oscillating straight round bar, for transmitting motion and torque. Usually supported by bearings, and connected to gears, wheels, propellers, or the like. Also drive shaft.

Shaft tachometer: *See* revolution counter.

Shaft tube: The watertight opening though which the propeller shaft exits the hull. Also stern tube.

Shaft tunnel: A housing surrounding and protecting the propeller shaft and providing a walkway for oilers. Also shaft alley.

Shag Harbour Incident: This airborne and underwater mystery is well-documented. On the night of 4th October 1967 the skies over Eastern Canada seemed unusually busy. Early in the evening the pilot and co-pilot of Air Canada flight 305 filed official reports of several unidentified flying objects sighted over the Canadian province of Québec. A little later, from near Shelburne in Nova Scotia, insurance salesman Grandy Irwin and 12-year-old Darrel Dorey independently called police to report strange lights in the sky. Then, at about 8:30 P.M. the 18-man crew of MV *Nickerson*—a dragger fishing off Sambro Island near Halifax—made a similar sighting and claimed to have used their radar to track four aerial objects for about two hours.

At about 11 P.M., half an hour after *Nickerson* stopped tracking, several residents of Shag Harbour—a tiny fishing village at the western tip of the Nova Scotia peninsula, opposite Portland, Maine—spotted strange orange lights in the sky. According to five teenage witnesses there were four of them, flashing in sequence. Royal Canadian Mounted Police (RCMP) Constable Ron Pound, driving toward Shag Harbour on the coast road, also saw four lights which seemed attached to an airborne object about sixty feet (18 meters) long with unusual flight characteristics. Suddenly, the lights changed shape and dived steeply into the water, striking about 900 meters (1000 yards) offshore with a loud roar and a bright flash, and then seeming to float. Convinced they had seen an airplane ditching, Constable Pound and several witnesses telephoned the nearest RCMP detachment, which dispatched Corporal Victor Werbieki and Constable Ron O'Brien to join Constable Pound. All three police officers and a number of local residents reported seeing at least one orange light moving slowly on the water, leaving yellowish foam in its wake.

Canadian Coast Guard *Cutter 101* and a number of fishing boats rushed to the scene only to find the light gone. However, an area of about 37 by 60 meters (120 × 300 feet) above the apparent point of submergence was densely covered by glowing yellow foam with a foul sulfurous smell. None of the local fishermen could recall ever having seen anything even vaguely like it. Meanwhile, the police had contacted Halifax Rescue Coordination Centre (HRCC), which had no reports of missing civilian or military aircraft, and it advised Canadian Armed Forces Headquarters that a flying object "of unknown origin" had hit the water just outside Shag Harbor. The military classified it as a UFO incident (which, as previously mentioned, does not imply alien origins). The HRCC report was forwarded to Canadian Armed Forces Maritime Command which ordered minesweeper HMCS *Granby* to investigate. However, extensive underwater search by seven naval divers found nothing.

(Up to this point the story is well-documented, much of it in Canada's National Archives. In contrast, the following is mostly anecdotal, much of it from officers and officials demanding anonymity to protect their jobs and pensions, and avoid public ridicule.)

The submerged craft is said to have been joined by another, apparently for underwater repairs or rescue, both being watched by *Granby* and other Canadian naval vessels for about a week. Then the small flotilla was diverted to challenge a Soviet submarine which had violated Canadian territorial waters in an apparent attempt to communicate with the submerged craft. Shortly afterward both underwater vehicles began moving into the Gulf of Maine, where they surfaced and became airborne. On that day, 11th October 1967, numerous independent witnesses reported strange flying objects in the sky over western Nova Scotia. No explanation has ever been given, but forty years later, at the end of April 2007, the Shag Harbor Incident Society opened a temporary museum dedicated to recording the event while eyewitnesses are still available. Fundraising for a permanent structure is ongoing.

Shake a cask: Take it to pieces and pack the staves (shakes).

Shake a leg!: Admonishment to move faster, hurry up! be quick! (not to be confused with show a leg).

Shake out: To undo reefs and spread a sail.

Shake the sails: To luff up in the wind, causing the sails to shiver.

Shakedown: A period for testing equipment and training a ship's company, frequently including a cruise to another port. Usually follows the construction or major repair of a vessel.

Shakes: [1] Shipwright's term for the cracks which appear in weathered timber. [2] *See* stave.

Shakings: Pieces of cordage, canvas, or oakum swept up from the decks.

Shallop: [1] Any of several types of sailing or rowing vessels formerly used in shallows. [2] A small cruising warship of the 17th/18th centuries, usually with two schooner-rigged masts.

Shallows: An area of sea with little depth of water.

Shanghai: To kidnap and enroll a seaman as crew by unscrupulous means such as drugs, liquor, or force. Named after the port city in eastern China, where such incidents were common.

Shank: That part of an instrument, tool, or other thing, which connects the working part with a handle, or other part by which it is held or moved. Hence: [1] An anchor shank is the long straight bar that connects the transverse bar called a stock with the crown, from which flukes branch out at a suitable angle to enter the ground. [2] A rudder shank is a long bar fastened on one side to the rudder blade and on the other to the sternpost of the vessel in such a way that it can be turned from side to side in the water by means of a tiller, wheel, or other steering mechanism.

Shanty/Shantey: [1] Properly, an 18th century working song of American lumbermen and railroad workers (after the shanties providing accommodation in their work camps). [2] Slightly incorrect, but in common usage, a seaman's working song (properly chanty or chantey).

Shape the course: To prescribe the direction to be steered. Also set the course.

Shape up: Instruction to begin to act properly or look smart.

Shape up or ship out: Instruction to improve performance; otherwise go away.

Shapes: Visual aids hung in the rigging of a vessel during daylight hours to indicate its navigational status. Day shapes, as they are properly called, include balls, baskets, cones, cylinders, and diamonds.

Share: [1] Piratical entitlement to participate in the division of booty. [2] Naval entitlement to receive prize money.

Sharp: [1] Command to make haste (look sharp!) or remain alert and vigilant (be sharp!). [2] Said of a square-rigger with sails trimmed as close as possible to the wind (also sharp up).

Sharpie: A long flat-bottomed centerboard boat with triangular sails on one or two masts. Used mainly for pleasure fishing and racing on the NE coast of USA.

She: All vessels are traditionally female.

Shear link: A connecting device designed to break at a specified mechanical load.

Shear pin: A soft metal pin used to attach a propeller to its shaft. If the propeller hits an obstacle the pin fractures minimizing damage to shaft and engine.

Shears: *See* sheerlegs.

Shearwater: This tube-nosed seabird of the petrel family flies with stiff wings, using a "shearing" technique to move across wave fronts with the minimum of active flight.

Sheathe: To cover a ship's underwater hull with copper as protection against shipworm damage.

Sheave: The grooved wheel in a block, over which the fall (rope, wire or chain) is led (pronounced "shiv").

Sheepshank: A versatile hitch for temporarily shortening a rope, taking up slack, or strengthening or bypassing a chafed line. It is made by taking two long bights and half-hitching each part over opposite ends of the resulting loop. This unknot remains secure under tension but — unlike ordinary knots that bind tightly under tension, becoming almost impossible to undo — easily comes apart when tension is removed. Also, the loops at each end can be used to pass another rope through.

Sheer: [1] To alter course sharply (sheer off). [2] The upward slope of a ship's hull towards bow (sheer stem) or stern (sheer counter). [3] The position a vessel assumes to stay clear of its own anchor cable (riding sheer). [4] To approach a ship or pier at an angle (sheer alongside).

Sheer batten: In shipbuilding, a long strip of wood to guide carpenters in following the sheer plan.

Sheer hulk: A sort of floating crane, used in the days of sail to position the heavy yards and lower masts of a ship under construction or repair. Masting sheers were suspended at an angle from the cut-off main mast of the hulk.

Sheer masted: Having a sheerlegs instead of a mast on which to hoist and sling the sail. Found on Malayan pirate prahus and Spanish riverine rafts.

Sheer off: To avoid a danger by turning the ship s head away from it.

Sheer plan: A diagrammatic fore-and-aft elevation of the hull of a vessel, showing bow and buttock lines, stations, water lines, diagonals, decks, bulwarks, etc. Also called profile plan.

Sheer strake: The uppermost plank in the side of a wooden vessel, just below the main deck and running the full length from stem to stern.

Sheerlegs: A hoisting apparatus of spars, joined at the top and separated at the bottom to form a triangle, supported by guys, and having purchases to install masts or raise cargo and other heavy objects. Also sheers, sheer legs, shears, shearlegs.

Sheet: A line attached to the corner of a sail and used to control its position.

Sheet anchor: [1] A heavy anchor stowed well forward on the waist of sailing ships and used only in emergencies. One of a pair, the other being called the spare. [2] Until the 1950s warships of cruiser size carried sheet anchors. [3] The term is sometimes used incorrectly for a bower.

Sheet bend: A knot which temporarily fastens one rope through the bight of another. Especially useful when the ropes are of different diameters. Also called becket bend and weaver's knot or hitch.

Sheet home: To haul in a sheet until curvature of the sail is minimized.

Sheet ice: A thin smooth covering of fresh ice.

Sheet winch: A pawled winch used for handling a sheet. The barrel is usually vertical on small boats and horizontal on larger ships.

Sheets: Small platforms or seats at the forward and after ends of a small boat, ahead and astern of the thwarts for oarsmen or boathandlers. Used mainly by passengers. Naval tradition requires junior officers to seat themselves on the bowsheets, leaving the drier sternsheets for their seniors.

Shelf: A submerged sandbank or rock ledge extending from the low water line to the depth at which there is usually a marked increase of downward slope (cf. continental shelf, insular shelf).

Shelf ice: Layers of compressed snow, which have become firm but have not yet turned to glacier ice.

Shell: [1] A hollow explosive-filled projectile, fused to explode in flight, upon impact, or after penetration. [2] To bombard with such projectiles. [3] The plates or planking forming the exterior hull of a ship. [4] The casing of a block in which its sheave rotates. [5] A long, light and narrow racing canoe, equipped with outriggers for oars, and sliding seats for one, two, four, or eight oarsmen.

Shellback: [1] An older, more experienced seaman (said to have been at sea so long that his back is encrusted with mollusks and barnacles). [2] Any sailor who has crossed the equator (cf. Polliwog).

Shellroom: Storage area for projectiles, usually at the base of a barbette.

Shellshock: World War I term for combat fatigue.

Shelter deck: A full or partial weather deck above the main deck.

Shelving: Said of a rocky beach which rises with a gradual slope making approach from seaward difficult.

Sheriff: USN slang for a warship's Master-at-Arms.

Shibah: A small Indian vessel.

Shift: [1] A change in the direction of wind or current. [2] To move a vessel from one berth to another. [3] An unintended movement of cargo, usually due to wave motion. [4] Shipwright's term for overlapping timbers that give strength and stability.

Shift colors: *See* shifting colors.

Shift rudder!: USN steering command to turn the helm to exactly the same angle on the opposite side.

Shifting: Movement of cargo which can unbalance and endanger the ship.

Shifting ballast: Bags of sand, pigs of iron, or other ballast which can easily be moved to trim the ship. Also shiftable or moveable ballast.

Shifting board: A temporary bulkhead, installed to prevent cargo shifting.

Shifting colors: When a British or United States warship is at anchor or on moorings it flies its national ensign on the flagstaff (ensign staff) at the stern and its union jack on the jackstaff at the prow. As soon as the ship gets under way, both are struck while a sailing (or steaming) ensign is simultaneously hoisted to the gaff (a spar projecting diagonally from the mainmast). The ensign is struck when out of sight of land, but raised to the gaff when falling in with other ships, cruising near land, or going into battle. The switch from one configuration to the other is known as "shifting colors."

The practice began in the late 18th century, when a loose-footed spanker sail on the mizzenmast was replaced by a gaffsail whose horizontal boom projected beyond the taffrail. This spar would have broken the ensign staff when it swung, so the latter was struck when getting under way. The practice continued in the USN as a matter of custom long after the practical need disappeared.

Colors are also switched in the RN, but nowadays in a slightly different manner. In peacetime, only the jack is struck when getting under way. With no gaffsail boom to worry about, the ensign normally remains on the ensign staff while at sea, only being switched to the gaff in wartime, during foul weather, or when clearing for action. However, if the ship has a helicopter landing pad or ASW mortars on its stern an ensign staff would impede their operation. In this case, colors are switched and the ensign staff is struck as soon as the vessel is under way.

Shifting sand: A sandbar subject to movement by wave motion or undercurrents, creating a possible hazard to navigation.

Shingle: [1] A loose accumulation of round and water-worn gravel, pebbles, or roundish stones, such as is common on the seashore. From Norwegian singling. [2] The code-name for an Allied amphibious assault on Anzio, Italy, in 1944.

Ship: [1] Historically: A large square-rigged sailing ship with three or more masts. [2] Colloquially: Any sizable oceangoing vessel: [3] Official: The U.S. Coast Guard defines a ship as 300 tons or more, anything smaller being a boat. [4] In American English: An aircraft or space vehicle. [5] To bring on board (ship the anchor). [6] To step or fix in place (ship the mast or rudder). [7] To take over the side (ship water). [8] To receive on board (ship cargo in the hold). [9] To cause to be transported by ship (ship goods to Europe). [10] To hire oneself out or enlist as crew (ship out). [11] To embark as a passenger (ship on a cruise). From the Anglo-Saxon scip.

Ship breaker: One who dismantles and disposes of old ships no longer fit for use.

Ship broker: A mercantile agent who transacts business for shipowners and merchants; buying and selling ships, procuring cargoes, and similar tasks.

Ship chandler: A retail and wholesale dealer in supplies and equipment for both individual seamen and vessels. Traditional sailing ship items would have included blocks, brooms and mops, carpenter's tools, cordage, galley supplies, hemp, lard, leather goods, linseed oil, oakum, paper, pitch, rope, rosin, shipwright's tools, tallow, tar, turpentine, twine, and varnish. A modern chandlery will carry items such as cabin stores, bridge and deck equipment, engine room spares and equipment, safety items, chemical stores, and marine paints. In both periods the chandlery would supply fresh fruits and vegetables, dairy products, meats and seafood, liquor, beer, and tobacco. Because commercial ships discharge and turn around quickly, delay is expensive and a dependable ship chandler must be able to fill demands rapidly, either from stock or local sources. Some chandlers also serve as ship's agents.

Ship classification: A system for safeguarding life, property, and the environment at sea that entails verification against a series of benchmarks during the design, construction and operation of ships and offshore structures. This process consists of:
• Before construction: A technical review of the design plans and related documents for a new vessel, to verify compliance with applicable rules and standards.
• During construction: Attendance of a Classification Society surveyor in the shipyard, and at production facilities making key components such as steel, engines, generators, and castings, to verify that the vessel is built in accordance with the classification rules.
• After delivery: Each classified vessel is subject to a program of periodic surveys, with the rigor of each survey increasing with the age of the vessel.

Ship classification societies: Organizations that establish and apply technical standards in relation to the design, construction, and survey of marine related facilities. Each society issues a Certificate of Classification upon completion of relevant surveys. This certificate does not confirm fitness for purpose, nor seaworthiness, merely that the vessel complies with the standards of the issuing Society. More than 50 organizations provide marine classification, but the "big three" are generally considered to be Lloyd's Register, the American Bureau of Shipping, and Det Norske Veritas. These three, along with seven other members and two associates, form the International Association of Classification Societies which, collectively, classifies about 94 percent of all commercial tonnage involved in international trade. With date of foundation these are:
• 1764 Lloyd's Register (LR)
• 1828 Bureau Veritas (BV)
• 1861 Registro Italiano Navale (RINA)
• 1862 American Bureau of Shipping (ABS)
• 1864 Det Norske Veritas (DNV)
• 1867 Germanischer Lloyd (GL)

- 1899 Nippon Kaiji Kyokai (NK)
- 1913 Russian Maritime Register of Shipping (RS)
- 1949 Croatian Register of Shipping (CRS) — Associate
- 1956 China Classification Society (CCS)
- 1960 Korean Register (KR)
- 1975 Indian Register of Shipping (IRS) — Associate

Ship fever: An old name for epidemic typhus, which was common in the crowded conditions aboard immigrant ships. Spread by lice, it produced frightful mortality. In 1847, seven thousand Irish emigrants died of typhus at sea and 10,000 more after arrival in Québec. The disease was endemic in other overcrowded places. Ashore it was known as hospital fever and jail fever.

Ship green water: To take heavy seas over the gunwale. *See also* pooped, ship water.

Ship measurement: *See* tonnage.

Ship money: A tax levied under early English law, requiring ports and maritime towns to provide funds to support the king's navy. An attempt to re-introduce this levy was one of many contributing factors to the English Civil War.

Ship motion: The movement imparted to a ship by a seaway is considerably greater than ground upheaval that would destroy even the stoutest earthquake-resistant building. Anyone who has been afloat when winds reach force 8 on the Beaufort Scale (about 47 knots; 30 mph) and waves rise to 7 on the Douglas Scale (9 meters; 30 ft high), has experienced the feeling of being the ice cube inside a cocktail shaker. Consequently, naval architects and oceanographers devote a great deal of time to studying the physics of the complex movements derived from interaction between vessel, wind, and water. In a real seaway it is difficult to consider ship motions as isolated phenomena. Most frequently they are closely interrelated and may be coupled with one or more other movements.

There are six "degrees of freedom" in which a floating vessel can move in response to wave action. Pitch, roll, and yaw are rotational oscillations, which tend to be produced by active open seas. They are relatively complex and are discussed separately. The other three involve linear displacement, which often occurs when the vessel is anchored or riding long widely-spaced swells. Compared to rotational oscillations, linear movements are straightforward and easy to explain. Heave is vertical hull displacement, moving up-and-down; surge is longitudinal hull displacement, sliding fore-and-aft; and sway is lateral hull displacement, sliding from side-to-side.

Ship oars!: Command to place oars in the rowlocks ready for use. Cf. oars! boat oars! toss oars! trail oars!

Ship of State: This frequently-quoted analogy originated in Plato's "Republic" (4th century BCE) where he likens civil governance to command of a naval vessel. The metaphor reappears in an English translation of Niccolò Machiavelli's *The Prince* (1675) and again in Henry Wadsworth Longfellow's nationalistic poem "The Building of the Ship" (1850), which contained the popular "Sail on, O Ship of State! Sail on, O UNION, strong and great!" (In 1941, President Roosevelt sent this stanza to Prime Minister Churchill, saying it expressed the spirit of the British people in the face of Nazi aggression. Churchill had it printed as a broadside which he and Roosevelt signed as attestation of the critical alliance between Britain and the U.S. during World War II.)

Ship-of-the-line: Formerly, a warship large enough to engage in fleet battles. In the 18th century these ranged from third-rate with at least 64 guns, to first-rate with at least 100. Occasionally a fifth-rate would join the line of battle, but was rarely of much use in that service. (*See* Warship rating.)

Ship over: USN term for re-enlistment.

Ship-rigged: Carrying three masts, each provided with three yards, spreading square-sails.

Ship route: A path across the sea that is regularly used by vessels. *See also* sea lane, seaway.

Ship size: *See* size escalation.

Ship-sloop: In the 19th century, a sloop-of-war would normally by captained by a commander. If, however, a post-captain was placed in command, the vessel would be up-rated to ship.

Ship water: To receive water over the side of a boat or ship, often due to wave action. Cf. ship green water.

Ship will adjust: A term in naval gunfire support indicating that the ship can see the target and does not require a spotter.

Shipboard: The situation of being on or in a seagoing vessel.

Shipborne: Transported by ship.

Shipbreaking: Dismantling and scrapping a vessel that is obsolete or unfit for service.

Shipbuilder: One whose occupation is that of a shipwright or naval architect.

Shipbuilding: The design, construction, and launching of ships.

Shiphandling: Refers to managing the effects of controllable and uncontrollable forces on a ship while on the high seas or in constricted waters, and while docking, and mooring; always with due consideration of the laws governing heavy bodies in motion. The uncontrollable forces to be considered are winds, currents, seas, tides, and draft, while those that can be controlled are propellers, rudders, thrusters, mooring lines, anchors, and tugboats.

Modern shiphandling has had to adapt to substantial changes. The average size of vessel has vastly increased, but not all ports have been enlarged. Until recently, the only large vessels were capital ships and passenger liners. Being better manned and more powerfully engined than many modern monsters, they were safely handled with primitive communications and limited assistance. Much of the former charm and likeable characteristics of those ships is now missing, but every new floating object presents a challenge. Large container ships with towering deck cargo cannot be treated the same way as small general cargo ships. Huge car carriers, gigantic cruise ships, and mammoth tankers require special attention. Colossal aircraft carriers demand meticulous handling.

Good shiphandling is a combination of art, science, and skill; with competency depending on thorough understanding of the physical principles involved, and sufficient experience at sea to be able to evaluate rapidly changing conditions. The proficient shiphandler must have both, plus inborn sensitivity and perception. Today, unfortunately, the masters and officers of large merchantmen seldom have the opportunity or necessity of handling their own ships in confined waters. Likewise, due to career tracking, many naval officers claim to be so overwhelmed by ever more complex technology that they have insufficient time to develop shiphandling skills. In consequence some warship captains, especially those promoted from a specialty, feel insecure docking on their own and rely on tugboats and pilots — assistance that might be unavailable at times of crisis.

Shipload: The quantity of goods and cargo that will bring a vessel to its appropriate load line.

Shipman: The ancient name for a mariner.

Shipmaster: An officer in command of, or certificated to command, a merchant vessel. Also sea captain.

Shipmate: Any person with whom one is sailing or has sailed, especially one who is a close friend or good colleague.

Shipment: [1] A quantity of goods shipped or consigned. [2] The act of shipping commodities.

Shipowner: A person who owns one or more ships.

Shipper: A person or business purchasing transportation for goods or commodities.

Shipping: [1] The business of transporting cargo or passengers by sea. [2] Having to do with ships. [3] Collectively, the vessels in a given body of water.

Shipping container: A large rectangular or square box, opening on one side for the loading of cargo and designed to withstand rough intermodal transfers between road, rail, and sea transport. Because container sizes are defined by the International Standards Organization (ISO), they are sometimes known as Isotainers. Standard container lengths are 20', 40', 45', 48', and 53' but the first two are by far the most common. Capacity was originally defined in terms of "Twenty-foot equivalent units" (teu) but "Forty-foot equivalent units" (1 feu = 2 teu) are rapidly becoming the standard shipping measurement.

Shipping lanes: Regulated pathways to ensure that vessels operating in congested waters can avoid collisions. As early as 1855 USN Lieutenant Mathew Maury recommended the separation of eastward and westbound transatlantic traffic. This suggestion even-

tually developed into a complex international system of designated routes (cf. Traffic separation).

Ship's agent: A person or company authorized by owners to manage their vessel's needs and demands while in a foreign port. The agent may be responsible for berthing and docking, will contract for provisions at the chandlery, also arrange freight, towage, minor repairs, and the hiring of officers and crew as required.

Ship's biscuit or bread: *See* hard tack.

Ship's company: The formal name referring to the entire crew of a vessel or naval shore establishment (in the USN, excluding the airwing). Also troops.

Ship's gender: *See* Gender.

Ship's husband: [1] Formerly, the dockyard worker in charge of repairs to a specific ship. [2] A representative of the owners who travels with and in a merchantman exercising authorities and responsibilities as dictated by the country of registration.

Ships in English metaphor: With so many English-speaking seafarers, it was inevitable for phrases and idioms involving ships to creep into common usage. "Spoil the ship for a ha'porth of tar" and "Don't give up the ship" are discussed separately, but other common metaphors include "Run a tight ship," which implies the enforcement of rigid discipline; and "Ship them off," which refers to getting rid of someone by sending them away. "When my ship comes in" means anticipating a time when anticipated fortune materializes; while to "Leave a sinking ship" or to "Jump ship" is to abandon a failing enterprise.

Ship's names: *See* naming and reptiles.

Ship's papers: Documents that every merchantman is required to carry under International Law. These include certificates of registry and clearance, charter party, manifest, logs, articles, bills of lading, and the like. In time of war a passport or sea letter will also be required.

Ships that pass in the night: Attempts to pass this off as a nautical metaphor are misguided. The phrase originated in "Tales of a Wayside Inn," the 1863 narrative poem by Henry Wadsworth Longfellow which reads: "Ships that pass in the night, and speak to each other in passing; Only a signal shown, and a distant voice in the darkness; So on the ocean of life we pass and speak to one another; Only a look and a voice, then darkness again and silence" ["The Theologian's Tale," part III, Elizabeth iv].

Ships versus buildings: Landspeople and seafarers use differing terminologies for their physical environment. Some examples are:

• Ceiling	=	Overhead (US) or Deckhead (Brit.)
• Corridor	=	Passageway (US) or Alley (Brit.)*
• Floor	=	Deck
• Stairs	=	Ladder
• Toilet	=	Head (US) or Heads (Brit.)

Since World War II the main corridor in RN ships has been known colloquially as The Burma Road, after the strategic supply route from Lashio in Burma to Kunming in China; and the main corridor in a USN nuclear submarine is called the peeway.

- Wall = Bulkhead
- Window = Port (US) or Scuttle (Brit.)

Shipshape: In good order, neat, clean and trim. *See* Bristol Fashion.

Shipway: [1] The structure that supports a ship during its construction. [2] A navigable canal.

Shipworm: Any of various wormlike mollusks which burrow into the submerged timbers of ships, piers, or wharfs (*see* teredo).

Shipwreck: [1] The loss or destruction of a vessel, usually by collision, fire, grounding, or storm. [2] The remains of a vessel so destroyed.

Shipwright: [1] One who builds and launches wooden ships. [2] A ship's carpenter skilled in the repair of wooden or steel vessels.

Shipyard: A place where ships are built or repaired.

Shiver my timbers!: This piratical expletive, although popular with playwrights and comedians, was probably never used at sea.

Shoal: [1] An area of shallow water, with substantially less clearance than the surrounding area, forming an offshore hazard to surface navigation. [2] A submerged sandbank or reef visible at low tide. [3] To become shallower [4] A group of swimming fish. (The first three are pronounced shole, from Old English sceald = shallow; the fourth is pronounced skool, from Middle Dutch shōle = school.)

Shoaling: [1] The increase in height and decrease in length of a wave as it approaches a shoal. [2] Becoming shallower.

Shod: Said of an anchor whose flukes are so mud-covered that they will not dig in to hold.

Shoe: [1] An anti-chafing fitting on a minesweeper or other ship's bow from which paravanes are towed. [2] A strut between keel and sternpost. [3] An outboard element of the cutwater. [4] A wooden piece fitting over an anchor fluke to protect the ship's side. [5] To put such a piece in position. [6] A sabot.

Shoot: [1] To discharge a weapon. [2] To send forth a missile. [3] To ignite an explosive charge. [4] To acquire momentum and luff to coast into the wind. [5] To take a sighting with a sextant. [6] To put out fishing nets. [7] The interval between strokes when rowing.

Shoot!: [1] RN command to discharge ordnance or launch missiles (the USN term is fire!). [2] Colloquialism for "say what you want to say."

Shoot Charlie Noble: When the galley funnel (Charlie Noble) became clogged with soot, the cook was frequently given a pistol and ordered to fire a blank shot inside the stack so that the blast would shake down the obstruction.

Shore: [1] The narrow strip of land in immediate contact with the sea. [2] To brace something. [3] A beam used in shipbuilding or for temporary damage control.

Shore establishment: Any land-based naval facility.

Shore leave: RN term for permission to be relieved of all duties and be absent from a ship or shore establishment for less than 48 hours (the USN term is liberty); longer periods of authorized absence are termed leave in both services.

Shore patrol: A detail assigned to maintain discipline and assist local police deal with naval personnel while ashore.

Shore station: *See* shore establishment.

Shore-pay: Refers to the pay of an officer employed on land. *See* half-pay.

Shores of Tripoli: During the First Barbary War, U.S. naval agent William Eaton determined to seize the fortified city of Derna. His force consisted of Lieutenant Presley O'Bannon's Marine detachment of a sergeant and six privates, supplemented by Midshipman George Mann with four bluejackets, plus ninety Arab cavalry, about a hundred nondescript Egyptian mercenary infantry, sixty-seven "Christian adventurers," and a few Greek "cannoniers" equipped with an ancient field gun.

On 26th April 1805, after a grueling 600 mile (960 km) march across the Libyan desert, Eaton posted the Arabs on the shoreward side of the city, called for supporting fire from the USN brigs *Argus*, *Hornet*, and *Nautilus*, and ordered O'Bannon to attack. The ancient field gun was put out of action when its over-excited gunners shot away their only ramrod, and, without close fire-support, O'Bannon's attack stalled. Eaton rushed forward with the reserves, and together they renewed the assault, but Eaton was wounded and had to fall out. Then, as he later reported:

> Mr O'Bannon, accompanied by Mr Mann of Annapolis, urged forward with his Marines (and) Greeks ... passed through a shower of musketry ... took possession of the Battery, planted the American Flag upon its ramparts, and turned its guns upon the Enemy.... A little after four o'clock we had compleat possession of the town.

For six weeks, Eaton's motley force withstood massive attempts to retake the city. In recognition of this achievement, United States Marine officers and NCOs were "Authorized to carry Swords of the Mameluke Pattern." They proudly added "The Shores of Tripoli" to the Corps' colors and, later, to its hymn (*see* march music). But President Thomas Jefferson ungraciously disavowed Eaton's contribution, and blocked O'Bannon's captaincy, leading him to resign his commission. Later he was honored by having three destroyers named after him — DD-177 (1919), DD-450 (1942) and DD-987 (1978).

Shoreward: Towards the land.

Short-arm inspection: A visual medical scan of the genitals for venereal diseases (military and naval slang).

Short blast: A sounding of the ship's whistle lasting about one second (cf. prolonged blast).

Short-handed: With insufficient or less than normal crew.

Short-landed: Said of a cargo delivery that is less than the quantity shown on the manifest.

Short seas: Waves bunched closely together. Usually a warning that the bottom is shoaling.

Short-shipped: Said of cargo that could not be loaded as scheduled, due to unavailability or lack of space on board.

Short splice: A quick way of connecting two pieces of same-size cordage, but in such a way that the diameter of the splice is larger than that of the original cordage, preventing it from passing through a block or thimble. A long splice is more time-consuming, but overcomes the problem.

Short-stayed: Said of an anchor when its chain or cable has been taken in until it is nearly up-and-down with the anchor almost atrip but still gripping the bottom. This is the final phase before being aweigh, and the length of cable deployed is usually less than 1.5 times the depth of water.

Short ton: *See* ton.

Shorten Sail: [1] To reduce the number of sails set. [2] To reduce the sail area by reefing or furling.

Shot: [1] A solid projectile for discharge from a cannon or other weapon. [2] The aimed discharge of a missile. [3] The distance traveled by a missile. [4] USN term for a 15-fathom length of anchor chain or cable (the RN calls this a shackle of cable). [5] The union of two or more cables to form one long one.

Shot across the bows: This is another obviously-nautical phrase, derived from the practice of forcing another vessel to stop by firing a cannon ball to splash just in front of it. Now it is a colloquialism for an action intended to caution someone against unwanted moves.

Shot garland: A wooden frame to contain round shot, secured to the coamings and ledges round the hatchways of a ship. *See* shot trough, brass monkey.

Shot gauge: An instrument for measuring the diameter of round shot.

Shot grommet: A ring of rope used as a wad to hold a cannonball in place in the barrel of a gun.

Shot-hole: The opening made in a hull or timber by round shot or a bullet passing through.

Shot in the locker: Sailor slang for money in the purse or pocket.

Shot locker: A strongly-built locker to contain shot, usually in the hold.

Shot-plug: A tampion in the form of a cone tapered to fit cannon of any bore.

Shot-prop: A wooden support covered with tarred hemp, used to seal a shot-hole from the inside.

Shot rack: Iron rods fitted about the hatches and along the deck, to contain shot.

Shot trough: Wooden receptacle for cannon balls, placed on the gun-deck during action. *See* shot garland.

Shoulder board: One of a pair of stiffened cloth strips carrying badges of rank, worn between the shoulder and collar of officer's uniforms. Also shoulder strap.

Shoulder the anchor: Said when the cable is too short and the anchor is lifted by wave or tide allowing the vessel to drift.

Shove an oar in: An old naval expression meaning to break into someone else's conversation.

Shove off: To push away from a ship's side, dock, or pier.

Shove off!: A rude request to go away.

Shovel: In former naval use: [1] A copper implement for removing the charge from a smoothbore muzzle-loading cannon without damaging the cartridge. [2] To use such an implement.

Show a leg!: In sailing ship navies, shore leave was severely restricted for fear of desertion, so it was not unusual to allow women to visit husbands, sweethearts, or clients in their quarters. From time to time some of these "wives" would contrive to remain on board when the ship sailed, often with the tacit connivance of captain or officers, because women were useful for sewing, darning, and tending the wounded. Hence it became the practice, when rousting out the watch below, to order a leg to be hung or waved over the side of the hammock. If it was smooth and female, its owner was allowed to sleep on in peace. If male and hairy, he was unceremoniously tipped out to run topside for duty. (Also Shake a Leg.)

Show true colors: Wearing a foreign flag to allay suspicion while approaching an enemy has long been an accepted ruse de guerre, provided the proper ensign is raised and broken out before undertaking any hostile act. Nowadays, the phrase means that a crisis has forced someone to reveal their real attitude or personality. (*See also* bamboozle, false colors, flag verification.)

Shrapnel: A thin-skinned hollow projectile, filed with bullets or the like, that is split open by a fused explosive charge shortly before reaching the objective. The bullets then proceed towards the target with the same velocity as the shell had at the moment of being split, spreading out as they go. This effective anti-personnel weapon, essentially a long-range version of case or canister, was invented by British Army Lieutenant (later General) Henry Shrapnel in 1784, but was not formally accepted by the Army until 1803 and never officially used at sea.

Shroud: [1] One of the ropes or wires laterally supporting the masts of a sailing ship, forming a key component of standing rigging. [2] A protective casing around turbine or propeller blades. [3] One of the lines attaching a parachute canopy to its harness.

Shroud rope: Superior-quality rope for shrouds and stays, made from the finest Russian hemp.

Shuta: A small, thirty-oared Viking cargo vessel.

Sicily invasion: This island, strategically-located at the toe of Italy, has been the target of amphibious assault by Etruscans, Carthaginians, Greeks, Romans, Byzantines, Fatamids, Saracens, Normans, Angevins, French, Spanish, and others. But the 1943 invasion, code-named "Husky," would be larger than any of them could have imagined — larger, perhaps, than all of them combined. The landings were preceded by an airdrop and, altogether, more than 3,300 vessels ferried 80,000 soldiers, 600 tanks, 300 trucks, and 600 artillery pieces in the biggest amphibious operation ever undertaken — bigger even than the famous "D-Day" landings in Normandy a year later.

The Royal Italian Navy (Regia Marina) had four battleships, six cruisers, and ten destroyers within easy sailing distance of the island. Their bases were screened by British "Force H" with six battleships, two carriers, six cruisers, and twenty-four destroyers under Vice-Admiral Sir Algernon Willis.

The Western Task Force, under U.S. Vice-Admiral Kent Hewitt, sailed from Oran and Algiers, carrying four divisions of the U.S. Seventh Army. The Eastern Task Force, under British Admiral Sir Bertram Ramsey, left Tripoli and Alexandria, with three divisions of British Eighth Army and was joined at sea by a Canadian division and a Royal Marines Commando brigade, sailing from Britain under Rear-Admiral Philip Vian. Despite rough seas the landings went well, although high winds caused heavy casualties among the parachute and glider troops.

Sick bay: A warship's hospital, infirmary or first-aid station (merchantmen and passenger liners call such facilities the clinic or dispensary).

Sick call: A daily formation for those requiring medical attention. *See* binnacle list.

Sick leave: Exemption from duty due to illness.

Side: That part of a vessel's hull that extends lengthwise from stem to stern and vertically from gunwale to bottom.

Side-arms: [1] Personal weapons such as cutlass, bayonet, sword, or pistol carried on a belt or in a holster. [2] The assembly of tools used for cleaning and servicing a ship's cannon, including rammer, spunge, and wadhook.

Side echo: A phenomenon similar to ghosting which interferes with the signal received by a sonar or fathometer. Side echo also affects seismic surveying.

Side honors: Refers to the ceremonial greeting of senior officers and important visitors as they board and leave naval vessels. May include piping the side, sideboys, a guard of honor, band music, or gun salutes. *See* attend the side (USN), man the side (RN).

Side-keels: A pair of keels, placed on either side of the centerline of a ship's bottom. Used to give greater stiffness to small vessels.

Side lights: The green starboard and red port lights required by Rules of the Road.

Side port: A watertight doorway in a ship's hull.

Side tackle: *See* gun tackle.

Sideboys: This term applies to members of a warship's crew (of any age or sex) who line up at the gangway as a mark of respect for a senior officer or distinguished visitor coming aboard or disembarking (*see* piping the side). The number of sideboys is always even — junior officers are entitled to two, Comman-

ders and Captains four, Rear Admirals six, Vice Admirals and above eight.

• In the **Royal Navy,** the ceremony is invoked only for heads of state, naval or marine officers when in uniform, and foreign naval officers in uniform. No military, consular, or civil dignitaries are so honored, nor are naval officers in plain clothes.

• The **United States Navy**, has extended the courtesy to military, diplomatic, and consular officers, and to certain members of the legislative and executive branches of government. Those entitled to three or four ruffles and flourishes get eight sideboys, others six.

When a Marine detachment is embarked and involved in side ceremonies, it assembles separately from the sideboys (*see* side honors and rainbow sideboys).

Sidereal time: Time measured by the apparent diurnal (daily) motion of the stars.

Sideslip: The tendency of a vessel to slide away from its course due to the action of wind or current. *See* Leeway.

Sidewheeler: A steamship propelled by paddle wheels on either side of its hull.

Sierra: NATO phonetic notation for the letter "S."

Sight: [1] An accurate navigational observation of a heavenly body. [2] To aim a weapon. [2] to see something for the first time visually (not sonar or radar).

SIGINT: Signals intelligence.

Sign-off: Merchant term for the discharge and final payment of seamen at the end of a voyage or completion of their contracts. Also pay-off.

Sign-on: Merchant term for the signing of articles (contracts) by seamen before a voyage.

Signal: [1] A short message conveyed by flags, light flashes, electrical impulses, sound or radio waves, or other means. (*see* tables 8–10). [2] To send such a message.

Signal book: A book containing the code of signals, or in which signals are recorded. They are bound with metal, so as to sink in case of capture.

Signal bridge: Area on or near the navigating bridge equipped for visual communication, including flags and signal lamps. Not to be confused with the flag bridge.

Signal flare: A pyrotechnic flare of distinct color or character used as a signal. *See* parachute flare, star shell, very light.

Signal lamp: A visual signaling device, of which there are several types. [1] Small hand-held versions known as Aldis lamps. [2] Lights on the mastheads of ships. [3] More powerful ones mounted on pedestals. These larger ones use carbon arcs as their light source, and produce beams strong enough to communicate by line-of-sight to the horizon, even in conditions of bright sunlight. Communication beyond the horizon is also possible by illuminating cloud bases at night or by day.

Signalman: A naval job rating. Signalmen (who

may be female despite the title) stand watches on signal bridges to send and receive messages by signal lamp, semaphore, and flag hoist. They prepare and encode or decode headings and addresses, render passing honors to ships and boats, display ensigns and personal flags during salutes and colors, repair signal flags, pennants and ensigns, and perform as lookouts. As navigator's assistants, they take bearings, and recognize visual navigational aids. Both RN and USN have phased out this rating, with visual signaling transferred to a quartermaster.

Signals crossed: In the noise, excitement, and physical danger of sailing ship combat, a nervous signalman might assemble the message flags of a hoist in the wrong order (crossed), resulting in confusion, delay, or disaster. The phrase moved on shore as a metaphor for failure to properly understand or interpret someone's intentions.

Signature: [1] The distinctive acoustic, thermal, magnetic, or other non-acoustic signals emitted by a surface vessel or submarine that make it detectable and (possibly) identifiable. [2] The distinctive "ping" of a sonar. [3] The "fist" of a radio operator. [4] The pattern of a cloud formation (*see* Dvorak technique).

Silence!: [1] Formerly, a command requiring a USN gun-crew to face their weapon, and await further orders in silence. [2] Exclamation given by any member of a USN weapons team who observes a casualty requiring immediate attention.

Silent running: A condition of submarine operation involving noise minimization to avoid discovery by hostile sound detectors.

Sill: [1] The timber at the base of a dock or lock against which the gates shut and seal. The measurement from its upper edge to the surface represents the depth of water required to float a vessel in or out. [2] The horizontal lower element of the frame of a port or hatch. [3] A sea floor barrier of relatively shallow depth restricting water movement between basins. Formerly spelled Cill (now rare).

Silt: Fine sand or soft earthy mud deposited as sediment by the flow of water.

Silver thaw: Flaking ice falling from sails and rigging when heavy frost is followed by a sudden thaw.

Sin Bosun: RN slang for a chaplain.

Sindbad the Sailor: This principal character in *1001 Arabian Nights* is not actually a seaman, but a Baghdad merchant who acquires great wealth by going on seven adventurous and miraculous voyages.

- On the first, his ship's crew goes ashore and lights a fire, but the island turns out to be a giant whale, which sounds, leaving them floundering in the water.
- On the second, he encounters rocs — birds so powerful that they can lift an elephant — and steals their stash of diamonds.
- During his third voyage, Sindbad is kidnapped by dwarfs, almost eaten by a Cyclops, and attacked by an immense serpent.

- On the fourth, he escapes from cannibals, marries a king's daughter, and barely escapes being buried alive when she dies.
- Fantastic adventures continue on the fifth voyage, when his ship is sunk by vengeful rocs who dive-bomb it with boulders. Thrown into the water, he barely escapes being strangled by Sheik-al-Bahr (the Old Man of the Sea) who clings to his back and can only be shaken off after Sindbad makes him drunk.
- On his penultimate voyage, Sindbad is shipwrecked on an barren island, but builds a raft and sails away down a subterranean river to the fabulous country of Sarandib (*see* serendipity), whose king bestows great riches on him and sends gifts to the Caliph.
- Finally, the Caliph sends the traveler back to Sarandib with thanks and greetings, but he is captured by pirates and sold as a slave to an ivory merchant. However, he locates the fabled "Elephant's Graveyard," finds a mountain of tusks, buys his freedom, and returns to Baghdad wealthier than ever.

Sing out: To call or announce loudly.

Singing: Refers to the high-pitched chant of a leadsman calling out the sounding after each cast. An old rhyme is cited by Admiral Smyth in his *Sailor's Word-Book*:

> To heave the lead the seaman sprung
> And to the pilot cheerly sung
> By the deep, nine

Single-banked: [1] A small boat in which a single oarsman mans each thwart and oar. [2] A galley with one row of oars. [3] A vessel with one row of broadside guns on a main gun deck.

Single Up: To throw off or bring inboard all doubled sections of mooring line, leaving the vessel secured only by single lines preparatory to casting off altogether.

Single whip: A tackle using only one fixed block.

Singlestick: A wooden sword, used in weapons training and exercise.

Sink: To fall below the surface and descend to the bottom, to founder. From Old Teutonic sincan.

SINS: Ship's Inertial Navigation System. An all-weather dead-reckoning system.

Sinuate: [1] To wind in and out around a base course. [2] To bend or curve.

Siren: [1] An acoustical instrument designed to emit a wailing sound as a fog signal or warning. [2] In Greek mythology, any of several sea nymphs, part-woman and part-bird, whose seductive singing lures mariners to destruction on the rocks.

Sisal rope: Made from leaves of the Agave sisalana cactus, it is as strong as second-grade manila, but less flexible, durable, and resistant to wear and weather. Hence, it is not used for boat falls, slings, or any purpose where parting of the line might endanger life.

Sister: To strengthen a weak or broken element by securing another beside it.

Sister Ship Clause: A marine insurance provision,

confirming that the underwriters will accept responsibility if two ships owned by the same company collide.

Sister ships: Vessels built to the same design or under common ownership.

SITREP: Situation **rep**ort.

Sitting: *See* position of honor.

SIU: Seafarers International Union.

SIV: Special Interest Vessel.

Six-on-four: Reduced ration scale with six men receiving only enough food for four.

Sixty: *See* rule of sixty.

Size escalation: With global merchandise trade growing at phenomenal speed there is a boom in container shipping and each generation of vessel tends to be about twice the size of the one before. Panamax was followed by Post-Panamax, and then by Malaccamax. Vessels capable of carrying over 10,000 TEU (*see* shipping container) are already in service and 18–20,000 TEU capacity ships are on the drawing board.

SK: Storekeeper (USN enlisted rating). *See* SA.

Skag: A heavy chain thrown over the stern of a barge as a drag to steady the tow.

Skeg: [1] An extension of the keel under the propeller to support the sternpost. [2] Any of various underwater fins or projections serving to stabilize an object.

Skeld: A medium-sized 64-oared Viking cargo vessel.

Skeleton: The hull of a vessel without its plates or planking (cf. frame, skin).

Skids: The forerunner of davits. Used to support lifeboats while on board and to slide them to the side for launching. It has been claimed that the phrases "on the skids" and "skid row"—meaning to be descending to, or have reached, the depths of depravity or poverty—are analogies for the descent of a lifeboat. However, other sources suggest the term is a corrupt reference to the corduroy log pathway used to skid (drag) felled timber through the woods and bogs of northwest Canada and the United States. Unemployed lumbermen would often be reduced to sleeping and begging on this so-called "skid road."

Skiff: General term for shallow-draft boats small enough to be sailed, poled, or rowed by a single person.

Skilly: A thin, weak broth, consisting of oatmeal boiled in water with just enough meat to flavor it. Usually served to naval prisoners.

Skillygalee: A drink of sugar and oatmeal stirred into water. Reputed to reduce the cramps suffered by stokers and firemen working in hot engine spaces (but salt would probably have worked better).

Skim sweep: In naval mine warfare, a wire-sweep at a fixed depth over deep-laid mines to cut the moorings of those shallow enough to endanger the minesweepers themselves.

Skimmer: USN submariner slang for a surface sailor or ship.

Skin: The outer planks or plating of a vessel.

Skin-friction: Also known as viscous drag, is one of the four principal causes of resistance to movement through water. It is created by the skin of the hull rubbing against the boundary layer of the water it is moving through. Near the stem this layer is usually relatively thin and laminar, but it becomes progressively thicker and more turbulent as it flows towards the stern. Overcoming it takes energy which is subtracted from the power available to drive the vessel forward. *See also* eddy-resistance, parasitic drag, profile-drag, and wave-resistance.

Skip-bomb: To release an airborne bomb from such low altitude that it slides or bounces along the surface of the water to strike the target at or near the waterline.

Skipjack: A wooden sailboat 40–50 feet (12–15 m) long used to dredge oysters from Chesapeake Bay and now available for cruises there. It was precursor of the bugeye and descendant of the log canoe.

Skipper: [1] Familiar and informal name for a ship's captain. [2] The master of a small craft, yacht, or fisher boat. (Either from the Old English scip = ship, or the Dutch schipper = captain.)

Skirmish: A brief period of light combat, usually following a chance encounter, or to clear the way for a more serious engagement.

Skivvies: USN slang for underwear.

Skosh: USN term for being perilously close to minimum level (e.g., of fuel). From the Japanese sukoshi = little.

Skunk: NATO term for an unidentified radar contact.

Sky pilot: Naval slang for a chaplain (*see* Holy Joe, Sin Bosun, Padre).

Skylark: [1] Seaman's term for horseplay, fooling around, or engaging in noisy chatter. [2] Originally referred to a midshipman's game of follow-the-leader, climbing up to the skysails and sliding down the backstays. (From Anglo-Saxon sky = sky + lac = play.)

Skylight: [1] An area of ice translucent from below and thin enough for a submarine to push through. [2] A hatch with a (usually hinged) glass-paneled cover to admit light.

Skysail: [1] A small sail set above the royal on a square-rigged ship. [2] The trade name of a kite sail propulsion system.

Skyscraper: [1] A small triangular sail set above the skysail (cf. moonraker). [2] Jocular slang for an officer's full-dress cocked hat.

SL: Sea level.

Slack: [1] That part of a rope or sail which hangs loosely without tension. [2] To ease off a rope or line. [3] To shirk or be remiss in doing something. (Sometimes followed by "off.")

Slack water: The moment at which a reversing current or tide changes direction so that it has no motion (cf. turn).

Slam: To hit waves or swell with violent impact.

Slant: A change of wind direction, usually favorable.

Slatting: The flapping of sails when a vessel is almost becalmed.

Slave: [1] A machine under the direct control of another machine. [2] In hyperbolic radio-navigation, a station whose transmissions are controlled by a master station. [3] A person in enforced bondage.

Slave trade: Holding human beings as property has been a worldwide phenomenon for as long as humankind has been "civilized." For centuries, African kings, chiefs, and warlords captured members of rival tribes and sold them into slavery — northward across the Sahara Desert, southward through the Red Sea, and eastward over the Indian Ocean.

Then, in the fifteenth century, a westward route opened up to provide cheap labor for Portuguese plantations in the Atlantic islands (especially Madeira which became the largest sugar producer in the western world). After they colonized Brazil (1500) the Portuguese increased their purchases of African slaves, operating essentially as a state monopoly. By contrast, the Spanish introduced the "asiento" system which retained government control of the trade, but gave individual merchants exclusive licenses to import slaves into the South American colonies.

Late in 1562, English captain John Hawkins bought 300 slaves in West Africa and carried them to the West Indies where he traded them for hides, ginger, sugar, and pearls, making a profit of 12 percent on his investment. Other European countries were building slave-dependent colonial empires in North America and the Caribbean and soon Denmark, France, the Netherlands, and Sweden joined Portugal and Spain as Britain's competitors for the inhumane but profitable trade.

Their burgeoning requirements changed trans–Atlantic slave traffic from government monopolies to private enterprise and turned the trade from a steady flow into a virtual torrent, beginning the worst and longest-lasting maritime crime against humanity (*see* middle passage and triangular trade).

Finally, after almost two-and-a-half centuries, the British realized (in the words of Prime Minister William Grenville) that the trade was "contrary to the principles of justice, humanity and sound policy" and Parliament passed a bill to abolish the purchase and sale of slaves (but not the institution of slavery itself). A special squadron of the Royal Navy was charged with enforcing the Act, under which British vessels caught transporting slaves were fined £100 per head — amounting to as much as £70,000 for a full load — this was such a substantial amount in the early 19th century that most slaver captains ordered their krumen to throw the iron-fettered slaves overboard as soon as a naval vessel hove into view (without evidence, there was no fine). Finally, in 1833 Britain outlawed slavery throughout its Empire, but it was decades before other European nations followed suit.

The United States abolished the slave trade in March 1807, but illegal importation continued overland, while ships continued to smuggle slaves into the South. In 1820, Congress passed a law making participation in the trade an act of piracy, punishable by death, but it was not strongly enforced. The British then asked for American cooperation in search and seizure, but Congress opposed this, not out of desire to continue the trade, but to preserve the principle of freedom of the seas. This U.S. refusal to enforce its own laws or cooperate with other nations allowed the slave trade to continue, and it was not until ratification of the Thirteenth Amendment on December 18, 1865, that it finally ended. The last Atlantic country to ban the trade was Brazil in 1888. However, the practice continues to the present day; *see* human trafficking.

Slaver: A ship or person engaged in the slave trade. Also Blackbirder.

SLBM: Submarine-launched ballistic missile.

Sled: A small and speedy towed target for surface gunnery practice.

Sleep: A well filled and quiet sail is said to "sleep."

Sleeping on watch: Considering that this serious offense could endanger the ship and the lives of all on board, the penalties specified in the 17th century Admiralty Black Book were surprisingly lenient, giving a malefactor three chances, before facing potentially lethal punishment. A first offender was merely humiliated by having a bucket of seawater poured over his head, and a second incident only resulted in his hands being tied over his head while a bucketful of water was poured down each sleeve.

After a third offense, the penalty was a bit more severe, the culprit being tied to the mast with heavy weights attached to his arms and left there for as long as the captain deemed appropriate. However, a fourth offense brought what was essentially a death sentence. The perpetrator was placed in a covered basket, given a loaf of bread, a flask of ale, and a sharp knife, and slung below the bowsprit. An armed marine was posted to ensure he could not clamber back on board, leaving him with three alternatives — he could starve to death, slice his veins with the knife, or cut the basket loose to drown in the sea.

Sleeve: [1] A fabric tube towed by an aircraft as an anti-aircraft practice target. Also drogue. [2] The narrows of a channel. [3] The Strait of Dover (obsolete in English, but still used by the French in La Manche).

Sleeve insignia: *See* breast and sleeve insignia.

SLEP: Service Life Extension Program (USN).

Slew: [1] To turn a ship or traverse a gun rapidly. [2] To yaw, especially when being towed. [3] To force a vessel between adjoining ice-floes. Also slue.

Slick: Any calm patch of water such as that caused by [1] oil on the surface. [2] a vessel's drift to leeward. [3] the wake of a passing ship. [4] lack of wind.

Slide: That part of a gun mount that supports the weapon and allows it to move.

Slime: Thin glutinous mud or ooze often found on the floor of channels.

Sling: [1] A looped strap, or bight of rope, used to lift heavy items. [2] A single load of cargo being moved by sling. [3] A short strap with a string on either side, used by hand to give impetus to a small missile such as a stone. [4] A strap of cloth used to support a broken limb.

Slip: [1] The difference between the theoretical and actual motion induced by a propeller. [2] To release the anchor by unbuckling its chain — only done in emergency since both chain and anchor will be lost. [3] The space or berth for a vessel between two piers or jetties. [4] A slipway.

Slip the cable: To die (lower deck slang).

Slipstream: The air driven backward by a rotating aircraft propeller.

Slipway: A ramp sloping towards the water for launching ships or hauling them up for repair.

SLOC: Sea line of communication.

Sloop: [1] World War II, a small British convoy escort armed with one or two 4-inch guns and depth charges. [2] Formerly, a small, single-masted, fore-and-aft-rigged sailing vessel. (Dutch sloep.)

Sloop-of-war: Small and nimble 18th century unrated fighting vessel with from one to three masts and twelve to twenty guns on the weather deck. Probably the most ambiguous class ever named, since the term included brigs, brigantines, ketches, ships and snows, as well as actual sloops. In the late 19th century sloops-of-war evolved into gun vessels.

Slop chest: [1] Originally a ship's compartment for storing clothing, bedding and personal items for issue or sale to naval or merchant seamen. In the seventeenth century, impressed seamen had only the clothes they were wearing at the time of seizure, while vagabonds and felons often came aboard in disgusting rags. In 1623, the Navy Slop Office was established to provide "clothinge to avoyde nastie beastliness by diseases and unwholsomme ill smells in everye ship." [2] Today, the slop chest has evolved into an on board commissary or retail store for the same purpose. Goods are duty free, so the chest is locked before coming into port. Navigation Laws of the United States (Title 46:11103) allow a 10 percent mark-up and require every merchant vessel to be:

... provided with a slop chest which shall contain a complement of clothing for the intended voyage for each seaman employed, including boots or shoes, hats or caps, under clothing and outer clothing, oiled clothing, and everything necessary for the wear of a seaman; also a full supply of tobacco and blankets.

Slop chute: An inclined channel hung over a ship's side for the disposal of garbage clear of the hull. Known as a gash chute in the RN.

Slop tank: A container for the storage of oily waste pending disposal.

Slope: To bring down the edges of an awning, so that they shed rainwater, which might otherwise form pools to overload and tear the canvas.

Slops: [1] Unappetizing watery food or soup. [2] cheap, ready-made clothing, bedding, etc. issued or sold to sailors. (Pursers officially received 5 percent on the sale of slops, but many milked the system by charging far more than the fixed price and even "selling" slops to dead men in order to pocket the commission.) [3] Loose fitting outer garments such as a smock or coveralls. (From Old English oferslop meaning a surplice, via Middle English sloppe referring to a loose-fitting shapeless blouse, frequently worn by seamen before uniforms were issued.) [4] Archaic, wide baggy pantaloons, trousers, or breeches.

Slot: The space between jib and mainsail. Wind passing through this opening creates a pressure differential across the mainsail, urging the ship ahead.

Slough: A side channel, backwater, bayou, or marsh (pronounced sloo).

Slow match: Slightly twisted hemp rope soaked in lime water and saltpeter. It burns at a rate of about four inches (100 mm) an hour and was formerly used to ignite the charge of gunpowder weapons. *See* gun firing, linstock, portfire, quick match.

SLP: Seaward launch point.

SLQ: Electronic Warfare System.

Slue: To turn something such as a boom, cask, gun, spar, or even an entire ship on its axis without moving it out of its place. (Also slew and pronounced sloo.)

Slush: [1] Grease and fat skimmed off the kettles in a ship's galley. [2] An oily preservative applied to wire, line, or standing rigging. [3] Semi-frozen seawater which is viscous but not solid.

Slush fund: A perquisite of the ship's cook was to keep all the slush he could skim off the kettles of boiling salted meat. When he had gathered enough, he would sell the better quality to the purser for making candles. Then he sold the poorer grease to the bos'n as a protective coating for spars. In the course of a voyage the cook would amass a useful sum of money which he called his slush fund. Today, in civilian life, the term refers to money secretly set aside for political bribery.

SM: Signalman (USN).

Smack: A single-masted, cutter-rigged, fishing vessel.

Small anchor: *See* best bower.

Small arms: Weapons small enough to be carried and controlled by a single user.

Small arms salutes: These honor individuals. [1] Sword salutes probably go back to the Crusades when the cruciform hilt would be raised to the lips and kissed, after which the point would be thrust into the ground so that it could not easily be used. Nowadays the weapon is merely lowered in submission. [2] Rifle salutes can be of several kinds. The most ceremonial is "present arms" in which the rifle is held vertically in front of the body, with the muzzle upward and the trigger guard forward. Less formal are salutes with the weapon in the "shoulder," "slope," "trail," or "order arms" positions.

Small-craft advisory: A radio message or visual display (red pennant by day; red light over white at night) alerting small or underpowered vessels that unfavorable or dangerous sea conditions are forecast.

Small helm: Said when — thanks to good seamanship and sail-handling — only minor movement of the wheel or tiller is required to keep a ship on course.

Small stores: Soap, needles and thread, tobacco, spices, razors, brushes, and the like, issued to the crew through their mess-cooks.

Small stowage: Refers to goods of size and shape that will fit into gaps between beams or spaces between cargo.

Small stuff: Cordage less than 2.5 centimeters (1 inch) in diameter used for light jobs such as whipping, serving, or seizing.

Smart money: Nowadays this term refers to knowledgeable investment or betting on "sure things." In the 17th century, however, the word smart was synonymous with pain or agony, and the term referred to the pension paid for wounds acquired during active naval service. This original meaning lives on in legal terminology, where "smart money" still means punitive or exemplary damages.

Smartly!: Nautical command to be quick.

Smasher: Sailing ship seaman's slang for a carronade.

SMG: Speed made good.

Smoke flare: A pyrotechnic device producing colored smoke as a daylight distress signal (*see* table 10).

Smoker: An informal shipboard gathering with entertainment such as boxing, movies, comic skits, etc.

Smokesail: A small canvas hoisted to deflect smoke from the galley away from the quarterdeck.

Smokescreen: A dense mass of fumes laid down to conceal a vessel, fleet, or convoy.

Smokestack: A tall chimney or pipe through which the exhaust fumes of a steam or diesel powered vessel are discharged. Also funnel.

Smoking lamp: The fire hazard aboard a wooden warship laden with combustibles and gunpowder was tremendous. At least as early as the 16th century, when tobacco came into widespread use, navies prohibited smoking except at designated times and, usually, in or near the galley or forecastle. In the U.S. Navy the area was indicated by a special "smoking lamp." When this was lit smoking was allowed; when it was out, it was not. Indeed, since it was generally forbidden to carry matches, it was impossible to ignite a pipe or cigar unless the lamp was alight. The physical artifact is long gone from shipboard, but it survives in the phrases "The smoking lamp is lighted" or "The smoking lamp is out" to indicate when the crews of modern USN warships may light up. The equivalent RN term is spitkid.

Smoking sponson: designated smoking area aboard aircraft carriers, usually right below the flight deck on the exterior of the ship's hull. A great place to catch up on scuttlebutt.

Smooth sea: Wind-Sea condition 2 on the Douglas Scale, with waves defined as long, low and smooth, between 10 and 50 cms (4" to 20") high.

Smoothbore: Any firearm the inside of whose barrel is without rifling.

Smother: To extinguish or deaden a fire, usually by blanketing it with foam to cut off its oxygen supply.

Smuggle: [1] To avoid payment of excise tax or duty by bringing goods secretly into a country. [2] To surreptitiously take something somewhere.

Snake: [1] To rig netting on lifelines to prevent objects falling overboard. [2] To wrap a small line around a larger one (cf. worm). [3] A long flexible wire used for clearing drains.

Snake eaters: USN slang for special forces personnel.

Snap hook: *See* safety hook.

Snaphaunce: An early firearm similar to a musket.

Snatch block: A single-sheaved block with a hinged side which can be opened to accept a bight without having to thread the whole length of the line.

Sneer: To carry too much canvas and overstrain the standing rigging.

Snekkjur: A sailed and oared Nordic raiding longboat that could be beached for assault landings or rowed far inland up rivers. Had ten to twenty oars on each side, and carried 60 to 120 warriors. These speedy oceangoing vessels could beat to windward and carry enough provisions for extended voyages. The name means serpent.

Snib: Another name for the dog (locking handle) on a watertight door .

Snipes: USN slang for engineering crew members (cf. Black Gang).

SNLR: Services no longer required. The RN equivalent of a USN bad conduct discharge.

Snore: To make good progress while sailing on a comfortable reach with a fair and steady wind.

Snorkel: [1] A retractable tube which allows a diesel-engined submarine to ventilate and run its engines while cruising slightly below the surface. [2] A breathing tube used while swimming face-down in the water. [3] To use such a tube. (German schnorchel = air-intake.)

Snorkers: RN slang for sausages.

Snorting: RN term for snorkeling.

Snotty: RN derogatory slang for a midshipman (also Snottie).

Snow: A large European 17th–18th century sailing vessel, rigged like a brig but with a trysail mast just abaft the mainmast.

Snowmast: *See* trysail mast.

Snub: [1] To slow down and stop a vessel by letting out only enough chain for the anchor to drag. [2] To slow down a running rope by taking a half turn around a cleat and easing it out. [3] A short length of elastic material used as a shock absorber on a mooring line.

Snug down: Prepare for a storm by taking in sail and lashing loose gear.

Snug harbor: A well-sheltered anchorage.

So!: Command to cease hauling when a rope has reached its required position.

SOA: [1] Speed of advance. [2] Sustained operations ashore.

Soe Orm: This amphibious sea monster was described by Olaus Magnus, Roman Catholic Archbishop of Uppsala in Sweden, in his book *Historia de Gentibus Septentrionalibus* (*History of the Northern Peoples*) published at Rome in 1555:

> Those who sail up along the coast of Norway to trade or to fish, all tell the remarkable story of how a serpent of fearsome size, 200 feet long and 20 feet wide, resides in rocks and caves outside Bergen. On bright summer nights this serpent leaves its cavern to eat calves, lambs and pigs, or it swims out into the sea and feeds on cuttle (fish), lobsters, crabs and similar marine animals. It has ell (forty-five inch) long hair hanging from its neck, sharp scales dark brown in color, and flaming red eyes. It attacks vessels, grabs and swallows people, as it lifts itself up like a column from the water.

SOF: Special Operations Force.

Sofar: Sound Fixing And Ranging.

Soft eye: An eye-splice made without the metallic thimble.

Soft tack: Slang for fresh bread (cf. hard tack).

Solar day: The time between two successive transits of the sun.

Solar ship: Vessel placed in an Egyptian Pharaoh's tomb for his voyage to the sun. *See* Egyptian naval architecture.

Solas: *See* International Convention for the Safety of Life at Sea.

Soldier: A person having enlisted to serve and fight in an army.

Soldier on: To persist steadfastly in executing a task.

Soldiering: Seaman's slang for malingering, or shirking while pretending to work.

Soldier's wind: Wind blowing from abeam on either side, making it so easy to sail in either direction that even a soldier (the ultimate landsman) could do it.

Sole: The inside deck of a ship, especially the floor of a cabin.

Soleplate: *See* bedplate.

Solomon Gundy: Seafarer's slang for salmagundi.

Solstice: Either of the two times of the year when the sun reaches its maximum declination (cf. equinox).

Soma: A Japanese trading junk.

Somali Current: A prominent surface current in the northern Indian Ocean. During the northeast monsoon it flows southward, joining the north Equatorial Current and discharging into the equatorial Countercurrent. During the southwest monsoon it develops into an intense surface flow, fed from the South Equatorial Current and flowing along the eastern coast of the Horn of Africa, part of it going along the Arabian Peninsula as the East Arabian Current. During its northward phase the Somali Current is associated with strong upwelling near Ras Hafun, forming an eddy with a diameter of about 500 km known as the Great Whirl.

The *Somers* Incident: After being dismissed from university during his freshman year, Philip Spencer, son of the Secretary of War, obtained an appointment as acting midshipman aboard the frigate USS *John Adams*, but was soon forced to resign, charged with dereliction of duty and drunkenness. Perhaps due to his father's political influence, he was reinstated and assigned to the brig USS *Somers*, Commander Alexander Mackenzie.

In September 1842, *Somers* set sail on a training mission carrying a large number of volunteer apprentices (young officer candidates sent directly aboard for hands-on training). During the voyage an informant reported that Spencer had approached some of the crew saying he had a fancy to seize the brig, sail her to the Caribbean and become a pirate. Mackenzie confronted the 18 year old who tried to pass it off as a joke, but the captain ordered him chained hand and foot on the quarterdeck where the officer of the deck could keep him under observation.

Next day a topmast crashed to the deck, and Mackenzie labeled it an act of sabotage by supporters of Spencer's potential mutiny. Although there was no evidence against them, he had Spencer's friends boatswain's mate Samuel Cromwell and seaman Elisha Small arrested and put in irons. He then noticed the crew exchanging "suspicious glances"— which may have been due to fear and confusion — so ordered his officers to arm themselves and issue pistols and cutlasses to the petty officers.

On 30th November, the brig's officers were ordered to assemble in the wardroom. No formal court-martial was held; the three defendants were not present, nor were they informed they were being tried. Thirteen witnesses were called, but none gave any concrete evidence, except the original informant and he only mentioned Spencer. However, according to the brig's log, the officers ruled that all three "were decidedly Guilty, and that the safety of the vessel required that they be immediately put to death." Spencer insisted Cromwell and Small were innocent, but Mackenzie ordered the executions carried out. The corpses hung at the yardarms all afternoon, but after dinner, were cut down and buried at sea.

Somers reached New York City 13 days later, and the incident created an instantaneous adverse reaction. In a pamphlet entitled "The Cruise of the *Somers*," famous author and naval historian James Fenimore Cooper charged that Mackenzie, "in an hysterically paranoid state of mind," had executed three innocent men for a mutiny that existed only in his own unbalanced mind. A naval court of inquiry exonerated the commander, but — fearing Spencer's influential family might lay charges for murder in civilian court — he requested and was granted a full court-martial. On 31st March 1843, the court handed down its findings: The charges of Conduct Unbecoming an Officer and Cruelty and Oppression of Crew were dismissed, while three counts each of Murder, Oppression, and Illegal Punishment were declared "Not proven."

In October 1845 the United States Navy opened its school at Annapolis, Maryland, to train young midshipmen in a formal academic setting. It is generally accepted that this was a direct result of the *Somers* incident having raised doubts about the wisdom of sending untrained officer candidates directly to sea.

Son of a gun: Not infrequently one of the women visitors to a warship would find herself pregnant, with no idea which of the crew was the father. Birth normally took place between two cannon, one of which might be fired to encourage a difficult delivery. Since the child would certainly have been conceived on the gundeck, and because seamen often referred to genitals as their armament, it was natural to call it the "son of a gun" as a synonym for "son of a whore."

Sonar: This acronym of **So**und **Na**vigation and **R**anging refers to a system for the detection of underwater objects by reflected sound (cf. asdic). The operational mode can be "active" (pinging) or "passive" (listening). Several mass strandings of cetaceans have occurred simultaneously in time and space with naval exercises using mid-frequency active sonar. This relationship could be causal rather than coincidental and, before starting an active sonar search, it is now standard USN operating procedure for surface vessels to mount visual lookouts, trained to spot marine mammals with high-powered binoculars (*see* beaked whales).

Sonar dome: A streamlined, watertight enclosure that provides protection for a sonar transducer, sonar projector, or hydrophone and associated equipment, while offering minimum interference to sound transmission and reception by reducing the effects of turbulence, wave slam, and minor collision. Early versions were keel-mounted, made of steel-reinforced "egg box" construction, but they have now evolved into high performance lightweight shells, bow-mounted, relying on the structural and acoustic properties of advanced fiber composites.

Sonar gap: An area astern of a vessel where the cavitation and wake left by the vessel's own propulsion system impedes the ability of hull-mounted sonar to detect any hostile vessel which may be following behind. *See* baffle zone.

Song of the Seabees: USN Construction Battalions have their own song, written in 1943 with words by Sam M. Lewis to music by Peter de Rose. The original wartime text made specific reference to Pearl Harbor; two verses of an updated and less specific version are:

We're Seabees of the Navy
We can build and we can fight
We'll pave the way to victory
And guard it day and night

No matter what our mission
we'll uphold our proud tradition
We're Seabees of the Navy
Bees of the Seven Seas.

Sonobuoy: An expendable, air-dropped, floating, sonar-type device that detects submarines, or underwater sound emitted by surface vessels, and radio-transmits collected data for evaluation.

SOP: Standard operating procedure.

SOPA: Senior officer present afloat.

Sortie: [1] A rapid outward movement of invested troops to attack their besiegers. [2] A combat mission flown by a single aircraft. [3] A naval force setting out from port.

SOS!: Radio (Morse code) distress signal internationally agreed in 1908 to replace the former CQD. Although commonly believed to represent "save our souls" the letters have no significance, having been chosen because three dots, followed by three dashes and another three dots, are easy to remember and transmit. *See also* table 10.

SOSUS: Sound **su**rveillance **s**ystem.

Sough: An ancient and poetical term for the murmuring and moaning noise of wave and wind.

Soul ships: Ethereal vessels that were believed to hover off the coast of Brittany, hoping to rescue the souls of recently-deceased seamen and carry them westward to paradise in the fabulous Islands of the Blessed (cf. Fiddler's Green). Sailing-ship mariners in that vicinity sighted them as frequently as they saw sea serpents or mermaids.

Souls (of sea creatures): Many cultures believed that animals had souls and took great pains to placate them. Greenlanders were always careful to avoid breaking the skulls of their seal harvest, piling them next to their front doors to placate the creatures' souls and ensure they would not warn living seals to stay away from the coast. When the natives of Sainte Marie Island (north of Madagascar) hunt young whales they beg the mother to forgive them, explaining they only kill out of necessity, and asking her to sound so that she will not see the actual slaughter. The Huron, Ottawa, and Kwakiutl Indians of Canada believe the souls of dead fish will come back to life, so they never burn or discard the bones, but throw them back into the sea or river to ensure the resurrected fish will return next year.

Sound: [1] To emit noise as a call or summons; sound the bugle. [2] To announce by means of noise; sound the alarm (Middle English soun = noise). [3] To measure the liquid in a tank or ship's bilge. [4] To test the depth or quality of the seabed by leadline or any other means: (Middle English sundgyrd = measuring stick). [5] To dive or plunge downward as a whale or other marine mammal (Middle English sund = sea).

[6] A narrow passage, usually between a mainland and an island and wider than a channel, connecting two bodies of water (Scandinavian sund = channel). [7] In good condition; free from defect, damage or decay; "a sound timber"; "the ship is sound" (Old English gesund = in good shape).

Sound Fixing and Ranging: A system that allows two or more shore stations to locate an underwater signal by triangulation. *See also* oceanic sound channel.

Sound off: [1] To call out one's name or otherwise respond to a military roll call (mainly U.S.). [2] To speak freely or frankly, especially to complain. [3] to exaggerate or boast.

Sound out: This phrase, meaning to inquire discretely or cautiously into the feelings or opinions of a person, is clearly derived from the nautical use of a weighted line to determine the depth and nature of the sea bed.

Sound-powered: Said of telephones activated by vocalization. A transducer converts sound pressure from the user's voice into a minute electrical current, which is converted back to sound by a transducer at the receiving end. They are used extensively in warships because they need no external power source or internal battery, cannot be picked up by hostile listeners, and allow communication between key locations during power-outages.

Sound signals: Depending on their length, all vessels are required by Colregs to carry specified forms of sound and/or light signaling equipment, to be used only when they are within sight of each and are meeting or crossing another. Table 9 gives a brief list of signals concerning powered vessels in international waters, but Colregs are lengthy and complex, so readers wanting more detail should consult one of the many relevant websites (for example, that of the U.S. Coast Guard at www.navcen.uscg.gov/mwv/navrules).

Sound Surveillance System: During the Cold War, the timely detection of undersea threats was a high priority. Starting in the early 1950s the Atlantic and Pacific oceans were monitored by a system of bottom-mounted high-gain receivers connected by undersea cables to facilities on land (shore-based monitoring stations are less prone to interference from foul weather and ambient or self-generated noise). The arrays were installed primarily on continental slopes and seamounts at locations optimized for undistorted long-range acoustic propagation along the oceanic sound channel. The relatively loud signature of a Soviet submarine could be detected and tracked across an entire ocean basin.

Eventually, with the help of information supplied by the Walker espionage ring, the Soviets learned about the arrays and how easily their submarines were being detected. Each generation of Soviet boats then became quieter and harder to find than its predecessor. Detection fell off dramatically and, to regain some of the acoustic advantage, the USN's integrated undersea surveillance system turned from long line arrays to individual hydrophones, each capable of detecting submarines in its immediate vicinity. The first such "Fixed Distributed System" was deployed in 1985. With the end of the Cold War, however, SOSUS was gradually phased out, although remaining segments are still used for oceanic research.

Sounding: [1] The act of measuring depth or examining the bottom with leadline, echosounder, or other instrument. [2] The depth of the sea bottom as so determined. [3] The height of liquid in a tank or bilge. [4] Said of a deeply diving whale (*see also* depth measurement).

Sounding line: A leadline.

Sounding rod: A long pole used to sound tanks or bilges.

Sounding tube: A pipe through which a sounding rod is lowered into a tank or bilge.

Soundings: Water shallow enough to be sounded with a standard 100-fathom deep sea line. This is referred to as "in soundings," while water beyond the 100-fathom limit is "off soundings."

Soundless: Water so deep that soundings cannot be taken by leadline. Formerly considered bottomless, but now easily measured.

South Atlantic current: An ocean current produced by the confluence of the warm and saline Brazil current and the cooler, less salty, Falklands Current, flowing eastward towards the Cape of Good Hope.

South Indian current: An easterly flow in the Indian Ocean, north of the West Wind Drift.

South Pacific current: An easterly flow in the South Pacific, north of the West Wind Drift.

South Seas: [1] Former name for the South Pacific. [2] Generic term for all waters south of the equator.

Southern Ocean: The southernmost waters of the World Ocean have traditionally been known to mariners as the Antarctic Ocean, the Great Southern Sea, or the South Polar Ocean. Geographers long disagreed on a northern boundary, while some contended they were merely the convergence of Pacific, Atlantic, and Indian Oceans. In 2000, however, the International Hydrographic Organization ended the arguments by naming the Southern Ocean the fourth-largest of five principal oceanic divisions. It completely surrounds Antarctica, extending from the coast to 60 degrees south latitude.

Southing: The distance actually made good in a southerly direction on any course which has a southerly component.

Southwester: [1] A gusty wind, gale, or storm coming from the south-west. [2] A waterproof foul-weather hat with a broad brim at the back. Pronounced "sow-wester."

Sovereignty: *See* territorial sovereignty.

SP: Shore Patrol (USN).

Space: Nautical term for a large room or compartment (e.g., machinery space). *See also* outer space.

Spade rudder: *See* underhung.

Span: A line made fast at both ends.

Spanish bowline: A knot with two loops into which a person can put their legs to be swayed between two ships or hauled up a mast.

Spanish burton: A burton with two single blocks in series.

Spanish fox: A single yarn twisted up tightly in a direction contrary to its natural lay and rubbed smooth. It makes a neat seizing, and is used for the ends of light standing rigging, and for small seizings generally.

Spanish Main: [1] Properly, the north-east coast of South America between the Orinoco River and Panama, plus adjacent Caribbean islands (main is an abbreviation of mainland). [2] Often (incorrectly) the Caribbean Sea.

Spanish march: To frogmarch by hustling a person forward while holding and lifting their arms from behind. Said to have been the way Caribbean pirates handled Spanish (and presumably other) captives.

Spanish mare: "Riding the Spanish mare" is an ancient nautical punishment that involved lashing the culprit to a boom and suspending it over the side, just above the waterline, so that he would be dipped into the sea with every roll of the ship. *See also* yardarm ducking.

Spanish reef: Derisory term for lowering the yards instead of reefing topsails. Considered by British sailors (usually incorrectly) to be the practice of lubberly Spaniards.

Spanish windlass: A small wooden device, turned by a marlinspike to bring two ropes together.

Spanish worm: A nail buried in a piece of timber.

Spanker: A quadrilateral fore-and-aft sail set on the aftermost mast of a square-rigged vessel.

Spanking: [1] To be blowing briskly as wind or breeze. [2] To be running under a quartering wind which fills the spanker. [3] Said of a vessel experiencing wave slam as it comes off a large wave.

Spar: [1] A long cylindrical member tapered at the ends, used to support sails and standing rigging. [2] The generic term for any mast, yard, boom, gaff, or bowsprit. Wooden ships in the age of sail often carried many extra spars of all types and sizes for repairs while at sea (*see* spar deck). [3] A main structural member in an airplane wing or a tail assembly.

Spar buoy: A long cylindrical buoy, anchored so as to project above the water. Especially useful in icy areas since less likely to be swept away.

Spar deck: [1] The upper weather deck of a sailing vessel where spars, sails, boats, and other topside gear were stowed and handled. [2] The deck from which sails, rigging and spars were controlled. [3] The deck of a frigate or double-banked vessel having no open waist or on which spare spars were carried. [4] The raised quarterdeck and forecastle of a deep-waisted vessel. [5] The top deck of an offshore drilling platform.

Spar fender: A spar suspended on a short rope to protect the side of a vessel.

Spar torpedo: An explosive device attached to a long pole and manually placed against an enemy ship before being detonated. In practice its user was a kamikaze (suicide bomber).

Spare anchor: *See* sheet anchor.

Sparks: Nickname for a merchantman's radio operator.

Spars: Female component of the United States Coast Guard in World War II. The acronym was contrived by combining the Latin and English versions of the Coast Guard motto Semper Paratus = Always Ready. Spars served ashore in the United States, Alaska, and Hawaii, mainly on administrative duties.

Speak: To converse with a vessel, usually while in visual contact (first one hails, then one speaks).

Speaking tube: A long pipe running between shipboard stations, serving to convey verbal messages without amplification or enhancement. Also voice tube.

Special cargo: Refers to shipments that require unusual handling or protection, such as pyrotechnics, detonators, and precision instruments.

Special duty: Term for a commissioned officer who is not necessarily qualified for command at sea, but specializes in a particular and limited field. (*See also* specialist officers and limited duty officers.)

Special forces: Highly trained and heavily-armed, élite military raiders, employing covert warfare and unconventional tactics to assault and disrupt hostile forces, or undertake counterterrorism and other specialized and dangerous missions. Examples include the United States Navy Seals, Marine Corps Raiders and Force Recon, and Army Rangers and Green Berets; the Royal Navy Special Boat Service, Royal Marine Commandos, and the Army Special Air Service.

Special interest vessel: One which has been identified by the Coast Guard as a potential security threat while in U.S. waters.

Special operations mobile environment team: A team of U.S. Navy personnel organized, trained, and equipped to support special forces by providing weather, oceanographic, mapping, charting, and geodesy information.

Special sea detail: USN term for a team which takes over from the regular watch to crew key positions during difficult evolutions, including mooring and getting under way. The RN refers to this team as special sea dutymen.

Special services: USN term for welfare and recreational activities.

Specialist officers: Commissioned officers in career fields which are professions unto themselves (accountants, doctors, dentists, lawyers, etc.) are not line or executive officers, but assigned to staff corps in the U.S. Navy and special duties (formerly non-executive) in the Royal Navy. They wear insignia which identify them as limited duty officers not qualified for command. In the USN, staff officers replace the line officer's star with a distinguishing corps device worn above the stripes. Between 1918 and 1956, all RN non-executive officers wore distinguishing colored cloth between their stripes or below a single stripe. Then the distinguishing cloth was eliminated for all specialists except surgeons (red cloth), dentists (pink), and medical services officers (Salmon).

Specialty mark: USN term for the insignia which denotes a petty officer's rating.

Speck: Whaler's term for blubber.

Speck falls: Ropes rove through blocks, at the masthead of a whaler, and used for hoisting flensed strips of blubber.

Specktioneer: The chief harpooner in a whaler's crew, also responsible supervising the flensing of blubber.

Speed made good: Refers to travel in the desired direction regardless of actual speed or course alterations. Calculated by dividing the distance between two fixes by the elapsed time between those fixes. Also known as speed over the ground.

Speed of advance: The average speed that must be maintained in order to arrive at a scheduled time.

Speed table: [1] A table showing the time required to make good a specific distance at a given speed. [2] A table showing the engine rpm needed to achieve a specified vessel speed.

Speedboat: A motor boat designed to be fast. Not generally in nautical use.

Spell: [1] A period of duty. Also turn or trick. [2] To give someone relief by temporarily taking over their duty.

Spencer: A large, loose-footed gaff sail, hooped to a mast.

Spewing: [1] Occurs when oakum is forced from the seams by the ship's motion. [2] Vomiting, a symptom of seasickness.

Spherical sailing: *See* sailings.

Spick and span: In the days of sail, a nail or spike was called a "spick," while a freshly-cut wooden chip was a "span" (from Old Norse). Hence, the term "all new spicks and spans" implied spotlessly clean and neat, as it still does, although "new" is now usually dropped and the objects are singular.

Spider: An outrigger used to hold a block clear of something.

Spiegelschip: Formerly, a large Dutch trading vessel with three or four masts and a distinctive flat stern. Used extensively in trade with the East Indies.

Spike: To disable a muzzle-loading cannon by forcing a special nail or spike into its touchhole (vent). From the Latin spica = pointed ear of corn. *See also* spring-spike.

Spile: [1] A small hole drilled in a cask or barrel to allow air to enter when draining it. [2] A shipwright's measuring rod. [3] A treenail.

Spill: To reduce wind pressure on a square-sail, usually by shaking, and especially to make it easier to secure.

Spindrift: Sea foam (spume) windswept along the surface of the water.

Spinnaker: A large lightweight triangular sail, set out to the side on a boom to catch even the slightest breeze. Invented by the owner of a racing yacht called Sphinx which semi-literate seamen pronounced "spinnicks," probably adding "acre" because the sail was so large.

Spirits in the USN: Rules for Regulation of the Navy of the United Colonies, issued by the revolutionary Congress on 28 November 1775, specified a daily issue of one half-pint of rum to each enlisted man. Following the British practice, it was diluted and known as "grog," but was still held in great regard by the troops, leading to the traditional enlisted saying: "Blow up the magazines; throw the bread over the side; sink the salt horse; but handle them spirits gentle like."

In 1806, the Navy Department introduced whiskey to replace the rum ration, but it was unpopular and grog was brought back. Later, enlisted were given the option of replacing grog with a quart of beer, while teetotalers could take a cash payment of three to five cents in lieu of alcohol. Then, on 1st September 1862, more than a century before the RN the USN had its own "Black Tot Day," Congress ruled, "The spirit ration in the Navy of the United States shall forever cease."

Liquor continued to be freely available to wardroom officers until 1st July 1914, when Secretary of the Navy Josephus Daniels proclaimed prohibition by his infamous Order #99, otherwise known as the "Bonedry Order" (*see* Cup of Joe). Navies around the world ridiculed the decision, but Daniels did not back down, writing, "Naval Officers always obey orders, whether they like them or not."

Spit: A narrow point of land or long narrow shoal projecting into the water.

Spithead: The eastern part of the Solent, a channel between England and the Isle of Wight that is protected from all winds, except those from the southeast. It receives its name from the Spit, a sandbank stretching south from the Hampshire shore, where the important commercial port of Southampton and major naval base of Portsmouth are located. The area has witnessed several naval battles, was the site of number of large naval reviews, and the "Great Mutiny" of 1797 began there.

Spithead nightingales: RN slang for the boatswain and his mates, after the "chirping" of their calls.

Spitkid: A large saucer-shaped galvanized iron receptacle, originally a spittoon but now an ashtray. In the RN, the pipe "place spitkids" signifies the start of a smoking period, while "clear out and stow spitkids" announces its end. Cf. smoking lamp.

Splash line: Amphibious operations term for the point at which underwater demolition teams disembark to swim to a hostile beach at night.

Splashboard: A plank that slides into grooves to prevent water entering a companionway.

Splice: [1] To join the ends of two ropes or cables by interweaving their strands (cf. braid). [2] The joint so created. *See* short splice and long splice.

Splice the mainbrace: [1] Enjoy an alcoholic drink. [2] Issue an extra ration of rum. The main brace was one of the biggest running lines in the ship, so splicing it was extremely arduous. Moreover, it ran high up the mainmast, making the task dangerous as well. The job was so disliked that it became traditional to give seamen performing it an extra tot of rum or brandy. Later the practice was extended to cover any special occasion, such as after combat or to celebrate an anniversary.

That being said, it is something of a mystery that the phrase refers to running rigging at all, since standing rigging was much heavier and therefore harder to splice. For example, the principal stay on a first-rate was six inches (15 cm) in diameter and would have been far more arduous to splice than even the biggest brace. On the other hand, a running line was more likely to chafe and snap.

Spliced: Colloquialism for married.

Splinter: A sharp sliver of wood. When caused by cannon fire splinters were the major cause of death or disablement in combat between wooden ships.

Splinter deck: The least protected of two armored decks, usually the uppermost (cf. protective deck).

Splinter net: Mesh spread horizontally between the masts of a sailing man-o'-war during combat, to prevent damaged top hamper falling on the open deck.

Splinter shield: Light armor protecting a ship's bridge or gun stations. Also splinter screen.

Split plant: Division of a warship's engineering and propulsion equipment into independent units, each of which could continue to operate if one or more of the others was damaged.

SPM: Single point mooring.

SPOD: Seaport of debarkation.

SPOE: Seaport of embarkation.

Spoil: The silt, earth, stones, etc. thrown up by dredging or excavation.

Spoil bank: A raised shelf created by dumping spoil from a nearby channel.

Spoil the ship for a ha'porth of tar: This phrase today means endangering an enterprise by skimping or neglecting minor details. It is popularly believed to refer to caulking the seams of a ship, where failure to fill a tiny strip (even one short enough to be covered by a half-penny's worth of pitch) could result in a fatal leak. However, the adage predates England's maritime age. In rural medieval dialect, "sheep" was pronounced "ship," and the allusion is to the shepherd's practice of smearing tar on an animal's wounds to promote healing and prevent infection.

Spoiler: [1] A hinged airfoil on the upper surface of an aircraft wing that is raised to reduce lift and increase drag, providing speed, bank, and descent control. [2] Trade name of a buoy claimed to provide op-

timal performance in longline and net set commercial fishing operations.

Spoiler board: A device temporarily attached to the leading edge of a wing to prevent unintended lift-off when the aircraft is secured on the open deck in windy weather.

Spoke: [1] One of the turning handles on the outer rim of a ship's steering wheel. [2] One of the inner rods supporting the rim of a wheel.

Sponge: *See* Spunge.

Sponson: [1] A gun-platform projecting over the side of a warship. [2] A projection supporting the paddle-wheel and paddle-box of a side-wheel steamer. [3] An appendage at the side of a canoe to prevent it capsizing. [4] A protuberance on a flying-boat's hull to increase its lateral stability on water.

Sponsor: [1] The person (traditionally female) who christens a newly-built ship as part of the launching ritual. [2] A member of the ship's company told off to help indoctrinate a newly-arrived shipmate (also "sea daddy").

Spontoon: The army name for a half pike. Often carried by sergeants as a symbol of rank and used for signaling rather than fighting.

Spook: Slang for an intelligence operative.

Spoon bow: An overhanging bow with a convex spoon-shaped stem.

Spoon in the mouth: In former naval slang, a person who had to struggle to earn promotion was said to have been "born with a wooden ladle in the mouth." This was in contrast to persons who obtained rank or advancement by virtue of birth or connections and were "born with a silver spoon in the mouth." The latter term is still used in Britain.

Spoondrift: Another term for spindrift (mainly American).

Spooning: [1] Running directly before both wind and sea. [2] Loading a slaver by making the slaves lie on their sides, packed closely together like nested spoons.

Spot: [1] To observe the fall of shot. [2] To position a ship at a wharf. [3] To position cargo in a hold. [4] To position an aircraft on the flight deck of a carrier.

Spot charter: A one-time (as opposed to long-term) charter party, the price being based on fluctuating supply and demand.

Spot rate: A contract price covering total operating expenses (i.e., bunkers, food, and wages for the crew, port charges, canal tolls, marine insurance, and repairs).

Spot voyage: A charter for a specific vessel to move a single cargo between specified ports at the spot rate.

Spotted dick: A steamed pudding, containing dried fruits, usually currants or raisins, and served either with custard or with butter and brown sugar. "Spotted" refers to the raisins (which appear as dots on the surface) and "dick" may be a progressive corruption and contraction of the word pudding (→pud-dink→puddick→dick). Closely-related or identical to figgie-dowdie and plum duff.

Spotter: An observer stationed for the purpose of observing and reporting the results of naval gunfire to the firing vessel. May also be required to designate targets.

Spotting board: [1] Miniature flight and hangar decks with aircraft models to scale; used to plan the placement of aircraft in or on a carrier. [2] A fall of shot trainer for gunnery spotters.

Spray: Fine particles of water blown or thrown into the air. *See* spume.

Spread: [1] The breadth of a sail or length of a yard. [2] A fan-like salvo of torpedoes.

Spreadeagling: This penalty for relatively minor transgressions involved tying the culprit to the shrouds, with arms and legs widely spread, to be left hanging in considerable discomfort for as long as the offense justified or the captain felt appropriate.

Spreader: [1] A strut for separating shrouds on a sailing ship mast (mainly American; the British term is crosstree). [2] A device to facilitate the lifting and handling of breakbulk cargo, vehicles, or containers.

Spring: [1] The tide of greatest rise and fall occurring twice each month (cf. Neap). [2] A mooring line, secured almost parallel to the ship's side to prevent forward or backward movement. [3] To develop a leak. [4] To crack a mast or yard making it unsafe. [5] A hawser laid out from the stern of a sailing man-o-war, attached to the anchor cable forward, and used to haul the ship to a desired position, especially to bring the broadside to bear.

Spring-spike: A spike for a gun, with a spring at the lower end to prevent its withdrawal.

Sprit: A small spar serving to hoist the peak and extend a sail that has neither gaff nor boom.

Spritsail: [1] A fore-and-aft quadrilateral sail held in position and extended by a sprit crossing diagonally from the foot of the mast to the peak of the sail. [2] Formerly, a small square-sail set below the bowsprit.

Spume: Windblown froth or foam generated by waves.

Spun yarn: Cordage made of several tarred yarns, laid up without twisting. Also spunyarn.

Spun yarn Sunday: RN term for a Sunday on which no divisions are held and Church attendance is not compulsory.

Spunge: [1] A pole-mounted wooden cylinder wrapped in lambswool or rags (also sponge). [2] To dampen such a cylinder and use it to clean out the bore of a muzzle-loading cannon extinguishing any remaining sparks.

Spunger: The member of a gun crew responsible for spunging and worming a muzzle-loading cannon, assisting the loader/rammer, and helping to run out and train the gun.

Spur: The prong on a stockless anchor.

Spyglass: Another name for a hand-held telescope or long glass.

Squadron: [1] An administrative and tactical military aviation unit. Typically three or four flights, with a total of 12 to 24 aircraft. [2] A detachment of warships or subdivision of a fleet on special duty. Usually fewer than ten ships. [3] An administrative group of similar type vessels, such as submarines or destroyers. [4] A company-size unit of horse or armored cavalry, or other military force.

Squall: A sudden localized violent wind gust, often accompanied by rain, sleet, or thunder.

Squall line: An extended narrow region along a cold front within which active thunderstorms and possible squalls occur.

Square: [1] To brace the yards at right angles to the keel. [2] The upper part of an anchor shank. [3] The area at the foot of a hatchway. [4] A rectangular tray on which seamen's victuals were served (*see* square meal).

Square away: [1] To set the yards for sailing before the wind. [2] To tidy up. [3] To adjust to a new assignment or ship. [4] To prepare to do something. [5] In the USN, to admonish sharply.

Square knot: [1] A reef knot. [2] A sailor who has crossed all four of the equator, arctic and Antarctic circles, and the international date line. Qualifiers frequently sport the tattoo of a reef knot.

Square meal: This term for a substantial and nourishing repast originated in the 19th century Royal Navy, when meals were served on a rectangular tray or platter, known as a square and subdivided into compartments, not unlike modern fast-food containers.

Square-rig: [1] RN slang for a bell-bottomed uniform. [2] Quadrilateral sails extended by yards.

Square-rigger: A vessel having square sails as its principal means of propulsion.

Square sail: A quadrilateral canvas set beneath a yard which pivots around the mast at its center and sits athwartships except when trimmed to the wind. To furl and unfurl a square sail, sailors would have to climb the rigging and walk out on footropes below the yard. From top to bottom the eight sails on each mast of a typical square-rigger are:

Moonraker

Skyscraper

Royals

Upper and Lower Topgallants

Upper and Lower Topsails

Course

Each is named after the mast it sits upon; for example the lowermost sails of a three-master are fore course, main course, and mizzen course. *See also* Sailing Rigs.

Square yards!: Command to get the yards horizontal and at right angles to the keel. When squaring yards, the boatswain goes ahead in a boat, and signals with flags, while his chief mate stands on a head-spar to interpret the signals to the other bosun's mates, who direct topmen working the lifts, and seamen on deck hauling the braces.

Squatting: Said of a power-driven vessel when the bite of its propellers makes the stern ride lower than the bow.

Squawk box: Slang for a ship's public address system.

Squid: [1] Derogatory slang for a member of the USN. [2] A British forward-throwing anti-submarine weapon. [3] A ten-armed marine cephalopod that may have given rise to some of the "kraken" myths (*see* appendix).

SR: Seaman Recruit (USN).

SRBM: Short range ballistic missile.

SRG: Seabee readiness group.

SRP: Sealift Readiness Program.

SS: [1] Sea state. [2] Steamship. [3] Sailing ship. [3] Submersible ship. [4] Strategic sealift.

SSBN: Ship, submersible, ballistic, nuclear.

SSGN: Ship, submersible, guided missile, nuclear.

SSM: Surface to surface missile.

SSN: Ship, submersible, nuclear.

SSS: Strategic Sealift Ship.

Stable element: A device for naval surface fire control that operates in the horizontal plane much as the stable vertical does in the other plane.

Stable vertical: A device for naval surface fire control. The stable vertical is provided with a pair of firing contacts wired in series with the firing circuit, and in parallel with a switch which can short the contacts. One of the contacts is fixed in space by the stable vertical's gyroscope while the other moves with the ship. The contacts can be adjusted to close and thus fire the guns automatically at the instant they are in the correct position.

Stability: The property of resisting change or of returning to an original position if disturbed. This requires a ship's center of gravity to be vertically below its center of buoyancy (cf. metacenter).

Stabilizer: [1] One of one or more pairs of stabilizer fins used to dampen a ship's rolling motion. [2] A Frahm tank system. [3] A gyrostabilizer. [4] Any of various devices used to keep a gun trained on its target when the ship moves. [5] Any device or system designed to control the underwater depth and stability of a submarine or torpedo. [6] Any device to maintain the horizontal or vertical stability of an aircraft.

Stabilizer fins: Anti-roll hydrofoil elements which extend transversely for up to ten meters (33 feet) from the vessel's side and rotate around their axes in response to the roll. Substantial costs include a mechanism to retract the fins within the hull for docking, and the electronics required to adjust them to the hydraulic flow. When their angle of attack is too shallow, they produce less than optimum lift, while when it is too steep cavitation can occur. Moreover, they depend on forward motion to create lift and hence lose their effectiveness at low speeds.

To counteract these shortcomings, more advanced

systems place transducers within each fin shaft to signal the lift force being generated. An inboard computer system tuned to the characteristics of the vessel and of the sea around it, including the amplitude and frequency of oscillation, then adjusts the angle of attack to produce the lift required to maximize stabilization.

Stack: [1] To set the yards of a square-rigged vessel parallel to each other. [2] The funnel of an engine-powered ship (abbreviation of chimney-stack or smokestack).

Stack wash: Funnel smoke or air turbulence hovering above the ship's wake.

Staff: [1] The spar on which a flag is worn (also flagstaff, flagpole). [2] A body or corps of officers without command (line or executive) authority who perform administrative (planning, logistical, etc.) or support (medical. dental, religious, legal) functions. [3] A body of officers appointed as aides to a flag officer.

Staff Captain: [1] An officer who supports the master of a large Oceangoing passenger liner with special responsibility for fire and safety precautions, lifeboat drills, and the like. [2] Formerly, the most senior rank in the now obsolete RN Navigating Branch.

Staff Corps: *See* specialist officers.

Staff officer: [1] An officer serving on the staff of a flag officer. [2] A specialist officer with nonmilitary duties in a staff corps.

Stage: [1] A platform hung over a ship's side for personnel working on its hull above the waterline. [2] The military term for a place or point where troops and supplies can be assembled for an operation.

Stagger: A ship is said to stagger when she carries as much canvas as she can bear and rolls heavily.

Staging: [1] The assembly and processing of troops preparatory to movement, especially embarkation and transport. [2] Scaffolding.

Stairs/Staircase/Stairway: The passenger liner or cruise ship terms for what mariners call a ladder.

Stamp-and-go!: An order to quicken and coordinate men working the capstan or hauling ropes. They bang their feet in unison and then heave together. Also stomp-and-go.

Stanch: A vessel which is firm, strong, and unlikely to leak. Also staunch. From Old French estanche.

Stanchion: A vertical bar, pillar, post, or support.

Stand: [1] To direct a vessel's course (e.g., stand into harbor; stand out to sea). [2] To perform a duty (e.g., stand watch). [3] The brief period of no tidal movement that occurs at high or low water.

Stand at ease!: RN command for those standing at attention to assume a more relaxed but still formal posture. (The equivalent USN command omits "stand.")

Stand by: [1] To wait. [2] To prepare or make ready. [3] The substitute for someone. [4] To be such a substitute.

Stand clear!: Command to keep away from a specified place or object (e.g., "stand clear of the gangway when the admiral comes aboard").

Stand easy!: RN command to adopt an informal stance. Posture is relaxed, right foot remains in place, but body movement and quiet talking are permitted. (the equivalent USN command is "at rest!").

Stand fast!: Command to [1] Stay in formation or position. [2] Hold firm under attack. [3] Cease artillery action. [4] *See* up spirits!

Stand of arms: A complete set of personal weapons for one person.

Stand off: Keep a distance away from.

Stand on: To continue on the same course and speed. When two vessels meet, the one with right of way under the rules of the road is known as the "stand-on" or "privileged" vessel, the other being the "give-way vessel."

Stand out: [1] To leave a port or anchorage. [2] To be conspicuous.

Stand watch: To remain at an assigned duty station for the duration of a watch.

Standard: The flag or ensign of a head of state or other important functionary.

Standard commands: Codified words or phrases, always used in the same format to ensure instant understanding and execution without the ambiguity or confusion which can arise from extemporaneous commands composed hastily during emergencies or in combat. *See* customary phraseology.

Standard compass: The specific magnetic compass designated by the navigating officer as the reference against which all other onboard compasses should be checked.

Standard rudder: USN term for the helm position which will result in a tactical turn of defined diameter (normally 750 yards) at a defined speed (usually 12 knots).

Standard speed: USN term for a speed through the water that is set by the officer in tactical command of the unit or formation. Standard speed is established or changed only on verbal orders from the ship's control station. The correct phraseology for a change of standard speed is, "Next time we ring the Engine Order Telegraph, standard speed will be (xx) knots." *See also* Full Speed, Emergency Speed, Flank Speed.

Standards of Training, Certification, and Watchkeeping for Seafarers: This treaty, established by an international convention in 1978, specifies uniform qualifications for the masters, officers, and other watchkeeping individuals of seagoing vessels, and requires each candidate to demonstrate competence through examinations and practical tests before being licensed, certificated, or assigned to shipboard duties.

Standing: Said of any object or assemblage of objects (e.g., rigging, part of a line, etc.) that are fixed in position and not normally moved unless for maintenance or repair. The converse is "running."

Standing mute: *See* mute.

Standing orders: Permanent or semi-permanent directives establishing uniform procedures applicable to an entire ship's company or divisions thereof.

Standing part: One of three divisions or segments of a line rove through a tackle, being the section that is neither a bight nor an end, but is made fast to a spar, deck, or block. *See also* fall, leading part, running part.

Standing rigging: Consists of permanently-secured heavy lines that are adjusted and made fast to support the masts from forward and aft (stays), and athwartships (shrouds). The system depends on achieving a delicate balance between pull and counterpull. For example, tightening a backstay might bend the mast in a slight curve towards the stern. This could be compensated by increasing tension on a forestay, but that might slacken the port and starboard shrouds which would have to be tightened equally to re-balance them. When the entire system has been tuned and is in equilibrium, lines and tackles can be permanently fixed in position and the excess ends cut off.

The shrouds are crossed horizontally by ratlines that provide topmen with a means of going aloft. When they get there, the yards are equipped with loops, called foot-ropes or horses, on which they can stand while handling sails. Standing rigging is usually protected with pitch giving it a black look which distinguishes it from lighter colored running rigging which is left naked for flexibility.

Standing warrants: Eighteenth century RN term for those warrant officers (usually, boatswain, carpenter, cook, and gunner) who remained aboard at full pay to maintain a ship laid up for the winter, in ordinary, or on the stocks.

Standing water: Where there is no current or tide.

STAR: Surveillance, Target Acquisition and Reconnaissance.

***Star of the West*:** The first shots of the American Civil War occurred on January 9, 1861, when *Star of the West*— a merchant ship hired by the United States government to carry supplies and reinforcements to the garrison in Fort Sumter — was fired upon by a battery on Morris Island as she entered Charleston Harbor. *Star* ignored a warning bowshot but, after being hit twice, turned around and headed for home.

Star shell: A pyrotechnic projectile which bursts in mid-air, releasing a shower of bright lights to provide illumination during a night action. *See also* flare.

Star shot: An American invention, intended to be an improvement on crossbar shot, consisting of a number of metal bars hinged to a central hub. When fired from smooth-bore cannon the folded bars spread out into a whirling star shape which cut rigging in the same way as chain shot, or bar shot.

Starboard: The right side of a vessel when looking forward.

Stargazer: A small sail set above the moonraker of a square-rigged vessel.

Starkey's squid: In 1944, A.G. Starkey, quartermaster of a Royal Navy minesweeping trawler, was standing anchor watch off the Maldive Islands, shining his quartermaster's light into the water when he noticed something glowing:

As I gazed, fascinated, a circle of green light glowed in my area of illumination. This green unwinking orb I suddenly realised was an eye. The surface of the water undulated with some strange disturbance. Gradually I realised I was gazing at almost point-blank range at a huge squid.... I climbed the ladder to the fo'c's'le and shone the torch downwards. There in the pool of light were its tentacles."

Starkey says these were about two feet (60 cms) thick, with clearly visible suction discs. Then he walked aft again, keeping the pulsating animal in view all the while, until he came to its body and head, of which "...every detail was visible — the valve through which the creature appeared to breathe, and the parrot-like beak." With the tentacles lying at the bow and the head at the stern of the 175 foot (53 meter) vessel he had a precise estimate of the animal's length. After fifteen minutes, "...it seemed to swell as its valve opened fully, and without any visible effort it zoomed into the night."

Skeptics have pointed out a lack of background detail in this story. No specific date is mentioned, nor is the name of his ship. He was alone with no other witnesses but, if he saw something so amazing, why didn't he call his shipmates? (Perhaps he did not want to wake the watch below.) Moreover, it was a remarkable coincidence (but by no means impossible) that the creature was aligned exactly with the ship. The chorus of doubt revived in August 1997, after a Discovery Channel television broadcast reported the ship to be only 60 feet long. However, this had to be a mistake; British oceangoing trawlers were seldom less than 145 feet in length and 175 would not be unusual (the Algerine Class minesweepers were 225 feet long).

Current estimates of colossal squid put its adult size at about 15 meters (50 feet) with a longer mantle (body) but shorter tentacles (arms) than giant squid. This is far smaller than Starkey's report, and does not even match a dead squid found in 1878. However, there may still be giants to match the Kraken lurking undiscovered in the deep-water darkness.

Start: [1] A point of departure. [2] To induce motion. [3] To slacken a sheet, tack, or rope. [4] To spring, slip, or work loose (e.g., planking). [5] To loosen the staves of a butt, by the working of the ship. [6] To pierce a cask and pour out some of its contents. [7] To use a rattan or starter. [8] The place a whale is expected to rise, after being harpooned and sounding.

Starter: A rattan stick or knotted rope's end, formerly used by British and American petty officers to thrash and encourage laggards. They firmly believed that immediate, rough and brutal corporal encouragement was essential to ensure that apprentices, landsmen, and even ordinary seamen learnt their trade rapidly. Starters were seldom used on qualified AB's and almost never on élite topmen. *See also* Unofficial Beating.

Starve: To sail so close to the wind that the sails do not fill properly.

Stash it!: Stop it! or Be quiet!

State funerals: These are ceremonial events, full of pomp and circumstance, to honor a deceased head of state or other person of national significance and importance:

• **In the United Kingdom:** A "State" funeral requires a motion or vote in Parliament and is usually reserved for the sovereign and surviving consorts, although eight commoners have been so honored. A "Ceremonial" funeral is virtually the same except that parliamentary approval is not needed. Each consists of a military procession escorting the coffin, which is borne on a gun-carriage drawn by horses for a ceremonial funeral, but by Royal Navy sailors for a state one.

The latter tradition began when Queen Victoria's funeral cortège was about to leave Windsor Station. Her coffin was placed on a Royal Horse Artillery gun-carriage (fitted with rubber tires for the purpose) drums began their muffled roll, and an RHA battery began its 81-gun salute (one for each year of her life). But, when the gun-horses took the strain, an eyelet on the splinter bar broke and the trace swung around to hit the wheel-horse on the rump. The shock made it rear and plunge (giving rise to the popular belief that the horses were badly trained and frightened by the gunfire).

Only a minor repair was needed, but before the army gunners could fix the damage, an enthusiastic detachment of naval ratings broke ranks, seized the drag ropes and hauled the gun-carriage on its way. To the anger and embarrassment of the army, the navy has been assigned that duty at every subsequent royal or state funeral, including that of Sir Winston Churchill. (Princess Diana had a ceremonial funeral, and so did HRH the Queen Mother, but her gun-carriage was pulled by naval ratings.) After the procession the body lies in state in Westminster Hall for (usually) three days of public viewing and mourning. A funeral service is then held in Westminster Abbey or Saint Paul's cathedral.

• **In the United States:** Initially, state funerals were relatively unimpressive, since the founding fathers found pomp and circumstance too reminiscent of monarchical customs. George Washington's funeral, for example, was a simple local affair at Mount Vernon. However, nationwide mourning after the assassination of Abraham Lincoln led to the introduction of more elaborate ceremonies on which all subsequent state funerals have been based (subject to specific changes when requested by the deceased or immediate family). State funerals are required by law for sitting Presidents, former Presidents, and Presidents-elect, and may be awarded to others by the President in office.

The procession starts at 16th Street and proceeds along Constitution Avenue to the Capitol building. The coffin is carried on a caisson, drawn by six horses of the same color, accompanied by three riders and a mounted section chief. It is followed by a riderless "caparisoned horse" with a pair of boots reversed in the stirrups to signify the deceased will never ride again. Members of all five armed services and their bands form the escort. The official funeral service is held in the Capitol Rotunda, where the body lies in state for 24 hours (on a black catafalque made for Lincoln). The body is then taken to the National Cathedral (or other designated church) for a national memorial service, after which there is often a private family funeral.

Stateroom: An officer's or passenger's sleeping accommodation or cabin. (So named because the first-class compartments on nineteenth century Mississippi River paddleboats were named after states of the Union — *Virginia, New York*, etc.) The term is not used in the RN.

Station: [1] The operational area assigned to a ship or squadron. [2] A post of duty (e.g., battle station). [3] A specific position within a formation of ships. [4] A fixed naval land base (e.g., air station). [5] To assign personnel or vessels to any of the foregoing. [6] A radio transmitter.

Station bill: A list showing the posts of all crew members during various emergencies and maneuvers. *See* watch bill.

Station-keeping: The art and science of holding a vessel at its assigned position in a formation. *See* shiphandling.

Statute mile: A distance of 1,760 yards, which is equal to 1.6093 kilometers and 0.8683 of a nautical mile.

Staunch: Alternate spelling of stanch.

Stave: [1] To break in or crush, especially a vessel's hull. [2] One of the thin narrow shaped strips of wood which form the side of a cask (also shake). [3] The pole of a boathook. [4] To avoid collision by pushing with a boathook or other pole (usually stave off). From Old English staef = staff or pole.

Stay: Any wire or cable supporting a mast or funnel, especially those running fore-and-aft.

Stays: A sailing ship is said to be "in stays" when head-on to the wind and hanging there. Also "in irons."

Staysail: Any sail set on a stay, especially a triangular one between two masts.

STCW: Standards of Training, Certification, and Watchkeeping for Seafarers.

Steady!: Command for the helmsman to follow whatever heading the ship comes to after the rudder is put amidships.

Steady as she goes!: Command for the helmsman to maintain the present course.

Steady bearing: [1] In navigation, an approaching or closing craft is said to be on a steady bearing if the relative compass bearing between the two ships does not appreciably change. This signifies that they are either running parallel, diverging, or on a collision course. [2] In industrial engineering, a steady (or

steadying) bearing serves to limit deflection and vibration of a vertical shaft.

Steadying line: *See* tagline.

Steadying sail: A small sail serving [1] to maintain a sailing ship's heading when lying to. [2] To reduce a powerboat's roll in a beam sea.

Steal: To move stealthily in anticipation of an order. For example, climb a ratline or two before being ordered aloft, or pick up a sail before the order to furl is given.

Steal ahead: To move gently forward under light winds.

Steal the wind: In modern usage this phrase signifies doing something to forestall someone else's intentions, but the original nautical meaning described a combat maneuver in which a ship would pass close to its opponent on the windward side so that its sails blocked the wind from the enemy's. Loss of propulsive force meant loss of headway and maneuverability, giving the first ship a fighting advantage. This was a favorite tactic of sailing navies, and is still used by racing yachtsmen.

Stealth technology: A combination of techniques designed to minimize the signature or visibility of ships, aircraft, or ground vehicles to the human eye, satellite observation, radar, sonar, pressure, magnetic, or infrared methods. These include such things as:

- External design that avoids radar-reflecting shapes and round protuberances in favor of sharp corners and flat surfaces. Protruding and retruding surfaces tend to deflect signals at different angles.
- Internal construction involving re-entrant triangles. Such structures trap signals by bouncing them to-and-fro between internal faces.
- Composite panels of laminated carbon fiber and plastic. These materials tend to absorb rather than reflect incoming signals.
- Final treatment with energy absorbent paints or coatings.
- Minimization of wake disturbance by hydrodynamic control surfaces or, especially in shallow (brown) waters, by water jet propulsion.

Stealthy submarines: Every submarine is essentially stealthy, but some new designs have radar signatures no greater than that of a dolphin and can remain virtually undetected by current methods of location. Submarines employing stealth technology are in service or being developed by almost every seafaring nation, including Britain (*Astute* class), China (types *0093* & *0094*), France (*Barracuda* class), Iran (*Ghadir* class), Russia (*Borei* class), Sweden (*Gotland* class), and the United States (*Seawolf* & *Virginia* classes).

Stealthy surface warships: An early prototype was *Sea Shadow*, a USN experimental platform introduced in the mid–1980s with a security classification so high that (until 1993) it was only allowed out at night. As of the mid–2000s, many classes of warship employ varying degrees of stealth technology, including

Britain's *Type 45* destroyers, France's *La Fayette* frigates, Germany's *Sachsen* frigates and *Braunschweig* corvettes, India's *Shivalik* frigates, Norway's *Skjold* patrol craft, Singapore's *Formidible* frigates, Sweden's *Visby* corvettes, and the USN's *Zumwalt* destroyers.

Steam: [1] The invisible vapor into which water is converted when heated to its boiling point. When kept under pressure it can supply energy for heating, cooking, or mechanical work. *See* saturated, superheated, and wet steam. [2] To emit visible vapor. [3] To be moved by steam power.

Steam fog: When very cold air passes over comparatively warm surface water, columns of dense water vapor obscure low-level visibility even when the sky is clear.

Steam in metaphor: Probably due to rail rather than water transport, a number of steam-related phrases entered the language in the 19th century, including:
- blow off steam = vent repressed emotions.
- full steam ahead = pursue a project with vigor.
- raise steam = summon up the energy for a task.
- run out of steam = lose impetus or energy.
- steamed up = angry or excited.
- under one's own steam = unaided.

Steamboat: A small steamship, often riverine.

Steamboat Gothic: A 19th century architectural style emulating the gingerbread decoration of steamboats.

Steaming light: Former term for a masthead light, now obsolete.

Steamship: A vessel using steam to power its propulsion system (cf. motor vessel, sailing ship, steamboat).

Steep seas: Short but tall waves, caused by waves and currents opposite to wind direction.

Steeping tub: *See* harness cask.

Steer: To guide or direct the course. From Old Norse stjorn.

Steer small!: Command for the helmsman to hold the wheel as steady as possible.

Steerage: [1] Formerly, the cheapest passenger accommodation in a ocean liner, frequently located near the stern where the noise of propulsion systems was loudest. [2] The act of steering. [3] A short form of steerageway. [4] A steerage officer was the sailing merchantman's equivalent of a naval gunroom officer.

Steerageway: The slowest speed at which the helmsman can maintain directional control.

Steering: Maintaining the required course by vigilant attention to the motion of the ship's head, so as to check every deviation as soon as it occurs. From the Anglo-Saxon stéoran.

Steering commands: *See* helm orders.

Steering engine: *See* steering mechanisms.

Steering evolution: Directional control has always been essential to the mariner.
- In prehistory both steering and propulsion of rafts and dugout canoes were probably achieved by using a long pole in shallow water and a paddle in deeper.
- By about 3,500 BCE, boats had grown larger and journeys longer; a single hand-held oar was no longer sufficient and Egyptian naval architecture featured twin steering oars firmly secured to each side of the stern.
- As boats grew to become ships, the steering oars had to be fitted with tillers to reduce the manual effort of controlling the vessel.
- When ships grew even larger, tillers had to be longer, requiring more men to handle them, and steering was erratic because rolling lifted the steering oars out of the water. The sternpost was then reinforced and a rudder was attached to it on the ship's centerline, making the vessel's response to steering faster and firmer. The first rudders appeared on Baltic Sea cogs around about 1240.
- In the 16th century, the helmsman had to move to a higher level so he could see over the forward castle, with rudder-control being achieved by attaching a long vertical pole (whipstaff) to the tiller.
- By the 18th century, even bigger ships had become increasingly hard to control with whipstaff technology and the steering wheel was introduced. The mechanical advantage of connecting to the tiller with blocks and tackles gave smoother rudder-operation with less effort.
- By the late 19th century, hand-powered steering gear was inadequate to control heavy iron vessels, leading to the introduction of steam-powered devices.
- In most modern vessels, the classic spoke-handled steering wheel is gone, replaced by one or both of a couple of devices that seem too small to handle the huge ships they control. One is a tiny wheel (similar to that of an airplane or automobile) that is used mainly in open waters. The other is a joystick, toggle, or lever, used principally for maneuvering in confined spaces. The rudder is controlled remotely by steering mechanisms that incorporate a position indicator to give feedback to the helmsperson who can no longer "feel" any response.

Steering mechanism: The combination of mechanical, electrical or hydraulic machinery that turns the rudder in response to movement of the helm. Electro-mechanical systems, which require large motors and considerable maintenance, have mostly been replaced by electro-hydraulic gear, with smaller vessels using single-ram steering engines, while aircraft carriers and other large ships use double-ram systems. Also steering engine.

Steering pole: A hinged spar with a lamp at the end that could be lowered to project forward of the bow to provide helmsman and watch officer with a reference point when conning the ship from well aft at night.

Steering sail: *See* studding sail.

Steering wheel: *See* helm, and steering evolution.

Steersman: Alternate and less-frequently used term for a helmsman. It has a long lineage, going back to stiremannus which is listed as a maritime occupation in the *Domesday Book* of 1086.

Steeve: [1] The angle of a bowsprit above horizontal. [2] To elevate a spar from the deck. [3] To stow cotton, wool, or similar cargo in a merchantman's hold by means of a jackscrew.

Steinke hood: An inflatable life jacket with a hood that completely encloses the wearer's head, trapping a bubble of air. This allows the wearer to breathe while escaping from a distressed submarine at moderate depths. Its predecessor was the Momsen lung, and its successor is submarine escape immersion equipment.

***Stein*'s Monster:** Knox class Ocean Escort USS *Stein* (DE-1065) was configured with a multi-mode bow-mounted sonar for optimum antisubmarine performance. She was commissioned in January 1972 at Puget Sound Naval Shipyard and, on April 1, left San Diego for a four-week 14,000 mile shakedown cruise, with scheduled visits to "show the flag" at ports in Ecuador, Peru, Panama, and Mexico. According to a widely reported media story, she was just south of the equator, heading for her first port of call, when her underwater tracking gear suddenly and mysteriously malfunctioned. After all attempts to bring it back on line failed, Commander Nepier V. Smith was forced to abort the cruise and return north for immediate inspection and repair.

As soon as water had been drained from the dry dock at Long Beach Naval Shipyard, the cause of the alleged problem is said to have became obvious. The tough anti-fouling cover of her large sonar dome, protruding below and in front of the bow, had been badly ripped and gouged. Closer inspection revealed several hundred inch-long, sharp, hollow teeth or claws imbedded in the cover and on the dome itself. Marine biologists and other scientists were immediately called in from San Diego Naval Oceans Systems Center to study the incident, coming to the conclusion that the frigate had been repeatedly attacked by "a creature that must have been extremely large and of a species still unknown to science." (The author has checked with the Space & Naval Warfare Systems Center — successor to the Naval Oceans Systems Center — which can trace no record of the event.)

This fascinating tale, undoubtedly expanded and embellished in telling and re-telling, can be traced to comments made by one of *Stein*'s crew during a television interview and picked up by the mass media. In contrast, Petty Officer Bob Tackett's recollection of the event as recounted to the author is far less mysterious:

> I was stationed aboard at the time as a member of the sonar team. My memory of the whole thing was a bit different than what was shown on the TV show. We were scheduled to sail to Ecuador for a good will visit, taking a pilot on board in the Gulf of Guaya- quil, and then continuing on up the wide Guayas river to the town of Guayaquil. We "hit" something in the river so hard that the ship shook. I was on deck at the time but personally didn't see anything in the water.

> Some people said it must have been a large log or something stuck in the mud on the bottom of the river, but other people said they saw "something" appear to swim away after the jolt. At the time I believe the bridge assumed we had struck and then cleared some inanimate object that the pilot didn't know was there. Later, when the ship went into dry dock and the marks were found on the dome, some people thought we must have encountered some large creature like a giant squid or something. Personally, I think we hit something hard imbedded in the river bottom. Sorry I can't confirm "Nessy" ripping apart our sonar dome or alien claw nails found bleeding and imbedded in the hull.

Other sonarmen on board at the time do not recall any equipment failures and point out that a naval sonar transmitter is physically separate from its protective dome, so even extensive damage to the latter would not have caused the system to malfunction as the story claims. In fact, *Stein* completed her cruise as planned and it seems certain this intriguing tale of the "dome monster" can be dismissed as apocryphal. It does, however, demonstrate how easily word of mouth, supplemented by media hype, can transform a mundane incident into an inexplicable mystery.

Stem: [1] To tamp, plug, or otherwise make tight a leaking hole or joint. [2] To maintain position or make headway against wind, tide, or current. [3] The vertical element at the front of a vessel to which the sides are attached. [4] A contract to load cargo on a specific date and within a specific time.

Stem fender: A hemp mat wrapped around the stem of a tugboat to prevent damage to the vessel or its tow when pushing.

Stem-to-stern: The full length of the vessel.

Step: [1] To raise and position a mast. [2] The socket or plate which holds a mast in position.

Stepped hull: A form of powerboat construction with one or more levels on the bottom that progressively rise out of the water to reduce friction as speed increases.

Stepping on board: In the old days, because of an ancient belief that the left signified unluck or harm (hence "sinister"), a seaman would always put his right foot on the gangplank first. This superstition, inverted, may explain why soldiers march off left foot first — to threaten their enemies.

Sterilize: [1] In naval mine warfare, to permanently render a mine incapable of firing by means of a device (sterilizer) within the mine. [2] In covert and clandestine operations, to remove any marks or devices which can identify the sponsoring nation or organization.

Sterilizer: A device now required by international

law, intended to automatically inactivate a mine after a specified period.

Stern: The after part of a ship or boat.

Stern anchor: [1] Any anchor carried aft. [2] The anchor used by a landing craft or ship to steady itself while discharging vehicles and personnel, and to kedge itself off when finished.

Stern chase: A pursuit in which the quarry flees directly away from the attacker.

Stern drive: A propulsion system for small boats in which the engine is inboard while gears and propeller are outboard and can be turned to steer the vessel.

Stern gallery: *See* sternwalk.

Stern light: A bright white light placed as close as possible to the stern and visible only over an unbroken arc of three points (67½°) on each quarter of the vessel.

Stern slipway: [1] A steep sloping surface leading from the water to the flensing deck of a whaler, to which slaughtered whales are winched up to be stripped of their blubber. [2] Part of the launch and recovery system of Royal Netherlands Navy ocean-capable patrol vessels, slipway rails guide superfast rigid-hull interceptor boats into and out of the water, while a water management system and specially-shaped opening allow space for the boat's stern thruster.

Stern tube: [1] A submarine's after torpedo tube. [2] The watertight bushing or bearing that supports the propeller shaft's exit through the hull. Also shaft tube.

Stern wave: The transverse wave propagated by motion of a ship's stern through the water.

Sternage: An obsolete term for [1] the after-part of a vessel, or [2] sternway.

Stern-chaser: A gun mounted so as to fire astern of the vessel (cf. Bow-chaser).

Sternpost: A vertical element at the rear of a vessel, to which the sides and usually the rudder are attached. Also rudder post.

Sternrope: *See* mooring lines.

Sternsheets: A platform or seat at the rear of a small boat (*see* sheets).

Sternwalk: An open gallery around the after part of a sailing line of battle ship. Usually reserved for the captain or embarked admiral.

Sternway: Backward motion (cf. headway).

Sternwheeler: a steamship propelled by a single paddle wheel at its stern.

Stevedore: A dockyard worker engaged in loading or unloading cargo. From the Spanish estibador = pack or stow (cf. longshoreman, lumper).

Steward: A person assigned to managing, preparing, or serving food on shipboard (from the Anglo-Saxon styweard = house-warden).

Stick: A spar or mast (colloquial).

Stiff: Said of a vessel which resists heeling (cf. tender, crank).

Stinkpot: [1] Pejorative slang for a powerboat.

[2] Eighteenth century chemical warfare device, consisting of a fused earthenware jar filled with gunpowder, combustibles, and noxious materials.

Stirling engine: Invented in 1816 by Robert Stirling (as an alternative to steam power), this engine has the potential to be more efficient than conventional internal-combustion. Instead of burning fuel inside the cylinders, heat from an external source is transferred to an enclosed working fluid (usually an inert gas).

In simplified form, there are two interconnected banks of cylinders, one heated and the other cooled. As the first cylinder is heated, the gas expands against a piston, forcing it down to drive a generator to produce electricity for propulsion. Simultaneously, a mechanical linkage draws the second cylinder down, pulling in the expanded gas and cooling it to lower its pressure. As the cycle continues, the piston in the second cylinder begins to move up, compressing the cooled gas which is drawn back into the first cylinder as its piston retreats. Then the cycle is repeated.

The gas never leaves the engine, there are no exhaust valves, and no explosions occur. This makes Stirling engines very quiet. However, because the heat source is external it has to be conducted through the cylinder walls before it can produce useful power, nor can it change its power output rapidly. These factors make the cycle impractical for use in many automotive applications, but appropriate for marine propulsion. Stirling engines were installed during the late 1990s on three *Gotland*-class Swedish submarines which are reported to have an underwater endurance of 14 days at five knots.

Stirrups: Lines supporting the foot-ropes on which topmen stand when working aloft.

Stitch: Colloquial term for sail(s), used in expressions such as "every stitch she can carry," meaning as much sail as possible.

Stock: The crossbar of a traditional anchor which prevents it from lying flat on the floor without digging in. However, most modern anchors and all large ones are stockless.

Stockfish: Dried cod, a staple food on sailing ships.

Stockless anchor: Any of several designs of anchor that have no stock to facilitate handling and stowage.

Stocks: Heavy timbers supporting a ship under construction.

Stoker: [1] Formerly, a member of a coal-fired steamship's black gang who shoveled coal into the furnaces, removed clinkers and ashes, and leveled the fire before adding new fuel. *See* furnace room and trimmer. [2] Nowadays, a rating responsible for firing oil-fueled furnaces and tending boilers. Also fireman.

Stoker's friend: Royal Navy slang for the ace of spades, said to resemble a coal shovel.

Stone fleets: Various old ships, loaded with field-stone and sand, deliberately sunk by the Union Navy during the American Civil War. In December 1861,

Captain Charles Henry Davis scuttled 24 whaleships in Charleston Harbor, hoping to stop Confederate blockade runners. A second, smaller, fleet was sunk in nearby Mafitt's Channel in 1862.

Stone frigate: British naval slang for a shore establishment. RN shore stations are considered to be warships and are named as such (for example, the School of Marine and Air Engineering at Gosport in Hampshire is HMS *Sultan*).

Stopper: [1] A chain, line, or other device to temporarily hold a larger chain or cable while it is being secured. [2] A knot forming a knob at the end of a line to prevent it running through a block, cleat, hole, or other small space.

Stops: [1] Projections on a mast that support a yard, gaff, or other spar. [2] Short lines used in securing awnings or furling sails.

Storekeeper: [1] In the USN, a supply corps petty officer specifically charged with clerical or manual work. [2] In RN usage, the term is not a rating but refers to any individual responsible for specific departmental supplies (e.g., the "engineering storekeeper" would normally be a Leading or First Class Stoker).

Stores: General term for the provisions, materials, and supplies carried aboard ship for navigation, propulsion, upkeep, and crew.

Storm: Force 10 on the Beaufort Scale (winds 48–55 knots = 55.3–63.3 mph = 88.9–101.9 km/h).

Storm anchor: An exceptionally heavy anchor reserved for use in heavy weather.

Storm surge: An abnormal rise in sea level along a coastline, occurring as it is approached by the onshore winds of a tropical rotating windstorm.

Stormsail: A sail of reduced size and extra-heavy canvas for use in gales.

Stormy petrel: These little seabirds, who have been called "the sailor's friends," are said to come to warn of an approaching storm, and it is most unlucky to kill them since each contains the soul of a dead seaman. The French call them Oiseaux de Notre Dame (Birds of Our Lady) or Aves Sanctæ Mariæ (Saint Mary's fowl), while English seamen call them Mother Carey's chickens, which is an Anglicization of Mater Cara (Latin for Beloved Mother, i.e., The Virgin Mary).

Stove: [1] The condition of being crushed or pushed in (past participle of stave). [2] A cooking device in a ship's galley.

Stow: [1] To put goods, cargo, or equipment in the proper place. [2] To furl a sail.

Stow it!: Sailor's slang for "shut up!"

Stowage: The placement of cargo so as to ensure the safety and stability of the ship when at sea.

Stowaway: A person who hides aboard ship in order to obtain free passage or to elude pursuit.

Straddle: A salvo of projectiles that fall evenly around the target, which thus lies at the mean point of impact.

Strafe: [1] In military use: To rake with fire at close range; especially as ground troops with machine-gun fire from low-flying aircraft. From the German World War I slogan Gott strafe England = God punish England. [2] In video games: To move sideways, usually for the purpose of dodging.

Straggler: [1] A merchantman that falls behind the rest of a convoy. [2] Formerly, a seamen who had deserted his ship.

Strait: A narrow waterway connecting two larger bodies of water.

Strake: A continuous line of planking or plating extending along the entire length of the vessel's hull.

Strand: [1] To drive or leave a vessel firmly aground. [2] To abandon a person without means of transport. [3] One of the component parts of a rope, wire, or cable. [3] The land bordering a body of water (mainly poetical).

Stranded: Said of [1] A vessel which has been driven ashore and is unable to move. [2] A person left behind. [3] A rope, wire, or cable with one or more stands broken by strain or chafing.

Strap: Originally a variation of strop which now has three slightly different meanings: [1] A metal band used to secure something. [2] A loop or circle of rope or wire made by splicing the ends together for use as a sling. [3] To make or use such a loop.

Strapping: [1] An operation by which cartons or boxes are reinforced by bands, metal straps, or wire, drawn taut and sealed or clamped by a machine. [2] Measurement of storage tanks to provide tables for the conversion of depth of product to volume of contents.

Stratagem: A plan, scheme, or trick designed to deceive an opponent.

Strategic sealift: The ocean movement and afloat pre-positioning of military materiel.

Strategy: The planning, coordination, and employment of armed forces using all available military, political, psychological and economic factors, while making optimum use of space and time (not including actual combat operations which fall under tactics). Naval strategy is generally concerned with controlling the sea lanes to facilitate the passage of friendly vessels and deny it to hostile ones.

Stream: [1] To drop something over the side and tow it (e.g., a paravane). [2] To tow a vessel away from its berth. [3] Water flowing in a channel or watercourse. [4] A major ocean current (e.g., Gulf Stream).

Stream ice: Ice forming in and flowing with a current.

Stretch out!: Command for oarsmen to bend forward to their utmost, in order to pull as strongly as possible.

Stretchers: Athwartships crosspieces against which rowers brace their feet.

Stretching hook: *See* benchhook.

Strike: [1] Surrender by lowering the ship's colors. [2] Take down a mast, sail, or flag. [3] Run aground. [4] Take something below deck. [5] Ring the ship's bell. [6] An attack by naval aircraft. [7] Strive for promotion (USN slang).

Strike Group: Formerly known as a Battle Group, this USN term refers to a small fleet usually centered on an aircraft carrier, with an escort force of cruisers, destroyers, frigates, and attack submarines, armed with surface-to-surface, surface-to-air, and cruise missiles. One is usually a combat-control ship with Aegis missile-tracking and fire-control systems which can direct weapons aboard the other ships in the group. Others carry helicopters armed with antisubmarine torpedoes and anti-ship missiles. Accompanying logistic-support vessels carry fuel, food, matériel, and munitions. An Expeditionary Strike Group is a similar formation, with the addition of an Amphibious Ready Group.

Strikedown: Describes the movement of naval aircraft from the flight deck to the hangar deck.

Striker: [1] USN term for an apprentice or learner, especially an enlisted person training for promotion to petty officer. [2] Whaler's term for the thrower of a harpoon. [3] An attacking player in association football (soccer).

Stringer: A longitudinal stiffener for a ship's side.

Strip Ship: To remove all non-essential flammable, explosive, or other potentially dangerous material from a warship about to go into combat (cf. clear ship).

Stripe: [1] One of the "rings" of lace in a naval officer's rank insignia. [2] A strip of material worn on uniform as a symbol of service, good conduct, wounds, etc. [3] A blow with a whip or rod as punishment.

Stripping: Removing cargo from a shipping container (cf. stuffing).

Stroke: [1] A single pull or sweep of the oars in rowing. [2] The oarsman from whom all others in the boat take their time. [3] In an engine, the motion of a piston in moving from one end of the cylinder to the other.

Strong breeze: Force 6 on the Beaufort Scale (winds 22–27 knots = 25.3–31.1 mph = 40.8–50 km/h).

Strong gale: Force 9 on the Beaufort Scale (winds 41–47 knots = 47.2–54.1 mph = 76–87.1 km/h).

Strongback: [1] A longitudinal rod, laid along the top of a ship's boat, to support a cover when not in use. [2] A moveable girder for supporting a hatch cover. [3] An arched timber bracing the uprights of a hand windlass. [4] A short, stout beam used as a shore in damage control.

Strongroom: A safe, or secure compartment for the storage of valuables in a passenger vessel.

Strop: [1] A metal or spliced-rope band surrounding a block or deadeye and forming a loop for suspension. [2] A grommet. [3] A strap. (Latin *stroppus*.)

Stroppy: British nautical slang for being irritable, difficult, or hard to deal with.

Structural bulkhead: A transverse interior wall or divider that contributes to hull strength and forms a watertight boundary between compartments.

Strut: [1] A bar forming part of a framework, designed to resist compression. [2] Part of an aircraft's landing gear. [3] A support for the after portion of a propeller shaft.

Studding sail: A lightweight sail, attached to a boom extending the yardarm of a square-sail. Pronounced "stun'sl."

Stuff: [1] Any of various protective mixtures applied to a wooden ship. Turpentine mixed with resin was used on lower masts, tallow on topmasts: for the sides it was turpentine, oil, and varnish; and for the bottom, tallow, sulfur, and resin. [2] Obsolete term for the fiber of flax, hemp, or jute (cf. small stuff).

Stuffing: Placing cargo in a shipping container (cf. stripping).

Stuffing box: A cylindrical device containing packing, compressed around a rotating shaft or reciprocating rod to prevent leakage.

S-twist: *See* rope and hawser lay.

Sub-caliber: A projectile that is smaller than the bore of the weapon it is to be fired from, requiring a bushing or sabot to enlarge it.

Subdivision: Naval architecture term referring to the compartmentalization of interior spaces by watertight bulkheads.

Sub-Lieutenant: In 1802, Admiral Lord St. Vincent introduced the semi-official title of sub-lieutenant for midshipmen and master's mates who had passed the examination for lieutenant and were awaiting promotion. This practice was dropped at the end of the Napoleonic Wars in 1814, but the title was officially re-introduced in 1861 as the lowest commissioned rank, replacing that of mate. The USN equivalent is lieutenant (jg). *See also* acting sub-lieutenant.

Submarine: [1] Generically, below the surface of the sea (e.g., submarine cable). [2] Colloquially, any submersible vessel. [3] Specifically, a craft (always called a boat) designed for underwater exploration or warfare, the latter usually being armed with torpedoes or guided missiles (*see also* attack, ballistic missile, and hunter-killer).

Submarine canyon: A steep-sided valley on the continental slope. After decades of uncertainty and debate, the major mechanisms of canyon formation are now thought to be underwater landslides and turbidity currents.

Submarine chaser: A small, fast, wooden-hulled naval patrol vessel specially designed for anti-submarine warfare using depth-charges. The sub-chaser (as it is popularly known) came into existence via an Act of Congress of 4th March 1917 which authorized President Woodrow Wilson "...to secure the more economic and expeditious delivery of ... submarine chasers...." It saw service in both World Wars, but during the latter was gradually replaced by the destroyer escort.

Submarine current: One that flows beneath the surface, often in a different direction to the surface current. *See also* deepwater circulation.

Submarine Escape Immersion Equipment: A whole-body suit combined with a personal life raft, which has replaced the Steinke Hood in the USN submarine service.

Submarine pen: World War II term for a strong enclosure or bunker designed to protect submarines from air attack.

Submarine watch stations: [1] The traditional submarine control party includes an officer who supervises two junior enlisted personnel — helmsman (for steering) and planesman (for diving) — who manage the main control panel, along with a Chief of the Watch, who manages the ballast control panel where hull integrity, trim, depth control, and other parameters, are monitored and controlled. [2] Today, with fly-by-wire these four watch stations can be reduced to two (usually chief petty officers).

Submariner: A member of a submarine's crew. Pronounced submareener (as in marine) by the USN and submariner (as in mariner) by the RN.

Submerge: To sink or plunge below the surface.

Submersible: Any vessel capable of submerging and operating underwater.

Submunitions: Smaller weapons carried inside the warhead of a missile or projectile to be released and scattered when the target is neared.

Subordinate: Of inferior rank.

Subsidiary landing: In amphibious operations, a landing outside the designated landing area, in support of the main landing.

Substantive: A rank held permanently as opposed to only while serving in a particular post. When relieved of a temporary or acting promotion the holder of substantive rank reverts to that grade.

Substitute pennant: *See* table 8.

Substitution clause: A charter party clause that allows the carrier to transport cargo in a vessel other than that named in the bill of lading.

Subsurface: Below the surface of the water, submerged, underwater.

Subtropical surface currents: Currents on either side of the equator, in all ocean basins.

- The north and south equatorial currents both run westward at about 5 kilometers (3 miles) a day, at depths of 100 to 200 meters (330–660 feet).
- The eastward-flowing equatorial counter-current represents partial return of these currents. In the Pacific Ocean it is intensified during El Niño events.
- Warm water Western boundary currents flowing from the equator towards higher latitudes — the best known of which is the North Atlantic Gulf Stream — are narrow jet-like flows extending some 1000 meters (3300 feet) below the ocean surface and traveling at between 40 and 120 kilometers (25–75 miles) a day.

- In contrast, eastern boundary currents, flowing in the opposite direction and carrying cold water towards the tropics, are generally broad and shallow, creeping along at 3 to 7 kilometers (2–5 miles) per day.
- Other surface currents include the North Pacific Current and North Atlantic Drift in the Northern Hemisphere, and the South Pacific, South Indian, and South Atlantic Currents in the Southern.
- Further south, the Antarctic Circumpolar Current flows continuously around that continent as a more or less closed system.
- The Somali Current off the horn of Africa is unusual because it reverses direction, running northward from May to September and southward from November to March.

Suck the monkey: So that seamen could smuggle liquor aboard, Jamaicans sold them coconut shells drained of milk and filled with rum. The end of the nut was said to look like a monkey's face, so the phrase was originally applied to imbibing rum from such a nut. Later, it came to mean illicitly inserting a straw or pipe into a cask in order to suck alcohol from it. This was also known as bleeding the monkey.

Suez Canal: An artificial waterway connecting the Mediterranean and Red Seas, providing a shorter route than Cape Agulhas for ships sailing from Europe or America to southern Asia, eastern Africa, or Oceania. Excavation begun in April 1859, and the canal opened to navigation in November 1869. It passes through three lakes, Manzala in the north, Timsah in the middle, and the Bitter Lakes further south, and has no locks due to minor sea level differences and flat terrain. There are several passing bays, but most of the canal is single lane. It can accommodate vessels of up to 16 m (53 ft) draft, and improvements are scheduled to increase this to 22 m (72 ft) by 2010. Currently, those that draw too much can offload part of their cargo onto a canal-owned boat and reload at the other end of the canal.

Suez Canal Rudder: *See* salmontail.

Sufferance wharf: A dock under the control of Customs authorities at which goods can be loaded or discharged without being subject to duty.

Suit: A complete set of sails for a vessel. Also suite.

Sullit: A broad-beamed Dutch fishing boat.

Summer tank: A tanker's compartment in which extra liquid cargo can be carried so as to lower the hull to its summer load line.

Sump: A low point or chamber in a well or bilge into which liquid drains for subsequent removal by a sump pump.

Sun deck: The uppermost deck on a passenger liner, usually reserved for tanning and games such as shuffleboard.

Sundowner: [1] In the RN, an early evening drink taken after a hard day's work. [2] In the USN, an excessively strict or bullying captain, who required all libertymen to be aboard before nightfall.

Sunrise ceremony: The morning flag-hoisting ceremony while in harbor is almost identical in the RN and USN. At 0800 hours each morning, with a guard and band (when available) on parade, the colors are hoisted — national flag at the ensign staff and union jack at the jackstaff. As soon as the band starts playing (or if there is no band, when the hoist begins) all within earshot turn to face the national ensign and hand salute until the flags reach their trucks, which they must do just as the Anthem ends. Either a bugle or voice command will then order "carry on!"

Sun's over the yardarm: Traditionally, this phrase indicated it was appropriate to imbibe an alcoholic drink. The spar in question is the foreyard as seen from the quarterdeck. In temperate latitudes the sun will rise above it at about 11 A.M.

Sunset ceremony: In both RN and USN, at about five minutes before sunset, "First Call" is made by voice, boatswain's pipe or bugle. Exactly at sunset, "Attention" is sounded and either the National Anthem or the bugle call "retreat" is played. Ensign and jack will be started down as soon as the music begins, with lowering timed to be complete exactly as the last note is played. If already at half-mast, they are hoisted smartly to the truck at the beginning of the music, and then lowered slowly. As at sunrise, all within earshot face the ensign and hand salute. (In special circumstances, "Official Sunset" may be delayed in order to render daytime honors to an important visitor.)

Super battleships: The most powerful battleships ever built were the Japanese *Yamato* and *Musashi*, each exceeding 72,000 tons and mounting 18-inch guns. The former was sunk during a suicide mission against the Okinawa invasion, and the latter in the Battle of Leyte Gulf. *Shinano*, the third vessel of the class, was converted to an aircraft carrier, but was sunk on her maiden voyage by American submarine *Archerfish*.

Super cruisers: *See* pocket battleships.

Super frigates: In 1794, Congress authorized the United States Navy to acquire six frigates which, although technically fifth-rates, don't really fit the warship ratings. Like the German pocket-battleships of World War II, they were strategically designed to be more powerful than anything fast enough to catch them, and speedy enough to outrun anything more heavily gunned. They were longer proportionally, had heavier scantling, and carried heavier batteries than any ships of equal rating in the world. Three were nominal 36-gunners and three nominal forty-fours, but they were actually much more heavily-armed. For example, USS *Constitution* carried one long 18-pounder and thirty long 24-pounder guns, plus twenty-four 32-pounder carronades. This so far outclassed all contemporary frigates that the British called them "Seventy-fours in disguise" and issued Fighting Instructions requiring more lightly-armed RN vessels to avoid engagement unless they enjoyed superiority of two-to-one (but *see* Chesapeake & Shannon). *See also* President.

Supercargo: The officer responsible for the consigned goods and commercial activity of a merchantman. (Spanish sobre = over + cargar = cargo.)

Superheated steam: Steam heated to a temperature higher than its boiling point. Hence it cannot exist in contact with water, nor contain water, and resembles a perfect gas. Also known as dry steam. Cf. saturated steam and wet steam.

Supernumerary: A person in excess of the normal or prescribed establishment.

Superstructure: All structures rising above the main deck.

Supertanker: An imprecise term covering bulk oil carriers in excess of 75,000 dwt (*see* VLCC, and ULCC).

Supplies: [1] In general and commercial use, consumable items such as fuel, food, clothing, and ammunition carried for use during a voyage (cf. furniture). [2] In military logistics, all matériel and items used in the equipment, support, and maintenance of military forces.

Supply Corps: This staff corps was founded in 1795 by President George Washington, making it one of the oldest in the United States Navy. Today a USN supply officer is responsible for such things as supply management, expeditionary logistics, inventory control, disbursements, financial management, contracting, information systems, operations analysis, material and operational logistics, fuel management, and food services. The official supply corps motto is Ready for Sea. The equivalent RN organization is the logistics branch.

Supply Officer: [1] Formerly, a member of the RN supply branch (now re-titled logistics officer and branch respectively). [2] A member of the USN supply corps. *See also* purser.

Support: The action of aiding, protecting, complementing, or sustaining another force or unit.

Surf: [1] The swell of the sea as it approaches a beach or shoal. [2] The line or mass of foamy water caused by breaking waves. [3] To ride on waves using a specially designed board. [4] To move from site to site on the Internet.

Surf line: The point offshore where incoming waves and swells are affected by the bottom and form breakers.

Surf zone: Amphibious operations term for that portion of the littoral where waves break.

Surface: [1] The upper boundary or air/liquid interface of the water in a river, lake, sea, or ocean. [2] To rise to that boundary.

Surface action group: A temporary or standing organization of surface combatant ships, tailored for a specific tactical mission that does not require the aircraft of a strike group.

Surface combatant: A warship constructed and armed for combat use against air, surface and subsurface threats, or onshore targets.

Surface current: Oceanic surface currents are of

great importance to mariners. Some are large and permanent, others local and transient. They can be defined as horizontal movement in the upper 220 fathoms (400 meters, 1320 feet), which represents somewhat less than 10 percent of all the water in the oceans. Solar heat and wind are the primary forces that start surface water moving. Secondary forces such as gravity and terrestrial rotation then determine which way the currents will flow.

The sun is most powerful at the equator, where its heat causes surface water to expand and rise about eight centimeters (3 inches) above the levels in temperate latitudes. Influenced by gravity, equatorial surface water tends to flow down this slight slope in both directions towards the north and south polar regions. Solar heat also affects the tropical atmosphere, creating winds which flow in the same north and south directions as the currents. Blowing across the air-ocean interface they create friction which tends to push the surface water into another small "hill" down which gravity pulls the water poleward. At this point Coriolis effect clicks in to amplify the movement. In the northern hemisphere the larger surface currents are constrained by land masses which force them into virtually closed rotational systems known as a Gyres. These do not develop in the southern hemisphere due to lack of bordering continents. *See also* subtropical surface currents, polar surface currents, and oceanic circulation.

Surface Deployment & Distribution Command: A U.S. Army unit that is the DoD's worldwide port manager and organizes global movement of military personnel and cargo. Formerly called Military Traffic Management Command.

Surface effect ship: A vessel supported by a cushion of downward-thrusting air, usually with twin hulls (like a catamaran). When it is "off-cushion" or "hull-borne," its full weight is supported by the buoyancy of the hulls. When "on-cushion," a small portion of each hull remains in the water, making it more resistant to slipping sideways and able to use underwater jets for propulsion: One type, which can move over land as well as water, is commonly known by the trade name "Hovercraft." *See also* air cushion vehicle and ground-effect vessel.

Surface fire support: Fire provided by naval surface gun, missile, and electronic warfare systems in support of a unit or units tasked with achieving the mission's objectives. *See also* gunfire support.

Surface layer: *See* mixed layer.

Surface-to-air: Shipboard weapons designed to attack aircraft and missiles.

Surface-to-surface: Shipboard weapons designed to attack surface ships.

Surface vessel: One that does not submerge.

Surface warfare: Naval combat operations excluding aviation and submarine activities.

Surge: [1] The difference between actual wave height and that considered normal or predictable (*see*

also storm surge). [2] A swelling wave or billow. [3] One of six possible responses of a vessel to movement of the sea (*see* linear displacement and ship motion). [4] The bight of a rope. [5] To slacken a line by allowing it to slip around (for example) a windlass or capstan drum. [6] USN term for the deployment of a strike group ahead of schedule. [7] A pulsating speed variation by an engine or gas turbine. [8] A sudden flow of electricity. [9] The swash of liquid in a container. [10] The 2007 deployment of additional U.S. troops to Iraq.

Surgeon: Formerly, a medical specialist assigned to RN ships by the Navy Board, warranted with wardroom rank and entitled to walk the quarterdeck. Appointment was originally subject to examination by one or more of the Worshipful Company of Barber-Surgeons, the Sick & Hurt Board, the Transport Board, and/or the Victualing Board; but after 1832 qualifications were examined by the Admiralty. Later in the nineteenth century, surgeons became commissioned officers. The surgeon was the only fully-qualified medical person on the ship, and was assisted by surgeon's mates who were inferior warrant officers with paramedical training.

On 9th March 1798 Dr. George Balfour of Virginia became the United States Navy's first medical officer. At that time the majority of ships' surgeons were appointed and served as civilians, although some commanding officers awarded temporary commissions the for the duration of a specific cruise. In 1872 USN doctors became commissioned officers. *See also* medical services.

Surtass: **Sur**veillance **T**owed **A**rray **S**ensor **S**ystem.

Surveillance: Is defined by DoD and NATO as "the systematic observation of aerospace, surface or subsurface areas, places, persons, or things, by visual, aural, electronic, photographic, or other means." *See also* sea surveillance and Integrated Undersea Surveillance Systems.

Surveillance Towed Array Sensor System: A passive, receive-only sonar system consisting of an array designed for the long range detection of submarines, and towed miles behind an ocean surveillance ship as the mobile component of U.S. Navy's network for deep ocean surveillance. *See* Integrated Undersea Surveillance Systems.

Suspension: To relieve an officer of his duties for up to ten days as a non-judicial punishment. A longer suspension may be allowed if court-martial is pending.

Swab: [1] A mop made of rope yarn. [2] To use such a mop to clean something. [3] A clumsy or contemptible person (only the lowest seaman would be assigned to swabbing duty). [4] USN slang for an officer's epaulette.

Swabbie: A disrespectful nickname for a USN enlisted person.

Swage: [1] To tighten a metal fitting around a wire rope. [2] The tool used for this purpose.

Swallow the anchor: Leave the seafaring life.

Swamp: To bring a vessel close to foundering by shipping water over its side.

Swarm: To climb rigging or a mast using legs, arms and hands to draw oneself aloft as rapidly as possible. Cf. hand over fist.

Swash: [1] The to-and-fro surge of water in a ship's tanks. [2]The rush of a broken wave up a beach. [3] A shoal over which the tide ripples.

Swashbuckler: [1] A term first recorded in 1560 to describe a noisy and boastful swordsman, based on the practice of using a sword in the fighting-hand to strike a buckler in the off-hand in order to intimidate an adversary. (Derived from the archaic words swash = strike violently + buckler = small shield). [2] Later, a boastful or noisy buccaneer or brigand.

Swashplate: [1] An inclined disc revolving on an shaft to give reciprocating motion to a part attached to it. [2] A metal baffle placed in a tank to inhibit the surge of liquid due to the vessel's motion.

Sway: [1] A sliding lateral movement across the water. One of six possible responses of a vessel to movement of the sea (*see* linear displacement, and ship motion). [2] To hoist or raise something such as a spar or cargo.

Sweat: To haul a rope until it is as taut as possible.

Sweat the glass: Attempt to shorten the watch by turning he glass before all the sand had run out.

Sweep: [1] To clear the decks for action. [2] To clear an area of mines. [3] A sortie by warships or aircraft. [4] The rotation of a radar antenna. [5] A long oar. [6] To drag for something underwater (e.g., a lost anchor). [7] A minesweeping operation.

Sweep rate: The number of times a radar antenna or sonar transducer rotates in a minute.

Sweepers: USN term for personnel assigned clean the decks with brooms.

Sweet Fanny Adams: This RN slang for "nothing at all," often abbreviated to "sweet eff eh," is commonly believed to be a euphemism for "fuck all," but in fact it refers to the non-existence of a murdered child (*see* Fanny).

Swell: Long unbroken heaves of the sea due to wind-generated waves that have advanced into calmer waters and acquired a more rounded form. Because of their length, swell waves do not break. The stronger the winds at the source area, the bigger will be the swell and the further will it travel; and the longer the wind blows in the source area, the longer will the swell persist, even long after the wind has ceased or changed direction. Experienced watch officers often report trains of swell waves, of differing periods and amplitudes, arriving simultaneously from two or even three directions.

Swept area: A channel or other waterway kept clear of mines.

Swift boat: A fast patrol craft used for inshore and riverine operations during the Vietnam War.

Swifter: [1] A rope threaded through holes in cap-stan bars to hold them in place. [2] Formerly a heavy rope circling a warship just below the gunwale to strengthen it when laying alongside in combat. [3] The aftermost shroud on either side of a sailing ship's masts.

Swing: [1] To ride at anchor with the bow pointing in different directions due to wind and tide. [2] A NATO enabling concept, based on the probability that the future strategic environment will be confused and unpredictable. "Swing" is defined as "the ability to configure a force, formation, or unit to operate successfully and cost-effectively across a wide range of mission types and roles." The concept is force-oriented and visualizes the seamless integration of Maritime, Land and Air components with multi-tasking versatility as a result of integrating key elements of doctrine, equipment, platform design, training, personnel, and force structure.

Swing out: To move an anchor or rotate a small boat's davits over the side preparatory to launching.

Swing ship: To follow various courses in order to check compass deviation.

Swing the lead: This British idiom, which refers to malingering, shirking duty, or feigning sickness, has an obvious nautical origin. Throwing and retrieving the heavy leadline was hard work, so a lazy sailor would stand there swinging it like a pendulum and shouting a fictitious depth from time to time. If an officer came by, the seaman would release the line on the next forward swing, appearing to have been properly casting all the while.

Swipes: Sailing ship seaman's slang for exceptionally weak beer. The first mayor of Melbourne, Australia, was the brewer of "Murphy's Swipes" — a beer so noxious that some drinkers needed medical attention.

Swivel-gun: A light firearm mounted on a pin or pivot, allowing it to sweep across a wide field of fire. Old English swifen = rotate.

Sword: The personal sidearm of an officer, consisting of a long straight or curved blade fixed to a hilt.

Synchro: An electromagnetic device for transmitting mechanical motion to a remote location. A transmitter emits an electrical signal corresponding to the angle of rotation of its shaft, and a receiver causes its own shaft to rotate to an angle corresponding to the signal. Used for the control of propulsion machinery and in fire-control. Also called selsyn.

Synchronous roll: An excessive movement which occurs when the oscillating period of the hull coincides with the ambient wave period. This is especially troublesome to seafarers because rocking from side-to-side, with high acceleration and rapid repetition, is disconcerting to the human inner ear and a primary cause of seasickness. Hence many roll control devices have been developed (*see* ship motion and rotational oscillation).

Synoptic chart: A depiction of meteorological conditions over a wide area at a given moment. The word is derived from the Greek sunoptikos = seen together.

Synoptic scale: In meteorology, a horizontal length

of some 1000 kilometres (620 miles) or more. This corresponds to the typical size of mid-latitude depressions. Most weather maps depicting high and low pressure areas are synoptic-scale systems. (also known as large scale or cyclonic scale).

T

T-124: [1] A form, signed during World War II by British merchant seamen agreeing to serve under Naval Articles and subjecting them to naval discipline. It was T-124 that allowed civilian yachtsmen to participate in the evacuation of Dunkirk. [2] A conference control protocol, issued by the United Nations International Telecommunications Union.

Tab: *See* trim tab.

Tabernacle: A device at the base of the deck-mounted mast of a small boat or barge, which both holds it in place and allows it to pivot to pass under bridges.

Table: [1] To make board hems in the skirts and bottoms of sails in order to strengthen them in the part attached to the boltrope. [2] *See* captain's table.

Tablemount: A flat-topped seamount or guyot.

Tabling: The reinforcing hem of a sail to which the boltrope is sewn.

TAC: Tactical air command (USMC).

Tachometer: An instrument that measures engine speed, usually in revolutions per minute.

Tack: [1] To come about by turning the bow through the wind (the opposite of wear). [2] The direction in which a vessel is moving as determined by the position of its sails in relation to the wind. [3] The lower forward corner of a fore-and-aft sail. [4] A line for extending the weather clew of a course. [5] A course run obliquely against the wind. [6] The equivalent of a dash in a flag signal (*see* tackline). [7] A separator in a radio signal. [8] Seaman's slang for food. [9] A short pointed nail with a broad flat head. [10] A sewing stitch used to temporarily fasten cloth together.

This is another nautical word that has found its way into common usage. To be "on the right tack" is to be following an appropriate course of action, while "on the wrong tack" implies being under a misapprehension, and to "change tack" is to abandon one course of action or argument for another. (The term "hard tack," meaning bad luck or substandard food, has a completely different origin, having originally referred to the coarse, rock-like, weevil-infested bread known as ship's biscuit).

Tackle: Any combination of ropes, pulleys, hooks etc., which provides a mechanical advantage for lifting weights or setting sails (from the Middle Dutch "taekel," and pronounced tay-kle).

Tackline: A short length of line inserted between two flags in a hoist. Usually to separate two signals in the same hoist, but sometimes serving the same purpose as a dash does in print.

T-ACS: Auxiliary crane ship (DoD).

Tactical Action Officer: USN designation of the person in charge of a warship's weapons and combat systems. Supervises the entire watch team staffing the ship's command center. Duties include tactical decision making, console operation, communications, and oversight of a variety of watchstander responsibilities in air, surface, and subsurface warfare areas. The RN equivalent is warfare officer.

Tactical air navigation: An electronic homing system that guides aircraft back to their carrier or shore base.

Tactical air officer (afloat): An officer assigned to an amphibious task force to coordinate all phases of tactical air support for the amphibious operation, plus the air operations of support forces en route to and in the objective area.

Tactical air support: Air operations carried out in coordination with surface forces and which directly assist land or maritime operations.

Tactical Command Support System: A USN information system for the management of ships, submarines, aviation squadrons, and intermediate maintenance activities afloat and ashore. It provides access to data on parts inventory, finances, technical manuals and drawings, personnel and medical information, crews mess, ships stores, and unit administration. It also facilitates the management of workload and resources for ship and aircraft repair and maintenance.

Tactical diameter: The lateral distance a ship has traveled from its original course after completing a 180° turn. When ships are in formation a uniform tactical diameter will be prescribed to ensure that each ship's "standard rudder" will produce the same arc of turn.

Tactical interval: The distance to be maintained between adjacent vessels in a formation.

Tactical loading: Placing military cargo on board ship so that it can be unloaded in the sequence required for combat (*see* cargo classification).

Tactics: The plans, means, and art of disposing and applying armed force while in actual contact with an enemy (cf. strategy). *See also* naval tactics in the age of sail.

Taffrail: [1] A guard rail around the uppermost part of a ship's stern. Possibly derived from "aft rail." [2] The flat upper part of a wooden ship's stern, often richly carved. From the Dutch tafereel = carved or painted panel.

Taffrail log: A patent log designed to be attached to the taffrail.

Tagline: A rope used to steady a load which is being swung inboard or outboard. Also steadying line.

T-AH: Hull classification symbol of a Hospital ship (DoD).

TAI: International Atomic Time (from the French Temps Atomique International). *See* Coordinated Universal Time.

Taifa: The association or union of Barbary Corsair captains.

Tail: [1] The orientation an anchored ship tends to adopt (e.g., she tails downstream). [2] To taper and wax the end of a rope. [3] The rope which replaces a hook on a block. [4] To prevent the end of a halyard or sheet from fouling while being winched. [5] The latter part of a gale as it tapers off.

Tail on!: USN command to lay hold of a line and haul away.

Tail splice: A method of connecting fiber rope to wire rope.

Tailblock: A block with a rope tail instead of a hook.

Tailhook: A device lowered from the lower fuselage of a carrier-based aircraft to engage the arrester gear and bring the aircraft to a controlled stop when landing.

Tailshaft: A rotating bar which transmits motion and torque from the engines to the propellers. Also propeller shaft.

Tainted goods: Under Admiralty Law, the discovery of contraband allows all other goods on board belonging to the owners of the contraband to be declared "tainted" and seized.

Tajaso: A kind of jerked beef supplied to vessels by Latin American ship chandlers (pronounced "tar-huso").

T-AK: Hull classification symbol of a cargo ship (DoD).

Take a turn: To wrap a line around something (e.g., cleat, bitts, winch, or capstan).

Take charge: Said of a rope or cable when it gets out of control and runs out under its own momentum.

Take down a peg or two: This idiom meaning to humble someone who is showing undue pride or ego has a nautical origin. The position of flags on sailing warships was regulated by a series of pegs at the base of the mast where the halyards were secured. If a flag officer was aboard, he had the right to fly his personal flag at the highest point to signify his power and prestige. If, however, a more senior admiral arrived, the first one's flag would have to be lowered by a peg or two to make place for the newcomer's.

Take in!: The command to [1] To lower and furl a sail. [2] To pull on a rope or hawser. [3] To bring a mooring line aboard.

Take on: To engage or hire.

Take over: [1] To relieve someone (e.g., at change of watch). [2] To assume command, especially in case of illness or incompetence.

Take the ground: Said of a vessel when a falling tide leaves it stranded. Also take the bottom.

Take the strain!: Command to apply light tension to a line without actually pulling it.

Take the wind out: Nowadays, this means winning a discussion by anticipating and discrediting the opponent's arguments. The phrase is derived from the former combat maneuver known as "stealing the wind."

Taken aback: To landlubbers this phrase describes someone who has been disconcerted by some unexpected news or happening, but it originally described a hazardous maritime event. When a square-rigged vessel was sailing with the wind and a sudden unexpected squall from a different direction blew the sails back against the masts, it threatened to snap them off, rendering the vessel helpless and un-maneuverable.

T-AKR: Hull classification symbol of a fast logistics ship (DoD).

Taku: During the early twentieth century, the British, French, German, and Russian navies each had a destroyer named *Taku*. This unusual coincidence came about as a result of the Third China War, commonly known as the Boxer Rebellion. A nationalist Chinese secret society, the Righteous Harmonious Fists (called "Boxers" by foreigners), mounted an insurgency against foreign occupation. Rape, pillage, and murder spread rapidly, and the international settlements at Tientsin and Peking (now Beijing) came under siege. An international relief force of Austrian, British, French, German, Italian, Japanese, Russian, and United States warships gathered offshore, but was held up by Chinese batteries in the Taku Forts guarding the Hai River Estuary. On 17th June 1900, nine shallow-draft warships were detached from the main fleet under the command of Lieutenant-Commander Roger Keyes (later Admiral Lord Keyes of Zeebrugge and Dover) to storm the forts with naval infantry. Four Chinese destroyers were captured and allotted to the navies mentioned above, each being re-named *Taku*.

Talker: A person assigned to repeat orders received via headphones.

Tall ship: Informal term for a square-rigged vessel with two or more masts irrespective of its sail plan.

Tally: [1] To inventory cargo being shipped or offloaded. [2] A notched stick used for this purpose especially in the Orient. [3] An RN seaman's cap ribbon carrying the name of his ship. [4] RN slang for a person's name (e.g., What's your tally?). From the French Taille = cut.

Tally-Ho!: Traditional cry of a fighter pilot on sighting a target. The term originated in fox-hunting and was adopted by RAF pilots during the Battle of Britain.

Tampion: The stopper inserted in the muzzle of a cannon, to keep corrosive salt water from getting into the barrel when the weapon is not in service. Also tompion, shot-plug.

Tampon: Nowadays, this is a plug or first-aid dressing used to stem hemorrhages or control menstrual flow, but the term is derived from tampion.

TAMY: Transportable Aircraft Maintenance Yard. A Royal Navy World War II unit designed to provide advanced servicing facilities comparable to a permanent installation. Only one was operational before atomic bombs ended the Pacific War. It was set up at Archerfield in Australia, where it assembled, repaired, and flight tested aircraft for the British Pacific Fleet. The U.S. Navy equivalent was the CASU (Carrier Aircraft Service Unit).

Tan: To preserve sailcloth by soaking it in tannin derived from tree bark. This slows the development of bacteria and mildew.

Tang: The metal fitting on a sailing ship's mast to which stays and shrouds are attached.

Tango: NATO phonetic notation for the letter "T."

Tank Landing Ship: A vessel designed to transport and land tanks and other large military vehicles to drive over the beach during an amphibious assault. Also Landing ship, tank.

Tanka: A covered Chinese rowing boat, used to ferry passengers to and from vessels.

Tanker: A ship, aircraft, or vehicle designed to carry liquids (especially crude oil and refined petroleum products) in bulk.

T-AP: Hull classification symbol of a troop transport (DoD).

Tap the Admiral: *See* Nelson's Blood.

Taps: The U.S. bugle call blown at military funerals and at sunset (cf. "Last Post"). The name refers to the fact that it originated as a drum beat and was only later transcribed for bugle. *See* Bugle calls.

TAR: Training and Administration Reserve (USN).

Tar: [1] A heavy dark distillate of coal or wood. [2] A seaman. 17th century sailors were nicknamed "Jack Tarpaulins" after the tar-impregnated cloth used to make their foul-weather coats, and this became abbreviated first to "Jack Tar" and then to "Jack" or "Tar."

Taranto: Was the principal fleet base of Regia Marina (Royal Italian Navy) in both World Wars. After the 1940 defeat of France and neutralization of its navy, previously allied to Britain, the Italians outnumbered Britain's Mediterranean Fleet in every class of warship except aircraft carriers. Their "fleet-in-being" at Taranto, deep in the "instep" of the Italian "boot," posed a serious threat to British convoys en route to Egypt. Determined to redress the balance, the Royal Navy mounted the second sea-launched naval air attack in history. (The first, on Christmas Day, 1914, had been an RNAS raid on the German naval base at Cuxhaven, launched from three fast cross–Channel packets converted into seaplane tenders.)

The night raid, of November 11/12, 1940, was one of the most daring episodes of World War II. A few obsolete, open-cockpit, biplane aircraft attacked the Italian fleet in heavily-defended Taranto harbor, transforming the balance of naval power in the Mediterranean and leading naval pundits around the world to predict the end of the battleship. The tactics employed were carefully studied by the Imperial Japanese Navy (*see* Pearl Harbor).

Tare: An allowance made for the weight of packaging, wrapping, or a container of goods.

Target: [1] The mark, point, or object to be aimed or fired at. [2] To identify or single out a person or thing as an objective.

Target angle: The relative direction (measured in degrees clockwise from the bow) of a target.

Target bearing: The true compass direction of a target.

Target discrimination: The ability of a surveillance or homing guidance system to identify or engage a specified target when multiple alternative targets are present.

Target grid: A framework of lines used to plan and control a sea-to-shore bombardment.

Tarpaulin: [1] A heavy canvas material treated with tar or other waterproofing substance. Formerly tarpawling (From "tar" + "pall" = cloak or cover). [2] A hat or coat made of or covered with such material. [3] A large sheet of any strong, flexible, water resistant or waterproof material, often with reinforced grommets as attachment points for rope, allowing it to be tied down or suspended. [4] A seaman (now rare).

Tarpaulin muster: Formerly, an informal gathering of the crew, who would throw cash onto a sheet of tarpaulin as donations to a charity (usually the widow of a deceased shipmate).

Tarring: [1] The application of tar to something (standing rigging, for example) as a protective. [2] Tarring and feathering is a very unpleasant form of punishment which was well-known in the revolutionary United States, but seldom applied at sea. Almost the only reference to it as a nautical practice is found in Ordinances or Usages of the Sea which specified:

> A lawfully convicted thief or felon shall have his head shorn, and boiling pitch poured upon his head, and feathers or down strewn upon it so that he may be known. And he is to be put ashore at the first landing place they come to.

Tartana: A single-masted lateen-sailed vessel of the Western Mediterranean and North African Atlantic coasts.

Task organization: A temporary formation of warships, assembled under unified command to accomplish a specific objective, or constituted on a more permanent basis to carry out a complete mission. Developed for the Pacific Campaigns of World War II, task organization provides a unit commander with a flexible and efficient command and control structure and is the standard operational format of the postwar U.S. Navy.

The largest task-oriented entity is the **Fleet**, identified by a single digit (e.g., 7th Fleet). The next largest is a **Task Force** identified by adding a second digit (e.g., TF 71). Each further subdivision is identified by a decimal point and a sequence number. For example (reading backward) TE 71.12.4.10 refers to the tenth **Task Element** of the fourth **Task Unit** of the twelfth **Task Group** in the first **Task Force** of the 7th **Fleet**. None of these formations has any prescribed structure and can be re-arranged or disbanded as operationally required.

Tattletale: A bight of (usually) colored manila

thread hanging between two fixed points on a working line. As the load increases, the line stretches, gradually tightening the thread, until it is taut, showing the line has reached its safe working load. Not to be confused with telltale.

Tattoo: [1] Originally, an evening drum or bugle signal (copied from the army) recalling sailors and marines from shore leave. From the Dutch doe den tiptoe, meaning "close the taps" (i.e., stop drinking). [2] Today, tattoo may be a more elaborate ceremony, staged as an outdoor pageant or display of marching and counter-marching to music. (*See also* last post and taps.) [3] To mark human skin with indelible designs or pictures. From the Tahitian tatau.

Tattooing: The mariners' obsession with body decoration began in the 17th century among Roman Catholic sailors who believed that a tattooed crucifix would serve to identify their corpses and ensure a proper funeral with all the churchly rites of burial. A century later sailors often had a pig tattooed on one foot and a rooster on the other, the superstition being that since neither of these creatures can swim, in the event of shipwreck, they would rush ashore taking the seaman with them. It is believed they got the idea from Polynesian natives, some of whom were tattooed with sacred pigs and other charms.

Taut: [1] Well-stayed (masts and rigging). [2] Said of masts that are tall in proportion to spread of yards or size of ship. [3] Tightly drawn, having no give or slack (a taut rope). [4] In proper order or condition (a taut ship). Also taunt.

Taut leg mooring: Chains or cables stretched tight to subject the anchors to vertical forces as well as horizontal. *See* Offshore mooring.

Taut-line hitch: An adjustable loop knot for use on lines under tension, made by tying a rolling hitch around the standing part after passing around an anchoring object. Tension is maintained by sliding the hitch, thus changing the effective length of the standing part without retying the knot. It is typically used for creating adjustable moorings in tidal areas, but has many non-nautical applications — even being used by astronauts to repair the Hubble Space Telescope.

TC: Tidal current.

TE: Task element.

Tea-wagon: Sailor slang for an Indiaman clipper.

Teaser: An 18-inch length of rope, knotted and dipped in tar, used to flog non-adult "boys" as punishment. Also known as a bimmy. *See* juvenile punishment.

Tectonic plate: Plates are like giant rafts of lithosphere (the earth's surface) which collide with and are forced underneath other plates. *See* oceanic trench, ring of fire, and oceanic deep.

Teeth: Fanciful nautical term for [1] the direction a wind is coming from (sailing into the teeth of a gale). [2] The broadside guns of a man-o-war (she opened the ports to show her teeth): The bows (she has a bone in her teeth).

Telegraph: [1] Generally, a device or system that transmits messages over distance. [2] Specifically, a shipboard apparatus, usually mechanical, that transmits speed and other orders from the bridge to the engine room. [3] Nowadays, the telegraph may directly control the propulsion machinery. (Also called engine-room telegraph or engine-order telegraph.)

Telegraph block: A block with multiple sheaves that allows signals to be sent using several halyards simultaneously.

Telemetry: The measurement of data at one location and their transmission to another for analysis or display.

Telescope: A long optical instrument, designed to make distant objects appear larger and nearer. Usually constructed in sections which slide within one-another to make it less cumbersome when not in use. Frequently carried by naval officers as a symbol of authority. Also "long glass" and, formerly, "bring-'em-near."

Tell off: To detail seamen for special duty.

Tell the Marines: The origin of this phrase, which indicates disbelief of a statement or story, has two widespread and mutually-exclusive interpretations. [1] In the first — no doubt advanced by seamen — marines are portrayed as thick-witted naïve greenhorns who, unlike intelligent and alert sailors, would believe any tale put to them, no matter how far-fetched. [2] In the second, Samuel Pepys, the famed diarist and admiralty official, writes of relaying reports of flying fish to King Charles II who scoffed at this unbelievable story. A Major of Marines, who happened to be at Court, assured the skeptical monarch he had personally seen them, whereupon the king is reputed to have said:

> No class of Our subjects can have so wide a knowledge of seas and lands as the officers and men of Our Loyal Maritime Regiment. Henceforth, before We ever cast doubts upon a tale which lacks likelihood, We shall first tell it to the Marines.

Telltale: [1] A short length of yarn or light line attached to the edge or belly of a sail to indicate wind direction. [2] Specifically, a remote instrument repeating the reading of the ship's main compass in the cabin of the captain or other senior officer. Often suspended over a bunk so that it can be read from below while resting. [3] Generically, any remote instrument repeating a reading or signal. Not to be confused with tattletale.

Temperature chimney: A pipe leading from the deck into the hold of a bulker, down which a thermometer can be lowered to determine heat build-up which might lead to spontaneous combustion.

Temperature gradient: The change of sea heat with increasing depth, recorded as positive if it rises. Except for anomalies such as hot vents on the sea floor, the gradient is almost always negative because cold water normally sinks. *See also* Thermocline.

Tempest: Force 11 on the Beaufort Scale (table 1)

with winds of 56 to 63 knots (64.5 to 72.6 mph; 103.8 to 116.7 km/h). Characterized by exceptionally high waves and seas covered in foam. Also violent storm.

Tenant: Said of a command which lies physically within the geographical limits of another command but is independent of it.

Tend: [1] To handle, take care of, or watch over something (e.g., a deck crew tends mooring lines, or an anchor watch tends the ship). [2] To lead in a given direction (e.g., the anchor cable tends forward). Also trend.

Tend the side: *See* attend the side.

Tender: [1] Said of a vessel with low stability, tending to yield easily to wind pressure. [2] An auxiliary vessel, serving others in the fleet. [3] A small boat or dinghy used to transfer crews and equipment to larger vessels.

Tensile strength: [1] The resistance of rope to a longitudinal force tending to break it. [2] The force that must be applied to break a rope.

Tensiometer: An instrument which measures the tension in a wire or cable.

Tent: To rig an awning as a catchment for rainwater.

Teredo: A marine worm with an auger-like head which bores into timber, forming a shell as it progresses. Each individual can attain a meter (three-feet) or more in length, and an infestation can eventually destroy a wooden ship.

Terminal: [1] A facility designed to transfer cargo from one means of transportation to another. [2] A petroleum tank farm or oil storage depot.

Terminal operations: [1] The reception, processing, and staging of passengers. [2] The receipt, transit, storage, and marshalling of cargo. [3] The loading and unloading of modes of transport. [4] The manifesting and forwarding of cargo and passengers to destination.

Tern: [1] A three-masted schooner found in Canada's maritime provinces. [2] A marine bird similar to a gull but smaller and with a long forked tail.

Terrestrial equator: The great circle on the earth's surface which is equidistant from the North and South poles. Commonly known as "the equator."

Territorial sea: *See* territorial waters.

Territorial sea baseline: Is generally the low tide mark, but runs from headland to headland when the coast is indented.

Territorial sovereignty: The Peace of Westphalia in 1648 established the doctrine of noninterference in the affairs of other nations. Since then there have been many attempts to clarify the concept of "territorial sovereignty," but a clear, universally agreed-upon definition has not emerged. According to the traditional Westphalian view, the power of a state to exercise supreme authority over all persons and things within its territory and territorial waters is unlimited, but today the picture is more complex with each state's freedom of action being limited by international law and diplomatic agreements such as United Nations

resolution 53/144: "Declaration on the Right and Responsibility of Individuals, Groups and Organs of Society to Promote and Protect Universally Recognized Human Rights and Fundamental Freedoms." *See also* exclusive economic zone, and right of fishery.

Territorial strait: When a narrow waterway separates two countries, it is generally agreed that the dividing line will run down the middle of the strait, equidistant from both.

Territorial waters: According to the UN Convention on Law of the Sea the sovereignty of a coastal state extends beyond its land and internal waters across an adjacent belt of sea up to a limit not exceeding 12 nautical miles (22.2 kilometers) from the baseline. This sovereignty includes the airspace over the sea as well as to its bed and subsoil. In territorial seas, submarines and other underwater vehicles are required to navigate on the surface showing their national flag. Some states have unilaterally claimed limits of up to 200 nautical miles. Also called "territorial sea."

Territory: *See* country.

Tertiate: To test the thickness of metal at the muzzle of a gun, in order to ascertain its strength.

Tether: A line attached to a safety harness at one end and fixed to a secure part of the ship at the other.

TEU: Twenty-foot Equivalent Unit.

Texas deck: An American riverboat term for the uppermost deck adjacent to the pilot house.

Texas Navy: Texas was an independent republic between 1835, when it seceded from Mexico, and 1844, when it joined the United States. A sea service was created at the time of secession to protect the trade route to New Orleans. In 1846 all its ships were transferred to the United States Navy, but the name was re-established in 1958 as a non-profit organization dedicated to preserving Texan maritime history.

TF: Task force.

TG: Task group.

Thach weave: An aerial combat maneuver developed by Lt.Cdr. (later Admiral) John (Jimmie) Thach in the summer of 1941 to counter the superior performance of Japanese naval fighters. Abandoning the traditional three-plane section favored by all the world's air forces, he devised a four-plane unit divided into two two-plane sections flying wide apart. Each section would watch the tails of the other. An enemy coming from astern would have to choose which section to attack. When one section saw the attacker it would immediately make a 90° inward turn. This would alert the other section it was under threat and it would also make a 90° inward turn. An enemy following the second section would then meet the guns of the first section head on. *See* Weave [2].

Thalweg: Term in international maritime law referring to the middle of the main navigable channel of a waterway separating two states. From the German thal = valley and weg = way and pronounced "tarl-vaig."

Thassalocracy: Naval, political, or economic domination of the seas. The Greek term Thassalokratia was first used in the fifth century BCE by both Herodotus and Thucydides.

Theater/Theatre: The geographical area for which the commander of a major combatant command has been assigned responsibility. Also Theater of Operations.

Theft: In marine insurance, theft is stealing the contents of an entire package or shipment. Taking only part is called pilferage.

There!: An attention-gathering suffix to a hail in the sailing navy (e.g., Mast-head there!).

There away!: A phrase used when pointing towards a sighted object, or in response to the query "where away?"

Thermal imaging: *See* forward-looking infrared.

Thermocline: A transition layer of varying thickness forming a temperature gradient between the relatively warm epilimnion (mixed or surface layer) and the much colder hypolimnion (deep water layer). The Thermocline varies with latitude and season, being permanent in the tropics and almost absent at the poles.

Thermocline effect: In the open ocean, the thermocline is characterized by a negative sound speed gradient, making the thermocline important in submarine warfare. Rapid changes in temperature and density over relatively little change of depth, create discontinuity in the acoustic impedance of water and tend to refract the sound waves of active sonar and other acoustic signals, complicating the problem of detection.

Thermohaline circulation: Refers to deepwater ocean currents created by differences of water density. This property of sea water is a factor of temperature and salinity (thermo = heat; haline = salt).

Thick: Said of weather with reduced visibility due to fog, haze, rain, or snow.

Thieve's cat: *See* running the gauntlet.

Thieve's knot: An extra knot tied in each of a cat's nine tails to increase the victim's suffering.

Thimble: [1] A metal ring, concave on the outside and fitting within a eyesplice to prevent chafing. [2] A protective shield worn on the finger or thumb during sewing. [3] *See* sail palm.

Third hand: Colloquialism for a benchhook.

Thole pin: A wooden peg or pair of pegs attached to the gunwale of a boat to hold oars in place and allow them to pivot and rotate while being pulled (cf. oarlock, rowlock).

Thousand-ship Navy: This imaginative and evocative name has been replaced by the more mundane Global maritime partnership.

Thread: The smallest component of a rope. *See* strand and yarn.

Threat axis: The direction or bearing from which hostile activity can be anticipated.

Three-figure compass: A gyrocompass whose card, instead of showing points, starts at 000° and ends at 359° with all three digits being used for course commands (e.g., steer zero-zero-six).

Three-island ship: A vessel with raised forecastle, midships house, and poop.

Three-letter compass: A compass whose card identifies the eight secondary intercardinal points as well as the cardinal and primary intercardinal points. (e.g., steer East-North-East).

Three sheets in the wind: The speed and direction of a sailing ship is controlled by the number of sails raised on each mast, the angle of the sails to the wind (trim), and the position of the rudder. If a sheet (line used to control a square-sail) has broken or been released, it is said to be "in the wind." It is extremely difficult to manage even a single sail thrashing wildly with its control ropes blowing about in a strong wind. With sheets on all three masts in this condition, the ship is essentially out of control. Hence this phrase — first recorded in Richard Henry Dana's 1840 book *Two Years Before the Mast*— has come to mean being too intoxicated to know what one is doing. Much less frequently "one sheet to the wind" is used to indicate slight inebriation.

Threefold purchase: A tackle containing a pair of three-sheaved blocks.

Throat: [1] The jaws of a gaff. [2] The forward upper corner of a square-sail. [3] The higher corner of a lugsail.

Throttle: A device that controls the speed of an engine by obstructing or checking the flow of a fluid such as fuel or steam. From Middle English throtelen = to strangle or cut the throat of (someone).

Throttle lever: A lever or pedal for controlling or manipulating a throttle valve.

Throttle valve: A valve moved by hand or by a governor for regulating the supply of steam to a steam engine or the flow of fuel to an internal-combustion engine.

Throttle watch: A throttleman who stands by the controls during foul weather to prevent the engine from racing when the rising stern lifts propeller(s) above the water.

Throttleman: The engine-room detail who controls the speed of the ship.

Through-hull: Any fittings that exit the hull, such as drains and outlet or intake pipes.

Through the cabin window: [1] In former RN slang, any naval officer who obtained rank or advancement by birth or connections had "Come aboard through the cabin window." [2] The term is still in USN use to describe an officer who reaches command status without broad qualifying experience.

Through the hawsepipe/hawseholes: [1] Approbatory USN slang for an officer who achieves command grade after passing through all ranks from enlisted. [2] RN slang for any officer commissioned from the lower deck, "He came aft through the hawsepipe." The USN equivalent is Mustang.

Through the hoop: Before hammocks were stowed

in storage nettings, it was the practice in some ships to pass them through a hoop gauge to ensure they met regulations as to size and appearance. The term is now in civilian use meaning to undergo an ordeal.

Throw off: [1] To release a line and let it run freely. [2] Gunnery term for putting guns a few degrees out of alignment, so that they can be aimed at another ship and practice-fired without hitting it.

Thrums: Short pieces of rope yarn used [1] for making mats; [2] for inserting into canvas to form an anti-chafing wrap; [3] to muffle oars.

Thrust: A reactive force resulting from Newton's second law of motion (which defines how velocity changes when force is applied) and his third law (that every action produces an equal and opposite reaction). Thus, [1] A powered vessel generates forward thrust when its propellers push water aft, and reverse thrust when they push it forward; and, [2] An aircraft generates forward thrust when air is pushed in the opposite direction of flight, whether by the spinning blades of a propeller, or the rotating turbine of a jet engine.

Thruster: A tunnel-mounted propeller or water jet at bow or stern to provide sideways propulsion and eliminate the need for tugboat assistance when docking. *See also* podded drive.

Thus!: The order by which a pilot directs the helmsman to keep the ship in her present situation.

Thwart: A seat or crossbeam in a small boat (from Old English thverr = transverse) (cf. bench, sheets).

Thwartships: Abbreviation of athwartships.

Ticket: [1] Slang for a merchant mariner's license. [2] A Royal Navy warrant or certificate of discharge. These were so prized in the days of impressment that blank copies were always kept under lock and key to avoid theft.

Ticklers: RN slang for tobacco, especially purser's issue. Named after the firm that originally supplied that product.

Tidal: Pertaining to, characterized by, or influenced by tides.

Tidal basin: British term for a tidal harbor in which the water level is kept constant by a floodgate or tidal gate.

Tidal bore: A phenomenon generated when the leading edge of a rising tide rides over the top of an outflowing river current and moves upstream in the form of a wave. This makes it a true tidal wave (not to be confused with tsunami). These phenomena are relatively rare, occurring only in a few locations where large incoming tides are funneled into a shallow narrowing river via a broad bay. The biggest in North America occurs in the otherwise lazy Shubenacadie River, off the Bay of Fundy where the tidal range is about 12 meters (40 feet). The Shubenacadie bore races upstream at a speed as high as 50 km/h (30 mph) and can rise to a height of 5 meters (16 feet) but is usually less. It has claimed the lives of several tourists who were in the riverbed when it came in. The word

derives from Old Norse bara, meaning wave or swell. (Also eagre.)

Tidal current: Horizontal movement of water caused by the influence of sun and moon. Also tidal stream.

Tidal cycle: As the water moves away from the shore and gets shallower, the tide is said to be going out, ebbing, or on the ebb. The moment at which the current begins to reverse direction and has no motion is known as turn of the tide or slack water. And as it comes back towards the shore the tide is coming in, rising, or on the rise.

Tidal datum: Mean low-water level, taken as the reference point from which all other heights and depths are measured or predicted.

Tidal day: One complete tidal cycle.

Tidal gate: A barrier through which water flows freely when the tidal current is in one direction and which closes automatically when the current reverses (cf. floodgate).

Tidal harbor: A harbor in which the depth of water is directly affected by the rise and fall of tides. Frequently the port can only be entered or exited at the flood.

Tidal pool: A rocky pool filled with seawater that can be small and shallow or large and deep. As the tide comes in over a rocky shore, water fills depressions that become isolated pools when the tide retreats. This process, repeated twice a day, replenishes the seawater in what would otherwise be a stagnant pond.

Tidal range: The average difference between successive high and low tides. Geographical position and local topography determine the scale of tidal movement, which is usually small in the middle of the ocean or enclosed bodies of water; for example, the waters around Hawaii, and the Baltic and Mediterranean Seas have hardly any tidal range at all. On the other hand, it can be very large when funneled into a bay or river estuary; in Canada's Bay of Fundy the tide rises and falls some 12–15 meters (40–50 feet) and very high ranges are also found in other coastal areas such as the Amazonian and the Patagonian shelves.

Tidal waters: All fresh or salt waters influenced by the ebb and flow of tides including affected river systems.

Tidal wave: [1] One of two ocean-water swellings, caused by the combined action of sun and moon, that travel around the globe on opposite sides inducing tide creation. [2] A tidal bore or eagre. [3] Popular but incorrect term for a tsunami or storm surge, neither of which is actually tidal.

Tiddly: [1] RN lower deck slang for smart or shipshape. [2] Colloquialism for slightly inebriated. Also tiddley.

Tiddy-oggy: RN slang for meat and spiced vegetables enclosed in a small, flat pastry shell (known ashore in Britain as a Cornish Pasty).

Tide: The cyclical rise and fall of sea level that occurs roughly every twelve hours (from Old English tid = time). These are of great importance to navigation, since significant errors in position will occur if they are not taken into account. Tidal range and height are also important, because many rivers and harbors have shallow bars that prevent vessels with significant draft from entering at certain states of the tidal cycle. *See also* tide creation.

Tide ball: A ball-shaped signal hoisted when the depth of water allows a vessel to enter a bar-restricted harbor.

Tide creation: All surfaces of the Earth are pulled toward the moon and sun by gravitational attraction. This has minor effect on solid land masses, but exerts great and obvious influence on the fluid oceans. Moon gravity pulls upwards on the water, while the stronger force of earth gravity simultaneously pulls downward.

The sun's gravity also has an impact, but its gravitational force on the earth is less than half that of the moon, making the latter the predominant factor in tide creation. As the moon rotates around the Earth, it pulls the water on the nearest side of the Earth outward into a bulge. A similar bulge on the opposite side of the Earth is caused by the water being thrown outward by the centrifugal force of the planet's spin. These two bulges travel around the globe as tidal waves, producing diurnal high tides (two each day).

When the sun→earth→moon line is straight (at new moon and full moon) their gravitational pulls combine to produce higher high tides and lower low tides, known as spring tides. When sun and moon are at right angles from the Earth (during the quarter phases of the moon) the gravitational pull on the oceans is less, producing a smaller range between high and low water, known as neap tides. There is about a seven day interval between springs and neaps. Tides also occur at slightly different times from one day to another, due to shifts in the relative orbits of earth, moon, and sun. Northern California has two unequal tides each day, while the Gulf of Mexico experiences only one high and one low tide each day.

Tide gate: [1] A restricted passage which produces a tide race. [2] A tidal gate.

Tide gauge: Any device for measuring or recording tides. May be as simple as a yardstick on the seawall or as complex as a marigraph.

Tide race: A rapid and hazardous tidal current, usually caused by a narrow channel (tide gate) or a submerged rock.

Tide rip: A stretch of turbulent water caused either by conflicting tidal currents or by a tidal current crossing a rough bottom.

Tide rode: Said of an anchored vessel which swings with the tide (cf. wind rode).

Tide table: A publication listing the predicted times and heights of tides at specific locations on specific dates.

Tidebound: Unable to move because of surrounding low water but not necessarily aground.

Tidehead: The furthest inland point affected by tidal action.

Tidesman: Former name for a customs officer who had to wait for the tide to turn before the revenue cutter could take him out to incoming ships. Also tide waiter.

Tidewater: Fresh water that is affected by tides. Not to be confused with tidal waters.

Tideway: [1] The rush of tidal water through a channel or stream. [2] A channel in which a tidal current runs.

Tie: *See* tye.

Tie beam: A heavy bar used to secure the tarpaulin covering a hatch cover.

Tie-for-tie: Formerly, a sailor's term for the mutual exchange of favors with no obligation on either side. Originally referred to the plaiting of pigtails by "tie mates."

Tie mate: A friend so intimate that he can help with personal matters such as plaiting (tying) the queue (pigtail).

Tie up: To attach to a buoy or other mooring.

Tiedown: A fitting used to secure aircraft on the flight deck or in the hangar of a carrier.

Tier: [1] One of several turns of rope. [2] To stow an anchor cable in the chain locker. [3] One of several layers of casks or barrels. [4] One bank of guns in the broadside of a man-o-war.

Tiered shot: A muzzle-loading projectile consisting of layers of grapeshot separated by circular metal discs.

Ties: The straps or strings used to tighten a life preserver.

Tiff or Tiffy: RN slang for an artificer.

Tiger: British slang for a shipmaster's oriental servant. In days of sail, the "Captain's Tiger" was frequently dressed appropriately in a striped outfit.

Tight: [1] Said of a wooden vessel which does not leak. (Old Norse thettr = watertight.) [2] Said of a vessel where discipline is strictly enforced. (German dicht = tight.) [3] A well-run business is often referred to as a "tight ship." [4] Common slang for inebriated (origin uncertain).

Tiller: A horizontal bar attached to the rudderhead and used to steer the vessel. As the size of sailing warships increased, the power needed to control the rudder became excessive and a helm (or wheel) was used to move the tiller with the mechanical advantage of a steering mechanism of ropes and pulleys. When this mechanism suffered battle damage, the tiller had to be moved manually and even with tackles the effort was prodigious. It took thirty men heaving to port and the same number to starboard to turn the rudder of a first-rate such as HMS *Victory*. *See also* steering evolution.

Timber hitch: A method of attaching a line to a spar.

Timberheads: The tops of poles or beams that project above the weather deck in pairs to form bitts.

Timbers: [1] The frames or ribs of a wooden ship. [2] Any large pieces of wood used in shipbuilding. [3] *See* "Shiver my timbers!"

Time ball: A visual signal consisting of a ball raised to the masthead and released to drop at the stroke of an important hour such as noon.

Time charter: A form of charter party where the owner leases a vessel and its crew for a fixed period. The charterer pays for bunkers and port charges in addition to the cost of the lease.

Time notation: *See* Date & Time Notation and table 12.

Time penalty: A marine insurance clause that relieves the insurer of claims against losses due to peril of the sea.

Time zones (civil): Internationally, the globe is divided into 24 one-hour time zones, each covering 15° of longitude and centered on a meridian (except for adjustments to accommodate political boundaries). Each zone thus has 7½° (representing 30 minutes of time) on either side of its meridian. Times around the world are expressed as positive or negative offsets from the Prime Meridian at Greenwich, England (known as "Z"). Thus Z + hhmm lies east of Greenwich and is ahead of Coordinated Universal Time (UTC), while Z-hhmm lies to the west and is behind. (*See also* date and time notation, and day.)

Some states span multiple time zones. For example, Australia runs from its Western Zone (at Z + 0800) to the Eastern (Z + 1000); North America covers six zones, from Atlantic (Z-0400) to Alaska (Z-0900); Russia spans eleven zones from Kaliningrad (Z + 0200) to Kamchatka (Z + 1200), extending from Eastern Europe to just short of the International Date Line. Domestically, zones are often adjusted to fit local circumstances, politics, or geography. For example, Newfoundland Time is Z-0430 (half way between Atlantic and Eastern time); Central Australian Time is also on the half-hour (Z + 0930); and Greenland, which actually spans five time zones, only uses one (Z-0300) throughout the country.

Time zones (military and naval): United States and NATO armed forces use UTC time zones, defined by a phonetic alphabet, in which "J" (Juliett) is not used, being reserved to identify current local (zone) time. As in civil usage the zones run eastward (positive) and westward (negative) from the Prime Meridian. This puts half of Zulu zone in the western hemisphere and half in the eastern, with reconciliation at the International Date Line, where time zones "Mike" (Z + 1200) and "Yankee" (Z-1200) are each only 7½° wide. For easier orientation, the following table shows one of the locations within each zone:

UTC Offset	Eastward Zones (+)	Westward Zones (-)
Z ± 0000	Z Zulu [½] (Lagos)	Z Zulu [½] (Iceland)
Z ± 0100	A Alpha (Vienna)	N November (Azores)
Z ± 0200	B Bravo (Athens)	O Oscar (E. Greenland)
Z ± 0300	C Charlie (Moscow)	P Papa (Rio de Janeiro)
Z ± 0400	D Delta (Abu Dhabi)	Q Quebec (Halifax)
Z ± 0500	E Echo (Karachi)	R Romeo (New York)
Z ± 0600	F Foxtrot (Rangoon)	S Sierra (Chicago)
Z ± 0700	G Golf (Jakarta)	T Tango (Calgary)
Z ± 0800	H Hotel (Beijing)	U Uniform (Vancouver)
Z ± 0900	I India (Tokyo)	V Victor (Anchorage)
Z ± 1000	K Kilo (Sydney)	W Whiskey (Hawaii)
Z ± 1100	L Lima (Guadalcanal)	X X-Ray (Samoa)
Z ± 1200	M Mike (Fiji)	Y Yankee (Tarawa)

Timekeeping: Time aboard ship is measured by the striking of a bell every thirty minutes. This practice originated in the 13th century, when the ship's boy kept time by turning a half-hour sand-glass. Each time the sand ran out and he turned the glass over he would yell "first turn," "second turn," and so on until "eighth turn" indicated the end of the watch. Because young voices did not always carry well, it became customary for him to strike the ship's bell to indicate the number of turns he had made. The watch ended with eight bells and the next boy started the cycle again. The number is still shouted out as well as rung and, unless there has been a significant untoward incident to report, it is traditional to signify the end of the watch with the call "Eight bells and all's well." *See also* bells, nautical day, and watchkeeping.

Timoneer: Former name for a helmsman. From the French timonier.

Tin can: USN slang for a destroyer.

Tin fish: Slang for a torpedo.

Tin hat: RN slang for a steel helmet (also battle bowler).

Tin tunas: USN slang for a submariner's dolphin insignia.

Tingle: Thin sheet metal used for temporary hull repairs.

Tip clearance: The smallest distance between a ship's propellers and its hull.

Tipping the nines: Colloquialism for foundering due to having set too much sail on all nine principal yards of a ship.

***Titanic* mailmen:** On the night of 14th April 1912, while on her maiden voyage, RMS *Titanic* struck an iceberg, sinking with tremendous loss of life. The largest ocean liner of her day and reputed to be unsinkable, *Titanic* did not carry sufficient lifeboats for all on board. The law at that time (issued eighteen years earlier when ships were much smaller) required her to have 16 lifeboats with space for 962 occupants. The White Star Line had exceeded this regulation by also carrying four collapsible Berthon boats, bringing total capacity to 1,178, but the liner carried close to 2,200 passengers and crew (there is no consensus on the exact number) of which only about 700 survived. Many books and movies have told the full story, but one of many individual acts of self-sacrifice which has received little publicity concerns two American and three British postal workers (RMS stands for Royal Mail Ship) who desperately tried to save 200 sacks of registered mail by dragging them to the upper decks and possible safety. All five perished in the freezing water, along with some 1500 others.

Title: Nomenclature or form of address indicating a person's rank or status.

Tjalk: A small single-masted Dutch sailing vessel of about 60 tons burthen.

TNT: Trinitrotoluene (an explosive).

To the bitter end: It has been postulated that this colloquial phrase, meaning to carry on until resources are exhausted, refers to the sour or acrid dregs at the end of a drink. However, a nautical origin seems more probable since the phrase is still in naval use, indicating that a cable has been let out until no more is available. Some sources suggest the term was originally the "better end" since the inboard end of a ship's hempen anchor cable was less worn than the outboard end.

TOA: Time of arrival.

Toasts in the Royal Navy: A unique privilege is said to have begun when King William IV, known as "The Sailor King," was inspecting the fleet at Spithead. Wooden warships had very little headroom, and the king noticed several tall officers banging against low beams when rising to drink his health. Having bumped his head all too often during his own sea service, he immediately ordered that naval officers could in future drink to their monarch while seated. This story is probably apocryphal, since it is also attributed to two other kings (Charles II and George IV) and such an important event would surely have been precisely recorded.

Most probably the custom arose simply because the spacing of overhead beams was such that every third wardroom officer would have been forced to crouch rather than stand erect. Whatever its origin, the dispensation did not apply when the national anthem was played, so many captains ordered their bands to remain silent during the Loyal Toast in order not to jeopardize the privilege. In 1964, on the 300th birthday of the corps, Queen Elizabeth II granted Royal Marine officers the privilege of also remaining seated for the Loyal Toast.

Although in civilian circles it is permissible to drink toasts in water, this is taboo in naval circles where it traditionally predicts a drowning death for the recipient (*see also* clinking glasses). Nowadays, no officer or guest is required to actually drink, but each is expected to raise a charged glass to their lips when a toast is proposed. With the exception of the toast to foreign heads of state (when their nationals are present) no toast may be proposed before the sovereign's health is drunk (*see* Passing the Port). After the Royal toast it was traditional to propose the toast of the day, a ritual which is still followed in some British warships. The standard toasts, for which officers rise, are:

• Monday: "Our ships at sea."
• Tuesday: "Our men."
• Wednesday: "Ourselves."
• Thursday: "A bloody war and a sickly season" (both guarantee rapid promotion).
• Friday: "A willing foe and sea room."
• Saturday: "Sweethearts and wives" (traditionally some wag responds "and may they never meet").
• Sunday: "Absent friends and those at sea."

Toasts in the United States Navy: Since 1914, when Navy Secretary Josephus Daniels banned alcohol aboard USN ships, formal "dining-in" has required special dispensation and is rare. Mess nights are usually held at an officers' club, a hotel, or another shore facility. Toasts are drunk standing, with the first normally being to "The Commander in Chief" (The President), during which the national anthem is played. However, as in the Royal Navy, when foreigners are guests of the wardroom this toast will be preceded by one to the country and the title (not name) of its head of state, accompanied by the foreign national anthem. When appropriate, these will be followed by one or more pre-arranged "Formal toasts." These are always proposed in the following sequence, and to an organization or a post (rather than its incumbent):

• The Army.
• The Marine Corps.
• The Coast Guard.
• The Air Force.
• The Secretary of the Navy.
• The Chief of Naval Operations.
• The Civil Engineer Corps.
• The Chief of Civil Engineers.
• The Seabees.
• Missing Comrades.

"Informal toasts" may then be introduced by individual members of the mess, with an introduction supposed (in the words of the directive) to show "inspired and subtle sarcasm." Finally, the dinner closes with a toast to "The United States Navy." Unlike earlier toasts, which may be sipped or feigned, the entire glass should be drained while the band plays "Anchors Aweigh."

TOD: Time of departure.

Toe the Line: [1] In sailing navies the entire ship's company was assembled at least once a week (usually Sunday) for formal inspection. The booted Marines were trained soldiers who knew how to form up in straight lines, but barefooted seamen were clueless in that respect. To get them into some semblance of order, petty officers wielding ropes-ends would push them to stand with their toes touching one of the oakum-filled seams that ran along the length of the weather deck. [2] Toeing the line could also be punitive. For some minor infraction of discipline an offender would be ordered to toe a seam and stay there without moving for a specified period of time, in fair weather or foul.

Toggle: A wooden or metal pin attached to a line

and used to connect items which need to be easily released. Typically used on signal flags, lifebuoys, and (in ornamental form) on duffle coats.

Tom Cox: Derogatory term describing a sailor who bustles about looking busy but achieving little. Now seldom used.

Tom Pepper: Obsolete term for a lying sailor.

Tomahawk: [1] A hand-held weapon with a steel blade on one side of a short wooden handle, and a sharp hook on the other. In the 17th–18th century, boarders used it to hang on to enemy bulwarks, and to cut away rigging, as well as in hand-to-hand combat. [2] A long-range, low-altitude, subsonic cruise missile, launched against land targets from submarines and surface vessels.

Tombola: A form of lottery similar to "bingo." It became the RN's most popular game when gambling games such as crown-and-anchor were outlawed. When the rules were relaxed, tombola was supplanted by uckers, a much more savage game of ancient British naval origin.

Tompion: *See* tampion.

Ton: Various units of weight or volume. [1] Metric tonne = 1000 kg = 2204.6 lbs. [2] Long ton = 1016.4 kg = 2240 lbs. [3] Short ton = 907.18 kg = 2000 lbs. [4] Cargo ton (or tun) = 252 wine gallons = 302.6 U.S. gallons = 1145.6 liters = 40 cu.ft. [5] Register ton = 100 cu.ft. (*see also* tonnage).

Ton-for-ton: A privateer's phrase indicating that ships sailing in consort will have equal shares in all prizes taken by any of them.

Ton-mile: A measurement in transportation economics, designating the movement of one ton of cargo over a distance of one mile.

Tongue: [1] A long narrow strip of land such as a cape or spit projecting into the water. [2] A submerged strip of ice projecting from an iceberg or floe. [3] A small wooden block inserted to help the jaws of a gaff to slide.

Tonnage: The term is derived from the Old English tunne and refers to [1] the fees or duty charged on ships and their cargoes; [2] the total amount of shipping in a fleet or of a country; [3] the cargo handling capacity of a port; [4] the carrying capacity or weight of an individual ship.

Tonnage measurement: The first English-language laws of ship measurement, issued in 1492, were straightforward — a ship that could carry 30 tunne casks in her hold had a burthen of 30 tunnes. Since then, there have been various other systems, many based on a ship's linear dimensions. Today there are two basic methods, each of which has a number of sub-divisions:

• **Volume measurement** applies almost exclusively to merchantmen, with 100 cubic feet being counted as one ton: (a) **Gross tonnage** is a measure of the total internal volume of the ship, with the exception of machinery spaces, bridge/navigation spaces, and other minor spaces essential to its operation; (b)

Net tonnage expresses the vessel's earning capacity by deducting space not available for the carriage of passengers or cargo; (c) **Freight tonnage** is another method of calculating volume capacity by determining the ship's container-carrying capability in terms of Twenty-foot Equivalent Units (two TEU = one freight ton).

• **Weight measurement** is expressed in long tons or in metric tonnes, calculated by multiplying the volume of the hull below the waterline (i.e., the quantity of water it displaces) by the density of that water. Weight measurements are not "tonnage" in the proper sense, although they are often referred to as such. (a) *Lightweight tonnage* is the weight of the merchantman's structure when empty; (b) *Deadweight tonnage* is the difference between loaded displacement and lightweight tonnage, thus representing the weight of cargo, fuel, water ballast, fresh water, stores, crew, passengers and luggage; (c) *Displacement tonnage* is almost exclusively used for warships. It is further subdivided by the Washington Naval Treaty as follows:

  i. *Standard*, which is defined as:

  Complete, fully manned, engined, and equipped ready for sea, including all armament and ammunition, equipment, outfit, provisions and fresh water for crew, miscellaneous stores and implements of every description that are intended to be carried in war, but without fuel or reserve feed water on board.

  ii. *Full load*, which adds fuel and reserve feed water to the standard definition.

  iii. *Normal*, as used by the USN and NATO, which allows two-thirds supply of stores and fuel, and is regarded as an average operational displacement.

Tonne: The proper spelling for a metric ton of 1,000 kilograms (0.9842 long tons; 1.1023 short tons).

Top dog: *See* underdog.

Top drawer: The highest level of rank or best available quality. The expression arose, some have said, because a ship's captain used to keep vital documents and charts in the top drawer of his desk for easy access in emergencies. That is possible, but the author suspects it more probably reflects the fact that a woman of quality always kept her finest jewelry in the top drawer of her dressing table.

Top Gun: The popular (semi-official) name of the United States Navy Strike Fighter Tactics Instructor school (formerly Fighter Weapons School). "Power Projection" classes train experienced Navy and Marine Corps aircrews in all aspects of fighter aircraft employment, including tactics, hardware, techniques, and current world threats. During concurrent "Adversary Training," pilots receive individual instruction in threat simulation, threat presentation, and adversary tactics.

Top hamper: [1] Collective term for a ship's superstructure including masts, spars, rigging, and antennae. [2] The spars, rigging, and gear aloft, considered as an encumbrance or the cause of windage. [3] Any unnecessary weight, either aloft or on the upper deck.

Top-lantern: A signal light hung aloft in a sailing flagship at night, replacing the admiral's flag and signifying his presence.

Top off: [1] Generically, to finish or fill something. [2] Specifically, to complete the loading of a partially laden vessel.

Top secret: The highest security classification.

Topgallant: [1] A square-sail mounted above the topsail to form the third sail above the deck. [2] The mast, yard, sail, and rigging mounted above and attached to the topmast, but forming a separate unit. Pronounced "t'gallant."

Topman: [1] Specifically, a highly-skilled and agile seaman assigned to sail-handling on the highest yards; the cream of a sailing-ship crew. [2] Generally, any sailor working aloft.

Topmast: A mast mounted between the lower mast and the topgallant mast to support the yards and rigging of a topsail.

TOPP: Technical Officer, Petroleum Products (RN).

Topping: The act of raising one extremity of a spar higher than the other.

Topping lift: [1] Standing rigging supporting a boom or spar. [2] Running rigging used to raise and support a boom. Also uphaul.

Tops: Platforms around the heads of the lower masts on a sailing ship, serving to spread the topmast shrouds. On warships they were large enough to carry small guns or marksmen and were often termed fighting tops.

Topsail: The second sail above the deck on a square-rigger. Pronounced tops'l.

Topsail schooner: A schooner with one or more square-sails on its foremast.

Topside: [1] On deck (cf. aloft). [2] The part of the hull above the waterline (cf. freeboard).

Topside tank: A side hopper tank above the hold of a bulker.

Torch: Code-name for the Anglo-American North Africa invasion of November 1942.

Tornado: A violent weather event in which rotating columns of air form into funnel-shaped clouds, often reaching the ground and causing severe damage. Tornadoes often form when warm, moist air rushes upward to meet cooler, drier air. As the moisture condenses, it forms a massive thundercloud or supercell. Variable winds at different altitudes then feed the updraft, causing the characteristic funnel shape to develop and spin downward to the surface. *See also* waterspout.

Torpedo: Originally referred to [1] a stationary explosive mine, then [2] an explosive charge mounted on the end of a long pole or spar, and finally [3] a self-propelled underwater missile detonated by contact, sound, or magnetism. The latter may be unguided, or maneuvered by commands passed along a wire during its run, or transmitted acoustically when it nears the target. Also fish, tin fish, and mouldy.

Torpedo belt: *See* armor belt.

Torpedo boat: A small, fast, maneuverable motorboat armed with torpedoes. *See also* motor torpedo boat, patrol torpedo boat.

Torpedo boat destroyer: A warship designed to be fast enough to catch torpedo boats, with armament to destroy them. Forerunner of the destroyer.

Torpedo juice: World War II USN slang for a potent drink distilled from the alcohol drained from torpedoes.

Torpedo mine: A deep-water bottom-moored lightweight torpedo launcher, equipped with an acoustic recognition system capable of differentiating surface craft and friendly submarines from hostile submersibles. The weapon lies dormant until one of the latter is detected, when it is launched from its capsule to follow a circular search pattern using active sonar to home in on the target. The USN version is called CAPTOR. *See also* Mine (Naval).

Torpedo tube: A device for launching torpedoes horizontally, having many of the characteristics of a naval gun. It has a barrel with breech and muzzle, and propels a torpedo much as the gun fires a shell, the major difference being that the shell is "reactive" while the torpedo is self-propelling. The launcher only has to supply initial impetus by compressed air or an explosive charge. There are two main types of launcher, both are which are normally called tubes. [1] Deck-mounted torpedo launchers have been installed on many warships, from patrol boats to battleships. They are usually designed to use a specific munition. [2] Submerged torpedo tubes are built in to submarines and some destroyers and frigates. Being integral to the vessel's hull, they are usually capable of handling different munitions; and, being designed to operate below water level, they have to be equipped with doors at both breech and muzzle; the former to seal against the escape of propulsion gasses into the vessel, and the latter to prevent the inrush of sea water. A cardinal principle of submerged torpedo tube operation is that one or the other of these doors must always be closed.

Torrid zone: That part of the Earth's surface lying between the Tropics of Cancer and Capricorn, in which the climate is extremely hot and parching.

Toss oars!: A command for the crew of a double-banked pulling boat to swiftly raise their oars to the vertical, with blades trimmed fore-and-aft, and handles resting on the bottom of the boat between their feet. Their outboard hands grasp the oars at chin level, their inboard hands at thigh level. Done as a salute or in preparation for landing. *See also* oars, boat oars, ship oars, trail oars.

Tossed: Thrown restlessly from side-to-side due to irregular wave movement (cf. pitch, roll).

Tot: RN term for a serving of rum or other spirit issued as a daily ration and on special occasions.

Total current: The combination of regular and tidal currents.

Touch of the tar brush: This unpleasant and racist expression, now used to denigrate a person whose ancestry includes an admixture of Caucasian and African, was once less offensive. It originated as the 18th century RN equivalent of the 20th century USN term "Mustang," describing an officer who served as a rating or enlisted seaman (i.e., working with tar) before being commissioned.

Touch-and-go: [1] Said of a practice carrier landing with the tailhook stowed so that the aircraft can take off for another circuit without stopping. [2] Said of a surface ship which runs aground, but immediately comes loose without damage. (Reporting such an incident is moot.) [3] Said colloquially of any risky venture whose outcome is uncertain.

Touchdown: The moment at which a naval aircraft makes contact with the flight deck when landing.

Touchhole: An opening in the breech of an old-time personal firearm through which the charge was ignited. In a cannon, this opening is called the vent.

Tow: [1] To drag or pull one or more vessels. [2] The vessel or chain of vessels so pulled. [3] A chain of barges being pushed may also be called a tow. From Old English togian.

Towage: Charges for the service of a tug or towboat.

Towboat: A vessel with powerful engines and a square steel-reinforced bow, specifically designed for pushing long tows of barges. Towboats are most frequently employed in inland waterways and on rivers. Also (and more logically) called push boat.

Towing & Salvage: A charter party clause that allows the chartered vessel to deviate from the terms of the charter to tow or otherwise help a vessel in distress.

Towing bar: See fog buoy.

Towing bitts: Cylindrical castings on the afterdeck of a tugboat at or near its pivot point used to secure the towing hawser(s).

Towing bows: Girders across the caprail of a tugboat, serving to hold towing hawsers above the heads of deck crew (pronounced to rhyme with toeing toes). Also called Dutch bars.

Towing bridle: A span of chain or cable attached across the bows of a tow or the transom of a tugboat to form a "Y" with the towing hawser and reduce yaw.

Towing hawser: An exceptionally strong and elastic pulling rope. The Military Sealift Command specification is reasonably typical — 2,400 feet (400 fathoms, 732 meters) in length, and 14 inch (35.6 cms) in circumference; made of double-braided, polyester sheath and core, with 36-inch eyes spliced in each end.

Towing lights: Two or three vertically-mounted lights required by the rules of the road when one vessel is towing another.

Towing machine: A winch-like device which automatically maintains safe tension by slacking off or retrieving lengths of towing hawser.

Towing spar: See fog buoy.

Towing wire: Steel-cored plow-steel wire rope, used instead of fiber rope for towing hawsers.

Trabaccolo: A trading craft of the Adriatic.

Tracer: [1] A projectile trailing smoke or glowing brightly to aid in correcting the aim of machine guns or automatic cannon. [2] A message sent to confirm delivery of a prior message. [3] An inquiry as to the whereabouts of a cargo shipment. [4] Color-coding to identify a specific wire in electrical cable. [5] Colored yarn inserted in a rope for identification.

Track: [1] to follow the movement of a target either visually or by radar. [2] To record such movement on a plotting or maneuvering board. [3] The desired or intended direction of travel with respect to the earth. [4] A vessel's ability to hold its course with minimum or temporarily unattended helm. [5] To haul a barge or ship along a canal or river bank. [6] The path followed by a storm or hurricane. [7] A metal guide or rail.

Trade: [1] In Middle English, the word meant a path or track, hence the obsolete nautical phrase "the wide blows trade," meaning in a consistent direction. However, by the 18th century, because of the importance of trade winds to merchantmen crossing the Atlantic, the term had come to mean [2] The act or process of buying, selling, or exchanging goods or commodities within a country (domestic trade) or between countries (international trade).

Trade lane: A sea route followed by merchant shipping.

Trade route: The path usually followed by merchantmen in the course of trade. See also sea lane, seaway, ship route, trade lane.

Trade wind: One of the nearly constant easterly winds which dominate tropical and subtropical latitudes, blowing mainly northeast in the Northern and southeast in the Southern hemisphere. In certain places they reverse direction every six months.

Trader: [1] A businessman or merchant engaged in trade. [2] Formerly, a merchantman that moved between ports bartering one cargo for another (cf. tramp).

The trades: Widely-accepted colloquial term for the trade winds.

Traffic separation: Exceptionally busy waterways such as the straits of Dover and Gibraltar are divided into shipping lanes or corridors which separate inbound from outbound traffic.

Trafficking: Buying and selling, especially illicit trade. See drug trafficking, human trafficking, and Palermo Protocol.

Trail oars: To allow oars to swing loosely in their locks without being held by the rowers. See also oars, boat oars, ship oars, toss oars.

Trailspike: A tool used to aim naval cannon. To train the weapon, a trailspike was inserted between gun carriage and deck as a lever to lift the carriage so that it could be inched to one side or the other. To control elevation, a trailspike on one of the carriage steps could lever the barrel off its quoins for re-positioning; but this was seldom required at sea where it was a matter of gauging the right moment to fire as the ship rolled. (Also handspike, and *see* gun crew.)

Train: To aim, direct, or bring to bear as, for example, a gun, radar, searchlight or telescope.

Train tackle: *See* Gun tackles.

Trainer: One of a pair of gunners who work as a team, the trainer controls deflection which is the horizontal direction of firing (cf. layer, pointer).

Trajectory: The curved flight path followed by a projectile.

Tramp: A merchant vessel operating without any fixed schedule or itinerary, picking up and delivering cargo opportunistically wherever trade can be found (cf. trader).

Trankeh: A barge-like sailing vessel of the Persian/ Arabian Gulf.

Transceiver: A radio device that can both send and receive, but not simultaneously.

Transducer: A device that converts one type of energy to another (e.g., water pressure to electricity, as in a speed recorder; or electrical to acoustic as in a loudspeaker).

Transship: To transfer cargo from one mode of transportation to another, or from one vessel to another. Unless contractually permitted, trans-shipment is a serious breach of agreement and may invalidate marine insurance.

Transit: [1] The act, process or instance of passing or journeying across, through, or over. [2] The conveyance of goods across a place or region. [3] The passage of a heavenly body over a meridian, or through the field of a telescope, or across the disk of a larger one. [4] One of a series of satellites providing positional data. [5] A pair of navigational aids spaced so that their alignment indicates a vessel is correctly positioned. [6] A surveying instrument. [7] An identification number assigned to banks and savings associations. [8] A system of (usually urban) public transportation. *See also* right of transit.

Transit cargo: Goods that are not to be offloaded at the current port of call, but carried on to another destination.

Transit port: A port where cargo is offloaded for onward movement by another carrier or mode of transportation.

Transition zone: *See* density levels.

Transom: [1] An horizontal timber or plating fixed across the sternpost of a vessel. [2] A boat's flat stern above the waterline. [3] Formerly, the couch across the after end of the Great Cabin in a sailing man-o-war. [4] A timber joining the cheeks of a gun-carriage (also axle tree). [5] Generic term for any wooden crosspiece.

Transponder: An electronic transmitter which identifies itself in response to interrogation by another transmitter.

Transport: [1] To carry, move, or convey goods or people from one place to another. [2] A private ship or aircraft employed in the movement of troops or

munitions of war. [3] Formerly, to send into banishment as a convict. [4] A person so banished.

Transverse: Perpendicular to the keel (athwartship).

Transverse wave: *See* wave motion.

Trap: To catch an aircraft with arrester gear when it lands on a carrier.

Traveler: [1] A metal ring or thimble fitted to move freely on a rope, spar, or rod. [2] A person who moves from place to place.

Traverse: [1] To swivel a gun laterally. [2] To brace yards fore-and-aft. [3] To determine the course resulting from several changes of direction.

Traverse sailing: *See* sailings.

Trawl: [1] A large conical fishing net. [2] To drag such a net along the bottom in such a way that fish cannot escape below it.

Trawler: A boat or person engaged in fishing with a trawl.

Trebling: Triple-planking a whaler's bows to protect against ice-damage.

Trebuchet: Ancient stone-casting artillery.

Treenail: A wooden peg used to fasten a ship's planks to its frame (pronounced "trennel"). Nicely described in Sir Henry Mainwaring's *Sea-Man's Dictionary* (1604) as:

> Long Woodden Pins made of the harte of Oake, wherewth they fasten all the Plancks vnto the Timbers ... for we doe vse as litle Iron vnder Water, as wee may conveniently, least the Shippe should grow Iron Sick. Theis Tree nailes must be well seasoned, and not sappy, for then the Shippe wil be continually Leakie.

Trench: [1] A long, narrow, steep-sided, depression in the ocean bottom. Trenches generally lie parallel to island arcs or littoral mountain ranges (*see also* oceanic trench). [2] A long cut in the ground, especially one used for military defense, often with the excavated dirt thrown up as a parapet in front.

Trend: *See* tend.

Trestletrees: A pair of timbers or metal shapes sitting on the hounds and serving to support the crosstrees of a sailing ship's mast.

Tret: [1] Formerly an allowance of extra weight to compensate for wastage of goods in transit. [2] An allowance made by insurance underwriters to cover depreciation of a vessel during a voyage. Pronounced "trait" after the Old English word for draft, from which it is derived.

Triage: Medical assignment of degrees of urgency to the treatment of sick or wounded patients. From the French for sorting-out or selection.

Triangular Trade: There were actually two "triangular" routes followed by slave traders: [1] The principal one involved the carriage of manufactured goods from England to West Africa, there to be traded for slaves to be carried via the middle passage to the West Indies, where they were sold. The slave ship was usually scuttled to wash away some of the obnoxious smell, then re-floated to carry island products (sugar, cotton, tobacco, rum, and molasses) back to England on the last leg of the triangle. [2] The "colonial" trade, which was much smaller, originated in New England and carried rum, molasses, candles, guns, and ironware to West Africa, took slaves on the middle passage to the West Indies, and then returned to the American colonies with island products. Both routes were hazardous, but highly profitable.

Triatic: A stay leading from one mast to another.

Trice: [1] To pull up or haul on a rope. [2] Former USN term for securing one's bedding (cf. lash up and stow). Also trice up.

Trick: A turn, stint, or spell of duty, especially at the helm or on lookout.

Tricolor lamp: A lantern combining the port (red), starboard (green), and stern (white) lights in a single housing. Used on yachts and other small vessels of less than 20 meters.

Tricorne: A broad brimmed hat, pinned up on sides and back to produce a triangular shape that was usually worn with the point facing forward. Between the late 17th and early 19th centuries, it served both as civilian dress and as part of military and naval uniforms. During the American Revolution it was a favorite headgear of "Patriots" and "Minutemen." A cocked hat is often incorrectly called a tricorne.

Trident: [1] A long, three-pronged fork or weapon, especially a three-pronged spear used for fishing. [2] In Greek & Roman Mythology; the three-pronged spear carried by Neptune or Poseidon. [3] A strategic weapon system consisting of a ballistic missile armed with a nuclear warhead. Usually launched from a nuclear-powered submarine of either the USN's *Ohio* Class or the RN's *Vanguard* Class.

Triemiola: A triple-banked version of the hemiola, designed by the Rhodian navy as a pirate-chaser.

Trierarch: [1] The commander of a trireme. [2] A rich or aristocratic Athenian whose civic duty was to equip and maintain a trireme.

Trigger bar: A device for quickly releasing the anchor to drop overboard.

Trim: [1] Neat and tidy. [2] The fore-and-aft attitude of a vessel. [3] To adjust the balance of a ship by moving cargo or ballast. [4] To evenly distribute the coal in a steamship's bunkers so as to keep the vessel in balance. [5] The buoyancy condition of a submarine. [6] To arrange sails to best exploit the wind.

Trim tab: A secondary control surface on the trailing edge of a marine rudder or aircraft control surface. When adjusted to deflect the flow of water or air it generates a force that holds the main control surface in the desired position, thus minimizing the effort that has to be exerted by the ship's coxswain or aircraft's pilot.

Trim tank: *See* trimming tanks.

Trimaran: [1] A vessel with floats on either side of a central hull. [2] A boat with three hulls.

Trimmer: The humblest, dirtiest, and most-de-

manding of all the arduous jobs in a steamship's black gang. Some worked inside the steel catacomb of a bunker, moving coal from upper to lower levels and thence to the furnace room doors, all the while, ensuring that the remaining fuel was properly trimmed (hence the job title). Others worked inside the furnace room, carrying coal from the bunker doors to provide each stoker with a constant supply of fuel, and carrying away ashes and clinker.

Trimming system: An assembly of pipes, valves, tanks, and pumps by means of which a submarine controls and maintains neutral buoyancy and stability when submerged. The balance of air and water in the tanks is adjusted so that the vessel's overall density is equal to the surrounding water.

Trimming tanks: [1] Receptacles at bow and stern of a surface vessel which can be filled or emptied to adjust its attitude. [2] Variable ballast tanks at bow, stern and amidships of a submarine, forming part of its trimming system and used to keep the boat level at any depth.

Trinity House: This British corporation, originally chartered in 1514 by King Henry VIII, is today responsible for navigational aids in the waters of England, Wales, Channel Islands, and Gibraltar (Independent Boards of Commissioners for Lights and Navigational Aids in Irish and Scottish waters were established in 1786). Trinity House also provides expert navigators for deep sea pilotage in North European waters, and acts as a charity with regard to the safety, welfare, and training of mariners. Its Directors — drawn from both the Royal and Merchant Navies and known quaintly as "Trinity Masters and Elder Brethren" — serve as assessors and expert witnesses in Admiralty Court.

Trip: [1] A passage between two ports. [2] To release a pelican hook. [3] To raise and swing a yard or spar into position for lowering. [4] To break out an anchor with a tripping line. [5] Said of a boom rolling underwater in a seaway [from Old French triper = to dance].

Triple-A: Colloquial term for anti-aircraft artillery.

Tripping line: A line attached to the fluke or crown of an anchor and used to break it out from the sea bed or loosen it from rocks.

Trireme: An ancient Phoenician, Greek, or Roman battle galley propelled by three banks of oars each pulled by a single man, called thalamite on the lower level, zygite on the middle bank, and thranite on the upper.

Troll: [1] A long fishing line with lures and hooks attached. [2] To fish by towing such a line. Because this activity does not reduce maneuverability, trolling craft are exempt from the Navigation Rules governing vessels engaged in fishing. [3] In Scandinavian folklore, a fabulous cave-dwelling giant (sometimes a dwarf).

Troops: [1] A body of soldiers. [2] Informal naval term for the crew or ship's company.

Tropic: Either of two parallels of terrestrial latitude lying roughly 23¼° from the Equator and enclosing the

Torrid Zone. The Summer Solstice occurs when the sun reaches the northern Tropic of Cancer, and the Winter Solstice when it arrives at the southern Tropic of Capricorn.

Tropic tide: A tide or current that occurs semi-monthly when the moon is at its maximum northern or southern declination. Diurnal inequality is then at a maximum.

Tropical rotating windstorm: A destructive circular storm that forms over tropical waters during late summer and autumn, and is very different from extra-tropical storms that form in winter, even though both are associated with powerful winds and drenching rain. Eight characteristics define a tropical cyclone (as such storms are generically known):

* It has no front
* It forms under weak high-altitude winds
* Its winds lessen with height
* Its center is warmer than its surroundings
* Air sinks at its center
* Its main energy source is the latent heat of condensation
* It rotates inward towards an area of low-pressure known as the eye
* It weakens rapidly over land

Formation begins when thunderstorms drift overhead, while warm air from the ocean surface begins rising, creating a column of low pressure. Trade winds blowing in opposing directions then cause this rising column to start spinning. Thanks to Coriolis Effect the rotation is clockwise in the southern hemisphere and counter-clockwise in the northern. As the spiral moves over the surface, the low pressure around the eye sucks in more and more warm damp air while, at the same time, cooler dryer air is sucked downward. If they last long enough, these conditions feed the cyclone so that it grows to produce violent winds, massive waves, and torrential rains. (*See* Dvorak technique.)

When sustained maximum surface winds are less than 17 meters/second (33 knots, 38 mph, 61 km/hr) the disturbance is called a tropical depression; when winds exceed this speed it becomes a tropical storm and is usually assigned a name. At 33 meters/second (64 knots, 74 mph, 119 km/hr) it is fully-fledged but, confusingly, no standard nomenclature has emerged so meteorologists have given it different names in discrete regions, even changing name within the confines of a single ocean. Cyclonic tropical storms which are otherwise identical are called:

* **Hurricanes**— In the North Atlantic, the North Pacific (E of the dateline), and the South Pacific (W of 160°E).
* **Typhoons**— In the North Pacific (W of the dateline).
* **Severe Tropical Cyclones**— In the South Pacific (W of 160°E) and the South Indian Ocean (E of 90°E).
* **Tropical Cyclones**— In the South Indian Ocean (W of 90°W).

* **Severe Cyclonic Storms**— In the North Indian Ocean.

There is general agreement that winds reach "hurricane strength" when their speeds exceed 33 meters/second, but these storms can go considerably faster (*see* tables 1–6). In consequence, they are extremely dangerous maritime hazards and, when they move onto land, can cause extensive damage due to high winds, heavy waves, severe flooding, and especially storm surge.

Tropospheric Forward Scatter: A former communications system that beamed high-frequency signals against the troposphere (8–16 kms /5–10 miles above earth), picked up part of the reflected signal with sensitive receivers and beamed it onward in the same way. These systems became obsolete with the advent of microwave-satellite communications technology in the 1980s.

Trot: [1] Buoys or moorings arranged to form a line. [2] RN term for a line of moored destroyers. [3] A long fishing line secured at both ends.

Trough: [1] In general, the low point of a wave, opposite to its crest. [2] The hollow between the crests of two waves. [3] In meteorology, an elongated area of low pressure. [4] In oceanography, a long depression of the sea floor, characteristically flat bottomed and steep sided and shallower than a trench.

Trowsers: Loose-fitting canvas breeches worn by common sailors in the age of sail.

Truce: A temporary cessation or suspension of hostilities by agreement of the opposing sides; an armistice.

Truck: [1] The top of the highest mast on a vessel, or a flagstaff. [2] A wooden disc protecting the head of such a staff or mast, usually provided with holes for halyards (similar discs at the top of lower masts are called caps). [3] The small solid wheel of a naval gun-carriage. (From Middle English trocle = wheel or roller.)

True: [1] Properly fitted, placed, or shaped. [2] To align, adjust, balance, or position something. [3] Determined with reference to the earth's axis rather than its magnetic poles (e.g., true North). [4] In accordance with fact; not false. [5] Exact, accurate; correct. [6] Faithful.

True bearing: The bearing of an object as shown by the ship's compass rather than its relative bearing based on the ship's heading.

True blue: This phrase, now describing a loyal and faithful person, is sometimes said to have referred originally to the old rhyme, "Jack Tar steadfast and true; true to his uniform, and uniformly blue." In fact, the term was originally coined by 17th-century Scottish Presbyterians, to distinguish themselves from the Royalists' red.

True course: A route based on true north as opposed to magnetic north (i.e., corrected for magnetic variation and compass deviation).

True North: The direction of the geographic North Pole.

True wind: The speed and direction of wind as observed from a stationary position (cf. apparent wind).

Trundlehead: [1] The upper section of a capstan, drilled with holes into which the turning bars are inserted. [2] The term is also used for the lantern gears of a windmill.

Trunk: A large encased pipe or passage through the decks or bulkheads of a vessel, for cooling, ventilation, or a ladder.

Trunk cabin: [1] The low-profile cabin of a yacht or small boat, extending both above and below the upper deck. [2] That part of a cabin rising above the upper deck of a larger vessel (seldom used today).

Trunnion: [1] Either of two cylindrical projections on either side of a muzzle-loading cannon, supporting it on its carriage and allowing its elevation to be adjusted. [2] One of the pins or gudgeons in a modern gun mount on which the weapon pivots. [3] A hinged hoop connecting an upper mast to a lower one.

Try-boiler: A large copper cauldron used by whalers to boil blubber.

Try down: To extract oil from blubber by boiling.

Trysail: A quadrilateral or triangular sail with its luff looped or otherwise bent to a mast. Used for lying to, for keeping a vessel headed into the wind, or as a course in heavy weather.

Trysail mast: An auxiliary mast that enables the gaff of a fore-and-aft sail to be raised higher than the yard of a course. Also called a snowmast.

Tsunami: An enormously destructive wave produced by a submarine earthquake, landslide, or volcanic action. (Japanese tsu = harbor + nami = wave). Unlike wind-generated waves, it often creates little more than a ripple on the surface of deep water, but travels with high velocity (up to about 435 kts = 500 mph = 806 km/h) and therefore holds a great deal of energy. As it approaches shallow coastal waters, much of the energy of movement is converted into raising the wave to a great height. The first sign of its approach is a withdrawal of water from the coast, as if the tide were retreating, but to unprecedented distances. Then the wave arrives, flooding well above normal high-tide level as it strikes the beach. After withdrawing again, the sea returns and the cycle is repeated several times.

Tsushima (battle): This pivotal naval battle began on May 14, 1905, in the strait between Japan and Korea. A Russian fleet of ancient obsolescent warships had sailed halfway around the world only to be overwhelmed by faster modern Japanese vessels, superior gunnery, discipline and admiralship. The fight went on through the night and, by morning, 43 Russian ships had been sunk with the loss over 5,000 men killed and another 6,000 taken prisoner. Czar Nicholas II was forced to sue for peace, resulting in the Portsmouth Treaty, signed on August 23, 1905. This gave Japan land concessions in Korea, especially the Liaodong peninsula, along with a variety of other arrangements which allowed Japan to become the major superpower of East Asia. It also seriously weakened the prestige of the Czar, paving the way for revolution a decade later.

Tsushima Current: Part of the kuroshio current, flowing through Tsushima Strait into the Sea of Japan.

TU: Task unit.

Tub: [1] Derogatory slang for an old and decrepit vessel. [2] A cylindrical band encircling a mast for securing a yard or gaff so that it can slide. [3] A round shallow open-topped wooden container.

Tuck: See chine.

Tugboat: A small, powerful craft, specifically designed for towing or pushing other ships or barges. See also towboat.

Tumblehome: Having sides that slope inward and upward from the lowest gundeck to the weather deck of a wooden man-o'-war, thus concentrating the weight of ordnance toward the centerline, improving stability and seaworthiness, making it possible to fire the upper guns while grappled alongside, and making the vessel difficult to board.

Tumbling: Said of a gyroscope that has lost stability and is moving erratically.

Tun: A large cask used for transporting wine or beer. It had a capacity of 252 wine gallons = 302.6 U.S. gallons = 1145.6 liters, which equals 40 cubic feet, and weighs about one long ton (2,240 lbs) (cf. Tonnage).

Tune: To adjust [1] standing rigging, sails, and hull for optimum performance; [2] an engine to run smoothly and efficiently; [3] the frequency of radio instruments or circuits.

Tungula: A small boat of the Moluccas and Borneo.

Tunne: See tun.

Turbidity: Cloudiness due to suspended sediment or the growth of phytoplankton. The phenomenon prevents light from reaching lower levels, inhibiting the growth of aquatic plants and the fish dependent on them (Latin turbidus = disordered).

Turbidity current: A flow of heavily-sedimented water, often caused by an underwater avalanche or earthquake. Also density current.

Turbine: A machine driven by the reactive force of a gas or liquid flowing through blades or vanes attached to a rotor. In marine service, steam or gas turbines are used as main propulsion systems and also for auxiliary purposes such as electrical generation.

Turbo-blower: A device used to complete the evacuation of a submarine's ballast tanks after the boat has surfaced. Colloquially, "blower."

Turbo-electric: A propulsion system consisting of a turbine connected to a generator whose electricity powers the propellers.

Turbosail propulsion: This system — invented by the research team of Lucien Malavard, Bertrand Charrier, and Jacques-Yves Cousteau — combines the principles of conventional sails with the aerodynamic design of airplane wings. A fan draws air into 33-foot aerofoil towers, boosting wind speed over the leeward side and creating forward pull more powerful than that of traditional sails. Computers control the angles, suction power, and rotation of the turbosails, which reduce the fuel consumption of standard engines while adding power and speed. A ship equipped with turbosails looks virtually identical to one with Flettner rotators.

Turbo-supercharger: A turbine driven by the exhaust gases of a reciprocating engine and attached to a blower which raises inflowing air above atmospheric pressure in order to increase the engine's power. Also "Turbocharger."

Turbulence: Disturbed motion of the sea or atmosphere, usually due to the confluence of water or air currents.

Turbulent flow: A term in fluid mechanics referring to movement in which particle velocity and direction are irregular in the boundary layer. Cf. laminar flow.

Turkish Straits: A term referring to two narrow waterways that connect the Aegean arm of the Mediterranean with the Black Sea, via the Sea of Marmara. At the western end of that sea, the Dardanelles (known in antiquity as the Hellespont) lie between the Gallipoli peninsula and Asia Minor. At the eastern end, the Bosphorus, which is straddled by the city of Istanbul, is a former river valley, drowned by the sea at the end of the Tertiary period. The Turkish Straits are an international waterway, governed by the Montreux Convention. They are conventionally considered the boundary between Europe and Asia.

Turk's head: A turban-like ornamental knot braided from small line.

Turn: [1] A tactical maneuver in which all ships go round simultaneously and maintain the same true bearings on each other while changing course (as opposed to a corpen in which they maintain relative bearings). [2] To put about or tack when sailing. [3] A trick or spell of duty. [4] To wrap a line about something. [5] The moment at which tide changes from flow to ebb and vice versa (cf. slack water).

Turn a blind eye: See blind eye.

Turn and turn about: To stand alternate spells of duty. See watch-and-watch.

Turn count: The number of propeller revolutions per minute.

Turn count masking: Random alterations of turn count to preclude a listening submarine from estimating the speed of its target or an attacker.

Turn in: [1] To go to bed. [2] To return items taken on loan or issued.

Turn in all standing: To go to bed fully-clothed (e.g., when a call to action stations is anticipated).

Turn of the bilge: See chine.

Turn out: [1] To awaken and get up from cot or hammock. [2] To assemble a guard or working party. [3] To unreef sails.

Turn to: To get to work.

Turn turtle: To overturn or capsize, so that the ship is upside down with its hull resembling the carapace of a turtle.

Turnaround: [1] The total time consumed by entering a port, and mooring, loading or unloading, casting-off, and returning to sea. [2] The elapsed time between aircraft touchdown and being ready to depart after refueling and rearming.

Turnbuckle: A metal link or sleeve internally threaded to accept opposite-threaded eyed screws at each end. Once a turnbuckle has been inserted in standing rigging or any other line, the sleeve can be turned to slacken-off or tighten the line.

Turning-bar: A wooden rod inserted into a socket and used to turn a capstan.

Turning basin: A wide section in or at the end of a narrow channel in which vessels can reverse direction.

Turning circle: The path followed by a vessel when the helm is hard over.

Turpentine: [1] An oleo-resin secreted by trees of the pine family. [2] A volatile pungent oil distilled from that resin. (Cf. Rosin.)

Turret: A rotating armored housing for artillery. Defined as single, twin, triple, or quadruple, depending on the number of guns it houses.

Turtle deck: A convex-arched forward deck, designed to minimize damage from shipping heavy seas.

Turtle ship: A Korean warship (*Kobukson*) designed by Admiral Yi Sun-sin in the early 16th century and in active service for some three centuries. Propelled by sail and oars, its convex upper deck was covered in thin iron plates with sharp spikes to repel borders. Offensive weaponry included fire-arrows, several types of cannon, and a ram.

Twaqo: A Malaysian variation of the junk.

Tween deck: [1] A space above the hold for supplementary cargo storage. [2] Any deck in a ship below the main deck. Abbreviation of "between."

Tween decks: Anywhere inside the ship below the weather deck.

Tweendecker: A general cargo or breakbulk merchantman with two or three decks. Small items such as bales, bags, or drums can be stacked in the tweendeck space atop the tweendeck. Below the tweendeck is the hold space, used for general cargo. *See also* multipurpose vessel.

Twenty-foot equivalent unit: An inexact measurement that cannot be converted precisely into other units. The most common dimensions for a TEU container are 20 feet long × 8 feet wide × 8.5 feet high. *See* container and tonnage.

Twiddling line: A short length of rope or cord used to secure a helm or tiller while the steersman is temporarily absent.

Twilight: A period of partial darkness immediately before sunrise and following sunset.

Twins: Double headsails worn on opposite sides of the mast when sailing downwind.

Two-block: [1] To bring blocks together by hauling on the fall. [2] To bring a flag or sail to the top of a mast. [3] USN slang, for adjusting the knot of a necktie to hide the collar.

Two for Seven: U.S. Naval Academy slang for the Commitment Papers a midshipman must sign, agreeing to seven years of active service in return for two years at the Academy.

Two-handed: Former USN enlisted slang for a man who had served as a marine as well as a sailor. (Marines who could qualify as able-seamen often transferred to enjoy higher pay.)

Tye: [1] A rope forming part of a purchase for hoisting an upper yard by its center, using the halyard tackle. [2] A pigtail.

Tymung: Cantonese name for a pirate-junk.

Type Command: All USN ships are organized into commands which have responsibility for the administration, training, maintenance, and readiness of all vessels or units of a specified type. Thus, submarines come under the administrative control of Commander Submarine Force; aircraft carriers, aircraft squadrons, and air stations under Commander Naval Air Force; and all other ships under Commander Naval Surface Force. Normally, the type commander controls the unit during its primary and intermediate training cycles, after which it falls under the operational control of a fleet commander.

Typhon: [1] A loud signal horn operated by steam or compressed-air. [2] In Greek mythology, Typhon was a monster who tried to overthrow the gods and wreck the earth with thunderbolts stolen from Zeus. He was defeated and thrown into the stormy pit of Tartarus from where he emits hot, dangerous winds. It has been suggested that the name was borrowed by the Persians as tufân to describe the cyclonic storms of the Indian Ocean.

Typhoon: A violent cyclonic storm of the northwest Pacific Ocean. Probably Cantonese Tai-Phong = enormous wind, but *see* Typhon for alternative etymology. *See also* tropical rotating windstorm.

U

UA: Unauthorized absence.

UAM: Underwater to air missile.

UAV: Unmanned aerial vehicle.

U-Boat: A German submarine of World Wars I and II. (Anglicized contraction of Unterseeboot.)

U-Bolt: An iron bar bent into the shape of a "U" and threaded for nuts at each end. Used as a connector. Also U-clip.

Uckers: A naval gambling game, similar to Backgammon, adapted from the ancient Indian game of Pachisi by 18th century British sailors anxious to pass the time on long voyages to and from the Orient. The children's game Ludo is a simplified and much less vicious version, using one die instead of two. (Possibly

derived from the Anglo-Saxon uck = send back to the start.)

UCMJ: Uniform Code of Military Justice (U.S.).

UCT: Underwater construction team.

UDT: Underwater demolition team.

UFO: Unidentified flying object.

Ugly: Said of threatening or dangerous seas or weather.

UHF: Ultra high frequency.

ULBC: Abbreviation of Ultra Large Bulk Carrier; defined as in excess of 300,000 dwt.

ULCC: Abbreviation of Ultra Large Crude Carrier; defined as a tanker in excess of 320,000 dwt.

Ullage: [1] The depth of free space above the liquid in a tank or container. [2] The amount of liquid lost from a cask or other container by leakage and evaporation. [3] The space provided for thermal expansion of the propellant in a liquid-fueled missile. [4] In the RN, any grog left over after all had received their tot. [5] Formerly, a lazy sailor. (Pronounced ull-idge.)

ULO: Unrestricted line officer.

Ultima Thule: Today referring to the highest degree or furthest point attainable, this term originally described an island at the most northerly reaches of the world. It was first mentioned by the Greek explorer Pytheas who claimed to have visited it between 330 and 320 B.C. His *On the Ocean* is now lost, but is quoted in the works of later authors. For example, Strabo's *Geography* (Book II, Chapter 5), written in the first century of the current era, tells us that Pytheas described Thule as "the most northerly of the Britannic Islands." This could refer to the Shetlands, Faeroes, or Iceland, but others have speculated it could be Greenland, or an island off Norway. It is generally pronounced "two-lay" rather than "tool" or "thool."

Ultra Mare: A Latin term in naval law meaning "overseas." Pronounced ultra mar-ray.

Ulu: Malayan for "headwaters" used in the RN as slang for any remote and undeveloped place (cf. boondocks).

Umbrella: [1] A shield of military aircraft covering a surface formation (*see* combat air patrol). [2] A cone-shaped cover to protect a smokestack against the weather. [3] A contrivance formerly used to warp wooden ships forward.

UMCM: Underwater mine countermeasures.

Umiak: A large Inuit or Eskimo boat made from skins.

UN: United Nations.

Unarm: To deprive or free of weapons or armor. Also de-arm or disarm.

Unarmed: Without offensive weapons or protective armor. In certain conditions merchant vessels carrying defensive weaponry may be considered legally unarmed.

Unattached: An officer not having a specific appointment.

Unauthorized absence: The current term for leaving the assigned vessel or place of duty without permission. Former terminology included absentee, straggler, and absent without official leave (AWOL).

Unbend: To cast off or untie.

Unclaimed: Refers to vessels found derelict (with neither humans nor domestic animals on board) which are not claimed by the owners within 366 days of discovery.

Uncle Sam's Confused Group: USN sailor's interpretation of the initials USCG.

UNCLOS: United Nations Convention on Law of the Sea.

Uncover: To doff one's headgear, usually as a sign of respect.

Uncovered: Said of reefs, wrecks, and other normally submerged objects that have temporarily appeared above the surface.

UNCTAD: United Nations Conference on Trade & Development.

Undecked: An open boat.

Under canvas: With sails set. Not to be confused with undercanvassed.

Under courses: Said of a fully square-rigged ship, having sails suspended only on its lowermost yards. *See* courses.

Under false colors: *See* false colors, bamboozle, flag verification.

Under hack: Said of a USN officer confined to quarters for disciplinary infraction.

Under power: Propelled by mechanical means. No to be confused with underpowered.

Under sail: Propelled by the action of wind on sails.

Under the captain's cloak: This 18th–19th century phrase refers to clause 36 in the British Articles of War which gives captains wide discretion in matters of punishment not previously specified, reading; "All other crimes ... shall be punished according to the laws and customs in such cases used at sea."

Under the weather: During times of rough seas, seasick passengers often retreat under the weather deck, partly for shelter, but just as importantly because the greatest swaying action is above deck and the most stable point is down near the keel. Hence they tend to feel better when below.

Under tow: A vessel being pulled along.

Under way: Said of a vessel which is floating freely neither anchored, moored, nor aground irrespective of whether it is stationary or moving. Also underway.

Undercanvassed: Carrying fewer sails than are appropriate for the vessel. Not to be confused with under canvas.

Undercarriage: An aircraft's landing gear.

Undercliff: A lower cliff or terrace, usually formed by a landslip or slide.

Undercurrent: [1] A subsurface flow below a calm surface or contrary current. Also underflow. [2] In common usage, a hidden meaning at variance with the outward significance of words or actions.

Underdog: This term — now referring to a person who is disadvantaged, or not expected to win — originated in a trade with close maritime connections. During the 17th through 19th centuries, shipbuilding was a major user of planking, which was cut from wooden logs by a two-man team using a long double-handled "whipsaw." The logs were secured above the "sawpit," by fanged metal supports called "dogs." The senior (or top) sawyer stood on the log to guide the cut, while the bottom sawyer clambered down into the pit to provide musclepower, often standing in ice-cold water and choking on a constant shower of sawdust. In sawpit jargon, they were known as "top dog" and "underdog." (This derivation is challenged by the dog-fighting fraternity, which claims the terms for itself.)

Underfoot: Said of an anchor when it is below the ship's forefoot and the cable is nearly straight up-and-down.

Underhauled: Lying at anchor in a direction contrary to the set of surface current and wind.

Underhung: Said of a rudder which is supported entirely within the hull without connection to the sternpost. Also spade rudder.

Undermanned: Said of a vessel whose crew is either below the level specified in its certification, or is too small to handle or navigate the ship safely (not necessarily the same thing).

Under-masted: Said of a ship whose masts are too short or too weak to carry the optimum amount of sail.

Underpowered: Said of a vessel whose propulsion system is inadequate to move the hull as designed, with or without sail assistance. Not the same as under power.

Underrigged: Said of a vessel whose masts or other rigging are either too light for its sails or too small to take full advantage of its hull capabilities.

Underrun: [1] To pass below or run underneath something, such as a rope, net, or bridge. [2] To inspect something from beneath in a water vessel. [3] To take-in a line on one side of the deck and pay out on the other. [4] Said of a log when it indicates less distance than the ship has actually run. [5] To lay out a tackle in its proper order for use.

Undersea: Beneath the surface, submarine.

Undersea warfare: Operations including offensive and defensive submarine, antisubmarine, and mine warfare activities conducted to establish underwater battlespace dominance.

Underset: An undercurrent.

Undershoot: To land an aircraft short of its runway or flight deck.

Understeer: The tendency of a vessel to turn less sharply than the helmsman intended.

Understowed: *See* flatted cargo.

Undertow: [1] The momentary downward and seaward thrust of a wave as it collapses and breaks on a beach. [2] A subsurface current flowing opposite to the surface current.

Underwater: Below the surface, submerged.

Underwater countercurrent: *See* undertow.

Underwater demolition: The location and destruction or neutralization of obstacles along an invasion beach prior to amphibious assault.

Underwater exploration: Along coastlines the water is usually shallow enough to be within the range of scuba diving. Beyond the continental slope, however, exploration becomes extremely difficult and hazardous. *See* Deep sea exploration.

Underway replenishment: Refers to the transfer of fuel, munitions, and stores from one ship to another while under way. Also known as replenishment at sea.

Underwrite: To sign and accept liability under an insurance policy for a vessel or a voyage. (*See* marine insurance.)

Undine: A female water spirit.

Undocumented: Said of a vessel which does not have the required certificates and clearances.

Unfurl: [1] To spread a furled sail. [2] To shake out a rolled flag.

Unhandy: Said of a clumsy vessel, one not easy to handle or manage.

Unidentified flying object: In military terminology, and contrary to popular belief, this term does not imply extraterrestrial incursion, but means exactly what it says — an airborne object of unknown origin.

Unified Command Structure: As a global superpower, the United States divides the entire world into military combatant commands, with an admiral or general as commander-in-chief (CINC) of all the armed forces in each designated region or function. The structure is flexible, and changes as required to meet national security needs. As of 2008, there are six established geographic commands:
- Central (Egypt, Arabia, Central Asia).
- Europe (including Greenland and the former Soviet Union, Central Asian republics excluded).
- Northern (America).
- Southern (America).
- Pacific.
- Africa.

There are also four functional commands not bounded by geography — Joint Forces, Special Operations, Strategic, and Transportation. The establishment of a Unified Medical command is under consideration.

Uniform: [1] NATO phonetic notation of the letter "U." [2] Always the same; not varying or changing. [3] The dress prescribed for naval, marine, or military personnel. *See* uniforms for naval officers and uniforms for enlisted and rated personnel.

Uniform buoyage systems: Two such systems are in worldwide use. They consist of aids to navigation in which the shape, number and coloring of buoys and their relative positions indicate the location of navigable waterways. [1] The cardinal system is best suited to coasts with many hazards to navigation. It is always used in conjunction with [2] The lateral system which works well in regions where channels are well-defined with few hazards.

Uniform Code of Military Justice: United States Congressional legislation concerning military criminal law that allows the President, as Commander-in-Chief, to prescribe rules and procedures to implement its provisions. He does this via the Manual for Courts-Martial, which has the status of an executive order, and contains detailed instructions for consistent implementation throughout the armed forces. *See also* articles of war, captain's mast, non-judicial punishment, and non-punitive disciplinary action.

Uniform oddities: The uniforms of both English-speaking navies have unusual incidents in their histories. In 1919, RN flag officers' sleeve stripes were narrowed without consulting the King as is traditionally required. Feeling insulted, he simply ignored the new rule and, to this day, members of the royal family wear the old style broad stripes.

Then, in 1941, someone belatedly realized that the Napoleonic eagle on the cap badges of USN officers (and the insignia of enlisted) faced to the left (sinister) in disregard of traditional heraldry. In May of that year it was changed to face right, towards the sword arm, which is the correct chivalric direction.

Uniform of the day: The uniform designated by a commanding officer or in standing orders to be worn at a specified time.

Uniform pitch: *See* fixed pitch.

Uniforms for enlisted personnel (U.S.): Sailors in the Continental Navy had no official uniform, but tended to dress alike, wearing pantaloons, usually tied at the knee, with a jumper or shirt, neckerchief, short-waisted jacket, and low crowned hat. The first sign of true uniformity came in January 1813, when Commodore Decatur arrived at New York with the crews of *United States* and *Macedonia* unofficially dressed in blue jackets buttoned loosely over waistcoats, blue bell-bottomed trousers and glazed canvas hats with stiff brims decked with streamers and ribbons.

Official regulations were not issued until September 1817. White duck jacket, trousers and vest made up the summer uniform, while the colorful winter outfit included blue jacket and trousers, red vest, yellow buttons and black hat. These regulations also provided that when men swabbed the decks they were to be barefooted with their trousers rolled up. This first attempt at standardization was loosely enforced, and sailors added their own buttons, striping, and accoutrements as they wished.

Not until 1841 were commanding officers required to ensure that personnel had the prescribed clothing, then consisting of blue woolen frock with white collar and cuffs, blue trousers and vest, black hat and handkerchief. In 1862, senior petty officers were authorized to wear officer style double-breasted jackets. In 1901, denim working uniforms were authorized.

In 1973, recognizing that the traditional enlisted dress uniform had originally evolved to meet the needs of operating a fully-rigged sailing ship, it was replaced with a suit and tie similar to those of officers and CPOs, so as to create a more modern appearance. This break with tradition was far from universally popular, sailors prefer to be distinctively dressed and many derisively called it the "bus driver's uniform." Even though jumper and bell-bottoms serve no nautical purpose today and are not related to anything worn in the civilian world, there was strong resistance to changing traditional garments that had identified sailors for a long time and were still retained by most of the world's other navies. In 1980, the Navy began to re-issue jumper-style dress uniforms. At the same time, women's uniforms underwent a sweeping change to increase their practicality and to make them more parallel to the men's.

Uniforms for naval officers (British): In medieval times it was customary for the masters of Royal ships to be issued with distinctive clothing. The following is extracted from a warrant issued by James I in 1604, the year after the Union of England and Scotland (the original is in the British Museum).

> Wee will and commaunde you ymediatile vpon the sight hereof, to delyuer or cause to be deliuered vnto our well-beloved servants ... principall Maisters of our ships by vs appointed to that office ... for theire Lyurie coat.... To eury of them two yards of fine red cloth ... two yards of velvet for gardinge the same coats ... ten ounces of silk lace for garrishing the same coats ... two ounces of sowinge silk ... two yards of passamayne lace ... two dozen buttons of silke and golde.... For imbroderinge of their coats with ships, roses, crownes ... richlie embrodered wth Venice golde, siluer and silke, and wth spangles....

These fancy clothes were shipmaster liveries rather than uniforms, and it would be generations before seamen began to dress in anything like standard fashion. In 1745 a group of British naval officers meeting at Wills Coffee House in London decided to petition the Admiralty for an official uniform similar to other navies. Several captains were directed to submit designs, the two most popular colors being grey or the traditional English military red. The final decision was left to King George II.

According to legend, he saw the Duchess of Bedford riding in Hyde Park wearing a new habit of dark blue with rows of gold buttons down the front, gold lace on the cuffs, and white facings, and was so impressed that he immediately ordered it be copied for naval officers' uniforms. However, records show that Captain Philip Saumarez had previously recommended blue with white facings, so this story is probably apocryphal. In fact, the choice may have been for practical reasons.

It was at about this time that indigo dye became freely and cheaply available from the East India Company. Compared to other contemporary dyes, this tropical plant extract offered greater color fastness to sunlight and wear and had less tendency to run when wet, so it would have made sense to select blue no matter what the king or the captain said. Whatever the reason, in April 1748 the Admiralty finally promulgated standardized blue-and-white uniforms for commissioned sea officers. The preamble to the Regulation read in part:

> Whereas we judge it necessary, in order to better distinguish the Rank of Sea Officers, to establish a Military Uniform clothing for Admirals, Captains, Commanders, and Lieutenants, and judging it also necessary to distinguish their Class to be in the Rank of Gentlemen ... you are hereby required and directed to conform yourself to the said Establishment by wearing clothing accordingly at all times; and to take care that such of the foresaid officers and midshipmen who may be from time to time under your command to do the like.

Initially, the "clothing" consisted of frocked coats and breeches, with differences in rank being reflected in the shape and cut of lapels and cuffs. However, many officers still dressed as they pleased, leading Admiral Jervis (later Lord St. Vincent) to comment in 1797:

> I have seen several officers of the Fleet on shore dressed like shop-keepers in colored cloaths ... in direct violation of the late order ... any officer offending against this ... regulation will be arrested and court-martialled and never allowed on shore so long as he serves under me.

In 1783 flag officers were further distinguished by gold embroidery decorating the fronts, skirts, cuffs, and pocket flaps of their coats. One row of embroidery signified a rear-admiral, two a vice-admiral, and three a full admiral. Later, rank was indicated by the number and positioning of epaulettes. In 1787 an official uniform for RN warrant officers was introduced. Further changes during the 19th and early 20th centuries led to the current uniforms, including those of the Merchant Navy which were standardized in 1918, modeled on the Royal Navy.

Uniforms for naval officers (United States): Officers' uniforms went through several iterations, starting in September 1776 when the Marine Committee of Congress resolved that the uniform for officers in the Continental Navy be "blue cloth with red lapels ... blue britches (and) red waistcoat." This design was unpopular and, in March 1777 a group of captains proposed a design based on that of the Royal Navy, consisting of "a blue coat ... trimmed with gold lace and gold buttons; white waistcoat, breeches, and stockings; and gold epaulettes." Neither of the foregoing was adopted, leaving American officers free to develop their own uniforms, most choosing the design proposed by the captains. But they went too far. Congress deemed the fancy trimmings and decoration to be excessively royalist and resolved in 1781 that "no officer whatsoever in the service of the United States shall ... wear ... any gold or lace embroidery or vellum."

The first official naval uniform regulations were issued by the Army-dominated War Department in August 1797 and prescribed officers' uniforms of "blue and buff." Following the establishment of a separate Navy Department in 1798, blue and gold uniforms were semi-officially recognized, but it was not until August 1802 that the Secretary of the Navy signed an instruction which made those colors mandatory.

Khaki made its debut in 1912 as a summer uniform for naval aviators, and in 1917 the "forestry green" uniform of the Marine Corps was authorized as aviators' winter working uniform. Aviation khaki was adopted by submariners in 1931. Ten years later the Navy approved khakis for on-station wear by senior officers and, soon after Pearl Harbor, chiefs and officers were authorized to wear khakis ashore on liberty. Gray uniforms in the same style as khaki were introduced for officers in 1943. Permission to wear gray uniform was later extended to Chief Petty Officers (and cooks and stewards), but the Navy abolished "grays" in 1949. The aviators' need for rank identification while wearing a flight jacket eventually evolved into metal shirt collar devices, rather than bulky hard shoulder boards for all officers.

Uniforms for rated personnel (British): As early as 1760, a group of RN officers petitioned the Admiralty to formalize seamen's uniforms, but nothing came of it and the sailors had to continue supplying their own clothing, often by purchase of cheap and shoddy items provided by the purser from the slop chest. The luckier ones served under a wealthy captain who outfitted his boat's crew (if rich enough, all deck crew as well), frequently choosing fancy patterns and colors to meet his personal taste. For example, the eccentric Captain Wilmott of HMS *Harlequin* dressed his boats crew in pantomime clown costumes, exposing the poor men to ridicule every time they came close to the shore.

The first official service-wide dress codes for petty officers, seamen, landsmen, and boys were not introduced in the RN until 1857, sixteen years after they had been prescribed in the USN. Even then, RN ratings had to tailor their own uniforms from cloth supplied by the purser. A standard item was a short double-breasted blue coat or peajacket that led to American and British sailors being known as "bluejackets." This coat was discontinued by the RN in 1890, but the nickname lived on in both RN and USN. Ready-made uniforms began to be issued by the RN in the early 20th century, but their rough cloth and poor fit led many sailors to buy "tiddly suits" — tailored uniforms of superior cloth — to be worn ashore when far from the eagle eyes of the master at arms. These were often so tight-fitting that a messmate's help was needed to pull the jumper on, and the trousers' bell-bottoms were frequently expanded until well beyond regulation width.

Uninterruptible power supply: A device which maintains a continuous supply of power to connected equipment by supplying electricity when the main power source is not available. It differs from auxiliary power or a standby generator, since it provides instant protection from momentary power interruptions or fluctuations. Integrated systems that have both UPS and a standby generator are often referred to as emergency power systems or continuous power supply.

Union: The upper quarter of an ensign, nearest to the mast. Often containing a small version of the national flag or some other national emblem. *See also* Canton.

Union down: Said of an ensign flown upside down as a distress signal.

Union Flag: The proper name of both the UK and U.S. national ensign. The former is formed by the superimposed crosses of Saints Andrew (Scotland), George (England), and Patrick (Ireland). The latter is composed of 50 stars in the union and 13 stripes on the fly.

Union Jack: [1] The union of the U.S. national flag flown at the jackstaff of USN warships. (*See also* First Navy Jack.) [2] The British union flag when flown at the jackstaff of an RN warship. [3] Incorrect but widespread terminology for the British union flag when flown as the national ensign.

Unit: A generic term for the military assets assigned to a single tactical commander. May be a single ship or aircraft, or a larger force.

Unit citation: A formal, honorary recognition by high authority of a naval or military unit's outstanding performance, usually but not exclusively in combat. Unit citations are not intended to recognize individual actions, but to acknowledge the combined efforts of the unit as a whole. A USN vessel receiving such a citation is entitled to fly an identifying pennant, and those on board at the time the service was performed are awarded a medal to be worn permanently on the right breast of their uniforms. (*See also* Award Flags & Pennants.)

Unit loading: The loading of troops with their equipment and supplies in the same vessels.

United Nations Conference on Trade & Development: Established in 1964, to promote the integration of developing countries into the world economy, with particular focus on ensuring that domestic policies and international action are mutually supportive in bringing about sustainable development.

United Nations Convention on the Law of the Sea: An international conference that convened in 1973 and ended in 1982. During those nine years, representatives of more than 160 sovereign States shuttled back and forth between New York and Geneva, discussing issues, bargaining and trading national rights and obligations, in a series of marathon negotiations that produced the Convention which came into force in November 1994. As of April 2008, it had been ratified by 155 coastal nations, excluding the United States. Its key features cover:

Navigational rights, territorial sea limits, economic jurisdiction, legal status of resources on the sea bed beyond the limits of national jurisdiction, passage of ships through narrow straits, conservation and management of living marine resources, protection of the marine environment, a marine research regime and, a more unique feature, a binding procedure for the settlement of disputes between States.

United States Army Transportation Corps: Established by Executive Order in July 1942, the Transportation Corps is charged with the operation of all vessels under War Department jurisdiction. Previously known as the Army Transportation Service, its motto is "Spearhead of Logistics." The concept of an Army-operated fleet had its origins during the Spanish-American War when U.S. flagged commercial shipping was unresponsive to the Army's needs for military sealift. During World War I the Army crewed in excess of fifty oceangoing ships to support the Expeditionary Force in France, but, in July 1918, the War Department requested the Navy's Overseas Transportation Service to take over the Army fleet.

Between the wars, the Army began taking back its historic sealift function until, with the beginning of World War II, the fleet was again expanded, reaching a peak of 170 large vessels (over 200' LOA) and 1360 medium (over 65' LOA). The craft operated under Army control and were manned partly by the Civilian Branch of the Water Division and in part by military crews. During the early 1950s, the Navy's Military Sealift Command took over the Army's prior role in oceangoing shipping. The Army Transportation Corps still operates a substantial fleet of small craft, the crews of which are now all military.

United States Coast Guard: *See* Coast Guard.

United States Department of Defense: Established in 1949, to reduce inter-service rivalry and improve overall economy and efficiency. Based at the Pentagon, and often referred to colloquially by that name, it is headed by a Secretary with Cabinet status. Like the British Ministry of Defence, it is both a policy-making department of state and the highest-level military command. It includes the departments of Navy, Army, and Air Force, and a number of non-combatant agencies including the National Security Agency, and the Defense Intelligence Agency. The Coast Guard, which is normally controlled by the Department of Homeland Security, comes under DoD authority in wartime.

United States Department of the Navy: Was established by Act of Congress in 1798, to replace the U.S. Board of Admiralty, and to provide civilian oversight and administrative and technical support to the Navy and Marine Corps. Previously a cabinet member, its Secretary now reports to the Secretary of Defense. With executive offices in the Pentagon, the Department is responsible for organizing, supplying, equipping, training, and mobilizing naval and marine personnel and assets. It oversees the construction, outfitting, and repair of naval ships, aircraft, equipment, and facilities, and is responsible for

shore establishments including dockyards, bases, depots, etc.

United States Marine Corps: This branch of the United States military was formed on November 10, 1775 — exactly four weeks after creation of the Continental Navy — when the Continental Congress resolved:

> That two battalions of Marines be raised consisting of one colonel, two lieutenant colonels, two majors and officers as usual in other regiments; That they consist of an equal number of privates with other battalions; that particular care be taken that no persons be appointed to office or inlisted into said battalions, but such as are good seamen, or so acquainted with Maritime affairs as to be able to serve to advantage by sea, when required.

Both navy and marines were disbanded after the War of Independence, not to be re-established until 1794 and 1798 respectively. The two most famous actions of this early period were in 1803, during the First Barbary War, and in 1847, during the War with Mexico. The former added "Shores of Tripoli," and the second "Halls of Montezuma" to the Corps' colors and eventually its hymn (*see* march music).

In 1834, President Andrew Jackson (a former army general) planned to transfer the Marines to the Army, but was thwarted by an Act of Congress. In 1917, the Corps acquired a marine aviation component. During World War II, the Pacific War "island-hopping" campaign firmly established the Marines as an élite unit and a leading exponent of amphibious warfare, but when the war ended, senior army generals again tried to gain control. Once more Congress came to the rescue and gave the Corps statutory protection under the National Security Act of 1947.

As in the British and most other 18th century navies, United States marines were originally conceived as infantry serving aboard warships with — in addition to combat duties — responsibility for defending the ship's officers from mutiny. This mission ended in the 1990s, when the last Marine security detachments were withdrawn from U.S. Navy ships, but the infantry focus continues with the doctrine "Every Marine a rifleman." Regardless of military specialization, all enlisted Marines are trained in ground combat and all officers are qualified infantry platoon commanders.

Today, the Corps relies on the U.S. Navy for sealift, but is otherwise a self-contained, combined-arms, rapid-deployment force that integrates ground combat units with an air combat component and a logistics element, to provide both expeditionary and amphibious capability. Like the British Royal Marines, the Corps badge is a globe, with the former showing the eastern hemisphere and the latter the western.

United States Maritime Service: In 1938, when a Second World War was imminent, President Franklin D. Roosevelt established the U.S. Maritime Service — the only racially integrated service of the time — to train men for the Merchant Marine and the Army Transportation Corps. Its ranks, grades, and ratings were the same as those of the United States Coast Guard. The training bases were closed in 1954, but the U.S. Merchant Marine Academy and the State Maritime Academies are still part of the USMS.

United States Merchant Marine: This service was formally established by the Merchant Marine Act of 1936 which mandated that...

... The United States shall have a merchant marine ... [to] serve as a naval or military auxiliary in time of war or national emergency ... [it] should be operated by highly trained and efficient citizens of the United States ... the United States Navy and the Merchant Marine of the United States should work closely together to promote the maximum integration of the total seapower forces of the United States.

United States Naval Institute: A private institution with strong ties to the USN. Publishes books, periodicals, and conducts seminars on naval affairs. Founded in 1873, it provides an independent forum to...

... Honor America's enduring sea services heritage; to support the professional development of United States Sailors, Marines, and Coast Guardsmen; to champion a strong national defense; and to challenge military conventionalism by encouraging debate on critical defense issues.

United States Naval Ship: A ship that is owned by the USN and operated by the Military Sealift Command, but not commissioned as a warship. Normally operated by a civilian crew with a small contingent of naval personnel. Usually abbreviated USNS and used as a prefix to the ship's name.

United States Navy: Most of the Continental Navy was disbanded after the War of Independence and, in spite of an active merchant marine, the Republic was effectively toothless at sea. Then, in 1794, Congress passed a "Bill to Provide a Naval Armament" and, four years later, established the Navy Department. Half a dozen well-built and powerful "super-frigates" were commissioned (*see* Warship Rating), and their crews were "blooded" during an undeclared naval war with France (1798–1800) and the first Barbary War (1803–1805).

In June 1812, knowing Britain to be preoccupied with the Napoleonic conflict, the United States opportunistically declared war on Britain, ostensibly to defend "Freedom of the Seas." They opened with a poorly-conceived triple-pronged invasion of Canada that went badly wrong and had to be aborted, but, in stunning contrast to the dismal performance of ground forces, the Navy opened the War brilliantly with a series of triumphant single-ship actions. The chastened and humiliated British struck back with the victory of an experienced crew over a green one (*see* Don't give up the ship), but were soon to lose a critical fleet action on Lake Erie and a smaller engagement on Lake Champlain.

At sea, however, British blockade soon restricted American naval action to guerre de course in which a few warships and numerous privateers preyed on British shipping with considerable success, capturing over 800 merchantmen and forcing the Royal Navy to mount a convoy system along the English and Irish coasts. The naval war ended as it had begun with an American victory in which USS *Hornet* captured HMS *Penguin* in a sloop-on-sloop action off Tristan da Cunha. Having successfully tweaked the lion's tail for almost three years, the USN rightfully felt it had come of age.

The navy played a significant role in the Civil War, doing much to advance naval architecture and technology, but then suffered neglect and decline until a modernization program began in the 1880s. By 1907, when President Teddy Roosevelt sent the Great White Fleet around the world, the United States had established itself as a major maritime power. In 1922 the Washington Naval Treaties gave the USN parity with the RN, a situation which ended with the exponential expansion of American naval power during World War II. Since then, in spite of a brief but serious challenge by Fleet Admiral Gorshkov's vastly expanded Soviet Navy, the USN has remained the world's predominant maritime force.

United States Navy Memorial: In 1791, when Pierre L'Enfant, a French-born American military engineer, designed the street layout of Washington, D.C., he included a Navy Memorial in his plans. But it was not until 1977 that a committee of prominent military and civilian leaders formed the Navy Memorial Foundation, which undertook the construction of such a memorial on Pennsylvania Avenue.

Its centerpiece is a granite map of the world, 100 feet in diameter, surrounded by relief sculptures of historic U.S. naval events. An adjacent Naval Historical Center houses a theatre, an electronic log of over half-a-million navy veterans, and other displays. The Foundation also follows a broad-based mission of public outreach and values-based education.

United States numbered fleets: The concept of numbered fleets was introduced by Admiral Ernest King in 1943. At that time even-numbered fleets served in the Atlantic and European theaters and odd-numbered in the Pacific. Eight such fleets were established, but the first, fourth, and eighth were deactivated after World War II. In April 2008 the fourth fleet was reactivated and six fleets were deployed as follows:

- Second Fleet   Atlantic Ocean
- Third Fleet   Eastern Pacific Ocean
- Fourth Fleet   Caribbean, Central & South America
- Fifth Fleet   Persian/Arabian Gulf, Red Sea, Gulf of Oman, Indian Ocean
- Sixth Fleet   Mediterranean Sea
- Seventh Fleet   Western Pacific Ocean

United States Ship: A commissioned warship of

the USN. Usually abbreviated USS and used as a prefix to the ship's name.

United States Transportation Command: Established in 1987, as one of nine unified commands, and is manager of the United States' global defense transportation system. It has three components — the Air Force's air mobility command, the Army's military traffic management command, and the Navy's military sealift command.

Universal time: *See* coordinated universal time.

Unknot: [1] To undo or untangle a knot. [2] A closed loop of rope without a binding knot (e.g., a sheepshank or a hobbling knot). [3] A concept in the mathematical theory of knots.

Unlash: To loosen or untie something.

Unlay: To untwist and separate the strands of a rope or cable.

Unload: To remove goods or cargo from a vessel. Also discharge.

Unmanned vehicles: Along with unmanned ("uninhabited" to be "politically correct") aerial vehicles (UAV) and unmanned underwater vehicles (UUV), unmanned surface vessels (USV)are likely to be vital components of future naval, coast guard, and homeland security forces. Most maritime activities carry an element of risk, but some — such as close inspection of suspected terrorist vessels; clearing shipping lanes; evaluation of chemical, biological, or radiation hazards; mine clearance and countermeasures; target identification and illumination; and underwater search — are especially hazardous. In such circumstances, an unmanned vessel or vehicle can be deployed without risking sailors' lives; can be designed for mission effectiveness, ignoring human comfort and crew space, and can remain on station without resupply or crew rotation. It can also be reconfigurable through "plug-and-play" design that allows the installation of specialized mission modules.

Unmoor: To weigh one anchor while continuing to ride on the other.

Unofficial beating: During the 17th and 18th centuries Royal Navy boatswain's mates normally carried small whips called "colts" or "starters" hidden in their hats. These were occasionally made of leather, somewhat like a Russian knout, but more often were lengths of knotted rope. They were seldom used on able seamen and almost never on elite upperyard men, but were wielded viciously to speed up clumsy landsmen and ordinary sailors who were slow to respond to orders. The boatswain openly carried a rattan (bamboo cane) with which he executed instant chastisement. These summary punishments were officially suppressed in 1811.

Unrated: Refers to any warship smaller than a frigate (*see* warship rating).

Unreeve: To pull the rope out of a block or fairlead.

Unrig: To remove all rigging, both standing and running from a vessel.

Unseaworthy: Said of any vessel incapable of meeting the ordinary perils of the sea due to its state of maintenance, the capability of its crew, or any other factor.

Unship: [1] To take out of a ship or vessel (unship cargo). [2] To remove or detach something from its usual or proper place or connection (unship the capstan bars). [3] To become detached (heavy seas unshipped the rudder).

Unstay: To destroy an enemy's stays by gunfire, thereby bringing down his masts.

Unstep: Intentional removal of a mast or spar (cf. dismast).

Unstow: *See* break out.

Up anchor!: [1] A boatswain's pipe calling the anchor detail to their stations. [2] The order to weigh the anchor.

Up-and-down: The condition of an anchor chain or cable when it is under the forefoot and the anchor is short-stayed.

Up behind!: Command to stop heaving and slacken off rapidly to facilitate cleating.

Up screw!: Former command to raise the propeller of an auxiliary-powered sailing-ship to reduce drag when planning to proceed under sailpower alone.

Up spirits!: The traditional RN boatswain's call for the troops to muster for their daily issue of rum or brandy at 12 noon precisely. Frequently the bosun added the sotto voce pun, "Stand fast the Holy Ghost."

Uphaul: *See* topping lift.

Upper deck: [1] The highest continuous deck of a passenger ship. [2] A partial deck above the main deck of a cargo ship. [3] A deck in the superstructure of a warship. [4] A non-naval term for the commissioned officers of a warship's company.

Upper masts: The top, topgallant, and royal masts. Spars higher than these were called "poles" rather than masts.

Upper yardman: In days of sail, the men who manned the upper yards formed an élite, generally regarded as the smartest men in the ship. In the Royal Navy, since about 1935 the term has described a seaman selected from the lower deck to become an officer candidate.

Upperworks: [1] That part of a ship which is above water when fully-laden. [2] The superstructure above a vessel's weather deck.

UPS: Uninterruptible power supply.

Upsetting angle: The degree of tilt beyond which a vessel will no longer right itself.

Upsetting moment: [1] The instant at which a vessel capsizes. [2] The force which causes it to do so.

Upstream: Toward or against the direction in which a current is flowing.

Uptake: [1] An exhaust trunk taking boiler gases to the stacks. [2] A forced-draft ventilator removing stale air from interior compartments.

Upwelling: The oceans are layered; with sun-warmed water on top, and colder water containing nutrients and dissolved gases below. Upwelling is a phenomenon that brings this deeper water to the surface. When nutrients rise towards the sunlight, microscopic plants (phytoplankton) combine them with carbon dioxide and solar energy by photosynthesis. The organic compounds thus produced form the basis of the oceanic food chain. Oceanographers have identified many different forms of this phenomenon, the more significant of which are:

- *Coastal Upwelling:* Coriolis effect causes wind-driven currents to move to the right of winds in the Northern Hemisphere. Thus winds blowing south along an eastern land-ocean boundary, or north along a western one, drive surface water away from the coast, allowing cold, nutrient-rich deep water to rise and replace it. In the Southern Hemisphere, these directions are reversed. Some of the world's most productive fishing grounds are in regions where coastal upwelling occurs.
- *Equatorial Upwelling:* A related phenomenon. The equatorial surface current flows from east to west in both the Atlantic and Pacific Basins. Coriolis force turns the flow away from the equator (north to the right, south to the left) once again clearing a path for colder water to rise from the depths. As phytoplankton feast on the rising nutrients they bloom, causing the water to become green and murky — to the extent that space travelers can visually locate the Pacific equatorial region by a line of high phytoplankton concentration.
- *Dynamic uplift:* Occurs in response to variations in coastal ocean currents and is independent of coastal wind conditions.
- *Tidal pumping:* Strong tidal currents produce upwelling through amplification and associated topographic turbulence. During flood tide, oceanic water mixes with and transfers part of its nutrient load to the shelf water before being removed again during ebb tide. Each flood tide brings another load of nutrients, and the resulting enrichment can be substantial. Marine life on the Great Barrier Reef benefits greatly from tidal pumping, as do similar geographical settings where tidal currents are amplified in channels between islands.
- *Eddy formation:* Western boundary currents spawn several eddies per year, each of which maintains its identity for two years or longer. Warm core eddies are characterized by a deep thermocline in the centre and shallow thermocline around the eddy fringe. As they impinge on the continental slope, the thermocline is lifted up, having the same effect as when the main current impinges on the shelf.

Upwind: Toward or against the direction from which the wind is blowing.

Urca: An armed Spanish fly-boat.

USA: [1] United States of America. [2] United States Army.

USAF: United States Air Force.

Usages: Habitual or customary practices that are legal precedents and have the force of law in admiralty courts and courts-martial. *See also* laws and usages of war.

USCG: United States Coast Guard.

USCGC: United States Coast Guard Cutter.

USCGS: United States Coast Guard Ship.

Usciere: Venetian horse transports. *See* Huissiers.

USMC: United States Marine Corps.

USMM: United States Merchant Marine.

USMS: United States Maritime Service.

USN: United States Navy.

USN Sailor's Creed: As part of their "Core Values" all officers and enlisted personnel are required to acknowledge and support the statement:

I am a United States sailor. I will support and defend the Constitution of the United States of America and **I will obey the orders of those appointed over me.** I represent the fighting spirit of the Navy and those who have gone before me to defend freedom and democracy around the world. I proudly serve my country's Navy combat team with Honor, Courage and commitment. I am committed to excellence and the fair treatment of all.

At time of writing (2008), there is unresolved controversy and argument over whether it is appropriate for commissioned officers to affirm the latter part of the second statement (highlighted above). The reason goes back to differences between the Oath of Enlistment and the officer's Oath of Appointment, both of which start in the same way:

I do solemnly swear that I will support and defend the Constitution of the United States against all enemies, foreign and domestic, that I will bear true faith and allegiance to the same; ...

But the enlistee's oath then says:

... I will obey the orders of the President of the United States and the orders of the officers appointed over me, according to regulations and the Uniform Code of Military Justice. So help me God.

Whereas the officer swears:

... I take this obligation freely, without any mental reservation or purpose of evasion, and that I will well and faithfully discharge the duties of the office upon which I am about to enter, so help me God.

Those who claim officers should not recite the Creed contend that confining their allegiance to the Constitution, while not requiring an oath to obey orders, is a deliberate Congressional attempt to ensure that they will refuse illegal commands to do things prohibited by the Constitution, even if ordered by senior officers up to and including the commander-in-chief (president). The debate continues.

USNA: United States Naval Academy.

USNI: United States Naval Institute.

USNR: United States Navy Reserve.

USNS: United States Naval Ship. Prefix preceding a ship's name and identifying it as a non-combatant vessel, such a hospital ship, ocean tug, fleet oiler, or replenishment vessel, owned or operated by the United States Military Sealift Command.

USNY: United States Navy Yard.

USS: United States Ship. Prefix identifying a U.S. warship in commission.

USV: Unmanned surface vessel.

USW: Undersea warfare. *See* UWW.

UTC: Coordinated Universal Time.

UTR: Underwater tracking range.

UUO: Unidentified underwater object.

UUV: Unmanned underwater vehicle

UWW: Underwater warfare. *See* USW.

UX: Unexploded. Suffix "B" = bomb; "M" = mine or munition; "O" = ordnance; "W" = weapon.

V

VA: [1] Air squadron (USN). [2] Veteran's Administration (U.S.).

Vail: Archaic term for hauling down a sail or flag in salute.

***Valhalla*'s serpent:** In 1905, off the Brazilian coast, the crew of research ship *Valhalla* reported another of many eel-like sightings. This time, they were supported by two British naturalists, both Fellows of the Zoological Society and equipped with binoculars, whose account is recorded in the 1906 edition of the Society's *Proceedings*. The sighting lasted for several minutes after which Edmund Meade-Waldo reported that the creature was dark seaweed-brown above, and whitish below, with a neck which was...

> about the thickness of a slight man's body, and from 7 to 8 feet was out of the water; head and neck were all about the same thickness. The head had a very turtle-like appearance.... It moved its head and neck from side to side in a peculiar manner...

The other scientist, Michael Nicoll, added, "This creature was an example, I consider, of what has been reported, for want of a better name, as the 'great sea serpent.'" Later, three crew members reported seeing the same animal overtaking *Valhalla* at a speed of about nine knots.

Valley: A relatively shallow, wide depression on the sea floor, the bottom of which usually has a continuous gradient. This term is generally not used for features that have canyon-like characteristics. Also called submarine valley or sea valley. Cf. Oceanic trench.

Valve: A tap-like device for controlling the passage of gas or fluid through a pipe.

Valve chest: A manifold.

Van/Vanguard: The leading ship or division of a fleet. (From Middle French avangarde = advance guard.)

Vane: [1] A piece of cloth (telltale) or sheet metal (weathervane) used to indicate wind direction. [2] The blade of a propeller, turbine, windmill, or similar device.

Vang: A rope, bar, or tackle used to steady a boom or spar.

Vanishing tide: A tide with only a single apparent high-to-low water cycle, the intermediate diurnal movement being too small to measure.

Variable fuse: A fuse that is activated by signals generated by the projectile and reflected off the target. Also proximity fuse.

Variable pitch: Said of an aerial or marine propeller in which the angle of the blades can be adjusted to optimize thrust. The mathematics of propulsion efficiency are extremely complex, but can be simplified by comparing propeller pitch to an automobile transmission. Low gear and fine pitch each provide good acceleration but limited speed. High gear and coarse pitch provide greater thrust, allowing higher speed but less acceleration.

Ships with engines that work most efficiently at a steady pace can vary their speed by changing the pitch of their propellers. In contrast, a fixed pitch propeller can be more efficient at its designed speed and load, but is less flexible than one which can be adjusted to absorb virtually all the power the engine can produce at any combination of speed and vessel loading. (Variable pitch is also called adjustable pitch or controllable pitch.)

Variation: The angle between true and magnetic north, expressed either in degrees easterly or westerly, or as positive when the compass card points to the east and negative when to the west. Known to earth scientists as magnetic declination.

Vast: Abbreviation of avast.

Vast heaving! Command to stop hauling (*see* "up behind.")

VBS: Visit, board, and search.

VBSS: Visit, board, search, and seizure.

Vector: [1] A straight line graphically representing the direction and magnitude of a force or movement. [2] To follow a designated compass direction to an amphibious landing beach. [3] To give an aircraft directions for its approach to set down on a flight deck or runway.

Vedette: [1] Naval: a small launch used for reconnaissance. [2] Military: a mounted scout or sentinel.

Veer: [1] The wind direction shifting clockwise (cf. back). [2] Said of a ship turning abruptly. [3] To wear. [4] To pay out a rope or line, especially an anchor cable.

Veer a buoy astern: To let out a float with attached line, in order to pull in a boat or rescue a person overboard.

Veer and haul: To pull and slacken alternately.

Vehicle cargo: Refers to military freight in the form of wheeled or tracked equipment, including weapons, that require special deck space, head room, and other clearances.

Vein: A lane of clear water between floes of ice. *See also* lead.

Velocity: The rate of motion in a given direction.

Vent: [1] An aperture or valve which allows air or steam to escape when pressure becomes excessive. [2] To open such a valve. [3] A large valve on top of a submarine's main ballast tank by which trapped air is released to facilitate diving. [4] The touchhole of a firearm or cannon.

Vent bit: An auger specially-designed for clearing the obstructed vent of a gun.

Vent stopper: A protective plug or cover (usually leather) for the vent of a cannon.

Ventilating trunk: A space between frames which acts as a duct to ventilate bilges.

Ventilation: The distribution of fresh air below decks.

Ventilator cowl: A mushroom- or hood-shaped deck fitting which catches the wind and directs air to below-deck spaces via ventilation tubes.

Venture: An undertaking or operation involving an element of risk, especially a speculative business enterprise of uncertain outcome.

Venturi: A tapered section of pipe that reduces pressure and increases rate of flow.

Veritas: The French equivalent of Lloyd's List.

Versailles (Treaty): In 1919 the vindictive victors of World War I imposed severe restrictions on the size and capacities of the German armed forces. The total naval forces allowed were six heavy cruisers of no more than 10,000 tons displacement, six light cruisers of no more than 6,000 tons displacement, 12 destroyers of no more than 800 tons displacement and 12 torpedo boats. There were to be no submarines, no naval aviation, and no battleships. In March 1935, Adolf Hitler violated the Treaty by introducing military conscription and rebuilding all the armed forces. Three months later, Britain reacted by negotiating the Anglo-German Naval Agreement, secretly giving Hitler a "green light" to ignore the Versailles naval restrictions.

Vertical launch: A system that dispenses with traditional launching rails and allows missiles to be launched directly from their magazines.

Vertical loading: Arranging similar items in vertical tiers in cargo holds so that they will be available at any stage of discharging (cf. horizontal loading).

Vertical replenishment: The transfer of supplies to or from a ship by helicopter.

Very good or Very well: The traditional acknowledgement by a senior naval officer of a junior's report. Unlike armies or air forces where "very good sir" is an acceptable response to an order, its use in place of "aye-aye sir" by a junior RN or USN officer would be likely to produce the retort "and who gave you permission to criticize my orders?"

Very high frequency: The radio frequency most frequently used by vessels at sea.

Very high sea: Wind-Sea condition 8 on the Douglas Scale (table 2), with waves defined as long, heavy and mountainous, between nine and fourteen meters (30 to 46 feet) high.

Very light: A colored flare, star-shell, or pyrotechnic fireball fired from a special gun called a Very pistol. Old, but still an excellent method of signaling, especially at night. (Pronounced veery.)

Very low sea: Wind-Sea condition 1 on the Douglas Scale (table 2), with waves defined as short, low and rippled, less than 10 centimeters (4 inches) high.

Very pistol: A snub-nosed, large-caliber (1½ inch or 12 gauge) hand-held flare gun, designed in 1877 by American naval officer Edward Very (pronounced veery), which shoots Very lights or parachute-flares. (Incorrectly, but often seen, Verey pistol. Properly, but seldom used, Very's pistol.) *See also* Coston gun.

Very rough sea: Wind-Sea condition 6 on the Douglas Scale (table 2) with waves defined as large, short and heavy, between four and six meters (13 to 20 feet) high.

Vessel: The generic term for any water vehicle larger than a rowboat irrespective of its size or method of propulsion. Not quite as all-embracing as craft, however. *See also* boat, ship.

Vessel size: *See* size escalation.

VHF: Very High Frequency.

Vicar: Slang for the ship's chaplain, whose cabin is sometimes called The Vicarage.

Vice Admiral: This three-star flag rank originally designated the deputy leader of a fleet or squadron (Latin vices = alternative) who also commanded the forward element or van. A vice admiral ranks below Admiral and above Rear Admiral (upper half). *See* tables 13 & 14.

Victor: NATO phonetic notation for the letter "V."

Victoria: The sole survivor of Ferdinand Magellan's five-ship 1519 expedition and the first European vessel to circumnavigate the globe (the Chinese may have succeeded earlier). Commanded by Basque adventurer Juan Sebastián de Eleano, *Victoria* returned to Spain on September 8, 1522, winning him a coat of arms showing the globe with the Latin motto Primus circumdedisti me = You went around me first.

Victory: Launched in 1765, Nelson's 104-gun flagship at the 1805 Battle of Trafalgar is the oldest naval ship still in commission. She sits in dry dock in Portsmouth as a museum ship.

Victory ship: A mass-producible World War II cargo ship of 15,200 displacement tons, designed by the U.S. Maritime Commission as a longer range, larger and faster replacement for the Liberty ship, with better post-war commercial potential. Their speed of 15 to 17 knots (28 to 31 km/h) — compared to 11 knots (20 km/h) — made them less easy prey to U-boats, They were oil fired, although some Canadian-built vessels were designed to use coal or oil. They also had strengthened hulls compared to Liberty ships, since some of the latter had suffered fractured hulls.

Victualer: [1] A supply ship. [2] A contractor supplying foodstuffs (rhymes with Hitler).

Victualing bill: A list of bonded goods taken on board for consumption during a voyage. Pronounced vittling.

Victualling stores: *See* naval supplies.

Victualling yard: A facility that supplies food and drink to Royal Navy ships.

Victuals: Food or provisions. Pronounced vittles. (From Latin victualia.)

Vigia: Notation on a chart warning of a hazard to navigation which cannot be exactly located. From the Spanish for a watchman and pronounced "vee-jee-ah."

Vikings: Generic name for early medieval (9th to 11th century) Scandinavian shipbuilders, seafarers, warriors, pillagers, and settlers, who first terrorized and later colonized Western Europe, then voyaged westward to Iceland, Greenland and North America, and southward around Iberia to North Africa. Other Norsemen moved eastward to colonize the Baltic shores, and some, known as the Rus, moved south to settle in Kiev and give their name to Russia. Others known as Varangians traveled down that country's great rivers to reach the Black Sea, Constantinople, and probably Baghdad. The name comes from Old Norse wik or vik, meaning a creek, bay, or estuary, and a naval raid was called "faro-i-viking" which can be loosely translated as "go-a-baying" (probably in reference to the Viking raiders' tendency to work their way inland via bays and rivers). *See also* Berserker.

Vintiner: A naval officer in Henry VIII's fleet, commanding a company of 20 men. From the Latin vigintinarius.

Violent storm: Alternate name for a Tempest.

VIP: Very important person.

Virginia Capes (battle): In the summer of 1781, British troops under Lord Charles Cornwallis were at Yorktown, Virginia, awaiting ocean transport to New York City where Sir Henry Clinton's army was threatened by Franco-American forces led by George Washington and Jean-Baptiste de Rochambeau. Another French force under Marie-Joseph de Lafayette was observing Cornwallis from south of Yorktown.

Recognizing the strategic possibility of defeating the British in detail, Washington sent a French frigate to ask Contre-Amiral François de Grasse to sail from the West Indies and seize control of Chesapeake Bay before British warships could arrive. Leaving a small force to contain Clinton, the combined forces moved toward Yorktown, first by forced march and then by sea in French transports.

On 30th August, de Grasse arrived in the Chesapeake with twenty-seven ships of the line and debarked 3,000 reinforcements for Lafayette. On 5th September, Rear-Admiral Thomas Graves with nineteen of the line arrived off Hampton Roads. De Grasse sallied to meet Graves with twenty-four of his ships and the fleets fought an inconclusive two-hour action off the Virginia capes.

They maneuvered at sea for another four days, during which eight French ships of the line under Commodore Paul de Barras slipped into the Chesapeake convoying transports carrying Washington's siege artillery. When Graves followed de Grasse back to the Bay, he found his nineteen ships, many of which had battle damage, facing thirty-five of the line. He wisely decided to return to New York to refit.

Although itself indecisive, this engagement — also known as the Battle of Chesapeake Bay — was pivotal because it ensured success for the American revolution. Cornwallis surrendered after a three-week siege, leading Britain to recognize United States independence.

Viscous drag: *See* skin-friction.

Visibility: [1] Visual range. [2] The atmospheric property that determines ability to see and identify objects. [3] In meteorology, the distance at which a standard object can be seen and identified by the unaided human eye.

Visit and search: Inspection of a private vessel to determine its nationality, the nature of its cargo, its destination, etc.

Visit, board, search, and seizure: Search and seizure is a legal procedure in many countries, under which police or other authorities may — provided they suspect a crime has been committed — search property and confiscate any relevant evidence. To combat suspected terrorism, piracy and smuggling, maritime law enforcement necessarily involves visitation and boarding as preliminaries.

Visitation: *See* Right of Visitation.

Visual aid: An aid to navigation that provides information through observation of a shape by day or a light by night.

Visual range: The maximum distance at which a given object can be seen. Also visibility.

Visual recognition of approaching boats: Both RN and USN boats use colors, flags, or symbols to indicate the status of their most senior passenger. A blue or green Royal Navy barge automatically signifies a flag officer, while an admiral's flag on its forward staff indicates that he is coming on a ceremonial visit; if so a guard and band will be paraded and the officers greeting him will wear swords and medals. However, if a red disc bearing a white cross is inserted in a slot on the staff, he's coming officially but not formally, and will be met by the captain and commander, but no guard or band. If it displays a white disc with a black cross, his visit is personal and informal, and he may even be in plain clothes (perhaps returning from a game of golf).

The U.S. Navy places polished brass devices at the truck of boat flagstaffs to indicate the rank of the most senior person aboard. A Spread Eagle represents an official entitled to a salute of 19 or more guns (Fleet Admiral, Chief of Naval Operations, Commandant of the Marine Corps, service secretaries, etc.). A Halberd (axe-like device) represents other flag and general officers and certain civil officials (assistant service secretaries, consuls general, etc.). A Ball represents a captain or civil official (such as first secretary of a legation). A Star signifies the presence of a commander or civil equivalent. For all other ranks the flagstaff has a flat truck with no distinguishing device. The head of the eagle and cutting edge of the halberd face forward, and the points of the star are aligned fore-and-aft.

Similar devices on flagstaffs ashore indicate the rank of the officer commanding a headquarters or other shore establishment.

Vivier: A French fishing boat with a well amidships for the storage of live catch.

VLBC: Acronym of Very Large Bulk Carrier; defined as a bulker of more than 200,000 but less than 300,000 dwt (Cf. ULBC).

VLCC: Acronym of Very Large Crude Carrier; defined as a tanker of more than 160,000 but less than 320,000 dwt (cf. ULCC).

VLF: Very low frequency.

Vlieboot: A small, speedy boat used by early boucanier pirates operating from Tortuga.

VM: Air squadron (USMC).

VMC: Visual meteorological conditions.

Vocal salutes: On special occasions, a ship's company may be called upon to salute by cheering, almost always in multiples of three and sometimes timed by the preceding call "Hip-hip." The naval cry is "Hooray!," but U.S. Marines shout "Oorah!," while "Huzzah!" is the army's cry, and "Hurrah!" is the civil version. According to a 17th century source, huzzah is the oldest, "being derived from the shouts seamen make when friends come aboard or go off." It may have originated with the sail-raising cry recorded in Chapter VI of the *Complaynt of Scotland*, published in 1541: "Than the master cryit ... nou heis, than the marynalis began to heis up the sail, crying heisau heisau." (Then the master cried ... now haul, then the mariners began to haul up the sail, crying huzzah, huzzah.)

VOD: Vertical onboard delivery.

Vogue: Now meaning to be in fashion in both French and English, the word was originally nautical, coming from the French voguer meaning to forge ahead under oars or sail. It is unclear how the change of meaning came about.

Voice tube: *See* speaking tube.

Void: A compartment within the hull designed and intended to remain empty as an aid to buoyancy.

Voith-Schneider Drive: A highly maneuverable patented marine propulsion system which can change its direction of thrust almost instantaneously, eliminating the need for a rudder. From a circular plate, rotating about a vertical axis, an array of aerofoil-shaped blades protrudes below the vessel's hull. Internal gearing changes their angles of attack in synchronization with rotation of the plate. This system, which is similar to that for the control of helicopter blades, gives complete freedom of motion when docking or maneuvering without changing the power input. It is the only current example of the propulsion system known generically as Cycloidal Drive.

Volley: The simultaneous discharge of a number of firearms.

Voluntary stranding: A marine insurance term referring to the beaching of a vessel in order to avoid serious harm. Such action is subject to general average.

Volunteer: A seaman who enters naval service willingly, as opposed being impressed.

Volunteer-per-Order: *See* Kings letter man.

Vortex: [1] Any fluid having a whirling or circular motion, tending to form a cavity or vacuum at its center. [2] A whirlpool or maelstrom having a pronounced downward-spiraling flow. [3] A circular region at the center of a tropical cyclone, where the weather is fair and winds relatively light. Otherwise known as the eye of the storm.

Voyage: A long journey (usually round-trip) to a distant port.

Voyage charter: A contract where the owner places his vessel at the disposal of a charterer for one or more voyages while retaining responsibility for the vessel's operation.

Voyo: A rope messenger.

V/STOL: Acronym for an aircraft capable of Vertical or Short Take-Off and Landing.

VSW: Very shallow water.

Vulture's Row: Naval aviators' slang for the catwalks and open gallery on an aircraft carrier island, where spectators often gather to view take-offs and landings. Cf. goofing stations.

W

Wad: One of two plugs, usually made of hay, old canvas, or condemned rope junk, that were rammed down the bore of a smoothbore cannon — one ahead of the charge to keep it in place and reduce windage; the other in front of the ball to prevent it rolling out due to heeling of the ship. Wads were slightly larger than the bore for a good fit. In action they were kept in a net close to the shot rack.

Wad former: A mold in which wads were beaten into shape, then removed and wound with worsted to keep their form.

Wadding: Any material from which gun wads can be made.

Wadhook: An iron tool shaped like a double corkscrew on the end of a long staff, used to withdraw wads or charges from muzzle-loading cannon. Also called a worm.

Waft: Obsolete term for [1] A sailing ship convoy. [2] A flag flown with the fly attached to the mast as a request for customs clearance. [3] A piece of clothing or a rolled and knotted flag flown as a signal (*see* weft).

Wages: Under old English maritime law, the wages of merchant seamen were contingent on safe delivery of freight or cargo. Hence a vessel had to make landfall, moor, and unload before the crew was paid. If the goods were lost by misfortune, jettison, tempest, enemy action, wreck, or fire, all earnings were forfeit. Hence freight became known as "The mother of wages." This harsh rule was intended to ensure that all hands strove to maintain the integrity of cargo and safety of the ship, but it was finally deemed unfair and impracticable.

Waggoner: Ancient name for a descriptive atlas giving sailing directions and charts showing ports and coastal features. Also known as a portolano or rutter. Waggoner is named after Dutch navigator Lucas Janszoon Wagenaer who published an atlas in 1584 with the Dutch title *Spieghel der Zeevaert* (Mirror of Seafaring). It was later translated into Latin and many vernacular editions, the English one of 1588 being titled *The Mariner's Mirrour.*

Waif: Obsolete term for [1] Derelict and unclaimed goods. [2] A waft or weft. [3] A buoy attached to a harpoon line — to establish title to the abandoned kill when the whalers set off after another quarry.

Waist: That part of the weather deck not covered by forecastle or quarterdeck and lying between them.

Waister: A disabled, inexperienced, incompetent, or superannuated seaman incapable of working aloft and confined to duty amidships on the main deck (i.e., at the waist).

Wait 'til you see the whites of their eyes: Commonly believed to be an infantry fire command, this phrase was actually coined by Horatio Nelson, who wanted to ensure that his gunners held their fire until the most effective range of 200 yards — half the usual distance at that time. *See* musket shot.

Waive: To forgo the right to court-martial.

Wake: The visible track left astern of a moving vessel, caused by the turbulence of its hull and rudder, plus that of the propeller(s) if any.

Wake light: A dim stern light shining on the wake of a warship in line-ahead (column) formation, to provide a station-keeping marker for the following vessel.

Wakey: A corruption of "awaken ye." (*See* bugle calls.)

Wale: A heavy longitudinal plank below the gunwale of a wooden ship. From the Anglo-Saxon wala = ridge or strip. Also rubbing strake.

Wale shore: An extra long and sturdy spar used to brace a ship upright when in dry dock.

Walk away!: Command to step briskly when hoisting a boat.

Walk back!: Command to move backwards when at the capstan bars.

Walk back the cat: USN term for re-starting a procedure from the beginning.

Walk Spanish: Obsolete term for leaving an assigned station without permission.

Walk the anchor: Means to drag it.

Walk the netting: As punishment for having missed muster, a sailing ship sailor would have to pace along the netting of the weather gangway in the wet and cold of the night.

Walk the plank: [1] Formerly, if a sailor was suspected of being drunk, he was required to walk a straight line along one of the quarterdeck planks. [2] A piratical method of execution that is supposedly intended to appear self-inflicted and absolve the pirate from murder charges. The victim is compelled to walk, bound and blindfolded, along a plank projecting over the ship's side, which overbalances to tip him into the sea and drown. This seems to have been a 19th century fiction, with only two authentic cases ever being recorded: (a) *The Times* of 23rd July 1829 reported that Dutch brig *Vhan Fredericka* had been boarded by pirates who pinioned and blindfolded the crew, tied shot to their feet, and forced them into the sea; (b) The second, which occurred on the Hudson River in the 1860s, was a copycat event based on fictional accounts read by "Sadie-the-goat," who described herself as "a blinkin' pirate queen."

Walking: *See* position of honor.

Wall knot: An ornamental stopper formed at the end of a line by looping each strand around the one behind and through the loop of the one in front.

Wallop: [1] To move along in a rapid, reckless, awkward way. In this sense the word is derived directly from the Middle English walopen meaning to gallop. [2] To beat soundly, thrash, or overwhelmingly defeat. It is hard to see how this second meaning could have developed from the former, and some sources suggest it arose spontaneously after 1514 when King Henry VIII, furious that French amphibious raiders had burned the English town of Brighton to the ground, ordered Admiral Wallop to retaliate. The English fleet then rampaged along the coast of France destroying twenty-one towns and villages and making the admiral's name a synonym for defeat or thrashing.

Wandering albatross: This is the largest of all flying birds, with a wingspan of up to five meters (15 feet), weighing up to 11 kilograms (24 lbs), and flying at up to 53 km/h (33 mph). Completely oceanic, it lands only to lay eggs and raise chicks. Sailors believe that killing one is an horrendous maritime crime that will bring disaster to the ship committing the murder. This is because seamen have long believed that when a shipmate dies, his body goes to Davy Jones' locker, but his soul is transferred to an albatross whose supernatural nature seems to be confirmed when it is seen to remain aloft without flapping its wings for days on end (using the technique of "dynamic soaring" to exploit and glide over cross-currents of air).

Wankel engine: An internal combustion engine that, instead of reciprocating pistons and cylinders, uses a triangular revolving rotor. The tips of the rotor remain in constant contact with the combustion walls forming combustion chambers as it turns. This design delivers smooth high-revolution power from a compact, lightweight engine with fewer moving parts. However, until very recently, the efficiency of rotary engines was inferior to conventional engines, while emissions were worse.

War Establishment: A complement of men and equipment higher than that required in peacetime.

Wardrobe: All the sails carried by a yacht.

Wardrobe Room: A sailing warship's locker originally used to store officers' spare uniforms and any loot secured from enemy ships (*see* wardroom).

Wardroom: During the 18th century, in an effort to have some privacy in a crowded ship, junior commissioned officers and senior warrants (such as sailing master, chaplain, and surgeon) began to take their meals and sling their hammocks in the wardrobe room. Gradually the original purpose was abandoned and the compartment evolved into an area where officers take their meals, relax, and socialize. "The wardroom" refers to those officers collectively.

Warehouse hulk: A hulk used for the storage of ship's stores and supplies.

Warfare Officer: RN position responsible for navigation, and bridge watchkeeping; running the computers in the operations room, plotting the positions of nearby surface vessels, aircraft, submarines, and land masses; making sure that weapons, communications, and sensor systems are used safely and correctly; and making some minor operational and tactical decisions. Warfare Officers can deviate from the General Service career path to specialize in surface, underwater, or electronic warfare; also in diving, mine clearance, fighter aircraft control, or meteorology and oceanography. *See also* Principal Warfare Officer and Tactical Action Officer.

Warfare/Weapons Qualification: A medal or other device issued to USN personnel in recognition of proficiency in a type of warfare (surface/submarine, etc.) or the use of weaponry (pistol, rifle, etc.).

Warhead: That part (usually the head or forward section) of a bomb, shell, missile, torpedo, or other munition, that contains an explosive charge, a nuclear weapon, chemical or biological agents, or harmful inert materials. *See also* peacehead.

Warm the bell: [1] Originally, striking the bell early to signal the end of a watch. [2] Today, RN slang for anything done ahead of time. *See also* watchkeeping manipulation.

Warm the glass: [1] Seamen believed they could shorten their spell of duty by heating the half-hour sand glass used to determine the passage of time during a watch (*see* watchkeeping manipulation). [2] Although the glass is no longer used, the term lives on, meaning to arrive early for an appointment.

Warning shot(s): The firing of one or more shots, or the delivery of ordnance in the vicinity of a vessel, aircraft, or person, as a signal to immediately cease activity, withdraw, or end threatening actions.

Warp: [1] A heavy rope used to shift vessels. [2] To move a vessel along a dock or quay with such a rope. [3] A bighted rope towed behind a small boat as a sea anchor. [4] The long strands of a rope, cloth, or canvas.

Warrant: [1] A writ of authority inferior to a commission, considered a patent of trust and honor but not an authority to command. [2] A document authorizing arrest, court-martial, or execution. [3] A guaran-

tee or pledge. (The word comes from Old French guarant, meaning "authorization.")

Warrant Officer: A naval person ranking above Petty Officer but below Commissioned Officer in warships, or below Mate in merchantmen, usually appointed because of specialized skills or knowledge.

Warrant Officers in the Royal Navy: The warrant rank was inaugurated in 1040 when, in return for certain privileges, the "Cinque Ports" began providing warships to King Edward the Confessor. Captains were then usually nobles with little or no seagoing experience, so they relied on the expertise of professionals who had nothing to do with fighting, but took care of the technical aspects of running and navigating the ship. The senior warrant was the master, and serving under him were the boatswain, carpenter and cook, also warranted. These four are the oldest purely naval titles.

By the 18th century, Captains and other commissioned officers were qualified seamen and the master had been renamed sailing master. Other warrant ranks had been established some, like the original four, being representatives of skilled maritime trades or specialties. They reported directly to the Captain, but for administration were responsible to one of the bodies which governed naval affairs such as the Navy Board, Victualling Board, and Ordnance Board. They were usually examined professionally by a body other than the Admiralty and had frequently served an apprenticeship. Others were professionally qualified landsmen such as the doctor (surgeon) and parson (chaplain). All were required to be able to "read, write, and cipher" (calculate), but had varying degrees of status and authority:

- **Warrant Officers of Wardroom Rank** had the privilege of standing on the quarterdeck and dining with the commissioned officers. They included sailing master, surgeon, chaplain, and purser.
- **Standing Warrant Officers** included boatswain, carpenter, and gunner. Unlike the rest of the crew who paid off or transferred to another vessel at the end of a commission, the standing officers were permanently attached to the vessel to provide maintenance and fittings even when it was "in ordinary." Standing warrant officers had their own mess.
- **Warrant Officers of Inferior Grade** were basically senior petty officers who could be demoted at the captain's whim and lost their jobs when their ship paid off. They included armorer, caulker, cook, master-at-arms, ropemaker, and sailmaker.

In 1843 the wardroom warrant officers were given commissioned status, while in 1853 the lower-grade warrant officers were absorbed into the new rate of Chief Petty Officer, both classes thereby ceasing to be warrant officers.

By the time of the First World War warrant officers had been divided into two grades: Warrant Officers and Chief (Commissioned) Warrant Officers and their ranks included technical trades such as telegraphist, electrician, shipwright, and artificer. Except in ships too small to have a separate mess, WOs and CWOs dined alone rather than in the wardroom. WOs and CWOs carried swords, were saluted by ratings, and ranked between Sub-Lieutenants and Midshipmen.

In 1949, all existing warrant officers were commissioned in regular and senior grades, with titles reflecting their specialty (Commissioned Gunner, Senior Commissioned Engineer, etc.), the former ranking with but behind Sub-Lieutenant, and the latter with but after Lieutenant. The WOs messes closed down, and they were admitted to the wardroom. Collectively these officers were known as "Branch Officers," being retitled "Special Duties" officers in 1956.

In 1970 the new warranted rate of Fleet Chief Petty Officer was introduced, being re-named Warrant Officer a few years later. In 2004, the title changed again to Warrant Officer First Class (WO.1) and the former Charge Chief Petty Officer was designated Warrant Officer Second class (WO.2). Both are senior non-commissioned officers, entitled to be addressed as "Sir" or "Ma'am" by subordinates, but not saluted.

Warrant Officers in the United States Navy: Technical specialists were appointed as warrant officers, starting with a purser in December 1775, and more or less followed the British pattern through the 19th century. Navy and Coast Guard Warrant Officers held positions as boatswains, carpenters, chaplains, masters mates, and surgeons.

Nowadays, there are no "warrant officers" in the U.S. Navy, all being "Chief Warrant Officers," who are commissioned and entitled to the corresponding courtesies and privileges. A sailor must be in one of the top three enlisted ranks to be eligible to become a CWO. Even when commissioned, they remain limited duty specialists, whose primary task is to serve as a technical experts, providing practical skills, guidance, and expertise to commanders and organizations in their particular field. Nevertheless, a CWO can command a detachment, unit, or even a vessel, and many fill lieutenant and lieutenant commander billets throughout the U.S. Navy.

Warranty: Assurance by a seller that goods are exactly as described in a contract. Breach of warranty can lead to cancellation of marine insurance.

Warship: An armed vessel, designed for combat, under the command of an officer commissioned by a national government, crewed by personnel under armed forces discipline, and bearing markings or an ensign identifying its nationality.

Warship rating: From the late 17th to early 19th century, ships of the Royal Navy were classified according to the number of cannon they carried. Until 1817, carronades were not counted, even though from one to a dozen of these heavy (24- or 32-pounder) weapons might be on board.

Complements were increased by 15 men for a Rear-

Rate	Guns	Decks	Complement
1st	100+	3	850+
2nd	90–98	3	700–750
3rd	64–80	2	500–650
4th	50–60	2	320–450
5th	32–40	1	200–300
6th	20–28	1	100–140

Vessels rated 1 to 3 were Ships of the line, while 4 to 6 were Frigates. Unrated single-decker vessels included Sloops of War with 16 to 18 guns and crews of 90 to 130, Gun Brigs carrying 1 to 18 guns and 30 to 50 men, and Cutters with 6 or more small guns and crews of up to 25 men.

Admiral's flagship, 20 for a Vice-Admiral's, and 25 for an Admiral's. All rated vessels (and post-ships) were commanded by a Post-Captain. The larger unrated ships and those en flute (rated vessels with some guns removed for use as transports) were captained by Commanders. Smaller vessels were usually commanded by Lieutenants, but very small craft might be commanded by Midshipmen or Masters Mates. (*See also* Super frigates.)

Wart: RN officer's nickname for a midshipman.

Wash: The rough or broken water left behind and spreading from a moving vessel. Less long-lived but more damaging to nearby property than a wake.

Washboard: [1] A thin plank placed on the gunwale of a boat to protect against spray. [2] A similar plank used to protect the sill of a hatch or companionway.

Washington Naval Treaties: After World War I, a naval arms race threatened to get out of hand, Britain still had the world's largest navy, closely followed by the United States, and more distantly by Japan. France and Italy had much smaller but growing navies, while the German fleet had been scuttled at Scapa Flow and new naval construction was tightly controlled by the Treaty of Versailles. In November 1921, U.S. President Harding convened a international conference on naval arms limitation, commonly known as the Washington Conference. At its conclusion in February 1922 nine treaties were executed, two of which directly controlled naval armament.

The first was a five-power agreement between Britain, France, Italy, Japan, and the United States, that restricted the use of submarines in naval warfare and outlawed asphyxiating gases. A second agreement between the same powers specified that no battleship could exceed 35,000 tons or carry a gun greater than 16-inch (406 mm), while aircraft carriers were limited to 27,000 tons (except that each signatory could have two of up to 33,000 tons each). The treaty also required the United States to scrap 845,000 tons of existing warships, Britain 583,000 tons, and Japan 480,000 tons, and it set the following limits on each signatory's total tonnage of major warships:

Signatories	Capital Ships	Aircraft Carriers
Britain & USA	525,000 tons	135,000 tons
Japan	315,000 tons	81,000 tons
France & Italy	175,000 tons	60,000 tons

The terms of the Washington treaty were modified by the London Naval Treaties of 1930 and 1936. Italy secretly exceeded the restrictions, and in 1936 Japan officially renounced them. Finally World War II made the whole concept of arms control obsolete.

Washington's Tomb: *See* Mount Vernon.

Waste: Cotton yarn used for cleaning purposes.

Watch: [1] One of the divisions of the nautical day as outlined below. [2] The members of a ship's company assigned to duty during such a division. [3] A spell of duty. It is inconceivable that an oceangoing ship could be operated around-the-clock without shift work and, from the earliest days of navigation there are records showing the division of crews into groups known as watches.

Nowadays, the merchantman's nautical day is most usually divided into six 4-hour time periods, but sometime follow the warship routine of five 4-hour and two 2-hour watches. The shorter periods — called "dogwatches" — ensure that seamen are not always on duty at the same time, whether the crew is divided into the usual three watches, which gives them eight hours between spells of duty, or in two (watch-and-watch) standing a grueling four hours on and four off.

The term originated in the 17th century and is of uncertain origin, though some say it is a corruption of "dodge watch."

British and U.S. watch terminology are slightly different:

USN	RN	Period
Mid Watch	Middle Watch	0000–0400 (Midnight–4 A.M.)
Morning Watch	Morning Watch	0400–0800 (4 A.M.–8 A.M.)
Forenoon Watch	Forenoon Watch	0800–1200 (8 A.M.–Noon)
Afternoon Watch	Afternoon Watch	1200–1600 (Noon–4 P.M.)
First Dogwatch	First Dogwatch	1600–1800 (4 P.M.–6 P.M.)
Second Dogwatch	Last Dogwatch	1800–2000 (6 P.M.–8 P.M.)
Evening Watch	First Watch	2000–2400 (8 P.M.–Midnight)

In the USN, normal bell routine continues through the dogwatches, with 1, 2, 3, 4 bells being rung in the first and 5, 6, 7, 8 in the second. The RN also rings 1, 2, 3, 4 bells in the first dogwatch, but 1, 2, 3, 8 in the last. This originated on 13th May 1797, when officers learned that five bells instead of four in the last dogwatch was to be the signal for launching a mutiny. *See also* "five and dimes."

Watch-and-watch: A watch bill based on only two duty sections, so that each has only four hours for eating, sleeping, and recreation before the next spell of duty.

This arduous schedule has also been called four-on-four-off, heel-and-toe, turn-and-turn, and watch-and-watch-about. The most usual naval terminology is port-and-starboard watches.

Watch below: Refers to watchkeepers who are not on duty; therefore free to eat, sleep, or otherwise amuse themselves.

Watch bill: A duty list for the crew. The RN calls it "Watch and Station Bill," the USN "Watch, Quarter, and Station Bill."

Watch buoy: A buoy moored near an anchored lightship so that its crew can visually ensure she has not moved by dragging.

Watch cap: [1] A form of knitted woolen headgear worn by seamen; full at the sides so that it can be pulled down over the ears without obscuring vision. [2] USN slang for the canvas cover of a smokestack.

Watch glass: [1] The 30-minute hour-glass used to measure the eight periods of a watch or four of a dogwatch. [2] A small clear glass disc, used to cover the face of a watch or clock. [3] A similar disc used in laboratories to hold experimental material.

Watch Officer: Generic USN term for the senior officer on duty during a watch, whether responsible for control and navigation (OOW), for engineering spaces (EOOW), for a vessel in harbor (OOD), or any other specialty or activity.

Watch station: The job or position assigned to an individual when on duty.

Watch stripes: These were lengths of material formerly worn round the shoulder seam of jumpers or frocks to identify each Royal Navy sailor's watch. On blue clothing the stripe was red, on white clothing it was blue. The starboard watch wore their stripes on the right shoulder, the port watch on the left. They were abolished about 1895.

Watchcon: Watch condition.

Watchkeeper: [1] Any person on watch at a given time (also watch stander). [2] An Israeli-developed, British unmanned aerial vehicle for all weather, Intelligence, Surveillance, Target Acquisition and Reconnaissance. Intended to enter service in 2010, it will be powered by a Wankel engine, have a payload capacity of 150 kg, and endurance of 17 hours.

Watchkeeping manipulation: Ingenious seamen constantly tried to find ways of shortening their spells of duty. "Sweating the glass" was turning it before all the sand had run out; "flogging the glass" involved shaking it in the hope that vibration would speed up the transfer of sand; while "warming the glass" was to hold it close to a lantern with similar expectations. None had any appreciable effect, but all were optimistically continued until sand-glasses were replaced by chronometers. *See also* warm the bell.

Water Bailiff: An officer formerly employed to search vessels at seaports.

Water battery: The broadside guns nearest to the waterline.

Water breaker: A container for fresh water. Also barricoe, beaker, butt, or scuttlebutt.

Water deities: Almost every culture has one or more gods devoted to water, usually covering rivers and lakes as well as seas, and frequently symbolizing cleansing and purification. Some of those who are chiefly concerned with seamen and oceans will be found under Gods of the Seas. A few of the others are:

Agwe = Haitian	Ahto = Finnish
Anguta = Inuit	Apam Napat = Hindu
Brighid = Irish	Dogon = Philistine
Hapi = Egyptian	Itzama = Mayan
Kul = Syrian	Llyr = Welsh
Mara = Latvian	Mo-Hou-Lo-Chia = Chinese
Njord = Scandanavian	Tiamat = Babylonian
Tlaloque = Aztec	Undine = Latin
Yemayah = Yoruba	Zurvan = Persian

Water-laid: The heaviest anchor cables were constructed by twisting three hawser-laid ropes together. Repeated twisting, clockwise and anticlockwise produced very strong lines, known as water-laid because they absorbed very little water.

Water taxi: A harbor boat available for short-term hire.

Water-tube: Refers to a type of boiler in which water circulates in tubes heated externally by hot gases from the furnace to produce the high-pressure steam needed for marine propulsion machinery. Saturated steam is recycled to become superheated for driving turbines. *See also* fire-tube.

Water wraith: The apparition or specter of a skinny old women with scowling features, always dressed in green, who appears to unsuspecting travelers on the coasts of Scotland and (especially) the Shetland Isles. Water wraiths are evil and should be avoided at all times, since they lure people into the sea to die by drowning.

Waterborne: Afloat.

Watercourse: [1] A natural or artificial channel through which water flows. [2] A stream or river. [3] A limber hole.

Watercraft: [1] Inclusive term for any boat, ship, or other waterborne vessel. [2] The art of sailing or boating.

Waterfront: [1] The wharf or dock area of a city. [2] Land at the edge of a stream, harbor, or other body of water.

Waterjet: Marine propulsion technology is moving quickly to offer alternatives to the venerable propeller, one of these being jet propulsion. Basically, this depends on differences in the mass-flow of water, which enters and exits a jet drive at differing velocities. A pump draws in water through a mesh that stops foreign objects from entering. An impeller then forces the water out of one or more nozzles at high pressure,

accelerating the craft in the opposite direction. In some systems, forward and reverse motion is infinitely controllable through a deflector that diverts thrust forward or aft; in others, the nozzle(s) can turn a full 360 degrees to achieve maximum thrust in either direction. Steering is accomplished by directing exit flow, much like directing the thrust of a submerged propeller system.

The exit jet does not have to be underwater, since propulsion will be equally good if it thrusts against the air. Provided engine and jet drive are well matched, water jet propulsion can be more efficient than conventional propellers. For vessels designed to go faster than 30 knots, especially those that can be called upon to operate in shallow waters, waterjets turned by diesels or gas turbines are often the preferred propulsion option. Also called hydrojet propulsion, and *see* cycloidal drive.

Waterline: Where the water surface touches the side of a ship.

Waterlogged: [1] In general, filled, flooded, or saturated with water. [2] Of a specific vessel, afloat but heavy and unmanageable.

Waterman: [1] A boatman plying for hire. [2] A general term encompassing all those who work on or around boats in inshore waters.

Waters: The sea or seas bordering a specified land mass (e.g., Mexican waters).

Waterspace management: The allocation of surface and underwater spaces as areas for antisubmarine warfare, together with the implementation of procedures to permit the rapid and effective engagement of hostile submarines, while preventing inadvertent attacks on friendly submarines.

Waterspout: A serious maritime hazard, capable of damaging or destroying ships and aircraft. As early as the first century BCE, Roman philosopher Titus Lucretius Carus wrote of "whirling columns that put sailors into great peril." Often thought of as tiny cyclonic storms or as tornadoes over water, waterspouts actually have somewhat different characteristics from either. They are relatively short-lived, have weaker wind speeds, and normally spin upward from the surface rather than downward as a tornado does. They are frequently, but not always, associated with tropical thunderstorms. Waterspouts begin when sun-heated humid air moves upward from the surface and condenses into tiny water droplets, releasing heat which makes the air rise faster, and swirl into a vortex that forms and dissipates in five distinct phases:

• The first indication, seldom visible from a ship's deck, but easily noticed by overflying aircraft, is the formation of a "dark spot" on the water.

• Many of these fade away, but those progressing to waterspout assume a spiral pattern of lighter and darker water. During this second stage, a shipboard observer will probably feel the wind begin to shift and increase in speed.

• When the rotating wind reaches about 35 knots it

begins to throw up water in a circular pattern. The spray vortex of this third stage is clearly visible to people afloat, who will sometimes see a "funnel" starting to head downward toward the rising vortex from a cloud overhead or off to one side. The funnel itself is a cloud of minute water droplets which are so fine that it can usually be seen through.

- In the fourth stage, the funnel, if any, links cloud to ocean, while the spinning vortex kicks up small waves and leaves a bubbly wake behind as it moves across the surface.
- In the fifth and final stage, rain begins to fall from the parent cloud, cooling the warm and humid air which feeds the waterspout. The spray vortex weakens, and the funnel becomes shorter, possibly more tapered and often twists around, so that the bottom of the spout moves out from under the cloud as it dissipates.

Watertender: The person, usually a petty officer, responsible for keeping boiler water at the proper level and pressure.

Watertight: Fitted, sealed, or constructed so as to be impervious to penetration by water.

Watertight closure log: A document recording the opening and closure of watertight doors.

Watertight door or hatch: A heavy, strongly constructed, hinged closure, either vertical or horizontal, sealed by a tightly-fitting gasket. Locked by individual dogs, or by single point activation (wheel or lever).

Watertight integrity: A vessel's degree of resistance to flooding.

Waterway: [1] A canal, river, or navigable channel on which vessels can travel. [2] A gutter along the edge of a ship's deck that drains into the scuppers.

Waterwings: USN derisive slang for surface warfare insignia.

Wave: [1] A surface disturbance in the form of a forward-moving ridge-and-trough which does not cause horizontal displacement of the water (*see* measurement of wind and wave). [2] A line of landing craft or section of an amphibious assault force on its way to the beach. [3] A disturbance, such as a pulse or vibration, which travels through an object, volume of matter, or space itself (e.g., radio wave, sonar wave).

Wave amplitude: One half of the wave height.

Wave attenuation: The reduction of wave height as it gets further form its source.

Wave basin: An area adjacent to the entry of an inner harbor in which the waves of the outer anchorage are depleted.

Wave characteristics: The kinetic energy of waves is tremendous. A relatively small 1.22 meter (4 foot) high wave striking a coast at 10 second intervals expends more than 26,000 kilowatts (35,000 horsepower) per mile of beach, meaning that the energy along a 56-mile stretch is equal to the power generated by Hoover Dam (Bowditch 1995 edition). Waves are defined by five characteristics:

- Height — the vertical distance from trough to crest;
- Length — the horizontal distance between crests;
- Period — the time interval between successive crests as they pass a specific point;
- Velocity — the speed of the wave-form's forward movement (which seldom exceeds 25 knots = 29 mph = 46 km/h);
- Surface drift — the actual advance of the water (usually about one-percent of the wave velocity).

The highest regular sinusoidal ocean wave (as opposed to an irregular rogue wave) was reliably measured by officers of 16,800 ton fleet oiler USS *Ramapo* in the North Pacific on 7th February 1933. Following an extraordinary week-long storm that stretched from New York City to the coast of Asia, powerful 60-knot (70 mph; 110 km/h) winds crossing thousands of kilometers of unobstructed ocean had produced mountainous waves. By triangulation based on the ship's superstructure, its officers calculated a height of 34 meters (112 feet) from trough to crest. The crest-to-crest length was calculated as 342 meters which explains why relatively short *Ramapo* (146 meters) was able to ride the waves without the severe structural distress which would have afflicted a longer vessel. *See also* measurement of wind and wave, wave formation, and wave motion.

Wave combination: There are statistics that give some support to the old rule of thumb about every seventh wave being a big one. Being caused by winds of varying strength, waves are of varying sizes and travel at different speeds. Over the open sea, faster moving waves catch up with slower ones, combining to produce a larger wave. Moreover, wind waves are often superimposed on swell and the combination can be critically important to cargo vessels, causing deck cargo to be washed overboard or bulk cargo to shift dangerously.

Wave crest: The highest part of a wave.

Wave formation: The friction of wind blowing across the surface causes particles of water to oscillate up and down in a rotary fashion, moving forward at the crest and backward in the trough. The result is that the wave-form moves across the surface of the water, while the water molecules themselves simply rise and fall, staying in almost the same position except for surface drift. Wave size is proportional to wind speed:

- A puff of wind (Beaufort 1) has very little grip on calm water (Beaufort 0).
- As it gets stronger it begins to make the surface move, forming small eddies and ripples at 70° to 80°angles to the wind direction.
- The ripples roughen the water, offering more surface area for the wind to work on until, a light breeze (Beaufort 2) produces small wavelets at about 30° from the wind.
- As the breeze freshens to moderate (Beaufort 3) the wavelets travel parallel to the wind direction, become choppy, and begin to break. The surface no

longer looks smooth and presents enough wind resistance to create turbulence, a condition that facilitates and accelerates wave formation.
- As wind speed continues to rise, wave size and fury also increase, reaching 14 meters (46 feet) or more by Beaufort 12.

See also measurement of wind and wave, wave characteristics, and wave motion.

Wave height: The vertical distance between a wave trough and the subsequent crest. Cf. wave amplitude.

Wave length: The horizontal distance between consecutive crests or troughs in any form of wave motion, including ocean and electrical. Also Wavelength.

Wave motion: "Mechanical" waves propagate through a physical medium (solid, liquid, or gas) at speeds depending on the elastic and inertial properties of that medium. Individual particles do not move with the waves, but are simply displaced in such a manner as to propagate the wave. (This is analogous to people standing up and sitting down in a sports stadium — they create a "wave" which travels around the arena, but each person remains where they started). There are two basic forms of mechanical wave motion, with ocean waves being a combination of the two.
- **Longitudinal Waves:** In this form, each particle oscillates back-and-forth about its equilibrium position, its displacement being parallel to the direction of wave propagation.
- **Transverse Waves**: As in longitudinal waves, individual particles oscillate around their equilibrium positions, but displacement is perpendicular to the direction of wave motion. Transverse waves are generated at the bow and stern of a vessel moving through water.
- **Ocean Waves:** Are essentially a combination of the foregoing motions. As the wave travels through the water, individual particles rotate in clockwise circles, with the radius of the circles decreasing as the depth of water increases.

Excellent animations illustrating each of these motions can be found on the Kettering University website at www.kettering.edu/~drussell/demos.html. (*See* wave formation and wave characteristics.)

Wave-off: Batsman's signal refusing an aircraft permission to land on a carrier.

Wave period: The duration of one complete cycle from crest-to-crest or trough-to-trough.

Wave-resistance: The stem of a vessel cutting through the water produces a bow wave and a similar phenomenon occurs at the stern. It takes energy to create these phenomena, and that energy is subtracted from the power available to drive the vessel forward. (*See also* eddy-resistance, skin-friction, parasitic drag, and profile-drag.)

Wave slam: Refers to the force exerted and noise generated by a wave striking a fixed or floating body. Also called wave impact.

Wave speed: The horizontal velocity of a wave's forward motion. This can be calculated by dividing wavelength by wave period. Also wave velocity.

Wave trough: The lowest part of the wave between its crests.

Waveguide: A hollow tube of conducting material, used as a directional transmitter of electromagnetic microwaves (in radar, for example).

Waves: A somewhat contrived acronym of Women Accepted for Volunteer Emergency Service, the World War II organization of women inducted into the U.S. Naval Reserve to perform mainly administrative duties ashore. By act of Congress, Waves could not serve at sea or outside the continental United States; could not exercise military command over men; and could not go beyond lieutenant commander on the promotion ladder. After the War Congress passed the Women's Armed Services Integration Act (Public Law 625, 1948) and females became part of the regular Navy.

Waveson: Term in old English Law referring to goods which, after shipwreck, appear floating on the waves or sea. Cf. flotsam, jetsam.

Wavy Navy: Derogatory reference to the Royal Naval Volunteer Reserve, officers of which used to be distinguished by undulating rank insignia, while ratings had three wavy stripes on their bibs.

Way: [1] Movement of a vessel through the water, as in gather way, under way, way enough, and way on. [2] *See* ways and slipway.

Way aloft!: Command for topmen to climb the rigging (abbreviation of away).

Way enough!: Coxswain's command for the oarsmen to stop rowing after one more stroke since the boat will then have enough way on to reach its destination.

Way on: A vessel that is moving is said to "have way on."

Waybill: A list of goods consigned to a common carrier.

Waypoint: A charted position or feature.

Ways: Two or more inclined tracks down which a hull slides when being launched (despite its "s" the word is singular). Also slipway.

Weapon: Anything (such as a club, knife, gun, or missile) employed to kill, injure, defeat, or destroy. From Old English wæ pen; akin to Old High German wǣffan.

Weapon system: The integrated assembly of a gun or missile launcher, including supporting sub-systems for target acquisition, ammunition supply, and the like.

Weapons free!: An anti-aircraft artillery control order under which weapons may be fired at any target not known to be friendly without waiting for a direct command to do so. (Cf. Weapons hold! and Weapons tight!)

Weapons hold!: An anti-aircraft artillery control order under which weapons may only be fired in self-defense or in response to a direct command. (Cf. Weapons free! and Weapons tight!)

Weapons Officer: The commissioned officer in charge of and responsible for a warship's armament including artillery, missiles, and other weaponry.

Weapons team: The personnel assigned to a crew-operated weapon.

Weapons qualification: *See* warfare/weapons qualification.

Weapons tight!: An anti-aircraft artillery control order under which weapons may only be fired at targets confirmed to be hostile. (Cf. Weapons free! and Weapons hold!)

Wear: [1] To use habitually for clothing (a coat), adornment (medals), or assistance (glasses). [2] To cause to deteriorate by use or attrition (wear out). [3] To go about with the stern presented to the wind (wear ship). [4] RN ships "wear" their flags, whereas USN ships "display" them, and merchantmen "fly" or "carry" them.

Wear ship!: Command for a sailing vessel to pass her stern through the wind to bring it to the other side and thus change course. A square-rigger usually wears, but a fore-and-after almost always tacks (passes her bow through the wind) instead.

Weather: [1] The state of the atmosphere (clear, rain, snow, fog, etc.). [2] The direction from which the wind blows (the weather side = to windward). [3] To be aged by exposure to the atmosphere (weathered timber). [4] To survive a difficult period (weather the storm). [5] To sail to windward of something (weather the headland).

Weather-bound: Confined to port by unfavorable weather.

Weather deck: The upper deck where open.

Weather eye: Said of [1] Sensitivity and alertness to changes in the weather. [2] By extension, general alertness, especially close observation and awareness of potential changes of circumstance. The phrase is undoubtedly of nautical origin. A landlubber forgetting to check the weather forecast before leaving home would probably face nothing worse than a heavy soaking. For the sailor, however, failing to check before leaving shore could have severe if not fatal consequences.

Weather gauge: To be upwind of an enemy is to hold the weather gauge.

Weather permitting: A charter party term that excludes (from the time specified in the contract) those days when weather conditions preclude working cargo.

Weather side: Towards the wind, the opposite of lee side.

Weather tide: A tide moving in the same direction as the wind.

Weathered: Permanently damaged by wind and weather. Said of old seamen as well as equipment.

Weatherly: Capable of sailing close to the wind with minimal drift to leeward.

Weatherproof: Resistant to the effects of weather, especially wind and rain. Also weathertight.

Weathertight: Fitted, sealed, or constructed so as to be impervious to penetration by wind, rain, or spray. Also weatherproof.

Weathervane: [1] A term used in dynamic positioning, referring to the tendency of a vessel to yaw under the influence of winds, waves, or currents. A weathervaning system is used to maintain the most favorable angle of approach to the combination of these external influences. [2] A pivoted sheet metal pointer used to indicate wind direction. *See also* telltale.

Weave: [1] A surface maneuver involving small tactical changes of direction as a form of zig-zag. [2] An aerial combat maneuver (*see* Thach Weave).

Web: [1] A net, mesh, or weave. [2] The World Wide Web (the universe of internet-accessible information).

Web belt: A wide waistband, made of cotton webbing and used to carry sidearms, water canteens, etc. Sometimes worn as a badge of office. Also (mainly British) webbing belt.

Web sling: A sling made of canvas or rope webbing, used with bagged cargo which might be broken open by a standard rope sling.

Webbing: A strong, narrow, closely-woven fabric.

Wedge: A pie-shaped wooden block hammered in to tighten a batten against its coaming so as to batten down the hatches.

Weep: To ooze through seams, pipe joints, or the like.

Weevil: A burrowing insect which perforates biscuits, and sometimes destroys wood.

Weft: [1] In common English usage, the thread or yarn which is shuttled back and forth across the warp to create a woven fabric (from the Old English wefan = to weave). [2] A 17th and 18th century naval term referring to a flag or ensign, lightly rolled up lengthwise and hoisted at various positions as a signal conveying orders to the fleet. For example, Prince Rupert's 1666 *Fighting Instructions* anticipate Nelson's famous signal "Engage the Enemy more closely" by saying:

> When the admiral of the fleet makes a weft with his flag, the rest of the flag officers are to do the like, and then all the best sailing ships are to make what way they can to engage the enemy.

However, the import of a weft was not fixed and, seven years later, orders issued by the Duke of York gave the signal a different meaning:

> Upon discovery of a (hostile) fleet and receiving of a signal from the admiral, which is to be the striking (lowering) of the admiral's ensign, and making (hoisting) a weft, such frigates as are appointed ... are to make sail and to stand with them (the enemy), as nigh as they can conveniently, the better to gain knowledge of ... what position their fleet is in; which being done the frigates are to speak together and conclude (agree on) the report they are to give....

By the late 18th century navies had developed better signaling systems, but the weft continued in merchant service — where it was also known as waft or waif— to describe any piece of cloth or clothing, or a rolled and knotted flag, flown as a signal. Different positions told which message applied. For example, a weft at the ensign staff signified "man overboard," at the peak it said "let's talk," and at the masthead it was the "recall" for small boats.

Weigh: To haul up, especially to raise an anchor. (Old English woegan = lift or carry.)

Well deck: [1] A section of weather deck bounded by superstructures fore and aft. [2] A weather deck with solid bulwarks which inhibit the drainage of water. [3] The flood-capable area of an amphibious ship that can be lowered to permit landing craft to enter and leave.

Well found: Said of a vessel which is solidly built, appropriately equipped, and properly maintained.

Well: [1] A vertical trunk or cofferdam through which pipes connect the bilge pump to a sump at the bottom of the ship. [2] A metal-lined compartment in a fishing boat, perforated to allow the entry of sea water to preserve live fish.

Well!: That's enough! Often followed by "belay!" (also "Well there!").

WEN: Web-enabled Navy.

Wend: Obsolete term for changing tack. (From Gothic wandjan = due to wind.)

West Wind Drift: An ocean current that flows eastward through all the oceans surrounding Antarctica (*see* seven seas).

Westerly: *See* Easterly.

Westing: The distance actually made good in a westerly direction on any course that has a westerly component.

Wet dock: A basin that is accessible only when the tide is in. Gates trap water inside when the tide falls, allowing ships to remain afloat during the loading and discharge of cargo. Unlike a dry dock, a wet dock cannot be drained or pumped out for hull repairs.

Wet locker: [1] A place for stowing dry foul weather gear. [2] A compartment equipped with drainage for wet clothing.

Wet ship: A vessel tending to take waves on board.

Wet steam: Steam containing particles of unevaporated or unevaporated water. Also saturated.

Wetsuit: Tight-fitting foam-rubber body covering, used by divers, surfers, and seamen to retain body heat when working in cold and wet conditions.

Wetting a commission: Formerly, a newly appointed officer's parchment commission was literally wetted; being rolled into a cornucopia, filled with wine, and passed around the wardroom for brother officers to drink his health from.
- **In the RN** this phrase still refers to entertaining shipmates to celebrate a promotion.
- **In the USN** it is now known as "wetting down" and officers' new rank insignia are usually placed at the bottom of a capacious glass and cannot be worn until it has been drained, preferably without pausing for breath.

Whack: A share of something, especially a seaman's ration of food. Also wack.

Whale catcher: A seaworthy self-propelled (steam or diesel) whaler with a bow-mounted harpoon gun. Catchers deliver their kill to an onshore whaling station, a factory ship anchored in a sheltered bay or inlet, or to a stern-slipway equipped factory ship operating in the open sea.

Whale chaser: An open boat launched from a whaler to catch and harpoon whales, bringing the captured animals to the mother ship. *See* whale processing.

Whale processing: After a kill the blubber is flensed into large strips known as blanket pieces, the head is cut off, and major body parts dissected. Any ambergris found is stored for refining ashore. The lower jaws are boiled until the teeth can be extracted for making scrimshaw. Bones, meat, and blubber are cut to fit cookers known as digesters where they are rendered into a gigantic "stew" in which oil floats to the surface and is "tapped" (drawn off) into storage tanks. The remainder is a mixture of bits of meat and "gluewater" containing bone pulverized to the size of pepper grains. After processing by centrifuge and hammer mill, the meat (65 percent protein) is bagged for animal fodder. The remaining gluewater is dried into "whale solubles" (85–90 percent protein) also used in feed mixes, but in limited quantity since such a high protein content can be toxic. Every part of the animal is used with no waste products whatsoever, and a typical 13-meter (43 foot) Sperm Whale yields roughly:

Oil	7,100 kg (7 tons)
Solubles	2,900 kg (2.9 tons)
Meat	1,700 kg (1.7 tons)
Teeth	54 kg (120 lbs)

Ambergris is sometimes found.

Whaleback: [1] A cargo vessel with the curve of its tumblehome side continued across the deck. Now seldom seen, but popular in the Great Lakes during the early 1900s. [2] A small rounded structure on stem or stern to protect against breaking seas.

Whaleboat: A small double-ended pulling or power boat, tapered and high at both bow and stern for good handling and stability, especially in a heavy seaway.

Whaler: A ship or seaman engaged in the harvesting of marine mammals.

Whales: Seaman's satirical slang for canned sardines.

Wharf: A quay built of open rather than solid construction.

Wharf rat: A dockyard worker engaged in petty theft or pilferage.

Wharfage: Charges for the use of a wharf, pier, or dock.

Wharfinger: The owner or operator of a wharf.

Wharfman: A shore laborer who catches lines and attaches them to bollards, secures gangways and ladders, but does not handle cargo.

What water? Question asking the leadsman to report the measured depth.

Wheel: [1] A tactical maneuver in which all ships in a line abreast maintain their relative positions, with inner vessels slowing down and outer ones speeding up (also corpen turn). [2] A ship's steering wheel, its helm. [3] The handwheel of a capstan. [4] A propeller or paddlewheel. [5] Any circular disc or frame that revolves on an axis.

Wheel-lock: A musket equipped with a small metal wheel which turns against iron pyrites to produce a spark and ignite the charge.

Wheelhouse: A structure enclosing the helmsman's station, usually containing the compass, engine speed controls, and communications equipment (cf. bridge; pilothouse).

Wheelropes: The lines connecting helm and rudder.

Wheelsman: Another name for helmsman or steersman.

When the balloon goes up: This slang expression, referring to an anticipated action or event, originated in World War I when the first visible sign of a naval operation was the sending up of observation balloons from ships fitted with them.

Where away?: The conventional deck officer's response to a lookout's call of "Sail Ho!" asking him to report the direction of the sighting.

Wherry: A small ship's boat rowed by two pairs of oars.

Whip: To wrap a line with small stuff to prevent it unraveling.

Whipstaff: A vertical lever attached to the tiller to give the steersman a mechanical advantage. Introduced in the early 16th century, and progressively replaced by the steering wheel (helm) during the 18th. Examination of the wreck of HMS *Stirling Castle* (built 1679, wrecked 1703) suggests she was equipped with both a whipstaff and a steering wheel, indicating there was probably an interim period.

Whirlpool: A large eddy in which water moves in a circle producing a cavity or depression in the center. One in which the cavity becomes a strong downward-spiraling flow is properly called a vortex or maelstrom. Whirlpools can be dangerous to small boats, but tales of large vessels being sucked under are purely fictional. As for the mythical whirlpool Charybdis, it is just that — a myth.

Whiskey: NATO phonetic notation for the letter "W."

Whistle: [1] A signaling device required on merchantmen, with its frequency, audible range, and other characteristics being determined by the type of vessel and its service. [2] Incorrectly, a boatswain's call.

Whistle up a wind: Sailing mariners believed that making a sound like the wind would conjure one up and blew accordingly when becalmed. Superstition required them to first stick a knife into the mainmast on the bearing from which wind was desired. They might also knot a short length of rope, with a single knot for a light breeze, two for fresh breezes, and three for strong winds.

Whistling: With the exception of a mess cook (*see* food distribution) and deliberately trying to whistle up a wind, whistling when the wind was fair was something no sailing ship sailor would even dream of doing for fear the wind god Boreas would think he was being mocked and bring up a full gale to demonstrate his power. Moreover, on ships of the Royal and United States Navies, whistling anywhere on board was (and still is) strictly forbidden because it might be confused with the piping of a boatswain's call. *See also* Pig.

White ensign: One of three United Kingdom naval flags carrying a centered cross of Saint George with the union in its upper left quadrant. Strictly reserved for use by ships of the RN and the Royal Yacht Squadron, with the exception of USS *Winston Churchill*. (*See also* British ensigns.)

White hat: USN slang for enlisted personnel below the rank of chief petty officer.

White horse: A fast-moving wave with a foamy crest. Also Neptune's sheep, sea horse, and whitecap.

White monkey: *See* black dog.

White rope: Said of line or rope that has not been tarred. It is used for log-lines and signal halyards.

White shirt: Personnel working on a USN aircraft carrier's flight deck wear colored shirts for easy identification. White shirts are worn by those not falling into one of the other color groups, including aircraft inspectors, landing signal officers, and medical personnel.

White squall: A sudden, localized tropical disturbance, characterized by turbulence, whitecaps, and spindrift.

White water: [1] A frothy sea surface covered in white horses. [2] Swiftly-flowing frothy water in river rapids. [3] Lightly-colored sea water above a shoal or sandy bottom.

Whitecap: A wave with a broken and foaming crest as a result of the action of strong winds. Also white horse.

WHO: World Health Organization (UN)

Whole nine yards: *See* nine yards.

Wich: An ancient name for a port, long obsolete but surviving in names such as Norwich and Greenwich.

Wide berth: To remain at a distance from another vessel or object.

Widow-maker: Slang for the bowsprit, off which many sailors fell to drown.

Widows' Man: A fictitious seaman, representing an early form of life insurance for naval officers. By a 1760 Act of George II, the purser was authorized to carry on the ship's books two extra men for every one-hundred of the vessel's complement. These men were given imaginary names known as "pusser's tallies," and their wages were paid into a fund for the relief of indigent widows of officers killed or died on active service. The practice lasted until 1832.

Wigwag: To use hand-held flags for a semaphore message.

Wilco: Voice communication shorthand (proword) meaning "message understood: will comply" (not to be confused with "roger" which only means "message received"). Abbreviation of **will** comply.

Wildfire: Term for an 18th–19th century version of Greek Fire.

Williamson Turn: *See* "Person Overboard."

Williwaw: A violent squall, typically encountered off mountainous coasts.

Winch: [1] A hand-cranked windlass used to increase hauling power when raising or trimming sails, or pulling lines. [2] A similar but larger steam or electric powered machine with a drum to coil cable, chain, or hawsers. A winch/windlass has a horizontal drum, while a capstan has a vertical one.

Wind: [1] To turn a ship by its mooring lines or previously laid-out anchors (pronounced wined). [2] Air in natural motion across the earth's surface (rhymes with pinned). *See also* ill wind, gods of the wind, and measurement of wind and wave.

Wind direction: It is conventional to define winds by the direction they are blowing from rather than towards. But *see* current flow.

Wind gods: *See* gods of the wind.

Wind in the teeth: Blowing dead against the ship.

Wind lop: Short choppy waves caused by local winds.

Wind rode: Said of an anchored vessel which is riding head-on to the wind and is unaffected by less-powerful tidal currents (cf. tide rode).

Wind scoop: A structural ventilation device consisting of metal funnel which can be rotated to catch the prevailing wind and is attached to a port leading below deck.

Wind shadow: The area of calm to leeward of an obstruction.

Windage: [1] Generally considered to be the difference between the bore of a gun and the diameter of its projectile. More correctly it is the difference in their cross-sectional areas. In either case this leaves a gap through which gas can escape. [2] The influence of the wind in deflecting a missile. [3] The degree to which a gun sight must be adjusted to allow for such deflection. [4] A ship's tendency to make leeway. [5] Frictional resistance of a hull to airflow. [6] The area of sail presented to the wind.

Windbound: Unable to leave port or an anchorage due to unfavorable winds.

Windfall: During the Napoleonic Wars, when timber for the Royal Navy was a vital strategic asset, it was illegal to cut down any tree of more than twenty-four inches in diameter. However, if one fell or was blown down naturally, it could legally be used by the property-owner. Hence "windfall" came to mean an unexpected gain or good fortune.

Winding: The act of blowing the boatswain's call. Pronounced wind-ing, not wine-ding.

Windjammer: [1] The word originally referred to a horn player or bugler. [2] By the 19th century it had come to mean a talkative person or windbag. [3] It was specifically applied to a large, usually square-rigged, sailing ship, with an iron or steel hull, copious cargo space, and three to five huge masts. Introduced during the 1870s to compete with steam-powered vessels. [4] Steamship sailors punned that old school sailors who kept bragging about the superiority of sail were "windjammers." [5] In popular usage, the word came to mean any large sailing ship.

Windlass: A horizontal revolving drum, turned by bars inserted in its rim, used for hauling the anchor or other cables (cf. Capstan, winch).

Windsail: A temporary ventilation device consisting of a canvas wind catcher attached to scoops which direct fresh air into the foul-smelling gundecks and orlop.

Windward: Towards the side from which the wind is blowing (cf. Leeward).

Wind-wave: [1] A wave produced by the action of wind on the ocean surface. [2] *See* Douglas Scale and table 2.

Wing: [1] Open area at each side of a bridge, used by lookouts and signalers. [2] Any extension beyond the side of a ship. [3] Two or more squadrons of aircraft.

Wing-and-wing: Sailing downwind with sails set on both sides. A square-rigger carries studding-sails on both sides; a fore-and-after runs with foresail out to one side and mainsail on the other.

Wing passage: An area in the wings of warships; always kept clear to allow the carpenter and his mates access for damage control.

Wing tank: An outboard ballast tank under the weather deck.

Wing turret: A gun housing that is on the extreme edge of a ship or protrudes from the ship's side

Wingman: A pilot who flies in formation with another to provide mutual support and protection.

Wings: [1] The extremities of a fleet or convoy dispersed in line-abreast or in a "V" formation. [2] The outboard sides of a sailing ship's hold or orlop. Used for storage in merchantmen or as wing passages in warships. [3] Slang for the insignia designating an aviator or parachutist.

Winkle-pickers: The winkle, also known as periwinkle, is a small soft-bodied marine mollusk, usually served pre-cooked in its shell. It is a popular delicacy at English seaports, but a long pin is needed to pry the tasty meat from inside the outer case. As a result, women's shoes with long pointed toes acquired the name winkle-pickers. The slang term is also applied to stiletto heels.

Winston Churchill: Named after Britain's World War II prime minister, DDG-81 is the fourth USN ship to be named after an Englishman and the only one currently in commission. As a unique courtesy to her namesake's country, an officer of the Royal Navy is assigned to the ship's company at all times, and the guided missile destroyer flies the White Ensign on its port yardarm along with the stars and stripes to starboard.

Wire: A metal strand or filament. *See* wire rope.

Wire rope: Wire rope or cable (the names are here interchangeable) refers to a number of metal strands twisted together, each consisting of individual wires laid helically about a central core. This produces metal in its strongest, yet most flexible form. It is unusual to think of rope as a machine, but it is composed of moving parts working in relation to one another. For example, a six-strand rope consisting of forty-nine wires per strand, laid around an independent wire rope core, contains a total of 343 individual wires, each of which must blend with and move relative to the others to give the flexibility necessary for successful operation.

Various types have been designed to meet a wide range of operating conditions. They are designated by the kind of core (fabric, metal, plastic, etc.); the number of strands; the number, size, and arrangement of the wires in each strand; and the way in which the wires and strands are wound, or laid.

Most ropes used for nautical duty are fabricated from plow-steel strands laid around a steel core. They must be easy to handle and able to withstand corrosion, but these traits tend to be mutually exclusive. A galvanized finish on individual wires can provide some corrosion protection, but relatively large diameters are needed to prolong resistance. Bigger wires usually mean less flexibility, reducing handling ease. To provide the desired combination of handling properties and corrosion resistance for marine service, the fiber content is normally increased. This reduces the strength, but the sacrifice is necessary.

Wire stopper: A device for gripping and securing wire hawser when it is too stiff to be easily secured on bitts.

Wireless: [1] An early (mainly British) name for radio. During World War II the British armed forces made a distinction between wireless telegraphy (WT), meaning Morse-coded messages, and radio telephony (RT), meaning voice communication. [2] Nowadays the term is used for a number of electronic devices, including computer mouses and mobile telephones.

Wireways: Passageways for electrical cables.

Wishbone: A V-shaped rod used to support the upper platform of an accommodation ladder.

Wishbone boom: A double-sided boom set at an angle to the mast and typically supported by line stays from the leading edge of the mast to each side of the boom. Tension of the sail's foot (outhaul) and luff (vang) are adjusted simultaneously by the use of a single line.

With a will!: Command for oarsmen to pull hard in unison.

With the sun: [1] From east to west. [2] Clockwise. [3] Said of rope laid-up right-handed.

Wives: Whenever a sailing warship was in port, it was common practice to allow sailors to bring their spouses on board for conjugal relations. Sweethearts and prostitutes frequently came aboard in the guise of wives. *See also* Women aboard ship.

WL: Water line.

WMD: Weapon(s) of mass destruction.

WMO: World Meteorological Organization.

WO: [1] Warrant Officer. [2] Work Order.

Wolfpack: An organized force of submarines coordinated for a specific mission or to attack a designated target. The concept was developed by the German Kriegsmarine for the Battle of the Atlantic, and the USN deployed similar but smaller groups in the latter part of the Pacific War.

Women aboard ship: [1] In the days of sail, superstitious seamen generally resented the presence of a female at sea, believing it was sure to produce foul weather or even gales. [2] On the other hand, many captains and some other officers took their wives on voyages, perhaps because a contrary superstition held that a pregnant woman was lucky for the ship. [3] *See* naked female.

Women and children first!: Aboard HMS *Birkenhead*, in the early hours of 26th February 1852, the troops were in their quarters, passengers in their bunks, and only the duty watch was on deck. The sea was calm, the skies were clear, and a course had been plotted to avoid treacherous offshore rocks, but no one had realized that an iron hull (a rarity at the time) would cause compass deviation.

With a terrible crunch, the brigantine-rigged transport impaled herself on Pinnacle Rock, just off Danger Point on the South African coast. The serious rent in her hull was enlarged when Captain Robert Salmond put her auxiliary paddle-wheels full astern in an attempt to back off the rocks. A hundred or more embarked troops drowned in their sleep, but the remainder rushed on deck where their sergeants formed them in parade order. Salmond shouted "Abandon ship! Every man for himself!" but Lieutenant-Colonel Alexander Seaton bellowed, "Stand fast the ranks — women and children first!" This is the first time this phrase, later to become a maritime tradition, is known to have been used.

All but three of the eight lifeboats stowed on her paddle-boxes were stuck there by multiple coats of paint, and one of these was crushed when the funnel collapsed. Seven of the 25 female passengers got into the two remaining boats, together with 13 of 31 children. Next day, the schooner *Lioness* rescued them along with 54 seamen, 6 marines, and 113 soldiers, who had been clinging to flotsam or hanging in the rigging of topmasts projecting above the water. An estimated 445 had drowned or been eaten by sharks, including Captain Salmond and Colonel Seaton with most of the troops who had steadfastly obeyed his order to stand fast. Rudyard Kipling immortalized their courage when he wrote:

To stand and be still
to the Birken'ead Drill
is a damn tough bullet to chew

Women Marines: The Navy and Marine Corps were the only United States armed forces to enlist women in World War I (1918), but the Marines were last to do so in World War II (1943). The Corps is the only sea service that does not identify its women by an acronym (*see* Spars, Waves, and Wrens); when the first World War II females were inducted, USMC Commandant Lt.Gen. Thomas Holcomb commented, "They don't have a nickname, and they don't need one.... They are Marines."

During World War II, in addition to clerical and administrative duties, women Marines served in over 200 military assignments, including radio operators, parachute riggers, vehicle drivers and mechanics, welders, and cartographers. They formed about one-third of personnel manning major posts in the United States and Hawaii. In 1948 Congress passed the Women's Armed Services Integration Act (Public Law 625) and women became part of the regular Marine Corps.

The USMC allows women in all occupational fields except infantry, artillery, armor, and aircrew. In contrast, the Royal Marines admits females only to its Band Service. They have a secondary role as field hospital orderlies but, not being commando trained, wear blue berets instead of the prestigious green ones.

Women sailors: During both World Wars, females played important roles in support of naval operations. Today they serve afloat alongside men. *See* Spars, Waves, Wrens, and Yeomanettes.

Wooden Wall: This 19th century British term for the fleet as protector of the nation is first recorded by fifth century BCE historian, Herodotus who tells U.S. that, threatened by Persian invasion, Athens consulted the Oracle at Delphi who forecast: "The headlong god of war shall bring you low." Rather than accept this dire prediction, the Athenians requested a second session, first giving the Delphic priests substantial gifts. This time the Oracle was more positive; "Though all else be taken, all-seeing Zeus grants that the wooden wall shall not fall." Athenians agonized over this pronouncement, some thinking it referred to fortifications on the Corinthian Isthmus, others that it alluded to a palisade on the Athenian Acropolis. But commander-in-chief, Themistocles, insisted it meant the ships of his fleet which, indeed, trounced the invaders at the naval battle of Salamis.

Woodlock: A wooden block, often copper-sheathed, placed under the pintle of a rudder to prevent it from being lifted or unshipped.

Woof: The transverse strand in a cloth or canvas (cf. warp).

Woold: To repair a broken spar by lashing the break (rhymes with cold).

Woolder: A spike used to tighten the lashing of a woold (rhymes with colder).

Woolly-pully: [1] RN slang for a navy-blue wool or cloth sweater with leather or suede reinforcement. [2] USMC slang for a similar knitted green sweater.

Work: [1] To tack into the wind. [2] To loosen at seams or joints due to the action of heavy seas. [3] To use engines, lines, and other gear to maneuver in tight situations. [4] In physics, work is done when a force acts to move an object. [5] In general, sustained physical or mental effort to do or perform something. [6] something produced or accomplished by effort, exertion, or exercise of skill.

Working load: Also known as working strength. The static weight that can safely be applied to new rope under normal service conditions, when it is in good condition with appropriate splices. Where dynamic loading is expected, the recommended working load should be reduced accordingly.

Working party: A detail assembled for a specific job.

World Geographic Reference System: A spatially referenced (linked to location) area-designation method that is suitable for reporting and plotting and can be applied to any map or chart that is graduated in latitude and longitude, regardless of its projection. The system divides the globe into twenty-four longitudinal zones, each 15 degrees wide, identified by the letters A to Z (I and O omitted). There are twelve bands of latitude, also 15 degrees wide, lettered A to M (omitting I). In referencing a location, the first letter is that of the longitude band and the second letter is that of the latitude. The "Georef" system is used for interservice reporting of strategic air operations, and in air defense. *See also* geographic referencing.

World grid: A network of horizontal and perpendicular lines that divides the entire world into one-thousand meter squares, used mainly for military target designation.

World Meteorological Organization: This specialized agency of the United Nations is the international authority on the state and behavior of the earth's atmosphere, its interaction with the oceans, the climate it produces, and the resulting distribution of water resources. It was created in 1950, to replace the International Meteorological Organization founded in 1873.

World Ocean: The interconnected waters that comprise the bulk of the hydrosphere and encircle most of the Earth. This continuity is of fundamental importance to oceanography and international trade. Customarily, the World Ocean is divided by the continents and various oceanographic features into five principal areas known as the Atlantic, Arctic, Indian, Pacific, and Southern (or Antarctic) Oceans. These are interspersed by many smaller seas and other bodies of water. The term was coined by Russian oceanographer Yuly Shokalsky early in the 20th century, but the notion dates back to classical antiquity in the form of Oceanus.

Worldscale: An index of the cost of chartering a

tanker for a specific voyage and time. The negotiated price is normally a percentage of Worldscale, expressed in US$/ton of oil.

Worm: [1] A wad-hook. [2] To pass a small line in a spiral between the lays of a rope, preparatory to parcelling and serving. An old aide-memoire says "Worm and parcel with the lay. Turn and serve the other way."

Worsted: A knitted material made from spun woolen thread.

WPB: Patrol boat (USCG)

Wrack: [1] Seaweed thrown ashore by the waves. [2] To destroy by wave action.

Wreck: [1] The ruin or destruction of a vessel in the course of navigation. [2] The remains of a vessel so ruined or destroyed whether sunk or aground.

Wreck master: The person in charge of a salvage operation. Also salvage master.

Wreckage: The debris and flotsam or waveson of a vessel which has been wrecked.

Wrecker: [1] One who illegally exhibits false signals to lure ships to destruction and then plunders the wreck. [2] A person who legally salvages and destroys wrecked vessels. [3] Derogatory RN slang for an artificer.

Wrens: Phoneticization of the initial letters in Women's Royal Naval Service. Established in 1914, disbanded after World War I and reinstated for World War II. Unlike the USN's Waves who were almost exclusively employed in administrative duties, Wrens served ashore as drivers, signals officers and ratings; aircraft, torpedo, and ordnance mechanics; and in many other specialties. Afloat they provided coxwains and crews for harbor boats, and served on oceangoing transports as cooks, stewards, and signals ratings.

Wring: To set shrouds too taut, thereby straining or crippling the mast.

Writer: A Royal Navy rating with administrative, secretarial, and clerical duties related to personnel records, accounting, filing, correspondence, and the like. The USN equivalent is Yeoman.

WRNS: Women's Royal Naval Service. *See* Wrens.

Wrong: Proword meaning "previous transmission was incorrect, correct version follows..."

WS: Weapon System.

WSES: Surface effect ship (USCG).

WTR: Writer (RN Clerical rating).

WvHt: Wave height.

WWI: World War One (1914–1918). Also World War 1.

WWII: World War Two (1937–1945). Also World War 2.

WWIS: World Weather Information Service. A WMO Website providing worldwide weather forecasts and climatological information.

X

Xebec: An oared and sailed Mediterranean vessel with up to three lateen-rigged masts (often square-rigged on the foremast). According to William Falconer's 1780 *Dictionary of the Marine*:

> the hull is extremely different from ... almost every other vessel. It is furnished with a strong prow, and the extremity of the stern, which is nothing more than a sort of railed platform or gallery, projects further behind the counter and buttock than that of any European ship. Being generally equipped as a corsair, the xebec is constructed with a narrow floor, to be more swift in pursuit of the enemy; and of a great breadth to enable her to carry a great force of sail ... there is a platform of grating extending along the deck ... whereon the crew may walk dry-footed, whilst the water is conveyed through the grating to the scuppers.

X-craft: British World War II midget submarine with a crew of four.

XO: Executive Officer.

X-ray: NATO phonetic notation for the letter "X." Also written without the hyphen.

Y

Yacht: [1] A pleasure craft. [2] A small, fast pirate ship. The word entered the English language in 1660 when the States General of Holland presented newly-restored Charles II of England with a jaght-schip = chase-ship (the "j" being pronounced "y" in Dutch).

Yacht ensigns: While in foreign waters and on the high seas United States yachts fly the national flag. In home waters they may wear that flag defaced by a fouled anchor in a ring of 13 stars. When this is dipped to USN vessels, they will acknowledge and return the salute. British practice is more complex. Members of the Royal Yacht Squadron are entitled to fly the white ensign, while the vessels of specified yacht clubs may wear the blue ensign, either plain or defaced with an emblem. RN vessels will always acknowledge and return the salute of these flags. Other yacht clubs may be authorized to fly the red ensign with a defacing badge or emblem, while any citizen may fly the undefaced red ensign. The RN is not required to, but normally will, respond to the dip of any red ensign.

Yankee: [1] American term for a foresail. [2] NATO phonetic notation for the letter "Y." [3] Properly, a native of New England. [4] Applied by Confederates to Union troops during the Civil War. [5] Often applied by foreigners to any citizen of the United States.

Yar: Describes a ship that is trim, responsive, lively, and answers readily to the helm. The term has been in use since the 13th century, but is seldom heard today (rhymes with care). Also yare.

Yard: [1] A cylindrical spar, tapered at each end and slung across a mast to support a sail. [2] A similar spar on a powered warship, supporting signal halyards, blinkers, and antennae. [3] A shore establishment which builds, repairs, or maintains ships. [4] The campus of the U.S. Naval Academy is sometimes called "The Yard."

Yard and stay: A handling rig in which one boom is positioned over the hatch, and another over the ship's side. Cargo is moved from one to the other by means of lines running between them.

Yard boom: A spar swung over the side to handle cargo.

Yardarm: The tapered outboard extremity of a yard extending beyond the sail. *See* clear the yardarm and sun's over the yardarm.

Yardarm blinkers: Signaling lights, placed at the end of yards for maximum visibility.

Yardarm ducking: A more severe version of the Spanish Mare. The culprit was lashed to a batten, hauled up to the main yardarm and immediately released to plunge violently into the sea. The sequence would be repeated several times with the actual number depending on the severity of the offense. This punishment was never practiced by the RN or USN, but was common in the French Navy.

Yardarm-to-yardarm: Said of warships in such close combat that the outboard tips of their yards are almost in contact.

Yardbird: [1] USN slang for a low-rank enlisted person with few nautical skills, a landlubber. [2] Someone who works on the docks or in a shipyard, often a retired seaman. [3] U.S. penitentiary slang for an inmate.

Yards apeak: Yards turned to form St. Andrew's crosses to create space when vessels are docked alongside one another. Also as a sign of mourning (*see* a-cockbill).

Yare: *See* Yar.

Yarn: [1] Fibers loosely twisted into strands for making rope. [2] A tall tale or embellished seafaring story. This originated in sailing ship days when old rope used to be separated into its yarns and then rewoven into new rope. Seamen assigned to this long and boring task would wile away the time by telling each other tales, which they called "spinning a yarn" or just plain "yarning."

Yaw: Deviation from a straight course in either direction. One of the six responses of a vessel to movement of the sea (*see* ship motion, rotational oscillation).

Yawl: [1] A two-masted sailing boat with the mizzen stepped abaft the rudder post. [2] A small fishing craft. [3] A merchant ship's jollyboat with four or six oars. [4] A twelve-oared warship's boat.

Yellow Admiral: When the British fleet was "color-coded" (*see* British Ensigns & Admirals) a captain who had patiently worked his way to the top of the seniority list, only to find there was no vacancy for another rear-admiral of the blue, could be "yellowed" — that is promoted to flag rank "without distinction of squadron" — a somewhat dubious honor.

Yellow Jack: [1] Yellow fever. [2] Seafarer's slang for the quarantine flag. [3] Slang name for a pensioner at Greenwich Naval Hospital when he was under punishment and forced to wear his uniform coat inside out with the yellow lining exposed.

Yellow Shirt: Personnel working on a USN aircraft carrier's flight deck wear colored shirts for easy identification. Yellow shirts are worn by 'plane directors, aircraft handling officers, catapult officers, and arrester gear officers.

Yemanja: This beautiful Brazilian sea goddess brings fish to fishermen, and good luck to all who attend her annual festival and throw her offerings of flowers, beads, and trinkets. Sometimes, when a man has ventured too far out to sea, she will appear, holding out her arms to him. If he then embraces the radiant goddess she will take him to her submarine palace to live as her happy husband forever.

Yeo-heave-ho! The traditional cry of merchant seamen working at a windlass or the falls of a purchase. It was not allowed in the navy.

Yeoman: [1] Originally RN and currently USN, a rating with administrative, secretarial, and clerical duties related to personnel records, accounting, filing, correspondence, and the like. (The RN rating is now Writer.) [2] Currently, an RN petty officer responsible for visual signaling, the senior signalman on board.

Yeomanette: On March 19, 1917, the Bureau of Navigation advised the commanders of U.S. naval districts they could recruit women into the Naval Coast Defense Reserve to be "utilized as radio operators, stenographers, nurses, messengers, chauffeurs, etc., and in many other capacities in the industrial line." The majority of enlisted women were designated Yeomen (F) — inevitably known as yeomanettes. (*See also* Waves.) One of them wrote a short jingle to eulogize the force:

I've been in frigid Greenland and in sunny Tennessee,
I've been in noisy London and in wicked, gay Paree,
I've seen the Latin Quarter, with its models,
wines, and tights,
I've hobnobbed oft with Broadway stars who
outshone Broadway lights;
But North or South or East or West,
the girls that I have met
Could never hold a candle to a Newport yeomanette.

Yesty: Elizabethan term for foamy breakers ("yesty seas unfound and swallow navigation up" — Shakespeare, *Macbeth*, IV, i, 52).

Y-Gun: A Y-shaped launcher that can throw depth charges forward on both sides of a vessel simultaneously.

Yoke: [1] A crosspiece on the head of a small boat's rudder, to which steering lines or chains are attached. [2] An airplane control operating the elevators and ailerons. [3] The frame from which a bell is hung. [4] A clamp or similar piece that embraces two parts to hold or unite them in position.

Yoke lines: *See* steering lines. Also yolk lines.

You, Sir!: Admiral Smyth relates that this arrogant phrase, once used by officers to address seamen, was forbidden by Admiral Lord Collingwood.

Young gentleman: A term formerly used to describe a midshipman.

Your number's up: This phrase, which today means "You've been caught," "You're in trouble," or even "You're about to die," comes from the days of fighting sail. For ease of signaling and identification, every warship was given a unique four-letter "number" which, when hoisted, was said to be "up." When the flagship flew a number with no other message, it was a peremptory summons for the captain to report immediately to the admiral. This frequently meant a reprimand for some lapse of conduct or dereliction of duty, so word from the officer on watch "Captain, your number's up" was seldom welcomed.

Yow-yow: A small Chinese sampan.

YTD: Year to Date.

Yureisen: An ancient Japanese fisherman's legend tells of this archaic war junk that appears from nowhere, moving rapidly despite its lack of sails and halyards. The sight can be extremely dangerous, but the remedy is to steer head-on towards the junk. As soon as it is rammed, the apparition will disappear, but the waters will immediately be filled with struggling men crying for scoops with which to bail out the sea. The wise fisherman will only throw them dippers with holes in them, for if they are given proper scoops they will throw water into the fishers' boat to sink it.

Z

Z: (1) Zenith: (2) Zero: (3) Zulu (time): (4) Flash, the highest military and diplomatic communications priority level (*see* ZO).

ZA: Zone Alarm.

Zaratan: This monstrous creature loves to doze on the ocean surface, sometimes floating long enough for vegetation and even trees to sprout on its back. When it reaches this state, mariners are said to mistake it for an island, cast their anchor to grip its scales, and go ashore for a meal. If the heat of their cooking fire penetrates its thick leathery scales, the beast jerks awake and plunges to the deep, dragging the men and their ship behind it. Similar events, involving fires being lit on the backs of whales rather than Zaratan himself, appear in the tales of Sindbad the Sailor and Brendan the Navigator.

Z-card: A USCG document issued to U.S. merchant seamen in lieu of a passport.

Zebec: A variation of xebec.

Zenith: The point of the celestial sphere directly overhead.

Zephyr: The slightest gentle breeze (once nautical, but now mainly poetic).

Zeroing: In naval fire-control, the process of setting a synchro to its zero position.

Zerox the log: USN submariner slang for copying the previous entries in the engineering record book instead of taking new readings. From Xerox, the proprietary name of a copying machine. (*See also* gundeck.)

ZIF: Zero Incident Frequency.

Zigzag: An evasive maneuver designed to confuse tracking submarines, consisting of a random series of small straight-line diversions from a base course.

Zincs: Small sacrificial anodes of zinc implanted in an iron hull to minimize oxidation.

Zizz: RN lower deck slang for a brief sleep.

ZO: Flash Override. Code allowing the U.S. President and designated senior officials and officers to pre-empt all other traffic irrespective of priority. Not a precedence code but a function of office.

Zodiac: [1] Although it is a registered trademark, this name is often used colloquially for any motorized, inflatable, rigid-bottomed boat used for recreational and military purposes, ranging from yacht tender to high-speed beach landing craft. [2] The heavenly belt that includes the apparent positions of sun, moon, and those planets known to ancient astronomers, who divided it into twelve equal "signs" (Aries, Taurus, Gemini, etc.).

Zodiacal light: A luminous cone-shaped area of sky seen at sunrise or sunset, mainly in the tropics.

Zonal wind: The component of a wind along the local parallel of latitude.

Zone: [1] One of seven longitudinal belts into which geographers divide the globe. A central equatorial or torrid zone is bordered by tropical zones, followed by temperate zones and, finally, polar or frigid zones. [2] One of twenty-four latitudinal time zones, each covering 15° of longitude and centered on a meridian (except for adjustments to accommodate political boundaries). [3] To be "in the zone" means eligible for promotion.

Zone of fire: An area into which a designated fire support ship delivers, or is prepared to deliver, long-range artillery fire.

Zone Time: Local or civilian time, known to the military as time zone Juliett.

Zopissa: Obsolete term for tar scraped off the bottom of old ships. Believed by sailing ship seamen to be a cure for ulcers.

Z-twist: *See* rope and hawser lay.

Zubian: This World War I British destroyer acquired its name thanks to the unusual distinction of having been constructed by welding together the bow section of HMS *Zulu*, whose stern had been blown off by a mine, and the after section of HMS *Nubian*, whose bow had been destroyed by a torpedo.

Zulu: [1] NATO phonetic notation for the letter "Z." [2] Used in NATO and commercial radio communications to signify Coordinated Universal Time using the 24-hour clock (e.g., 1700 Zulu signifies 5:00 P.M. GMT). [3] Sometimes also used to signify Greenwich Mean Time. [4] A type of Scottish fishing vessel with a straight upright bow, a sharply-raked stern, a dipping lugsail, and mizzen.

Zumbra: A small Spanish yawl-like boat.

Zyglo: An extremely sensitive fluorescent penetrant produced by the Magnaflux division of Illinois Tool Works Inc. After the product is applied, ultraviolet light reveals cracks and other surface discontinuities in virtually any non-porous material.

Zzz's: A (usually written) colloquialism for sleep. *See* zizz.

APPENDIX:
REAL AND SPECULATIVE SEA MONSTERS

Far far beneath in the abysmal sea,
His ancient, dreamless, uninvaded sleep
The Kraken sleepeth: faintest sunlights flee
About his shadowy sides; above him swell
Huge sponges of millennial growth and height;
And far away into the sickly light,
From many a wondrous grot and secret cell

Unnumber'd and enormous polypi
Winnow with giant arms the slumbering green.
There hath he lain for ages, and will lie
Battening upon huge seaworms in his sleep,
Until the latter fire shall heat the deep;
Then once by man and angels to be seen,
In roaring he shall rise and on the surface die.
—Alfred, Lord Tennyson, 1830

There are a few known animals that could have been mistaken for sea serpents or monsters, but the most probable are cryptids — hypothetical creatures such as colossal squid and super eels — whose existence is speculative but correspond to eyewitness descriptions. Other candidates can be called "living fossils" — the descendents of aquatic dinosaurs that lived in the world's oceans during the Jurassic (208–146 million years ago) or of fish-like reptiles *(ichthyosaurs)* from the same era. Cryptozoologists also propose the survival of primitive whales *(archeocetes)* that thrived in the much more recent Eocene (54–30 mya).

Frilled sharks: These very primitive animals are so different from other sharks that it has been suggested they should be given their own order. Superficially, they resemble dark brown or grey eels with dorsal fins which can look like manes. It has been suggested that sightings could have been reported as sea serpents, but this seems unlikely, since no specimen much over two meters (six feet) long has ever been documented. On the other hand, bigger ones may exist in the depths. In 1880, Captain S.W. Hanna claimed to have netted one which measured over twenty-five feet (almost 8 meters) but no similar-sized specimen has since been reported in spite of intensive fishing operations.

Basking sharks: Are responsible for almost all the many reports of "sea serpent" corpses discovered washed onto the shore. This is because of the way in which they decay, as described by writers Simon Welfare and John Fairley: "First the jaws, which are attached by only a small piece of flesh, drop off leaving what looks like a small skull and thin serpentlike neck. Then, as only the upper half of the tail fin carries the spine, the lower half rots away leaving the lower fins which look like legs. Time after time this monsterlike relic has been the cause of a sea serpent 'flap.'"

Oarfish: This is the largest bony fish in the sea, and could be one of the real creatures most frequently mistaken for sea serpents. It is possible the Loch Ness Monster is one (if it exists at all). Oarfish are found in all the world's oceans and are believed to live at depths between 100 and 500 fathoms (600–3000 feet). Only sick or dying specimens are known to have surfaced, and none has been taken alive. Sightings are common, with reliable observers estimating lengths between 15 and 17 meters (50–55 feet), but the largest to be accurately measured (taken in 1996 by U.S. Navy Seals off Coronado Island, California) was only 7 meters (23 feet) long. In May 1996, diver Jonathan Bird sighted one swimming underwater off the Bahamas. He noted that its coloration was different from dead specimens and, interestingly, that it swam like a seahorse with its long slender silver body aligned vertically, propelling itself by undulating its bright red crestlike dorsal fin.

Giant octopus: Cephalopods, a class which includes octopus and squid, share a number of features, including an invertebrate body, sometimes with multiple hearts; the largest eyes in the animal kingdom; a mouth surrounded by oversize lips in the form of prehensile arms or tentacles; one or more parrot-like beaks for tearing food apart; a muscular siphon for jet propulsion; an ink sac to produce a protective "smokescreen"; and the ability to change color for camouflage or to express emotion. They are also believed to be extremely intelligent. There are numerous species varying from tiny to immense.

The Giant Pacific Octopus is the largest known member of the species, usually weighing about 23 kg (50 lbs) at maturity. One large specimen, captured off British Columbia in 1967, weighed 70 kg (156 lbs) and measured almost 7½ meters (23 feet) from arm tip to arm tip. The Santa Barbara Museum of Natural History has an apparently well documented record of one weighing more than 180 kg (400 lbs).

In 1896, a bloated, mutilated, and decomposing corpse of incredible size washed up on a beach in Florida. Dr DeWitt Webb, President of the St Augustine Historical Society and Institute of Science, examined and photographed the monster, which he estimated to weigh between six and seven tons (6100–7100 kg) with skin 3½ inches (89 mm) thick. Only the stubs of tentacles were extant but, based on the dimensions of the body, he estimated their span would have been some 200 feet (61 m) matching that reported for the Kraken.

Webb sent samples preserved in formaldehyde to the National (now Smithsonian) Museum where, based on visual examination only, they were pronounced to have come from a sperm whale. However, in 1957, a team of biologists from the Naval Undersea Research Laboratory in San Diego, led by biologist Dr Joseph Gennaro, tracked down and examined the sixty-one year old samples under polarized light, reporting: "We decided at once and beyond any doubt, that the sample was not whale blubber. Further, the connective tissue pattern was ... similar to, if not identical with, that in my octopus sample.... The evidence appears unmistakable that the St. Augustine sea monster was in fact an octopus, but the implications (of its size) are fantastic."

With its eight writhing arms, alien appearance, and uncanny reasoning ability, this animal (which, having no bones, can squeeze through any opening the size of its own eye) has long had an evil reputation. Tales of bloodthirsty octopuses surfacing to tear ships apart have been heard around the globe, but divers report finding the creature shy and more inclined to hide than attack. Moreover, it is a bottom feeder with no reason to surface and assault an object considerably larger than itself. More than likely the reports of oc-

topus attack actually arose from seeing the tentacles of a large squid.

On the other hand, on 18th November 2005, the remotely operated submarine *Seaeye Falcon,* owned by SubOceanic Sciences, was conducting a salmon survey off British Columbia's Brooks Peninsula when, at a depth of 30 fathoms (55 meters, 180 feet), a large Giant Pacific Octopus appeared. Even though it was broad daylight, the normally retiring nocturnal creature took hold of the Falcon's cable with two of its tentacles and then reached for the body of the submarine with the other six.

According to Director of Operations Mike D. Wood, who feared the animal might damage the vehicle with its beak, "I go full reverse and blast him with all these seabed particles." The octopus flared its mantle in anger and, for a moment, it looked as though it was going to intensify its attack, but "Finally he lets go and disappears into the gloom." Wood captured the entire event on the *Falcon*'s digital video recorder.

Giant squid: Squid in general have a large head (called the mantle), eight arms with sucker discs, like an octopus, for holding their prey, and two longer tentacles for catching it. Inside the discs are claws that dig in to secure the grip, while a beak powerful enough to cut steel cable rips off chunks of flesh to be chewed by rows of teeth inside the mouth. Those encountered or caught by fishers are normally far too small to threaten shipping and widespread tales of attacks by larger specimens were long dismissed as mythical sailor-yarns.

Alecton's monster of 1861, of which only a part was recovered, was probably a giant squid. Then, on 2nd November 1878, the first complete specimen washed ashore at Glover's Harbor in Newfoundland. Its dead body was about six meters (20 feet) long, and one of its tentacles measured 10.7 meters (35 feet). Two years later an 18.5 meter (60.7 foot) creature was caught at Island Bay, New Zealand. This is still the record, although upwards of six hundred dead specimens have since have been recovered, about 20 percent of them off Newfoundland.

Underwater photographs and videotape have captured images of the giant squid, but most of what was known came from corpses and body parts. Some scientists believe a squid's blood can only carry oxygen at low temperatures and that long exposure to surface conditions might cause suffocation. Others think warm water affects the animal's buoyancy mechanism making it unable to re-submerge. If this is the case, a surfaced giant squid moving from a cold ocean current to a warm one would be doomed.

Then, late in 1997, a 7.6 meter (25 foot) giant squid was hauled up in a New Zealand fisherman's net. It was flash-frozen on board and shipped to The American Museum of Natural History in New York, where it went on display in October 1999. A slightly bigger specimen, 8.62 meters (28 feet) long, was taken by a trawler off the Falkland Islands in March 2004. It too was fast-frozen, then taken to London's Natural History Museum where (whimsically nicknamed "Archie") it went on display in February 2006.

Squid are carnivorous and quite aggressive. Humbolt squid, a smaller species, have been known to attack human swimmers, and giant squid have been witnessed furiously fighting sperm whales, which are one of their predators. It is probable that the Norwegian tanker incident (see Brunswick's kraken) occurred because the vessel was mistaken for a whale. An unauthenticated World War II account claims that a giant squid ate one of the survivors of a torpedoing.

Saltwater crocodiles: These creatures, which today are widely distributed around the Indian Ocean, the Coral Sea, and the East and South China Seas, can make long sea voyages, and have been sighted as far apart as Australia, Japan and India. They are the largest living reptiles, with adult males normally ranging from five to seven meters (17–23 feet) in length and weighing over a ton. One unusually large specimen, measuring 8.6 meters (28 feet), was shot by hunter Krystina Pawoski in the Norman River, Queensland, Australia in July 1957.

The crocodilian structure of articulated armor plates provides structural support for large heavy bodies, especially when supported by the buoyancy of a waterborne habitat. Fossil evidence of prehistoric "super-crocs" has been found on almost every continent. For example, *sarcosuchus imperator* of West Africa seems to have been about twelve meters (40 feet) long and weighed about nine tons, while North American *deinosuchus* was somewhat bigger at fifteen meters (50 feet) and twelve tons.

It has been hypothesized that such large specimens may still make their habitat in the oceans far from human eyes. (See Iberian's crocodilian.)

Sirenia: Mermaids and mermen are a far cry from deep sea monsters, but their folklore may have arisen from sightings of actual aquatic mammals. Members of the sirenia often take on a human appearance, and can seem touchingly feminine when breast-feeding their young.

There are three members of the order, all being large, herbivorous, grey-brown aquatic animals which inhabit coastal waters and slow-flowing rivers. Manatees can be found on both sides of the Atlantic, dugongs throughout the Southern Indo-Pacific region, and Steller's Sea Cow lived in the North Pacific until hunted to extinction during the 1760's. Somewhat amazingly, their nearest land relatives are the huge elephant and the tiny hyrax.

Adults of the extant species are about 3 meters (10 feet) long and weigh some 450 kgs (1,000 lbs) but the sea cow was somewhat bigger. They have a life expectancy of 60–70 years. Their streamlined bodies taper to a flat paddle-shaped tail, and females are distinguished by large teats between their flippers. Heads are rounded, with small eyes and wrinkled faces,

which could perhaps be mistaken for ugly witch-like mermaids or unsightly mermen.

Dolphins: It would take a lively imagination for a seafarer to look at an ill-favored sirenian and turn it into a blonde-haired beauty, but it would be easy for him to stare into a bright sun and mistake a pod of leaping, spinning, and glistening dolphins for mermaids gamboling playfully through the waves, green-gold tresses flowing, and silvery fishtails glinting in the rays.

Super eels: Known oceanic eels seldom grow longer than three meters (9 feet) but a considerable number of "sea serpent" descriptions, many of them made by impeccable witnesses, have led to widespread speculation that larger ones may exist, so far undiscovered. Two of the most famous giant eel sightings were reported by Captain Peter M'Quahe on 6th August 1848 (see *Daedelus'* Creature) and less than two months later by Captain Henderson (see *Daphne's* Serpent).

In 1833, four British army officers from the Halifax garrison were fishing off the Nova Scotia coast when their boatman, Jack Dowling, a retired "old salt," cried out "Oh sirs, look at that ... this is the queerest thing I ever did see!" All six aboard the boat later testified to seeing the head of a serpent, rising about six feet above the surface, with a "neck as thick as the trunk of a moderate-size tree." It was colored brown and white in an irregular pattern.

In 1875, off the north-eastern coast of Brazil, Captain George Drevar of British collier *Pauline* watched a huge snake-like creature wrap its coils around a sperm whale "which it proceeded to crush in the fashion of a boa-constrictor." Two years later, in June 1877, officers of the Royal Yacht *Osborne*, sailing off the Sicilian coast in good visibility, saw a sea monster for long enough for Lieutenant W. P. Hynes to make a quick pencil sketch. The sketch seems to have disappeared, but the accounts of the deck officers, all trained observers, agree that it was of immense length (Lt. Hynes estimated 150 feet) with a ridge of fins, each about fifteen feet long and six feet apart. It was fifteen or twenty feet wide at the shoulders, with smooth skin and a head and mouth resembling an alligator. It appeared to scull itself along by large fins or flippers.

Another well-documented sighting was made by Captain Platt and the crew of United States Coastal Survey vessel *Drift* on August 29, 1878. She was lying becalmed off Cape Cod's Race Point, with the crew lounging under the shade of the sails, when what looked like a thick spar rose about fifteen feet out of the calm water about 400 yards away. Suddenly the "spar" bent over in a curve and plunged below. The crew watched excitedly for another glimpse of the creature and, after roughly thirty minutes about forty feet of spar-shaped body rose again, this time standing erect like a monstrous worm with a round, dark brown body. No mouth, eye, or ear could be seen, indicating it was probably the tail that had emerged.

Again, it curved over and submerged and, as it did so, a dorsal fin, estimated to be at least fifteen feet high was exposed. Captain Platt submitted a written report to the Superintendent of Survey in Washington but, mindful of possible ridicule, the sighting was unreported until 1886 when the story was published in the magazine *Science*. Equally difficult to dismiss out of hand are the *Décidée* incident of 1904 and *Valhalla*'s serpent in the following year.

There have been subsequent sightings of other serpent-like animals. Early in the 20th century, Captain Ballard reported a large creature off the Scottish coast (see Craig-Gowan monster), and in 1912, Kapitan Ruser of *Kaiserin Victoria* saw a sinuous creature off the English coast, claiming it to be about twenty feet long and eighteen inches thick. In 1937, Alfred Peterson, aboard a British troopship in the China Sea, saw a 25 foot long grey-black body with a giraffe-like head. And in 1947, Grace liner *Santa Clara* ran over a brown eel-like creature, estimated to be at least 60 feet long.

Dinosaur survivors: The question of whether dinosaurs could swim has been debated for years, but no firm evidence had come to light until 2005, when the tracks of six-foot-tall, bipedal creature, about the size of an ostrich, were discovered at a number of sites in northern Wyoming. The tracks suggest it waded along the shoreline and swam offshore, perhaps to feed on fish or carrion. Then, in 2007, a 15-meter track, found in Spain's Cameros Basin, contained the first long and continuous record of swimming by a therapod dinosaur. Both of these finds concern creatures that hunted in the water, but lived on land, and there is no reason to believe dinosaurs ever adapted to a full-time aquatic life, or ventured far enough offshore to be mistaken for sea monsters. Many believe the "Loch Ness Monster" to be a surviving dinosaur.

Ichthyosaurs: These aquatic reptiles, which lived between 240 and 90 million years ago, averaged 5 meters (16 feet) in length, but some of the largest reached an astounding 23 meters (75 feet). However, they resembled modern dolphins (except for an upright tail fin) which does not fit well with most descriptions of sea serpents.

Archeocetes: Ancient whales came in many varieties, of which three possible survivors have been postulated as sea monster candidates. The first, known as *plesiosaurus elasmosaur*, had a small head at the end of a very long neck with up to 72 vertebrae (a giraffe has seven). This matches eyewitness descriptions of Scotland's mythical Loch Ness monster, but it would have been impossible for it to lift head and neck above the surface in the swan-like pose usually depicted. Even if it had had the muscles and conformation to bend so far upward, gravity would have tipped the body forward and kept most of the heavy neck in the water.

In contrast, another genus of archaic whale, *pliosaursus,* had large heads and very short necks. The fossils indicate that they swam by undulating their vertebral columns, thus forcing their feet up and down in a way similar to modern otters, while their movement on land probably resembled those of sea lions to some degree, involving protraction and retraction of the abducted limbs. The genus contained several species, most of which averaged 5–6 meters (16–20 feet) in length, but the species *Kronosaurus* measures 10–11 meters (33–36 feet) long.

On Spitsbergen, in August 2007, a team from the Natural History Museum of Norway excavated the almost complete skeleton of an immense *pliosaur* that would have measured 15m (50ft) from nose to tail — about half the length of the largest whale ever measured. A preliminary analysis of the bones suggests this beast belongs to a previously unknown species. It must have been an awesomely powerful predator. Two sets of its massive skull with huge, wide-opening, robust jaws, worked by big, powerful muscles should have been capable of picking up a small boat and biting it in half. If a specimen has survived it would certainly qualify as a potential ocean monster.

However, the most likely sea serpent candidate is the most advanced and largest of the archaeocetes, the *basilosaurus* or *zeuglodon,* which was about the size of a modern sperm whale, averaging 18 meters (60 feet) in length. Its most notable physical feature was unparalleled elongation of the vertebrae, making it the closest a whale ever came to a snake. It must have been fully aquatic, because its thoracic, lumbar, sacral and caudal vertebrae were similar, whereas creatures living in terrestrial gravity have to have different size vertebrae to distribute the load of head and limbs. These vertebrae were hollow, and probably fluid-filled for buoyancy, implying that *basilosaurus* only operated in two dimensions at the surface, compared with the three dimensional diving practices of most other cetaceans. In fact, judging from relatively weak axial musculature, it was probably incapable of deep diving.

Moreover, unlike other archeocetes and modern cetaceans, its spine was not fused but free to move. This implies that *basilosaurus* swam in an anguilliform (eel-like) fashion, undulating vertically (dorsoventral or spine-to-belly) rather than laterally (side-to-side), thus conforming exactly to the movement reported in most sea serpent sightings. It is supposed to have been extinct for 37 million years. But in the ocean depths, who knows what can survive?

TABLES

Table 1: *A*— Beaufort's Original Scale

Force	Wind	Condition	Speed/Sails
0	Calm	Becalmed	Not going anywhere
1	Light air	Just sufficient to give steerage way	Less than a knot
2	Light breeze	That in which a man-of-war with all sails set and clean full, would go in smooth water	From 1 to 2 knots
3	Gentle breeze		From 3 to 4 knots
4	Moderate breeze		From 5 to 6 knots
5	Fresh breeze	That in which a well-conditioned man-of-war could just carry when in chase full and bye	Royals, etc.
6	Strong breeze		Single-reefed topsails and topgallant sails
7	Moderate gale		Double-reefed topsails, jib, etc.
8	Fresh gale		Triple-reefed topsails, etc.
9	Strong gale		Close-reefed topsails and courses
10	Whole gale	That in which she could scarcely bear	Close-reefed main topsail and reefed foresail
11	Storm	That which would reduce her to	Storm staysails
12	Hurricane	That which no canvas could withstand	

Table 1: *B*— The Modern Beaufort Scale

Force	Wind Type[1]	Knots	Visual Appearance of the Sea[2]
0	Calm	<1	Like a mirror
1	Puff of Wind	1–3	A few ripples without foamy crests
2	Light Breeze	4–6	Small wavelets which do not break
3	Moderate Breeze	7–10	Large wavelets beginning to break
4	Lively Breeze	11–16	Small waves with white horses
5	Stiff Breeze	17–21	Pronounced long waves with many white horses
6	Squall	22–27	Large waves, extensive foam crests, and some spray
7	Near Gale	28–33	Sea heaps up and foam begins to blow in streaks
8	Gale	34–40	Moderately high waves, crests break into spindrift
9	Strong Gale	41–47	High waves, dense foam streaks, crests start to topple
10	Storm	48–55	Very high waves, overhanging crests, big foam patches
11	Tempest	56–63	Exceptionally high waves, sea covered in foam
12	Hurricane[3]	>64	Air filled with foam and driving spray, little visibility

1. There are several different and inconsistent naming conventions for wind type and some of them are mutually exclusive. As just one example, *Moderate Breeze* and *Gentle Breeze* have each been used to describe both force 3 and force 4.

2. There is a different set of visual descriptions for use on land.

3. In 1946, the World Meteorological Organization (WMO) added five more hurricane force wind speeds. These are not shown here but will be found in Table 6.

Table 2: The Douglas Scales

Table 2(a)

Wind-Sea	Condition	Average Wave Height
0	Calm	No measurable wind or swell
1	Rippled	Less than 10 cm waves
2	Smooth	Waves between 10 and 50 cms

Wind-Sea	Condition	Average Wave Height
3	Moved	Waves rising from 50 cms to 1.25 m
4	Moderate	Wave heights from 1.25 to 2.5 m
5	Rough	Disturbed waves from 2.5 to 4 m
6	Very rough	Large waves of 4 to 6 m high
7	High	Rough waves between 6 and 9 m
8	Very high	Mountainous seas of 9 to 14 m
9	Confused	Maximum wave disturbance, over 14 m

Table 2(b)

Swell	Description	Wave Characteristics
0	No swell	Not noticeable
1	Very low	Short and low
2	Low	Long and low
3	Light	Short and moderate
4	Moderate	Average and moderate
5	Moderate rough	Long and moderate
6	Rough	Short and heavy
7	High	Average and heavy
8	Very high	Long and heavy
9	Confused	Indefinable

Table 3: Pierson-Moskowitch Sea State

Wind Speed (Kts)	Sea State	Significant Wave (Ft)	Significant Range of Periods (Sec)	Average Period (Sec)	Average Length of Waves (FT)
3	0	<.5	<.5–1	0.5	1.5
4	0	<.5	.5–1	1	2
5	1	0.5	1–2.5	1.5	9.5
7	1	1	1–3.5	2	13
8	1	1	1–4	2	16
9	2	1.5	1.5–4	2.5	20
10	2	2	1.5–5	3	26
11	2.5	2.5	1.5–5.5	3	33
13	2.5	3	2–6	3.5	39.5
14	3	3.5	2–6.5	3.5	46
15	3	4	2–7	4	52.5
16	3.5	4.5	2.5–7	4	59
17	3.5	5	2.5–7.5	4.5	65.5
18	4	6	2.5–8.5	5	79
19	4	7	3–9	5	92
20	4	7.5	3–9.5	5.5	99
21	5	8	3–10	5.5	105
22	5	9	3.5–10.5	6	118
23	5	10	3.5–11	6	131.5
25	5	12	4–12	7	157.5
27	6	14	4–13	7.5	184
29	6	16	4.5–13.5	8	210
31	6	18	4.5–14.5	8.5	236.5
33	6	20	5–15.5	9	262.5
37	7	25	5.5–17	10	328.5
40	7	30	6–19	11	394
43	7	35	6.5–21	12	460
46	7	40	7–22	12.5	525.5
49	8	45	7.5–23	13	591
52	8	50	7.5–24	14	566
54	8	55	8–25.5	14.5	722.5
57	8	60	8.5–26.5	15	788
61	9	70	9–28.5	16.5	920
65	9	80	10–30.5	17.5	1099
69	9	90	**10.5–32.5**	**18.5**	**1182**

Table 4: World Meteorological Organization Sea State Codes

Sea state and wave size

0	Calm (glassy)	0 m
1	Calm (rippled)	0 to 0.1 m
2	Smooth (wavelets)	0.1 to 0.5 m
3	Slight	0.5 to 1.25 m
4	Moderate	1.25 to 2.5 m
5	Rough	2.5 to 4 m
6	Very rough	4 to 6 m
7	High	6 to 9 m
8	Very high	9 to 14 m
9	Phenomenal	Over 14 m

Character of the sea swell

	0. None
Low	1. Short or average
	2. Long
Moderate	3. Short
	4. Average
	5. Long
Heavy	6. Short
	7. Average
	8. Long
	9. Confused

Direction from which swell is coming should be recorded as "character + direction" (e.g., "Confused northeast")

Table 5: The Saffir-Simpson Hurricane Scale

Category	Wind Speed	General Extent of Property Damage and Flooding[1]
1— Minimal	74–95 mph	No real damage to buildings. Small trees blown down. Some flooding of coastal roads.
2 — Moderate	96–110 mph	Considerable damage to mobile homes. Some roofs damaged. Many trees fall. Small craft break moorings.
3 — Extensive	111–130 mph	Coastal floods destroy small structures, larger ones damaged by floating debris. Large trees topple. Land less than 5 feet above sea level (ASL) flooded 8 miles or more from the shore.[2]
4 — Extreme	131–155 mph	Extensive curtain wall and some roof structure failure. Major erosion of beaches. Land lower than 10 feet ASL flooded.
5 — Catastrophic	>155 mph	Complete roof failures and some complete building failures. Severe damage to structures less than 15 feet ASL. Evacuation may be required up to 10 miles inland.

1. Descriptions of damage are condensed
2. Hurricane Katrina was Category 3.

Table 6: Wind Speed Scales Compared
(rounded to nearest whole number)

Scale	Level	Generic Description	Wind Speed Greater Than		
			Kts	mph	km/h
Beaufort	0	Calm	-	-	-
Beaufort	1	Puff of Wind	1	1	2
Beaufort	2	Light Breeze	4	5	7
Beaufort	3	Moderate Breeze	7	8	13
Beaufort	4	Lively Breeze	11	13	20
Beaufort	5	Stiff Breeze	17	20	32
Beaufort	6	Squall	22	25	41
Beaufort	7	Near Gale	28	32	52
Beaufort	8	Gale	34	39	62
Fujita	0	Gale Tornado	36	40	64
Beaufort	9	Strong Gale	41	47	75
Beaufort	10	Storm	48	55	89

Scale	Level	Generic Description	Wind Speed Greater Than		
			Kts	*mph*	*km/h*
Beaufort	11	Tempest	56	64	103
Fujita	1	Moderate Tornado	63	73	117
Beaufort	12	Hurricane	64	73	118
Saffir-Simpson	1	Category 1	65	74	119
Beaufort	13	1st extra level	72	83	133
Beaufort	14	2nd extra level	81	93	150
Saffir-Simpson	2	Category 2	84	96	154
Beaufort	15	3rd extra level	90	104	167
Saffir-Simpson	3	Category 3	96	111	178
Fujita	2	Significant Tornado	98	113	181
Beaufort	16	4th extra level	100	115	185
Beaufort	17	5th extra level	109	125	202
Saffir-Simpson	4	Category 4	114	131	210
Saffir-Simpson	5	Category 5	135	155	249
Fujita	3	Severe Tornado	137	158	254
Fujita	4	Devastating Tornado	180	207	333
Fujita	5	Incredible Tornado	227	261	420
Fujita	6	Inconceivable Tornado	277	319	513

Table 7: COLREGS (Navigation Rules or Rules of the Road)

There are 38 Rules, divided into Parts and Subparts as follow. Only the headings are given here, but details can be found on various IMO websites, including: The Admiralty Law Guide at *www.admiraltylawguide.com/conven/collisions 1972* and United States Coast Guard Navigation Center at *<www.navcen.uscg.gov/mwv/navrules>*.

Part A — General

Rule 1— Application (International/Inland)
Rule 2 — Responsibility
Rule 3 — General Definitions

Part B — Steering and Sailing

Subpart 1— Conduct of Vessels in any Condition of Visibility

Rule 4 — Application
Rule 5 — Look-out
Rule 6 — Safe Speed
Rule 7 — Risk of Collision
Rule 8 — Action to Avoid Collision
Rule 9 — Narrow Channels
Rule 10 — Traffic Separation Schemes

Subpart 2 — Conduct of Vessels in Sight of One Another

Rule 11— Application
Rule 12 — Sailing Vessels
Rule 13 — Overtaking
Rule 14 — Head-on Situation
Rule 15 — Crossing Situation
Rule 16 — Action by Give-way Vessel
Rule 17 — Action by Stand-on Vessel
Rule 18 — Responsibilities Between Vessels

Subpart 3 — Conduct of Vessels in Restricted Visibility

Rule 19 — Conduct of Vessels in Restricted Visibility.

Part C — Lights and Shapes

Rule 20 — Application
Rule 21— Definitions
Rule 22 — Visibility of Lights
Rule 23 — Power-driven Vessels Underway
Rule 24 — Towing and pushing
Rule 25 — Sailing Vessels Underway and Vessels Under Oars

Table 8: International Flag Signals

The *International Signaling Code* consists of 26 alphabetical flags, 10 numeral pendants, an answering pendant, and three substitutes or repeaters.

Only a few colors can be easily distinguished from one another at sea so, for clarity, besides plain red, white, and blue, combinations are red-and-white, yellow-and-blue, black, or red, blue-and-white, or white-and-black.

Sentences can be spelled out word-by-word, but there are also standard abbreviations for commonly used phrases, using up to seven flags in a hoist. Their general characteristics are as follow:

Code Flag: A red-and-white striped pennant used to signal that International Code will be used for the subsequent message.

Single flag hoists: Are either urgent or extremely common. They are all shown below under the appropriate letter.

Double hoists: Are mostly distress and maneuvering signals. Some of the more important are shown immediately after the single flag signals.

Triple hoists: Cover points of the compass, relative bearings, standard times, verbs, punctuation, and general code and decode signals.

Quadruple hoists: Are used mainly for geographic signals, ship names, and bearings.

Five-flag hoists: Cover times and positions.

Six-flag hoists: Indicate north, south, east, or west in latitude and longitude signals.

Seven-flag hoists: Are used for longitude signals containing more than 100°

Substitute Flags

Single-pointed pennants are used to repeat letters when spelling-out words. Without them, ships would have to carry several sets of signal flags, but the substitutes allow any letter to be represented up to four times.

The first substitute repeats the first (top) letter in the hoist, the next repeats the second letter, and the third the third letter in the hoist. Thus, for example, the word "*mamma*" would be Signaled as; M-flag, A-flag, 1st Sub (1st letter = M), 3rd Sub (3rd letter = M), 2nd Sub (2nd letter = A). The USN calls substitute pennants "repeaters."

Single Flag Codes

A-flag: A vertically divided burgee, with white on the hoist and blue on the fly. Flown alone it means (1) When stationary "I have a diver down — keep well clear of me at slow speed" (2) When under way "I am undergoing a speed trial."

B-flag: A red burgee. Flown alone means "I am taking on, discharging, or carrying dangerous cargo." Since this covers explosives and ammunition, it is colloquially known as the "powder flag" in naval circles.

C-flag: Square, equally divided into blue-white-red-white-blue horizontal stripes. Flown alone means "Yes" or "Affirmative."

D-flag: Square, horizontally divided yellow-blue-yellow in the ratio 1:2:1. Flown alone means "I am maneuvering with difficulty — keep clear."

E-flag: Square, horizontally divided blue over red. Flown as a single signal means "I am altering course to starboard."

F-flag: White square with a red square superimposed on it at 45° rotation. Flown alone means (1) In general use "I am disabled — communicate with me": (2) On USN & NATO aircraft carriers "Flight operations underway."

G-flag: Square, vertically divided (from the hoist) into six equal stripes alternately yellow and blue. (1) Flown alone means "I require a pilot" (2) Worn by a fishing vessel means "I am handling nets."

H-flag: Vertically divided square with white on hoist and red on fly. Flown alone means "Pilot on board."

I-flag: Square with a small black circle on a yellow background. Flown alone means (1) In general use "I am altering course to port" (2) USN & NATO "Coming alongside. "

J-flag: Square, equally divided horizontally blue-white-blue. Flown alone means "Keep clear I am on fire with dangerous cargo."

K-flag: Square, vertically divided yellow on hoist, blue on fly. Flown alone means "I wish to communicate with you."

L-flag: Quartered square, hoist yellow over black, fly black over yellow. Flown alone means "You should stop your vessel immediately."

M-flag: Square with a white saltire-style cross on a blue background. Flown alone means (1) In general use "I have a doctor on board" (2) USN "My vessel is stopped making no way."

N-flag: Square checkered flag with four rows and columns, alternating blue and white, starting with blue in the upper hoist. Flown alone means "No" or "Negative."

O-flag: Square diagonally divided with yellow in the lower hoist and red in the upper fly. Flown alone means "Person overboard." (See also double hoist "G over W").

P-flag: Square with a small white square on a blue ground. Conventionally called the "Blue Peter," When hoisted in port means (1) "Return to ship — we are about to depart." At sea it usually means (2) "Your lights are out or burning badly" but in daylight may mean (3) "Fishing nets are an obstruction."

Q-flag: A yellow square. (1) In general use it is the quarantine flag, meaning "My ship is healthy, I request free pratique" (2) In the USN & NATO it is the recall "All boats return to ship."

R-flag: Square with a narrow yellow cross on a red field. Flown alone it means (1) In general use "The way is off my ship — You may feel your way past" (2) USN & NATO at sea "Preparing to replenish" (3) USN & NATO in port identifies a ready-duty ship.

S-flag: Square with a blue cross of a white field. Flown alone means (1) In general use "My engines are full astern" (2) USN & NATO "Conducting flag hoist drill."

T-flag: Square, equally divided vertically red-white-blue from hoist to fly. Flown alone means (1) "Do not pass ahead of me" or, if flown by a fishing vessel (2) "Keep clear I am engaged in trawling."

U-flag: Square, quartered red over white at hoist, white over red at fly. Flown alone warns "You are standing into danger."

V-flag: Square with a red saltire-style cross on a white ground. Flown alone means "I need assistance." This is *not* a distress signal (See C over D and N over C).

W-flag: Square with a white square centered on a blue field and a small red square centered on the white. Flown alone means "I require medical assistance."

X-flag: Square with a blue cross on a white field. Flown alone means "Stop carrying out your intentions and watch for my signals."

Y-flag: Square with ten diagonal stripes alternating yellow and red, rising from lower fly to upper hoist. (1) Flown alone when at sea or coming into port means "I am carrying mails." (2) When anchored it means "My anchor is dragging." (3) USN & NATO "Ship has visual communications duty."

Z-flag: Square, diagonally quartered with yellow in the upper sector, black along hoist, blue on the fly, and red in the bottom sector. (1) Flown alone by a ship coming in to port means "I require a tug." (2) Flown alone by a fisherboat at sea means "I am fishing or casting nets." (3) May be used to attract the attention of shore stations.

Some Common Double Flag Hoists

A over C: "I am abandoning ship."
A over N: "I need a doctor."
B over R: "I require a helicopter"
C over D: I require immediate assistance."
D over V: "I am drifting."
E over F: "Cancel my distress signal."
F-over-A: "Can you give me my position?"
F-over-O: "I am standing by."
G over W: "Please rescue my man overboard."
J over L: "You run the risk of going aground."
K over P: "Can you tow me into port."
K over N: "I am unable to tow you."
L over O: Flown by a lightship "I am not in my correct position."

N over C: "I am in distress and require immediate assistance."
P over D: "Your navigation lights cannot be seen."
P over P: "Keep well clear of me."
P over M: "Follow me."
Q over D: "I am going ahead."
Q over L: "I have had infectious disease on board less than 5 days ago."
Q over Q: "I require health clearance" (Either the ship's health is suspect, or there has been unusual mortality among rats on board, or the ship had infectious diseases aboard more than five days ago).
Q over T: "I am going astern."
Q over U: "Anchoring prohibited."
Q over X: "Request permission to anchor."
R over U: "Keep clear I am maneuvering with difficulty."
S over O: "You should stop immediately."
U over M: "The harbor is closed to traffic."
U over P: "Emergency — permission to enter harbor is urgently requested."
Y over U: "I am going to communicate by means of the International Code."
Z over L: "Your signal has been received but not understood."

Table 9: Sound and Light Signals

Depending on their length, all vessels are required to carry specified forms of sound and/or light signaling equipment, to be used only when vessels are within sight of each other and are meeting or crossing. Because these rules are lengthy and complex, this appendix will only give a brief indication of those concerning power-driven vessels in international waters. Other signals apply to vessels under tow, being pushed, at anchor (riding), aground, trawling, or engaged on pilot duties. Readers wanting more detail on these rules, other classes of vessel, or inland waters should consult one of the many relevant websites, for example that of the U.S. Coast Guard at: <www.navcen.uscg.gov/mwv/navrules>.

In the regulations, a "short blast" of the whistle is defined as being about one second in duration, a "prolonged blast" being from four to six seconds. These signals may be supplemented by light flashes of about one second, with the interval between flashes also being one second.

When maneuvering:
- One short blast (+ one flash) = *I am altering course to starboard.*
- Two short blasts (+ two flashes) = *I am altering course to port.*
- Three short blasts (+ three flashes) = *I am operating astern propulsion.*

In a narrow channel:
- Two prolonged blasts followed by one short blast = *I intend to overtake you on your starboard side.*
- Two prolonged blasts followed by two short blasts = *I intend to overtake you on your port side.*
- The vessel being overtaken shall acknowledge her agreement with one prolonged, one short, one prolonged, and one short blast in that sequence.

When in doubt:
- If either vessel fails to understand the intentions of the other, or fears collision, the vessel in doubt shall give at least five short blasts, which may be supplemented by at least five flashes.

Limitation:
- The foregoing signals may never be used in fog or other conditions where vessels are not visible to each other by eye. The following then apply.

Obstructed vision:
- A vessel nearing a bend or an area where vision is obstructed shall sound one prolonged blast as a warning. Any vessel around the bend or behind the obstruction shall respond with one prolonged blast.

Restricted visibility (e.g., fog):
- One prolonged blast sounded at two-minute intervals = *I am making way through the water.*
- Two prolonged blasts sounded at two-minute intervals = *I am underway but stopped and making no way through the water.*
- One prolonged followed by two short blasts at two-minute intervals = *I am not under command or am restricted in ability to maneuver.*

Table 10: Distress Signals

Requests for help at sea may be made by a wide range of flag signals, morse code, voice radio, pyrotechnic devices, and other means. Some of these are:

Flag Signals: (1) Flying the ship's ensign at half-mast or upside down. (2) Flying the international code signal flags "N" over "C." (3) Flying a flag with a black square above a black ball on an orange background. (4) Hoisting a square flag above a ball.

Morse Signals: (1) Originally "CQD," popularly believed to signify "Come Quick Danger," but actually meaningless, consisting of the standard prefix "CQ" followed by "D," possibly for "danger." (2) In 1906 "SOS" was adopted, this time popular belief thought it stood for "Save Our Ship (or Souls)" but it was in fact chosen because three dots and three dashes were easy to transmit, easy to remember, and difficult to misinterpret.

Radio Voice Signals: (1) "Pan-pan" repeated means that a problem exists on board posing no immediate danger to life or the vessel: (2) "Mayday," derived from the French *m'aidez* (help me) means the matter is extremely urgent with imminent danger to life or the vessel.

Visual Signals: Include red flares, lights flashing at specified frequencies, and various pyrotechnics such as red star shells or parachute flares.

Triple Signals: Traditionally, signals repeated in groups of three, such as gunshots, puffs of smoke, whistle blasts, and the like.

Other Distress Signals: Include:
- Continuously-sounding the fog horn.
- Firing a gun at one-minute intervals.
- Showing flames on the vessel.
- Dropping any color of dye marker.
- Lighting a smoke generator.
- Waving the arms.

Attention-seeking Signals: If necessary to attract the attention of another vessel, any vessel may make light or sound signals so long as they cannot be mistaken for any other signal (especially distress) authorized by the rules and regulations. It may also direct a searchlight beam in the direction of a hazard in such a way as not to embarrass another vessel or be mistaken for any aid to navigation.

Table 11: Examples of Phonetic Alphabets

World War I U.S. Navy	World War I Royal Navy	World War I British Army	1932 ITU International	World War II Allied Forces	Current NYC Police Department	Current NATO, ICAO, IMO
Able	Apples	Ack	Amsterdam	Abel	Adam	**Alfa**
Boy	Butter	Beer	Baltimore	Baker	Boy	**Bravo**
Cast	Charlie	Charlie	Casablanca	Charlie	Charlie	**Charlie**
Dog	Duff	Don	Denmark	Dog	David	**Delta**
Easy	Edward	Edward	Edison	Easy	Edward	**Echo**
Fox	Freddie	Freddy	Florida	Fox	Frank	**Foxtrot**
George	George	Gee	Gallipoli	George	George	**Golf**
Have	Harry	Harry	Havana	How	Henry	**Hotel**
Item	Ink	Ink	Italia	Item	Ida	**India**
Jig	Johnnie	Johnnie	Jerusalem	Jig	John	**Juliett**
King	King	King	Kilogramme	King	King	**Kilo**
Love	London	London	Liverpool	Love	Lincoln	**Lima**
Mike	Monkey	Emma	Magagascar	Mike	Mary	**Mike**
Nan	Nuts	Nuts	New York	Nan	Nora	**November**
Oboe	Orange	Oranges	Oslo	Oboe	Ocean	**Oscar**
Pup	Pudding	Pip	Paris	Peter	Peter	**Papa**
Quack	Queenie	Queen	Quebec	Queen	Queen	**Quebec**
Rush	Robert	Robert	Roma	Roger	Robert	**Romeo**
Sail	Sugar	Esses	Santiago	Sugar	Sam	**Sierra**
Tare	Tommy	Toc	Tripoli	Tare	Tom	**Tango**
Unit	Uncle	Uncle	Upsala	Uncle	Union	**Uniform**
Vice	Vinegar	Vic	Valencia	Victor	Victor	**Victor**
Watch	Willie	William	Washington	William	William	**Whisky**
X-Ray	Xerxes	X-Ray	Xanthippe	X-Ray	X-Ray	**X-Ray**
Yoke	Yellow	Yorker	Yokohama	Yoke	Young	**Yankee**
Zed	Zebra	Zebra	Zurich	Zebra	Zebra	**Zulu**

Table 12: International Standard 8601

Promulgated by the International Standards Organization in 1988 (see Date & Time Notation) this standard runs to some 35 pages, but only its salient points will be covered here.

Date notation: Is required to be in the numerical format **YYYY-MM-DD,** where YYYY is the Gregorian calendar year, MM is the month, and DD the day. This offers the advantages of:

- Being easily readable and writeable by computer software, with no alpha-numeric conversions required (e.g. for months).
- Easily comparable and sortable by string comparison, especially if separators are eliminated as in **YYYYM-MDD.**
- Simplified keyboard entry and table layout due to constant length.
- Language-independent.
- Cannot be confused with other date notations.
- Identical to notations already used in China, Hungary, Japan, Korea, Scandinavia, and elsewhere.
- Consistent with time notation by moving progressively from larger to smaller units.

The standard also allows the Gregorian format to be replaced by ordinal dates, shown as **YYYY-DDD** where DDD is day of the year. For example, **2008-366** is the last day of the leap year starting **2008-001.**

In some areas of industrial planning (shift scheduling, delivery timing, packaging date, for example) it is preferable to know the week and day. ISO 8601 expresses this as **YYYY-Wd** where d is day-of-the-week, and W is week-of-the-year (usually 52, but some years go into a 53rd). For example, reading right-to-left, **2006W152** signifies Tuesday (the 2nd day) in the fifteenth week of 2006. The system can easily be expanded — for historians and archaeologists, for example — by adding digits to the year field while "BC" or "BCE" can be replaced by a minus sign (**-10000** for instance).

Time notation: ISO 8601 specifies the format **hh:mm**, where hh is the number of complete hours since midnight (from 00 to 24), and mm is the number of complete minutes since the start of the incomplete hour (from 00 to 59). For example, 4:30 AM becomes **04:30** (or **0430**) while 4:30 PM becomes **16:30** (or **1630**). This is the notation traditionally used by military forces and in virtually all parts of the world beyond English-speaking countries, since many other languages do not even have equivalents for "AM/PM"). Its advantages include most of those listed under date notation, plus:
- The number of complete seconds since the start of the minute (also from 00 to 59) can be appended when this level of precision is required, making the format **hh:mm:ss**. If this is not sufficient, the notation can be made infinitely precise by using decimals. For example, **hh:mm:ss.sss** would be accurate to the nearest one-thousandth of a second.
- The notation also allows distinction between beginning and ending midnights. For example, **2006-03-05 24:00** and **2006-03-06 00:00** refer to precisely the same moment in time. (In practice, however, this distinction is seldom required, and it is conventional to avoid ambiguity by using **00:00** rather than **24:00** to represent midnight).
- It is consistent with date notation and can be combined with it to move progressively from most significant to least significant unit, the combined format to the nearest second being **YYYY-MM-DD hh:mm:ss**. When date and time are stored together in a single data field without dashes, colons, or a space as separators, ISO suggests dividing them with a capital "T" as in **20060731T1745** (5:45 PM on 31st July 2006).

Table 13: Comparative Officer Ranks

British Royal Navy	*U.S. Navy and Coast Guard*	*British Army & Royal Marines[1]*	*U.S. Army & Marine Corps*
Cadet[2]	Midshipman (USN)[2] Cadet (USCG)[2]	Cadet[2]	Cadet (USA) Midshipman (USMC)
Midshipman[2]	Ensign	2nd Lieutenant	2nd Lieutenant
Sub-Lieutenant	Lieutenant (junior grade)	Lieutenant	1st Lieutenant
Lieutenant	Lieutenant	Captain	Captain
Lt-Commander	Lt-Commander	Major	Major
Commander	Commander	Lt-Colonel	Lt-Colonel
Captain	Captain	Colonel	Colonel
Commodore	Rear Admiral (lower half)	Brigadier	Brigadier General
Rear Admiral	Rear Admiral (upper half)	Major General	Major General
Vice-Admiral	Vice-Admiral	Lt-General[3]	Lt-General
Admiral	Admiral	General	General
Admiral of the Fleet[4]	Fleet Admiral[4]	Field Marshal[4]	General of the Army[4]

1. Royal Marines rank one grade higher when afloat.
2. Not a commissioned rank.
3. The Commandant of Royal Marines is normally a Lieutenant General.
4. Currently dormant.

Table 14: NATO and United States Rank Codes

NATO Rank Code	Royal Navy	British Army & Royal Marines	U.S. Rank Code	U.S. Navy	U.S. Army & Marine Corps
OF-10	Admiral of the Fleet	Field Marshal	O-11	Fleet Admiral	General of the Army
OF-9	Admiral	General	O-10	Admiral	General
OF-8	Vice-Admiral	Lieutenant General	O-9	Vice Admiral	Lieutenant General
OF-7	Rear-Admiral	Major General	O-8	Rear Admiral Upper Half	Major General
OF-6	Commodore captain[1]	Brigadier	O-7	Rear Admiral Lower Half	Brigadier General
OF-5	Captain	Colonel[2]	O-6	Captain	Colonel
OF-4	Commander	Lieutenant Colonel[2]	O-5	Commander	Lieutenant Colonel
OF-3	Lieutenant Commander	Major[2]	O-4	Lieutenant Commander	Major
OF-2	Lieutenant	Captain[2]	O-3	Lieutenant	Captain
OF-1	Sub-Lieutenant Midshipman	Second Lieutenant[2]	O-2	Lieutenant (jg)	First Lieutenant
			O-1	Ensign	Second Lieutenant
WO-5			W-5	Chief Warrant Officer (5)	
WO-4			W-4	Chief Warrant Officer (4)	
WO-3			W-3	Chief Warrant Officer (3)	
WO-2			W-2	Chief Warrant Officer (2)	
OR-9	Warrant Officer (1)	Warrant Officer (1)	E-9	Master Chief Petty Officer	Sergeant Major
OR-8	Warrant Officer (2)	Quartermaster Sergeant	E-8	Senior Chief Petty Officer	Master/First Sergeant
OR-7	Chief Petty Officer	Colour Sergeant	E-7	Chief Petty Officer	Gunnery Sergeant
OR-6	Petty Officer	Sergeant	E-6	Petty Officer First Class	Staff Sergeant
OR-5			E-5	Petty Officer Second Class	Sergeant
OR-4	Leading Rate	Corporal	E-4	Petty Officer Third Class	Corporal
OR-3	Able Rate	Lance Corporal	E-3	Seaman	Lance Corporal
OR-2	Ordinary Rate	Marine	E-2	Seaman Apprentice	Private First Class
OR-1	Junior Rate		E-1	Seaman Recruit	Private

1. With six years seniority.
2. Royal Marines rank one grade higher when afloat.

Table 15: The Evolution of United States Navy Officer Titles
Listed in Order of Seniority and Succession to Command

1775: Captain, Lieutenants,[1] Boatswain,[2] Master's Mate. Gunner,[2] Carpenter,[2] Midshipman.

1794: Captain, Lieutenants, *Sailing Master*, Boatswain, Master's Mate, Gunner, Carpenter, Midshipman.

1806: Captain, *Master Commandant,* Lieutenants, Sailing Master, Master's Mate, Boatswain, Gunner, Carpenter, Midshipman.

1815: Captain, *Commander,*[3] Lieutenants, *Master,*[4] Master's Mate, Boatswain, Gunner, Carpenter, Midshipman.

1837: Captain, Commander, Lieutenants, Master, *Passed Midshipman, Warranted Master's Mate,* Boatswain, Midshipman.

1852: Captain, Commander, Lieutenants, Master, Passed Midshipman, Midshipman, Boatswain.

1862: *Rear Admiral, Commodore,*[5] Captain, Commander, *Lieutenant Commander,*[6] Lieutenants, Master, *Ensign*, Passed Midshipman, Midshipman.

1882: *Admiral, Vice-Admiral,* Commodore,[7] Captain, Commander, Lieutenant, *Lieutenant (jg),*[8] Ensign, *Ensign (jg),*[9] Naval Cadet.[10]

1902: *Admiral of the Navy,*[11] Admiral, Vice-Admiral, Rear Admiral, Captain, Commander, Lieutenant Commander, Lieutenants, Lieutenant (jg), Ensign, *Midshipman.*[12]

1944: *Fleet Admiral,*[13] Admiral, Vice-Admiral, Rear Admiral, *Commodore,*[14] Captain, Commander, Lieutenant Commander, Lieutenant, Lieutenant (jg), Ensign, Midshipman.

1982: Admiral, Vice-Admiral, Rear Admiral, *Commodore Admiral,*[15] Captain, Commander, Lieutenant Commander, Lieutenants, Lieutenant (jg), Ensign, Midshipman.

2008: Admiral, Vice-Admiral, Rear Admiral, *Rear Admiral (lower half),* Captain, Commander, Lieutenant Commander, Lieutenants, Lieutenant (jg), Ensign, Midshipman.

1. Listed in order of seniority (succession to command).
2. Note progressively diminishing status of traditional standing officers.
3. Formerly master commandant.
4. Formerly sailing master.
5. Previously the courtesy title of a captain commanding a squadron.
6. Previously a senior lieutenant in charge of a smaller vessel had been called lieutenant commanding.

7. The rank was abolished in 1899.
8. Formerly master.
9. Formerly passed midshipman, the rank was later abandoned
10. Formerly midshipman.
11. Special rank created for Admiral Dewey, never again awarded.
12. Title reinstated.
13. Special rank created for the victorious commanders of World War II. Placed in abeyance thereafter. See section 8.
14. Reinstated for World War II and abandoned in 1947.
15. Created in response to Army and Air Force complaints that naval promotions leapfrogged one-star rank. Changed to commodore in 1983 and rear admiral (lower half) in 1985.

Table 16: Equivalent U.S. and Foreign Naval Officer Ranks

NATO	United States	France	Germany	Italy	Russia	China
OF-10	Fleet Admiral		Grossadmiral	Grande Amiraglio	Admiral Flota	
OF-9	Admiral	Amiral	Admiral	Ammiraglio d'Armata	Admiral	Shang Jiang
OF-8	Vice Admiral	Vice Amiral	Vizadmiral	Ammariglio di Squadra	Vitse-Admiral	Zhong Jiang
OF-7	Rear Admiral	Contre Amiral	Konteradmiral	Contrammiraglio	Kontr-Admiral	Shao Jiang
OF-6	Rear Admiral (Lower half)	Chef d'Escadre	Kommodore	Commodoro		Da Xiao
OF-5	Captain	Capitaine de Vaisseau	Kapitän zur See	Capitano di Vascello	Kapitan pervogo ranga	Shang Xiao
OF-4	Commander	Capitaine de Frégate	Fregatten Kapitän	Capitano di Fregatta	Kapitan vtorogo ranga	Zhong Xiao
OF-3	Lieutenant Commander	Capitaine de Corvette	Korvettenkapitän Kapitänleutnant	Capitano di Corvetta	Kapitan-leytenant	Kapitan tret'yego ranga
OF-2	Lieutenant	Lieutenant de Vaisseau	Oberleutnant zur See	Tenente di Vascello	Starshiy leytenant	Shang Wei
OF-1	Lieutenant (jg)	Enseigne de Vaisseau	Leutnant zur See	Sottotenente di Vascello	Leytenant	Zhong Wei
	Ensign	Aspirant	Fähnrich	Guardiamarina	Mladshiy	Shao Wei

Table 17: Boxing the Compass

#	Compass point	Abbreviation	True heading
1	North	N	0.00°
2	North by east	NbE	11.25°
3	North-northeast	NNE	22.50°
4	Northeast by north	NEbN	33.75°
5	Northeast	NE	45.00°
6	Northeast by east	NEbE	56.25°
7	East-northeast	ENE	67.50°
8	East by north	EbN	78.75°
9	East	E	90.00°
10	East by south	EbS	101.25°
11	East-southeast	ESE	112.50°
12	Southeast by east	SEbE	123.75°
13	Southeast	SE	135.00°
14	Southeast by south	SEbS	146.25°
15	South-southeast	SSE	157.50°
16	South by east	SbE	168.75°
17	South	S	180.00°
18	South by west	SbW	191.25°
19	South-southwest	SSW	202.50°
20	Southwest by south	SWbS	213.75°
21	Southwest	SW	225.00°
22	Southwest by west	SWbW	236.25°
23	West-southwest	WSW	247.50°
24	West by south	WbS	258.75°
25	West	W	270.00°
26	West by north	WbN	281.25°
27	West-northwest	WNW	292.50°
28	Northwest by west	NWbW	303.75°

#	Compass point	Abbreviation	True heading
29	Northwest	NW	315.00°
30	Northwest by north	NWbN	326.25°
31	North-northwest	NNW	337.50°
32	North by west	NbW	348.75°

BIBLIOGRAPHY

Beavis, Bill. *Salty Dog Talk: The Nautical Origins of Everyday Expressions.* London: Grenada, 1983.

Bowen, Frank Charles. *Sea Slang: A Dictionary of Old Timers' Expressions and Epithets.* London: Samson Low, Marston, 1929.

Bridges, T.C. *The Book of the Sea.* London: Harrap, 1928.

Burgess, Robert. *We Joined the Navy: Traditions, Customs and Nomenclature of the Royal Navy.* London: Black, 1943.

Cutler, Deborah W. & Thomas J. *A Dictionary of Naval Terms.* Annapolis, MD: Naval Institute, 2005.

Degler, Teri. *Scuttlebutt and Other Expressions of Nautical Origin.* Saskatoon, Saskatchewan: Eastern Producers Prairie, 1989.

Department of Defense. *Dictionary of Military and Associated Terms.* Washington, D.C., 2007.

Falconer, William. *An Universal Dictionary of the Marine.* London, 1780, rptd. National Library of Australia, 2004.

Hamersly, Lewis Randolph. *A Naval Encyclopædia: Comprising a Dictionary of Nautical Words and Phrases; Biographical Notices, and Records of Naval Officers; Special Articles of Naval Art and Science. Boston (?),* 1884.

Hendrickson, Robert. *Encyclopedia of Word and Phrase Origins.* New York: Facts on File, 1987.

Isil, Olivia A. *When a Loose Cannon Flogs a Dead Horse There's the Devil to Pay: Seafaring Words in Everyday Speech.* Campden, ME: International Marine, 1956.

Jeans, Peter D. *Seafaring Lore & Legend: A Miscellany of Maritime Myth, Superstition, Fable, and Fact.* Campden, ME: International Marine, 2004.

_____. *Ship to Shore: A Dictionary of Everyday Words and Phrases Derived from the Sea.* Campden, ME: International Marine, 1993, rptd. 2004.

Kemp, Peter, ed. *The Oxford Companion to Ships & the Sea:* London: Oxford University Press, 1976.

Layton, Cyril Walter Thomas. *Dictionary of Nautical Words and Phrases.* Glasgow, Scotland: Brown Sons & Ferguson, 1955.

Lenfestey, Tom, and Tom Lenfestey. *Dictionary of Nautical Terms.* New York: Facts on File, 1993.

Mack, William P. *Naval Ceremonies, Customs, and Traditions.* Annapolis, MD: Naval Institute, 1980.

McKenna, Robert. *Dictionary of Nautical Literacy.* Camden, ME: International Marine, 2001.

Morris, James, and Kearns, Patricia. *Historical Dictionary of the U.S. Navy.* London: Scarecrow, 1998.

NATO Standardization Agency. *Glossary of Terms and Definitions.* Brussels, Belgium, 2007.

Paré, Ambroise. *On Monsters and Marvels.* Chicago: University of Chicago Press, 1982.

Parry, M.H. *Aak to Zumbra: A Dictionary of the World's Watercraft.* Newport News, VA: Mariners Museum, 2000.

Smyth, Admiral W.H. *The Sailor's Word-book.* London, 1887, rptd. Conway Maritime, 2005.

Stein, Jess, ed. *Dictionary of the English Language,* unabridged edition. New York: Random House, 1966.

Watson, Bruce, and Susan Watson. *United States Navy: A Dictionary.* New York: Garland, 1991.

INDEX

This index references items such as people, ships, and deities, many of which will not be found through the alphabetical sequencing of dictionary entries. It also provides pointers to groups of like items, such as "Sea Serpents and monsters" and "Laws and conventions of the sea."